ESSENTIAL

VOLUME 5

CAPTAIN AMERICA

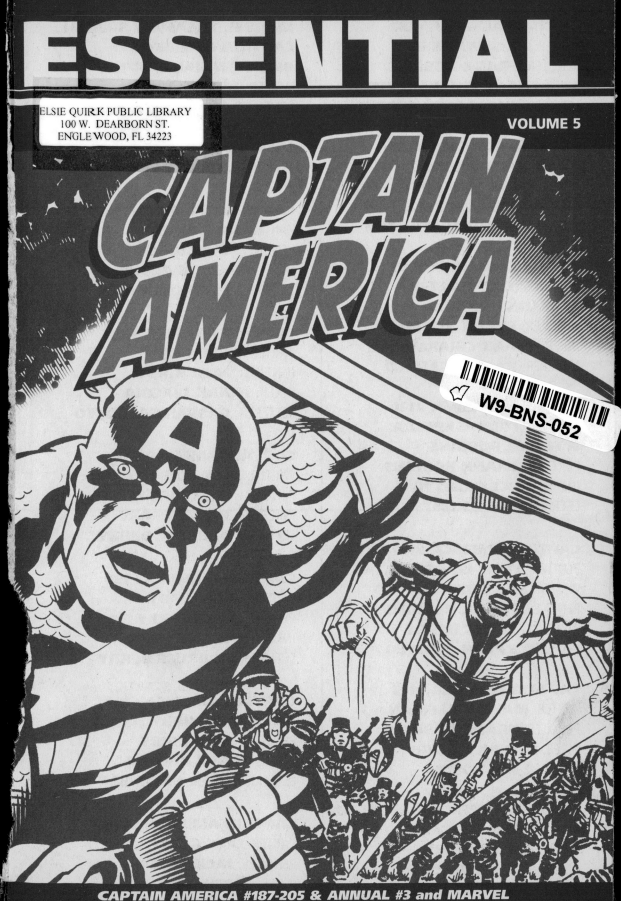

CAPTAIN AMERICA #187-205 & ANNUAL #3 and MARVEL TREASURY SPECIAL: CAPTAIN AMERICA'S BICENTENNIAL BATTLES

CAPTAIN AMERICA #187
WRITER: **JOHN WARNER**
PENCILER: **FRANK ROBBINS**
INKER: **FRANK CHIARMONTE**
LETTERER: **CHARLOTTE JETTER**

CAPTAIN AMERICA #188
WRITER: **JOHN WARNER**
PENCILER: **SAL BUSCEMA**
INKER: **VINCE COLLETTA**
LETTERER: **IRVING WATANABE**

CAPTAIN AMERICA #189
WRITERS: **TONY ISABELLA
& FRANK ROBBINS**
PENCILER: **FRANK ROBBINS**
INKER: **FRANK CHIARMONTE**
LETTERER: **KAREN MANTLO**

CAPTAIN AMERICA #190
WRITERS: **TONY ISABELLA
& FRANK ROBBINS**
PENCILER: **FRANK ROBBINS**
INKER: **VINCE COLETTA**
LETTERER: **DAVE HUNT**

CAPTAIN AMERICA #191
PLOTTER: **TONY ISABELLA**
WRITER: **BILL MANTLO**
PENCILER: **FRANK ROBBINS**
INKER: **D. BRUCE BERRY**
LETTERER: **KAREN MANTLO**

CAPTAIN AMERICA #192
WRITER: **MARV WOLFMAN**
PENCILER: **FRANK ROBBINS**
INKER: **D. BRUCE BERRY**
LETTERER: **JOE ROSEN**

CAPTAIN AMERICA ANNUAL #3
WRITER: **JACK KIRBY**
PENCILER: **JACK KIRBY**
INKERS: **FRANK GIACOIA
& JOHN VERPOORTEN**
LETTERER: **GASPAR SALADINO**

**MARVEL TREASURY SPECIAL:
CAPTAIN AMERICA'S
BICENTENNIAL BATTLES**
WRITER: **JACK KIRBY**
PENCILER: **JACK KIRBY**
INKERS: **HERB TRIMPE,
JOHN ROMITA & BOB SMITH**
LETTERER: **JOHN COSTANZA**

CAPTAIN AMERICA #193
WRITER: **JACK KIRBY**
PENCILER: **JACK KIRBY**
INKER: **FRANK GIACOIA**
LETTERER: **JOHN COSTANZA**

CAPTAIN AMERICA #194
WRITER: **JACK KIRBY**
PENCILER: **JACK KIRBY**
INKER: **FRANK GIACOIA**
LETTERER: **GASPAR SALADINO**

CAPTAIN AMERICA #195
WRITER: **JACK KIRBY**
PENCILER: **JACK KIRBY**
INKER: **D. BRUCE BERRY**
LETTERER: **D. BRUCE BERRY**

CAPTAIN AMERICA #196
WRITER: **JACK KIRBY**
PENCILER: **JACK KIRBY**
INKER: **D. BRUCE BERRY**
LETTERER: **D. BRUCE BERRY**

CAPTAIN AMERICA #197
WRITER: **JACK KIRBY**
PENCILER: **JACK KIRBY**
INKER: **FRANK GIACOIA**
LETTERER: **JOHN COSTANZA**

CAPTAIN AMERICA #198
WRITER: **JACK KIRBY**
PENCILER: **JACK KIRBY**
INKER: **FRANK GIACOIA**
LETTERER: **GASPAR SALADINO**

CAPTAIN AMERICA #199
WRITER: **JACK KIRBY**
PENCILER: **JACK KIRBY**
INKER: **FRANK GIACOIA**
LETTERER: **GASPAR SALADINO**

CAPTAIN AMERICA #200
WRITER: **JACK KIRBY**
PENCILER: **JACK KIRBY**
INKER: **FRANK GIACOIA**
LETTERER: **JOHN COSTANZA**

CAPTAIN AMERICA #201
WRITER: **JACK KIRBY**
PENCILER: **JACK KIRBY**
INKER: **FRANK GIACOIA**
LETTERER: **JOHN COSTANZA**

CAPTAIN AMERICA #202
WRITER: **JACK KIRBY**
PENCILER: **JACK KIRBY**
INKER: **FRANK GIACOIA**
LETTERER: **JOHN COSTANZA**

CAPTAIN AMERICA #203
WRITERS: **JACK KIRBY**
PENCILER: **JACK KIRBY**
INKER: **FRANK GIACOIA**
LETTERER: **GASPAR SALADINO**

CAPTAIN AMERICA #204
WRITER: **JACK KIRBY**
PENCILER: **JACK KIRBY**
INKER: **FRANK GIACOIA**
LETTERER: **GASPAR SALADINO**

CAPTAIN AMERICA #205
WRITER: **JACK KIRBY**
PENCILER: **JACK KIRBY**
INKER: **JOHN VERPOORTEN**
LETTERER: **JIM NOVAK**

REPRINT CREDITS

COVER ART:
JACK KIRBY

FRONT COVER COLORS:
THOMAS MASON

BACK COVER COLORS:
AVALON'S ANDY TROY

COLLECTION EDITOR:
MARK D. BEAZLEY

ASSOCIATE EDITOR:
JOHN DENNING

EDITORIAL ASSISTANTS:
**JOE HOCHSTEIN
& JAMES EMMETT**

EDITOR, SPECIAL PROJECT:
JENNIFER GRÜNWALD

SENIOR EDITOR, SPECIAL PROJECTS:
JEFF YOUNGQUIST

SENIOR VICE PRESIDENT OF SALES:
DAVID GABRIEL

RESEARCH:
CHAD ANDERSON

BOOK DESIGNER:
MICHAEL CHATHAM

PRODUCTION:
RYAN DEVALL & COLORTEK

EDITOR IN CHIEF:
JOE QUESADA

PUBLISHER:
DAN BUCKLEY

EXECUTIVE PRODUCER:
ALAN FINE

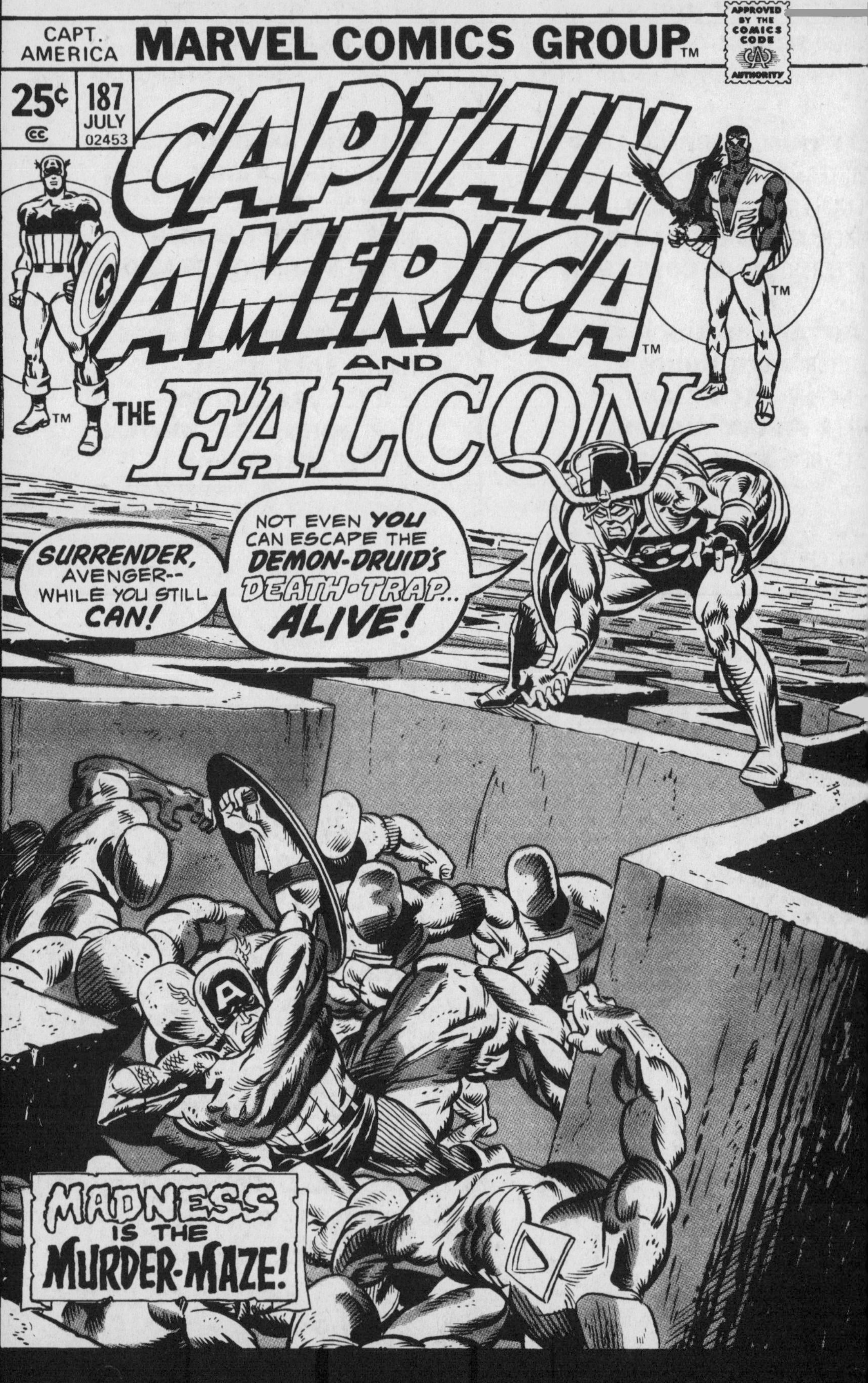
CAPT. AMERICA
MARVEL COMICS GROUP™
APPROVED BY THE COMICS CODE AUTHORITY
25¢
187
JULY
02453
CAPTAIN AMERICA™
AND
THE FALCON™
SURRENDER, AVENGER-- WHILE YOU STILL CAN!
NOT EVEN YOU CAN ESCAPE THE DEMON-DRUID'S DEATH-TRAP... ALIVE!
MADNESS IS THE MURDER-MAZE!

1941! The world at war! And in a full-security laboratory, frail *Steve Rogers* became *Captain America*, the American *super-soldier!* For four thrilling years, he struck back at the Axis' treacherous attack— until a freak stroke of fate threw him into *suspended animation*... to awaken in the *mid-1960's*, a man *twenty years out of his time.* Since that day, *Captain America* has sought his destiny in this *brave new world.*

Stan Lee PRESENTS: CAPTAIN AMERICA AND THE FALCON™

JOHN WARNER, SCRIPT • FRANK ROBBINS, ART • F. CHIARAMONTE, INKS • C. JETTER, LETTERING • G. ROUSSOS, COLORIST • LEN WEIN, EDITOR

The Madness Maze!

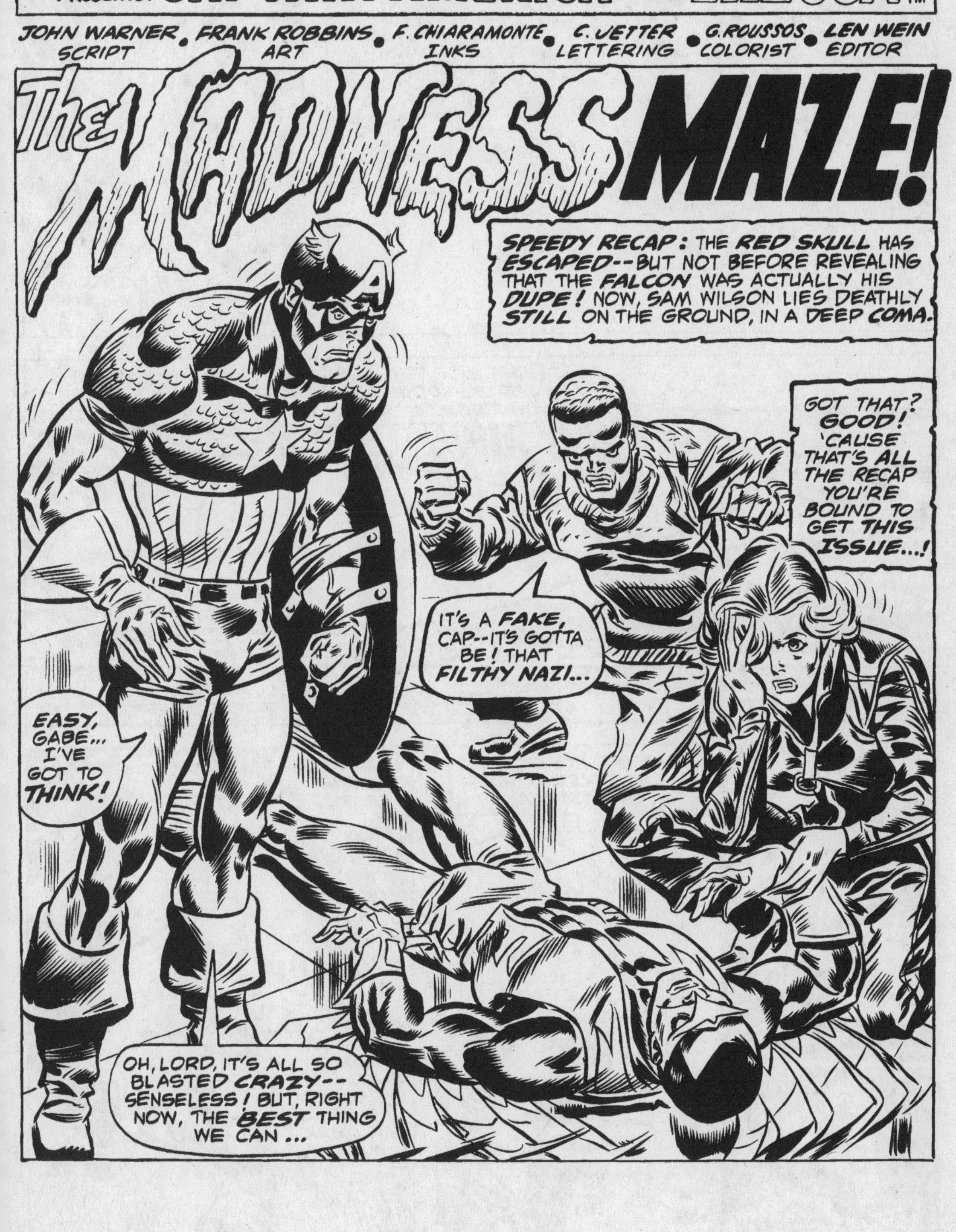
SPEEDY RECAP: THE RED SKULL HAS ESCAPED--BUT NOT BEFORE REVEALING THAT THE FALCON WAS ACTUALLY HIS DUPE! NOW, SAM WILSON LIES DEATHLY STILL ON THE GROUND, IN A DEEP COMA.
GOT THAT? GOOD! 'CAUSE THAT'S ALL THE RECAP YOU'RE BOUND TO GET THIS ISSUE...!
IT'S A FAKE, CAP--IT'S GOTTA BE! THAT FILTHY NAZI...
EASY, GABE... I'VE GOT TO THINK!
OH, LORD, IT'S ALL SO BLASTED CRAZY--SENSELESS! BUT, RIGHT NOW, THE BEST THING WE CAN...

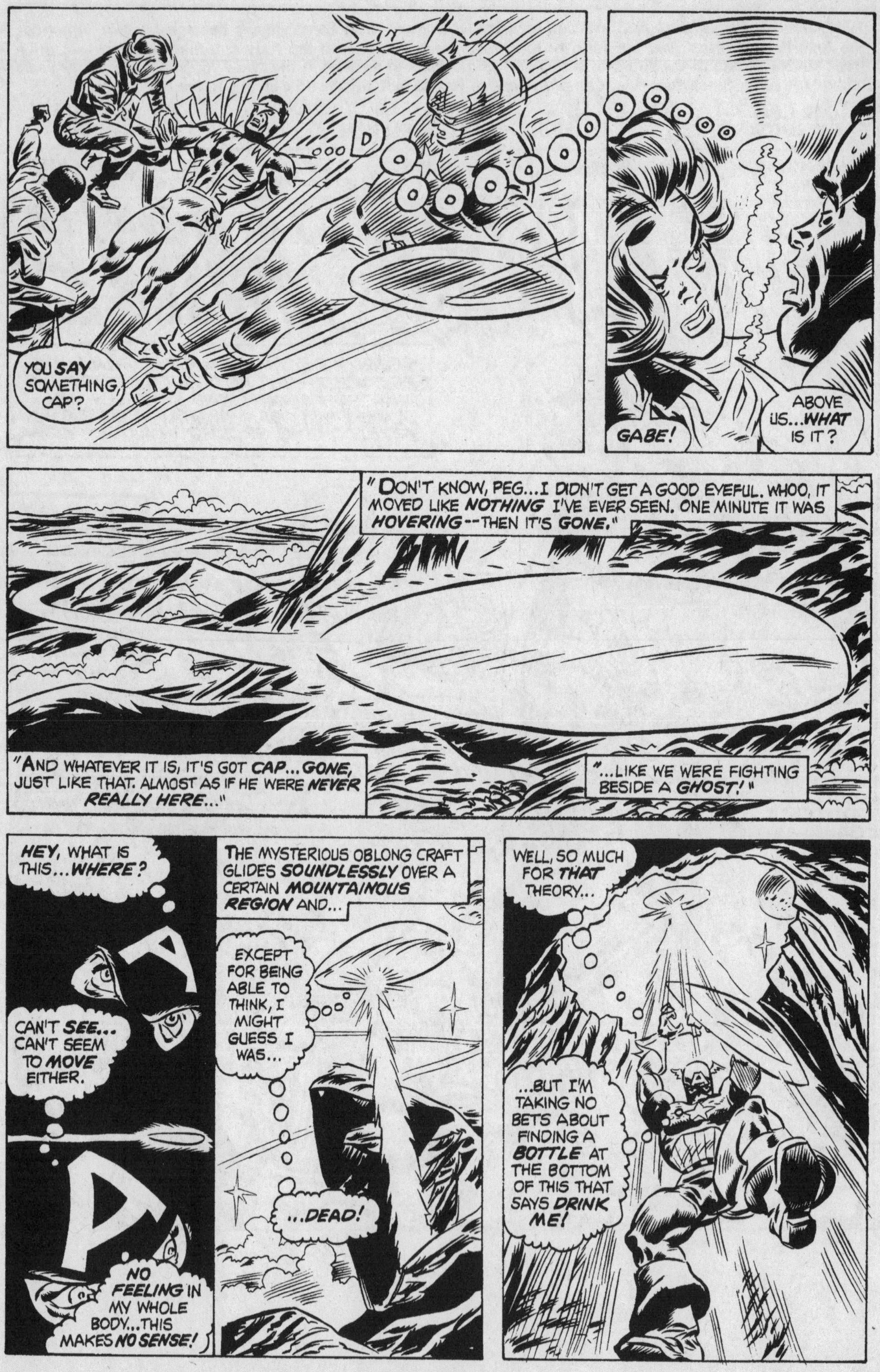
...DOOOOOOOOOOOOOOO
YOU SAY SOMETHING, CAP?
GABE!
ABOVE US...WHAT IS IT?
"DON'T KNOW, PEG...I DIDN'T GET A GOOD EYEFUL. WHOO, IT MOVED LIKE NOTHING I'VE EVER SEEN. ONE MINUTE IT WAS HOVERING--THEN IT'S GONE."
"AND WHATEVER IT IS, IT'S GOT CAP... GONE, JUST LIKE THAT. ALMOST AS IF HE WERE NEVER REALLY HERE..."
"...LIKE WE WERE FIGHTING BESIDE A GHOST!"
HEY, WHAT IS THIS...WHERE?
CAN'T SEE... CAN'T SEEM TO MOVE EITHER.
NO FEELING IN MY WHOLE BODY...THIS MAKES NO SENSE!
THE MYSTERIOUS OBLONG CRAFT GLIDES SOUNDLESSLY OVER A CERTAIN MOUNTAINOUS REGION AND...
EXCEPT FOR BEING ABLE TO THINK, I MIGHT GUESS I WAS...
...DEAD!
WELL, SO MUCH FOR THAT THEORY...
...BUT I'M TAKING NO BETS ABOUT FINDING A BOTTLE AT THE BOTTOM OF THIS THAT SAYS DRINK ME!

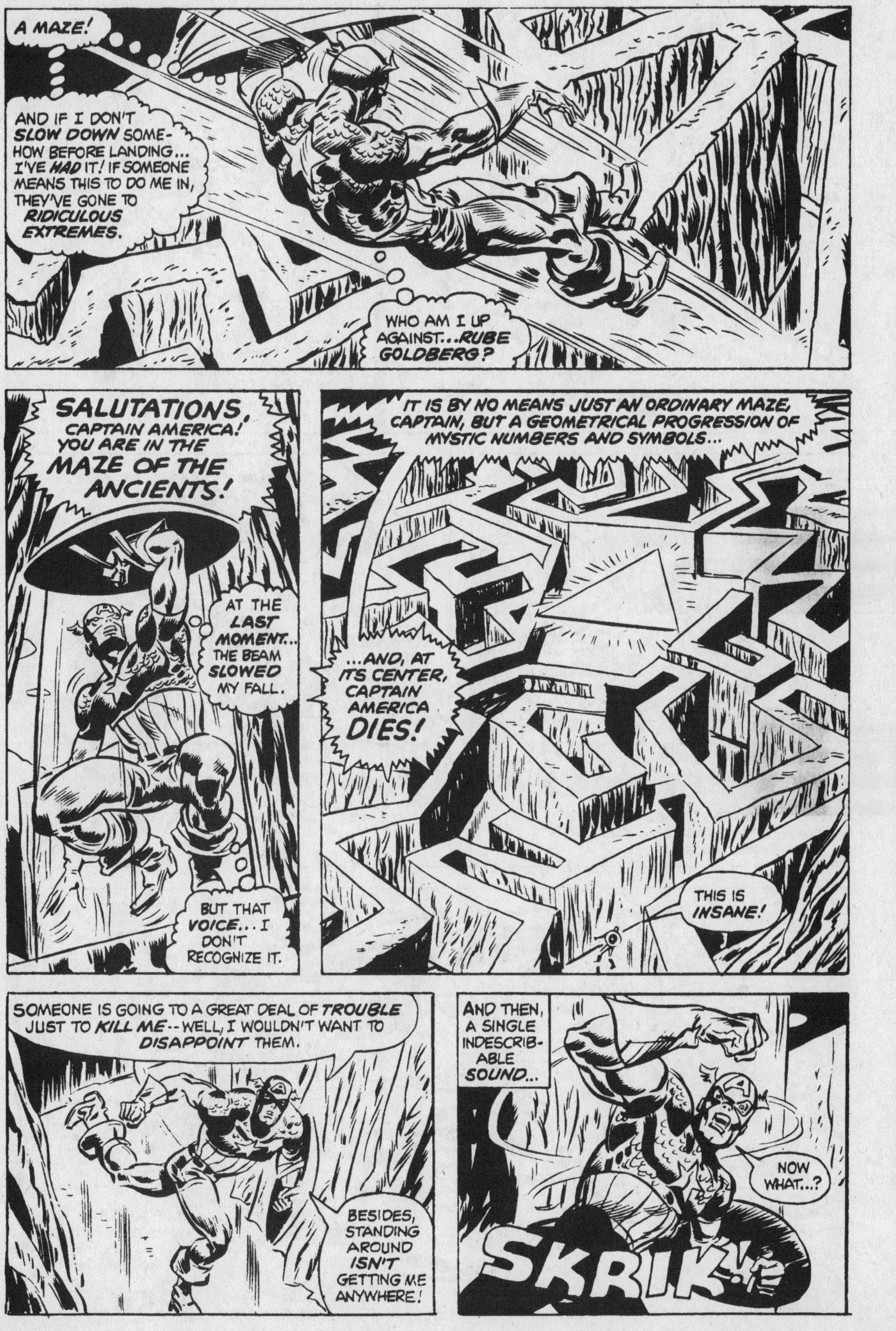
A MAZE!
AND IF I DON'T SLOW DOWN SOMEHOW BEFORE LANDING... I'VE HAD IT! IF SOMEONE MEANS THIS TO DO ME IN, THEY'VE GONE TO RIDICULOUS EXTREMES.
WHO AM I UP AGAINST...RUBE GOLDBERG?
SALUTATIONS, CAPTAIN AMERICA! YOU ARE IN THE MAZE OF THE ANCIENTS!
AT THE LAST MOMENT... THE BEAM SLOWED MY FALL.
BUT THAT VOICE... I DON'T RECOGNIZE IT.
IT IS BY NO MEANS JUST AN ORDINARY MAZE, CAPTAIN, BUT A GEOMETRICAL PROGRESSION OF MYSTIC NUMBERS AND SYMBOLS...
...AND, AT ITS CENTER, CAPTAIN AMERICA DIES!
THIS IS INSANE!
SOMEONE IS GOING TO A GREAT DEAL OF TROUBLE JUST TO KILL ME--WELL, I WOULDN'T WANT TO DISAPPOINT THEM.
BESIDES, STANDING AROUND ISN'T GETTING ME ANYWHERE!
AND THEN, A SINGLE INDESCRIBABLE SOUND...
NOW WHAT...?
SKRIK!

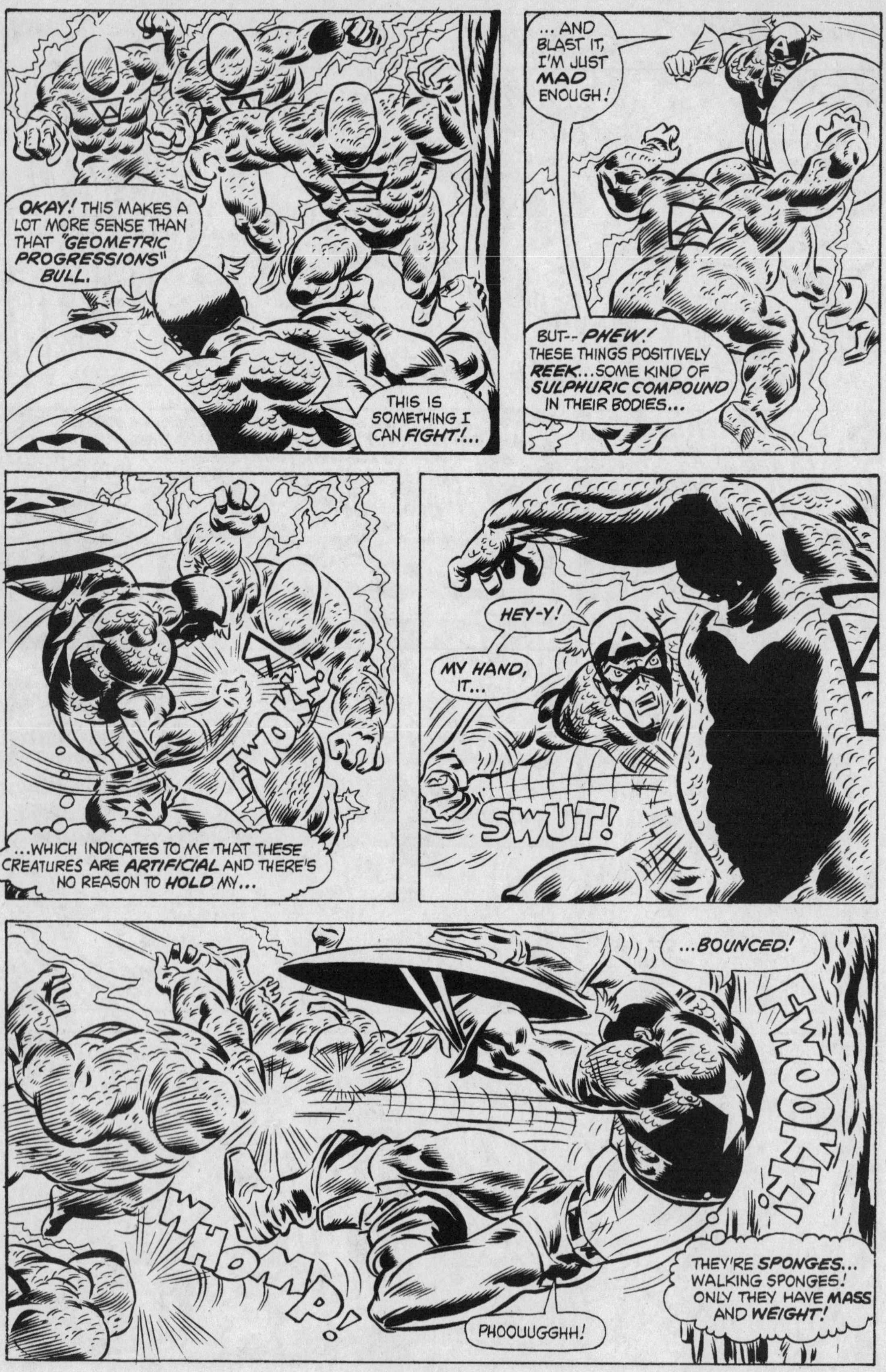
OKAY! THIS MAKES A LOT MORE SENSE THAN THAT "GEOMETRIC PROGRESSIONS" BULL.
THIS IS SOMETHING I CAN FIGHT!...
...AND BLAST IT, I'M JUST MAD ENOUGH!
BUT-- PHEW! THESE THINGS POSITIVELY REEK...SOME KIND OF SULPHURIC COMPOUND IN THEIR BODIES...
FWOK!
...WHICH INDICATES TO ME THAT THESE CREATURES ARE ARTIFICIAL AND THERE'S NO REASON TO HOLD MY...
HEY-Y!
MY HAND, IT...
SWUT!
...BOUNCED!
FWOOKK!
WHOMP!
PHOOUUGGHH!
THEY'RE SPONGES... WALKING SPONGES! ONLY THEY HAVE MASS AND WEIGHT!

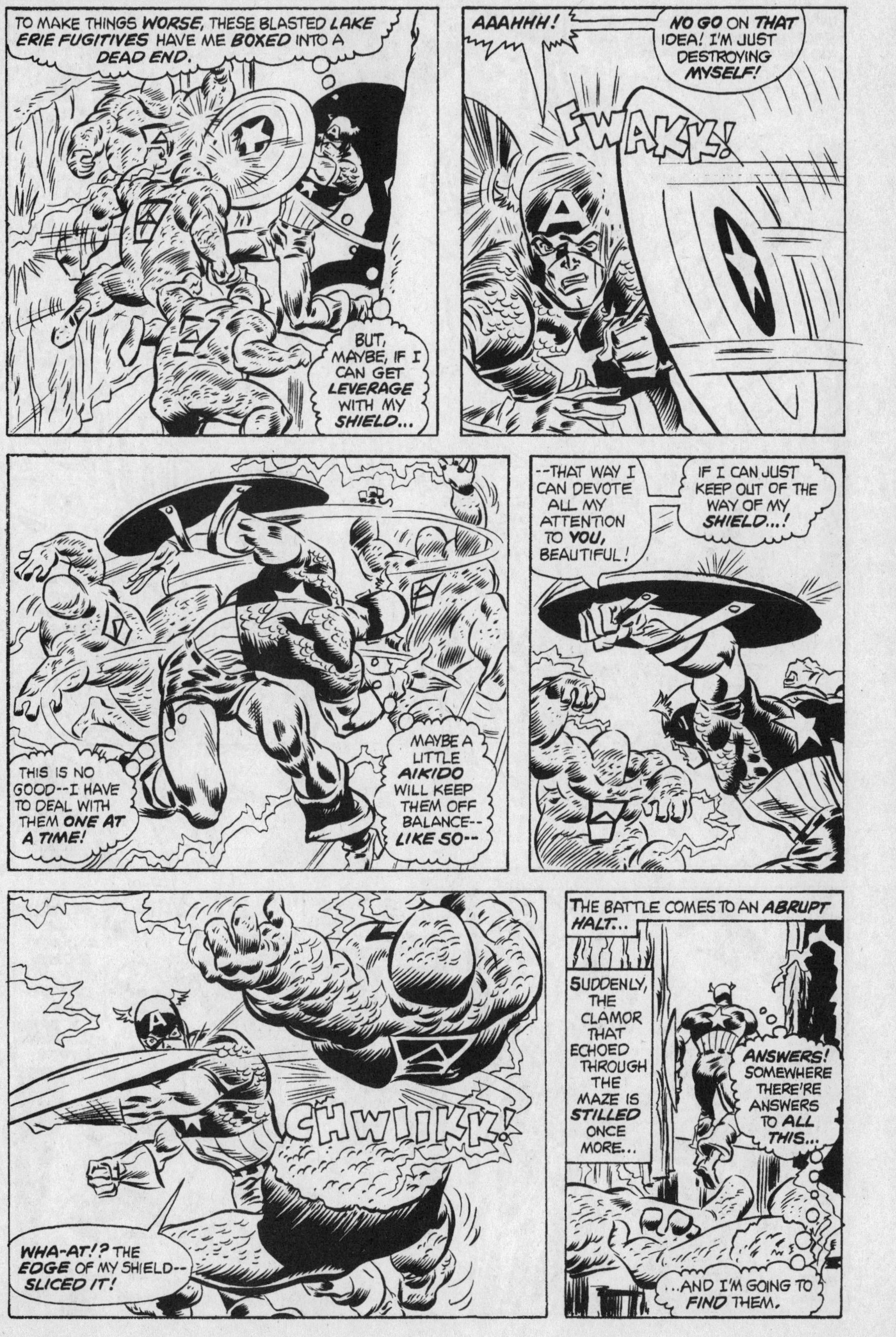
TO MAKE THINGS WORSE, THESE BLASTED LAKE ERIE FUGITIVES HAVE ME BOXED INTO A DEAD END.
BUT, MAYBE, IF I CAN GET LEVERAGE WITH MY SHIELD...
AAAHHH!
NO GO ON THAT IDEA! I'M JUST DESTROYING MYSELF!
FWAKK!
THIS IS NO GOOD--I HAVE TO DEAL WITH THEM ONE AT A TIME!
MAYBE A LITTLE AIKIDO WILL KEEP THEM OFF BALANCE-- LIKE SO--
--THAT WAY I CAN DEVOTE ALL MY ATTENTION TO YOU, BEAUTIFUL!
IF I CAN JUST KEEP OUT OF THE WAY OF MY SHIELD...!
CHWIIKK!
WHA-AT!? THE EDGE OF MY SHIELD-- SLICED IT!
THE BATTLE COMES TO AN ABRUPT HALT...
SUDDENLY, THE CLAMOR THAT ECHOED THROUGH THE MAZE IS STILLED ONCE MORE...
ANSWERS! SOMEWHERE THERE'RE ANSWERS TO ALL THIS...
...AND I'M GOING TO FIND THEM.

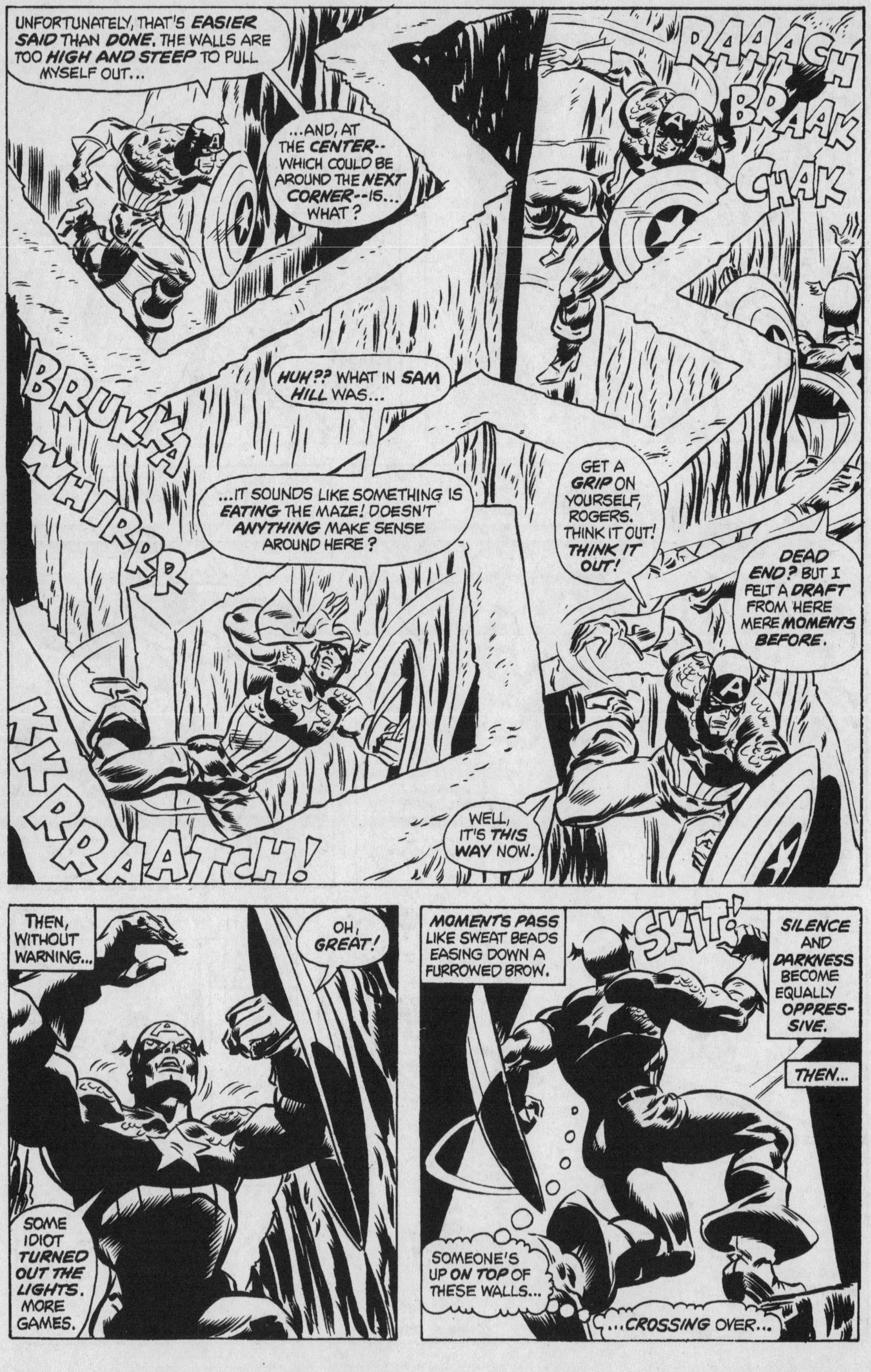
UNFORTUNATELY, THAT'S EASIER SAID THAN DONE. THE WALLS ARE TOO HIGH AND STEEP TO PULL MYSELF OUT...
...AND, AT THE CENTER-- WHICH COULD BE AROUND THE NEXT CORNER--IS... WHAT?
RAAACH
BRAAK
CHAK
BRUKKA
HUH?? WHAT IN SAM HILL WAS...
WHIRRR
...IT SOUNDS LIKE SOMETHING IS EATING THE MAZE! DOESN'T ANYTHING MAKE SENSE AROUND HERE?
GET A GRIP ON YOURSELF, ROGERS. THINK IT OUT! THINK IT OUT!
DEAD END? BUT I FELT A DRAFT FROM HERE MERE MOMENTS BEFORE.
KKRRAATCH!
WELL, IT'S THIS WAY NOW.
THEN, WITHOUT WARNING...
OH, GREAT!
SOME IDIOT TURNED OUT THE LIGHTS. MORE GAMES.
MOMENTS PASS LIKE SWEAT BEADS EASING DOWN A FURROWED BROW.
SKIT!
SILENCE AND DARKNESS BECOME EQUALLY OPPRESSIVE.
THEN...
SOMEONE'S UP ON TOP OF THESE WALLS...
...CROSSING OVER...

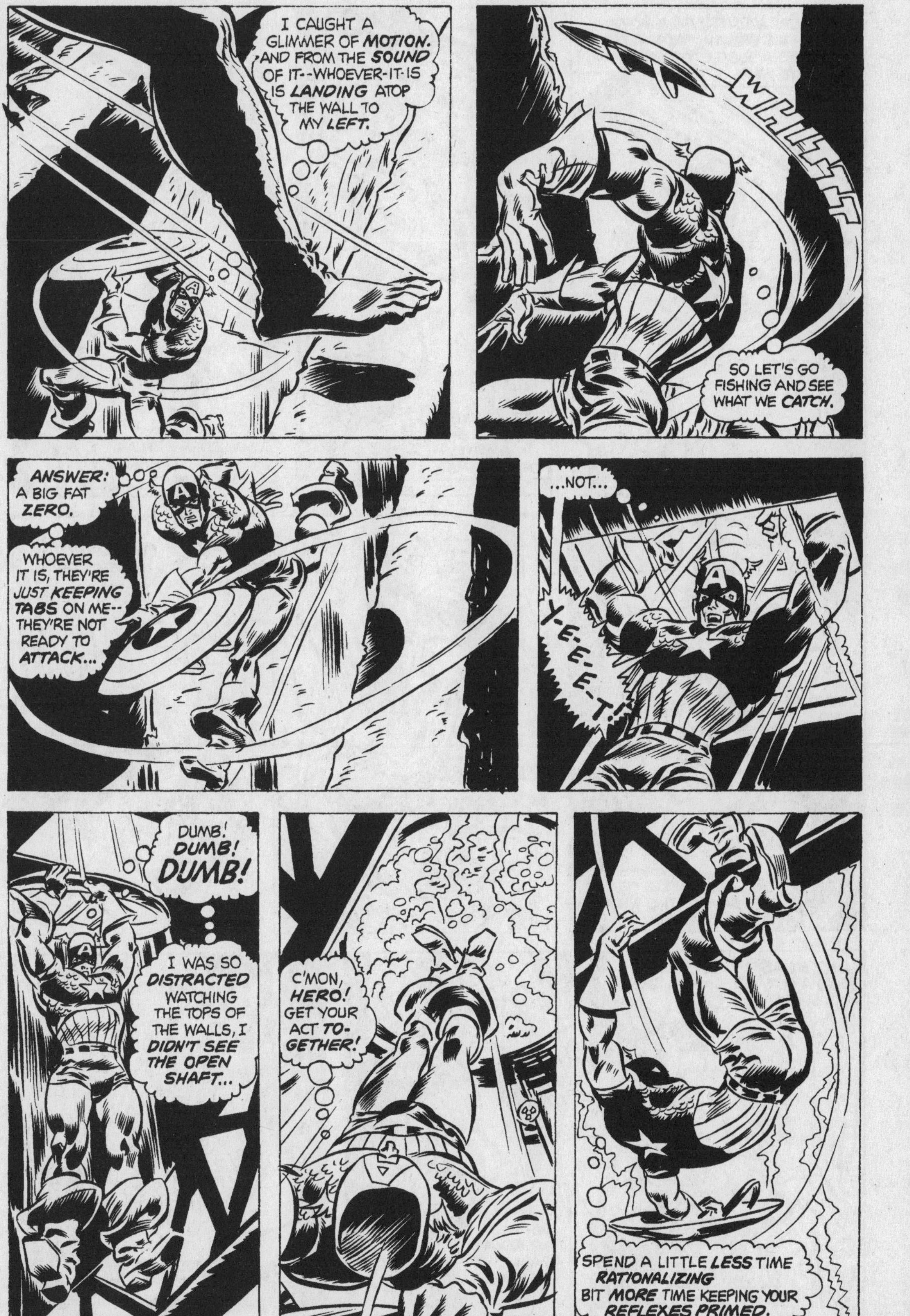

I CAUGHT A GLIMMER OF MOTION. AND FROM THE SOUND OF IT--WHOEVER-IT-IS IS LANDING ATOP THE WALL TO MY LEFT.
WHISTTT
SO LET'S GO FISHING AND SEE WHAT WE CATCH.
ANSWER: A BIG FAT ZERO.
WHOEVER IT IS, THEY'RE JUST KEEPING TABS ON ME-- THEY'RE NOT READY TO ATTACK...
...NOT...
Y-E-E-E-T!
DUMB! DUMB! DUMB!
I WAS SO DISTRACTED WATCHING THE TOPS OF THE WALLS, I DIDN'T SEE THE OPEN SHAFT...
C'MON, HERO! GET YOUR ACT TO-GETHER!
SPEND A LITTLE LESS TIME RATIONALIZING
BIT MORE TIME KEEPING YOUR REFLEXES PRIMED.

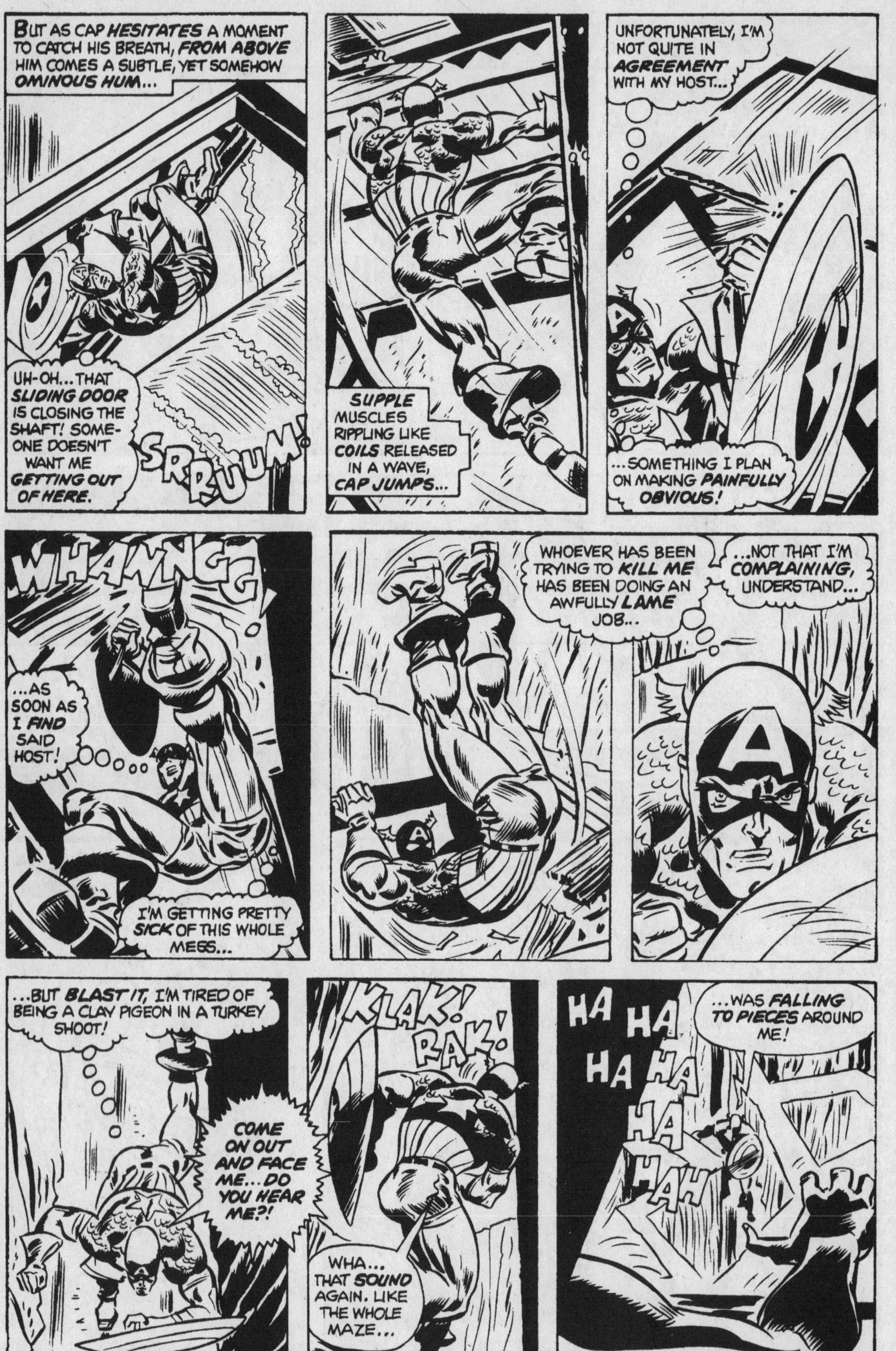
BUT AS CAP HESITATES A MOMENT TO CATCH HIS BREATH, FROM ABOVE HIM COMES A SUBTLE, YET SOMEHOW OMINOUS HUM...
UH-OH... THAT SLIDING DOOR IS CLOSING THE SHAFT! SOME-ONE DOESN'T WANT ME GETTING OUT OF HERE.
SRRUUUM!
SUPPLE MUSCLES RIPPLING LIKE COILS RELEASED IN A WAVE, CAP JUMPS...
UNFORTUNATELY, I'M NOT QUITE IN AGREEMENT WITH MY HOST...
...SOMETHING I PLAN ON MAKING PAINFULLY OBVIOUS!
WHANNGG!
...AS SOON AS I FIND SAID HOST!
I'M GETTING PRETTY SICK OF THIS WHOLE MESS...
WHOEVER HAS BEEN TRYING TO KILL ME HAS BEEN DOING AN AWFULLY LAME JOB...
...NOT THAT I'M COMPLAINING, UNDERSTAND...
...BUT BLAST IT, I'M TIRED OF BEING A CLAY PIGEON IN A TURKEY SHOOT!
COME ON OUT AND FACE ME... DO YOU HEAR ME?!
KLAK! RAK!
WHA... THAT SOUND AGAIN. LIKE THE WHOLE MAZE...
...WAS FALLING TO PIECES AROUND ME!
HA HA HA HA HA HA HAH!

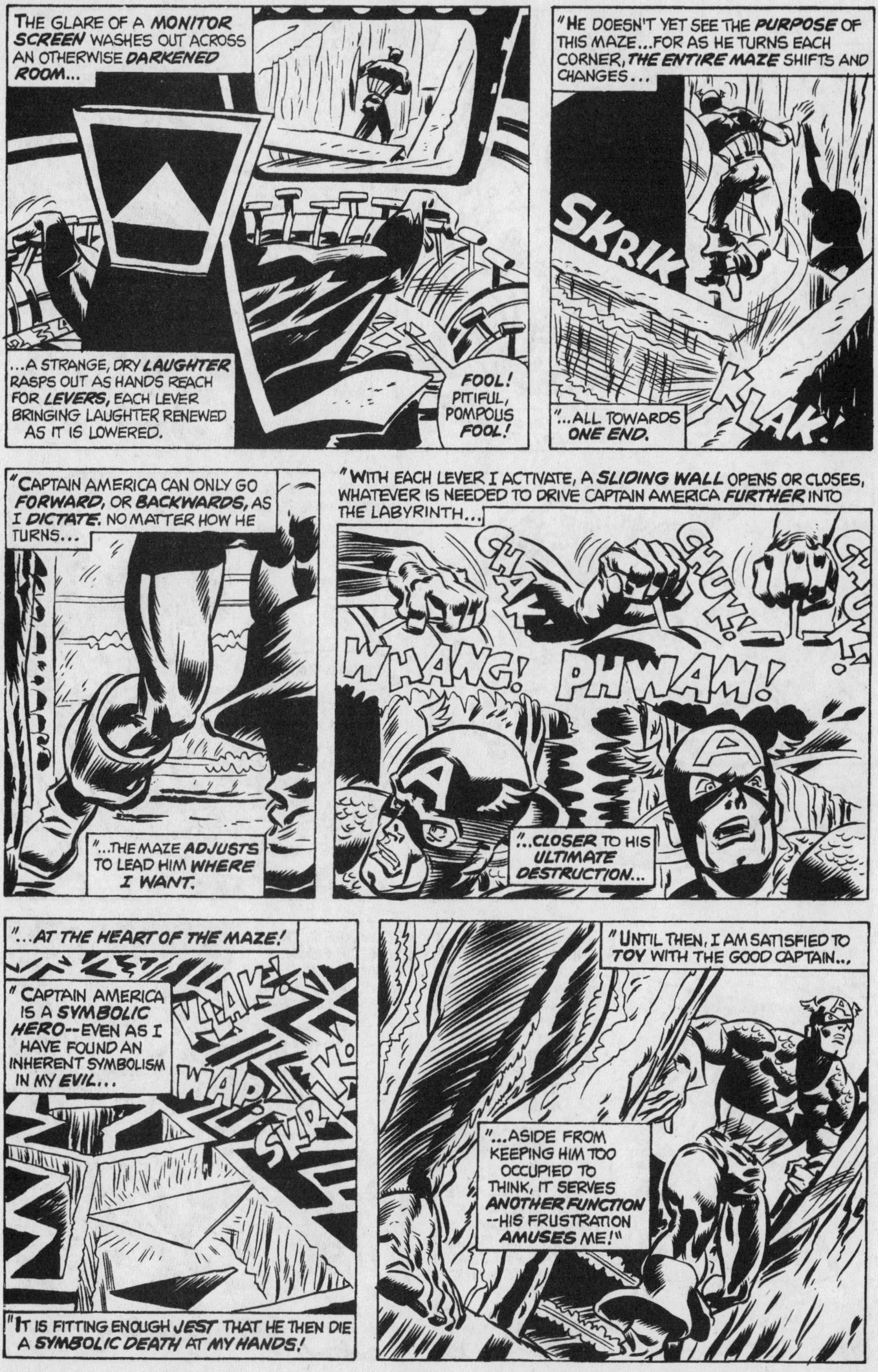
THE GLARE OF A MONITOR SCREEN WASHES OUT ACROSS AN OTHERWISE DARKENED ROOM...
...A STRANGE, DRY LAUGHTER RASPS OUT AS HANDS REACH FOR LEVERS, EACH LEVER BRINGING LAUGHTER RENEWED AS IT IS LOWERED.
FOOL! PITIFUL, POMPOUS FOOL!
"HE DOESN'T YET SEE THE PURPOSE OF THIS MAZE...FOR AS HE TURNS EACH CORNER, THE ENTIRE MAZE SHIFTS AND CHANGES...
SKRIK
KLAK!
"...ALL TOWARDS ONE END.
"CAPTAIN AMERICA CAN ONLY GO FORWARD, OR BACKWARDS, AS I DICTATE. NO MATTER HOW HE TURNS...
"...THE MAZE ADJUSTS TO LEAD HIM WHERE I WANT.
"WITH EACH LEVER I ACTIVATE, A SLIDING WALL OPENS OR CLOSES, WHATEVER IS NEEDED TO DRIVE CAPTAIN AMERICA FURTHER INTO THE LABYRINTH...
CHAK
CHUK!
CHUK!
WHANG!
PHWAM!
"...CLOSER TO HIS ULTIMATE DESTRUCTION...
"...AT THE HEART OF THE MAZE!
"CAPTAIN AMERICA IS A SYMBOLIC HERO--EVEN AS I HAVE FOUND AN INHERENT SYMBOLISM IN MY EVIL...
KLAK!
WAP
SKRIK
"IT IS FITTING ENOUGH JEST THAT HE THEN DIE A SYMBOLIC DEATH AT MY HANDS!
"UNTIL THEN, I AM SATISFIED TO TOY WITH THE GOOD CAPTAIN...
"...ASIDE FROM KEEPING HIM TOO OCCUPIED TO THINK, IT SERVES ANOTHER FUNCTION --HIS FRUSTRATION AMUSES ME!"

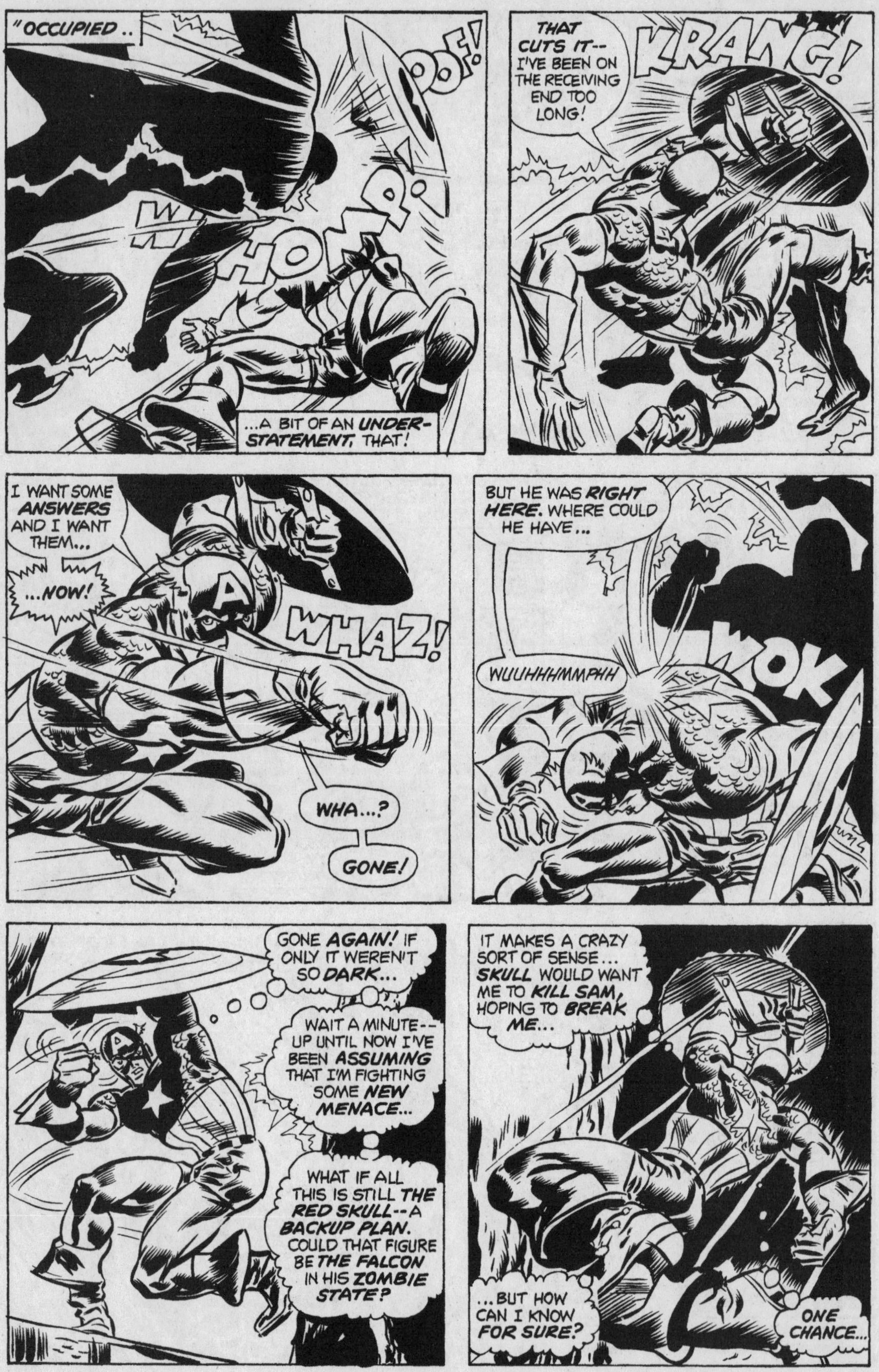
"OCCUPIED ..
WHOOF!
WHOMP!
...A BIT OF AN UNDER-STATEMENT, THAT!
THAT CUTS IT-- I'VE BEEN ON THE RECEIVING END TOO LONG!
KRANG!
I WANT SOME ANSWERS AND I WANT THEM...
...NOW!
WHAZ!
WHA...?
GONE!
BUT HE WAS RIGHT HERE. WHERE COULD HE HAVE...
WUUHHHMMPHH
WOK
GONE AGAIN! IF ONLY IT WEREN'T SO DARK...
WAIT A MINUTE-- UP UNTIL NOW I'VE BEEN ASSUMING THAT I'M FIGHTING SOME NEW MENACE...
WHAT IF ALL THIS IS STILL THE RED SKULL--A BACKUP PLAN. COULD THAT FIGURE BE THE FALCON IN HIS ZOMBIE STATE?
IT MAKES A CRAZY SORT OF SENSE... SKULL WOULD WANT ME TO KILL SAM, HOPING TO BREAK ME...
...BUT HOW CAN I KNOW FOR SURE?
ONE CHANCE...

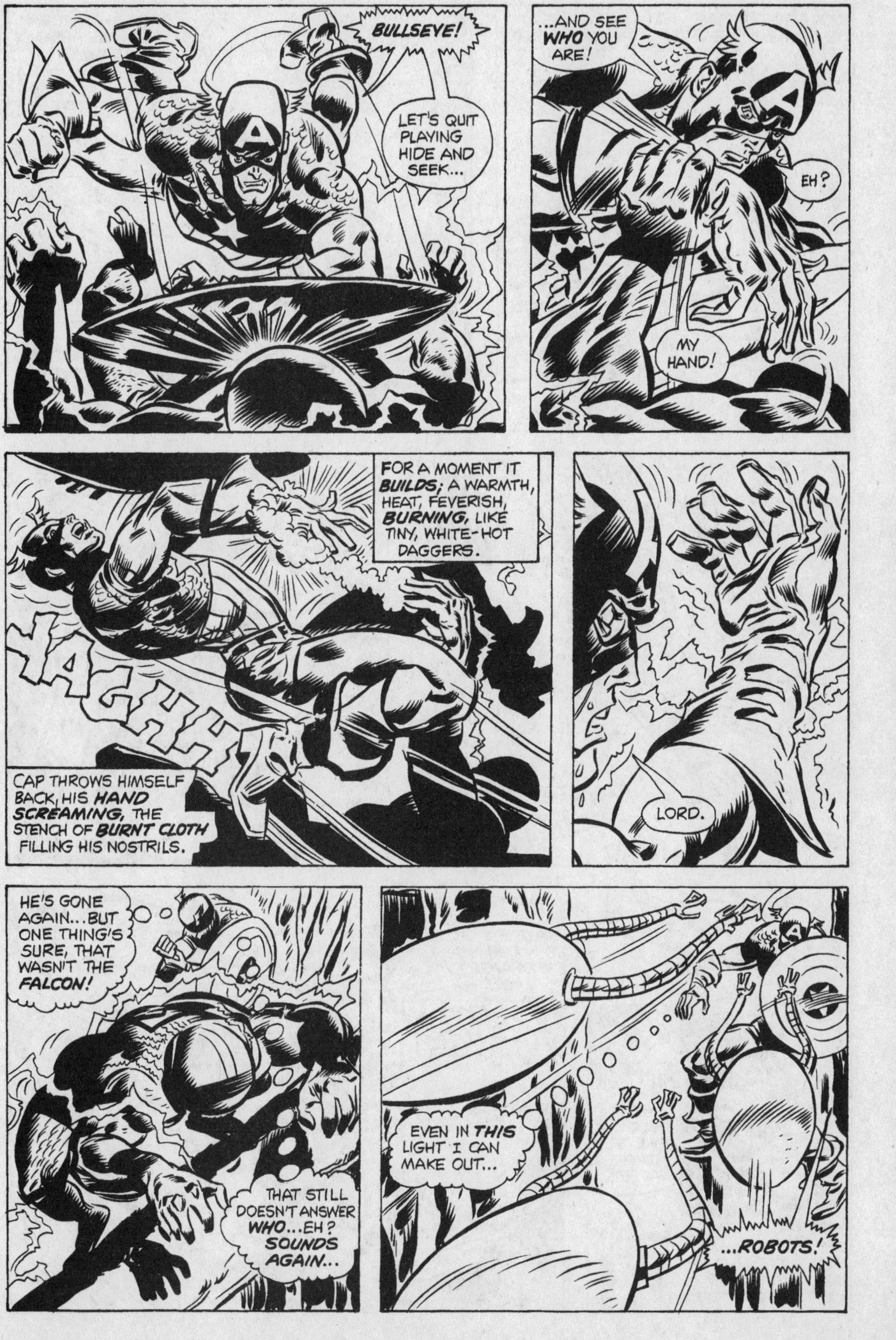
BULLSEYE!
LET'S QUIT PLAYING HIDE AND SEEK...
...AND SEE WHO YOU ARE!
EH?
MY HAND!
FOR A MOMENT IT BUILDS; A WARMTH, HEAT, FEVERISH, BURNING, LIKE TINY, WHITE-HOT DAGGERS.
YAGHH
CAP THROWS HIMSELF BACK, HIS HAND SCREAMING, THE STENCH OF BURNT CLOTH FILLING HIS NOSTRILS.
LORD.
HE'S GONE AGAIN... BUT ONE THING'S SURE, THAT WASN'T THE FALCON!
THAT STILL DOESN'T ANSWER WHO... EH? SOUNDS AGAIN...
EVEN IN THIS LIGHT I CAN MAKE OUT...
...ROBOTS!

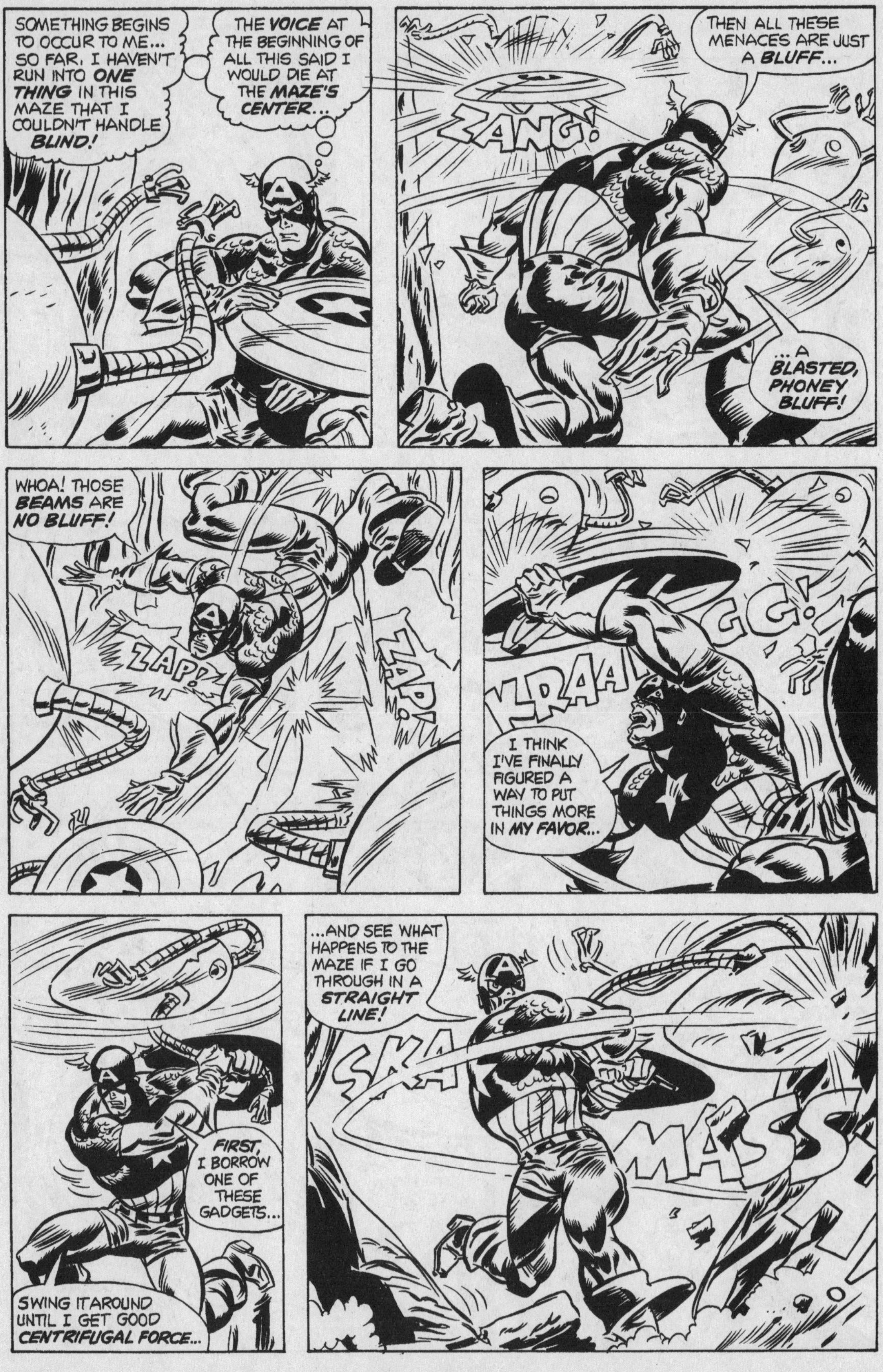
SOMETHING BEGINS TO OCCUR TO ME... SO FAR, I HAVEN'T RUN INTO ONE THING IN THIS MAZE THAT I COULDN'T HANDLE BLIND!
THE VOICE AT THE BEGINNING OF ALL THIS SAID I WOULD DIE AT THE MAZE'S CENTER...
THEN ALL THESE MENACES ARE JUST A BLUFF...
ZANG!
...A BLASTED, PHONEY BLUFF!
WHOA! THOSE BEAMS ARE NO BLUFF!
ZAP!
ZAP!
KRAAAGG!
I THINK I'VE FINALLY FIGURED A WAY TO PUT THINGS MORE IN MY FAVOR...
FIRST, I BORROW ONE OF THESE GADGETS...
SWING IT AROUND UNTIL I GET GOOD CENTRIFUGAL FORCE...
...AND SEE WHAT HAPPENS TO THE MAZE IF I GO THROUGH IN A STRAIGHT LINE!
SKA-MASS!

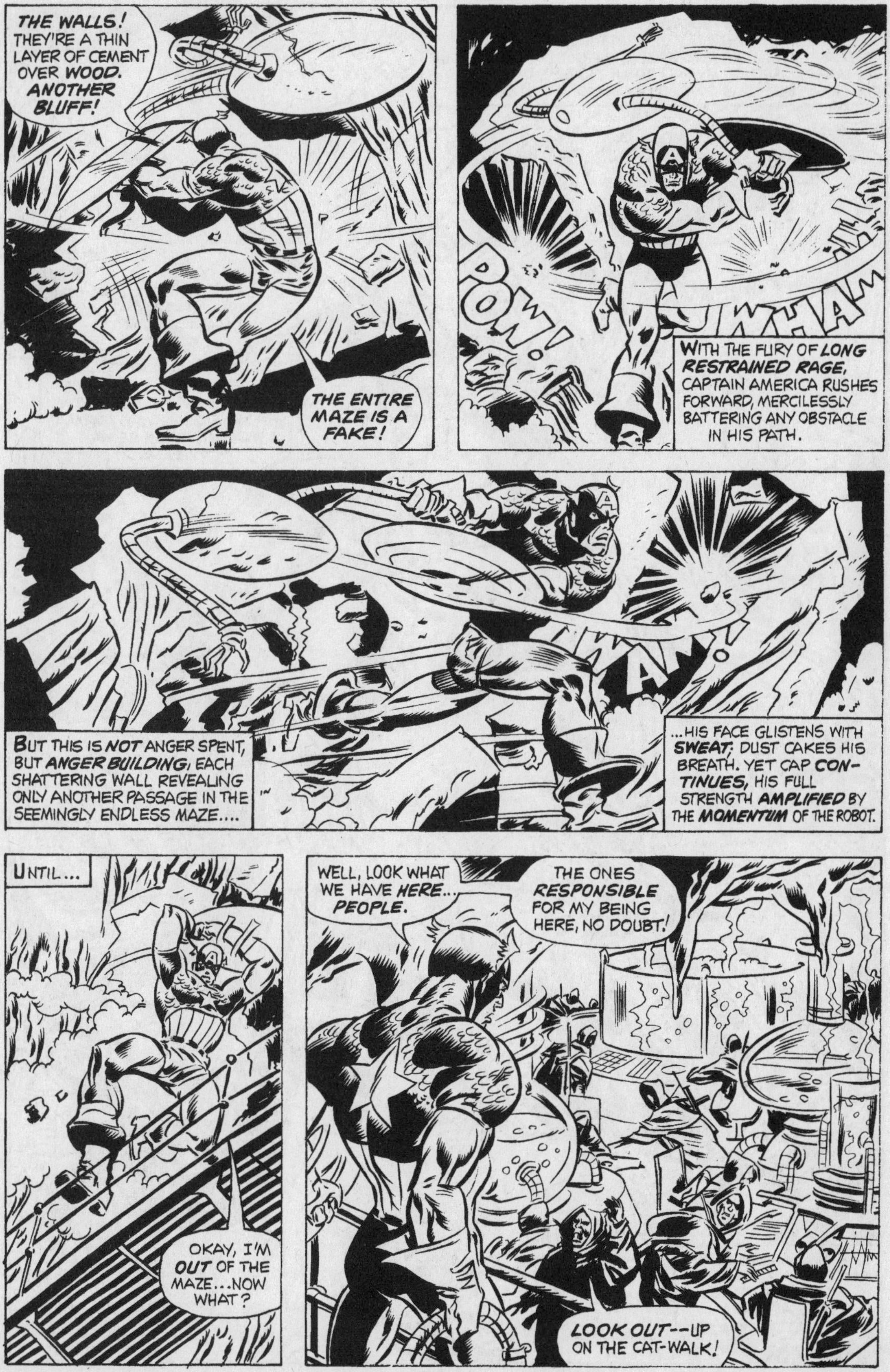
THE WALLS! THEY'RE A THIN LAYER OF CEMENT OVER WOOD. ANOTHER BLUFF!
THE ENTIRE MAZE IS A FAKE!
POW!
WHAM!
WITH THE FURY OF LONG RESTRAINED RAGE, CAPTAIN AMERICA RUSHES FORWARD, MERCILESSLY BATTERING ANY OBSTACLE IN HIS PATH.
BUT THIS IS NOT ANGER SPENT, BUT ANGER BUILDING; EACH SHATTERING WALL REVEALING ONLY ANOTHER PASSAGE IN THE SEEMINGLY ENDLESS MAZE....
WAM!
...HIS FACE GLISTENS WITH SWEAT; DUST CAKES HIS BREATH. YET CAP CONTINUES, HIS FULL STRENGTH AMPLIFIED BY THE MOMENTUM OF THE ROBOT.
UNTIL...
OKAY, I'M OUT OF THE MAZE...NOW WHAT?
WELL, LOOK WHAT WE HAVE HERE... PEOPLE.
THE ONES RESPONSIBLE FOR MY BEING HERE, NO DOUBT!
LOOK OUT--UP ON THE CAT-WALK!

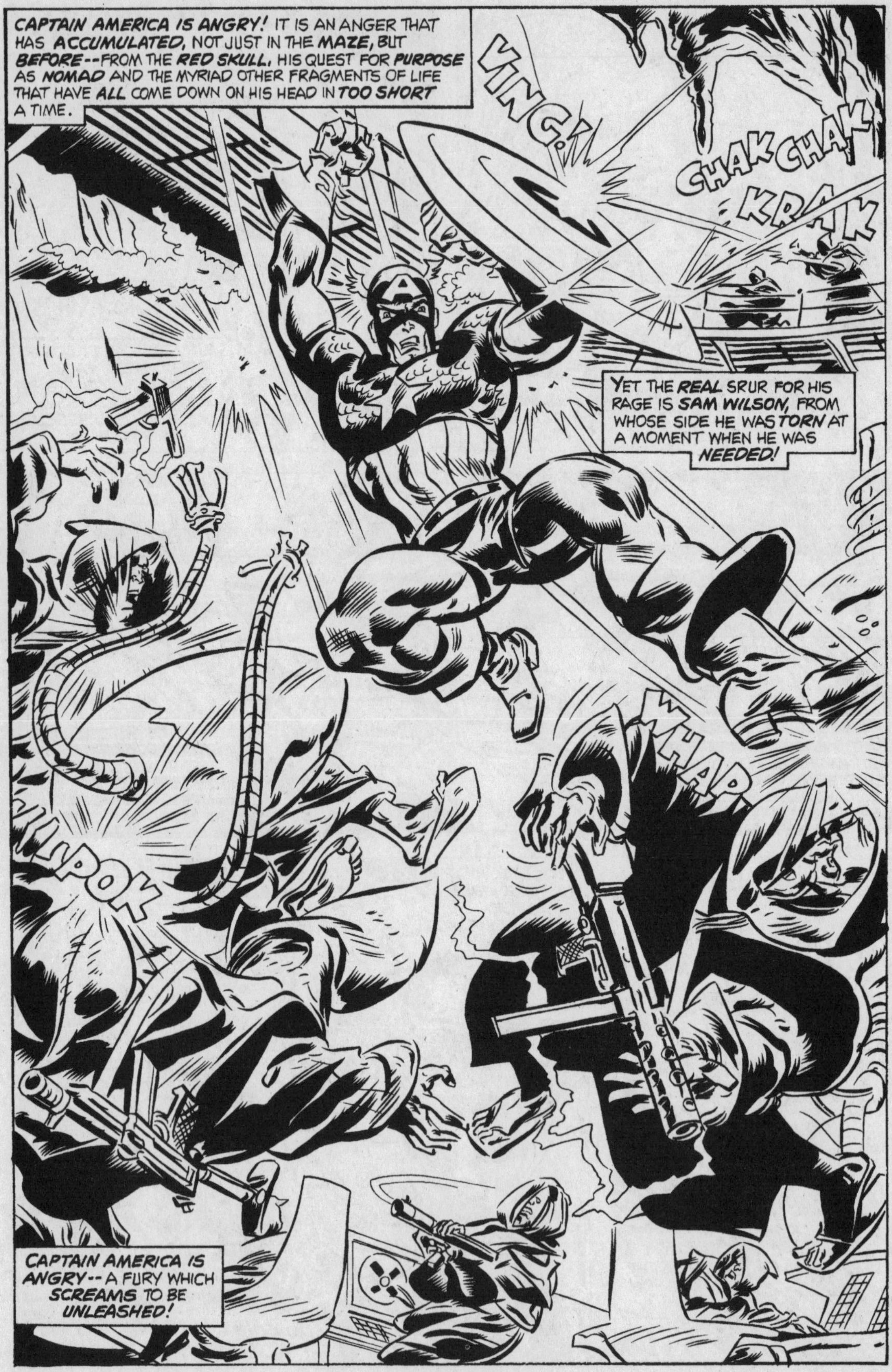
CAPTAIN AMERICA IS ANGRY! IT IS AN ANGER THAT HAS ACCUMULATED, NOT JUST IN THE MAZE, BUT BEFORE--FROM THE RED SKULL. HIS QUEST FOR PURPOSE AS NOMAD AND THE MYRIAD OTHER FRAGMENTS OF LIFE THAT HAVE ALL COME DOWN ON HIS HEAD IN TOO SHORT A TIME.
VING!
CHAKCHAK
KRAK
YET THE REAL SPUR FOR HIS RAGE IS SAM WILSON, FROM WHOSE SIDE HE WAS TORN AT A MOMENT WHEN HE WAS NEEDED!
WHAP
POK
CAPTAIN AMERICA IS ANGRY-- A FURY WHICH SCREAMS TO BE UNLEASHED!

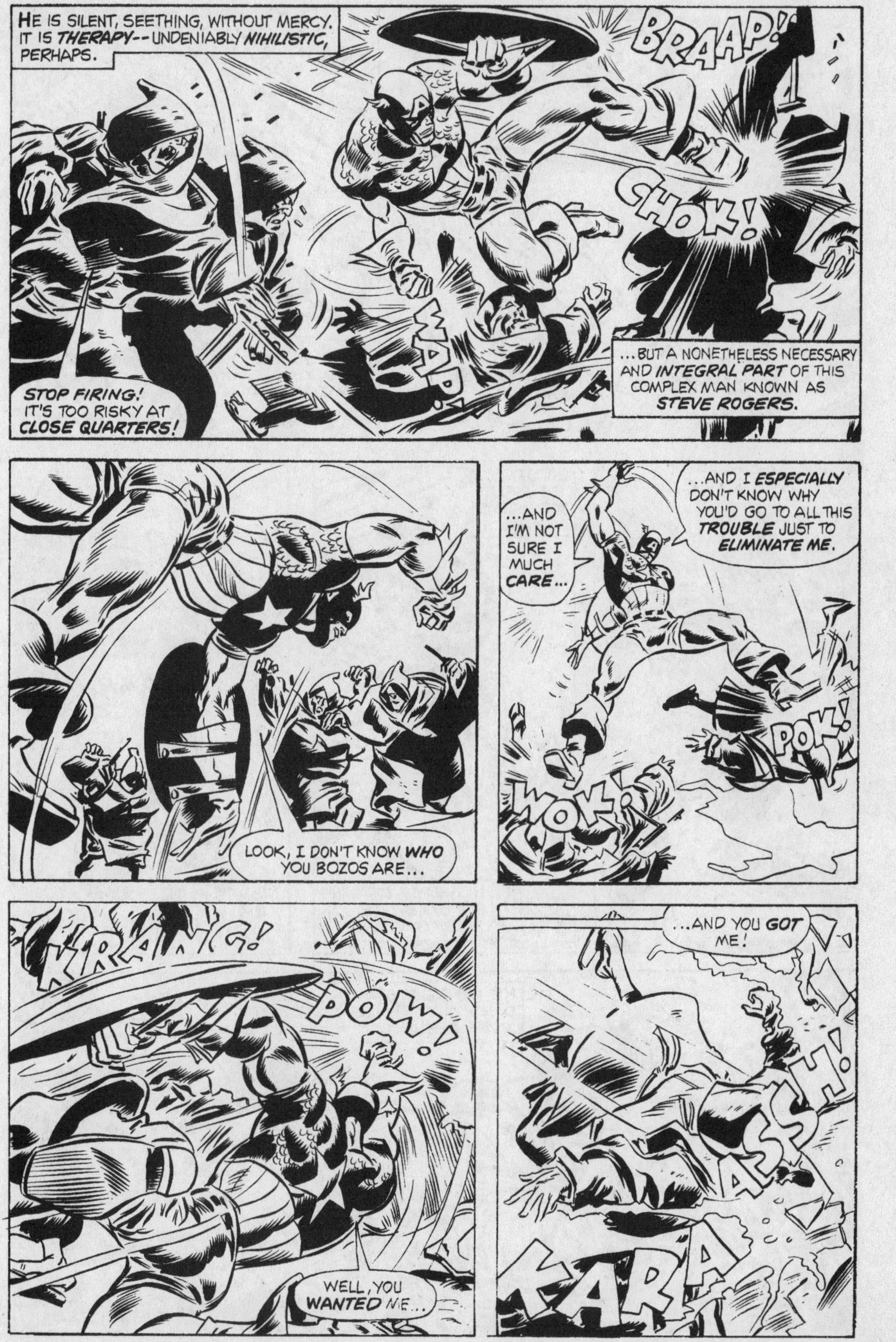
HE IS SILENT, SEETHING, WITHOUT MERCY. IT IS THERAPY-- UNDENIABLY NIHILISTIC, PERHAPS.
BRAAP!
CHOK!
WAP!
STOP FIRING! IT'S TOO RISKY AT CLOSE QUARTERS!
...BUT A NONETHELESS NECESSARY AND INTEGRAL PART OF THIS COMPLEX MAN KNOWN AS STEVE ROGERS.
LOOK, I DON'T KNOW WHO YOU BOZOS ARE...
...AND I ESPECIALLY DON'T KNOW WHY YOU'D GO TO ALL THIS TROUBLE JUST TO ELIMINATE ME.
...AND I'M NOT SURE I MUCH CARE...
POK!
WOK!
KRANG!
POW!
WELL, YOU WANTED ME...
...AND YOU GOT ME!
KRASSH!
KARA

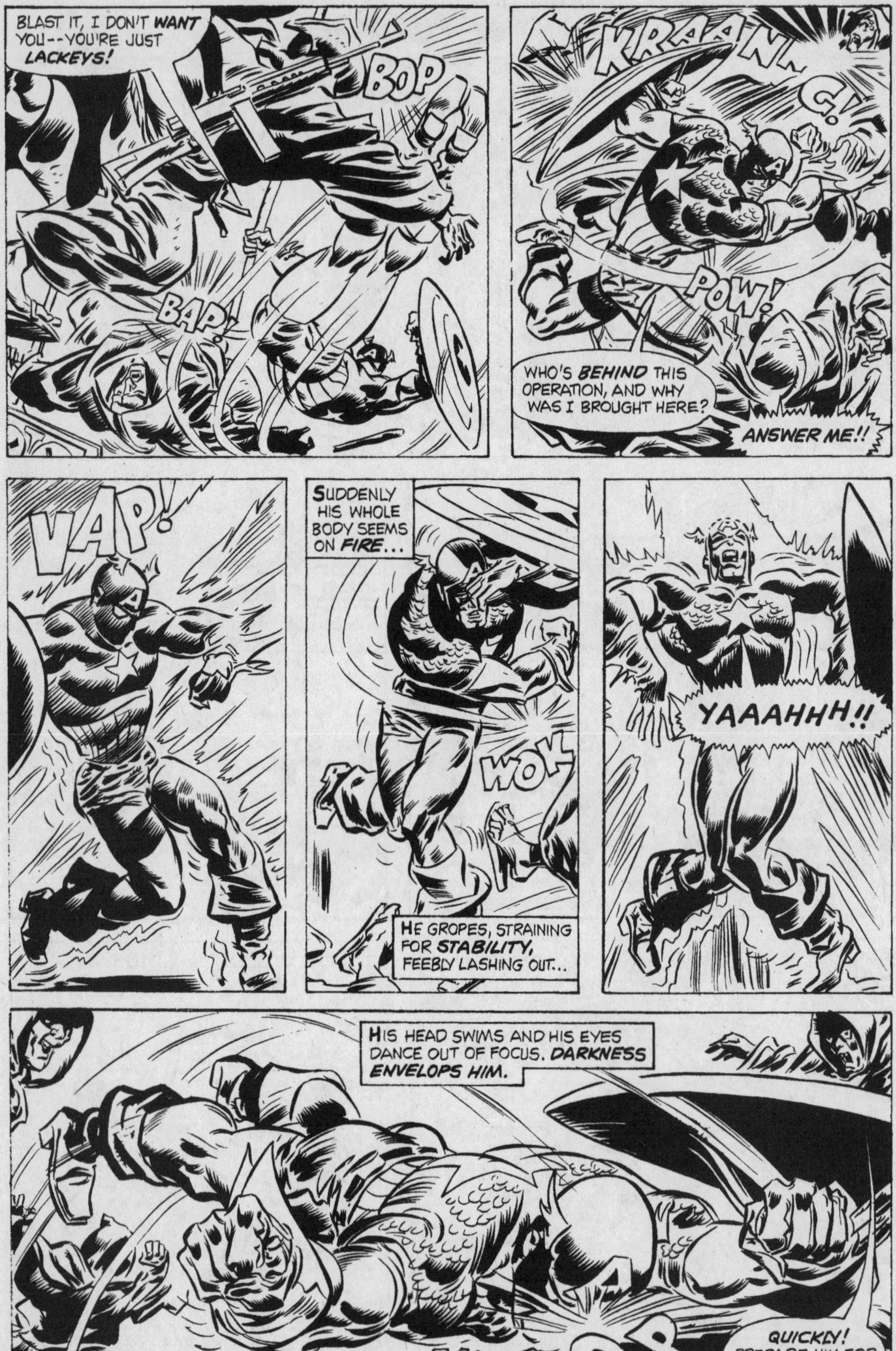
BLAST IT, I DON'T WANT YOU--YOU'RE JUST LACKEYS!
BOP
BAP
KRAANNG!
POW!
WHO'S BEHIND THIS OPERATION, AND WHY WAS I BROUGHT HERE?
ANSWER ME!!
VAP!
SUDDENLY HIS WHOLE BODY SEEMS ON FIRE...
WOK
HE GROPES, STRAINING FOR STABILITY, FEEBLY LASHING OUT...
YAAAHHH!!
HIS HEAD SWIMS AND HIS EYES DANCE OUT OF FOCUS. DARKNESS ENVELOPS HIM.
WHOP
QUICKLY! PREPARE HIM FOR THE MASTER!

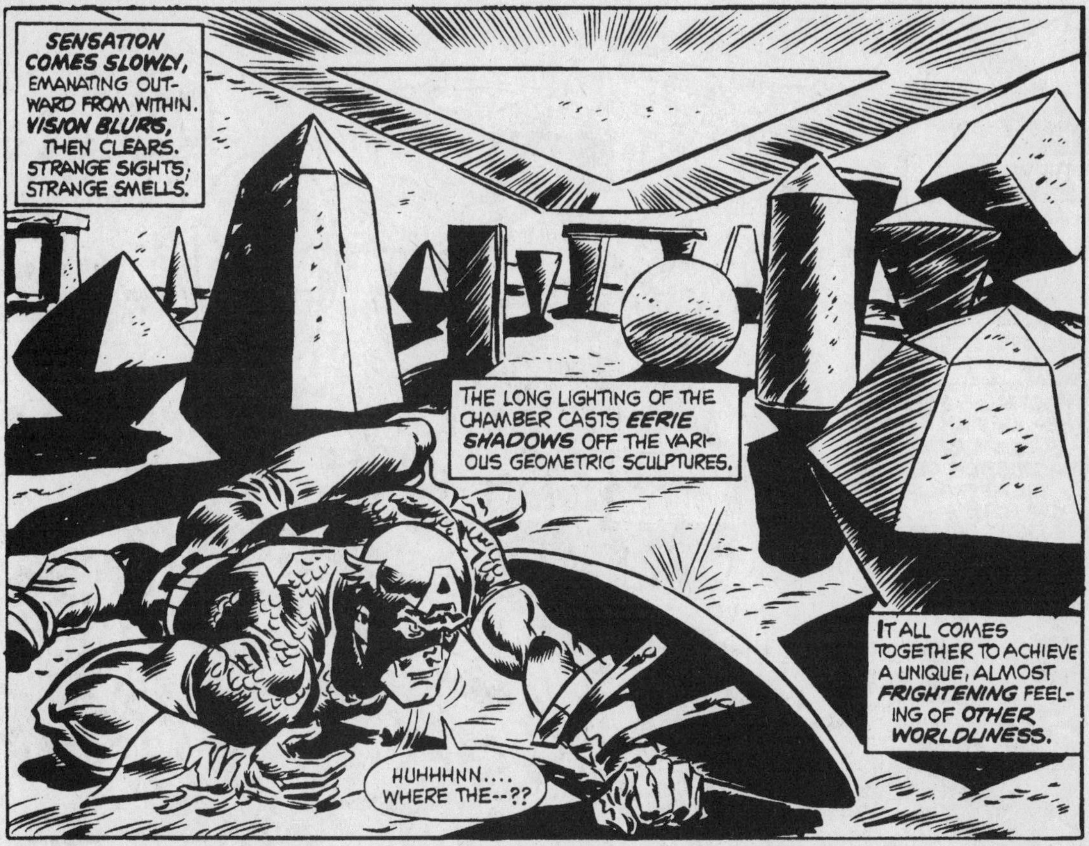
SENSATION COMES SLOWLY, EMANATING OUTWARD FROM WITHIN. VISION BLURS, THEN CLEARS. STRANGE SIGHTS; STRANGE SMELLS.
THE LONG LIGHTING OF THE CHAMBER CASTS EERIE SHADOWS OFF THE VARIOUS GEOMETRIC SCULPTURES.
IT ALL COMES TOGETHER TO ACHIEVE A UNIQUE, ALMOST FRIGHTENING FEELING OF OTHER WORLDLINESS.
HUHHHNN.... WHERE THE--??

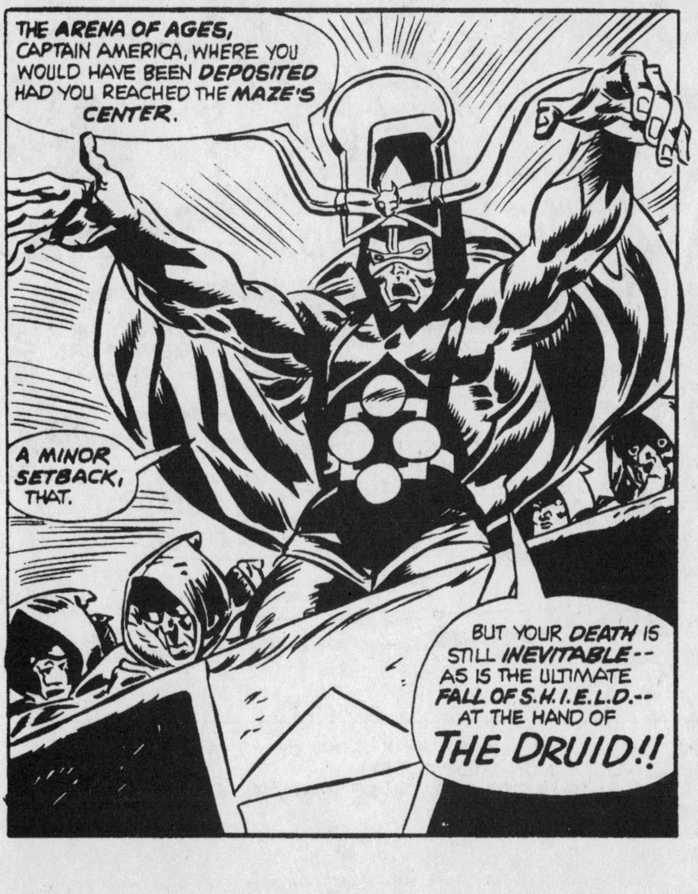
THE ARENA OF AGES, CAPTAIN AMERICA, WHERE YOU WOULD HAVE BEEN DEPOSITED HAD YOU REACHED THE MAZE'S CENTER.
A MINOR SETBACK, THAT.
BUT YOUR DEATH IS STILL INEVITABLE-- AS IS THE ULTIMATE FALL OF S.H.I.E.L.D.-- AT THE HAND OF THE DRUID!!

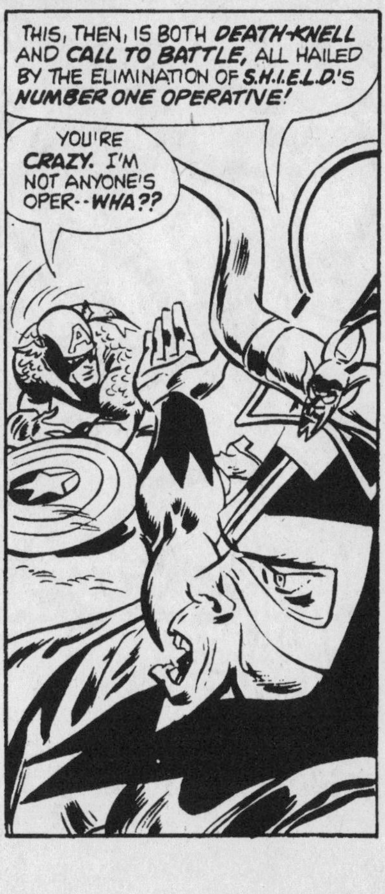
THIS, THEN, IS BOTH DEATH-KNELL AND CALL TO BATTLE, ALL HAILED BY THE ELIMINATION OF S.H.I.E.L.D.'S NUMBER ONE OPERATIVE!
YOU'RE CRAZY. I'M NOT ANYONE'S OPER--WHA??

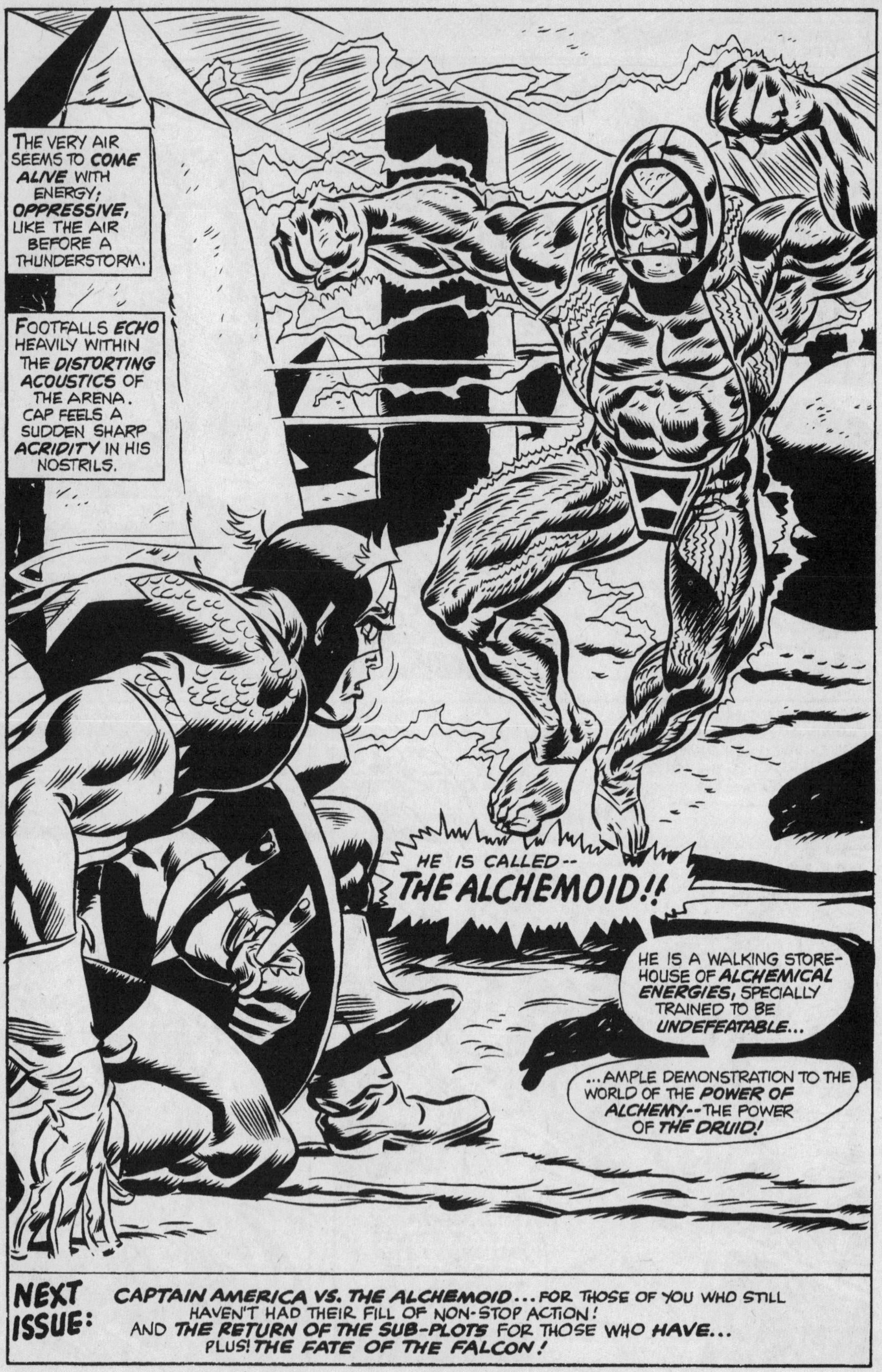
THE VERY AIR SEEMS TO COME ALIVE WITH ENERGY; OPPRESSIVE, LIKE THE AIR BEFORE A THUNDERSTORM.
FOOTFALLS ECHO HEAVILY WITHIN THE DISTORTING ACOUSTICS OF THE ARENA. CAP FEELS A SUDDEN SHARP ACRIDITY IN HIS NOSTRILS.
HE IS CALLED-- THE ALCHEMOID!!
HE IS A WALKING STORE-HOUSE OF ALCHEMICAL ENERGIES, SPECIALLY TRAINED TO BE UNDEFEATABLE...
...AMPLE DEMONSTRATION TO THE WORLD OF THE POWER OF ALCHEMY--THE POWER OF THE DRUID!

NEXT ISSUE: **CAPTAIN AMERICA VS. THE ALCHEMOID**... FOR THOSE OF YOU WHO STILL HAVEN'T HAD THEIR FILL OF NON-STOP ACTION! AND **THE RETURN OF THE SUB-PLOTS** FOR THOSE WHO **HAVE**... PLUS! **THE FATE OF THE FALCON!**

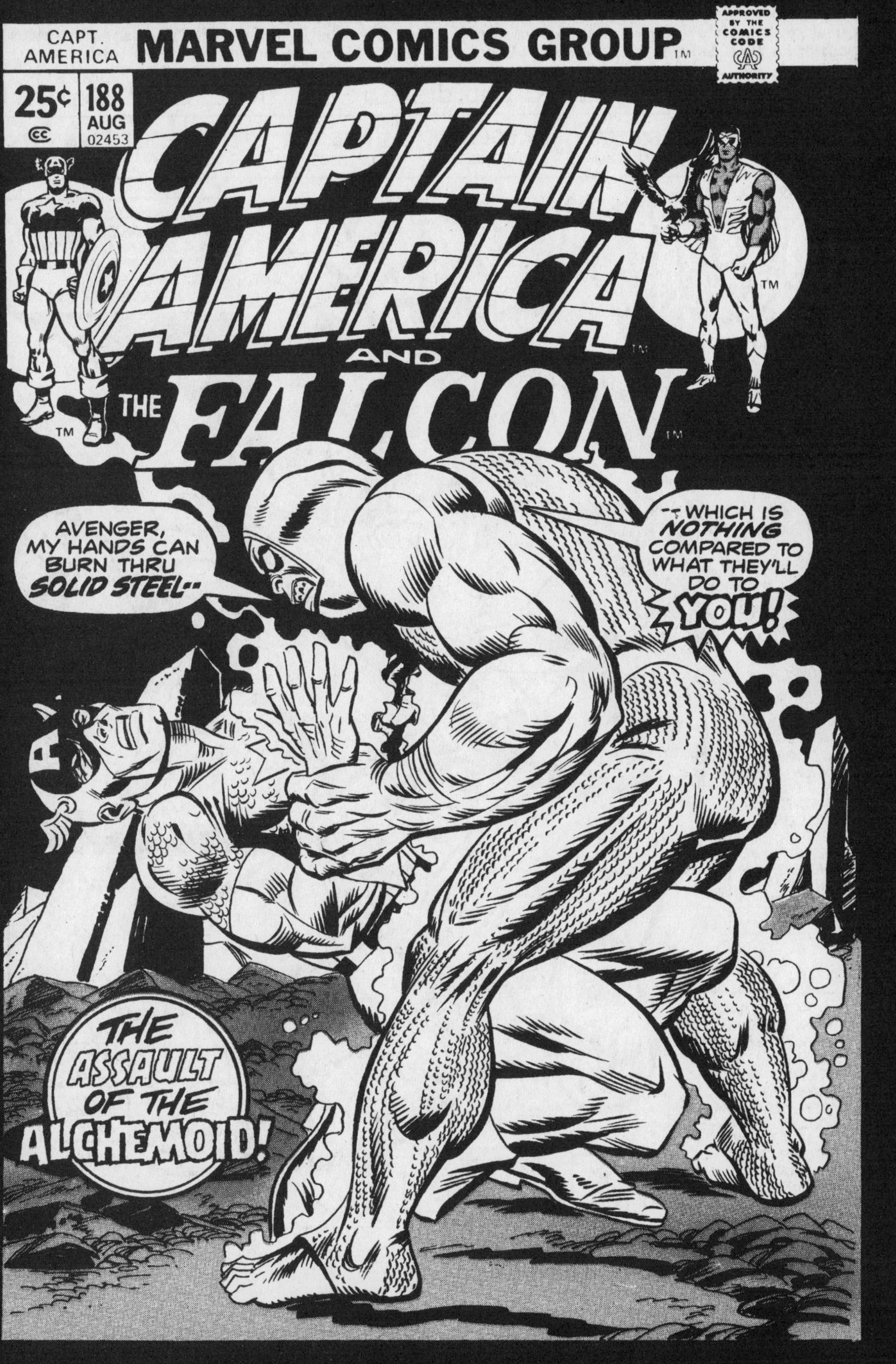
CAPT. AMERICA
MARVEL COMICS GROUP
APPROVED BY THE COMICS CODE AUTHORITY
25¢
188
AUG
02453
CAPTAIN AMERICA AND THE FALCON
AVENGER, MY HANDS CAN BURN THRU SOLID STEEL--
--WHICH IS NOTHING COMPARED TO WHAT THEY'LL DO TO YOU!
THE ASSAULT OF THE ALCHEMOID!

1941! The world at war! And in a full-security laboratory, frail *Steve Rogers* became *Captain America*, the American *super-soldier!* For four thrilling years, he struck back at the Axis' treacherous attack— until a freak stroke of fate threw him into *suspended animation*... to awaken in the *mid-1960's*, a man *twenty years out of his time.* Since that day, *Captain America* has sought his destiny in this *brave new world.*

Stan Lee PRESENTS: CAPTAIN AMERICA AND THE FALCON™

JOHN WARNER • SAL BUSCEMA • V. COLLETTA • I. WATANABE • DON WARFIELD & LEN WEIN
WRITER • BREAKDOWNS • FINISHED ART • LETTERER • COLORIST • EDITOR

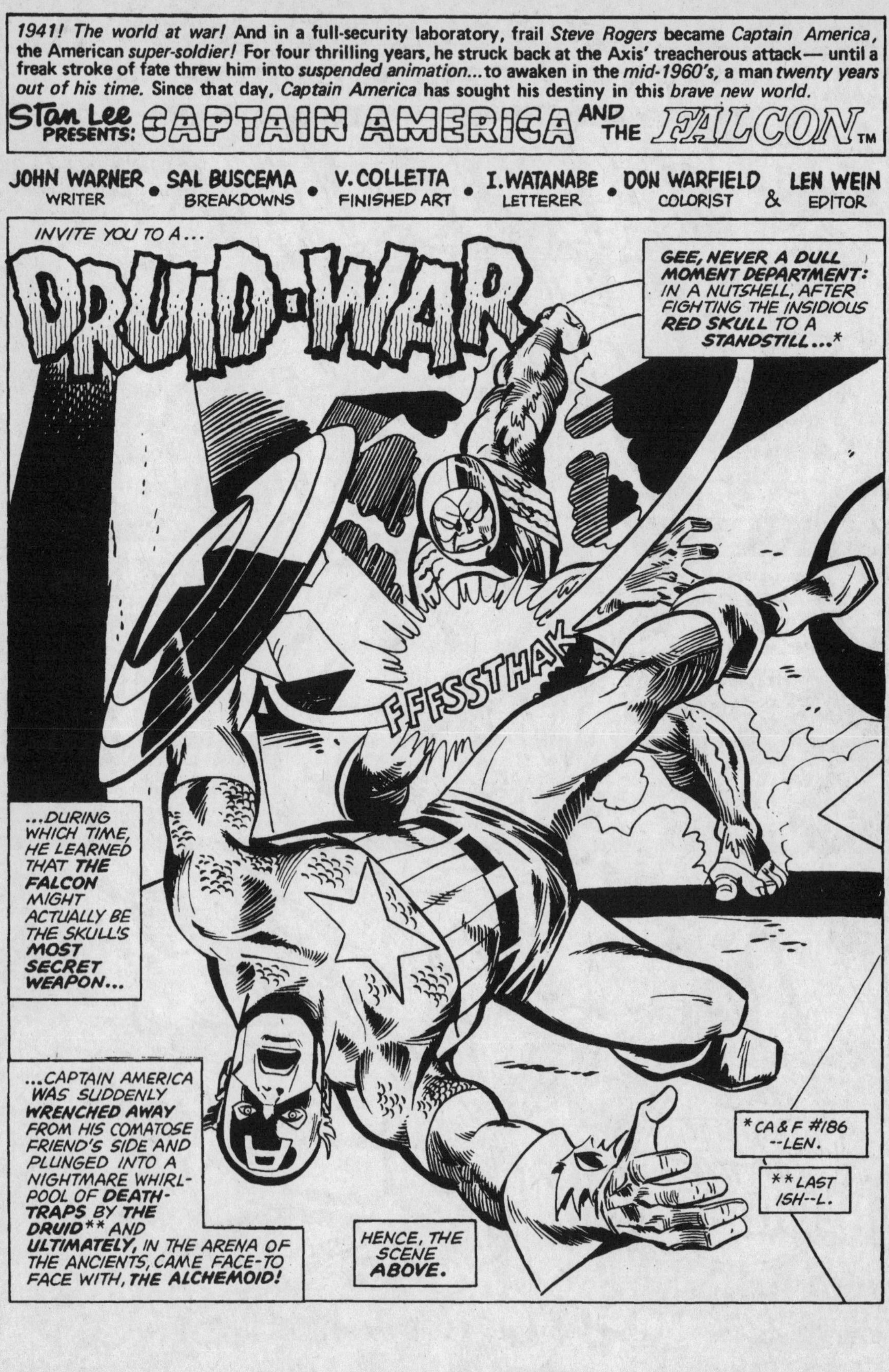
INVITE YOU TO A...
DRUID-WAR
GEE, NEVER A DULL MOMENT DEPARTMENT: IN A NUTSHELL, AFTER FIGHTING THE INSIDIOUS RED SKULL TO A STANDSTILL...*
FFFSSTHAK
...DURING WHICH TIME, HE LEARNED THAT THE FALCON MIGHT ACTUALLY BE THE SKULL'S MOST SECRET WEAPON...
...CAPTAIN AMERICA WAS SUDDENLY WRENCHED AWAY FROM HIS COMATOSE FRIEND'S SIDE AND PLUNGED INTO A NIGHTMARE WHIRL-POOL OF DEATH-TRAPS BY THE DRUID** AND ULTIMATELY, IN THE ARENA OF THE ANCIENTS, CAME FACE-TO FACE WITH, THE ALCHEMOID!
HENCE, THE SCENE ABOVE.
*CA&F #186 --LEN.
**LAST ISH--L.

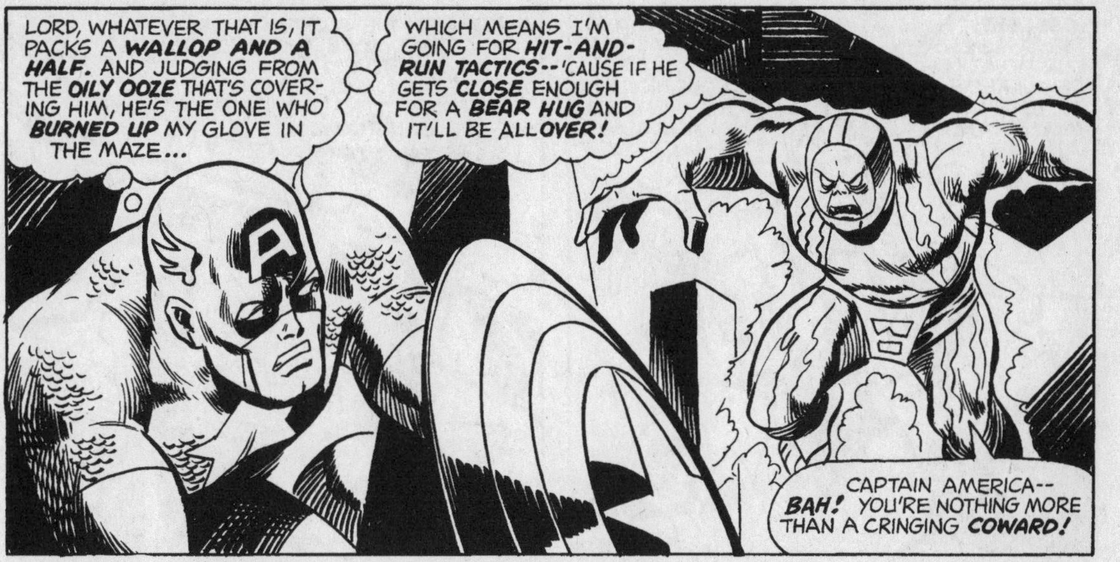
LORD, WHATEVER THAT IS, IT PACKS A **WALLOP AND A HALF.** AND JUDGING FROM THE **OILY OOZE** THAT'S COVERING HIM, HE'S THE ONE WHO **BURNED UP** MY GLOVE IN THE MAZE...
WHICH MEANS I'M GOING FOR **HIT-AND-RUN TACTICS**--'CAUSE IF HE GETS **CLOSE** ENOUGH FOR A **BEAR HUG** AND IT'LL BE ALL **OVER!**
CAPTAIN AMERICA-- **BAH!** YOU'RE NOTHING MORE THAN A CRINGING **COWARD!**

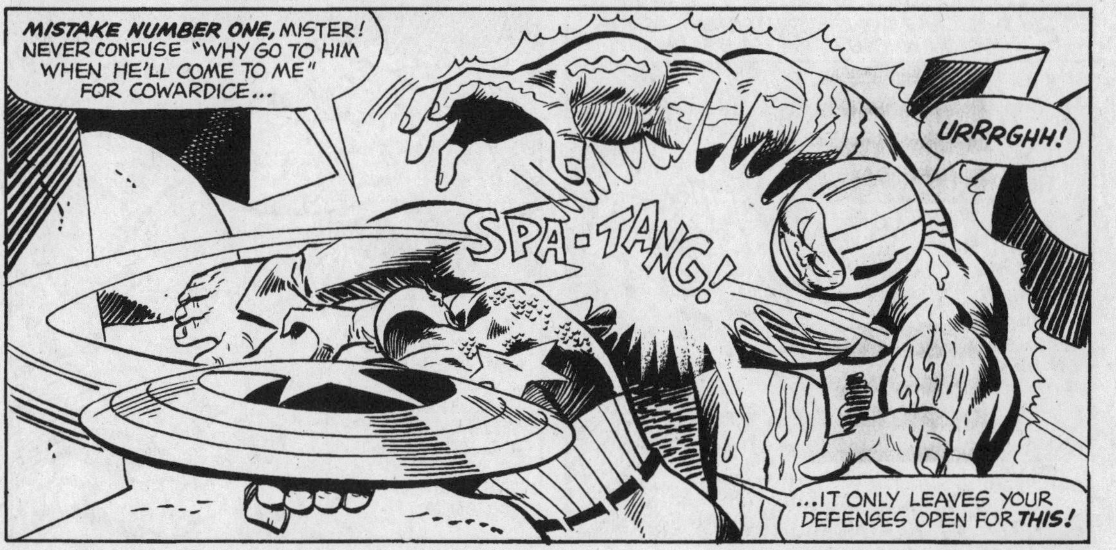
MISTAKE NUMBER ONE, MISTER! NEVER CONFUSE "WHY GO TO HIM WHEN HE'LL COME TO ME" FOR COWARDICE...
URRRGHH!
SPA-TANG!
...IT ONLY LEAVES YOUR DEFENSES OPEN FOR **THIS!**

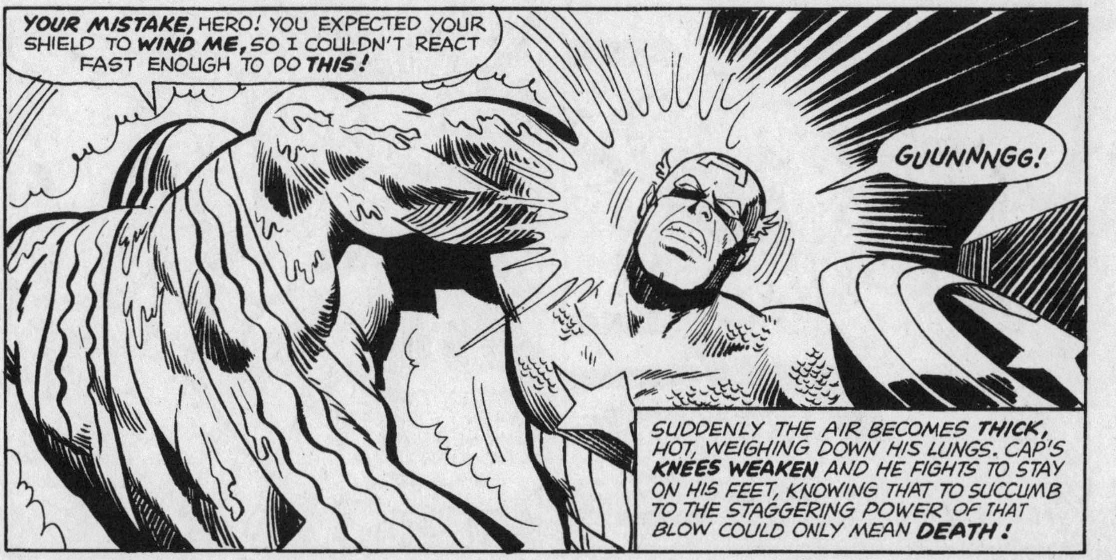
YOUR MISTAKE, HERO! YOU EXPECTED YOUR SHIELD TO **WIND ME,** SO I COULDN'T REACT FAST ENOUGH TO DO **THIS!**
GUUNNNGG!
SUDDENLY THE AIR BECOMES **THICK,** HOT, WEIGHING DOWN HIS LUNGS. CAP'S **KNEES WEAKEN** AND HE FIGHTS TO STAY ON HIS FEET, KNOWING THAT TO SUCCUMB TO THE STAGGERING POWER OF THAT BLOW COULD ONLY MEAN **DEATH!**

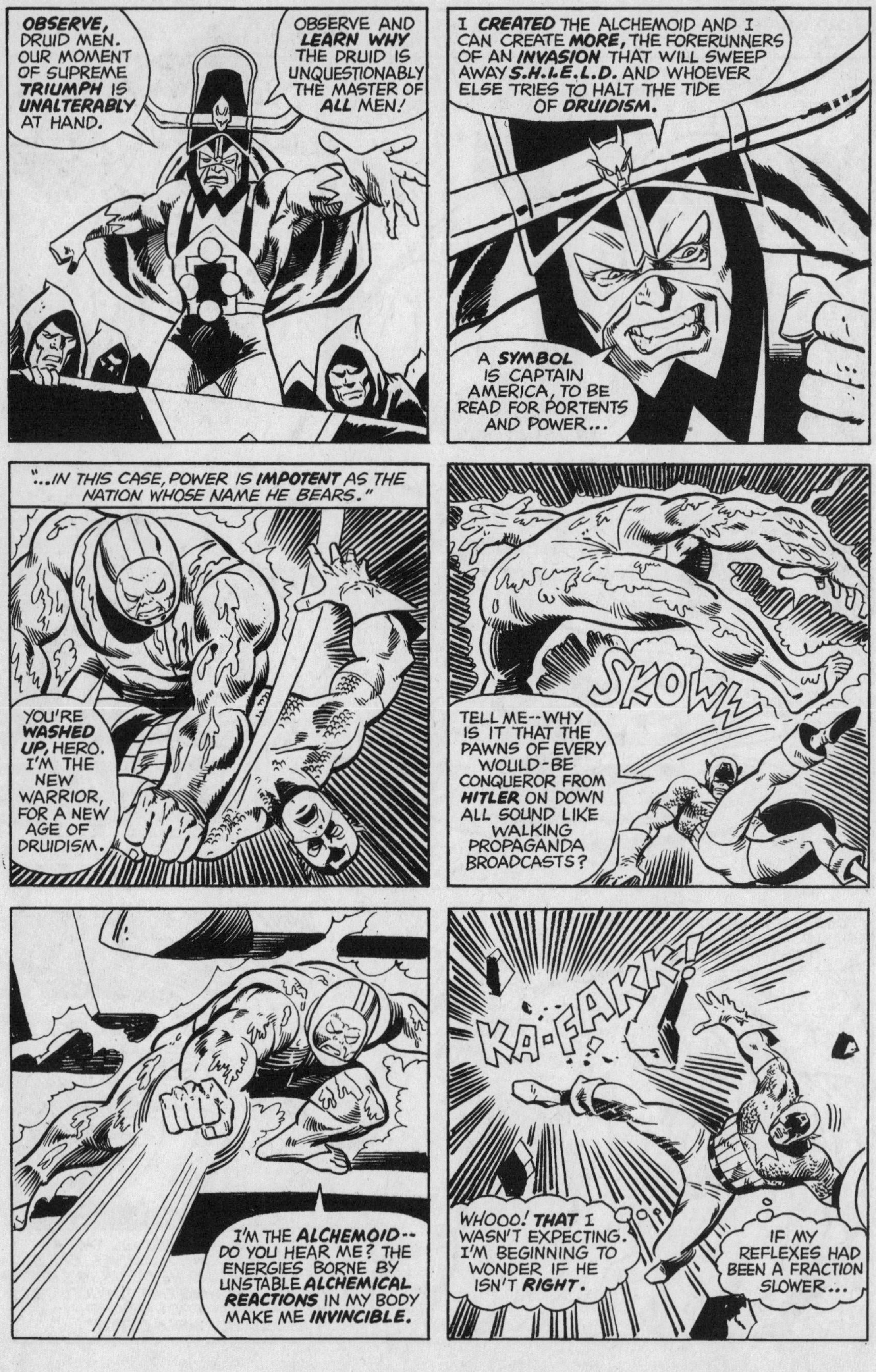
OBSERVE, DRUID MEN. OUR MOMENT OF SUPREME TRIUMPH IS UNALTERABLY AT HAND.
OBSERVE AND LEARN WHY THE DRUID IS UNQUESTIONABLY THE MASTER OF ALL MEN!
I CREATED THE ALCHEMOID AND I CAN CREATE MORE, THE FORERUNNERS OF AN INVASION THAT WILL SWEEP AWAY S.H.I.E.L.D. AND WHOEVER ELSE TRIES TO HALT THE TIDE OF DRUIDISM.
A SYMBOL IS CAPTAIN AMERICA, TO BE READ FOR PORTENTS AND POWER...
"...IN THIS CASE, POWER IS IMPOTENT AS THE NATION WHOSE NAME HE BEARS."
YOU'RE WASHED UP, HERO. I'M THE NEW WARRIOR, FOR A NEW AGE OF DRUIDISM.
SKOWW
TELL ME--WHY IS IT THAT THE PAWNS OF EVERY WOULD-BE CONQUEROR FROM HITLER ON DOWN ALL SOUND LIKE WALKING PROPAGANDA BROADCASTS?
I'M THE ALCHEMOID--DO YOU HEAR ME? THE ENERGIES BORNE BY UNSTABLE ALCHEMICAL REACTIONS IN MY BODY MAKE ME INVINCIBLE.
KA-FAKK!
WHOOO! THAT I WASN'T EXPECTING. I'M BEGINNING TO WONDER IF HE ISN'T RIGHT.
IF MY REFLEXES HAD BEEN A FRACTION SLOWER...

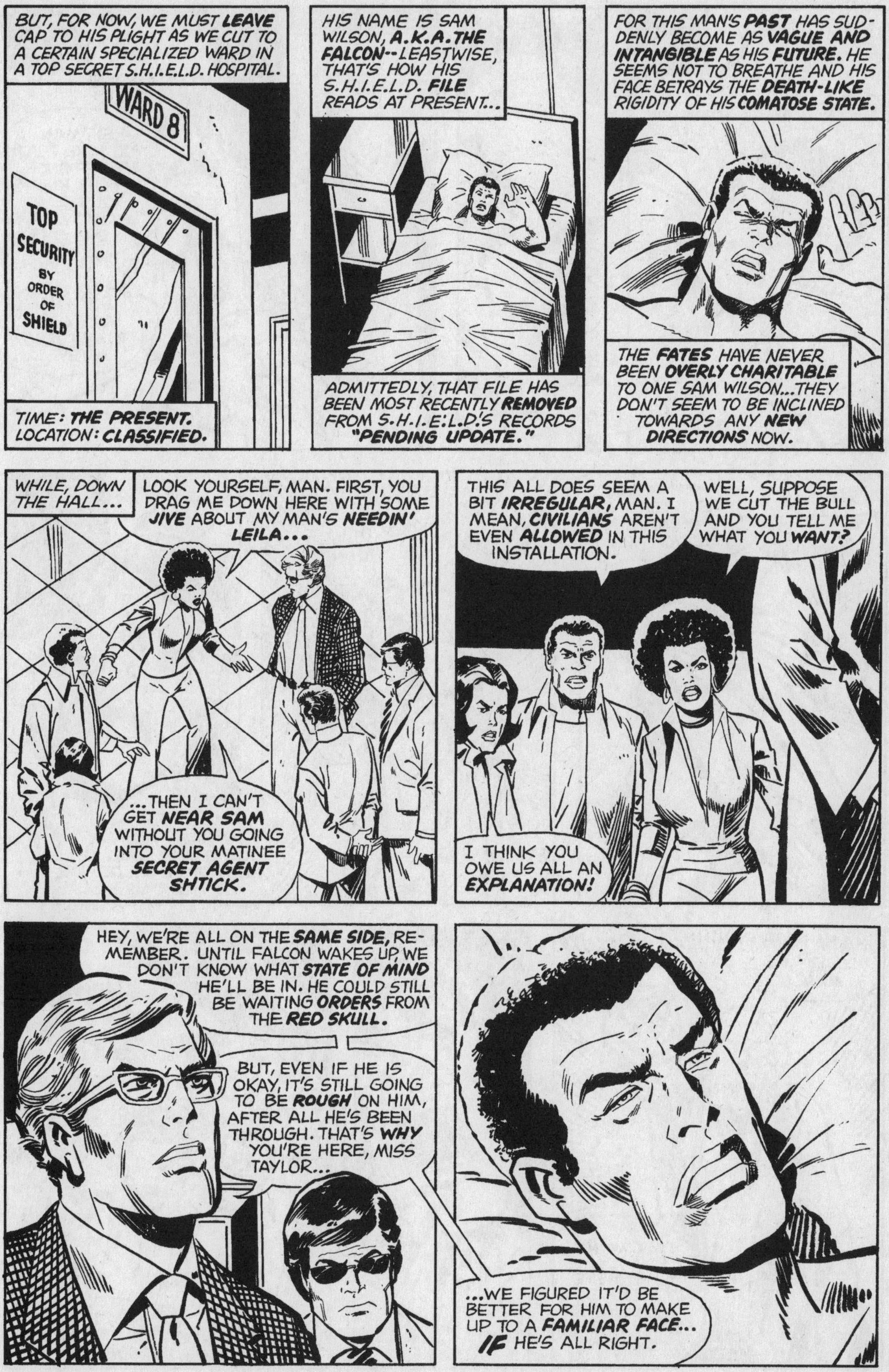
BUT, FOR NOW, WE MUST LEAVE CAP TO HIS PLIGHT AS WE CUT TO A CERTAIN SPECIALIZED WARD IN A TOP SECRET S.H.I.E.L.D. HOSPITAL.
WARD 8
TOP SECURITY BY ORDER OF SHIELD
TIME: THE PRESENT. LOCATION: CLASSIFIED.
HIS NAME IS SAM WILSON, A.K.A. THE FALCON--LEASTWISE, THAT'S HOW HIS S.H.I.E.L.D. FILE READS AT PRESENT...
ADMITTEDLY, THAT FILE HAS BEEN MOST RECENTLY REMOVED FROM S.H.I.E.L.D.'S RECORDS "PENDING UPDATE."
FOR THIS MAN'S PAST HAS SUDDENLY BECOME AS VAGUE AND INTANGIBLE AS HIS FUTURE. HE SEEMS NOT TO BREATHE AND HIS FACE BETRAYS THE DEATH-LIKE RIGIDITY OF HIS COMATOSE STATE.
THE FATES HAVE NEVER BEEN OVERLY CHARITABLE TO ONE SAM WILSON...THEY DON'T SEEM TO BE INCLINED TOWARDS ANY NEW DIRECTIONS NOW.
WHILE, DOWN THE HALL...
LOOK YOURSELF, MAN. FIRST, YOU DRAG ME DOWN HERE WITH SOME JIVE ABOUT MY MAN'S NEEDIN' LEILA...
...THEN I CAN'T GET NEAR SAM WITHOUT YOU GOING INTO YOUR MATINEE SECRET AGENT SHTICK.
THIS ALL DOES SEEM A BIT IRREGULAR, MAN. I MEAN, CIVILIANS AREN'T EVEN ALLOWED IN THIS INSTALLATION.
WELL, SUPPOSE WE CUT THE BULL AND YOU TELL ME WHAT YOU WANT?
I THINK YOU OWE US ALL AN EXPLANATION!
HEY, WE'RE ALL ON THE SAME SIDE, REMEMBER. UNTIL FALCON WAKES UP, WE DON'T KNOW WHAT STATE OF MIND HE'LL BE IN. HE COULD STILL BE WAITING ORDERS FROM THE RED SKULL.
BUT, EVEN IF HE IS OKAY, IT'S STILL GOING TO BE ROUGH ON HIM, AFTER ALL HE'S BEEN THROUGH. THAT'S WHY YOU'RE HERE, MISS TAYLOR...
...WE FIGURED IT'D BE BETTER FOR HIM TO MAKE UP TO A FAMILIAR FACE... IF HE'S ALL RIGHT.

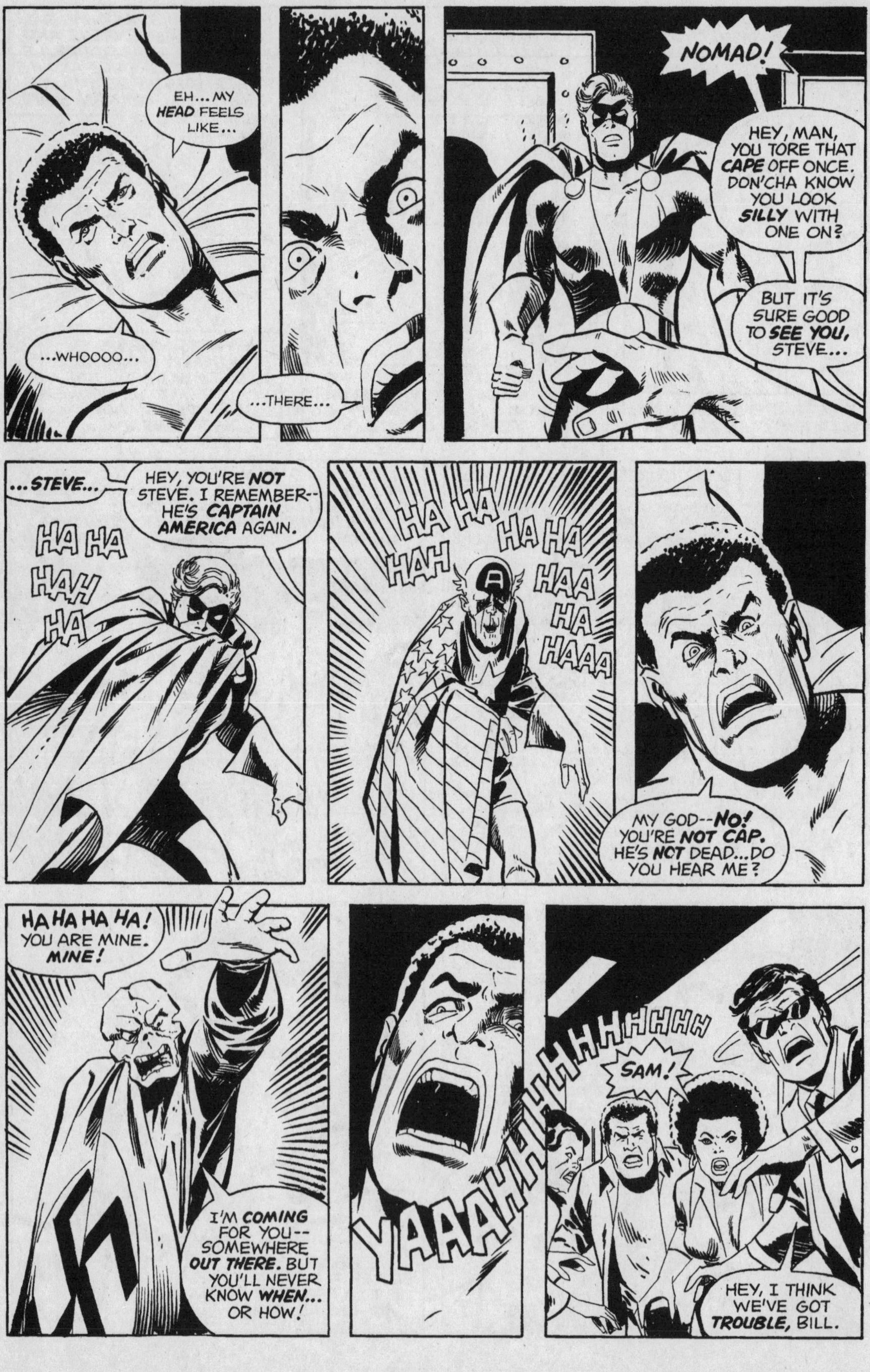
EH... MY HEAD FEELS LIKE...
...WHOOOO...
...THERE...
NOMAD!
HEY, MAN, YOU TORE THAT CAPE OFF ONCE. DON'CHA KNOW YOU LOOK SILLY WITH ONE ON?
BUT IT'S SURE GOOD TO SEE YOU, STEVE...
...STEVE...
HEY, YOU'RE NOT STEVE. I REMEMBER-- HE'S CAPTAIN AMERICA AGAIN.
HA HA HAH HA
HA HA HAH HA HA HAA HA HAAA
MY GOD--NO! YOU'RE NOT CAP. HE'S NOT DEAD...DO YOU HEAR ME?
HA HA HA HA! YOU ARE MINE. MINE!
I'M COMING FOR YOU-- SOMEWHERE OUT THERE. BUT YOU'LL NEVER KNOW WHEN... OR HOW!
YAAAHHHHHHHHHHHHH
SAM!
HEY, I THINK WE'VE GOT TROUBLE, BILL.

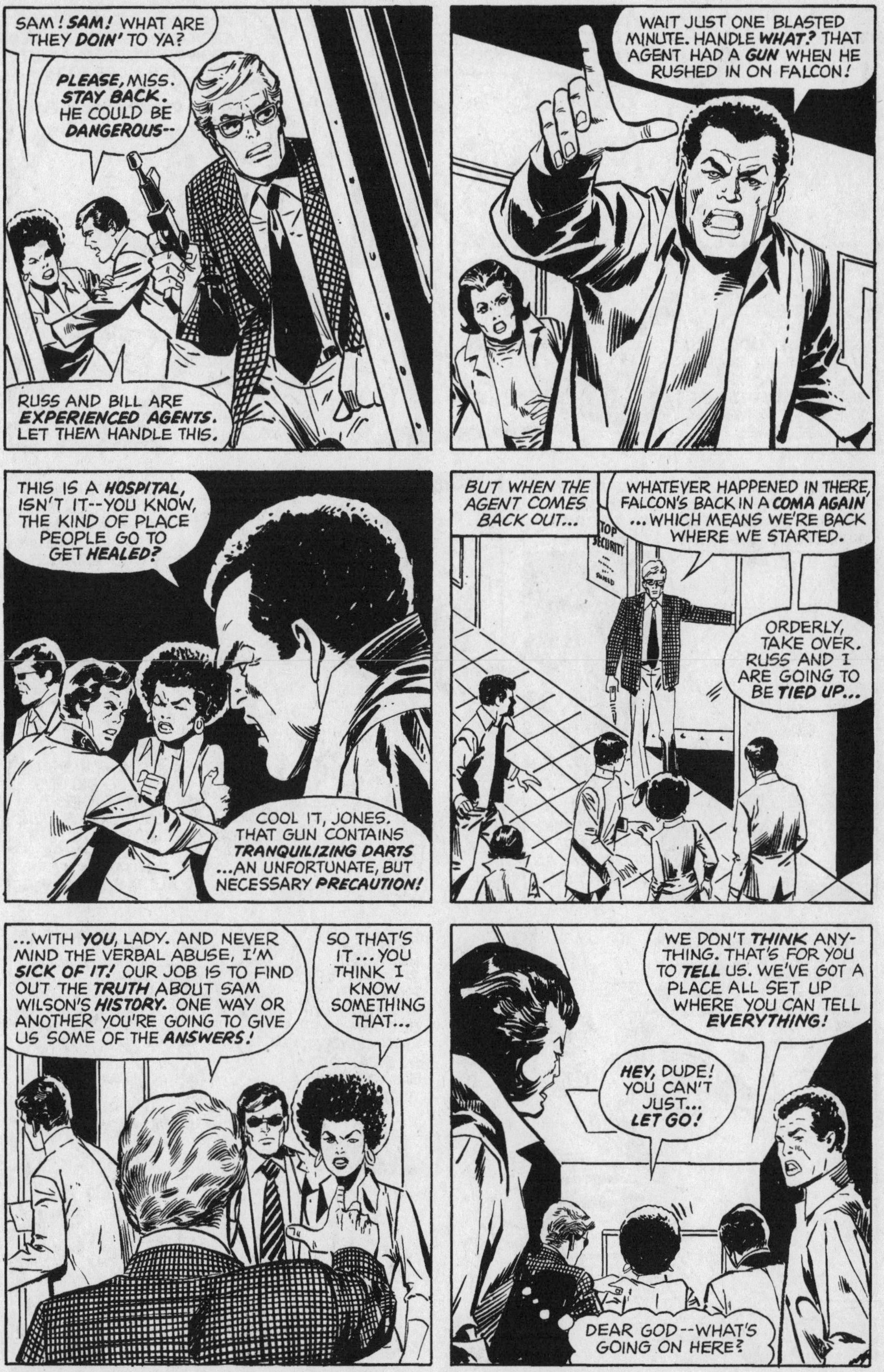
SAM! SAM! WHAT ARE THEY DOIN' TO YA?
PLEASE, MISS. STAY BACK. HE COULD BE DANGEROUS--
RUSS AND BILL ARE EXPERIENCED AGENTS. LET THEM HANDLE THIS.
WAIT JUST ONE BLASTED MINUTE. HANDLE WHAT? THAT AGENT HAD A GUN WHEN HE RUSHED IN ON FALCON!
THIS IS A HOSPITAL, ISN'T IT--YOU KNOW, THE KIND OF PLACE PEOPLE GO TO GET HEALED?
COOL IT, JONES. THAT GUN CONTAINS TRANQUILIZING DARTS ...AN UNFORTUNATE, BUT NECESSARY PRECAUTION!
BUT WHEN THE AGENT COMES BACK OUT...
WHATEVER HAPPENED IN THERE, FALCON'S BACK IN A COMA AGAIN ...WHICH MEANS WE'RE BACK WHERE WE STARTED.
TOP SECURITY
ORDERLY, TAKE OVER. RUSS AND I ARE GOING TO BE TIED UP...
...WITH YOU, LADY. AND NEVER MIND THE VERBAL ABUSE, I'M SICK OF IT! OUR JOB IS TO FIND OUT THE TRUTH ABOUT SAM WILSON'S HISTORY. ONE WAY OR ANOTHER YOU'RE GOING TO GIVE US SOME OF THE ANSWERS!
SO THAT'S IT...YOU THINK I KNOW SOMETHING THAT...
WE DON'T THINK ANYTHING. THAT'S FOR YOU TO TELL US. WE'VE GOT A PLACE ALL SET UP WHERE YOU CAN TELL EVERYTHING!
HEY, DUDE! YOU CAN'T JUST... LET GO!
DEAR GOD--WHAT'S GOING ON HERE?

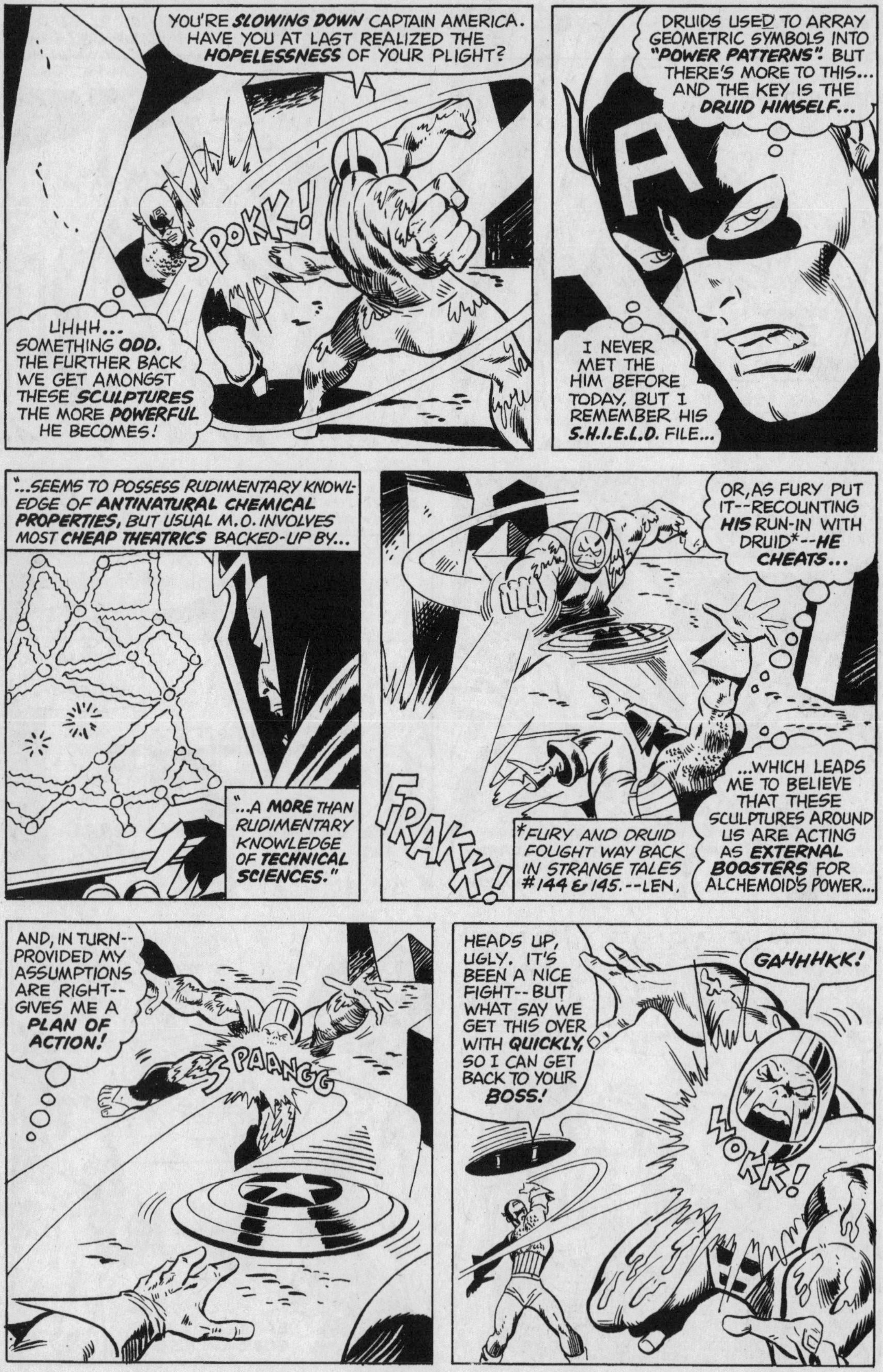
YOU'RE SLOWING DOWN CAPTAIN AMERICA. HAVE YOU AT LAST REALIZED THE HOPELESSNESS OF YOUR PLIGHT?
SPOKK!
UHHH... SOMETHING ODD. THE FURTHER BACK WE GET AMONGST THESE SCULPTURES THE MORE POWERFUL HE BECOMES!
DRUIDS USED TO ARRAY GEOMETRIC SYMBOLS INTO "POWER PATTERNS". BUT THERE'S MORE TO THIS... AND THE KEY IS THE DRUID HIMSELF...
I NEVER MET THE HIM BEFORE TODAY, BUT I REMEMBER HIS S.H.I.E.L.D. FILE...
"...SEEMS TO POSSESS RUDIMENTARY KNOWLEDGE OF ANTINATURAL CHEMICAL PROPERTIES, BUT USUAL M.O. INVOLVES MOST CHEAP THEATRICS BACKED-UP BY...
"...A MORE THAN RUDIMENTARY KNOWLEDGE OF TECHNICAL SCIENCES."
OR, AS FURY PUT IT--RECOUNTING HIS RUN-IN WITH DRUID*--HE CHEATS...
FRAKKK!
*FURY AND DRUID FOUGHT WAY BACK IN STRANGE TALES #144 & 145.--LEN.
...WHICH LEADS ME TO BELIEVE THAT THESE SCULPTURES AROUND US ARE ACTING AS EXTERNAL BOOSTERS FOR ALCHEMOID'S POWER...
AND, IN TURN--PROVIDED MY ASSUMPTIONS ARE RIGHT--GIVES ME A PLAN OF ACTION!
SPAANGG
HEADS UP, UGLY. IT'S BEEN A NICE FIGHT--BUT WHAT SAY WE GET THIS OVER WITH QUICKLY, SO I CAN GET BACK TO YOUR BOSS!
GAHHHKK!
WOKK!

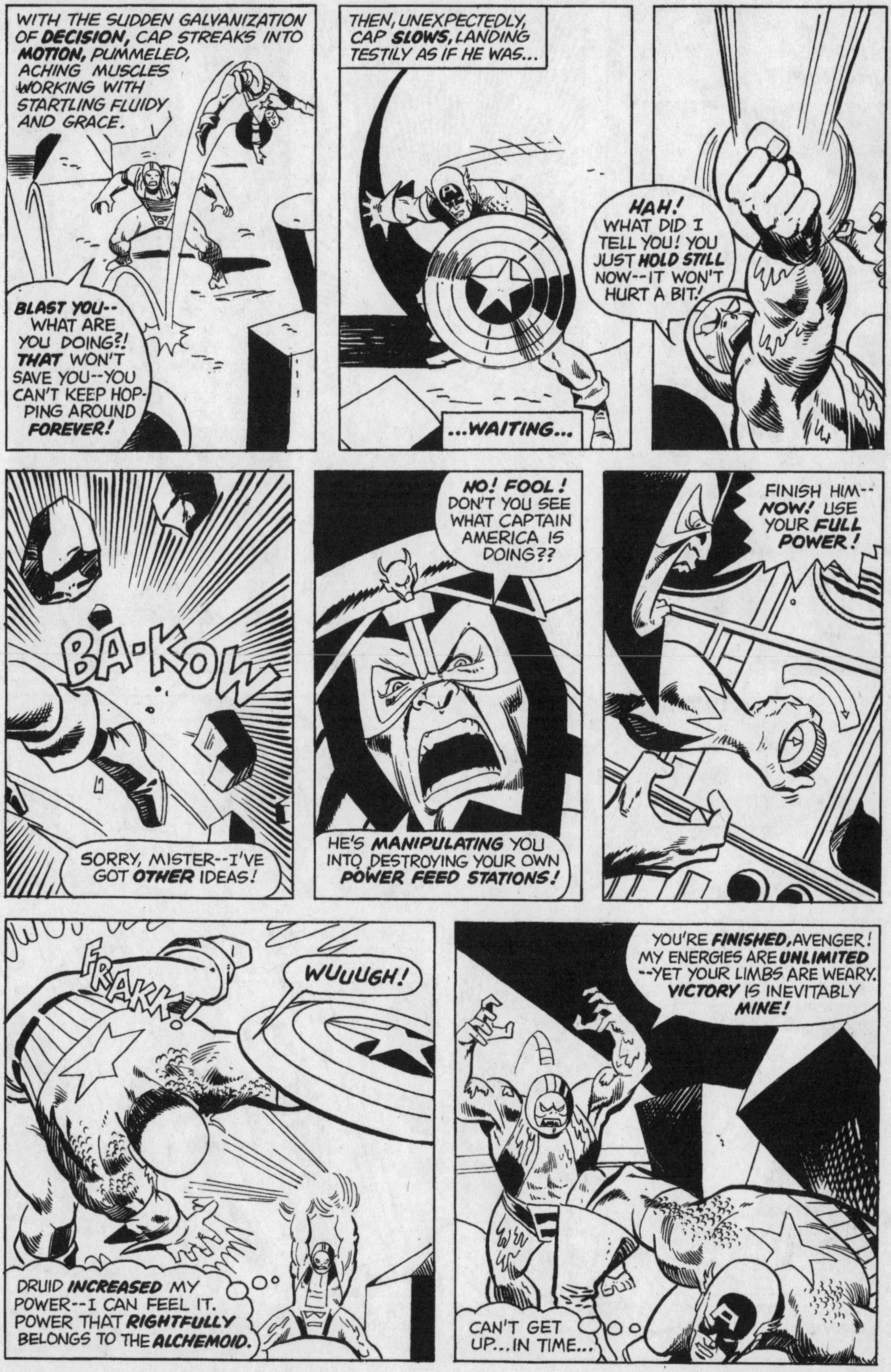
WITH THE SUDDEN GALVANIZATION OF DECISION, CAP STREAKS INTO MOTION, PUMMELED, ACHING MUSCLES WORKING WITH STARTLING FLUIDY AND GRACE.
BLAST YOU-- WHAT ARE YOU DOING?! THAT WON'T SAVE YOU--YOU CAN'T KEEP HOP-PING AROUND FOREVER!
THEN, UNEXPECTEDLY, CAP SLOWS, LANDING TESTILY AS IF HE WAS...
...WAITING...
HAH! WHAT DID I TELL YOU! YOU JUST HOLD STILL NOW--IT WON'T HURT A BIT!
BA-KOW
SORRY, MISTER--I'VE GOT OTHER IDEAS!
NO! FOOL! DON'T YOU SEE WHAT CAPTAIN AMERICA IS DOING??
HE'S MANIPULATING YOU INTO DESTROYING YOUR OWN POWER FEED STATIONS!
FINISH HIM-- NOW! USE YOUR FULL POWER!
FRAKK!
WUUUGH!
DRUID INCREASED MY POWER--I CAN FEEL IT. POWER THAT RIGHTFULLY BELONGS TO THE ALCHEMOID.
YOU'RE FINISHED, AVENGER! MY ENERGIES ARE UNLIMITED --YET YOUR LIMBS ARE WEARY. VICTORY IS INEVITABLY MINE!
CAN'T GET UP...IN TIME...

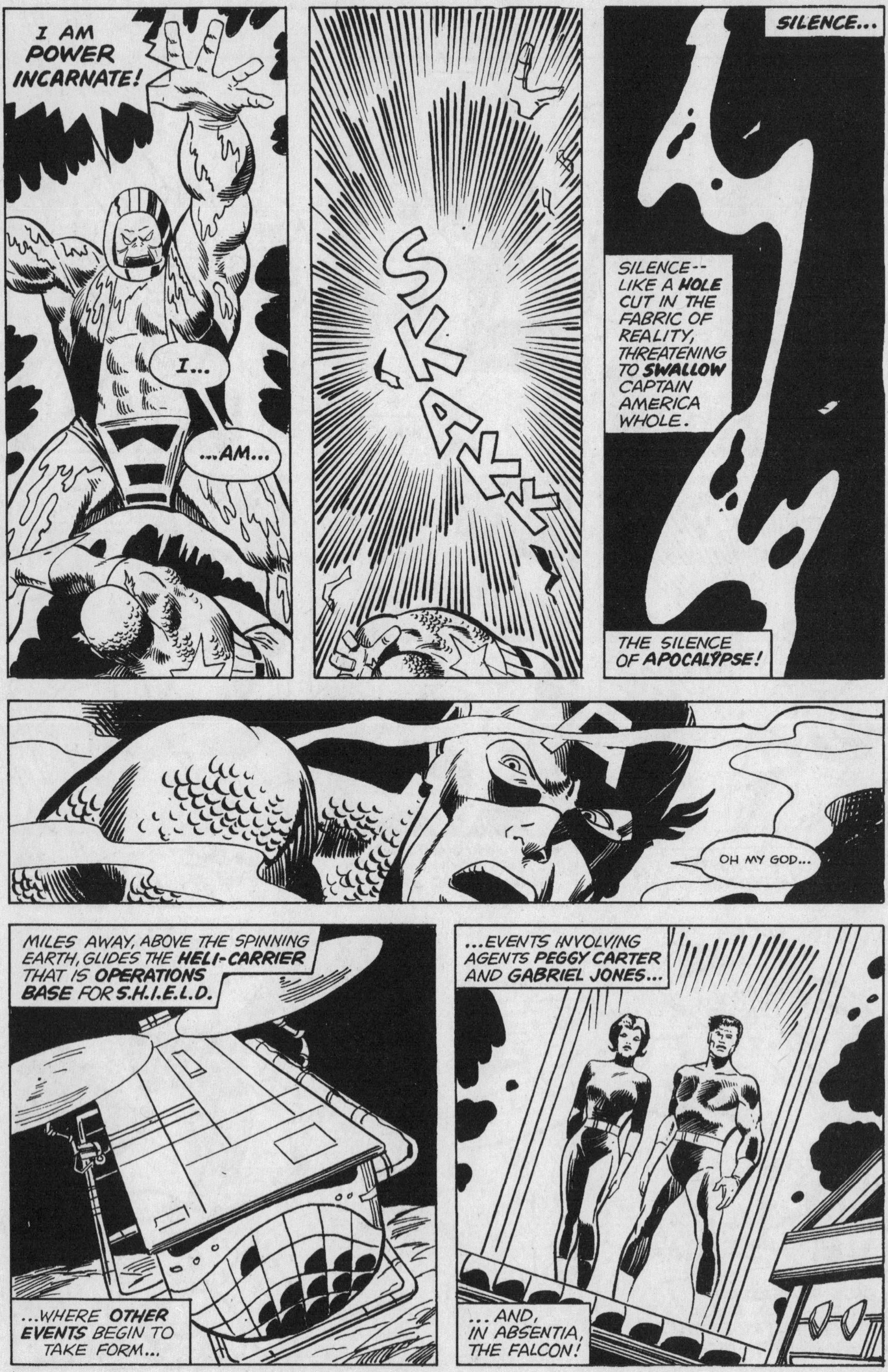
I AM POWER INCARNATE!
I...
...AM...
SKAKKK
SILENCE...
SILENCE-- LIKE A HOLE CUT IN THE FABRIC OF REALITY, THREATENING TO SWALLOW CAPTAIN AMERICA WHOLE.
THE SILENCE OF APOCALYPSE!
OH MY GOD...
MILES AWAY, ABOVE THE SPINNING EARTH, GLIDES THE HELI-CARRIER THAT IS OPERATIONS BASE FOR S.H.I.E.L.D.
...WHERE OTHER EVENTS BEGIN TO TAKE FORM...
...EVENTS INVOLVING AGENTS PEGGY CARTER AND GABRIEL JONES...
...AND, IN ABSENTIA, THE FALCON!

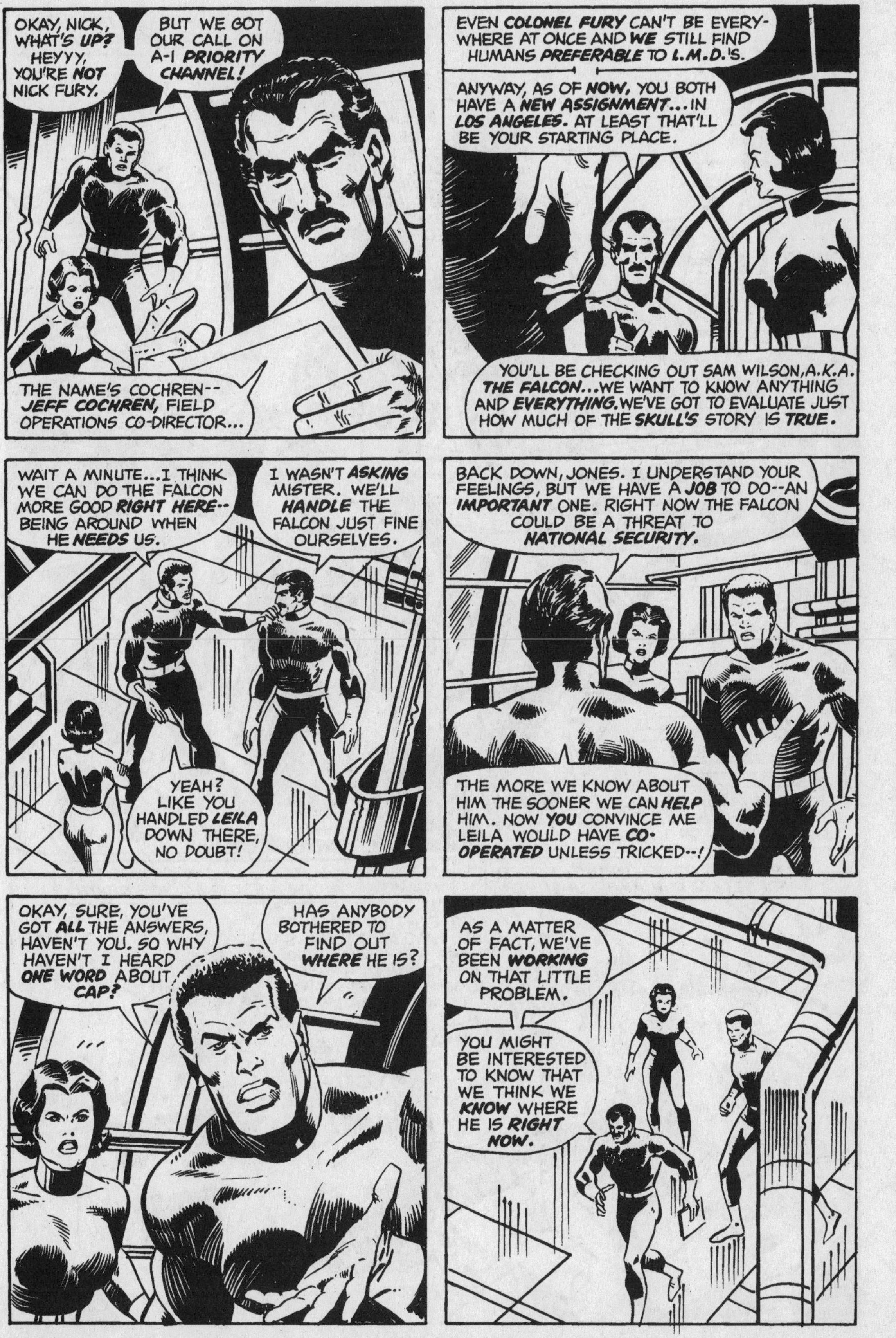
OKAY, NICK, WHAT'S UP? HEYYY, YOU'RE NOT NICK FURY.
BUT WE GOT OUR CALL ON A-1 PRIORITY CHANNEL!
THE NAME'S COCHREN-- JEFF COCHREN, FIELD OPERATIONS CO-DIRECTOR...
EVEN COLONEL FURY CAN'T BE EVERYWHERE AT ONCE AND WE STILL FIND HUMANS PREFERABLE TO L.M.D.'S.
ANYWAY, AS OF NOW, YOU BOTH HAVE A NEW ASSIGNMENT... IN LOS ANGELES. AT LEAST THAT'LL BE YOUR STARTING PLACE.
YOU'LL BE CHECKING OUT SAM WILSON, A.K.A. THE FALCON... WE WANT TO KNOW ANYTHING AND EVERYTHING. WE'VE GOT TO EVALUATE JUST HOW MUCH OF THE SKULL'S STORY IS TRUE.
WAIT A MINUTE... I THINK WE CAN DO THE FALCON MORE GOOD RIGHT HERE-- BEING AROUND WHEN HE NEEDS US.
I WASN'T ASKING MISTER. WE'LL HANDLE THE FALCON JUST FINE OURSELVES.
YEAH? LIKE YOU HANDLED LEILA DOWN THERE, NO DOUBT!
BACK DOWN, JONES. I UNDERSTAND YOUR FEELINGS, BUT WE HAVE A JOB TO DO--AN IMPORTANT ONE. RIGHT NOW THE FALCON COULD BE A THREAT TO NATIONAL SECURITY.
THE MORE WE KNOW ABOUT HIM THE SOONER WE CAN HELP HIM. NOW YOU CONVINCE ME LEILA WOULD HAVE CO-OPERATED UNLESS TRICKED--!
OKAY, SURE, YOU'VE GOT ALL THE ANSWERS, HAVEN'T YOU. SO WHY HAVEN'T I HEARD ONE WORD ABOUT CAP?
HAS ANYBODY BOTHERED TO FIND OUT WHERE HE IS?
AS A MATTER OF FACT, WE'VE BEEN WORKING ON THAT LITTLE PROBLEM.
YOU MIGHT BE INTERESTED TO KNOW THAT WE KNOW WHERE HE IS RIGHT NOW.

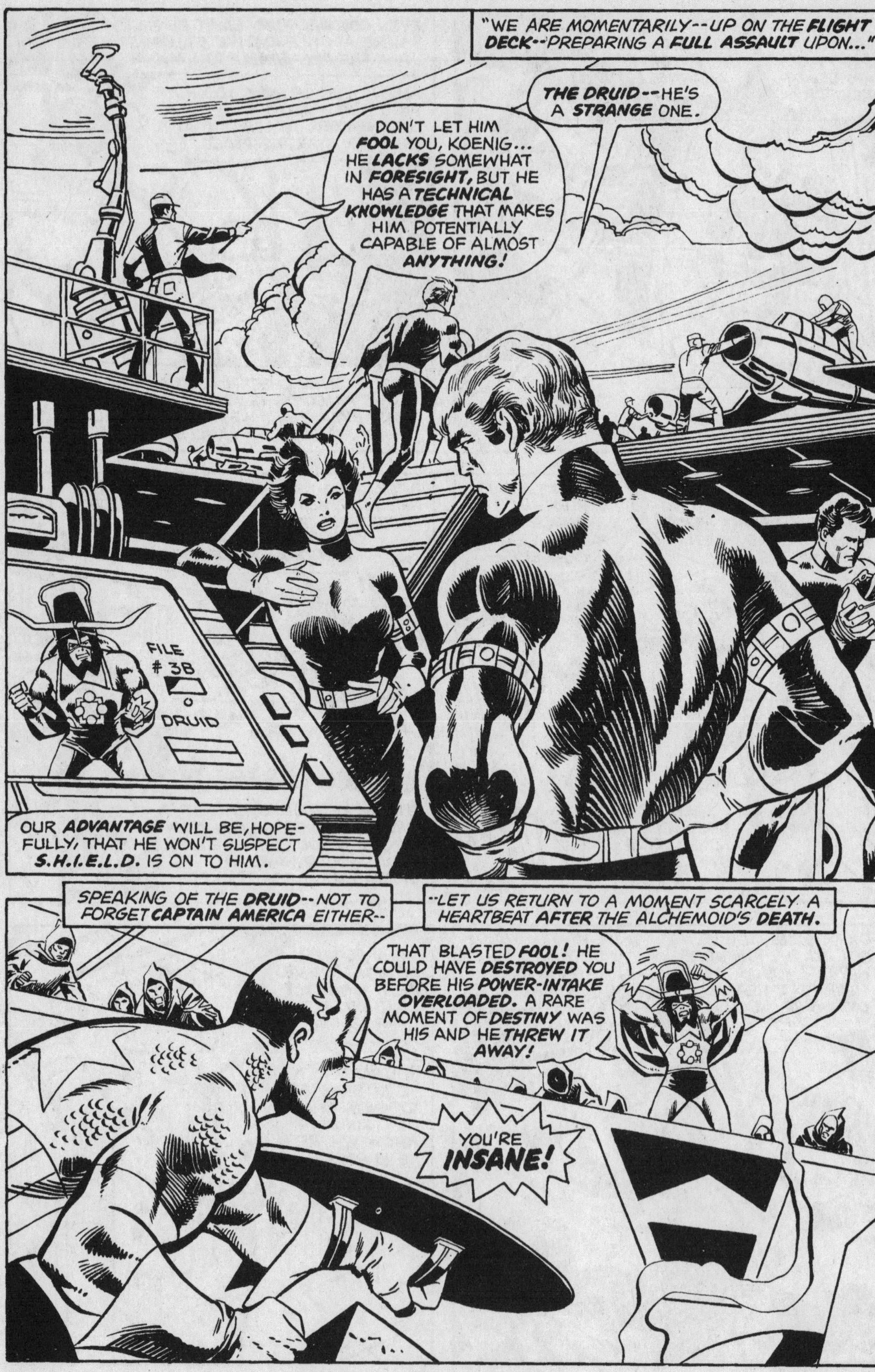
"WE ARE MOMENTARILY--UP ON THE FLIGHT DECK--PREPARING A FULL ASSAULT UPON..."
THE DRUID--HE'S A STRANGE ONE.
DON'T LET HIM FOOL YOU, KOENIG... HE LACKS SOMEWHAT IN FORESIGHT, BUT HE HAS A TECHNICAL KNOWLEDGE THAT MAKES HIM POTENTIALLY CAPABLE OF ALMOST ANYTHING!
FILE #38
DRUID
OUR ADVANTAGE WILL BE, HOPEFULLY, THAT HE WON'T SUSPECT S.H.I.E.L.D. IS ON TO HIM.
SPEAKING OF THE DRUID--NOT TO FORGET CAPTAIN AMERICA EITHER--
--LET US RETURN TO A MOMENT SCARCELY A HEARTBEAT AFTER THE ALCHEMOID'S DEATH.
THAT BLASTED FOOL! HE COULD HAVE DESTROYED YOU BEFORE HIS POWER-INTAKE OVERLOADED. A RARE MOMENT OF DESTINY WAS HIS AND HE THREW IT AWAY!
YOU'RE INSANE!

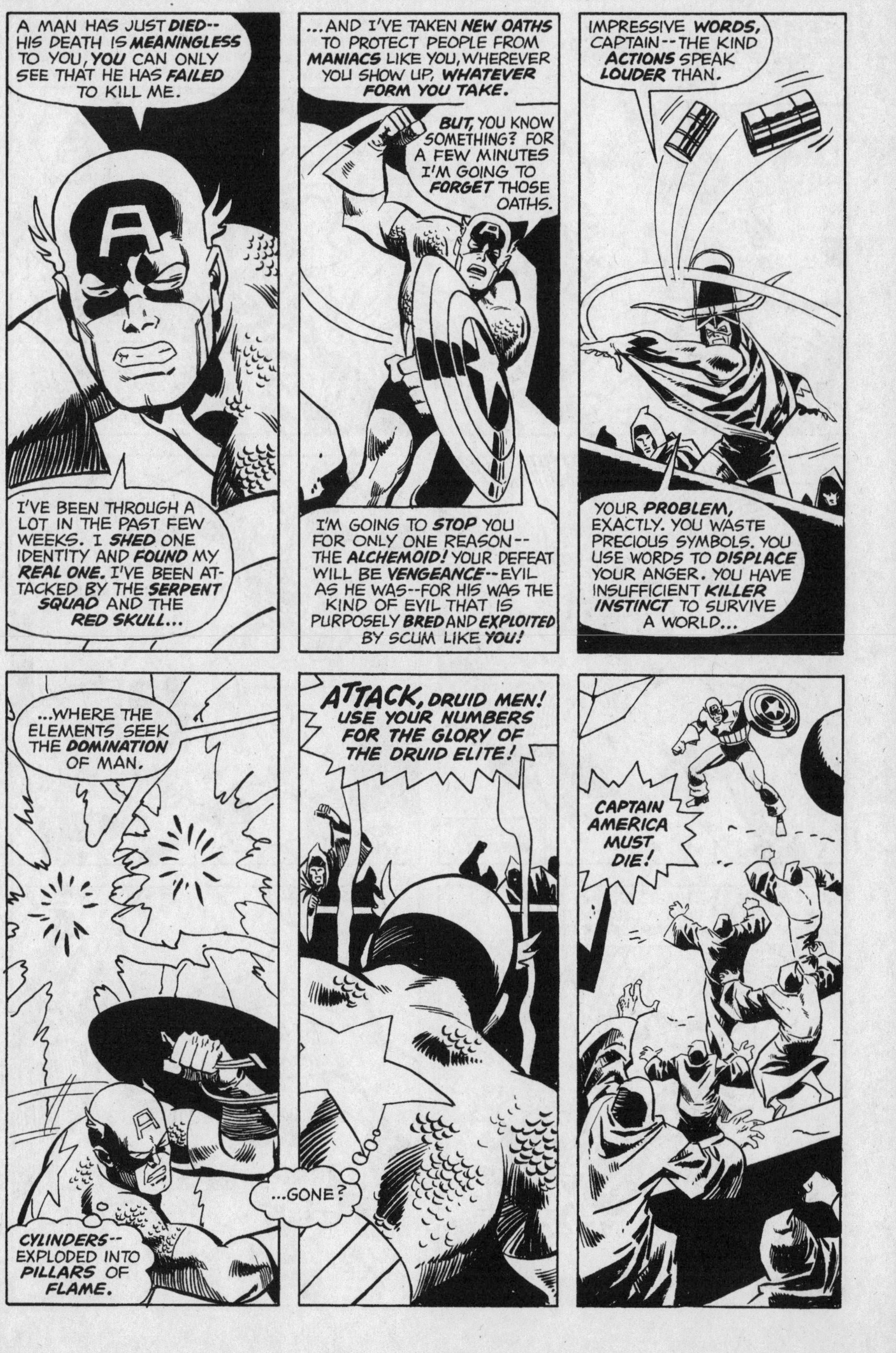
A MAN HAS JUST DIED-- HIS DEATH IS MEANINGLESS TO YOU, YOU CAN ONLY SEE THAT HE HAS FAILED TO KILL ME.
I'VE BEEN THROUGH A LOT IN THE PAST FEW WEEKS. I SHED ONE IDENTITY AND FOUND MY REAL ONE. I'VE BEEN ATTACKED BY THE SERPENT SQUAD AND THE RED SKULL...
...AND I'VE TAKEN NEW OATHS TO PROTECT PEOPLE FROM MANIACS LIKE YOU, WHEREVER YOU SHOW UP, WHATEVER FORM YOU TAKE.
BUT, YOU KNOW SOMETHING? FOR A FEW MINUTES I'M GOING TO FORGET THOSE OATHS.
I'M GOING TO STOP YOU FOR ONLY ONE REASON-- THE ALCHEMOID! YOUR DEFEAT WILL BE VENGEANCE--EVIL AS HE WAS--FOR HIS WAS THE KIND OF EVIL THAT IS PURPOSELY BRED AND EXPLOITED BY SCUM LIKE YOU!
IMPRESSIVE WORDS, CAPTAIN--THE KIND ACTIONS SPEAK LOUDER THAN.
YOUR PROBLEM, EXACTLY. YOU WASTE PRECIOUS SYMBOLS. YOU USE WORDS TO DISPLACE YOUR ANGER. YOU HAVE INSUFFICIENT KILLER INSTINCT TO SURVIVE A WORLD...
...WHERE THE ELEMENTS SEEK THE DOMINATION OF MAN.
CYLINDERS-- EXPLODED INTO PILLARS OF FLAME.
...GONE?
ATTACK, DRUID MEN! USE YOUR NUMBERS FOR THE GLORY OF THE DRUID ELITE!
CAPTAIN AMERICA MUST DIE!

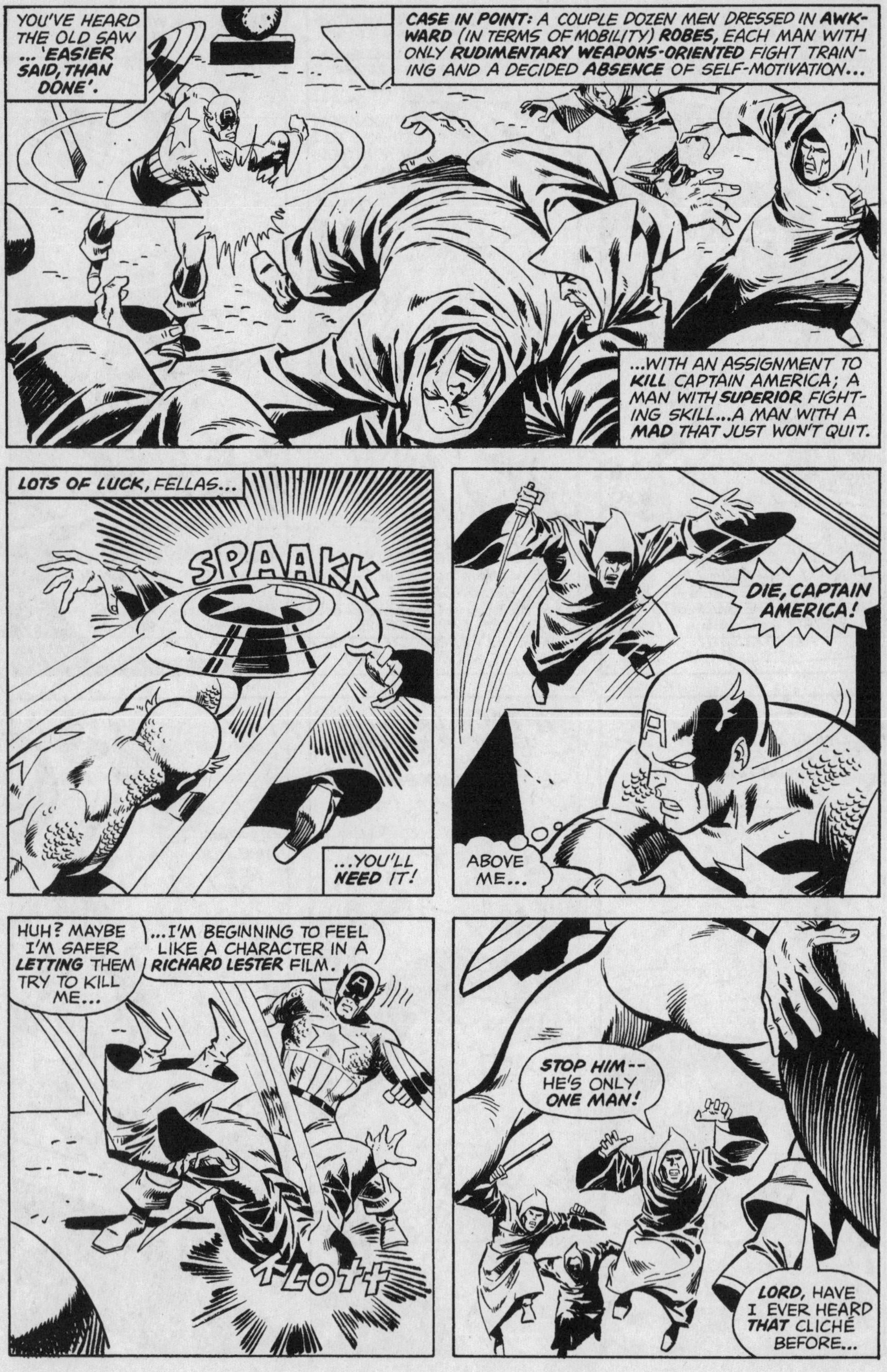
YOU'VE HEARD THE OLD SAW ...'EASIER SAID, THAN DONE'.
CASE IN POINT: A COUPLE DOZEN MEN DRESSED IN AWKWARD (IN TERMS OF MOBILITY) ROBES, EACH MAN WITH ONLY RUDIMENTARY WEAPONS-ORIENTED FIGHT TRAINING AND A DECIDED ABSENCE OF SELF-MOTIVATION...
...WITH AN ASSIGNMENT TO KILL CAPTAIN AMERICA; A MAN WITH SUPERIOR FIGHTING SKILL...A MAN WITH A MAD THAT JUST WON'T QUIT.
LOTS OF LUCK, FELLAS...
SPAAKK
...YOU'LL NEED IT!
DIE, CAPTAIN AMERICA!
ABOVE ME...
HUH? MAYBE I'M SAFER LETTING THEM TRY TO KILL ME...
...I'M BEGINNING TO FEEL LIKE A CHARACTER IN A RICHARD LESTER FILM.
TLOTT
STOP HIM-- HE'S ONLY ONE MAN!
LORD, HAVE I EVER HEARD THAT CLICHÉ BEFORE...

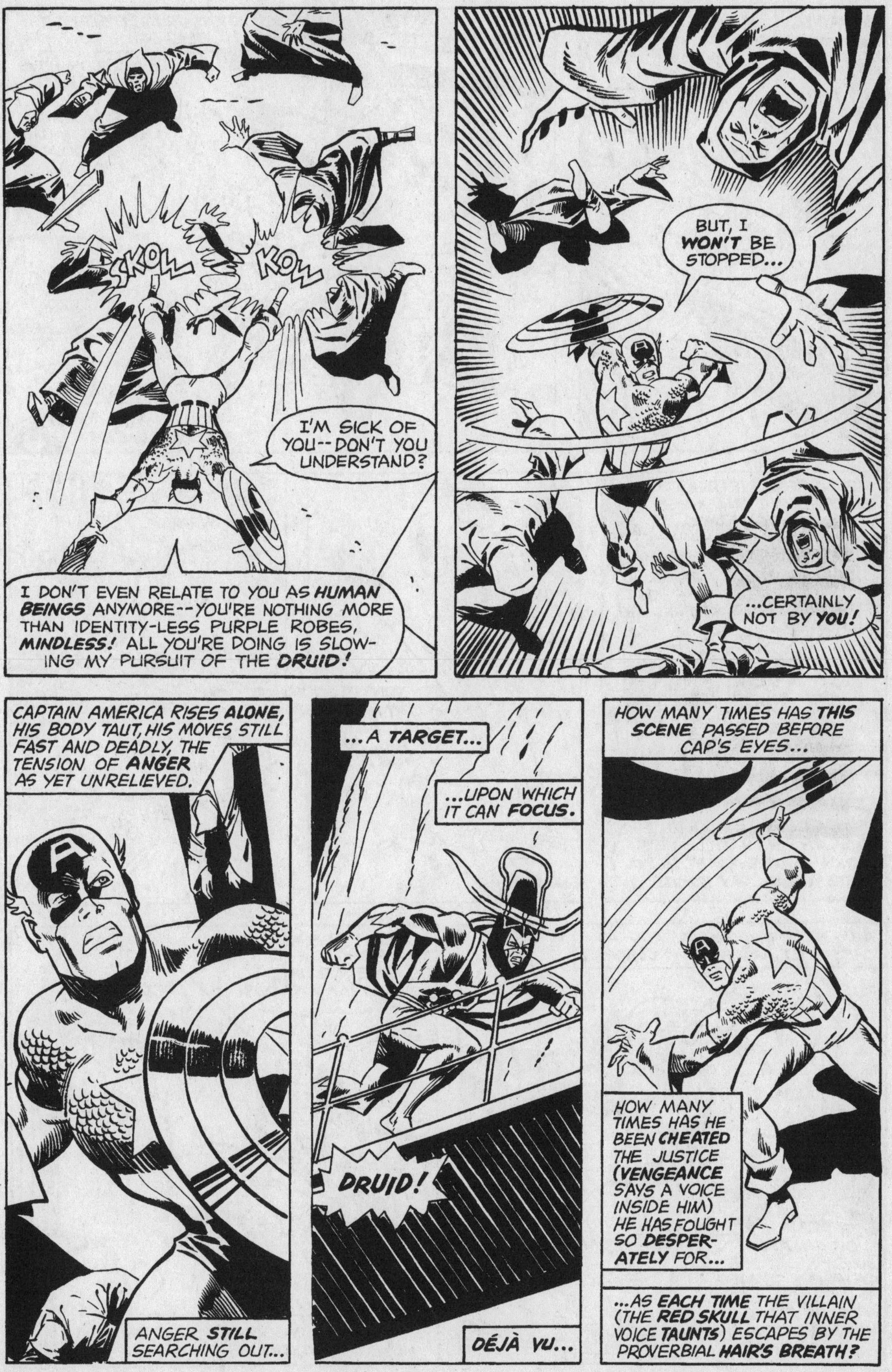
SKOW
KOW
I'M SICK OF YOU--DON'T YOU UNDERSTAND?
I DON'T EVEN RELATE TO YOU AS HUMAN BEINGS ANYMORE--YOU'RE NOTHING MORE THAN IDENTITY-LESS PURPLE ROBES, MINDLESS! ALL YOU'RE DOING IS SLOWING MY PURSUIT OF THE DRUID!
BUT, I WON'T BE STOPPED...
...CERTAINLY NOT BY YOU!
CAPTAIN AMERICA RISES ALONE, HIS BODY TAUT, HIS MOVES STILL FAST AND DEADLY, THE TENSION OF ANGER AS YET UNRELIEVED.
ANGER STILL SEARCHING OUT...
...A TARGET...
...UPON WHICH IT CAN FOCUS.
DRUID!
DÉJÀ VU...
HOW MANY TIMES HAS THIS SCENE PASSED BEFORE CAP'S EYES...
HOW MANY TIMES HAS HE BEEN CHEATED THE JUSTICE (VENGEANCE SAYS A VOICE INSIDE HIM) HE HAS FOUGHT SO DESPERATELY FOR...
...AS EACH TIME THE VILLAIN (THE RED SKULL THAT INNER VOICE TAUNTS) ESCAPES BY THE PROVERBIAL HAIR'S BREATH?

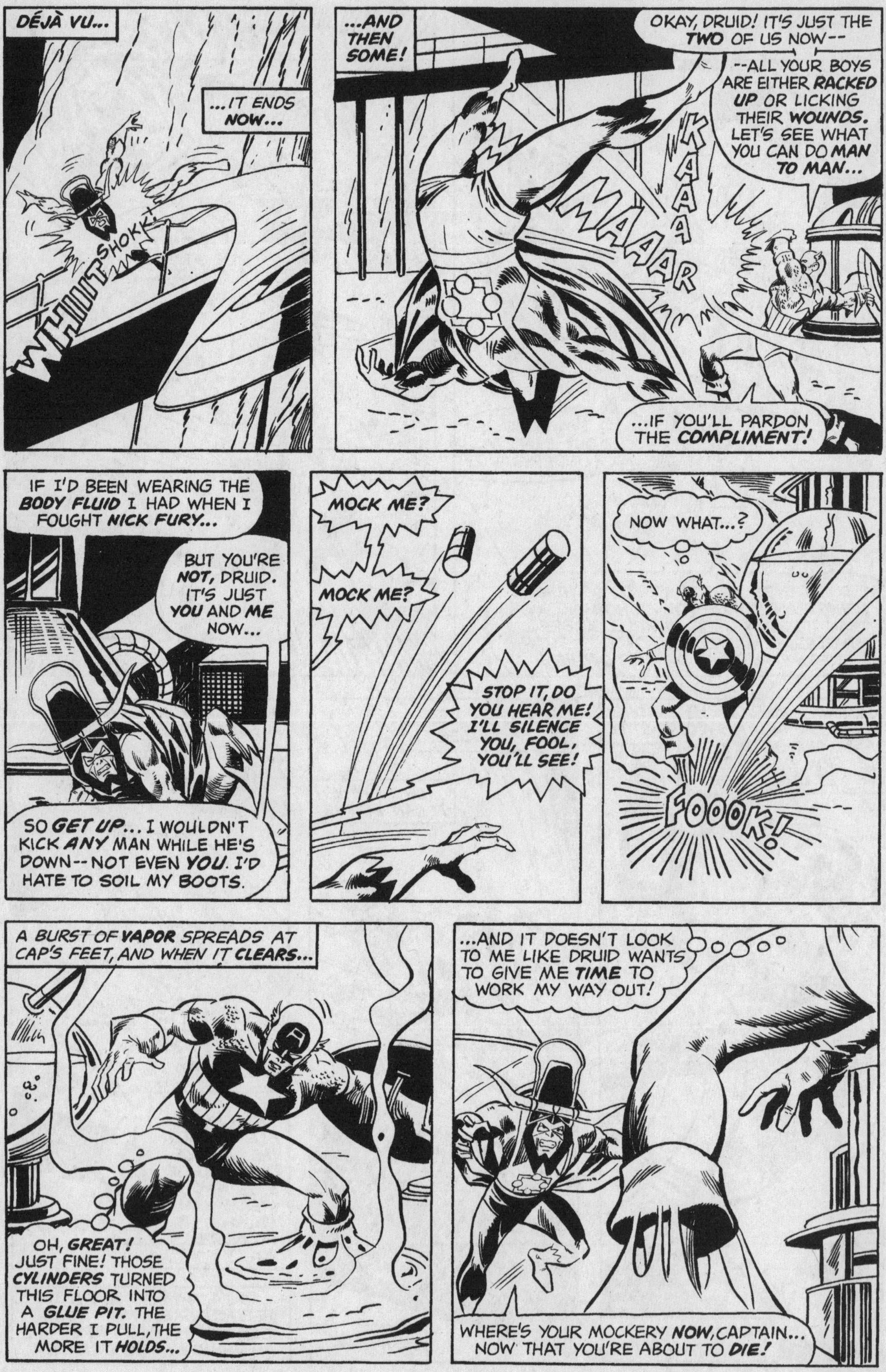
DÉJÀ VU...
...IT ENDS NOW...
WHIIT
SHOKK
...AND THEN SOME!
OKAY, DRUID! IT'S JUST THE TWO OF US NOW--
--ALL YOUR BOYS ARE EITHER RACKED UP OR LICKING THEIR WOUNDS. LET'S SEE WHAT YOU CAN DO MAN TO MAN...
KAAAA
MAAAAR
...IF YOU'LL PARDON THE COMPLIMENT!
IF I'D BEEN WEARING THE BODY FLUID I HAD WHEN I FOUGHT NICK FURY...
BUT YOU'RE NOT, DRUID. IT'S JUST YOU AND ME NOW...
SO GET UP... I WOULDN'T KICK ANY MAN WHILE HE'S DOWN--NOT EVEN YOU. I'D HATE TO SOIL MY BOOTS.
MOCK ME?
MOCK ME?
STOP IT, DO YOU HEAR ME! I'LL SILENCE YOU, FOOL, YOU'LL SEE!
NOW WHAT...?
FOOOK!
A BURST OF VAPOR SPREADS AT CAP'S FEET, AND WHEN IT CLEARS...
OH, GREAT! JUST FINE! THOSE CYLINDERS TURNED THIS FLOOR INTO A GLUE PIT. THE HARDER I PULL, THE MORE IT HOLDS...
...AND IT DOESN'T LOOK TO ME LIKE DRUID WANTS TO GIVE ME TIME TO WORK MY WAY OUT!
WHERE'S YOUR MOCKERY NOW, CAPTAIN... NOW THAT YOU'RE ABOUT TO DIE!

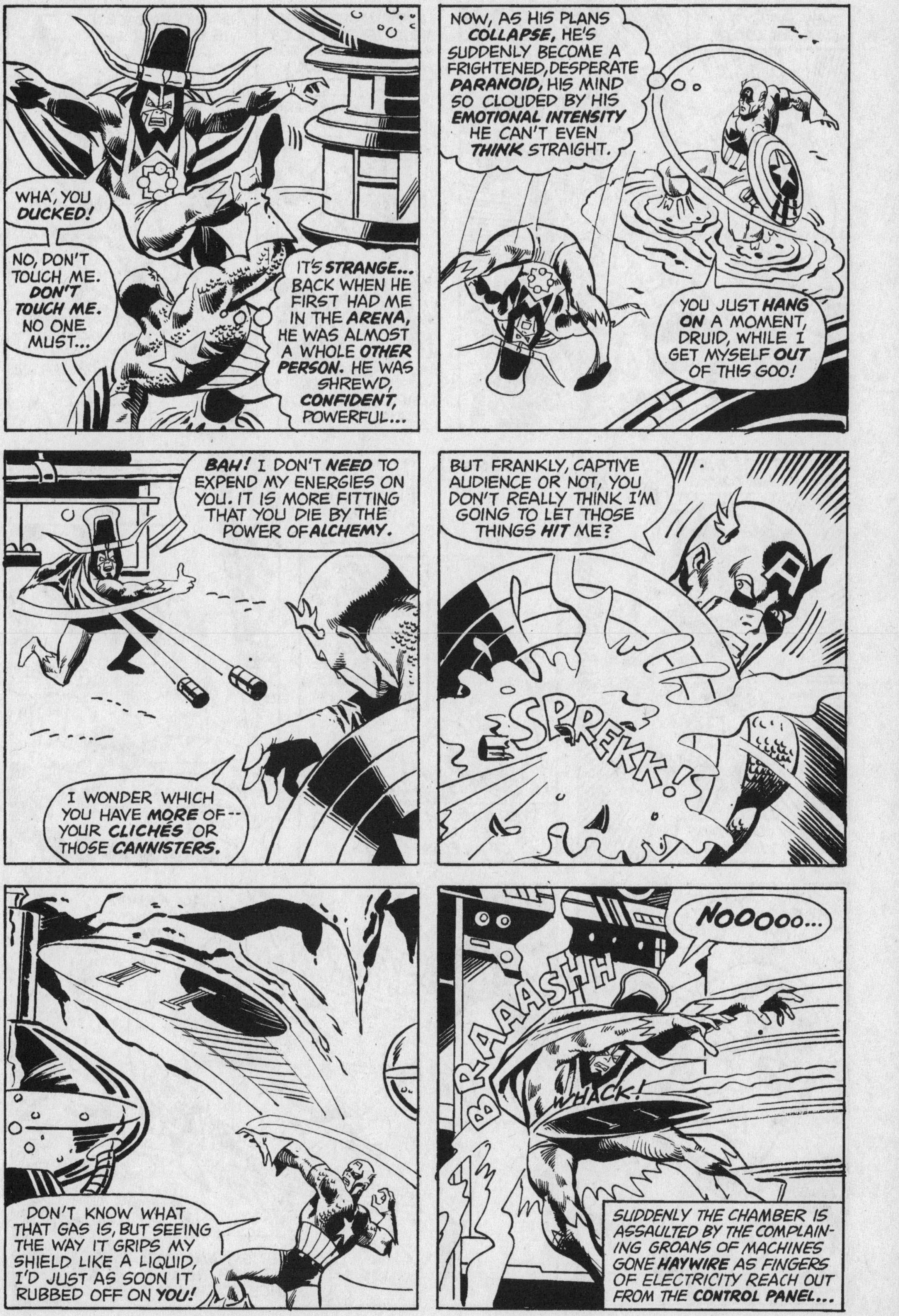
WHA', YOU DUCKED!
NO, DON'T TOUCH ME. DON'T TOUCH ME. NO ONE MUST...
IT'S STRANGE... BACK WHEN HE FIRST HAD ME IN THE ARENA, HE WAS ALMOST A WHOLE OTHER PERSON. HE WAS SHREWD, CONFIDENT, POWERFUL...
NOW, AS HIS PLANS COLLAPSE, HE'S SUDDENLY BECOME A FRIGHTENED, DESPERATE PARANOID, HIS MIND SO CLOUDED BY HIS EMOTIONAL INTENSITY HE CAN'T EVEN THINK STRAIGHT.
YOU JUST HANG ON A MOMENT, DRUID, WHILE I GET MYSELF OUT OF THIS GOO!
BAH! I DON'T NEED TO EXPEND MY ENERGIES ON YOU. IT IS MORE FITTING THAT YOU DIE BY THE POWER OF ALCHEMY.
I WONDER WHICH YOU HAVE MORE OF-- YOUR CLICHÉS OR THOSE CANNISTERS.
BUT FRANKLY, CAPTIVE AUDIENCE OR NOT, YOU DON'T REALLY THINK I'M GOING TO LET THOSE THINGS HIT ME?
SPREKKK!
DON'T KNOW WHAT THAT GAS IS, BUT SEEING THE WAY IT GRIPS MY SHIELD LIKE A LIQUID, I'D JUST AS SOON IT RUBBED OFF ON YOU!
NOOOOO...
BRAAAASHH
WHACK!
SUDDENLY THE CHAMBER IS ASSAULTED BY THE COMPLAINING GROANS OF MACHINES GONE HAYWIRE AS FINGERS OF ELECTRICITY REACH OUT FROM THE CONTROL PANEL...

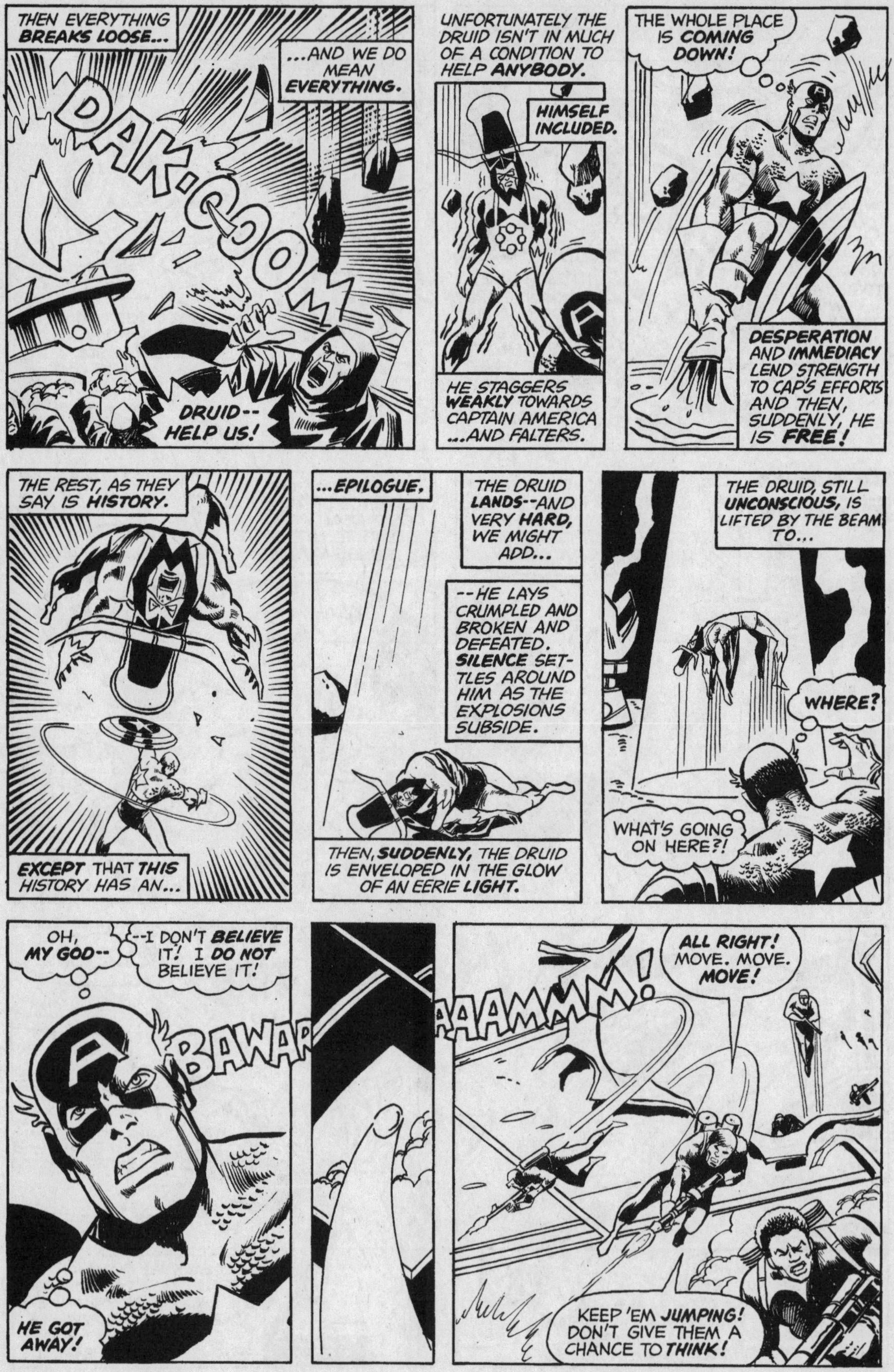
THEN EVERYTHING BREAKS LOOSE...
...AND WE DO MEAN EVERYTHING.
DAK-COOOM
DRUID-- HELP US!
UNFORTUNATELY THE DRUID ISN'T IN MUCH OF A CONDITION TO HELP ANYBODY.
HIMSELF INCLUDED.
HE STAGGERS WEAKLY TOWARDS CAPTAIN AMERICA ...AND FALTERS.
THE WHOLE PLACE IS COMING DOWN!
DESPERATION AND IMMEDIACY LEND STRENGTH TO CAP'S EFFORTS AND THEN, SUDDENLY, HE IS FREE!
THE REST, AS THEY SAY IS HISTORY.
EXCEPT THAT THIS HISTORY HAS AN...
...EPILOGUE.
THE DRUID LANDS--AND VERY HARD, WE MIGHT ADD...
--HE LAYS CRUMPLED AND BROKEN AND DEFEATED. SILENCE SET-TLES AROUND HIM AS THE EXPLOSIONS SUBSIDE.
THEN, SUDDENLY, THE DRUID IS ENVELOPED IN THE GLOW OF AN EERIE LIGHT.
THE DRUID, STILL UNCONSCIOUS, IS LIFTED BY THE BEAM TO...
WHERE?
WHAT'S GOING ON HERE?!
OH, MY GOD--
--I DON'T BELIEVE IT! I DO NOT BELIEVE IT!
HE GOT AWAY!
BAWAR AAAMMMM!
ALL RIGHT! MOVE. MOVE. MOVE!
KEEP 'EM JUMPING! DON'T GIVE THEM A CHANCE TO THINK!

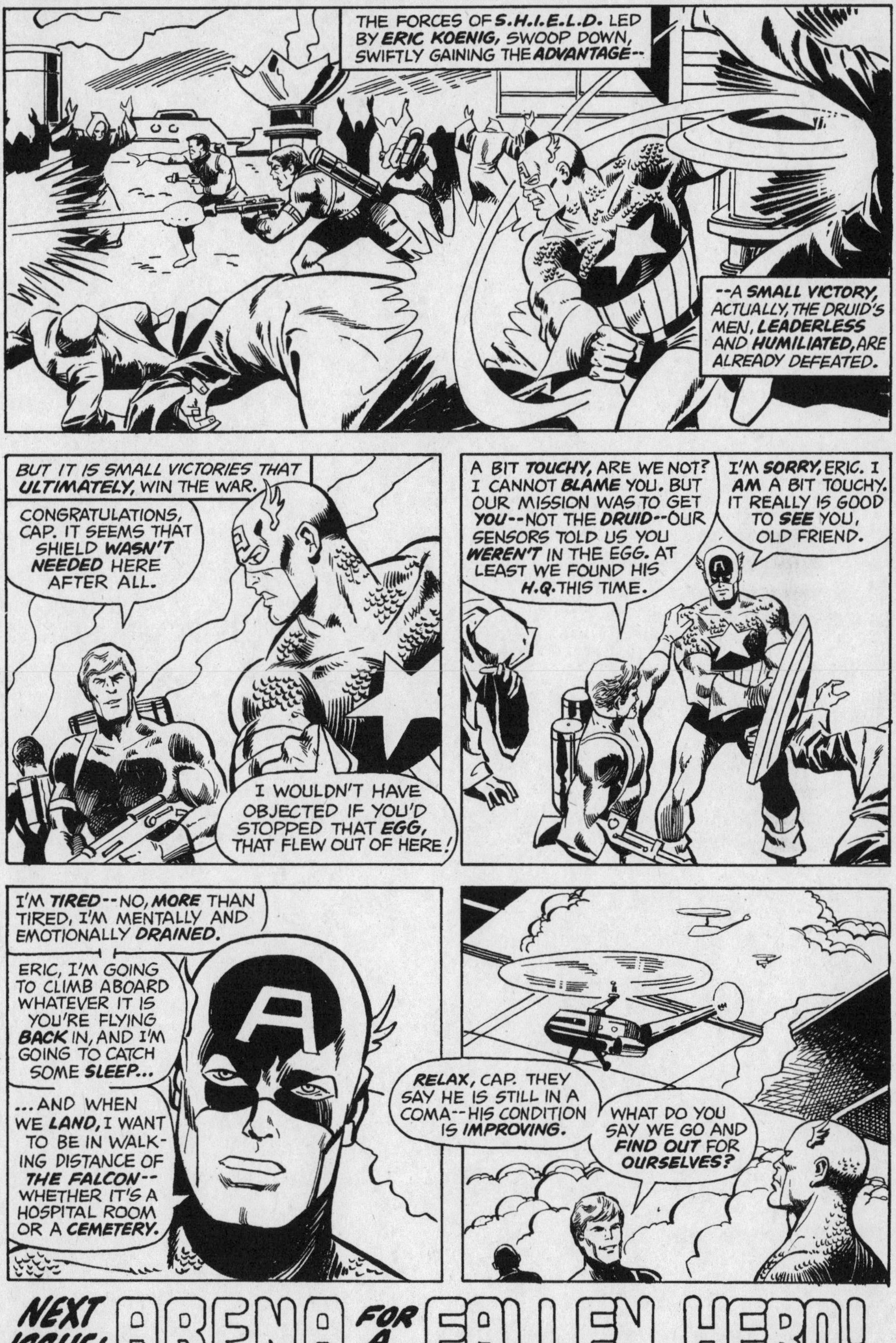
THE FORCES OF S.H.I.E.L.D. LED BY ERIC KOENIG, SWOOP DOWN, SWIFTLY GAINING THE ADVANTAGE--
--A SMALL VICTORY, ACTUALLY, THE DRUID'S MEN, LEADERLESS AND HUMILIATED, ARE ALREADY DEFEATED.
BUT IT IS SMALL VICTORIES THAT ULTIMATELY, WIN THE WAR.
CONGRATULATIONS, CAP. IT SEEMS THAT SHIELD WASN'T NEEDED HERE AFTER ALL.
I WOULDN'T HAVE OBJECTED IF YOU'D STOPPED THAT EGG, THAT FLEW OUT OF HERE!
A BIT TOUCHY, ARE WE NOT? I CANNOT BLAME YOU. BUT OUR MISSION WAS TO GET YOU--NOT THE DRUID--OUR SENSORS TOLD US YOU WEREN'T IN THE EGG. AT LEAST WE FOUND HIS H.Q. THIS TIME.
I'M SORRY, ERIC. I AM A BIT TOUCHY. IT REALLY IS GOOD TO SEE YOU, OLD FRIEND.
I'M TIRED--NO, MORE THAN TIRED, I'M MENTALLY AND EMOTIONALLY DRAINED.
ERIC, I'M GOING TO CLIMB ABOARD WHATEVER IT IS YOU'RE FLYING BACK IN, AND I'M GOING TO CATCH SOME SLEEP...
...AND WHEN WE LAND, I WANT TO BE IN WALKING DISTANCE OF THE FALCON--WHETHER IT'S A HOSPITAL ROOM OR A CEMETERY.
RELAX, CAP. THEY SAY HE IS STILL IN A COMA--HIS CONDITION IS IMPROVING.
WHAT DO YOU SAY WE GO AND FIND OUT FOR OURSELVES?

NEXT ISSUE: ARENA FOR A FALLEN HERO!

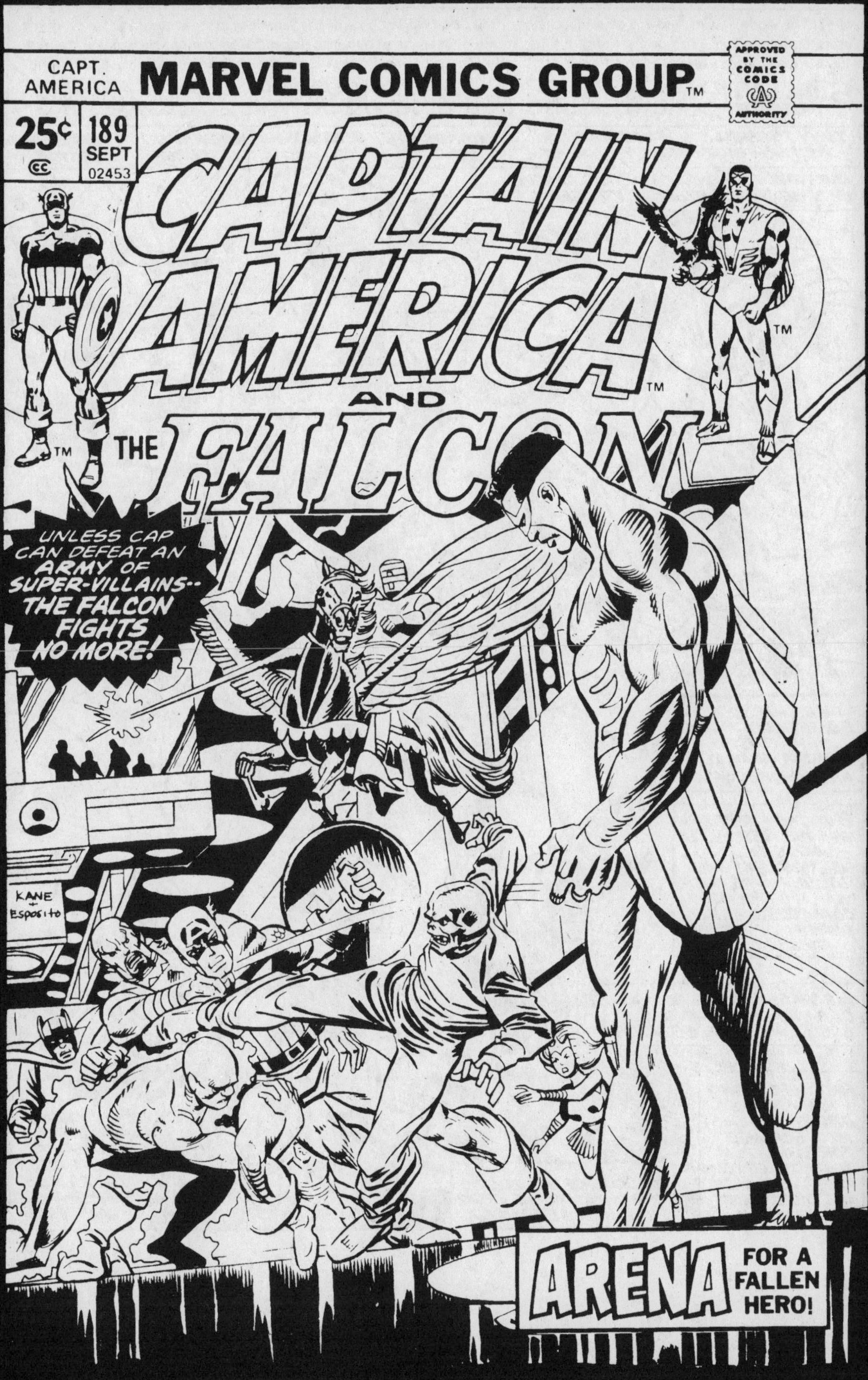

CAPT. AMERICA
MARVEL COMICS GROUP
APPROVED BY THE COMICS CODE AUTHORITY
25¢
189 SEPT
02453
CAPTAIN AMERICA AND THE FALCON
UNLESS CAP CAN DEFEAT AN ARMY OF SUPER-VILLAINS-- THE FALCON FIGHTS NO MORE!
KANE + Esposito
ARENA FOR A FALLEN HERO!

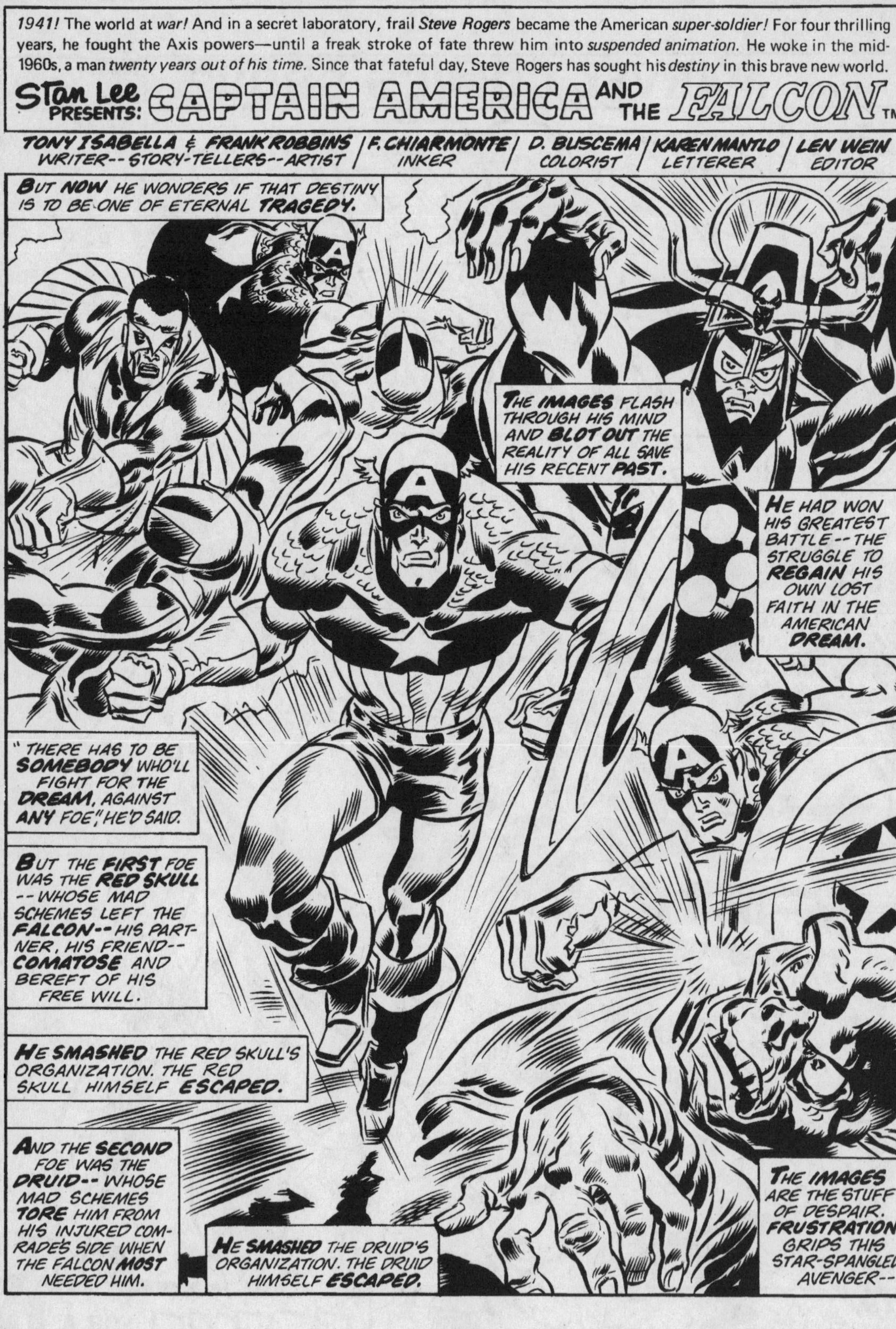
1941! The world at war! And in a secret laboratory, frail Steve Rogers became the American super-soldier! For four thrilling years, he fought the Axis powers—until a freak stroke of fate threw him into suspended animation. He woke in the mid-1960s, a man twenty years out of his time. Since that fateful day, Steve Rogers has sought his destiny in this brave new world.
Stan Lee PRESENTS: CAPTAIN AMERICA AND THE FALCON™
TONY ISABELLA & FRANK ROBBINS WRITER-- STORY-TELLERS--ARTIST | F. CHIARMONTE INKER | D. BUSCEMA COLORIST | KAREN MANTLO LETTERER | LEN WEIN EDITOR
BUT NOW HE WONDERS IF THAT DESTINY IS TO BE ONE OF ETERNAL TRAGEDY.
THE IMAGES FLASH THROUGH HIS MIND AND BLOT OUT THE REALITY OF ALL SAVE HIS RECENT PAST.
HE HAD WON HIS GREATEST BATTLE -- THE STRUGGLE TO REGAIN HIS OWN LOST FAITH IN THE AMERICAN DREAM.
"THERE HAS TO BE SOMEBODY WHO'LL FIGHT FOR THE DREAM, AGAINST ANY FOE", HE'D SAID.
BUT THE FIRST FOE WAS THE RED SKULL -- WHOSE MAD SCHEMES LEFT THE FALCON-- HIS PARTNER, HIS FRIEND-- COMATOSE AND BEREFT OF HIS FREE WILL.
HE SMASHED THE RED SKULL'S ORGANIZATION. THE RED SKULL HIMSELF ESCAPED.
AND THE SECOND FOE WAS THE DRUID-- WHOSE MAD SCHEMES TORE HIM FROM HIS INJURED COMRADE'S SIDE WHEN THE FALCON MOST NEEDED HIM.
HE SMASHED THE DRUID'S ORGANIZATION. THE DRUID HIMSELF ESCAPED.
THE IMAGES ARE THE STUFF OF DESPAIR. FRUSTRATION GRIPS THIS STAR-SPANGLED AVENGER--

Panel 1:

--UNTIL A PAIR OF STRONG ARMS GRIPS HIM WITH *EQUAL* FIRMNESS AND PULLS HIM AWAY FROM HIS *MEMORIES** AND INTO THE *REALITY.*

WAIT! YOU CAN'T GO ANY *FURTHER!*

HUH?

*SAID MEMORIES HAVING ENCOMPASSED --IN GREATLY CONDENSED FORM--THE EVENTS OF ISSUES #176-188--LEN.

Panel 2:

I'M *SORRY,* CAPTAIN, BUT YOUR PARTNER'S ROOM IS *OFF LIMITS* TO ALL BUT *AUTHORIZED* PERSONNEL-- AND OUR LIST OF SAID PERSONNEL DOES NOT *INCLUDE* YOU.

THAT'S AN *OFFICIAL* SHIELD ORDER, MISTER.

FURY WOULDN'T GIVE AN ORDER LIKE *THAT!*

Panel 3:

HE DIDN'T -- *I* DID. UNTIL AGENTS CARTER AND JONES RETURN FROM THEIR MISSION TO PROBE THE FALCON'S *PAST,* YOUR PARTNER IS A POTENTIAL *SECURITY THREAT!* NOBODY SEES HIM--

--ESPECIALLY YOU!

LISTEN, FRIEND. I'VE KNOWN SAM WILSON FOR *SIX* YEARS! HE'S NO CRIMINAL -- *DESPITE* THE SKULL'S CONTROL OVER HIM!*

*ISSUES #185 & 186--LEN.

Panel 4:

SO UNLESS YOU CAN *BACK UP* YOUR ASININE ORDER WITH SOME PRETTY *HEFTY* CREDENTIALS, I'M GOING *IN* THERE-- EVEN IF I HAVE TO WALK RIGHT *OVER* YOU!

WOULDN'T *ADVISE* IT, PAL. I'M *JEFF COCHREN,* SHIELD CO-DIRECTOR. WHEN FURY'S GONE, *I'M* IN CHARGE -- AND *NOBODY* DISREGARDS *MY* ORDERS.

NOT STURE

Panel 5:

LOOK, DO YOU THINK *SHIELD* ISN'T AS CONCERNED ABOUT THE FALCON AS *YOU* ARE? HE'S WORKED WITH *US,* TOO.

WE *THINK* WE'VE COME UP WITH A POSSIBLE *TREATMENT* FOR HIS CONDITION. BUT WE'LL NEED *YOUR* HELP TO MAKE IT *WORK!*

IF THERE'S *ANYTHING* I CAN DO TO HELP SAM WILSON, I'LL *DO* IT!

JUST *NAME* IT, MISTER!

GOOD! ALL YOU HAVE TO DO IS--

Panel 6:

--BATTLE THE *FALCON* TO THE DEATH!

WHAT?!

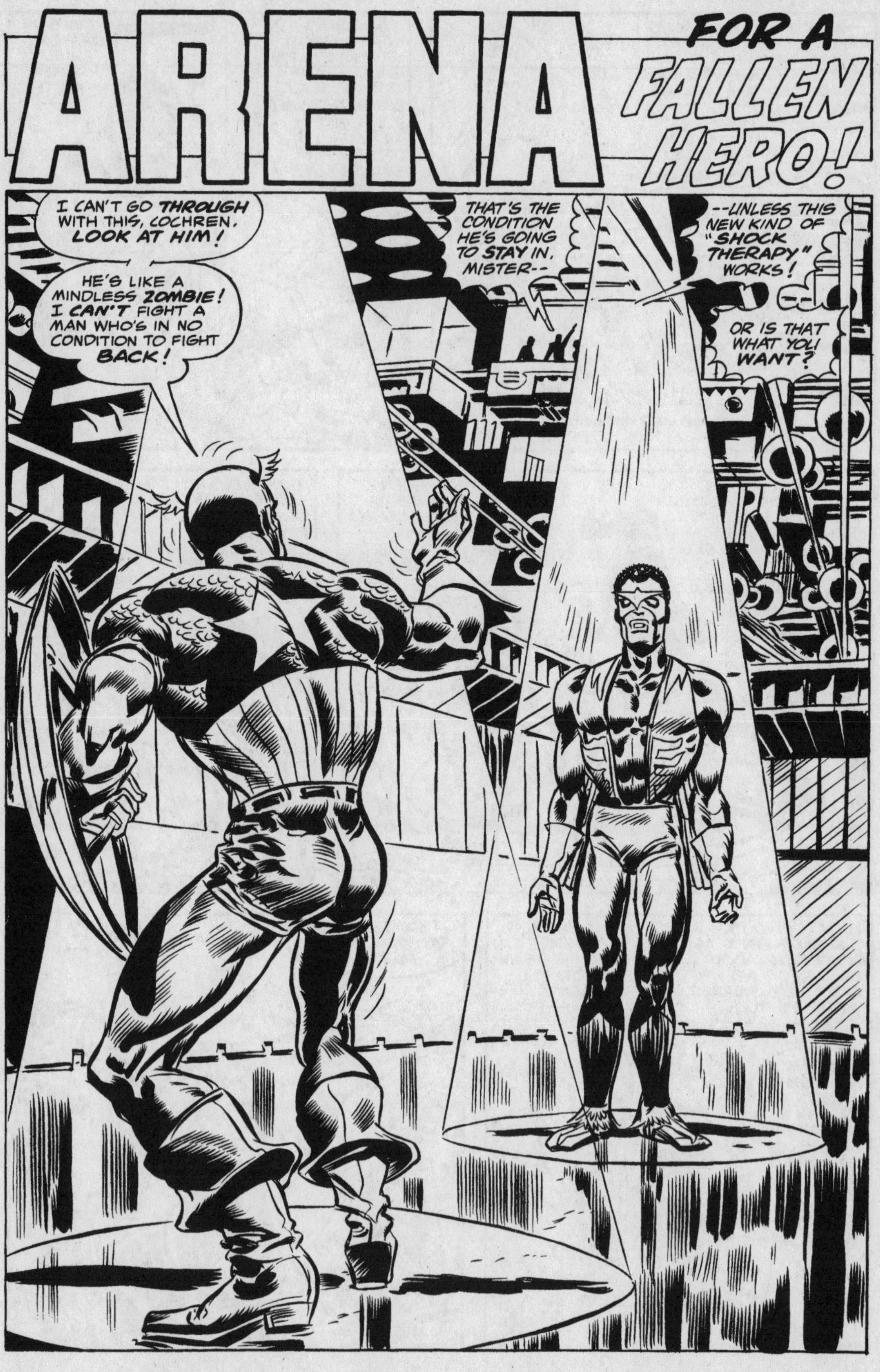
ARENA FOR A FALLEN HERO!
I CAN'T GO THROUGH WITH THIS, COCHREN. LOOK AT HIM!
HE'S LIKE A MINDLESS ZOMBIE! I CAN'T FIGHT A MAN WHO'S IN NO CONDITION TO FIGHT BACK!
THAT'S THE CONDITION HE'S GOING TO STAY IN, MISTER--
--UNLESS THIS NEW KIND OF "SHOCK THERAPY" WORKS!
OR IS THAT WHAT YOU WANT?

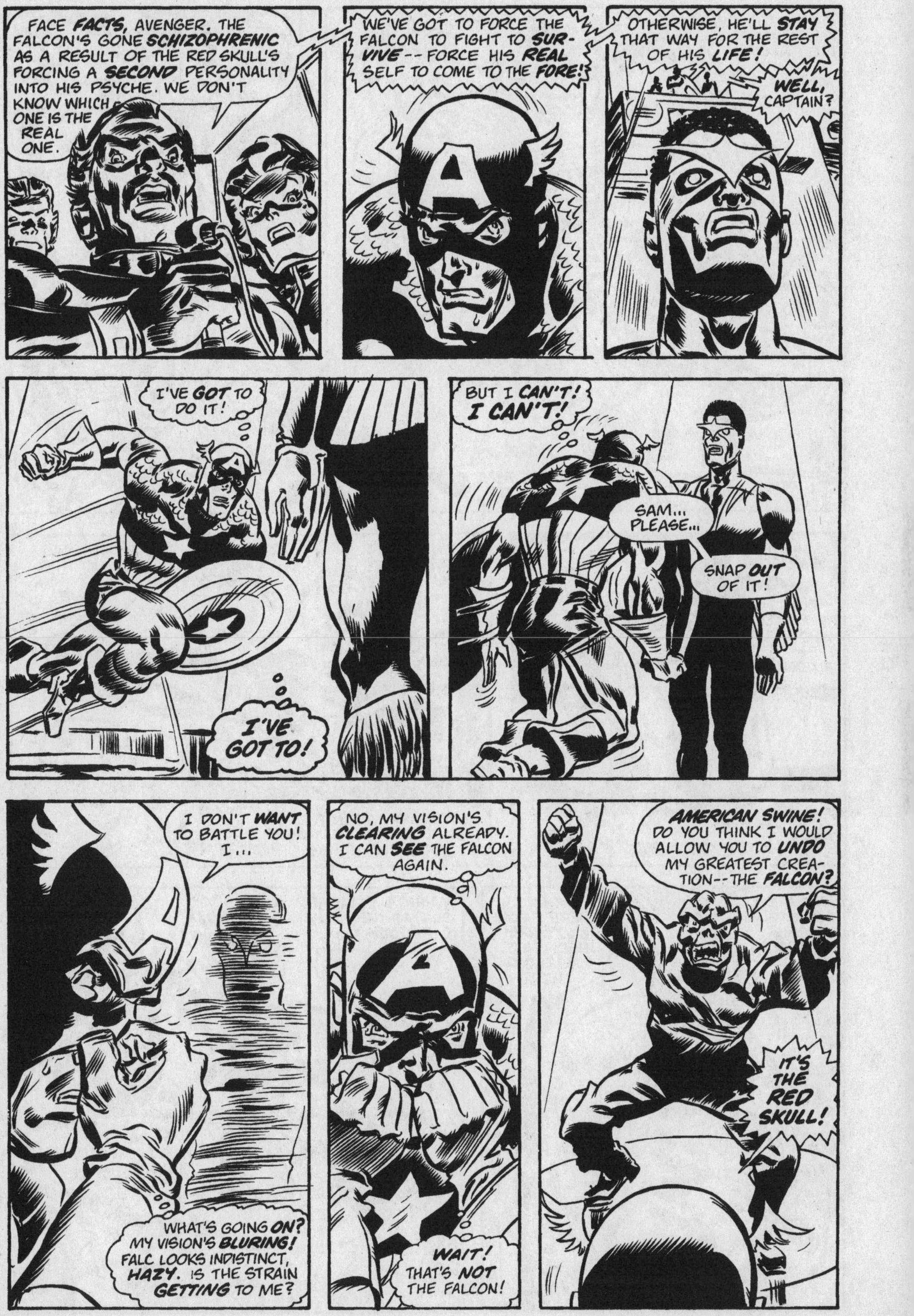

FACE FACTS, AVENGER. THE FALCON'S GONE SCHIZOPHRENIC AS A RESULT OF THE RED SKULL'S FORCING A SECOND PERSONALITY INTO HIS PSYCHE. WE DON'T KNOW WHICH ONE IS THE REAL ONE.
WE'VE GOT TO FORCE THE FALCON TO FIGHT TO SURVIVE -- FORCE HIS REAL SELF TO COME TO THE FORE!
OTHERWISE, HE'LL STAY THAT WAY FOR THE REST OF HIS LIFE!
WELL, CAPTAIN?
I'VE GOT TO DO IT!
I'VE GOT TO!
BUT I CAN'T! I CAN'T!
SAM... PLEASE...
SNAP OUT OF IT!
I DON'T WANT TO BATTLE YOU! I...
WHAT'S GOING ON? MY VISION'S BLURING! FALC LOOKS INDISTINCT, HAZY. IS THE STRAIN GETTING TO ME?
NO, MY VISION'S CLEARING ALREADY. I CAN SEE THE FALCON AGAIN.
WAIT! THAT'S NOT THE FALCON!
AMERICAN SWINE! DO YOU THINK I WOULD ALLOW YOU TO UNDO MY GREATEST CREATION--THE FALCON?
IT'S THE RED SKULL!

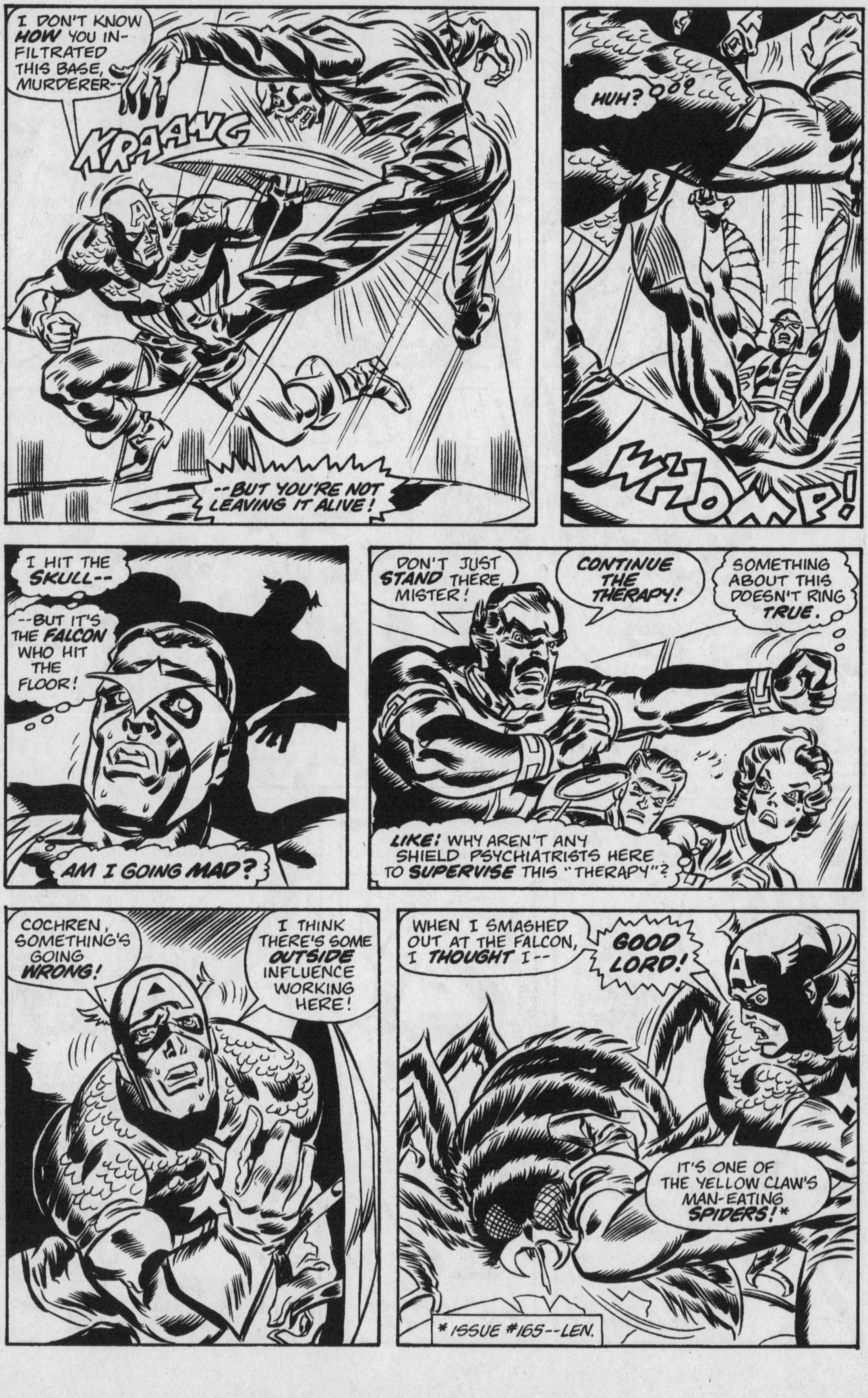
I DON'T KNOW HOW YOU IN-FILTRATED THIS BASE, MURDERER--
KRAAANG
--BUT YOU'RE NOT LEAVING IT ALIVE!
HUH?
WHOMP!
I HIT THE SKULL--
--BUT IT'S THE FALCON WHO HIT THE FLOOR!
AM I GOING MAD?
DON'T JUST STAND THERE, MISTER!
CONTINUE THE THERAPY!
SOMETHING ABOUT THIS DOESN'T RING TRUE.
LIKE: WHY AREN'T ANY SHIELD PSYCHIATRISTS HERE TO SUPERVISE THIS "THERAPY"?
COCHREN, SOMETHING'S GOING WRONG!
I THINK THERE'S SOME OUTSIDE INFLUENCE WORKING HERE!
WHEN I SMASHED OUT AT THE FALCON, I THOUGHT I--
GOOD LORD!
IT'S ONE OF THE YELLOW CLAW'S MAN-EATING SPIDERS!*
* ISSUE #165--LEN.

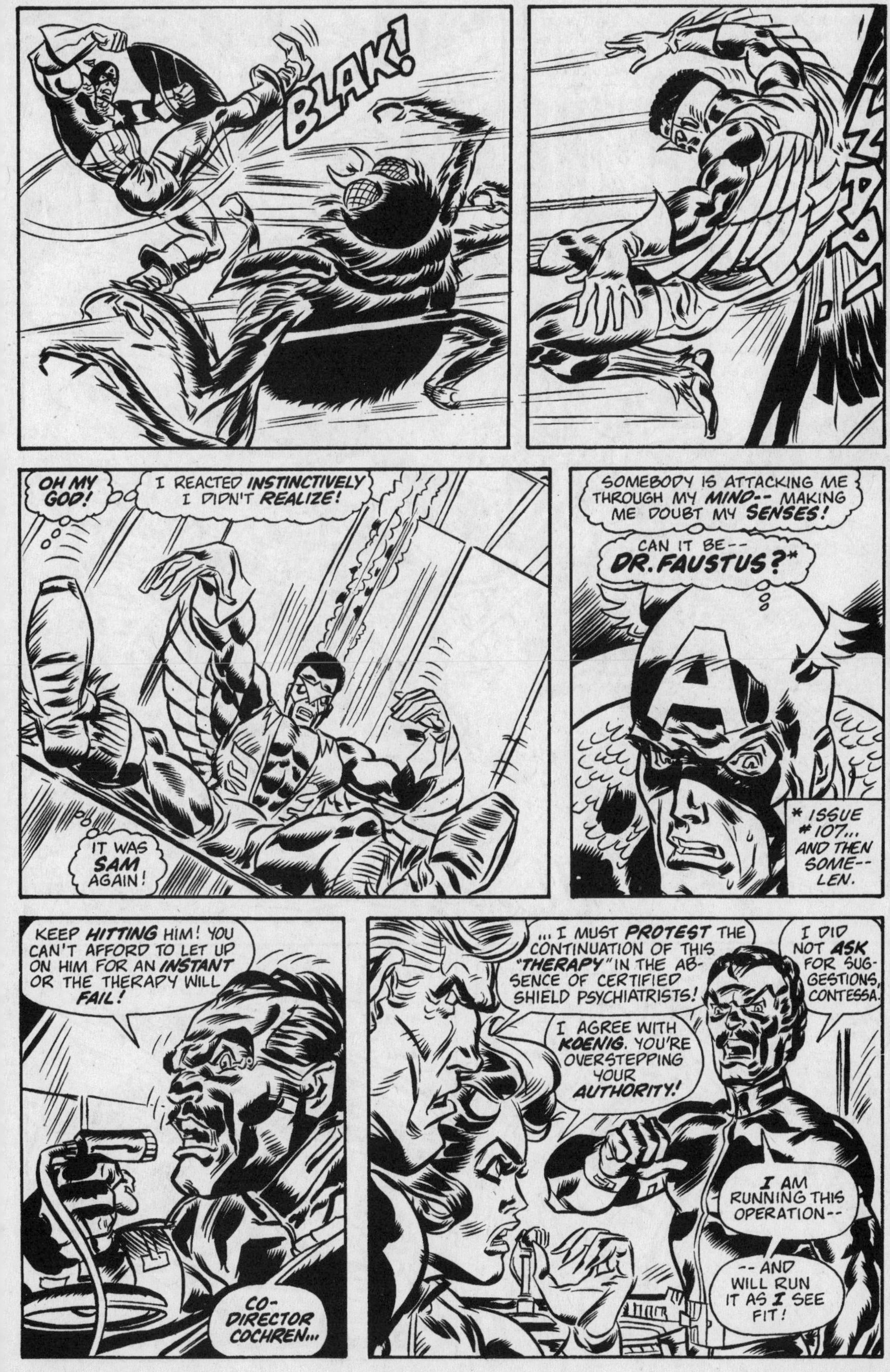
BLAK!
WHAP!
OH MY GOD!
I REACTED INSTINCTIVELY I DIDN'T REALIZE!
IT WAS SAM AGAIN!
SOMEBODY IS ATTACKING ME THROUGH MY MIND-- MAKING ME DOUBT MY SENSES!
CAN IT BE-- DR. FAUSTUS?*
* ISSUE #107... AND THEN SOME-- LEN.
KEEP HITTING HIM! YOU CAN'T AFFORD TO LET UP ON HIM FOR AN INSTANT OR THE THERAPY WILL FAIL!
CO-DIRECTOR COCHREN...
... I MUST PROTEST THE CONTINUATION OF THIS "THERAPY" IN THE ABSENCE OF CERTIFIED SHIELD PSYCHIATRISTS!
I AGREE WITH KOENIG. YOU'RE OVERSTEPPING YOUR AUTHORITY!
I DID NOT ASK FOR SUGGESTIONS, CONTESSA.
I AM RUNNING THIS OPERATION--
-- AND WILL RUN IT AS I SEE FIT!

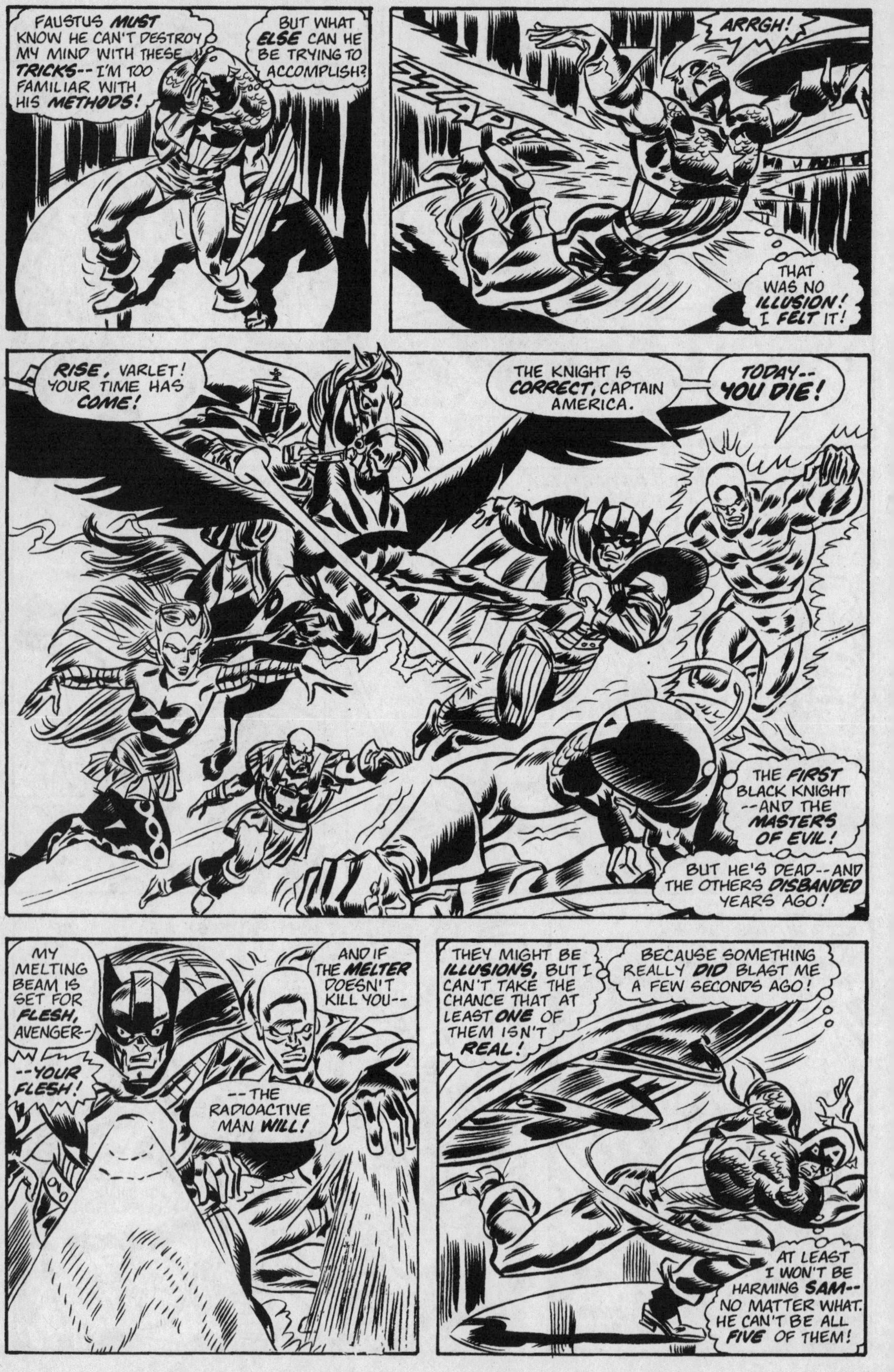
FAUSTUS MUST KNOW HE CAN'T DESTROY MY MIND WITH THESE TRICKS-- I'M TOO FAMILIAR WITH HIS METHODS!
BUT WHAT ELSE CAN HE BE TRYING TO ACCOMPLISH?
ARRGH!
THAT WAS NO ILLUSION! I FELT IT!
RISE, VARLET! YOUR TIME HAS COME!
THE KNIGHT IS CORRECT, CAPTAIN AMERICA.
TODAY-- YOU DIE!
THE FIRST BLACK KNIGHT --AND THE MASTERS OF EVIL!
BUT HE'S DEAD--AND THE OTHERS DISBANDED YEARS AGO!
MY MELTING BEAM IS SET FOR FLESH, AVENGER--
--YOUR FLESH!
AND IF THE MELTER DOESN'T KILL YOU--
--THE RADIOACTIVE MAN WILL!
THEY MIGHT BE ILLUSIONS, BUT I CAN'T TAKE THE CHANCE THAT AT LEAST ONE OF THEM ISN'T REAL!
BECAUSE SOMETHING REALLY DID BLAST ME A FEW SECONDS AGO!
AT LEAST I WON'T BE HARMING SAM-- NO MATTER WHAT. HE CAN'T BE ALL FIVE OF THEM!

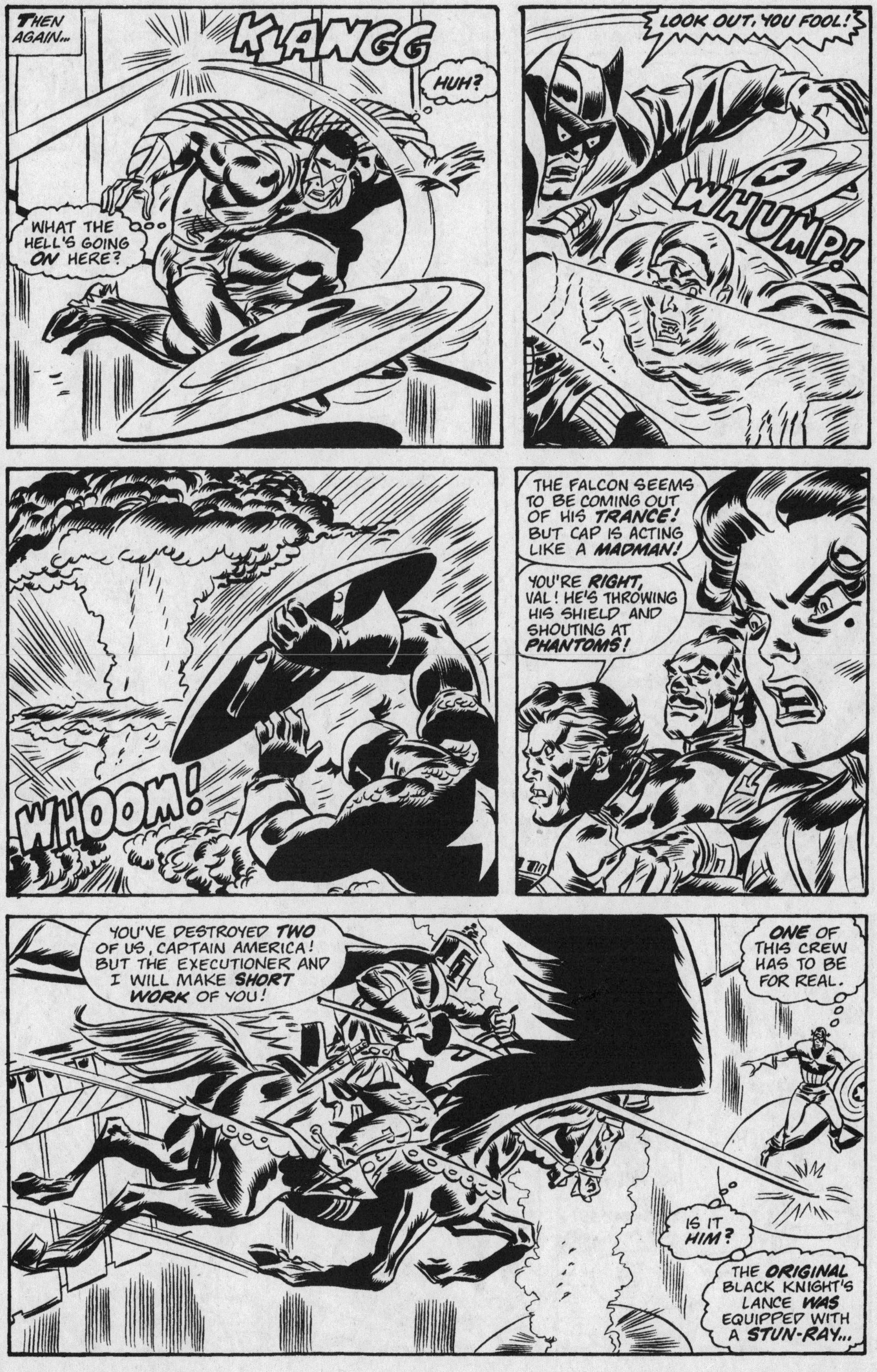
THEN AGAIN...
KLANGG
HUH?
WHAT THE HELL'S GOING ON HERE?
LOOK OUT, YOU FOOL!
WHUMP!
WHOOM!
THE FALCON SEEMS TO BE COMING OUT OF HIS TRANCE! BUT CAP IS ACTING LIKE A MADMAN!
YOU'RE RIGHT, VAL! HE'S THROWING HIS SHIELD AND SHOUTING AT PHANTOMS!
YOU'VE DESTROYED TWO OF US, CAPTAIN AMERICA! BUT THE EXECUTIONER AND I WILL MAKE SHORT WORK OF YOU!
ONE OF THIS CREW HAS TO BE FOR REAL.
IS IT HIM?
THE ORIGINAL BLACK KNIGHT'S LANCE WAS EQUIPPED WITH A STUN-RAY...

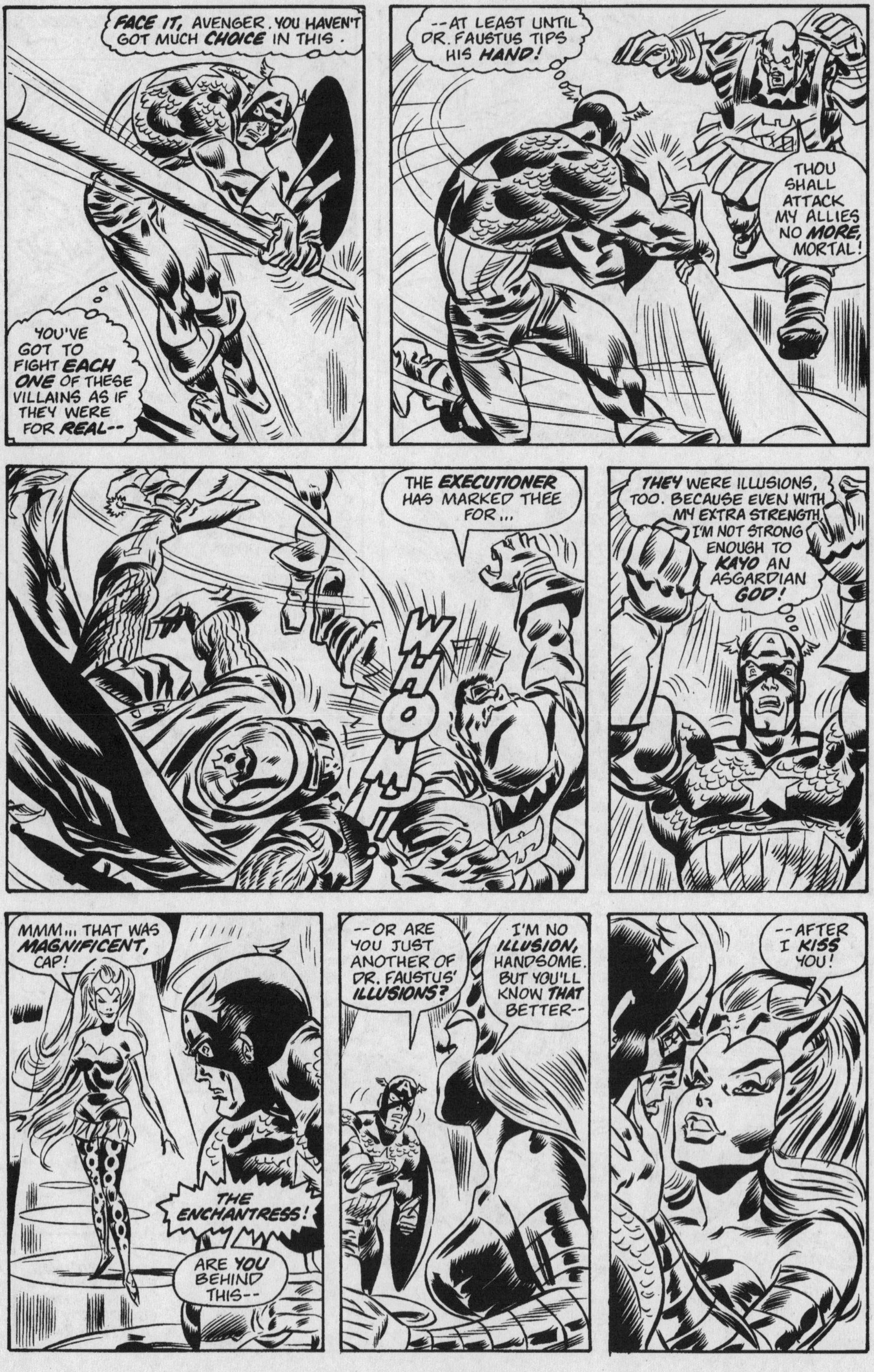
FACE IT, AVENGER. YOU HAVEN'T GOT MUCH CHOICE IN THIS.
YOU'VE GOT TO FIGHT EACH ONE OF THESE VILLAINS AS IF THEY WERE FOR REAL--
--AT LEAST UNTIL DR. FAUSTUS TIPS HIS HAND!
THOU SHALL ATTACK MY ALLIES NO MORE, MORTAL!
THE EXECUTIONER HAS MARKED THEE FOR...
WHOOMP
THEY WERE ILLUSIONS, TOO. BECAUSE EVEN WITH MY EXTRA STRENGTH, I'M NOT STRONG ENOUGH TO KAYO AN ASGARDIAN GOD!
MMM... THAT WAS MAGNIFICENT, CAP!
THE ENCHANTRESS!
ARE YOU BEHIND THIS--
--OR ARE YOU JUST ANOTHER OF DR. FAUSTUS' ILLUSIONS?
I'M NO ILLUSION, HANDSOME. BUT YOU'LL KNOW THAT BETTER--
--AFTER I KISS YOU!

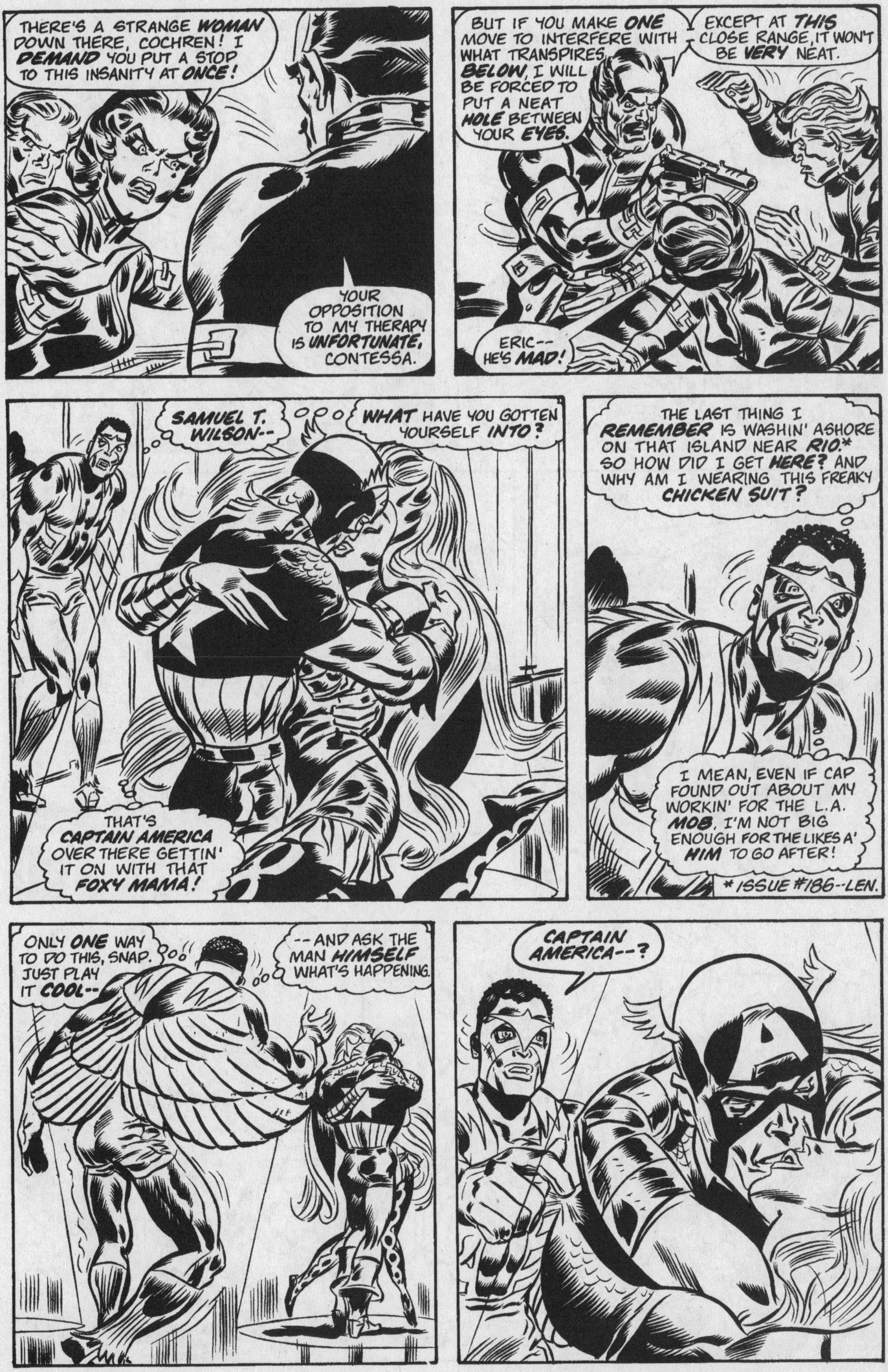
THERE'S A STRANGE WOMAN DOWN THERE, COCHREN! I DEMAND YOU PUT A STOP TO THIS INSANITY AT ONCE!
YOUR OPPOSITION TO MY THERAPY IS UNFORTUNATE, CONTESSA.
BUT IF YOU MAKE ONE MOVE TO INTERFERE WITH WHAT TRANSPIRES BELOW, I WILL BE FORCED TO PUT A NEAT HOLE BETWEEN YOUR EYES.
EXCEPT AT THIS CLOSE RANGE, IT WON'T BE VERY NEAT.
ERIC-- HE'S MAD!
SAMUEL T. WILSON--
WHAT HAVE YOU GOTTEN YOURSELF INTO?
THAT'S CAPTAIN AMERICA OVER THERE GETTIN' IT ON WITH THAT FOXY MAMA!
THE LAST THING I REMEMBER IS WASHIN' ASHORE ON THAT ISLAND NEAR RIO.* SO HOW DID I GET HERE? AND WHY AM I WEARING THIS FREAKY CHICKEN SUIT?
I MEAN, EVEN IF CAP FOUND OUT ABOUT MY WORKIN' FOR THE L.A. MOB, I'M NOT BIG ENOUGH FOR THE LIKES A' HIM TO GO AFTER!
* ISSUE #186--LEN.
ONLY ONE WAY TO DO THIS, SNAP. JUST PLAY IT COOL--
--AND ASK THE MAN HIMSELF WHAT'S HAPPENING.
CAPTAIN AMERICA--?

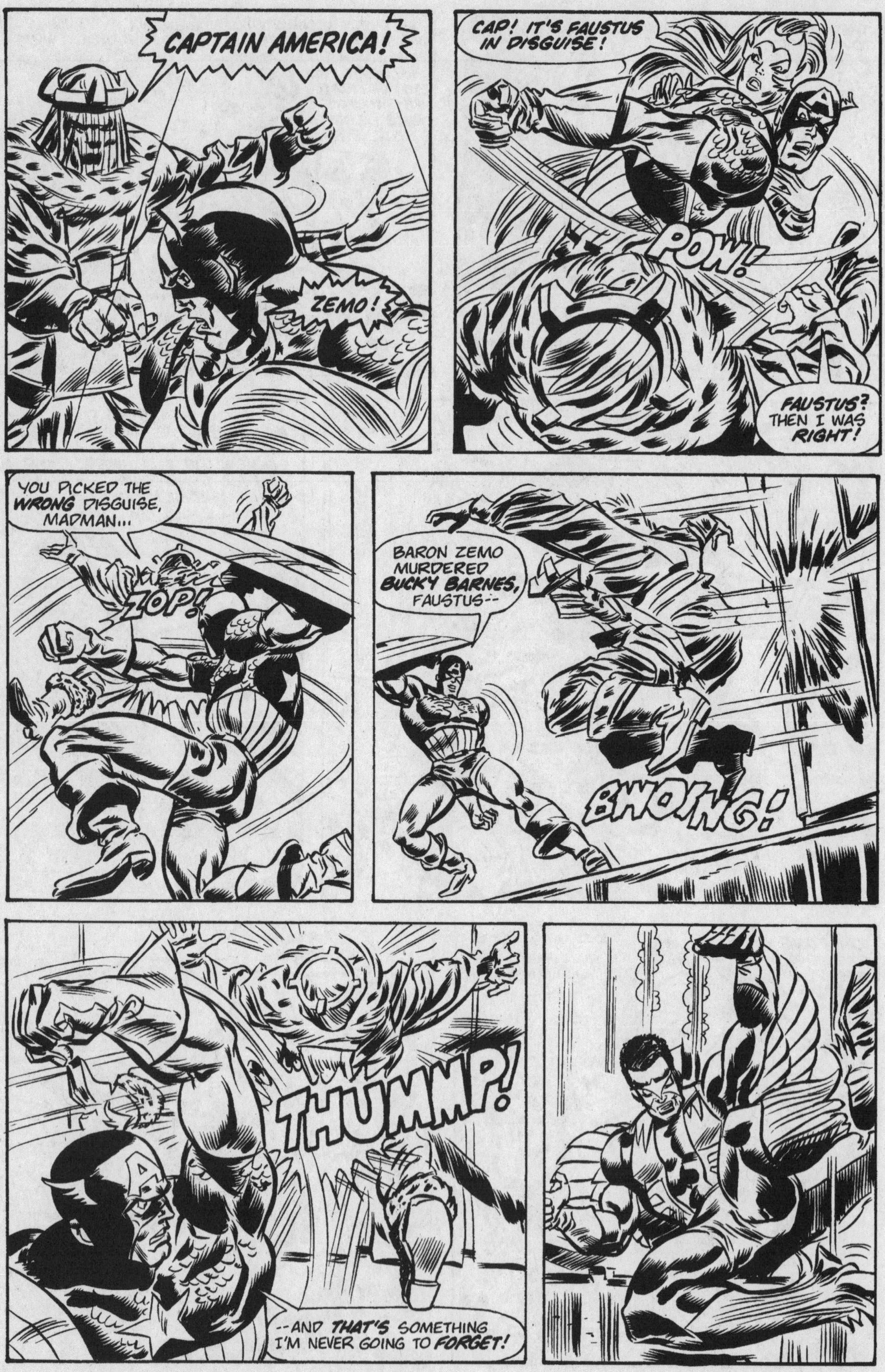
CAPTAIN AMERICA!
ZEMO!
CAP! IT'S FAUSTUS IN DISGUISE!
POW!
FAUSTUS? THEN I WAS RIGHT!
YOU PICKED THE WRONG DISGUISE, MADMAN...
ZOP!
BARON ZEMO MURDERED BUCKY BARNES, FAUSTUS--
BWOING!
THUMMP!
--AND THAT'S SOMETHING I'M NEVER GOING TO FORGET!

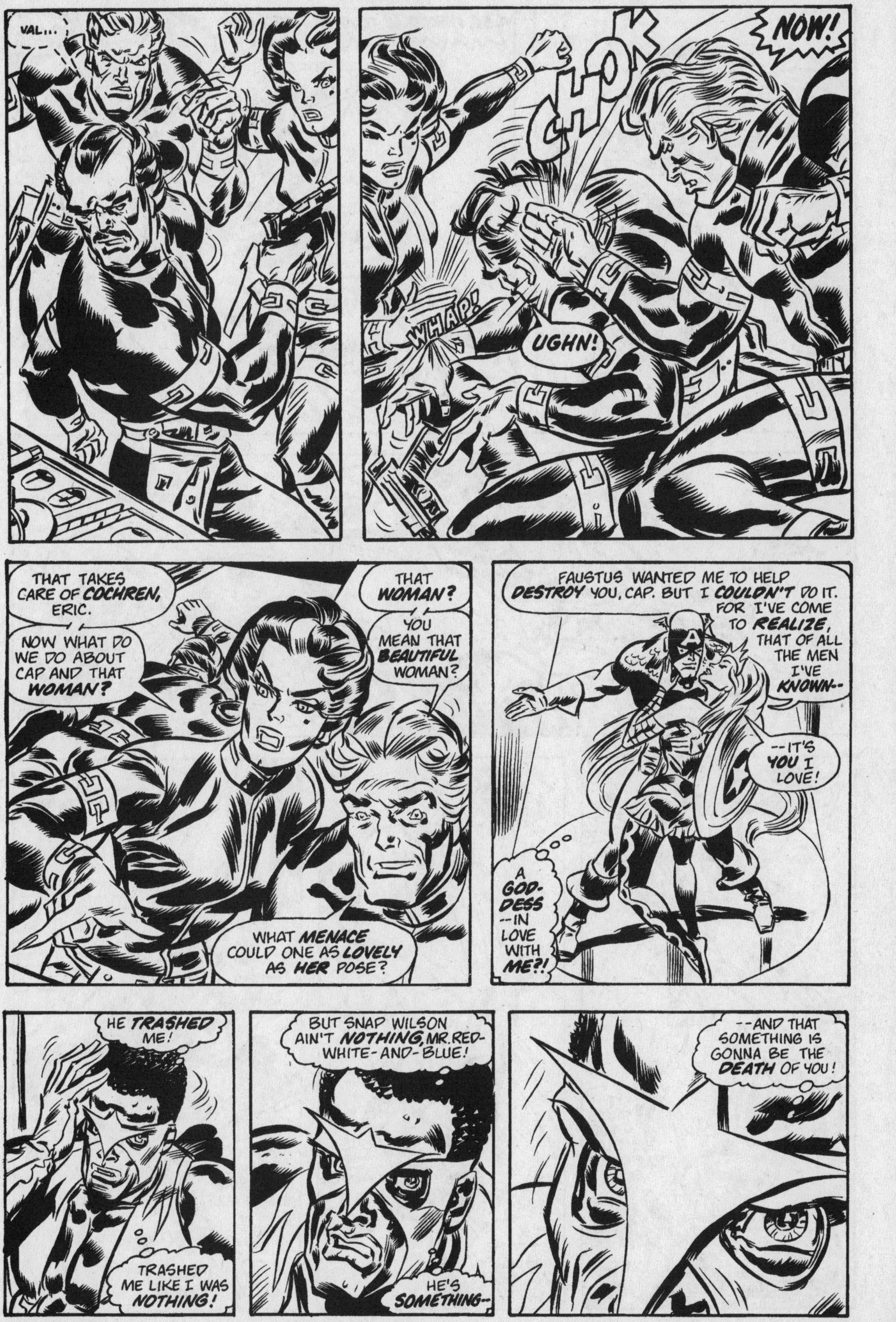
VAL...
CHOK
NOW!
WHAP!
UGHN!
THAT TAKES CARE OF COCHREN, ERIC.
NOW WHAT DO WE DO ABOUT CAP AND THAT WOMAN?
THAT WOMAN?
YOU MEAN THAT BEAUTIFUL WOMAN?
WHAT MENACE COULD ONE AS LOVELY AS HER POSE?
FAUSTUS WANTED ME TO HELP DESTROY YOU, CAP. BUT I COULDN'T DO IT. FOR I'VE COME TO REALIZE, THAT OF ALL THE MEN I'VE KNOWN--
--IT'S YOU I LOVE!
A GOD-DESS --IN LOVE WITH ME?!
HE TRASHED ME!
TRASHED ME LIKE I WAS NOTHING!
BUT SNAP WILSON AIN'T NOTHING, MR. RED-WHITE-AND-BLUE!
HE'S SOMETHING--
--AND THAT SOMETHING IS GONNA BE THE DEATH OF YOU!

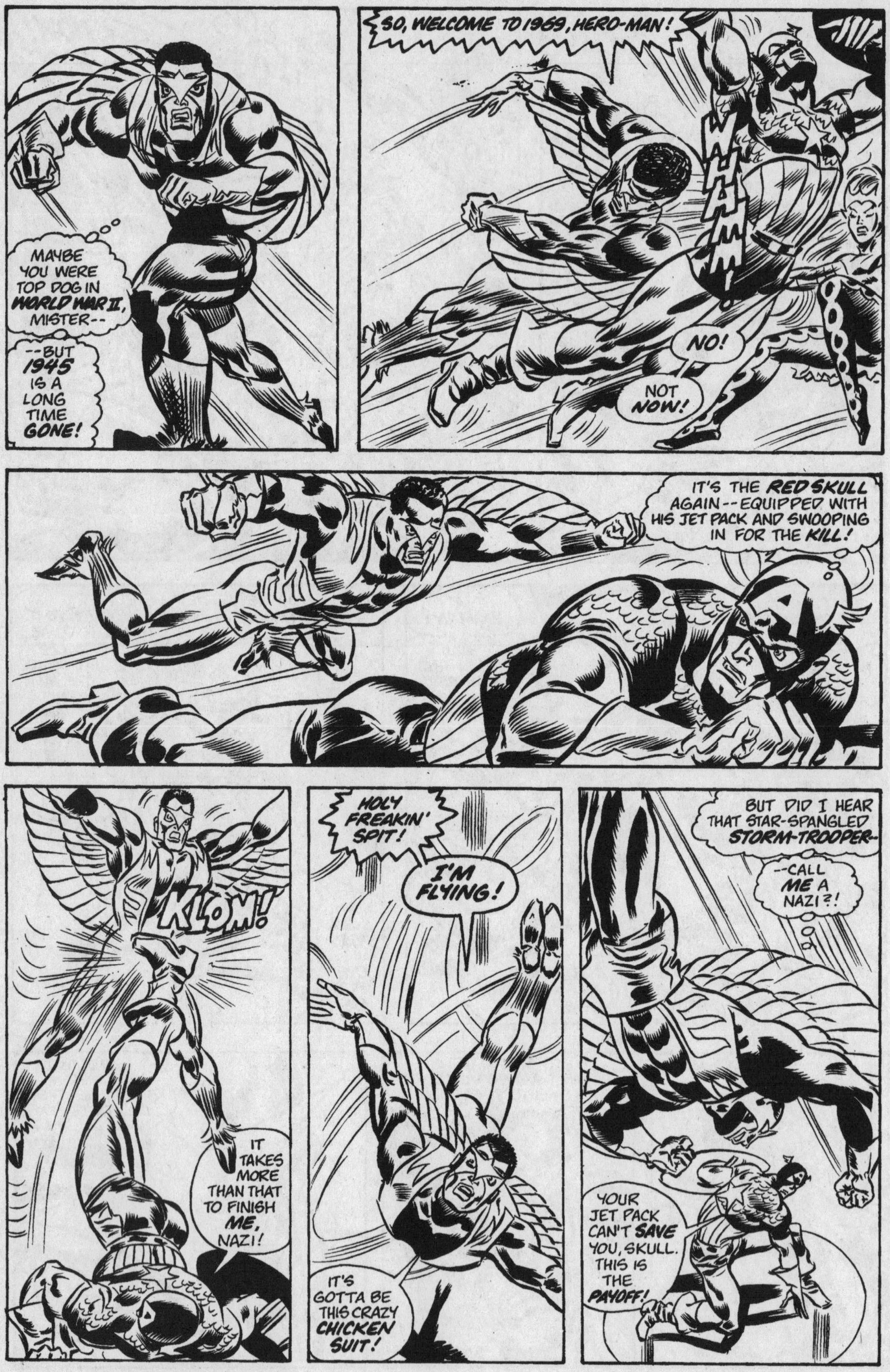
MAYBE YOU WERE TOP DOG IN WORLD WAR II, MISTER--
--BUT 1945 IS A LONG TIME GONE!
SO, WELCOME TO 1969, HERO-MAN!
WHAM!
NO!
NOT NOW!
IT'S THE RED SKULL AGAIN--EQUIPPED WITH HIS JET PACK AND SWOOPING IN FOR THE KILL!
KLOM!
IT TAKES MORE THAN THAT TO FINISH ME, NAZI!
HOLY FREAKIN' SPIT!
I'M FLYING!
IT'S GOTTA BE THIS CRAZY CHICKEN SUIT!
BUT DID I HEAR THAT STAR-SPANGLED STORM-TROOPER--
--CALL ME A NAZI?!
YOUR JET PACK CAN'T SAVE YOU, SKULL. THIS IS THE PAYOFF!

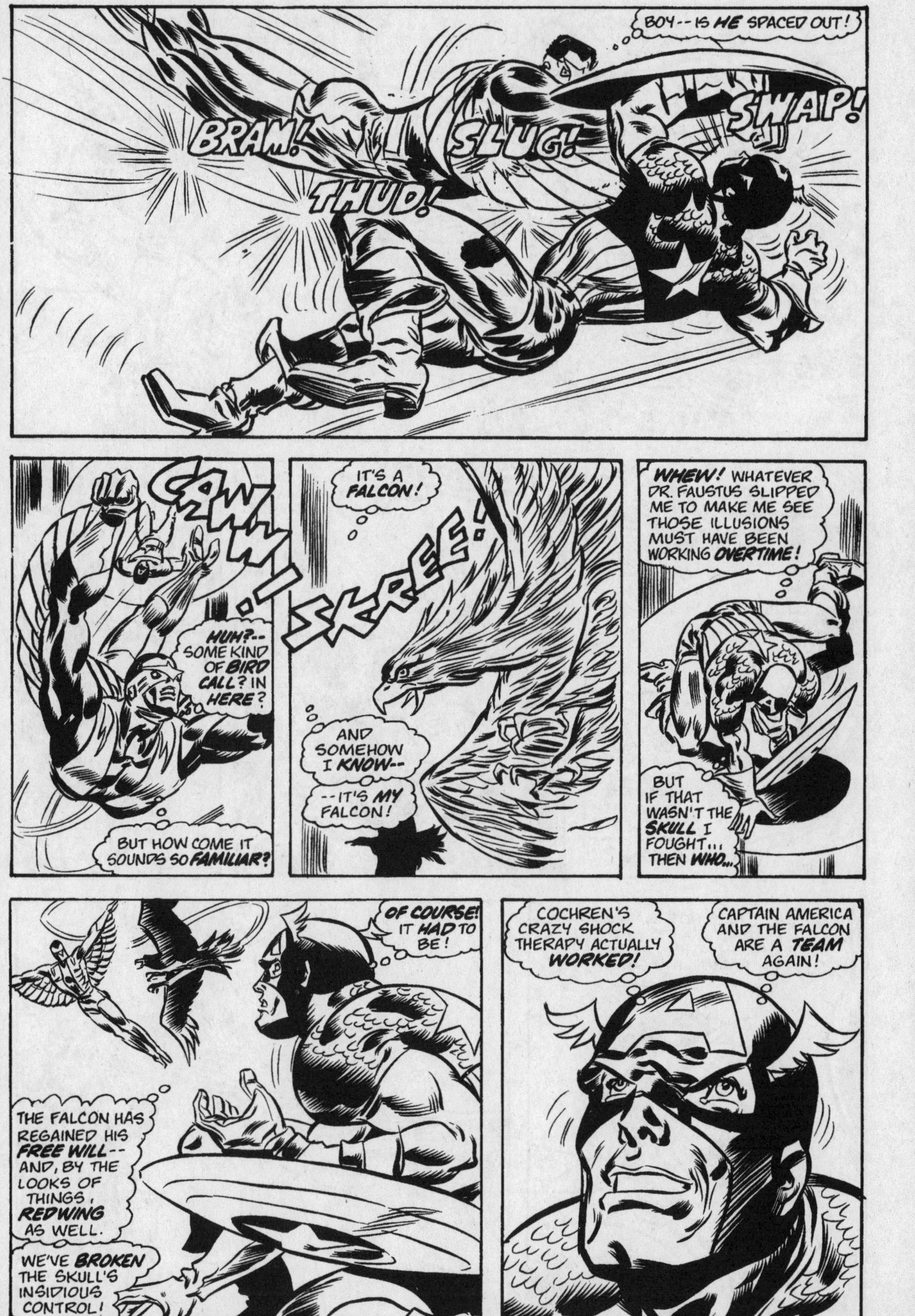
BOY--IS HE SPACED OUT!
BRAM!
SLUG!
SWAP!
THUD!
CAWW!
HUH?--SOME KIND OF BIRD CALL? IN HERE?
BUT HOW COME IT SOUNDS SO FAMILIAR?
IT'S A FALCON!
SKREEE!
AND SOMEHOW I KNOW--
--IT'S MY FALCON!
WHEW! WHATEVER DR. FAUSTUS SLIPPED ME TO MAKE ME SEE THOSE ILLUSIONS MUST HAVE BEEN WORKING OVERTIME!
BUT IF THAT WASN'T THE SKULL I FOUGHT... THEN WHO...
OF COURSE! IT HAD TO BE!
THE FALCON HAS REGAINED HIS FREE WILL--AND, BY THE LOOKS OF THINGS, REDWING AS WELL.
WE'VE BROKEN THE SKULL'S INSIDIOUS CONTROL!
COCHREN'S CRAZY SHOCK THERAPY ACTUALLY WORKED!
CAPTAIN AMERICA AND THE FALCON ARE A TEAM AGAIN!

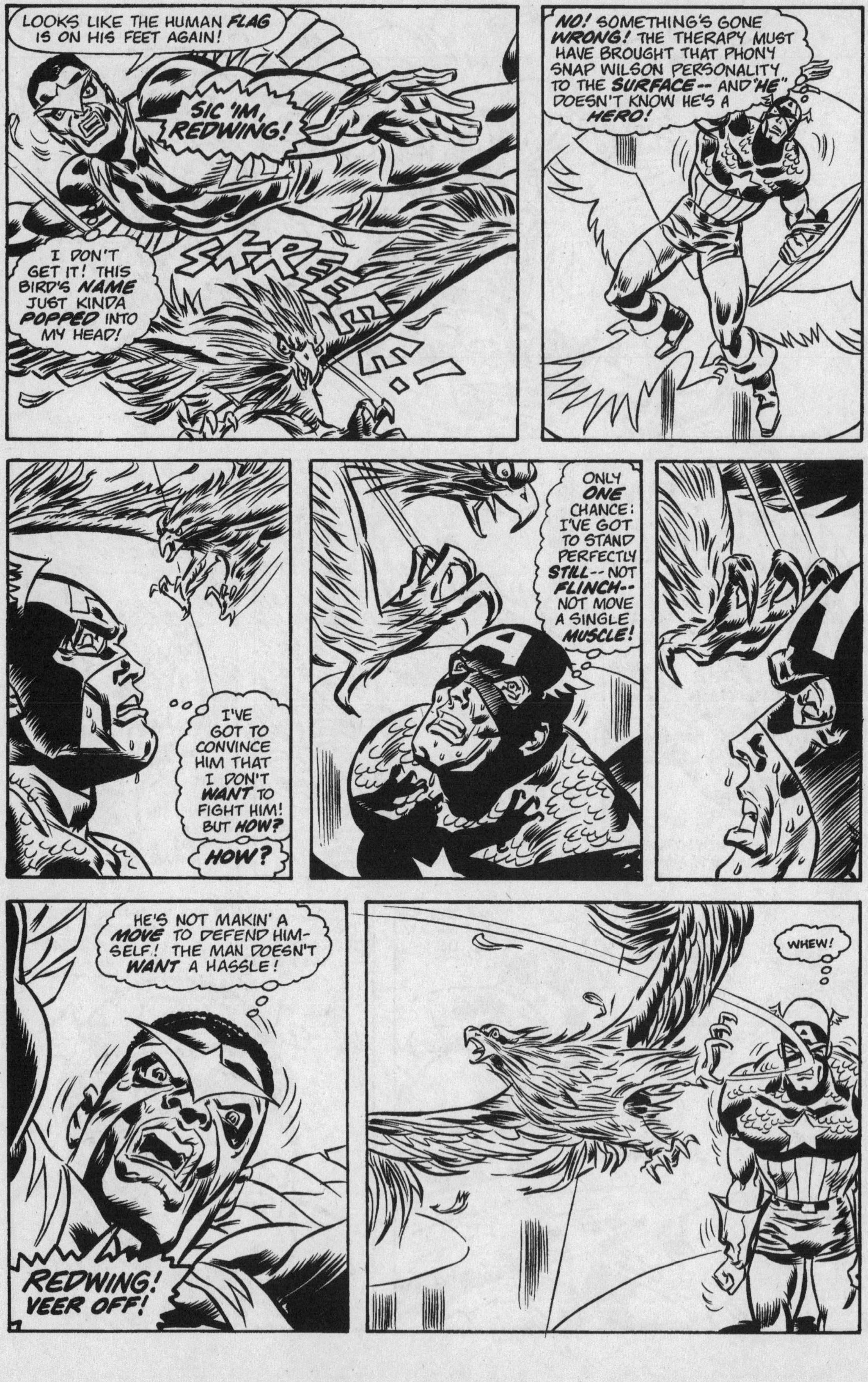

LOOKS LIKE THE HUMAN FLAG IS ON HIS FEET AGAIN!
SIC 'IM, REDWING!
SKREEEEE!
I DON'T GET IT! THIS BIRD'S NAME JUST KINDA POPPED INTO MY HEAD!
NO! SOMETHING'S GONE WRONG! THE THERAPY MUST HAVE BROUGHT THAT PHONY SNAP WILSON PERSONALITY TO THE SURFACE -- AND "HE" DOESN'T KNOW HE'S A HERO!
I'VE GOT TO CONVINCE HIM THAT I DON'T WANT TO FIGHT HIM! BUT HOW? HOW?
ONLY ONE CHANCE: I'VE GOT TO STAND PERFECTLY STILL -- NOT FLINCH -- NOT MOVE A SINGLE MUSCLE!
HE'S NOT MAKIN' A MOVE TO DEFEND HIM-SELF! THE MAN DOESN'T WANT A HASSLE!
REDWING! VEER OFF!
WHEW!

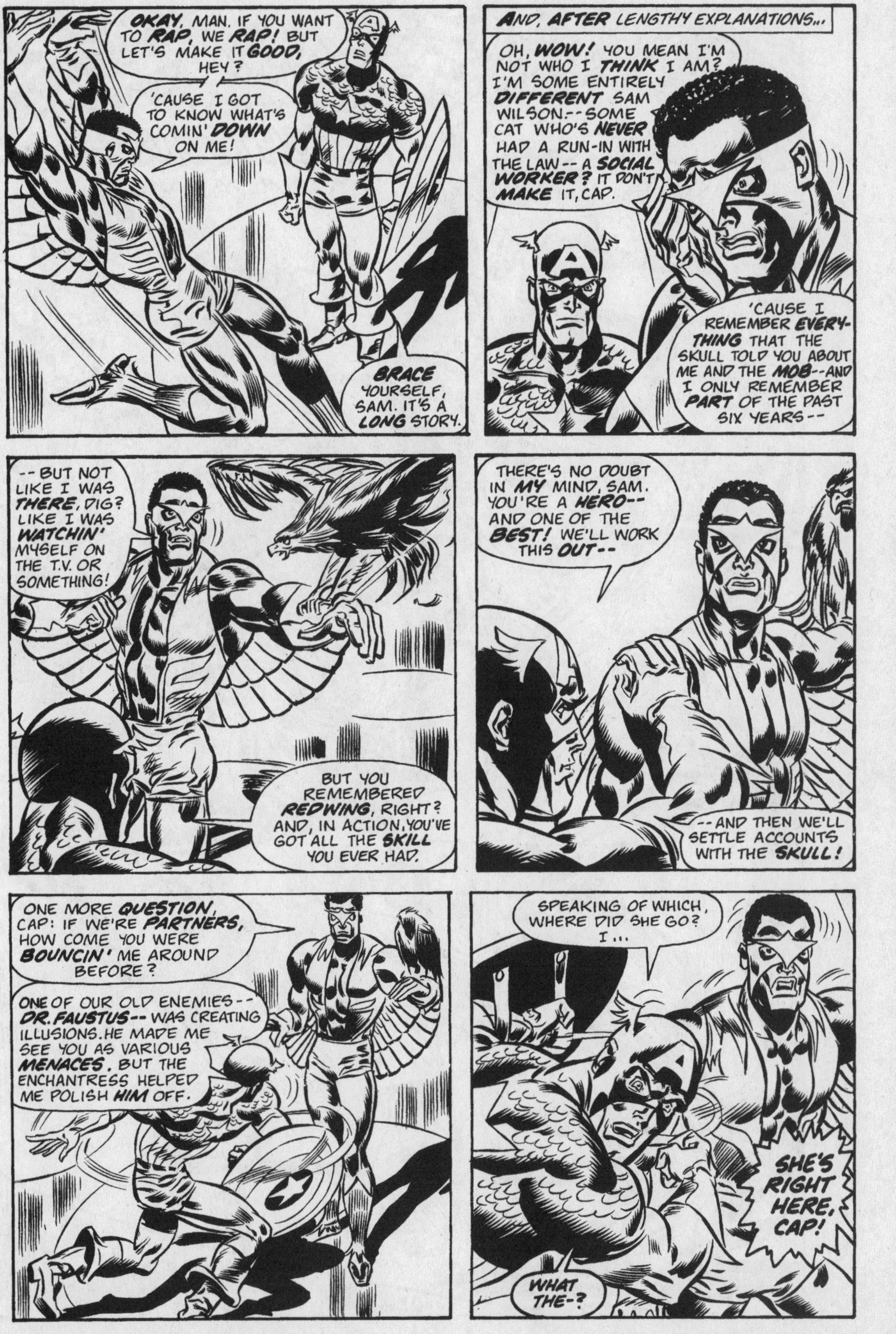
OKAY, MAN. IF YOU WANT TO RAP, WE RAP! BUT LET'S MAKE IT GOOD, HEY?
'CAUSE I GOT TO KNOW WHAT'S COMIN' DOWN ON ME!
BRACE YOURSELF, SAM. IT'S A LONG STORY.
AND, AFTER LENGTHY EXPLANATIONS...
OH, WOW! YOU MEAN I'M NOT WHO I THINK I AM? I'M SOME ENTIRELY DIFFERENT SAM WILSON.--SOME CAT WHO'S NEVER HAD A RUN-IN WITH THE LAW--A SOCIAL WORKER? IT DON'T MAKE IT, CAP.
'CAUSE I REMEMBER EVERYTHING THAT THE SKULL TOLD YOU ABOUT ME AND THE MOB--AND I ONLY REMEMBER PART OF THE PAST SIX YEARS--
--BUT NOT LIKE I WAS THERE, DIG? LIKE I WAS WATCHIN' MYSELF ON THE T.V. OR SOMETHING!
BUT YOU REMEMBERED REDWING, RIGHT? AND, IN ACTION, YOU'VE GOT ALL THE SKILL YOU EVER HAD.
THERE'S NO DOUBT IN MY MIND, SAM. YOU'RE A HERO--AND ONE OF THE BEST! WE'LL WORK THIS OUT--
--AND THEN WE'LL SETTLE ACCOUNTS WITH THE SKULL!
ONE MORE QUESTION, CAP: IF WE'RE PARTNERS, HOW COME YOU WERE BOUNCIN' ME AROUND BEFORE?
ONE OF OUR OLD ENEMIES--DR. FAUSTUS--WAS CREATING ILLUSIONS. HE MADE ME SEE YOU AS VARIOUS MENACES. BUT THE ENCHANTRESS HELPED ME POLISH HIM OFF.
SPEAKING OF WHICH, WHERE DID SHE GO? I...
SHE'S RIGHT HERE, CAP!
WHAT THE-?

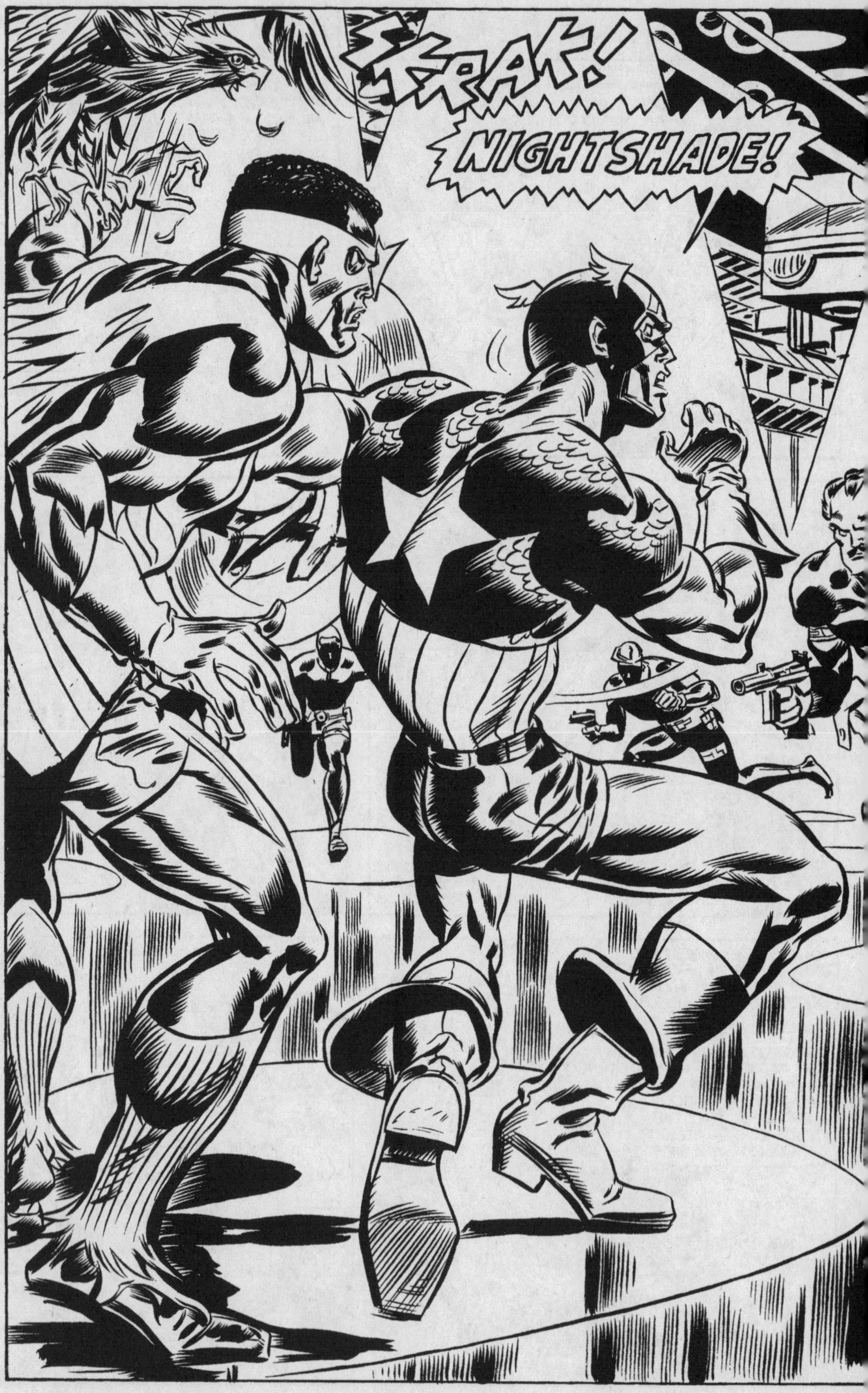
SKRAK!
NIGHTSHADE!

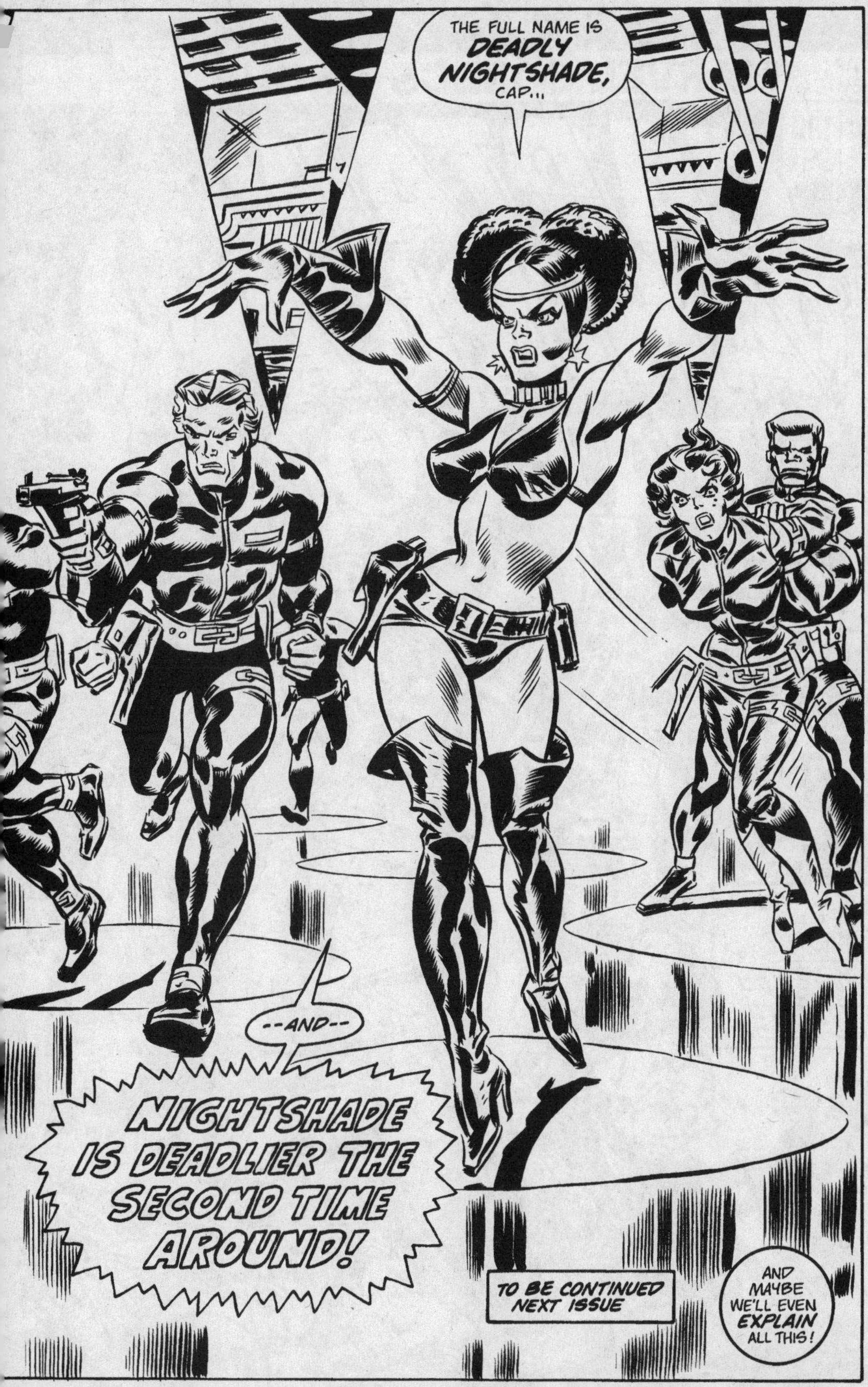
THE FULL NAME IS DEADLY NIGHTSHADE, CAP...
--AND--
NIGHTSHADE IS DEADLIER THE SECOND TIME AROUND!
TO BE CONTINUED NEXT ISSUE
AND MAYBE WE'LL EVEN EXPLAIN ALL THIS!

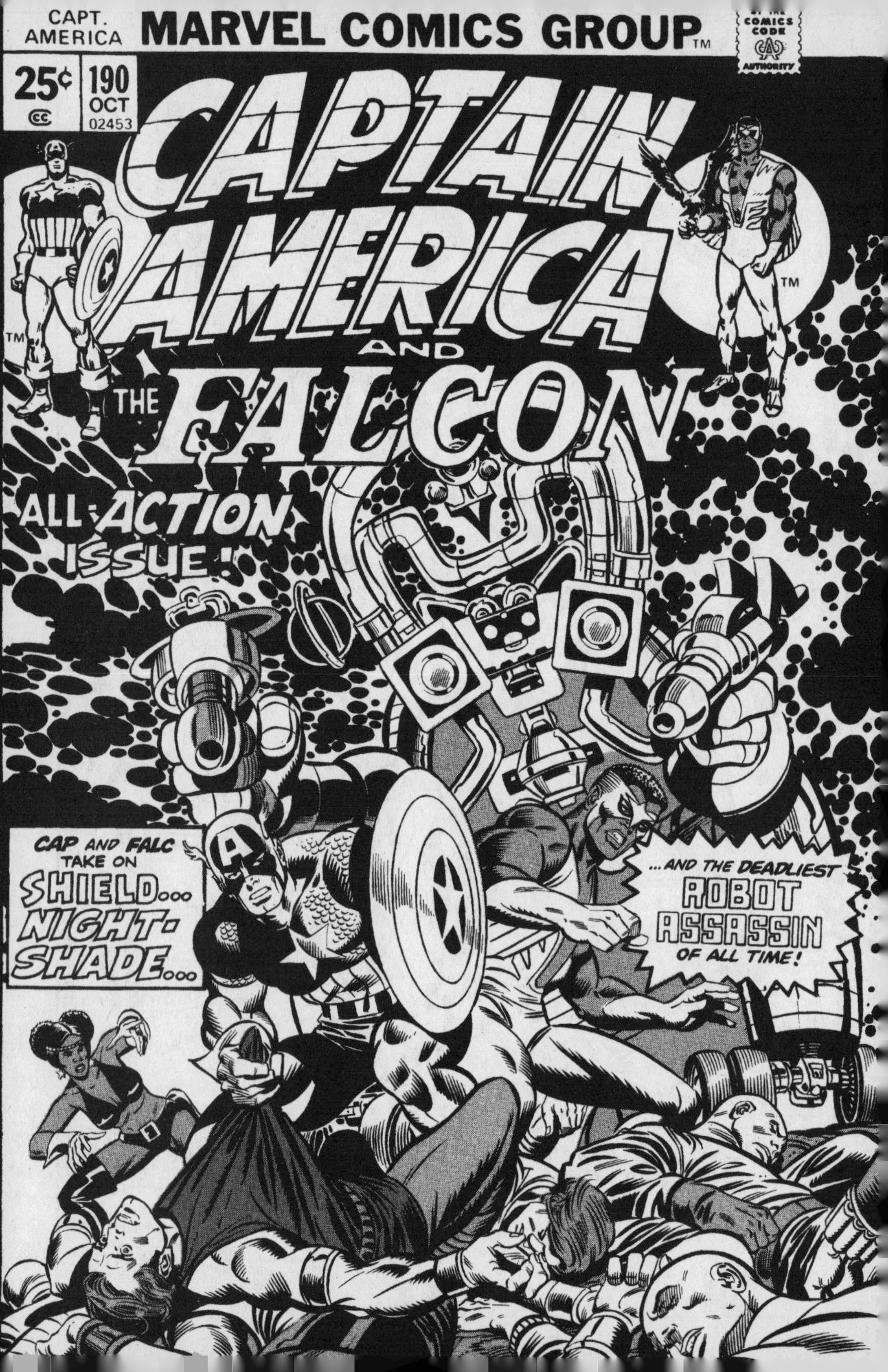
CAPT. AMERICA
MARVEL COMICS GROUP™
COMICS CODE
AUTHORITY
25¢
190
OCT
02453
CAPTAIN AMERICA™
AND
THE FALCON
ALL-ACTION ISSUE!
CAP AND FALC TAKE ON SHIELD... NIGHT-SHADE...
...AND THE DEADLIEST ROBOT ASSASSIN OF ALL TIME!

1941! The world at *war!* And in a secret laboratory, frail *Steve Rogers* became the American *super-soldier!* For four thrilling years, he fought the Axis powers—until a freak stroke of fate threw him into *suspended animation.* He woke in the mid-1960s, a man *twenty years out of his time.* Since that fateful day, Steve Rogers has sought his *destiny* in this brave new world.

Stan Lee PRESENTS: CAPTAIN AMERICA AND THE FALCON™

| TONY ISABELLA & FRANK ROBBINS | VINCE COLLETTA | DAVE HUNT, LETTERS | MARV WOLFMAN |
| WRITER-STORY TELLERS-ARTIST | INKER | MICHELE W., COLORS | EDITOR |

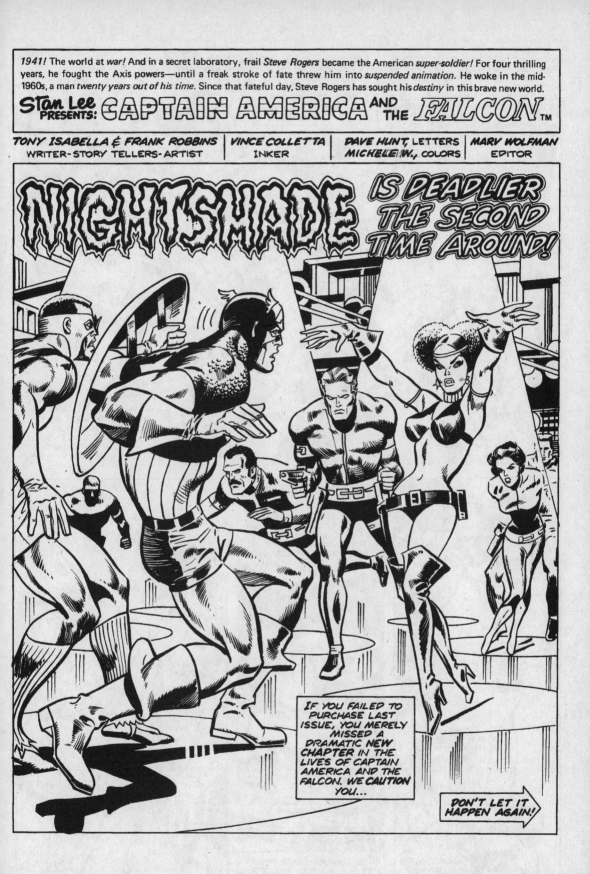

NIGHTSHADE IS DEADLIER THE SECOND TIME AROUND!

IF YOU FAILED TO PURCHASE LAST ISSUE, YOU MERELY MISSED A DRAMATIC NEW CHAPTER IN THE LIVES OF CAPTAIN AMERICA AND THE FALCON. WE CAUTION YOU...

DON'T LET IT HAPPEN AGAIN!

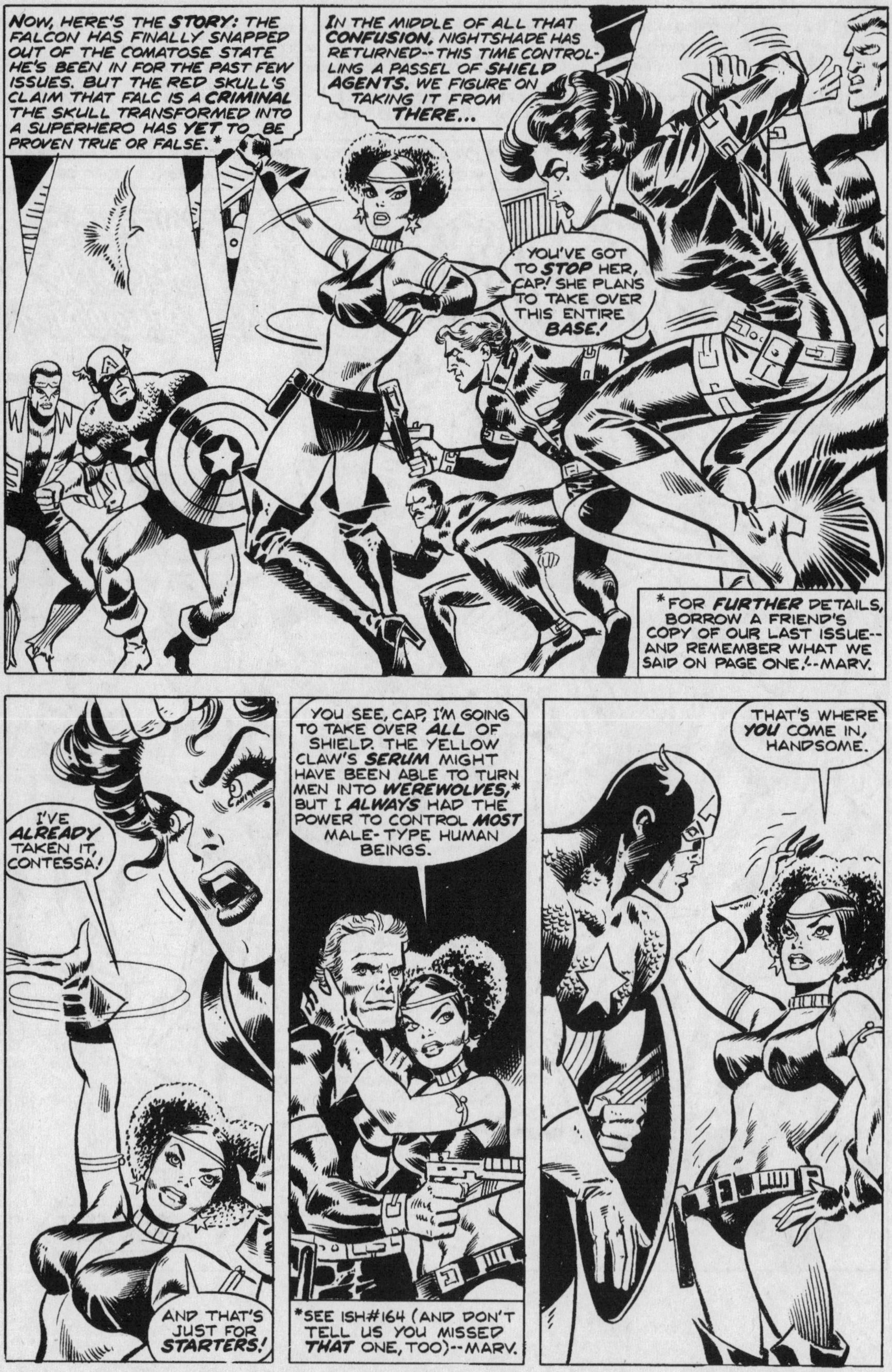
NOW, HERE'S THE STORY: THE FALCON HAS FINALLY SNAPPED OUT OF THE COMATOSE STATE HE'S BEEN IN FOR THE PAST FEW ISSUES. BUT THE RED SKULL'S CLAIM THAT FALC IS A CRIMINAL THE SKULL TRANSFORMED INTO A SUPERHERO HAS YET TO BE PROVEN TRUE OR FALSE.*
IN THE MIDDLE OF ALL THAT CONFUSION, NIGHTSHADE HAS RETURNED-- THIS TIME CONTROLLING A PASSEL OF SHIELD AGENTS. WE FIGURE ON TAKING IT FROM THERE...
YOU'VE GOT TO STOP HER, CAP! SHE PLANS TO TAKE OVER THIS ENTIRE BASE!
*FOR FURTHER DETAILS, BORROW A FRIEND'S COPY OF OUR LAST ISSUE-- AND REMEMBER WHAT WE SAID ON PAGE ONE!--MARV.
I'VE ALREADY TAKEN IT, CONTESSA!
AND THAT'S JUST FOR STARTERS!
YOU SEE, CAP, I'M GOING TO TAKE OVER ALL OF SHIELD. THE YELLOW CLAW'S SERUM MIGHT HAVE BEEN ABLE TO TURN MEN INTO WEREWOLVES,* BUT I ALWAYS HAD THE POWER TO CONTROL MOST MALE-TYPE HUMAN BEINGS.
*SEE ISH#164 (AND DON'T TELL US YOU MISSED THAT ONE, TOO)--MARV.
THAT'S WHERE YOU COME IN, HANDSOME.

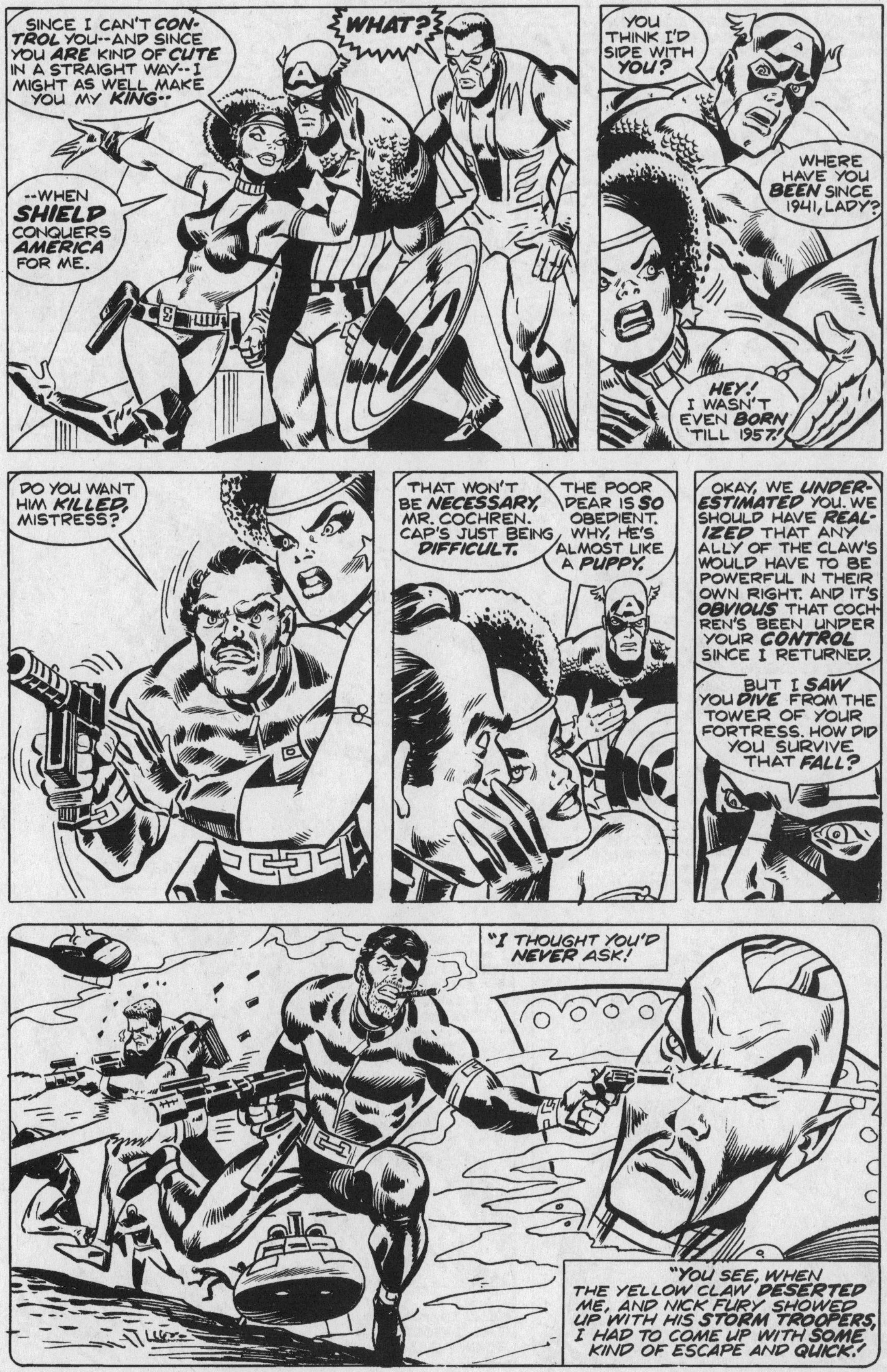
SINCE I CAN'T CONTROL YOU--AND SINCE YOU ARE KIND OF CUTE IN A STRAIGHT WAY--I MIGHT AS WELL MAKE YOU MY KING--
--WHEN SHIELD CONQUERS AMERICA FOR ME.
WHAT?
YOU THINK I'D SIDE WITH YOU?
WHERE HAVE YOU BEEN SINCE 1941, LADY?
HEY! I WASN'T EVEN BORN 'TILL 1957!
DO YOU WANT HIM KILLED, MISTRESS?
THAT WON'T BE NECESSARY, MR. COCHREN. CAP'S JUST BEING DIFFICULT.
THE POOR DEAR IS SO OBEDIENT. WHY, HE'S ALMOST LIKE A PUPPY.
OKAY, WE UNDERESTIMATED YOU. WE SHOULD HAVE REALIZED THAT ANY ALLY OF THE CLAW'S WOULD HAVE TO BE POWERFUL IN THEIR OWN RIGHT. AND IT'S OBVIOUS THAT COCHREN'S BEEN UNDER YOUR CONTROL SINCE I RETURNED.
BUT I SAW YOU DIVE FROM THE TOWER OF YOUR FORTRESS. HOW DID YOU SURVIVE THAT FALL?
"I THOUGHT YOU'D NEVER ASK!
"YOU SEE, WHEN THE YELLOW CLAW DESERTED ME, AND NICK FURY SHOWED UP WITH HIS STORM TROOPERS, I HAD TO COME UP WITH SOME KIND OF ESCAPE AND QUICK!

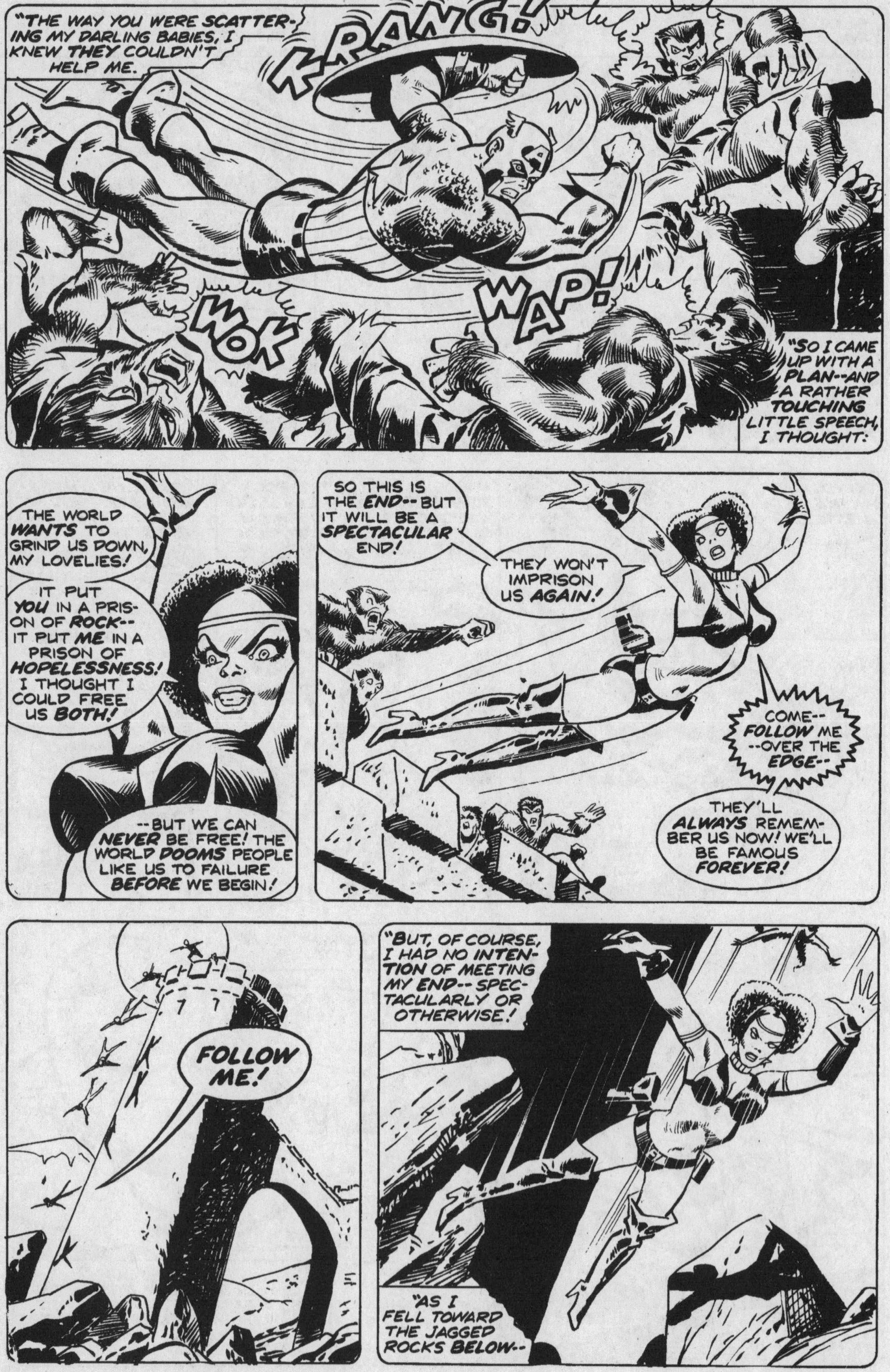
"THE WAY YOU WERE SCATTERING MY DARLING BABIES, I KNEW THEY COULDN'T HELP ME.
KRANG!
WOK
WAP!
"SO I CAME UP WITH A PLAN--AND A RATHER TOUCHING LITTLE SPEECH, I THOUGHT:
THE WORLD WANTS TO GRIND US DOWN, MY LOVELIES!
IT PUT YOU IN A PRISON OF ROCK-- IT PUT ME IN A PRISON OF HOPELESSNESS! I THOUGHT I COULD FREE US BOTH!
--BUT WE CAN NEVER BE FREE! THE WORLD DOOMS PEOPLE LIKE US TO FAILURE BEFORE WE BEGIN!
SO THIS IS THE END-- BUT IT WILL BE A SPECTACULAR END!
THEY WON'T IMPRISON US AGAIN!
COME-- FOLLOW ME --OVER THE EDGE--
THEY'LL ALWAYS REMEMBER US NOW! WE'LL BE FAMOUS FOREVER!
FOLLOW ME!
"BUT, OF COURSE, I HAD NO INTENTION OF MEETING MY END-- SPECTACULARLY OR OTHERWISE!
"AS I FELL TOWARD THE JAGGED ROCKS BELOW--

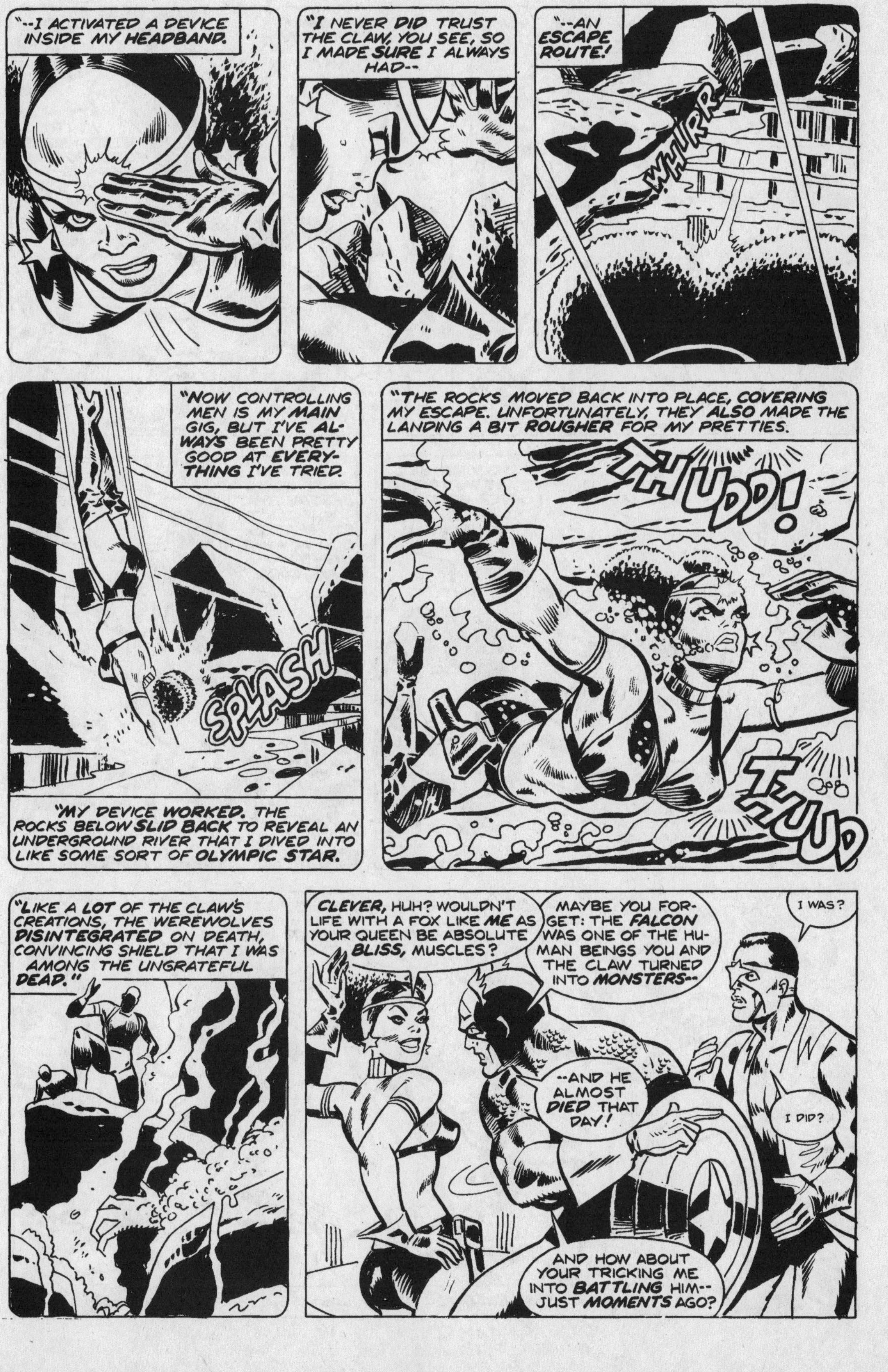
"--I ACTIVATED A DEVICE INSIDE MY HEADBAND.
"I NEVER DID TRUST THE CLAW, YOU SEE, SO I MADE SURE I ALWAYS HAD--
"--AN ESCAPE ROUTE!
WHIRR
"NOW CONTROLLING MEN IS MY MAIN GIG, BUT I'VE ALWAYS BEEN PRETTY GOOD AT EVERYTHING I'VE TRIED.
SPLASH
"MY DEVICE WORKED. THE ROCKS BELOW SLID BACK TO REVEAL AN UNDERGROUND RIVER THAT I DIVED INTO LIKE SOME SORT OF OLYMPIC STAR.
"THE ROCKS MOVED BACK INTO PLACE, COVERING MY ESCAPE. UNFORTUNATELY, THEY ALSO MADE THE LANDING A BIT ROUGHER FOR MY PRETTIES.
THUDD!
THUUD
"LIKE A LOT OF THE CLAW'S CREATIONS, THE WEREWOLVES DISINTEGRATED ON DEATH, CONVINCING SHIELD THAT I WAS AMONG THE UNGRATEFUL DEAD."
CLEVER, HUH? WOULDN'T LIFE WITH A FOX LIKE ME AS YOUR QUEEN BE ABSOLUTE BLISS, MUSCLES?
MAYBE YOU FORGET: THE FALCON WAS ONE OF THE HUMAN BEINGS YOU AND THE CLAW TURNED INTO MONSTERS--
I WAS?
--AND HE ALMOST DIED THAT DAY!
I DID?
AND HOW ABOUT YOUR TRICKING ME INTO BATTLING HIM--JUST MOMENTS AGO?

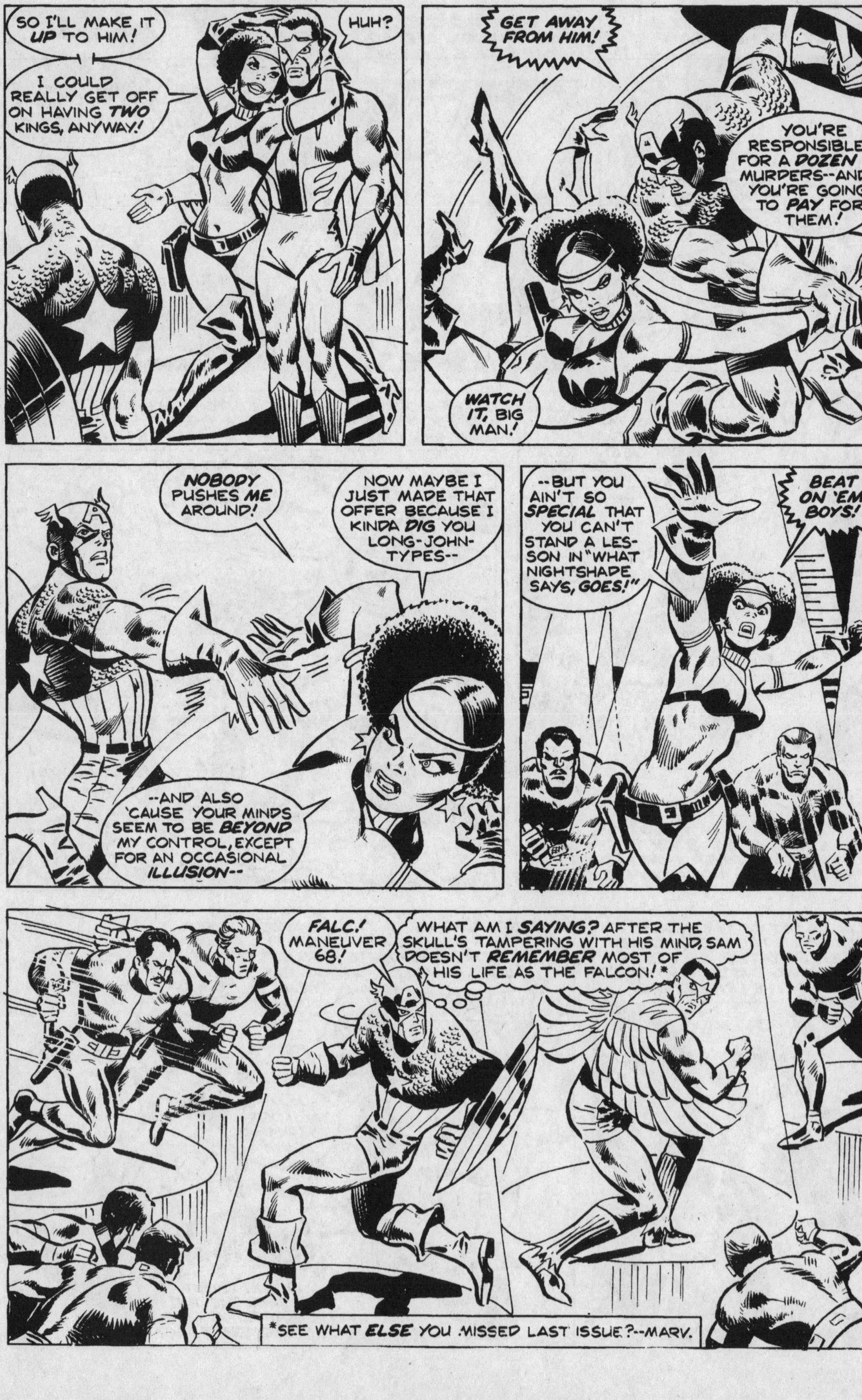
SO I'LL MAKE IT UP TO HIM!
I COULD REALLY GET OFF ON HAVING TWO KINGS, ANYWAY!
HUH?
GET AWAY FROM HIM!
YOU'RE RESPONSIBLE FOR A DOZEN MURDERS--AND YOU'RE GOING TO PAY FOR THEM!
WATCH IT, BIG MAN!
NOBODY PUSHES ME AROUND!
NOW MAYBE I JUST MADE THAT OFFER BECAUSE I KINDA DIG YOU LONG-JOHN-TYPES--
--AND ALSO 'CAUSE YOUR MINDS SEEM TO BE BEYOND MY CONTROL, EXCEPT FOR AN OCCASIONAL ILLUSION--
--BUT YOU AIN'T SO SPECIAL THAT YOU CAN'T STAND A LES-SON IN "WHAT NIGHTSHADE SAYS, GOES!"
BEAT ON 'EM, BOYS!
FALC! MANEUVER 68!
WHAT AM I SAYING? AFTER THE SKULL'S TAMPERING WITH HIS MIND, SAM DOESN'T REMEMBER MOST OF HIS LIFE AS THE FALCON! *
*SEE WHAT ELSE YOU MISSED LAST ISSUE?--MARV.

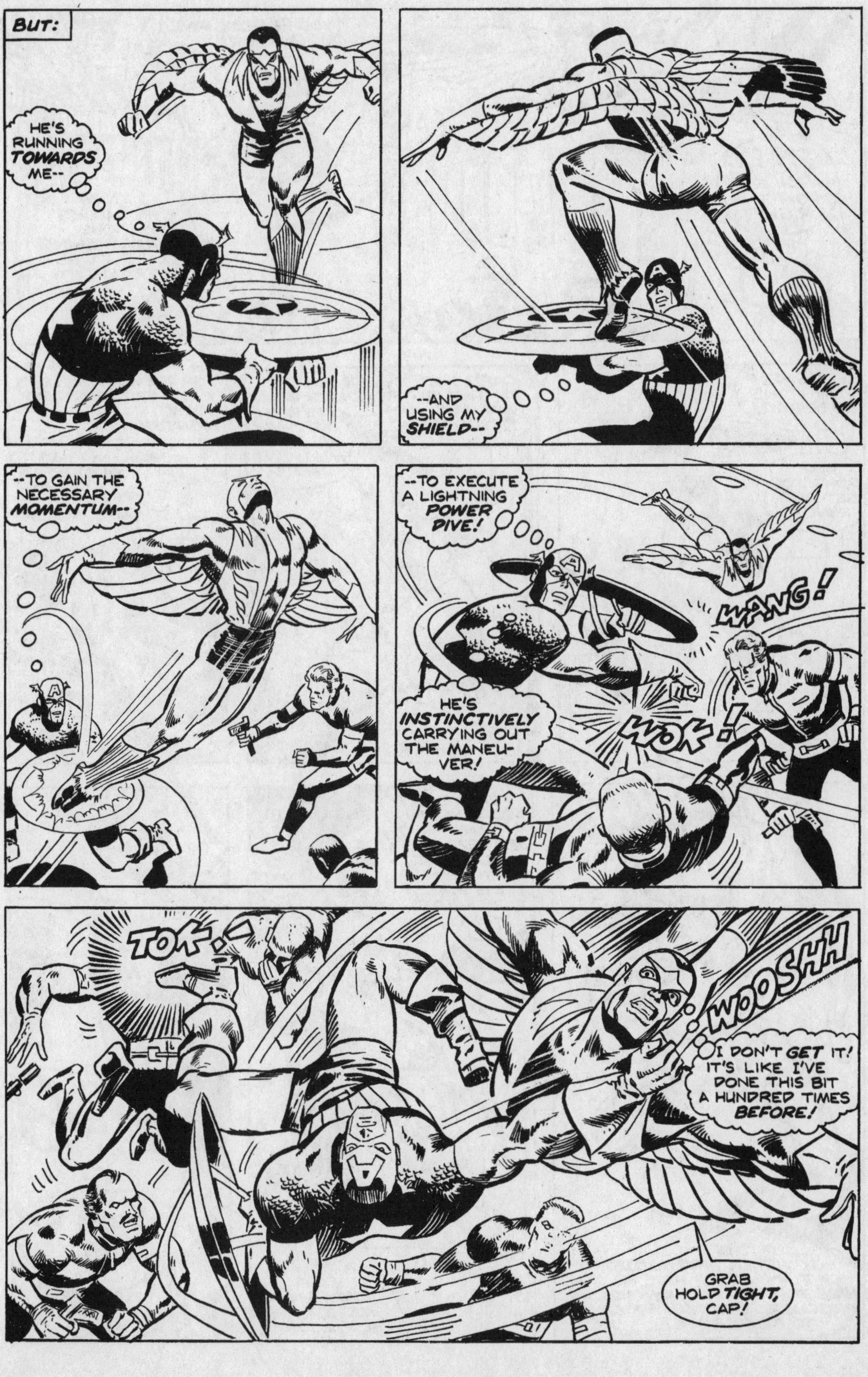
BUT:
HE'S RUNNING TOWARDS ME--
--AND USING MY SHIELD--
--TO GAIN THE NECESSARY MOMENTUM--
--TO EXECUTE A LIGHTNING POWER DIVE!
WANG!
HE'S INSTINCTIVELY CARRYING OUT THE MANEU-VER!
WOK!
TOK!
WOOSHH
I DON'T GET IT! IT'S LIKE I'VE DONE THIS BIT A HUNDRED TIMES BEFORE!
GRAB HOLD TIGHT, CAP!

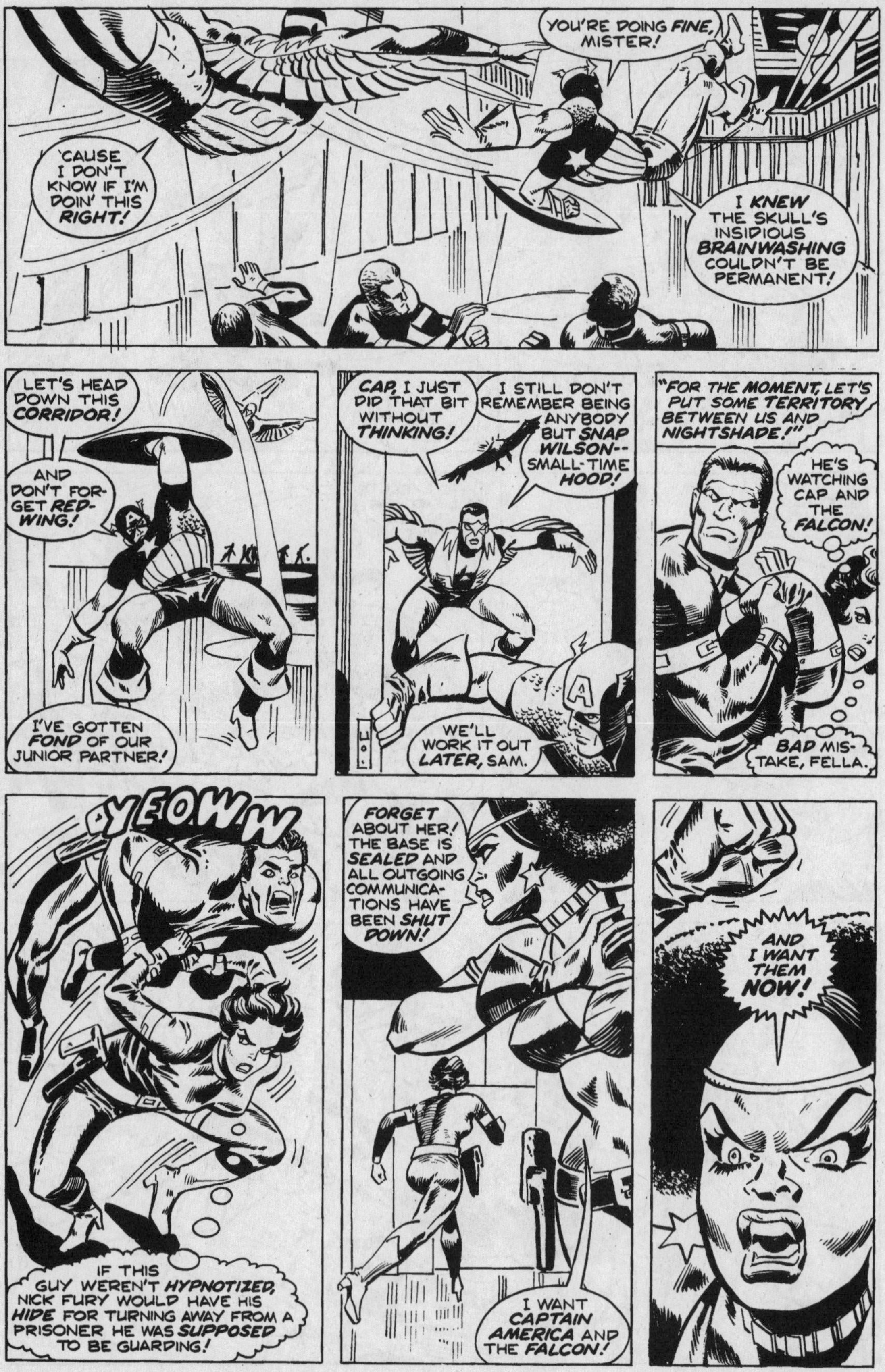

YOU'RE DOING FINE, MISTER!
'CAUSE I DON'T KNOW IF I'M DOIN' THIS RIGHT!
I KNEW THE SKULL'S INSIDIOUS BRAINWASHING COULDN'T BE PERMANENT!
LET'S HEAD DOWN THIS CORRIDOR!
AND DON'T FORGET RED-WING!
I'VE GOTTEN FOND OF OUR JUNIOR PARTNER!
CAP, I JUST DID THAT BIT WITHOUT THINKING!
I STILL DON'T REMEMBER BEING ANYBODY BUT SNAP WILSON--SMALL-TIME HOOD!
WE'LL WORK IT OUT LATER, SAM.
"FOR THE MOMENT, LET'S PUT SOME TERRITORY BETWEEN US AND NIGHTSHADE!"
HE'S WATCHING CAP AND THE FALCON!
BAD MISTAKE, FELLA.
YEOWW
IF THIS GUY WEREN'T HYPNOTIZED, NICK FURY WOULD HAVE HIS HIDE FOR TURNING AWAY FROM A PRISONER HE WAS SUPPOSED TO BE GUARDING!
FORGET ABOUT HER! THE BASE IS SEALED AND ALL OUTGOING COMMUNICATIONS HAVE BEEN SHUT DOWN!
I WANT CAPTAIN AMERICA AND THE FALCON!
AND I WANT THEM NOW!

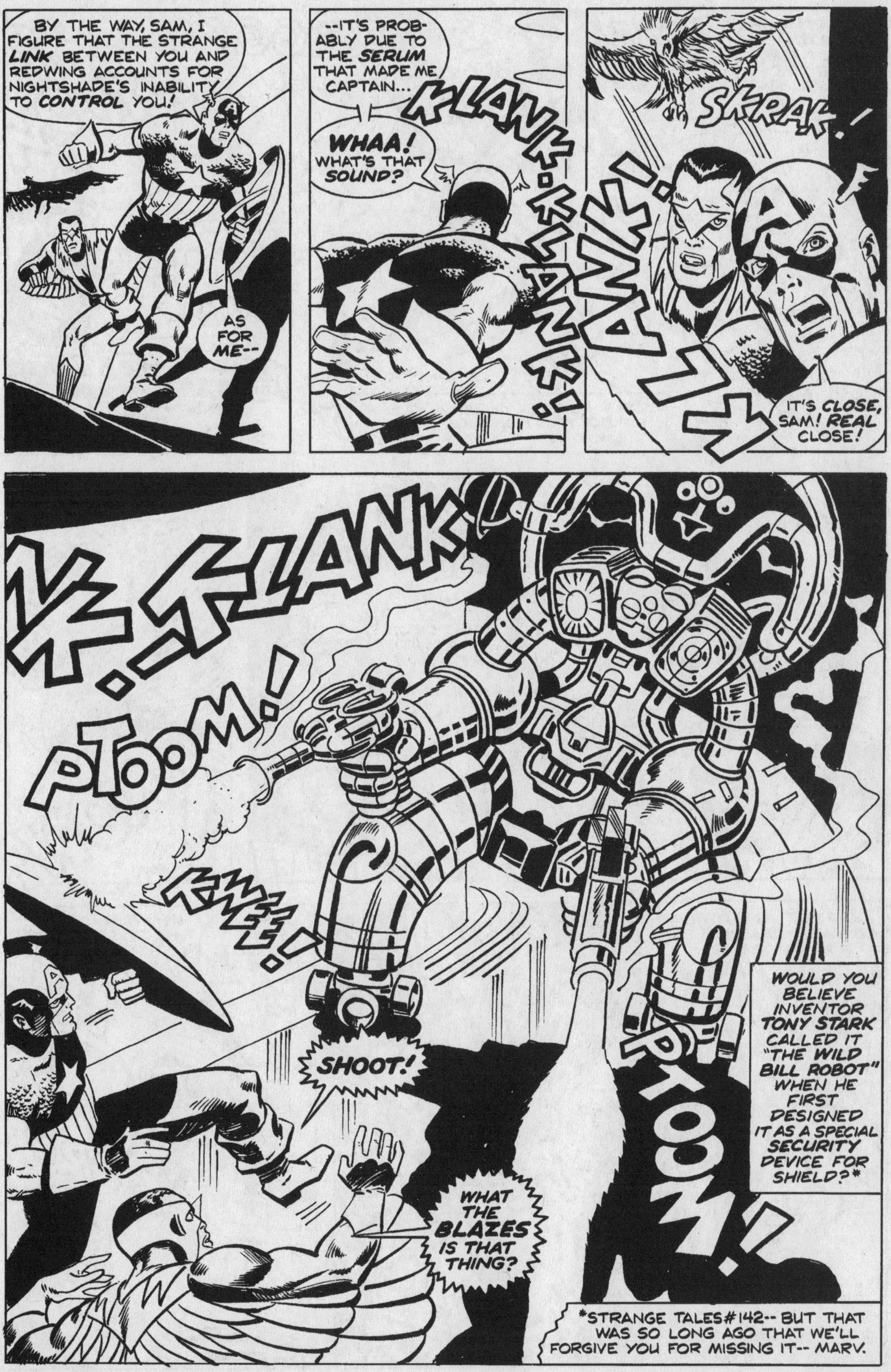
BY THE WAY, SAM, I FIGURE THAT THE STRANGE LINK BETWEEN YOU AND REDWING ACCOUNTS FOR NIGHTSHADE'S INABILITY TO CONTROL YOU!
AS FOR ME--
--IT'S PROBABLY DUE TO THE SERUM THAT MADE ME CAPTAIN...
WHAA! WHAT'S THAT SOUND?
KLANK-KLANK-KLANK!
SKRAK!
KLANK!
IT'S CLOSE, SAM! REAL CLOSE!
NK-KLANK-KLANK
PTOOM!
KWEE!
SHOOT!
WHAT THE BLAZES IS THAT THING?
PTOOM!
WOULD YOU BELIEVE INVENTOR TONY STARK CALLED IT "THE WILD BILL ROBOT" WHEN HE FIRST DESIGNED IT AS A SPECIAL SECURITY DEVICE FOR SHIELD?*
*STRANGE TALES #142-- BUT THAT WAS SO LONG AGO THAT WE'LL FORGIVE YOU FOR MISSING IT-- MARV.

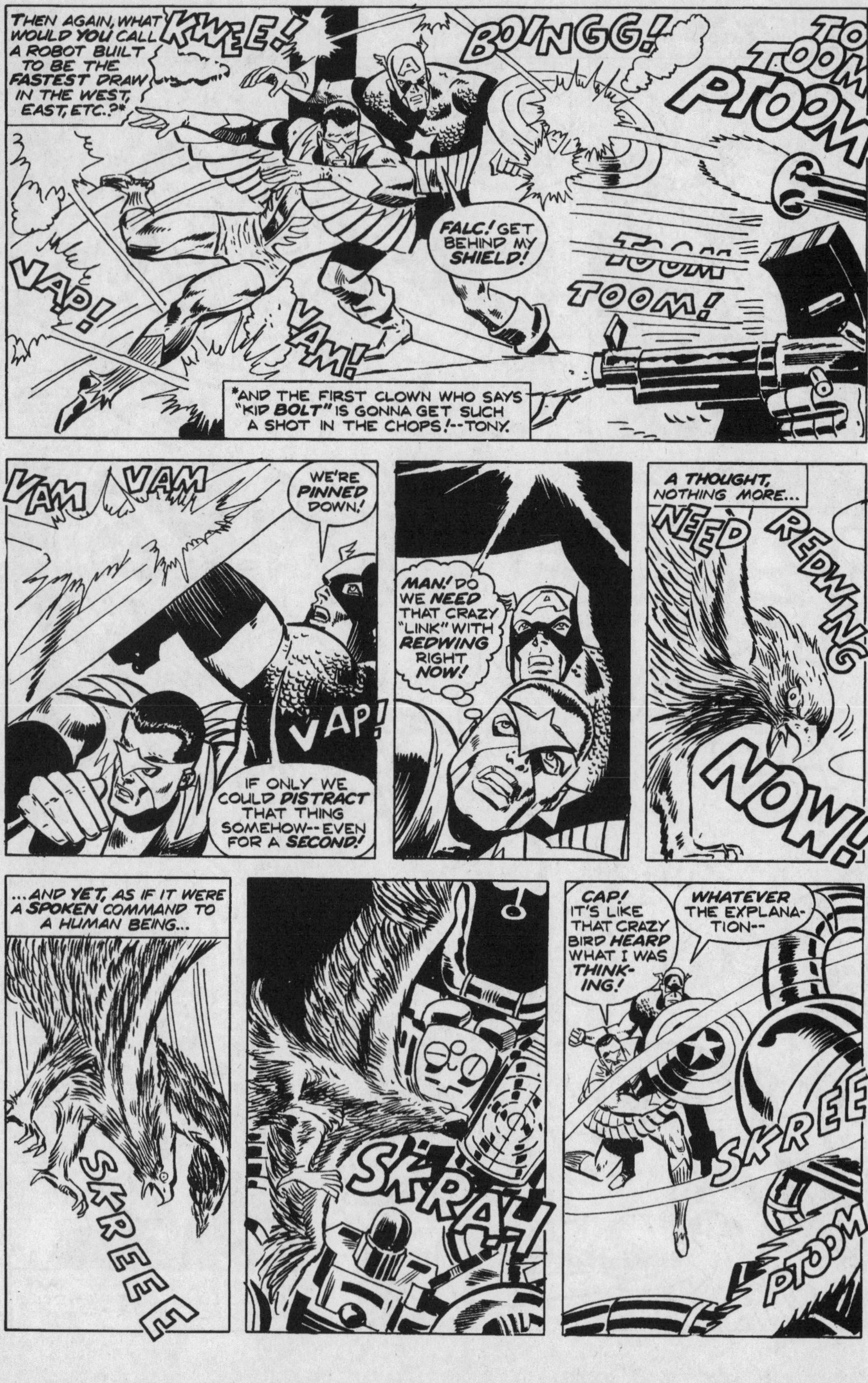
THEN AGAIN, WHAT WOULD YOU CALL A ROBOT BUILT TO BE THE FASTEST DRAW IN THE WEST, EAST, ETC.?*
KWEE!
BOINGG!
TOOM TOOM
PTOOM
FALC! GET BEHIND MY SHIELD!
TOOM
TOOM!
VAP!
VAM!
*AND THE FIRST CLOWN WHO SAYS "KID BOLT" IS GONNA GET SUCH A SHOT IN THE CHOPS!--TONY.
VAM VAM
WE'RE PINNED DOWN!
VAP!
IF ONLY WE COULD DISTRACT THAT THING SOMEHOW--EVEN FOR A SECOND!
MAN! DO WE NEED THAT CRAZY "LINK" WITH REDWING RIGHT NOW!
A THOUGHT, NOTHING MORE...
NEED REDWING
NOW!
...AND YET, AS IF IT WERE A SPOKEN COMMAND TO A HUMAN BEING...
SKREEE
SKRAAY
CAP! IT'S LIKE THAT CRAZY BIRD HEARD WHAT I WAS THINKING!
WHATEVER THE EXPLANATION--
SKREEE
PTOOM

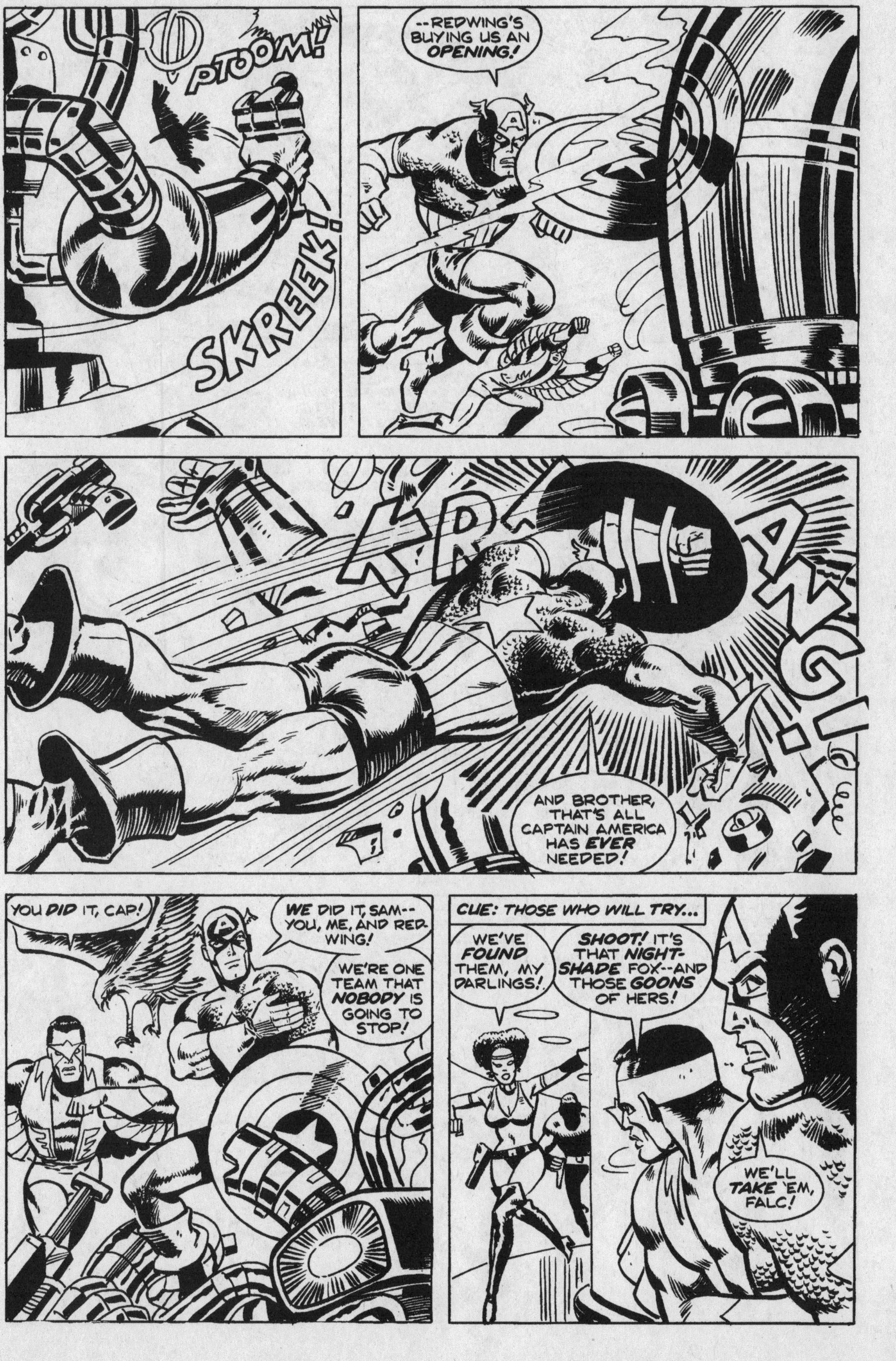
PTOOM!
SKREEK!
--REDWING'S BUYING US AN OPENING!
KRANG!
AND BROTHER, THAT'S ALL CAPTAIN AMERICA HAS EVER NEEDED!
YOU DID IT, CAP!
WE DID IT, SAM-- YOU, ME, AND RED-WING!
WE'RE ONE TEAM THAT NOBODY IS GOING TO STOP!
CUE: THOSE WHO WILL TRY...
WE'VE FOUND THEM, MY DARLINGS!
SHOOT! IT'S THAT NIGHT-SHADE FOX--AND THOSE GOONS OF HERS!
WE'LL TAKE 'EM, FALC!

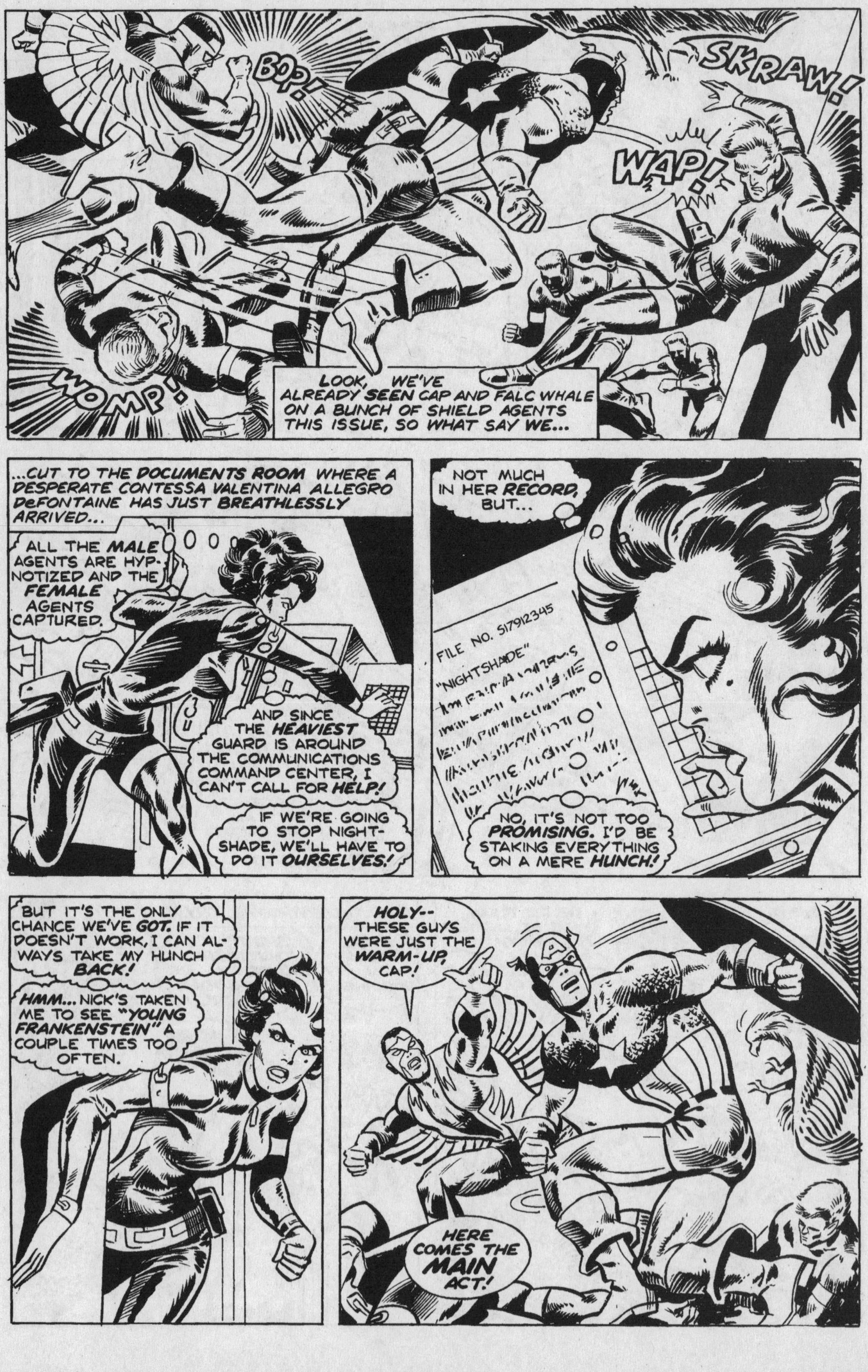
BOP!
SKRAW!
WAP!
WOMP!
LOOK, WE'VE ALREADY SEEN CAP AND FALC WHALE ON A BUNCH OF SHIELD AGENTS THIS ISSUE, SO WHAT SAY WE...
...CUT TO THE DOCUMENTS ROOM WHERE A DESPERATE CONTESSA VALENTINA ALLEGRO DeFONTAINE HAS JUST BREATHLESSLY ARRIVED...
ALL THE MALE AGENTS ARE HYPNOTIZED AND THE FEMALE AGENTS CAPTURED.
AND SINCE THE HEAVIEST GUARD IS AROUND THE COMMUNICATIONS COMMAND CENTER, I CAN'T CALL FOR HELP!
IF WE'RE GOING TO STOP NIGHTSHADE, WE'LL HAVE TO DO IT OURSELVES!
NOT MUCH IN HER RECORD, BUT...
FILE NO. 517912345
"NIGHTSHADE"
NO, IT'S NOT TOO PROMISING. I'D BE STAKING EVERYTHING ON A MERE HUNCH!
BUT IT'S THE ONLY CHANCE WE'VE GOT. IF IT DOESN'T WORK, I CAN ALWAYS TAKE MY HUNCH BACK!
HMM... NICK'S TAKEN ME TO SEE "YOUNG FRANKENSTEIN" A COUPLE TIMES TOO OFTEN.
HOLY-- THESE GUYS WERE JUST THE WARM-UP, CAP!
HERE COMES THE MAIN ACT!

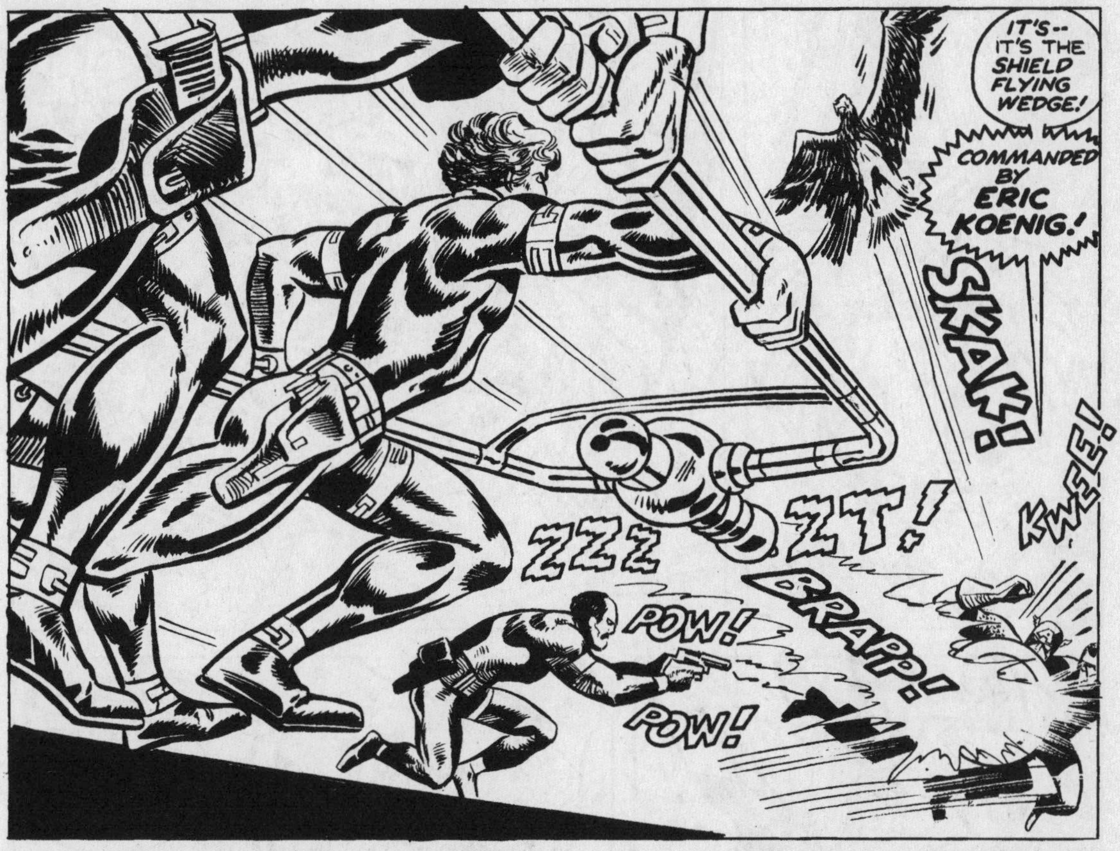
IT'S-- IT'S THE SHIELD FLYING WEDGE!
COMMANDED BY ERIC KOENIG!
SKAK!
KWEE!
ZZZ ZT!
BRAPP!
POW!
POW!
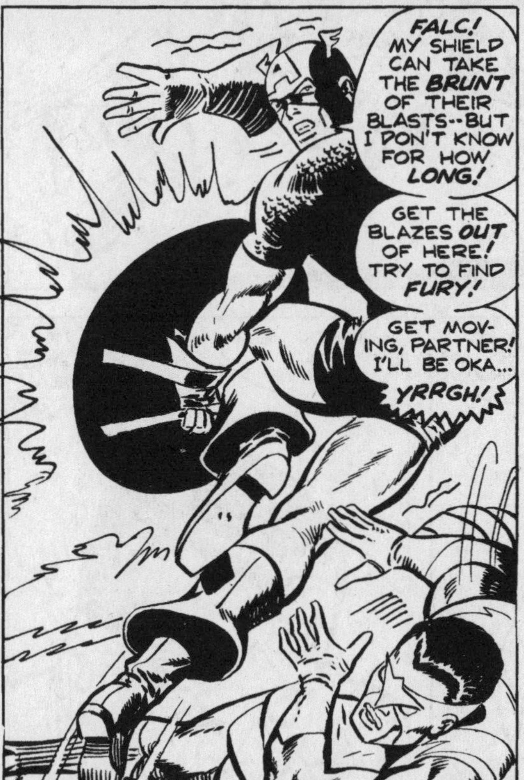
FALC! MY SHIELD CAN TAKE THE BRUNT OF THEIR BLASTS--BUT I DON'T KNOW FOR HOW LONG!
GET THE BLAZES OUT OF HERE! TRY TO FIND FURY!
GET MOV- ING, PARTNER! I'LL BE OKA...
YRRGH!
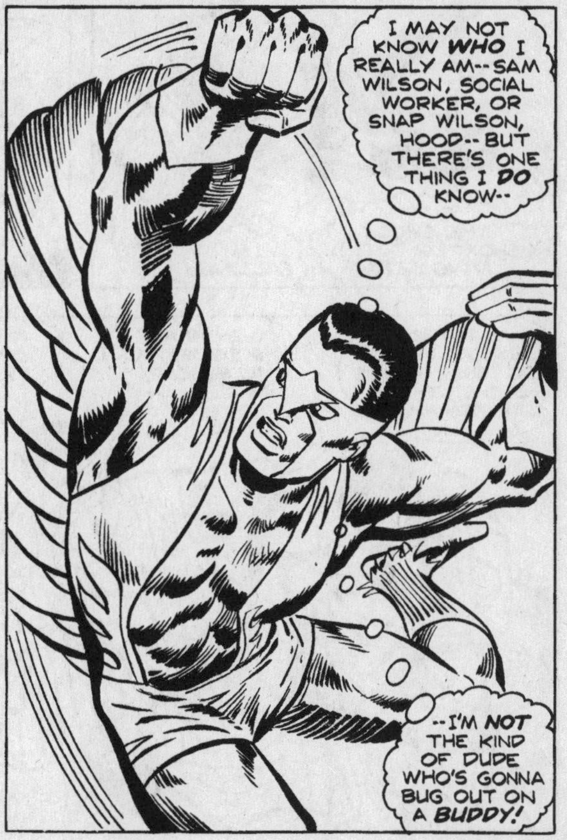
I MAY NOT KNOW WHO I REALLY AM--SAM WILSON, SOCIAL WORKER, OR SNAP WILSON, HOOD--BUT THERE'S ONE THING I DO KNOW--
--I'M NOT THE KIND OF DUDE WHO'S GONNA BUG OUT ON A BUDDY!

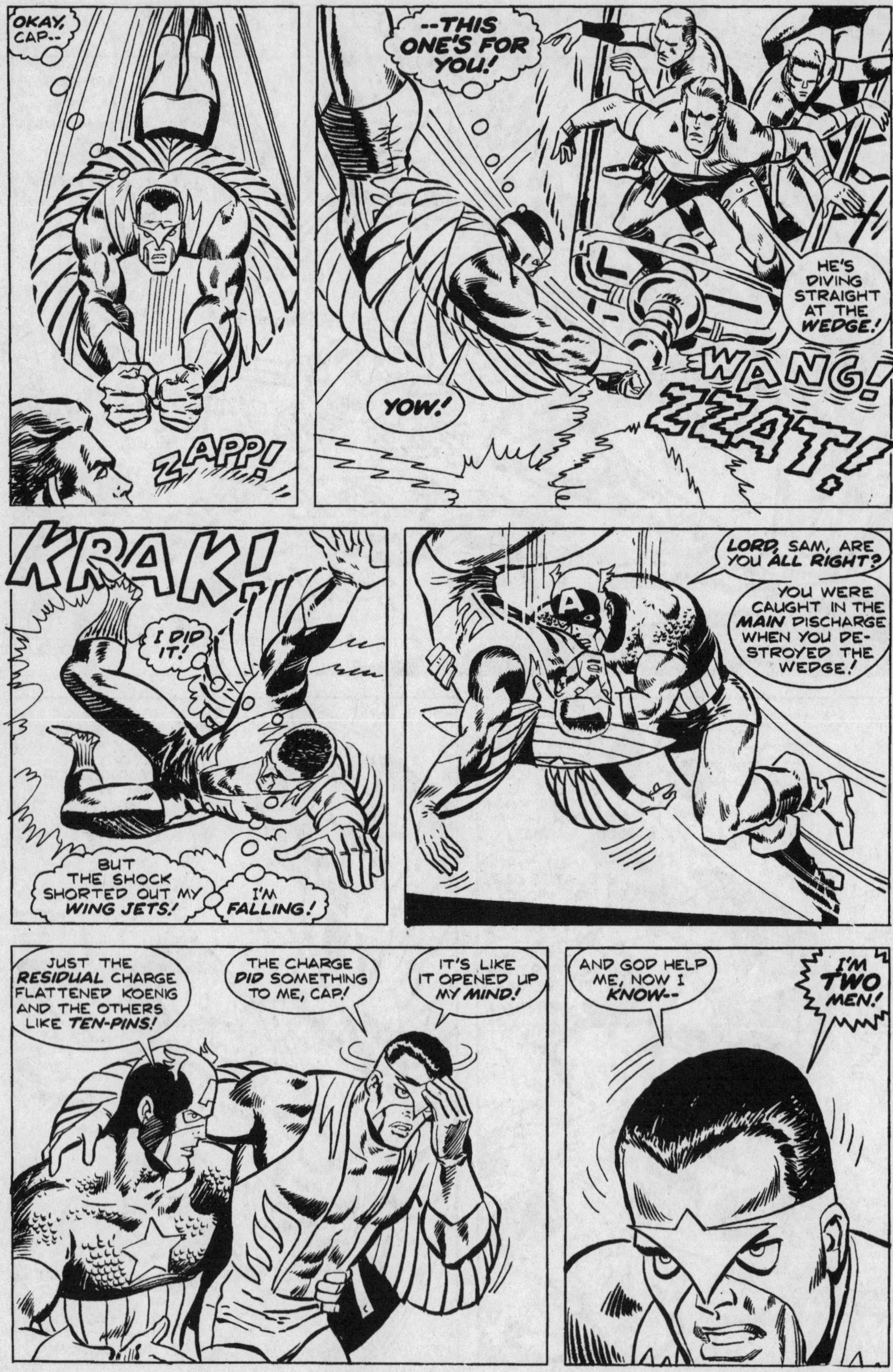
OKAY, CAP--
ZAPP!
--THIS ONE'S FOR YOU!
HE'S DIVING STRAIGHT AT THE WEDGE!
YOW!
WANG!
ZZAT!
KRAK!
I DID IT!
BUT THE SHOCK SHORTED OUT MY WING JETS!
I'M FALLING!
LORD, SAM, ARE YOU ALL RIGHT?
YOU WERE CAUGHT IN THE MAIN DISCHARGE WHEN YOU DESTROYED THE WEDGE!
JUST THE RESIDUAL CHARGE FLATTENED KOENIG AND THE OTHERS LIKE TEN-PINS!
THE CHARGE DID SOMETHING TO ME, CAP!
IT'S LIKE IT OPENED UP MY MIND!
AND GOD HELP ME, NOW I KNOW--
I'M TWO MEN!

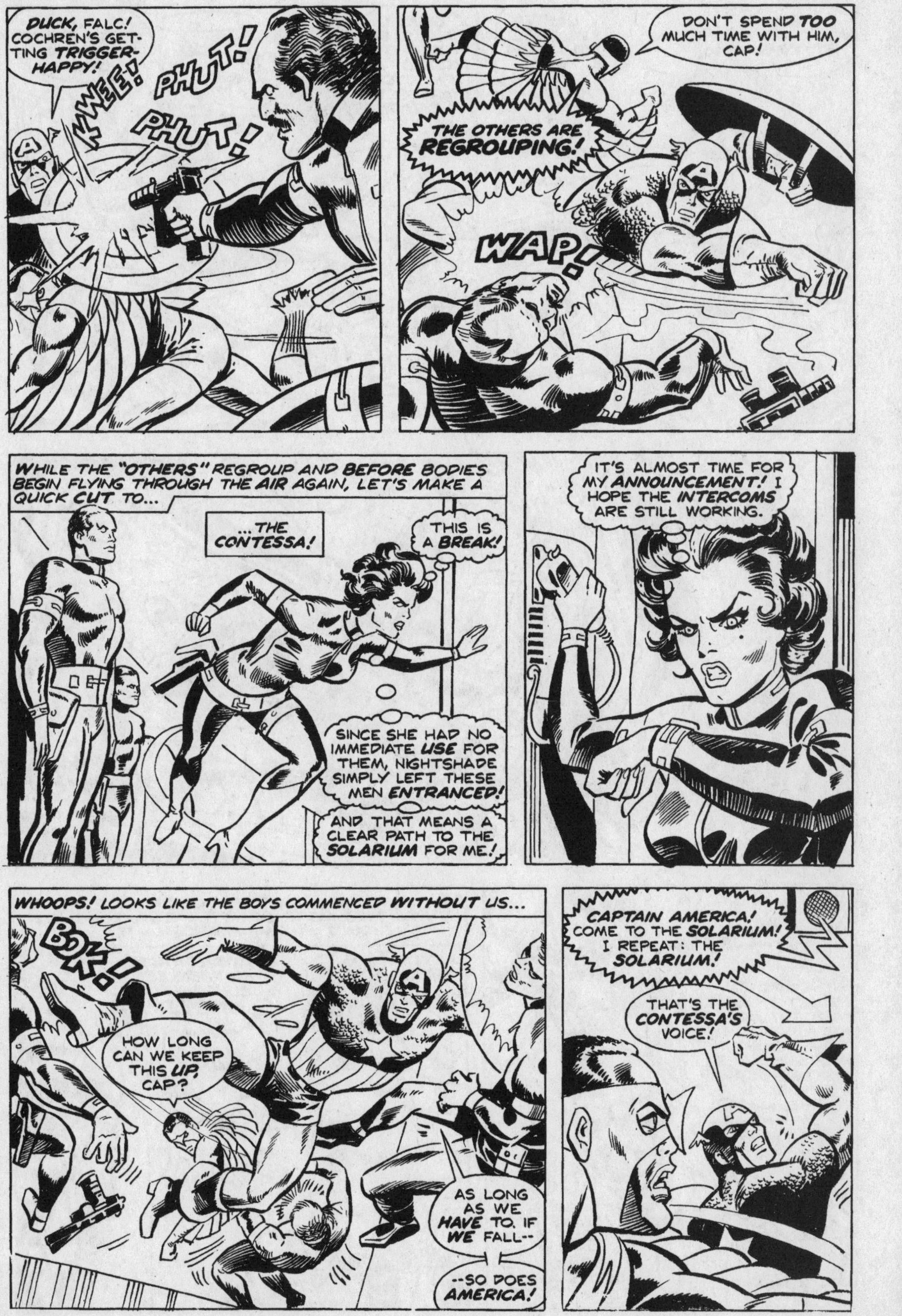
DUCK, FALC! COCHREN'S GETTING TRIGGER-HAPPY!
K'WEE!
PHUT!
PHUT!
DON'T SPEND TOO MUCH TIME WITH HIM, CAP!
THE OTHERS ARE REGROUPING!
WAP!
WHILE THE "OTHERS" REGROUP AND BEFORE BODIES BEGIN FLYING THROUGH THE AIR AGAIN, LET'S MAKE A QUICK CUT TO...
...THE CONTESSA!
THIS IS A BREAK!
SINCE SHE HAD NO IMMEDIATE USE FOR THEM, NIGHTSHADE SIMPLY LEFT THESE MEN ENTRANCED!
AND THAT MEANS A CLEAR PATH TO THE SOLARIUM FOR ME!
IT'S ALMOST TIME FOR MY ANNOUNCEMENT! I HOPE THE INTERCOMS ARE STILL WORKING.
WHOOPS! LOOKS LIKE THE BOYS COMMENCED WITHOUT US...
BOK!
HOW LONG CAN WE KEEP THIS UP, CAP?
AS LONG AS WE HAVE TO. IF WE FALL--
--SO DOES AMERICA!
CAPTAIN AMERICA! COME TO THE SOLARIUM! I REPEAT: THE SOLARIUM!
THAT'S THE CONTESSA'S VOICE!

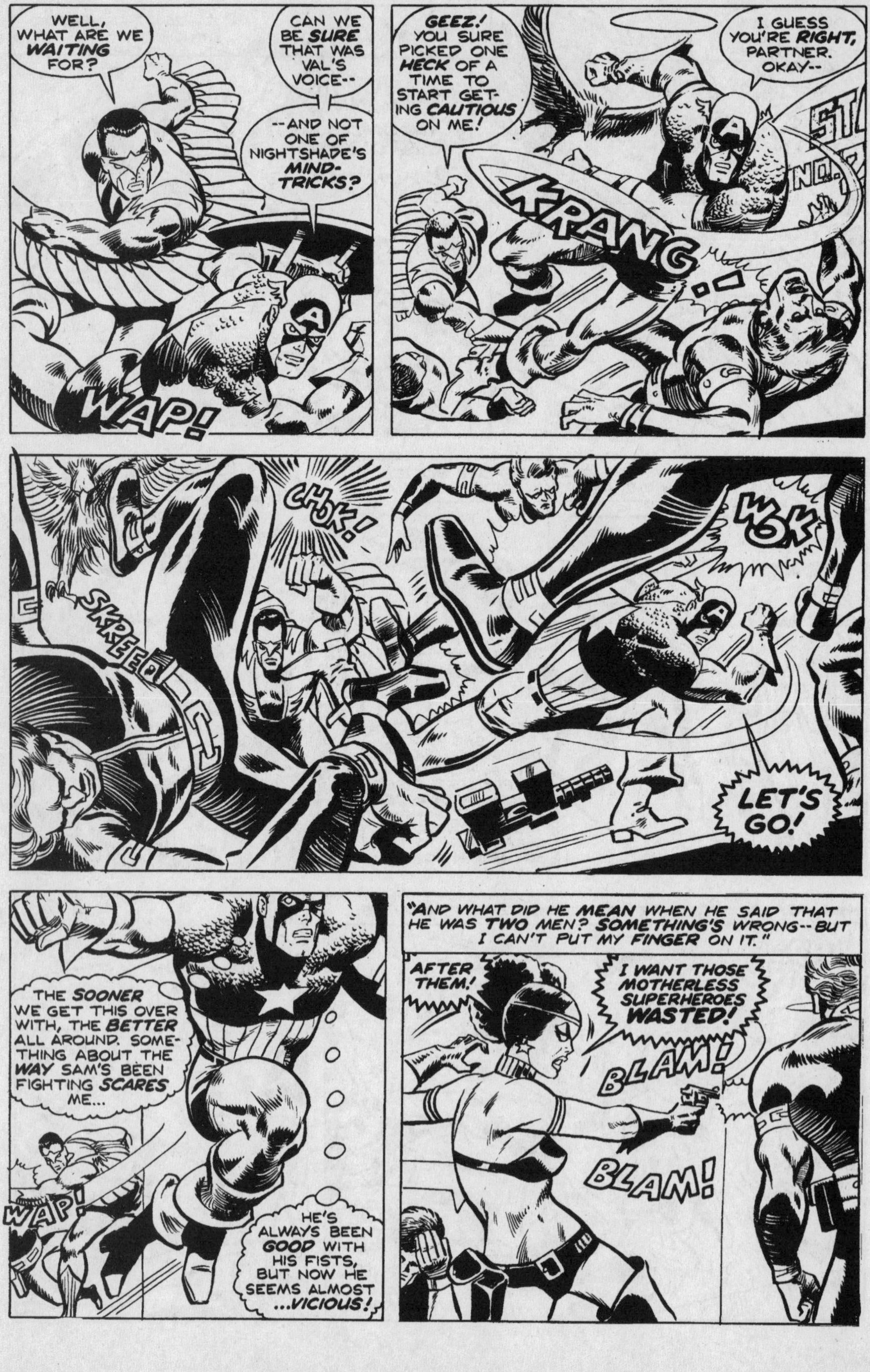
WELL, WHAT ARE WE WAITING FOR?
CAN WE BE SURE THAT WAS VAL'S VOICE--
--AND NOT ONE OF NIGHTSHADE'S MIND-TRICKS?
WAP!
GEEZ! YOU SURE PICKED ONE HECK OF A TIME TO START GETTING CAUTIOUS ON ME!
I GUESS YOU'RE RIGHT, PARTNER. OKAY--
KRANG
CHUK!
WOK
SKREEE
LET'S GO!
THE SOONER WE GET THIS OVER WITH, THE BETTER ALL AROUND. SOMETHING ABOUT THE WAY SAM'S BEEN FIGHTING SCARES ME...
WAP!
HE'S ALWAYS BEEN GOOD WITH HIS FISTS, BUT NOW HE SEEMS ALMOST ...VICIOUS!
"AND WHAT DID HE MEAN WHEN HE SAID THAT HE WAS TWO MEN? SOMETHING'S WRONG-- BUT I CAN'T PUT MY FINGER ON IT."
AFTER THEM!
I WANT THOSE MOTHERLESS SUPERHEROES WASTED!
BLAM!
BLAM!

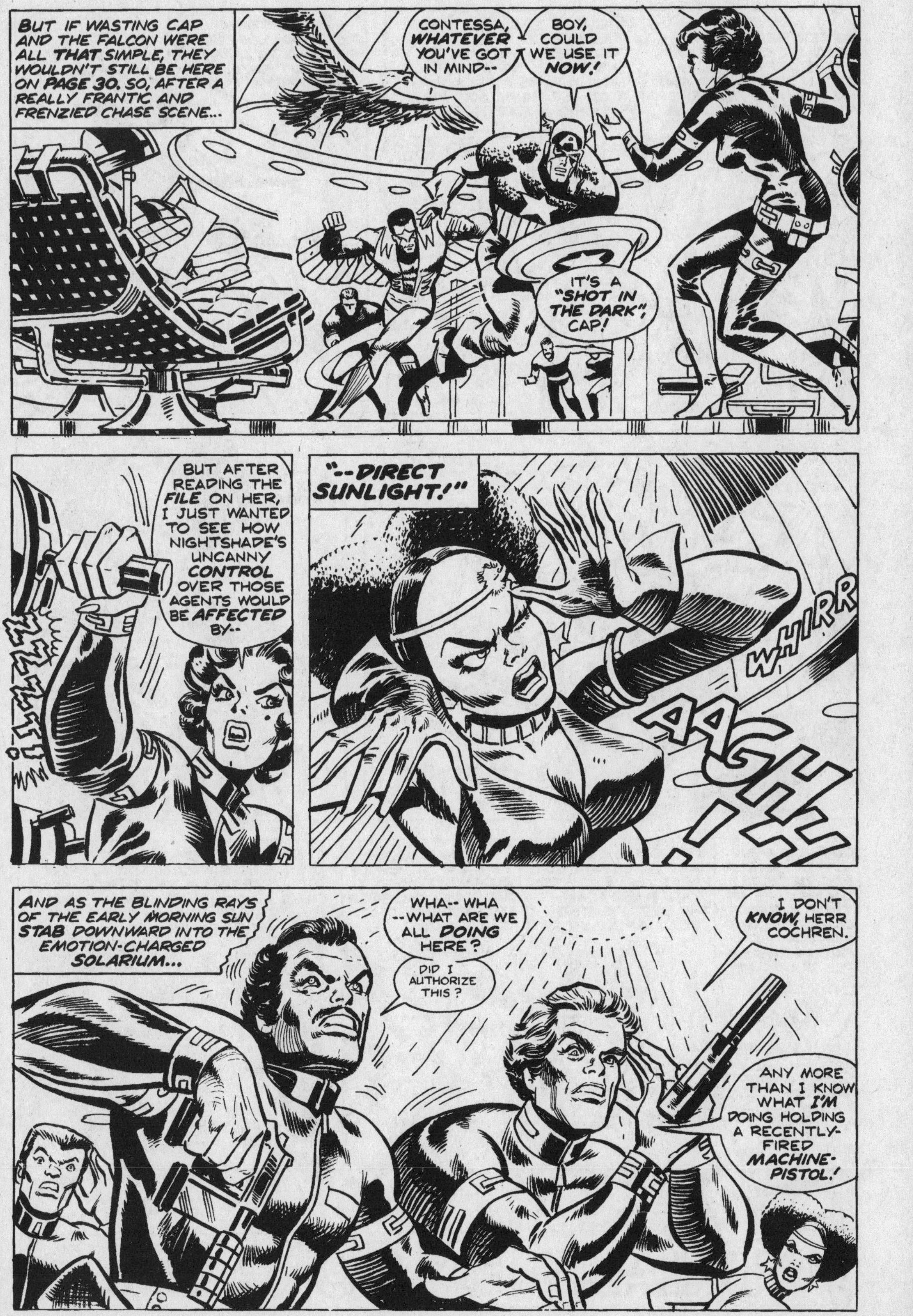
BUT IF WASTING CAP AND THE FALCON WERE ALL THAT SIMPLE, THEY WOULDN'T STILL BE HERE ON PAGE 30. SO, AFTER A REALLY FRANTIC AND FRENZIED CHASE SCENE...
CONTESSA, WHATEVER YOU'VE GOT IN MIND--
BOY, COULD WE USE IT NOW!
IT'S A "SHOT IN THE DARK", CAP!
BUT AFTER READING THE FILE ON HER, I JUST WANTED TO SEE HOW NIGHTSHADE'S UNCANNY CONTROL OVER THOSE AGENTS WOULD BE AFFECTED BY--
ZZZTTT!
"--DIRECT SUNLIGHT!"
WHIRR
AAGHH!!
AND AS THE BLINDING RAYS OF THE EARLY MORNING SUN STAB DOWNWARD INTO THE EMOTION-CHARGED SOLARIUM...
WHA-- WHA --WHAT ARE WE ALL DOING HERE?
DID I AUTHORIZE THIS?
I DON'T KNOW, HERR COCHREN.
ANY MORE THAN I KNOW WHAT I'M DOING HOLDING A RECENTLY-FIRED MACHINE-PISTOL!

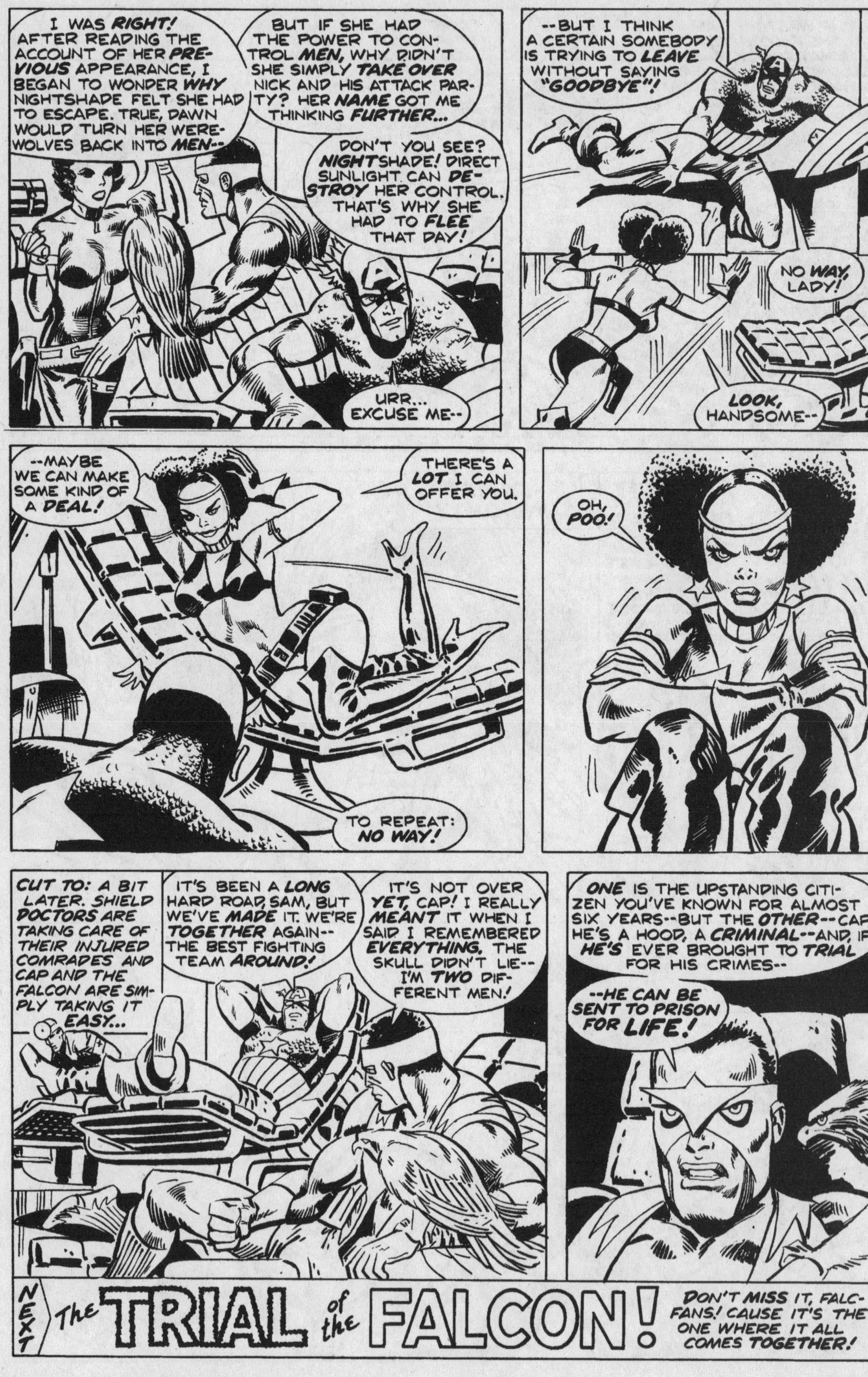
I WAS RIGHT! AFTER READING THE ACCOUNT OF HER PREVIOUS APPEARANCE, I BEGAN TO WONDER WHY NIGHTSHADE FELT SHE HAD TO ESCAPE. TRUE, DAWN WOULD TURN HER WEREWOLVES BACK INTO MEN--
BUT IF SHE HAD THE POWER TO CONTROL MEN, WHY DIDN'T SHE SIMPLY TAKE OVER NICK AND HIS ATTACK PARTY? HER NAME GOT ME THINKING FURTHER...
DON'T YOU SEE? NIGHTSHADE! DIRECT SUNLIGHT CAN DESTROY HER CONTROL. THAT'S WHY SHE HAD TO FLEE THAT DAY!
URR... EXCUSE ME--
--BUT I THINK A CERTAIN SOMEBODY IS TRYING TO LEAVE WITHOUT SAYING "GOODBYE"!
NO WAY, LADY!
LOOK, HANDSOME--
--MAYBE WE CAN MAKE SOME KIND OF A DEAL!
THERE'S A LOT I CAN OFFER YOU.
TO REPEAT: NO WAY!
OH, POO!
CUT TO: A BIT LATER. SHIELD DOCTORS ARE TAKING CARE OF THEIR INJURED COMRADES AND CAP AND THE FALCON ARE SIMPLY TAKING IT EASY...
IT'S BEEN A LONG HARD ROAD, SAM, BUT WE'VE MADE IT. WE'RE TOGETHER AGAIN-- THE BEST FIGHTING TEAM AROUND!
IT'S NOT OVER YET, CAP! I REALLY MEANT IT WHEN I SAID I REMEMBERED EVERYTHING. THE SKULL DIDN'T LIE-- I'M TWO DIFFERENT MEN!
ONE IS THE UPSTANDING CITIZEN YOU'VE KNOWN FOR ALMOST SIX YEARS--BUT THE OTHER--CAP, HE'S A HOOD, A CRIMINAL--AND, IF HE'S EVER BROUGHT TO TRIAL FOR HIS CRIMES--
--HE CAN BE SENT TO PRISON FOR LIFE!
NEXT
The TRIAL of the FALCON!
DON'T MISS IT, FALC-FANS! CAUSE IT'S THE ONE WHERE IT ALL COMES TOGETHER!

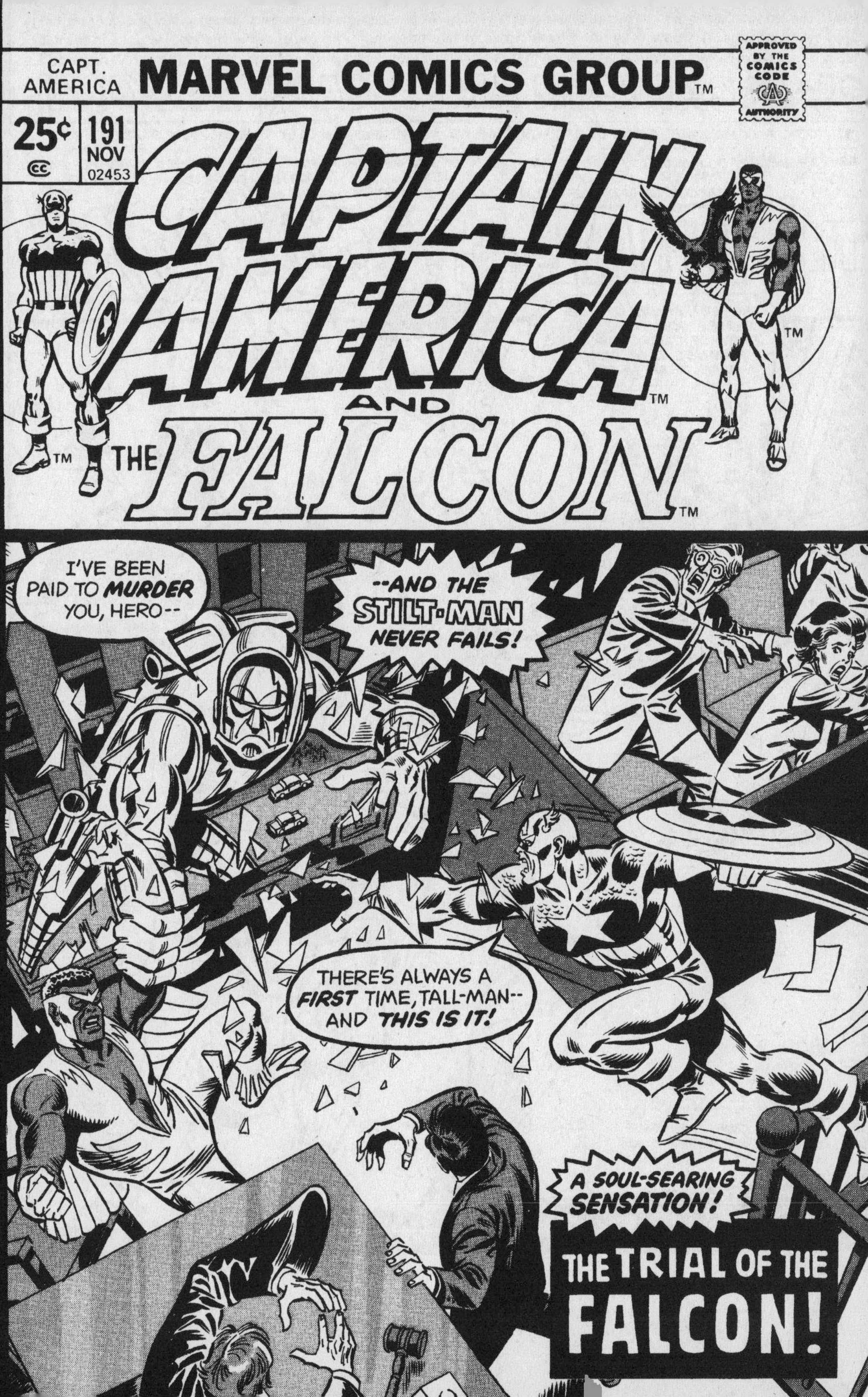

CAPT. AMERICA
MARVEL COMICS GROUP
APPROVED BY THE COMICS CODE AUTHORITY
25¢
191 NOV
02453
CAPTAIN AMERICA
AND
THE FALCON
I'VE BEEN PAID TO MURDER YOU, HERO--
--AND THE STILT-MAN NEVER FAILS!
THERE'S ALWAYS A FIRST TIME, TALL-MAN-- AND THIS IS IT!
A SOUL-SEARING SENSATION!
THE TRIAL OF THE FALCON!

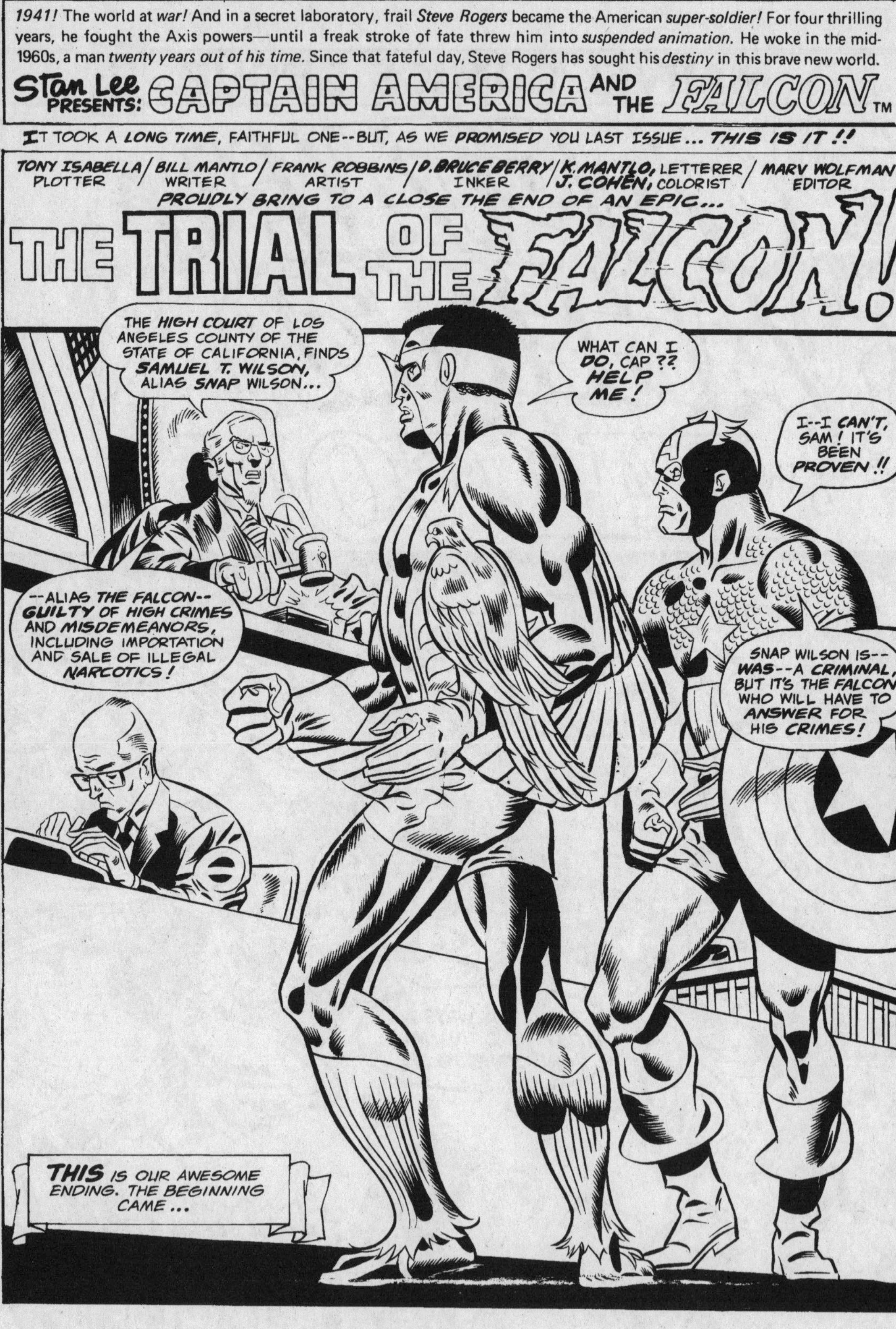

1941! The world at war! And in a secret laboratory, frail Steve Rogers became the American super-soldier! For four thrilling years, he fought the Axis powers—until a freak stroke of fate threw him into suspended animation. He woke in the mid-1960s, a man twenty years out of his time. Since that fateful day, Steve Rogers has sought his destiny in this brave new world.
Stan Lee PRESENTS: CAPTAIN AMERICA AND THE FALCON TM
IT TOOK A LONG TIME, FAITHFUL ONE--BUT, AS WE PROMISED YOU LAST ISSUE... THIS IS IT !!
TONY ISABELLA PLOTTER / BILL MANTLO WRITER / FRANK ROBBINS ARTIST / D. BRUCE BERRY INKER / K. MANTLO, LETTERER / J. COHEN, COLORIST / MARV WOLFMAN EDITOR
PROUDLY BRING TO A CLOSE THE END OF AN EPIC...
THE TRIAL OF THE FALCON!
THE HIGH COURT OF LOS ANGELES COUNTY OF THE STATE OF CALIFORNIA, FINDS SAMUEL T. WILSON, ALIAS SNAP WILSON...
WHAT CAN I DO, CAP ?? HELP ME!
I--I CAN'T, SAM! IT'S BEEN PROVEN !!
--ALIAS THE FALCON--GUILTY OF HIGH CRIMES AND MISDEMEANORS, INCLUDING IMPORTATION AND SALE OF ILLEGAL NARCOTICS!
SNAP WILSON IS--WAS--A CRIMINAL, BUT IT'S THE FALCON WHO WILL HAVE TO ANSWER FOR HIS CRIMES!
THIS IS OUR AWESOME ENDING. THE BEGINNING CAME...

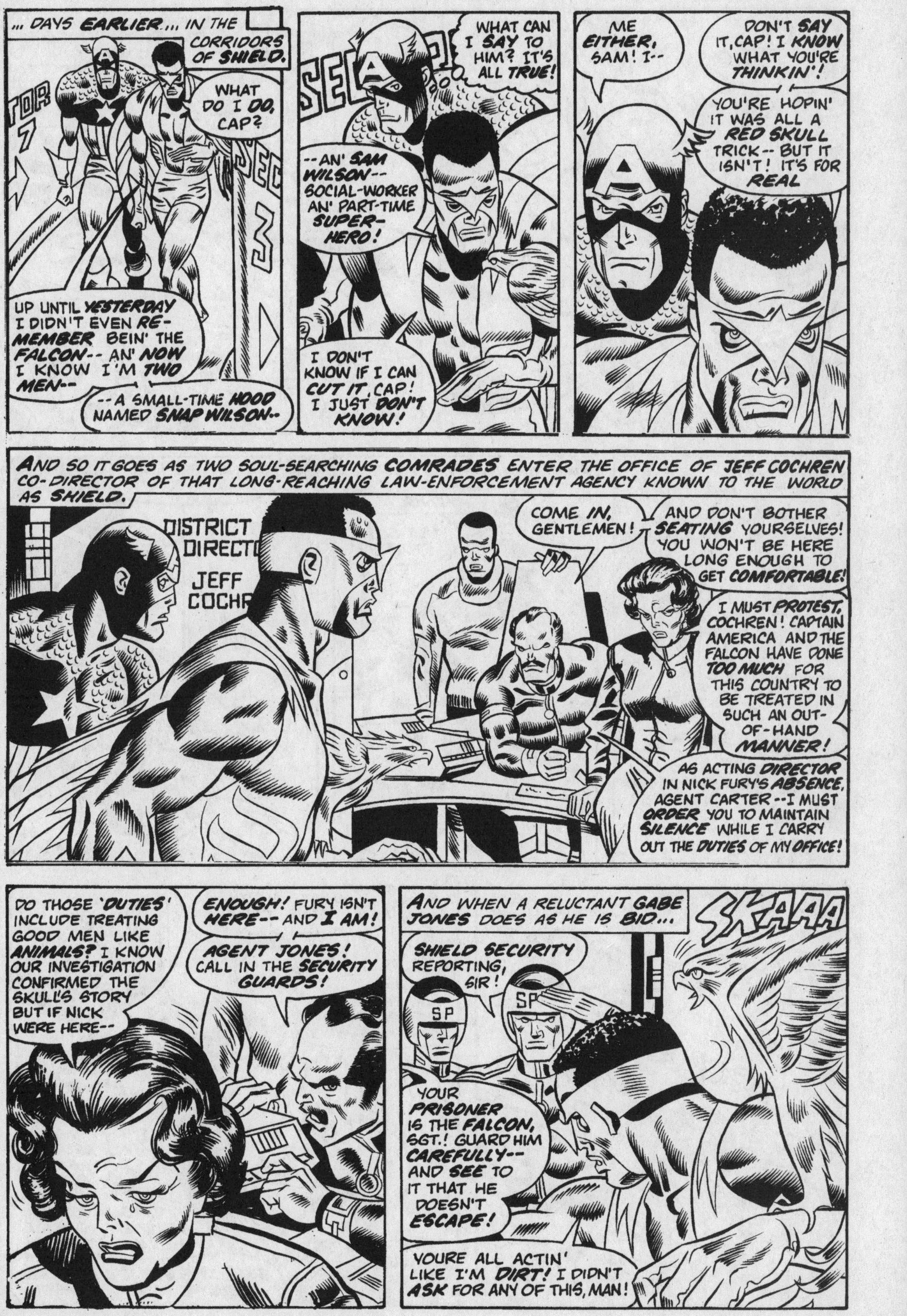
... DAYS EARLIER ... IN THE CORRIDORS OF SHIELD.
WHAT DO I DO, CAP?
UP UNTIL YESTERDAY I DIDN'T EVEN REMEMBER BEIN' THE FALCON-- AN' NOW I KNOW I'M TWO MEN--
--A SMALL-TIME HOOD NAMED SNAP WILSON--
WHAT CAN I SAY TO HIM? IT'S ALL TRUE!
--AN' SAM WILSON-- SOCIAL-WORKER AN' PART-TIME SUPER-HERO!
I DON'T KNOW IF I CAN CUT IT, CAP! I JUST DON'T KNOW!
ME EITHER, SAM! I--
DON'T SAY IT, CAP! I KNOW WHAT YOU'RE THINKIN'!
YOU'RE HOPIN' IT WAS ALL A RED SKULL TRICK-- BUT IT ISN'T! IT'S FOR REAL
AND SO IT GOES AS TWO SOUL-SEARCHING COMRADES ENTER THE OFFICE OF JEFF COCHREN CO-DIRECTOR OF THAT LONG-REACHING LAW-ENFORCEMENT AGENCY KNOWN TO THE WORLD AS SHIELD.
DISTRICT DIRECTO
JEFF COCHR
COME IN, GENTLEMEN!
AND DON'T BOTHER SEATING YOURSELVES! YOU WON'T BE HERE LONG ENOUGH TO GET COMFORTABLE!
I MUST PROTEST, COCHREN! CAPTAIN AMERICA AND THE FALCON HAVE DONE TOO MUCH FOR THIS COUNTRY TO BE TREATED IN SUCH AN OUT-OF-HAND MANNER!
AS ACTING DIRECTOR IN NICK FURY'S ABSENCE, AGENT CARTER --I MUST ORDER YOU TO MAINTAIN SILENCE WHILE I CARRY OUT THE DUTIES OF MY OFFICE!
DO THOSE 'DUTIES' INCLUDE TREATING GOOD MEN LIKE ANIMALS? I KNOW OUR INVESTIGATION CONFIRMED THE SKULL'S STORY BUT IF NICK WERE HERE--
ENOUGH! FURY ISN'T HERE-- AND I AM!
AGENT JONES! CALL IN THE SECURITY GUARDS!
AND WHEN A RELUCTANT GABE JONES DOES AS HE IS BID...
SKAAAA
SHIELD SECURITY REPORTING, SIR!
SP
SP
YOUR PRISONER IS THE FALCON, SGT.! GUARD HIM CAREFULLY-- AND SEE TO IT THAT HE DOESN'T ESCAPE!
YOURE ALL ACTIN' LIKE I'M DIRT! I DIDN'T ASK FOR ANY OF THIS, MAN!

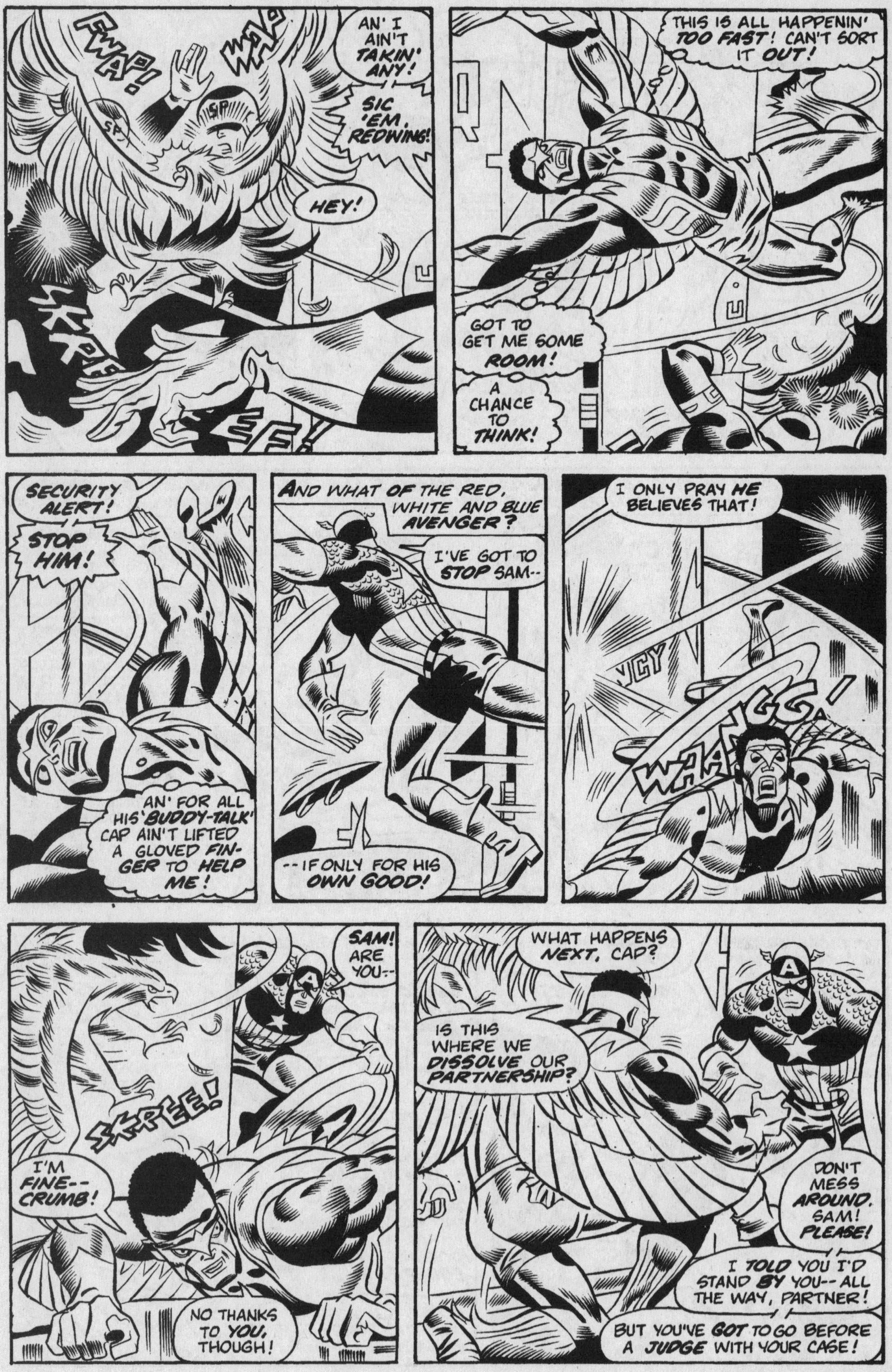
FWAP!
WAP!
AN' I AIN'T TAKIN' ANY!
SIC 'EM, REDWING!
HEY!
SKREE
THIS IS ALL HAPPENIN' TOO FAST! CAN'T SORT IT OUT!
GOT TO GET ME SOME ROOM!
A CHANCE TO THINK!
SECURITY ALERT!
STOP HIM!
AN' FOR ALL HIS 'BUDDY-TALK' CAP AIN'T LIFTED A GLOVED FINGER TO HELP ME!
AND WHAT OF THE RED, WHITE AND BLUE AVENGER?
I'VE GOT TO STOP SAM--
--IF ONLY FOR HIS OWN GOOD!
I ONLY PRAY HE BELIEVES THAT!
WHANGG!
SAM! ARE YOU--
SKREEE!
I'M FINE-- CRUMB!
NO THANKS TO YOU, THOUGH!
WHAT HAPPENS NEXT, CAP?
IS THIS WHERE WE DISSOLVE OUR PARTNERSHIP?
DON'T MESS AROUND, SAM! PLEASE!
I TOLD YOU I'D STAND BY YOU-- ALL THE WAY, PARTNER!
BUT YOU'VE GOT TO GO BEFORE A JUDGE WITH YOUR CASE!

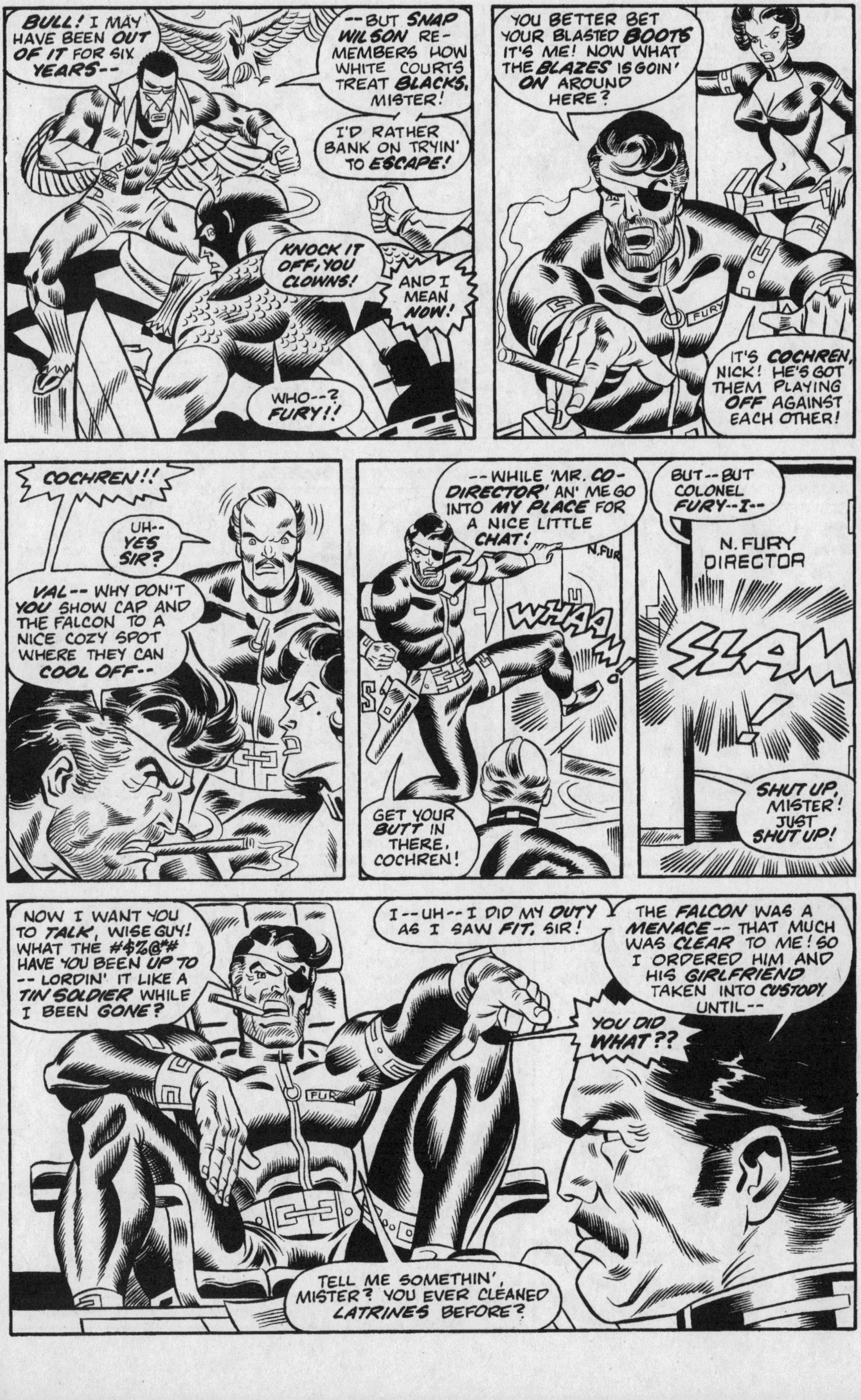
BULL! I MAY HAVE BEEN OUT OF IT FOR SIX YEARS--
--BUT SNAP WILSON REMEMBERS HOW WHITE COURTS TREAT BLACKS, MISTER!
I'D RATHER BANK ON TRYIN' TO ESCAPE!
KNOCK IT OFF, YOU CLOWNS!
AND I MEAN NOW!
WHO--? FURY!!
YOU BETTER BET YOUR BLASTED BOOTS IT'S ME! NOW WHAT THE BLAZES IS GOIN' ON AROUND HERE?
FURY
IT'S COCHREN, NICK! HE'S GOT THEM PLAYING OFF AGAINST EACH OTHER!
COCHREN!!
UH-- YES SIR?
VAL-- WHY DON'T YOU SHOW CAP AND THE FALCON TO A NICE COZY SPOT WHERE THEY CAN COOL OFF--
--WHILE 'MR. CO-DIRECTOR' AN' ME GO INTO MY PLACE FOR A NICE LITTLE CHAT!
N. FUR
WHAAM!
GET YOUR BUTT IN THERE, COCHREN!
BUT--BUT COLONEL FURY--I--
N. FURY DIRECTOR
SLAM!
SHUT UP, MISTER! JUST SHUT UP!
NOW I WANT YOU TO TALK, WISE GUY! WHAT THE #$%@*# HAVE YOU BEEN UP TO -- LORDIN' IT LIKE A TIN SOLDIER WHILE I BEEN GONE?
I--UH--I DID MY DUTY AS I SAW FIT, SIR!
THE FALCON WAS A MENACE -- THAT MUCH WAS CLEAR TO ME! SO I ORDERED HIM AND HIS GIRLFRIEND TAKEN INTO CUSTODY UNTIL--
YOU DID WHAT??
FUR
TELL ME SOMETHIN', MISTER? YOU EVER CLEANED LATRINES BEFORE?

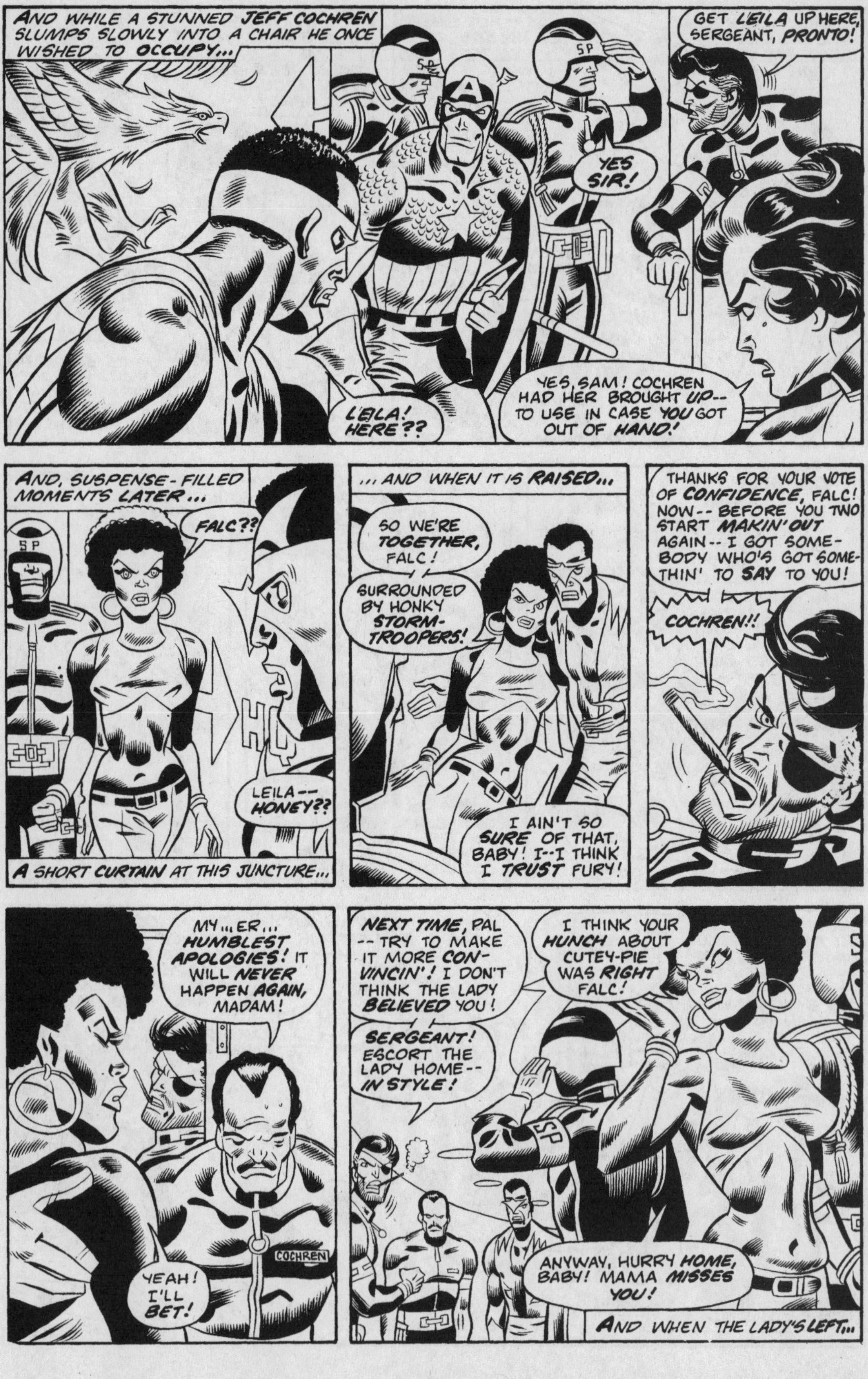
AND WHILE A STUNNED JEFF COCHREN SLUMPS SLOWLY INTO A CHAIR HE ONCE WISHED TO OCCUPY...
GET LEILA UP HERE, SERGEANT, PRONTO!
YES SIR!
LEILA! HERE??
YES, SAM! COCHREN HAD HER BROUGHT UP-- TO USE IN CASE YOU GOT OUT OF HAND!
A SHORT CURTAIN AT THIS JUNCTURE...
...AND WHEN IT IS RAISED...
AND, SUSPENSE-FILLED MOMENTS LATER...
FALC??
LEILA-- HONEY??
SO WE'RE TOGETHER, FALC!
SURROUNDED BY HONKY STORM-TROOPERS!
I AIN'T SO SURE OF THAT, BABY! I--I THINK I TRUST FURY!
THANKS FOR YOUR VOTE OF CONFIDENCE, FALC! NOW-- BEFORE YOU TWO START MAKIN' OUT AGAIN-- I GOT SOME-BODY WHO'S GOT SOME-THIN' TO SAY TO YOU!
COCHREN!!
MY... ER... HUMBLEST APOLOGIES! IT WILL NEVER HAPPEN AGAIN, MADAM!
YEAH! I'LL BET!
COCHREN
NEXT TIME, PAL -- TRY TO MAKE IT MORE CON-VINCIN'! I DON'T THINK THE LADY BELIEVED YOU!
SERGEANT! ESCORT THE LADY HOME-- IN STYLE!
I THINK YOUR HUNCH ABOUT CUTEY-PIE WAS RIGHT FALC!
ANYWAY, HURRY HOME, BABY! MAMA MISSES YOU!
AND WHEN THE LADY'S LEFT...

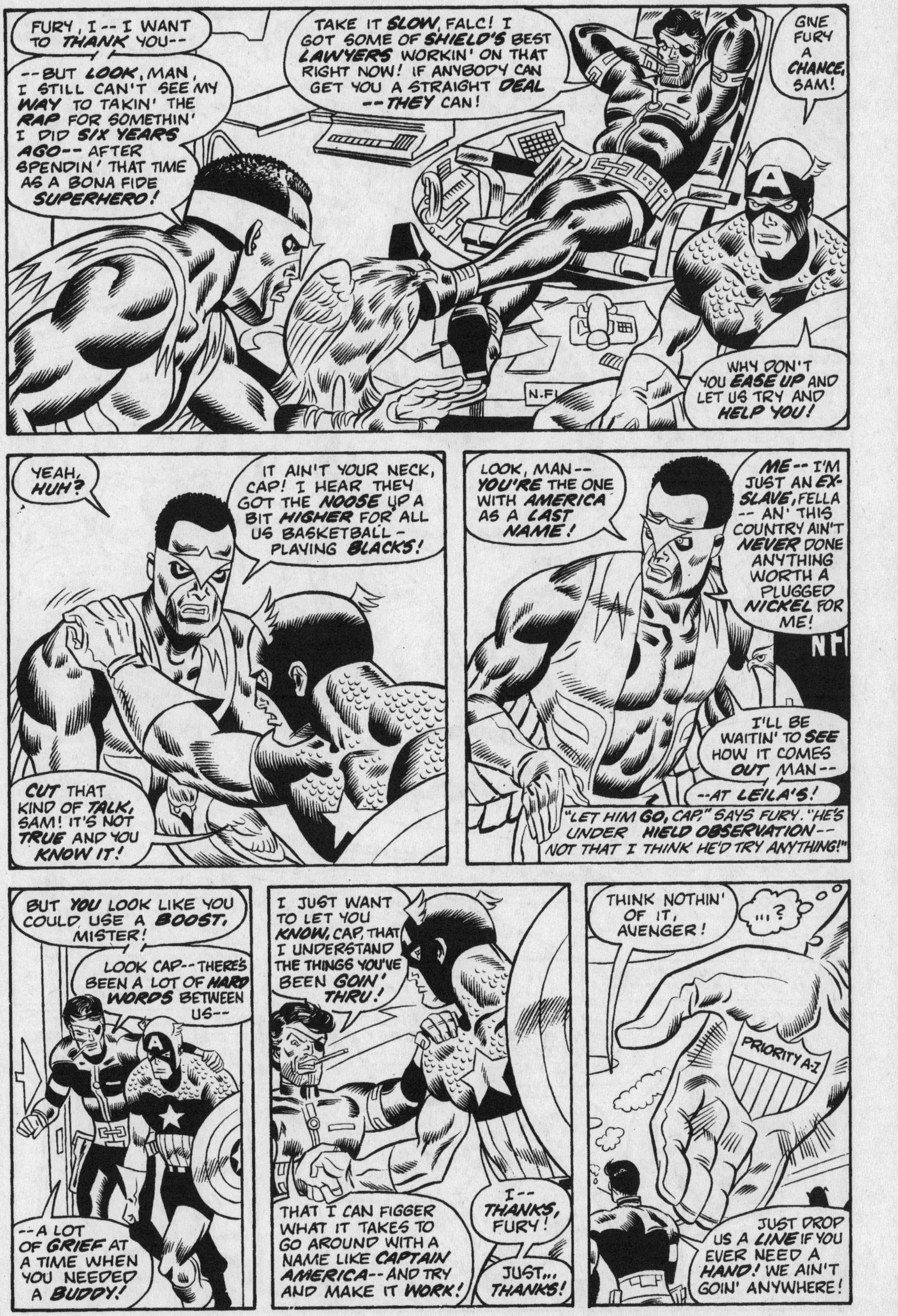

FURY, I -- I WANT TO THANK YOU--
--BUT LOOK, MAN, I STILL CAN'T SEE MY WAY TO TAKIN' THE RAP FOR SOMETHIN' I DID SIX YEARS AGO-- AFTER SPENDIN' THAT TIME AS A BONA FIDE SUPERHERO!
TAKE IT SLOW, FALC! I GOT SOME OF SHIELD'S BEST LAWYERS WORKIN' ON THAT RIGHT NOW! IF ANYBODY CAN GET YOU A STRAIGHT DEAL --THEY CAN!
GIVE FURY A CHANCE, SAM!
WHY DON'T YOU EASE UP AND LET US TRY AND HELP YOU!
N.F.
YEAH, HUH?
IT AIN'T YOUR NECK, CAP! I HEAR THEY GOT THE NOOSE UP A BIT HIGHER FOR ALL US BASKETBALL-PLAYING BLACKS!
CUT THAT KIND OF TALK, SAM! IT'S NOT TRUE AND YOU KNOW IT!
LOOK, MAN-- YOU'RE THE ONE WITH AMERICA AS A LAST NAME!
ME -- I'M JUST AN EX-SLAVE, FELLA -- AN' THIS COUNTRY AIN'T NEVER DONE ANYTHING WORTH A PLUGGED NICKEL FOR ME!
N.F.
I'LL BE WAITIN' TO SEE HOW IT COMES OUT MAN--
--AT LEILA'S!
"LET HIM GO, CAP," SAYS FURY. "HE'S UNDER HIELD OBSERVATION-- NOT THAT I THINK HE'D TRY ANYTHING!"
BUT YOU LOOK LIKE YOU COULD USE A BOOST, MISTER!
LOOK CAP-- THERE'S BEEN A LOT OF HARD WORDS BETWEEN US--
--A LOT OF GRIEF AT A TIME WHEN YOU NEEDED A BUDDY!
I JUST WANT TO LET YOU KNOW, CAP, THAT I UNDERSTAND THE THINGS YOU'VE BEEN GOIN' THRU!
THAT I CAN FIGGER WHAT IT TAKES TO GO AROUND WITH A NAME LIKE CAPTAIN AMERICA-- AND TRY AND MAKE IT WORK!
I-- THANKS, FURY!
JUST... THANKS!
THINK NOTHIN' OF IT, AVENGER!
...?
PRIORITY A-1
JUST DROP US A LINE IF YOU EVER NEED A HAND! WE AIN'T GOIN' ANYWHERE!

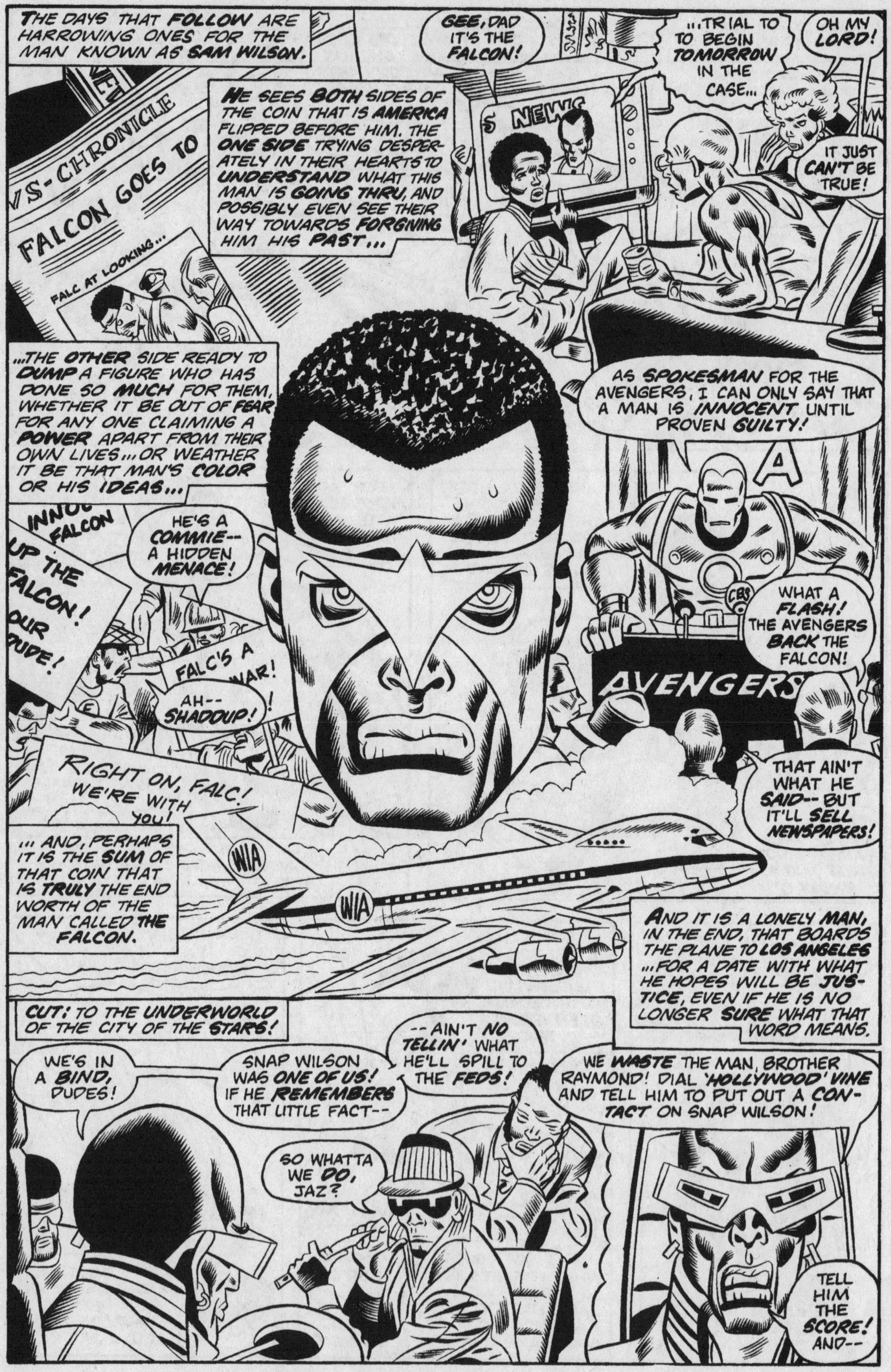

THE DAYS THAT FOLLOW ARE HARROWING ONES FOR THE MAN KNOWN AS SAM WILSON.
NEWS-CHRONICLE
FALCON GOES TO
FALC AT LOOKING...
HE SEES BOTH SIDES OF THE COIN THAT IS AMERICA FLIPPED BEFORE HIM. THE ONE SIDE TRYING DESPERATELY IN THEIR HEARTS TO UNDERSTAND WHAT THIS MAN IS GOING THRU, AND POSSIBLY EVEN SEE THEIR WAY TOWARDS FORGIVING HIM HIS PAST...
GEE, DAD IT'S THE FALCON!
NEWS
...TRIAL TO TO BEGIN TOMORROW IN THE CASE...
OH MY LORD!
IT JUST CAN'T BE TRUE!
...THE OTHER SIDE READY TO DUMP A FIGURE WHO HAS DONE SO MUCH FOR THEM, WHETHER IT BE OUT OF FEAR FOR ANY ONE CLAIMING A POWER APART FROM THEIR OWN LIVES...OR WEATHER IT BE THAT MAN'S COLOR OR HIS IDEAS...
AS SPOKESMAN FOR THE AVENGERS, I CAN ONLY SAY THAT A MAN IS INNOCENT UNTIL PROVEN GUILTY!
A
FALCON
UP THE FALCON!
OUR DUDE!
HE'S A COMMIE-- A HIDDEN MENACE!
FALC'S A WAR!
AH-- SHADDUP!
CBS
WHAT A FLASH! THE AVENGERS BACK THE FALCON!
AVENGERS
RIGHT ON, FALC! WE'RE WITH YOU!
THAT AIN'T WHAT HE SAID-- BUT IT'LL SELL NEWSPAPERS!
... AND, PERHAPS IT IS THE SUM OF THAT COIN THAT IS TRULY THE END WORTH OF THE MAN CALLED THE FALCON.
WIA
WIA
AND IT IS A LONELY MAN, IN THE END, THAT BOARDS THE PLANE TO LOS ANGELES ...FOR A DATE WITH WHAT HE HOPES WILL BE JUSTICE, EVEN IF HE IS NO LONGER SURE WHAT THAT WORD MEANS.
CUT: TO THE UNDERWORLD OF THE CITY OF THE STARS!
WE'S IN A BIND, DUDES!
SNAP WILSON WAS ONE OF US! IF HE REMEMBERS THAT LITTLE FACT--
--AIN'T NO TELLIN' WHAT HE'LL SPILL TO THE FEDS!
WE WASTE THE MAN, BROTHER RAYMOND! DIAL 'HOLLYWOOD' VINE AND TELL HIM TO PUT OUT A CONTACT ON SNAP WILSON!
SO WHATTA WE DO, JAZ?
TELL HIM THE SCORE! AND--

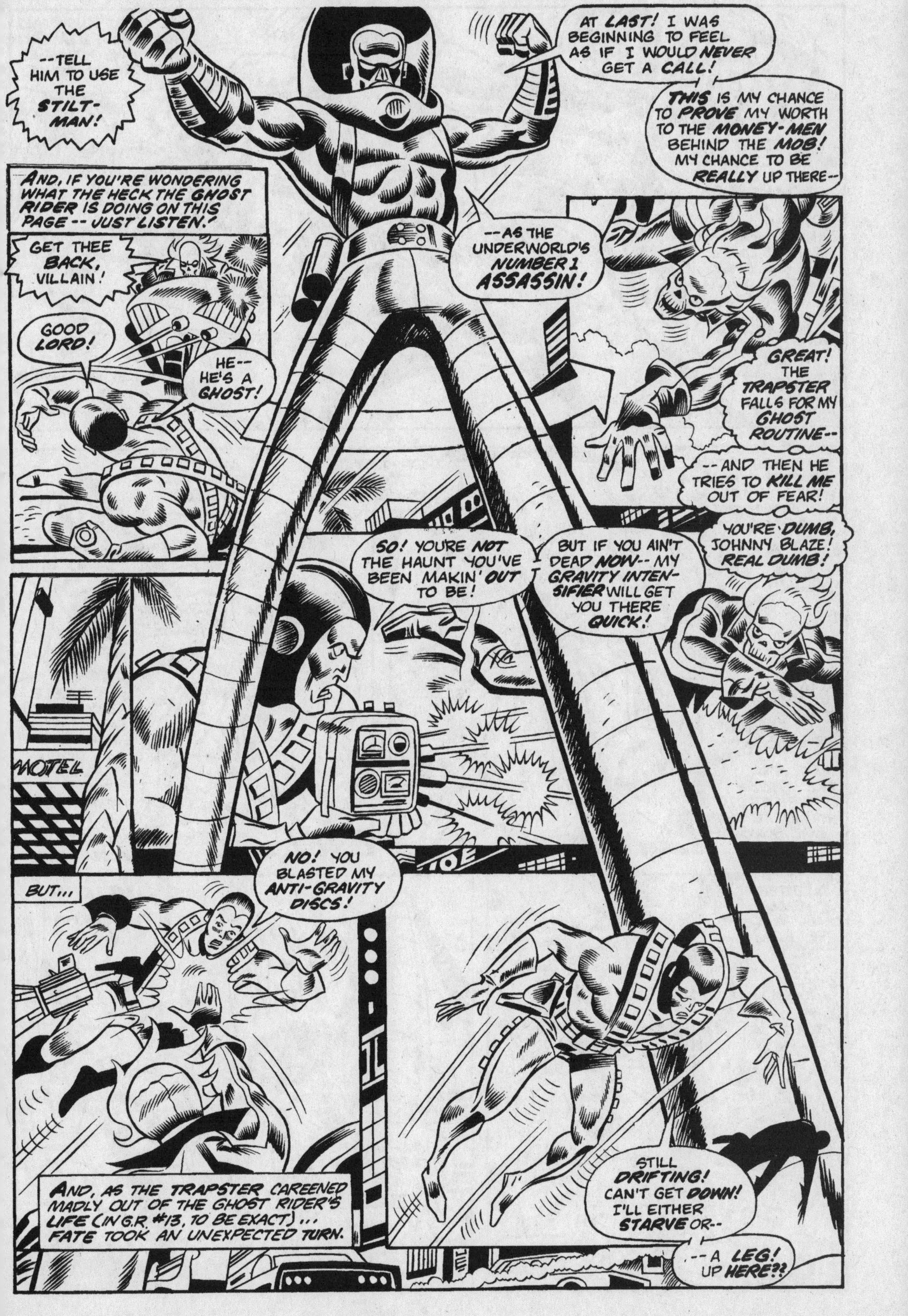

--TELL HIM TO USE THE STILT-MAN!
AT LAST! I WAS BEGINNING TO FEEL AS IF I WOULD NEVER GET A CALL!
THIS IS MY CHANCE TO PROVE MY WORTH TO THE MONEY-MEN BEHIND THE MOB! MY CHANCE TO BE REALLY UP THERE--
--AS THE UNDERWORLD'S NUMBER 1 ASSASSIN!
AND, IF YOU'RE WONDERING WHAT THE HECK THE GHOST RIDER IS DOING ON THIS PAGE -- JUST LISTEN!
GET THEE BACK, VILLAIN!
GOOD LORD!
HE-- HE'S A GHOST!
GREAT! THE TRAPSTER FALLS FOR MY GHOST ROUTINE--
--AND THEN HE TRIES TO KILL ME OUT OF FEAR!
SO! YOU'RE NOT THE HAUNT YOU'VE BEEN MAKIN' OUT TO BE!
BUT IF YOU AIN'T DEAD NOW-- MY GRAVITY INTENSIFIER WILL GET YOU THERE QUICK!
YOU'RE DUMB, JOHNNY BLAZE! REAL DUMB!
MOTEL
BUT...
NO! YOU BLASTED MY ANTI-GRAVITY DISCS!
AND, AS THE TRAPSTER CAREENED MADLY OUT OF THE GHOST RIDER'S LIFE (IN G.R. #13, TO BE EXACT)... FATE TOOK AN UNEXPECTED TURN.
STILL DRIFTING! CAN'T GET DOWN! I'LL EITHER STARVE OR--
--A LEG! UP HERE??

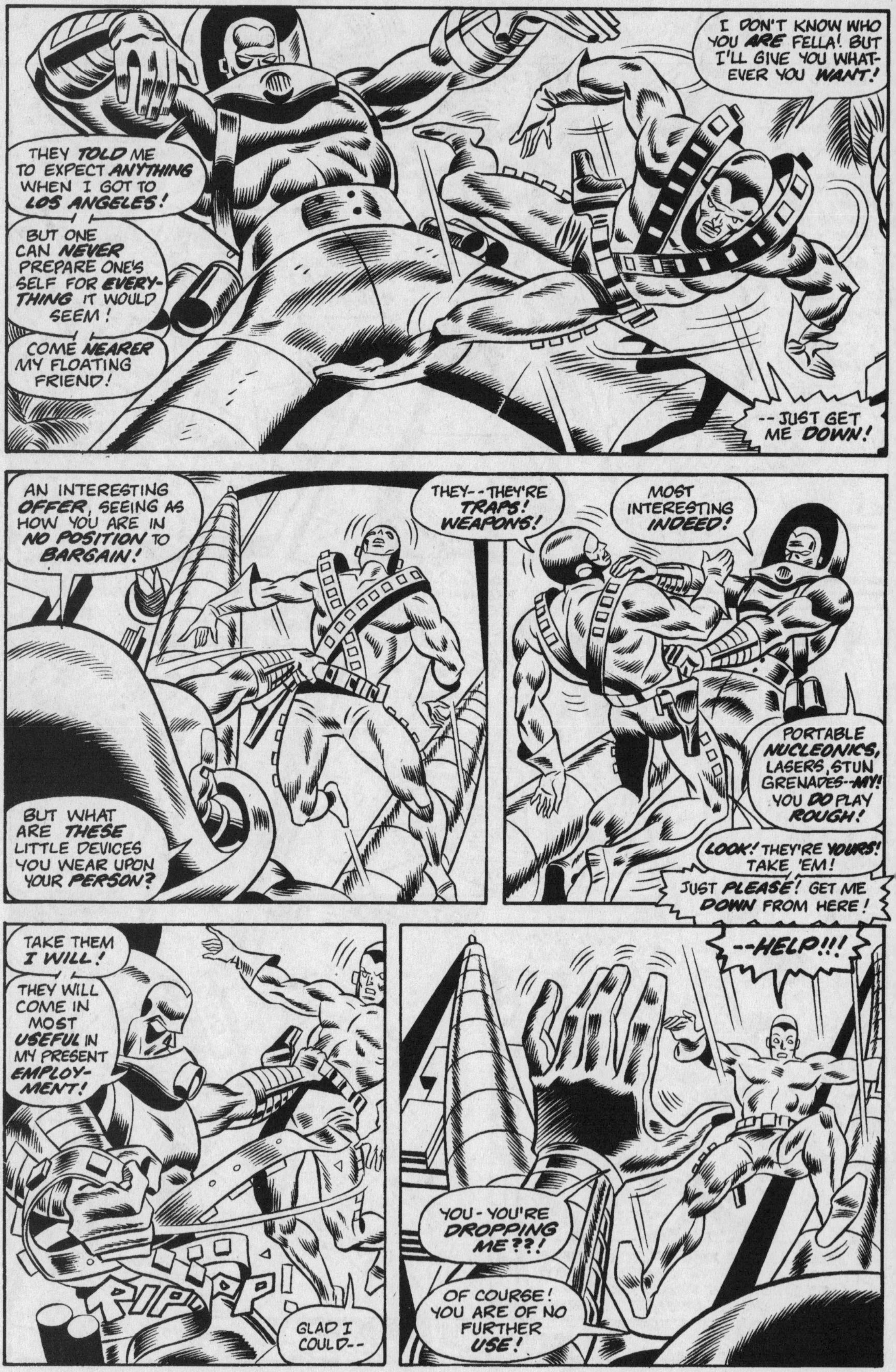
I DON'T KNOW WHO YOU ARE FELLA! BUT I'LL GIVE YOU WHAT-EVER YOU WANT!
THEY TOLD ME TO EXPECT ANYTHING WHEN I GOT TO LOS ANGELES!
BUT ONE CAN NEVER PREPARE ONE'S SELF FOR EVERY-THING IT WOULD SEEM!
COME NEARER MY FLOATING FRIEND!
--JUST GET ME DOWN!
AN INTERESTING OFFER, SEEING AS HOW YOU ARE IN NO POSITION TO BARGAIN!
BUT WHAT ARE THESE LITTLE DEVICES YOU WEAR UPON YOUR PERSON?
THEY--THEY'RE TRAPS! WEAPONS!
MOST INTERESTING INDEED!
PORTABLE NUCLEONICS, LASERS, STUN GRENADES--MY! YOU DO PLAY ROUGH!
LOOK! THEY'RE YOURS! TAKE 'EM!
JUST PLEASE! GET ME DOWN FROM HERE!
TAKE THEM I WILL!
THEY WILL COME IN MOST USEFUL IN MY PRESENT EMPLOY-MENT!
RIPPP!
GLAD I COULD--
--HELP!!!
YOU-YOU'RE DROPPING ME??!
OF COURSE! YOU ARE OF NO FURTHER USE!

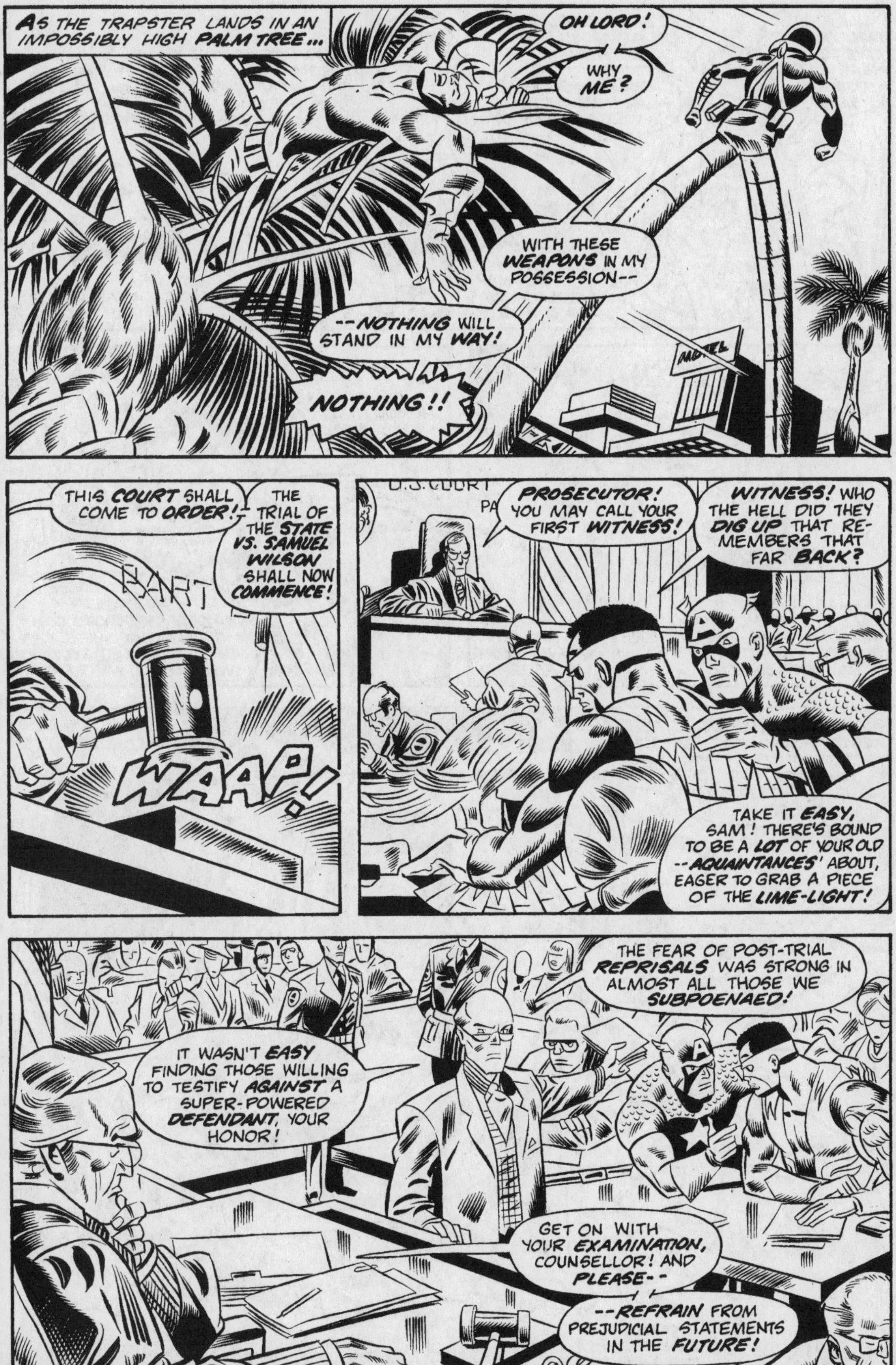
AS THE TRAPSTER LANDS IN AN IMPOSSIBLY HIGH PALM TREE...
OH LORD!
WHY ME?
WITH THESE WEAPONS IN MY POSSESSION--
--NOTHING WILL STAND IN MY WAY!
NOTHING!!
MOTEL
THIS COURT SHALL COME TO ORDER!
THE TRIAL OF THE STATE VS. SAMUEL WILSON SHALL NOW COMMENCE!
WAAP!
U.S. COURT
PROSECUTOR! YOU MAY CALL YOUR FIRST WITNESS!
WITNESS! WHO THE HELL DID THEY DIG UP THAT REMEMBERS THAT FAR BACK?
TAKE IT EASY, SAM! THERE'S BOUND TO BE A LOT OF YOUR OLD --AQUAINTANCES' ABOUT, EAGER TO GRAB A PIECE OF THE LIME-LIGHT!
THE FEAR OF POST-TRIAL REPRISALS WAS STRONG IN ALMOST ALL THOSE WE SUBPOENAED!
IT WASN'T EASY FINDING THOSE WILLING TO TESTIFY AGAINST A SUPER-POWERED DEFENDANT, YOUR HONOR!
GET ON WITH YOUR EXAMINATION, COUNSELLOR! AND PLEASE--
--REFRAIN FROM PREJUDICIAL STATEMENTS IN THE FUTURE!

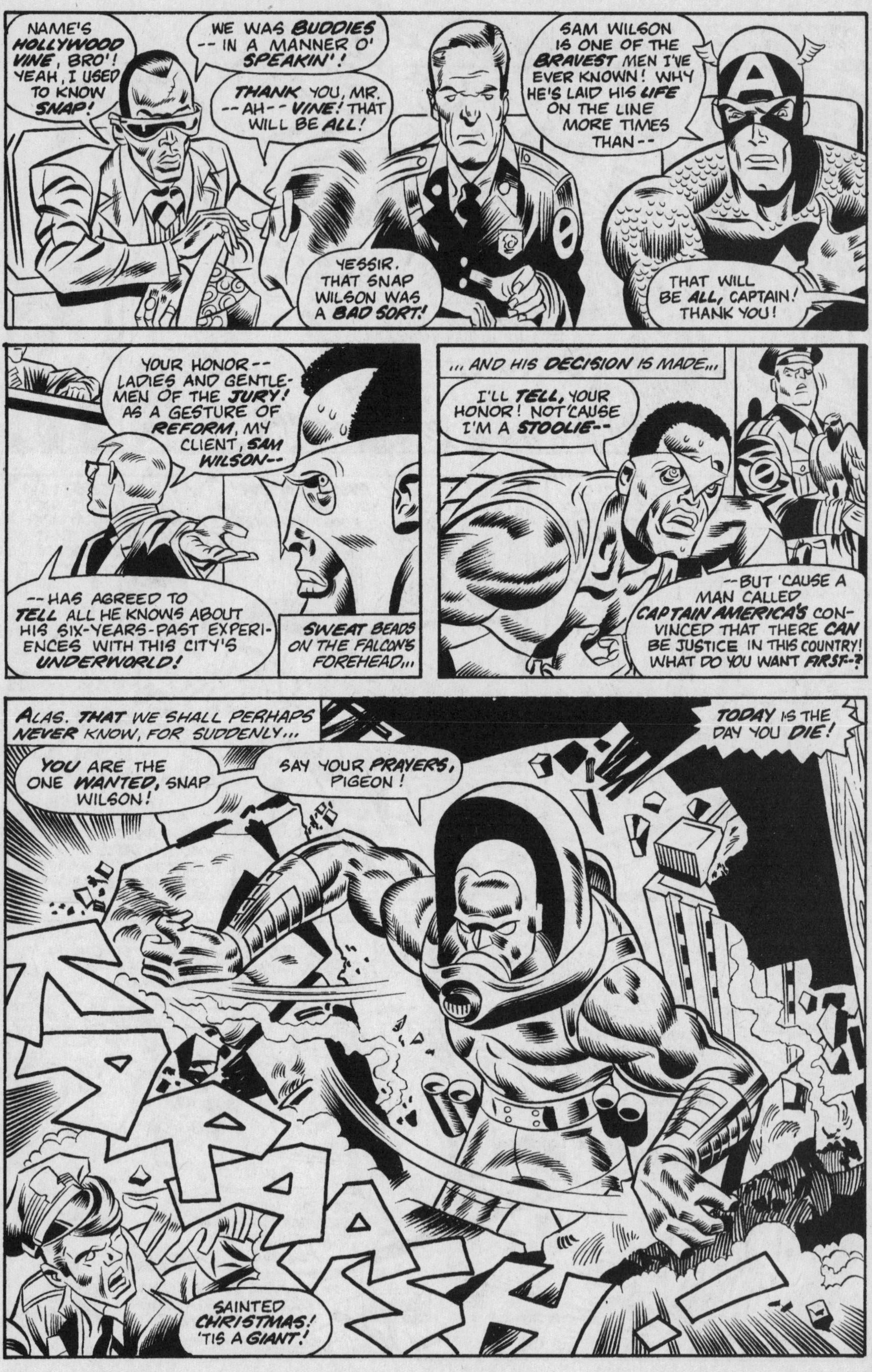
NAME'S HOLLYWOOD VINE, BRO'! YEAH, I USED TO KNOW SNAP!
WE WAS BUDDIES -- IN A MANNER O' SPEAKIN'!
THANK YOU, MR. --AH-- VINE! THAT WILL BE ALL!
YESSIR. THAT SNAP WILSON WAS A BAD SORT!
SAM WILSON IS ONE OF THE BRAVEST MEN I'VE EVER KNOWN! WHY HE'S LAID HIS LIFE ON THE LINE MORE TIMES THAN--
THAT WILL BE ALL, CAPTAIN! THANK YOU!
YOUR HONOR-- LADIES AND GENTLEMEN OF THE JURY! AS A GESTURE OF REFORM, MY CLIENT, SAM WILSON--
--HAS AGREED TO TELL ALL HE KNOWS ABOUT HIS SIX-YEARS-PAST EXPERIENCES WITH THIS CITY'S UNDERWORLD!
SWEAT BEADS ON THE FALCON'S FOREHEAD...
... AND HIS DECISION IS MADE...
I'LL TELL, YOUR HONOR! NOT 'CAUSE I'M A STOOLIE--
--BUT 'CAUSE A MAN CALLED CAPTAIN AMERICA'S CONVINCED THAT THERE CAN BE JUSTICE IN THIS COUNTRY! WHAT DO YOU WANT FIRST--?
ALAS. THAT WE SHALL PERHAPS NEVER KNOW, FOR SUDDENLY...
YOU ARE THE ONE WANTED, SNAP WILSON!
SAY YOUR PRAYERS, PIGEON!
TODAY IS THE DAY YOU DIE!
SAINTED CHRISTMAS! 'TIS A GIANT!

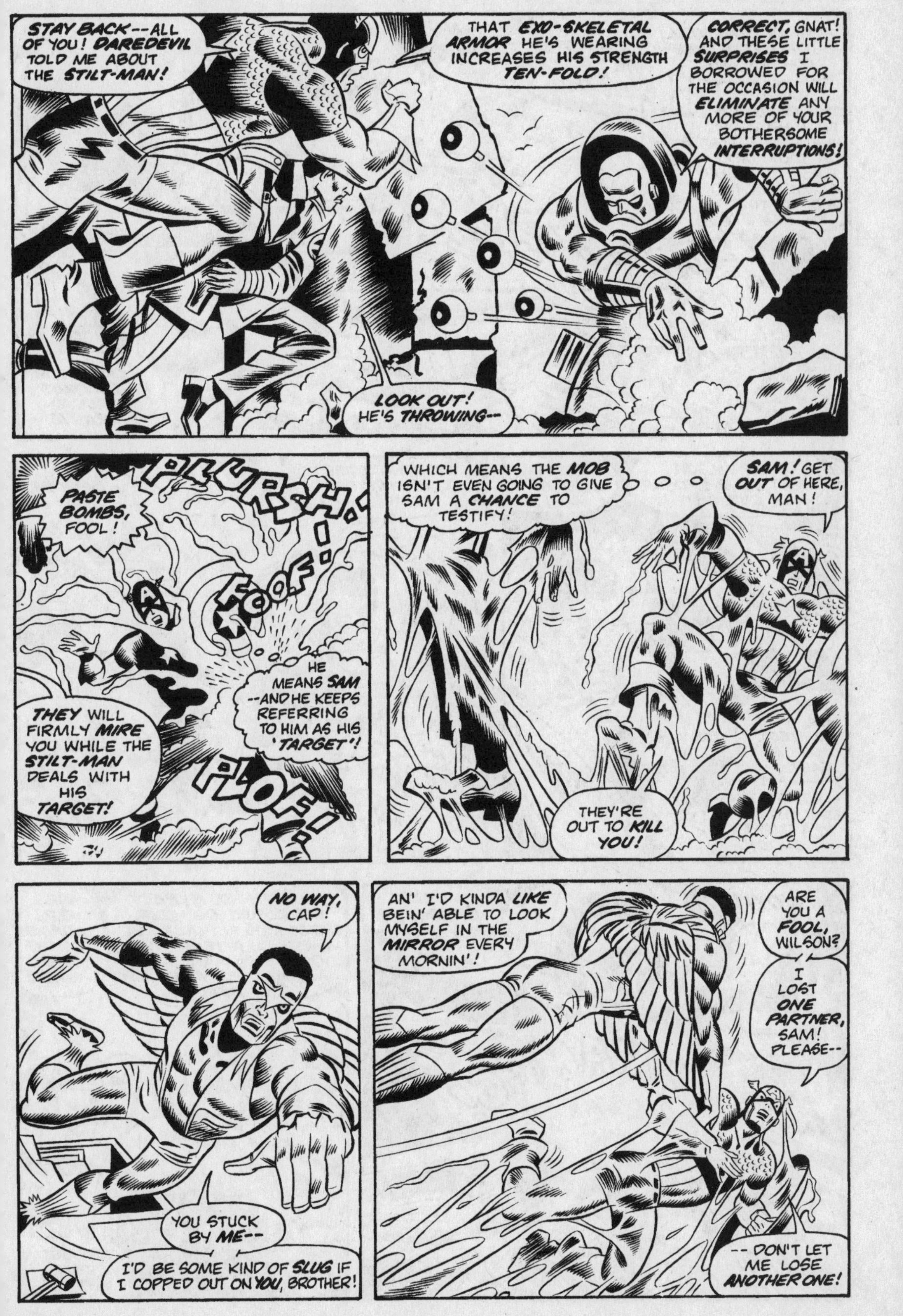
STAY BACK--ALL OF YOU! DAREDEVIL TOLD ME ABOUT THE STILT-MAN!
THAT EXO-SKELETAL ARMOR HE'S WEARING INCREASES HIS STRENGTH TEN-FOLD!
CORRECT, GNAT! AND THESE LITTLE SURPRISES I BORROWED FOR THE OCCASION WILL ELIMINATE ANY MORE OF YOUR BOTHERSOME INTERRUPTIONS!
LOOK OUT! HE'S THROWING--
PLURSH!
PASTE BOMBS, FOOL!
FOOF!
THEY WILL FIRMLY MIRE YOU WHILE THE STILT-MAN DEALS WITH HIS TARGET!
HE MEANS SAM --AND HE KEEPS REFERRING TO HIM AS HIS 'TARGET'!
PLOF!
WHICH MEANS THE MOB ISN'T EVEN GOING TO GIVE SAM A CHANCE TO TESTIFY!
SAM! GET OUT OF HERE, MAN!
THEY'RE OUT TO KILL YOU!
NO WAY, CAP!
YOU STUCK BY ME--
I'D BE SOME KIND OF SLUG IF I COPPED OUT ON YOU, BROTHER!
AN' I'D KINDA LIKE BEIN' ABLE TO LOOK MYSELF IN THE MIRROR EVERY MORNIN'!
ARE YOU A FOOL, WILSON?
I LOST ONE PARTNER, SAM! PLEASE--
--DON'T LET ME LOSE ANOTHER ONE!

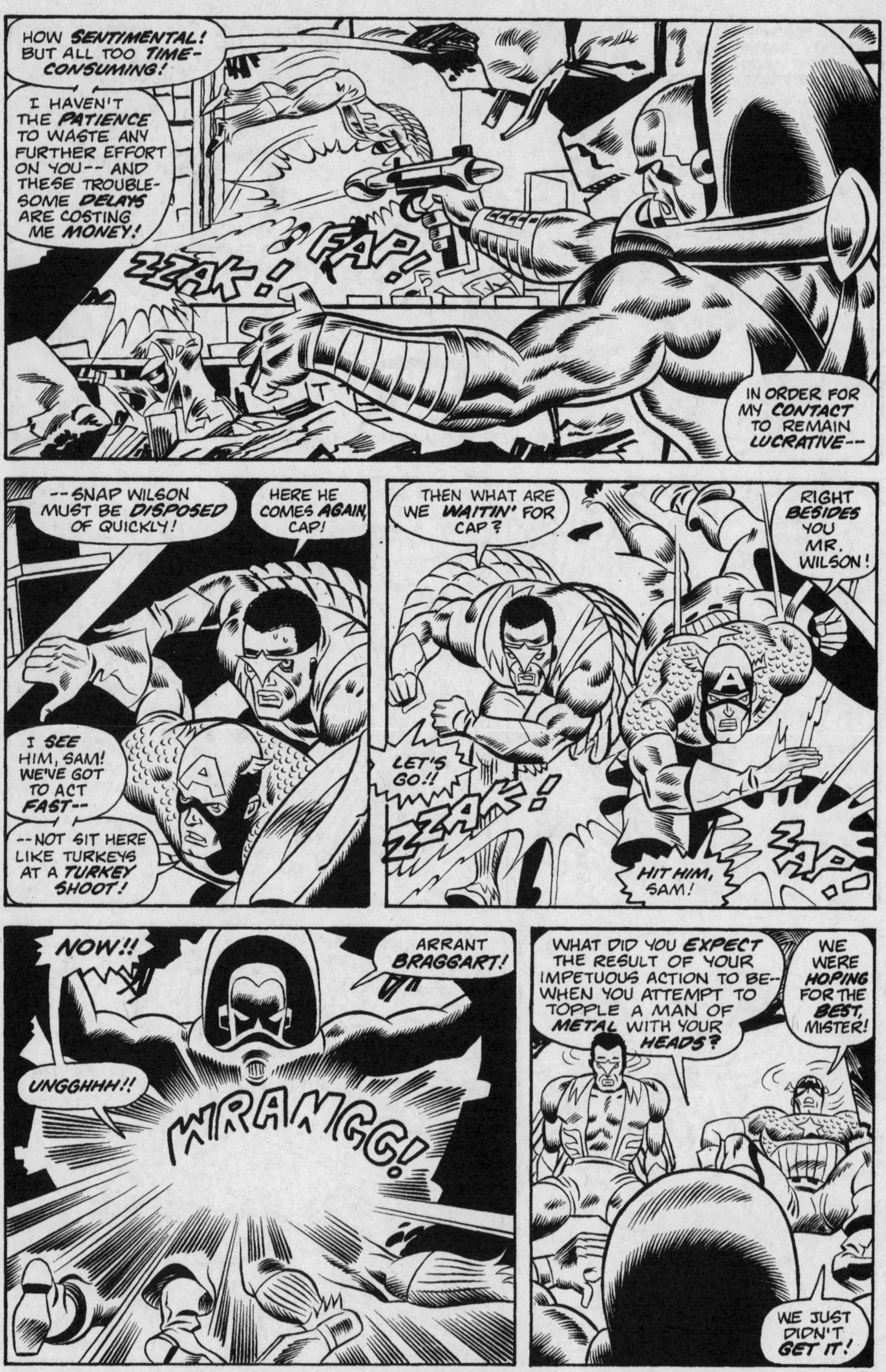
HOW SENTIMENTAL! BUT ALL TOO TIME-CONSUMING!
I HAVEN'T THE PATIENCE TO WASTE ANY FURTHER EFFORT ON YOU-- AND THESE TROUBLE-SOME DELAYS ARE COSTING ME MONEY!
ZZAK!
FAP!
IN ORDER FOR MY CONTACT TO REMAIN LUCRATIVE--
--SNAP WILSON MUST BE DISPOSED OF QUICKLY!
HERE HE COMES AGAIN, CAP!
I SEE HIM, SAM! WE'VE GOT TO ACT FAST--
--NOT SIT HERE LIKE TURKEYS AT A TURKEY SHOOT!
THEN WHAT ARE WE WAITIN' FOR CAP?
RIGHT BESIDES YOU MR. WILSON!
LET'S GO!!
ZZAK!
HIT HIM, SAM!
ZAP!
NOW!!
ARRANT BRAGGART!
UNGGHHH!!
WRANGG!
WHAT DID YOU EXPECT THE RESULT OF YOUR IMPETUOUS ACTION TO BE-- WHEN YOU ATTEMPT TO TOPPLE A MAN OF METAL WITH YOUR HEADS?
WE WERE HOPING FOR THE BEST, MISTER!
WE JUST DIDN'T GET IT!

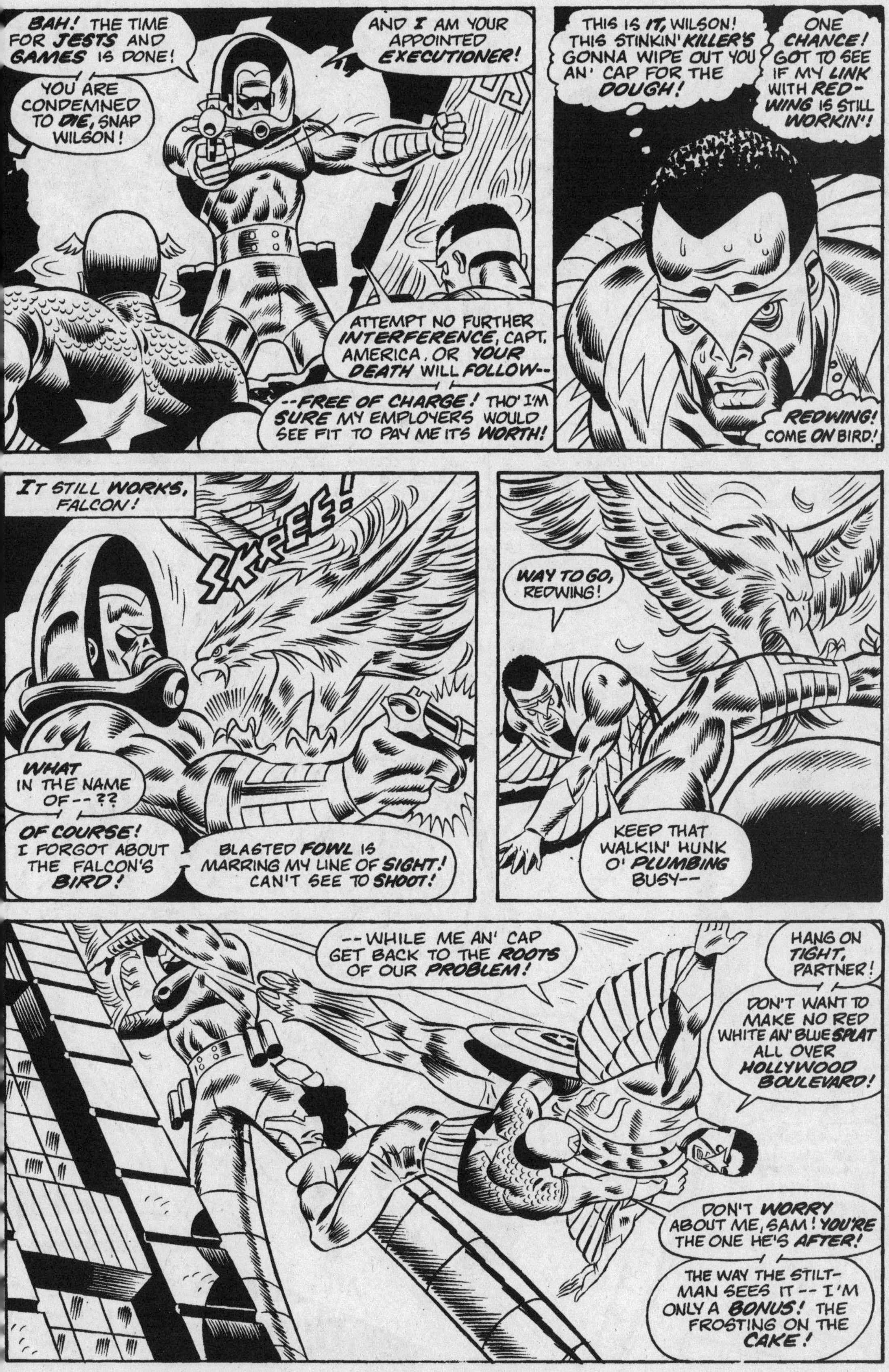
BAH! THE TIME FOR JESTS AND GAMES IS DONE!
YOU ARE CONDEMNED TO DIE, SNAP WILSON!
AND I AM YOUR APPOINTED EXECUTIONER!
ATTEMPT NO FURTHER INTERFERENCE, CAPT. AMERICA, OR YOUR DEATH WILL FOLLOW--
--FREE OF CHARGE! THO' I'M SURE MY EMPLOYERS WOULD SEE FIT TO PAY ME ITS WORTH!
THIS IS IT, WILSON! THIS STINKIN' KILLER'S GONNA WIPE OUT YOU AN' CAP FOR THE DOUGH!
ONE CHANCE! GOT TO SEE IF MY LINK WITH RED-WING IS STILL WORKIN'!
REDWING! COME ON BIRD!
IT STILL WORKS, FALCON!
SKREEE!
WHAT IN THE NAME OF--??
OF COURSE! I FORGOT ABOUT THE FALCON'S BIRD!
BLASTED FOWL IS MARRING MY LINE OF SIGHT! CAN'T SEE TO SHOOT!
WAY TO GO, REDWING!
KEEP THAT WALKIN' HUNK O' PLUMBING BUSY--
--WHILE ME AN' CAP GET BACK TO THE ROOTS OF OUR PROBLEM!
HANG ON TIGHT, PARTNER!
DON'T WANT TO MAKE NO RED WHITE AN' BLUE SPLAT ALL OVER HOLLYWOOD BOULEVARD!
DON'T WORRY ABOUT ME, SAM! YOU'RE THE ONE HE'S AFTER!
THE WAY THE STILT-MAN SEES IT -- I'M ONLY A BONUS! THE FROSTING ON THE CAKE!

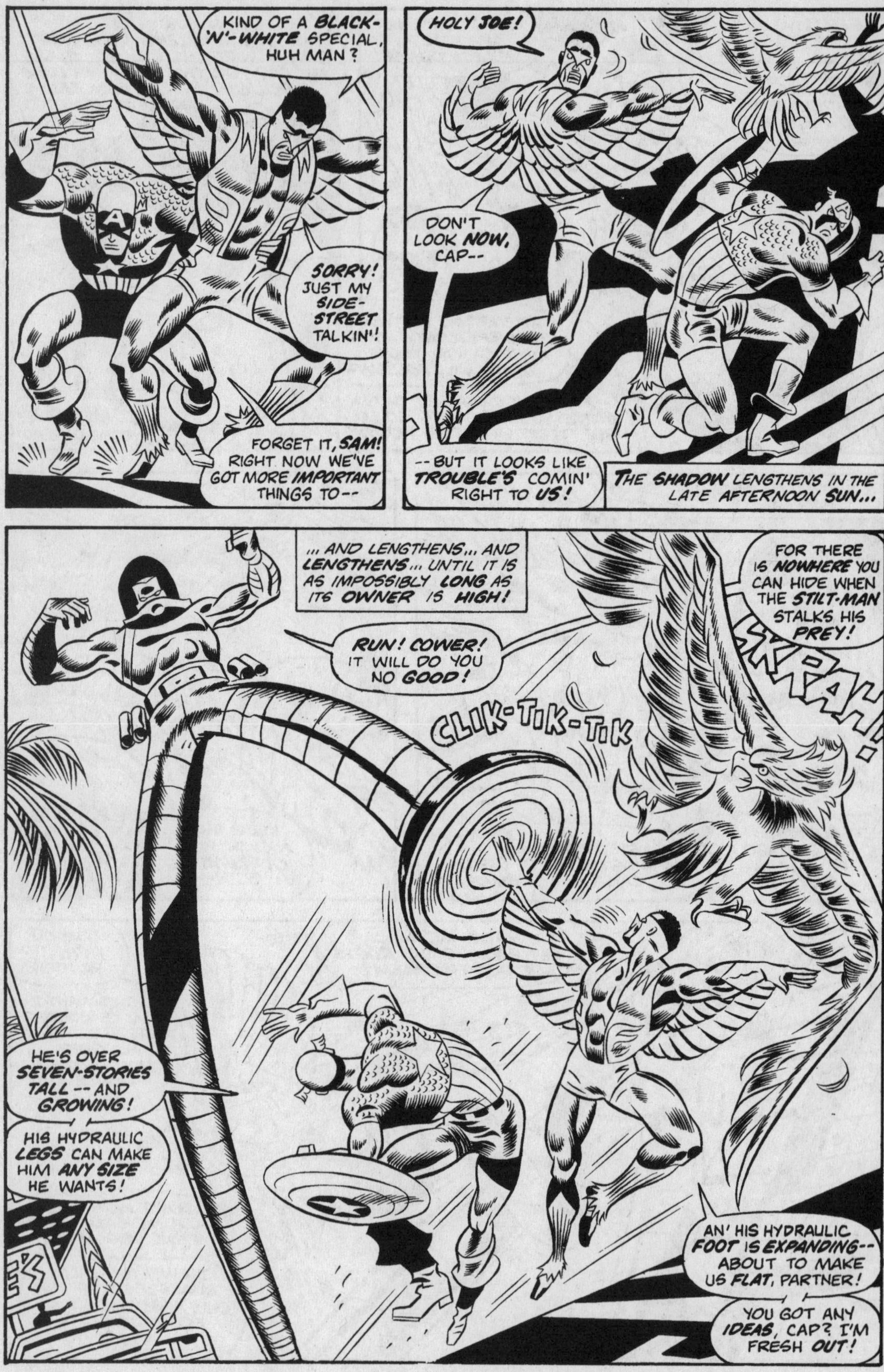
KIND OF A BLACK-'N'-WHITE SPECIAL, HUH MAN?
SORRY! JUST MY SIDE-STREET TALKIN'!
FORGET IT, SAM! RIGHT NOW WE'VE GOT MORE IMPORTANT THINGS TO--
HOLY JOE!
DON'T LOOK NOW, CAP--
--BUT IT LOOKS LIKE TROUBLE'S COMIN' RIGHT TO US!
THE SHADOW LENGTHENS IN THE LATE AFTERNOON SUN...
... AND LENGTHENS... AND LENGTHENS... UNTIL IT IS AS IMPOSSIBLY LONG AS ITS OWNER IS HIGH!
FOR THERE IS NOWHERE YOU CAN HIDE WHEN THE STILT-MAN STALKS HIS PREY!
RUN! COWER! IT WILL DO YOU NO GOOD!
SKRAH!
CLIK-TIK-TIK
HE'S OVER SEVEN-STORIES TALL -- AND GROWING!
HIS HYDRAULIC LEGS CAN MAKE HIM ANY SIZE HE WANTS!
AN' HIS HYDRAULIC FOOT IS EXPANDING-- ABOUT TO MAKE US FLAT, PARTNER!
YOU GOT ANY IDEAS, CAP? I'M FRESH OUT!

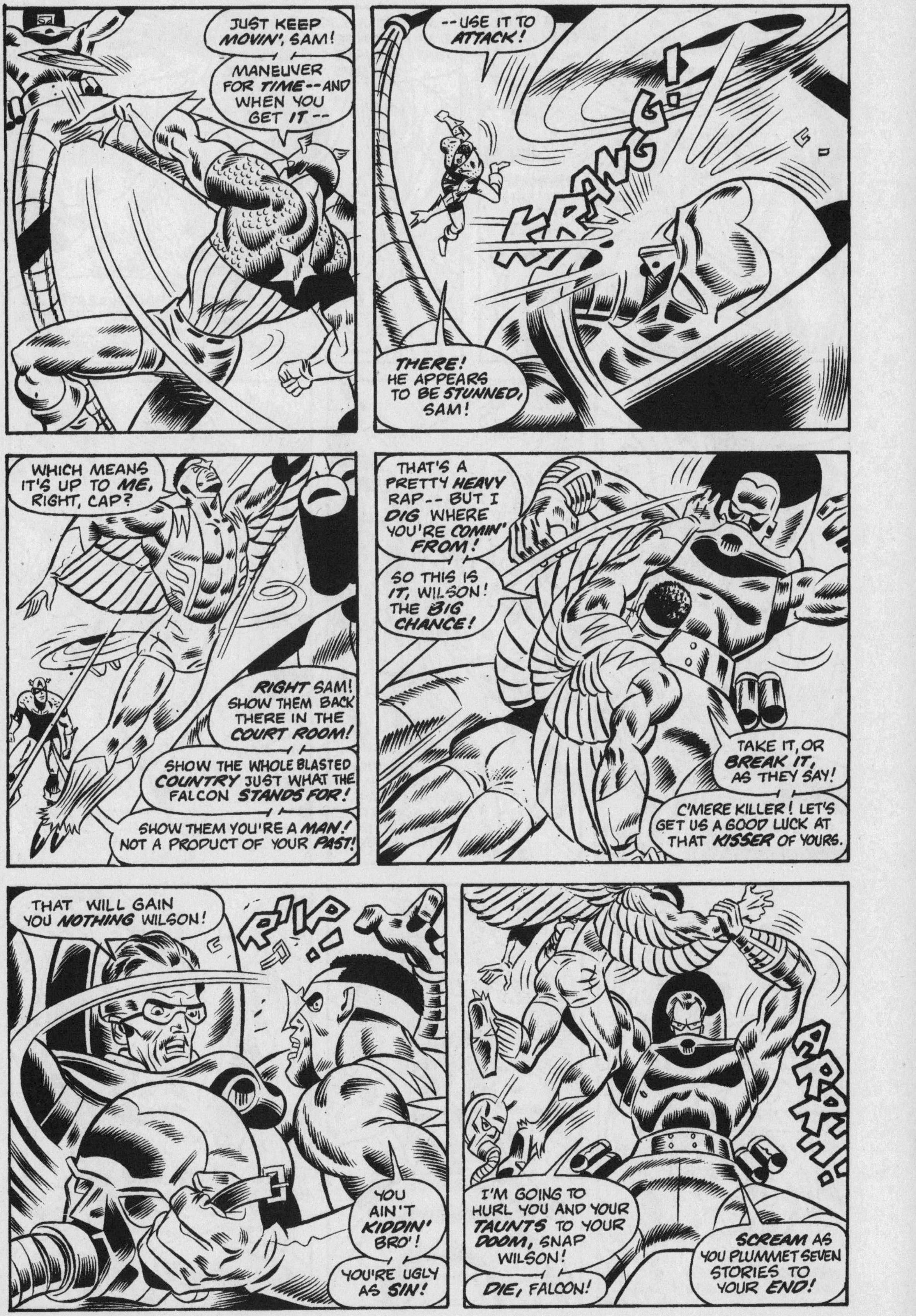
JUST KEEP MOVIN', SAM!
MANEUVER FOR TIME--AND WHEN YOU GET IT --
--USE IT TO ATTACK!
KRANG!
THERE! HE APPEARS TO BE STUNNED, SAM!
WHICH MEANS IT'S UP TO ME, RIGHT, CAP?
RIGHT SAM! SHOW THEM BACK THERE IN THE COURT ROOM!
SHOW THE WHOLE BLASTED COUNTRY JUST WHAT THE FALCON STANDS FOR!
SHOW THEM YOU'RE A MAN! NOT A PRODUCT OF YOUR PAST!
THAT'S A PRETTY HEAVY RAP-- BUT I DIG WHERE YOU'RE COMIN' FROM!
SO THIS IS IT, WILSON! THE BIG CHANCE!
TAKE IT, OR BREAK IT, AS THEY SAY!
C'MERE KILLER! LET'S GET US A GOOD LUCK AT THAT KISSER OF YOURS.
THAT WILL GAIN YOU NOTHING WILSON!
R!IP!
YOU AIN'T KIDDIN' BRO'!
YOU'RE UGLY AS SIN!
ARRR!
I'M GOING TO HURL YOU AND YOUR TAUNTS TO YOUR DOOM, SNAP WILSON!
DIE, FALCON!
SCREAM AS YOU PLUMMET SEVEN STORIES TO YOUR END!

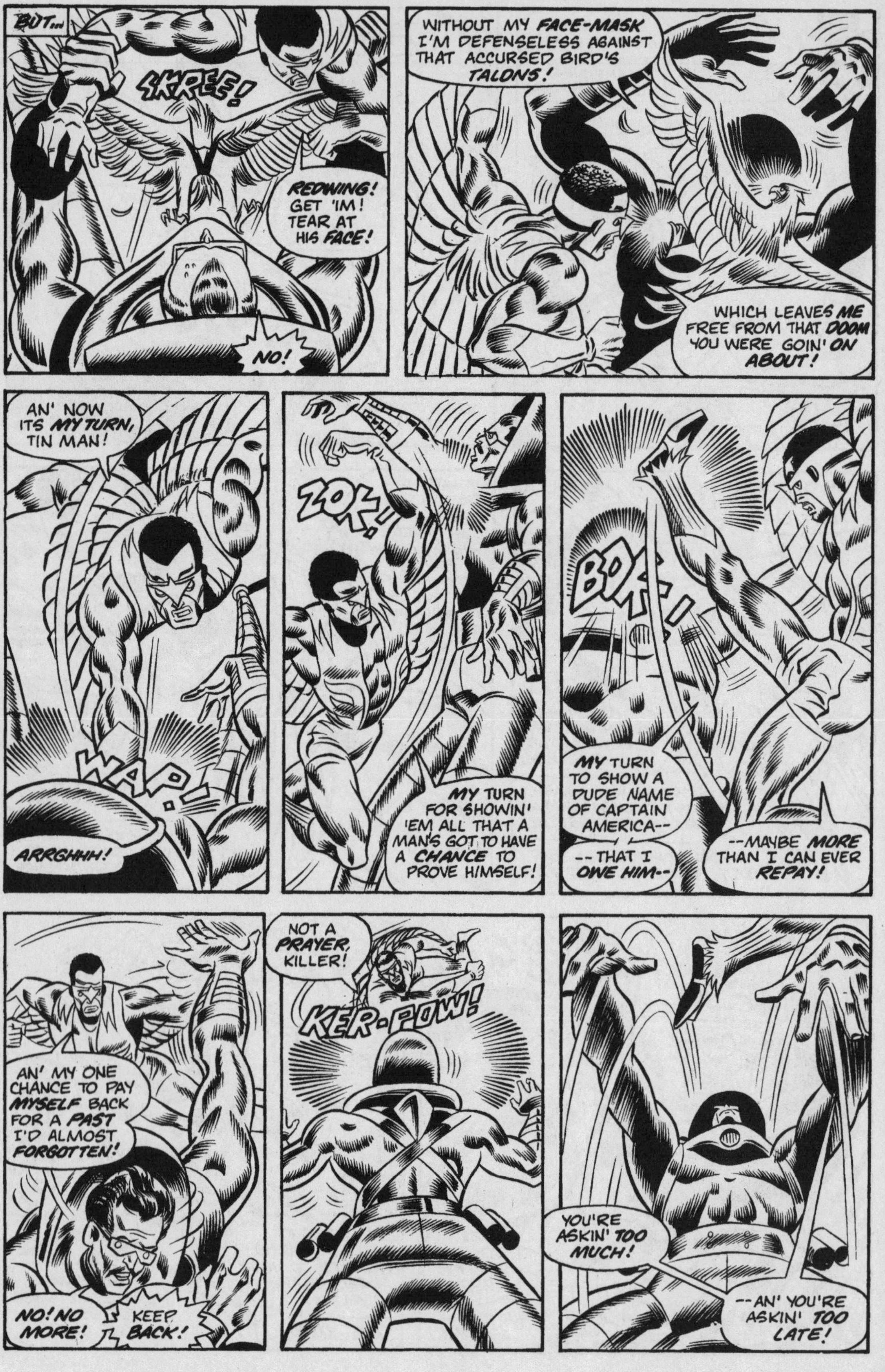
BUT...
SKREEE!
REDWING! GET 'IM! TEAR AT HIS FACE!
NO!
WITHOUT MY FACE-MASK I'M DEFENSELESS AGAINST THAT ACCURSED BIRD'S TALONS!
WHICH LEAVES ME FREE FROM THAT DOOM YOU WERE GOIN' ON ABOUT!
AN' NOW ITS MY TURN, TIN MAN!
WAP!
ARRGHHH!
ZOK!
MY TURN FOR SHOWIN' 'EM ALL THAT A MAN'S GOT TO HAVE A CHANCE TO PROVE HIMSELF!
BOK!
MY TURN TO SHOW A DUDE NAME OF CAPTAIN AMERICA--
--THAT I OWE HIM--
--MAYBE MORE THAN I CAN EVER REPAY!
AN' MY ONE CHANCE TO PAY MYSELF BACK FOR A PAST I'D ALMOST FORGOTTEN!
NO! NO MORE!
KEEP BACK!
NOT A PRAYER, KILLER!
KER-POW!
YOU'RE ASKIN' TOO MUCH!
--AN' YOU'RE ASKIN' TOO LATE!

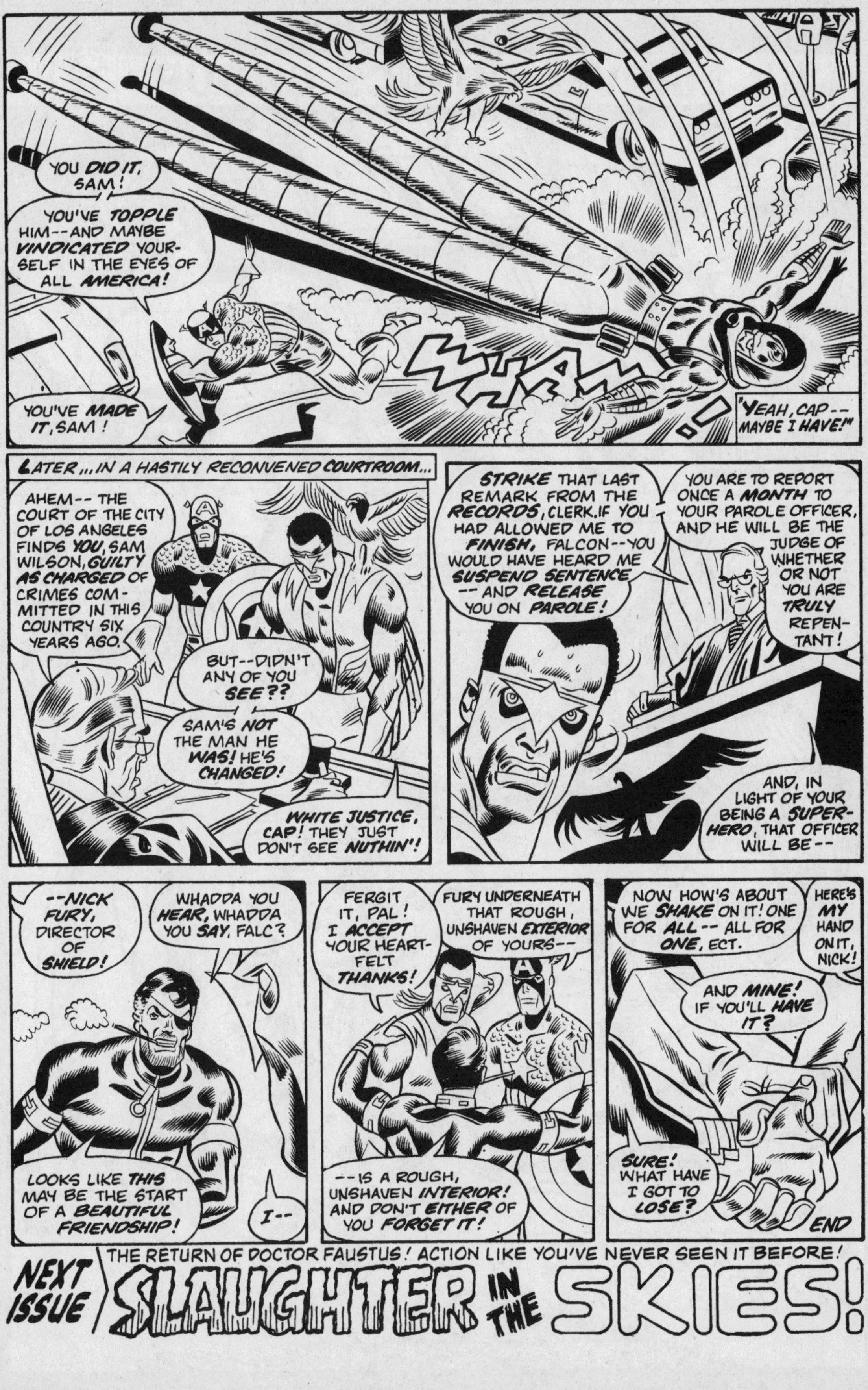
YOU DID IT, SAM!
YOU'VE TOPPLE HIM--AND MAYBE VINDICATED YOURSELF IN THE EYES OF ALL AMERICA!
YOU'VE MADE IT, SAM!
WHAM!
"YEAH, CAP--MAYBE I HAVE!"
LATER... IN A HASTILY RECONVENED COURTROOM...
AHEM-- THE COURT OF THE CITY OF LOS ANGELES FINDS YOU, SAM WILSON, GUILTY AS CHARGED OF CRIMES COMMITTED IN THIS COUNTRY SIX YEARS AGO.
BUT--DIDN'T ANY OF YOU SEE??
SAM'S NOT THE MAN HE WAS! HE'S CHANGED!
WHITE JUSTICE, CAP! THEY JUST DON'T SEE NUTHIN'!
STRIKE THAT LAST REMARK FROM THE RECORDS, CLERK. IF YOU HAD ALLOWED ME TO FINISH, FALCON--YOU WOULD HAVE HEARD ME SUSPEND SENTENCE --AND RELEASE YOU ON PAROLE!
YOU ARE TO REPORT ONCE A MONTH TO YOUR PAROLE OFFICER, AND HE WILL BE THE JUDGE OF WHETHER OR NOT YOU ARE TRULY REPENTANT!
AND, IN LIGHT OF YOUR BEING A SUPER-HERO, THAT OFFICER WILL BE--
--NICK FURY, DIRECTOR OF SHIELD!
WHADDA YOU HEAR, WHADDA YOU SAY, FALC?
LOOKS LIKE THIS MAY BE THE START OF A BEAUTIFUL FRIENDSHIP!
I--
FERGIT IT, PAL! I ACCEPT YOUR HEART-FELT THANKS!
FURY UNDERNEATH THAT ROUGH, UNSHAVEN EXTERIOR OF YOURS--
--IS A ROUGH, UNSHAVEN INTERIOR! AND DON'T EITHER OF YOU FORGET IT!
NOW HOW'S ABOUT WE SHAKE ON IT! ONE FOR ALL-- ALL FOR ONE, ECT.
HERE'S MY HAND ON IT, NICK!
AND MINE! IF YOU'LL HAVE IT?
SURE! WHAT HAVE I GOT TO LOSE?
END
NEXT ISSUE
THE RETURN OF DOCTOR FAUSTUS! ACTION LIKE YOU'VE NEVER SEEN IT BEFORE!
SLAUGHTER IN THE SKIES!

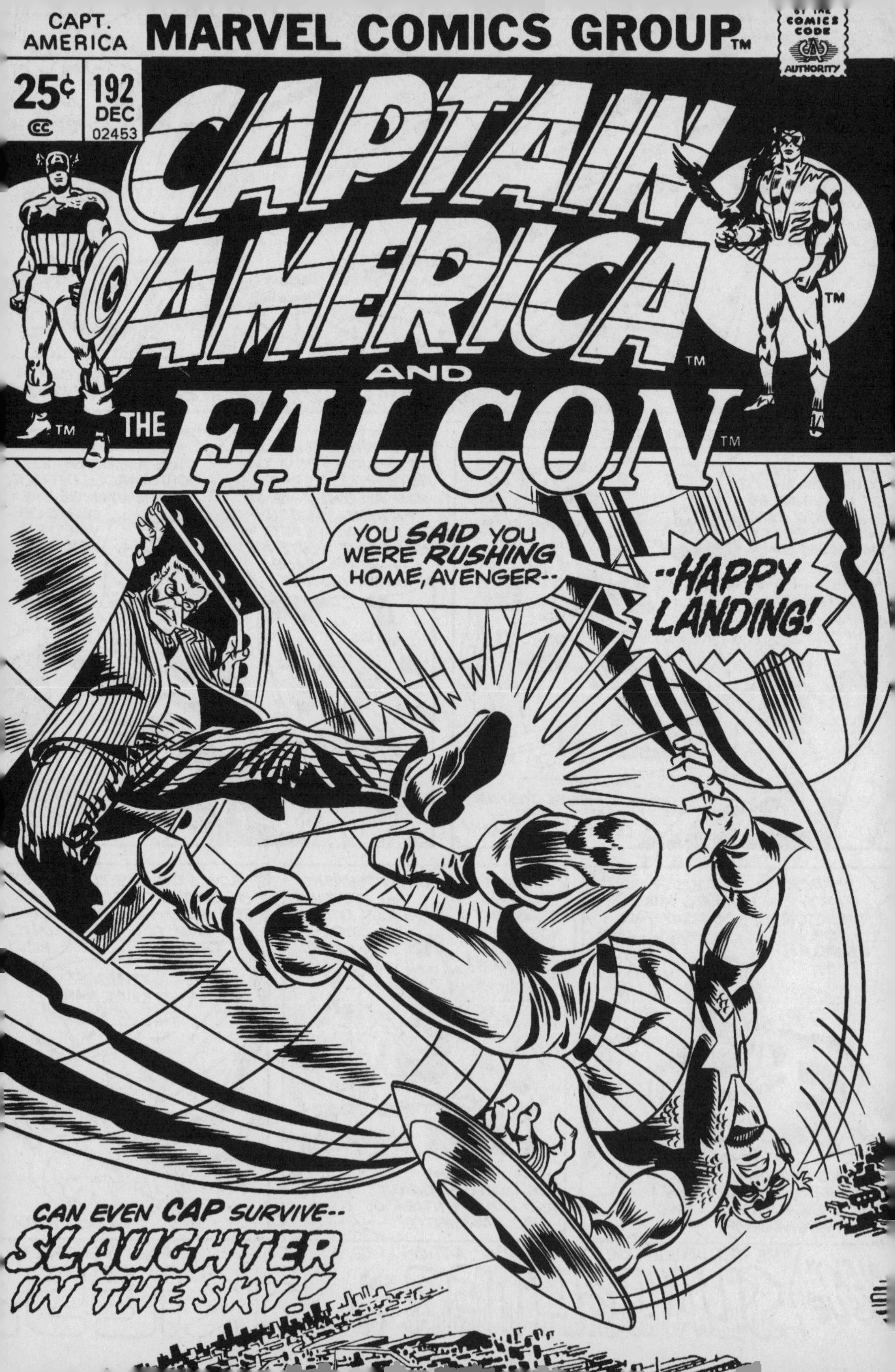
CAPT. AMERICA
MARVEL COMICS GROUP™
25¢
192 DEC
02453
CAPTAIN AMERICA™
AND
THE FALCON™
YOU SAID YOU WERE RUSHING HOME, AVENGER--
--HAPPY LANDING!
CAN EVEN CAP SURVIVE--
SLAUGHTER IN THE SKY!

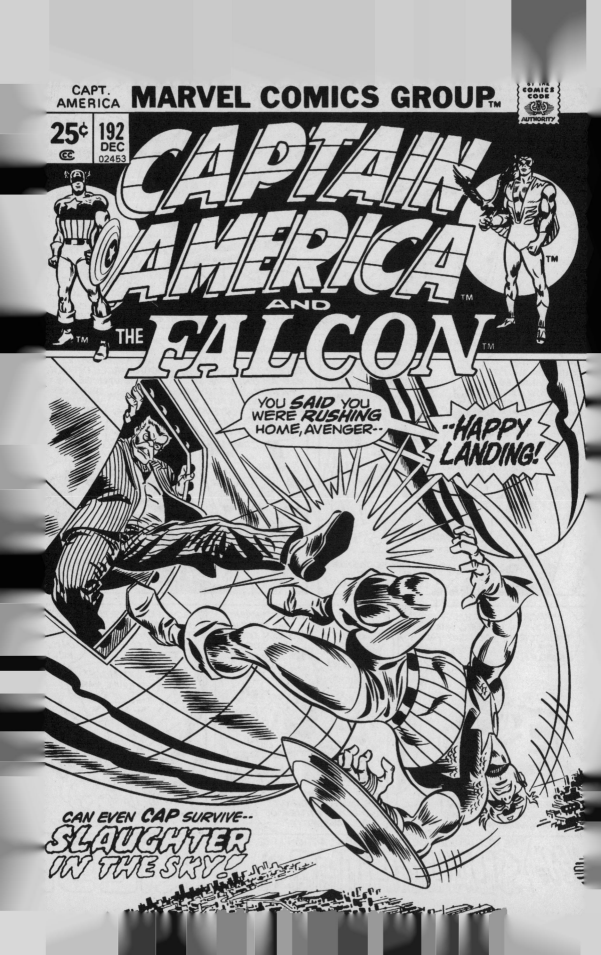

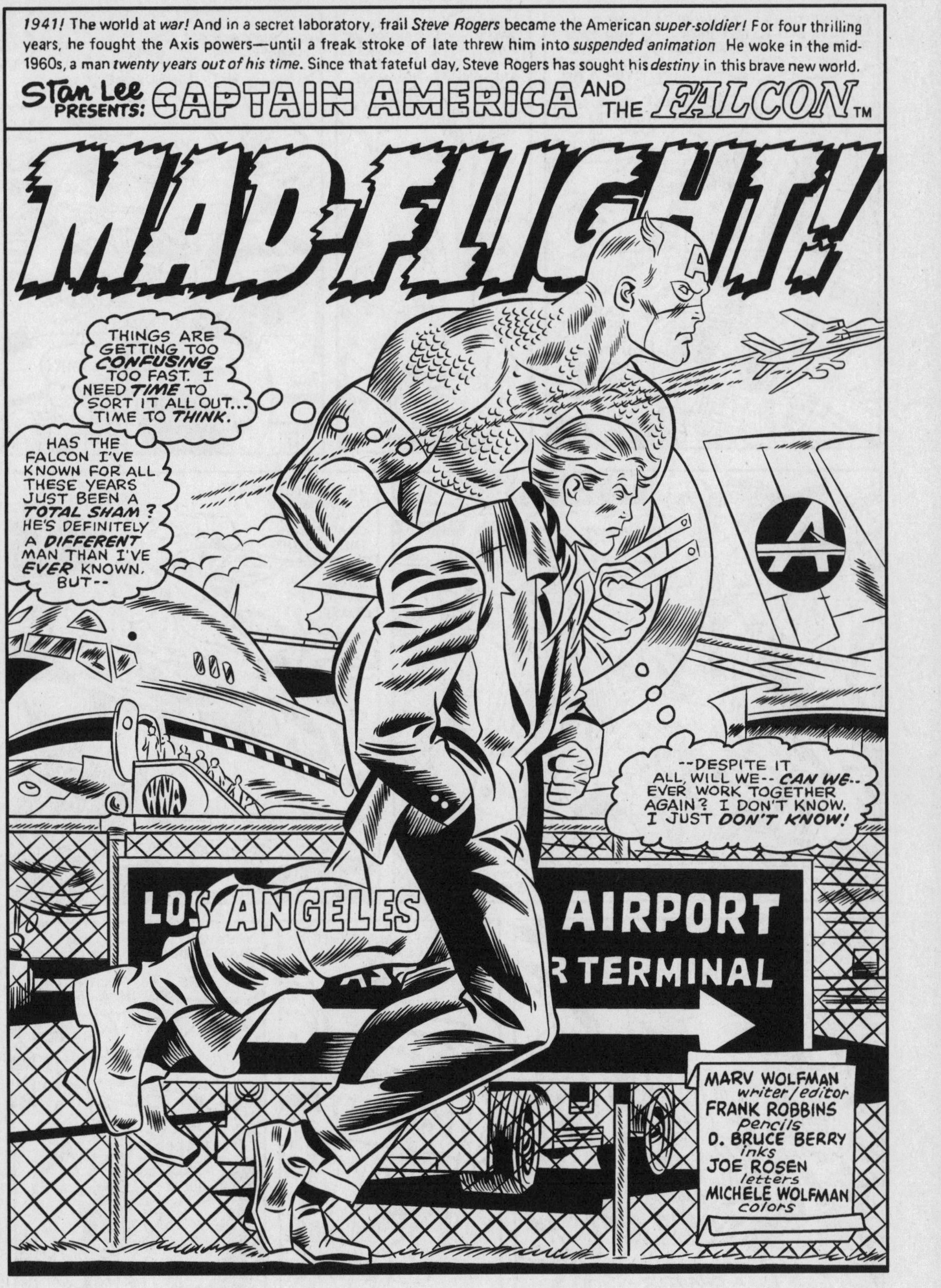

1941! The world at war! And in a secret laboratory, frail Steve Rogers became the American super-soldier! For four thrilling years, he fought the Axis powers—until a freak stroke of fate threw him into suspended animation He woke in the mid-1960s, a man twenty years out of his time. Since that fateful day, Steve Rogers has sought his destiny in this brave new world.
Stan Lee PRESENTS: CAPTAIN AMERICA AND THE FALCON TM
MAD-FLIGHT!
THINGS ARE GETTING TOO CONFUSING TOO FAST. I NEED TIME TO SORT IT ALL OUT... TIME TO THINK.
HAS THE FALCON I'VE KNOWN FOR ALL THESE YEARS JUST BEEN A TOTAL SHAM? HE'S DEFINITELY A DIFFERENT MAN THAN I'VE EVER KNOWN. BUT--
--DESPITE IT ALL, WILL WE-- CAN WE-- EVER WORK TOGETHER AGAIN? I DON'T KNOW. I JUST DON'T KNOW!
LOS ANGELES AIRPORT
R TERMINAL
MARV WOLFMAN writer/editor
FRANK ROBBINS pencils
D. BRUCE BERRY inks
JOE ROSEN letters
MICHELE WOLFMAN colors

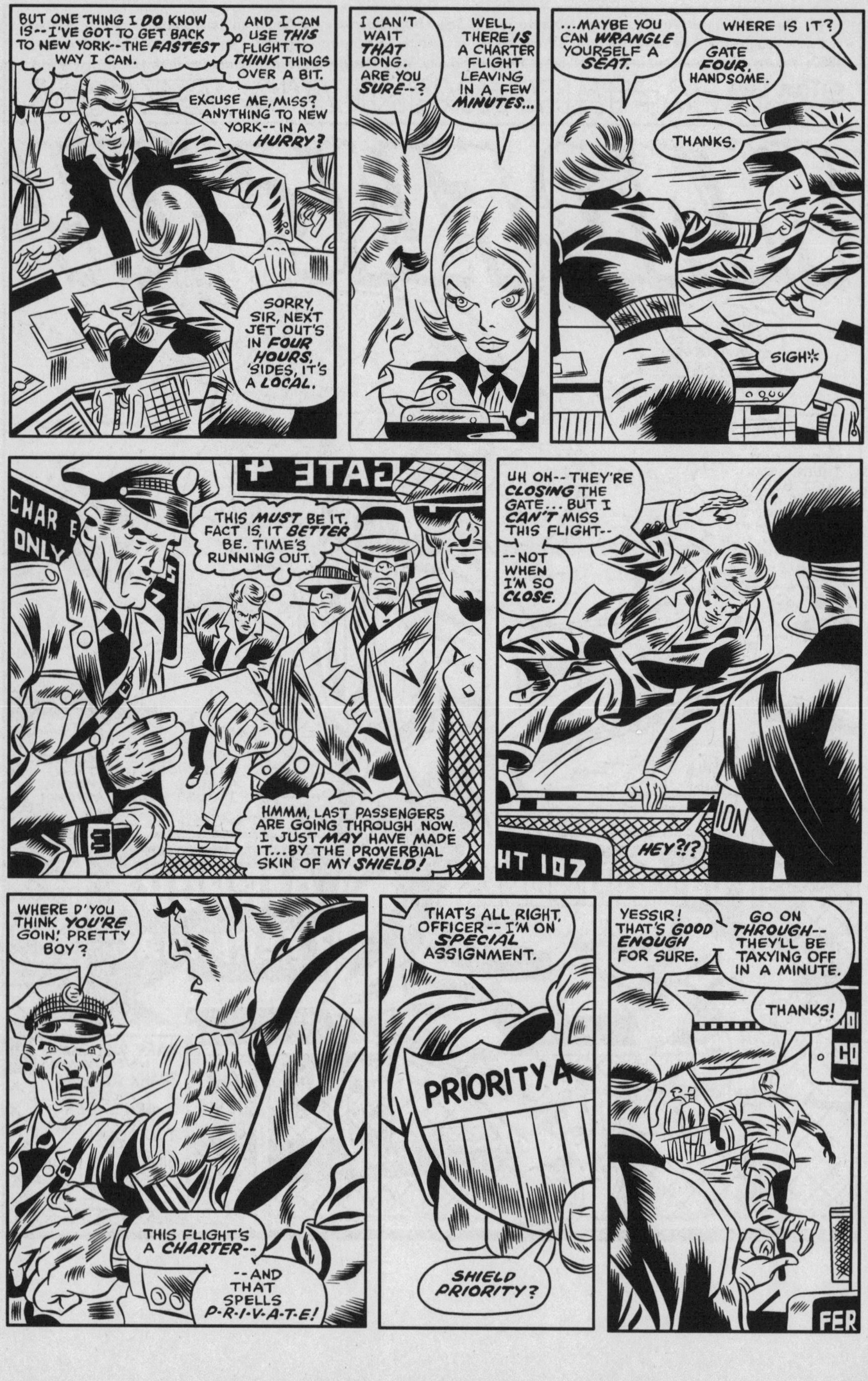

BUT ONE THING I DO KNOW IS--I'VE GOT TO GET BACK TO NEW YORK--THE FASTEST WAY I CAN.
AND I CAN USE THIS FLIGHT TO THINK THINGS OVER A BIT.
EXCUSE ME, MISS? ANYTHING TO NEW YORK-- IN A HURRY?
SORRY, SIR, NEXT JET OUT'S IN FOUR HOURS. 'SIDES, IT'S A LOCAL.
I CAN'T WAIT THAT LONG. ARE YOU SURE--?
WELL, THERE IS A CHARTER FLIGHT LEAVING IN A FEW MINUTES...
...MAYBE YOU CAN WRANGLE YOURSELF A SEAT.
WHERE IS IT?
GATE FOUR, HANDSOME.
THANKS.
SIGH*
THIS MUST BE IT. FACT IS, IT BETTER BE. TIME'S RUNNING OUT.
HMMM, LAST PASSENGERS ARE GOING THROUGH NOW. I JUST MAY HAVE MADE IT...BY THE PROVERBIAL SKIN OF MY SHIELD!
UH OH-- THEY'RE CLOSING THE GATE... BUT I CAN'T MISS THIS FLIGHT--
--NOT WHEN I'M SO CLOSE.
HEY?!?
WHERE D'YOU THINK YOU'RE GOIN', PRETTY BOY?
THIS FLIGHT'S A CHARTER--
--AND THAT SPELLS P-R-I-V-A-T-E!
THAT'S ALL RIGHT, OFFICER -- I'M ON SPECIAL ASSIGNMENT.
PRIORITY A
SHIELD PRIORITY?
YESSIR! THAT'S GOOD ENOUGH FOR SURE.
GO ON THROUGH-- THEY'LL BE TAXYING OFF IN A MINUTE.
THANKS!
FER

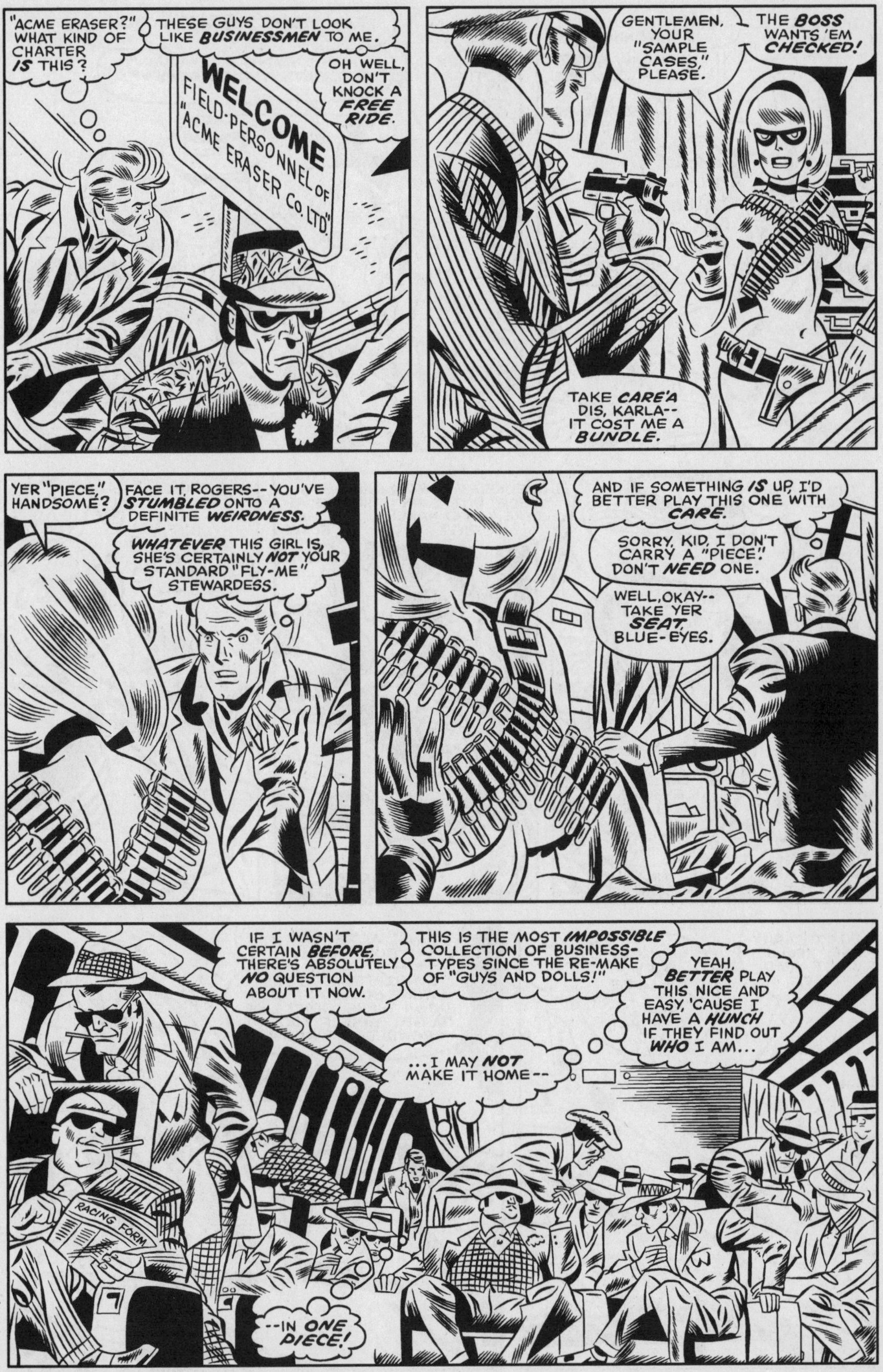
"ACME ERASER?" WHAT KIND OF CHARTER IS THIS?
THESE GUYS DON'T LOOK LIKE BUSINESSMEN TO ME.
OH WELL, DON'T KNOCK A FREE RIDE.
WELCOME FIELD-PERSONNEL OF "ACME ERASER Co. LTD."
GENTLEMEN, YOUR "SAMPLE CASES," PLEASE.
THE BOSS WANTS 'EM CHECKED!
TAKE CARE'A DIS, KARLA-- IT COST ME A BUNDLE.
YER "PIECE," HANDSOME?
FACE IT, ROGERS-- YOU'VE STUMBLED ONTO A DEFINITE WEIRDNESS.
WHATEVER THIS GIRL IS, SHE'S CERTAINLY NOT YOUR STANDARD "FLY-ME" STEWARDESS.
AND IF SOMETHING IS UP, I'D BETTER PLAY THIS ONE WITH CARE.
SORRY, KID, I DON'T CARRY A "PIECE." DON'T NEED ONE.
WELL, OKAY-- TAKE YER SEAT, BLUE-EYES.
IF I WASN'T CERTAIN BEFORE, THERE'S ABSOLUTELY NO QUESTION ABOUT IT NOW.
THIS IS THE MOST IMPOSSIBLE COLLECTION OF BUSINESS-TYPES SINCE THE RE-MAKE OF "GUYS AND DOLLS!"
YEAH, BETTER PLAY THIS NICE AND EASY, 'CAUSE I HAVE A HUNCH IF THEY FIND OUT WHO I AM...
...I MAY NOT MAKE IT HOME--
--IN ONE PIECE!
RACING FORM

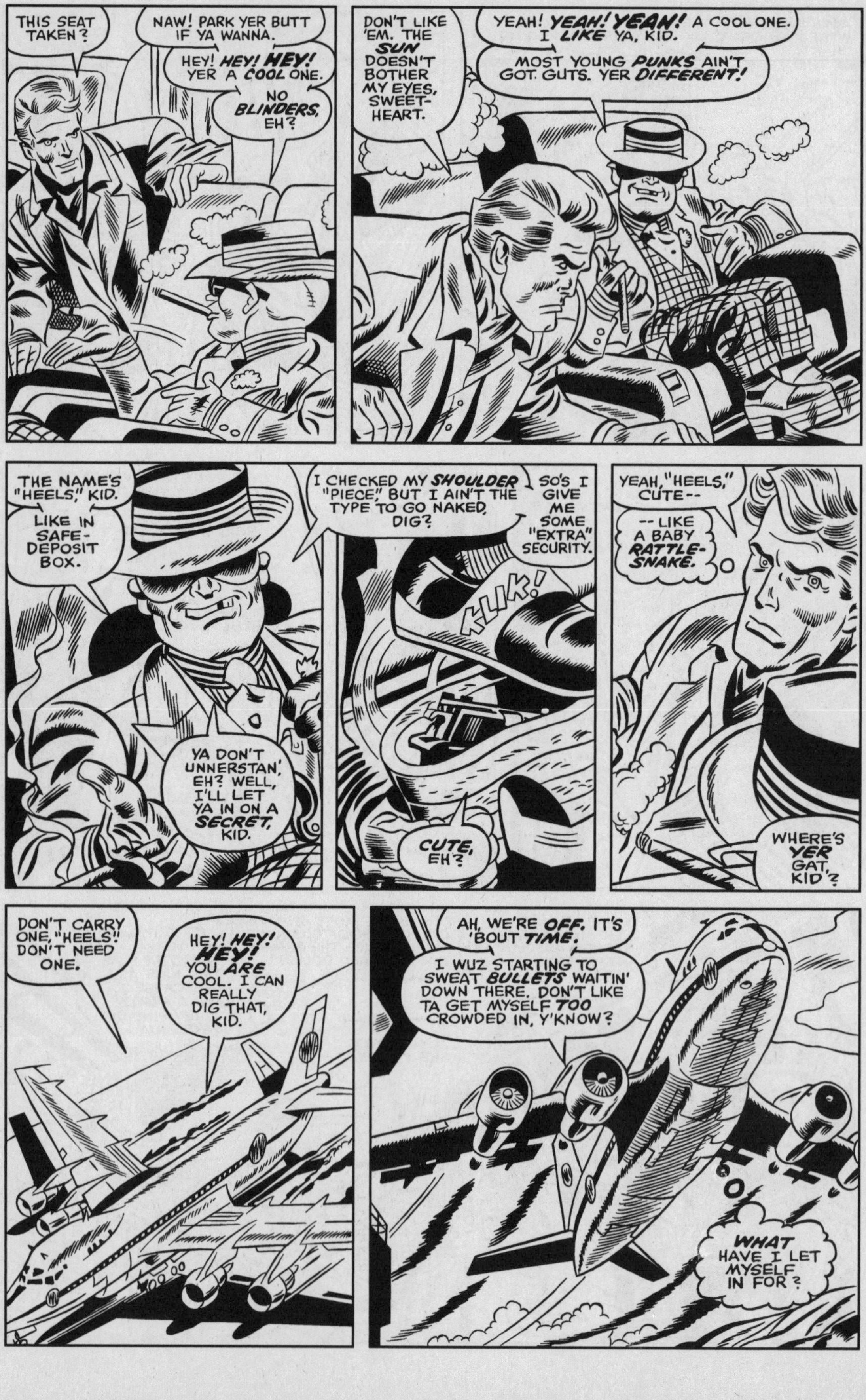
THIS SEAT TAKEN?
NAW! PARK YER BUTT IF YA WANNA.
HEY! HEY! HEY! YER A COOL ONE.
NO BLINDERS, EH?
DON'T LIKE 'EM. THE SUN DOESN'T BOTHER MY EYES, SWEET-HEART.
YEAH! YEAH! YEAH! A COOL ONE. I LIKE YA, KID.
MOST YOUNG PUNKS AIN'T GOT. GUTS. YER DIFFERENT!
THE NAME'S "HEELS," KID.
LIKE IN SAFE-DEPOSIT BOX.
YA DON'T UNNERSTAN', EH? WELL, I'LL LET YA IN ON A SECRET, KID.
I CHECKED MY SHOULDER "PIECE," BUT I AIN'T THE TYPE TO GO NAKED, DIG?
SO'S I GIVE ME SOME "EXTRA" SECURITY.
KLIK!
CUTE, EH?
YEAH, "HEELS," CUTE--
--LIKE A BABY RATTLE-SNAKE.
WHERE'S YER GAT, KID?
DON'T CARRY ONE, "HEELS." DON'T NEED ONE.
HEY! HEY! HEY! YOU ARE COOL. I CAN REALLY DIG THAT, KID.
AH, WE'RE OFF. IT'S 'BOUT TIME.
I WUZ STARTING TO SWEAT BULLETS WAITIN' DOWN THERE. DON'T LIKE TA GET MYSELF TOO CROWDED IN, Y'KNOW?
WHAT HAVE I LET MYSELF IN FOR?

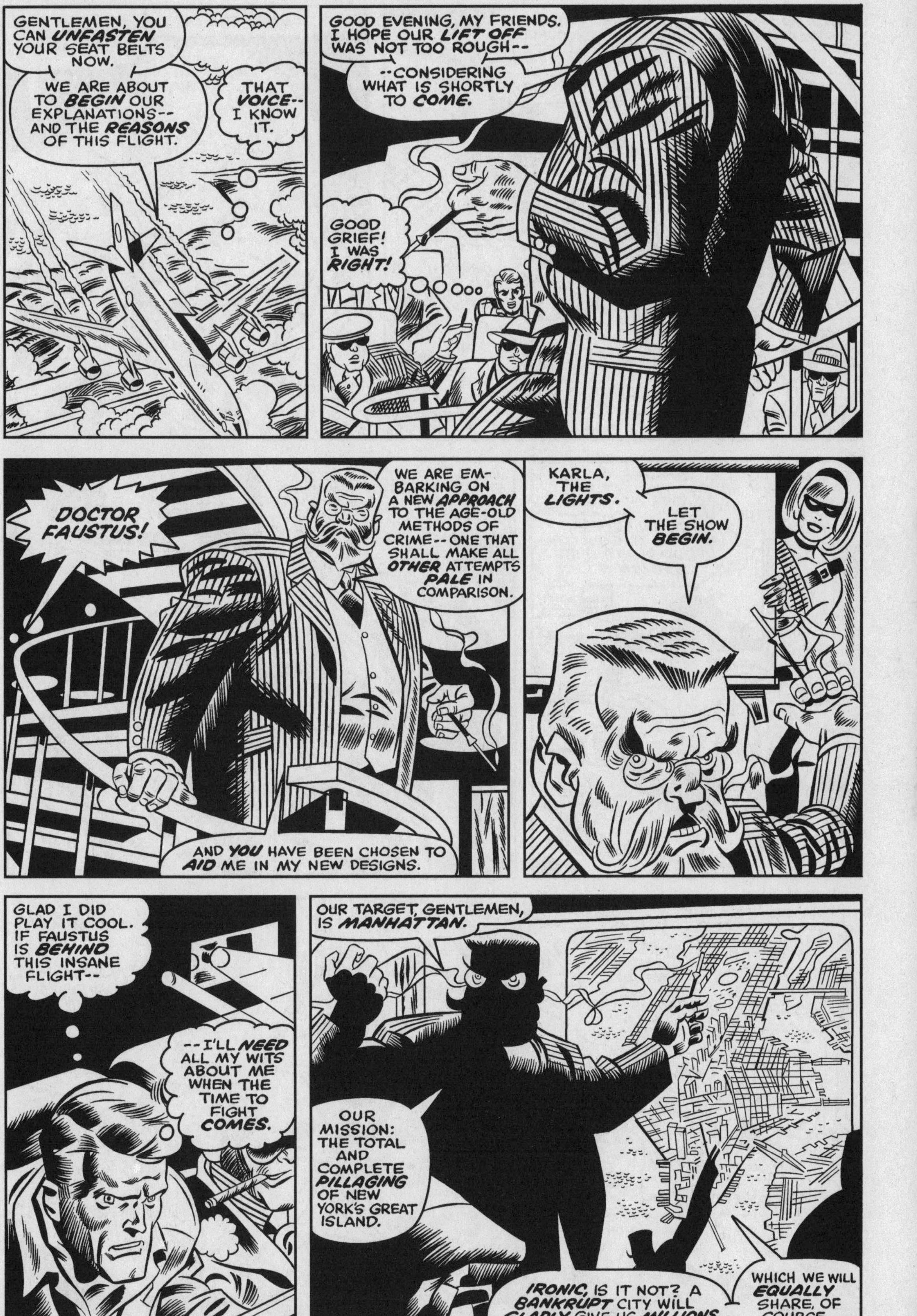
GENTLEMEN, YOU CAN UNFASTEN YOUR SEAT BELTS NOW.
WE ARE ABOUT TO BEGIN OUR EXPLANATIONS-- AND THE REASONS OF THIS FLIGHT.
THAT VOICE-- I KNOW IT.
GOOD EVENING, MY FRIENDS. I HOPE OUR LIFT OFF WAS NOT TOO ROUGH--
--CONSIDERING WHAT IS SHORTLY TO COME.
GOOD GRIEF! I WAS RIGHT!
DOCTOR FAUSTUS!
WE ARE EMBARKING ON A NEW APPROACH TO THE AGE-OLD METHODS OF CRIME-- ONE THAT SHALL MAKE ALL OTHER ATTEMPTS PALE IN COMPARISON.
AND YOU HAVE BEEN CHOSEN TO AID ME IN MY NEW DESIGNS.
KARLA, THE LIGHTS.
LET THE SHOW BEGIN.
GLAD I DID PLAY IT COOL. IF FAUSTUS IS BEHIND THIS INSANE FLIGHT--
--I'LL NEED ALL MY WITS ABOUT ME WHEN THE TIME TO FIGHT COMES.
OUR TARGET, GENTLEMEN, IS MANHATTAN.
OUR MISSION: THE TOTAL AND COMPLETE PILLAGING OF NEW YORK'S GREAT ISLAND.
IRONIC, IS IT NOT? A BANKRUPT CITY WILL GLADLY GIVE US MILLIONS.
WHICH WE WILL EQUALLY SHARE, OF COURSE.

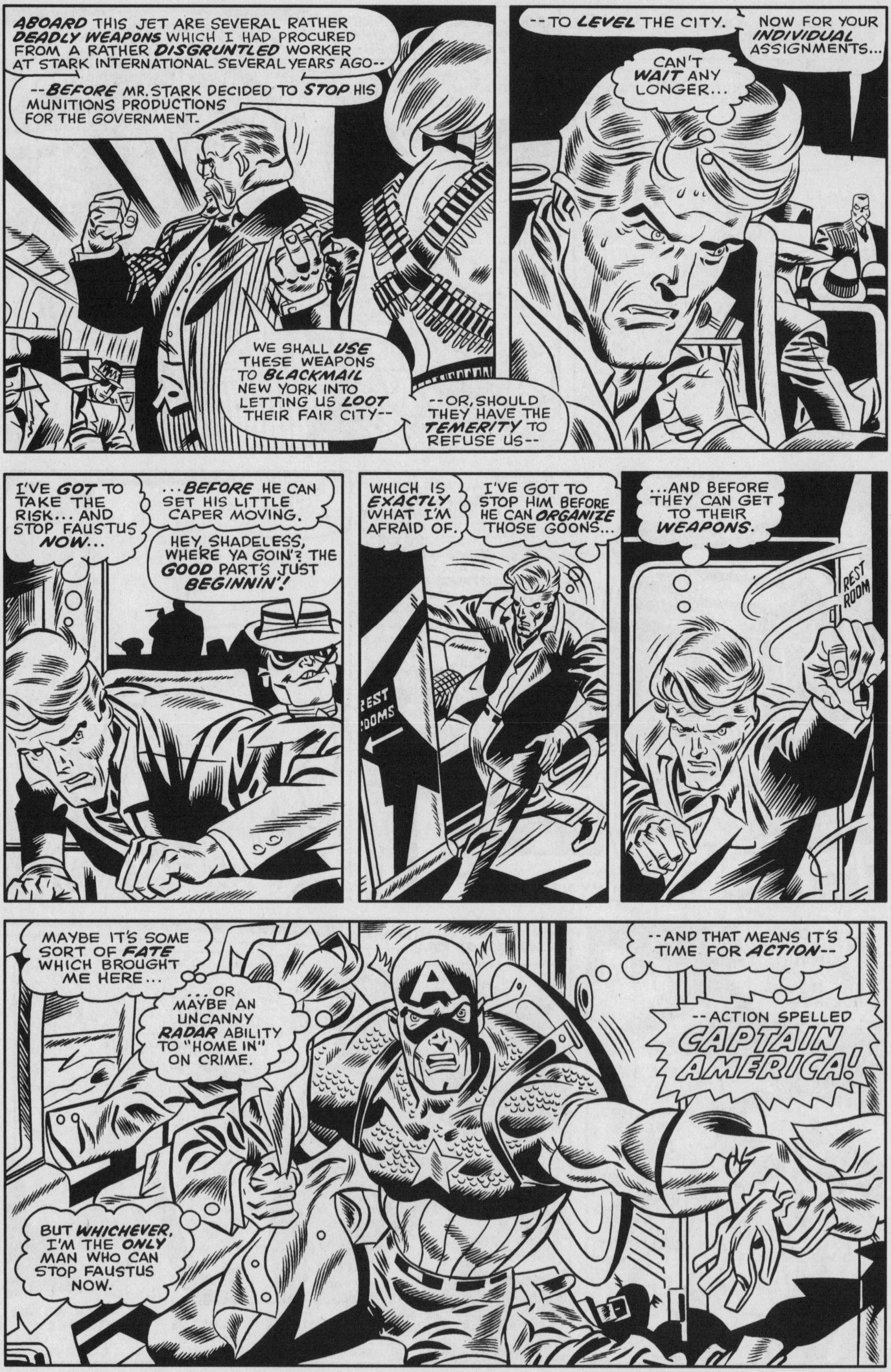
ABOARD THIS JET ARE SEVERAL RATHER DEADLY WEAPONS WHICH I HAD PROCURED FROM A RATHER DISGRUNTLED WORKER AT STARK INTERNATIONAL SEVERAL YEARS AGO--
--BEFORE MR. STARK DECIDED TO STOP HIS MUNITIONS PRODUCTIONS FOR THE GOVERNMENT.
WE SHALL USE THESE WEAPONS TO BLACKMAIL NEW YORK INTO LETTING US LOOT THEIR FAIR CITY--
--OR, SHOULD THEY HAVE THE TEMERITY TO REFUSE US--
--TO LEVEL THE CITY.
NOW FOR YOUR INDIVIDUAL ASSIGNMENTS...
CAN'T WAIT ANY LONGER...
I'VE GOT TO TAKE THE RISK... AND STOP FAUSTUS NOW...
...BEFORE HE CAN SET HIS LITTLE CAPER MOVING.
HEY, SHADELESS, WHERE YA GOIN'? THE GOOD PART'S JUST BEGINNIN'!
WHICH IS EXACTLY WHAT I'M AFRAID OF.
I'VE GOT TO STOP HIM BEFORE HE CAN ORGANIZE THOSE GOONS...
REST ROOMS
...AND BEFORE THEY CAN GET TO THEIR WEAPONS.
REST ROOM
MAYBE IT'S SOME SORT OF FATE WHICH BROUGHT ME HERE...
...OR MAYBE AN UNCANNY RADAR ABILITY TO "HOME IN" ON CRIME.
BUT WHICHEVER, I'M THE ONLY MAN WHO CAN STOP FAUSTUS NOW.
--AND THAT MEANS IT'S TIME FOR ACTION--
--ACTION SPELLED CAPTAIN AMERICA!

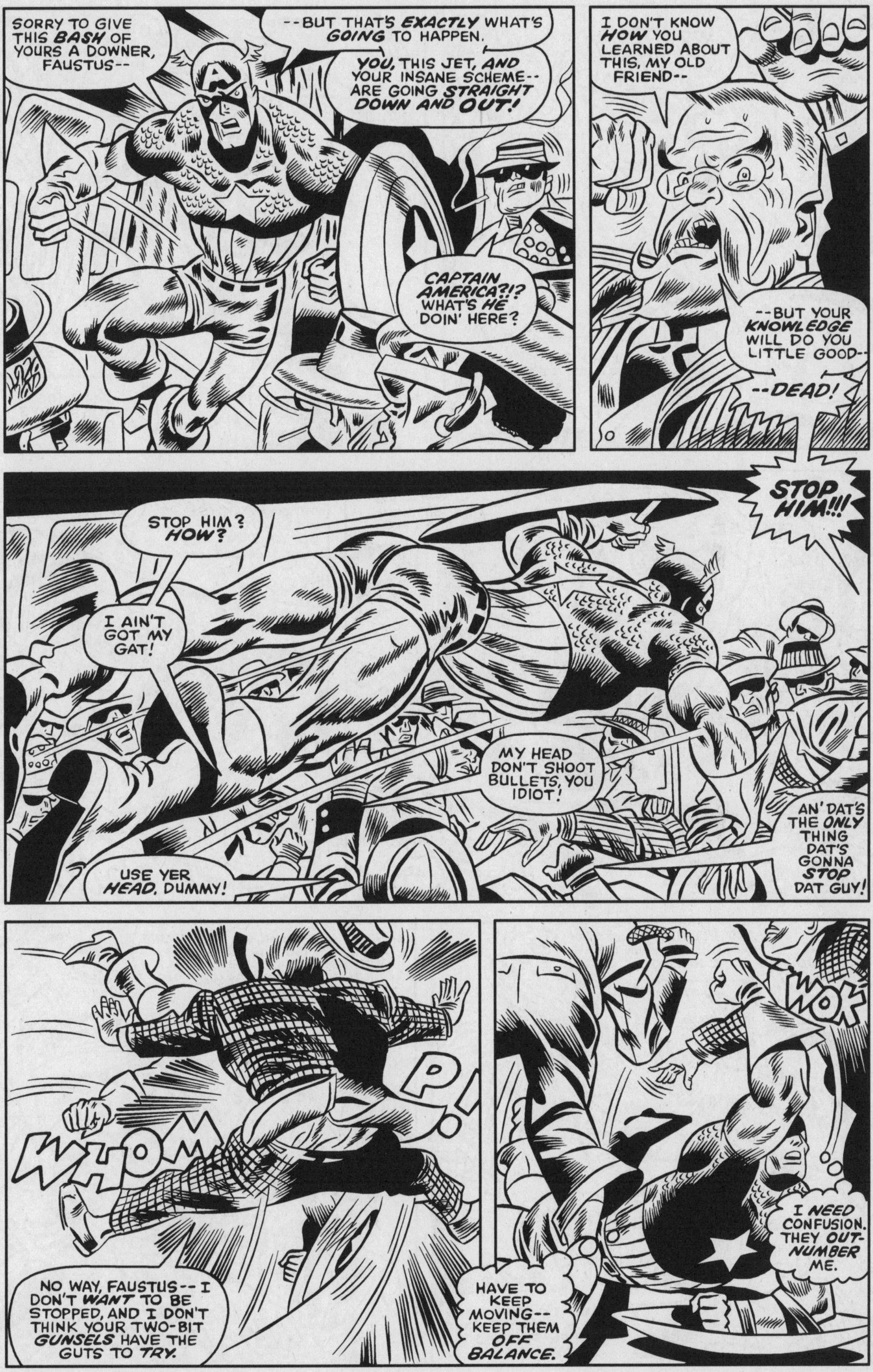
SORRY TO GIVE THIS BASH OF YOURS A DOWNER, FAUSTUS--
--BUT THAT'S EXACTLY WHAT'S GOING TO HAPPEN.
YOU, THIS JET, AND YOUR INSANE SCHEME-- ARE GOING STRAIGHT DOWN AND OUT!
CAPTAIN AMERICA?!? WHAT'S HE DOIN' HERE?
I DON'T KNOW HOW YOU LEARNED ABOUT THIS, MY OLD FRIEND--
--BUT YOUR KNOWLEDGE WILL DO YOU LITTLE GOOD--
--DEAD!
STOP HIM!!!
STOP HIM? HOW?
I AIN'T GOT MY GAT!
MY HEAD DON'T SHOOT BULLETS, YOU IDIOT!
USE YER HEAD, DUMMY!
AN' DAT'S THE ONLY THING DAT'S GONNA STOP DAT GUY!
P!
WHOM
NO WAY, FAUSTUS-- I DON'T WANT TO BE STOPPED, AND I DON'T THINK YOUR TWO-BIT GUNSELS HAVE THE GUTS TO TRY.
WOK
I NEED CONFUSION. THEY OUT-NUMBER ME.
HAVE TO KEEP MOVING-- KEEP THEM OFF BALANCE.

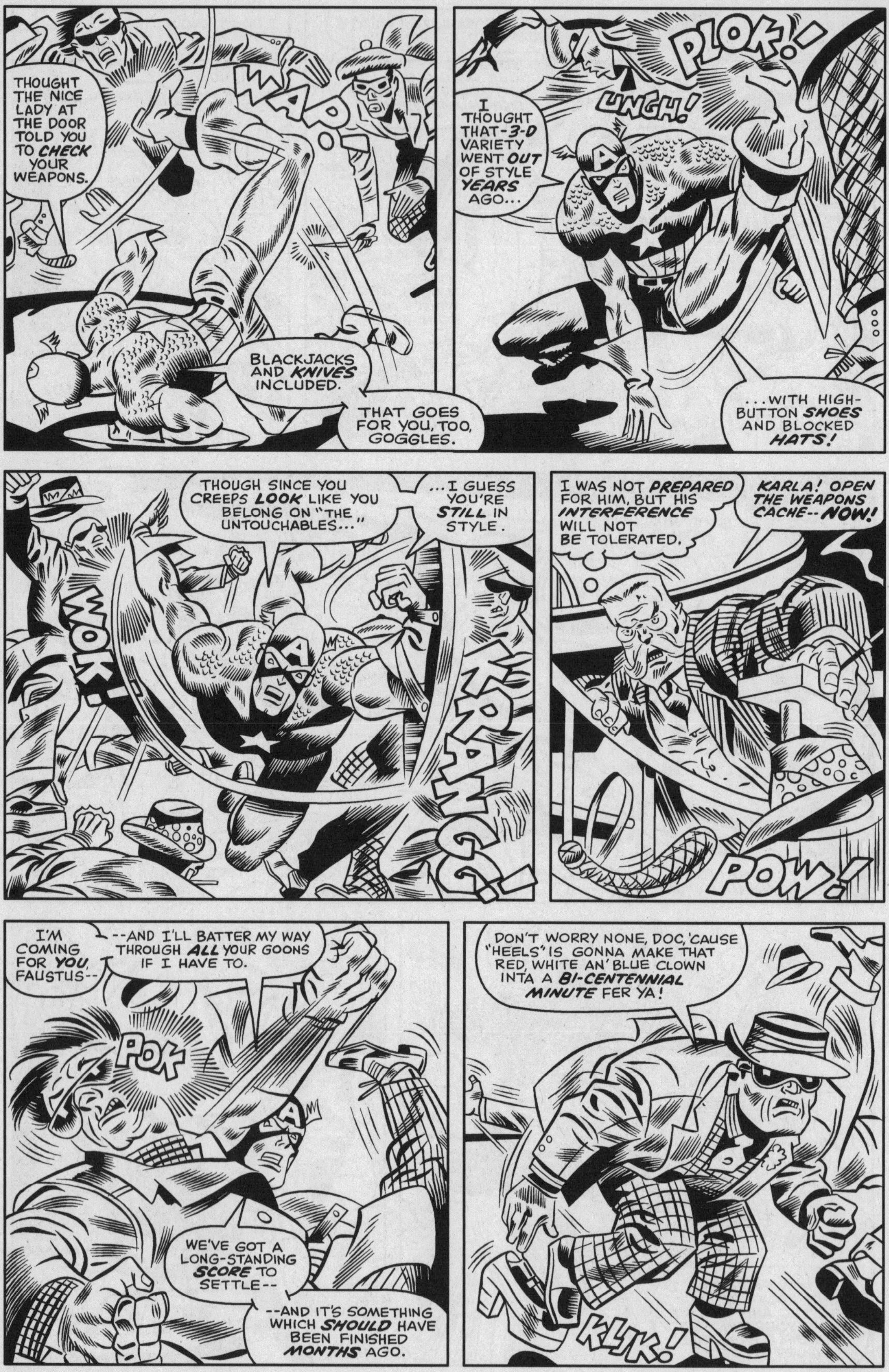
THOUGHT THE NICE LADY AT THE DOOR TOLD YOU TO CHECK YOUR WEAPONS.
WAP
BLACKJACKS AND KNIVES INCLUDED.
THAT GOES FOR YOU, TOO, GOGGLES.
PLOK!
UNGH!
I THOUGHT THAT 3-D VARIETY WENT OUT OF STYLE YEARS AGO...
...WITH HIGH-BUTTON SHOES AND BLOCKED HATS!
THOUGH SINCE YOU CREEPS LOOK LIKE YOU BELONG ON "THE UNTOUCHABLES..."
...I GUESS YOU'RE STILL IN STYLE.
WOK!
KRANG!
I WAS NOT PREPARED FOR HIM, BUT HIS INTERFERENCE WILL NOT BE TOLERATED.
KARLA! OPEN THE WEAPONS CACHE--NOW!
POW!
I'M COMING FOR YOU, FAUSTUS--
--AND I'LL BATTER MY WAY THROUGH ALL YOUR GOONS IF I HAVE TO.
POK
WE'VE GOT A LONG-STANDING SCORE TO SETTLE--
--AND IT'S SOMETHING WHICH SHOULD HAVE BEEN FINISHED MONTHS AGO.
DON'T WORRY NONE, DOC, 'CAUSE "HEELS" IS GONNA MAKE THAT RED, WHITE AN' BLUE CLOWN INTA A BI-CENTENNIAL MINUTE FER YA!
KLIK!

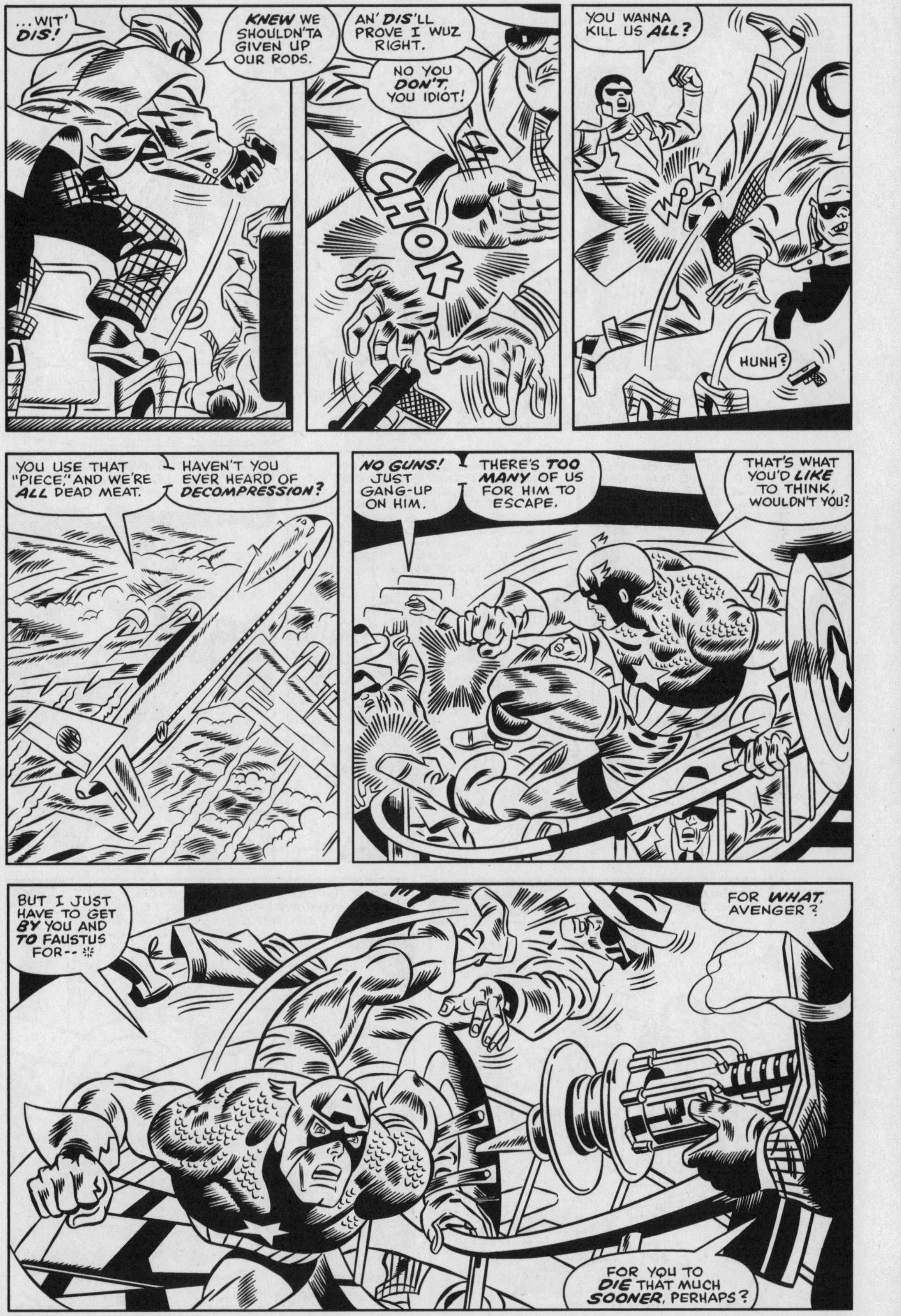
...WIT' DIS!
KNEW WE SHOULDN'TA GIVEN UP OUR RODS.
AN' DIS'LL PROVE I WUZ RIGHT.
NO YOU DON'T, YOU IDIOT!
CHOK
YOU WANNA KILL US ALL?
WOK
HUNH?
YOU USE THAT "PIECE," AND WE'RE ALL DEAD MEAT.
HAVEN'T YOU EVER HEARD OF DECOMPRESSION?
NO GUNS! JUST GANG-UP ON HIM.
THERE'S TOO MANY OF US FOR HIM TO ESCAPE.
THAT'S WHAT YOU'D LIKE TO THINK, WOULDN'T YOU?
BUT I JUST HAVE TO GET BY YOU AND TO FAUSTUS FOR--
FOR WHAT, AVENGER?
FOR YOU TO DIE THAT MUCH SOONER, PERHAPS?

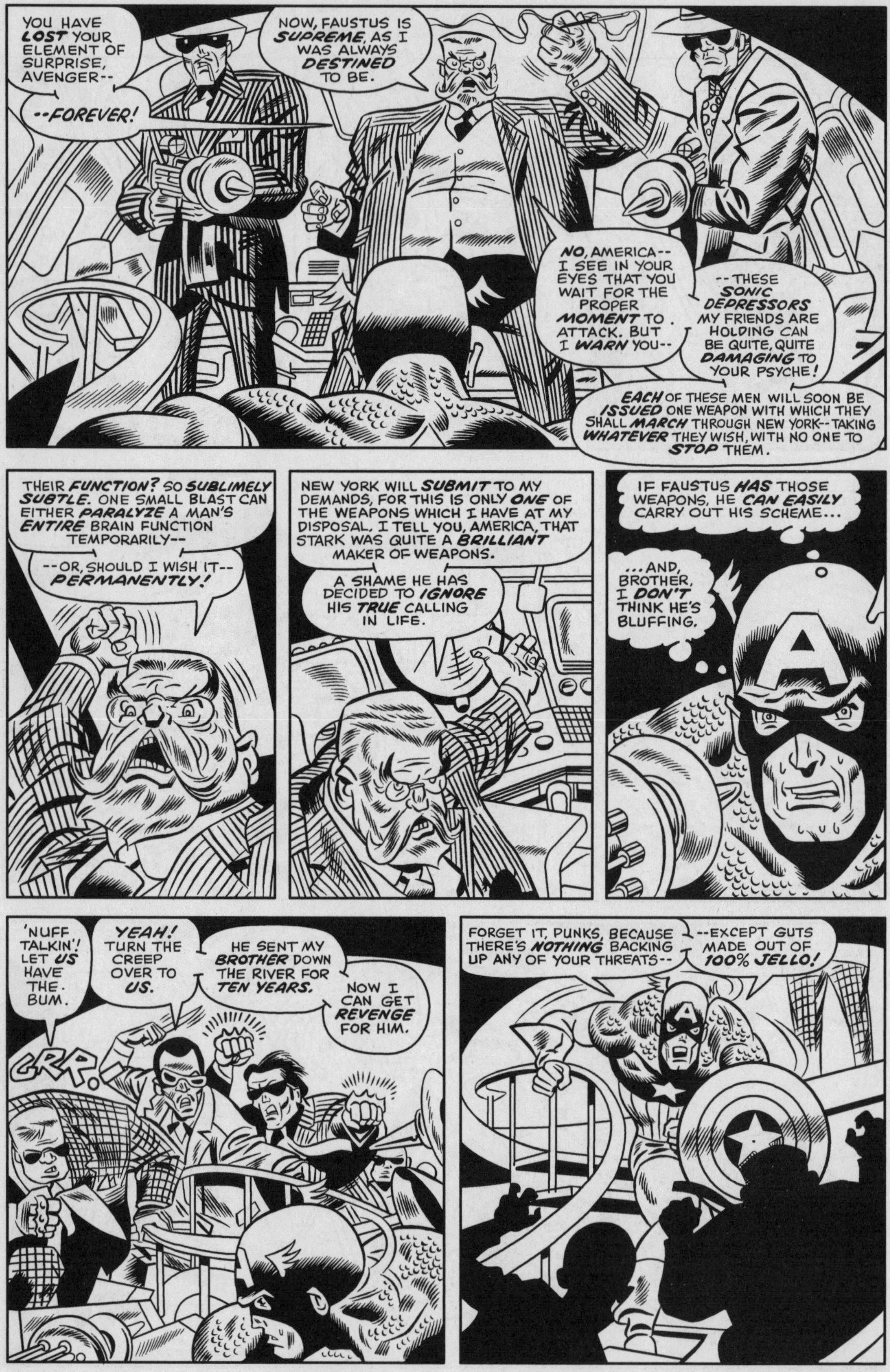

YOU HAVE LOST YOUR ELEMENT OF SURPRISE, AVENGER--
--FOREVER!
NOW, FAUSTUS IS SUPREME, AS I WAS ALWAYS DESTINED TO BE.
NO, AMERICA-- I SEE IN YOUR EYES THAT YOU WAIT FOR THE PROPER MOMENT TO ATTACK. BUT I WARN YOU--
--THESE SONIC DEPRESSORS MY FRIENDS ARE HOLDING CAN BE QUITE, QUITE DAMAGING TO YOUR PSYCHE!
EACH OF THESE MEN WILL SOON BE ISSUED ONE WEAPON WITH WHICH THEY SHALL MARCH THROUGH NEW YORK--TAKING WHATEVER THEY WISH, WITH NO ONE TO STOP THEM.
THEIR FUNCTION? SO SUBLIMELY SUBTLE. ONE SMALL BLAST CAN EITHER PARALYZE A MAN'S ENTIRE BRAIN FUNCTION TEMPORARILY--
--OR, SHOULD I WISH IT-- PERMANENTLY!
NEW YORK WILL SUBMIT TO MY DEMANDS, FOR THIS IS ONLY ONE OF THE WEAPONS WHICH I HAVE AT MY DISPOSAL. I TELL YOU, AMERICA, THAT STARK WAS QUITE A BRILLIANT MAKER OF WEAPONS.
A SHAME HE HAS DECIDED TO IGNORE HIS TRUE CALLING IN LIFE.
IF FAUSTUS HAS THOSE WEAPONS, HE CAN EASILY CARRY OUT HIS SCHEME...
...AND, BROTHER, I DON'T THINK HE'S BLUFFING.
'NUFF TALKIN'! LET US HAVE THE BUM.
YEAH! TURN THE CREEP OVER TO US.
HE SENT MY BROTHER DOWN THE RIVER FOR TEN YEARS.
NOW I CAN GET REVENGE FOR HIM.
GRR.
FORGET IT, PUNKS, BECAUSE THERE'S NOTHING BACKING UP ANY OF YOUR THREATS--
--EXCEPT GUTS MADE OUT OF 100% JELLO!

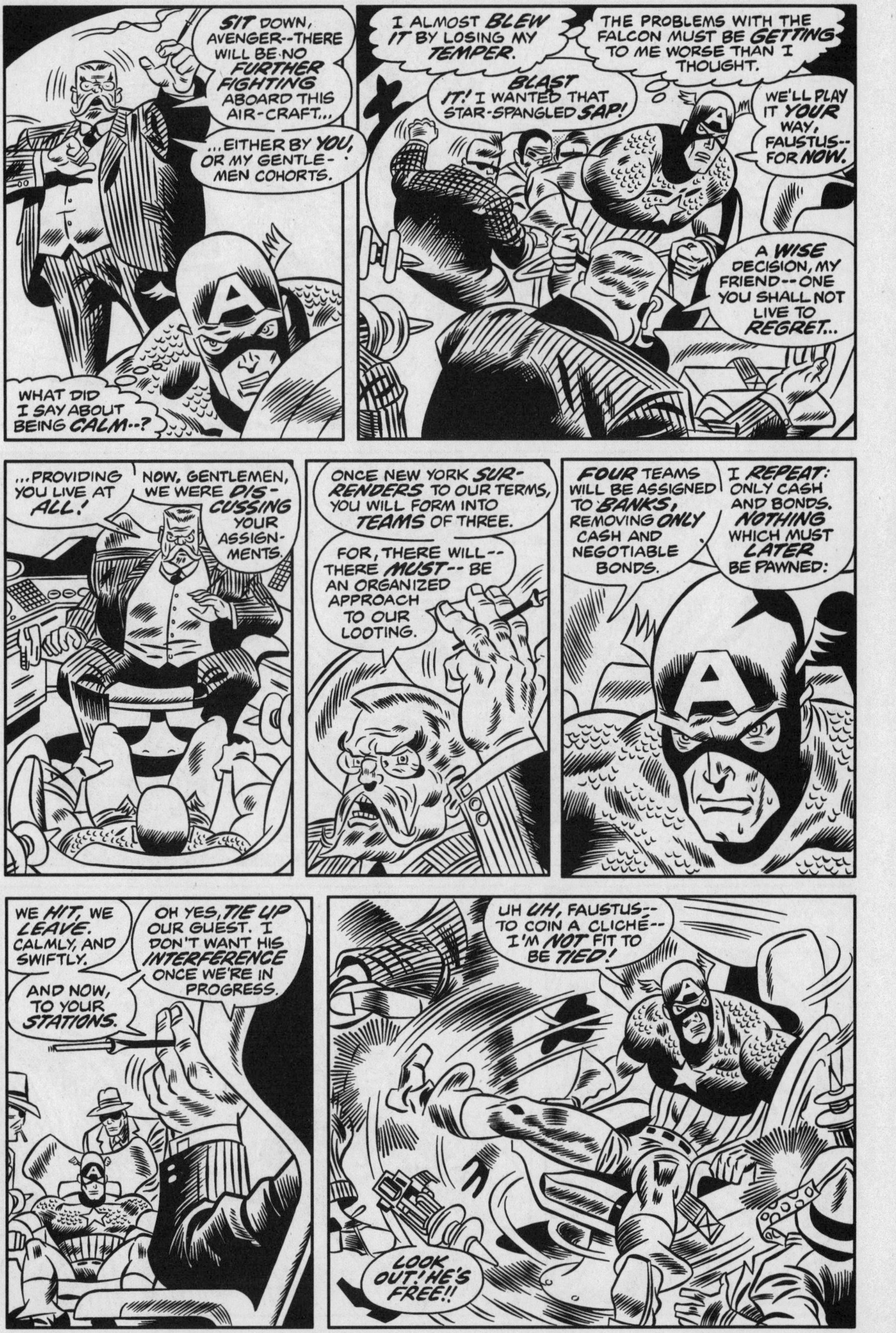
SIT DOWN, AVENGER--THERE WILL BE NO FURTHER FIGHTING ABOARD THIS AIR-CRAFT...
...EITHER BY YOU, OR MY GENTLE-MEN COHORTS.
WHAT DID I SAY ABOUT BEING CALM--?
I ALMOST BLEW IT BY LOSING MY TEMPER.
THE PROBLEMS WITH THE FALCON MUST BE GETTING TO ME WORSE THAN I THOUGHT.
BLAST IT! I WANTED THAT STAR-SPANGLED SAP!
WE'LL PLAY IT YOUR WAY, FAUSTUS--FOR NOW.
A WISE DECISION, MY FRIEND--ONE YOU SHALL NOT LIVE TO REGRET...
...PROVIDING YOU LIVE AT ALL!
NOW, GENTLEMEN, WE WERE DIS-CUSSING YOUR ASSIGN-MENTS.
ONCE NEW YORK SUR-RENDERS TO OUR TERMS, YOU WILL FORM INTO TEAMS OF THREE.
FOR, THERE WILL--THERE MUST--BE AN ORGANIZED APPROACH TO OUR LOOTING.
FOUR TEAMS WILL BE ASSIGNED TO BANKS, REMOVING ONLY CASH AND NEGOTIABLE BONDS.
I REPEAT: ONLY CASH AND BONDS. NOTHING WHICH MUST LATER BE PAWNED:
WE HIT, WE LEAVE. CALMLY, AND SWIFTLY.
OH YES, TIE UP OUR GUEST. I DON'T WANT HIS INTERFERENCE ONCE WE'RE IN PROGRESS.
AND NOW, TO YOUR STATIONS.
UH UH, FAUSTUS--TO COIN A CLICHÉ--I'M NOT FIT TO BE TIED!
LOOK OUT! HE'S FREE!!

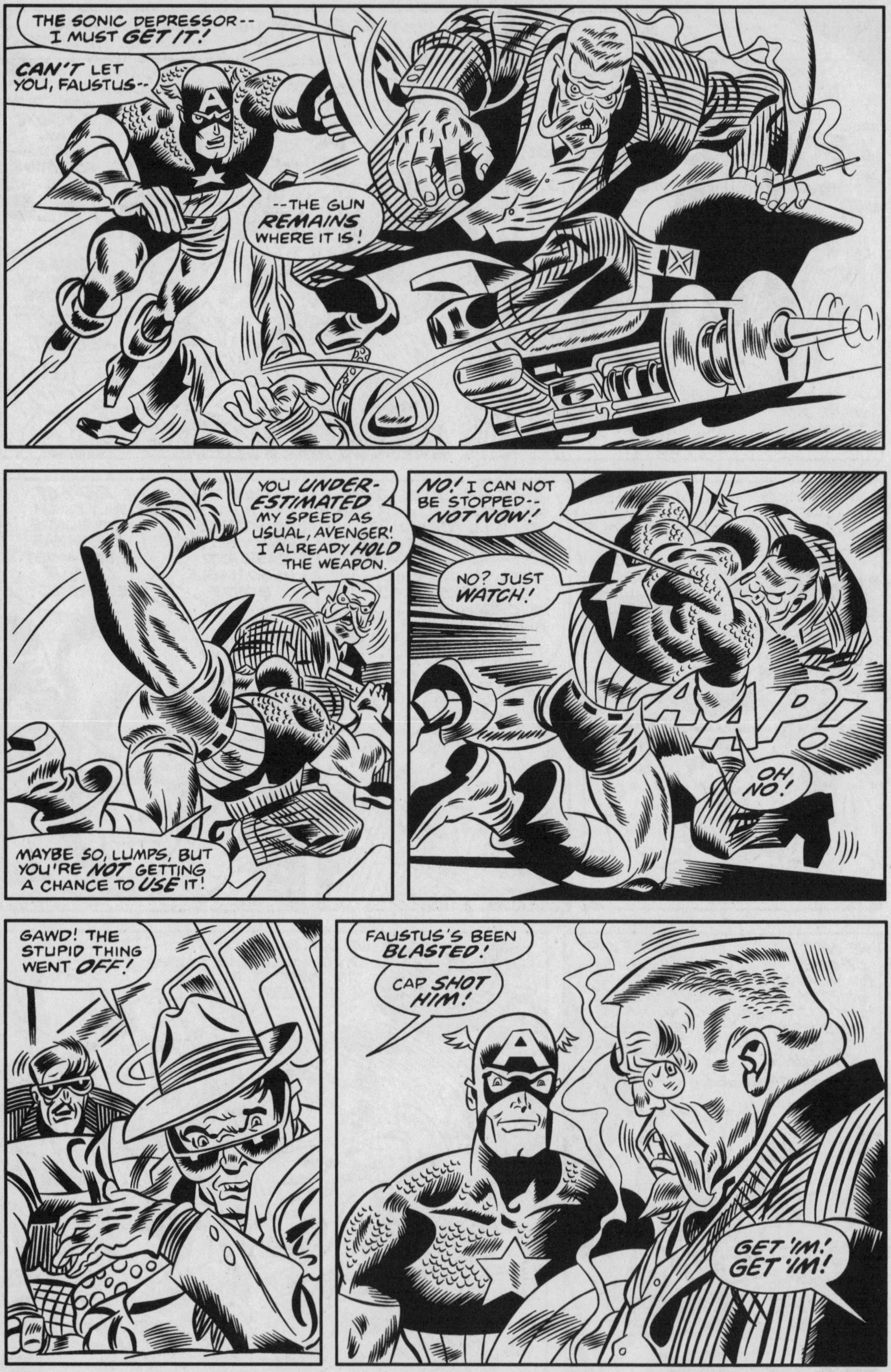
THE SONIC DEPRESSOR-- I MUST GET IT!
CAN'T LET YOU, FAUSTUS--
--THE GUN REMAINS WHERE IT IS!
YOU UNDER-ESTIMATED MY SPEED AS USUAL, AVENGER! I ALREADY HOLD THE WEAPON.
MAYBE SO, LUMPS, BUT YOU'RE NOT GETTING A CHANCE TO USE IT!
NO! I CAN NOT BE STOPPED-- NOT NOW!
NO? JUST WATCH!
AAP!
OH, NO!
GAWD! THE STUPID THING WENT OFF!
FAUSTUS'S BEEN BLASTED!
CAP SHOT HIM!
GET 'IM! GET 'IM!

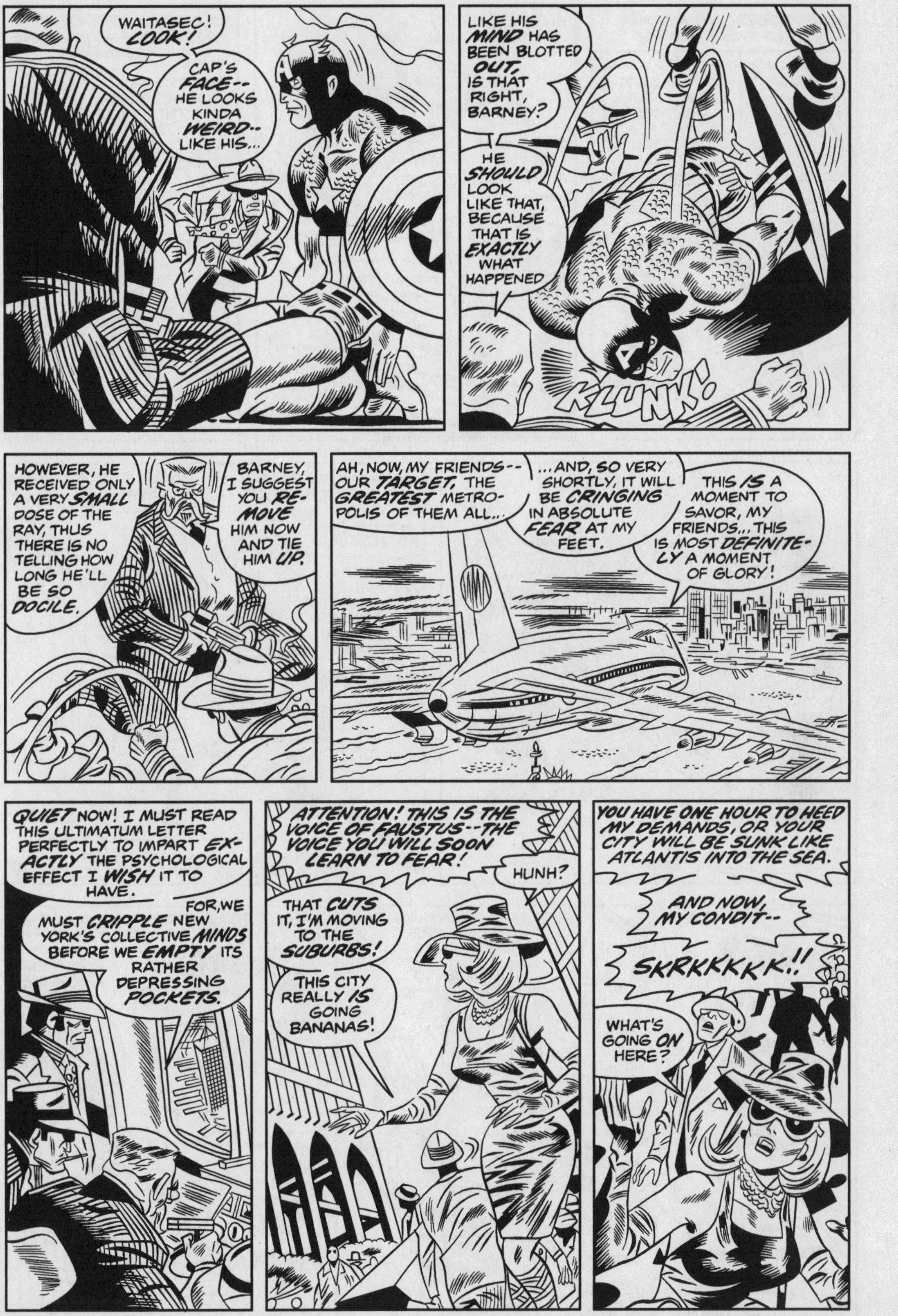
WAITASEC! LOOK!
CAP'S FACE-- HE LOOKS KINDA WEIRD-- LIKE HIS...
LIKE HIS MIND HAS BEEN BLOTTED OUT, IS THAT RIGHT, BARNEY?
HE SHOULD LOOK LIKE THAT, BECAUSE THAT IS EXACTLY WHAT HAPPENED
KLUNK!
HOWEVER, HE RECEIVED ONLY A VERY SMALL DOSE OF THE RAY, THUS THERE IS NO TELLING HOW LONG HE'LL BE SO DOCILE.
BARNEY, I SUGGEST YOU RE-MOVE HIM NOW AND TIE HIM UP.
AH, NOW, MY FRIENDS-- OUR TARGET, THE GREATEST METRO-POLIS OF THEM ALL...
...AND, SO VERY SHORTLY, IT WILL BE CRINGING IN ABSOLUTE FEAR AT MY FEET.
THIS IS A MOMENT TO SAVOR, MY FRIENDS... THIS IS MOST DEFINITE-LY A MOMENT OF GLORY!
QUIET NOW! I MUST READ THIS ULTIMATUM LETTER PERFECTLY TO IMPART EX-ACTLY THE PSYCHOLOGICAL EFFECT I WISH IT TO HAVE.
FOR, WE MUST CRIPPLE NEW YORK'S COLLECTIVE MINDS BEFORE WE EMPTY ITS RATHER DEPRESSING POCKETS.
ATTENTION! THIS IS THE VOICE OF FAUSTUS--THE VOICE YOU WILL SOON LEARN TO FEAR!
HUNH?
THAT CUTS IT, I'M MOVING TO THE SUBURBS!
THIS CITY REALLY IS GOING BANANAS!
YOU HAVE ONE HOUR TO HEED MY DEMANDS, OR YOUR CITY WILL BE SUNK LIKE ATLANTIS INTO THE SEA.
AND NOW, MY CONDIT--
SKRKKKKK!!
WHAT'S GOING ON HERE?

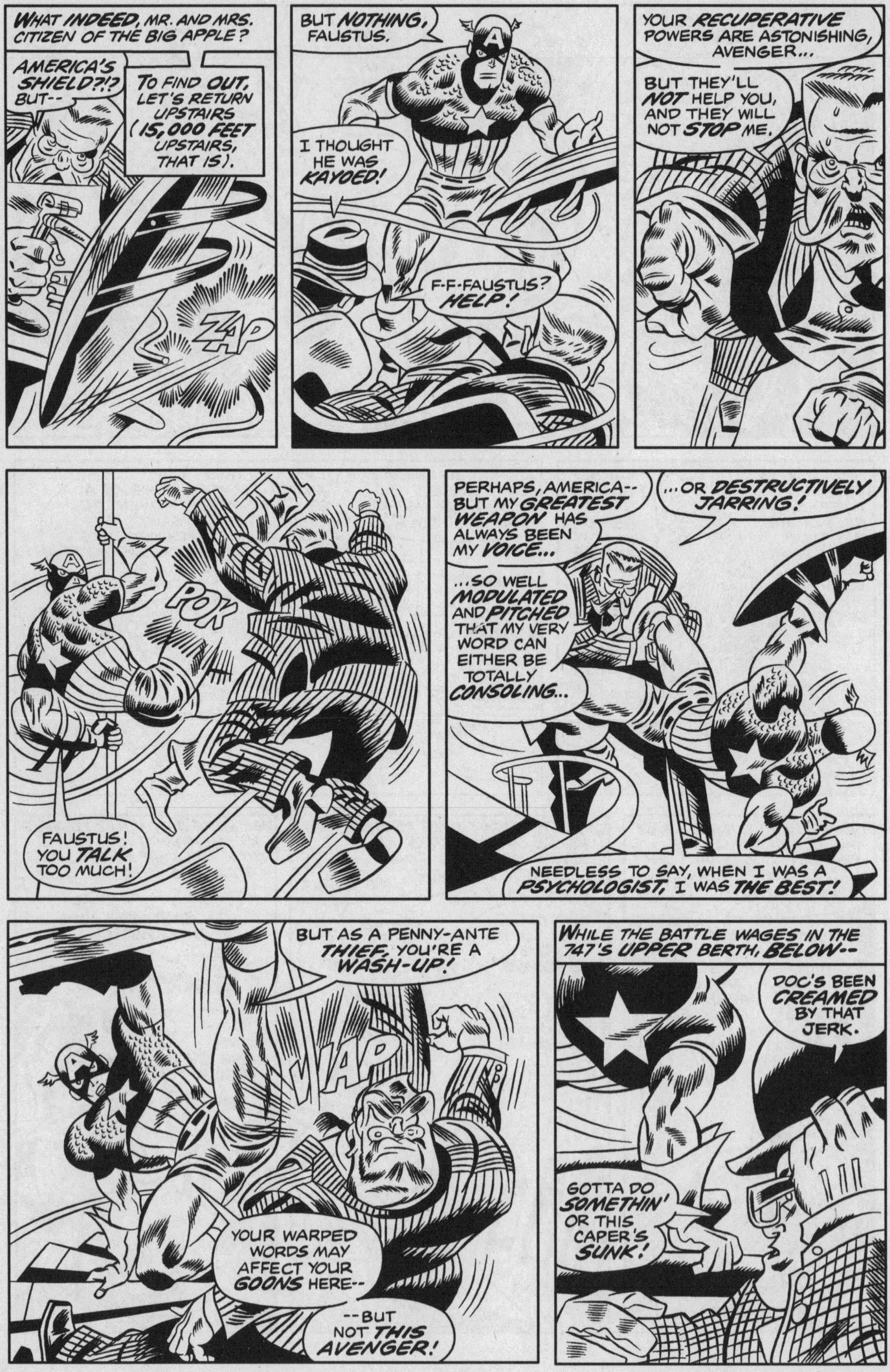
WHAT INDEED, MR. AND MRS. CITIZEN OF THE BIG APPLE?
AMERICA'S SHIELD?!? BUT--
TO FIND OUT, LET'S RETURN UPSTAIRS (15,000 FEET UPSTAIRS, THAT IS).
ZAP
BUT NOTHING, FAUSTUS.
I THOUGHT HE WAS KAYOED!
F-F-FAUSTUS? HELP!
YOUR RECUPERATIVE POWERS ARE ASTONISHING, AVENGER...
BUT THEY'LL NOT HELP YOU, AND THEY WILL NOT STOP ME.
POK
FAUSTUS! YOU TALK TOO MUCH!
PERHAPS, AMERICA-- BUT MY GREATEST WEAPON HAS ALWAYS BEEN MY VOICE...
...SO WELL MODULATED AND PITCHED THAT MY VERY WORD CAN EITHER BE TOTALLY CONSOLING...
...OR DESTRUCTIVELY JARRING!
NEEDLESS TO SAY, WHEN I WAS A PSYCHOLOGIST, I WAS THE BEST!
BUT AS A PENNY-ANTE THIEF, YOU'RE A WASH-UP!
WAP
YOUR WARPED WORDS MAY AFFECT YOUR GOONS HERE--
--BUT NOT THIS AVENGER!
WHILE THE BATTLE WAGES IN THE 747'S UPPER BERTH, BELOW--
DOC'S BEEN CREAMED BY THAT JERK.
GOTTA DO SOMETHIN' OR THIS CAPER'S SUNK!

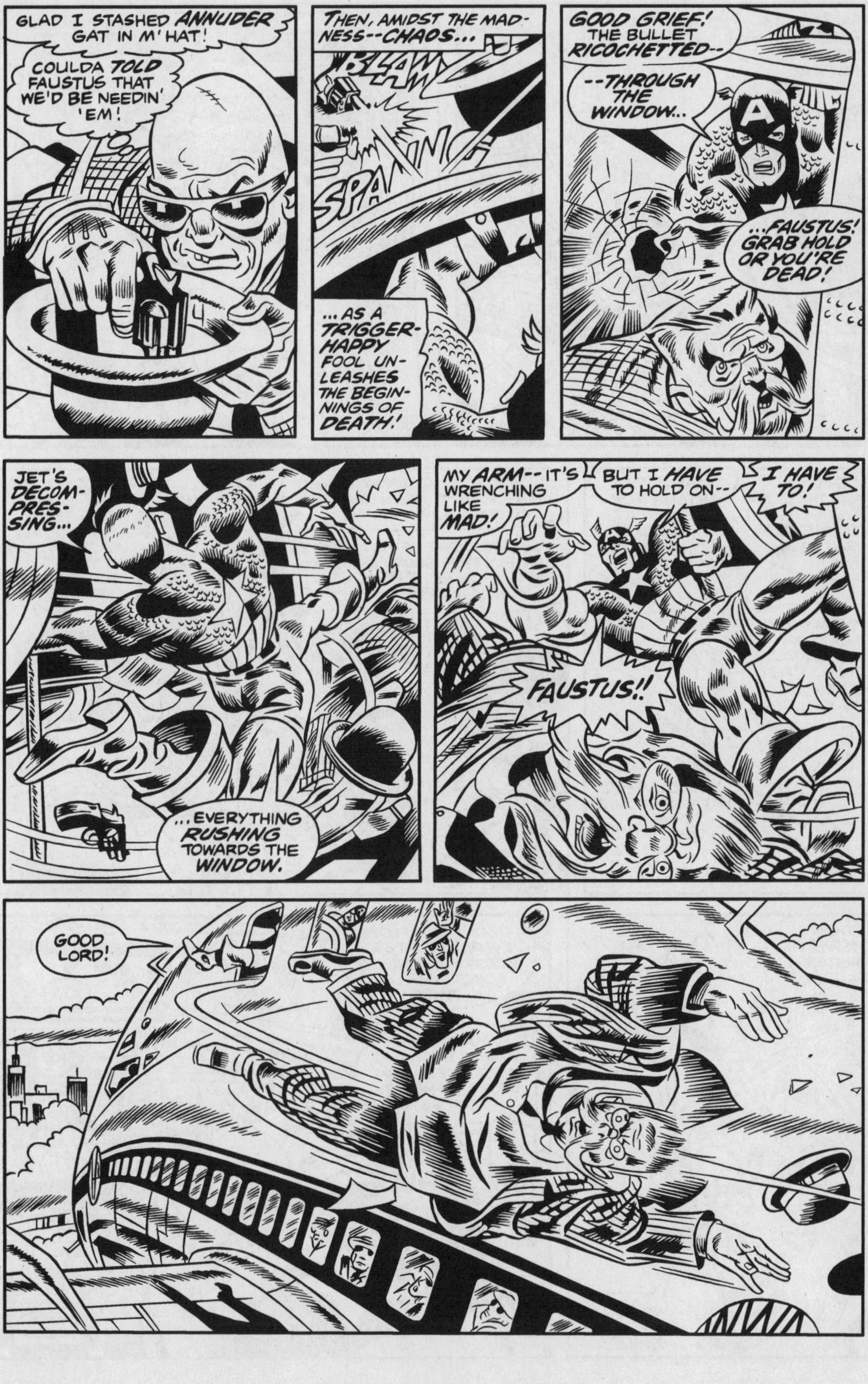

GLAD I STASHED ANNUDER GAT IN M' HAT!
COULDA TOLD FAUSTUS THAT WE'D BE NEEDIN' 'EM!
THEN, AMIDST THE MADNESS--CHAOS...
BLAM
SPANNG
...AS A TRIGGER-HAPPY FOOL UNLEASHES THE BEGINNINGS OF DEATH!
GOOD GRIEF! THE BULLET RICOCHETTED--
--THROUGH THE WINDOW...
...FAUSTUS! GRAB HOLD OR YOU'RE DEAD!
JET'S DECOMPRESSING...
...EVERYTHING RUSHING TOWARDS THE WINDOW.
MY ARM--IT'S WRENCHING LIKE MAD!
BUT I HAVE TO HOLD ON--
I HAVE TO!
FAUSTUS!!
GOOD LORD!

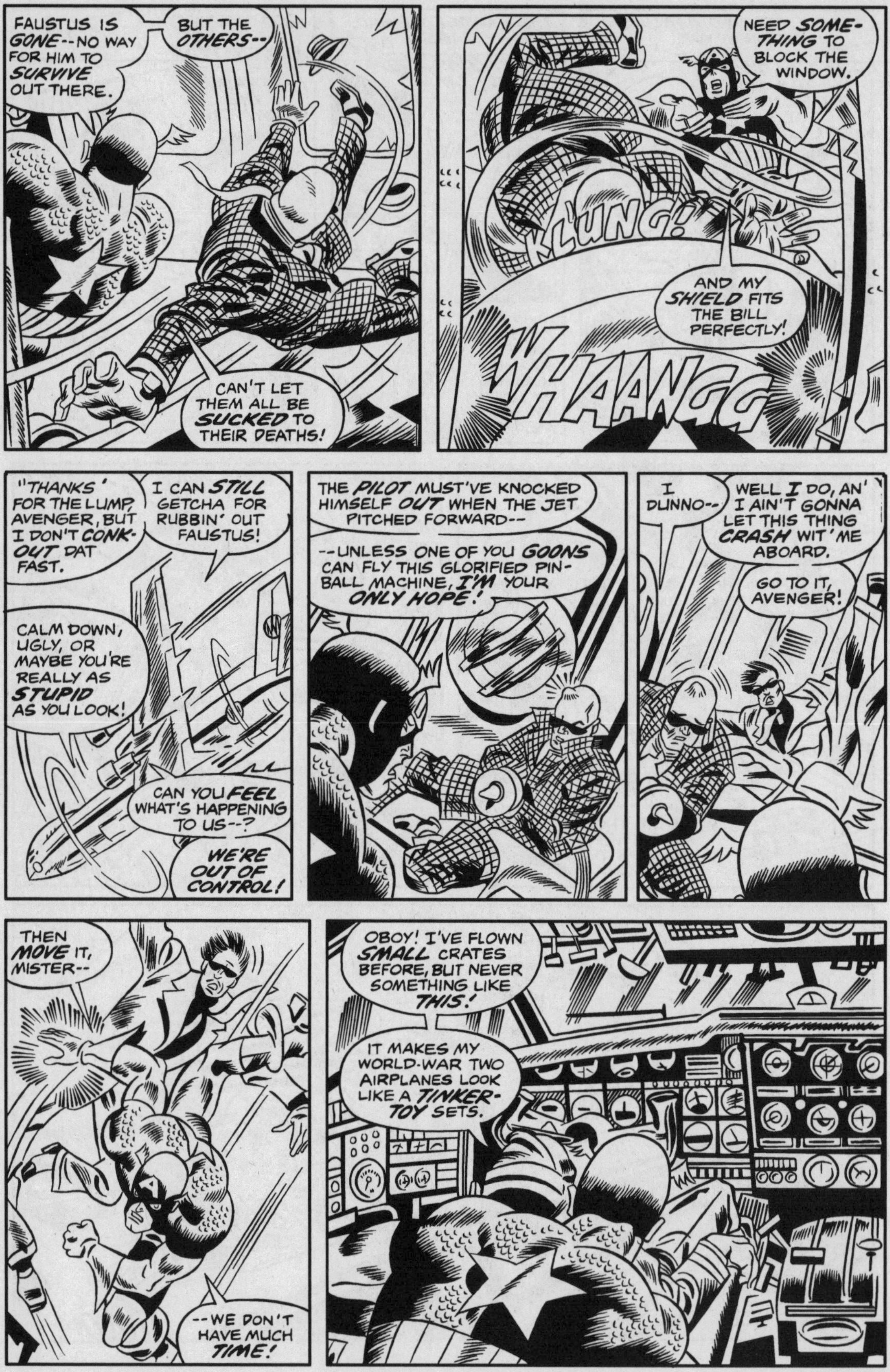
FAUSTUS IS GONE--NO WAY FOR HIM TO SURVIVE OUT THERE.
BUT THE OTHERS--
CAN'T LET THEM ALL BE SUCKED TO THEIR DEATHS!
NEED SOME-THING TO BLOCK THE WINDOW.
KLUNG!
AND MY SHIELD FITS THE BILL PERFECTLY!
WHAANGG
"THANKS' FOR THE LUMP, AVENGER, BUT I DON'T CONK-OUT DAT FAST.
I CAN STILL GETCHA FOR RUBBIN' OUT FAUSTUS!
CALM DOWN, UGLY, OR MAYBE YOU'RE REALLY AS STUPID AS YOU LOOK!
CAN YOU FEEL WHAT'S HAPPENING TO US--?
WE'RE OUT OF CONTROL!
THE PILOT MUST'VE KNOCKED HIMSELF OUT WHEN THE JET PITCHED FORWARD--
--UNLESS ONE OF YOU GOONS CAN FLY THIS GLORIFIED PIN-BALL MACHINE, I'M YOUR ONLY HOPE!
I DUNNO--
WELL I DO, AN' I AIN'T GONNA LET THIS THING CRASH WIT' ME ABOARD.
GO TO IT, AVENGER!
THEN MOVE IT, MISTER--
--WE DON'T HAVE MUCH TIME!
OBOY! I'VE FLOWN SMALL CRATES BEFORE, BUT NEVER SOMETHING LIKE THIS!
IT MAKES MY WORLD-WAR TWO AIRPLANES LOOK LIKE A TINKER-TOY SETS.

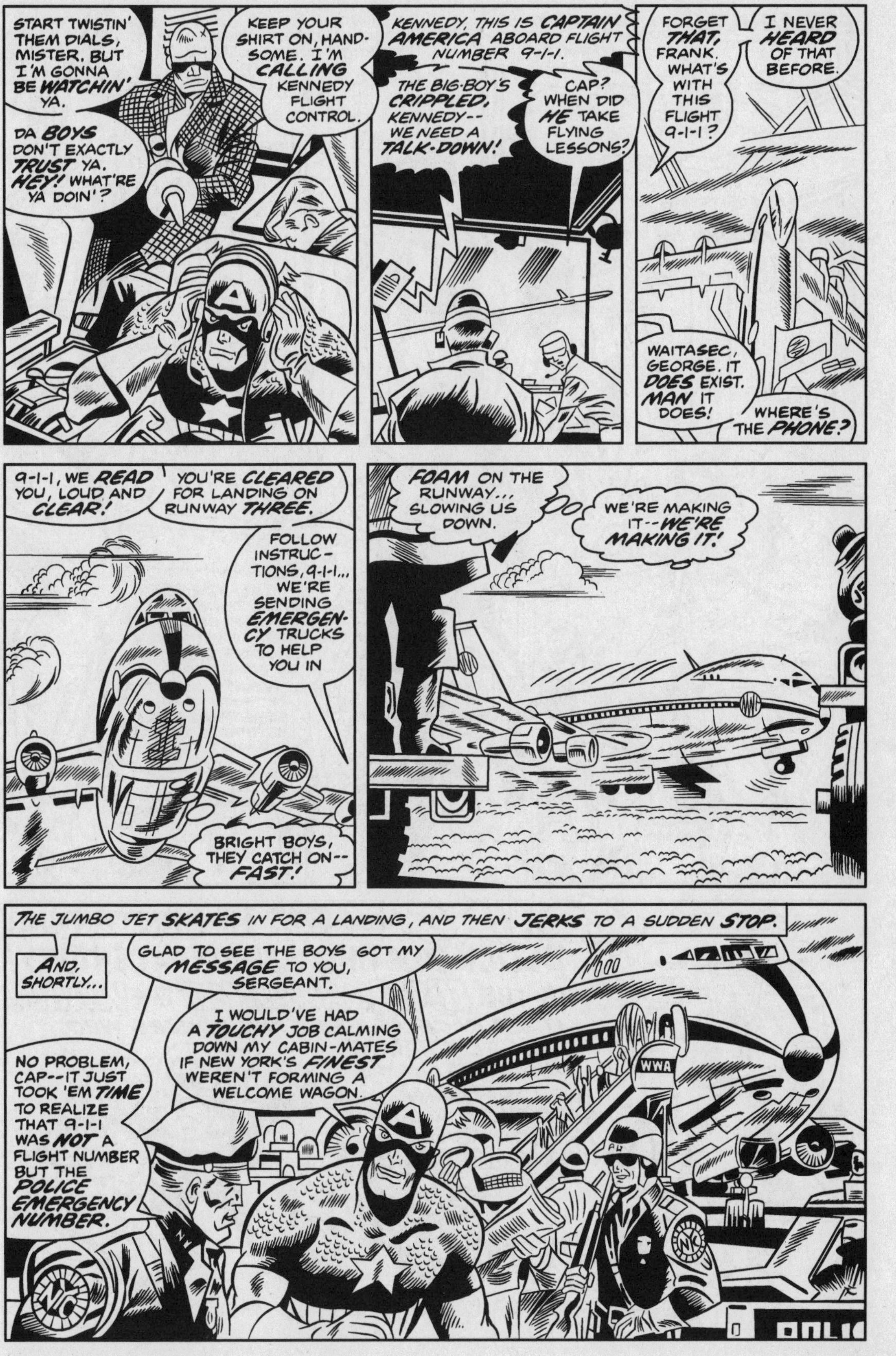
START TWISTIN' THEM DIALS, MISTER. BUT I'M GONNA BE WATCHIN' YA.
DA BOYS DON'T EXACTLY TRUST YA. HEY! WHAT'RE YA DOIN'?
KEEP YOUR SHIRT ON, HAND-SOME. I'M CALLING KENNEDY FLIGHT CONTROL.
KENNEDY, THIS IS CAPTAIN AMERICA ABOARD FLIGHT NUMBER 9-1-1.
THE BIG-BOY'S CRIPPLED, KENNEDY-- WE NEED A TALK-DOWN!
CAP? WHEN DID HE TAKE FLYING LESSONS?
FORGET THAT, FRANK. WHAT'S WITH THIS FLIGHT 9-1-1?
I NEVER HEARD OF THAT BEFORE.
WAITASEC, GEORGE. IT DOES EXIST. MAN IT DOES!
WHERE'S THE PHONE?
9-1-1, WE READ YOU, LOUD AND CLEAR!
YOU'RE CLEARED FOR LANDING ON RUNWAY THREE.
FOLLOW INSTRUC-TIONS, 9-1-1... WE'RE SENDING EMERGEN-CY TRUCKS TO HELP YOU IN
BRIGHT BOYS, THEY CATCH ON-- FAST!
FOAM ON THE RUNWAY... SLOWING US DOWN.
WE'RE MAKING IT--WE'RE MAKING IT!
THE JUMBO JET SKATES IN FOR A LANDING, AND THEN JERKS TO A SUDDEN STOP.
AND, SHORTLY...
GLAD TO SEE THE BOYS GOT MY MESSAGE TO YOU, SERGEANT.
I WOULD'VE HAD A TOUCHY JOB CALMING DOWN MY CABIN-MATES IF NEW YORK'S FINEST WEREN'T FORMING A WELCOME WAGON.
NO PROBLEM, CAP--IT JUST TOOK 'EM TIME TO REALIZE THAT 9-1-1 WAS NOT A FLIGHT NUMBER BUT THE POLICE EMERGENCY NUMBER.

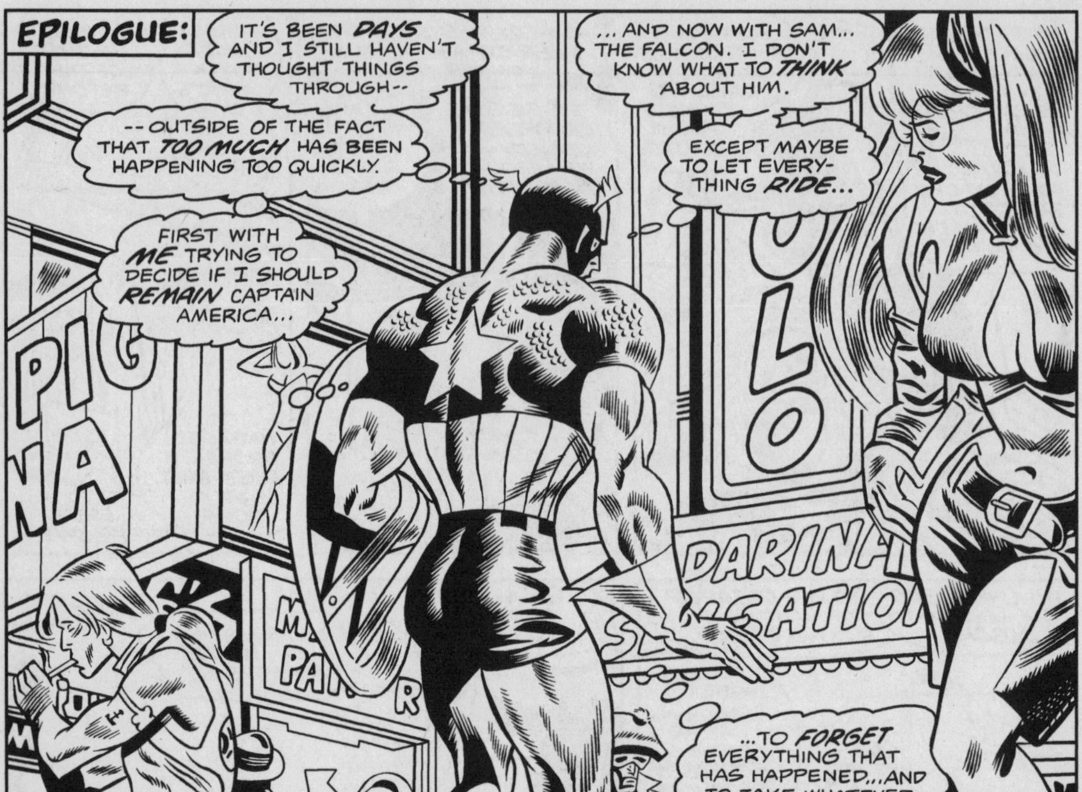
EPILOGUE:
IT'S BEEN DAYS AND I STILL HAVEN'T THOUGHT THINGS THROUGH--
--OUTSIDE OF THE FACT THAT TOO MUCH HAS BEEN HAPPENING TOO QUICKLY.
FIRST WITH ME TRYING TO DECIDE IF I SHOULD REMAIN CAPTAIN AMERICA...
...AND NOW WITH SAM... THE FALCON. I DON'T KNOW WHAT TO THINK ABOUT HIM.
EXCEPT MAYBE TO LET EVERYTHING RIDE...
...TO FORGET EVERYTHING THAT HAS HAPPENED,..AND TO TAKE WHATEVER IS GOING TO HAPPEN AS SOMETHING NEW.
YEAH, SOMETHING TELLS ME THAT IS THE ONLY ROAD TO WALK.
WE'LL SEE. LORD, WE'LL SEE.

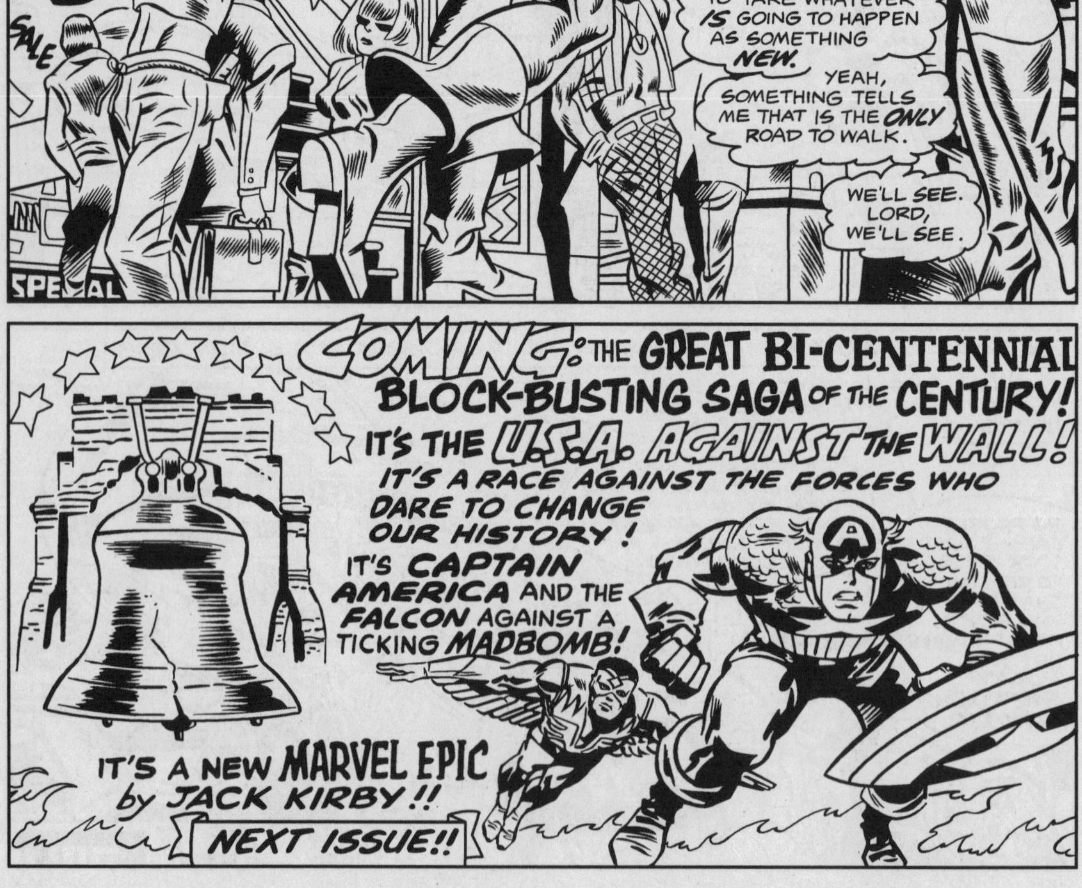
COMING: THE GREAT BI-CENTENNIAL BLOCK-BUSTING SAGA OF THE CENTURY!
IT'S THE U.S.A. AGAINST THE WALL!
IT'S A RACE AGAINST THE FORCES WHO DARE TO CHANGE OUR HISTORY!
IT'S CAPTAIN AMERICA AND THE FALCON AGAINST A TICKING MADBOMB!
IT'S A NEW MARVEL EPIC by JACK KIRBY!!
NEXT ISSUE!!

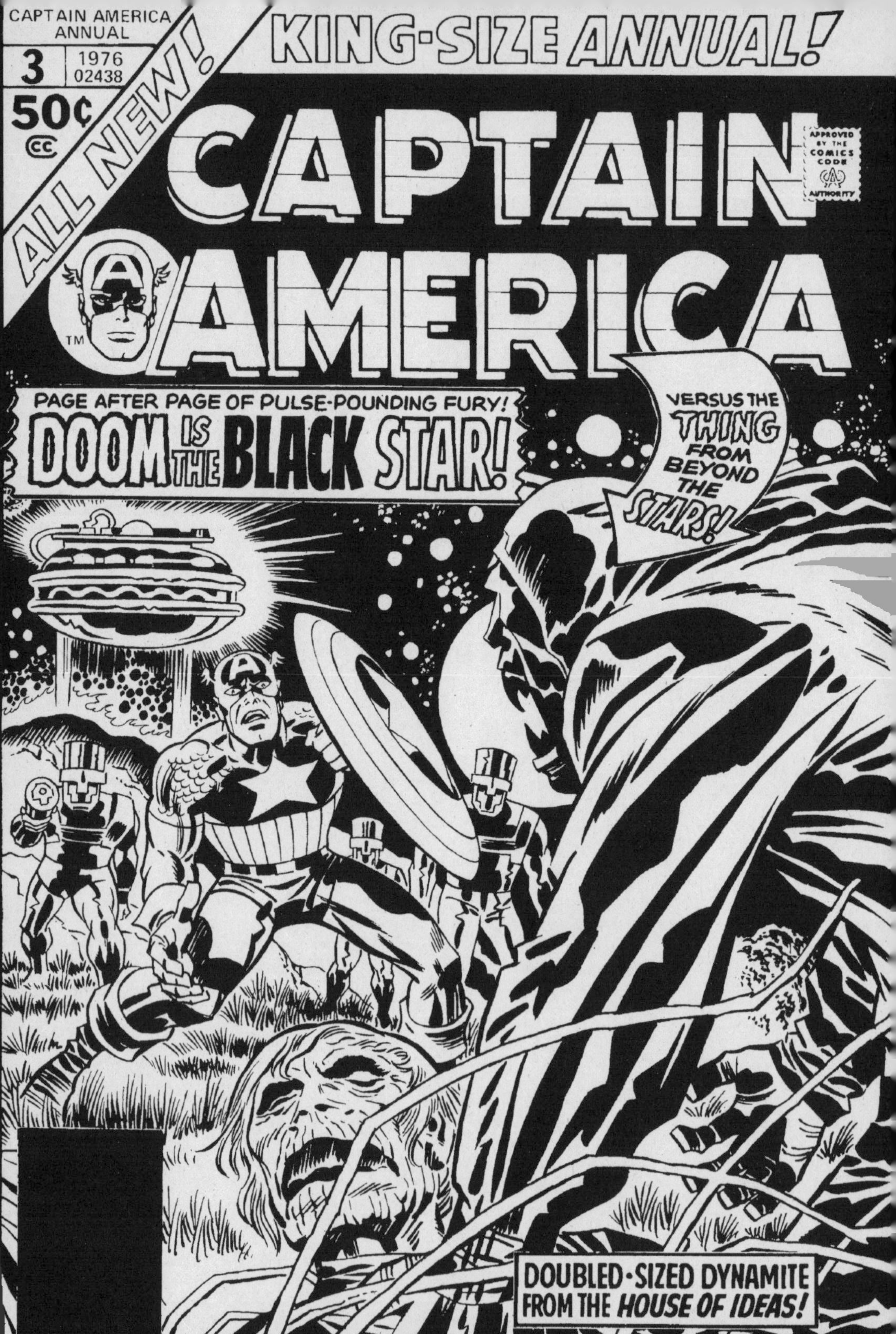

CAPTAIN AMERICA ANNUAL
3
1976
02438
50¢
CC
ALL NEW!
KING-SIZE ANNUAL!
CAPTAIN AMERICA
APPROVED BY THE COMICS CODE AUTHORITY
PAGE AFTER PAGE OF PULSE-POUNDING FURY!
DOOM IS THE BLACK STAR!
VERSUS THE THING FROM BEYOND THE STARS!
DOUBLED-SIZED DYNAMITE FROM THE HOUSE OF IDEAS!

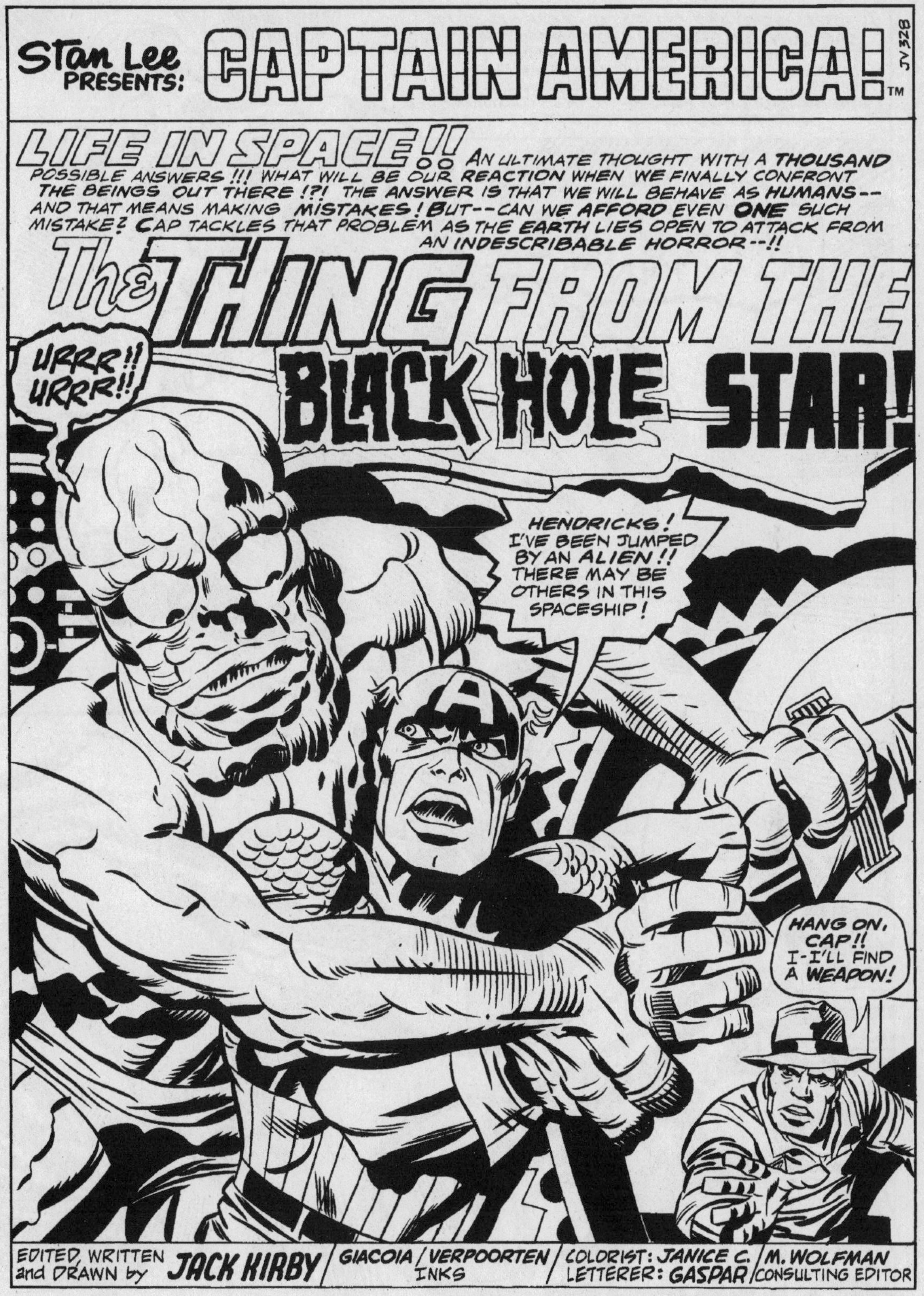
Stan Lee PRESENTS: CAPTAIN AMERICA!™
JV 328
LIFE IN SPACE!! AN ULTIMATE THOUGHT WITH A THOUSAND POSSIBLE ANSWERS!!! WHAT WILL BE OUR REACTION WHEN WE FINALLY CONFRONT THE BEINGS OUT THERE!?! THE ANSWER IS THAT WE WILL BEHAVE AS HUMANS-- AND THAT MEANS MAKING MISTAKES! BUT--CAN WE AFFORD EVEN ONE SUCH MISTAKE? CAP TACKLES THAT PROBLEM AS THE EARTH LIES OPEN TO ATTACK FROM AN INDESCRIBABLE HORROR--!!
The THING FROM THE BLACK HOLE STAR!
URRR!! URRR!!
HENDRICKS! I'VE BEEN JUMPED BY AN ALIEN!! THERE MAY BE OTHERS IN THIS SPACESHIP!
HANG ON, CAP!! I-I'LL FIND A WEAPON!
EDITED, WRITTEN and DRAWN by JACK KIRBY / GIACOIA / VERPOORTEN INKS / COLORIST: JANICE C. LETTERER: GASPAR / M. WOLFMAN CONSULTING EDITOR

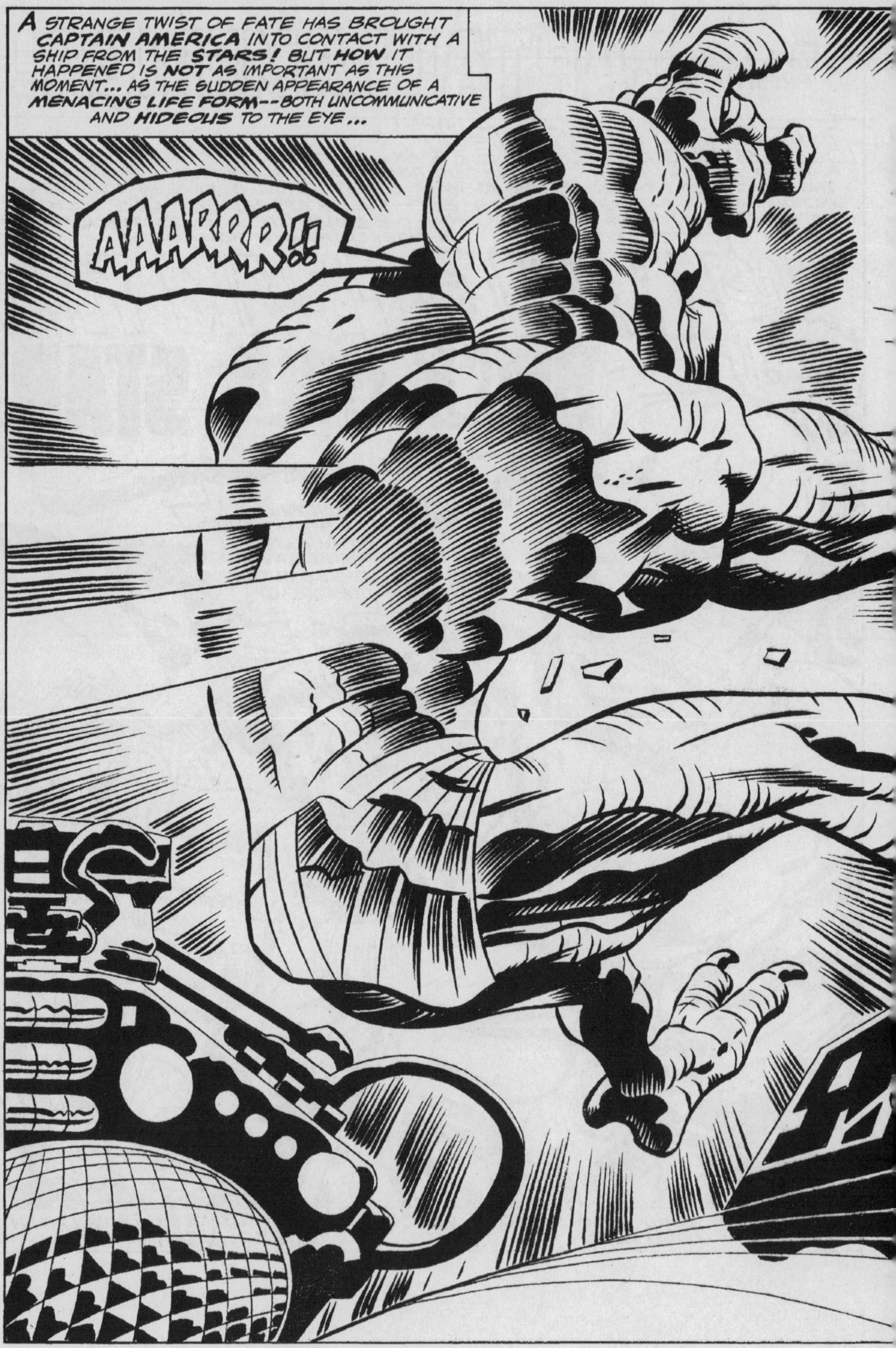
A STRANGE TWIST OF FATE HAS BROUGHT CAPTAIN AMERICA INTO CONTACT WITH A SHIP FROM THE STARS! BUT HOW IT HAPPENED IS NOT AS IMPORTANT AS THIS MOMENT... AS THE SUDDEN APPEARANCE OF A MENACING LIFE FORM--BOTH UNCOMMUNICATIVE AND HIDEOUS TO THE EYE...
AAARRR!!

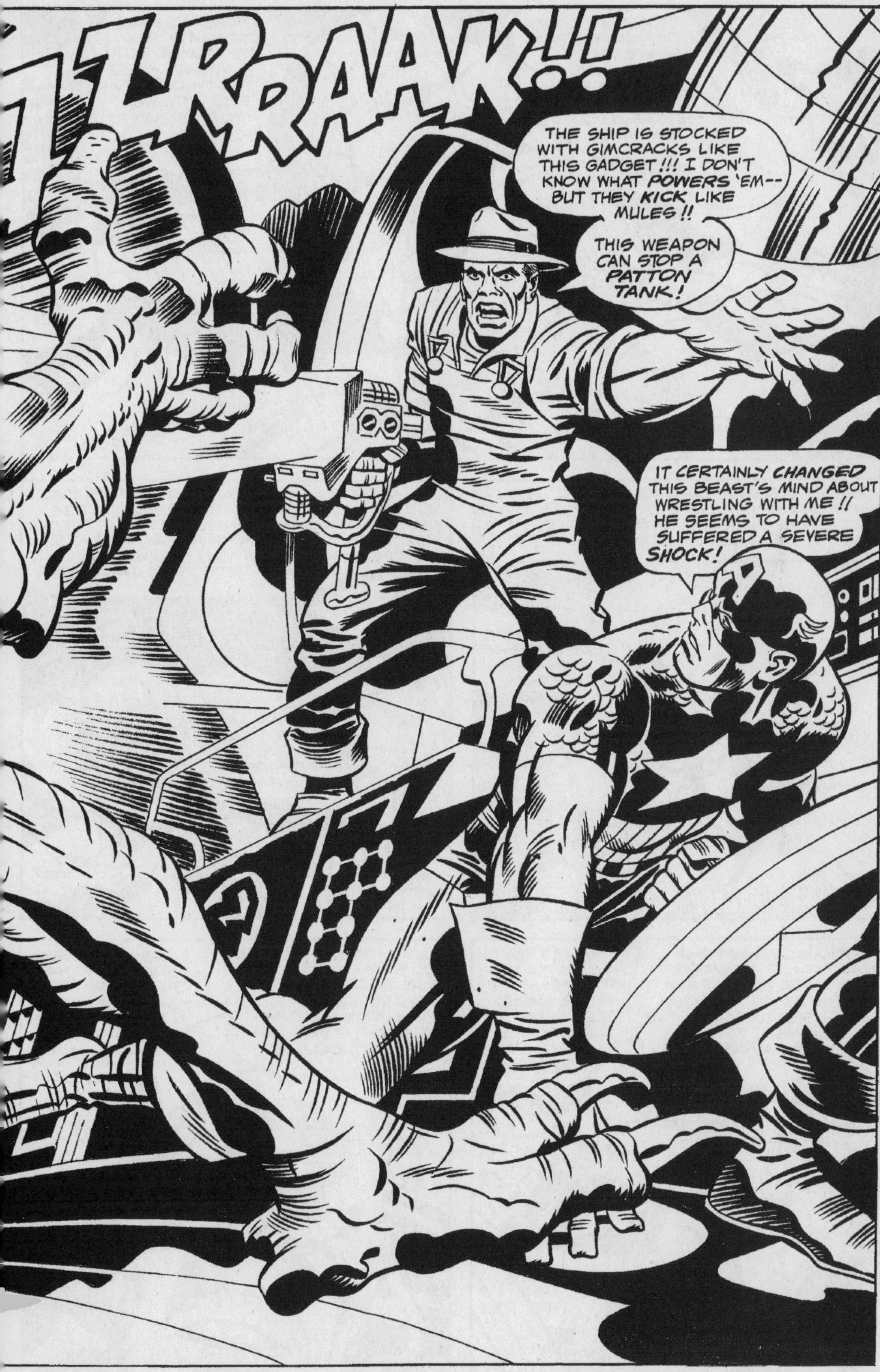

ZZRRAAK!!!
THE SHIP IS STOCKED WITH GIMCRACKS LIKE THIS GADGET!!! I DON'T KNOW WHAT POWERS 'EM-- BUT THEY KICK LIKE MULES!!
THIS WEAPON CAN STOP A PATTON TANK!
IT CERTAINLY CHANGED THIS BEAST'S MIND ABOUT WRESTLING WITH ME!! HE SEEMS TO HAVE SUFFERED A SEVERE SHOCK!

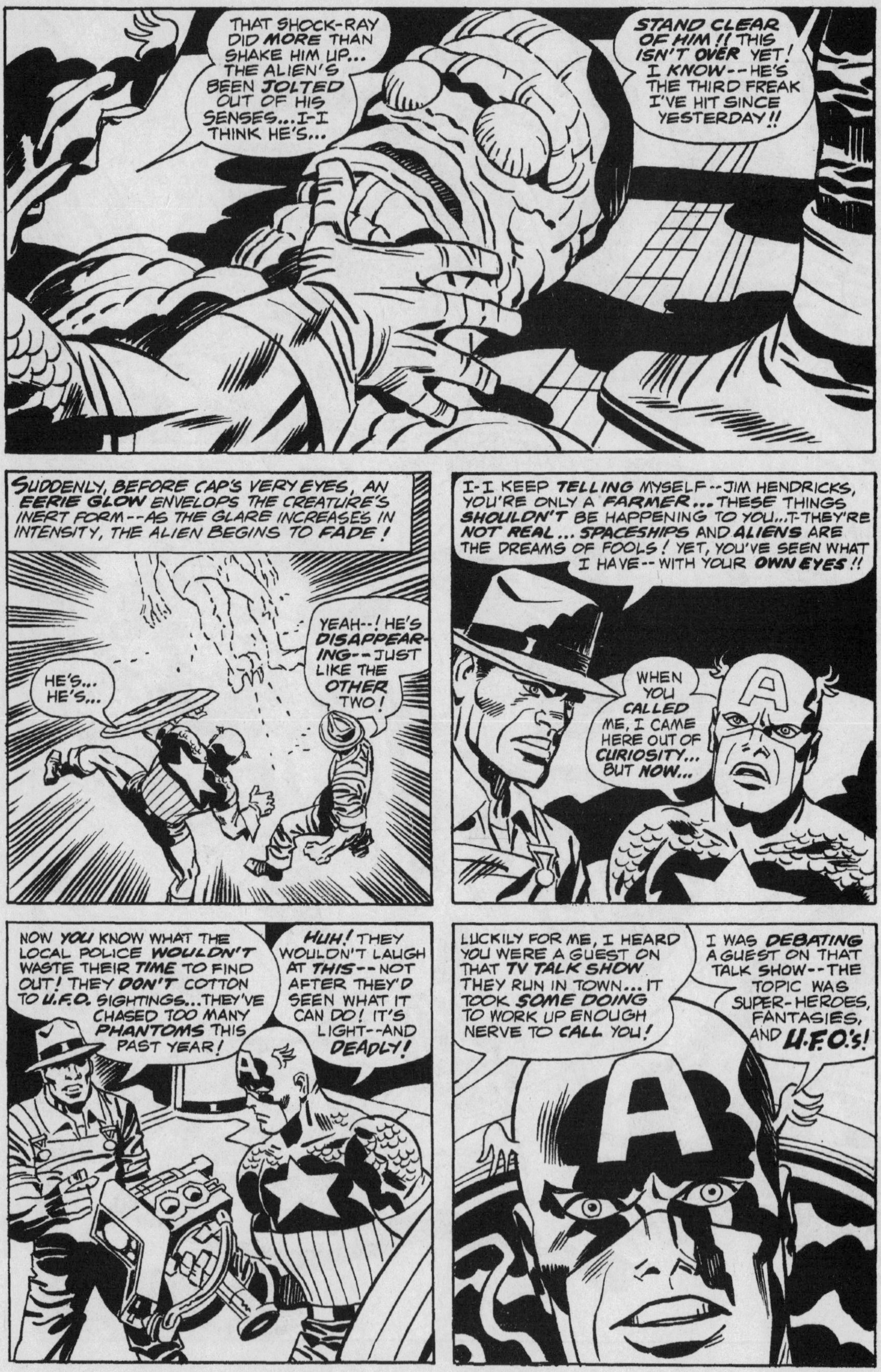
THAT SHOCK-RAY DID MORE THAN SHAKE HIM UP... THE ALIEN'S BEEN JOLTED OUT OF HIS SENSES...I-I THINK HE'S...
STAND CLEAR OF HIM!! THIS ISN'T OVER YET! I KNOW--HE'S THE THIRD FREAK I'VE HIT SINCE YESTERDAY!!
SUDDENLY, BEFORE CAP'S VERY EYES, AN EERIE GLOW ENVELOPS THE CREATURE'S INERT FORM--AS THE GLARE INCREASES IN INTENSITY, THE ALIEN BEGINS TO FADE!
HE'S... HE'S...
YEAH--! HE'S DISAPPEARING--JUST LIKE THE OTHER TWO!
I-I KEEP TELLING MYSELF--JIM HENDRICKS, YOU'RE ONLY A FARMER... THESE THINGS SHOULDN'T BE HAPPENING TO YOU...T-THEY'RE NOT REAL... SPACESHIPS AND ALIENS ARE THE DREAMS OF FOOLS! YET, YOU'VE SEEN WHAT I HAVE--WITH YOUR OWN EYES!!
WHEN YOU CALLED ME, I CAME HERE OUT OF CURIOSITY... BUT NOW...
NOW YOU KNOW WHAT THE LOCAL POLICE WOULDN'T WASTE THEIR TIME TO FIND OUT! THEY DON'T COTTON TO U.F.O. SIGHTINGS...THEY'VE CHASED TOO MANY PHANTOMS THIS PAST YEAR!
HUH! THEY WOULDN'T LAUGH AT THIS--NOT AFTER THEY'D SEEN WHAT IT CAN DO! IT'S LIGHT--AND DEADLY!
LUCKILY FOR ME, I HEARD YOU WERE A GUEST ON THAT TV TALK SHOW THEY RUN IN TOWN... IT TOOK SOME DOING TO WORK UP ENOUGH NERVE TO CALL YOU!
I WAS DEBATING A GUEST ON THAT TALK SHOW--THE TOPIC WAS SUPER-HEROES, FANTASIES, AND U.F.O.'s!

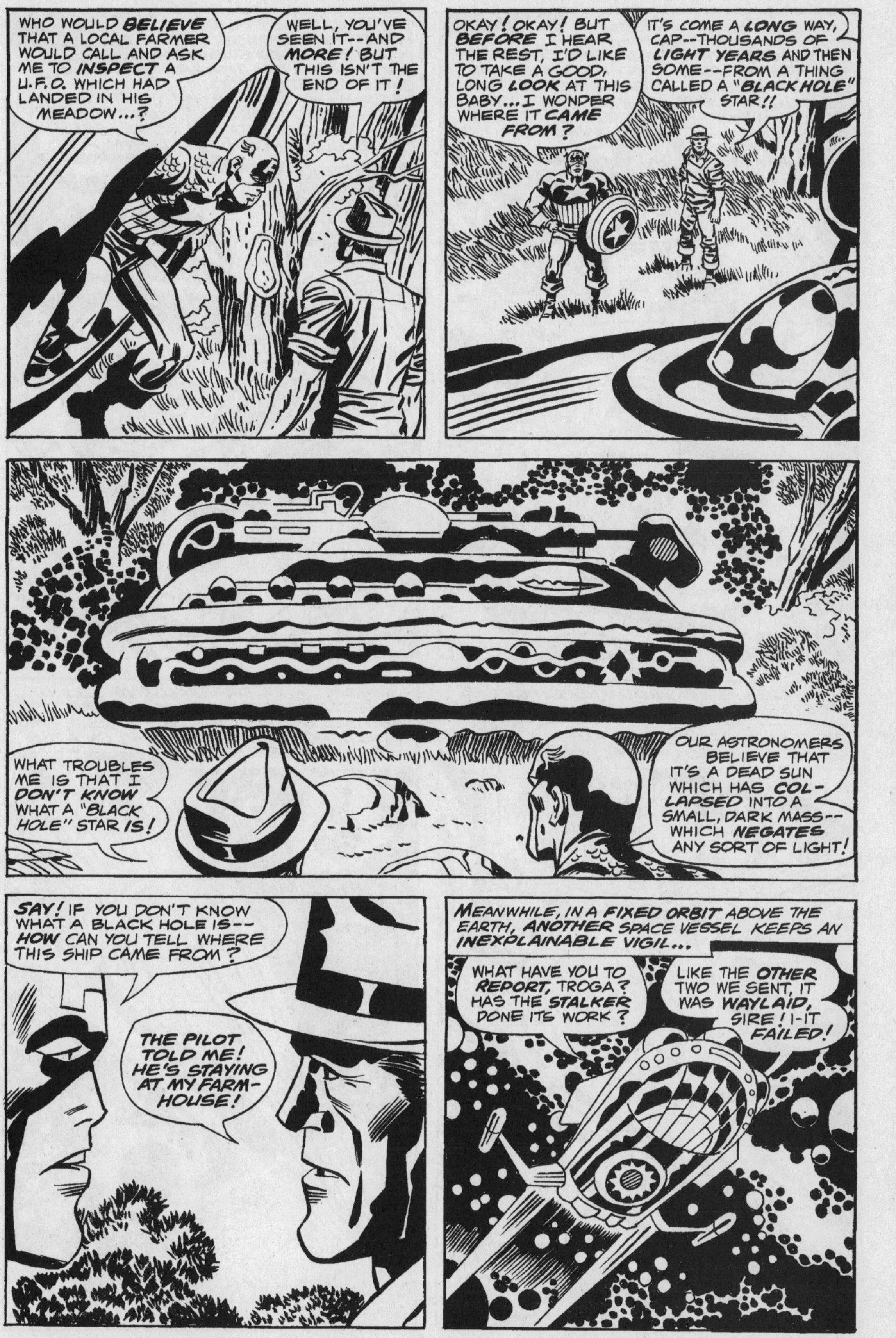
WHO WOULD BELIEVE THAT A LOCAL FARMER WOULD CALL AND ASK ME TO INSPECT A U.F.O. WHICH HAD LANDED IN HIS MEADOW...?
WELL, YOU'VE SEEN IT--AND MORE! BUT THIS ISN'T THE END OF IT!
OKAY! OKAY! BUT BEFORE I HEAR THE REST, I'D LIKE TO TAKE A GOOD, LONG LOOK AT THIS BABY... I WONDER WHERE IT CAME FROM?
IT'S COME A LONG WAY, CAP--THOUSANDS OF LIGHT YEARS AND THEN SOME--FROM A THING CALLED A "BLACK HOLE" STAR!!
WHAT TROUBLES ME IS THAT I DON'T KNOW WHAT A "BLACK HOLE" STAR IS!
OUR ASTRONOMERS BELIEVE THAT IT'S A DEAD SUN WHICH HAS COL-LAPSED INTO A SMALL, DARK MASS--WHICH NEGATES ANY SORT OF LIGHT!
SAY! IF YOU DON'T KNOW WHAT A BLACK HOLE IS--HOW CAN YOU TELL WHERE THIS SHIP CAME FROM?
THE PILOT TOLD ME! HE'S STAYING AT MY FARM-HOUSE!
MEANWHILE, IN A FIXED ORBIT ABOVE THE EARTH, ANOTHER SPACE VESSEL KEEPS AN INEXPLAINABLE VIGIL...
WHAT HAVE YOU TO REPORT, TROGA? HAS THE STALKER DONE ITS WORK?
LIKE THE OTHER TWO WE SENT, IT WAS WAYLAID, SIRE! I-IT FAILED!

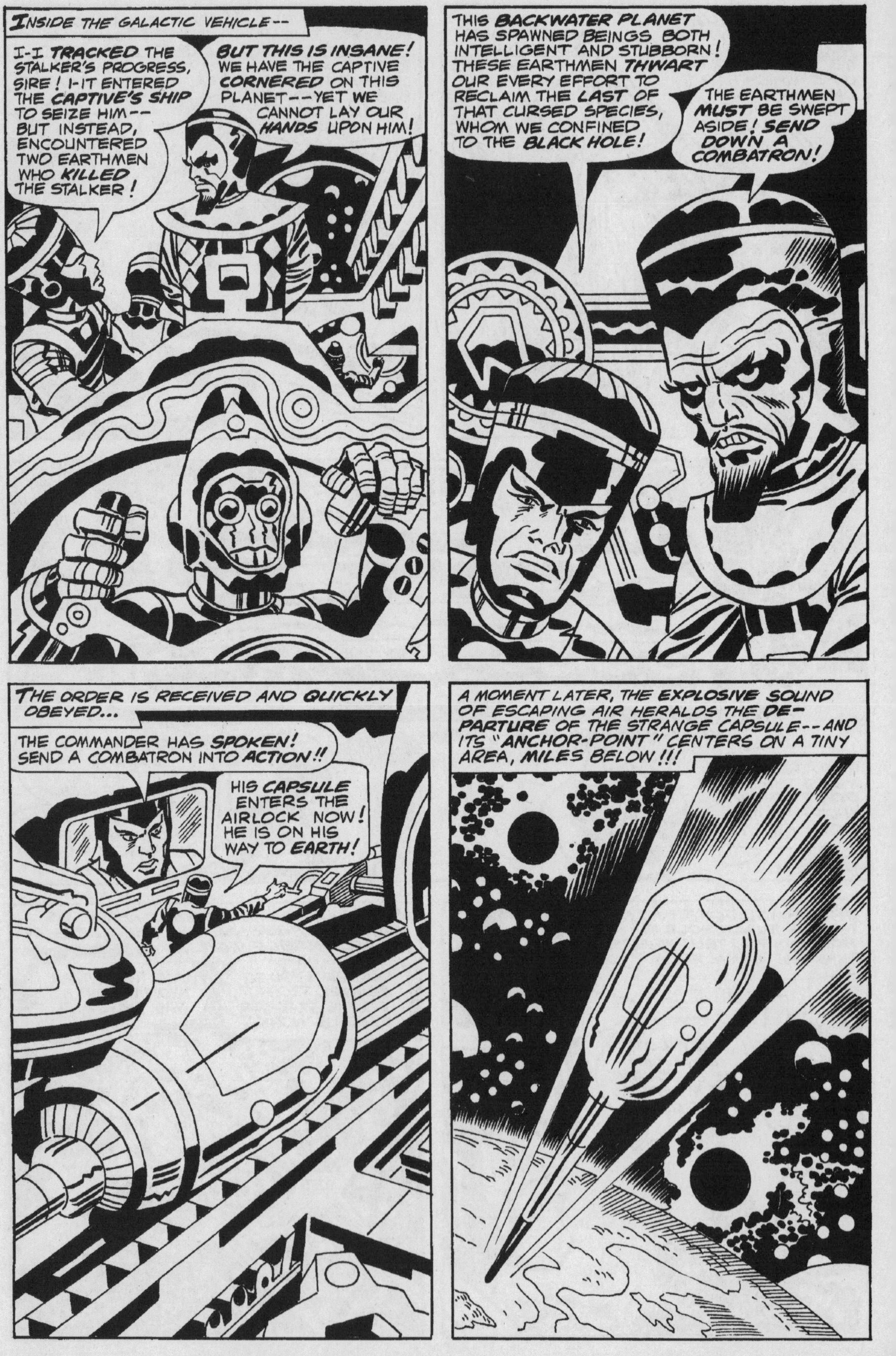
INSIDE THE GALACTIC VEHICLE--
I-I TRACKED THE STALKER'S PROGRESS, SIRE! I-IT ENTERED THE CAPTIVE'S SHIP TO SEIZE HIM--BUT INSTEAD, ENCOUNTERED TWO EARTHMEN WHO KILLED THE STALKER!
BUT THIS IS INSANE! WE HAVE THE CAPTIVE CORNERED ON THIS PLANET--YET WE CANNOT LAY OUR HANDS UPON HIM!
THIS BACKWATER PLANET HAS SPAWNED BEINGS BOTH INTELLIGENT AND STUBBORN! THESE EARTHMEN THWART OUR EVERY EFFORT TO RECLAIM THE LAST OF THAT CURSED SPECIES, WHOM WE CONFINED TO THE BLACK HOLE!
THE EARTHMEN MUST BE SWEPT ASIDE! SEND DOWN A COMBATRON!
THE ORDER IS RECEIVED AND QUICKLY OBEYED...
THE COMMANDER HAS SPOKEN! SEND A COMBATRON INTO ACTION!!
HIS CAPSULE ENTERS THE AIRLOCK NOW! HE IS ON HIS WAY TO EARTH!
A MOMENT LATER, THE EXPLOSIVE SOUND OF ESCAPING AIR HERALDS THE DEPARTURE OF THE STRANGE CAPSULE--AND ITS "ANCHOR-POINT" CENTERS ON A TINY AREA, MILES BELOW!!!

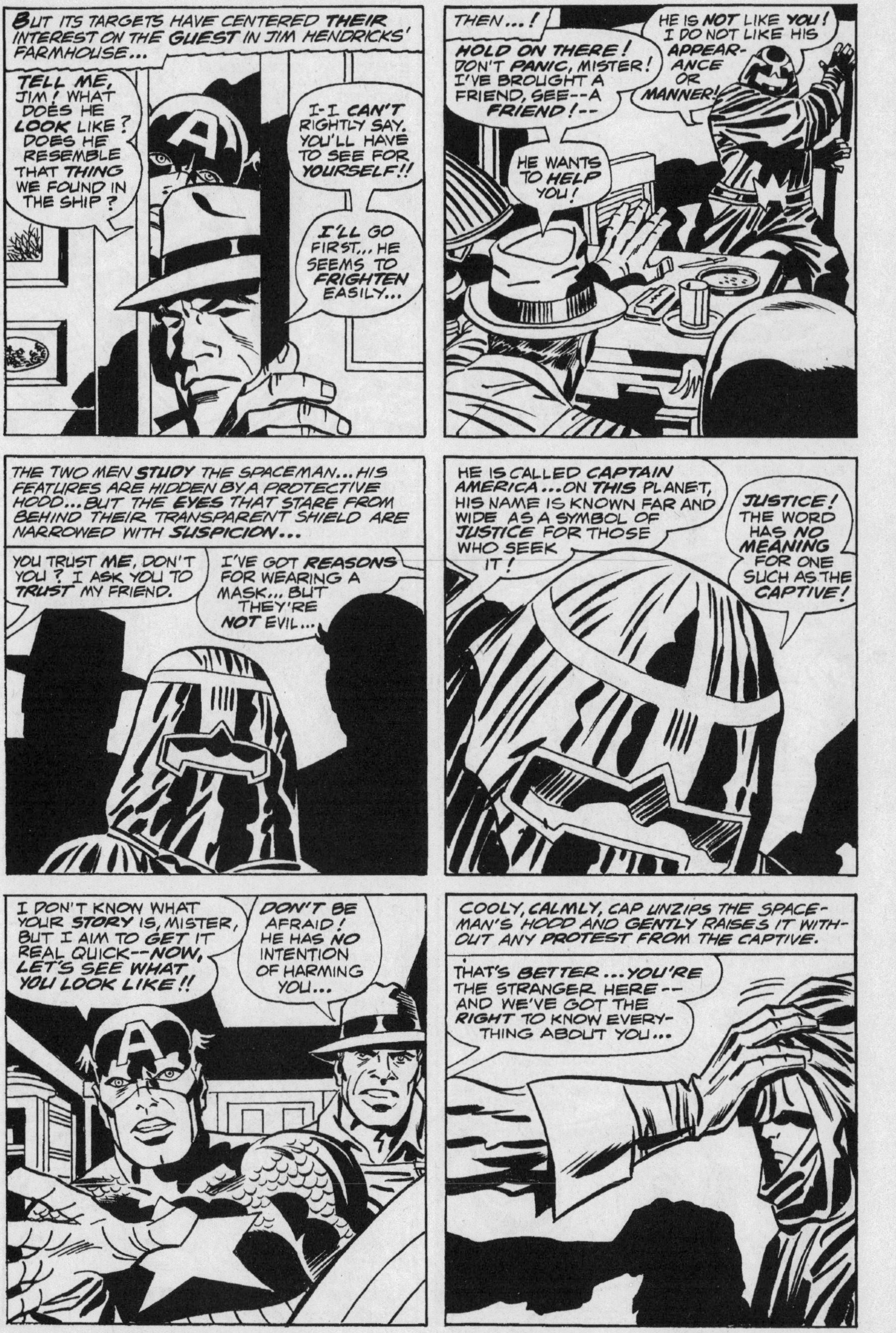
BUT ITS TARGETS HAVE CENTERED THEIR INTEREST ON THE GUEST IN JIM HENDRICKS' FARMHOUSE...
TELL ME, JIM! WHAT DOES HE LOOK LIKE? DOES HE RESEMBLE THAT THING WE FOUND IN THE SHIP?
I-I CAN'T RIGHTLY SAY. YOU'LL HAVE TO SEE FOR YOURSELF!!
I'LL GO FIRST... HE SEEMS TO FRIGHTEN EASILY...
THEN...!
HOLD ON THERE! DON'T PANIC, MISTER! I'VE BROUGHT A FRIEND, SEE--A FRIEND!--
HE IS NOT LIKE YOU! I DO NOT LIKE HIS APPEAR-ANCE OR MANNER!
HE WANTS TO HELP YOU!
THE TWO MEN STUDY THE SPACEMAN... HIS FEATURES ARE HIDDEN BY A PROTECTIVE HOOD... BUT THE EYES THAT STARE FROM BEHIND THEIR TRANSPARENT SHIELD ARE NARROWED WITH SUSPICION...
YOU TRUST ME, DON'T YOU? I ASK YOU TO TRUST MY FRIEND.
I'VE GOT REASONS FOR WEARING A MASK... BUT THEY'RE NOT EVIL...
HE IS CALLED CAPTAIN AMERICA... ON THIS PLANET, HIS NAME IS KNOWN FAR AND WIDE AS A SYMBOL OF JUSTICE FOR THOSE WHO SEEK IT!
JUSTICE! THE WORD HAS NO MEANING FOR ONE SUCH AS THE CAPTIVE!
I DON'T KNOW WHAT YOUR STORY IS, MISTER, BUT I AIM TO GET IT REAL QUICK--NOW, LET'S SEE WHAT YOU LOOK LIKE!!
DON'T BE AFRAID! HE HAS NO INTENTION OF HARMING YOU...
COOLY, CALMLY, CAP UNZIPS THE SPACE-MAN'S HOOD AND GENTLY RAISES IT WITH-OUT ANY PROTEST FROM THE CAPTIVE.
THAT'S BETTER... YOU'RE THE STRANGER HERE-- AND WE'VE GOT THE RIGHT TO KNOW EVERY-THING ABOUT YOU...

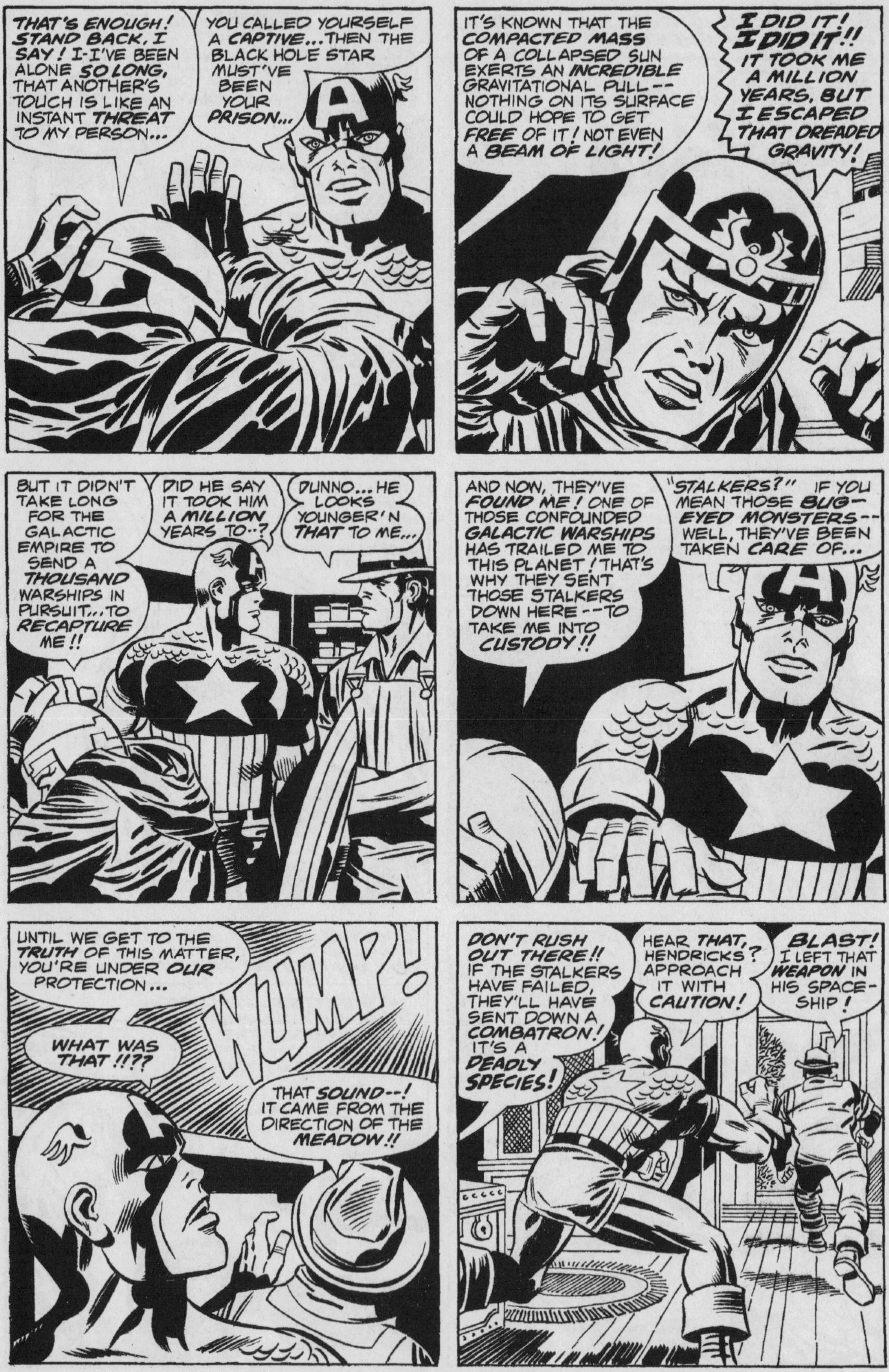
THAT'S ENOUGH! STAND BACK, I SAY! I-I'VE BEEN ALONE SO LONG, THAT ANOTHER'S TOUCH IS LIKE AN INSTANT THREAT TO MY PERSON...
YOU CALLED YOURSELF A CAPTIVE...THEN THE BLACK HOLE STAR MUST'VE BEEN YOUR PRISON...
IT'S KNOWN THAT THE COMPACTED MASS OF A COLLAPSED SUN EXERTS AN INCREDIBLE GRAVITATIONAL PULL-- NOTHING ON ITS SURFACE COULD HOPE TO GET FREE OF IT! NOT EVEN A BEAM OF LIGHT!
I DID IT! I DID IT!! IT TOOK ME A MILLION YEARS, BUT I ESCAPED THAT DREADED GRAVITY!
BUT IT DIDN'T TAKE LONG FOR THE GALACTIC EMPIRE TO SEND A THOUSAND WARSHIPS IN PURSUIT... TO RECAPTURE ME!!
DID HE SAY IT TOOK HIM A MILLION YEARS TO··?
DUNNO... HE LOOKS YOUNGER'N THAT TO ME...
AND NOW, THEY'VE FOUND ME! ONE OF THOSE CONFOUNDED GALACTIC WARSHIPS HAS TRAILED ME TO THIS PLANET! THAT'S WHY THEY SENT THOSE STALKERS DOWN HERE --TO TAKE ME INTO CUSTODY!!
"STALKERS?" IF YOU MEAN THOSE BUG-EYED MONSTERS-- WELL, THEY'VE BEEN TAKEN CARE OF...
UNTIL WE GET TO THE TRUTH OF THIS MATTER, YOU'RE UNDER OUR PROTECTION...
WUMP!
WHAT WAS THAT!!??
THAT SOUND--! IT CAME FROM THE DIRECTION OF THE MEADOW!!
DON'T RUSH OUT THERE!! IF THE STALKERS HAVE FAILED, THEY'LL HAVE SENT DOWN A COMBATRON! IT'S A DEADLY SPECIES!
HEAR THAT, HENDRICKS? APPROACH IT WITH CAUTION!
BLAST! I LEFT THAT WEAPON IN HIS SPACE-SHIP!

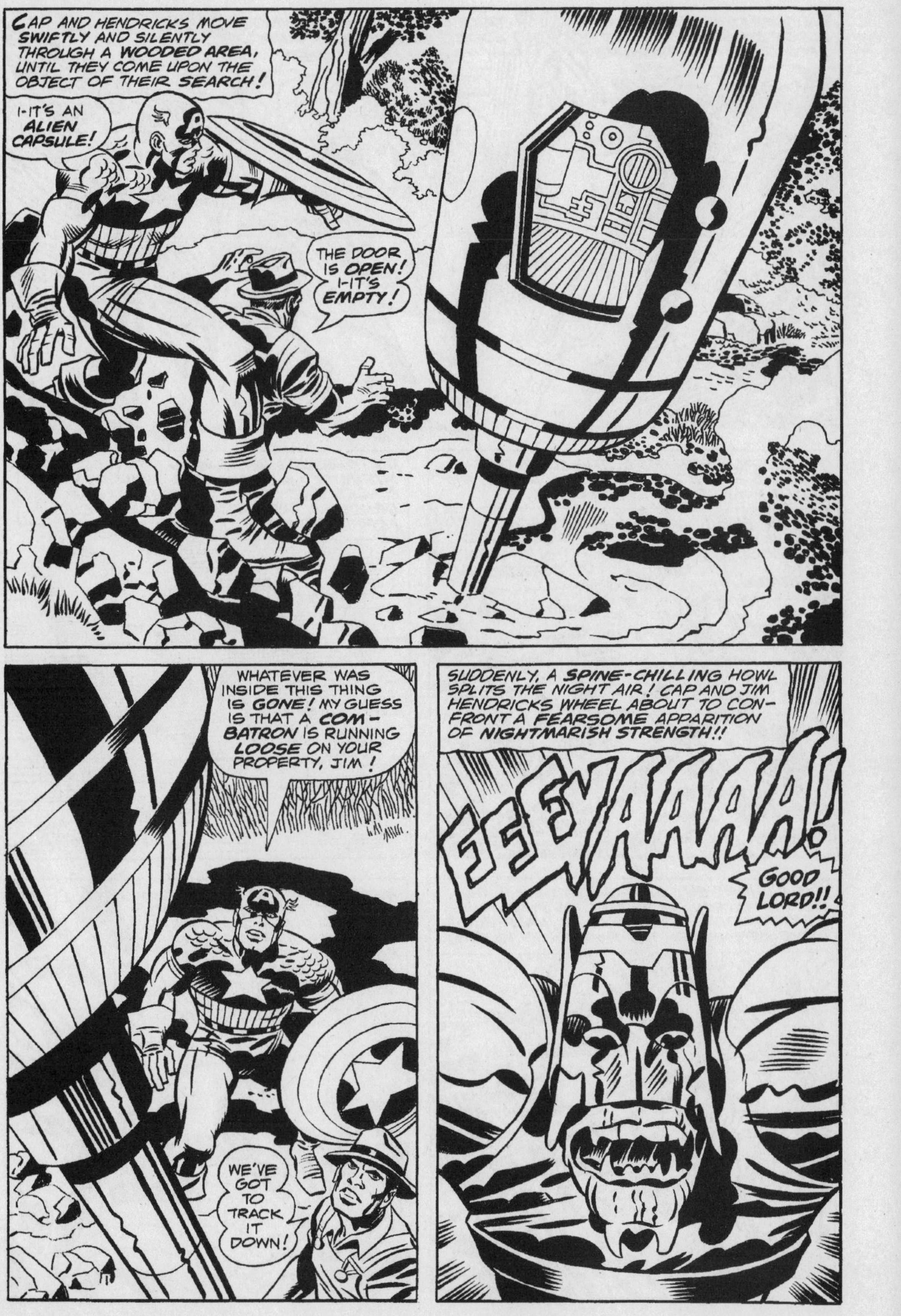
CAP AND HENDRICKS MOVE SWIFTLY AND SILENTLY THROUGH A WOODED AREA, UNTIL THEY COME UPON THE OBJECT OF THEIR SEARCH!
I-IT'S AN ALIEN CAPSULE!
THE DOOR IS OPEN! I-IT'S EMPTY!
WHATEVER WAS INSIDE THIS THING IS GONE! MY GUESS IS THAT A COM-BATRON IS RUNNING LOOSE ON YOUR PROPERTY, JIM!
WE'VE GOT TO TRACK IT DOWN!
SUDDENLY, A SPINE-CHILLING HOWL SPLITS THE NIGHT AIR! CAP AND JIM HENDRICKS WHEEL ABOUT TO CON-FRONT A FEARSOME APPARITION OF NIGHTMARISH STRENGTH!!
EEEYAAAA!
GOOD LORD!!

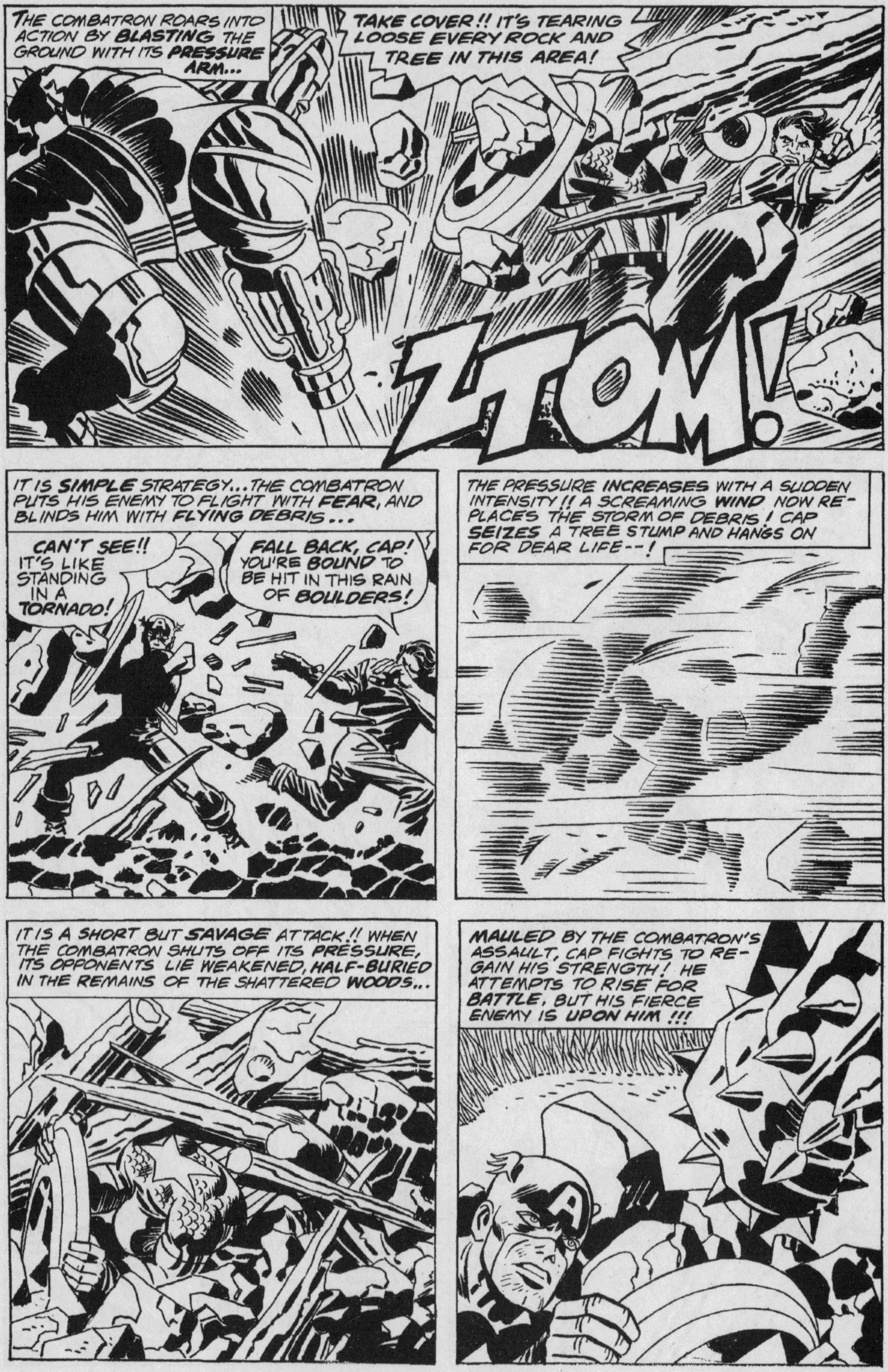
THE COMBATRON ROARS INTO ACTION BY BLASTING THE GROUND WITH ITS PRESSURE ARM...
TAKE COVER!! IT'S TEARING LOOSE EVERY ROCK AND TREE IN THIS AREA!
ZTOM!
IT IS SIMPLE STRATEGY...THE COMBATRON PUTS HIS ENEMY TO FLIGHT WITH FEAR, AND BLINDS HIM WITH FLYING DEBRIS...
CAN'T SEE!! IT'S LIKE STANDING IN A TORNADO!
FALL BACK, CAP! YOU'RE BOUND TO BE HIT IN THIS RAIN OF BOULDERS!
THE PRESSURE INCREASES WITH A SUDDEN INTENSITY!! A SCREAMING WIND NOW REPLACES THE STORM OF DEBRIS! CAP SEIZES A TREE STUMP AND HANGS ON FOR DEAR LIFE--!
IT IS A SHORT BUT SAVAGE ATTACK!! WHEN THE COMBATRON SHUTS OFF ITS PRESSURE, ITS OPPONENTS LIE WEAKENED, HALF-BURIED IN THE REMAINS OF THE SHATTERED WOODS...
MAULED BY THE COMBATRON'S ASSAULT, CAP FIGHTS TO REGAIN HIS STRENGTH! HE ATTEMPTS TO RISE FOR BATTLE, BUT HIS FIERCE ENEMY IS UPON HIM!!!

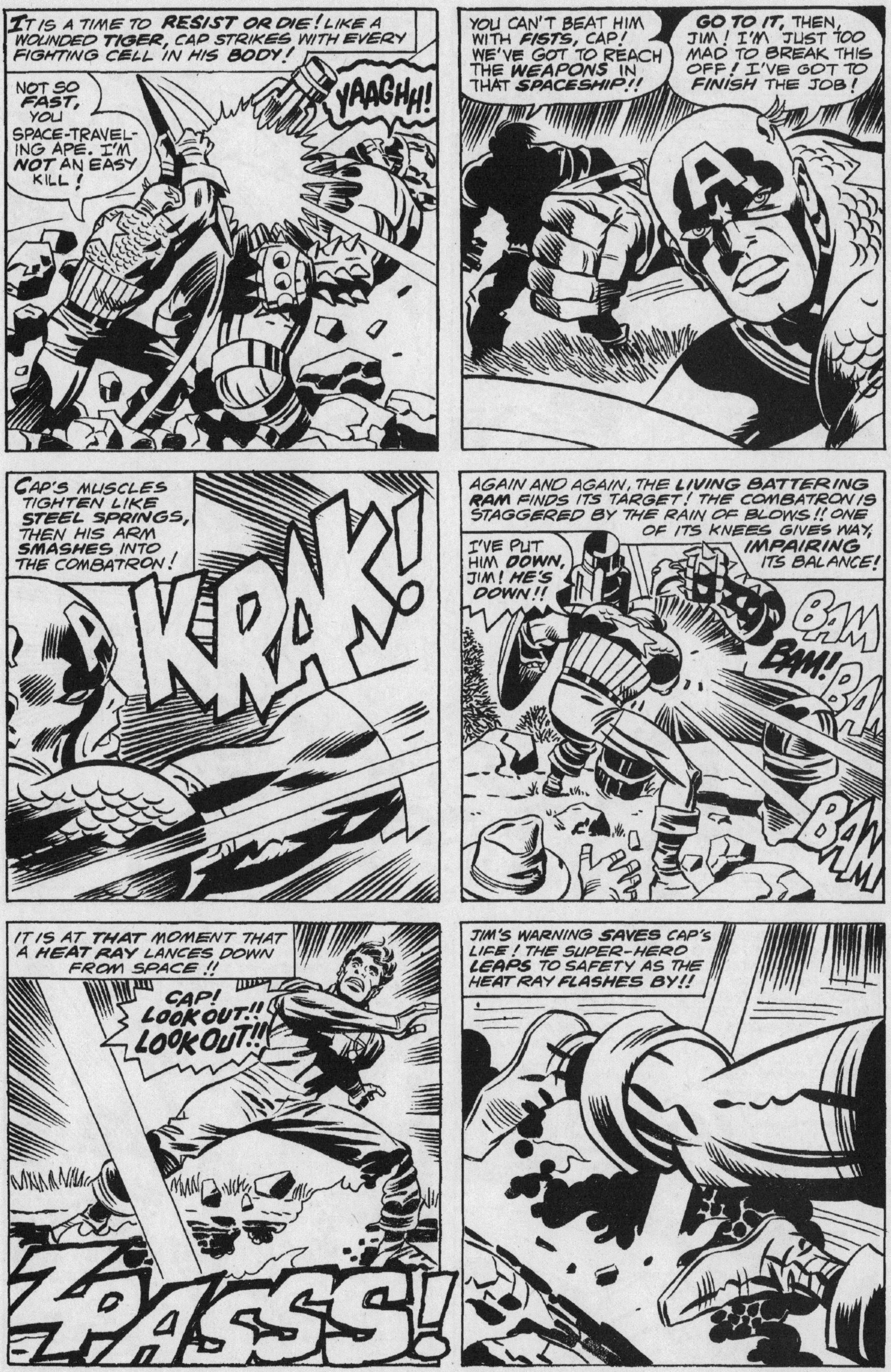
IT IS A TIME TO RESIST OR DIE! LIKE A WOUNDED TIGER, CAP STRIKES WITH EVERY FIGHTING CELL IN HIS BODY!
NOT SO FAST, YOU SPACE-TRAVELING APE. I'M NOT AN EASY KILL!
YAAGHH!
YOU CAN'T BEAT HIM WITH FISTS, CAP! WE'VE GOT TO REACH THE WEAPONS IN THAT SPACESHIP!!
GO TO IT, THEN, JIM! I'M JUST TOO MAD TO BREAK THIS OFF! I'VE GOT TO FINISH THE JOB!
CAP'S MUSCLES TIGHTEN LIKE STEEL SPRINGS, THEN HIS ARM SMASHES INTO THE COMBATRON!
KRAK!
AGAIN AND AGAIN, THE LIVING BATTERING RAM FINDS ITS TARGET! THE COMBATRON IS STAGGERED BY THE RAIN OF BLOWS!! ONE OF ITS KNEES GIVES WAY, IMPAIRING ITS BALANCE!
I'VE PUT HIM DOWN, JIM! HE'S DOWN!!
BAM
BAM!
IT IS AT THAT MOMENT THAT A HEAT RAY LANCES DOWN FROM SPACE!!
CAP! LOOK OUT!! LOOK OUT!!
ZPASSS!
JIM'S WARNING SAVES CAP'S LIFE! THE SUPER-HERO LEAPS TO SAFETY AS THE HEAT RAY FLASHES BY!!

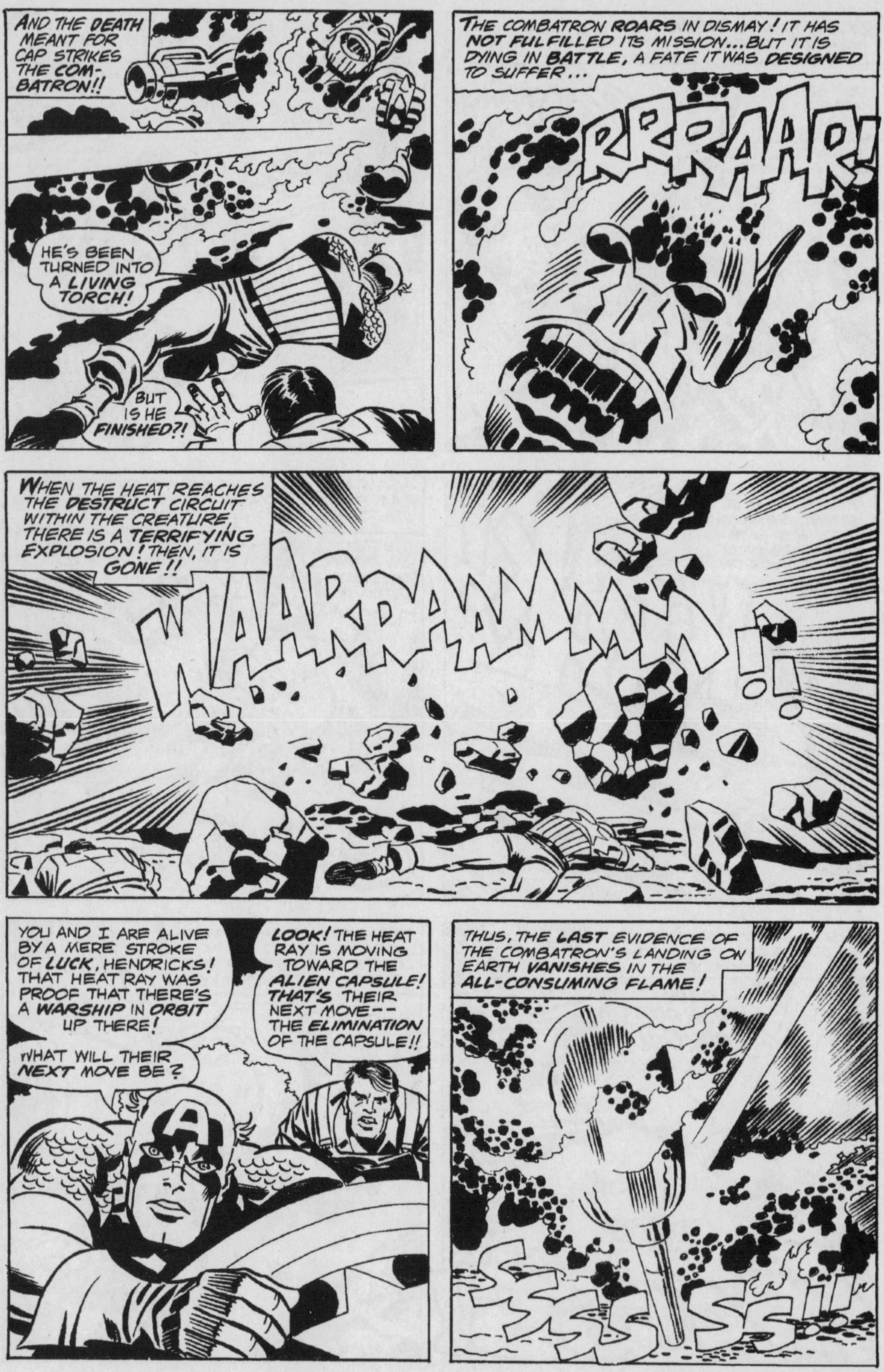
AND THE DEATH MEANT FOR CAP STRIKES THE COMBATRON!!
HE'S BEEN TURNED INTO A LIVING TORCH!
BUT IS HE FINISHED?!
THE COMBATRON ROARS IN DISMAY! IT HAS NOT FULFILLED ITS MISSION... BUT IT IS DYING IN BATTLE, A FATE IT WAS DESIGNED TO SUFFER...
RRRAAR!
WHEN THE HEAT REACHES THE DESTRUCT CIRCUIT WITHIN THE CREATURE, THERE IS A TERRIFYING EXPLOSION! THEN, IT IS GONE!!
WAARRAAMMM!!!
YOU AND I ARE ALIVE BY A MERE STROKE OF LUCK, HENDRICKS! THAT HEAT RAY WAS PROOF THAT THERE'S A WARSHIP IN ORBIT UP THERE!
WHAT WILL THEIR NEXT MOVE BE?
LOOK! THE HEAT RAY IS MOVING TOWARD THE ALIEN CAPSULE! THAT'S THEIR NEXT MOVE-- THE ELIMINATION OF THE CAPSULE!!
THUS, THE LAST EVIDENCE OF THE COMBATRON'S LANDING ON EARTH VANISHES IN THE ALL-CONSUMING FLAME!
SSSSSS!!

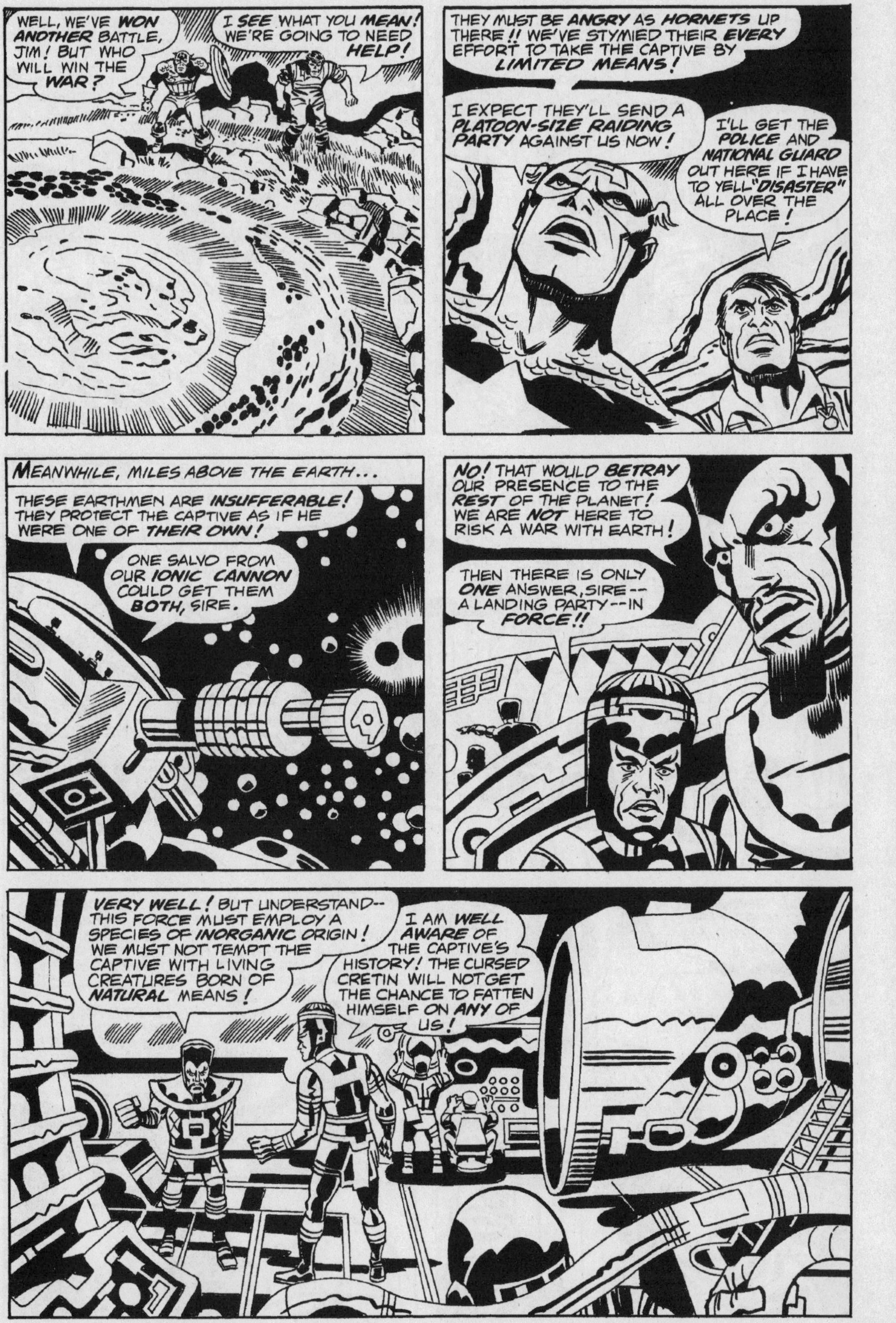
WELL, WE'VE WON ANOTHER BATTLE, JIM! BUT WHO WILL WIN THE WAR?
I SEE WHAT YOU MEAN! WE'RE GOING TO NEED HELP!
THEY MUST BE ANGRY AS HORNETS UP THERE!! WE'VE STYMIED THEIR EVERY EFFORT TO TAKE THE CAPTIVE BY LIMITED MEANS!
I EXPECT THEY'LL SEND A PLATOON-SIZE RAIDING PARTY AGAINST US NOW!
I'LL GET THE POLICE AND NATIONAL GUARD OUT HERE IF I HAVE TO YELL "DISASTER" ALL OVER THE PLACE!
MEANWHILE, MILES ABOVE THE EARTH...
THESE EARTHMEN ARE INSUFFERABLE! THEY PROTECT THE CAPTIVE AS IF HE WERE ONE OF THEIR OWN!
ONE SALVO FROM OUR IONIC CANNON COULD GET THEM BOTH, SIRE.
NO! THAT WOULD BETRAY OUR PRESENCE TO THE REST OF THE PLANET! WE ARE NOT HERE TO RISK A WAR WITH EARTH!
THEN THERE IS ONLY ONE ANSWER, SIRE -- A LANDING PARTY -- IN FORCE!!
VERY WELL! BUT UNDERSTAND -- THIS FORCE MUST EMPLOY A SPECIES OF INORGANIC ORIGIN! WE MUST NOT TEMPT THE CAPTIVE WITH LIVING CREATURES BORN OF NATURAL MEANS!
I AM WELL AWARE OF THE CAPTIVE'S HISTORY! THE CURSED CRETIN WILL NOT GET THE CHANCE TO FATTEN HIMSELF ON ANY OF US!

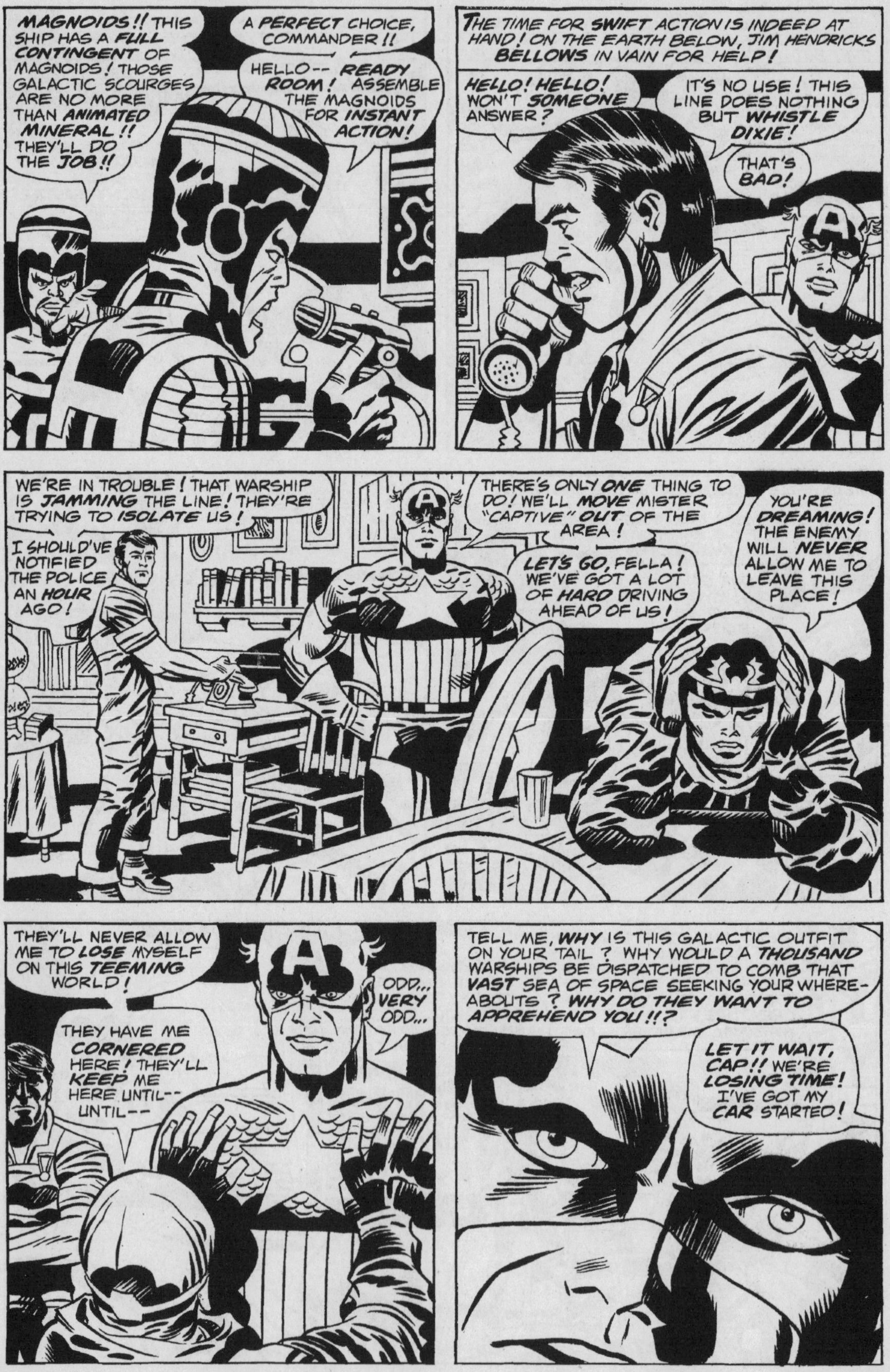

MAGNOIDS!! THIS SHIP HAS A FULL CONTINGENT OF MAGNOIDS! THOSE GALACTIC SCOURGES ARE NO MORE THAN ANIMATED MINERAL!! THEY'LL DO THE JOB!!
A PERFECT CHOICE, COMMANDER!!
HELLO-- READY ROOM! ASSEMBLE THE MAGNOIDS FOR INSTANT ACTION!
THE TIME FOR SWIFT ACTION IS INDEED AT HAND! ON THE EARTH BELOW, JIM HENDRICKS BELLOWS IN VAIN FOR HELP!
HELLO! HELLO! WON'T SOMEONE ANSWER?
IT'S NO USE! THIS LINE DOES NOTHING BUT WHISTLE DIXIE!
THAT'S BAD!
WE'RE IN TROUBLE! THAT WARSHIP IS JAMMING THE LINE! THEY'RE TRYING TO ISOLATE US!
I SHOULD'VE NOTIFIED THE POLICE AN HOUR AGO!
THERE'S ONLY ONE THING TO DO! WE'LL MOVE MISTER "CAPTIVE" OUT OF THE AREA!
LET'S GO, FELLA! WE'VE GOT A LOT OF HARD DRIVING AHEAD OF US!
YOU'RE DREAMING! THE ENEMY WILL NEVER ALLOW ME TO LEAVE THIS PLACE!
THEY'LL NEVER ALLOW ME TO LOSE MYSELF ON THIS TEEMING WORLD!
THEY HAVE ME CORNERED HERE! THEY'LL KEEP ME HERE UNTIL-- UNTIL--
ODD... VERY ODD...
TELL ME, WHY IS THIS GALACTIC OUTFIT ON YOUR TAIL? WHY WOULD A THOUSAND WARSHIPS BE DISPATCHED TO COMB THAT VAST SEA OF SPACE SEEKING YOUR WHERE-ABOUTS? WHY DO THEY WANT TO APPREHEND YOU!!?
LET IT WAIT, CAP!! WE'RE LOSING TIME! I'VE GOT MY CAR STARTED!

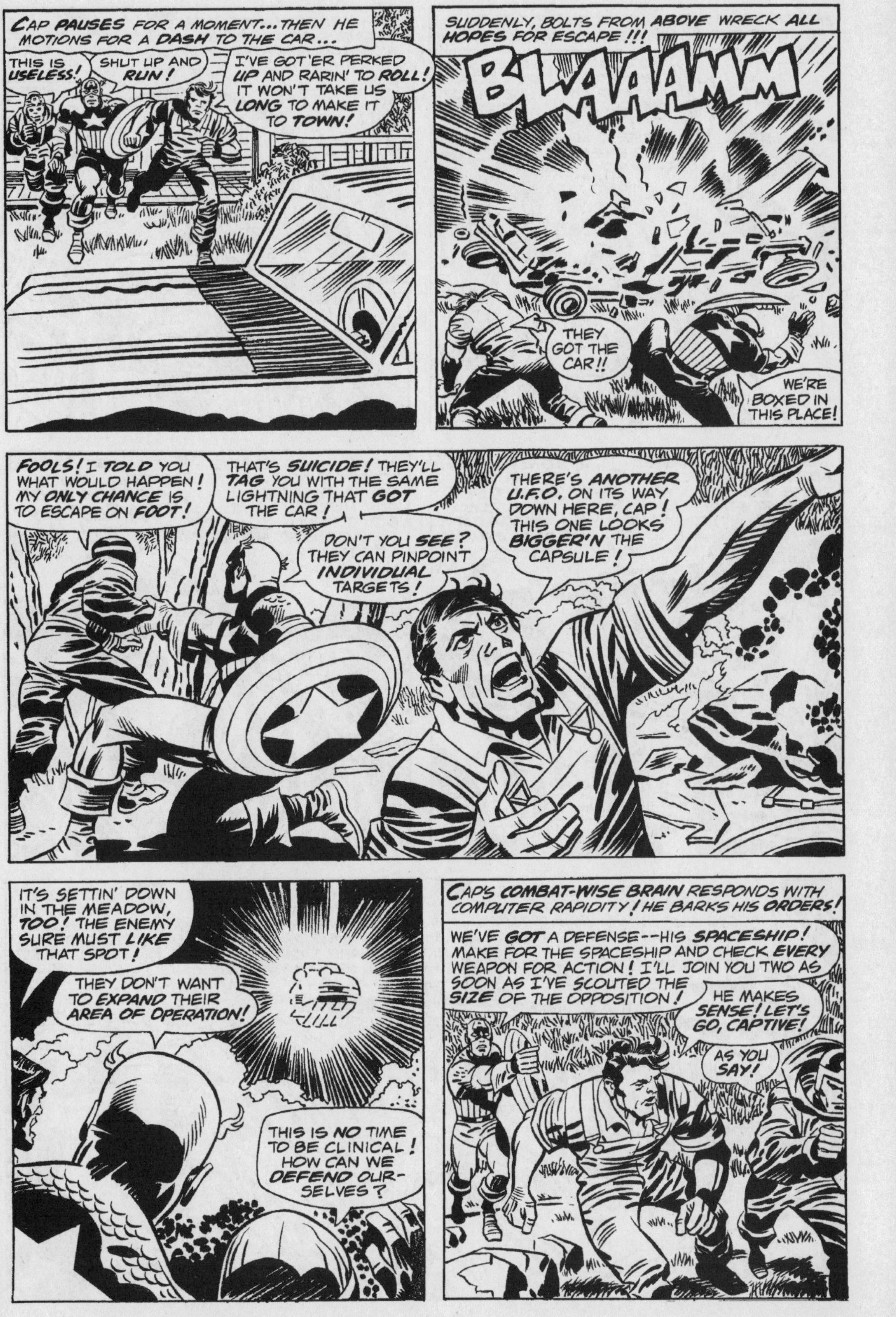
CAP PAUSES FOR A MOMENT...THEN HE MOTIONS FOR A DASH TO THE CAR...
THIS IS USELESS!
SHUT UP AND RUN!
I'VE GOT 'ER PERKED UP AND RARIN' TO ROLL! IT WON'T TAKE US LONG TO MAKE IT TO TOWN!
SUDDENLY, BOLTS FROM ABOVE WRECK ALL HOPES FOR ESCAPE!!!
BLAAAMM
THEY GOT THE CAR!!
WE'RE BOXED IN THIS PLACE!
FOOLS! I TOLD YOU WHAT WOULD HAPPEN! MY ONLY CHANCE IS TO ESCAPE ON FOOT!
THAT'S SUICIDE! THEY'LL TAG YOU WITH THE SAME LIGHTNING THAT GOT THE CAR!
DON'T YOU SEE? THEY CAN PINPOINT INDIVIDUAL TARGETS!
THERE'S ANOTHER U.F.O. ON ITS WAY DOWN HERE, CAP! THIS ONE LOOKS BIGGER'N THE CAPSULE!
IT'S SETTIN' DOWN IN THE MEADOW, TOO! THE ENEMY SURE MUST LIKE THAT SPOT!
THEY DON'T WANT TO EXPAND THEIR AREA OF OPERATION!
THIS IS NO TIME TO BE CLINICAL! HOW CAN WE DEFEND OURSELVES?
CAP'S COMBAT-WISE BRAIN RESPONDS WITH COMPUTER RAPIDITY! HE BARKS HIS ORDERS!
WE'VE GOT A DEFENSE--HIS SPACESHIP! MAKE FOR THE SPACESHIP AND CHECK EVERY WEAPON FOR ACTION! I'LL JOIN YOU TWO AS SOON AS I'VE SCOUTED THE SIZE OF THE OPPOSITION!
HE MAKES SENSE! LET'S GO, CAPTIVE!
AS YOU SAY!

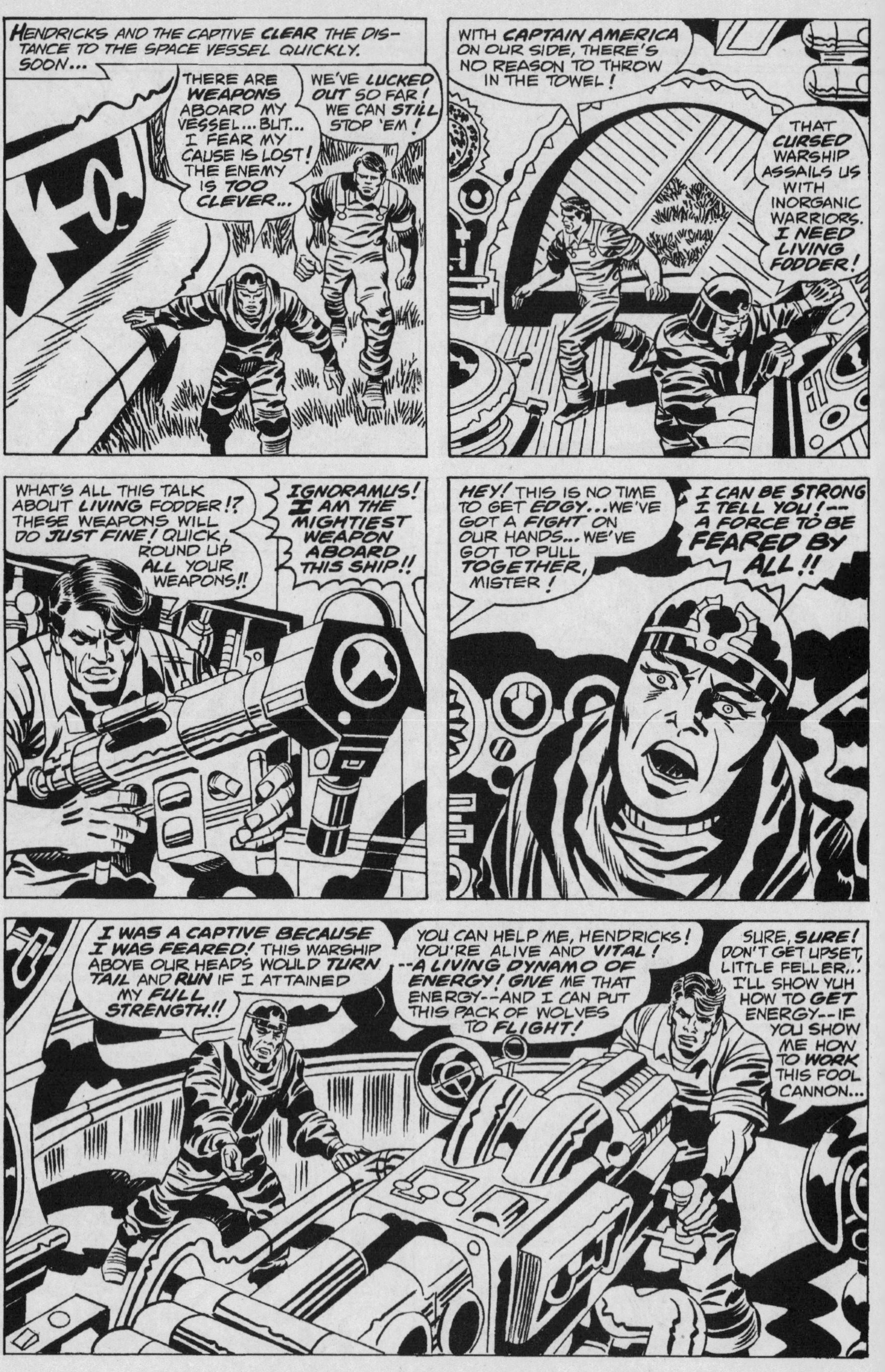

HENDRICKS AND THE CAPTIVE CLEAR THE DISTANCE TO THE SPACE VESSEL QUICKLY. SOON...
THERE ARE WEAPONS ABOARD MY VESSEL... BUT... I FEAR MY CAUSE IS LOST! THE ENEMY IS TOO CLEVER...
WE'VE LUCKED OUT SO FAR! WE CAN STILL STOP 'EM!
WITH CAPTAIN AMERICA ON OUR SIDE, THERE'S NO REASON TO THROW IN THE TOWEL!
THAT CURSED WARSHIP ASSAILS US WITH INORGANIC WARRIORS. I NEED LIVING FODDER!
WHAT'S ALL THIS TALK ABOUT LIVING FODDER!? THESE WEAPONS WILL DO JUST FINE! QUICK, ROUND UP ALL YOUR WEAPONS!!
IGNORAMUS! I AM THE MIGHTIEST WEAPON ABOARD THIS SHIP!!
HEY! THIS IS NO TIME TO GET EDGY... WE'VE GOT A FIGHT ON OUR HANDS... WE'VE GOT TO PULL TOGETHER, MISTER!
I CAN BE STRONG I TELL YOU!-- A FORCE TO BE FEARED BY ALL!!
I WAS A CAPTIVE BECAUSE I WAS FEARED! THIS WARSHIP ABOVE OUR HEADS WOULD TURN TAIL AND RUN IF I ATTAINED MY FULL STRENGTH!!
YOU CAN HELP ME, HENDRICKS! YOU'RE ALIVE AND VITAL! --A LIVING DYNAMO OF ENERGY! GIVE ME THAT ENERGY--AND I CAN PUT THIS PACK OF WOLVES TO FLIGHT!
SURE, SURE! DON'T GET UPSET, LITTLE FELLER... I'LL SHOW YUH HOW TO GET ENERGY--IF YOU SHOW ME HOW TO WORK THIS FOOL CANNON...

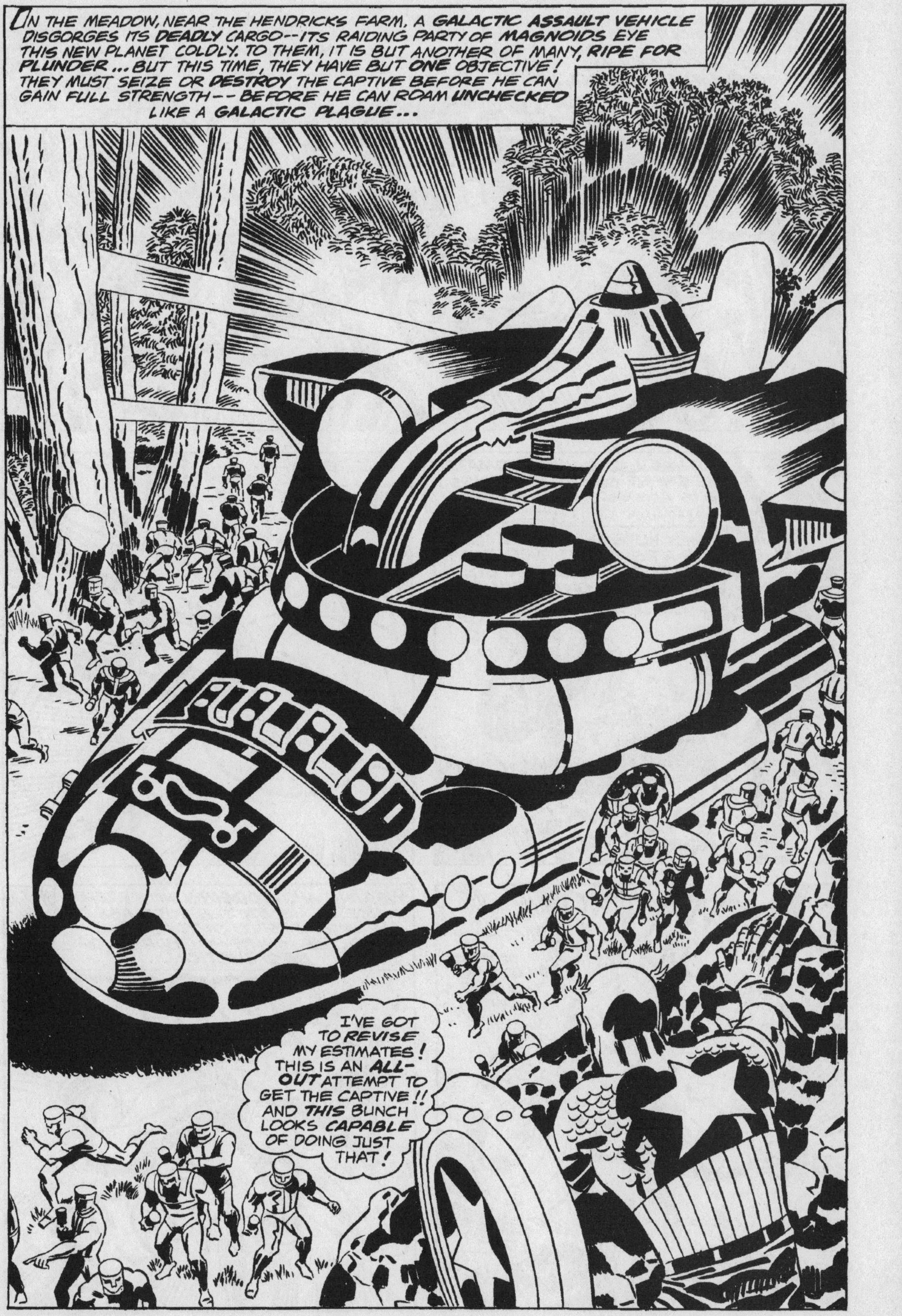
ON THE MEADOW, NEAR THE HENDRICKS FARM, A GALACTIC ASSAULT VEHICLE DISGORGES ITS DEADLY CARGO--ITS RAIDING PARTY OF MAGNOIDS EYE THIS NEW PLANET COLDLY. TO THEM, IT IS BUT ANOTHER OF MANY, RIPE FOR PLUNDER ... BUT THIS TIME, THEY HAVE BUT ONE OBJECTIVE! THEY MUST SEIZE OR DESTROY THE CAPTIVE BEFORE HE CAN GAIN FULL STRENGTH-- BEFORE HE CAN ROAM UNCHECKED LIKE A GALACTIC PLAGUE...
I'VE GOT TO REVISE MY ESTIMATES! THIS IS AN ALL-OUT ATTEMPT TO GET THE CAPTIVE!! AND THIS BUNCH LOOKS CAPABLE OF DOING JUST THAT!

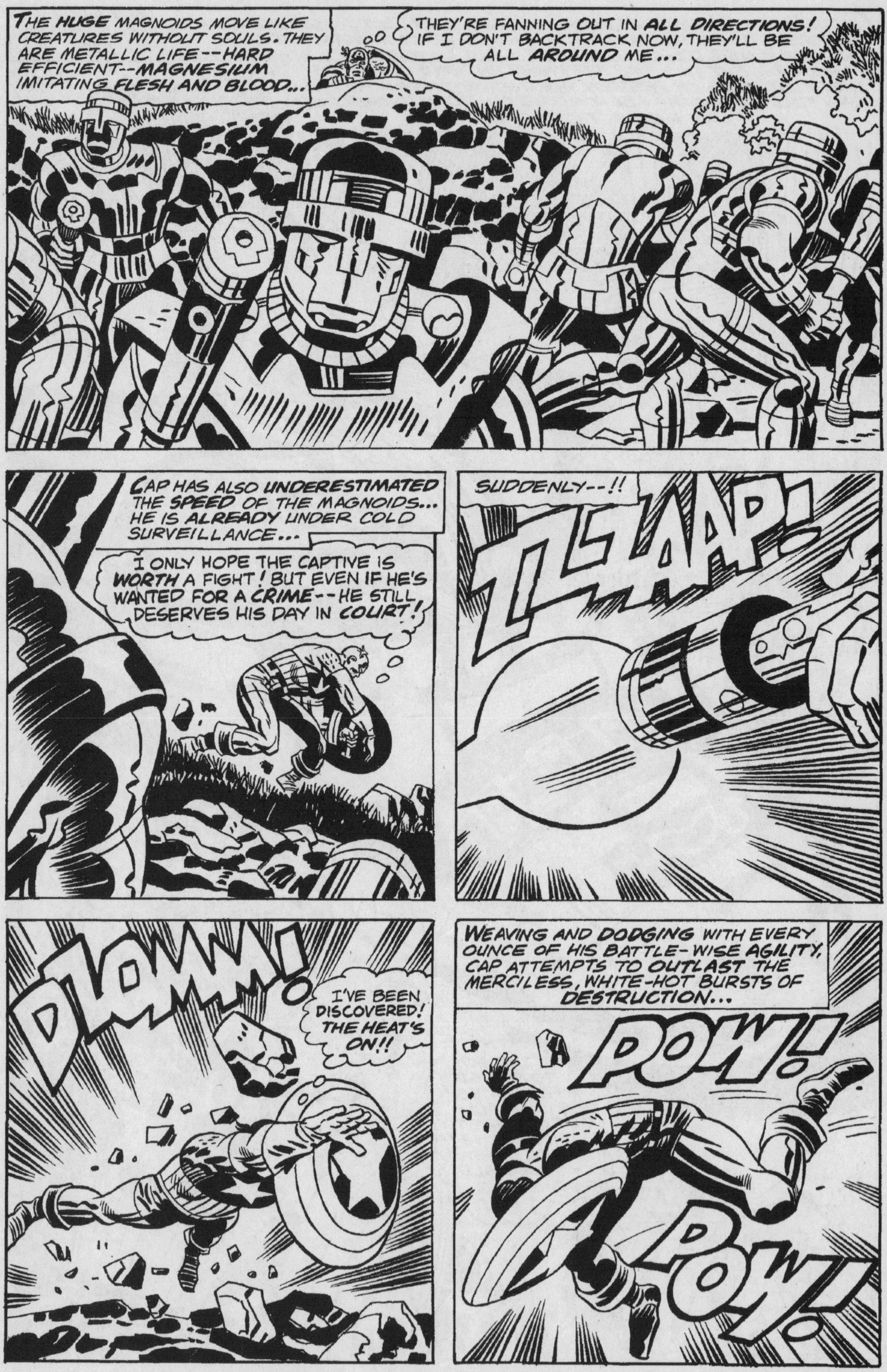
THE HUGE MAGNOIDS MOVE LIKE CREATURES WITHOUT SOULS. THEY ARE METALLIC LIFE--HARD EFFICIENT--MAGNESIUM IMITATING FLESH AND BLOOD...
THEY'RE FANNING OUT IN ALL DIRECTIONS! IF I DON'T BACKTRACK NOW, THEY'LL BE ALL AROUND ME...
CAP HAS ALSO UNDERESTIMATED THE SPEED OF THE MAGNOIDS... HE IS ALREADY UNDER COLD SURVEILLANCE...
I ONLY HOPE THE CAPTIVE IS WORTH A FIGHT! BUT EVEN IF HE'S WANTED FOR A CRIME--HE STILL DESERVES HIS DAY IN COURT!
SUDDENLY--!!
ZZZAAP!
DZOWW!
I'VE BEEN DISCOVERED! THE HEAT'S ON!!
WEAVING AND DODGING WITH EVERY OUNCE OF HIS BATTLE-WISE AGILITY, CAP ATTEMPTS TO OUTLAST THE MERCILESS, WHITE-HOT BURSTS OF DESTRUCTION...
POW!
POW!

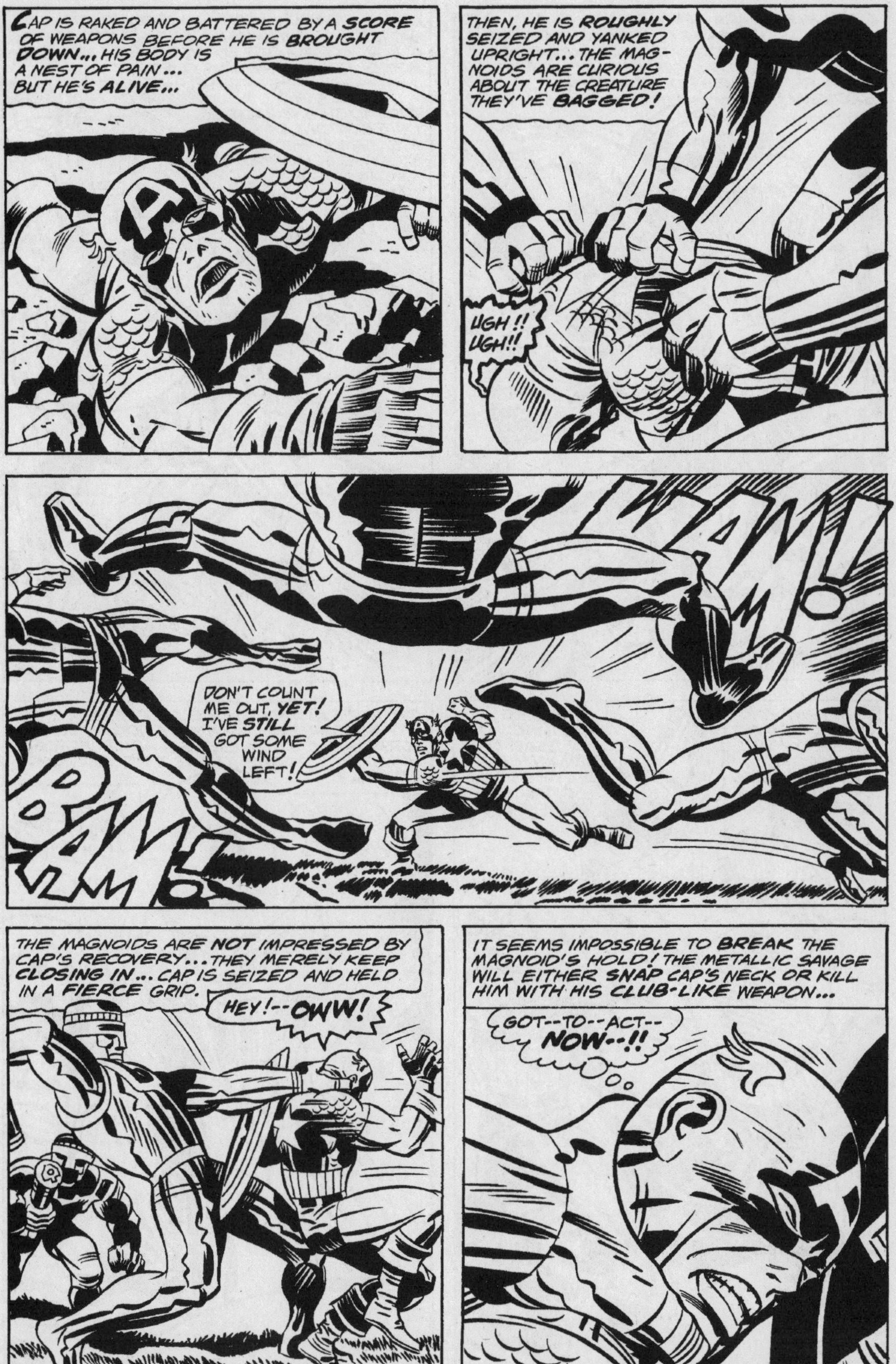
CAP IS RAKED AND BATTERED BY A SCORE OF WEAPONS BEFORE HE IS BROUGHT DOWN... HIS BODY IS A NEST OF PAIN... BUT HE'S ALIVE...
THEN, HE IS ROUGHLY SEIZED AND YANKED UPRIGHT... THE MAGNOIDS ARE CURIOUS ABOUT THE CREATURE THEY'VE BAGGED!
UGH!! UGH!!
WAM!
DON'T COUNT ME OUT, YET! I'VE STILL GOT SOME WIND LEFT!
BAM!
THE MAGNOIDS ARE NOT IMPRESSED BY CAP'S RECOVERY... THEY MERELY KEEP CLOSING IN... CAP IS SEIZED AND HELD IN A FIERCE GRIP.
HEY!--OWW!
IT SEEMS IMPOSSIBLE TO BREAK THE MAGNOID'S HOLD! THE METALLIC SAVAGE WILL EITHER SNAP CAP'S NECK OR KILL HIM WITH HIS CLUB-LIKE WEAPON...
GOT--TO--ACT--NOW--!!

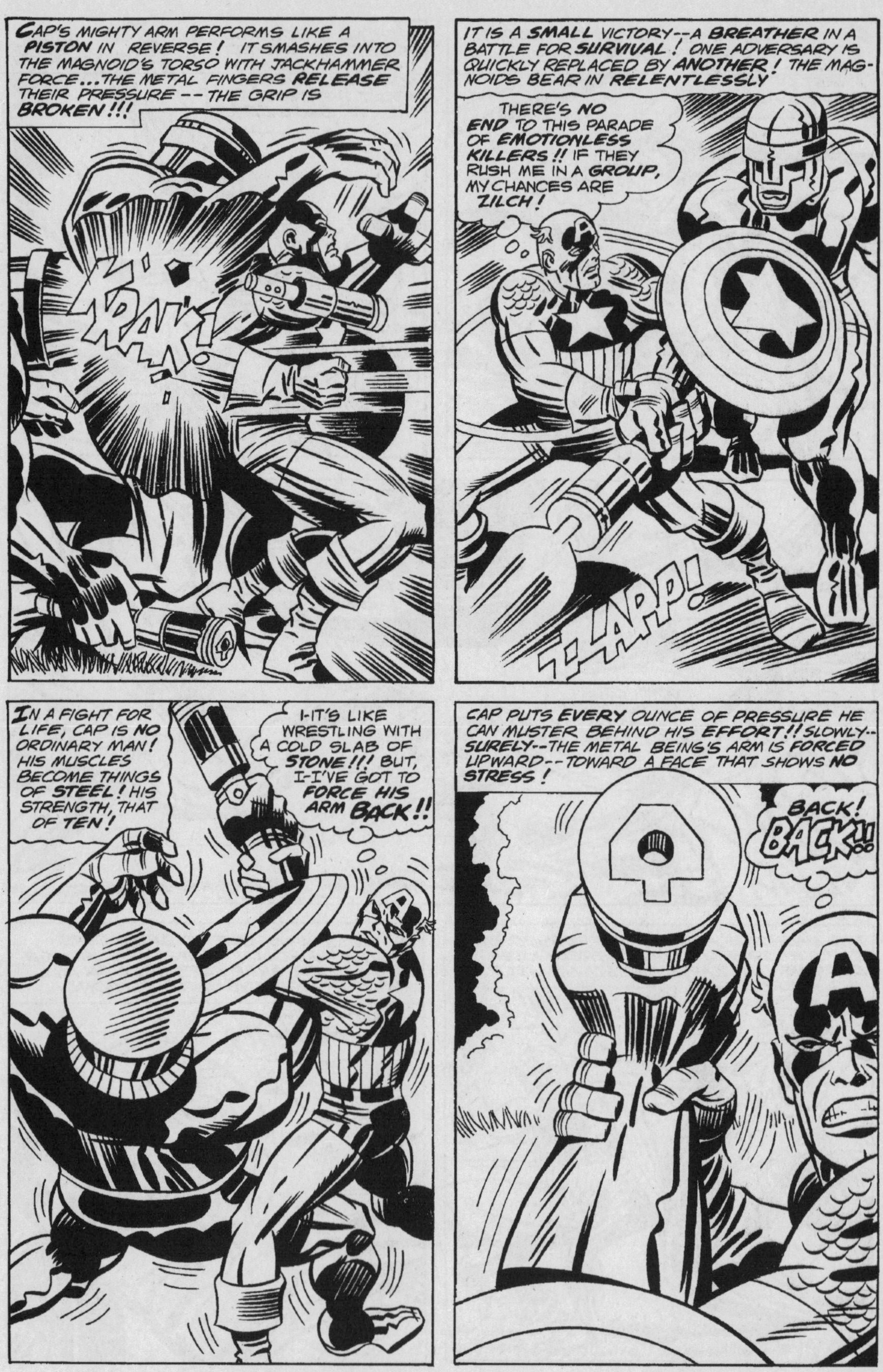
CAP'S MIGHTY ARM PERFORMS LIKE A PISTON IN REVERSE! IT SMASHES INTO THE MAGNOID'S TORSO WITH JACKHAMMER FORCE...THE METAL FINGERS RELEASE THEIR PRESSURE -- THE GRIP IS BROKEN!!!
KRAK!
IT IS A SMALL VICTORY--A BREATHER IN A BATTLE FOR SURVIVAL! ONE ADVERSARY IS QUICKLY REPLACED BY ANOTHER! THE MAGNOIDS BEAR IN RELENTLESSLY
THERE'S NO END TO THIS PARADE OF EMOTIONLESS KILLERS!! IF THEY RUSH ME IN A GROUP, MY CHANCES ARE ZILCH!
T-ZAPP!
IN A FIGHT FOR LIFE, CAP IS NO ORDINARY MAN! HIS MUSCLES BECOME THINGS OF STEEL! HIS STRENGTH, THAT OF TEN!
I-IT'S LIKE WRESTLING WITH A COLD SLAB OF STONE!!! BUT, I-I'VE GOT TO FORCE HIS ARM BACK!!
CAP PUTS EVERY OUNCE OF PRESSURE HE CAN MUSTER BEHIND HIS EFFORT!! SLOWLY--SURELY--THE METAL BEING'S ARM IS FORCED UPWARD--TOWARD A FACE THAT SHOWS NO STRESS!
BACK! BACK!!

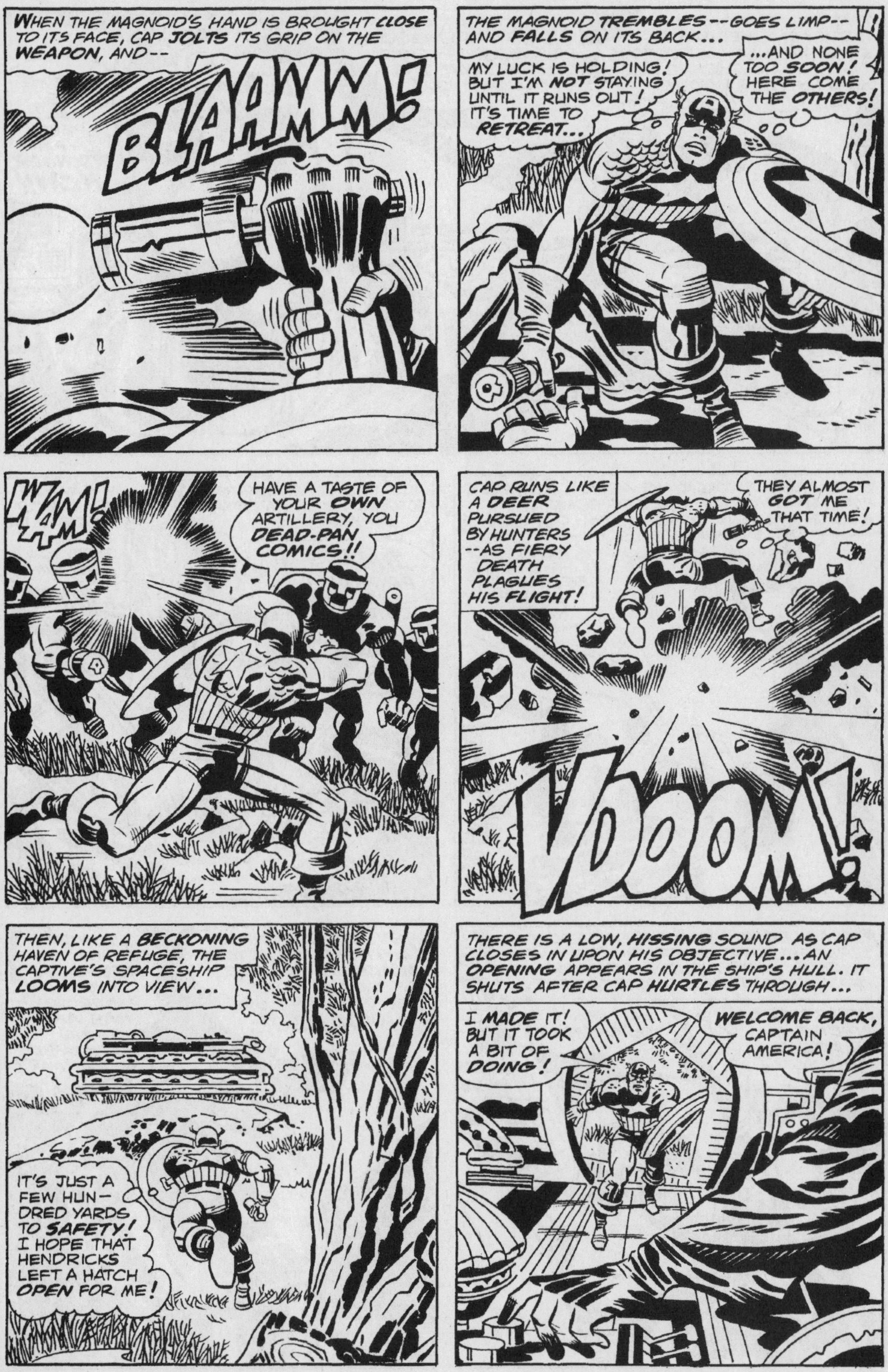
WHEN THE MAGNOID'S HAND IS BROUGHT CLOSE TO ITS FACE, CAP JOLTS ITS GRIP ON THE WEAPON, AND--
BLAAMM!
THE MAGNOID TREMBLES--GOES LIMP--AND FALLS ON ITS BACK...
MY LUCK IS HOLDING! BUT I'M NOT STAYING UNTIL IT RUNS OUT! IT'S TIME TO RETREAT...
...AND NONE TOO SOON! HERE COME THE OTHERS!
WAM!
HAVE A TASTE OF YOUR OWN ARTILLERY, YOU DEAD-PAN COMICS!!
CAP RUNS LIKE A DEER PURSUED BY HUNTERS --AS FIERY DEATH PLAGUES HIS FLIGHT!
THEY ALMOST GOT ME THAT TIME!
VDOOM!
THEN, LIKE A BECKONING HAVEN OF REFUGE, THE CAPTIVE'S SPACESHIP LOOMS INTO VIEW...
IT'S JUST A FEW HUN-DRED YARDS TO SAFETY! I HOPE THAT HENDRICKS LEFT A HATCH OPEN FOR ME!
THERE IS A LOW, HISSING SOUND AS CAP CLOSES IN UPON HIS OBJECTIVE... AN OPENING APPEARS IN THE SHIP'S HULL. IT SHUTS AFTER CAP HURTLES THROUGH...
I MADE IT! BUT IT TOOK A BIT OF DOING!
WELCOME BACK, CAPTAIN AMERICA!

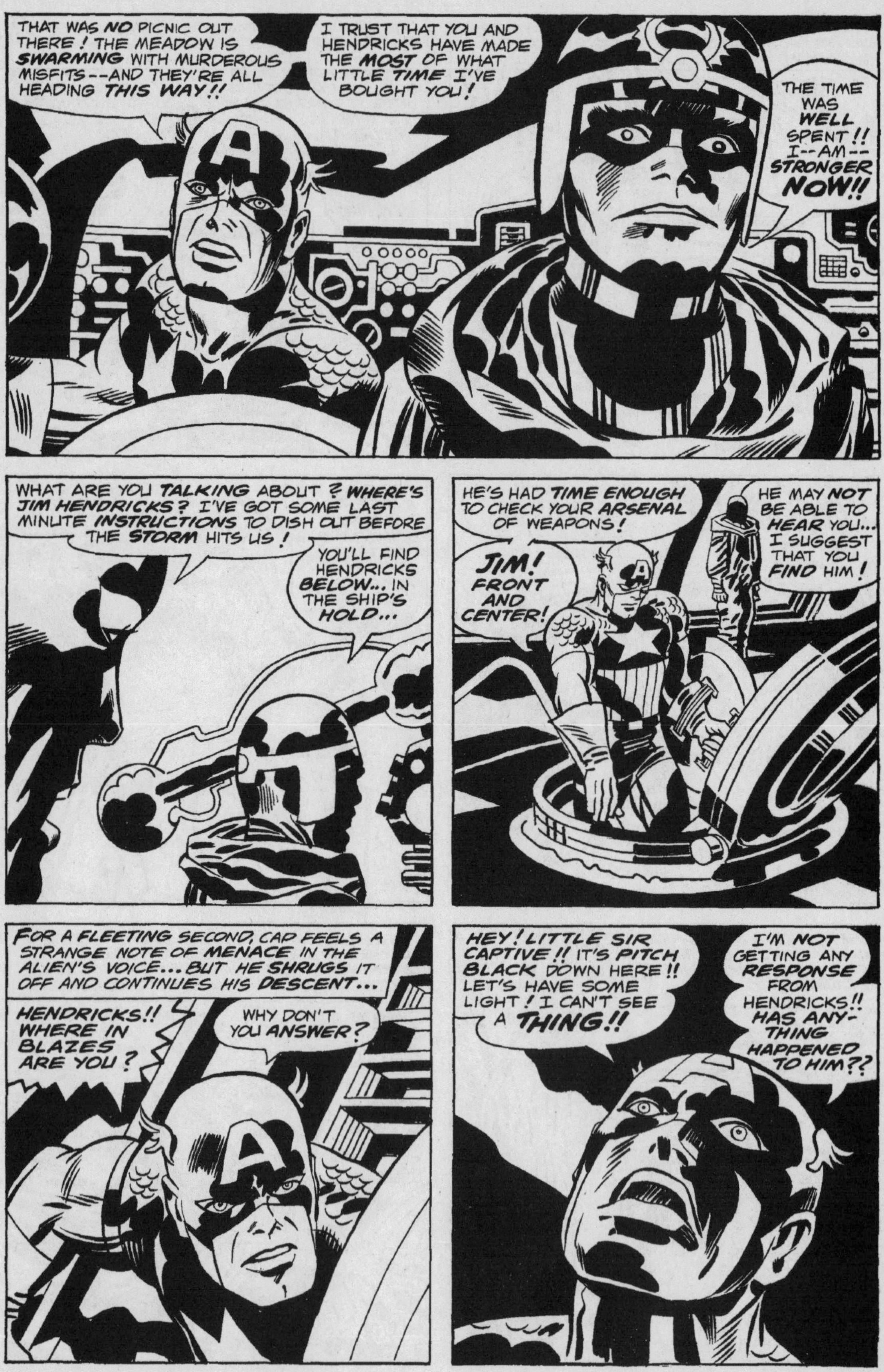
THAT WAS NO PICNIC OUT THERE! THE MEADOW IS SWARMING WITH MURDEROUS MISFITS--AND THEY'RE ALL HEADING THIS WAY!!
I TRUST THAT YOU AND HENDRICKS HAVE MADE THE MOST OF WHAT LITTLE TIME I'VE BOUGHT YOU!
THE TIME WAS WELL SPENT!! I--AM--STRONGER NOW!!
WHAT ARE YOU TALKING ABOUT? WHERE'S JIM HENDRICKS? I'VE GOT SOME LAST MINUTE INSTRUCTIONS TO DISH OUT BEFORE THE STORM HITS US!
YOU'LL FIND HENDRICKS BELOW... IN THE SHIP'S HOLD...
HE'S HAD TIME ENOUGH TO CHECK YOUR ARSENAL OF WEAPONS!
JIM! FRONT AND CENTER!
HE MAY NOT BE ABLE TO HEAR YOU... I SUGGEST THAT YOU FIND HIM!
FOR A FLEETING SECOND, CAP FEELS A STRANGE NOTE OF MENACE IN THE ALIEN'S VOICE... BUT HE SHRUGS IT OFF AND CONTINUES HIS DESCENT...
HENDRICKS!! WHERE IN BLAZES ARE YOU?
WHY DON'T YOU ANSWER?
HEY! LITTLE SIR CAPTIVE!! IT'S PITCH BLACK DOWN HERE!! LET'S HAVE SOME LIGHT! I CAN'T SEE A THING!!
I'M NOT GETTING ANY RESPONSE FROM HENDRICKS!! HAS ANYTHING HAPPENED TO HIM??

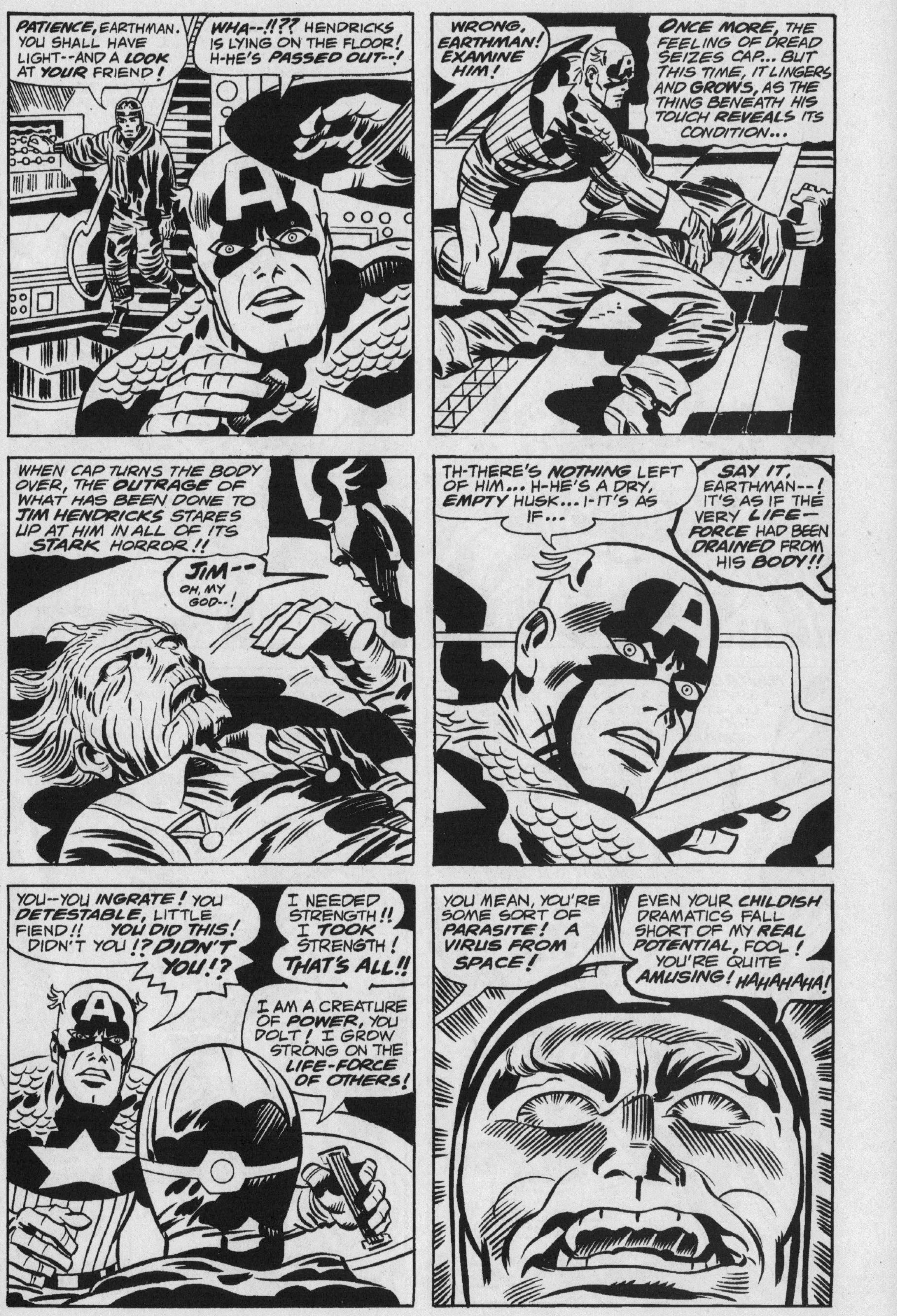
PATIENCE, EARTHMAN. YOU SHALL HAVE LIGHT--AND A LOOK AT YOUR FRIEND!
WHA--!!?? HENDRICKS IS LYING ON THE FLOOR! H-HE'S PASSED OUT--!
WRONG, EARTHMAN! EXAMINE HIM!
ONCE MORE, THE FEELING OF DREAD SEIZES CAP... BUT THIS TIME, IT LINGERS AND GROWS, AS THE THING BENEATH HIS TOUCH REVEALS ITS CONDITION...
WHEN CAP TURNS THE BODY OVER, THE OUTRAGE OF WHAT HAS BEEN DONE TO JIM HENDRICKS STARES UP AT HIM IN ALL OF ITS STARK HORROR!!
JIM-- OH, MY GOD--!
TH-THERE'S NOTHING LEFT OF HIM... H-HE'S A DRY, EMPTY HUSK... I-IT'S AS IF...
SAY IT, EARTHMAN--! IT'S AS IF THE VERY LIFE-FORCE HAD BEEN DRAINED FROM HIS BODY!!
YOU--YOU INGRATE! YOU DETESTABLE, LITTLE FIEND!! YOU DID THIS! DIDN'T YOU!? DIDN'T YOU!?
I NEEDED STRENGTH!! I TOOK STRENGTH! THAT'S ALL!!
I AM A CREATURE OF POWER, YOU DOLT! I GROW STRONG ON THE LIFE-FORCE OF OTHERS!
YOU MEAN, YOU'RE SOME SORT OF PARASITE! A VIRUS FROM SPACE!
EVEN YOUR CHILDISH DRAMATICS FALL SHORT OF MY REAL POTENTIAL, FOOL! YOU'RE QUITE AMUSING! HAHAHAHA!

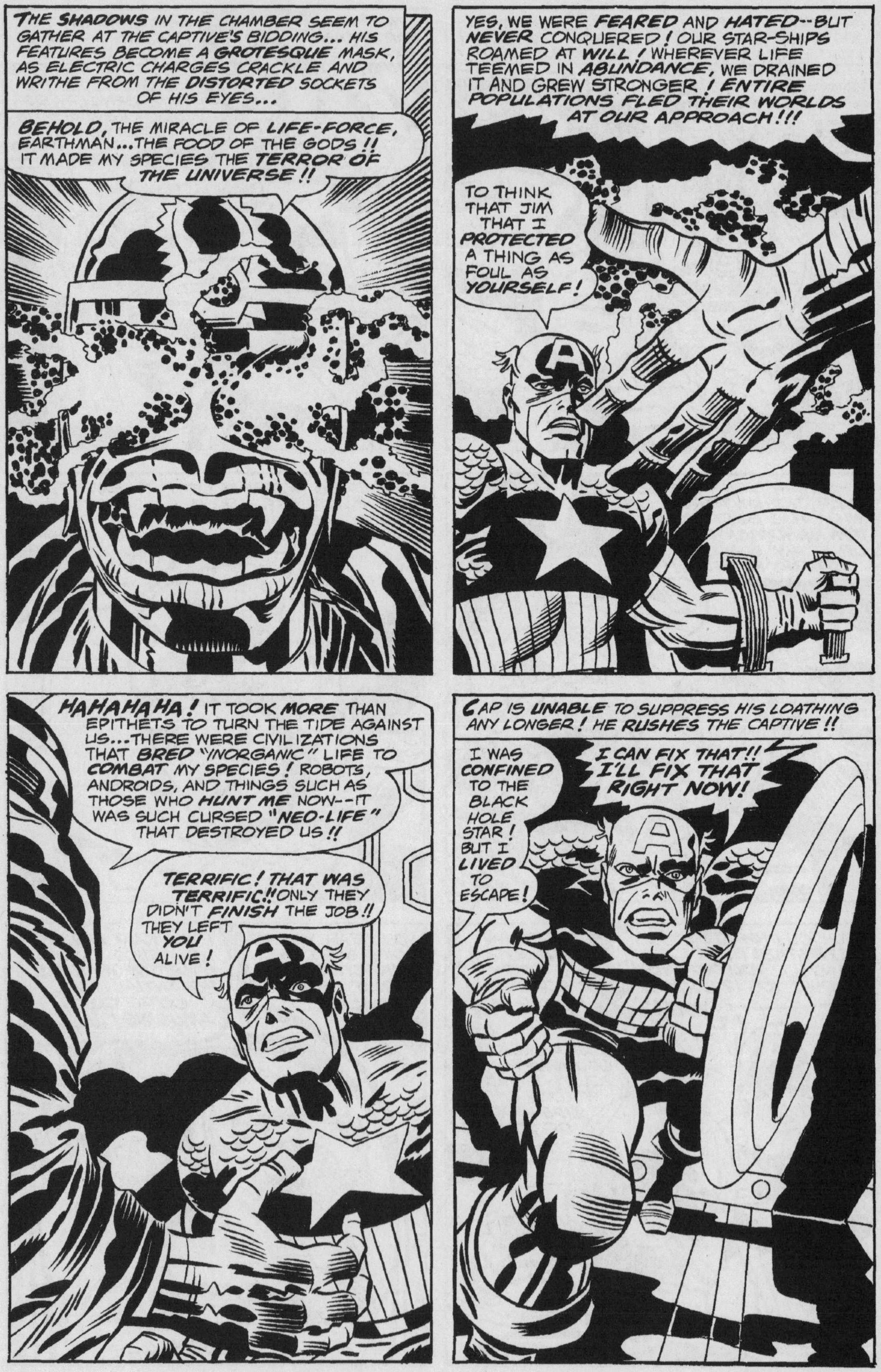
THE SHADOWS IN THE CHAMBER SEEM TO GATHER AT THE CAPTIVE'S BIDDING... HIS FEATURES BECOME A GROTESQUE MASK, AS ELECTRIC CHARGES CRACKLE AND WRITHE FROM THE DISTORTED SOCKETS OF HIS EYES...
BEHOLD, THE MIRACLE OF LIFE-FORCE, EARTHMAN...THE FOOD OF THE GODS!! IT MADE MY SPECIES THE TERROR OF THE UNIVERSE!!
YES, WE WERE FEARED AND HATED--BUT NEVER CONQUERED! OUR STAR-SHIPS ROAMED AT WILL! WHEREVER LIFE TEEMED IN ABUNDANCE, WE DRAINED IT AND GREW STRONGER! ENTIRE POPULATIONS FLED THEIR WORLDS AT OUR APPROACH!!!
TO THINK THAT JIM THAT I PROTECTED A THING AS FOUL AS YOURSELF!
HAHAHAHA! IT TOOK MORE THAN EPITHETS TO TURN THE TIDE AGAINST US...THERE WERE CIVILIZATIONS THAT BRED "INORGANIC" LIFE TO COMBAT MY SPECIES! ROBOTS, ANDROIDS, AND THINGS SUCH AS THOSE WHO HUNT ME NOW--IT WAS SUCH CURSED "NEO-LIFE" THAT DESTROYED US!!
TERRIFIC! THAT WAS TERRIFIC!! ONLY THEY DIDN'T FINISH THE JOB!! THEY LEFT YOU ALIVE!
CAP IS UNABLE TO SUPPRESS HIS LOATHING ANY LONGER! HE RUSHES THE CAPTIVE!!
I WAS CONFINED TO THE BLACK HOLE STAR! BUT I LIVED TO ESCAPE!
I CAN FIX THAT!! I'LL FIX THAT RIGHT NOW!

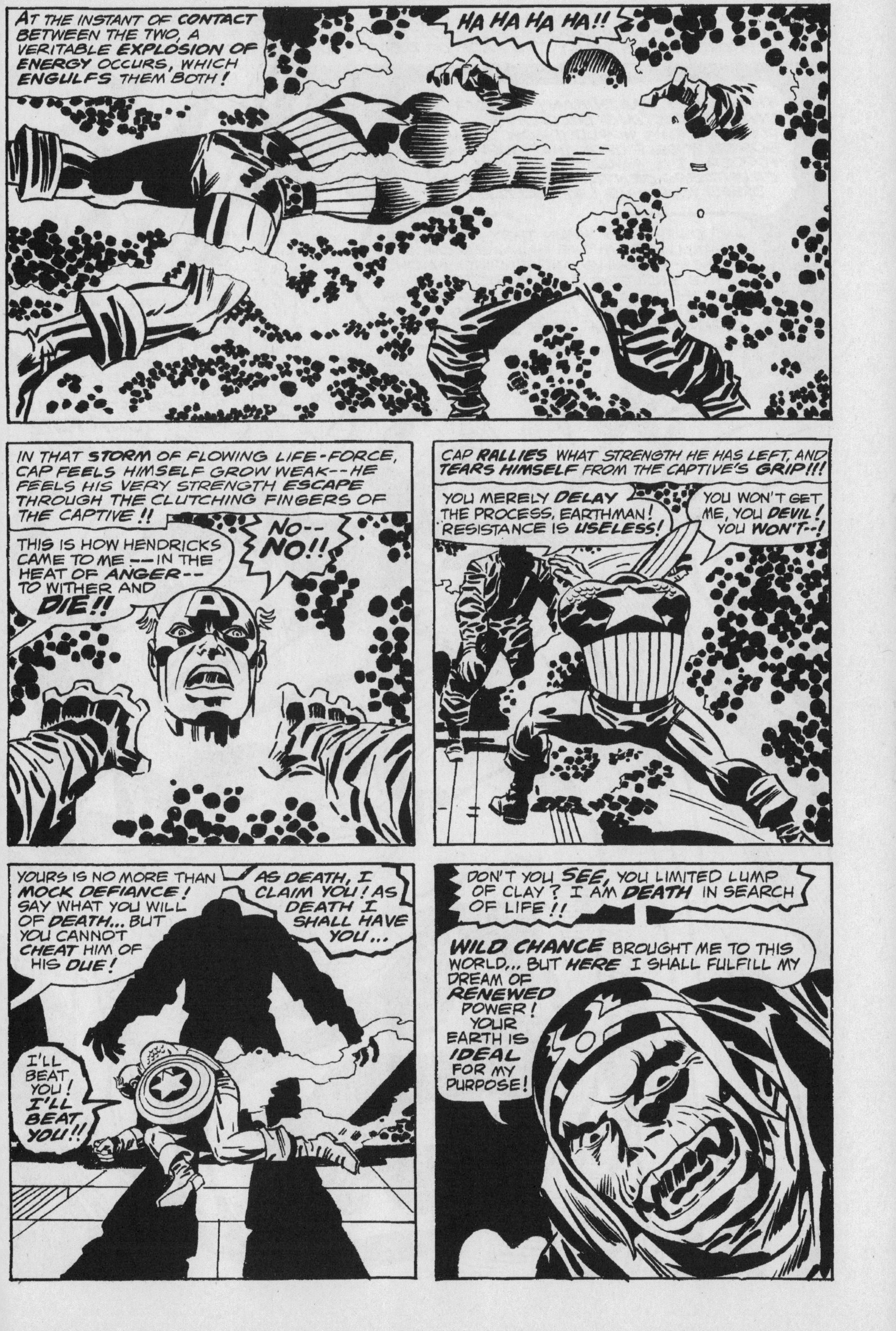

AT THE INSTANT OF CONTACT BETWEEN THE TWO, A VERITABLE EXPLOSION OF ENERGY OCCURS, WHICH ENGULFS THEM BOTH!
HA HA HA HA HA!!
IN THAT STORM OF FLOWING LIFE-FORCE, CAP FEELS HIMSELF GROW WEAK--HE FEELS HIS VERY STRENGTH ESCAPE THROUGH THE CLUTCHING FINGERS OF THE CAPTIVE!!
THIS IS HOW HENDRICKS CAME TO ME --IN THE HEAT OF ANGER-- TO WITHER AND DIE!!
NO-- NO!!
CAP RALLIES WHAT STRENGTH HE HAS LEFT, AND TEARS HIMSELF FROM THE CAPTIVE'S GRIP!!!
YOU MERELY DELAY THE PROCESS, EARTHMAN! RESISTANCE IS USELESS!
YOU WON'T GET ME, YOU DEVIL! YOU WON'T--!
YOURS IS NO MORE THAN MOCK DEFIANCE! SAY WHAT YOU WILL OF DEATH... BUT YOU CANNOT CHEAT HIM OF HIS DUE!
AS DEATH, I CLAIM YOU! AS DEATH I SHALL HAVE YOU...
I'LL BEAT YOU! I'LL BEAT YOU!!
DON'T YOU SEE, YOU LIMITED LUMP OF CLAY? I AM DEATH IN SEARCH OF LIFE!!
WILD CHANCE BROUGHT ME TO THIS WORLD,.. BUT HERE I SHALL FULFILL MY DREAM OF RENEWED POWER! YOUR EARTH IS IDEAL FOR MY PURPOSE!

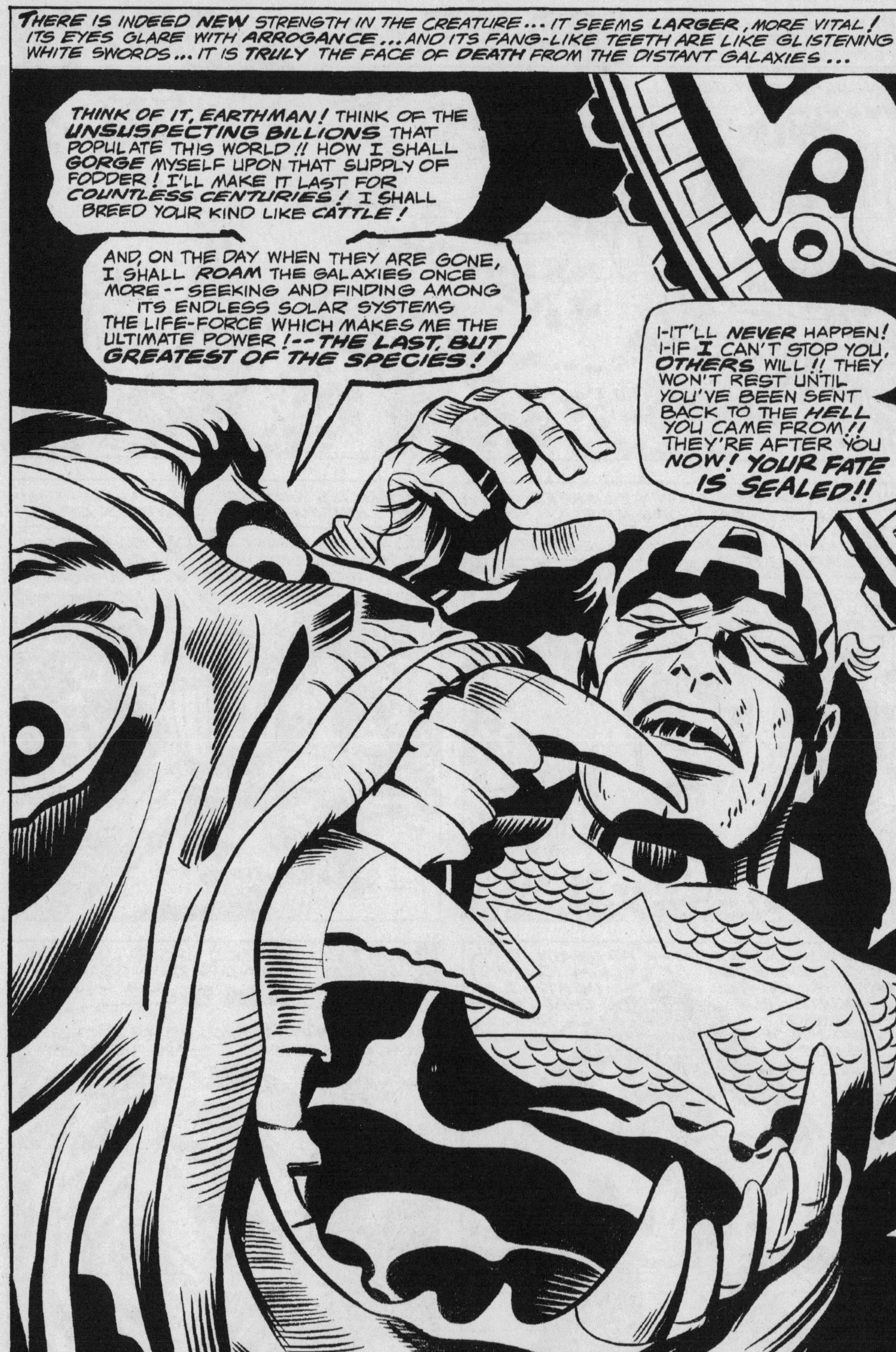
THERE IS INDEED NEW STRENGTH IN THE CREATURE... IT SEEMS LARGER, MORE VITAL! ITS EYES GLARE WITH ARROGANCE... AND ITS FANG-LIKE TEETH ARE LIKE GLISTENING WHITE SWORDS... IT IS TRULY THE FACE OF DEATH FROM THE DISTANT GALAXIES...
THINK OF IT, EARTHMAN! THINK OF THE UNSUSPECTING BILLIONS THAT POPULATE THIS WORLD!! HOW I SHALL GORGE MYSELF UPON THAT SUPPLY OF FODDER! I'LL MAKE IT LAST FOR COUNTLESS CENTURIES! I SHALL BREED YOUR KIND LIKE CATTLE!
AND, ON THE DAY WHEN THEY ARE GONE, I SHALL ROAM THE GALAXIES ONCE MORE--SEEKING AND FINDING AMONG ITS ENDLESS SOLAR SYSTEMS THE LIFE-FORCE WHICH MAKES ME THE ULTIMATE POWER!--THE LAST, BUT GREATEST OF THE SPECIES!
I-IT'LL NEVER HAPPEN! I-IF I CAN'T STOP YOU, OTHERS WILL!! THEY WON'T REST UNTIL YOU'VE BEEN SENT BACK TO THE HELL YOU CAME FROM!! THEY'RE AFTER YOU NOW! YOUR FATE IS SEALED!!

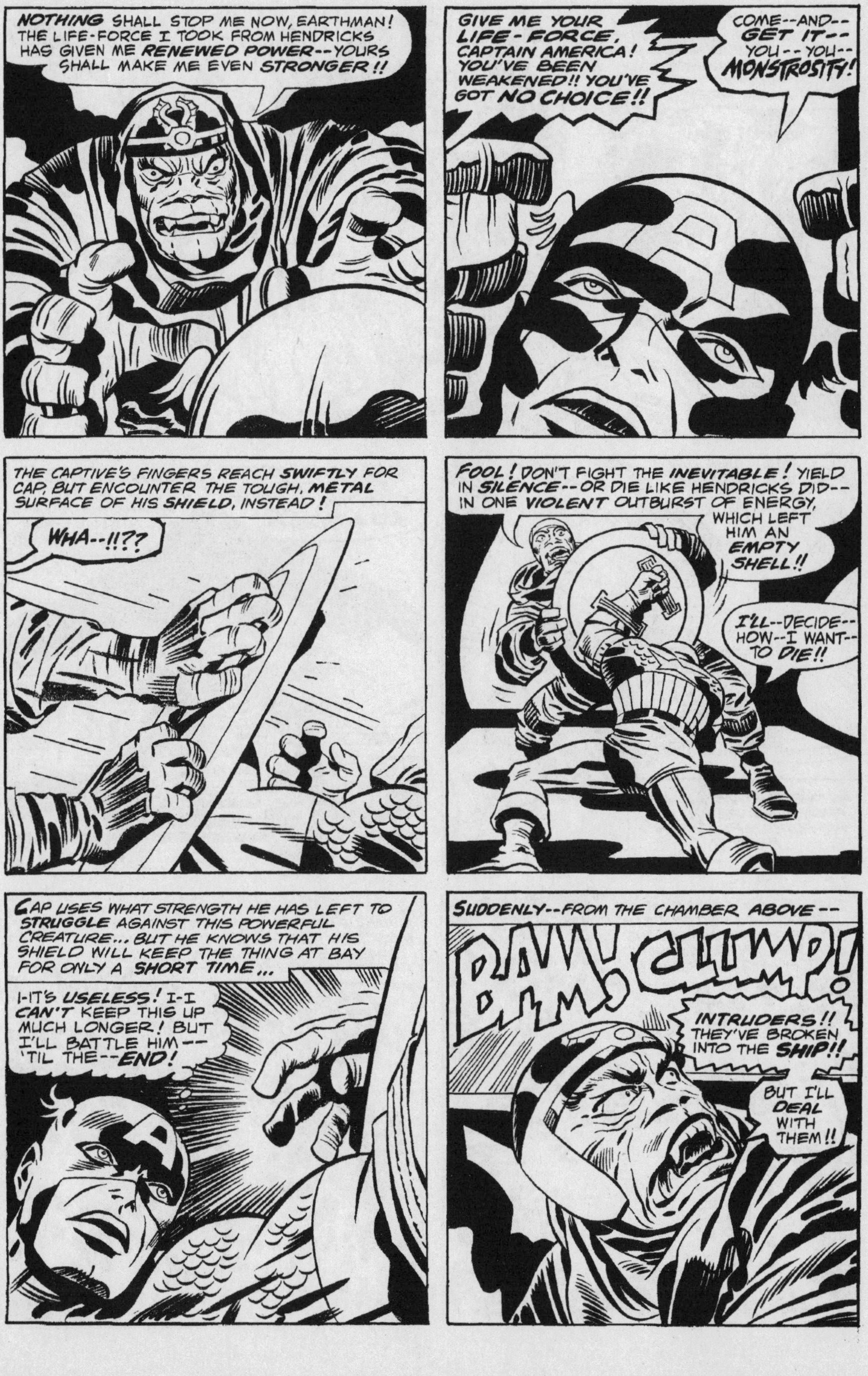
NOTHING SHALL STOP ME NOW, EARTHMAN! THE LIFE-FORCE I TOOK FROM HENDRICKS HAS GIVEN ME RENEWED POWER--YOURS SHALL MAKE ME EVEN STRONGER!!
GIVE ME YOUR LIFE-FORCE, CAPTAIN AMERICA! YOU'VE BEEN WEAKENED!! YOU'VE GOT NO CHOICE!!
COME--AND--GET IT--YOU--YOU--MONSTROSITY!
THE CAPTIVE'S FINGERS REACH SWIFTLY FOR CAP, BUT ENCOUNTER THE TOUGH, METAL SURFACE OF HIS SHIELD, INSTEAD!
WHA--!!??
FOOL! DON'T FIGHT THE INEVITABLE! YIELD IN SILENCE--OR DIE LIKE HENDRICKS DID--IN ONE VIOLENT OUTBURST OF ENERGY, WHICH LEFT HIM AN EMPTY SHELL!!
I'LL--DECIDE--HOW--I WANT--TO DIE!!
CAP USES WHAT STRENGTH HE HAS LEFT TO STRUGGLE AGAINST THIS POWERFUL CREATURE... BUT HE KNOWS THAT HIS SHIELD WILL KEEP THE THING AT BAY FOR ONLY A SHORT TIME...
I-IT'S USELESS! I-I CAN'T KEEP THIS UP MUCH LONGER! BUT I'LL BATTLE HIM--'TIL THE--END!
SUDDENLY--FROM THE CHAMBER ABOVE--
BAM! CLUMP!
INTRUDERS!! THEY'VE BROKEN INTO THE SHIP!!
BUT I'LL DEAL WITH THEM!!

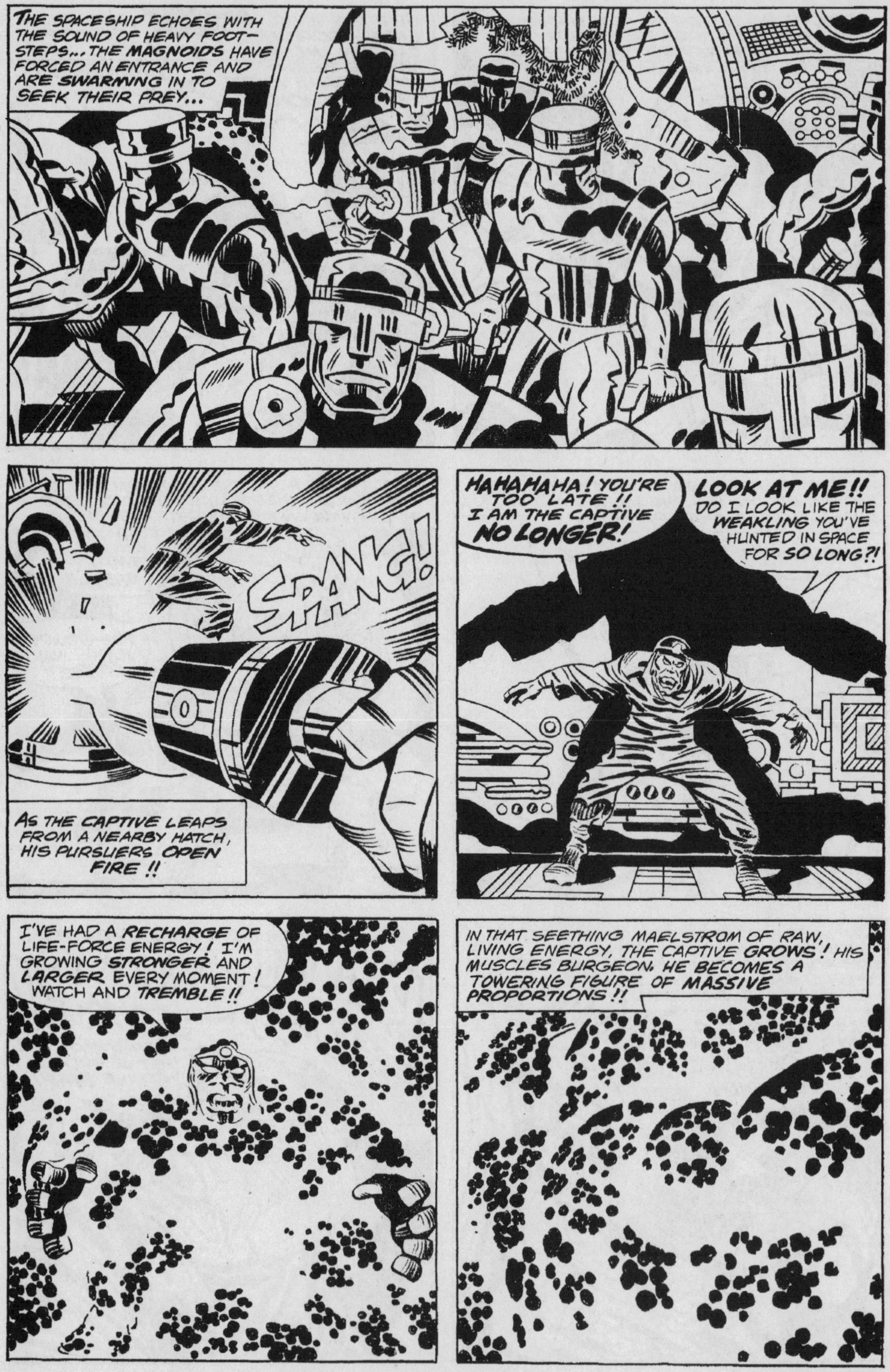
THE SPACESHIP ECHOES WITH THE SOUND OF HEAVY FOOT-STEPS... THE MAGNOIDS HAVE FORCED AN ENTRANCE AND ARE SWARMING IN TO SEEK THEIR PREY...
SPANG!
AS THE CAPTIVE LEAPS FROM A NEARBY HATCH, HIS PURSUERS OPEN FIRE !!
HAHAHAHA! YOU'RE TOO LATE !! I AM THE CAPTIVE NO LONGER!
LOOK AT ME!! DO I LOOK LIKE THE WEAKLING YOU'VE HUNTED IN SPACE FOR SO LONG?!
I'VE HAD A RECHARGE OF LIFE-FORCE ENERGY! I'M GROWING STRONGER AND LARGER EVERY MOMENT! WATCH AND TREMBLE!!
IN THAT SEETHING MAELSTROM OF RAW, LIVING ENERGY, THE CAPTIVE GROWS! HIS MUSCLES BURGEON. HE BECOMES A TOWERING FIGURE OF MASSIVE PROPORTIONS!!

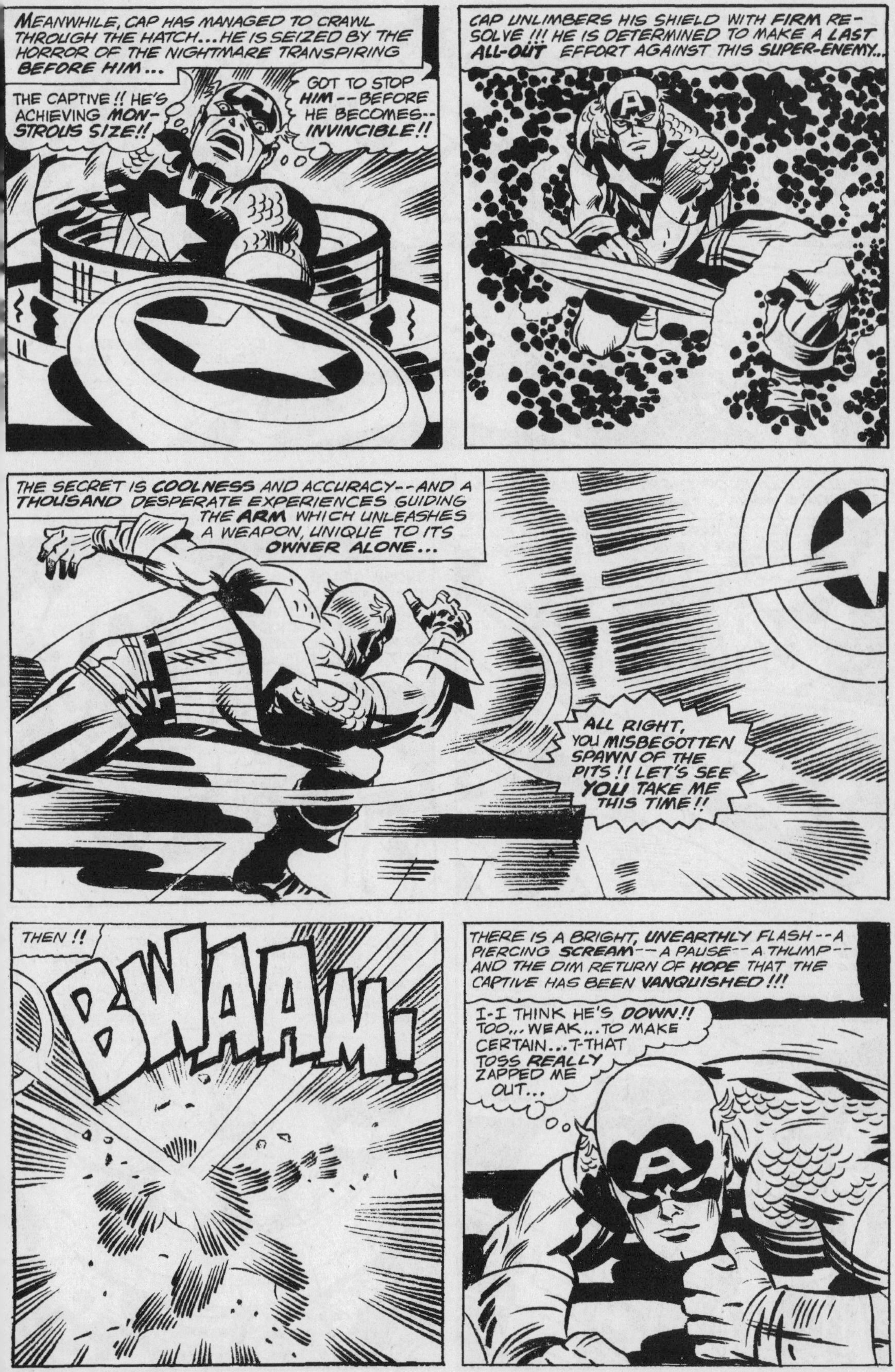
MEANWHILE, CAP HAS MANAGED TO CRAWL THROUGH THE HATCH... HE IS SEIZED BY THE HORROR OF THE NIGHTMARE TRANSPIRING BEFORE HIM...
THE CAPTIVE!! HE'S ACHIEVING MON-STROUS SIZE!!
GOT TO STOP HIM--BEFORE HE BECOMES--INVINCIBLE!!
CAP UNLIMBERS HIS SHIELD WITH FIRM RE-SOLVE!!! HE IS DETERMINED TO MAKE A LAST ALL-OUT EFFORT AGAINST THIS SUPER-ENEMY...
THE SECRET IS COOLNESS AND ACCURACY--AND A THOUSAND DESPERATE EXPERIENCES GUIDING THE ARM WHICH UNLEASHES A WEAPON, UNIQUE TO ITS OWNER ALONE...
ALL RIGHT, YOU MISBEGOTTEN SPAWN OF THE PITS!! LET'S SEE YOU TAKE ME THIS TIME!!
THEN!!
BWAAM!
THERE IS A BRIGHT, UNEARTHLY FLASH--A PIERCING SCREAM--A PAUSE--A THUMP--AND THE DIM RETURN OF HOPE THAT THE CAPTIVE HAS BEEN VANQUISHED!!!
I-I THINK HE'S DOWN!! TOO... WEAK... TO MAKE CERTAIN... T-THAT TOSS REALLY ZAPPED ME OUT...

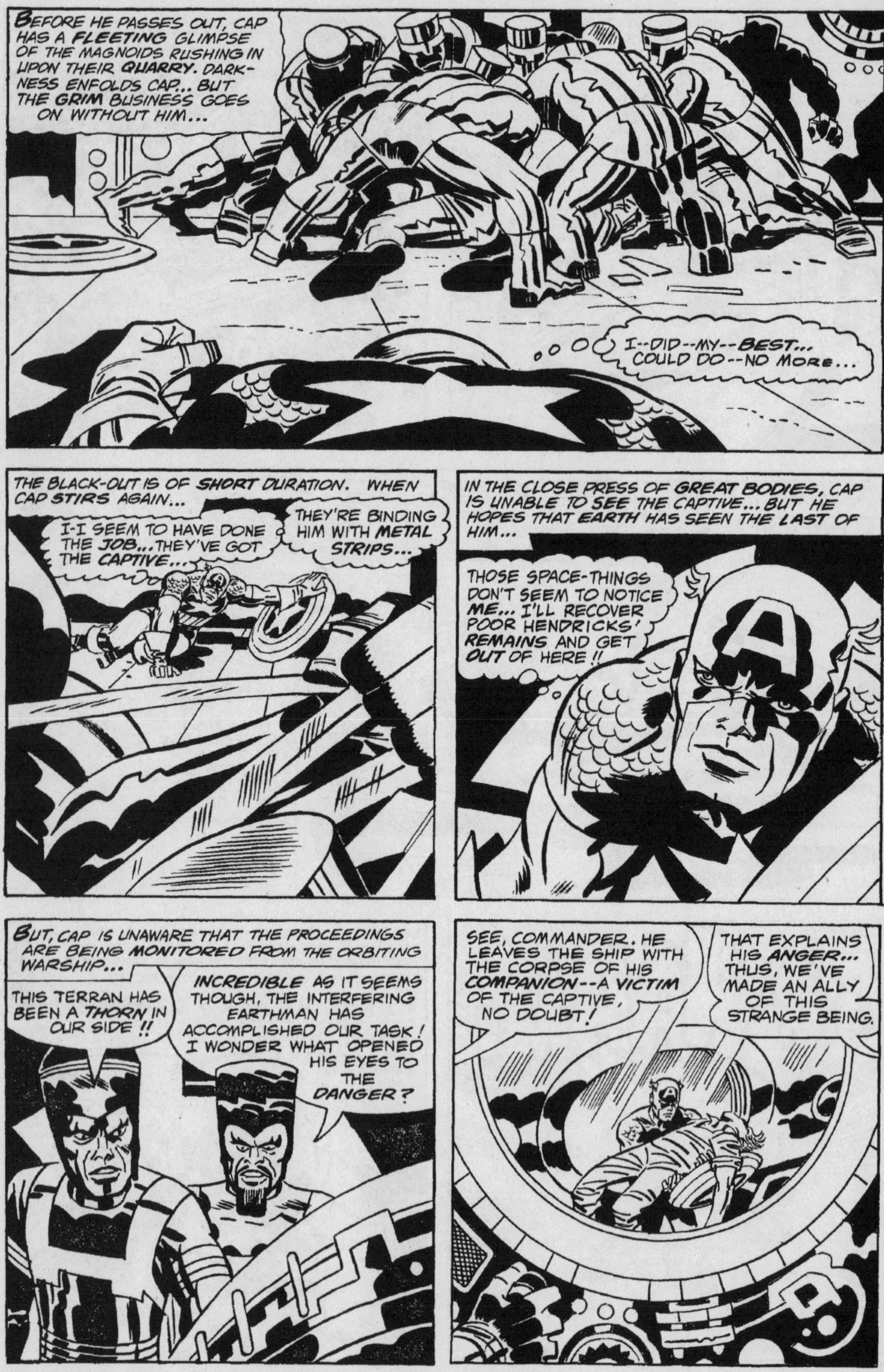
BEFORE HE PASSES OUT, CAP HAS A FLEETING GLIMPSE OF THE MAGNOIDS RUSHING IN UPON THEIR QUARRY. DARKNESS ENFOLDS CAP... BUT THE GRIM BUSINESS GOES ON WITHOUT HIM...
I--DID--MY--BEST... COULD DO--NO MORE...
THE BLACK-OUT IS OF SHORT DURATION. WHEN CAP STIRS AGAIN...
I-I SEEM TO HAVE DONE THE JOB... THEY'VE GOT THE CAPTIVE...
THEY'RE BINDING HIM WITH METAL STRIPS...
IN THE CLOSE PRESS OF GREAT BODIES, CAP IS UNABLE TO SEE THE CAPTIVE... BUT HE HOPES THAT EARTH HAS SEEN THE LAST OF HIM...
THOSE SPACE-THINGS DON'T SEEM TO NOTICE ME... I'LL RECOVER POOR HENDRICKS' REMAINS AND GET OUT OF HERE!!
BUT, CAP IS UNAWARE THAT THE PROCEEDINGS ARE BEING MONITORED FROM THE ORBITING WARSHIP...
THIS TERRAN HAS BEEN A THORN IN OUR SIDE!!
INCREDIBLE AS IT SEEMS THOUGH, THE INTERFERING EARTHMAN HAS ACCOMPLISHED OUR TASK! I WONDER WHAT OPENED HIS EYES TO THE DANGER?
SEE, COMMANDER. HE LEAVES THE SHIP WITH THE CORPSE OF HIS COMPANION--A VICTIM OF THE CAPTIVE, NO DOUBT!
THAT EXPLAINS HIS ANGER... THUS, WE'VE MADE AN ALLY OF THIS STRANGE BEING.

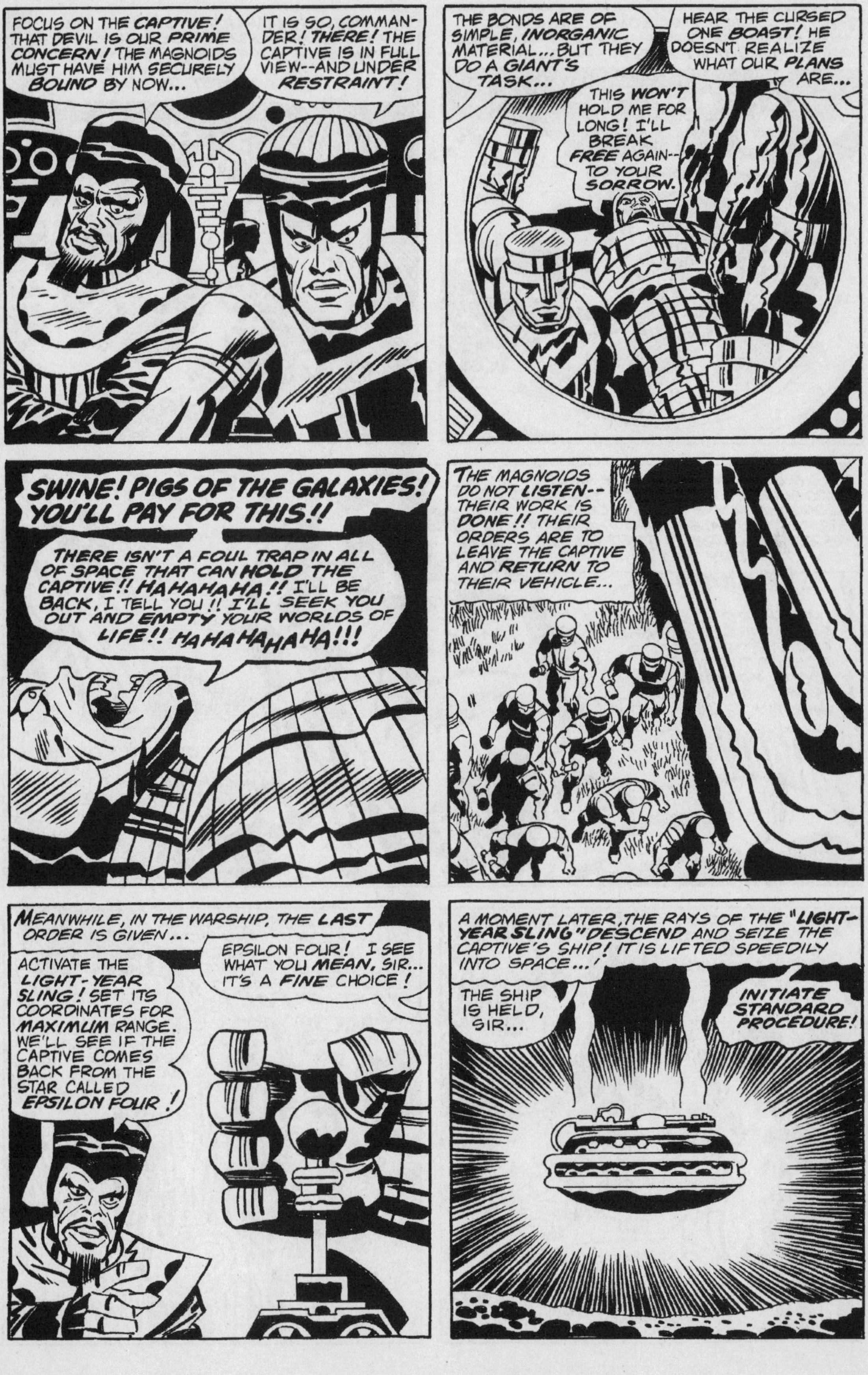
FOCUS ON THE CAPTIVE! THAT DEVIL IS OUR PRIME CONCERN! THE MAGNOIDS MUST HAVE HIM SECURELY BOUND BY NOW...
IT IS SO, COMMANDER! THERE! THE CAPTIVE IS IN FULL VIEW--AND UNDER RESTRAINT!
THE BONDS ARE OF SIMPLE, INORGANIC MATERIAL... BUT THEY DO A GIANT'S TASK...
HEAR THE CURSED ONE BOAST! HE DOESN'T REALIZE WHAT OUR PLANS ARE...
THIS WON'T HOLD ME FOR LONG! I'LL BREAK FREE AGAIN--TO YOUR SORROW.
SWINE! PIGS OF THE GALAXIES! YOU'LL PAY FOR THIS!!
THERE ISN'T A FOUL TRAP IN ALL OF SPACE THAT CAN HOLD THE CAPTIVE!! HAHAHAHA!! I'LL BE BACK, I TELL YOU!! I'LL SEEK YOU OUT AND EMPTY YOUR WORLDS OF LIFE!! HAHAHAHAHA!!!
THE MAGNOIDS DO NOT LISTEN--THEIR WORK IS DONE!! THEIR ORDERS ARE TO LEAVE THE CAPTIVE AND RETURN TO THEIR VEHICLE...
MEANWHILE, IN THE WARSHIP, THE LAST ORDER IS GIVEN...
ACTIVATE THE LIGHT-YEAR SLING! SET ITS COORDINATES FOR MAXIMUM RANGE. WE'LL SEE IF THE CAPTIVE COMES BACK FROM THE STAR CALLED EPSILON FOUR!
EPSILON FOUR! I SEE WHAT YOU MEAN, SIR... IT'S A FINE CHOICE!
A MOMENT LATER, THE RAYS OF THE "LIGHT-YEAR SLING" DESCEND AND SEIZE THE CAPTIVE'S SHIP! IT IS LIFTED SPEEDILY INTO SPACE...!
THE SHIP IS HELD, SIR...
INITIATE STANDARD PROCEDURE!

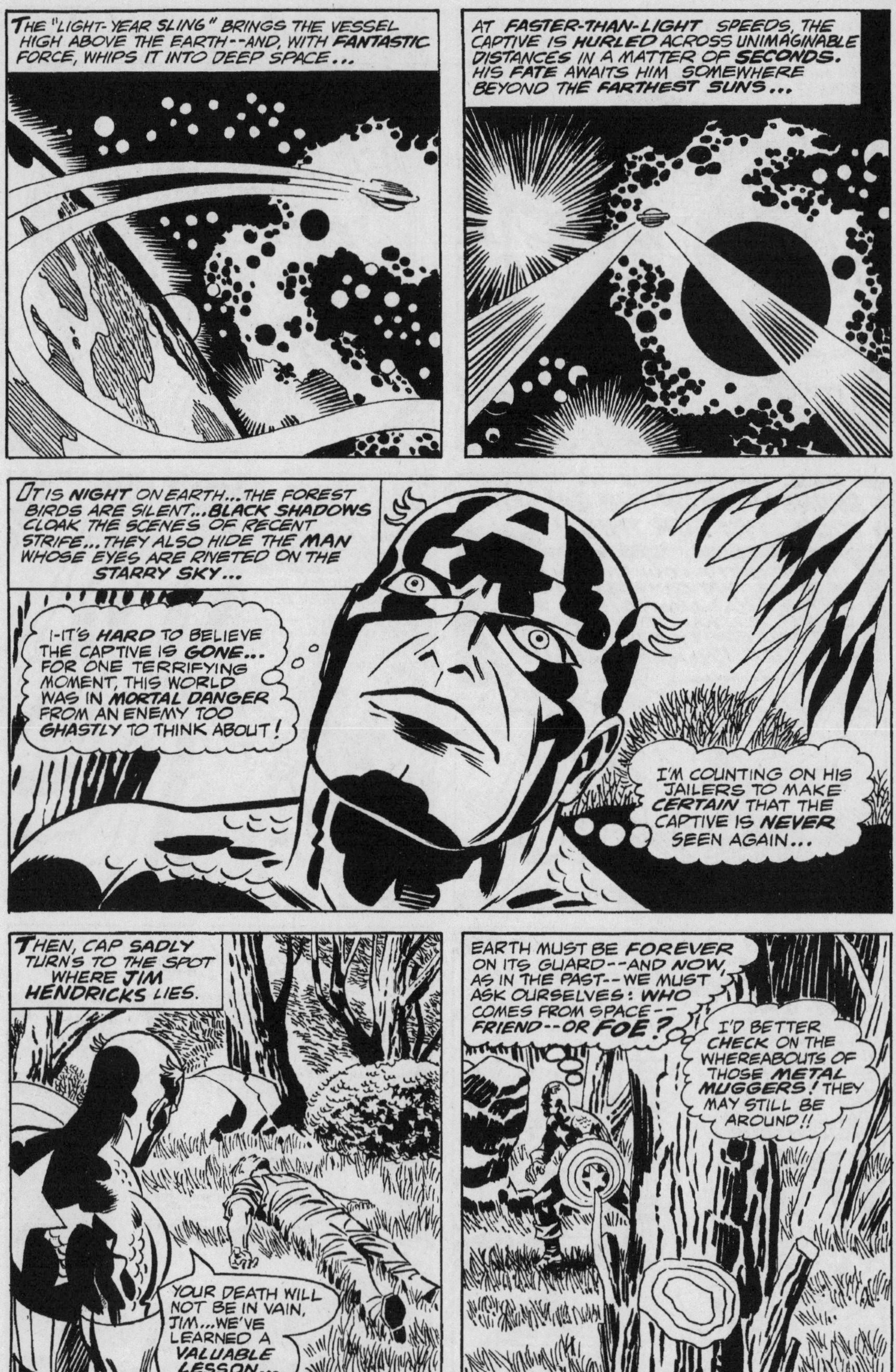
THE "LIGHT-YEAR SLING" BRINGS THE VESSEL HIGH ABOVE THE EARTH--AND, WITH FANTASTIC FORCE, WHIPS IT INTO DEEP SPACE...
AT FASTER-THAN-LIGHT SPEEDS, THE CAPTIVE IS HURLED ACROSS UNIMAGINABLE DISTANCES IN A MATTER OF SECONDS. HIS FATE AWAITS HIM SOMEWHERE BEYOND THE FARTHEST SUNS...
IT IS NIGHT ON EARTH...THE FOREST BIRDS ARE SILENT...BLACK SHADOWS CLOAK THE SCENES OF RECENT STRIFE...THEY ALSO HIDE THE MAN WHOSE EYES ARE RIVETED ON THE STARRY SKY...
I-IT'S HARD TO BELIEVE THE CAPTIVE IS GONE... FOR ONE TERRIFYING MOMENT, THIS WORLD WAS IN MORTAL DANGER FROM AN ENEMY TOO GHASTLY TO THINK ABOUT!
I'M COUNTING ON HIS JAILERS TO MAKE CERTAIN THAT THE CAPTIVE IS NEVER SEEN AGAIN...
THEN, CAP SADLY TURNS TO THE SPOT WHERE JIM HENDRICKS LIES.
YOUR DEATH WILL NOT BE IN VAIN, JIM...WE'VE LEARNED A VALUABLE LESSON...
EARTH MUST BE FOREVER ON ITS GUARD--AND NOW, AS IN THE PAST--WE MUST ASK OURSELVES: WHO COMES FROM SPACE-- FRIEND--OR FOE?
I'D BETTER CHECK ON THE WHEREABOUTS OF THOSE METAL MUGGERS! THEY MAY STILL BE AROUND!!

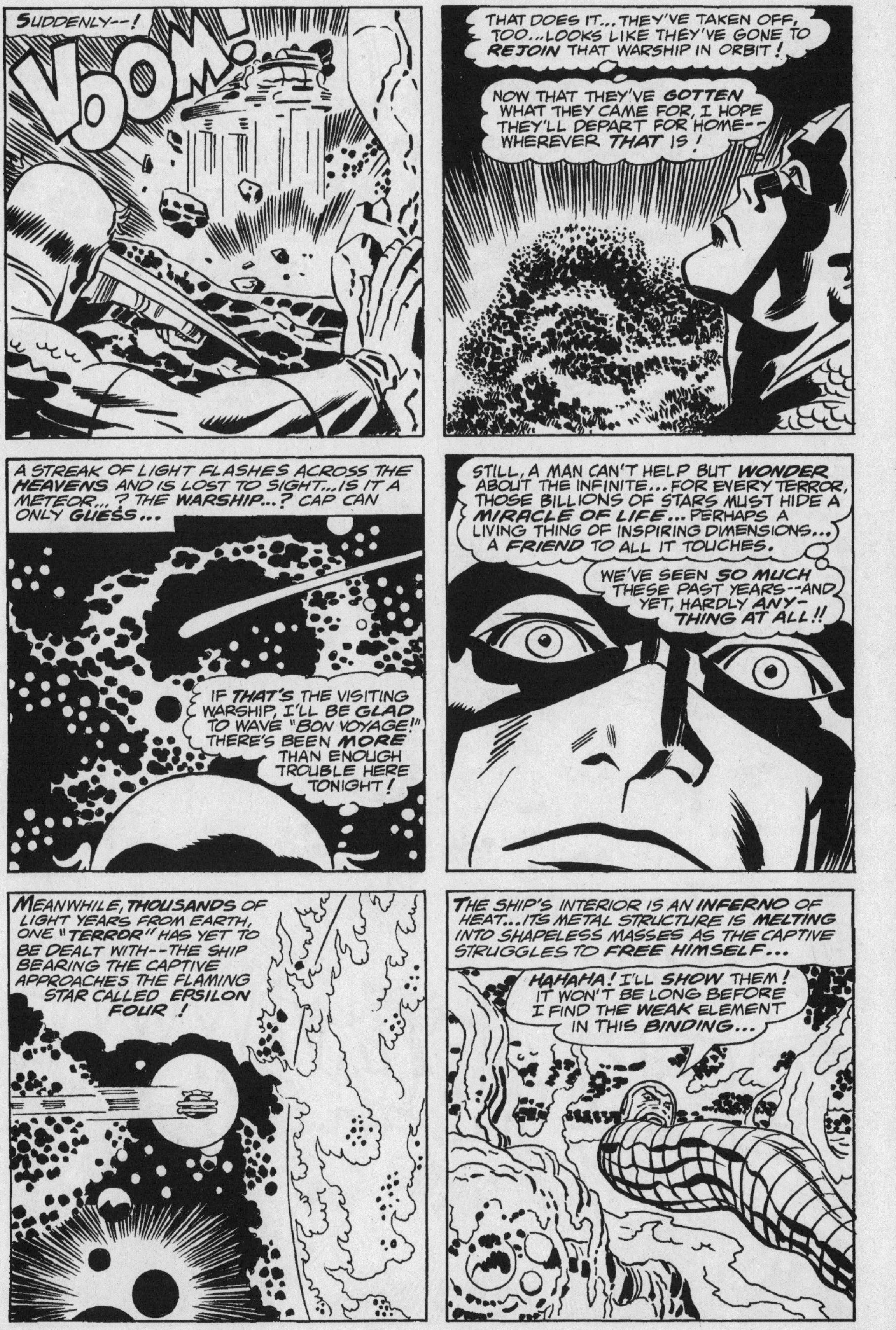
SUDDENLY--!
VOOM!
THAT DOES IT... THEY'VE TAKEN OFF, TOO... LOOKS LIKE THEY'VE GONE TO REJOIN THAT WARSHIP IN ORBIT!
NOW THAT THEY'VE GOTTEN WHAT THEY CAME FOR, I HOPE THEY'LL DEPART FOR HOME-- WHEREVER THAT IS!
A STREAK OF LIGHT FLASHES ACROSS THE HEAVENS AND IS LOST TO SIGHT... IS IT A METEOR...? THE WARSHIP...? CAP CAN ONLY GUESS...
IF THAT'S THE VISITING WARSHIP, I'LL BE GLAD TO WAVE "BON VOYAGE!" THERE'S BEEN MORE THAN ENOUGH TROUBLE HERE TONIGHT!
STILL, A MAN CAN'T HELP BUT WONDER ABOUT THE INFINITE... FOR EVERY TERROR, THOSE BILLIONS OF STARS MUST HIDE A MIRACLE OF LIFE... PERHAPS A LIVING THING OF INSPIRING DIMENSIONS... A FRIEND TO ALL IT TOUCHES.
WE'VE SEEN SO MUCH THESE PAST YEARS--AND YET, HARDLY ANY-THING AT ALL!!
MEANWHILE, THOUSANDS OF LIGHT YEARS FROM EARTH, ONE "TERROR" HAS YET TO BE DEALT WITH--THE SHIP BEARING THE CAPTIVE APPROACHES THE FLAMING STAR CALLED EPSILON FOUR!
THE SHIP'S INTERIOR IS AN INFERNO OF HEAT... ITS METAL STRUCTURE IS MELTING INTO SHAPELESS MASSES AS THE CAPTIVE STRUGGLES TO FREE HIMSELF...
HAHAHA! I'LL SHOW THEM! IT WON'T BE LONG BEFORE I FIND THE WEAK ELEMENT IN THIS BINDING...

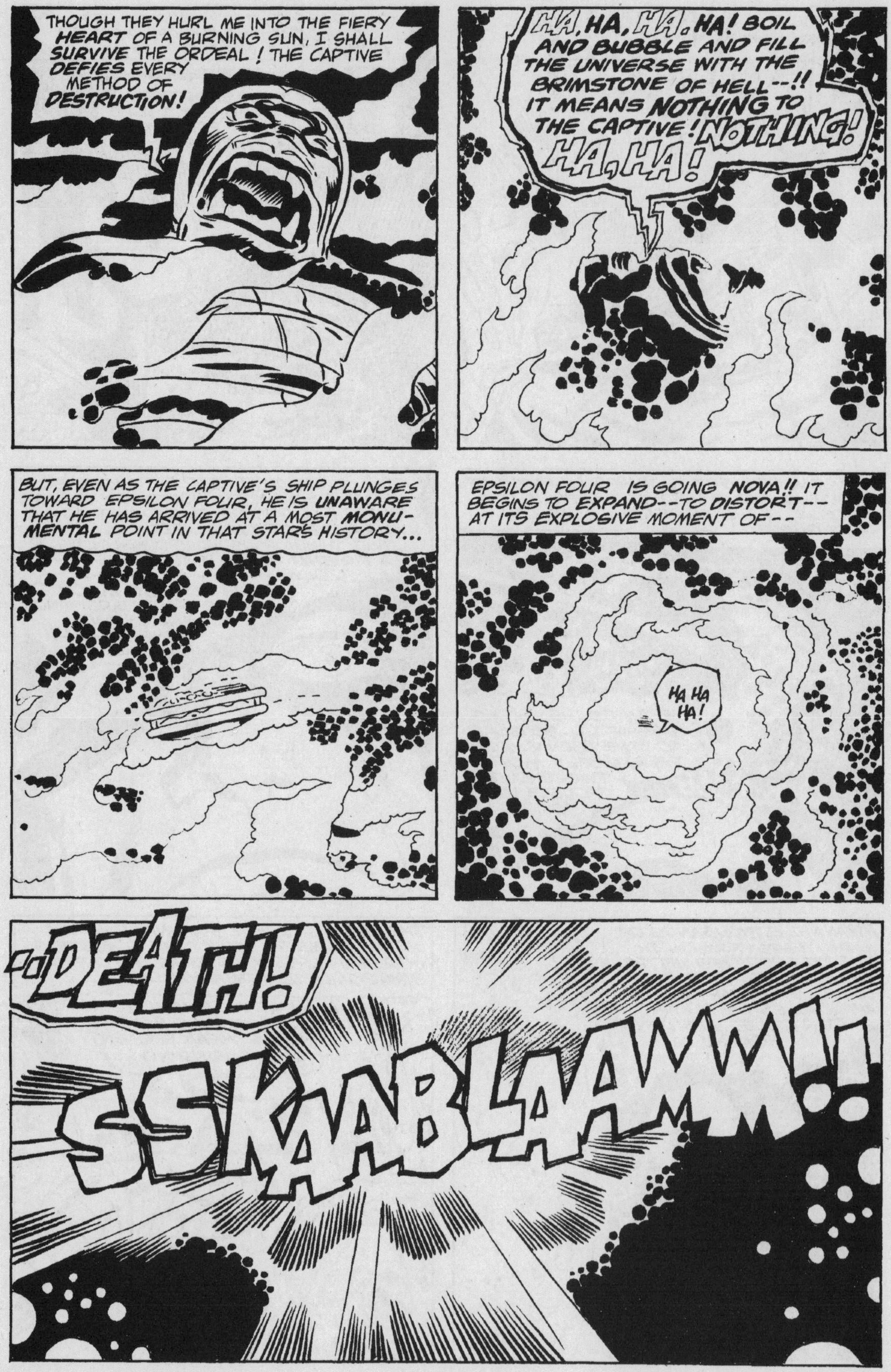
THOUGH THEY HURL ME INTO THE FIERY HEART OF A BURNING SUN, I SHALL SURVIVE THE ORDEAL ! THE CAPTIVE DEFIES EVERY METHOD OF DESTRUCTION!
HA, HA, HA. HA! BOIL AND BUBBLE AND FILL THE UNIVERSE WITH THE BRIMSTONE OF HELL--!! IT MEANS NOTHING TO THE CAPTIVE! NOTHING! HA, HA!
BUT, EVEN AS THE CAPTIVE'S SHIP PLUNGES TOWARD EPSILON FOUR, HE IS UNAWARE THAT HE HAS ARRIVED AT A MOST MONUMENTAL POINT IN THAT STAR'S HISTORY...
EPSILON FOUR IS GOING NOVA!! IT BEGINS TO EXPAND--TO DISTORT--AT ITS EXPLOSIVE MOMENT OF--
HA HA HA!
..DEATH!
S-SKAABLAAMM!!

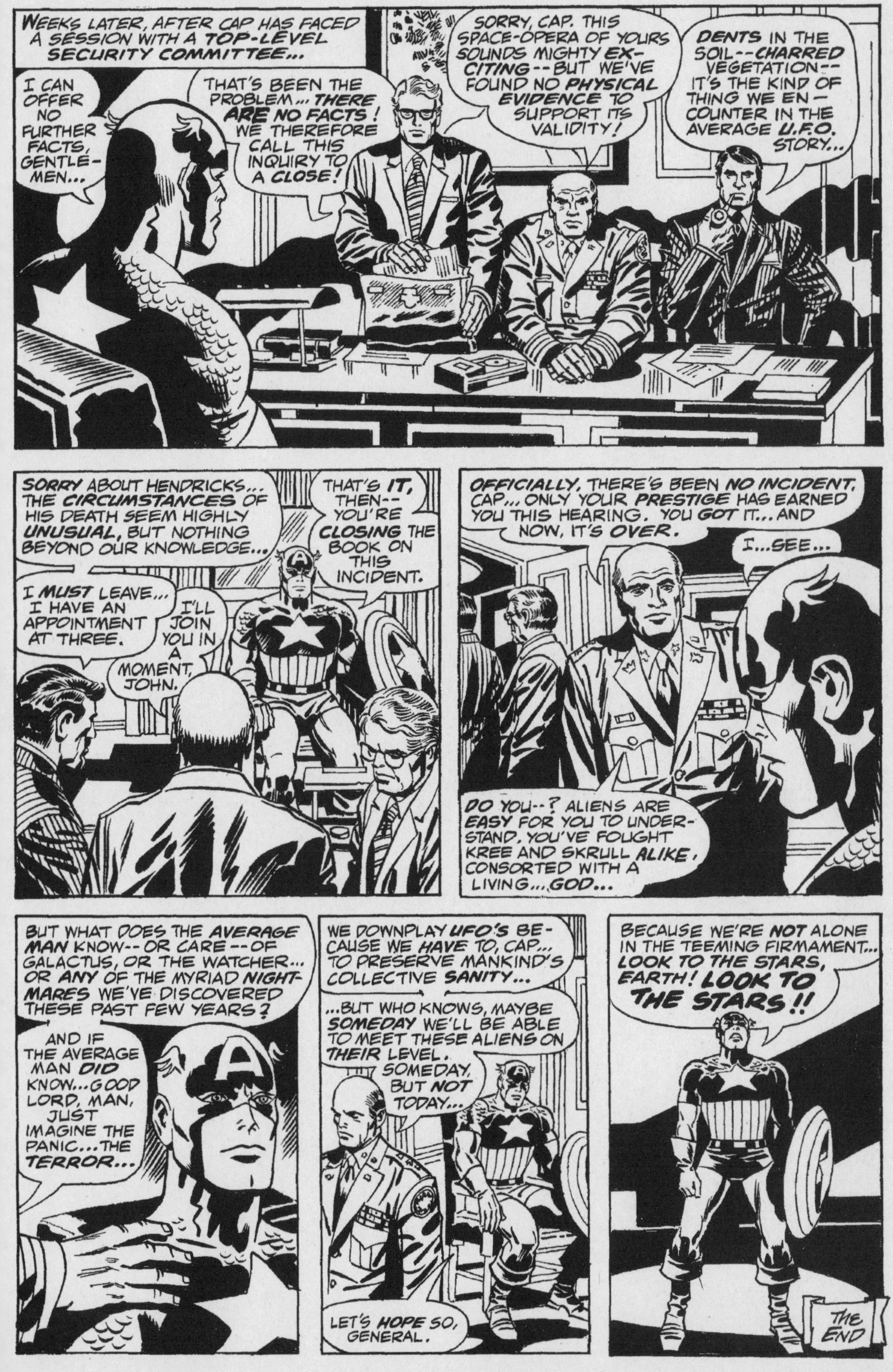
WEEKS LATER, AFTER CAP HAS FACED A SESSION WITH A TOP-LEVEL SECURITY COMMITTEE...
I CAN OFFER NO FURTHER FACTS, GENTLEMEN...
THAT'S BEEN THE PROBLEM... THERE ARE NO FACTS! WE THEREFORE CALL THIS INQUIRY TO A CLOSE!
SORRY, CAP. THIS SPACE-OPERA OF YOURS SOUNDS MIGHTY EXCITING--BUT WE'VE FOUND NO PHYSICAL EVIDENCE TO SUPPORT ITS VALIDITY!
DENTS IN THE SOIL--CHARRED VEGETATION--IT'S THE KIND OF THING WE ENCOUNTER IN THE AVERAGE U.F.O. STORY...
SORRY ABOUT HENDRICKS... THE CIRCUMSTANCES OF HIS DEATH SEEM HIGHLY UNUSUAL, BUT NOTHING BEYOND OUR KNOWLEDGE...
THAT'S IT, THEN--YOU'RE CLOSING THE BOOK ON THIS INCIDENT.
I MUST LEAVE... I HAVE AN APPOINTMENT AT THREE.
I'LL JOIN YOU IN A MOMENT, JOHN.
OFFICIALLY, THERE'S BEEN NO INCIDENT, CAP... ONLY YOUR PRESTIGE HAS EARNED YOU THIS HEARING. YOU GOT IT... AND NOW, IT'S OVER.
I...SEE...
DO YOU--? ALIENS ARE EASY FOR YOU TO UNDERSTAND. YOU'VE FOUGHT KREE AND SKRULL ALIKE, CONSORTED WITH A LIVING... GOD...
BUT WHAT DOES THE AVERAGE MAN KNOW--OR CARE--OF GALACTUS, OR THE WATCHER... OR ANY OF THE MYRIAD NIGHTMARES WE'VE DISCOVERED THESE PAST FEW YEARS?
AND IF THE AVERAGE MAN DID KNOW...GOOD LORD, MAN, JUST IMAGINE THE PANIC...THE TERROR...
WE DOWNPLAY UFO'S BECAUSE WE HAVE TO, CAP... TO PRESERVE MANKIND'S COLLECTIVE SANITY...
...BUT WHO KNOWS, MAYBE SOMEDAY WE'LL BE ABLE TO MEET THESE ALIENS ON THEIR LEVEL.
SOMEDAY, BUT NOT TODAY...
LET'S HOPE SO, GENERAL.
BECAUSE WE'RE NOT ALONE IN THE TEEMING FIRMAMENT... LOOK TO THE STARS, EARTH! LOOK TO THE STARS!!
THE END

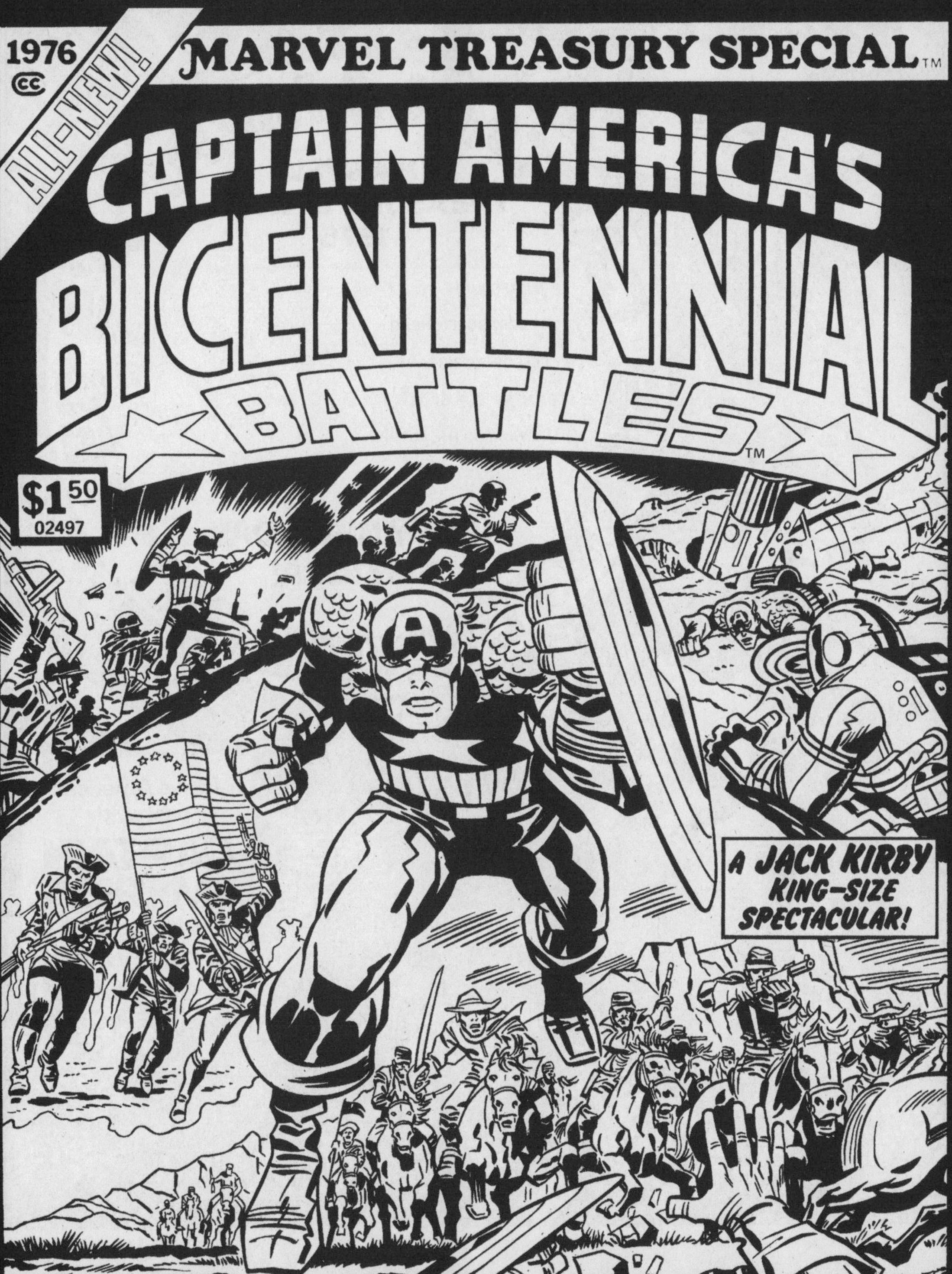
1976
CC
ALL-NEW!
MARVEL TREASURY SPECIAL
CAPTAIN AMERICA'S
BICENTENNIAL
BATTLES
$1.50
02497
A JACK KIRBY
KING-SIZE
SPECTACULAR!

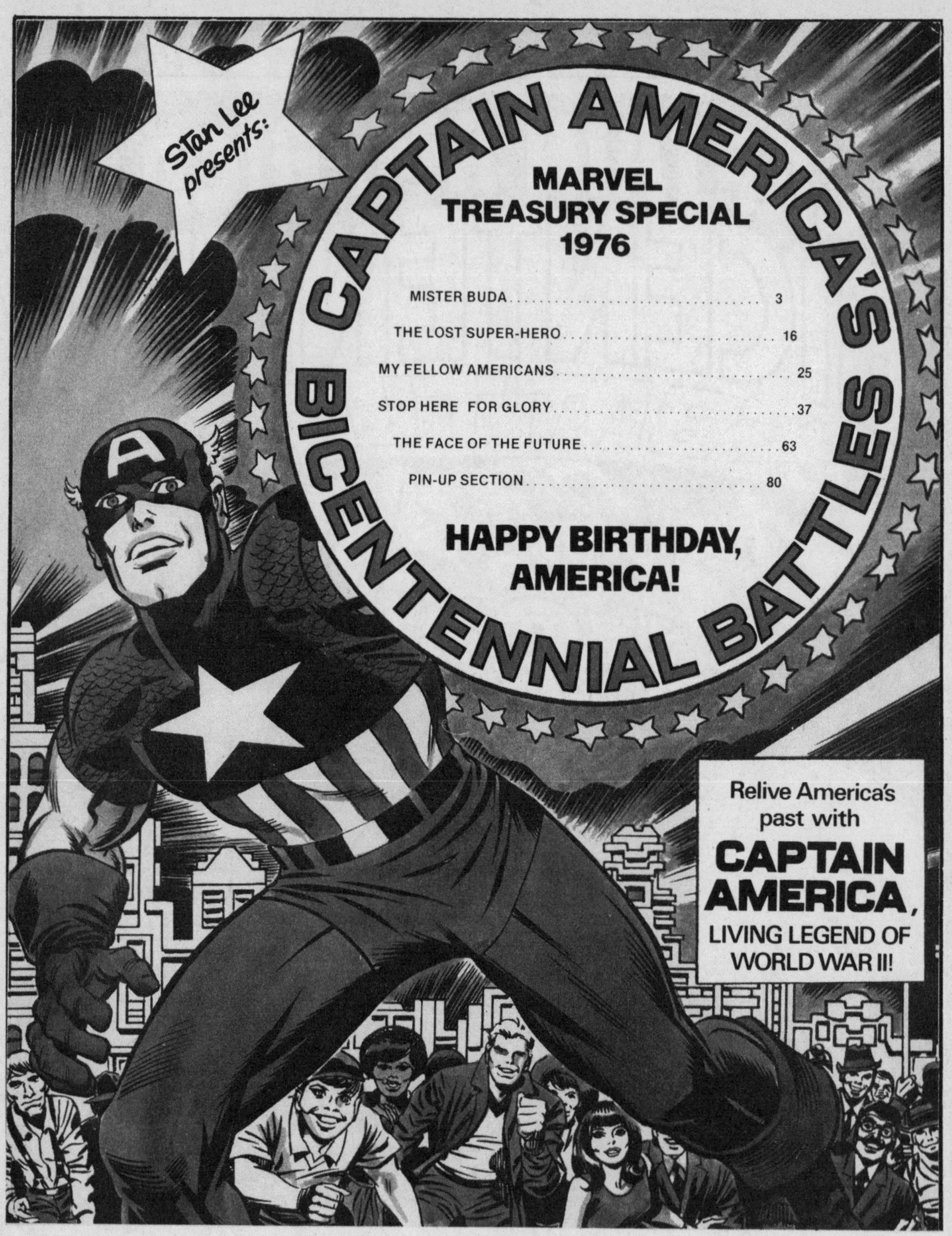
Stan Lee presents:
CAPTAIN AMERICA'S BICENTENNIAL BATTLES
MARVEL TREASURY SPECIAL 1976
MISTER BUDA 3
THE LOST SUPER-HERO 16
MY FELLOW AMERICANS 25
STOP HERE FOR GLORY 37
THE FACE OF THE FUTURE 63
PIN-UP SECTION 80
HAPPY BIRTHDAY, AMERICA!
Relive America's past with CAPTAIN AMERICA, LIVING LEGEND OF WORLD WAR II!

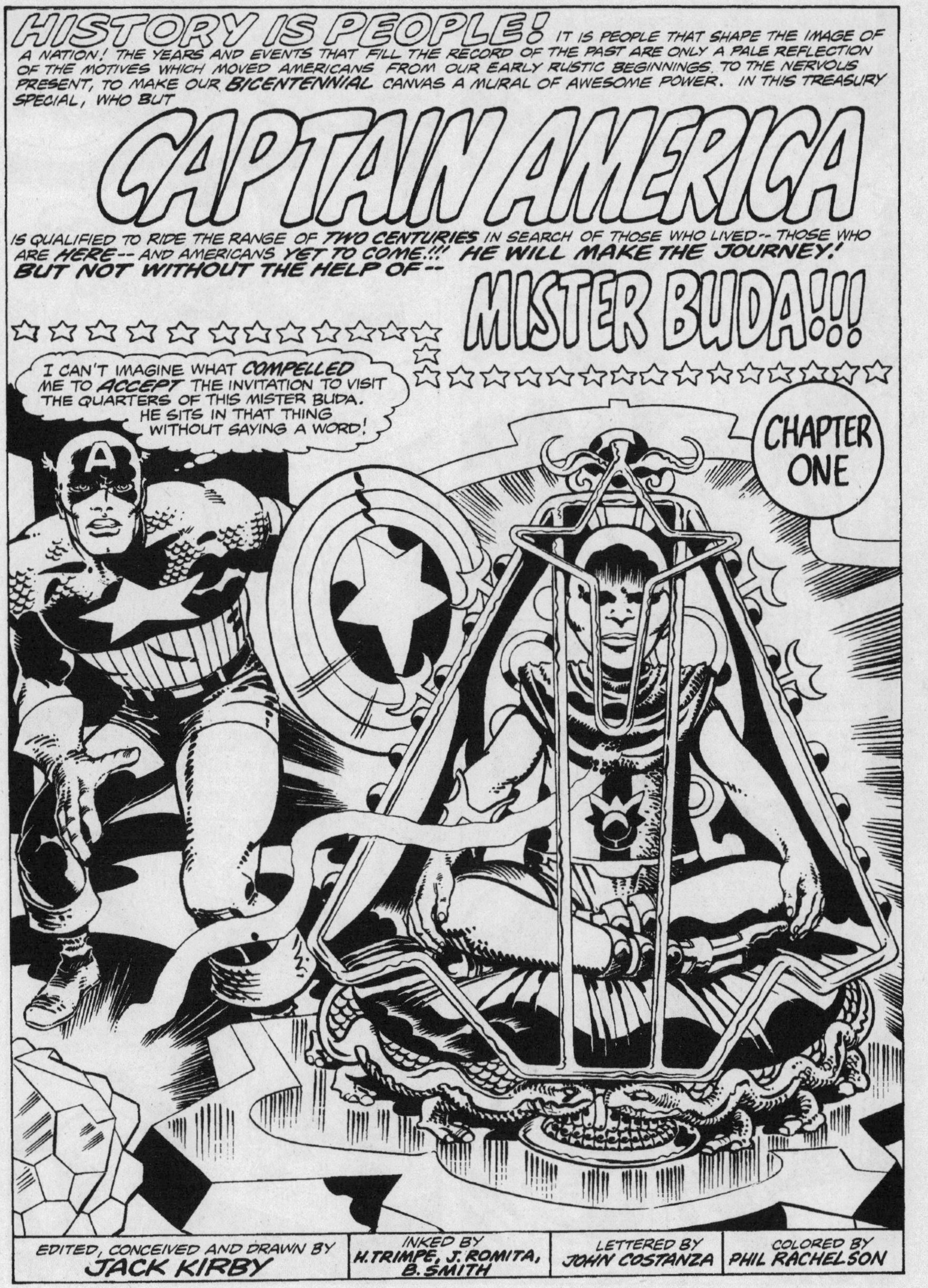
HISTORY IS PEOPLE! IT IS PEOPLE THAT SHAPE THE IMAGE OF A NATION! THE YEARS AND EVENTS THAT FILL THE RECORD OF THE PAST ARE ONLY A PALE REFLECTION OF THE MOTIVES WHICH MOVED AMERICANS FROM OUR EARLY RUSTIC BEGINNINGS TO THE NERVOUS PRESENT, TO MAKE OUR BICENTENNIAL CANVAS A MURAL OF AWESOME POWER. IN THIS TREASURY SPECIAL, WHO BUT
CAPTAIN AMERICA
IS QUALIFIED TO RIDE THE RANGE OF TWO CENTURIES IN SEARCH OF THOSE WHO LIVED-- THOSE WHO ARE HERE-- AND AMERICANS YET TO COME!!! HE WILL MAKE THE JOURNEY! BUT NOT WITHOUT THE HELP OF--
MISTER BUDA!!!
I CAN'T IMAGINE WHAT COMPELLED ME TO ACCEPT THE INVITATION TO VISIT THE QUARTERS OF THIS MISTER BUDA. HE SITS IN THAT THING WITHOUT SAYING A WORD!
CHAPTER ONE
EDITED, CONCEIVED AND DRAWN BY JACK KIRBY
INKED BY H. TRIMPE, J. ROMITA, B. SMITH
LETTERED BY JOHN COSTANZA
COLORED BY PHIL RACHELSON

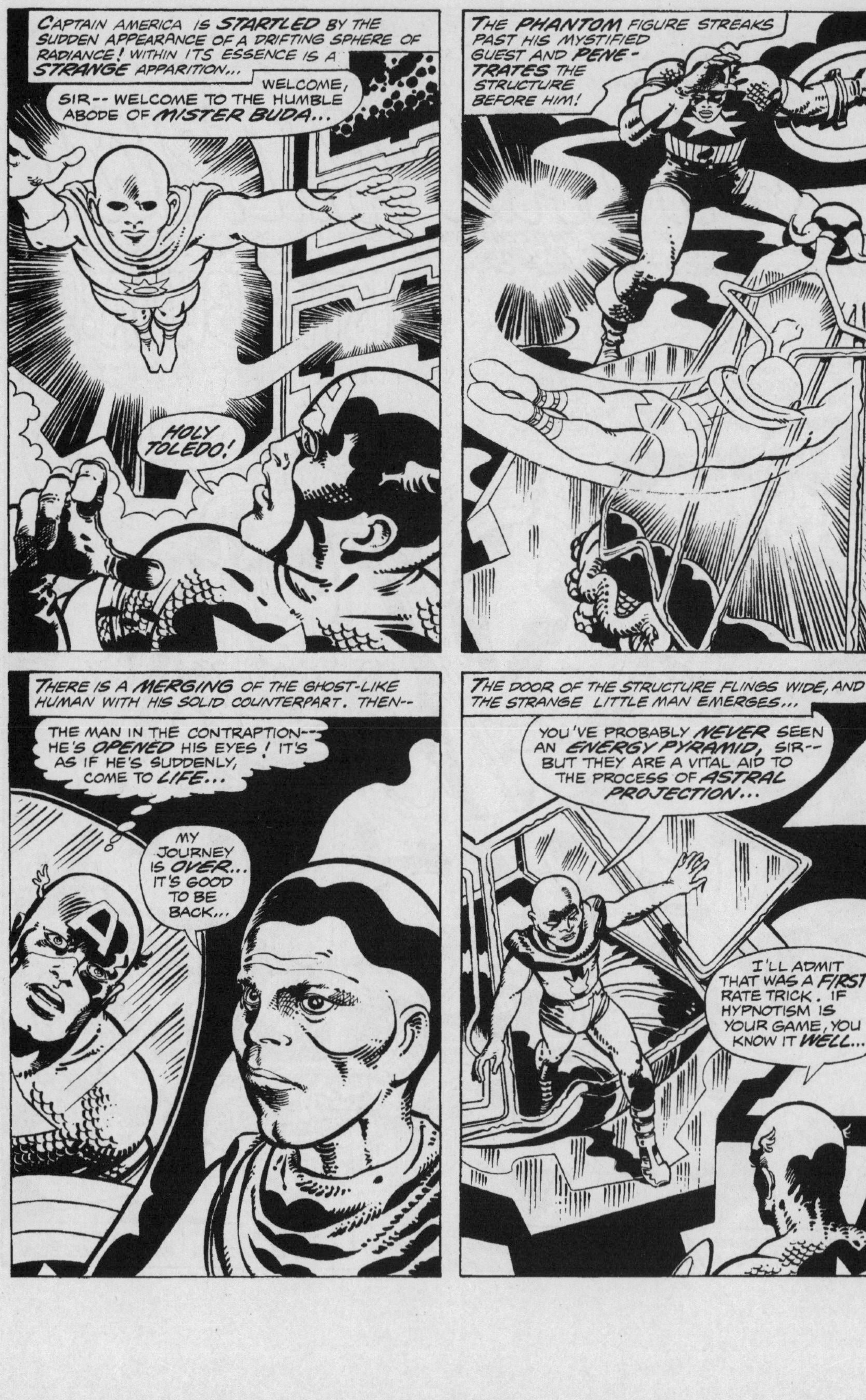

CAPTAIN AMERICA IS STARTLED BY THE SUDDEN APPEARANCE OF A DRIFTING SPHERE OF RADIANCE! WITHIN ITS ESSENCE IS A STRANGE APPARITION...
WELCOME, SIR-- WELCOME TO THE HUMBLE ABODE OF MISTER BUDA...
HOLY TOLEDO!
THE PHANTOM FIGURE STREAKS PAST HIS MYSTIFIED GUEST AND PENE-TRATES THE STRUCTURE BEFORE HIM!
THERE IS A MERGING OF THE GHOST-LIKE HUMAN WITH HIS SOLID COUNTERPART. THEN--
THE MAN IN THE CONTRAPTION-- HE'S OPENED HIS EYES! IT'S AS IF HE'S SUDDENLY, COME TO LIFE...
MY JOURNEY IS OVER... IT'S GOOD TO BE BACK...
THE DOOR OF THE STRUCTURE FLINGS WIDE, AND THE STRANGE LITTLE MAN EMERGES...
YOU'VE PROBABLY NEVER SEEN AN ENERGY PYRAMID, SIR-- BUT THEY ARE A VITAL AID TO THE PROCESS OF ASTRAL PROJECTION...
I'LL ADMIT THAT WAS A FIRST RATE TRICK. IF HYPNOTISM IS YOUR GAME, YOU KNOW IT WELL...

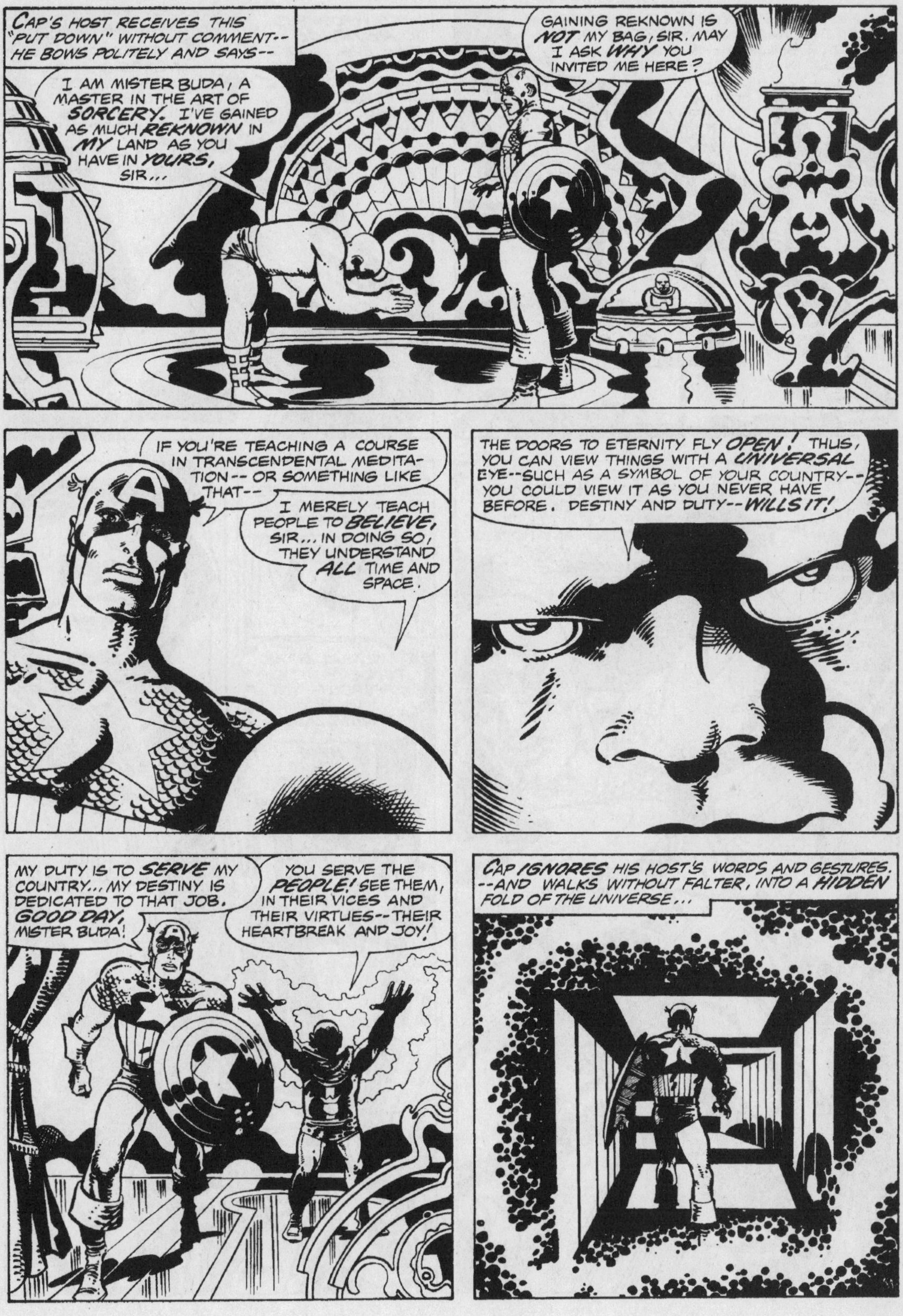
CAP'S HOST RECEIVES THIS "PUT DOWN" WITHOUT COMMENT-- HE BOWS POLITELY AND SAYS--
I AM MISTER BUDA, A MASTER IN THE ART OF SORCERY. I'VE GAINED AS MUCH REKNOWN IN MY LAND AS YOU HAVE IN YOURS, SIR...
GAINING REKNOWN IS NOT MY BAG, SIR. MAY I ASK WHY YOU INVITED ME HERE?
IF YOU'RE TEACHING A COURSE IN TRANSCENDENTAL MEDITATION-- OR SOMETHING LIKE THAT--
I MERELY TEACH PEOPLE TO BELIEVE, SIR... IN DOING SO, THEY UNDERSTAND ALL TIME AND SPACE.
THE DOORS TO ETERNITY FLY OPEN! THUS, YOU CAN VIEW THINGS WITH A UNIVERSAL EYE--SUCH AS A SYMBOL OF YOUR COUNTRY-- YOU COULD VIEW IT AS YOU NEVER HAVE BEFORE. DESTINY AND DUTY--WILLS IT!
MY DUTY IS TO SERVE MY COUNTRY... MY DESTINY IS DEDICATED TO THAT JOB. GOOD DAY, MISTER BUDA!
YOU SERVE THE PEOPLE! SEE THEM, IN THEIR VICES AND THEIR VIRTUES--THEIR HEARTBREAK AND JOY!
CAP IGNORES HIS HOST'S WORDS AND GESTURES. --AND WALKS WITHOUT FALTER, INTO A HIDDEN FOLD OF THE UNIVERSE...

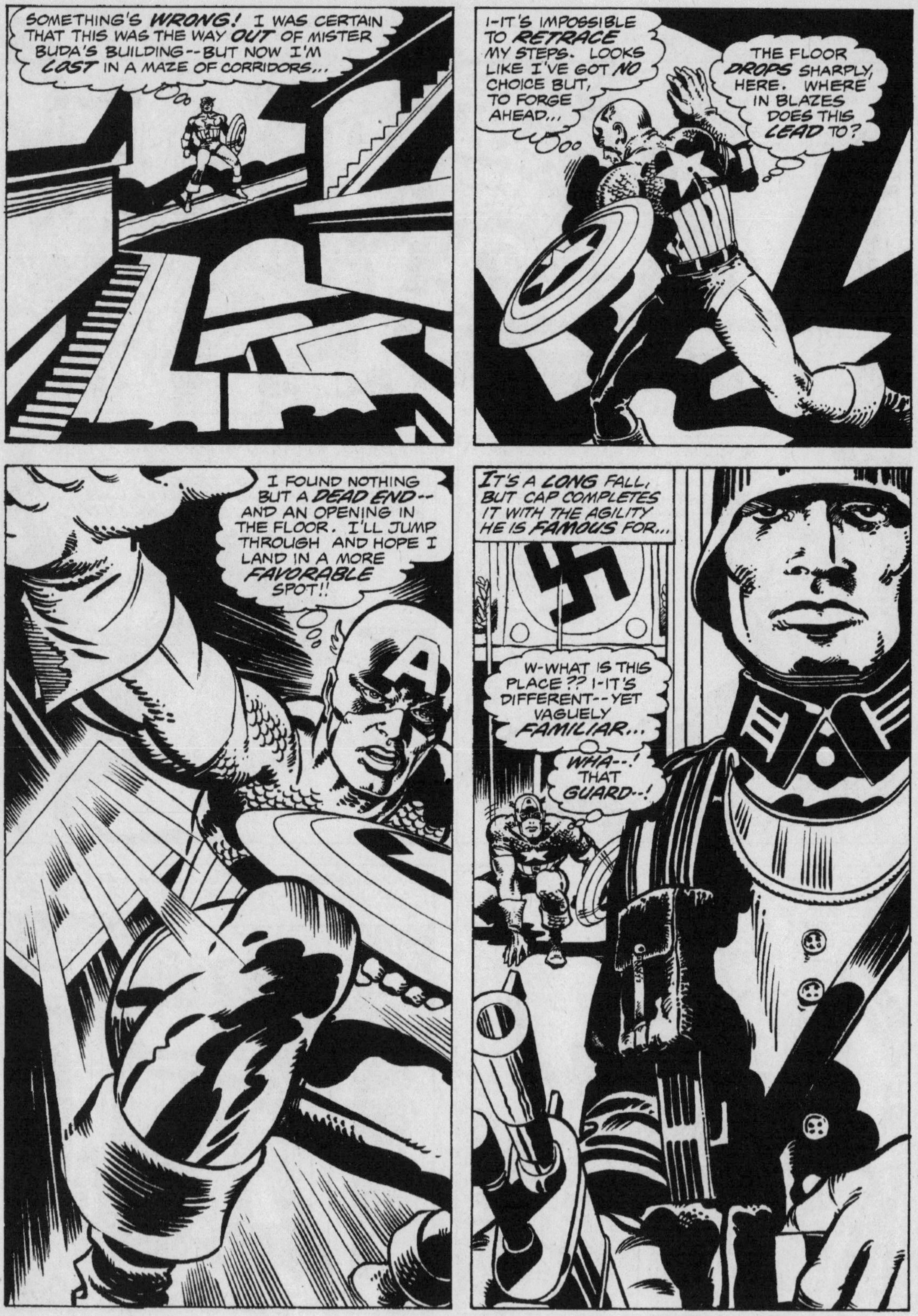
SOMETHING'S WRONG! I WAS CERTAIN THAT THIS WAS THE WAY OUT OF MISTER BUDA'S BUILDING--BUT NOW I'M LOST IN A MAZE OF CORRIDORS...
I-IT'S IMPOSSIBLE TO RETRACE MY STEPS. LOOKS LIKE I'VE GOT NO CHOICE BUT, TO FORGE AHEAD...
THE FLOOR DROPS SHARPLY, HERE. WHERE IN BLAZES DOES THIS LEAD TO?
I FOUND NOTHING BUT A DEAD END--AND AN OPENING IN THE FLOOR. I'LL JUMP THROUGH AND HOPE I LAND IN A MORE FAVORABLE SPOT!!
IT'S A LONG FALL, BUT CAP COMPLETES IT WITH THE AGILITY HE IS FAMOUS FOR...
W-WHAT IS THIS PLACE?? I-IT'S DIFFERENT--YET VAGUELY FAMILIAR...
WHA--! THAT GUARD--!

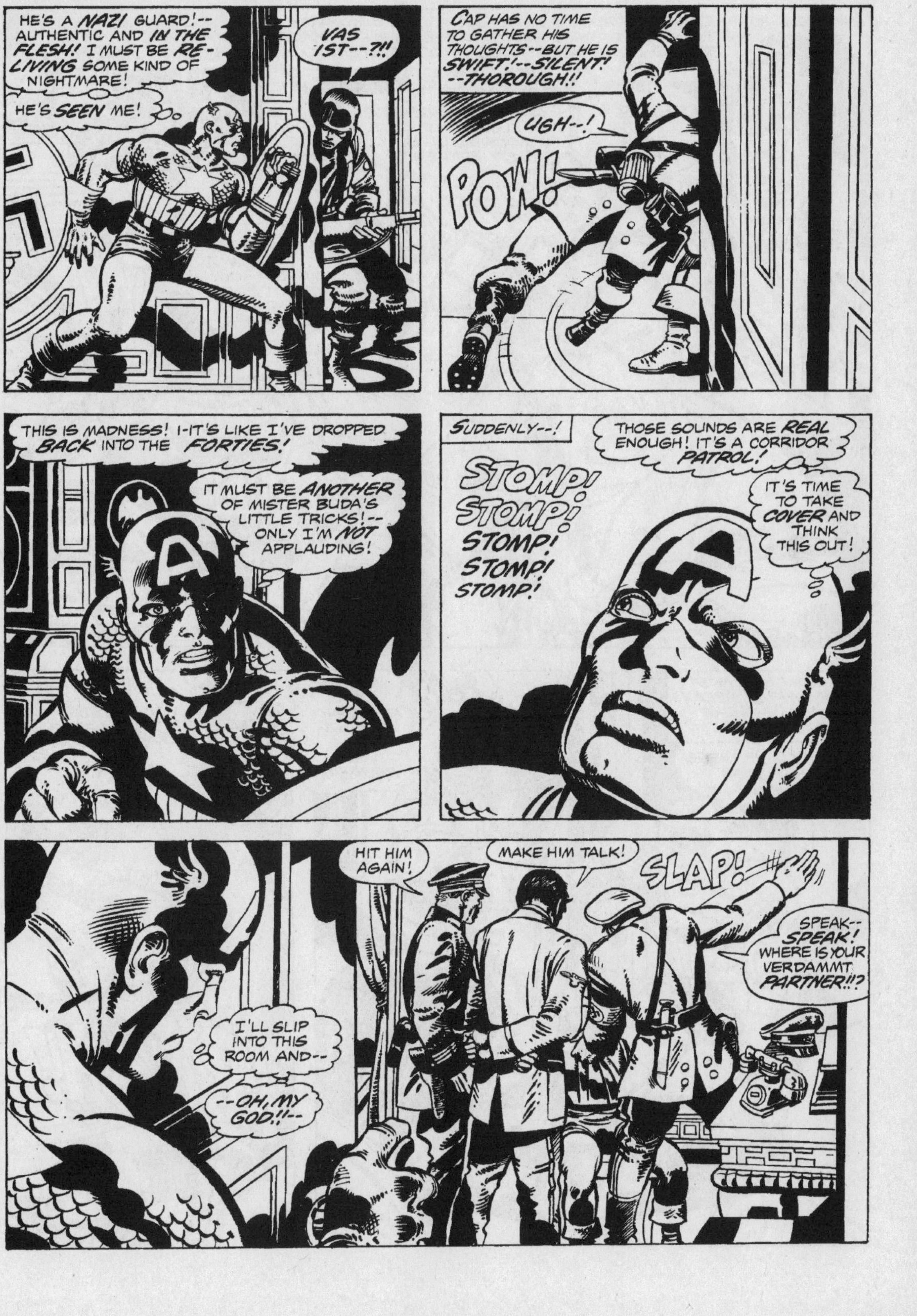
HE'S A NAZI GUARD!-- AUTHENTIC AND IN THE FLESH! I MUST BE RE-LIVING SOME KIND OF NIGHTMARE!
HE'S SEEN ME!
VAS IST--?!!
CAP HAS NO TIME TO GATHER HIS THOUGHTS--BUT HE IS SWIFT!--SILENT! --THOROUGH!!
UGH--!
POW!
THIS IS MADNESS! I-IT'S LIKE I'VE DROPPED BACK INTO THE FORTIES!
IT MUST BE ANOTHER OF MISTER BUDA'S LITTLE TRICKS!-- ONLY I'M NOT APPLAUDING!
SUDDENLY--!
THOSE SOUNDS ARE REAL ENOUGH! IT'S A CORRIDOR PATROL!
STOMP! STOMP! STOMP! STOMP! STOMP!
IT'S TIME TO TAKE COVER AND THINK THIS OUT!
I'LL SLIP INTO THIS ROOM AND--
--OH, MY GOD!!--
HIT HIM AGAIN!
MAKE HIM TALK!
SLAP!
SPEAK-- SPEAK! WHERE IS YOUR VERDAMMT PARTNER!!?

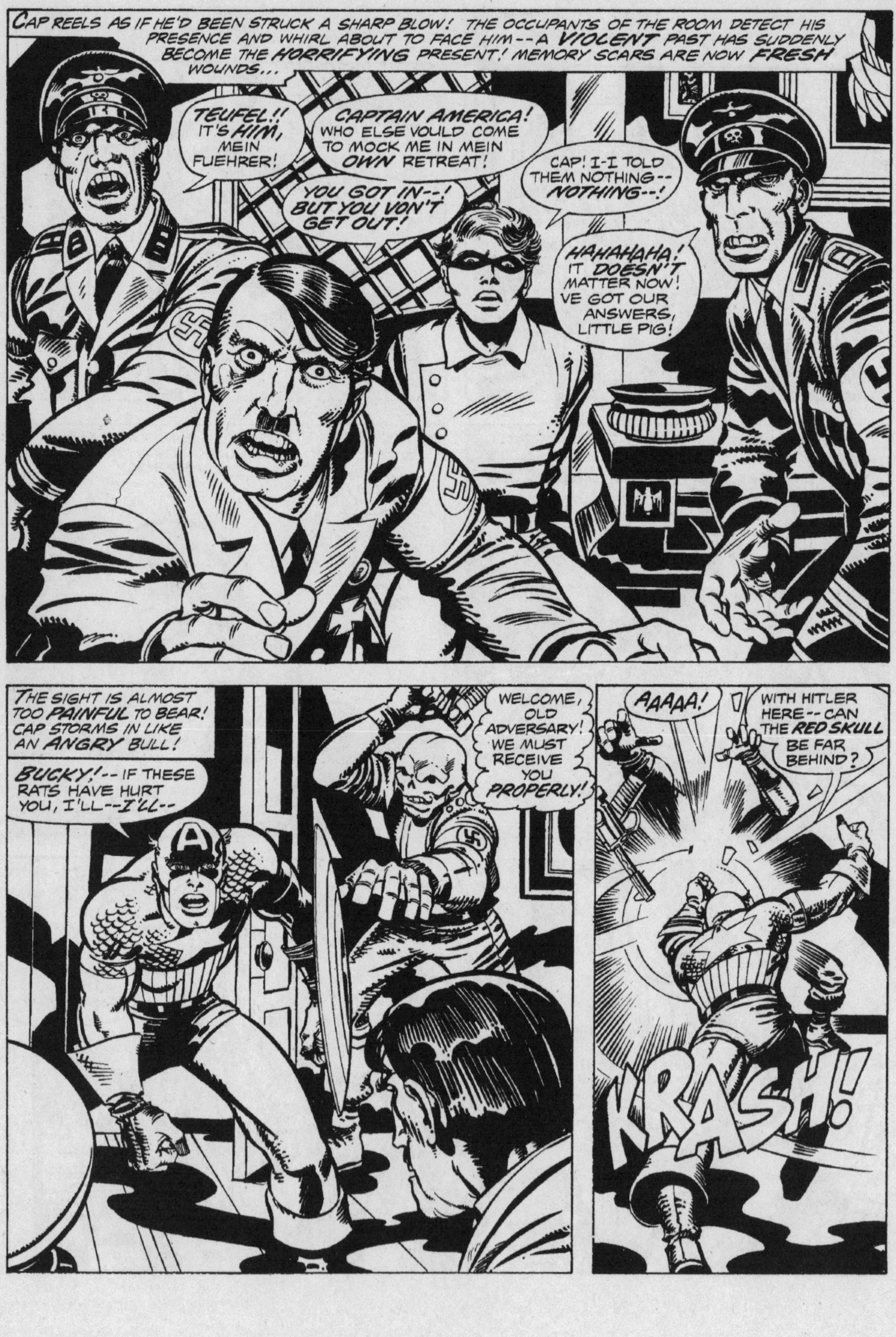
CAP REELS AS IF HE'D BEEN STRUCK A SHARP BLOW! THE OCCUPANTS OF THE ROOM DETECT HIS PRESENCE AND WHIRL ABOUT TO FACE HIM--A VIOLENT PAST HAS SUDDENLY BECOME THE HORRIFYING PRESENT! MEMORY SCARS ARE NOW FRESH WOUNDS...
TEUFEL!! IT'S HIM, MEIN FUEHRER!
CAPTAIN AMERICA! WHO ELSE VOULD COME TO MOCK ME IN MEIN OWN RETREAT!
YOU GOT IN--! BUT YOU VON'T GET OUT!
CAP! I-I TOLD THEM NOTHING-- NOTHING--!
HAHAHAHA! IT DOESN'T MATTER NOW! VE GOT OUR ANSWERS, LITTLE PIG!
THE SIGHT IS ALMOST TOO PAINFUL TO BEAR! CAP STORMS IN LIKE AN ANGRY BULL!
BUCKY!-- IF THESE RATS HAVE HURT YOU, I'LL--I'LL--
WELCOME, OLD ADVERSARY! WE MUST RECEIVE YOU PROPERLY!
AAAAA!
WITH HITLER HERE--CAN THE RED SKULL BE FAR BEHIND?
KRASH!

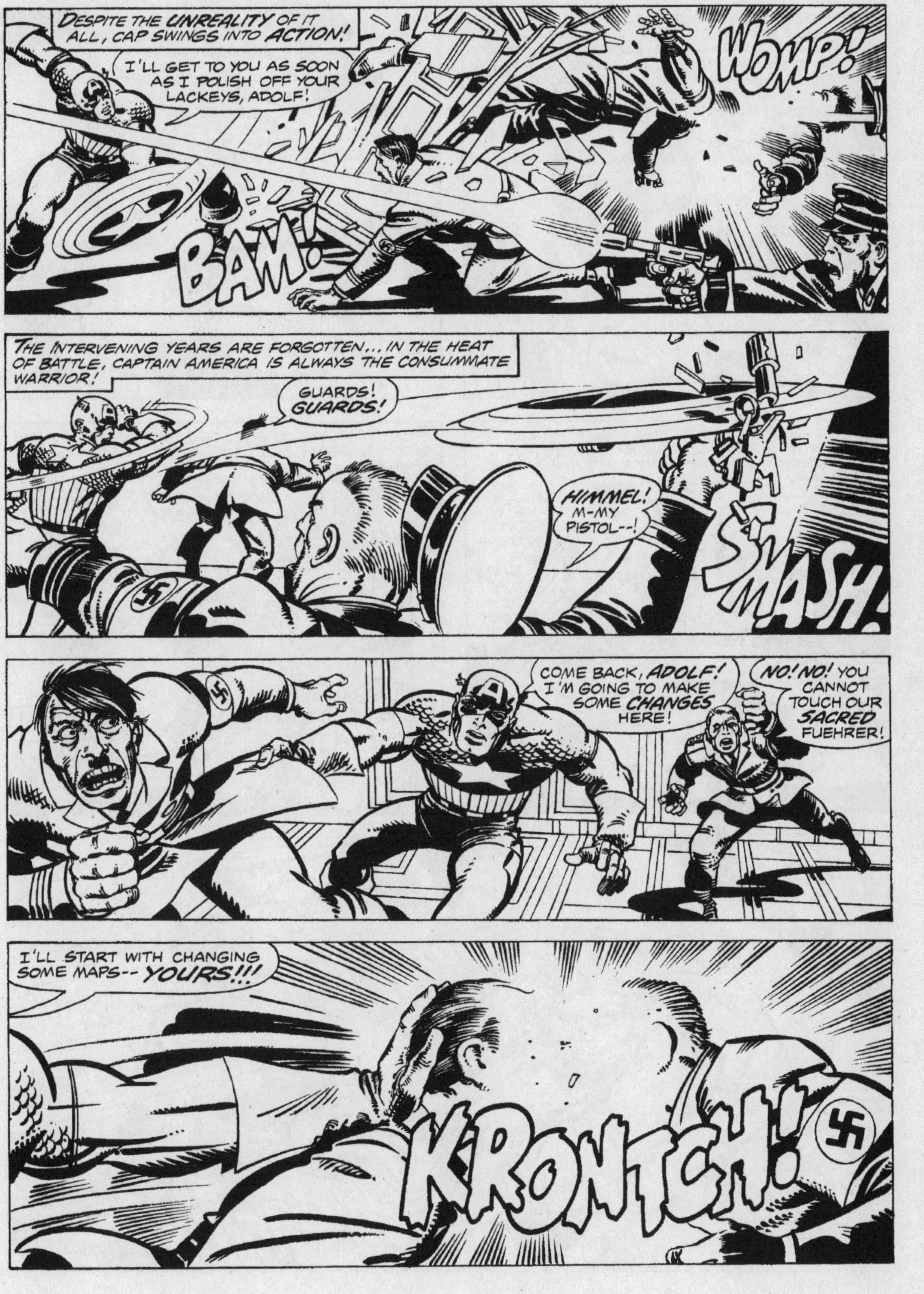
DESPITE THE UNREALITY OF IT ALL, CAP SWINGS INTO ACTION!
I'LL GET TO YOU AS SOON AS I POLISH OFF YOUR LACKEYS, ADOLF!
WOMP!
BAM!
THE INTERVENING YEARS ARE FORGOTTEN... IN THE HEAT OF BATTLE, CAPTAIN AMERICA IS ALWAYS THE CONSUMMATE WARRIOR!
GUARDS! GUARDS!
HIMMEL! M-MY PISTOL--!
SMASH!
COME BACK, ADOLF! I'M GOING TO MAKE SOME CHANGES HERE!
NO! NO! YOU CANNOT TOUCH OUR SACRED FUEHRER!
I'LL START WITH CHANGING SOME MAPS-- YOURS!!!
KRONTCH!

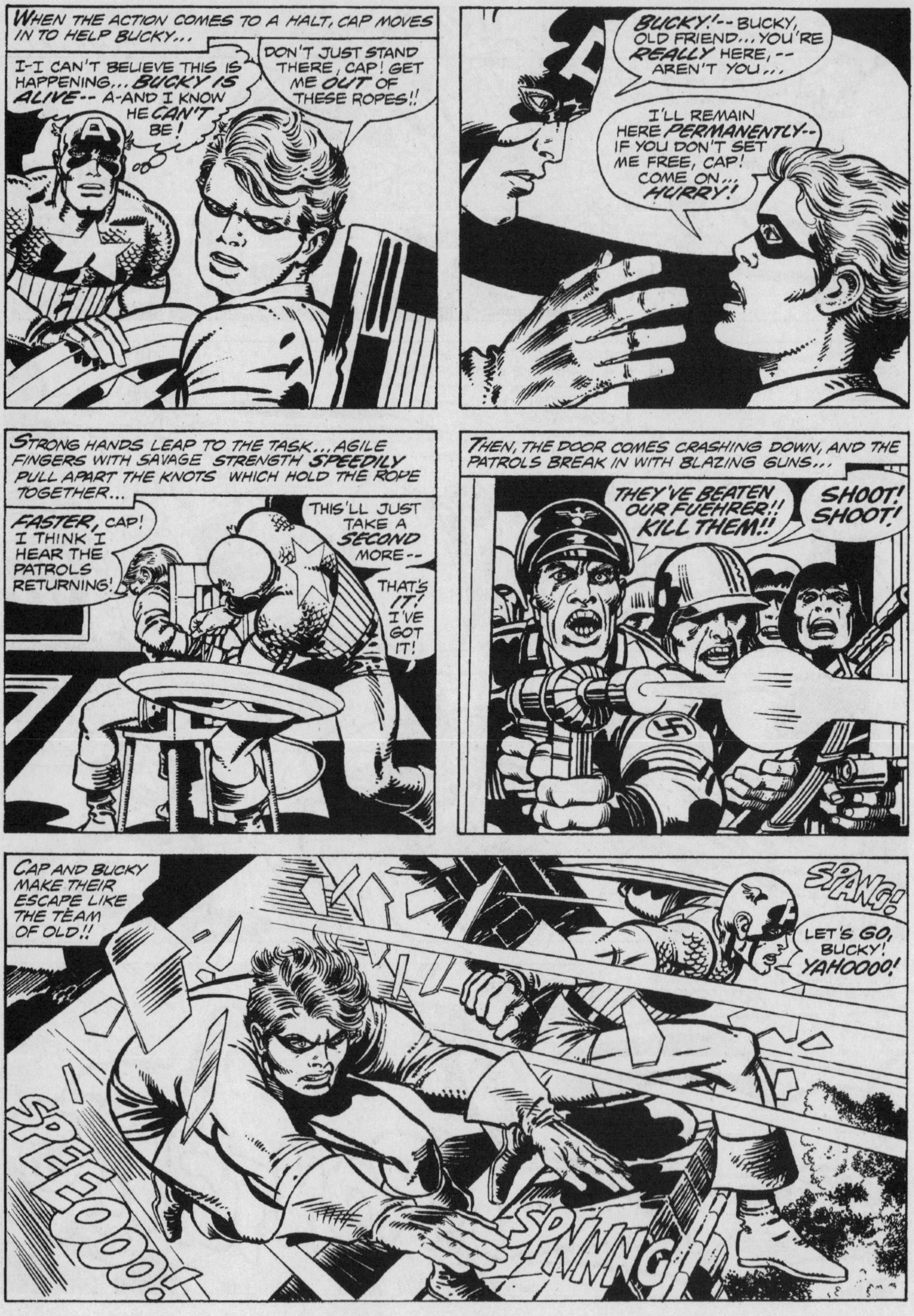

WHEN THE ACTION COMES TO A HALT, CAP MOVES IN TO HELP BUCKY...
I-I CAN'T BELIEVE THIS IS HAPPENING... BUCKY IS ALIVE-- A-AND I KNOW HE CAN'T BE!
DON'T JUST STAND THERE, CAP! GET ME OUT OF THESE ROPES!!
BUCKY!--BUCKY, OLD FRIEND... YOU'RE REALLY HERE,-- AREN'T YOU...
I'LL REMAIN HERE PERMANENTLY-- IF YOU DON'T SET ME FREE, CAP! COME ON... HURRY!
STRONG HANDS LEAP TO THE TASK... AGILE FINGERS WITH SAVAGE STRENGTH SPEEDILY PULL APART THE KNOTS WHICH HOLD THE ROPE TOGETHER...
FASTER, CAP! I THINK I HEAR THE PATROLS RETURNING!
THIS'LL JUST TAKE A SECOND MORE--
THAT'S IT! I'VE GOT IT!
THEN, THE DOOR COMES CRASHING DOWN, AND THE PATROLS BREAK IN WITH BLAZING GUNS...
THEY'VE BEATEN OUR FUEHRER!! KILL THEM!!
SHOOT! SHOOT!
CAP AND BUCKY MAKE THEIR ESCAPE LIKE THE TEAM OF OLD!!
SPANG!
LET'S GO, BUCKY! YAHOOOO!
SPEEOOO!
SPNNNG!

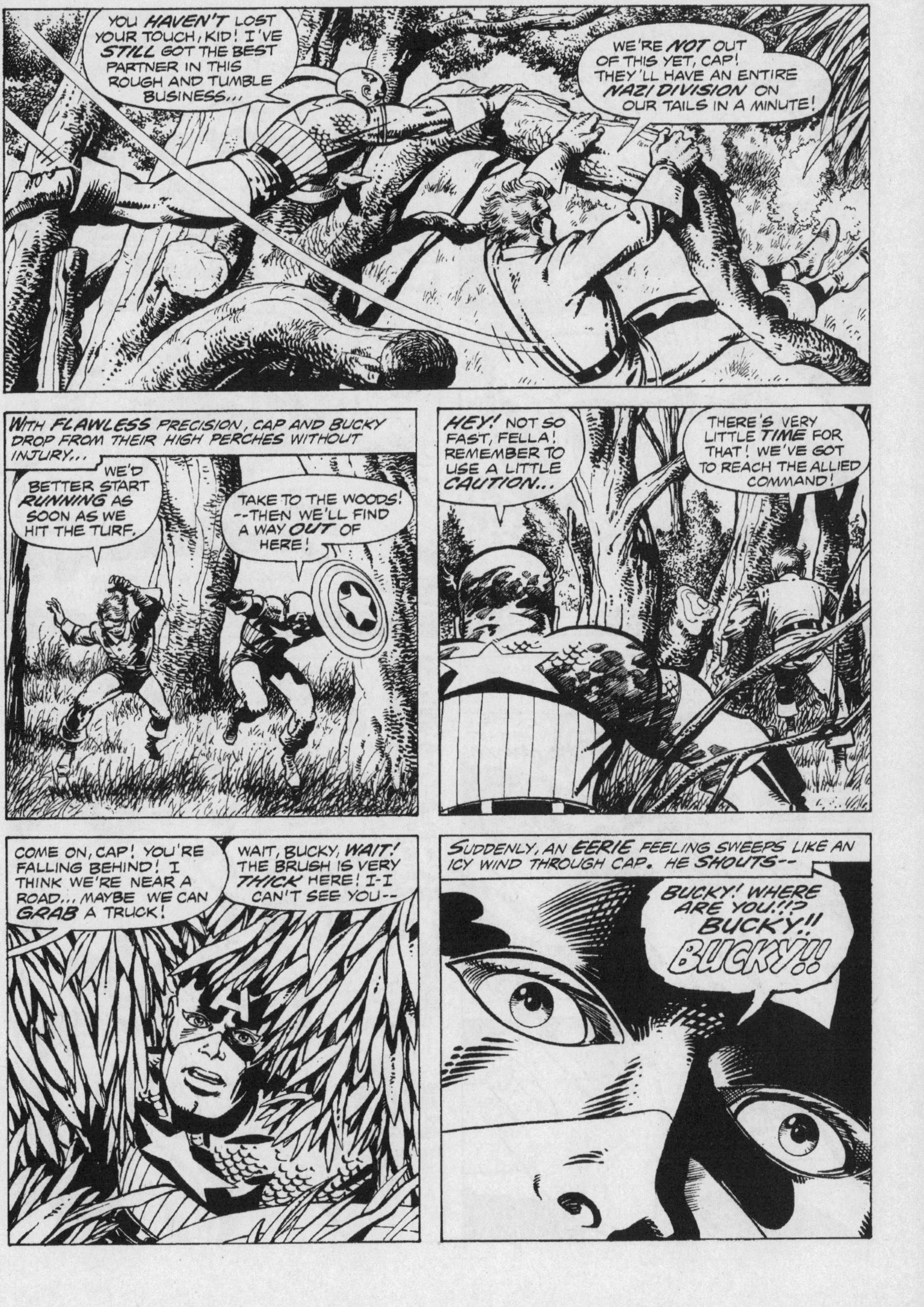

YOU HAVEN'T LOST YOUR TOUCH, KID! I'VE STILL GOT THE BEST PARTNER IN THIS ROUGH AND TUMBLE BUSINESS...
WE'RE NOT OUT OF THIS YET, CAP! THEY'LL HAVE AN ENTIRE NAZI DIVISION ON OUR TAILS IN A MINUTE!
WITH FLAWLESS PRECISION, CAP AND BUCKY DROP FROM THEIR HIGH PERCHES WITHOUT INJURY...
WE'D BETTER START RUNNING AS SOON AS WE HIT THE TURF.
TAKE TO THE WOODS! --THEN WE'LL FIND A WAY OUT OF HERE!
HEY! NOT SO FAST, FELLA! REMEMBER TO USE A LITTLE CAUTION...
THERE'S VERY LITTLE TIME FOR THAT! WE'VE GOT TO REACH THE ALLIED COMMAND!
COME ON, CAP! YOU'RE FALLING BEHIND! I THINK WE'RE NEAR A ROAD... MAYBE WE CAN GRAB A TRUCK!
WAIT, BUCKY, WAIT! THE BRUSH IS VERY THICK HERE! I-I CAN'T SEE YOU--
SUDDENLY, AN EERIE FEELING SWEEPS LIKE AN ICY WIND THROUGH CAP. HE SHOUTS--
BUCKY! WHERE ARE YOU!!? BUCKY!! BUCKY!!

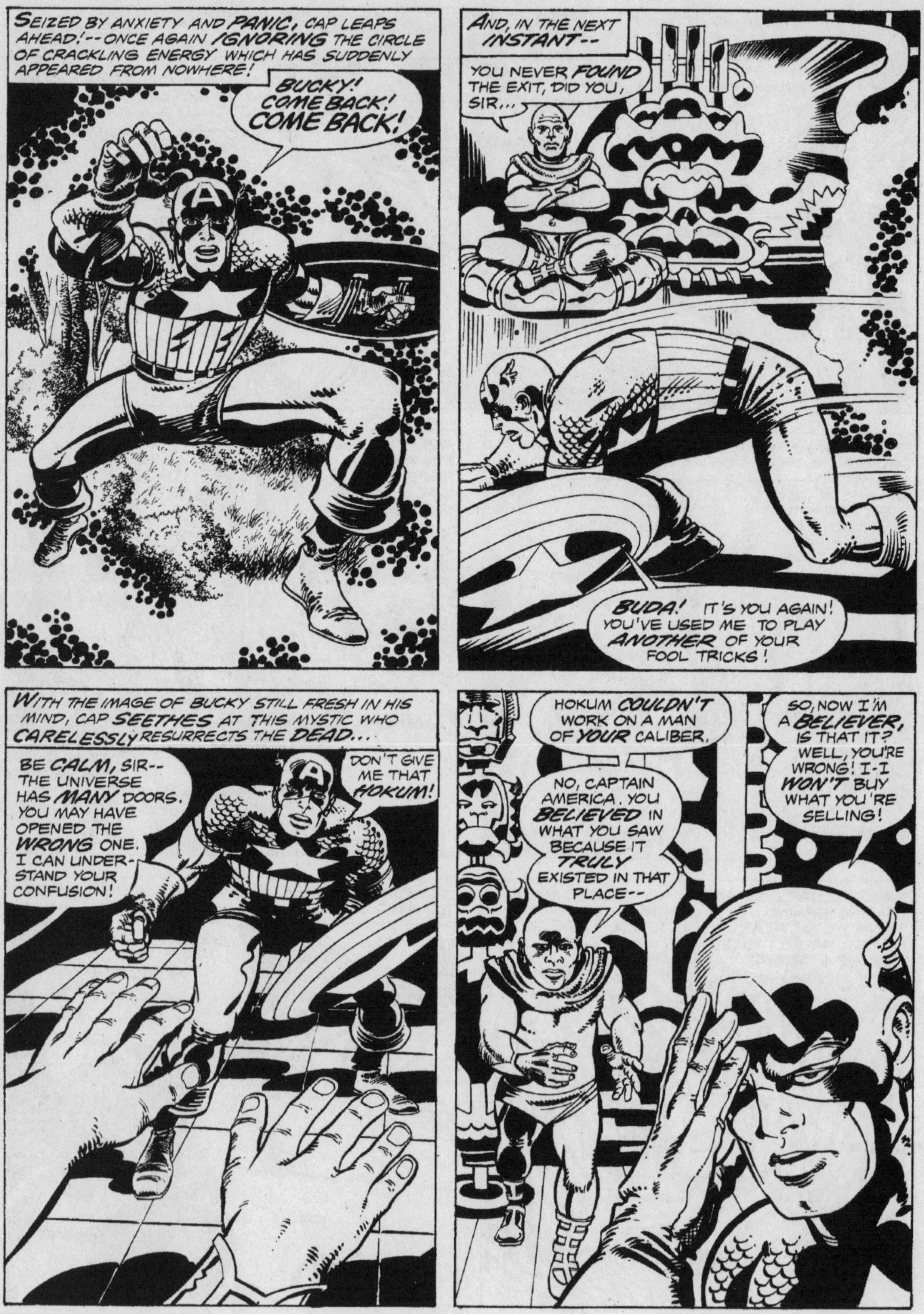
SEIZED BY ANXIETY AND PANIC, CAP LEAPS AHEAD!--ONCE AGAIN IGNORING THE CIRCLE OF CRACKLING ENERGY WHICH HAS SUDDENLY APPEARED FROM NOWHERE!
BUCKY! COME BACK! COME BACK!
AND, IN THE NEXT INSTANT--
YOU NEVER FOUND THE EXIT, DID YOU, SIR...
BUDA! IT'S YOU AGAIN! YOU'VE USED ME TO PLAY ANOTHER OF YOUR FOOL TRICKS!
WITH THE IMAGE OF BUCKY STILL FRESH IN HIS MIND, CAP SEETHES AT THIS MYSTIC WHO CARELESSLY RESURRECTS THE DEAD...
BE CALM, SIR-- THE UNIVERSE HAS MANY DOORS. YOU MAY HAVE OPENED THE WRONG ONE. I CAN UNDERSTAND YOUR CONFUSION!
DON'T GIVE ME THAT HOKUM!
HOKUM COULDN'T WORK ON A MAN OF YOUR CALIBER,
NO, CAPTAIN AMERICA. YOU BELIEVED IN WHAT YOU SAW BECAUSE IT TRULY EXISTED IN THAT PLACE--
SO, NOW I'M A BELIEVER, IS THAT IT? WELL, YOU'RE WRONG! I-I WON'T BUY WHAT YOU'RE SELLING!

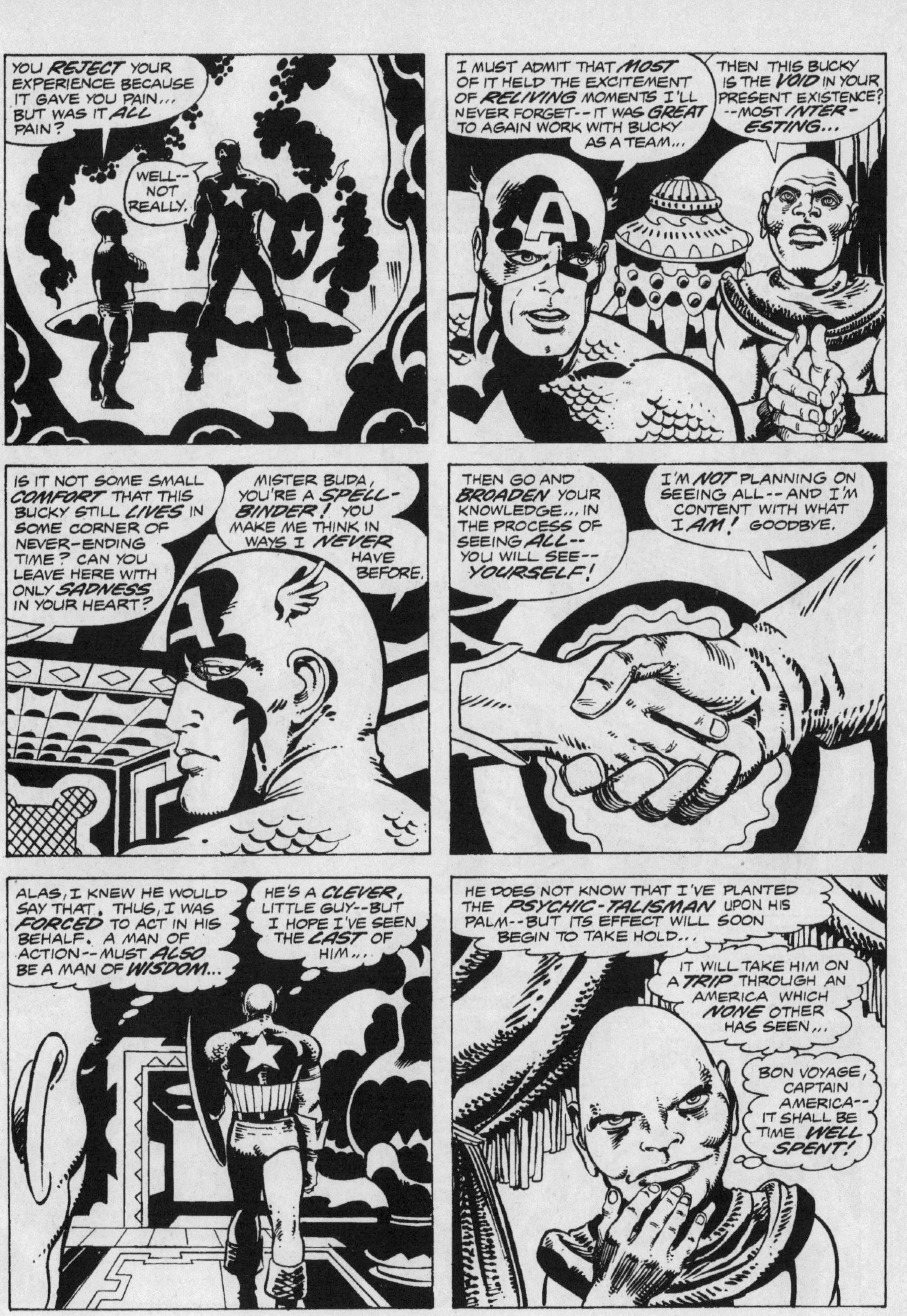

YOU REJECT YOUR EXPERIENCE BECAUSE IT GAVE YOU PAIN... BUT WAS IT ALL PAIN?
WELL-- NOT REALLY.
I MUST ADMIT THAT MOST OF IT HELD THE EXCITEMENT OF RELIVING MOMENTS I'LL NEVER FORGET-- IT WAS GREAT TO AGAIN WORK WITH BUCKY AS A TEAM...
THEN THIS BUCKY IS THE VOID IN YOUR PRESENT EXISTENCE? --MOST INTER-ESTING...
IS IT NOT SOME SMALL COMFORT THAT THIS BUCKY STILL LIVES IN SOME CORNER OF NEVER-ENDING TIME? CAN YOU LEAVE HERE WITH ONLY SADNESS IN YOUR HEART?
MISTER BUDA, YOU'RE A SPELL-BINDER! YOU MAKE ME THINK IN WAYS I NEVER HAVE BEFORE.
THEN GO AND BROADEN YOUR KNOWLEDGE... IN THE PROCESS OF SEEING ALL-- YOU WILL SEE-- YOURSELF!
I'M NOT PLANNING ON SEEING ALL-- AND I'M CONTENT WITH WHAT I AM! GOODBYE.
ALAS, I KNEW HE WOULD SAY THAT. THUS, I WAS FORCED TO ACT IN HIS BEHALF. A MAN OF ACTION-- MUST ALSO BE A MAN OF WISDOM...
HE'S A CLEVER, LITTLE GUY--BUT I HOPE I'VE SEEN THE LAST OF HIM...
HE DOES NOT KNOW THAT I'VE PLANTED THE PSYCHIC-TALISMAN UPON HIS PALM--BUT ITS EFFECT WILL SOON BEGIN TO TAKE HOLD...
IT WILL TAKE HIM ON A TRIP THROUGH AN AMERICA WHICH NONE OTHER HAS SEEN...
BON VOYAGE, CAPTAIN AMERICA-- IT SHALL BE TIME WELL SPENT!

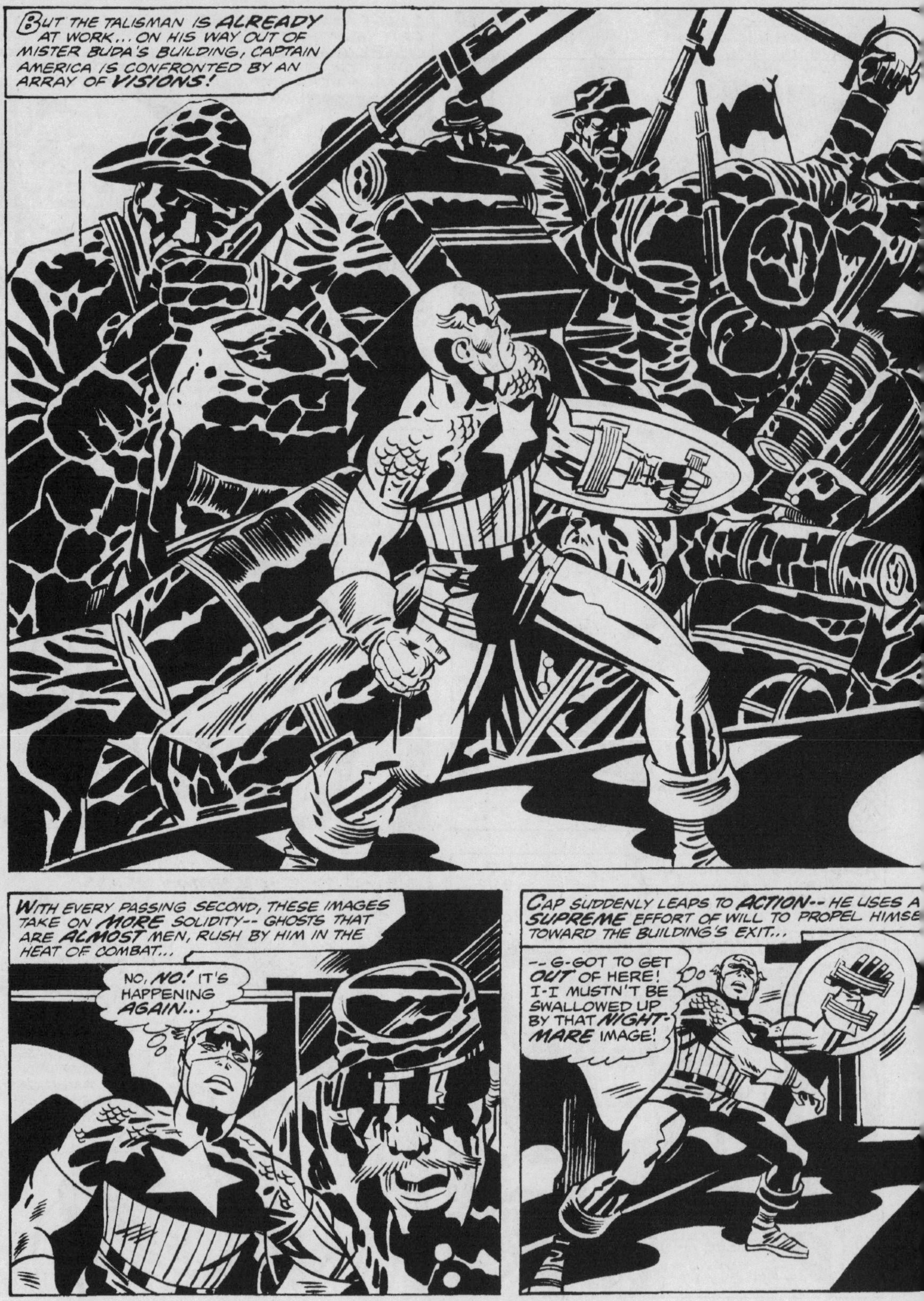
BUT THE TALISMAN IS ALREADY AT WORK... ON HIS WAY OUT OF MISTER BUDA'S BUILDING, CAPTAIN AMERICA IS CONFRONTED BY AN ARRAY OF VISIONS!
WITH EVERY PASSING SECOND, THESE IMAGES TAKE ON MORE SOLIDITY-- GHOSTS THAT ARE ALMOST MEN, RUSH BY HIM IN THE HEAT OF COMBAT...
NO, NO! IT'S HAPPENING AGAIN...
CAP SUDDENLY LEAPS TO ACTION-- HE USES A SUPREME EFFORT OF WILL TO PROPEL HIMSE
TOWARD THE BUILDING'S EXIT...
-- G-GOT TO GET OUT OF HERE! I-I MUSTN'T BE SWALLOWED UP BY THAT NIGHT-MARE IMAGE!

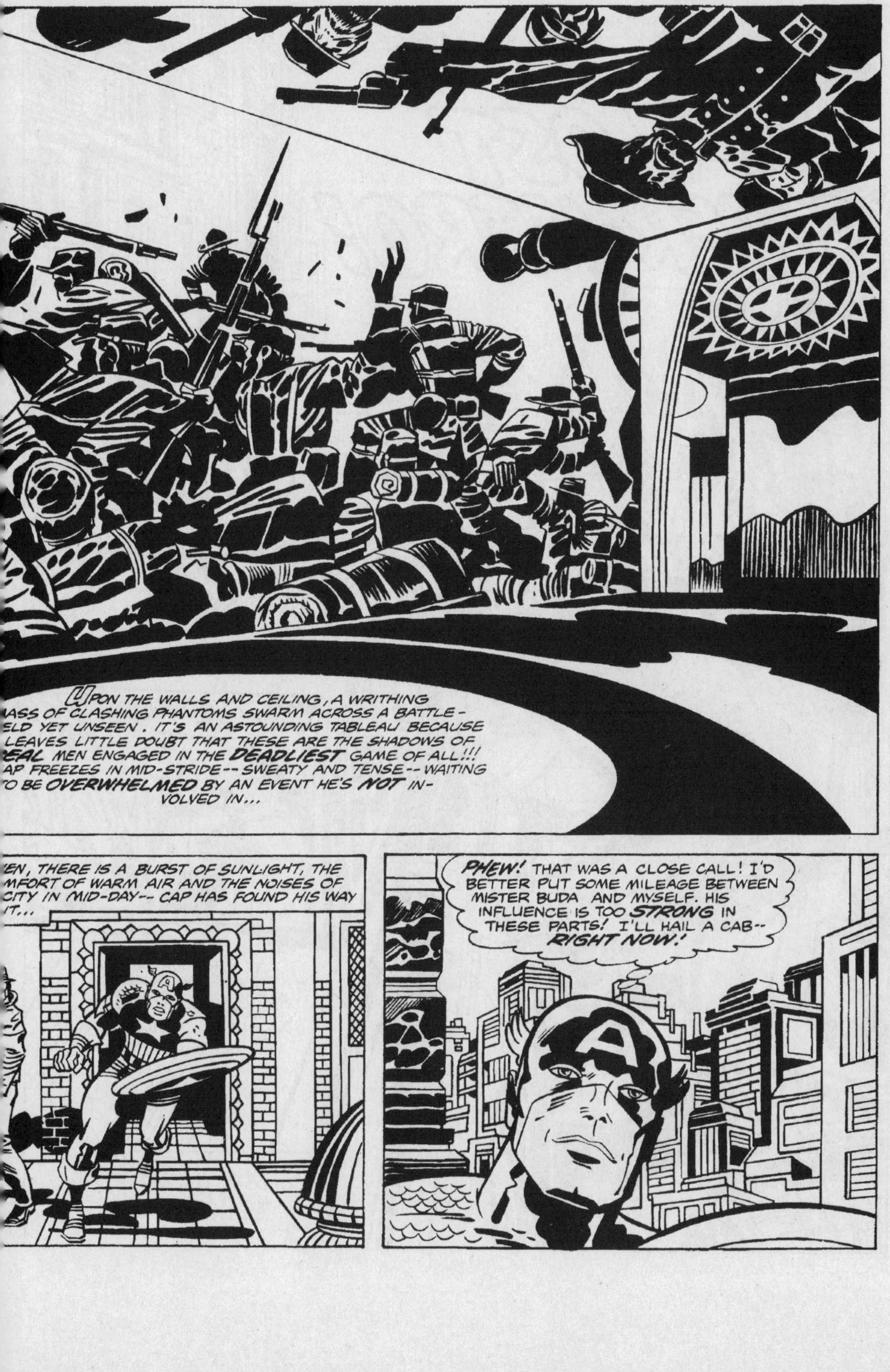
UPON THE WALLS AND CEILING, A WRITHING
ASS OF CLASHING PHANTOMS SWARM ACROSS A BATTLE-
ELD YET UNSEEN. IT'S AN ASTOUNDING TABLEAU BECAUSE
LEAVES LITTLE DOUBT THAT THESE ARE THE SHADOWS OF
REAL MEN ENGAGED IN THE DEADLIEST GAME OF ALL!!!
AP FREEZES IN MID-STRIDE-- SWEATY AND TENSE-- WAITING
TO BE OVERWHELMED BY AN EVENT HE'S NOT IN-
VOLVED IN...
EN, THERE IS A BURST OF SUNLIGHT, THE
MFORT OF WARM AIR AND THE NOISES OF
CITY IN MID-DAY-- CAP HAS FOUND HIS WAY
T...
PHEW! THAT WAS A CLOSE CALL! I'D BETTER PUT SOME MILEAGE BETWEEN MISTER BUDA AND MYSELF. HIS INFLUENCE IS TOO STRONG IN THESE PARTS! I'LL HAIL A CAB-- RIGHT NOW!

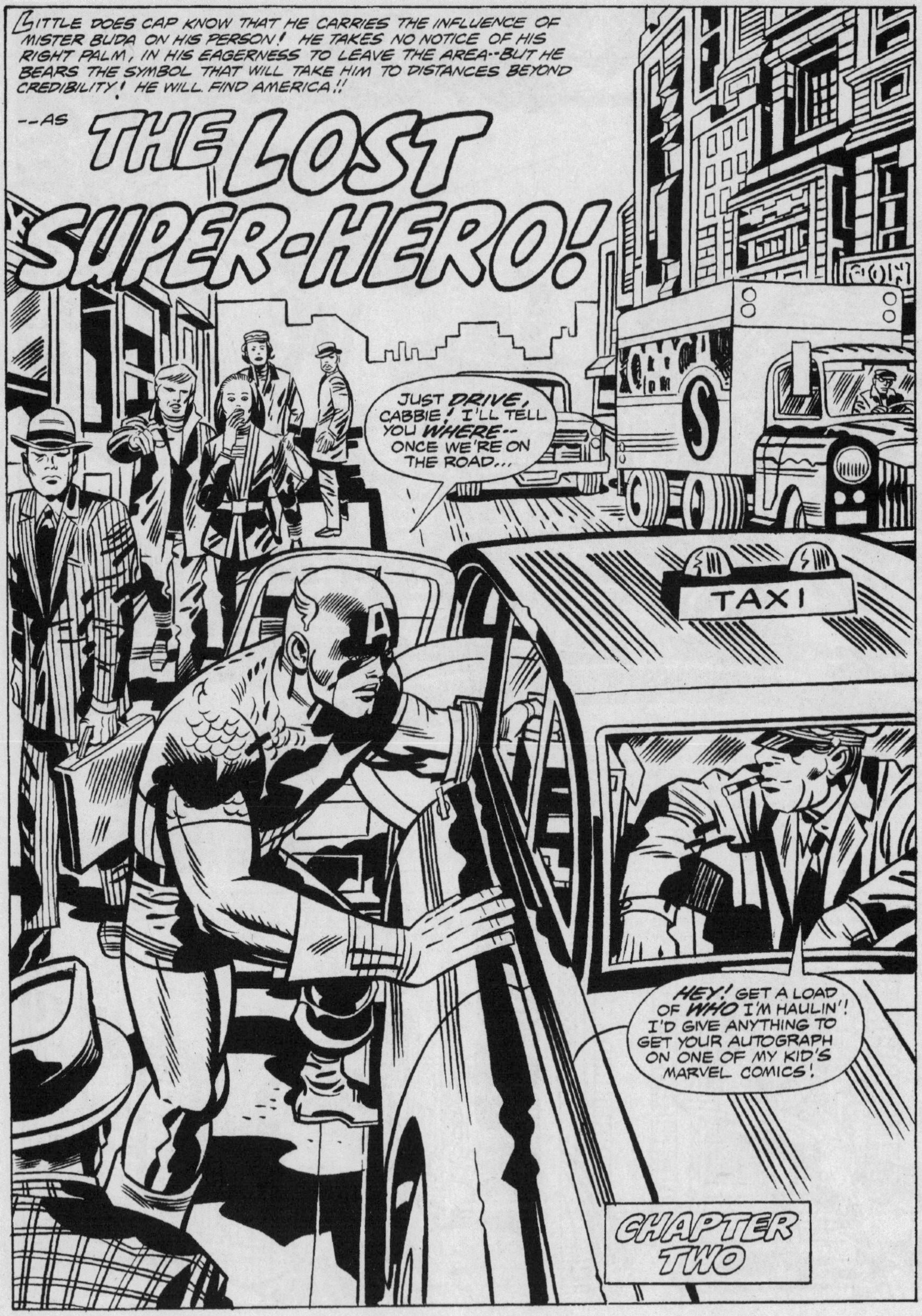
LITTLE DOES CAP KNOW THAT HE CARRIES THE INFLUENCE OF MISTER BUDA ON HIS PERSON! HE TAKES NO NOTICE OF HIS RIGHT PALM, IN HIS EAGERNESS TO LEAVE THE AREA--BUT HE BEARS THE SYMBOL THAT WILL TAKE HIM TO DISTANCES BEYOND CREDIBILITY! HE WILL FIND AMERICA!!
--AS THE LOST SUPER-HERO!
JUST DRIVE, CABBIE! I'LL TELL YOU WHERE-- ONCE WE'RE ON THE ROAD...
TAXI
HEY! GET A LOAD OF WHO I'M HAULIN'! I'D GIVE ANYTHING TO GET YOUR AUTOGRAPH ON ONE OF MY KID'S MARVEL COMICS!
CHAPTER TWO

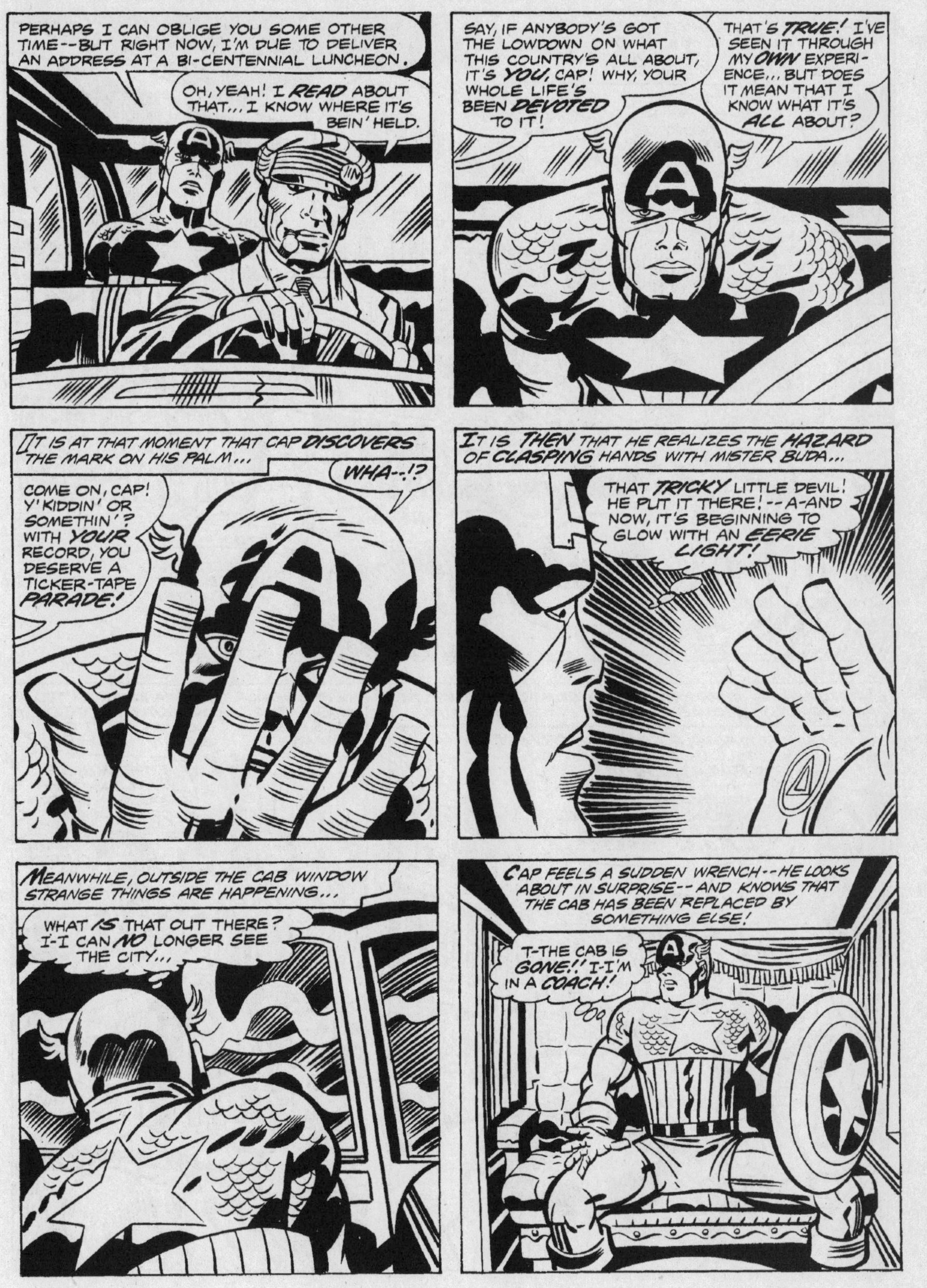
PERHAPS I CAN OBLIGE YOU SOME OTHER TIME--BUT RIGHT NOW, I'M DUE TO DELIVER AN ADDRESS AT A BI-CENTENNIAL LUNCHEON.
OH, YEAH! I READ ABOUT THAT... I KNOW WHERE IT'S BEIN' HELD.
SAY, IF ANYBODY'S GOT THE LOWDOWN ON WHAT THIS COUNTRY'S ALL ABOUT, IT'S YOU, CAP! WHY, YOUR WHOLE LIFE'S BEEN DEVOTED TO IT!
THAT'S TRUE! I'VE SEEN IT THROUGH MY OWN EXPERIENCE... BUT DOES IT MEAN THAT I KNOW WHAT IT'S ALL ABOUT?
IT IS AT THAT MOMENT THAT CAP DISCOVERS THE MARK ON HIS PALM...
WHA--!?
COME ON, CAP! Y'KIDDIN' OR SOMETHIN'? WITH YOUR RECORD, YOU DESERVE A TICKER-TAPE PARADE!
IT IS THEN THAT HE REALIZES THE HAZARD OF CLASPING HANDS WITH MISTER BUDA...
THAT TRICKY LITTLE DEVIL! HE PUT IT THERE! --A-AND NOW, IT'S BEGINNING TO GLOW WITH AN EERIE LIGHT!
MEANWHILE, OUTSIDE THE CAB WINDOW STRANGE THINGS ARE HAPPENING...
WHAT IS THAT OUT THERE? I-I CAN NO LONGER SEE THE CITY...
CAP FEELS A SUDDEN WRENCH--HE LOOKS ABOUT IN SURPRISE--AND KNOWS THAT THE CAB HAS BEEN REPLACED BY SOMETHING ELSE!
T-THE CAB IS GONE!! I-I'M IN A COACH!

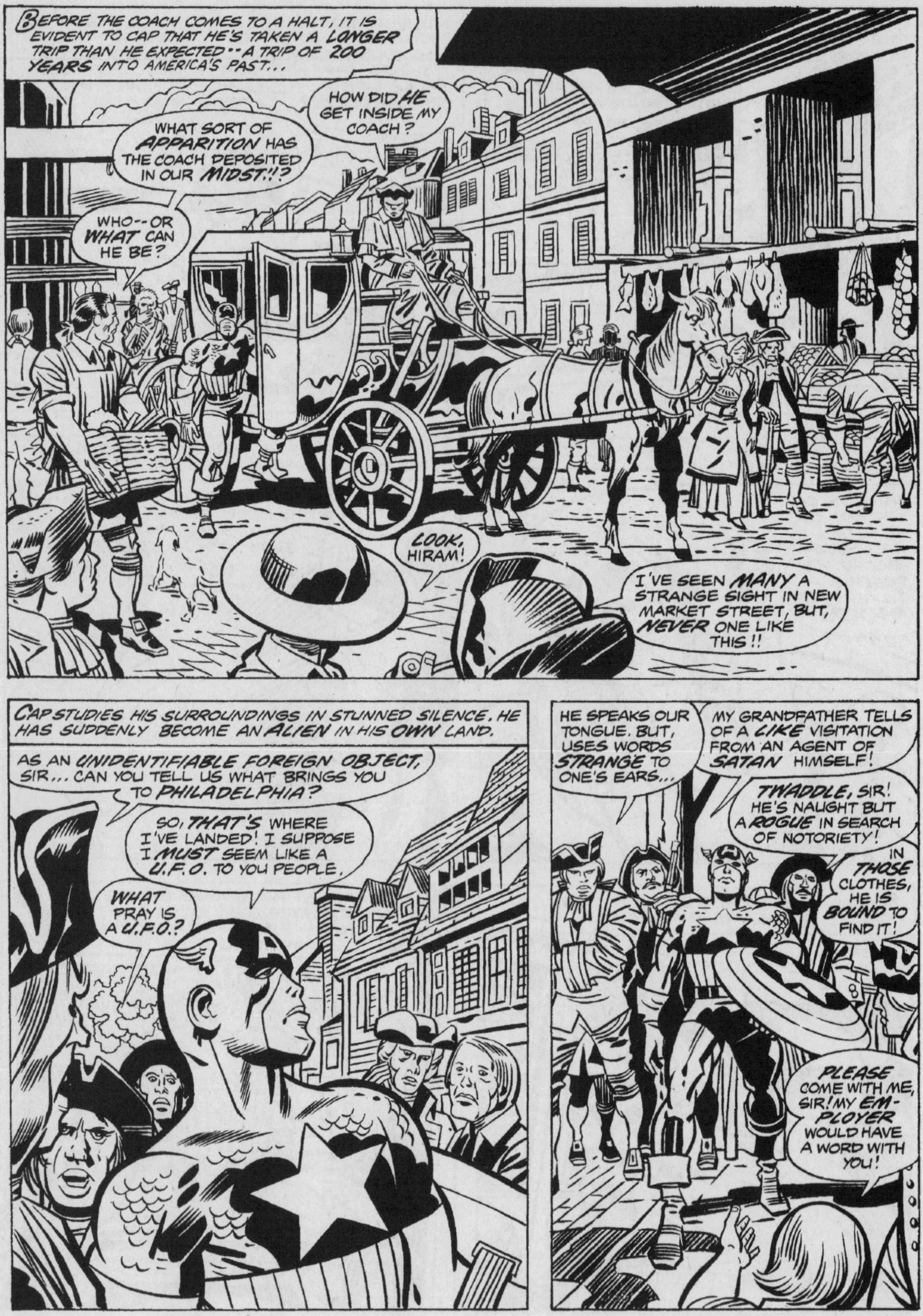
BEFORE THE COACH COMES TO A HALT, IT IS EVIDENT TO CAP THAT HE'S TAKEN A LONGER TRIP THAN HE EXPECTED -- A TRIP OF 200 YEARS INTO AMERICA'S PAST...
HOW DID HE GET INSIDE MY COACH?
WHAT SORT OF APPARITION HAS THE COACH DEPOSITED IN OUR MIDST!!?
WHO--OR WHAT CAN HE BE?
LOOK, HIRAM!
I'VE SEEN MANY A STRANGE SIGHT IN NEW MARKET STREET, BUT, NEVER ONE LIKE THIS!!
CAP STUDIES HIS SURROUNDINGS IN STUNNED SILENCE. HE HAS SUDDENLY BECOME AN ALIEN IN HIS OWN LAND.
AS AN UNIDENTIFIABLE FOREIGN OBJECT, SIR... CAN YOU TELL US WHAT BRINGS YOU TO PHILADELPHIA?
SO, THAT'S WHERE I'VE LANDED! I SUPPOSE I MUST SEEM LIKE A U.F.O. TO YOU PEOPLE.
WHAT PRAY IS A U.F.O.?
HE SPEAKS OUR TONGUE. BUT, USES WORDS STRANGE TO ONE'S EARS...
MY GRANDFATHER TELLS OF A LIKE VISITATION FROM AN AGENT OF SATAN HIMSELF!
TWADDLE, SIR! HE'S NAUGHT BUT A ROGUE IN SEARCH OF NOTORIETY!
IN THOSE CLOTHES, HE IS BOUND TO FIND IT!
PLEASE COME WITH ME, SIR! MY EMPLOYER WOULD HAVE A WORD WITH YOU!

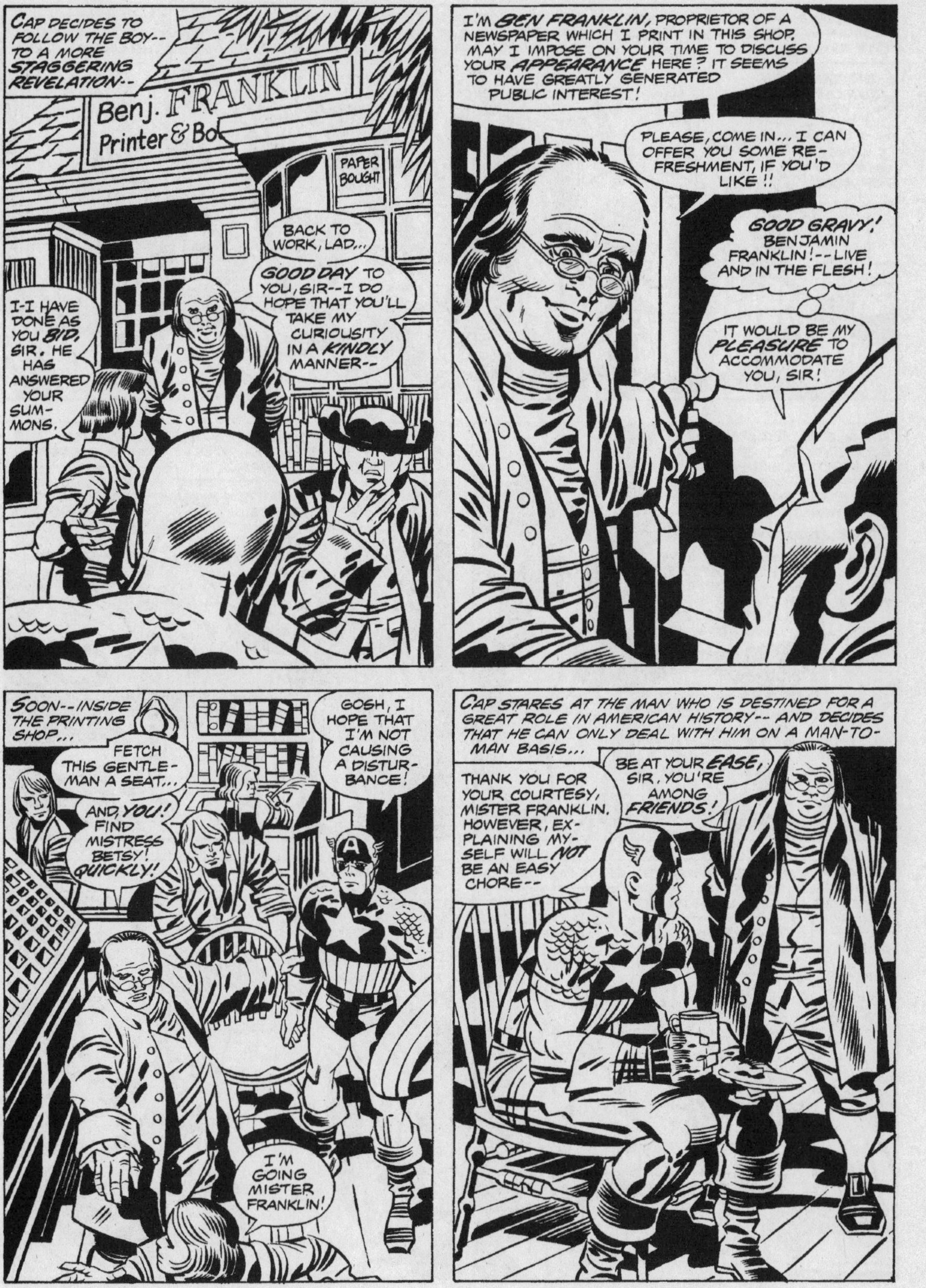
CAP DECIDES TO FOLLOW THE BOY-- TO A MORE STAGGERING REVELATION--
Benj. FRANKLIN
Printer & Bo
PAPER BOUGHT
BACK TO WORK, LAD...
GOOD DAY TO YOU, SIR--I DO HOPE THAT YOU'LL TAKE MY CURIOUSITY IN A KINDLY MANNER--
I-I HAVE DONE AS YOU BID, SIR. HE HAS ANSWERED YOUR SUMMONS.
I'M BEN FRANKLIN, PROPRIETOR OF A NEWSPAPER WHICH I PRINT IN THIS SHOP. MAY I IMPOSE ON YOUR TIME TO DISCUSS YOUR APPEARANCE HERE? IT SEEMS TO HAVE GREATLY GENERATED PUBLIC INTEREST!
PLEASE, COME IN... I CAN OFFER YOU SOME REFRESHMENT, IF YOU'D LIKE!!
GOOD GRAVY! BENJAMIN FRANKLIN!--LIVE AND IN THE FLESH!
IT WOULD BE MY PLEASURE TO ACCOMMODATE YOU, SIR!
SOON--INSIDE THE PRINTING SHOP...
FETCH THIS GENTLEMAN A SEAT...
AND, YOU! FIND MISTRESS BETSY! QUICKLY!
GOSH, I HOPE THAT I'M NOT CAUSING A DISTURBANCE!
I'M GOING MISTER FRANKLIN!
CAP STARES AT THE MAN WHO IS DESTINED FOR A GREAT ROLE IN AMERICAN HISTORY-- AND DECIDES THAT HE CAN ONLY DEAL WITH HIM ON A MAN-TO-MAN BASIS...
BE AT YOUR EASE, SIR, YOU'RE AMONG FRIENDS!
THANK YOU FOR YOUR COURTESY, MISTER FRANKLIN. HOWEVER, EXPLAINING MYSELF WILL NOT BE AN EASY CHORE--

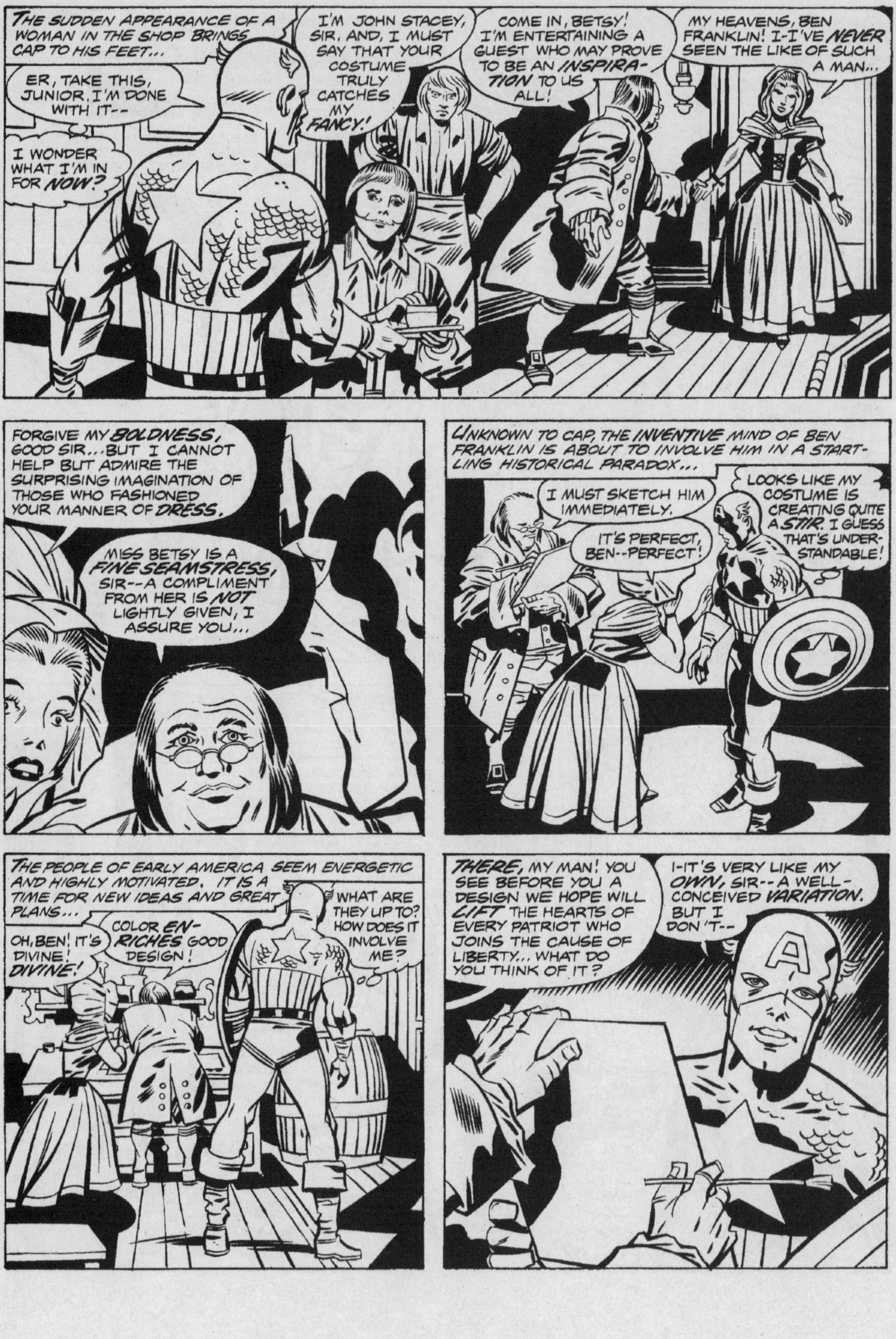
THE SUDDEN APPEARANCE OF A WOMAN IN THE SHOP BRINGS CAP TO HIS FEET...
ER, TAKE THIS, JUNIOR. I'M DONE WITH IT--
I WONDER WHAT I'M IN FOR NOW?
I'M JOHN STACEY, SIR. AND, I MUST SAY THAT YOUR COSTUME TRULY CATCHES MY FANCY!
COME IN, BETSY! I'M ENTERTAINING A GUEST WHO MAY PROVE TO BE AN INSPIRATION TO US ALL!
MY HEAVENS, BEN FRANKLIN! I-I'VE NEVER SEEN THE LIKE OF SUCH A MAN...
FORGIVE MY BOLDNESS, GOOD SIR... BUT I CANNOT HELP BUT ADMIRE THE SURPRISING IMAGINATION OF THOSE WHO FASHIONED YOUR MANNER OF DRESS.
MISS BETSY IS A FINE SEAMSTRESS, SIR--A COMPLIMENT FROM HER IS NOT LIGHTLY GIVEN, I ASSURE YOU...
UNKNOWN TO CAP, THE INVENTIVE MIND OF BEN FRANKLIN IS ABOUT TO INVOLVE HIM IN A STARTLING HISTORICAL PARADOX...
I MUST SKETCH HIM IMMEDIATELY.
IT'S PERFECT, BEN--PERFECT!
LOOKS LIKE MY COSTUME IS CREATING QUITE A STIR. I GUESS THAT'S UNDERSTANDABLE!
THE PEOPLE OF EARLY AMERICA SEEM ENERGETIC AND HIGHLY MOTIVATED. IT IS A TIME FOR NEW IDEAS AND GREAT PLANS...
OH, BEN! IT'S DIVINE! DIVINE!
COLOR ENRICHES GOOD DESIGN!
WHAT ARE THEY UP TO? HOW DOES IT INVOLVE ME?
THERE, MY MAN! YOU SEE BEFORE YOU A DESIGN WE HOPE WILL LIFT THE HEARTS OF EVERY PATRIOT WHO JOINS THE CAUSE OF LIBERTY... WHAT DO YOU THINK OF IT?
I-IT'S VERY LIKE MY OWN, SIR--A WELL-CONCEIVED VARIATION. BUT I DON'T--
A

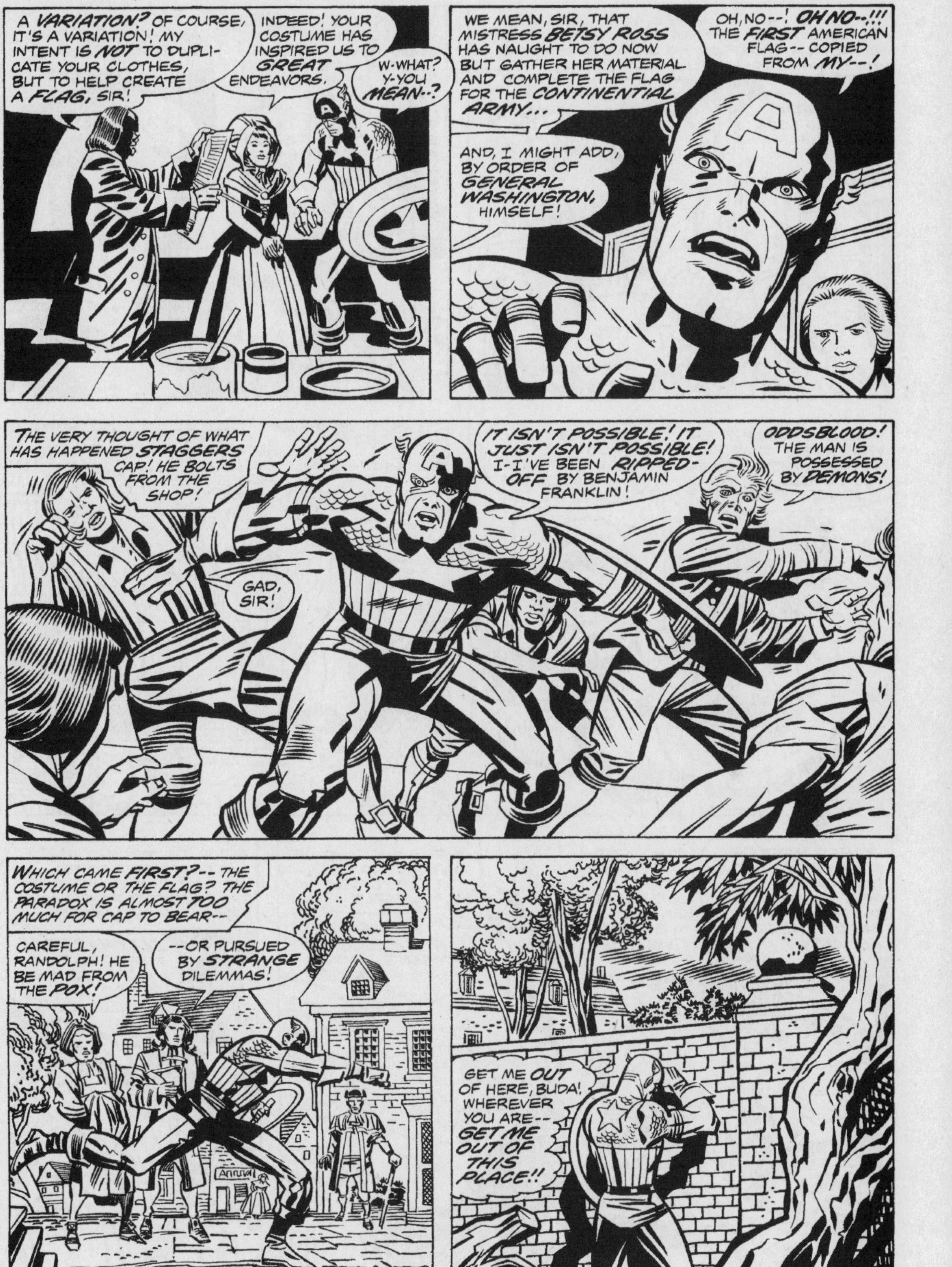
A VARIATION? OF COURSE, IT'S A VARIATION! MY INTENT IS NOT TO DUPLICATE YOUR CLOTHES, BUT TO HELP CREATE A FLAG, SIR!
INDEED! YOUR COSTUME HAS INSPIRED US TO GREAT ENDEAVORS.
W-WHAT? Y-YOU MEAN--?
WE MEAN, SIR, THAT MISTRESS BETSY ROSS HAS NAUGHT TO DO NOW BUT GATHER HER MATERIAL AND COMPLETE THE FLAG FOR THE CONTINENTIAL ARMY...
AND, I MIGHT ADD, BY ORDER OF GENERAL WASHINGTON, HIMSELF!
OH, NO--! OH NO--!!! THE FIRST AMERICAN FLAG-- COPIED FROM MY--!
THE VERY THOUGHT OF WHAT HAS HAPPENED STAGGERS CAP! HE BOLTS FROM THE SHOP!
IT ISN'T POSSIBLE! IT JUST ISN'T POSSIBLE! I-I'VE BEEN RIPPED-OFF BY BENJAMIN FRANKLIN!
GAD, SIR!
ODDSBLOOD! THE MAN IS POSSESSED BY DEMONS!
WHICH CAME FIRST?-- THE COSTUME OR THE FLAG? THE PARADOX IS ALMOST TOO MUCH FOR CAP TO BEAR--
CAREFUL, RANDOLPH! HE BE MAD FROM THE POX!
--OR PURSUED BY STRANGE DILEMMAS!
GET ME OUT OF HERE, BUDA! WHEREVER YOU ARE-- GET ME OUT OF THIS PLACE!!

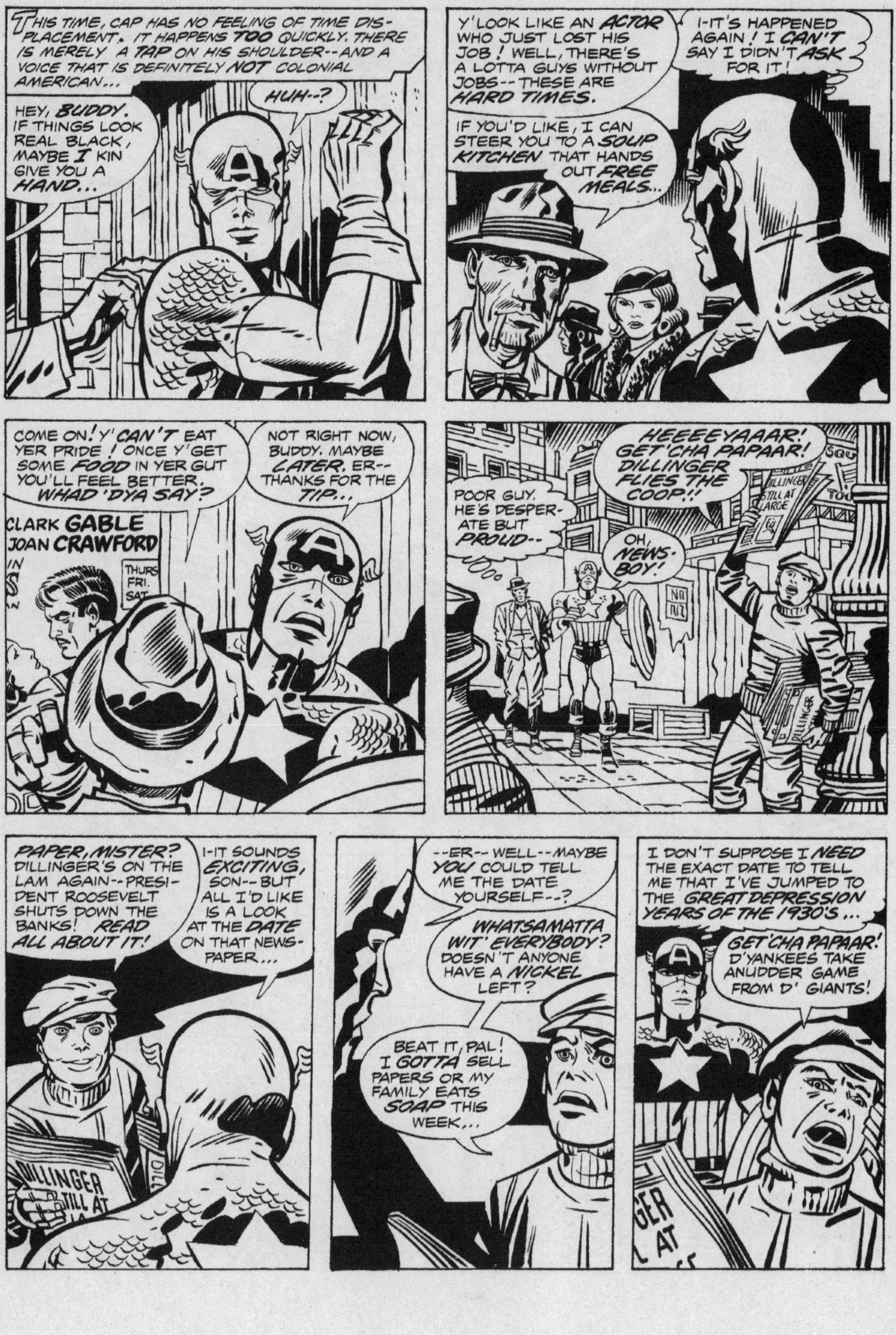
THIS TIME, CAP HAS NO FEELING OF TIME DISPLACEMENT. IT HAPPENS TOO QUICKLY. THERE IS MERELY A TAP ON HIS SHOULDER--AND A VOICE THAT IS DEFINITELY NOT COLONIAL AMERICAN...
HEY, BUDDY. IF THINGS LOOK REAL BLACK, MAYBE I KIN GIVE YOU A HAND...
HUH--?
Y'LOOK LIKE AN ACTOR WHO JUST LOST HIS JOB! WELL, THERE'S A LOTTA GUYS WITHOUT JOBS--THESE ARE HARD TIMES.
I-IT'S HAPPENED AGAIN! I CAN'T SAY I DIDN'T ASK FOR IT!
IF YOU'D LIKE, I CAN STEER YOU TO A SOUP KITCHEN THAT HANDS OUT FREE MEALS...
COME ON! Y' CAN'T EAT YER PRIDE! ONCE Y'GET SOME FOOD IN YER GUT YOU'LL FEEL BETTER. WHAD'DYA SAY?
NOT RIGHT NOW, BUDDY. MAYBE LATER. ER--THANKS FOR THE TIP...
CLARK GABLE
JOAN CRAWFORD
THURS FRI. SAT
HEEEEYAAAR! GET'CHA PAPAAR! DILLINGER FLIES THE COOP!!
DILLINGER STILL AT LARGE
POOR GUY. HE'S DESPERATE BUT PROUD--
OH, NEWS-BOY!
PAPER, MISTER? DILLINGER'S ON THE LAM AGAIN--PRESIDENT ROOSEVELT SHUTS DOWN THE BANKS! READ ALL ABOUT IT!
I-IT SOUNDS EXCITING, SON--BUT ALL I'D LIKE IS A LOOK AT THE DATE ON THAT NEWSPAPER...
--ER--WELL--MAYBE YOU COULD TELL ME THE DATE YOURSELF--?
WHATSAMATTA WIT' EVERYBODY? DOESN'T ANYONE HAVE A NICKEL LEFT?
BEAT IT, PAL! I GOTTA SELL PAPERS OR MY FAMILY EATS SOAP THIS WEEK...
I DON'T SUPPOSE I NEED THE EXACT DATE TO TELL ME THAT I'VE JUMPED TO THE GREAT DEPRESSION YEARS OF THE 1930'S...
GET'CHA PAPAAR! D'YANKEES TAKE ANUDDER GAME FROM D' GIANTS!

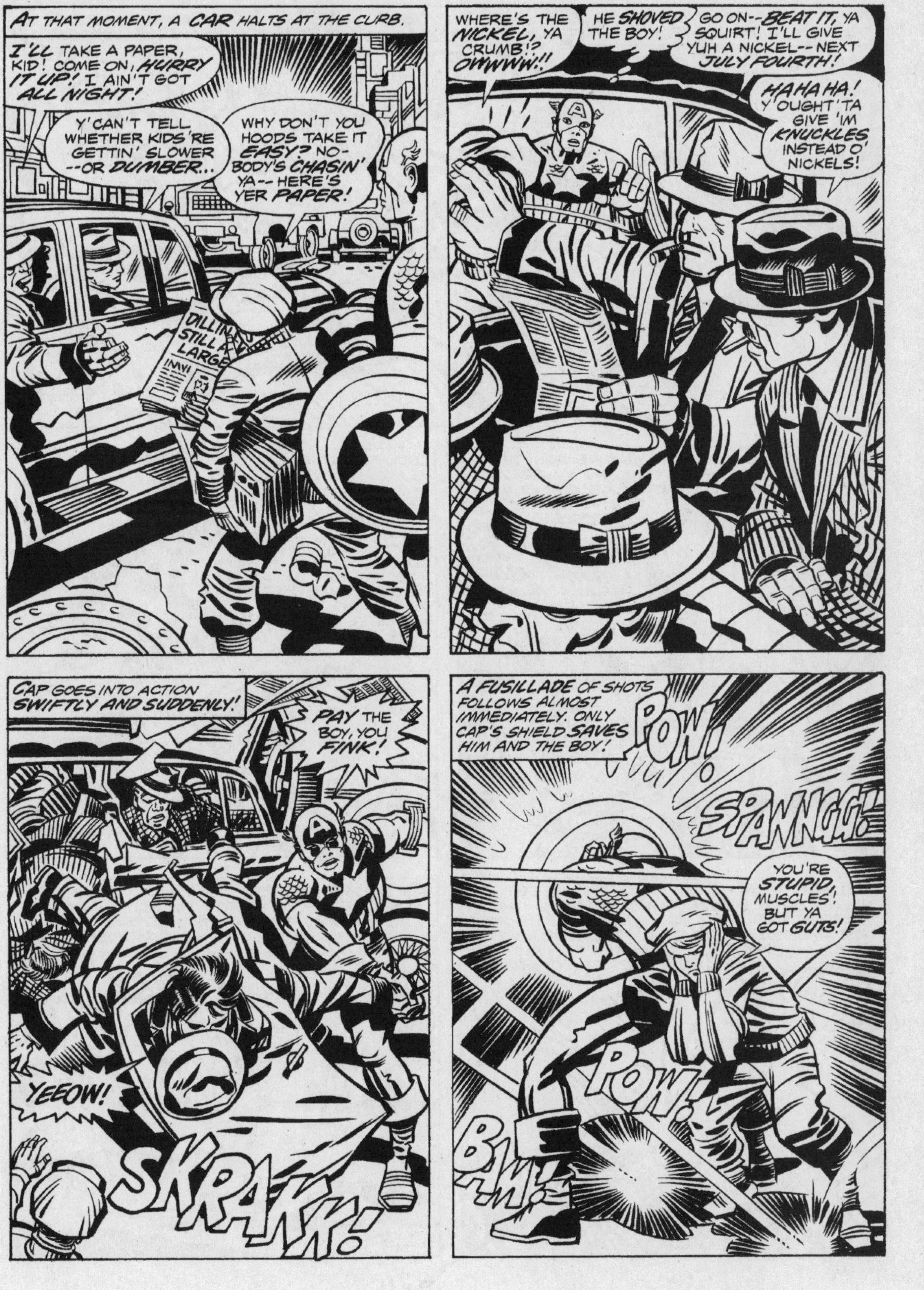
AT THAT MOMENT, A CAR HALTS AT THE CURB.
I'LL TAKE A PAPER, KID! COME ON, HURRY IT UP! I AIN'T GOT ALL NIGHT!
Y'CAN'T TELL WHETHER KIDS'RE GETTIN' SLOWER --OR DUMBER...
WHY DON'T YOU HOODS TAKE IT EASY? NO-BODY'S CHASIN' YA-- HERE'S YER PAPER!
WHERE'S THE NICKEL, YA CRUMB!? OWWWW!!
HE SHOVED THE BOY!
GO ON--BEAT IT, YA SQUIRT! I'LL GIVE YUH A NICKEL-- NEXT JULY FOURTH!
HAHAHA! Y'OUGHT 'TA GIVE 'IM KNUCKLES, INSTEAD O' NICKELS!
CAP GOES INTO ACTION SWIFTLY AND SUDDENLY!
PAY THE BOY, YOU FINK!
YEEOW!
SKRAKK!
A FUSILLADE OF SHOTS FOLLOWS ALMOST IMMEDIATELY. ONLY CAP'S SHIELD SAVES HIM AND THE BOY!
POW!
SPANNGG!
YOU'RE STUPID, MUSCLES! BUT YA GOT GUTS!
POW!

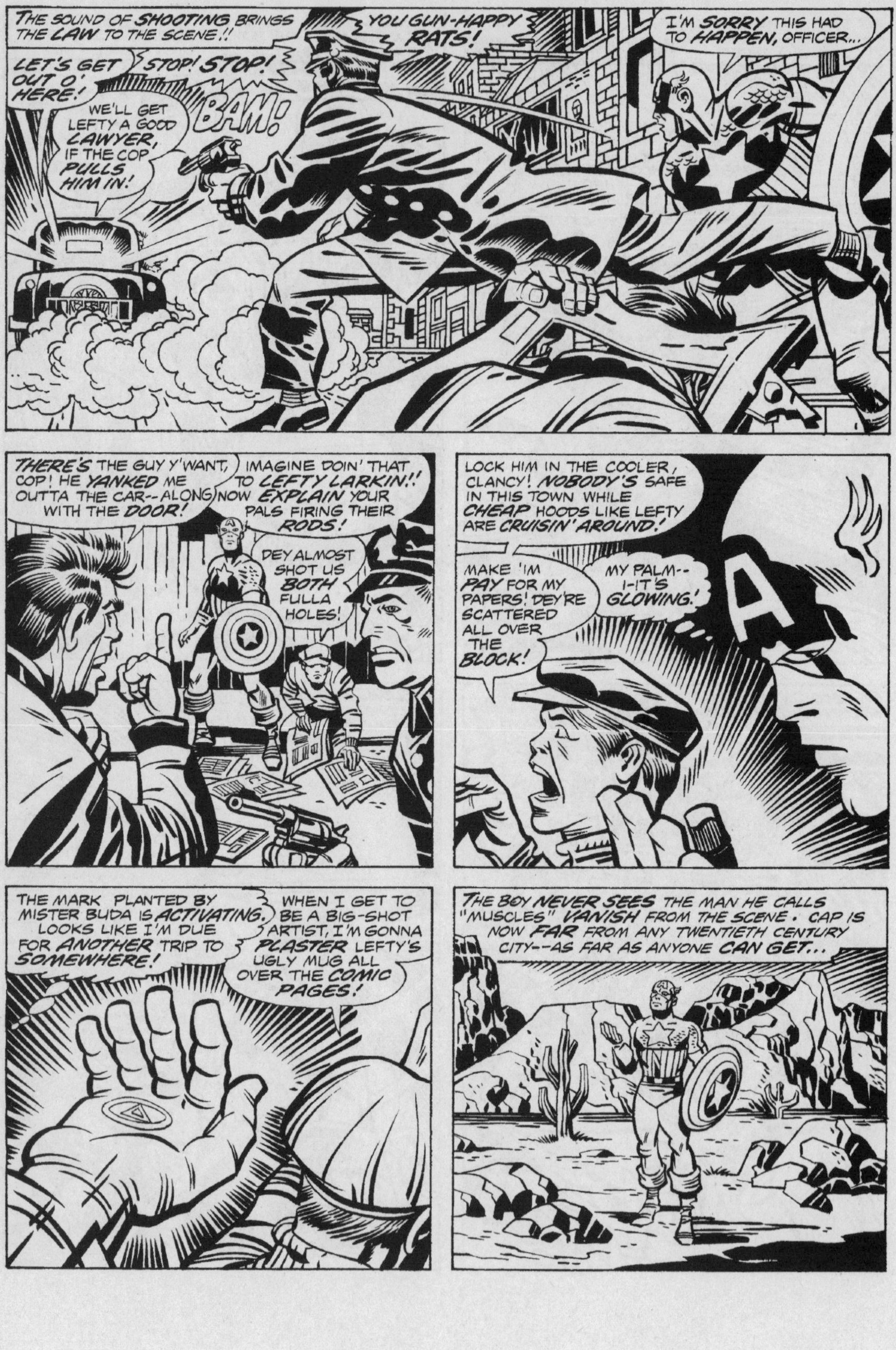
THE SOUND OF SHOOTING BRINGS THE LAW TO THE SCENE!!
YOU GUN-HAPPY RATS!
I'M SORRY THIS HAD TO HAPPEN, OFFICER...
LET'S GET OUT O' HERE!
STOP! STOP!
WE'LL GET LEFTY A GOOD LAWYER, IF THE COP PULLS HIM IN!
BAM!
THERE'S THE GUY Y'WANT, COP! HE YANKED ME OUTTA THE CAR--ALONG WITH THE DOOR!
IMAGINE DOIN' THAT TO LEFTY LARKIN!! NOW EXPLAIN YOUR PALS FIRING THEIR RODS!
DEY ALMOST SHOT US BOTH FULLA HOLES!
LOCK HIM IN THE COOLER, CLANCY! NOBODY'S SAFE IN THIS TOWN WHILE CHEAP HOODS LIKE LEFTY ARE CRUISIN' AROUND!
MAKE 'IM PAY FOR MY PAPERS! DEY'RE SCATTERED ALL OVER THE BLOCK!
MY PALM-- I-IT'S GLOWING!
THE MARK PLANTED BY MISTER BUDA IS ACTIVATING. LOOKS LIKE I'M DUE FOR ANOTHER TRIP TO SOMEWHERE!
WHEN I GET TO BE A BIG-SHOT ARTIST, I'M GONNA PLASTER LEFTY'S UGLY MUG ALL OVER THE COMIC PAGES!
THE BOY NEVER SEES THE MAN HE CALLS "MUSCLES" VANISH FROM THE SCENE. CAP IS NOW FAR FROM ANY TWENTIETH CENTURY CITY--AS FAR AS ANYONE CAN GET...

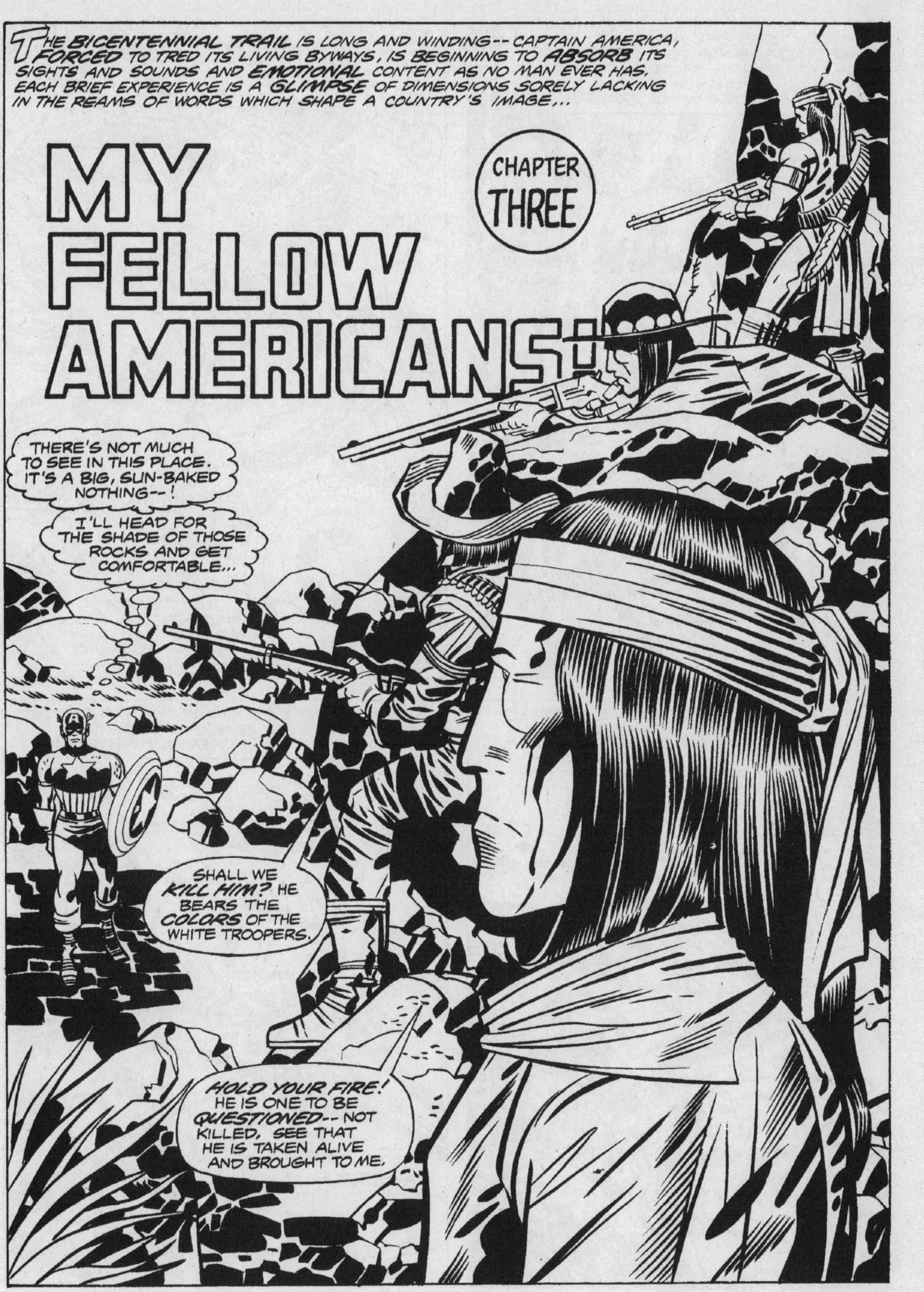
THE BICENTENNIAL TRAIL IS LONG AND WINDING-- CAPTAIN AMERICA, FORCED TO TRED ITS LIVING BYWAYS, IS BEGINNING TO ABSORB ITS SIGHTS AND SOUNDS AND EMOTIONAL CONTENT AS NO MAN EVER HAS. EACH BRIEF EXPERIENCE IS A GLIMPSE OF DIMENSIONS SORELY LACKING IN THE REAMS OF WORDS WHICH SHAPE A COUNTRY'S IMAGE...
MY FELLOW AMERICANS!
CHAPTER THREE
THERE'S NOT MUCH TO SEE IN THIS PLACE. IT'S A BIG, SUN-BAKED NOTHING--!
I'LL HEAD FOR THE SHADE OF THOSE ROCKS AND GET COMFORTABLE...
SHALL WE KILL HIM? HE BEARS THE COLORS OF THE WHITE TROOPERS.
HOLD YOUR FIRE! HE IS ONE TO BE QUESTIONED-- NOT KILLED. SEE THAT HE IS TAKEN ALIVE AND BROUGHT TO ME.

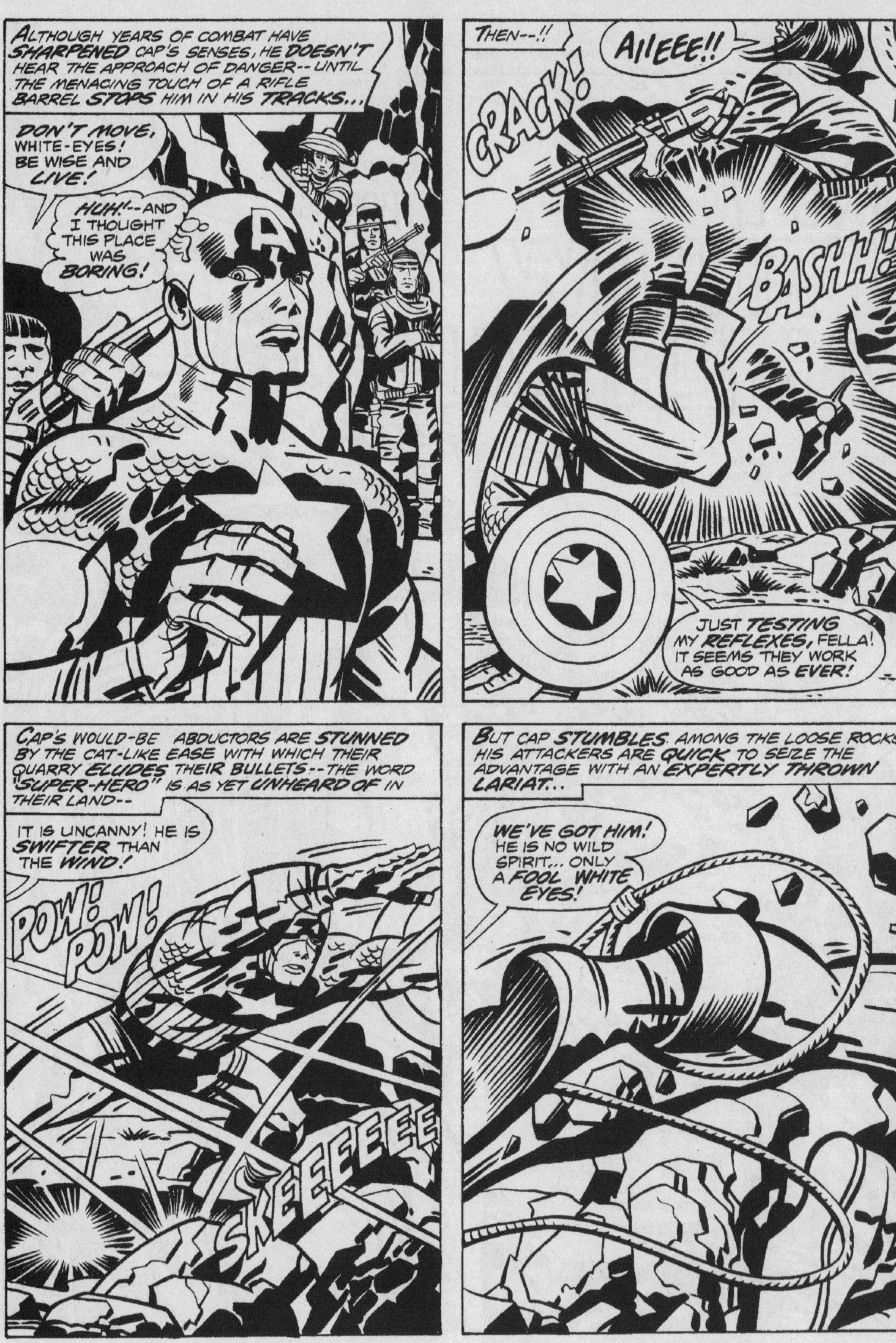
ALTHOUGH YEARS OF COMBAT HAVE SHARPENED CAP'S SENSES, HE DOESN'T HEAR THE APPROACH OF DANGER-- UNTIL THE MENACING TOUCH OF A RIFLE BARREL STOPS HIM IN HIS TRACKS...
DON'T MOVE, WHITE-EYES! BE WISE AND LIVE!
HUH!--AND I THOUGHT THIS PLACE WAS BORING!
THEN--!!
AIIEEE!!
CRACK!
BASHH!
JUST TESTING MY REFLEXES, FELLA! IT SEEMS THEY WORK AS GOOD AS EVER!
CAP'S WOULD-BE ABDUCTORS ARE STUNNED BY THE CAT-LIKE EASE WITH WHICH THEIR QUARRY ELUDES THEIR BULLETS--THE WORD "SUPER-HERO" IS AS YET UNHEARD OF IN THEIR LAND--
IT IS UNCANNY! HE IS SWIFTER THAN THE WIND!
POW! POW!
SKEEEEEEE
BUT CAP STUMBLES AMONG THE LOOSE ROCKS! HIS ATTACKERS ARE QUICK TO SEIZE THE ADVANTAGE WITH AN EXPERTLY THROWN LARIAT...
WE'VE GOT HIM! HE IS NO WILD SPIRIT... ONLY A FOOL WHITE EYES!

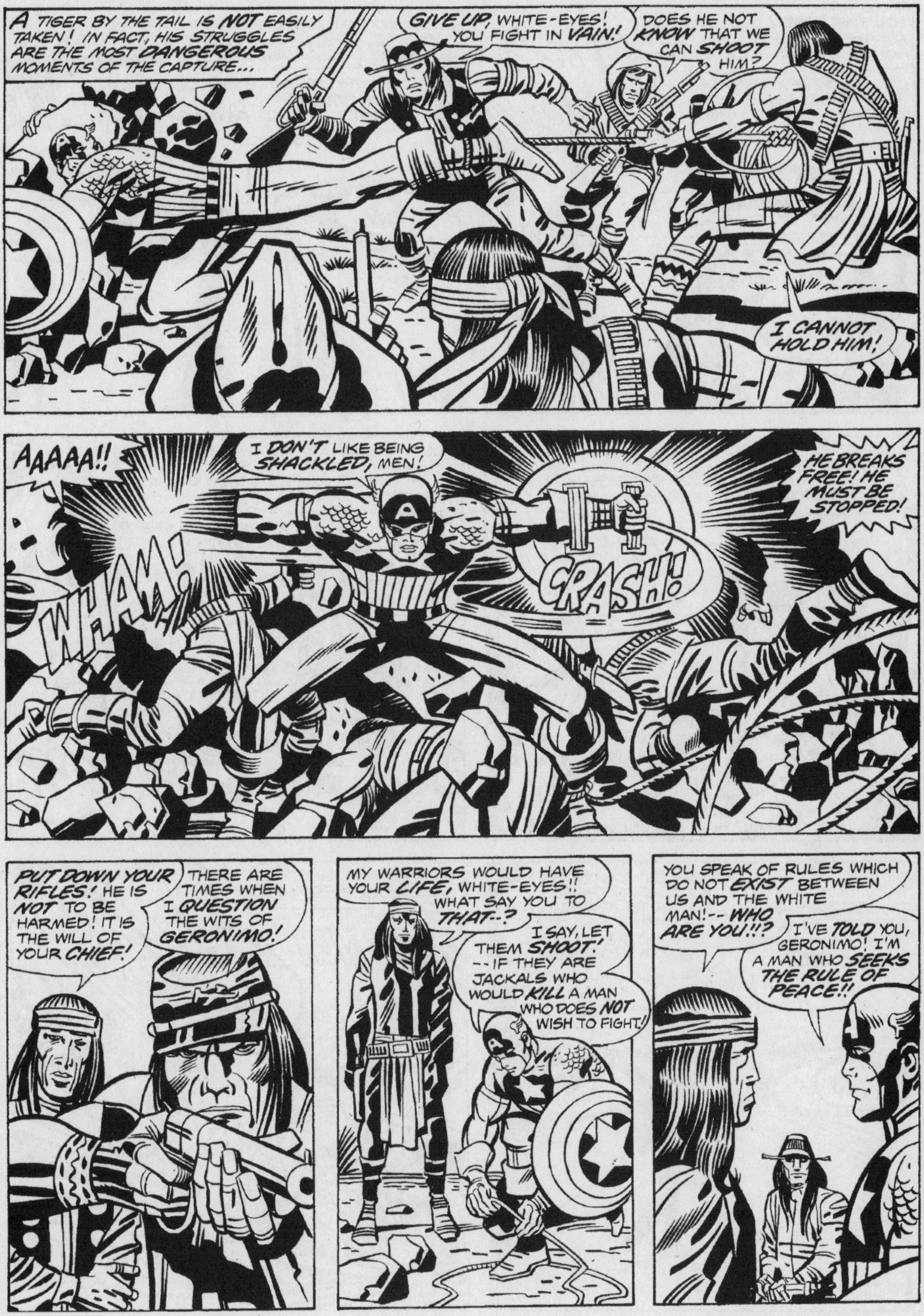
A TIGER BY THE TAIL IS NOT EASILY TAKEN! IN FACT, HIS STRUGGLES ARE THE MOST DANGEROUS MOMENTS OF THE CAPTURE...
GIVE UP, WHITE-EYES! YOU FIGHT IN VAIN!
DOES HE NOT KNOW THAT WE CAN SHOOT HIM?
I CANNOT HOLD HIM!
AAAAA!!
I DON'T LIKE BEING SHACKLED, MEN!
HE BREAKS FREE! HE MUST BE STOPPED!
WHAM!
CRASH!
PUT DOWN YOUR RIFLES! HE IS NOT TO BE HARMED! IT IS THE WILL OF YOUR CHIEF!
THERE ARE TIMES WHEN I QUESTION THE WITS OF GERONIMO!
MY WARRIORS WOULD HAVE YOUR LIFE, WHITE-EYES!! WHAT SAY YOU TO THAT--?
I SAY, LET THEM SHOOT! --IF THEY ARE JACKALS WHO WOULD KILL A MAN WHO DOES NOT WISH TO FIGHT!
YOU SPEAK OF RULES WHICH DO NOT EXIST BETWEEN US AND THE WHITE MAN!-- WHO ARE YOU!!?
I'VE TOLD YOU, GERONIMO! I'M A MAN WHO SEEKS THE RULE OF PEACE!!

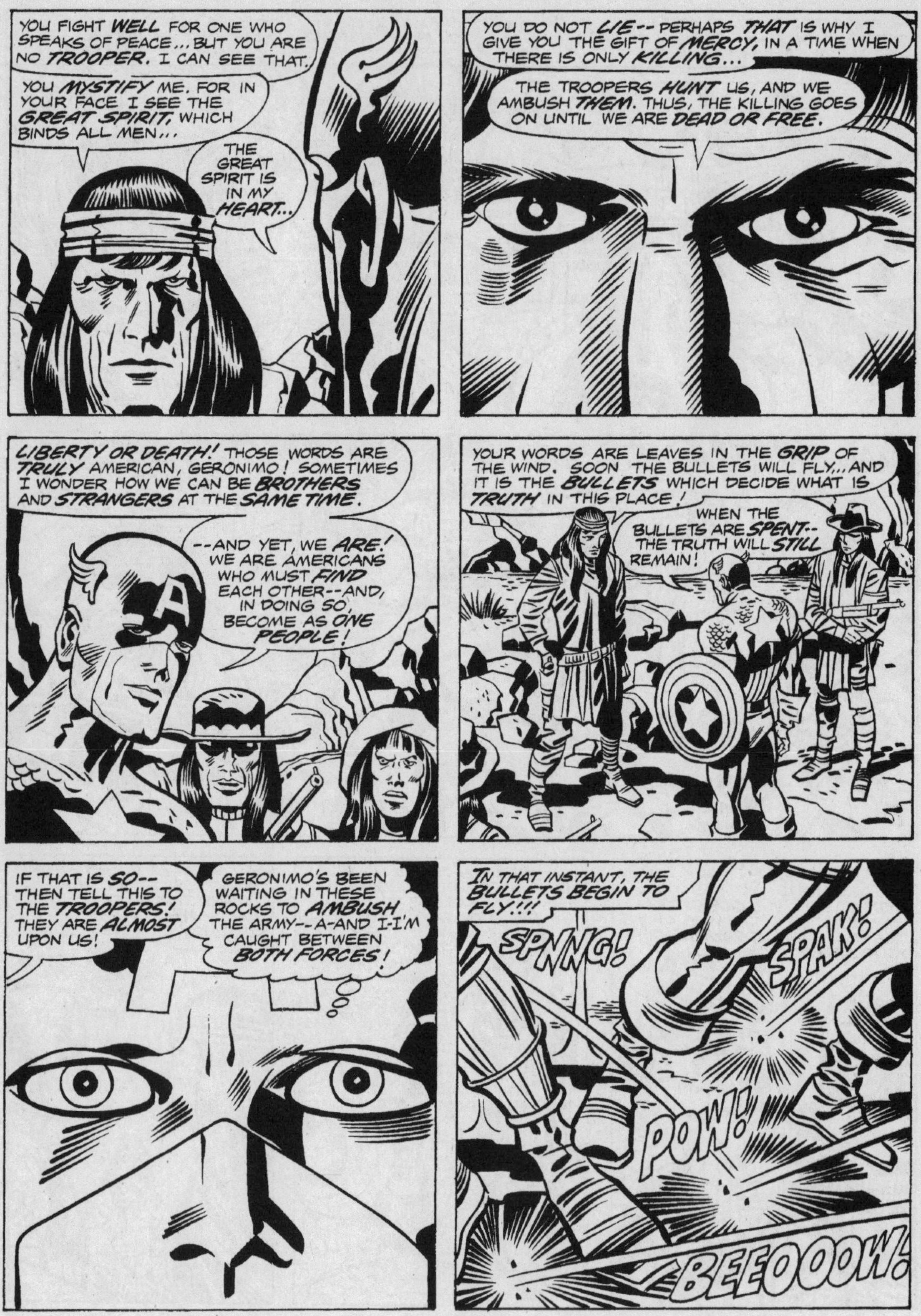
YOU FIGHT WELL FOR ONE WHO SPEAKS OF PEACE... BUT YOU ARE NO TROOPER. I CAN SEE THAT.
YOU MYSTIFY ME. FOR IN YOUR FACE I SEE THE GREAT SPIRIT, WHICH BINDS ALL MEN...
THE GREAT SPIRIT IS IN MY HEART...
YOU DO NOT LIE-- PERHAPS THAT IS WHY I GIVE YOU THE GIFT OF MERCY, IN A TIME WHEN THERE IS ONLY KILLING...
THE TROOPERS HUNT US, AND WE AMBUSH THEM. THUS, THE KILLING GOES ON UNTIL WE ARE DEAD OR FREE.
LIBERTY OR DEATH! THOSE WORDS ARE TRULY AMERICAN, GERONIMO! SOMETIMES I WONDER HOW WE CAN BE BROTHERS AND STRANGERS AT THE SAME TIME.
--AND YET, WE ARE! WE ARE AMERICANS WHO MUST FIND EACH OTHER--AND, IN DOING SO, BECOME AS ONE PEOPLE!
YOUR WORDS ARE LEAVES IN THE GRIP OF THE WIND. SOON THE BULLETS WILL FLY... AND IT IS THE BULLETS WHICH DECIDE WHAT IS TRUTH IN THIS PLACE!
WHEN THE BULLETS ARE SPENT-- THE TRUTH WILL STILL REMAIN!
IF THAT IS SO-- THEN TELL THIS TO THE TROOPERS! THEY ARE ALMOST UPON US!
GERONIMO'S BEEN WAITING IN THESE ROCKS TO AMBUSH THE ARMY-- A-AND I-I'M CAUGHT BETWEEN BOTH FORCES!
IN THAT INSTANT, THE BULLETS BEGIN TO FLY!!!
SPNNG!
SPAK!
POW!
BEEOOOW!

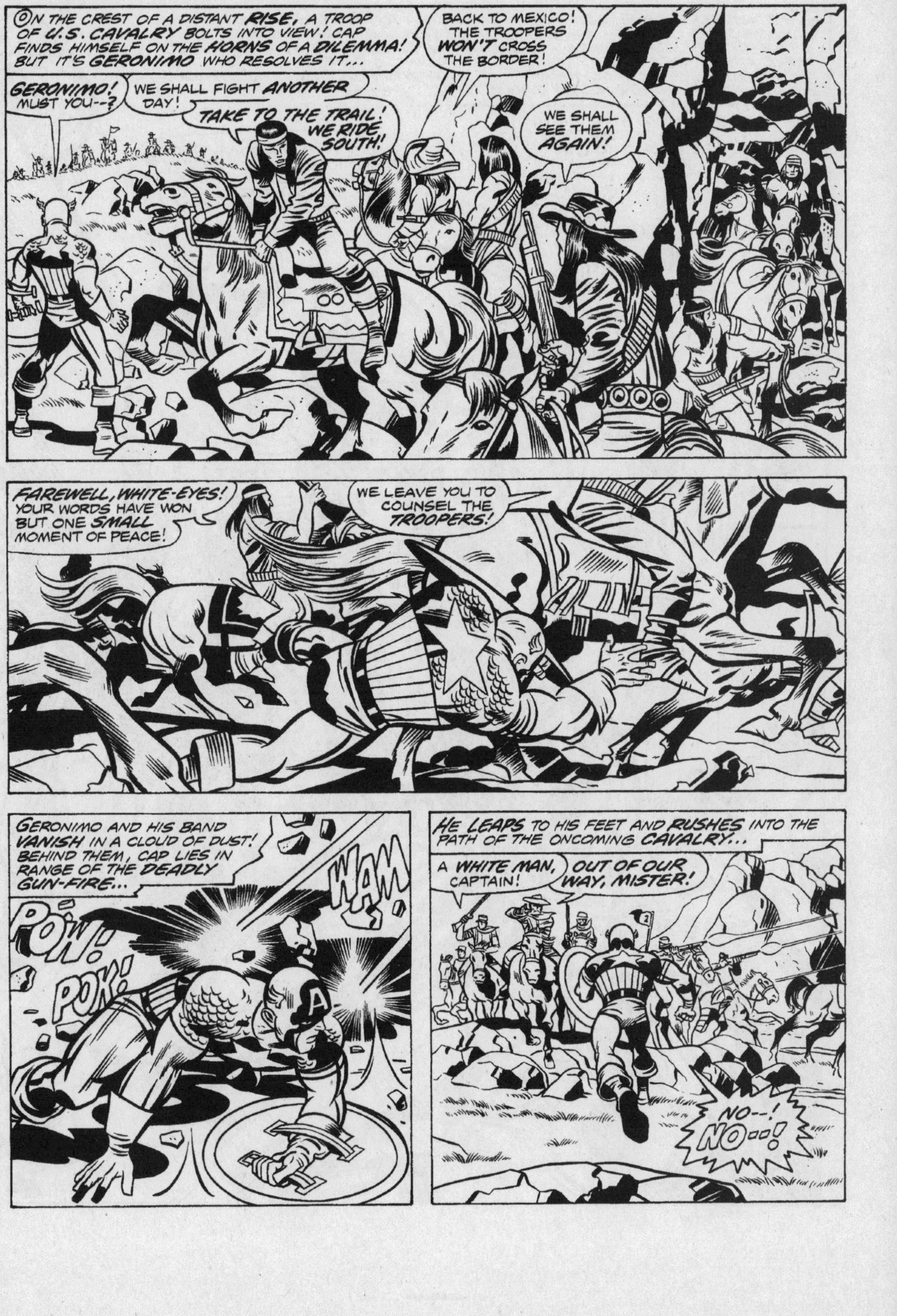
ON THE CREST OF A DISTANT RISE, A TROOP OF U.S. CAVALRY BOLTS INTO VIEW! CAP FINDS HIMSELF ON THE HORNS OF A DILEMMA! BUT IT'S GERONIMO WHO RESOLVES IT...
BACK TO MEXICO! THE TROOPERS WON'T CROSS THE BORDER!
GERONIMO! MUST YOU--?
WE SHALL FIGHT ANOTHER DAY!
TAKE TO THE TRAIL! WE RIDE SOUTH!
WE SHALL SEE THEM AGAIN!
FAREWELL, WHITE-EYES! YOUR WORDS HAVE WON BUT ONE SMALL MOMENT OF PEACE!
WE LEAVE YOU TO COUNSEL THE TROOPERS!
GERONIMO AND HIS BAND VANISH IN A CLOUD OF DUST! BEHIND THEM, CAP LIES IN RANGE OF THE DEADLY GUN-FIRE...
WAM
POW!
POK!
HE LEAPS TO HIS FEET AND RUSHES INTO THE PATH OF THE ONCOMING CAVALRY...
A WHITE MAN, CAPTAIN!
OUT OF OUR WAY, MISTER!
NO--! NO--!

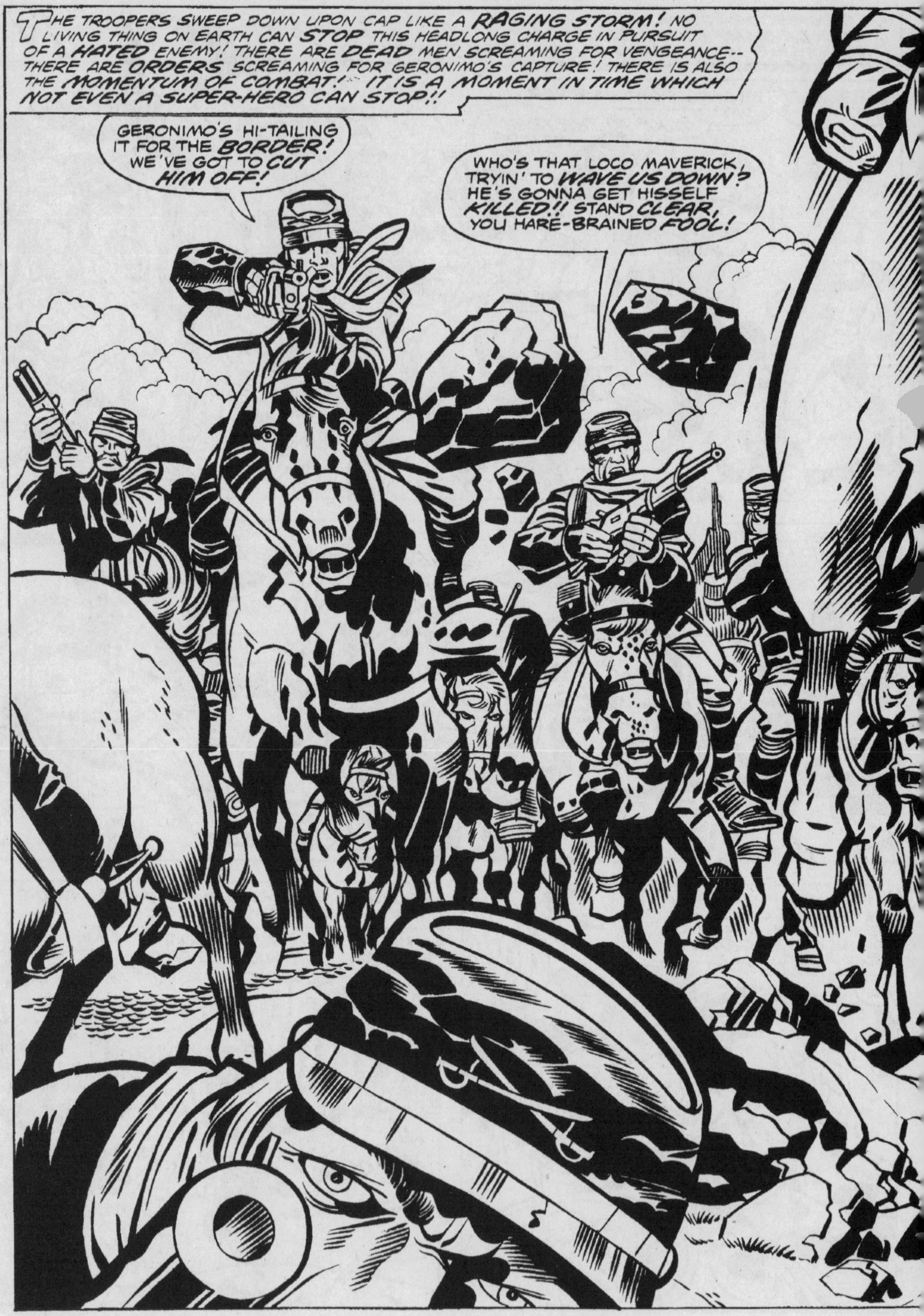
THE TROOPERS SWEEP DOWN UPON CAP LIKE A RAGING STORM! NO LIVING THING ON EARTH CAN STOP THIS HEADLONG CHARGE IN PURSUIT OF A HATED ENEMY! THERE ARE DEAD MEN SCREAMING FOR VENGEANCE-- THERE ARE ORDERS SCREAMING FOR GERONIMO'S CAPTURE! THERE IS ALSO THE MOMENTUM OF COMBAT! -- IT IS A MOMENT IN TIME WHICH NOT EVEN A SUPER-HERO CAN STOP!!
GERONIMO'S HI-TAILING IT FOR THE BORDER! WE'VE GOT TO CUT HIM OFF!
WHO'S THAT LOCO MAVERICK, TRYIN' TO WAVE US DOWN? HE'S GONNA GET HISSELF KILLED!! STAND CLEAR, YOU HARE-BRAINED FOOL!

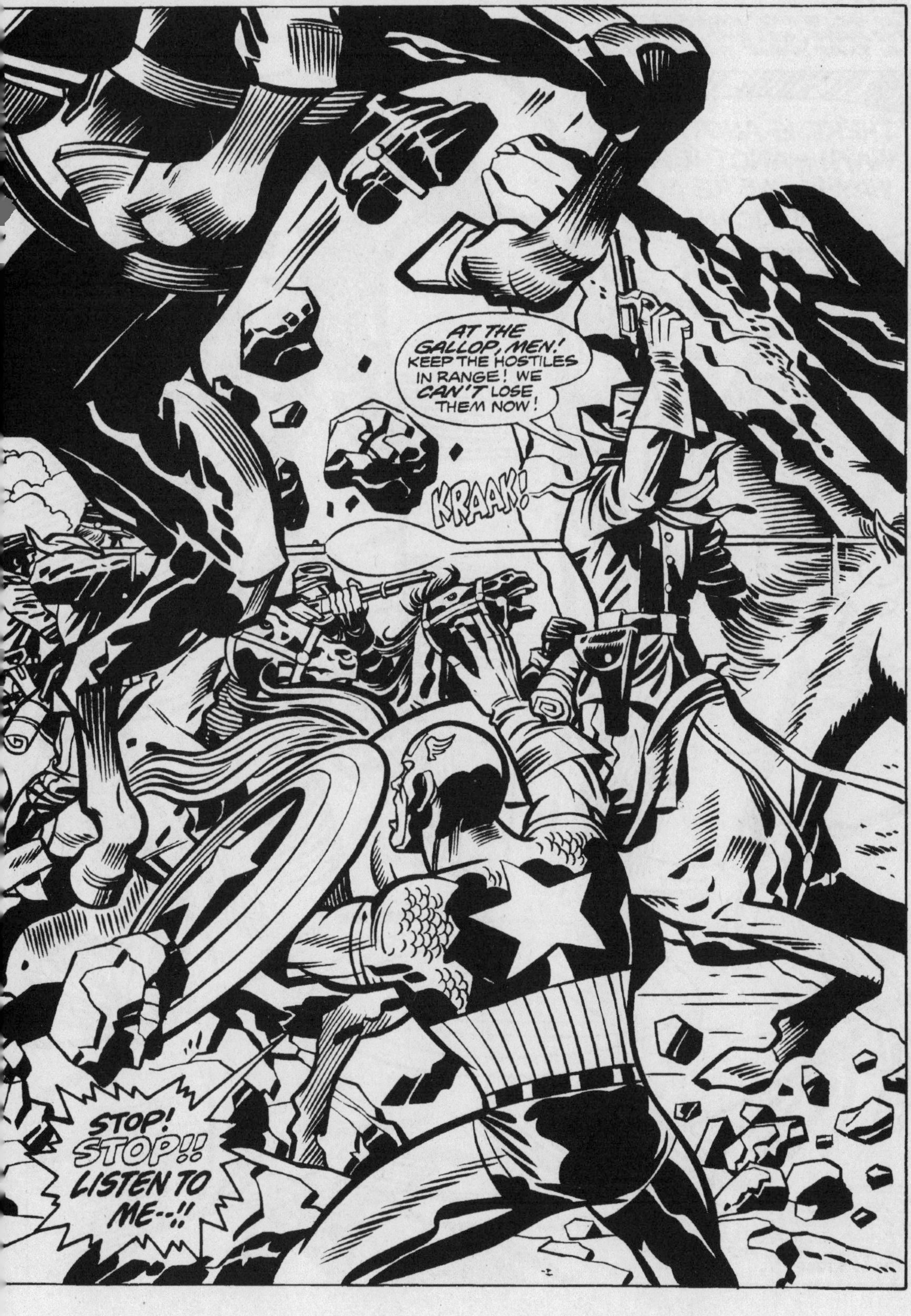
AT THE GALLOP, MEN! KEEP THE HOSTILES IN RANGE! WE CAN'T LOSE THEM NOW!
KRAAK!
STOP! STOP!! LISTEN TO ME--!!

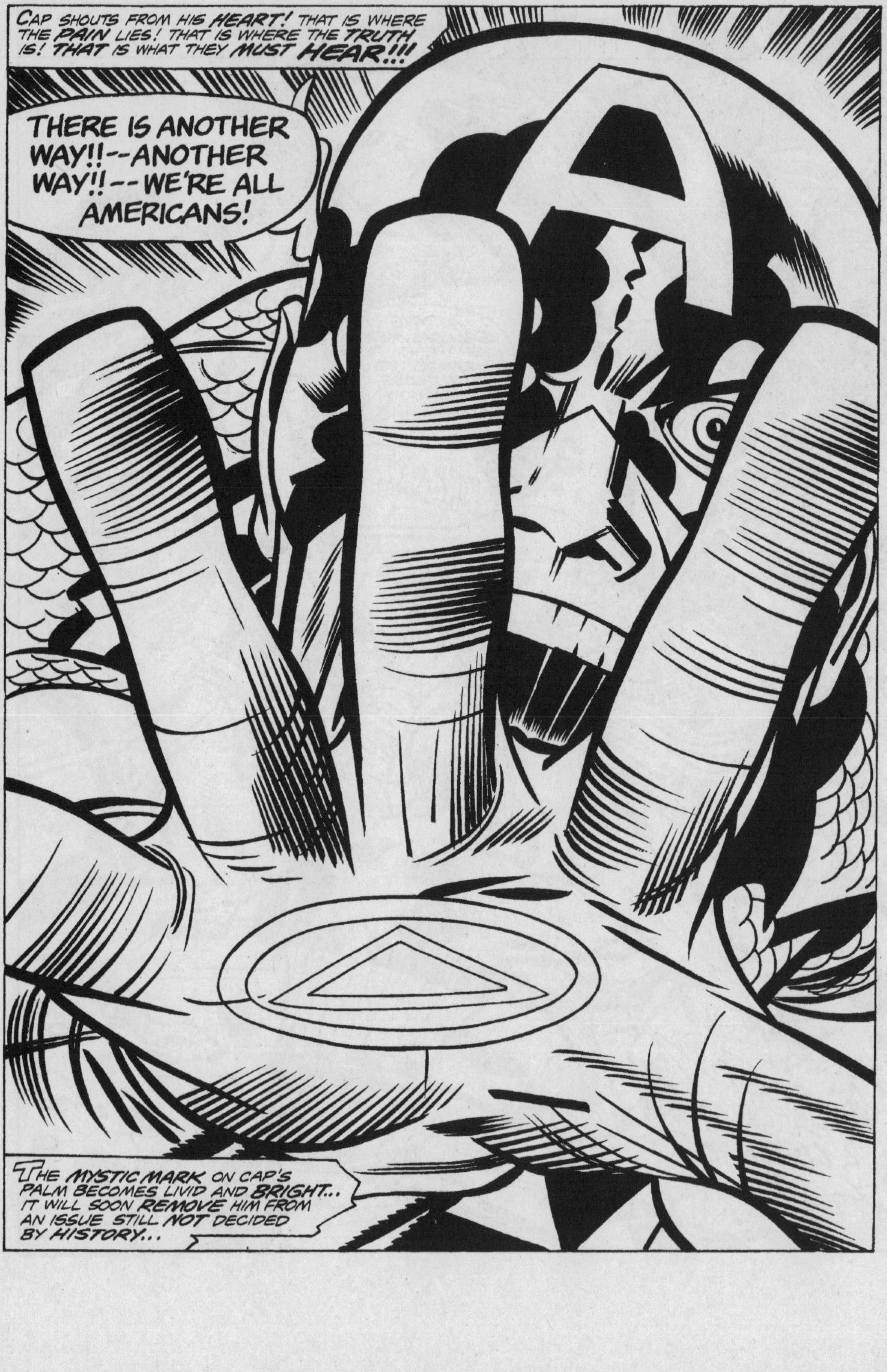
CAP SHOUTS FROM HIS HEART! THAT IS WHERE THE PAIN LIES! THAT IS WHERE THE TRUTH IS! THAT IS WHAT THEY MUST HEAR!!!
THERE IS ANOTHER WAY!!--ANOTHER WAY!!--WE'RE ALL AMERICANS!
THE MYSTIC MARK ON CAP'S PALM BECOMES LIVID AND BRIGHT... IT WILL SOON REMOVE HIM FROM AN ISSUE STILL NOT DECIDED BY HISTORY...

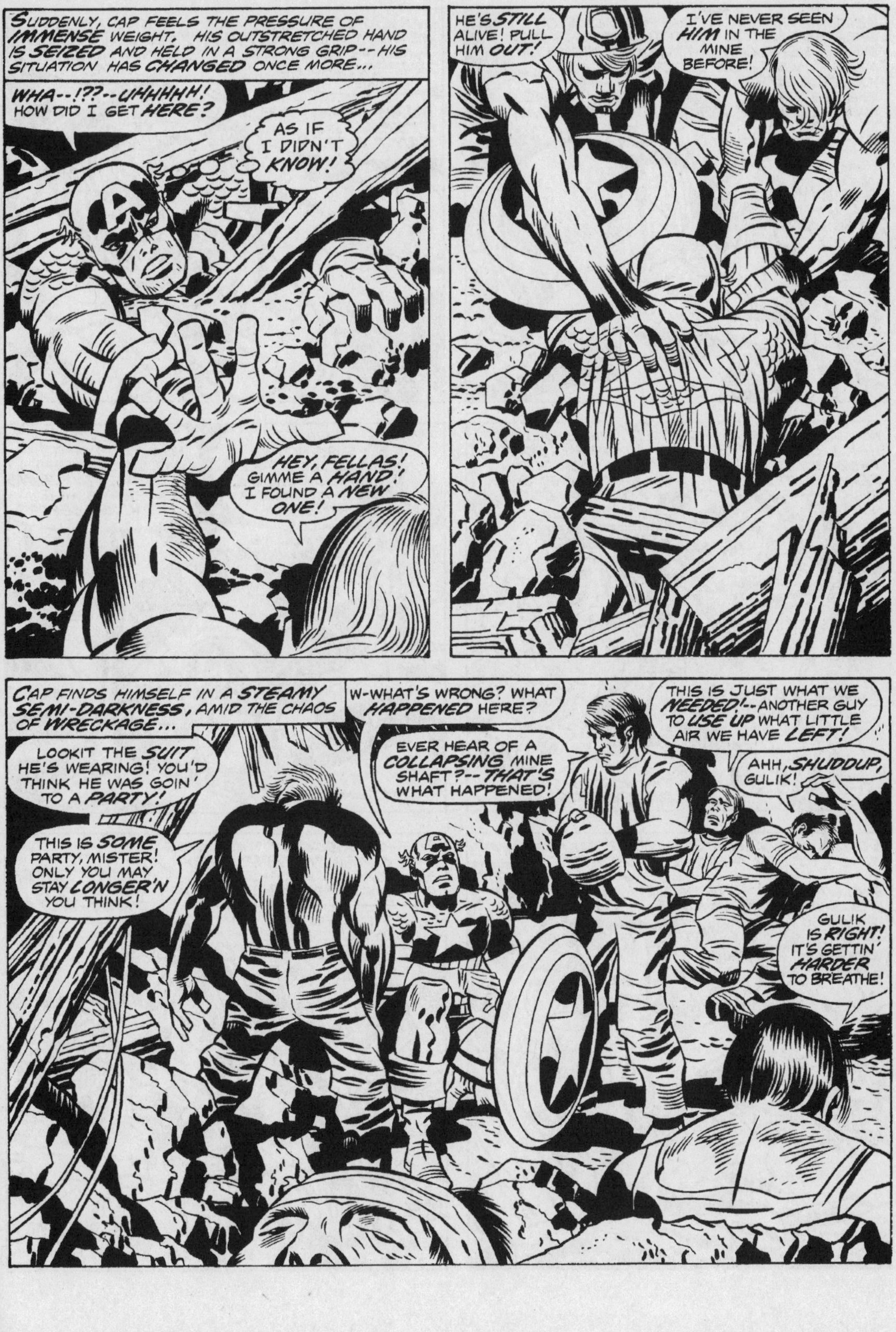

SUDDENLY, CAP FEELS THE PRESSURE OF IMMENSE WEIGHT. HIS OUTSTRETCHED HAND IS SEIZED AND HELD IN A STRONG GRIP--HIS SITUATION HAS CHANGED ONCE MORE...
WHA--!??--UHHHHH! HOW DID I GET HERE?
AS IF I DIDN'T KNOW!
HEY, FELLAS! GIMME A HAND! I FOUND A NEW ONE!
HE'S STILL ALIVE! PULL HIM OUT!
I'VE NEVER SEEN HIM IN THE MINE BEFORE!
CAP FINDS HIMSELF IN A STEAMY SEMI-DARKNESS, AMID THE CHAOS OF WRECKAGE...
W-WHAT'S WRONG? WHAT HAPPENED HERE?
LOOKIT THE SUIT HE'S WEARING! YOU'D THINK HE WAS GOIN' TO A PARTY!
EVER HEAR OF A COLLAPSING MINE SHAFT?--THAT'S WHAT HAPPENED!
THIS IS SOME PARTY, MISTER! ONLY YOU MAY STAY LONGER'N YOU THINK!
THIS IS JUST WHAT WE NEEDED!--ANOTHER GUY TO USE UP WHAT LITTLE AIR WE HAVE LEFT!
AHH, SHUDDUP, GULIK!
GULIK IS RIGHT! IT'S GETTIN' HARDER TO BREATHE!

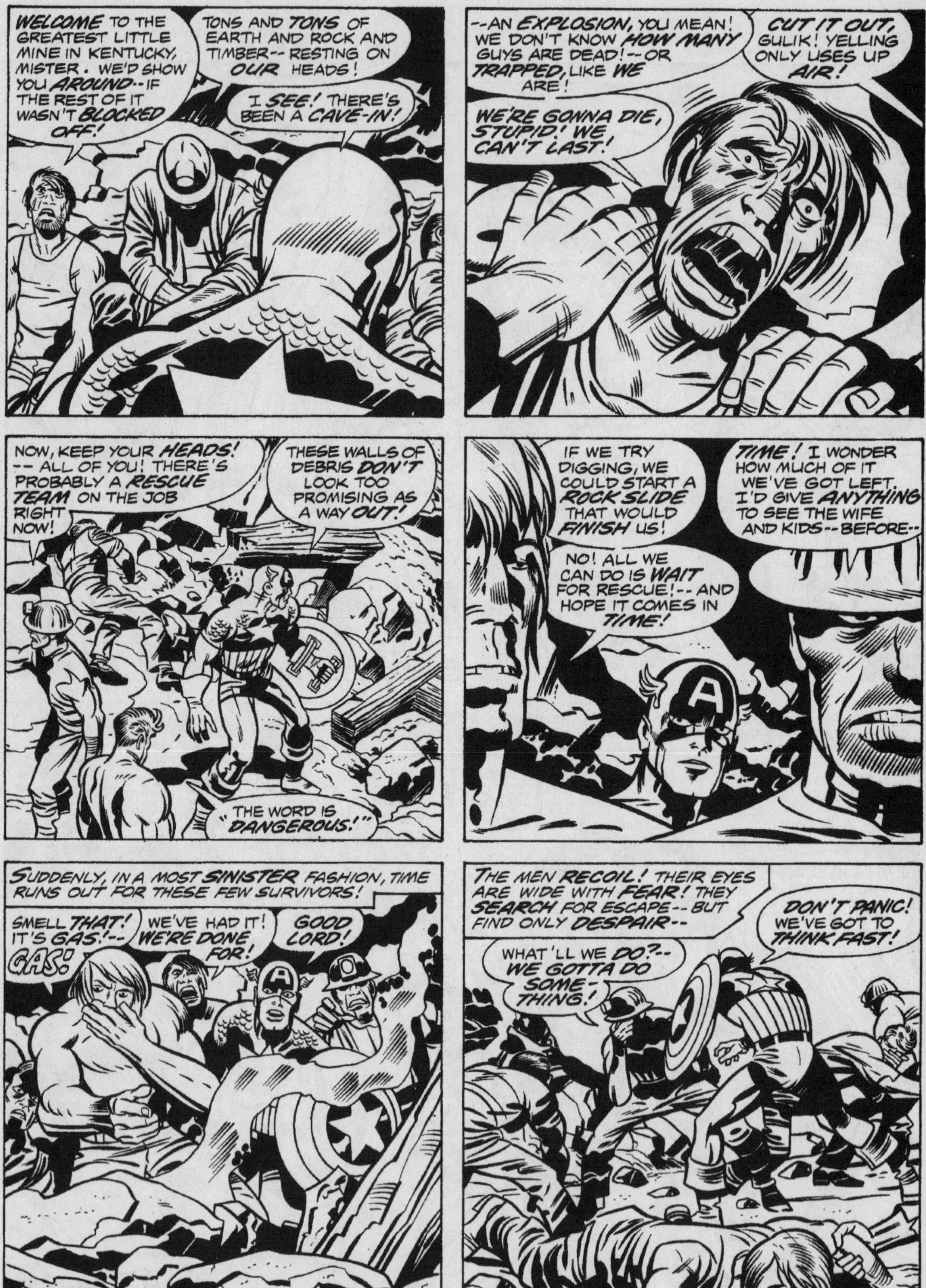
WELCOME TO THE GREATEST LITTLE MINE IN KENTUCKY, MISTER. WE'D SHOW YOU AROUND--IF THE REST OF IT WASN'T BLOCKED OFF!
TONS AND TONS OF EARTH AND ROCK AND TIMBER--RESTING ON OUR HEADS!
I SEE! THERE'S BEEN A CAVE-IN!
--AN EXPLOSION, YOU MEAN! WE DON'T KNOW HOW MANY GUYS ARE DEAD!--OR TRAPPED, LIKE WE ARE!
CUT IT OUT, GULIK! YELLING ONLY USES UP AIR!
WE'RE GONNA DIE, STUPID! WE CAN'T LAST!
NOW, KEEP YOUR HEADS! -- ALL OF YOU! THERE'S PROBABLY A RESCUE TEAM ON THE JOB RIGHT NOW!
THESE WALLS OF DEBRIS DON'T LOOK TOO PROMISING AS A WAY OUT!
"THE WORD IS "DANGEROUS!"
IF WE TRY DIGGING, WE COULD START A ROCK SLIDE THAT WOULD FINISH US!
NO! ALL WE CAN DO IS WAIT FOR RESCUE!--AND HOPE IT COMES IN TIME!
TIME! I WONDER HOW MUCH OF IT WE'VE GOT LEFT. I'D GIVE ANYTHING TO SEE THE WIFE AND KIDS--BEFORE--
SUDDENLY, IN A MOST SINISTER FASHION, TIME RUNS OUT FOR THESE FEW SURVIVORS!
SMELL THAT! IT'S GAS!-- GAS!
WE'VE HAD IT! WE'RE DONE FOR!
GOOD LORD!
THE MEN RECOIL! THEIR EYES ARE WIDE WITH FEAR! THEY SEARCH FOR ESCAPE--BUT FIND ONLY DESPAIR--
DON'T PANIC! WE'VE GOT TO THINK FAST!
WHAT'LL WE DO?--WE GOTTA DO SOME-THING!

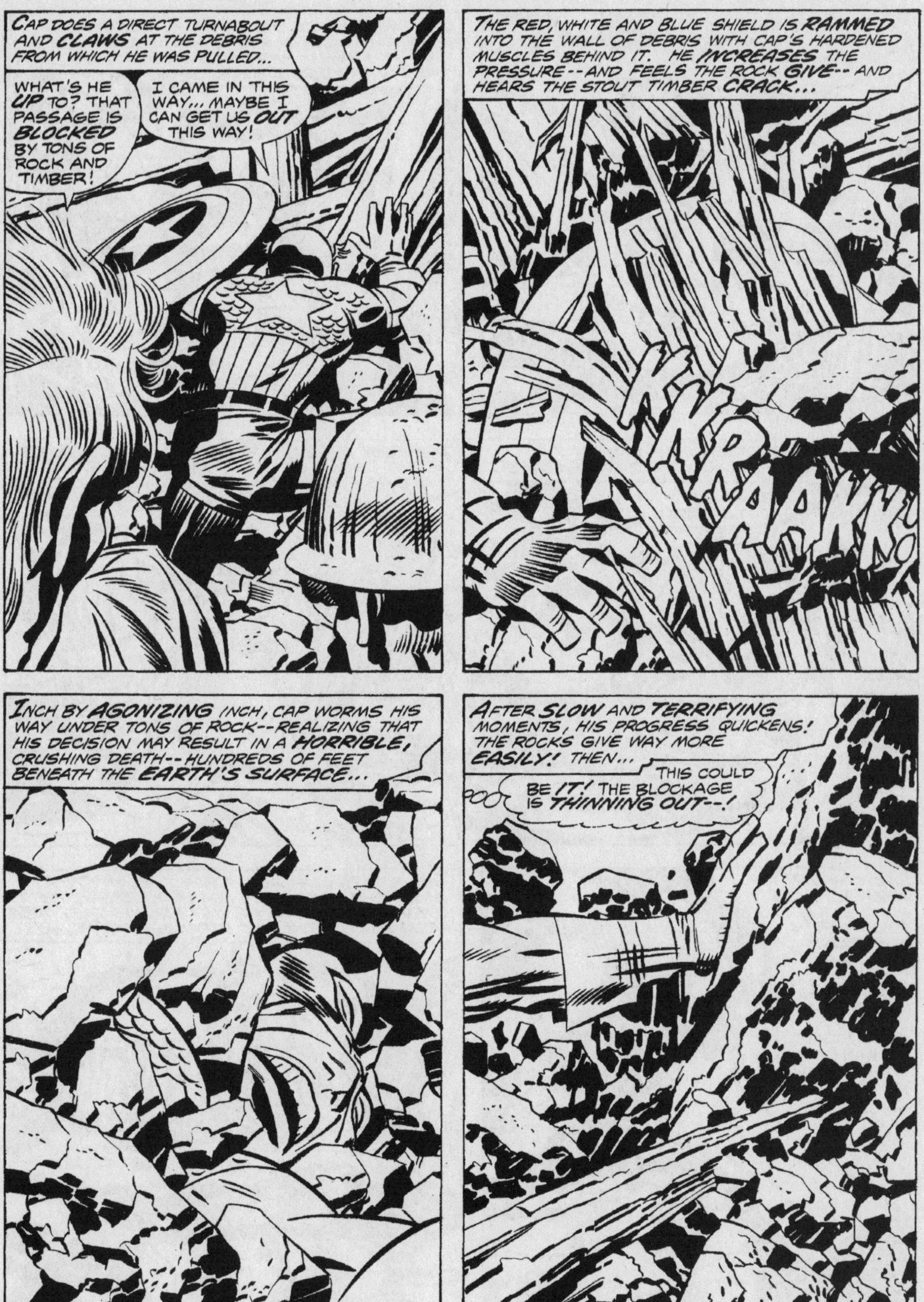
CAP DOES A DIRECT TURNABOUT AND CLAWS AT THE DEBRIS FROM WHICH HE WAS PULLED...
WHAT'S HE UP TO? THAT PASSAGE IS BLOCKED BY TONS OF ROCK AND TIMBER!
I CAME IN THIS WAY... MAYBE I CAN GET US OUT THIS WAY!
THE RED, WHITE AND BLUE SHIELD IS RAMMED INTO THE WALL OF DEBRIS WITH CAP'S HARDENED MUSCLES BEHIND IT. HE INCREASES THE PRESSURE--AND FEELS THE ROCK GIVE--AND HEARS THE STOUT TIMBER CRACK...
KKRAAKK
INCH BY AGONIZING INCH, CAP WORMS HIS WAY UNDER TONS OF ROCK--REALIZING THAT HIS DECISION MAY RESULT IN A HORRIBLE, CRUSHING DEATH--HUNDREDS OF FEET BENEATH THE EARTH'S SURFACE...
AFTER SLOW AND TERRIFYING MOMENTS, HIS PROGRESS QUICKENS! THE ROCKS GIVE WAY MORE EASILY! THEN...
THIS COULD BE IT! THE BLOCKAGE IS THINNING OUT--!

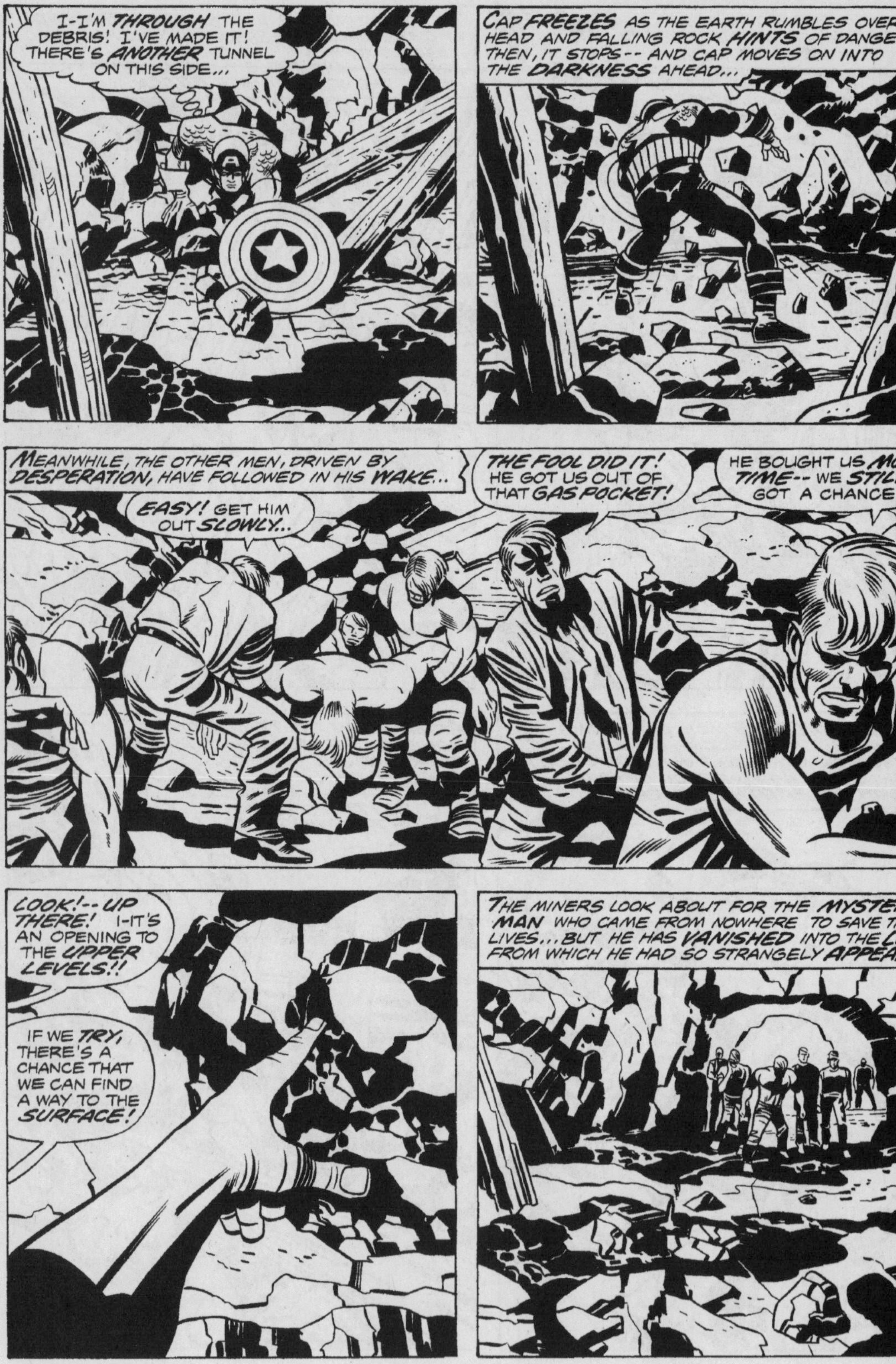

I-I'M THROUGH THE DEBRIS! I'VE MADE IT! THERE'S ANOTHER TUNNEL ON THIS SIDE...
CAP FREEZES AS THE EARTH RUMBLES OVER HEAD AND FALLING ROCK HINTS OF DANGER! THEN, IT STOPS-- AND CAP MOVES ON INTO THE DARKNESS AHEAD...
MEANWHILE, THE OTHER MEN, DRIVEN BY DESPERATION, HAVE FOLLOWED IN HIS WAKE...
EASY! GET HIM OUT SLOWLY...
THE FOOL DID IT! HE GOT US OUT OF THAT GAS POCKET!
HE BOUGHT US MORE TIME-- WE STILL GOT A CHANCE!
LOOK!-- UP THERE! I-IT'S AN OPENING TO THE UPPER LEVELS!!
IF WE TRY, THERE'S A CHANCE THAT WE CAN FIND A WAY TO THE SURFACE!
THE MINERS LOOK ABOUT FOR THE MYSTERY MAN WHO CAME FROM NOWHERE TO SAVE THEIR LIVES... BUT HE HAS VANISHED INTO THE LIMBO FROM WHICH HE HAD SO STRANGELY APPEARED...

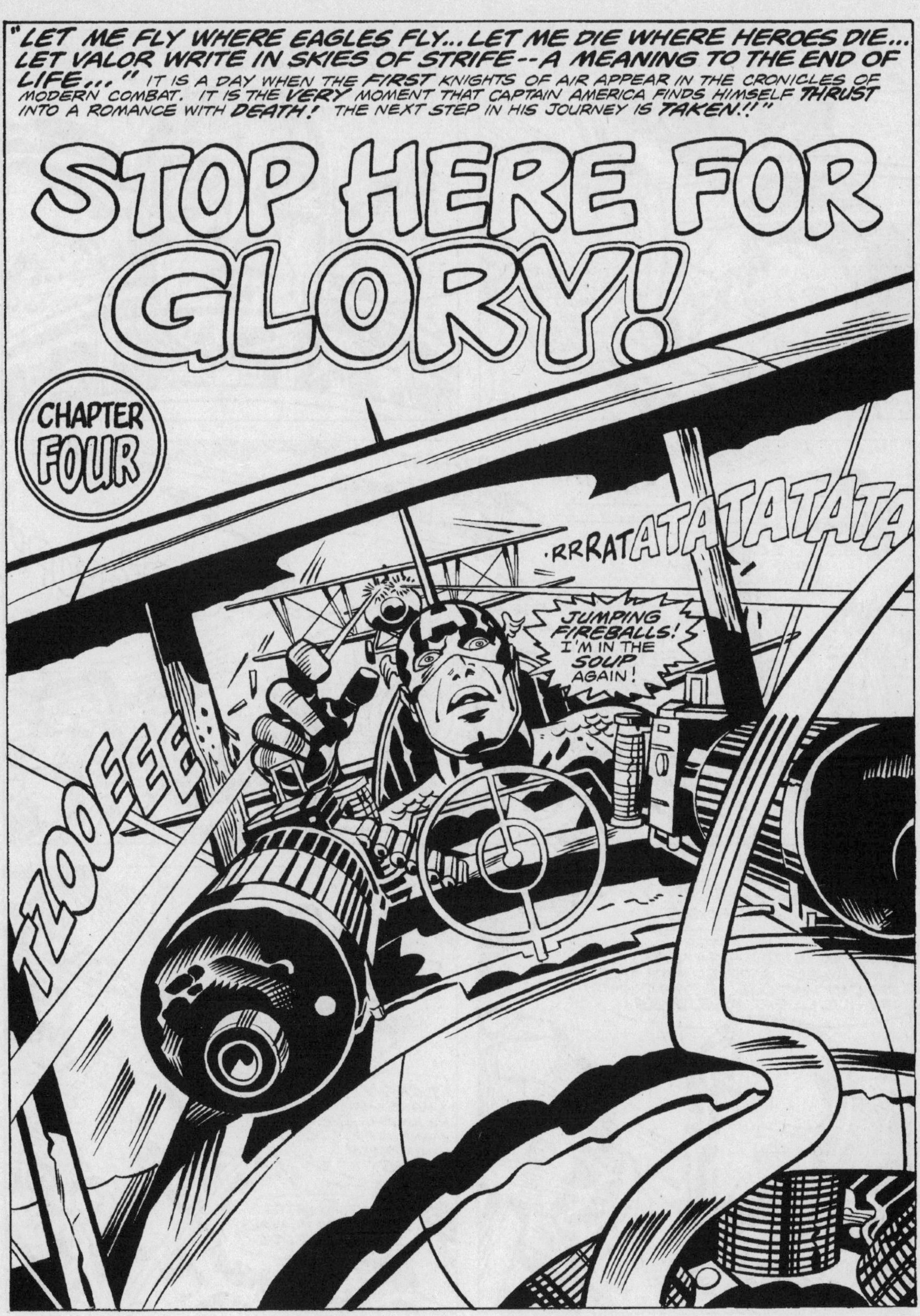
"LET ME FLY WHERE EAGLES FLY... LET ME DIE WHERE HEROES DIE... LET VALOR WRITE IN SKIES OF STRIFE--A MEANING TO THE END OF LIFE..." IT IS A DAY WHEN THE FIRST KNIGHTS OF AIR APPEAR IN THE CRONICLES OF MODERN COMBAT. IT IS THE VERY MOMENT THAT CAPTAIN AMERICA FINDS HIMSELF THRUST INTO A ROMANCE WITH DEATH! THE NEXT STEP IN HIS JOURNEY IS TAKEN!!"
STOP HERE FOR GLORY!
CHAPTER FOUR
RRRATATATATATATA
JUMPING FIREBALLS! I'M IN THE SOUP AGAIN!
TZOOEEE

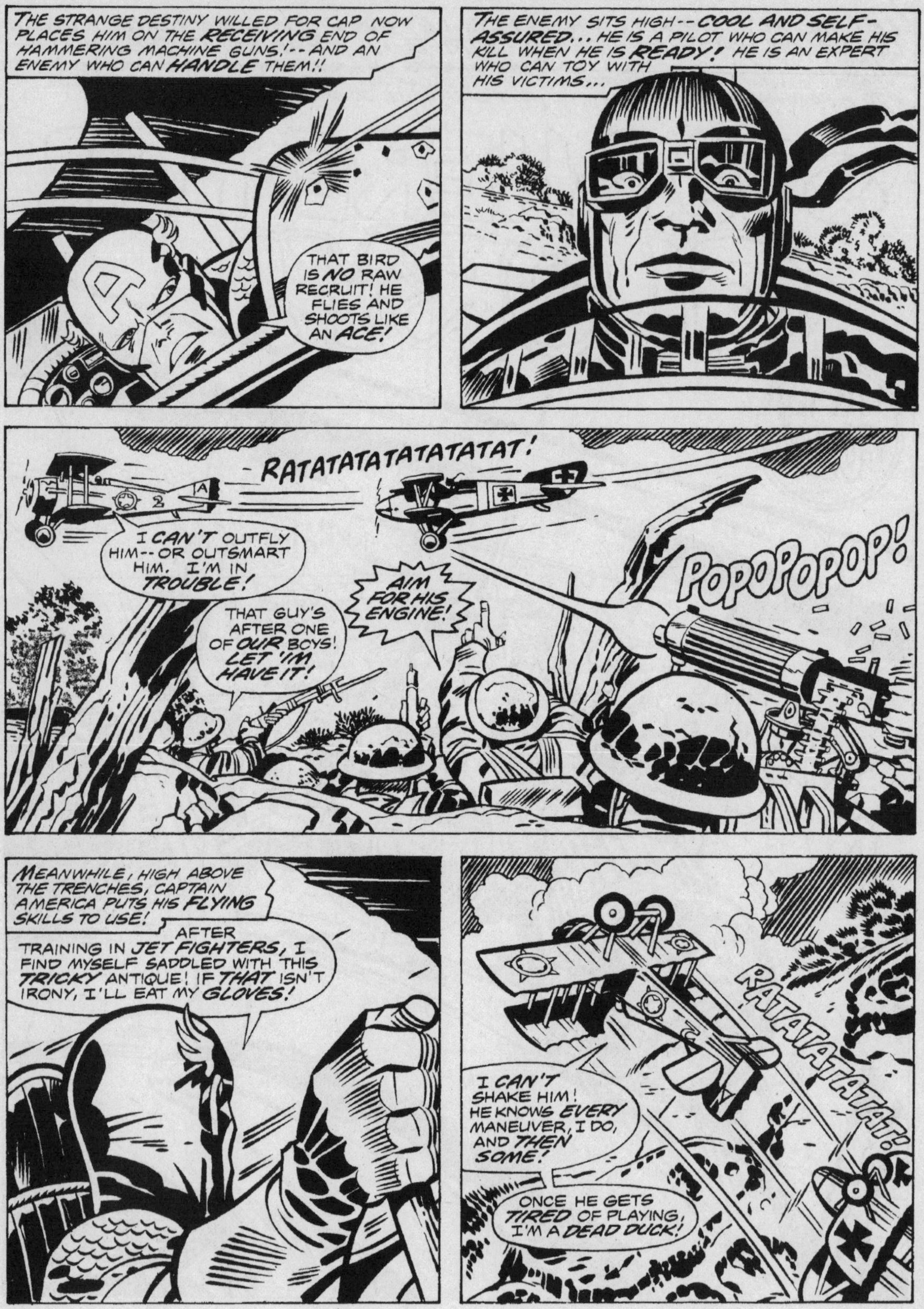
THE STRANGE DESTINY WILLED FOR CAP NOW PLACES HIM ON THE RECEIVING END OF HAMMERING MACHINE GUNS!--AND AN ENEMY WHO CAN HANDLE THEM!!
THAT BIRD IS NO RAW RECRUIT! HE FLIES AND SHOOTS LIKE AN ACE!
THE ENEMY SITS HIGH--COOL AND SELF-ASSURED... HE IS A PILOT WHO CAN MAKE HIS KILL WHEN HE IS READY! HE IS AN EXPERT WHO CAN TOY WITH HIS VICTIMS...
RATATATATATATATAT!
I CAN'T OUTFLY HIM--OR OUTSMART HIM. I'M IN TROUBLE!
THAT GUY'S AFTER ONE OF OUR BOYS! LET 'IM HAVE IT!
AIM FOR HIS ENGINE!
POPOPOPOP!
MEANWHILE, HIGH ABOVE THE TRENCHES, CAPTAIN AMERICA PUTS HIS FLYING SKILLS TO USE!
AFTER TRAINING IN JET FIGHTERS, I FIND MYSELF SADDLED WITH THIS TRICKY ANTIQUE! IF THAT ISN'T IRONY, I'LL EAT MY GLOVES!
RATATATATATAT!
I CAN'T SHAKE HIM! HE KNOWS EVERY MANEUVER I DO, AND THEN SOME!
ONCE HE GETS TIRED OF PLAYING, I'M A DEAD DUCK!

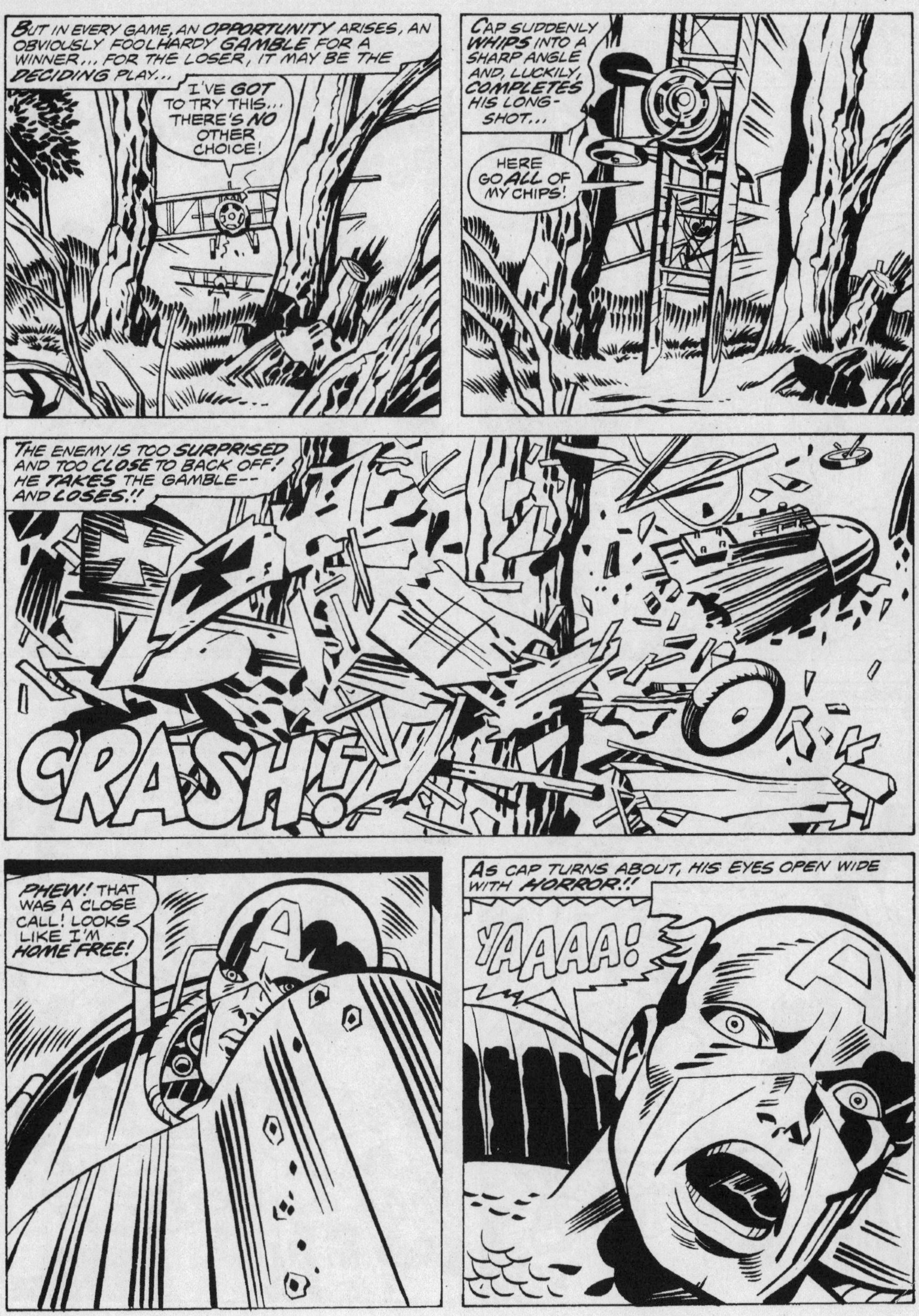

BUT IN EVERY GAME, AN OPPORTUNITY ARISES, AN OBVIOUSLY FOOLHARDY GAMBLE FOR A WINNER... FOR THE LOSER, IT MAY BE THE DECIDING PLAY...
I'VE GOT TO TRY THIS... THERE'S NO OTHER CHOICE!
CAP SUDDENLY WHIPS INTO A SHARP ANGLE AND, LUCKILY, COMPLETES HIS LONG-SHOT...
HERE GO ALL OF MY CHIPS!
THE ENEMY IS TOO SURPRISED AND TOO CLOSE TO BACK OFF! HE TAKES THE GAMBLE-- AND LOSES!!
CRASH!!
PHEW! THAT WAS A CLOSE CALL! LOOKS LIKE I'M HOME FREE!
AS CAP TURNS ABOUT, HIS EYES OPEN WIDE WITH HORROR!!
YAAAA!

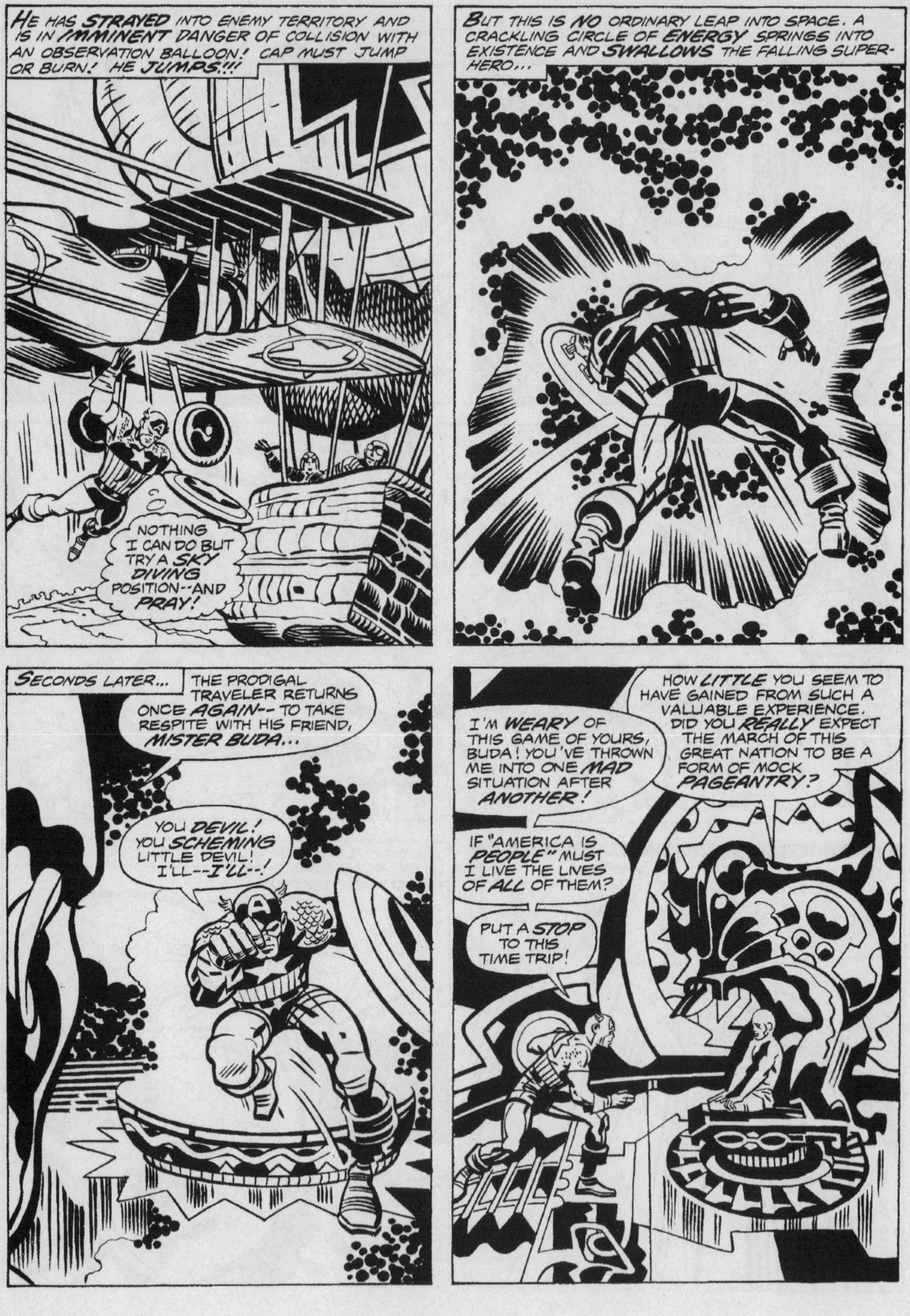
HE HAS STRAYED INTO ENEMY TERRITORY AND IS IN IMMINENT DANGER OF COLLISION WITH AN OBSERVATION BALLOON! CAP MUST JUMP OR BURN! HE JUMPS!!!
NOTHING I CAN DO BUT TRY A SKY DIVING POSITION--AND PRAY!
BUT THIS IS NO ORDINARY LEAP INTO SPACE. A CRACKLING CIRCLE OF ENERGY SPRINGS INTO EXISTENCE AND SWALLOWS THE FALLING SUPER-HERO...
SECONDS LATER...
THE PRODIGAL TRAVELER RETURNS ONCE AGAIN-- TO TAKE RESPITE WITH HIS FRIEND, MISTER BUDA...
YOU DEVIL! YOU SCHEMING LITTLE DEVIL! I'LL--I'LL--!
I'M WEARY OF THIS GAME OF YOURS, BUDA! YOU'VE THROWN ME INTO ONE MAD SITUATION AFTER ANOTHER!
IF "AMERICA IS PEOPLE" MUST I LIVE THE LIVES OF ALL OF THEM?
PUT A STOP TO THIS TIME TRIP!
HOW LITTLE YOU SEEM TO HAVE GAINED FROM SUCH A VALUABLE EXPERIENCE. DID YOU REALLY EXPECT THE MARCH OF THIS GREAT NATION TO BE A FORM OF MOCK PAGEANTRY?

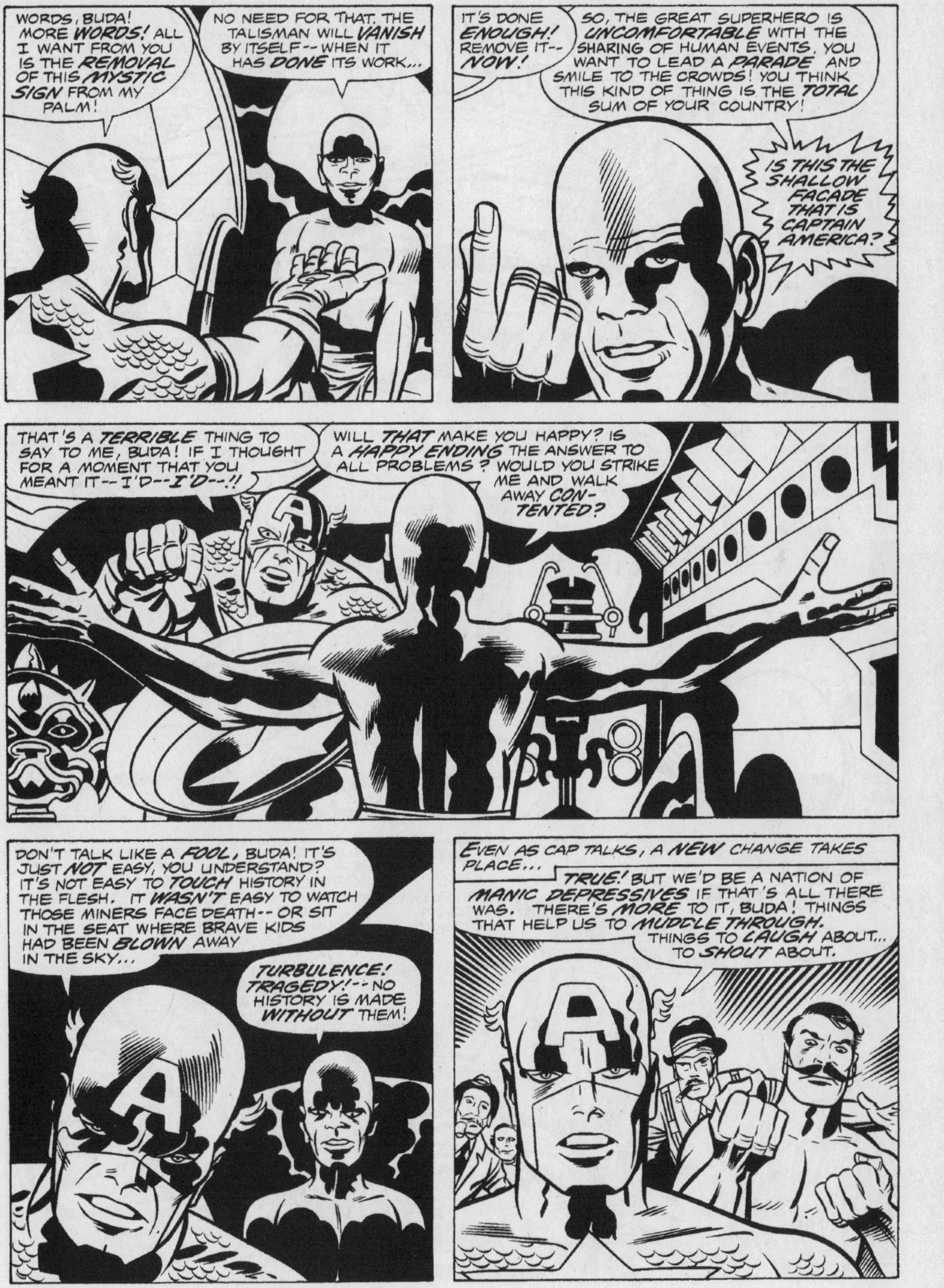
WORDS, BUDA! MORE WORDS! ALL I WANT FROM YOU IS THE REMOVAL OF THIS MYSTIC SIGN FROM MY PALM!
NO NEED FOR THAT. THE TALISMAN WILL VANISH BY ITSELF--WHEN IT HAS DONE ITS WORK...
IT'S DONE ENOUGH! REMOVE IT--NOW!
SO, THE GREAT SUPERHERO IS UNCOMFORTABLE WITH THE SHARING OF HUMAN EVENTS. YOU WANT TO LEAD A PARADE AND SMILE TO THE CROWDS! YOU THINK THIS KIND OF THING IS THE TOTAL SUM OF YOUR COUNTRY!
IS THIS THE SHALLOW FACADE THAT IS CAPTAIN AMERICA?
THAT'S A TERRIBLE THING TO SAY TO ME, BUDA! IF I THOUGHT FOR A MOMENT THAT YOU MEANT IT--I'D--I'D--!!
WILL THAT MAKE YOU HAPPY? IS A HAPPY ENDING THE ANSWER TO ALL PROBLEMS? WOULD YOU STRIKE ME AND WALK AWAY CONTENTED?
DON'T TALK LIKE A FOOL, BUDA! IT'S JUST NOT EASY, YOU UNDERSTAND? IT'S NOT EASY TO TOUCH HISTORY IN THE FLESH. IT WASN'T EASY TO WATCH THOSE MINERS FACE DEATH--OR SIT IN THE SEAT WHERE BRAVE KIDS HAD BEEN BLOWN AWAY IN THE SKY...
TURBULENCE! TRAGEDY!--NO HISTORY IS MADE WITHOUT THEM!
EVEN AS CAP TALKS, A NEW CHANGE TAKES PLACE...
TRUE! BUT WE'D BE A NATION OF MANIC DEPRESSIVES IF THAT'S ALL THERE WAS. THERE'S MORE TO IT, BUDA! THINGS THAT HELP US TO MUDDLE THROUGH. THINGS TO LAUGH ABOUT... TO SHOUT ABOUT.

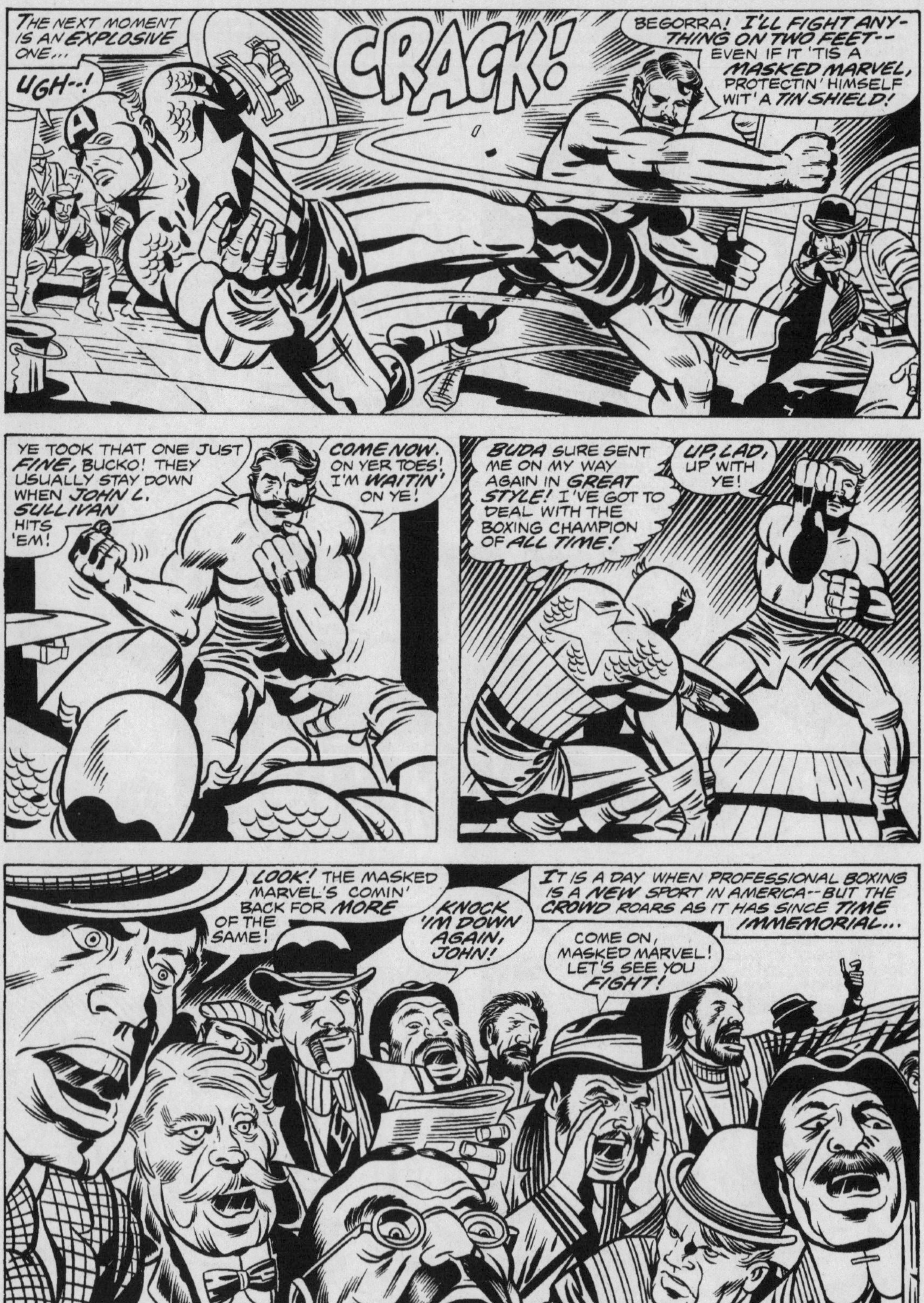
THE NEXT MOMENT IS AN EXPLOSIVE ONE...
UGH--!
CRACK!
BEGORRA! I'LL FIGHT ANYTHING ON TWO FEET-- EVEN IF IT 'TIS A MASKED MARVEL, PROTECTIN' HIMSELF WIT' A TIN SHIELD!
YE TOOK THAT ONE JUST FINE, BUCKO! THEY USUALLY STAY DOWN WHEN JOHN L. SULLIVAN HITS 'EM!
COME NOW. ON YER TOES! I'M WAITIN' ON YE!
BUDA SURE SENT ME ON MY WAY AGAIN IN GREAT STYLE! I'VE GOT TO DEAL WITH THE BOXING CHAMPION OF ALL TIME!
UP, LAD, UP WITH YE!
LOOK! THE MASKED MARVEL'S COMIN' BACK FOR MORE OF THE SAME!
KNOCK 'IM DOWN AGAIN, JOHN!
IT IS A DAY WHEN PROFESSIONAL BOXING IS A NEW SPORT IN AMERICA--BUT THE CROWD ROARS AS IT HAS SINCE TIME IMMEMORIAL...
COME ON, MASKED MARVEL! LET'S SEE YOU FIGHT!

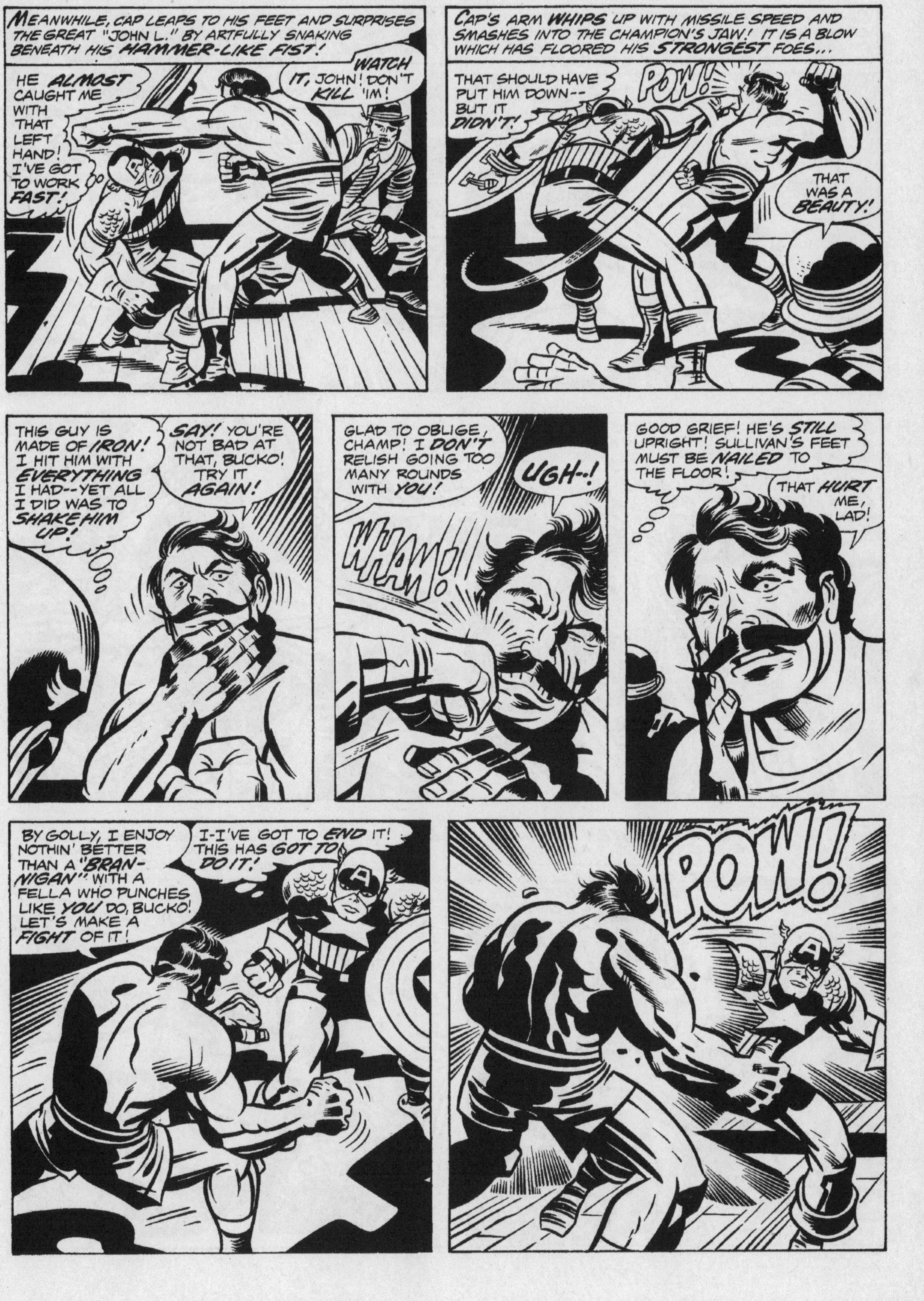
MEANWHILE, CAP LEAPS TO HIS FEET AND SURPRISES THE GREAT "JOHN L." BY ARTFULLY SNAKING BENEATH HIS HAMMER-LIKE FIST!
HE ALMOST CAUGHT ME WITH THAT LEFT HAND! I'VE GOT TO WORK FAST!
WATCH IT, JOHN! DON'T KILL 'IM!
CAP'S ARM WHIPS UP WITH MISSILE SPEED AND SMASHES INTO THE CHAMPION'S JAW! IT IS A BLOW WHICH HAS FLOORED HIS STRONGEST FOES...
THAT SHOULD HAVE PUT HIM DOWN-- BUT IT DIDN'T!
POW!
THAT WAS A BEAUTY!
THIS GUY IS MADE OF IRON! I HIT HIM WITH EVERYTHING I HAD--YET ALL I DID WAS TO SHAKE HIM UP!
SAY! YOU'RE NOT BAD AT THAT, BUCKO! TRY IT AGAIN!
GLAD TO OBLIGE, CHAMP! I DON'T RELISH GOING TOO MANY ROUNDS WITH YOU!
UGH--!
WHAM!
GOOD GRIEF! HE'S STILL UPRIGHT! SULLIVAN'S FEET MUST BE NAILED TO THE FLOOR!
THAT HURT ME, LAD!
BY GOLLY, I ENJOY NOTHIN' BETTER THAN A "BRAN-NIGAN" WITH A FELLA WHO PUNCHES LIKE YOU DO, BUCKO! LET'S MAKE A FIGHT OF IT!
I-I'VE GOT TO END IT! THIS HAS GOT TO DO IT!
POW!

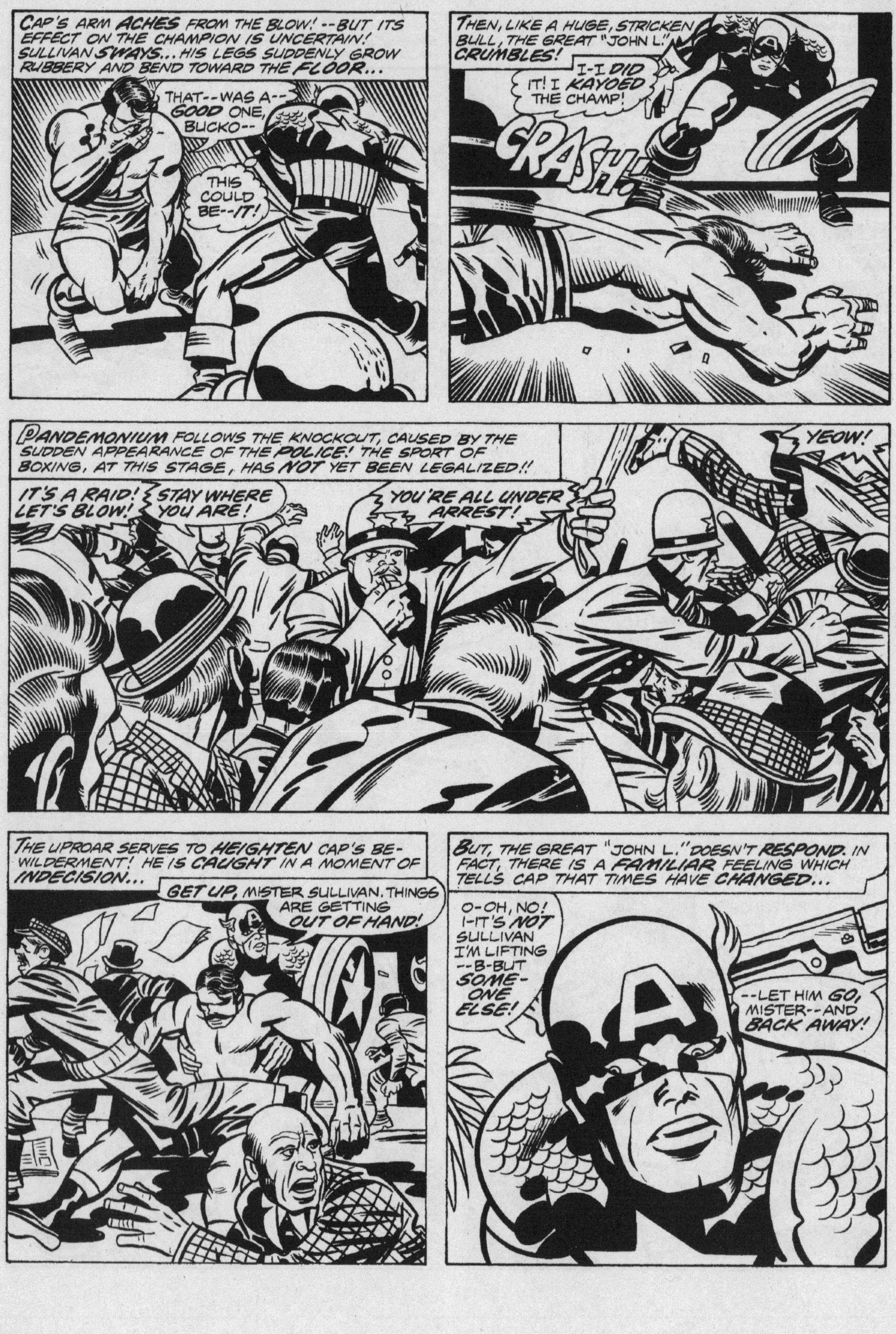
CAP'S ARM ACHES FROM THE BLOW! --BUT ITS EFFECT ON THE CHAMPION IS UNCERTAIN! SULLIVAN SWAYS... HIS LEGS SUDDENLY GROW RUBBERY AND BEND TOWARD THE FLOOR...
THAT--WAS A-- GOOD ONE, BUCKO--
THIS COULD BE--IT!
THEN, LIKE A HUGE, STRICKEN BULL, THE GREAT "JOHN L." CRUMBLES!
I-I DID IT! I KAYOED THE CHAMP!
CRASH!
PANDEMONIUM FOLLOWS THE KNOCKOUT, CAUSED BY THE SUDDEN APPEARANCE OF THE POLICE! THE SPORT OF BOXING, AT THIS STAGE, HAS NOT YET BEEN LEGALIZED!!
YEOW!
IT'S A RAID! LET'S BLOW!
STAY WHERE YOU ARE!
YOU'RE ALL UNDER ARREST!
THE UPROAR SERVES TO HEIGHTEN CAP'S BE-WILDERMENT! HE IS CAUGHT IN A MOMENT OF INDECISION...
GET UP, MISTER SULLIVAN. THINGS ARE GETTING OUT OF HAND!
BUT, THE GREAT "JOHN L." DOESN'T RESPOND. IN FACT, THERE IS A FAMILIAR FEELING WHICH TELLS CAP THAT TIMES HAVE CHANGED...
O-OH, NO! I-IT'S NOT SULLIVAN I'M LIFTING --B-BUT SOME-ONE ELSE!
--LET HIM GO, MISTER--AND BACK AWAY!

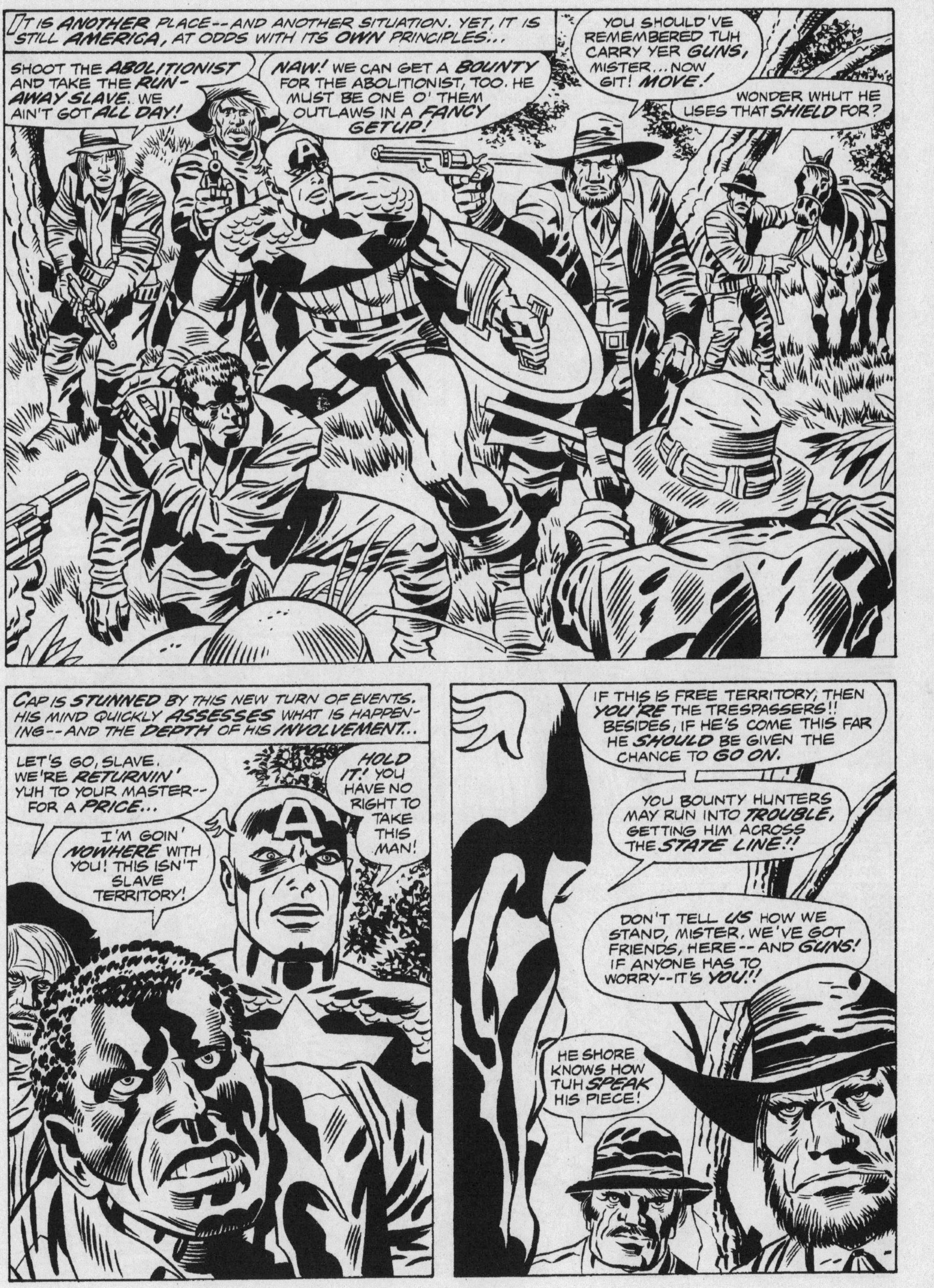
IT IS ANOTHER PLACE-- AND ANOTHER SITUATION. YET, IT IS STILL AMERICA, AT ODDS WITH ITS OWN PRINCIPLES...
SHOOT THE ABOLITIONIST AND TAKE THE RUN-AWAY SLAVE. WE AIN'T GOT ALL DAY!
NAW! WE CAN GET A BOUNTY FOR THE ABOLITIONIST, TOO. HE MUST BE ONE O' THEM OUTLAWS IN A FANCY GETUP!
YOU SHOULD'VE REMEMBERED TUH CARRY YER GUNS, MISTER... NOW GIT! MOVE!
WONDER WHUT HE USES THAT SHIELD FOR?
CAP IS STUNNED BY THIS NEW TURN OF EVENTS. HIS MIND QUICKLY ASSESSES WHAT IS HAPPENING-- AND THE DEPTH OF HIS INVOLVEMENT...
LET'S GO, SLAVE. WE'RE RETURNIN' YUH TO YOUR MASTER-- FOR A PRICE...
I'M GOIN' NOWHERE WITH YOU! THIS ISN'T SLAVE TERRITORY!
HOLD IT! YOU HAVE NO RIGHT TO TAKE THIS MAN!
IF THIS IS FREE TERRITORY, THEN YOU'RE THE TRESPASSERS!! BESIDES, IF HE'S COME THIS FAR HE SHOULD BE GIVEN THE CHANCE TO GO ON.
YOU BOUNTY HUNTERS MAY RUN INTO TROUBLE, GETTING HIM ACROSS THE STATE LINE!!
DON'T TELL US HOW WE STAND, MISTER. WE'VE GOT FRIENDS, HERE -- AND GUNS! IF ANYONE HAS TO WORRY--IT'S YOU!!
HE SHORE KNOWS HOW TUH SPEAK HIS PIECE!

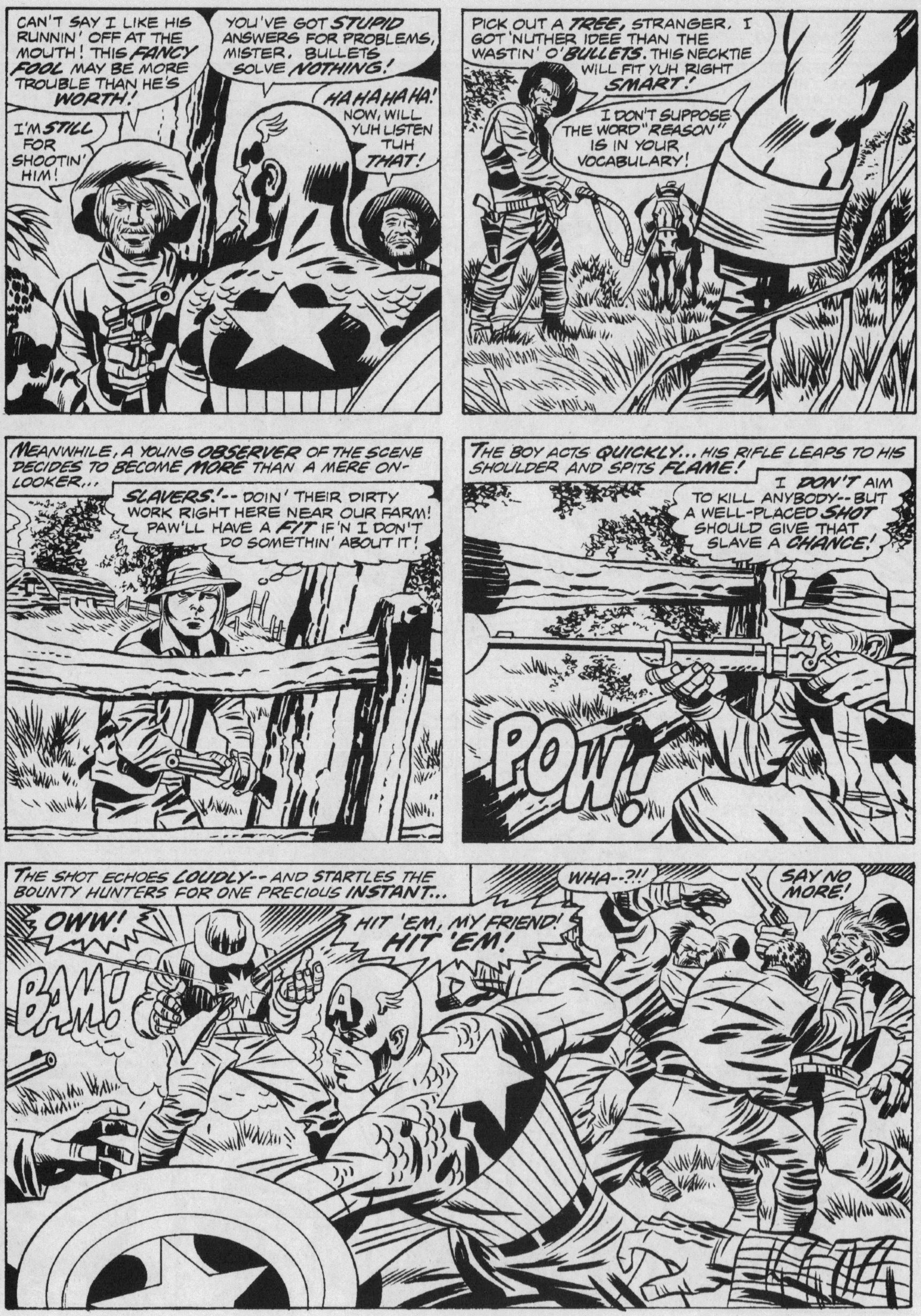

CAN'T SAY I LIKE HIS RUNNIN' OFF AT THE MOUTH! THIS FANCY FOOL MAY BE MORE TROUBLE THAN HE'S WORTH!
YOU'VE GOT STUPID ANSWERS FOR PROBLEMS, MISTER. BULLETS SOLVE NOTHING!
I'M STILL FOR SHOOTIN' HIM!
HA HA HA HA HA! NOW, WILL YUH LISTEN TUH THAT!
PICK OUT A TREE, STRANGER. I GOT 'NUTHER IDEE THAN THE WASTIN' O' BULLETS. THIS NECKTIE WILL FIT YUH RIGHT SMART!
I DON'T SUPPOSE THE WORD "REASON" IS IN YOUR VOCABULARY!
MEANWHILE, A YOUNG OBSERVER OF THE SCENE DECIDES TO BECOME MORE THAN A MERE ON-LOOKER...
SLAVERS!--DOIN' THEIR DIRTY WORK RIGHT HERE NEAR OUR FARM! PAW'LL HAVE A FIT IF'N I DON'T DO SOMETHIN' ABOUT IT!
THE BOY ACTS QUICKLY... HIS RIFLE LEAPS TO HIS SHOULDER AND SPITS FLAME!
I DON'T AIM TO KILL ANYBODY--BUT A WELL-PLACED SHOT SHOULD GIVE THAT SLAVE A CHANCE!
POW!
THE SHOT ECHOES LOUDLY--AND STARTLES THE BOUNTY HUNTERS FOR ONE PRECIOUS INSTANT...
WHA--?!!
SAY NO MORE!
OWW!
HIT 'EM, MY FRIEND! HIT 'EM!
BAM!

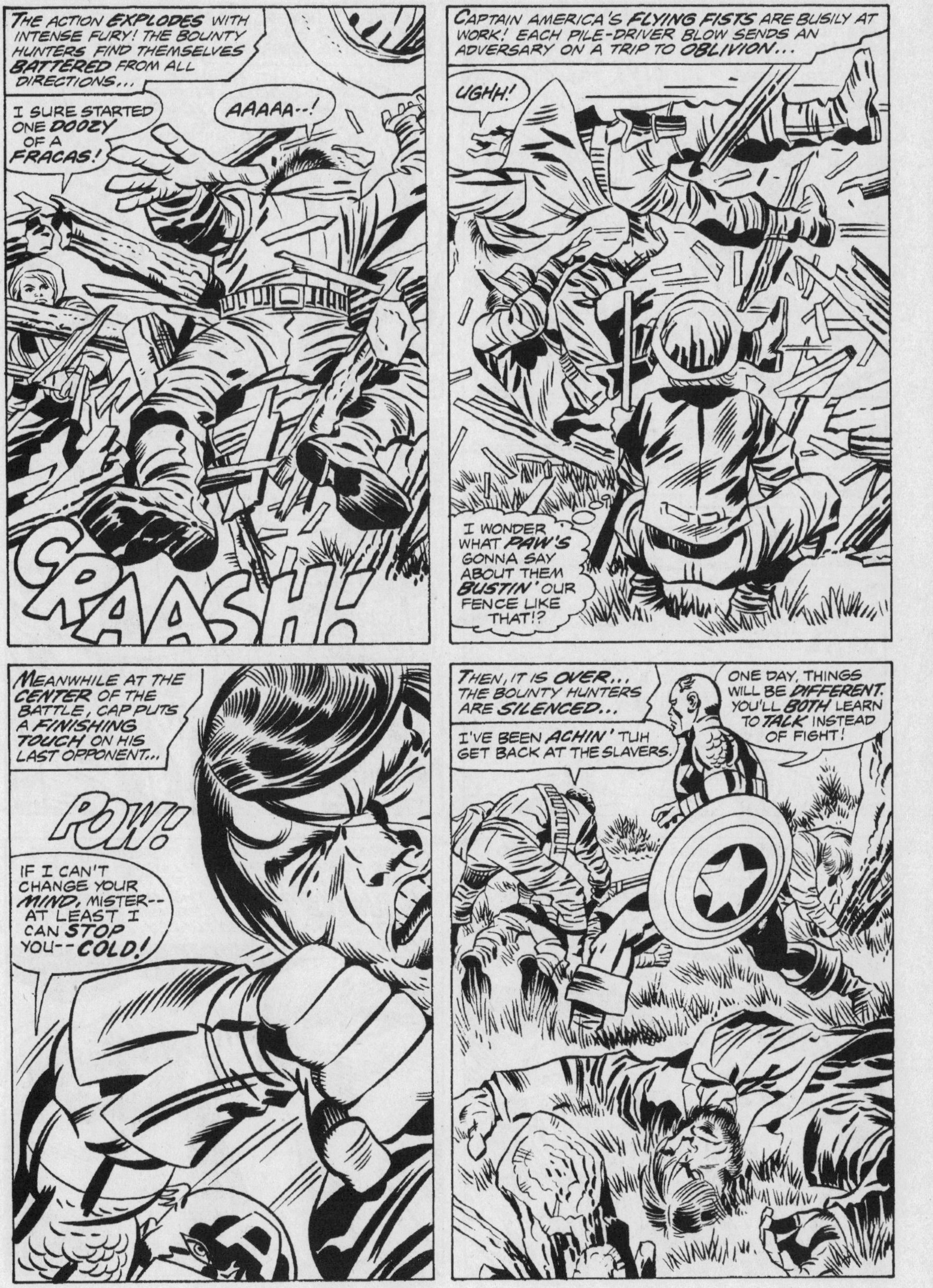
THE ACTION EXPLODES WITH INTENSE FURY! THE BOUNTY HUNTERS FIND THEMSELVES BATTERED FROM ALL DIRECTIONS...
I SURE STARTED ONE DOOZY OF A FRACAS!
AAAAA--!
CRAASH!
CAPTAIN AMERICA'S FLYING FISTS ARE BUSILY AT WORK! EACH PILE-DRIVER BLOW SENDS AN ADVERSARY ON A TRIP TO OBLIVION...
UGHH!
I WONDER WHAT PAW'S GONNA SAY ABOUT THEM BUSTIN' OUR FENCE LIKE THAT!?
MEANWHILE AT THE CENTER OF THE BATTLE, CAP PUTS A FINISHING TOUCH ON HIS LAST OPPONENT...
POW!
IF I CAN'T CHANGE YOUR MIND, MISTER-- AT LEAST I CAN STOP YOU--COLD!
THEN, IT IS OVER... THE BOUNTY HUNTERS ARE SILENCED...
I'VE BEEN ACHIN' TUH GET BACK AT THE SLAVERS.
ONE DAY, THINGS WILL BE DIFFERENT. YOU'LL BOTH LEARN TO TALK INSTEAD OF FIGHT!

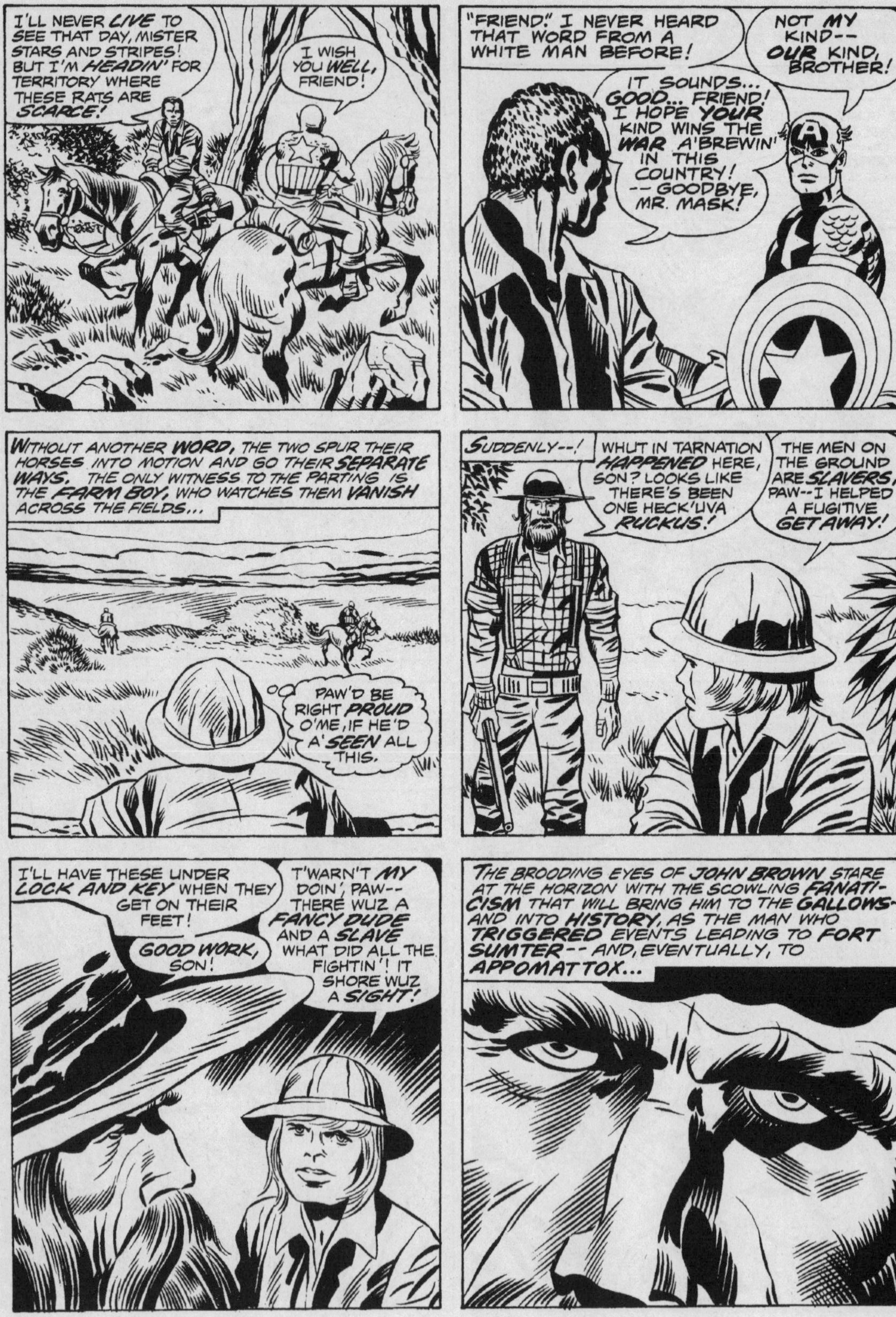
I'LL NEVER LIVE TO SEE THAT DAY, MISTER STARS AND STRIPES! BUT I'M HEADIN' FOR TERRITORY WHERE THESE RATS ARE SCARCE!
I WISH YOU WELL, FRIEND!
"FRIEND!" I NEVER HEARD THAT WORD FROM A WHITE MAN BEFORE!
IT SOUNDS... GOOD... FRIEND! I HOPE YOUR KIND WINS THE WAR A'BREWIN' IN THIS COUNTRY! -- GOODBYE, MR. MASK!
NOT MY KIND-- OUR KIND, BROTHER!
WITHOUT ANOTHER WORD, THE TWO SPUR THEIR HORSES INTO MOTION AND GO THEIR SEPARATE WAYS. THE ONLY WITNESS TO THE PARTING IS THE FARM BOY, WHO WATCHES THEM VANISH ACROSS THE FIELDS...
PAW'D BE RIGHT PROUD O'ME, IF HE'D A'SEEN ALL THIS.
SUDDENLY--!
WHUT IN TARNATION HAPPENED HERE, SON? LOOKS LIKE THERE'S BEEN ONE HECK'UVA RUCKUS!
THE MEN ON THE GROUND ARE SLAVERS, PAW--I HELPED A FUGITIVE GET AWAY!
I'LL HAVE THESE UNDER LOCK AND KEY WHEN THEY GET ON THEIR FEET!
GOOD WORK, SON!
T'WARN'T MY DOIN', PAW-- THERE WUZ A FANCY DUDE AND A SLAVE WHAT DID ALL THE FIGHTIN'! IT SHORE WUZ A SIGHT!
THE BROODING EYES OF JOHN BROWN STARE AT THE HORIZON WITH THE SCOWLING FANATICISM THAT WILL BRING HIM TO THE GALLOWS-- AND INTO HISTORY, AS THE MAN WHO TRIGGERED EVENTS LEADING TO FORT SUMTER-- AND, EVENTUALLY, TO APPOMATTOX...

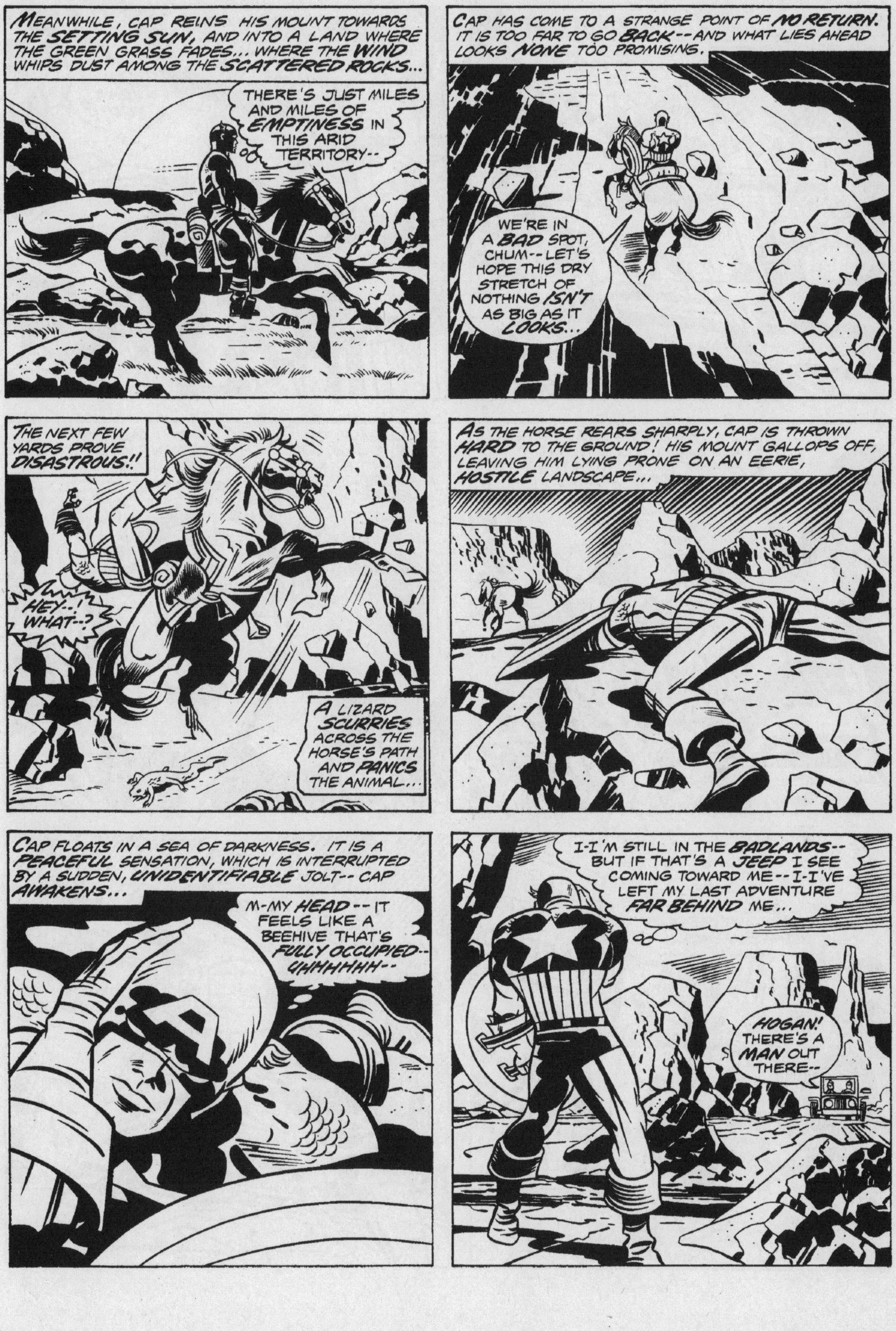
MEANWHILE, CAP REINS HIS MOUNT TOWARDS THE SETTING SUN, AND INTO A LAND WHERE THE GREEN GRASS FADES... WHERE THE WIND WHIPS DUST AMONG THE SCATTERED ROCKS...
THERE'S JUST MILES AND MILES OF EMPTINESS IN THIS ARID TERRITORY--
CAP HAS COME TO A STRANGE POINT OF NO RETURN. IT IS TOO FAR TO GO BACK--AND WHAT LIES AHEAD LOOKS NONE TOO PROMISING.
WE'RE IN A BAD SPOT, CHUM--LET'S HOPE THIS DRY STRETCH OF NOTHING ISN'T AS BIG AS IT LOOKS...
THE NEXT FEW YARDS PROVE DISASTROUS!!
HEY..! WHAT..?
A LIZARD SCURRIES ACROSS THE HORSE'S PATH AND PANICS THE ANIMAL...
AS THE HORSE REARS SHARPLY, CAP IS THROWN HARD TO THE GROUND! HIS MOUNT GALLOPS OFF, LEAVING HIM LYING PRONE ON AN EERIE, HOSTILE LANDSCAPE...
CAP FLOATS IN A SEA OF DARKNESS. IT IS A PEACEFUL SENSATION, WHICH IS INTERRUPTED BY A SUDDEN, UNIDENTIFIABLE JOLT-- CAP AWAKENS...
M-MY HEAD--IT FEELS LIKE A BEEHIVE THAT'S FULLY OCCUPIED-- UHHHHHH--
I-I'M STILL IN THE BADLANDS-- BUT IF THAT'S A JEEP I SEE COMING TOWARD ME--I-I'VE LEFT MY LAST ADVENTURE FAR BEHIND ME...
HOGAN! THERE'S A MAN OUT THERE--

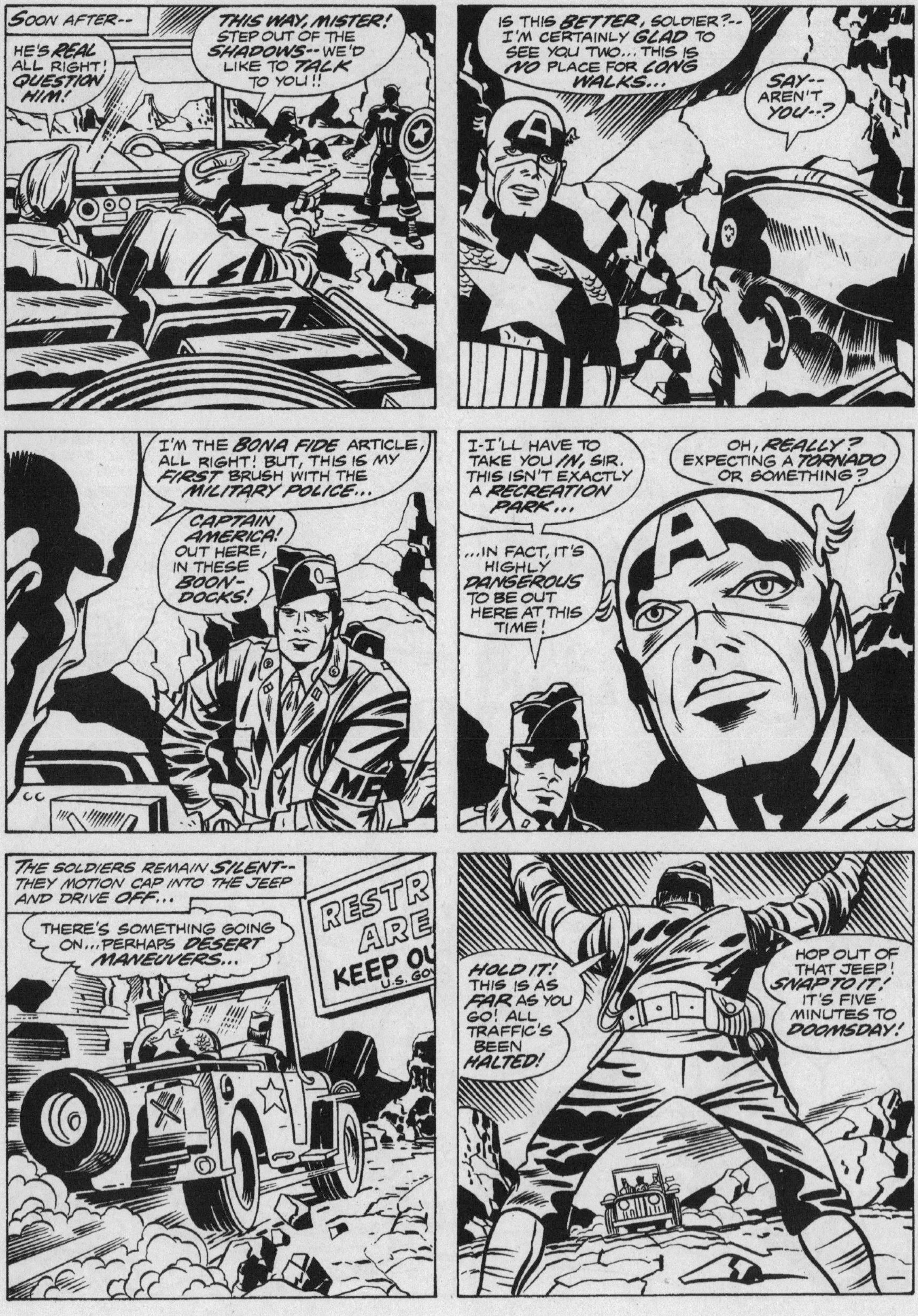
SOON AFTER--
THIS WAY, MISTER! STEP OUT OF THE SHADOWS-- WE'D LIKE TO TALK TO YOU!!
HE'S REAL ALL RIGHT! QUESTION HIM!
IS THIS BETTER, SOLDIER?-- I'M CERTAINLY GLAD TO SEE YOU TWO... THIS IS NO PLACE FOR LONG WALKS...
SAY-- AREN'T YOU--?
I'M THE BONA FIDE ARTICLE, ALL RIGHT! BUT, THIS IS MY FIRST BRUSH WITH THE MILITARY POLICE...
CAPTAIN AMERICA! OUT HERE, IN THESE BOON-DOCKS!
MP
I-I'LL HAVE TO TAKE YOU IN, SIR. THIS ISN'T EXACTLY A RECREATION PARK...
...IN FACT, IT'S HIGHLY DANGEROUS TO BE OUT HERE AT THIS TIME!
OH, REALLY? EXPECTING A TORNADO OR SOMETHING?
THE SOLDIERS REMAIN SILENT-- THEY MOTION CAP INTO THE JEEP AND DRIVE OFF...
THERE'S SOMETHING GOING ON... PERHAPS DESERT MANEUVERS...
RESTR
ARE
KEEP OU
U.S. GOV
HOLD IT! THIS IS AS FAR AS YOU GO! ALL TRAFFIC'S BEEN HALTED!
HOP OUT OF THAT JEEP! SNAP TO IT! IT'S FIVE MINUTES TO DOOMSDAY!

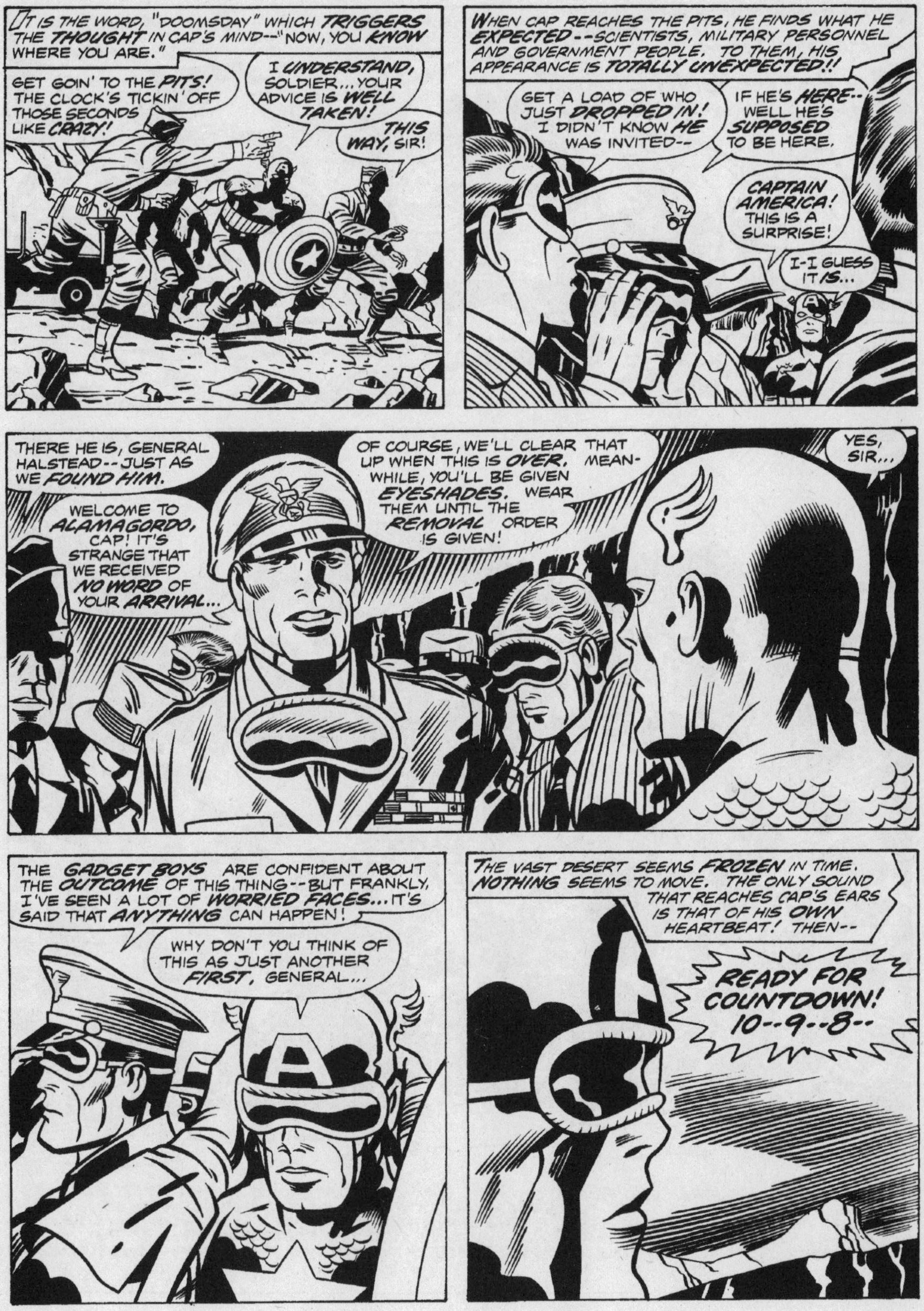
IT IS THE WORD, "DOOMSDAY" WHICH TRIGGERS THE THOUGHT IN CAP'S MIND--"NOW, YOU KNOW WHERE YOU ARE."
GET GOIN' TO THE PITS! THE CLOCK'S TICKIN' OFF THOSE SECONDS LIKE CRAZY!
I UNDERSTAND, SOLDIER...YOUR ADVICE IS WELL TAKEN!
THIS WAY, SIR!
WHEN CAP REACHES THE PITS, HE FINDS WHAT HE EXPECTED--SCIENTISTS, MILITARY PERSONNEL AND GOVERNMENT PEOPLE. TO THEM, HIS APPEARANCE IS TOTALLY UNEXPECTED!!
GET A LOAD OF WHO JUST DROPPED IN! I DIDN'T KNOW HE WAS INVITED--
IF HE'S HERE--WELL HE'S SUPPOSED TO BE HERE.
CAPTAIN AMERICA! THIS IS A SURPRISE!
I-I GUESS IT IS...
THERE HE IS, GENERAL HALSTEAD--JUST AS WE FOUND HIM.
WELCOME TO ALAMAGORDO, CAP! IT'S STRANGE THAT WE RECEIVED NO WORD OF YOUR ARRIVAL...
OF COURSE, WE'LL CLEAR THAT UP WHEN THIS IS OVER. MEAN-WHILE, YOU'LL BE GIVEN EYESHADES. WEAR THEM UNTIL THE REMOVAL ORDER IS GIVEN!
YES, SIR...
THE GADGET BOYS ARE CONFIDENT ABOUT THE OUTCOME OF THIS THING--BUT FRANKLY, I'VE SEEN A LOT OF WORRIED FACES...IT'S SAID THAT ANYTHING CAN HAPPEN!
WHY DON'T YOU THINK OF THIS AS JUST ANOTHER FIRST, GENERAL...
THE VAST DESERT SEEMS FROZEN IN TIME. NOTHING SEEMS TO MOVE. THE ONLY SOUND THAT REACHES CAP'S EARS IS THAT OF HIS OWN HEARTBEAT! THEN--
READY FOR COUNTDOWN! 10--9--8--

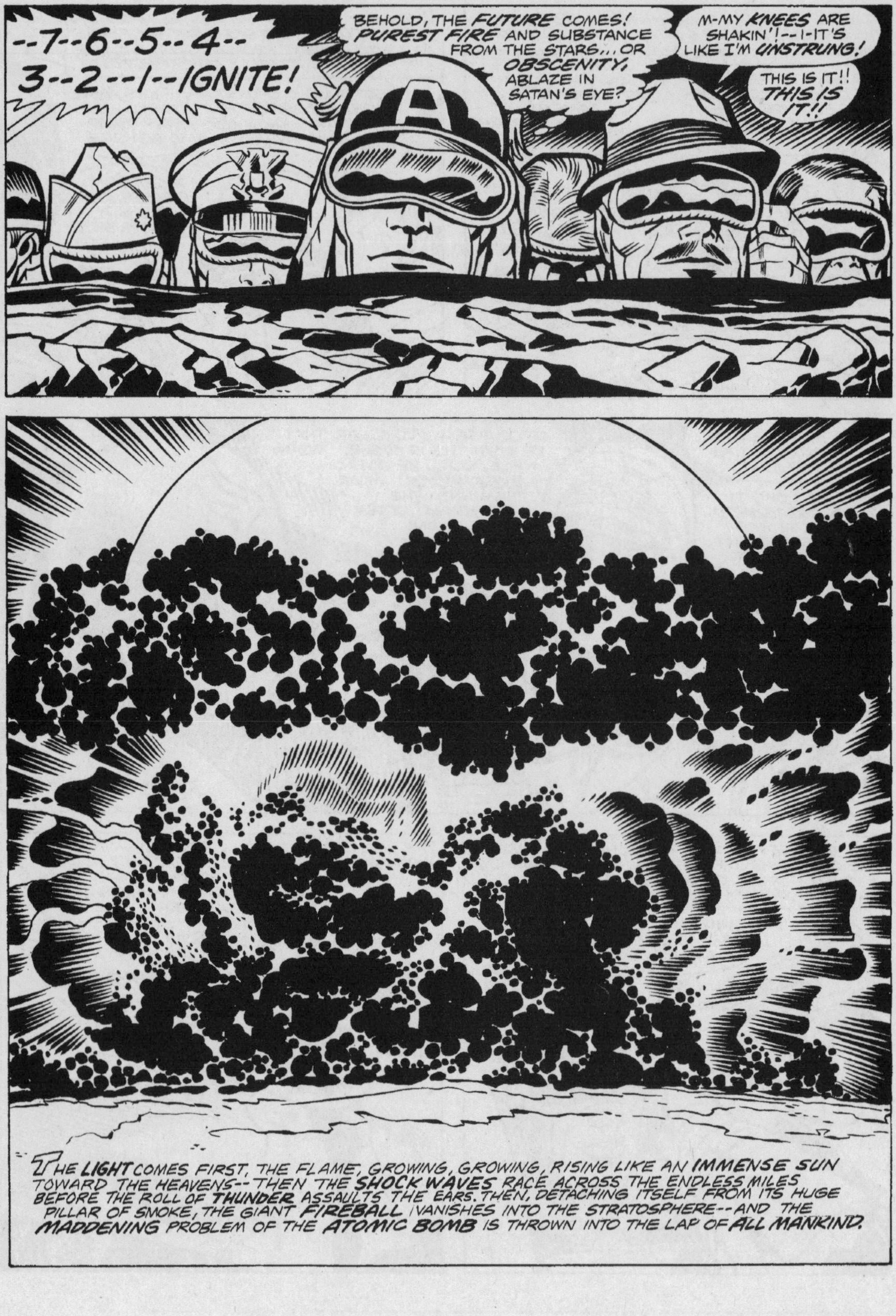
--7--6--5--4--
3--2--1--IGNITE!
BEHOLD, THE FUTURE COMES! PUREST FIRE AND SUBSTANCE FROM THE STARS... OR OBSCENITY, ABLAZE IN SATAN'S EYE?
M-MY KNEES ARE SHAKIN'!--I-IT'S LIKE I'M UNSTRUNG!
THIS IS IT!! THIS IS IT!!
THE LIGHT COMES FIRST, THE FLAME, GROWING, GROWING, RISING LIKE AN IMMENSE SUN TOWARD THE HEAVENS--THEN THE SHOCK WAVES RACE ACROSS THE ENDLESS MILES BEFORE THE ROLL OF THUNDER ASSAULTS THE EARS. THEN, DETACHING ITSELF FROM ITS HUGE PILLAR OF SMOKE, THE GIANT FIREBALL VANISHES INTO THE STRATOSPHERE--AND THE MADDENING PROBLEM OF THE ATOMIC BOMB IS THROWN INTO THE LAP OF ALL MANKIND.

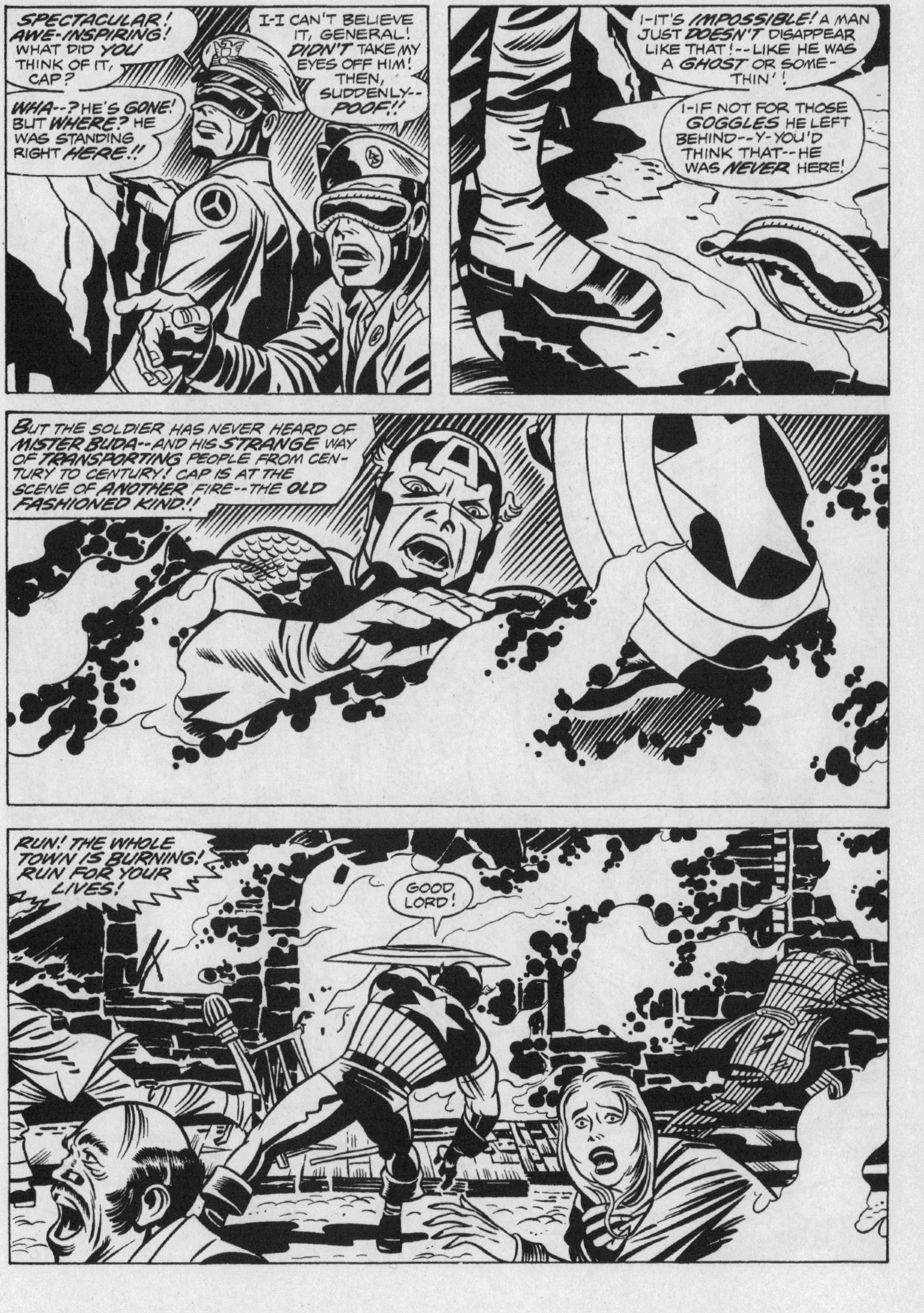
SPECTACULAR! AWE-INSPIRING! WHAT DID YOU THINK OF IT, CAP?
I-I CAN'T BELIEVE IT, GENERAL! DIDN'T TAKE MY EYES OFF HIM! THEN, SUDDENLY-- POOF!!
WHA--? HE'S GONE! BUT WHERE? HE WAS STANDING RIGHT HERE!!
I-IT'S IMPOSSIBLE! A MAN JUST DOESN'T DISAPPEAR LIKE THAT!--LIKE HE WAS A GHOST OR SOME-THIN'!
I-IF NOT FOR THOSE GOGGLES HE LEFT BEHIND--Y-YOU'D THINK THAT--HE WAS NEVER HERE!
BUT THE SOLDIER HAS NEVER HEARD OF MISTER BUDA--AND HIS STRANGE WAY OF TRANSPORTING PEOPLE FROM CENTURY TO CENTURY! CAP IS AT THE SCENE OF ANOTHER FIRE--THE OLD FASHIONED KIND!!
RUN! THE WHOLE TOWN IS BURNING! RUN FOR YOUR LIVES!
GOOD LORD!

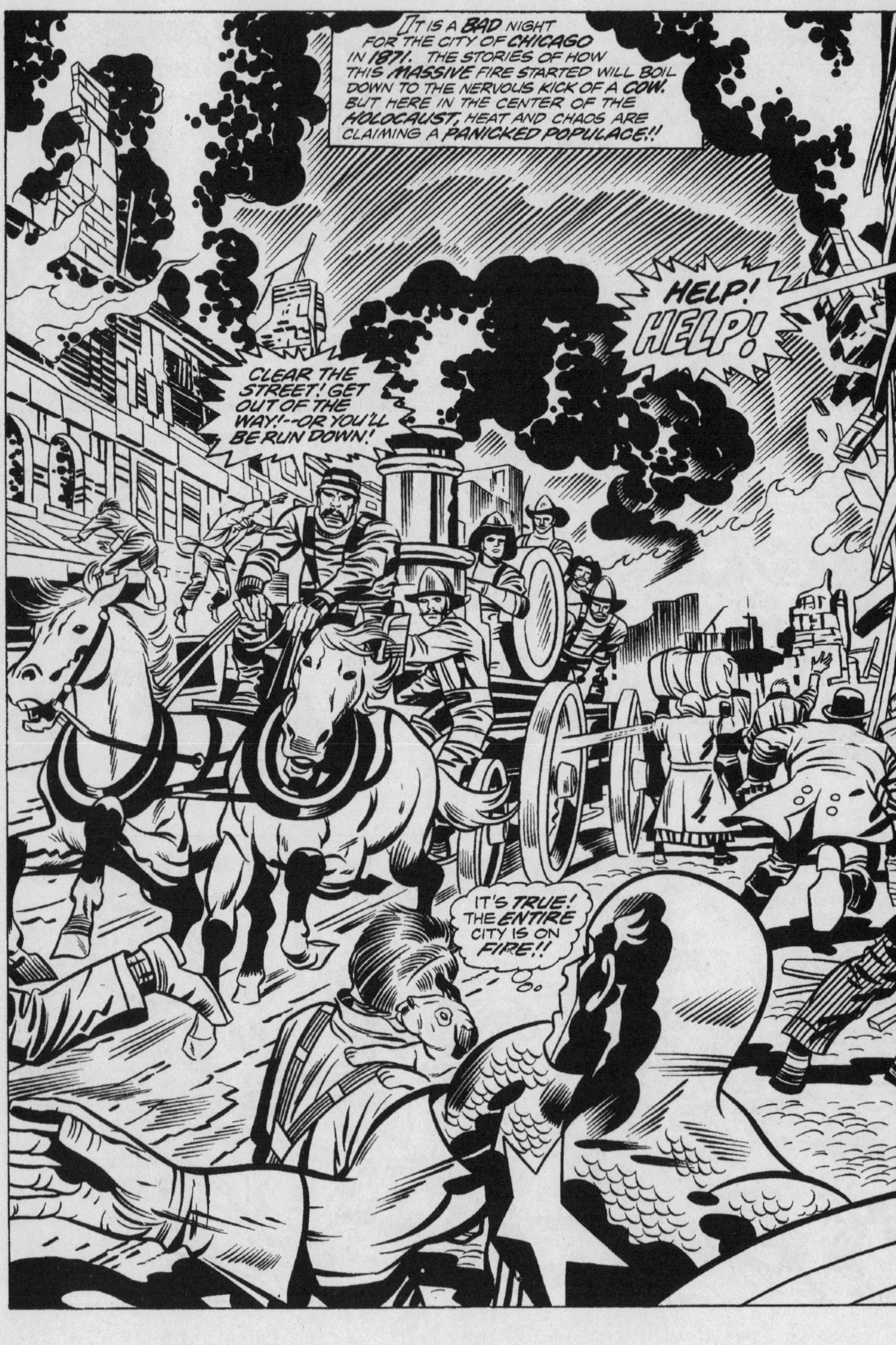
IT IS A BAD NIGHT FOR THE CITY OF CHICAGO IN 1871. THE STORIES OF HOW THIS MASSIVE FIRE STARTED WILL BOIL DOWN TO THE NERVOUS KICK OF A COW. BUT HERE IN THE CENTER OF THE HOLOCAUST, HEAT AND CHAOS ARE CLAIMING A PANICKED POPULACE!!
HELP! HELP!
CLEAR THE STREET! GET OUT OF THE WAY!--OR YOU'LL BE RUN DOWN!
IT'S TRUE! THE ENTIRE CITY IS ON FIRE!!

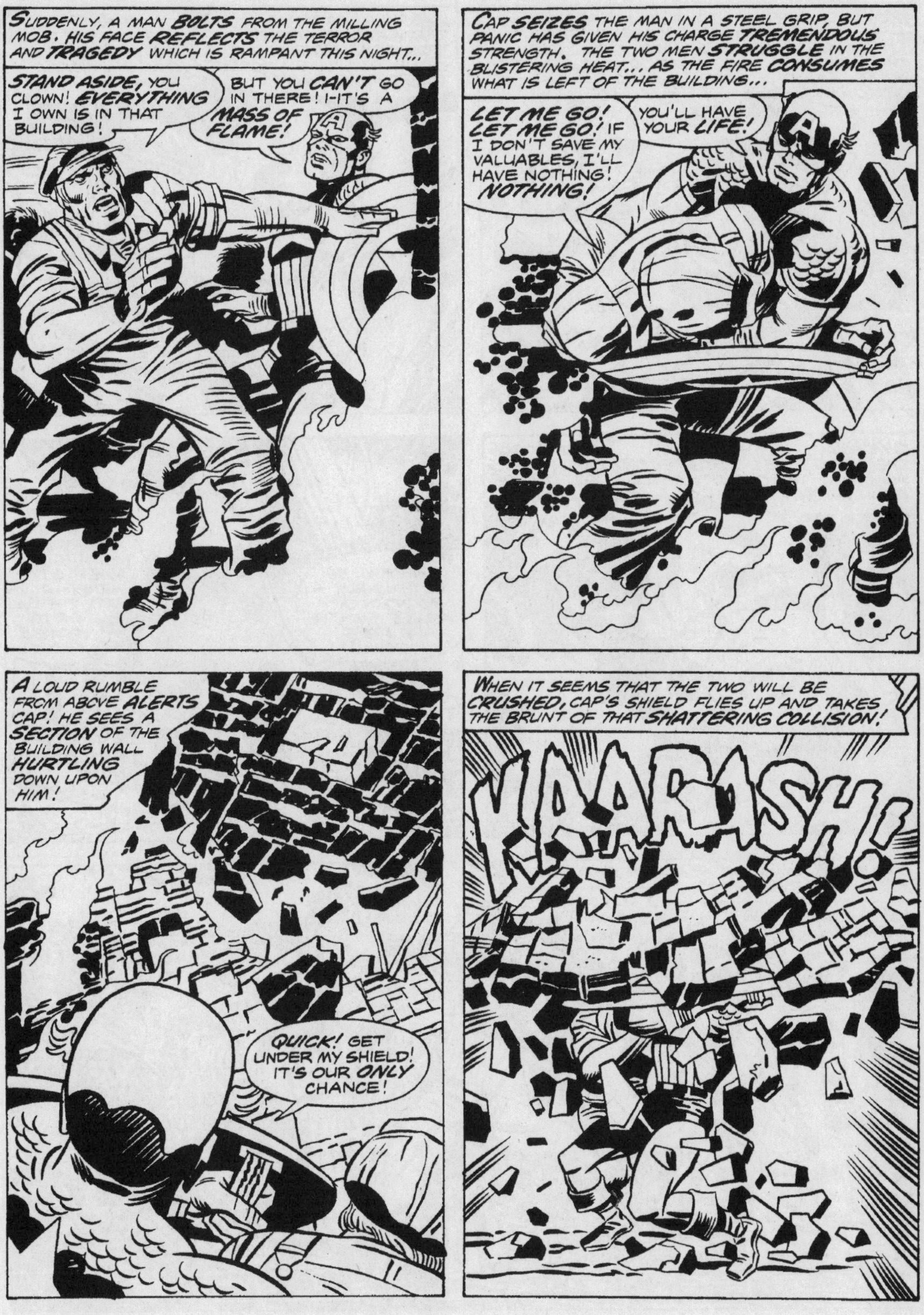
SUDDENLY, A MAN BOLTS FROM THE MILLING MOB. HIS FACE REFLECTS THE TERROR AND TRAGEDY WHICH IS RAMPANT THIS NIGHT...
STAND ASIDE, YOU CLOWN! EVERYTHING I OWN IS IN THAT BUILDING!
BUT YOU CAN'T GO IN THERE! I-IT'S A MASS OF FLAME!
CAP SEIZES THE MAN IN A STEEL GRIP, BUT PANIC HAS GIVEN HIS CHARGE TREMENDOUS STRENGTH. THE TWO MEN STRUGGLE IN THE BLISTERING HEAT... AS THE FIRE CONSUMES WHAT IS LEFT OF THE BUILDINGS...
LET ME GO! LET ME GO! IF I DON'T SAVE MY VALUABLES, I'LL HAVE NOTHING! NOTHING!
YOU'LL HAVE YOUR LIFE!
A LOUD RUMBLE FROM ABOVE ALERTS CAP! HE SEES A SECTION OF THE BUILDING WALL HURTLING DOWN UPON HIM!
QUICK! GET UNDER MY SHIELD! IT'S OUR ONLY CHANCE!
WHEN IT SEEMS THAT THE TWO WILL BE CRUSHED, CAP'S SHIELD FLIES UP AND TAKES THE BRUNT OF THAT SHATTERING COLLISION!
KRAARASH!

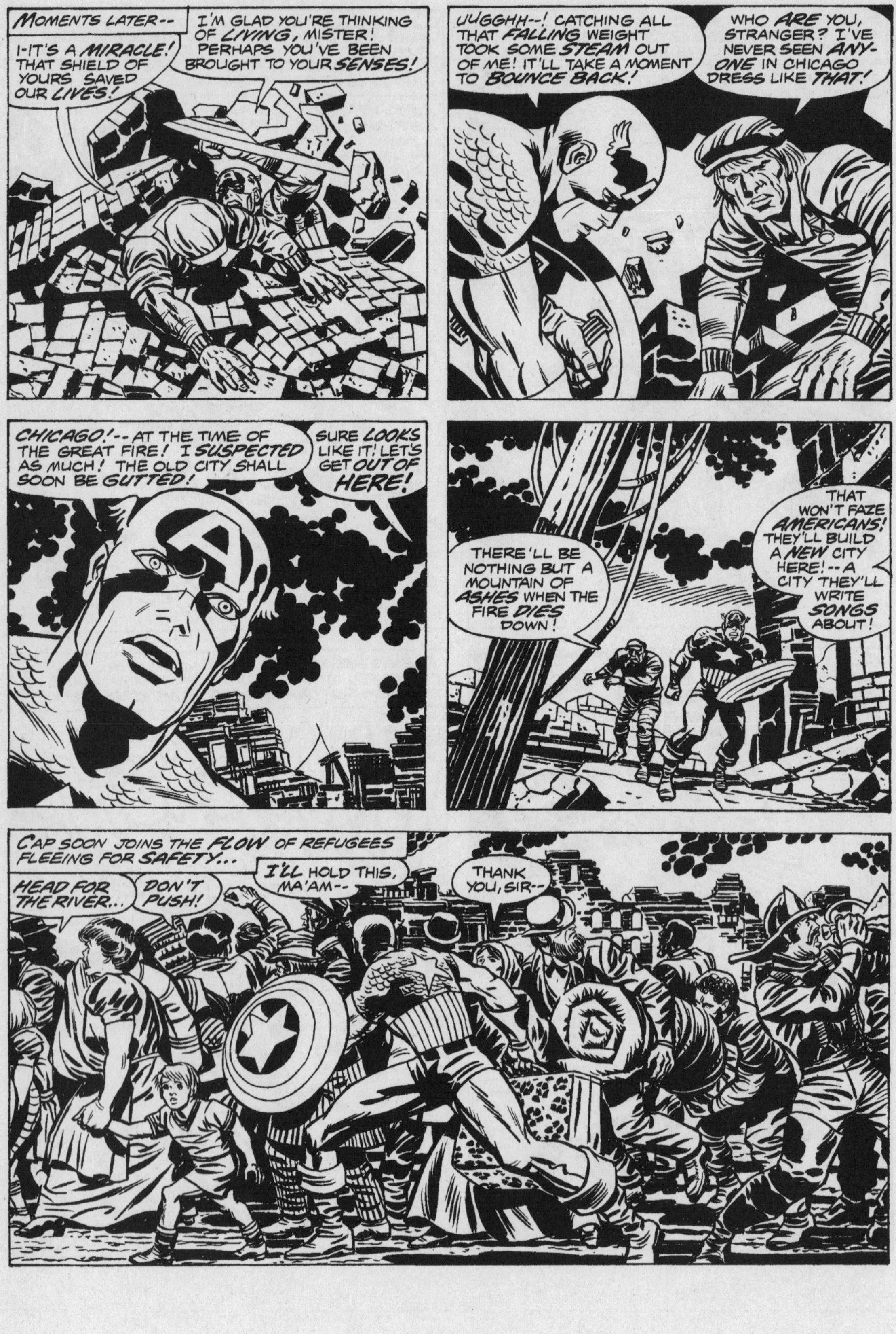
MOMENTS LATER--
I-IT'S A MIRACLE! THAT SHIELD OF YOURS SAVED OUR LIVES!
I'M GLAD YOU'RE THINKING OF LIVING, MISTER! PERHAPS YOU'VE BEEN BROUGHT TO YOUR SENSES!
UUGGHH--! CATCHING ALL THAT FALLING WEIGHT TOOK SOME STEAM OUT OF ME! IT'LL TAKE A MOMENT TO BOUNCE BACK!
WHO ARE YOU, STRANGER? I'VE NEVER SEEN ANY-ONE IN CHICAGO DRESS LIKE THAT!
CHICAGO!--AT THE TIME OF THE GREAT FIRE! I SUSPECTED AS MUCH! THE OLD CITY SHALL SOON BE GUTTED!
SURE LOOKS LIKE IT! LET'S GET OUT OF HERE!
THERE'LL BE NOTHING BUT A MOUNTAIN OF ASHES WHEN THE FIRE DIES DOWN!
THAT WON'T FAZE AMERICANS! THEY'LL BUILD A NEW CITY HERE!--A CITY THEY'LL WRITE SONGS ABOUT!
CAP SOON JOINS THE FLOW OF REFUGEES FLEEING FOR SAFETY...
HEAD FOR THE RIVER...
DON'T PUSH!
I'LL HOLD THIS, MA'AM--
THANK YOU, SIR--

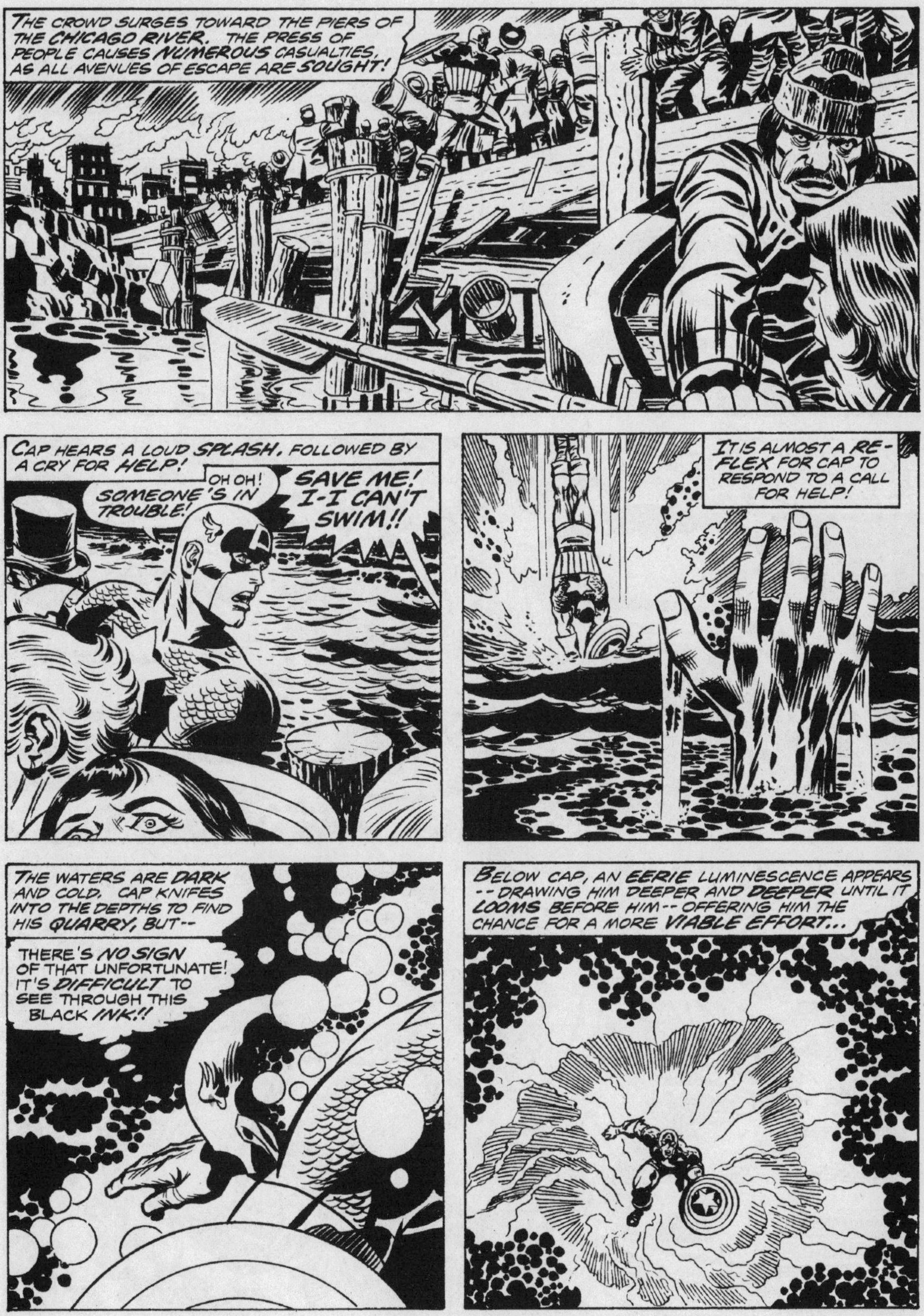
THE CROWD SURGES TOWARD THE PIERS OF THE CHICAGO RIVER. THE PRESS OF PEOPLE CAUSES NUMEROUS CASUALTIES AS ALL AVENUES OF ESCAPE ARE SOUGHT!
CAP HEARS A LOUD SPLASH, FOLLOWED BY A CRY FOR HELP!
OH OH! SOMEONE'S IN TROUBLE!
SAVE ME! I-I CAN'T SWIM!!
IT IS ALMOST A RE-FLEX FOR CAP TO RESPOND TO A CALL FOR HELP!
THE WATERS ARE DARK AND COLD. CAP KNIFES INTO THE DEPTHS TO FIND HIS QUARRY, BUT--
THERE'S NO SIGN OF THAT UNFORTUNATE! IT'S DIFFICULT TO SEE THROUGH THIS BLACK INK!!
BELOW CAP, AN EERIE LUMINESCENCE APPEARS -- DRAWING HIM DEEPER AND DEEPER UNTIL IT LOOMS BEFORE HIM -- OFFERING HIM THE CHANCE FOR A MORE VIABLE EFFORT...

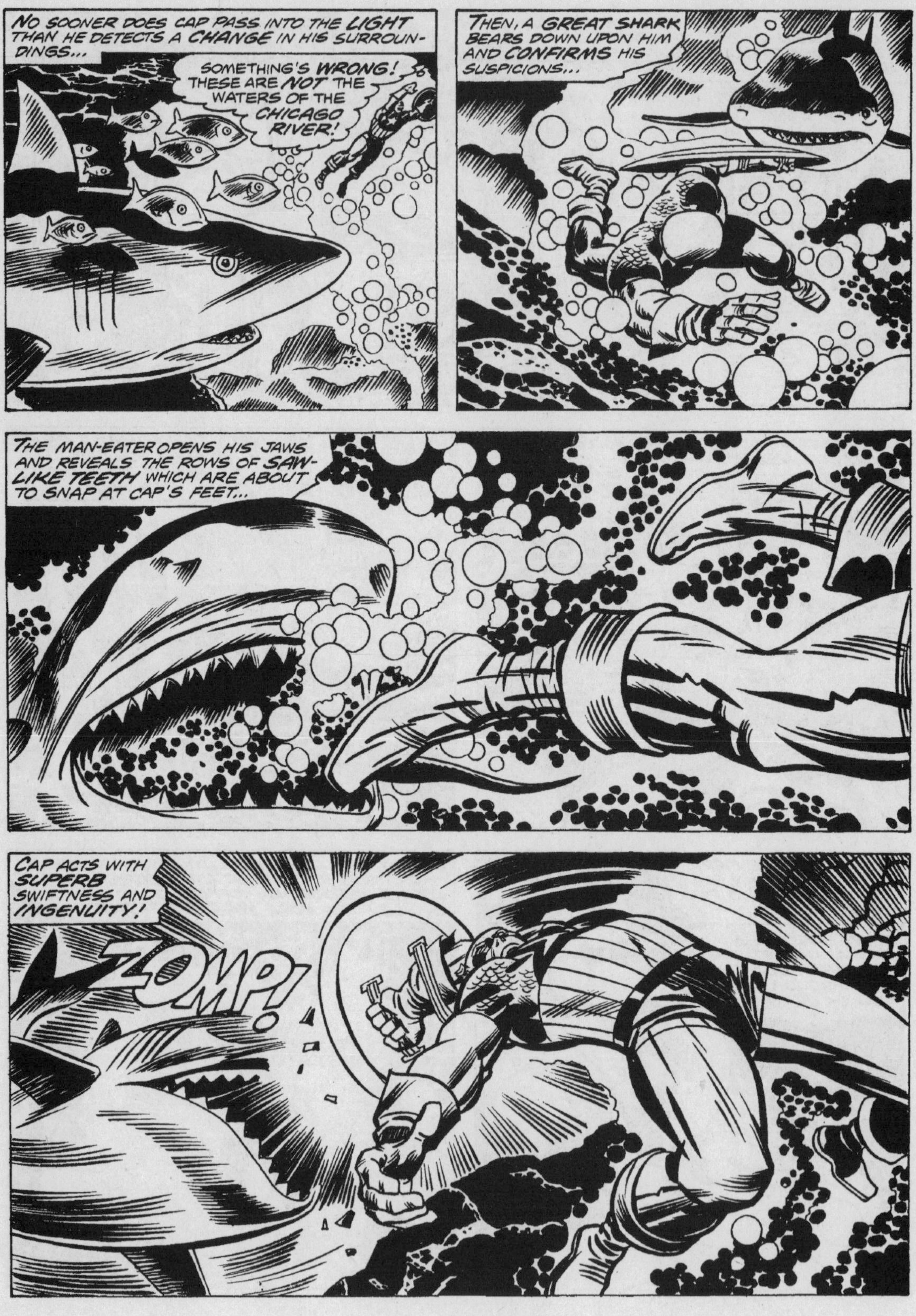
NO SOONER DOES CAP PASS INTO THE LIGHT THAN HE DETECTS A CHANGE IN HIS SURROUNDINGS...
SOMETHING'S WRONG! THESE ARE NOT THE WATERS OF THE CHICAGO RIVER!
THEN, A GREAT SHARK BEARS DOWN UPON HIM AND CONFIRMS HIS SUSPICIONS...
THE MAN-EATER OPENS HIS JAWS AND REVEALS THE ROWS OF SAW-LIKE TEETH WHICH ARE ABOUT TO SNAP AT CAP'S FEET...
CAP ACTS WITH SUPERB SWIFTNESS AND INGENUITY!
ZOMP!

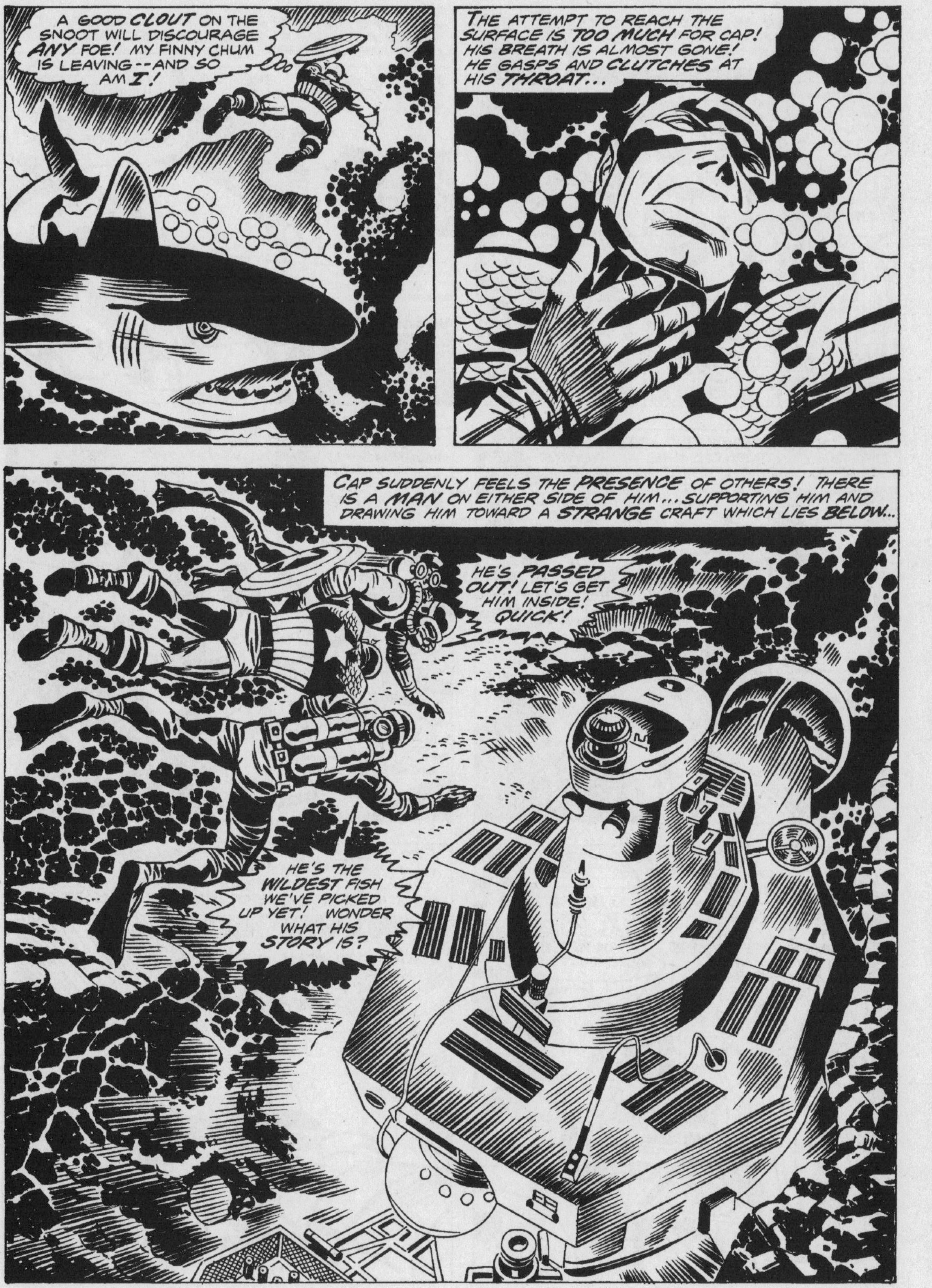
A GOOD CLOUT ON THE SNOOT WILL DISCOURAGE ANY FOE! MY FINNY CHUM IS LEAVING--AND SO AM I!
THE ATTEMPT TO REACH THE SURFACE IS TOO MUCH FOR CAP! HIS BREATH IS ALMOST GONE! HE GASPS AND CLUTCHES AT HIS THROAT...
CAP SUDDENLY FEELS THE PRESENCE OF OTHERS! THERE IS A MAN ON EITHER SIDE OF HIM... SUPPORTING HIM AND DRAWING HIM TOWARD A STRANGE CRAFT WHICH LIES BELOW...
HE'S PASSED OUT! LET'S GET HIM INSIDE! QUICK!
HE'S THE WILDEST FISH WE'VE PICKED UP YET! WONDER WHAT HIS STORY IS?

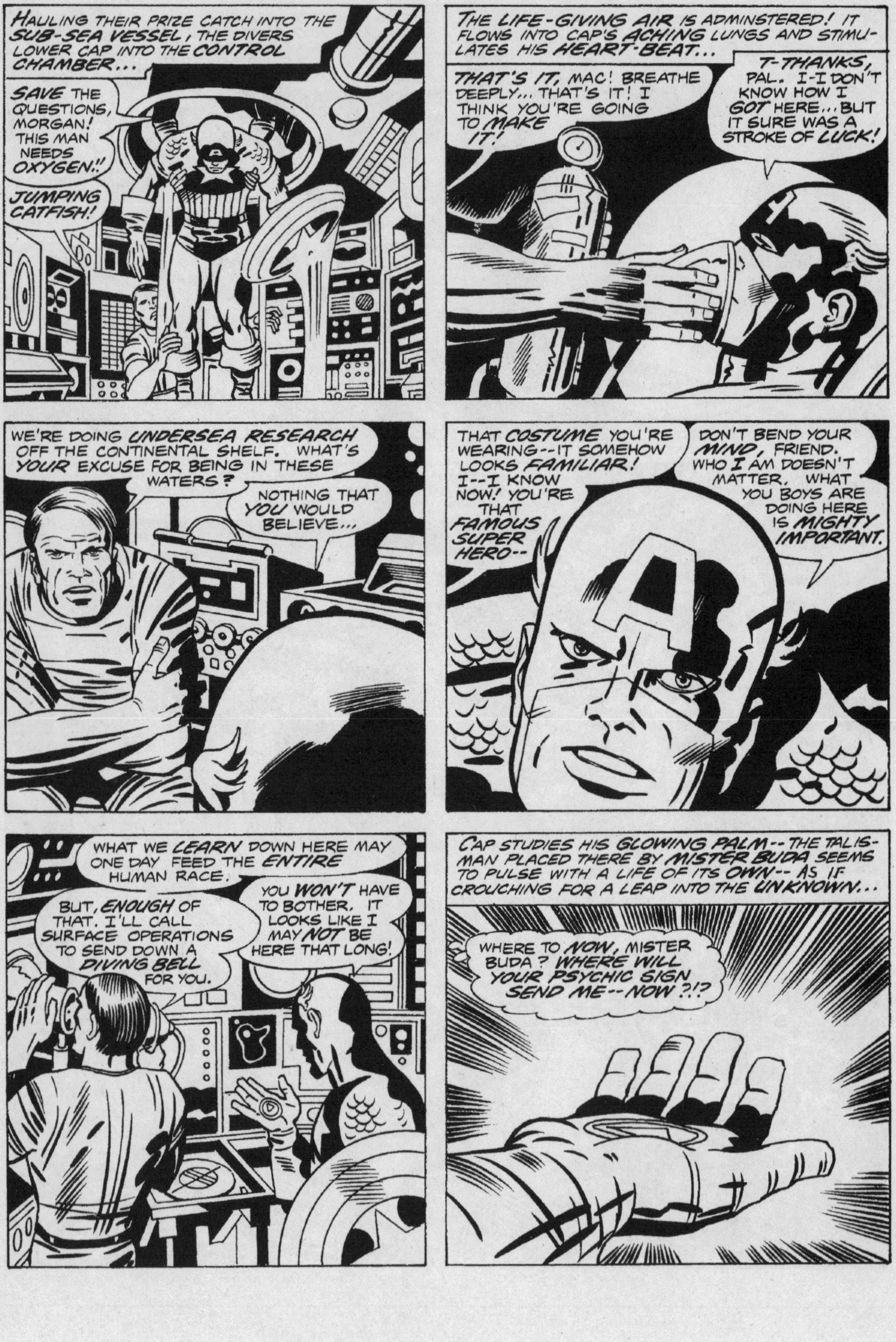

HAULING THEIR PRIZE CATCH INTO THE SUB-SEA VESSEL, THE DIVERS LOWER CAP INTO THE CONTROL CHAMBER...
SAVE THE QUESTIONS, MORGAN! THIS MAN NEEDS OXYGEN!!
JUMPING CATFISH!
THE LIFE-GIVING AIR IS ADMINSTERED! IT FLOWS INTO CAP'S ACHING LUNGS AND STIMULATES HIS HEART-BEAT...
THAT'S IT, MAC! BREATHE DEEPLY... THAT'S IT! I THINK YOU'RE GOING TO MAKE IT!
T-THANKS, PAL. I-I DON'T KNOW HOW I GOT HERE... BUT IT SURE WAS A STROKE OF LUCK!
WE'RE DOING UNDERSEA RESEARCH OFF THE CONTINENTAL SHELF. WHAT'S YOUR EXCUSE FOR BEING IN THESE WATERS?
NOTHING THAT YOU WOULD BELIEVE...
THAT COSTUME YOU'RE WEARING--IT SOMEHOW LOOKS FAMILIAR! I--I KNOW NOW! YOU'RE THAT FAMOUS SUPER HERO--
DON'T BEND YOUR MIND, FRIEND. WHO I AM DOESN'T MATTER. WHAT YOU BOYS ARE DOING HERE IS MIGHTY IMPORTANT.
WHAT WE LEARN DOWN HERE MAY ONE DAY FEED THE ENTIRE HUMAN RACE.
BUT, ENOUGH OF THAT. I'LL CALL SURFACE OPERATIONS TO SEND DOWN A DIVING BELL FOR YOU.
YOU WON'T HAVE TO BOTHER. IT LOOKS LIKE I MAY NOT BE HERE THAT LONG!
CAP STUDIES HIS GLOWING PALM--THE TALISMAN PLACED THERE BY MISTER BUDA SEEMS TO PULSE WITH A LIFE OF ITS OWN--AS IF CROUCHING FOR A LEAP INTO THE UNKNOWN...
WHERE TO NOW, MISTER BUDA? WHERE WILL YOUR PSYCHIC SIGN SEND ME--NOW?!?

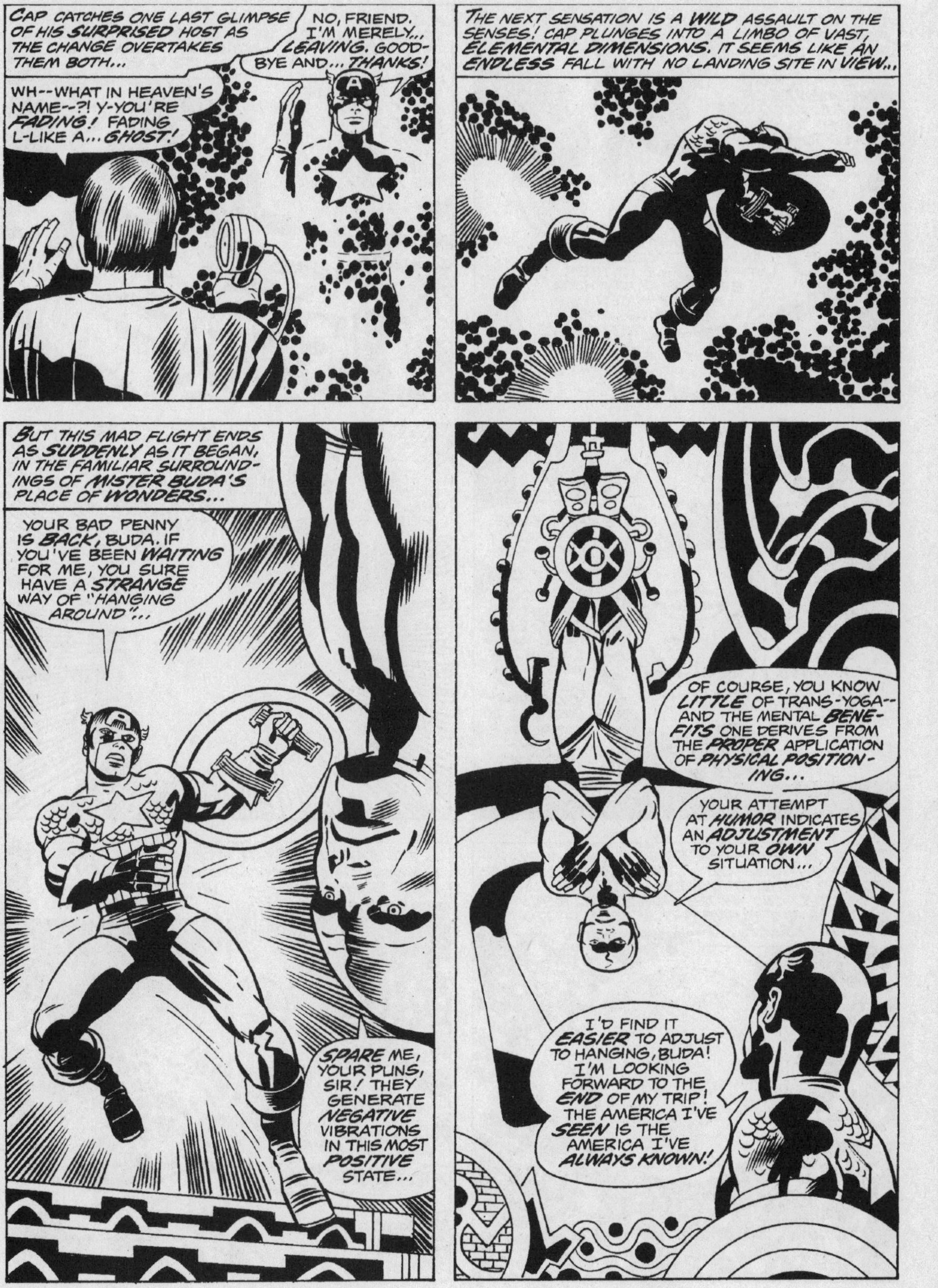

CAP CATCHES ONE LAST GLIMPSE OF HIS SURPRISED HOST AS THE CHANGE OVERTAKES THEM BOTH...
NO, FRIEND. I'M MERELY... LEAVING. GOOD-BYE AND... THANKS!
WH--WHAT IN HEAVEN'S NAME--?! Y-YOU'RE FADING! FADING L-LIKE A... GHOST!
THE NEXT SENSATION IS A WILD ASSAULT ON THE SENSES! CAP PLUNGES INTO A LIMBO OF VAST, ELEMENTAL DIMENSIONS. IT SEEMS LIKE AN ENDLESS FALL WITH NO LANDING SITE IN VIEW...
BUT THIS MAD FLIGHT ENDS AS SUDDENLY AS IT BEGAN, IN THE FAMILIAR SURROUNDINGS OF MISTER BUDA'S PLACE OF WONDERS...
YOUR BAD PENNY IS BACK, BUDA. IF YOU'VE BEEN WAITING FOR ME, YOU SURE HAVE A STRANGE WAY OF "HANGING AROUND"...
SPARE ME, YOUR PUNS, SIR! THEY GENERATE NEGATIVE VIBRATIONS IN THIS MOST POSITIVE STATE...
OF COURSE, YOU KNOW LITTLE OF TRANS-YOGA--AND THE MENTAL BENEFITS ONE DERIVES FROM THE PROPER APPLICATION OF PHYSICAL POSITIONING...
YOUR ATTEMPT AT HUMOR INDICATES AN ADJUSTMENT TO YOUR OWN SITUATION...
I'D FIND IT EASIER TO ADJUST TO HANGING, BUDA! I'M LOOKING FORWARD TO THE END OF MY TRIP! THE AMERICA I'VE SEEN IS THE AMERICA I'VE ALWAYS KNOWN!

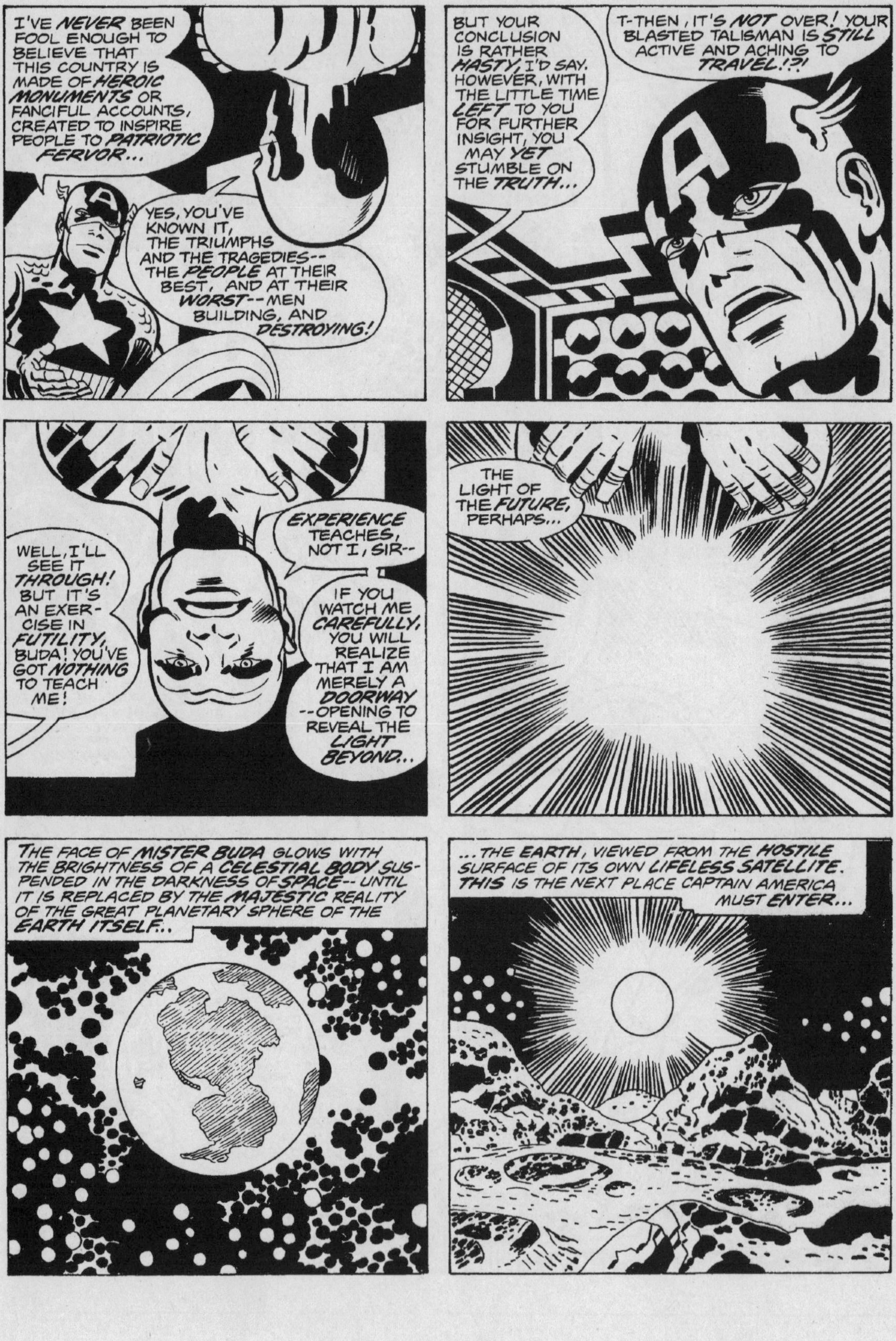
I'VE NEVER BEEN FOOL ENOUGH TO BELIEVE THAT THIS COUNTRY IS MADE OF HEROIC MONUMENTS OR FANCIFUL ACCOUNTS, CREATED TO INSPIRE PEOPLE TO PATRIOTIC FERVOR...
YES, YOU'VE KNOWN IT, THE TRIUMPHS AND THE TRAGEDIES-- THE PEOPLE AT THEIR BEST, AND AT THEIR WORST--MEN BUILDING, AND DESTROYING!
BUT YOUR CONCLUSION IS RATHER HASTY, I'D SAY. HOWEVER, WITH THE LITTLE TIME LEFT TO YOU FOR FURTHER INSIGHT, YOU MAY YET STUMBLE ON THE TRUTH...
T-THEN, IT'S NOT OVER! YOUR BLASTED TALISMAN IS STILL ACTIVE AND ACHING TO TRAVEL!?!
WELL, I'LL SEE IT THROUGH! BUT IT'S AN EXER-CISE IN FUTILITY, BUDA! YOU'VE GOT NOTHING TO TEACH ME!
EXPERIENCE TEACHES, NOT I, SIR--
IF YOU WATCH ME CAREFULLY, YOU WILL REALIZE THAT I AM MERELY A DOORWAY --OPENING TO REVEAL THE LIGHT BEYOND..
THE LIGHT OF THE FUTURE, PERHAPS...
THE FACE OF MISTER BUDA GLOWS WITH THE BRIGHTNESS OF A CELESTIAL BODY SUS-PENDED IN THE DARKNESS OF SPACE-- UNTIL IT IS REPLACED BY THE MAJESTIC REALITY OF THE GREAT PLANETARY SPHERE OF THE EARTH ITSELF..
...THE EARTH, VIEWED FROM THE HOSTILE SURFACE OF ITS OWN LIFELESS SATELLITE. THIS IS THE NEXT PLACE CAPTAIN AMERICA MUST ENTER...

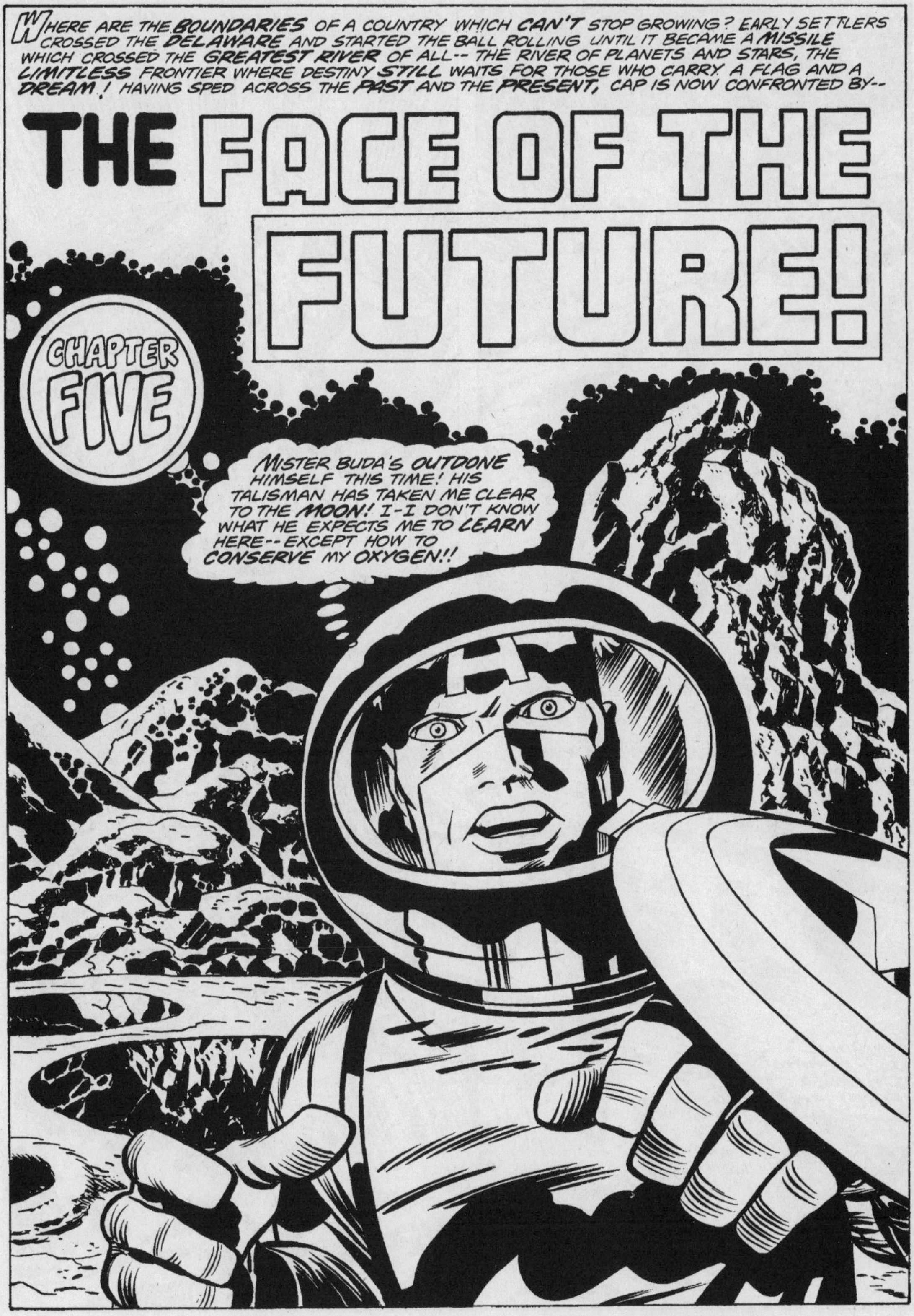
WHERE ARE THE BOUNDARIES OF A COUNTRY WHICH CAN'T STOP GROWING? EARLY SETTLERS CROSSED THE DELAWARE AND STARTED THE BALL ROLLING UNTIL IT BECAME A MISSILE WHICH CROSSED THE GREATEST RIVER OF ALL-- THE RIVER OF PLANETS AND STARS, THE LIMITLESS FRONTIER WHERE DESTINY STILL WAITS FOR THOSE WHO CARRY A FLAG AND A DREAM! HAVING SPED ACROSS THE PAST AND THE PRESENT, CAP IS NOW CONFRONTED BY--
THE FACE OF THE FUTURE!
CHAPTER FIVE
MISTER BUDA'S OUTDONE HIMSELF THIS TIME! HIS TALISMAN HAS TAKEN ME CLEAR TO THE MOON! I-I DON'T KNOW WHAT HE EXPECTS ME TO LEARN HERE--EXCEPT HOW TO CONSERVE MY OXYGEN!!

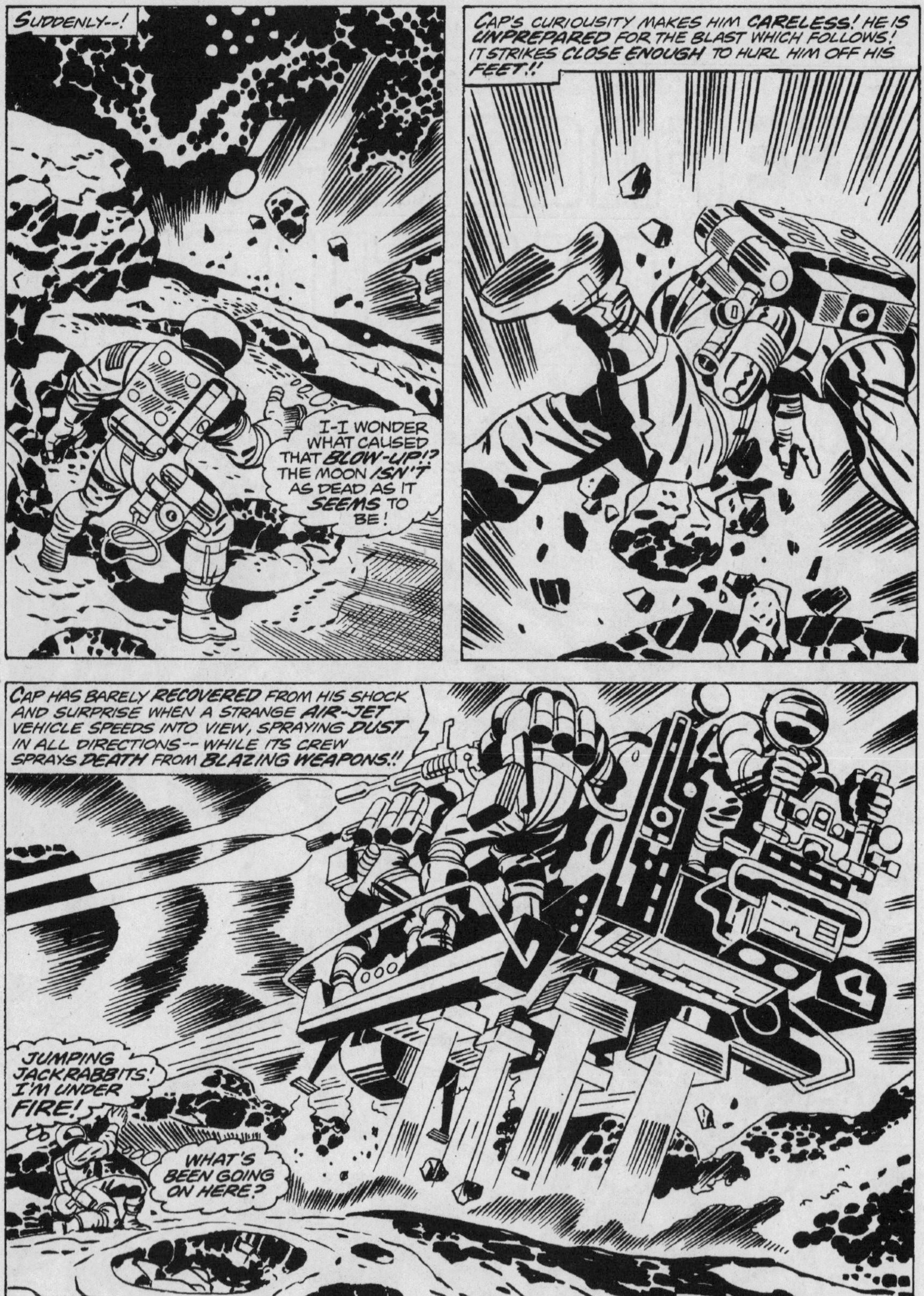
SUDDENLY--!
I-I WONDER WHAT CAUSED THAT BLOW-UP!? THE MOON ISN'T AS DEAD AS IT SEEMS TO BE!
CAP'S CURIOUSITY MAKES HIM CARELESS! HE IS UNPREPARED FOR THE BLAST WHICH FOLLOWS! IT STRIKES CLOSE ENOUGH TO HURL HIM OFF HIS FEET!!
CAP HAS BARELY RECOVERED FROM HIS SHOCK AND SURPRISE WHEN A STRANGE AIR-JET VEHICLE SPEEDS INTO VIEW, SPRAYING DUST IN ALL DIRECTIONS-- WHILE ITS CREW SPRAYS DEATH FROM BLAZING WEAPONS!!
JUMPING JACKRABBITS! I'M UNDER FIRE!
WHAT'S BEEN GOING ON HERE?

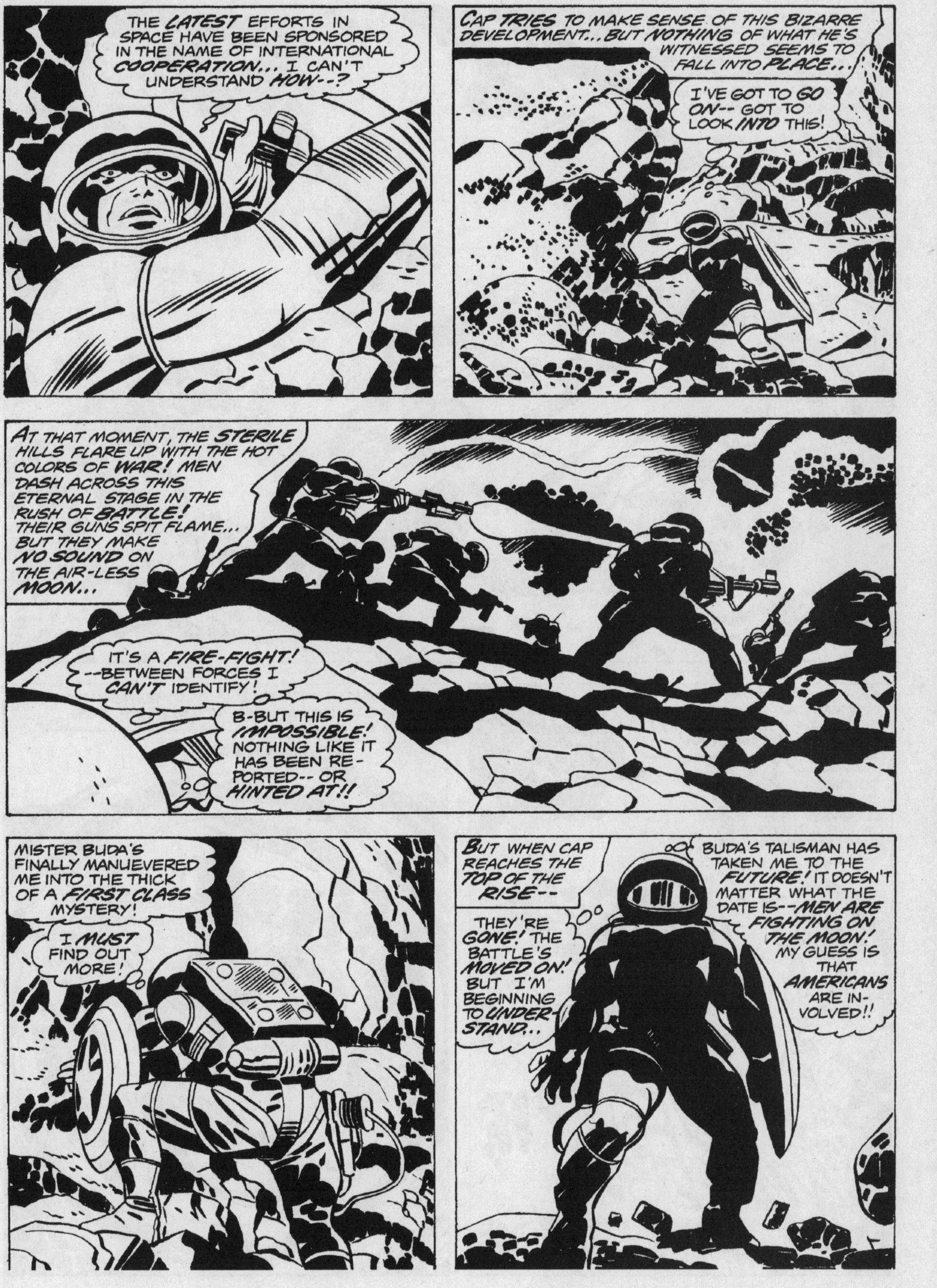
THE LATEST EFFORTS IN SPACE HAVE BEEN SPONSORED IN THE NAME OF INTERNATIONAL COOPERATION... I CAN'T UNDERSTAND HOW--?
CAP TRIES TO MAKE SENSE OF THIS BIZARRE DEVELOPMENT... BUT NOTHING OF WHAT HE'S WITNESSED SEEMS TO FALL INTO PLACE...
I'VE GOT TO GO ON-- GOT TO LOOK INTO THIS!
AT THAT MOMENT, THE STERILE HILLS FLARE UP WITH THE HOT COLORS OF WAR! MEN DASH ACROSS THIS ETERNAL STAGE IN THE RUSH OF BATTLE! THEIR GUNS SPIT FLAME... BUT THEY MAKE NO SOUND ON THE AIR-LESS MOON...
IT'S A FIRE-FIGHT! --BETWEEN FORCES I CAN'T IDENTIFY!
B-BUT THIS IS IMPOSSIBLE! NOTHING LIKE IT HAS BEEN RE-PORTED-- OR HINTED AT!!
MISTER BUDA'S FINALLY MANUEVERED ME INTO THE THICK OF A FIRST CLASS MYSTERY!
I MUST FIND OUT MORE!
BUT WHEN CAP REACHES THE TOP OF THE RISE--
THEY'RE GONE! THE BATTLE'S MOVED ON! BUT I'M BEGINNING TO UNDER-STAND...
BUDA'S TALISMAN HAS TAKEN ME TO THE FUTURE! IT DOESN'T MATTER WHAT THE DATE IS--MEN ARE FIGHTING ON THE MOON! MY GUESS IS THAT AMERICANS ARE IN-VOLVED!!

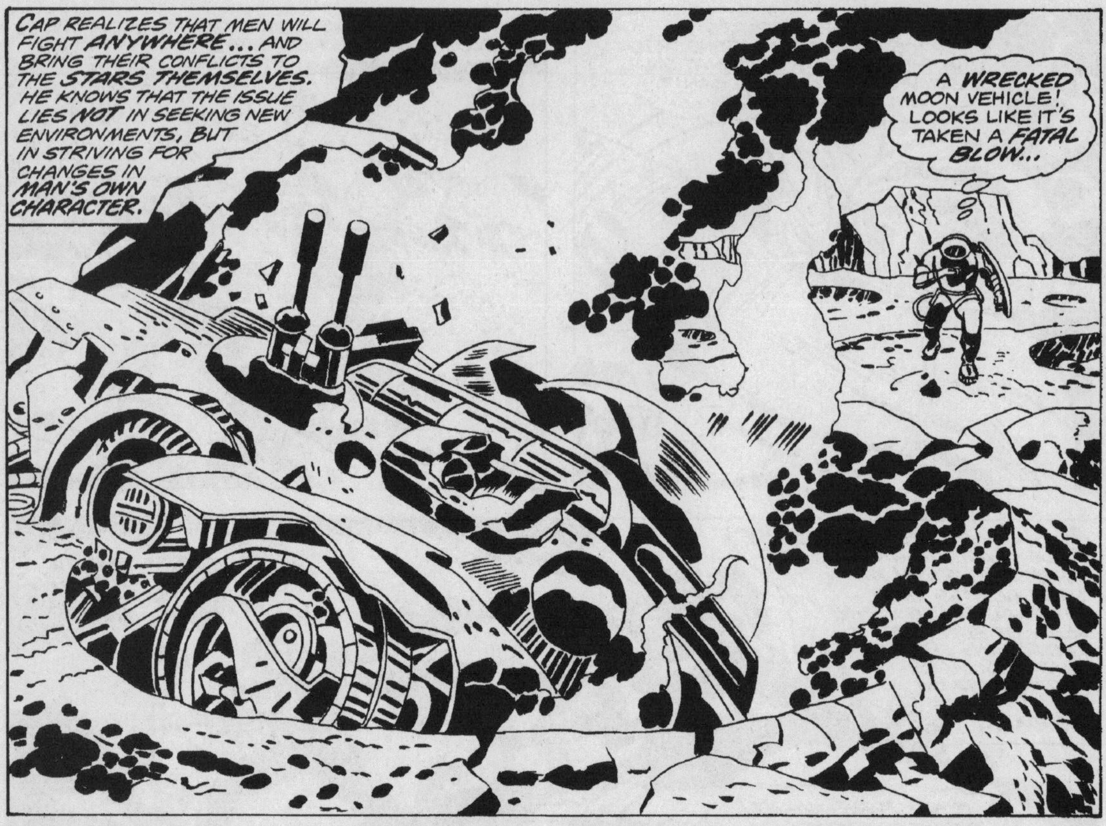
CAP REALIZES THAT MEN WILL FIGHT ANYWHERE... AND BRING THEIR CONFLICTS TO THE STARS THEMSELVES. HE KNOWS THAT THE ISSUE LIES NOT IN SEEKING NEW ENVIRONMENTS, BUT IN STRIVING FOR CHANGES IN MAN'S OWN CHARACTER.
A WRECKED MOON VEHICLE! LOOKS LIKE IT'S TAKEN A FATAL BLOW...

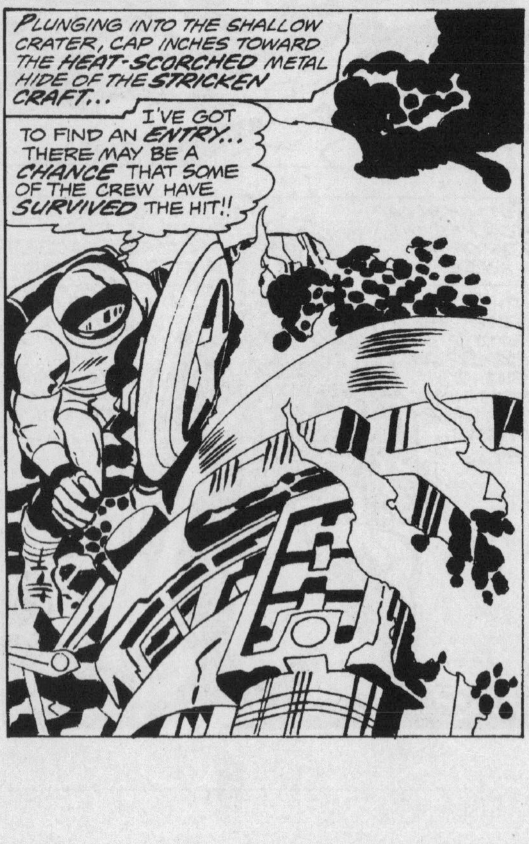
PLUNGING INTO THE SHALLOW CRATER, CAP INCHES TOWARD THE HEAT-SCORCHED METAL HIDE OF THE STRICKEN CRAFT...
I'VE GOT TO FIND AN ENTRY... THERE MAY BE A CHANCE THAT SOME OF THE CREW HAVE SURVIVED THE HIT!!

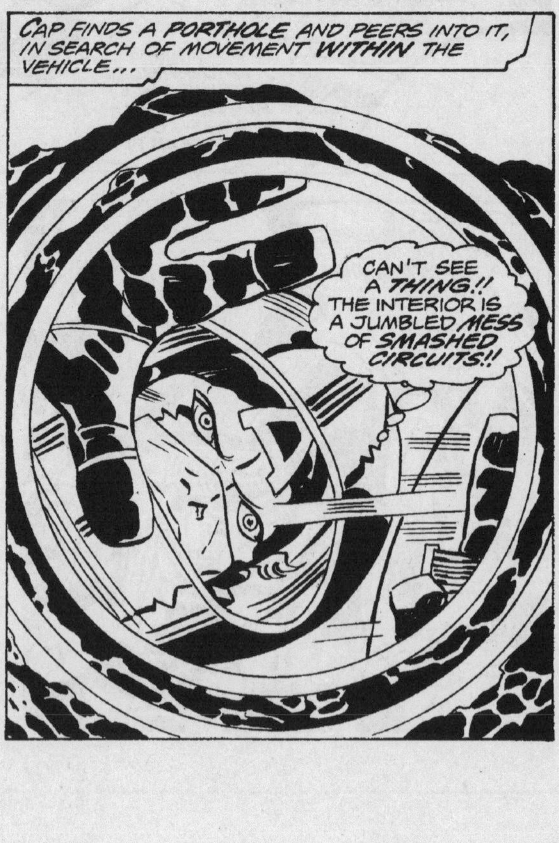
CAP FINDS A PORTHOLE AND PEERS INTO IT, IN SEARCH OF MOVEMENT WITHIN THE VEHICLE...
CAN'T SEE A THING!! THE INTERIOR IS A JUMBLED MESS OF SMASHED CIRCUITS!!

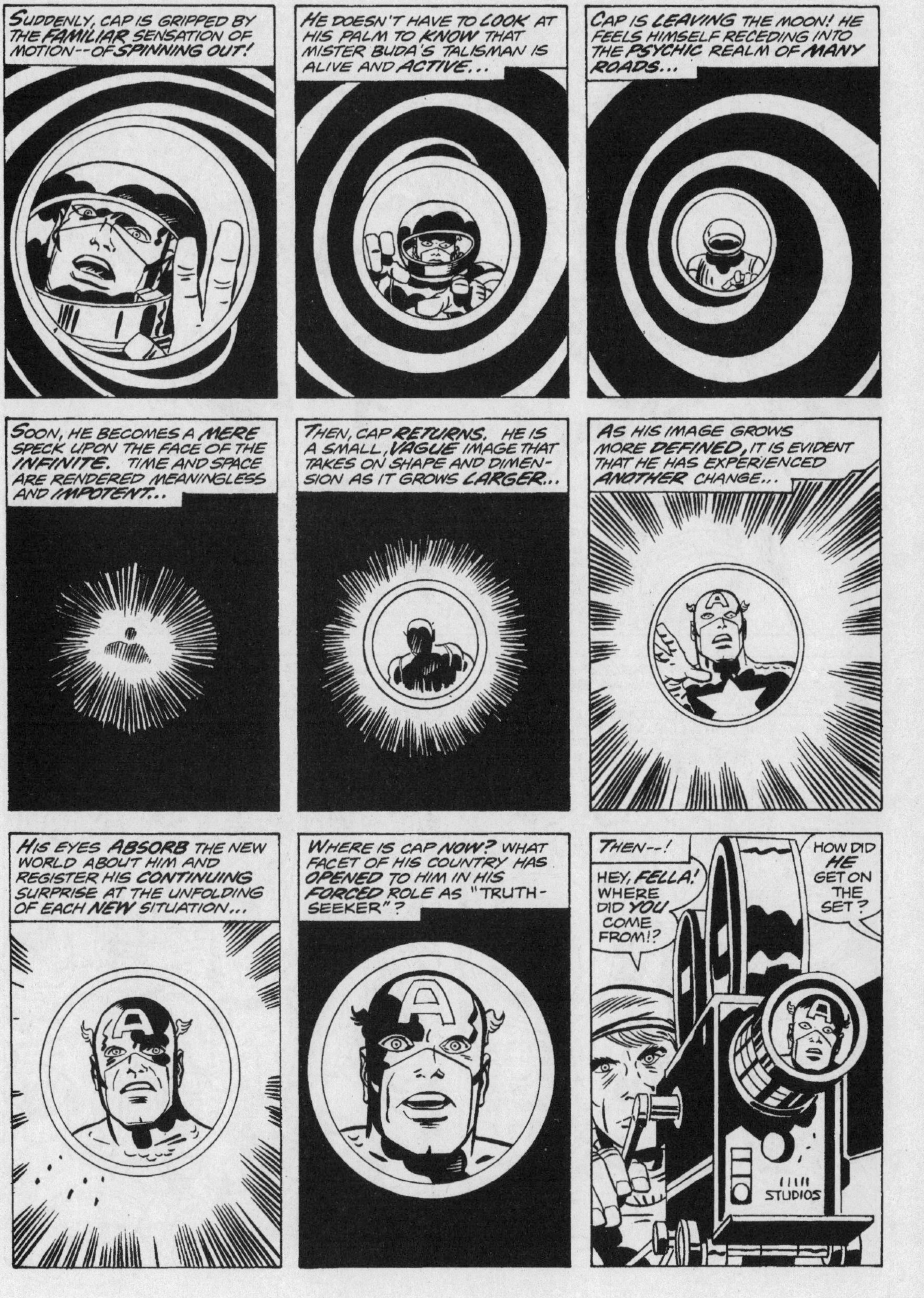
SUDDENLY, CAP IS GRIPPED BY THE FAMILIAR SENSATION OF MOTION--OF SPINNING OUT!
HE DOESN'T HAVE TO LOOK AT HIS PALM TO KNOW THAT MISTER BUDA'S TALISMAN IS ALIVE AND ACTIVE...
CAP IS LEAVING THE MOON! HE FEELS HIMSELF RECEDING INTO THE PSYCHIC REALM OF MANY ROADS...
SOON, HE BECOMES A MERE SPECK UPON THE FACE OF THE INFINITE. TIME AND SPACE ARE RENDERED MEANINGLESS AND IMPOTENT...
THEN, CAP RETURNS. HE IS A SMALL, VAGUE IMAGE THAT TAKES ON SHAPE AND DIMENSION AS IT GROWS LARGER...
AS HIS IMAGE GROWS MORE DEFINED, IT IS EVIDENT THAT HE HAS EXPERIENCED ANOTHER CHANGE...
HIS EYES ABSORB THE NEW WORLD ABOUT HIM AND REGISTER HIS CONTINUING SURPRISE AT THE UNFOLDING OF EACH NEW SITUATION...
WHERE IS CAP NOW? WHAT FACET OF HIS COUNTRY HAS OPENED TO HIM IN HIS FORCED ROLE AS "TRUTH-SEEKER"?
THEN--!
HEY, FELLA! WHERE DID YOU COME FROM!?
HOW DID HE GET ON THE SET?
STUDIOS

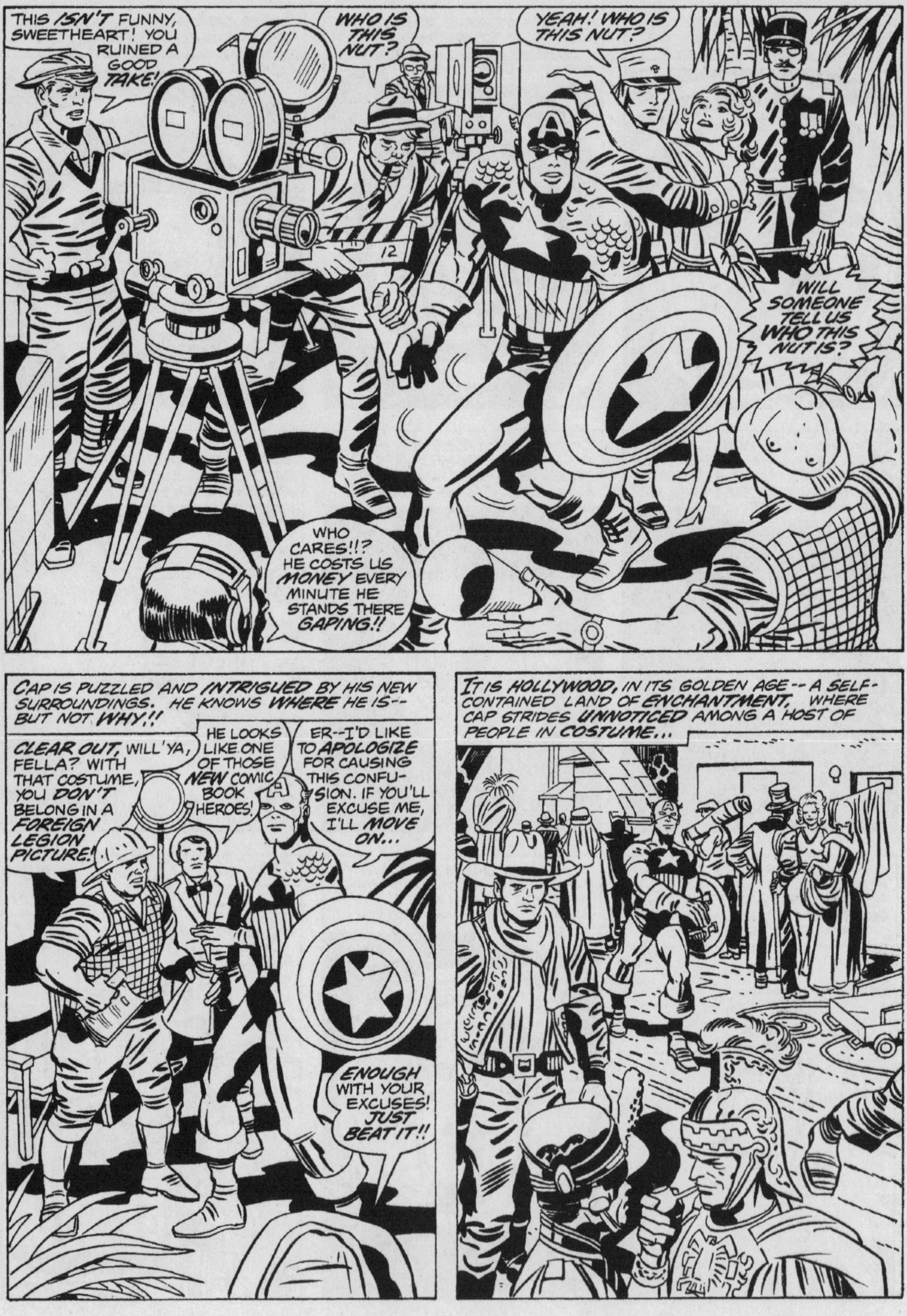
THIS ISN'T FUNNY, SWEETHEART! YOU RUINED A GOOD TAKE!
WHO IS THIS NUT?
YEAH! WHO IS THIS NUT?
WILL SOMEONE TELL US WHO THIS NUT IS?
WHO CARES!!? HE COSTS US MONEY EVERY MINUTE HE STANDS THERE GAPING!!
12
CAP IS PUZZLED AND INTRIGUED BY HIS NEW SURROUNDINGS. HE KNOWS WHERE HE IS-- BUT NOT WHY!!
CLEAR OUT, WILL'YA, FELLA? WITH THAT COSTUME, YOU DON'T BELONG IN A FOREIGN LEGION PICTURE!
HE LOOKS LIKE ONE OF THOSE NEW COMIC BOOK HEROES!
ER--I'D LIKE TO APOLOGIZE FOR CAUSING THIS CONFUSION. IF YOU'LL EXCUSE ME, I'LL MOVE ON...
ENOUGH WITH YOUR EXCUSES! JUST BEAT IT!!
IT IS HOLLYWOOD, IN ITS GOLDEN AGE -- A SELF-CONTAINED LAND OF ENCHANTMENT, WHERE CAP STRIDES UNNOTICED AMONG A HOST OF PEOPLE IN COSTUME...

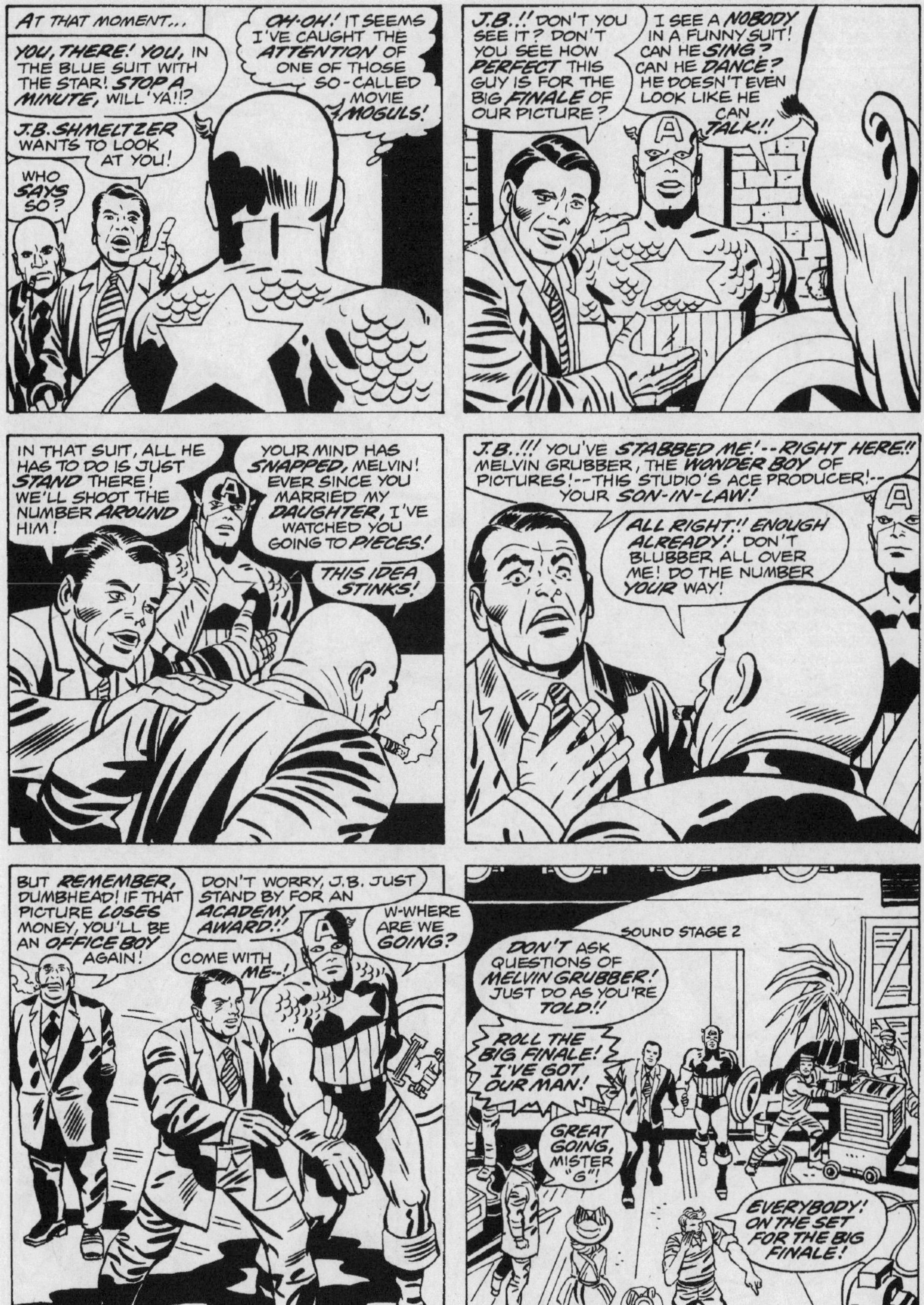
AT THAT MOMENT...
YOU, THERE! YOU, IN THE BLUE SUIT WITH THE STAR! STOP A MINUTE, WILL 'YA!!?
OH-OH! IT SEEMS I'VE CAUGHT THE ATTENTION OF ONE OF THOSE SO-CALLED MOVIE MOGULS!
J.B. SHMELTZER WANTS TO LOOK AT YOU!
WHO SAYS SO?
J.B.!! DON'T YOU SEE IT? DON'T YOU SEE HOW PERFECT THIS GUY IS FOR THE BIG FINALE OF OUR PICTURE?
I SEE A NOBODY IN A FUNNY SUIT! CAN HE SING? CAN HE DANCE? HE DOESN'T EVEN LOOK LIKE HE CAN TALK!!
IN THAT SUIT, ALL HE HAS TO DO IS JUST STAND THERE! WE'LL SHOOT THE NUMBER AROUND HIM!
YOUR MIND HAS SNAPPED, MELVIN! EVER SINCE YOU MARRIED MY DAUGHTER, I'VE WATCHED YOU GOING TO PIECES!
THIS IDEA STINKS!
J.B.!!! YOU'VE STABBED ME!--RIGHT HERE!! MELVIN GRUBBER, THE WONDER BOY OF PICTURES!--THIS STUDIO'S ACE PRODUCER!--YOUR SON-IN-LAW!
ALL RIGHT!! ENOUGH ALREADY! DON'T BLUBBER ALL OVER ME! DO THE NUMBER YOUR WAY!
BUT REMEMBER, DUMBHEAD! IF THAT PICTURE LOSES MONEY, YOU'LL BE AN OFFICE BOY AGAIN!
DON'T WORRY, J.B. JUST STAND BY FOR AN ACADEMY AWARD!!
COME WITH ME--!
W-WHERE ARE WE GOING?
SOUND STAGE 2
DON'T ASK QUESTIONS OF MELVIN GRUBBER! JUST DO AS YOU'RE TOLD!!
ROLL THE BIG FINALE! I'VE GOT OUR MAN!
GREAT GOING, MISTER "G"!
EVERYBODY! ON THE SET FOR THE BIG FINALE!

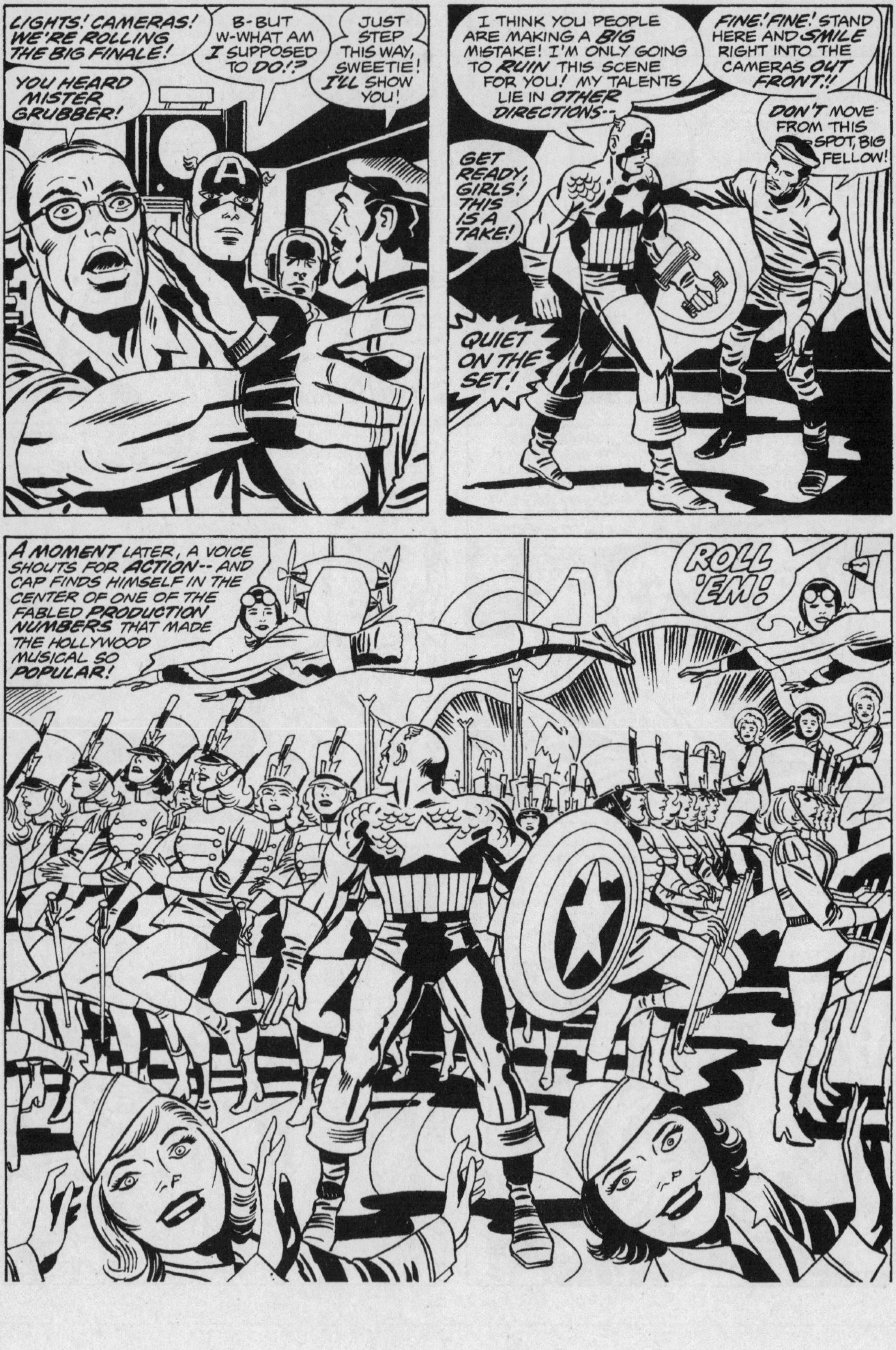
LIGHTS! CAMERAS! WE'RE ROLLING THE BIG FINALE!
YOU HEARD MISTER GRUBBER!
B-BUT W-WHAT AM I SUPPOSED TO DO!?
JUST STEP THIS WAY, SWEETIE! I'LL SHOW YOU!
I THINK YOU PEOPLE ARE MAKING A BIG MISTAKE! I'M ONLY GOING TO RUIN THIS SCENE FOR YOU! MY TALENTS LIE IN OTHER DIRECTIONS--
FINE! FINE! STAND HERE AND SMILE RIGHT INTO THE CAMERAS OUT FRONT!!
DON'T MOVE FROM THIS SPOT, BIG FELLOW!
GET READY, GIRLS! THIS IS A TAKE!
QUIET ON THE SET!
A MOMENT LATER, A VOICE SHOUTS FOR ACTION-- AND CAP FINDS HIMSELF IN THE CENTER OF ONE OF THE FABLED PRODUCTION NUMBERS THAT MADE THE HOLLYWOOD MUSICAL SO POPULAR!
ROLL 'EM!

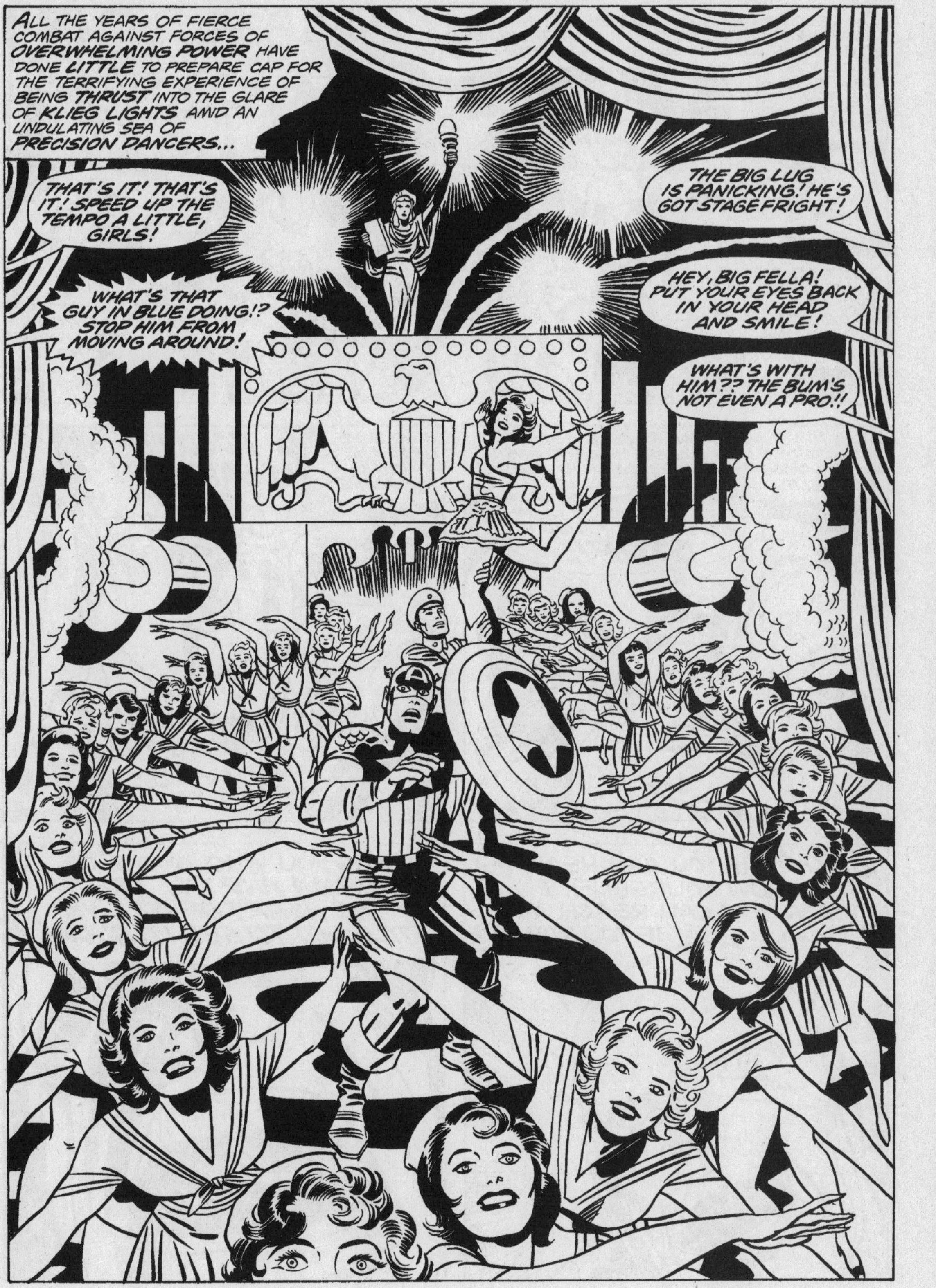
ALL THE YEARS OF FIERCE COMBAT AGAINST FORCES OF OVERWHELMING POWER HAVE DONE LITTLE TO PREPARE CAP FOR THE TERRIFYING EXPERIENCE OF BEING THRUST INTO THE GLARE OF KLIEG LIGHTS AMID AN UNDULATING SEA OF PRECISION DANCERS...
THAT'S IT! THAT'S IT! SPEED UP THE TEMPO A LITTLE, GIRLS!
THE BIG LUG IS PANICKING! HE'S GOT STAGE FRIGHT!
WHAT'S THAT GUY IN BLUE DOING!? STOP HIM FROM MOVING AROUND!
HEY, BIG FELLA! PUT YOUR EYES BACK IN YOUR HEAD AND SMILE!
WHAT'S WITH HIM?? THE BUM'S NOT EVEN A PRO!!

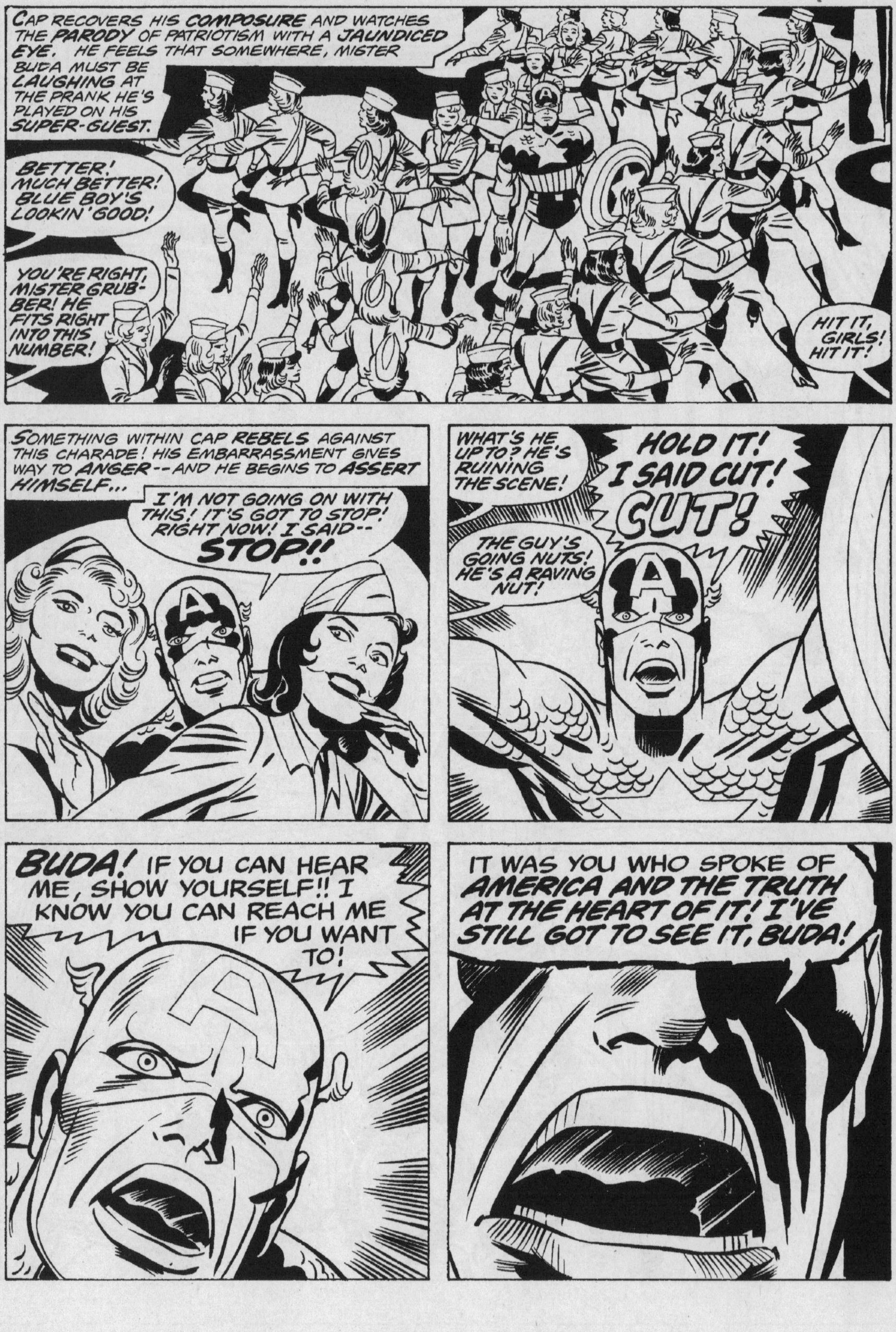
CAP RECOVERS HIS COMPOSURE AND WATCHES THE PARODY OF PATRIOTISM WITH A JAUNDICED EYE. HE FEELS THAT SOMEWHERE, MISTER BUDA MUST BE LAUGHING AT THE PRANK HE'S PLAYED ON HIS SUPER-GUEST.
BETTER! MUCH BETTER! BLUE BOY'S LOOKIN' GOOD!
YOU'RE RIGHT, MISTER GRUBBER! HE FITS RIGHT INTO THIS NUMBER!
HIT IT, GIRLS! HIT IT!
SOMETHING WITHIN CAP REBELS AGAINST THIS CHARADE! HIS EMBARRASSMENT GIVES WAY TO ANGER--AND HE BEGINS TO ASSERT HIMSELF...
I'M NOT GOING ON WITH THIS! IT'S GOT TO STOP! RIGHT NOW! I SAID-- STOP!!
WHAT'S HE UP TO? HE'S RUINING THE SCENE!
HOLD IT! I SAID CUT! CUT!
THE GUY'S GOING NUTS! HE'S A RAVING NUT!
BUDA! IF YOU CAN HEAR ME, SHOW YOURSELF!! I KNOW YOU CAN REACH ME IF YOU WANT TO!
IT WAS YOU WHO SPOKE OF AMERICA AND THE TRUTH AT THE HEART OF IT! I'VE STILL GOT TO SEE IT, BUDA!

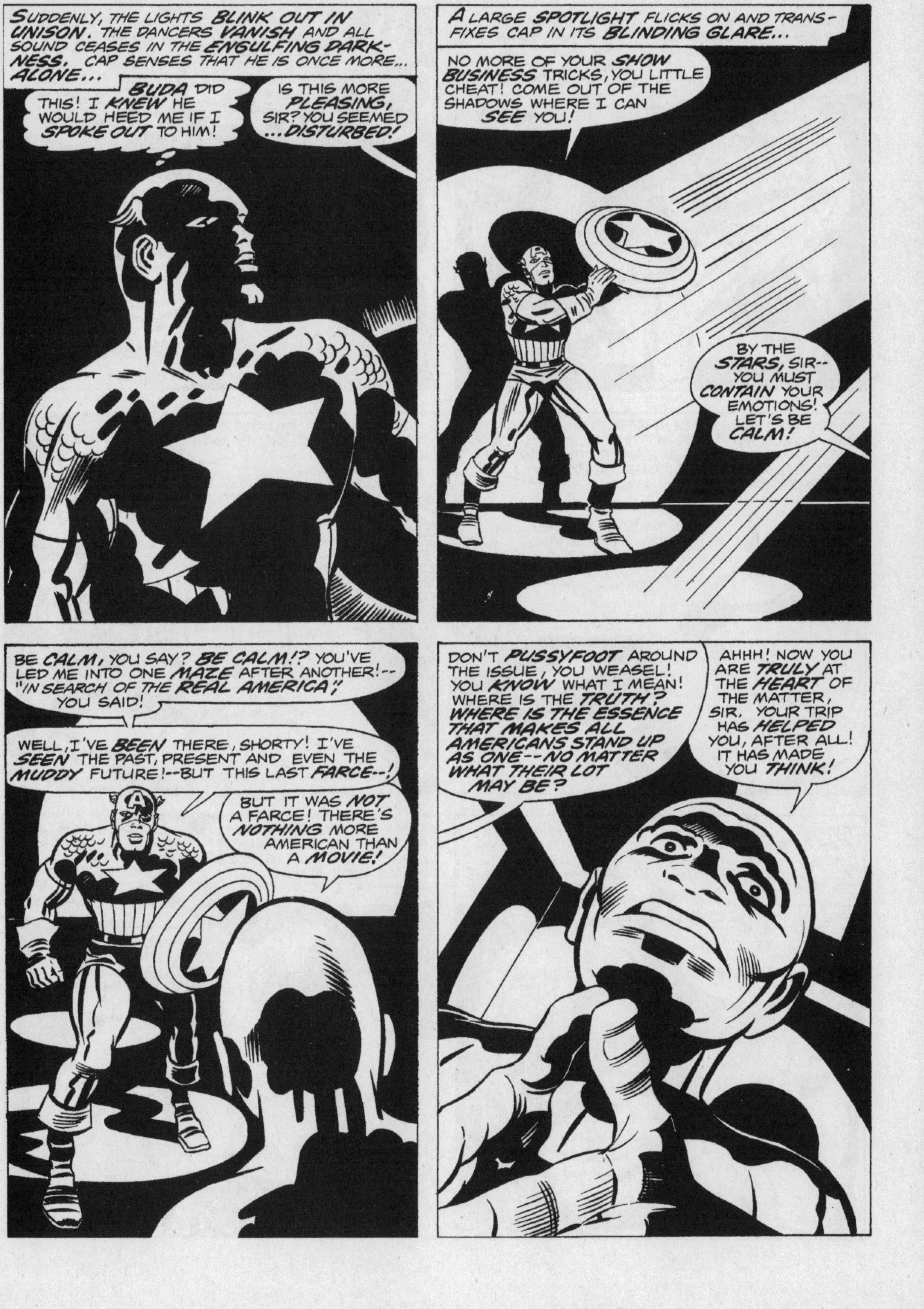
SUDDENLY, THE LIGHTS BLINK OUT IN UNISON. THE DANCERS VANISH AND ALL SOUND CEASES IN THE ENGULFING DARKNESS. CAP SENSES THAT HE IS ONCE MORE... ALONE...
BUDA DID THIS! I KNEW HE WOULD HEED ME IF I SPOKE OUT TO HIM!
IS THIS MORE PLEASING, SIR? YOU SEEMED ...DISTURBED!
A LARGE SPOTLIGHT FLICKS ON AND TRANSFIXES CAP IN ITS BLINDING GLARE...
NO MORE OF YOUR SHOW BUSINESS TRICKS, YOU LITTLE CHEAT! COME OUT OF THE SHADOWS WHERE I CAN SEE YOU!
BY THE STARS, SIR-- YOU MUST CONTAIN YOUR EMOTIONS! LET'S BE CALM!
BE CALM, YOU SAY? BE CALM!? YOU'VE LED ME INTO ONE MAZE AFTER ANOTHER!-- "IN SEARCH OF THE REAL AMERICA," YOU SAID!
WELL, I'VE BEEN THERE, SHORTY! I'VE SEEN THE PAST, PRESENT AND EVEN THE MUDDY FUTURE!--BUT THIS LAST FARCE--!
BUT IT WAS NOT A FARCE! THERE'S NOTHING MORE AMERICAN THAN A MOVIE!
DON'T PUSSYFOOT AROUND THE ISSUE, YOU WEASEL! YOU KNOW WHAT I MEAN! WHERE IS THE TRUTH? WHERE IS THE ESSENCE THAT MAKES ALL AMERICANS STAND UP AS ONE--NO MATTER WHAT THEIR LOT MAY BE?
AHHH! NOW YOU ARE TRULY AT THE HEART OF THE MATTER, SIR. YOUR TRIP HAS HELPED YOU, AFTER ALL! IT HAS MADE YOU THINK!

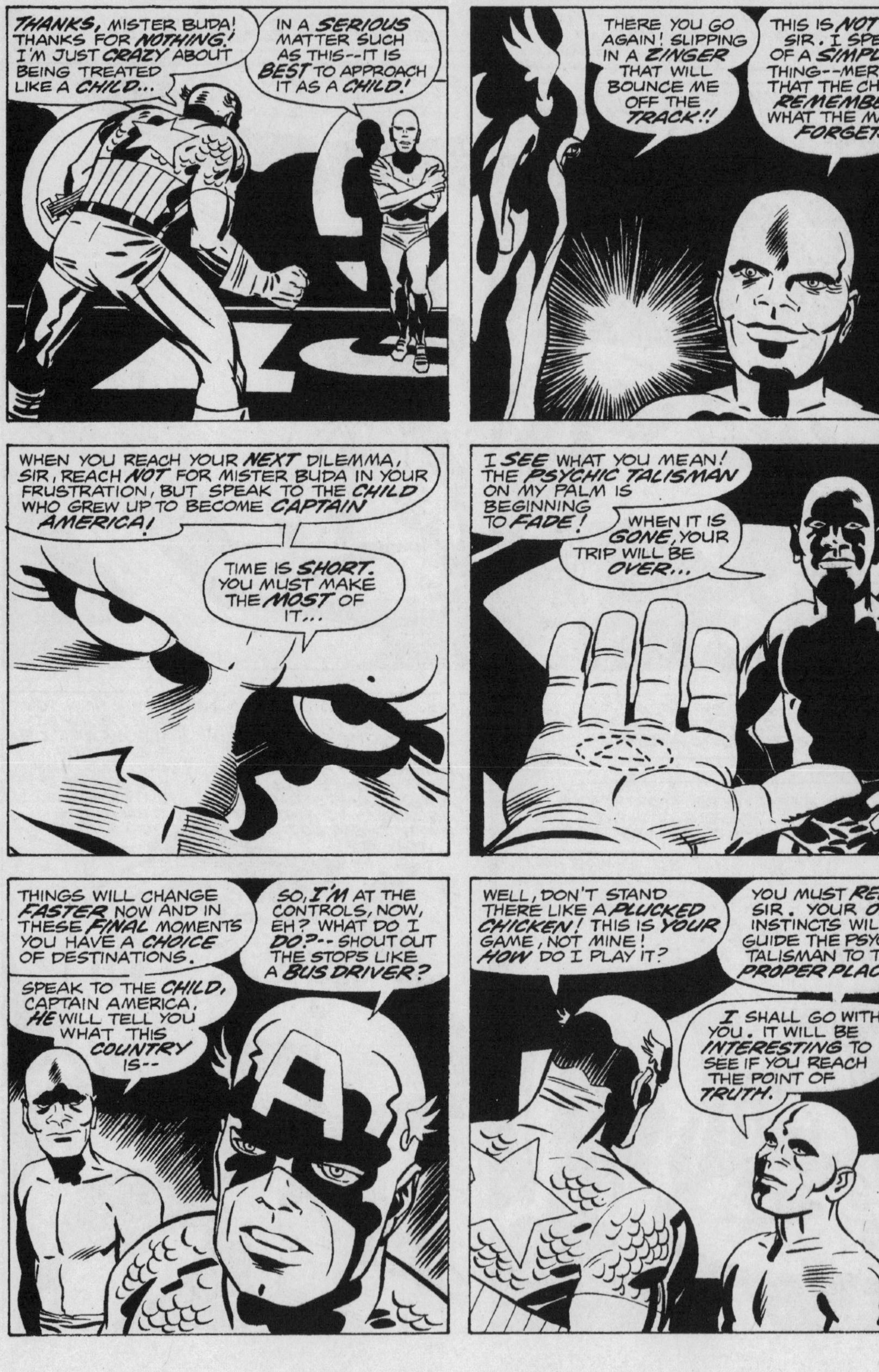
THANKS, MISTER BUDA! THANKS FOR NOTHING! I'M JUST CRAZY ABOUT BEING TREATED LIKE A CHILD...
IN A SERIOUS MATTER SUCH AS THIS--IT IS BEST TO APPROACH IT AS A CHILD!
THERE YOU GO AGAIN! SLIPPING IN A ZINGER THAT WILL BOUNCE ME OFF THE TRACK!!
THIS IS NOT SO, SIR. I SPEAK OF A SIMPLE THING--MERELY THAT THE CHILD REMEMBERS WHAT THE MAN FORGETS!
WHEN YOU REACH YOUR NEXT DILEMMA, SIR, REACH NOT FOR MISTER BUDA IN YOUR FRUSTRATION, BUT SPEAK TO THE CHILD WHO GREW UP TO BECOME CAPTAIN AMERICA!
TIME IS SHORT. YOU MUST MAKE THE MOST OF IT...
I SEE WHAT YOU MEAN! THE PSYCHIC TALISMAN ON MY PALM IS BEGINNING TO FADE!
WHEN IT IS GONE, YOUR TRIP WILL BE OVER...
THINGS WILL CHANGE FASTER NOW AND IN THESE FINAL MOMENTS YOU HAVE A CHOICE OF DESTINATIONS.
SO, I'M AT THE CONTROLS, NOW, EH? WHAT DO I DO?-- SHOUT OUT THE STOPS LIKE A BUS DRIVER?
SPEAK TO THE CHILD, CAPTAIN AMERICA. HE WILL TELL YOU WHAT THIS COUNTRY IS--
WELL, DON'T STAND THERE LIKE A PLUCKED CHICKEN! THIS IS YOUR GAME, NOT MINE! HOW DO I PLAY IT?
YOU MUST RELAX, SIR. YOUR OWN INSTINCTS WILL GUIDE THE PSYCHIC TALISMAN TO THE PROPER PLACES...
I SHALL GO WITH YOU. IT WILL BE INTERESTING TO SEE IF YOU REACH THE POINT OF TRUTH.

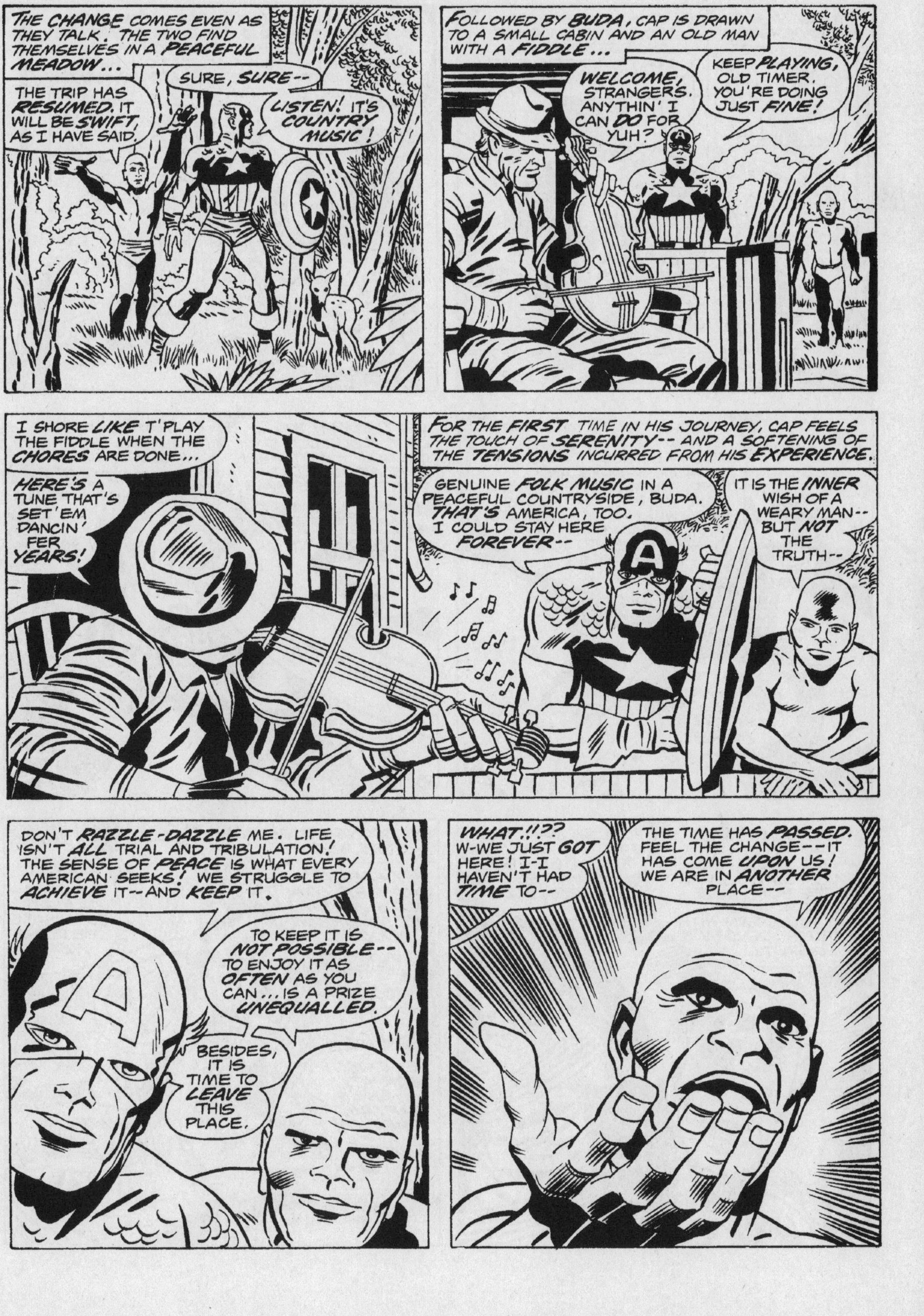
THE CHANGE COMES EVEN AS THEY TALK. THE TWO FIND THEMSELVES IN A PEACEFUL MEADOW...
THE TRIP HAS RESUMED. IT WILL BE SWIFT, AS I HAVE SAID.
SURE, SURE--
LISTEN! IT'S COUNTRY MUSIC!
FOLLOWED BY BUDA, CAP IS DRAWN TO A SMALL CABIN AND AN OLD MAN WITH A FIDDLE...
WELCOME, STRANGERS. ANYTHIN' I CAN DO FOR YUH?
KEEP PLAYING, OLD TIMER. YOU'RE DOING JUST FINE!
I SHORE LIKE T'PLAY THE FIDDLE WHEN THE CHORES ARE DONE...
HERE'S A TUNE THAT'S SET 'EM DANCIN' FER YEARS!
FOR THE FIRST TIME IN HIS JOURNEY, CAP FEELS THE TOUCH OF SERENITY-- AND A SOFTENING OF THE TENSIONS INCURRED FROM HIS EXPERIENCE.
GENUINE FOLK MUSIC IN A PEACEFUL COUNTRYSIDE, BUDA. THAT'S AMERICA, TOO. I COULD STAY HERE FOREVER--
IT IS THE INNER WISH OF A WEARY MAN-- BUT NOT THE TRUTH--
DON'T RAZZLE-DAZZLE ME. LIFE ISN'T ALL TRIAL AND TRIBULATION! THE SENSE OF PEACE IS WHAT EVERY AMERICAN SEEKS! WE STRUGGLE TO ACHIEVE IT--AND KEEP IT.
TO KEEP IT IS NOT POSSIBLE-- TO ENJOY IT AS OFTEN AS YOU CAN... IS A PRIZE UNEQUALLED.
BESIDES, IT IS TIME TO LEAVE THIS PLACE.
WHAT!!?? W-WE JUST GOT HERE! I-I HAVEN'T HAD TIME TO--
THE TIME HAS PASSED. FEEL THE CHANGE--IT HAS COME UPON US! WE ARE IN ANOTHER PLACE--

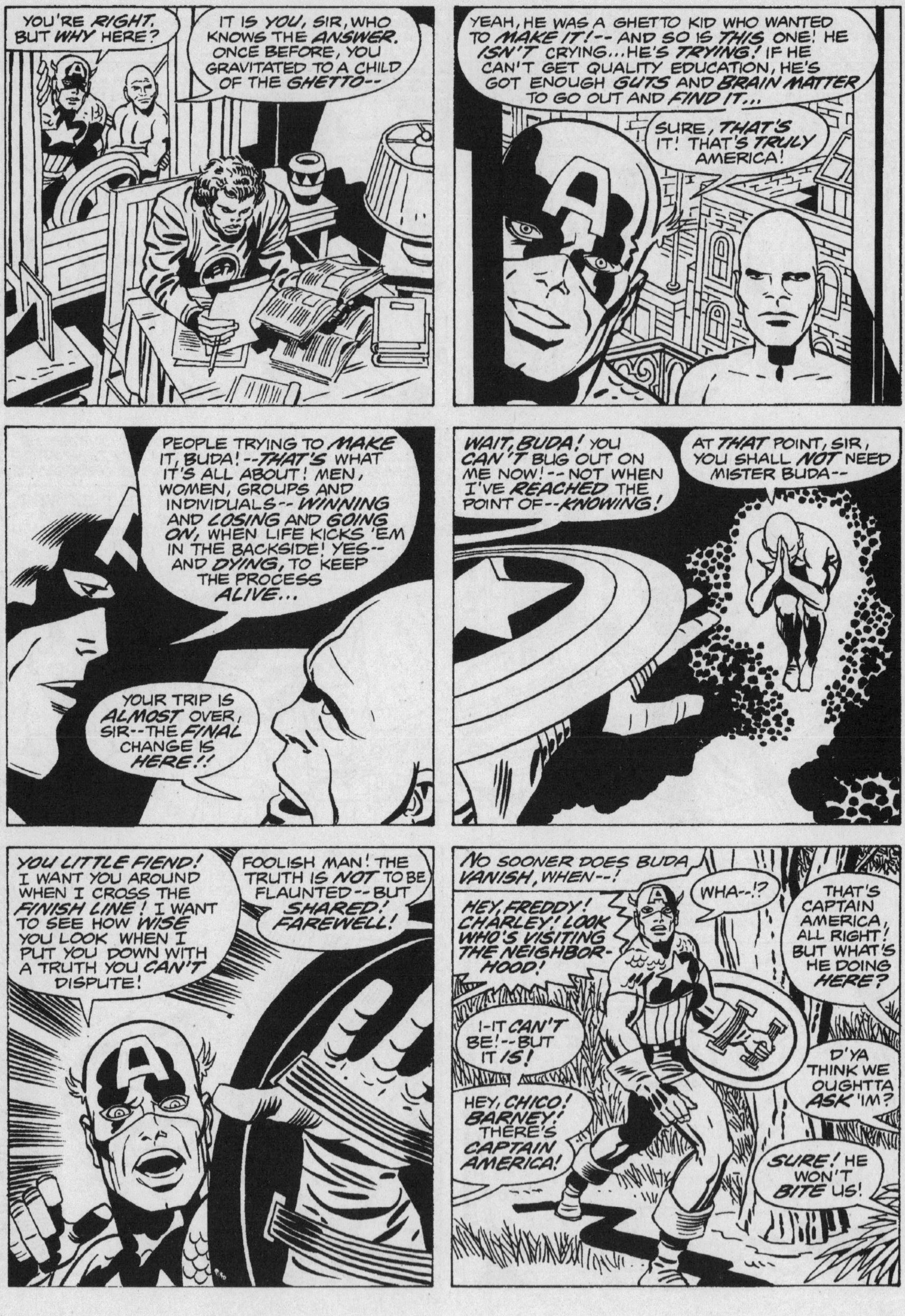
YOU'RE RIGHT. BUT WHY HERE?
IT IS YOU, SIR, WHO KNOWS THE ANSWER. ONCE BEFORE, YOU GRAVITATED TO A CHILD OF THE GHETTO--
YEAH, HE WAS A GHETTO KID WHO WANTED TO MAKE IT!-- AND SO IS THIS ONE! HE ISN'T CRYING...HE'S TRYING! IF HE CAN'T GET QUALITY EDUCATION, HE'S GOT ENOUGH GUTS AND BRAIN MATTER TO GO OUT AND FIND IT...
SURE, THAT'S IT! THAT'S TRULY AMERICA!
PEOPLE TRYING TO MAKE IT, BUDA! --THAT'S WHAT IT'S ALL ABOUT! MEN, WOMEN, GROUPS AND INDIVIDUALS-- WINNING AND LOSING AND GOING ON, WHEN LIFE KICKS 'EM IN THE BACKSIDE! YES-- AND DYING, TO KEEP THE PROCESS ALIVE...
YOUR TRIP IS ALMOST OVER, SIR--THE FINAL CHANGE IS HERE!!
WAIT, BUDA! YOU CAN'T BUG OUT ON ME NOW!--NOT WHEN I'VE REACHED THE POINT OF--KNOWING!
AT THAT POINT, SIR, YOU SHALL NOT NEED MISTER BUDA--
YOU LITTLE FIEND! I WANT YOU AROUND WHEN I CROSS THE FINISH LINE! I WANT TO SEE HOW WISE YOU LOOK WHEN I PUT YOU DOWN WITH A TRUTH YOU CAN'T DISPUTE!
FOOLISH MAN! THE TRUTH IS NOT TO BE FLAUNTED--BUT SHARED! FAREWELL!
NO SOONER DOES BUDA VANISH, WHEN--!
HEY, FREDDY! CHARLEY! LOOK WHO'S VISITING THE NEIGHBOR-HOOD!
WHA--!?
THAT'S CAPTAIN AMERICA, ALL RIGHT! BUT WHAT'S HE DOING HERE?
I-IT CAN'T BE!--BUT IT IS!
HEY, CHICO! BARNEY! THERE'S CAPTAIN AMERICA!
D'YA THINK WE OUGHTTA ASK 'IM?
SURE! HE WON'T BITE US!

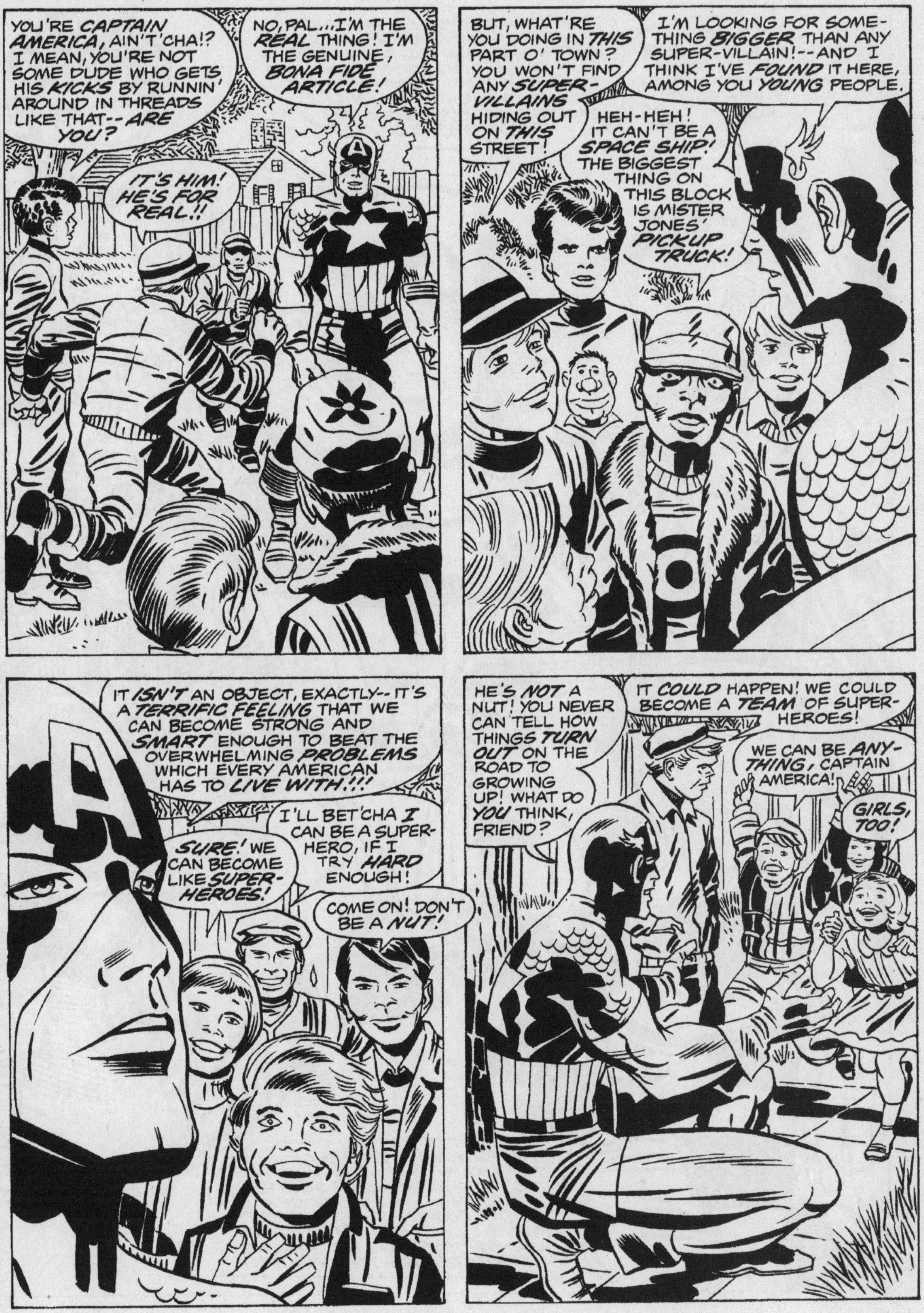
YOU'RE CAPTAIN AMERICA, AIN'T'CHA!? I MEAN, YOU'RE NOT SOME DUDE WHO GETS HIS KICKS BY RUNNIN' AROUND IN THREADS LIKE THAT-- ARE YOU?
NO, PAL...I'M THE REAL THING! I'M THE GENUINE, BONA FIDE ARTICLE!
IT'S HIM! HE'S FOR REAL!!
BUT, WHAT'RE YOU DOING IN THIS PART O' TOWN? YOU WON'T FIND ANY SUPER-VILLAINS HIDING OUT ON THIS STREET!
I'M LOOKING FOR SOMETHING BIGGER THAN ANY SUPER-VILLAIN!--AND I THINK I'VE FOUND IT HERE, AMONG YOU YOUNG PEOPLE.
HEH-HEH! IT CAN'T BE A SPACE SHIP! THE BIGGEST THING ON THIS BLOCK IS MISTER JONES' PICKUP TRUCK!
IT ISN'T AN OBJECT, EXACTLY-- IT'S A TERRIFIC FEELING THAT WE CAN BECOME STRONG AND SMART ENOUGH TO BEAT THE OVERWHELMING PROBLEMS WHICH EVERY AMERICAN HAS TO LIVE WITH!!!
SURE! WE CAN BECOME LIKE SUPER-HEROES!
I'LL BET'CHA I CAN BE A SUPER-HERO, IF I TRY HARD ENOUGH!
COME ON! DON'T BE A NUT!
HE'S NOT A NUT! YOU NEVER CAN TELL HOW THINGS TURN OUT ON THE ROAD TO GROWING UP! WHAT DO YOU THINK, FRIEND?
IT COULD HAPPEN! WE COULD BECOME A TEAM OF SUPER-HEROES!
WE CAN BE ANY-THING, CAPTAIN AMERICA!
GIRLS, TOO!

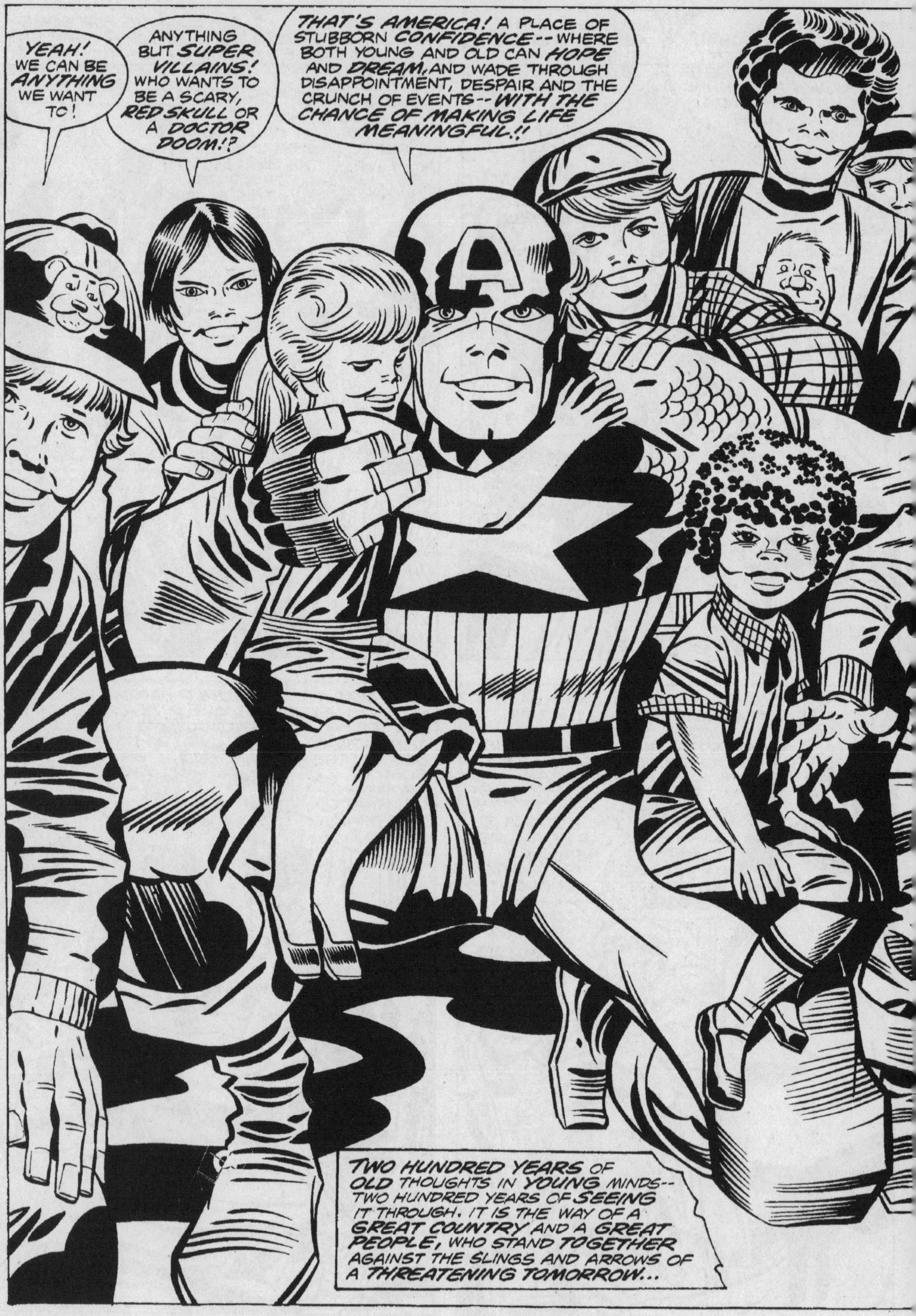
YEAH! WE CAN BE ANYTHING WE WANT TO!
ANYTHING BUT SUPER VILLAINS! WHO WANTS TO BE A SCARY, RED SKULL OR A DOCTOR DOOM!?
THAT'S AMERICA! A PLACE OF STUBBORN CONFIDENCE-- WHERE BOTH YOUNG AND OLD CAN HOPE AND DREAM, AND WADE THROUGH DISAPPOINTMENT, DESPAIR AND THE CRUNCH OF EVENTS-- WITH THE CHANCE OF MAKING LIFE MEANINGFUL!!
TWO HUNDRED YEARS OF OLD THOUGHTS IN YOUNG MINDS-- TWO HUNDRED YEARS OF SEEING IT THROUGH. IT IS THE WAY OF A GREAT COUNTRY AND A GREAT PEOPLE, WHO STAND TOGETHER AGAINST THE SLINGS AND ARROWS OF A THREATENING TOMORROW...

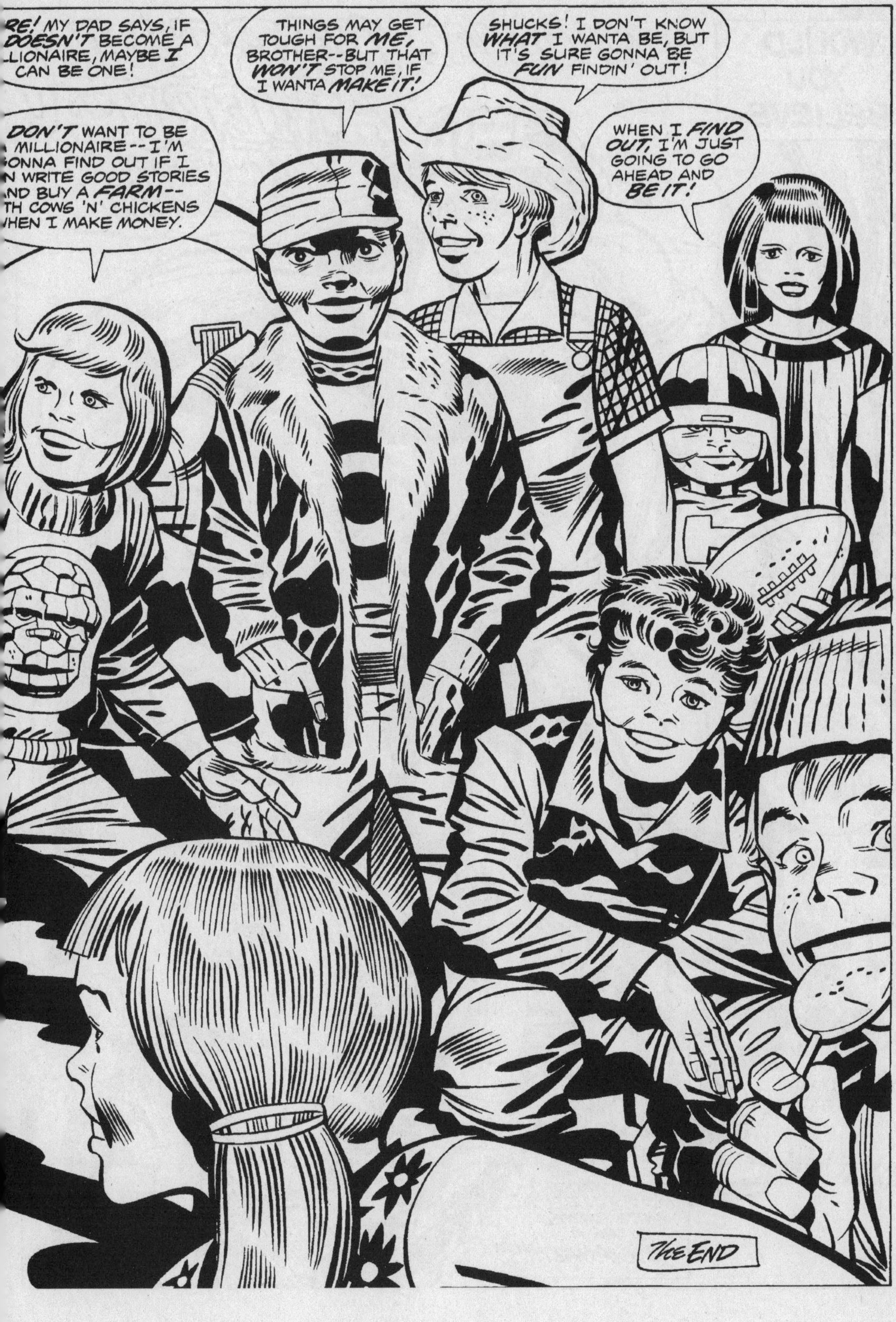
RE! MY DAD SAYS, IF DOESN'T BECOME A LLIONAIRE, MAYBE I CAN BE ONE!
DON'T WANT TO BE MILLIONAIRE--I'M GONNA FIND OUT IF I N WRITE GOOD STORIES ND BUY A FARM-- TH COWS 'N' CHICKENS WHEN I MAKE MONEY.
THINGS MAY GET TOUGH FOR ME, BROTHER--BUT THAT WON'T STOP ME, IF I WANTA MAKE IT!
SHUCKS! I DON'T KNOW WHAT I WANTA BE, BUT IT'S SURE GONNA BE FUN FINDIN' OUT!
WHEN I FIND OUT, I'M JUST GOING TO GO AHEAD AND BE IT!
THE END

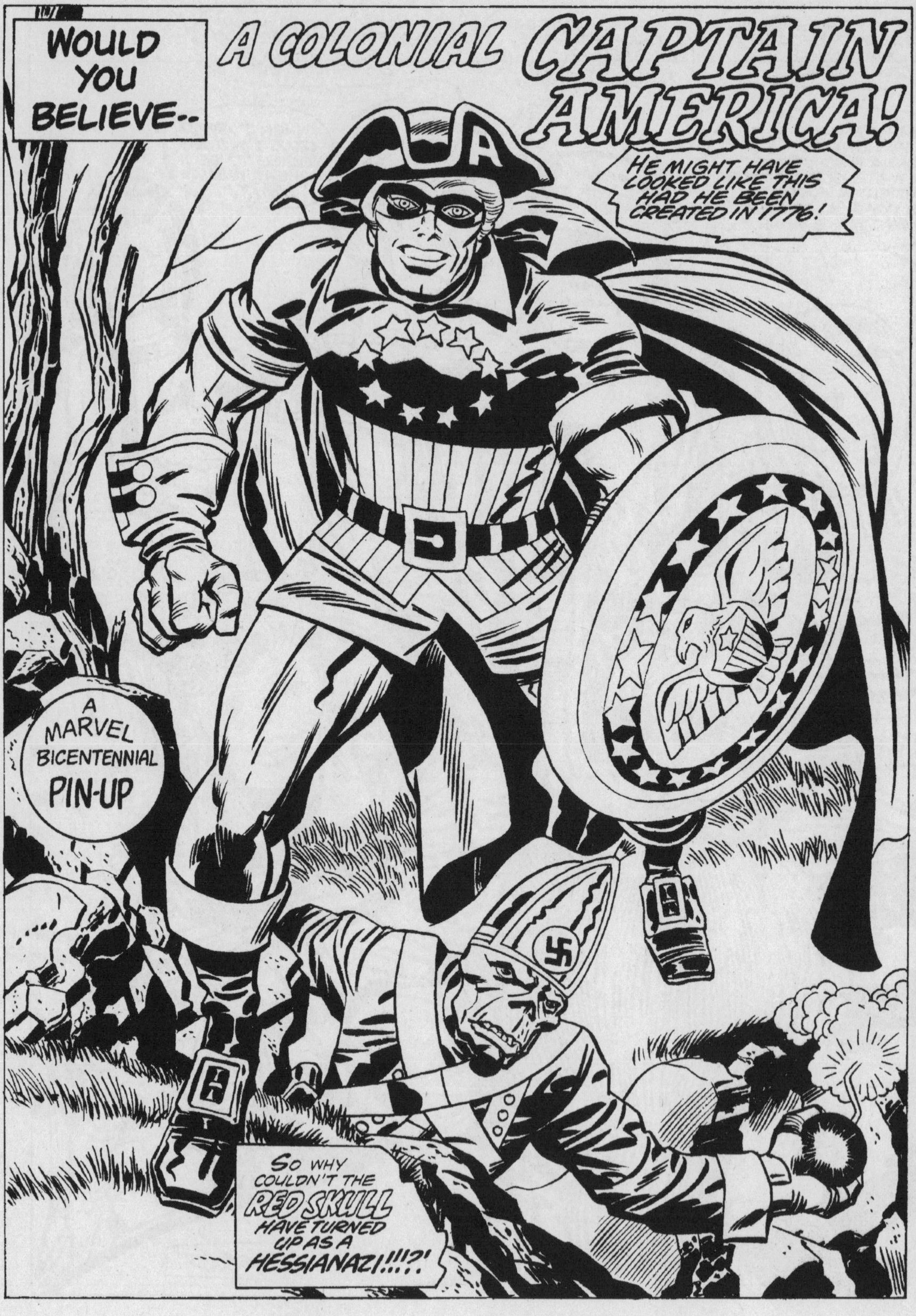
WOULD YOU BELIEVE--
A COLONIAL CAPTAIN AMERICA!
HE MIGHT HAVE LOOKED LIKE THIS HAD HE BEEN CREATED IN 1776!
A MARVEL BICENTENNIAL PIN-UP
SO WHY COULDN'T THE RED SKULL HAVE TURNED UP AS A HESSIANAZI!!!?!

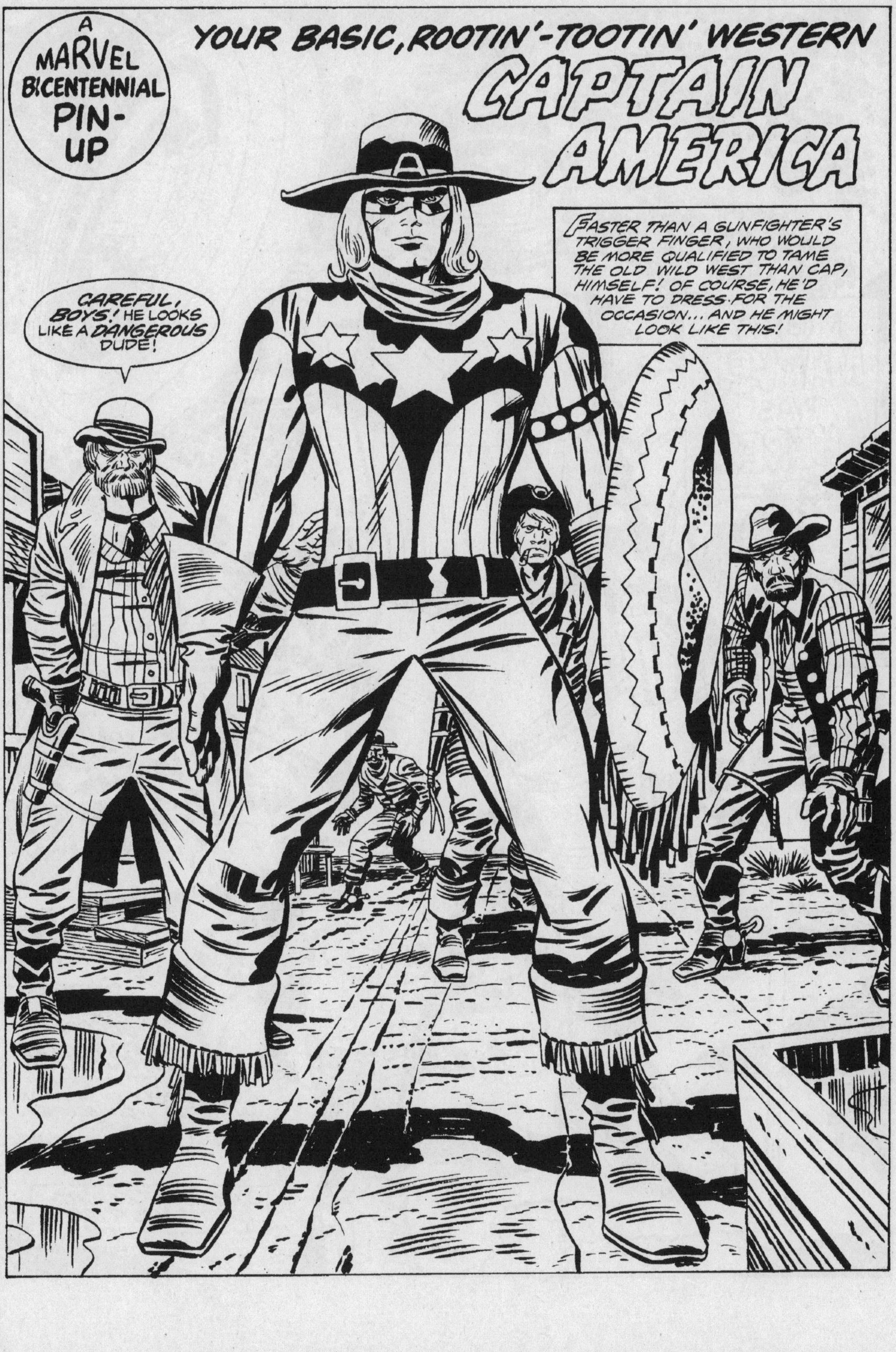
A MARVEL BICENTENNIAL PIN-UP
YOUR BASIC, ROOTIN'-TOOTIN' WESTERN
CAPTAIN AMERICA
FASTER THAN A GUNFIGHTER'S TRIGGER FINGER, WHO WOULD BE MORE QUALIFIED TO TAME THE OLD WILD WEST THAN CAP, HIMSELF! OF COURSE, HE'D HAVE TO DRESS FOR THE OCCASION... AND HE MIGHT LOOK LIKE THIS!
CAREFUL, BOYS! HE LOOKS LIKE A DANGEROUS DUDE!

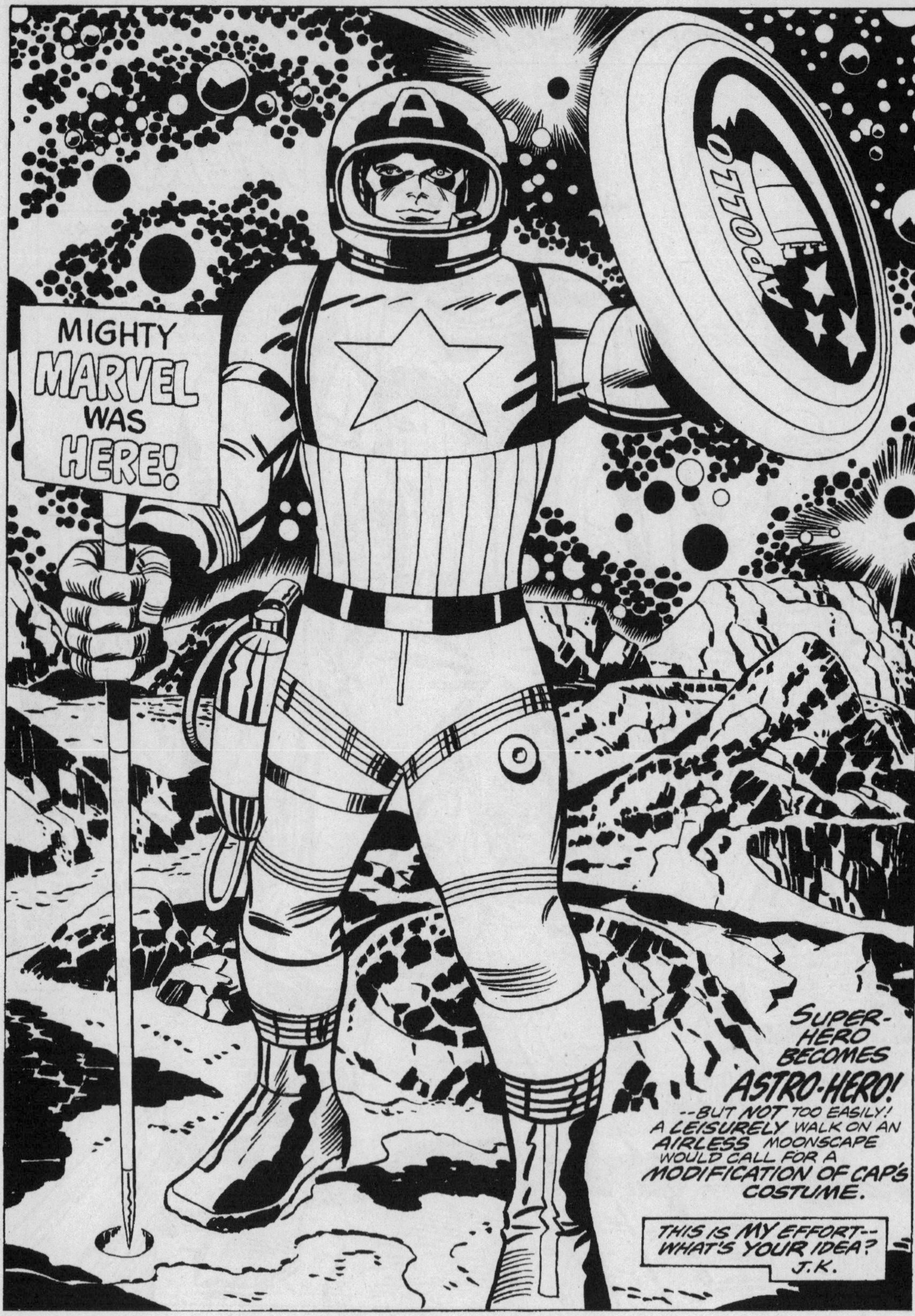

MIGHTY MARVEL WAS HERE!
APOLLO
SUPER-HERO BECOMES ASTRO-HERO! --BUT NOT TOO EASILY! A LEISURELY WALK ON AN AIRLESS MOONSCAPE WOULD CALL FOR A MODIFICATION OF CAP'S COSTUME.
THIS IS MY EFFORT-- WHAT'S YOUR IDEA? J.K.

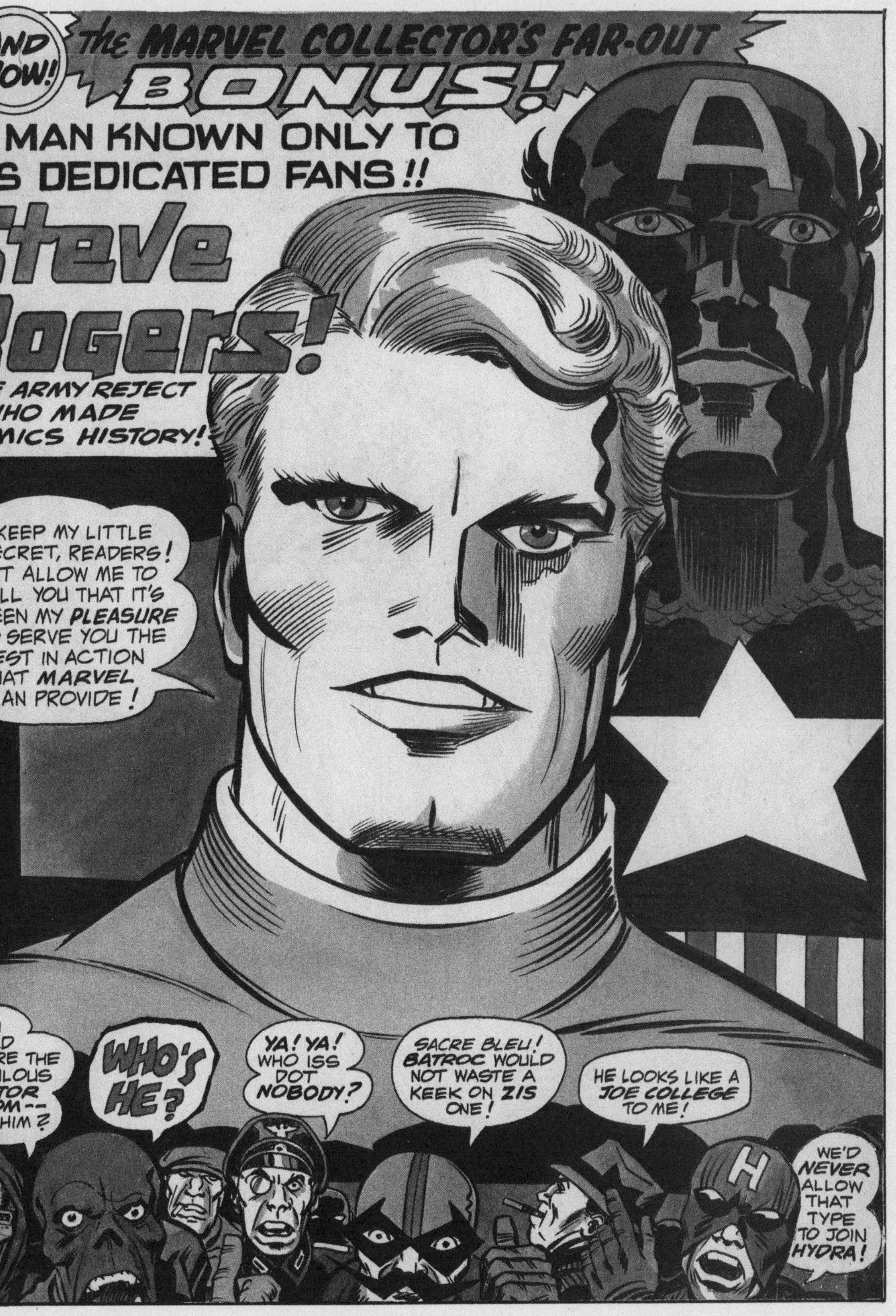
AND NOW!
the MARVEL COLLECTOR'S FAR-OUT
BONUS!
A MAN KNOWN ONLY TO HIS DEDICATED FANS!!
Steve Rogers!
THE ARMY REJECT WHO MADE COMICS HISTORY!
KEEP MY LITTLE SECRET, READERS! BUT ALLOW ME TO TELL YOU THAT IT'S BEEN MY PLEASURE TO SERVE YOU THE BEST IN ACTION THAT MARVEL CAN PROVIDE!
YOU WOULD IGNORE THE FABULOUS DOCTOR DOOM-- FOR HIM?
WHO'S HE?
YA! YA! WHO ISS DOT NOBODY?
SACRE BLEU! BATROC WOULD NOT WASTE A KEEK ON ZIS ONE!
HE LOOKS LIKE A JOE COLLEGE TO ME!
WE'D NEVER ALLOW THAT TYPE TO JOIN HYDRA!

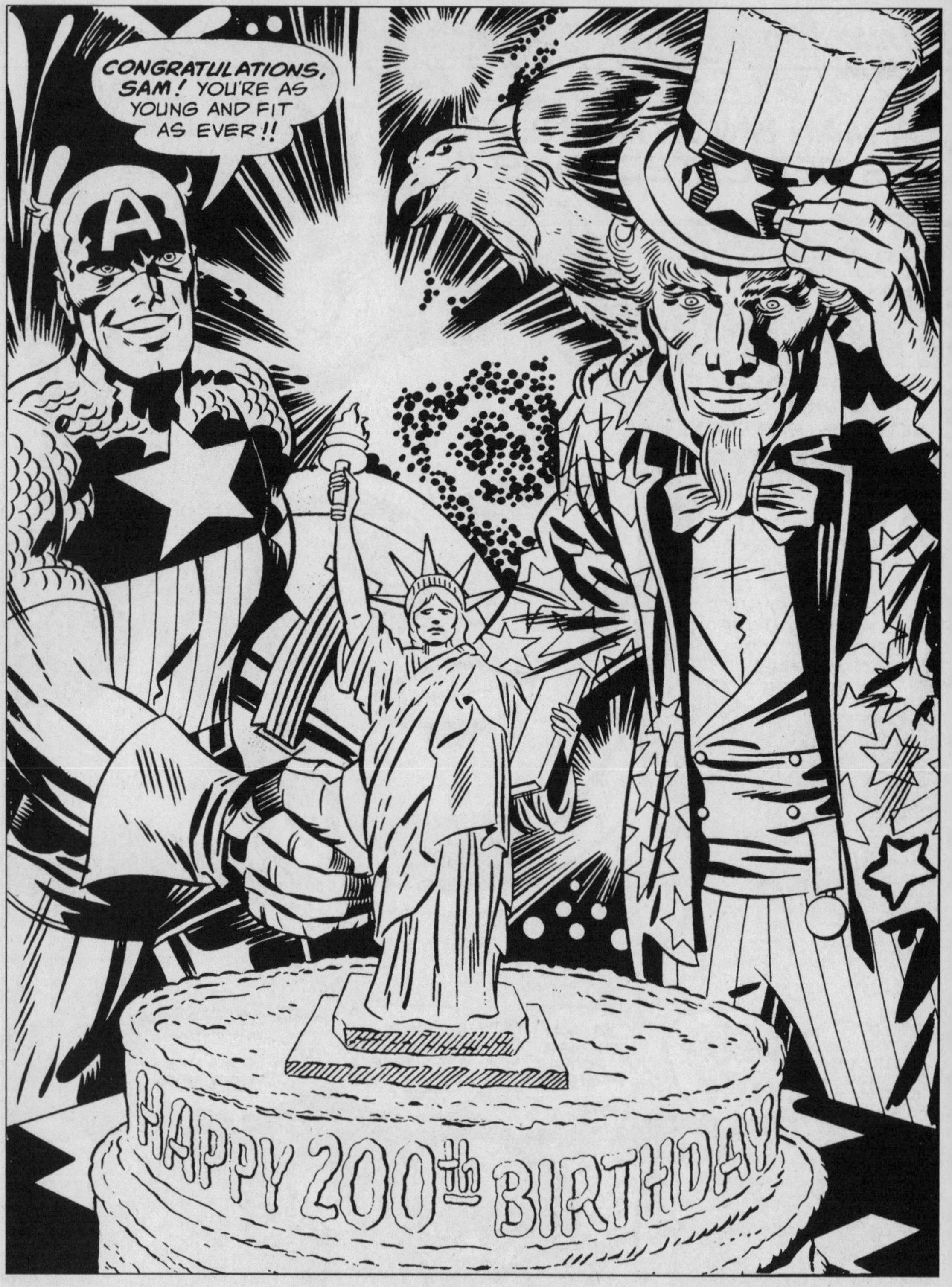
CONGRATULATIONS, SAM! YOU'RE AS YOUNG AND FIT AS EVER!!
HAPPY 200th BIRTHDAY

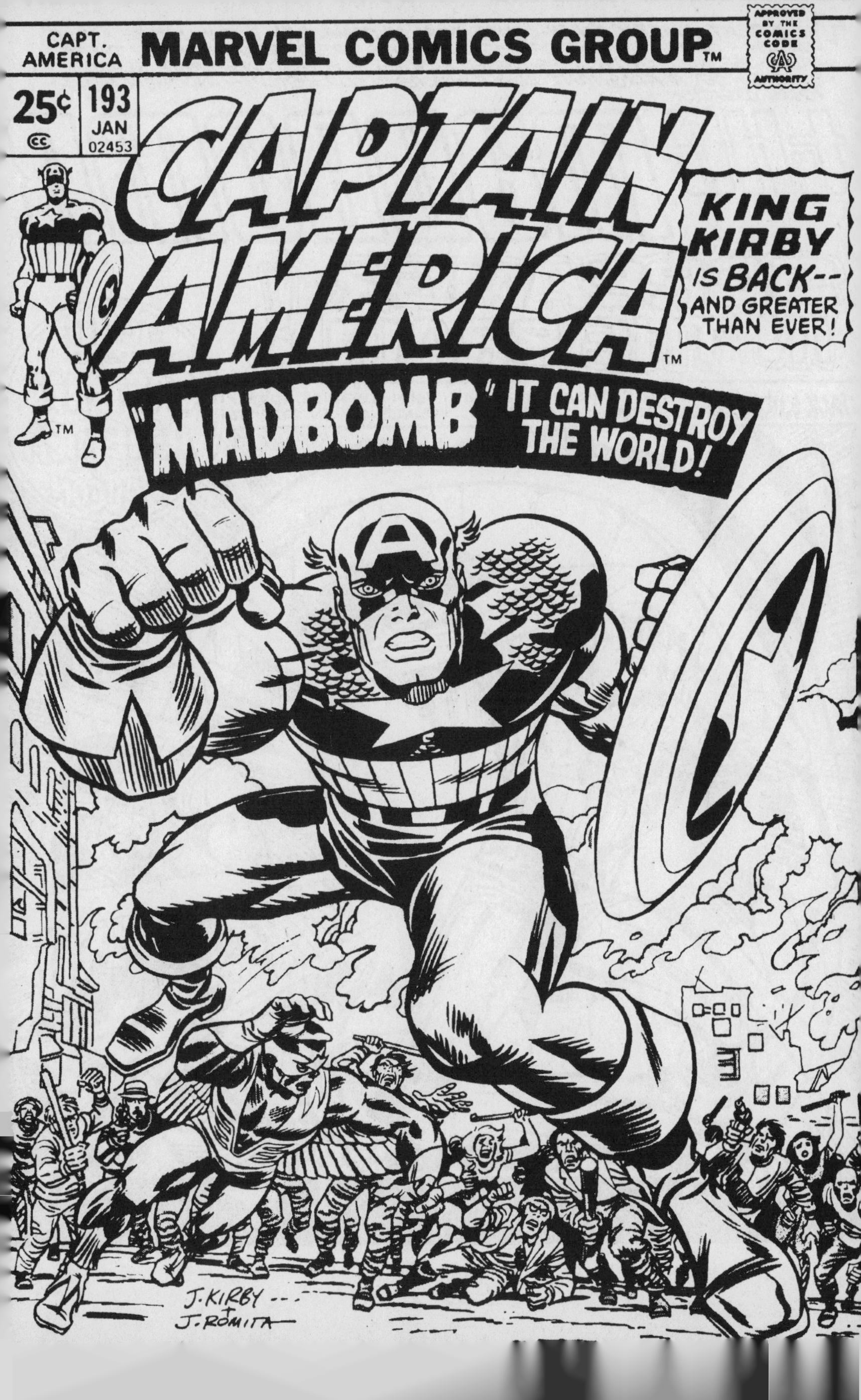
CAPT. AMERICA
MARVEL COMICS GROUP™
APPROVED BY THE COMICS CODE AUTHORITY
25¢
193
JAN
02453
CAPTAIN AMERICA™
KING KIRBY IS BACK-- AND GREATER THAN EVER!
"MADBOMB" IT CAN DESTROY THE WORLD!
J. KIRBY + J. ROMITA

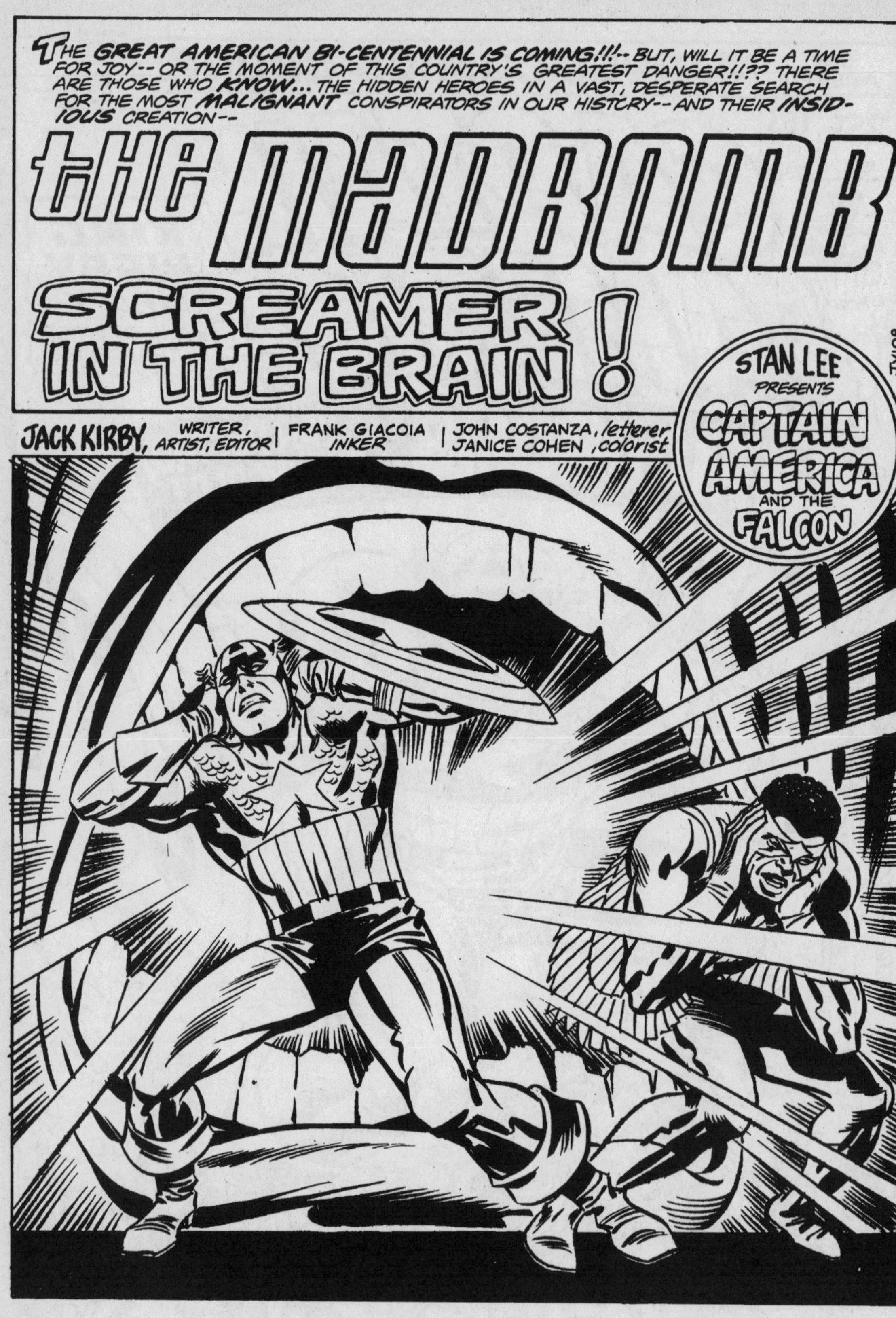
THE GREAT AMERICAN BI-CENTENNIAL IS COMING!!!-- BUT, WILL IT BE A TIME FOR JOY-- OR THE MOMENT OF THIS COUNTRY'S GREATEST DANGER!!?? THERE ARE THOSE WHO KNOW... THE HIDDEN HEROES IN A VAST, DESPERATE SEARCH FOR THE MOST MALIGNANT CONSPIRATORS IN OUR HISTORY-- AND THEIR INSIDIOUS CREATION--
THE MADBOMB
SCREAMER IN THE BRAIN!
JV108
STAN LEE PRESENTS CAPTAIN AMERICA AND THE FALCON
JACK KIRBY, WRITER, ARTIST, EDITOR | FRANK GIACOIA INKER | JOHN COSTANZA, letterer JANICE COHEN, colorist

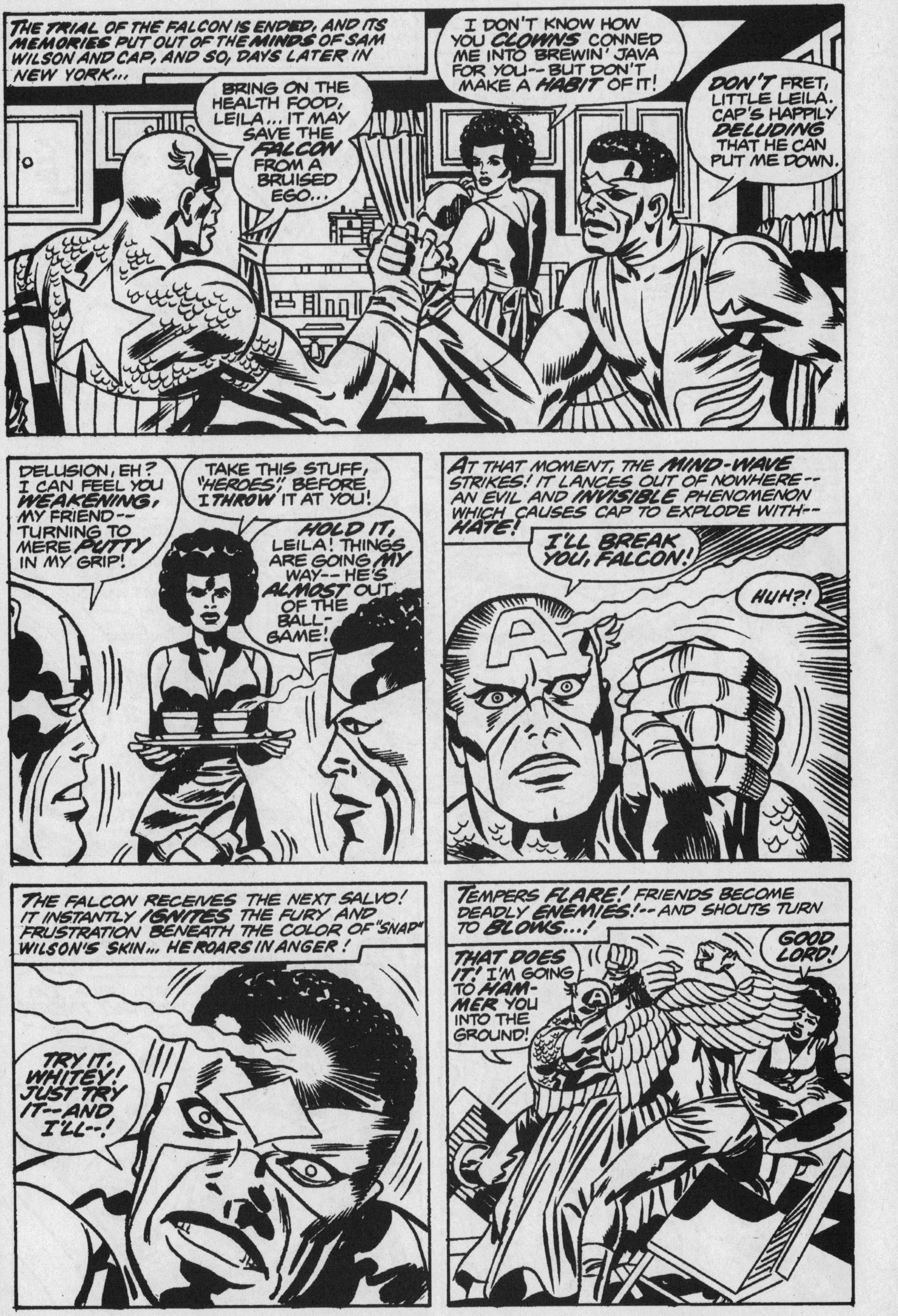

THE TRIAL OF THE FALCON IS ENDED, AND ITS MEMORIES PUT OUT OF THE MINDS OF SAM WILSON AND CAP, AND SO, DAYS LATER IN NEW YORK...
BRING ON THE HEALTH FOOD, LEILA... IT MAY SAVE THE FALCON FROM A BRUISED EGO...
I DON'T KNOW HOW YOU CLOWNS CONNED ME INTO BREWIN' JAVA FOR YOU-- BUT DON'T MAKE A HABIT OF IT!
DON'T FRET, LITTLE LEILA. CAP'S HAPPILY DELUDING THAT HE CAN PUT ME DOWN.
DELUSION, EH? I CAN FEEL YOU WEAKENING, MY FRIEND-- TURNING TO MERE PUTTY IN MY GRIP!
TAKE THIS STUFF, "HEROES", BEFORE I THROW IT AT YOU!
HOLD IT, LEILA! THINGS ARE GOING MY WAY-- HE'S ALMOST OUT OF THE BALL-GAME!
AT THAT MOMENT, THE MIND-WAVE STRIKES! IT LANCES OUT OF NOWHERE-- AN EVIL AND INVISIBLE PHENOMENON WHICH CAUSES CAP TO EXPLODE WITH-- HATE!
I'LL BREAK YOU, FALCON!
HUH?!
THE FALCON RECEIVES THE NEXT SALVO! IT INSTANTLY IGNITES THE FURY AND FRUSTRATION BENEATH THE COLOR OF "SNAP" WILSON'S SKIN... HE ROARS IN ANGER!
TRY IT, WHITEY! JUST TRY IT-- AND I'LL--!
TEMPERS FLARE! FRIENDS BECOME DEADLY ENEMIES!-- AND SHOUTS TURN TO BLOWS...!
THAT DOES IT! I'M GOING TO HAM-MER YOU INTO THE GROUND!
GOOD LORD!

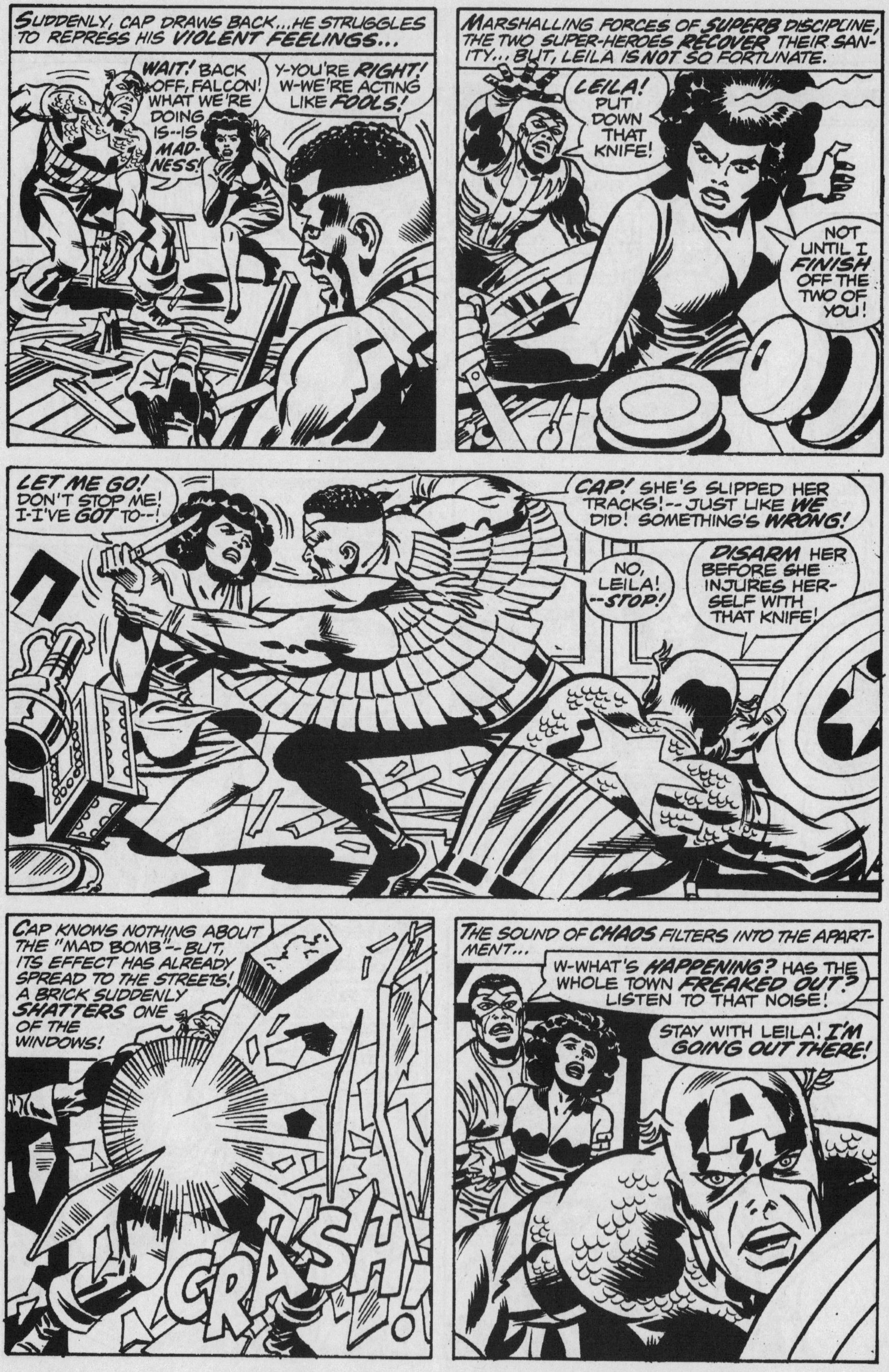
SUDDENLY, CAP DRAWS BACK... HE STRUGGLES TO REPRESS HIS VIOLENT FEELINGS...
WAIT! BACK OFF, FALCON! WHAT WE'RE DOING IS--IS MADNESS!
Y-YOU'RE RIGHT! W-WE'RE ACTING LIKE FOOLS!
MARSHALLING FORCES OF SUPERB DISCIPLINE, THE TWO SUPER-HEROES RECOVER THEIR SANITY... BUT, LEILA IS NOT SO FORTUNATE.
LEILA! PUT DOWN THAT KNIFE!
NOT UNTIL I FINISH OFF THE TWO OF YOU!
LET ME GO! DON'T STOP ME! I-I'VE GOT TO--!
CAP! SHE'S SLIPPED HER TRACKS!--JUST LIKE WE DID! SOMETHING'S WRONG!
NO, LEILA! --STOP!
DISARM HER BEFORE SHE INJURES HERSELF WITH THAT KNIFE!
CAP KNOWS NOTHING ABOUT THE "MAD BOMB"--BUT, ITS EFFECT HAS ALREADY SPREAD TO THE STREETS! A BRICK SUDDENLY SHATTERS ONE OF THE WINDOWS!
CRASH!
THE SOUND OF CHAOS FILTERS INTO THE APARTMENT...
W-WHAT'S HAPPENING? HAS THE WHOLE TOWN FREAKED OUT? LISTEN TO THAT NOISE!
STAY WITH LEILA! I'M GOING OUT THERE!

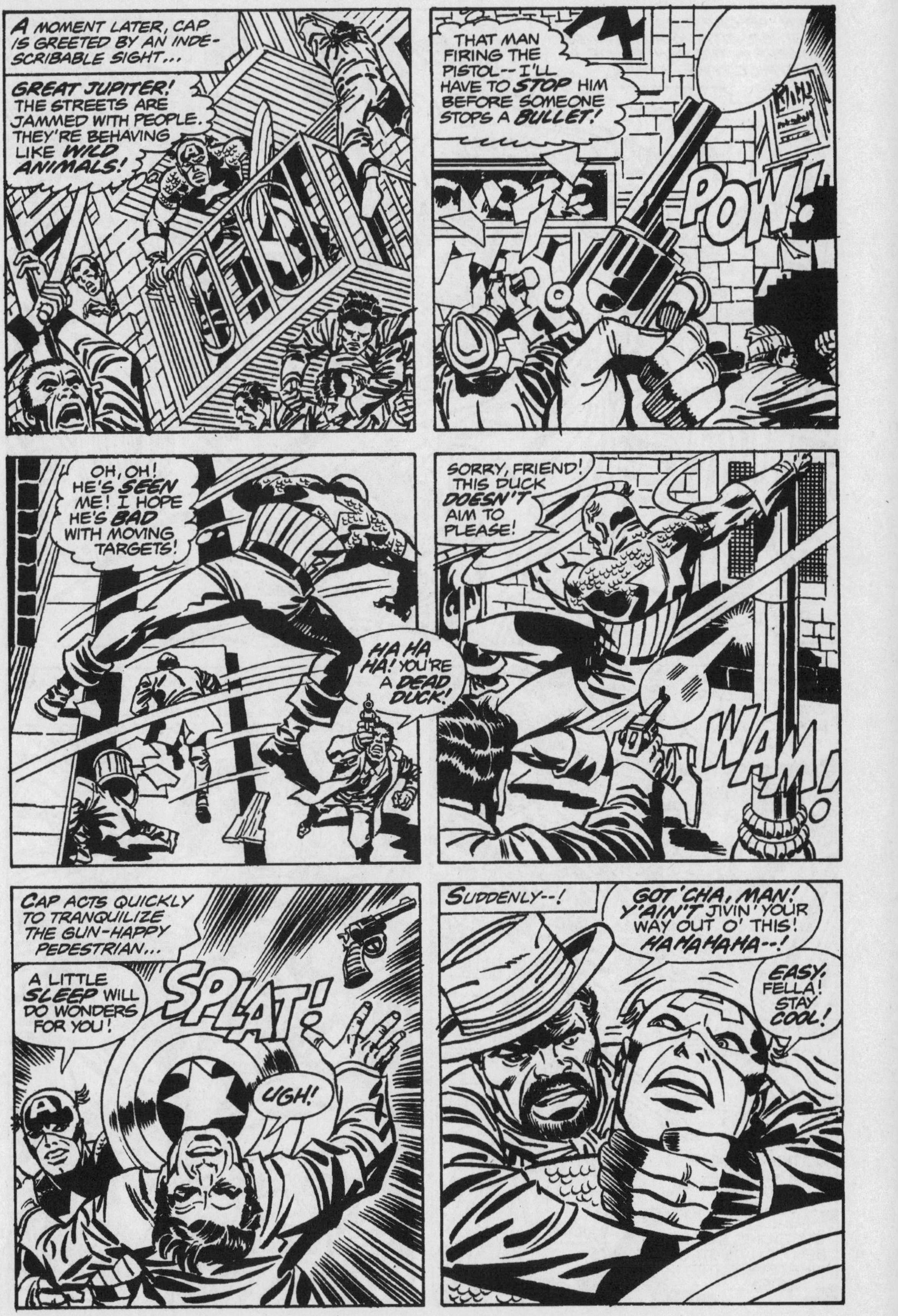
A MOMENT LATER, CAP IS GREETED BY AN INDESCRIBABLE SIGHT...
GREAT JUPITER! THE STREETS ARE JAMMED WITH PEOPLE. THEY'RE BEHAVING LIKE WILD ANIMALS!
THAT MAN FIRING THE PISTOL--I'LL HAVE TO STOP HIM BEFORE SOMEONE STOPS A BULLET!
POW!
OH, OH! HE'S SEEN ME! I HOPE HE'S BAD WITH MOVING TARGETS!
HA HA HA! YOU'RE A DEAD DUCK!
SORRY, FRIEND! THIS DUCK DOESN'T AIM TO PLEASE!
WAM!
CAP ACTS QUICKLY TO TRANQUILIZE THE GUN-HAPPY PEDESTRIAN...
A LITTLE SLEEP WILL DO WONDERS FOR YOU!
SPLAT!
UGH!
SUDDENLY--!
GOT 'CHA, MAN! Y'AIN'T JIVIN' YOUR WAY OUT O' THIS! HAHAHAHA--!
EASY, FELLA! STAY COOL!

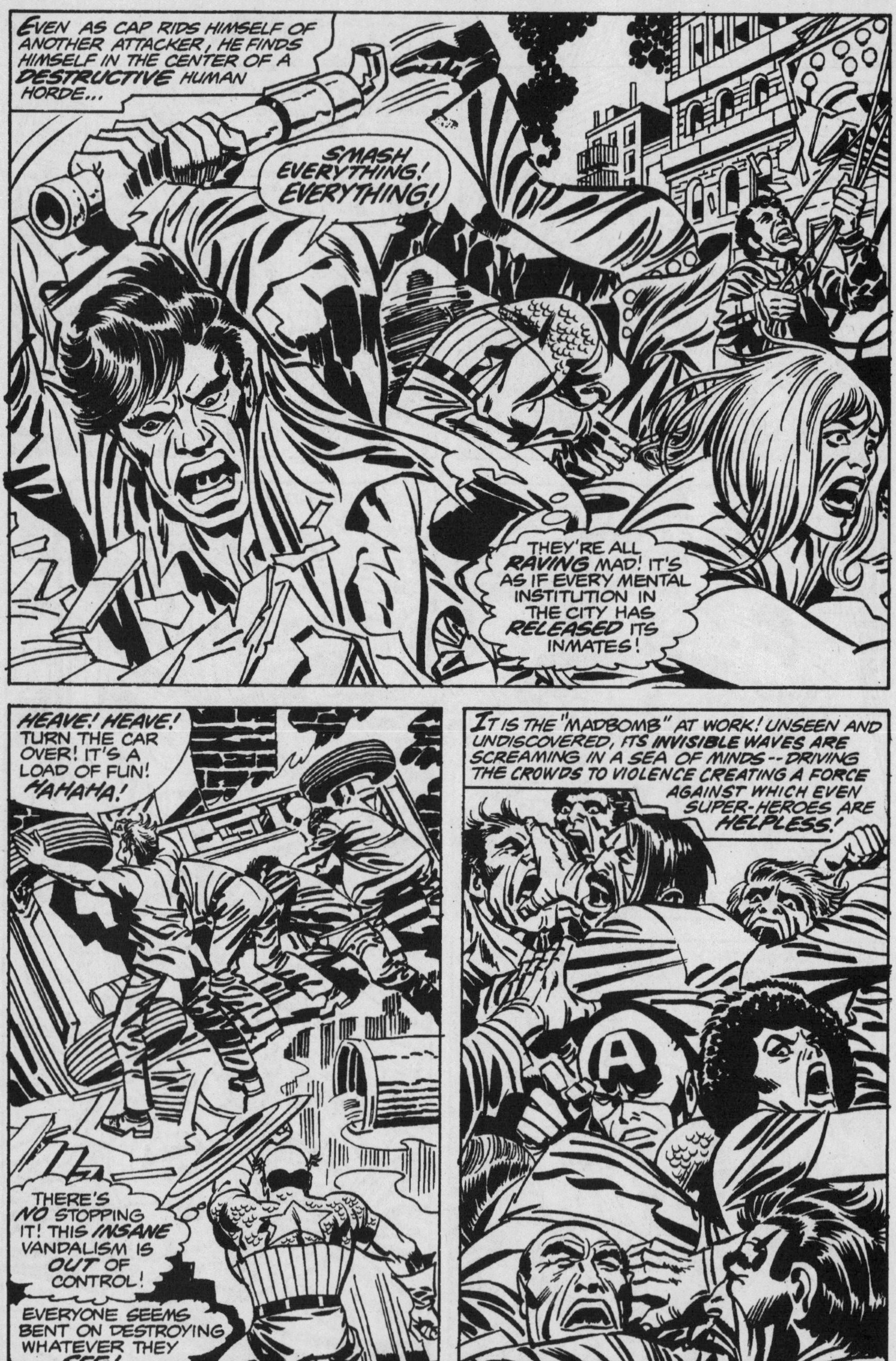
EVEN AS CAP RIDS HIMSELF OF ANOTHER ATTACKER, HE FINDS HIMSELF IN THE CENTER OF A DESTRUCTIVE HUMAN HORDE...
SMASH EVERYTHING! EVERYTHING!
THEY'RE ALL RAVING MAD! IT'S AS IF EVERY MENTAL INSTITUTION IN THE CITY HAS RELEASED ITS INMATES!
HEAVE! HEAVE! TURN THE CAR OVER! IT'S A LOAD OF FUN! HAHAHA!
THERE'S NO STOPPING IT! THIS INSANE VANDALISM IS OUT OF CONTROL!
EVERYONE SEEMS BENT ON DESTROYING WHATEVER THEY SEE!
IT IS THE "MADBOMB" AT WORK! UNSEEN AND UNDISCOVERED, ITS INVISIBLE WAVES ARE SCREAMING IN A SEA OF MINDS--DRIVING THE CROWDS TO VIOLENCE CREATING A FORCE AGAINST WHICH EVEN SUPER-HEROES ARE HELPLESS!

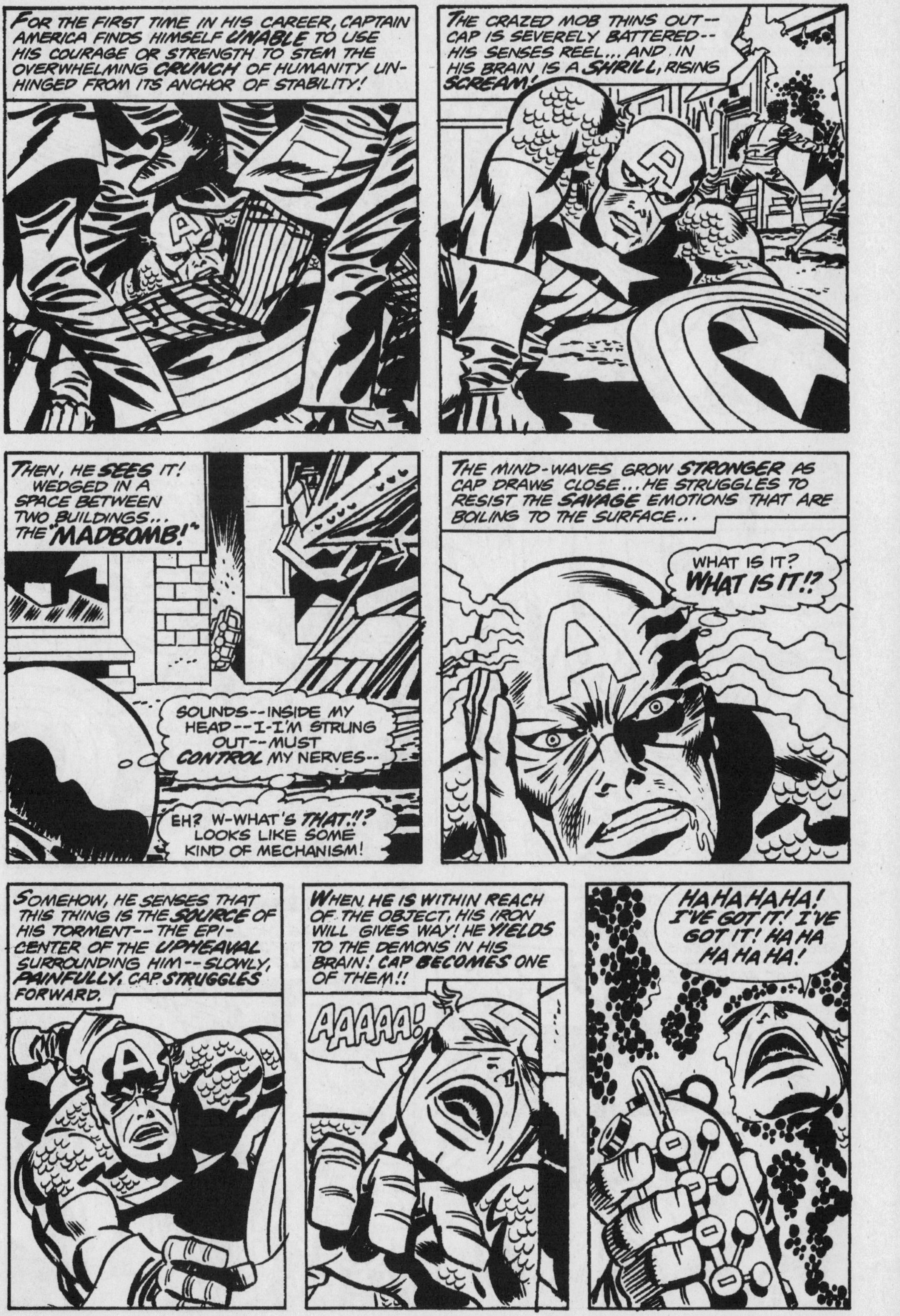
FOR THE FIRST TIME IN HIS CAREER, CAPTAIN AMERICA FINDS HIMSELF UNABLE TO USE HIS COURAGE OR STRENGTH TO STEM THE OVERWHELMING CRUNCH OF HUMANITY UN-HINGED FROM ITS ANCHOR OF STABILITY!
THE CRAZED MOB THINS OUT-- CAP IS SEVERELY BATTERED-- HIS SENSES REEL... AND IN HIS BRAIN IS A SHRILL, RISING SCREAM!
THEN, HE SEES IT! WEDGED IN A SPACE BETWEEN TWO BUILDINGS... THE "MADBOMB!"
SOUNDS--INSIDE MY HEAD--I-I'M STRUNG OUT--MUST CONTROL MY NERVES--
EH? W-WHAT'S THAT!!? LOOKS LIKE SOME KIND OF MECHANISM!
THE MIND-WAVES GROW STRONGER AS CAP DRAWS CLOSE... HE STRUGGLES TO RESIST THE SAVAGE EMOTIONS THAT ARE BOILING TO THE SURFACE...
WHAT IS IT? WHAT IS IT!?
SOMEHOW, HE SENSES THAT THIS THING IS THE SOURCE OF HIS TORMENT-- THE EPI-CENTER OF THE UPHEAVAL SURROUNDING HIM--SLOWLY, PAINFULLY, CAP STRUGGLES FORWARD.
WHEN HE IS WITHIN REACH OF THE OBJECT, HIS IRON WILL GIVES WAY! HE YIELDS TO THE DEMONS IN HIS BRAIN! CAP BECOMES ONE OF THEM!!
AAAAA!
HAHAHAHA! I'VE GOT IT! I'VE GOT IT! HA HA HA HA HA!

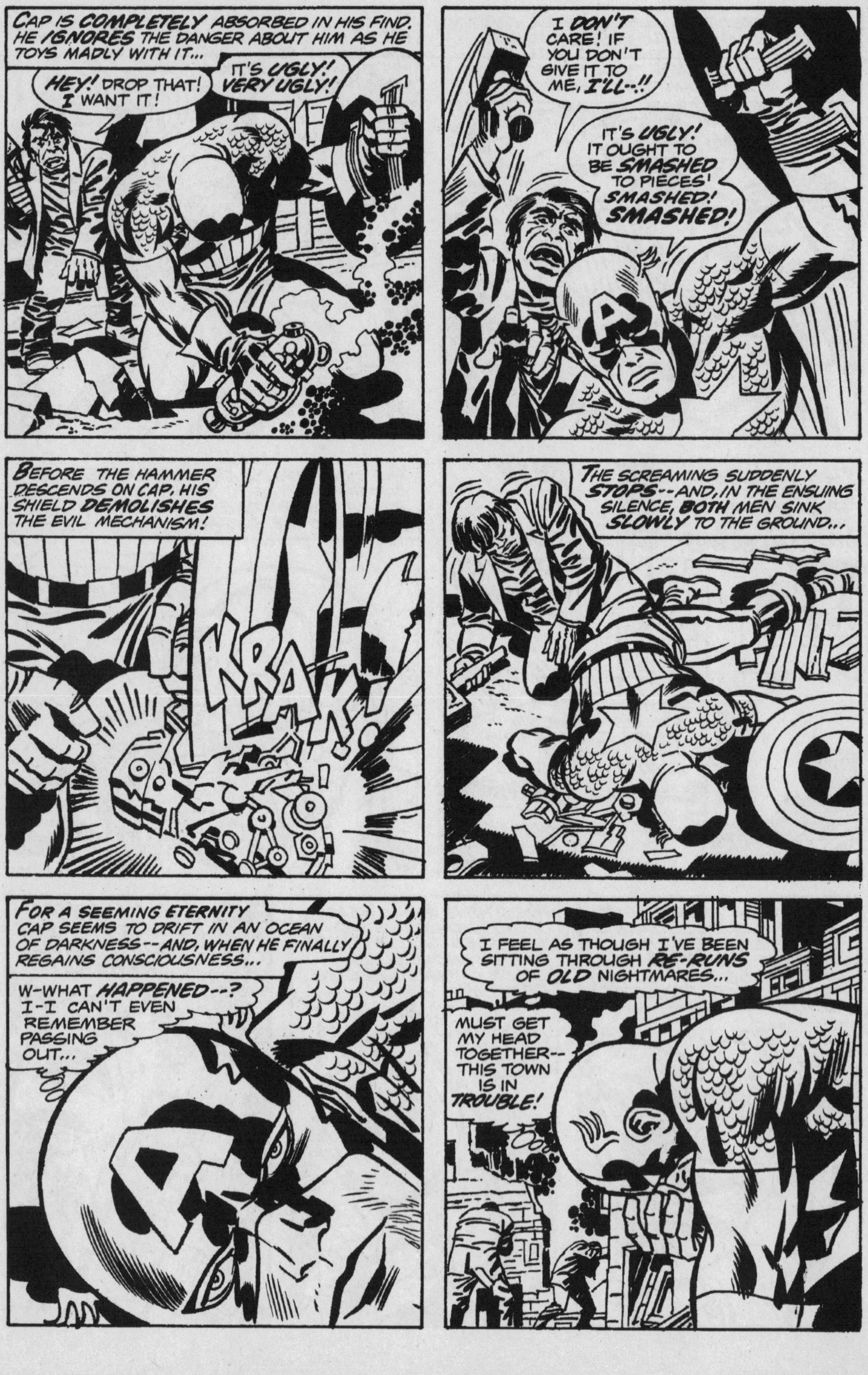

CAP IS COMPLETELY ABSORBED IN HIS FIND. HE IGNORES THE DANGER ABOUT HIM AS HE TOYS MADLY WITH IT...
HEY! DROP THAT! I WANT IT!
IT'S UGLY! VERY UGLY!
I DON'T CARE! IF YOU DON'T GIVE IT TO ME, I'LL--!!
IT'S UGLY! IT OUGHT TO BE SMASHED TO PIECES! SMASHED! SMASHED!
BEFORE THE HAMMER DESCENDS ON CAP, HIS SHIELD DEMOLISHES THE EVIL MECHANISM!
KRAK!
THE SCREAMING SUDDENLY STOPS--AND, IN THE ENSUING SILENCE, BOTH MEN SINK SLOWLY TO THE GROUND...
FOR A SEEMING ETERNITY CAP SEEMS TO DRIFT IN AN OCEAN OF DARKNESS--AND, WHEN HE FINALLY REGAINS CONSCIOUSNESS...
W-WHAT HAPPENED--? I-I CAN'T EVEN REMEMBER PASSING OUT...
I FEEL AS THOUGH I'VE BEEN SITTING THROUGH RE-RUNS OF OLD NIGHTMARES...
MUST GET MY HEAD TOGETHER-- THIS TOWN IS IN TROUBLE!

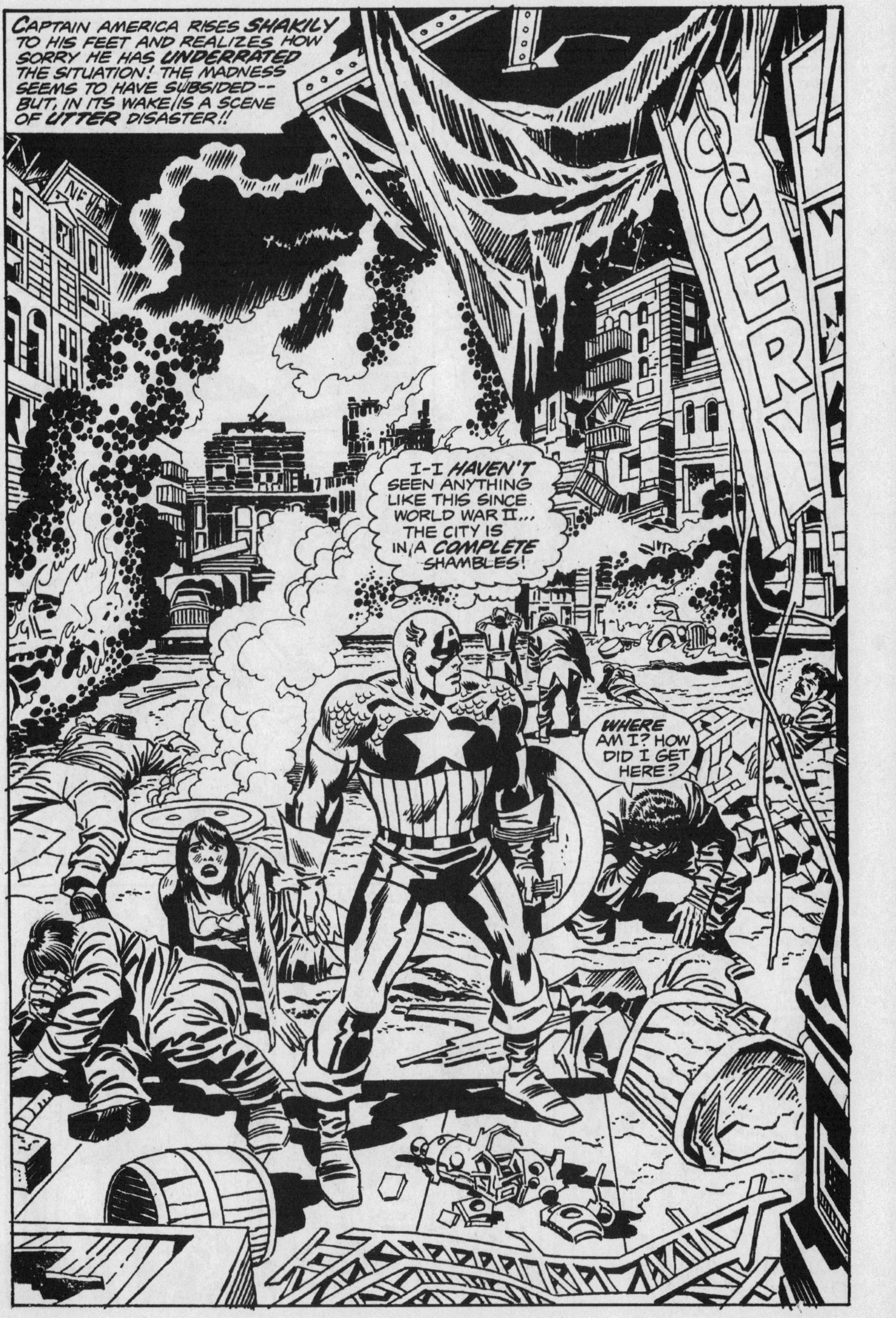
CAPTAIN AMERICA RISES SHAKILY TO HIS FEET AND REALIZES HOW SORRY HE HAS UNDERRATED THE SITUATION! THE MADNESS SEEMS TO HAVE SUBSIDED-- BUT, IN ITS WAKE IS A SCENE OF UTTER DISASTER!!
I-I HAVEN'T SEEN ANYTHING LIKE THIS SINCE WORLD WAR II... THE CITY IS IN A COMPLETE SHAMBLES!
WHERE AM I? HOW DID I GET HERE?
OCERY

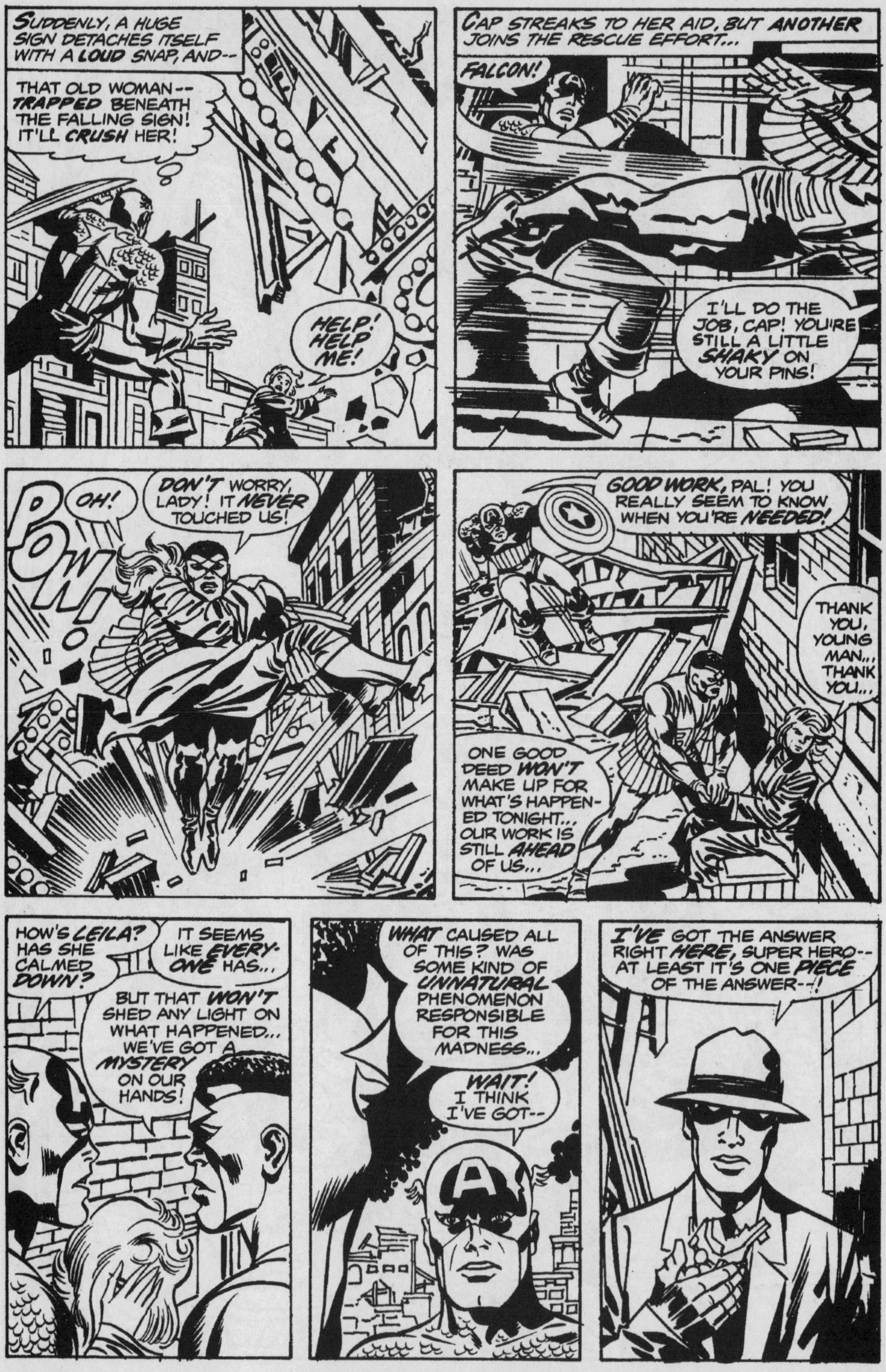
SUDDENLY, A HUGE SIGN DETACHES ITSELF WITH A LOUD SNAP, AND--
THAT OLD WOMAN-- TRAPPED BENEATH THE FALLING SIGN! IT'LL CRUSH HER!
HELP! HELP ME!
CAP STREAKS TO HER AID, BUT ANOTHER JOINS THE RESCUE EFFORT...
FALCON!
I'LL DO THE JOB, CAP! YOU'RE STILL A LITTLE SHAKY ON YOUR PINS!
POW!
OH!
DON'T WORRY, LADY! IT NEVER TOUCHED US!
GOOD WORK, PAL! YOU REALLY SEEM TO KNOW WHEN YOU'RE NEEDED!
THANK YOU, YOUNG MAN... THANK YOU...
ONE GOOD DEED WON'T MAKE UP FOR WHAT'S HAPPEN-ED TONIGHT... OUR WORK IS STILL AHEAD OF US...
HOW'S LEILA? HAS SHE CALMED DOWN?
IT SEEMS LIKE EVERY-ONE HAS...
BUT THAT WON'T SHED ANY LIGHT ON WHAT HAPPENED... WE'VE GOT A MYSTERY ON OUR HANDS!
WHAT CAUSED ALL OF THIS? WAS SOME KIND OF UNNATURAL PHENOMENON RESPONSIBLE FOR THIS MADNESS...
WAIT! I THINK I'VE GOT--
I'VE GOT THE ANSWER RIGHT HERE, SUPER HERO-- AT LEAST IT'S ONE PIECE OF THE ANSWER--!

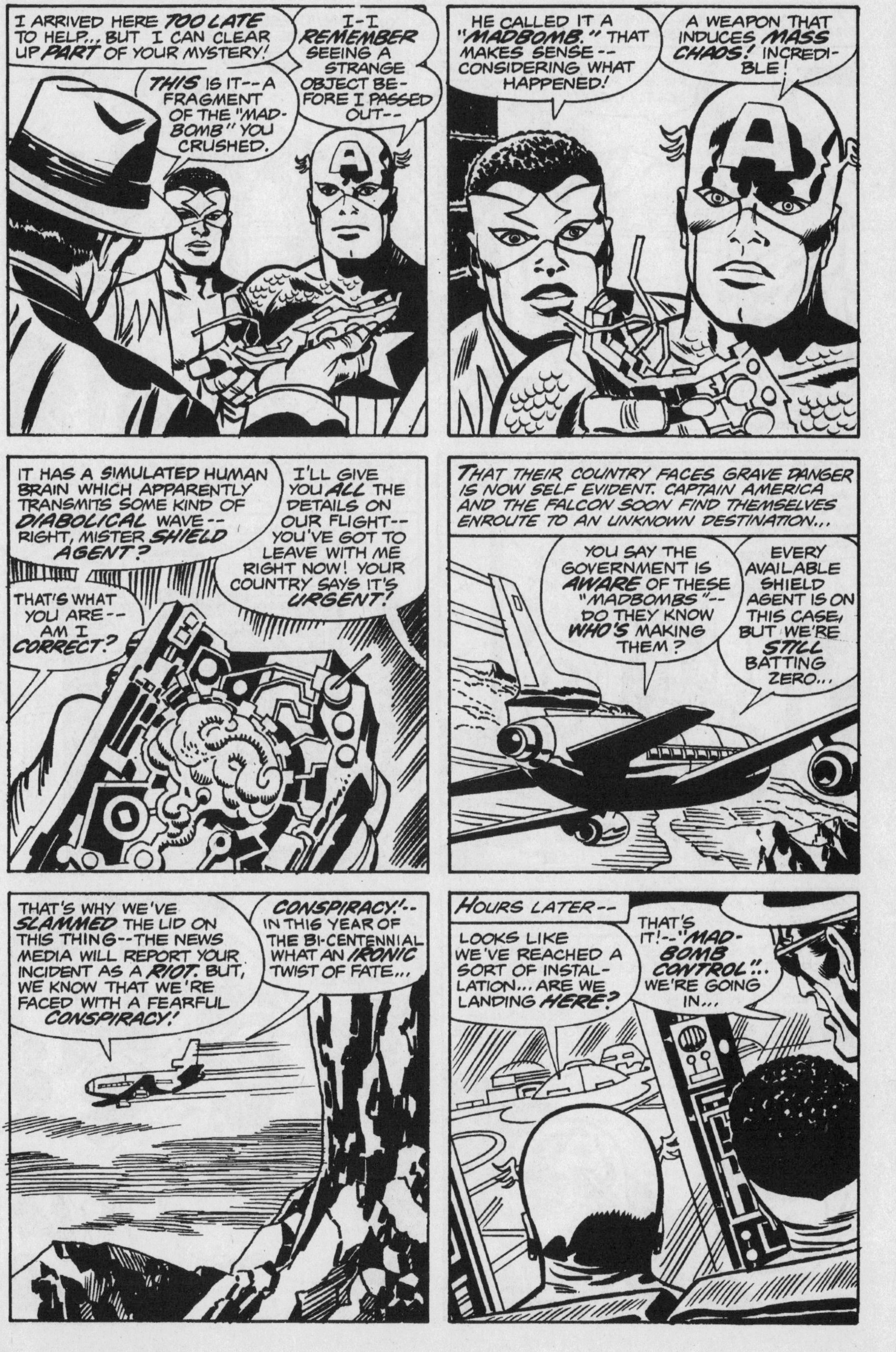
I ARRIVED HERE TOO LATE TO HELP... BUT I CAN CLEAR UP PART OF YOUR MYSTERY!
I-I REMEMBER SEEING A STRANGE OBJECT BEFORE I PASSED OUT--
THIS IS IT--A FRAGMENT OF THE "MAD-BOMB" YOU CRUSHED.
HE CALLED IT A "MADBOMB." THAT MAKES SENSE--CONSIDERING WHAT HAPPENED!
A WEAPON THAT INDUCES MASS CHAOS! INCREDIBLE!
IT HAS A SIMULATED HUMAN BRAIN WHICH APPARENTLY TRANSMITS SOME KIND OF DIABOLICAL WAVE--RIGHT, MISTER SHIELD AGENT?
THAT'S WHAT YOU ARE--AM I CORRECT?
I'LL GIVE YOU ALL THE DETAILS ON OUR FLIGHT--YOU'VE GOT TO LEAVE WITH ME RIGHT NOW! YOUR COUNTRY SAYS IT'S URGENT!
THAT THEIR COUNTRY FACES GRAVE DANGER IS NOW SELF EVIDENT. CAPTAIN AMERICA AND THE FALCON SOON FIND THEMSELVES ENROUTE TO AN UNKNOWN DESTINATION...
YOU SAY THE GOVERNMENT IS AWARE OF THESE "MADBOMBS"--DO THEY KNOW WHO'S MAKING THEM?
EVERY AVAILABLE SHIELD AGENT IS ON THIS CASE, BUT WE'RE STILL BATTING ZERO...
THAT'S WHY WE'VE SLAMMED THE LID ON THIS THING--THE NEWS MEDIA WILL REPORT YOUR INCIDENT AS A RIOT. BUT, WE KNOW THAT WE'RE FACED WITH A FEARFUL CONSPIRACY!
CONSPIRACY!--IN THIS YEAR OF THE BI-CENTENNIAL WHAT AN IRONIC TWIST OF FATE...
HOURS LATER--
LOOKS LIKE WE'VE REACHED A SORT OF INSTALLATION... ARE WE LANDING HERE?
THAT'S IT!--"MAD-BOMB CONTROL"... WE'RE GOING IN...

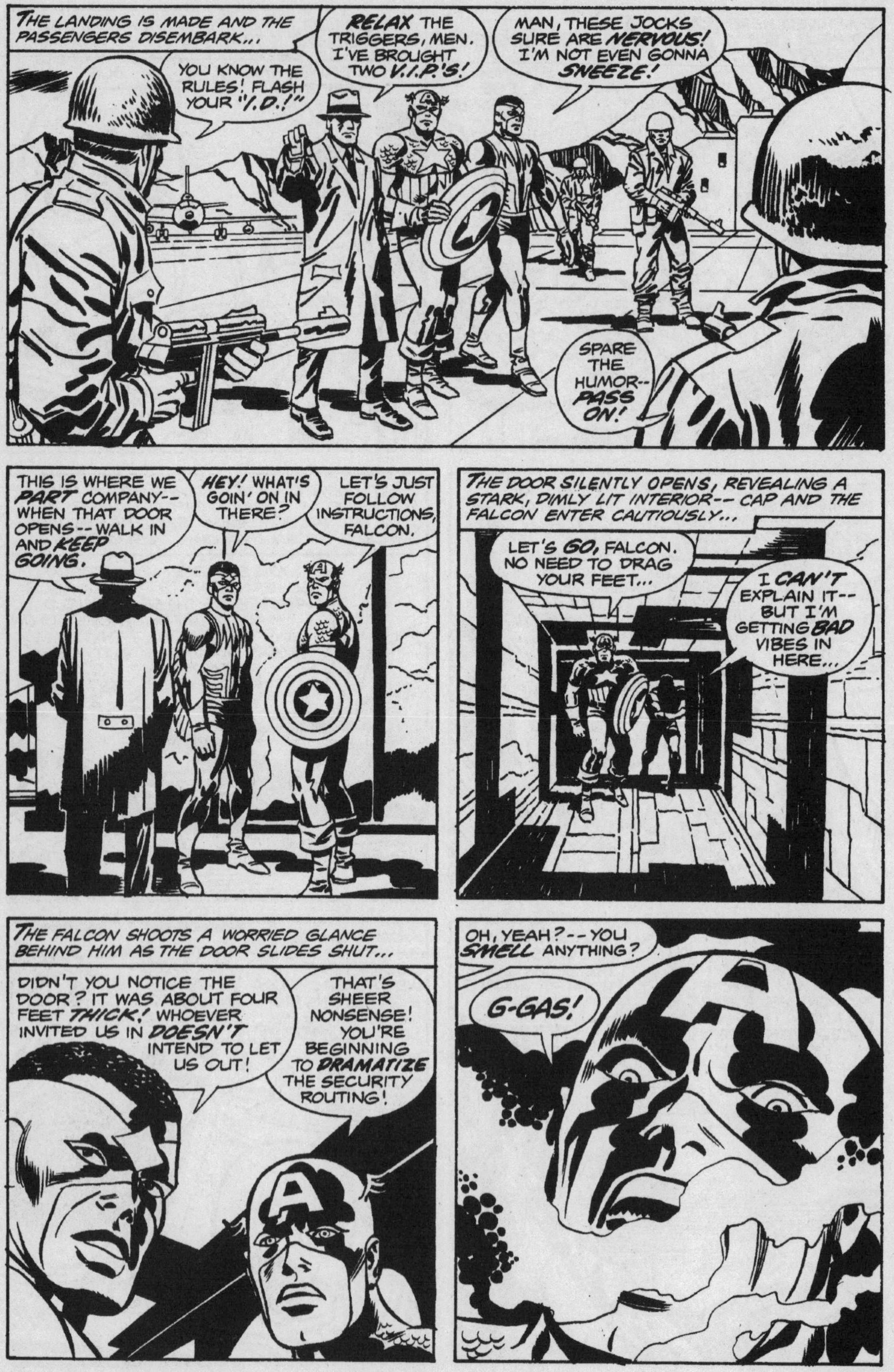
THE LANDING IS MADE AND THE PASSENGERS DISEMBARK...
YOU KNOW THE RULES! FLASH YOUR "I.D.!"
RELAX THE TRIGGERS, MEN. I'VE BROUGHT TWO V.I.P.'S!
MAN, THESE JOCKS SURE ARE NERVOUS! I'M NOT EVEN GONNA SNEEZE!
SPARE THE HUMOR-- PASS ON!
THIS IS WHERE WE PART COMPANY-- WHEN THAT DOOR OPENS--WALK IN AND KEEP GOING.
HEY! WHAT'S GOIN' ON IN THERE?
LET'S JUST FOLLOW INSTRUCTIONS, FALCON.
THE DOOR SILENTLY OPENS, REVEALING A STARK, DIMLY LIT INTERIOR-- CAP AND THE FALCON ENTER CAUTIOUSLY...
LET'S GO, FALCON. NO NEED TO DRAG YOUR FEET...
I CAN'T EXPLAIN IT-- BUT I'M GETTING BAD VIBES IN HERE...
THE FALCON SHOOTS A WORRIED GLANCE BEHIND HIM AS THE DOOR SLIDES SHUT...
DIDN'T YOU NOTICE THE DOOR? IT WAS ABOUT FOUR FEET THICK! WHOEVER INVITED US IN DOESN'T INTEND TO LET US OUT!
THAT'S SHEER NONSENSE! YOU'RE BEGINNING TO DRAMATIZE THE SECURITY ROUTING!
OH, YEAH?--YOU SMELL ANYTHING?
G-GAS!

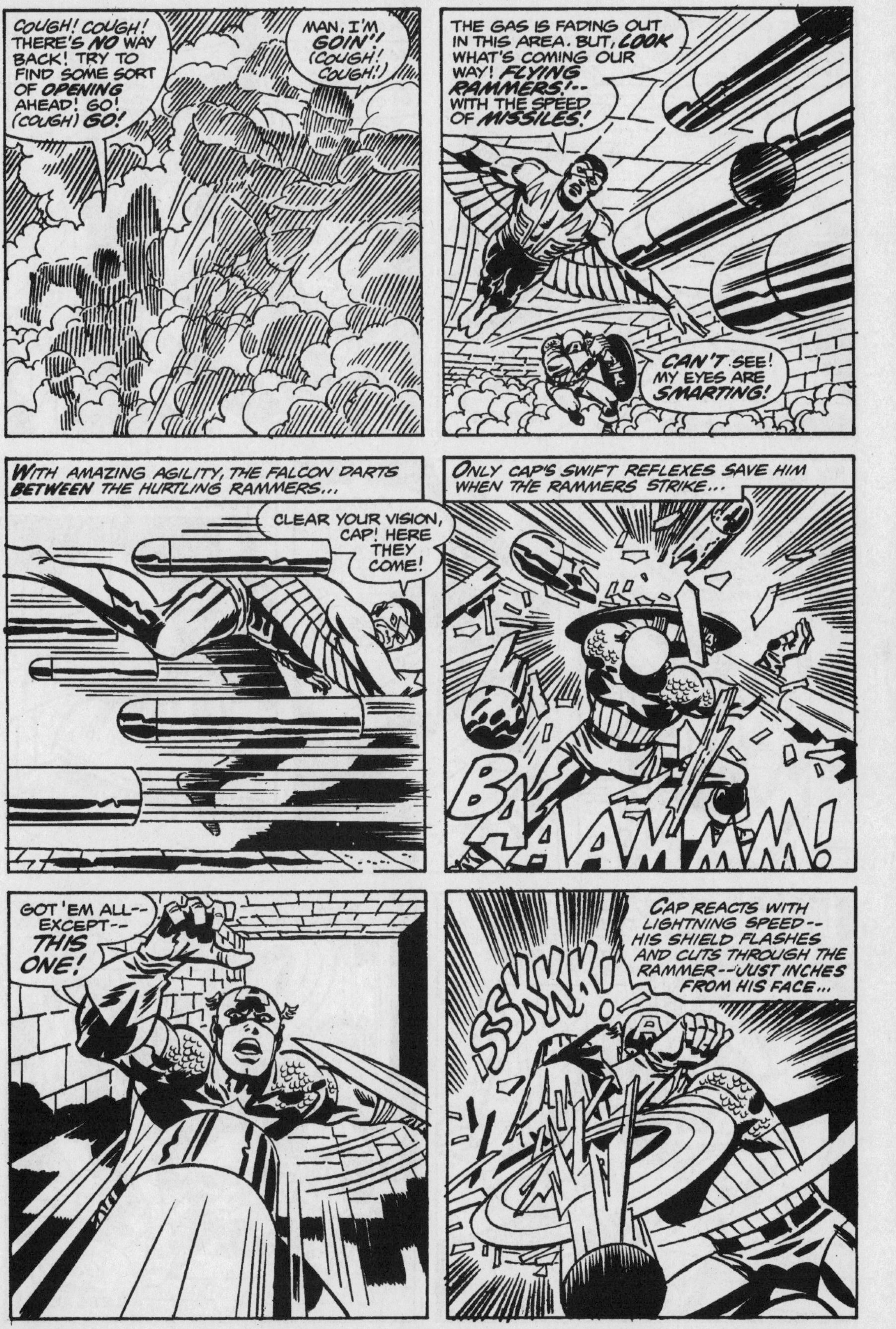
COUGH! COUGH! THERE'S NO WAY BACK! TRY TO FIND SOME SORT OF OPENING AHEAD! GO! (COUGH) GO!
MAN, I'M GOIN'! (COUGH! COUGH!)
THE GAS IS FADING OUT IN THIS AREA. BUT, LOOK WHAT'S COMING OUR WAY! FLYING RAMMERS!-- WITH THE SPEED OF MISSILES!
CAN'T SEE! MY EYES ARE SMARTING!
WITH AMAZING AGILITY, THE FALCON DARTS BETWEEN THE HURTLING RAMMERS...
CLEAR YOUR VISION, CAP! HERE THEY COME!
ONLY CAP'S SWIFT REFLEXES SAVE HIM WHEN THE RAMMERS STRIKE...
BAAAMMM!
GOT 'EM ALL-- EXCEPT-- THIS ONE!
CAP REACTS WITH LIGHTNING SPEED-- HIS SHIELD FLASHES AND CUTS THROUGH THE RAMMER--JUST INCHES FROM HIS FACE...
SSKKK!

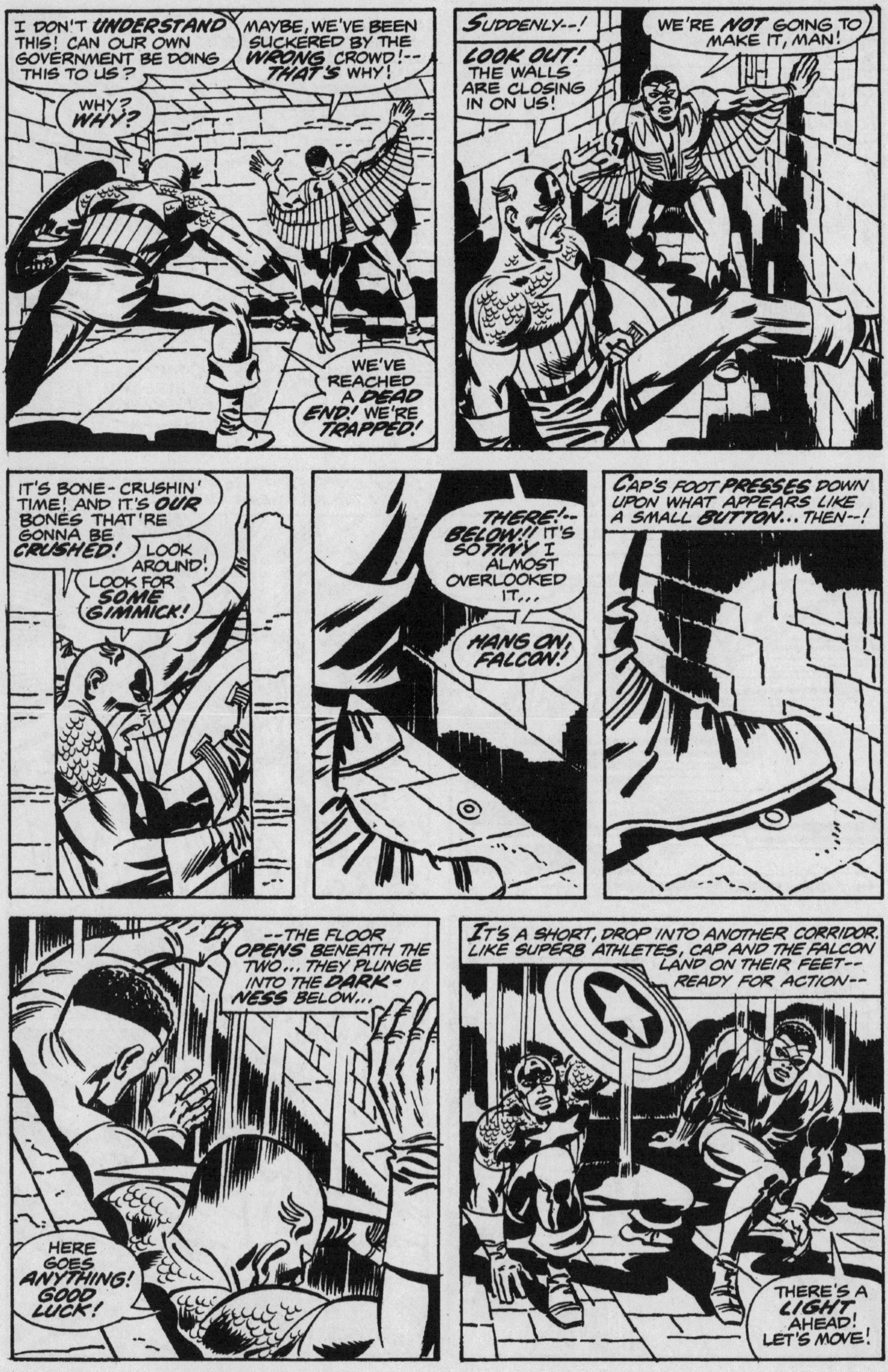

I DON'T UNDERSTAND THIS! CAN OUR OWN GOVERNMENT BE DOING THIS TO US?
MAYBE, WE'VE BEEN SUCKERED BY THE WRONG CROWD!-- THAT'S WHY!
WHY? WHY?
WE'VE REACHED A DEAD END! WE'RE TRAPPED!
SUDDENLY--!
WE'RE NOT GOING TO MAKE IT, MAN!
LOOK OUT! THE WALLS ARE CLOSING IN ON US!
IT'S BONE-CRUSHIN' TIME! AND IT'S OUR BONES THAT'RE GONNA BE CRUSHED!
LOOK AROUND! LOOK FOR SOME GIMMICK!
THERE!-- BELOW!! IT'S SO TINY I ALMOST OVERLOOKED IT...
HANG ON, FALCON!
CAP'S FOOT PRESSES DOWN UPON WHAT APPEARS LIKE A SMALL BUTTON... THEN--!
--THE FLOOR OPENS BENEATH THE TWO... THEY PLUNGE INTO THE DARK-NESS BELOW...
HERE GOES ANYTHING! GOOD LUCK!
IT'S A SHORT, DROP INTO ANOTHER CORRIDOR. LIKE SUPERB ATHLETES, CAP AND THE FALCON LAND ON THEIR FEET-- READY FOR ACTION--
THERE'S A LIGHT AHEAD! LET'S MOVE!

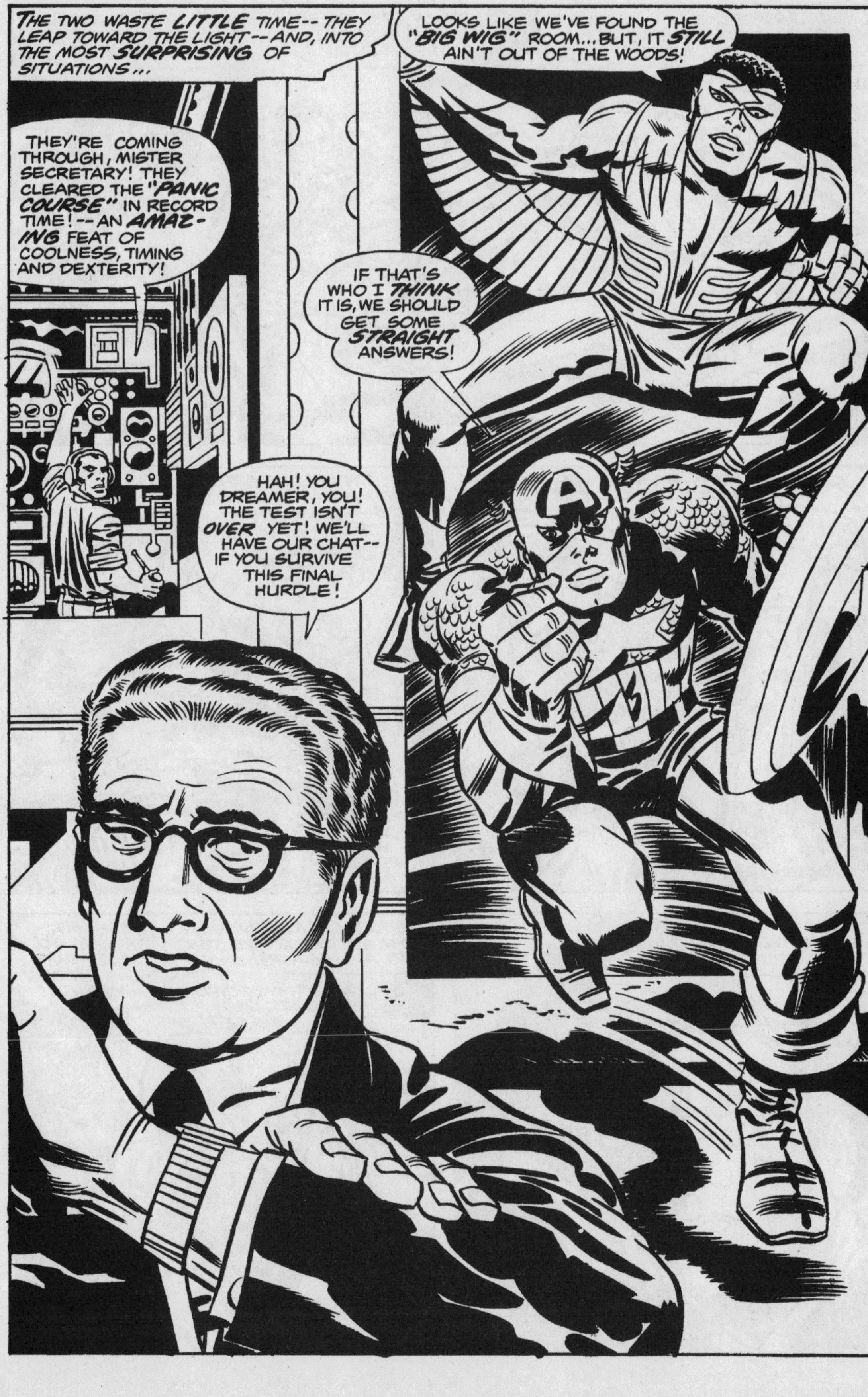
THE TWO WASTE LITTLE TIME-- THEY LEAP TOWARD THE LIGHT-- AND, INTO THE MOST SURPRISING OF SITUATIONS...
LOOKS LIKE WE'VE FOUND THE "BIG WIG" ROOM... BUT, IT STILL AIN'T OUT OF THE WOODS!
THEY'RE COMING THROUGH, MISTER SECRETARY! THEY CLEARED THE "PANIC COURSE" IN RECORD TIME! -- AN AMAZ-ING FEAT OF COOLNESS, TIMING AND DEXTERITY!
IF THAT'S WHO I THINK IT IS, WE SHOULD GET SOME STRAIGHT ANSWERS!
HAH! YOU DREAMER, YOU! THE TEST ISN'T OVER YET! WE'LL HAVE OUR CHAT-- IF YOU SURVIVE THIS FINAL HURDLE!

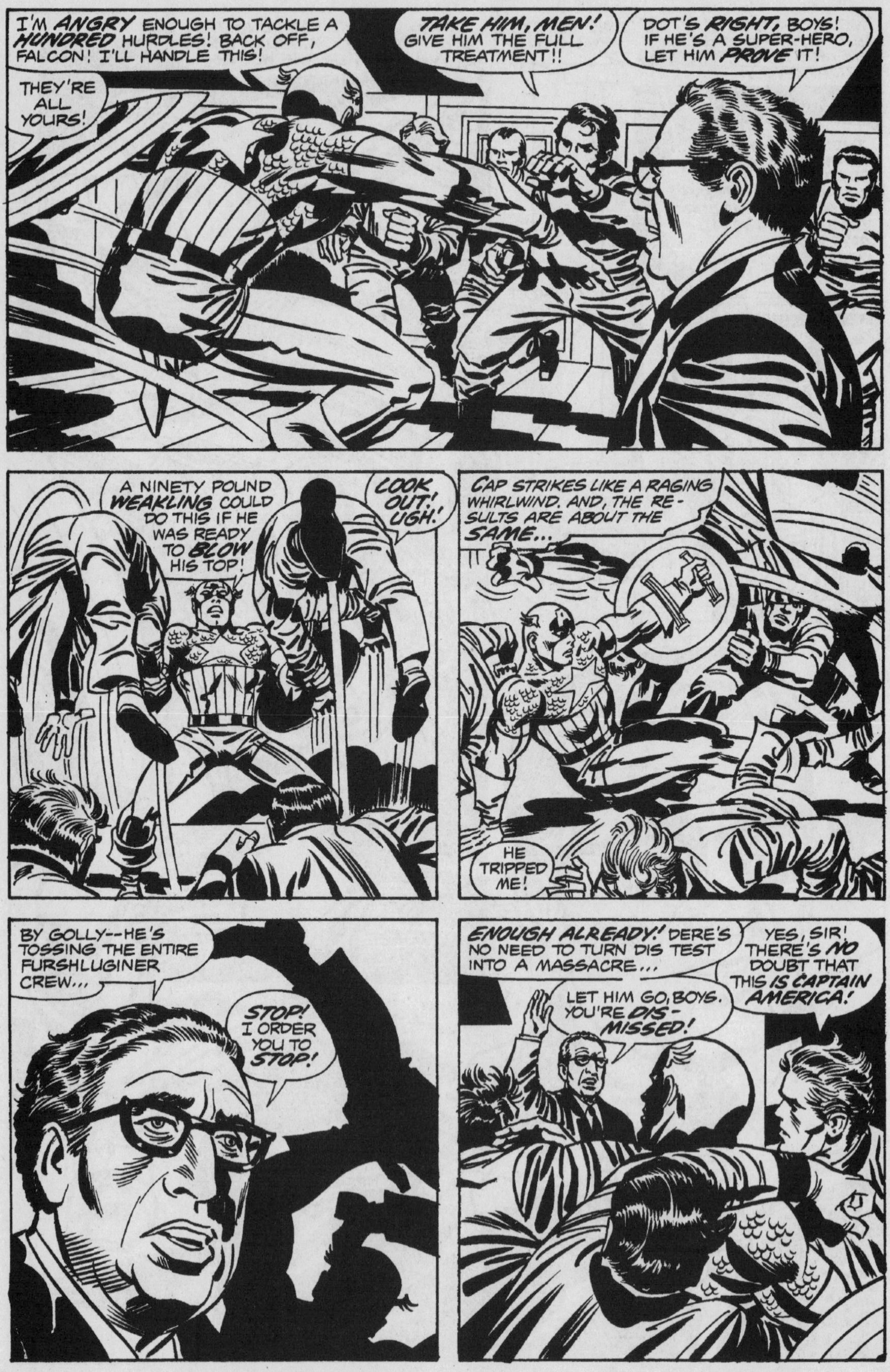
I'M ANGRY ENOUGH TO TACKLE A HUNDRED HURDLES! BACK OFF, FALCON! I'LL HANDLE THIS!
THEY'RE ALL YOURS!
TAKE HIM, MEN! GIVE HIM THE FULL TREATMENT!!
DOT'S RIGHT, BOYS! IF HE'S A SUPER-HERO, LET HIM PROVE IT!
A NINETY POUND WEAKLING COULD DO THIS IF HE WAS READY TO BLOW HIS TOP!
LOOK OUT! UGH!
CAP STRIKES LIKE A RAGING WHIRLWIND. AND, THE RESULTS ARE ABOUT THE SAME...
HE TRIPPED ME!
BY GOLLY--HE'S TOSSING THE ENTIRE FURSHLUGINER CREW...
STOP! I ORDER YOU TO STOP!
ENOUGH ALREADY! DERE'S NO NEED TO TURN DIS TEST INTO A MASSACRE...
LET HIM GO, BOYS. YOU'RE DIS-MISSED!
YES, SIR! THERE'S NO DOUBT THAT THIS IS CAPTAIN AMERICA!

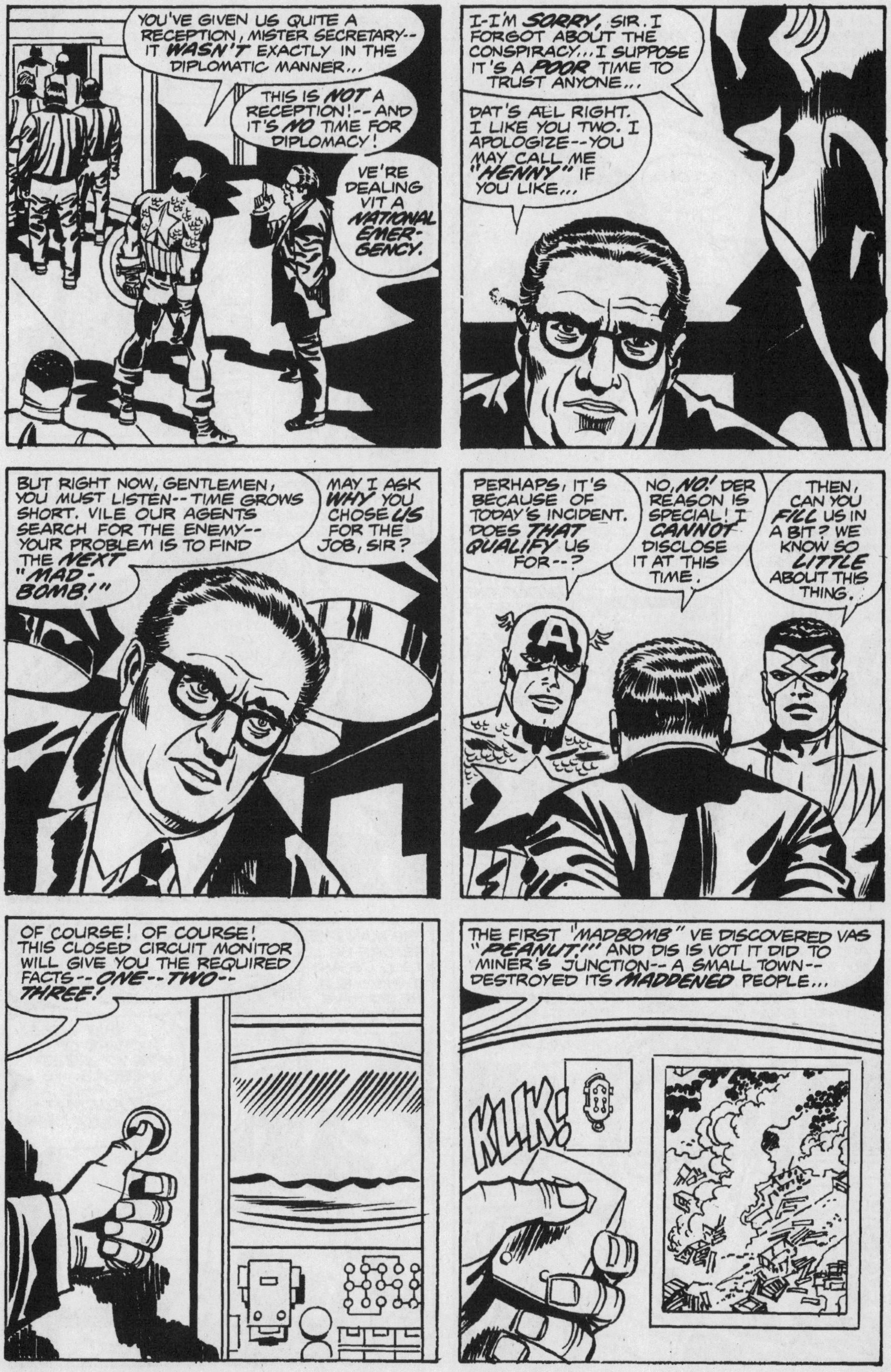

YOU'VE GIVEN US QUITE A RECEPTION, MISTER SECRETARY-- IT WASN'T EXACTLY IN THE DIPLOMATIC MANNER...
THIS IS NOT A RECEPTION!-- AND IT'S NO TIME FOR DIPLOMACY!
VE'RE DEALING VIT A NATIONAL EMERGENCY.
I-I'M SORRY, SIR. I FORGOT ABOUT THE CONSPIRACY... I SUPPOSE IT'S A POOR TIME TO TRUST ANYONE...
DAT'S ALL RIGHT. I LIKE YOU TWO. I APOLOGIZE--YOU MAY CALL ME "HENNY" IF YOU LIKE...
BUT RIGHT NOW, GENTLEMEN, YOU MUST LISTEN-- TIME GROWS SHORT. VILE OUR AGENTS SEARCH FOR THE ENEMY-- YOUR PROBLEM IS TO FIND THE NEXT "MAD-BOMB!"
MAY I ASK WHY YOU CHOSE US FOR THE JOB, SIR?
PERHAPS, IT'S BECAUSE OF TODAY'S INCIDENT. DOES THAT QUALIFY US FOR--?
NO, NO! DER REASON IS SPECIAL! I CANNOT DISCLOSE IT AT THIS TIME.
THEN, CAN YOU FILL US IN A BIT? WE KNOW SO LITTLE ABOUT THIS THING.
OF COURSE! OF COURSE! THIS CLOSED CIRCUIT MONITOR WILL GIVE YOU THE REQUIRED FACTS--ONE--TWO--THREE!
THE FIRST "MADBOMB" VE DISCOVERED VAS "PEANUT!" AND DIS IS VOT IT DID TO MINER'S JUNCTION-- A SMALL TOWN-- DESTROYED ITS MADDENED PEOPLE...
KLIK!

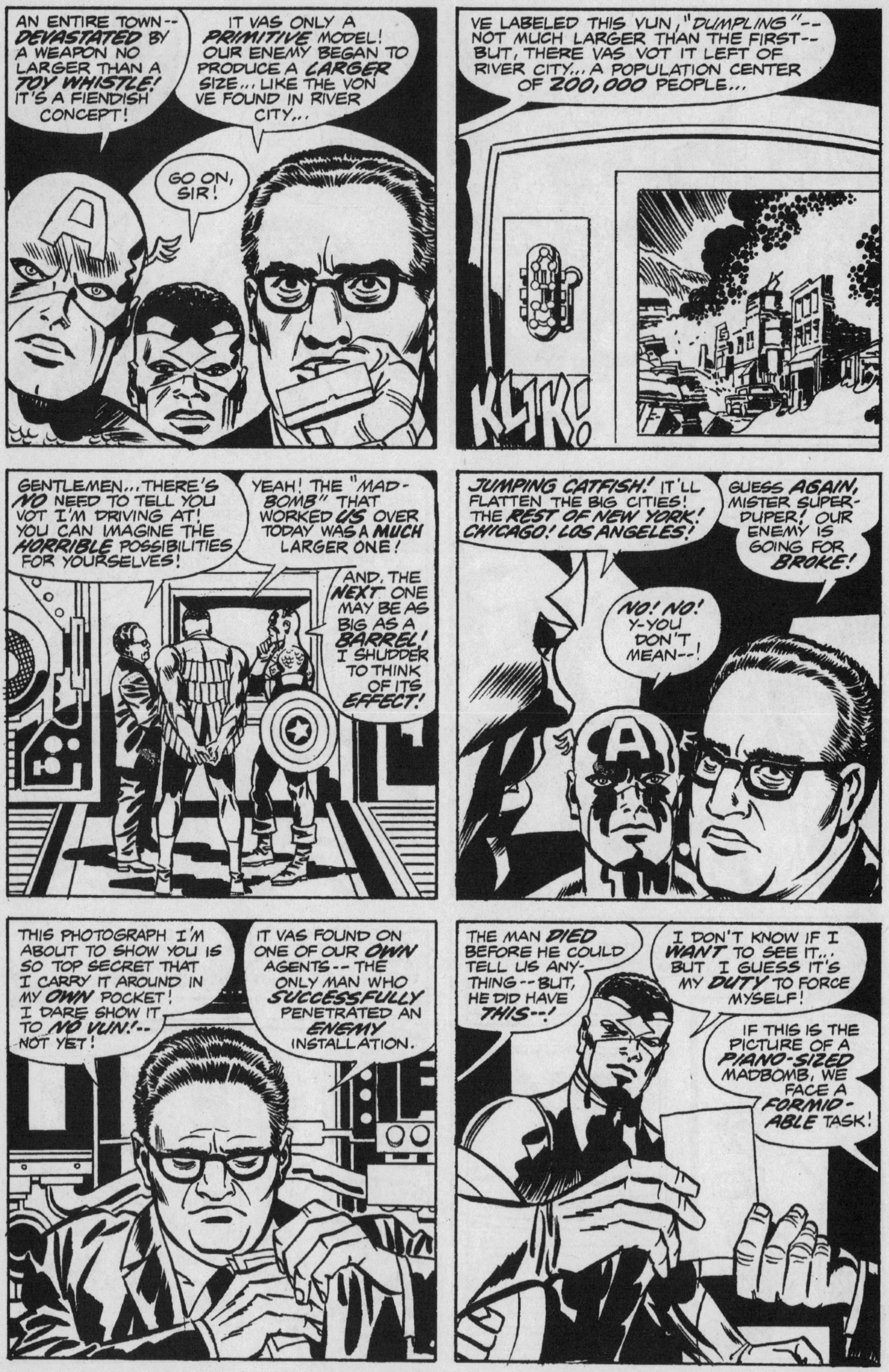
AN ENTIRE TOWN-- DEVASTATED BY A WEAPON NO LARGER THAN A TOY WHISTLE! IT'S A FIENDISH CONCEPT!
IT VAS ONLY A PRIMITIVE MODEL! OUR ENEMY BEGAN TO PRODUCE A LARGER SIZE... LIKE THE VON VE FOUND IN RIVER CITY...
GO ON, SIR!
VE LABELED THIS VUN, "DUMPLING"-- NOT MUCH LARGER THAN THE FIRST-- BUT, THERE VAS VOT IT LEFT OF RIVER CITY... A POPULATION CENTER OF 200,000 PEOPLE...
KLIK!
GENTLEMEN... THERE'S NO NEED TO TELL YOU VOT I'M DRIVING AT! YOU CAN IMAGINE THE HORRIBLE POSSIBILITIES FOR YOURSELVES!
YEAH! THE "MAD-BOMB" THAT WORKED US OVER TODAY WAS A MUCH LARGER ONE!
AND, THE NEXT ONE MAY BE AS BIG AS A BARREL! I SHUDDER TO THINK OF ITS EFFECT!
JUMPING CATFISH! IT'LL FLATTEN THE BIG CITIES! THE REST OF NEW YORK! CHICAGO! LOS ANGELES!
GUESS AGAIN, MISTER SUPER-DUPER! OUR ENEMY IS GOING FOR BROKE!
NO! NO! Y-YOU DON'T MEAN--!
THIS PHOTOGRAPH I'M ABOUT TO SHOW YOU IS SO TOP SECRET THAT I CARRY IT AROUND IN MY OWN POCKET! I DARE SHOW IT TO NO VUN!-- NOT YET!
IT VAS FOUND ON ONE OF OUR OWN AGENTS-- THE ONLY MAN WHO SUCCESSFULLY PENETRATED AN ENEMY INSTALLATION.
THE MAN DIED BEFORE HE COULD TELL US ANY-THING--BUT, HE DID HAVE THIS--!
I DON'T KNOW IF I WANT TO SEE IT... BUT I GUESS IT'S MY DUTY TO FORCE MYSELF!
IF THIS IS THE PICTURE OF A PIANO-SIZED MADBOMB, WE FACE A FORMID-ABLE TASK!

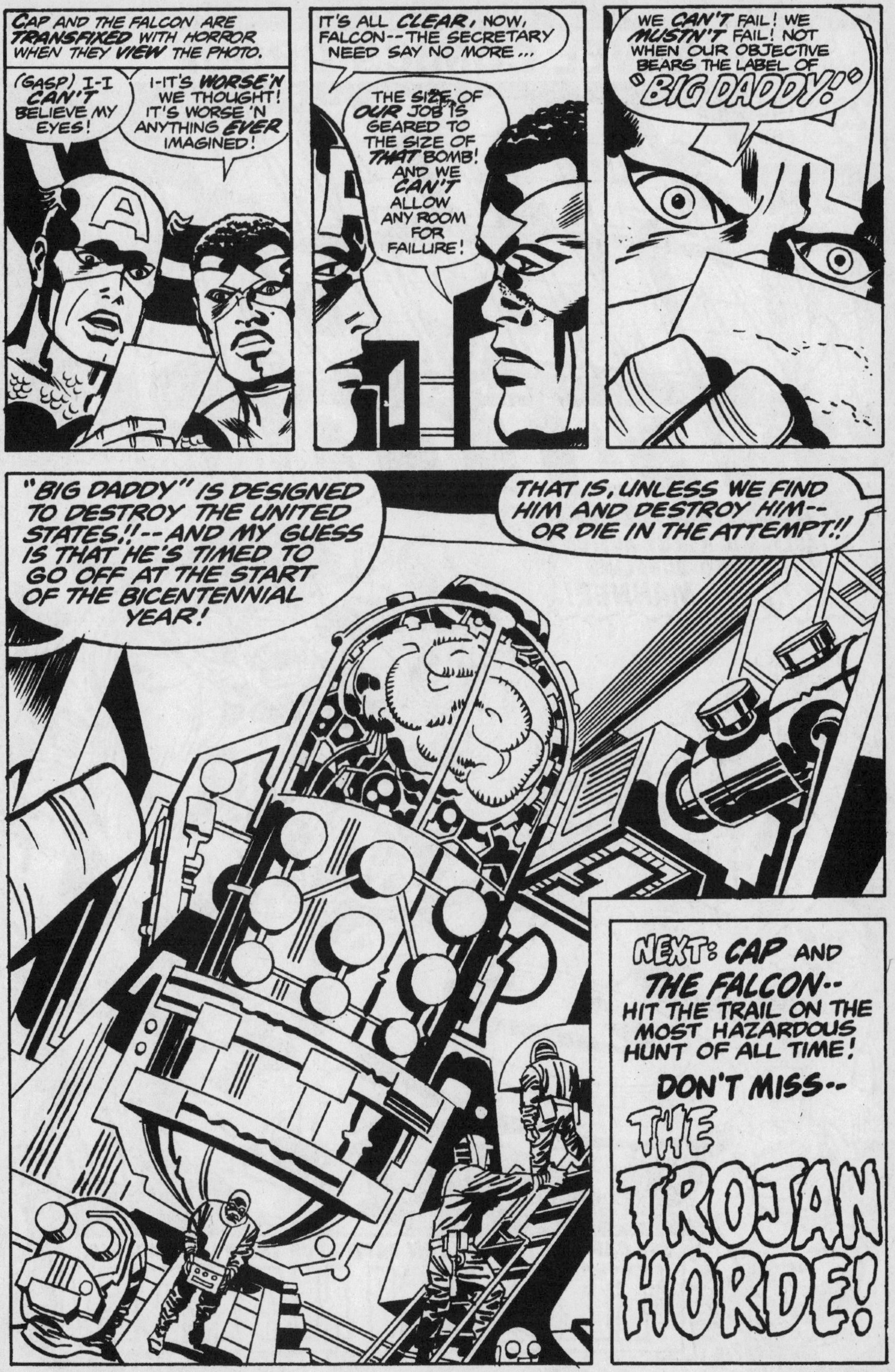
CAP AND THE FALCON ARE TRANSFIXED WITH HORROR WHEN THEY VIEW THE PHOTO.
(GASP) I-I CAN'T BELIEVE MY EYES!
I-IT'S WORSE'N WE THOUGHT! IT'S WORSE 'N ANYTHING EVER IMAGINED!
IT'S ALL CLEAR, NOW, FALCON--THE SECRETARY NEED SAY NO MORE...
THE SIZE OF OUR JOB IS GEARED TO THE SIZE OF THAT BOMB! AND WE CAN'T ALLOW ANY ROOM FOR FAILURE!
WE CAN'T FAIL! WE MUSTN'T FAIL! NOT WHEN OUR OBJECTIVE BEARS THE LABEL OF "BIG DADDY!"
"BIG DADDY" IS DESIGNED TO DESTROY THE UNITED STATES!!--AND MY GUESS IS THAT HE'S TIMED TO GO OFF AT THE START OF THE BICENTENNIAL YEAR!
THAT IS, UNLESS WE FIND HIM AND DESTROY HIM--OR DIE IN THE ATTEMPT!!
NEXT: CAP AND THE FALCON-- HIT THE TRAIL ON THE MOST HAZARDOUS HUNT OF ALL TIME!
DON'T MISS--
THE TROJAN HORDE!

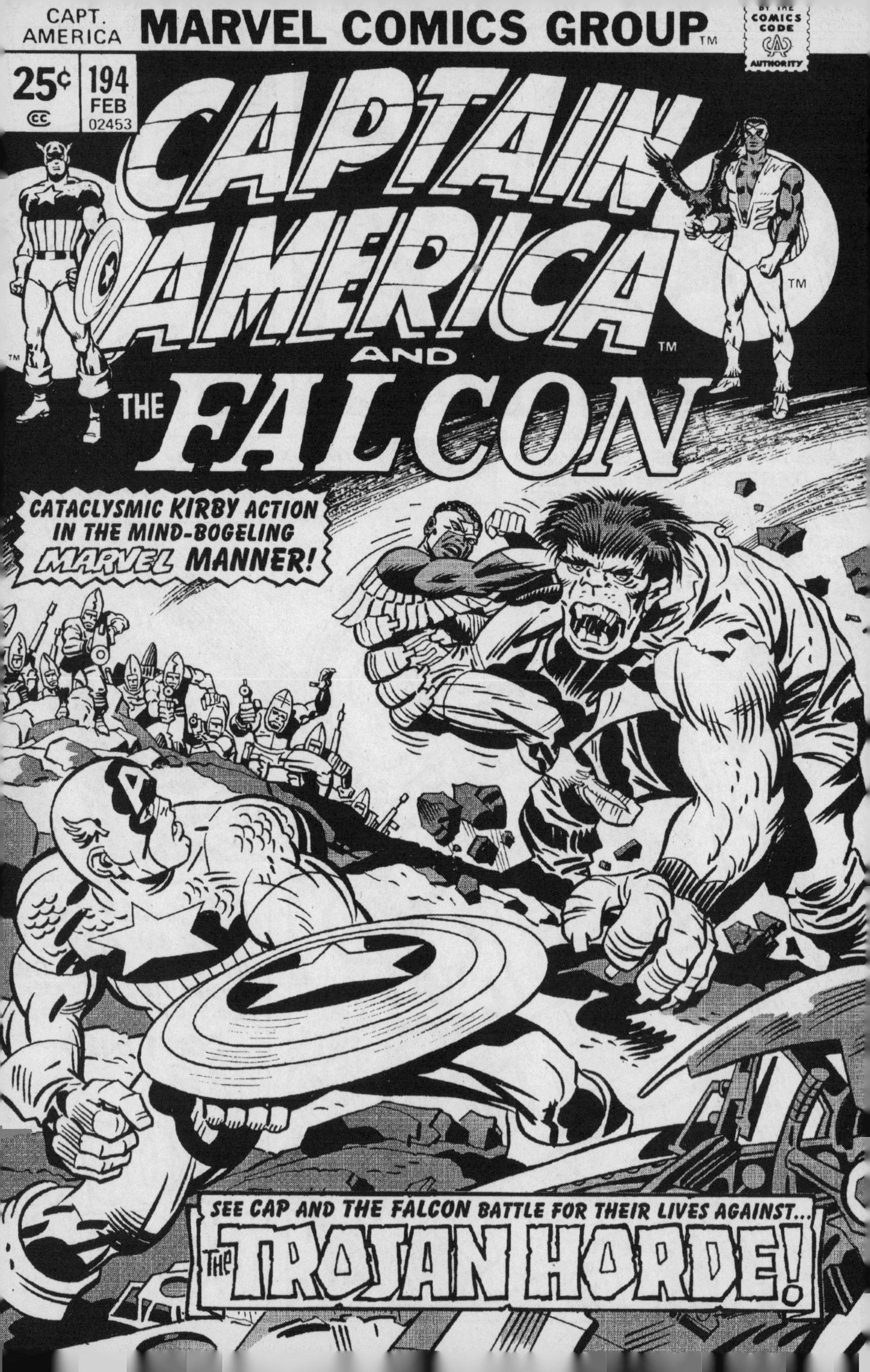
CAPT. AMERICA
MARVEL COMICS GROUP™
BY THE COMICS CODE
AUTHORITY
25¢
194
FEB
02453
CAPTAIN AMERICA™
AND
THE FALCON™
CATACLYSMIC KIRBY ACTION IN THE MIND-BOGELING MARVEL MANNER!
SEE CAP AND THE FALCON BATTLE FOR THEIR LIVES AGAINST...
The TROJAN HORDE!

1941! The world at *war!* And in a secret laboratory, frail *Steve Rogers* became the American *super-soldier!* For four thrilling years, he fought the Axis powers—until a freak stroke of fate threw him into *suspended animation.* He woke in the mid-1960s, a man *twenty years out of his time.* Since that fateful day, Steve Rogers has sought his *destiny* in this brave new world.

STAN LEE PRESENTS: CAPTAIN AMERICA AND THE FALCON™

"DON'T FIRE UNTIL YOU SEE THE WHITES OF THEIR EYES!"

AN AMERICAN HERO SAID THAT IN **SIMPLER** DAYS-- WHEN MEN CONFRONTED EACH OTHER IN ARMED COMBAT... BUT, THIS IS THE AGE OF THE **SUPER-HERO** VERSUS THE **SUPER-THREAT!**-- AND, NO MENACE EVER DEVISED BY **CONSPIRATORS** HAS BEGUN TO LOOM AS LARGE AS THE PLOT UNCOVERED IN THE HEART OF THE UNITED STATES...

THE TROJAN HORDE

JACK KIRBY	FRANK GIACOIA	GASPAR SALADINO	JANICE COHEN
WRITER·ARTIST·EDITOR	INKER	LETTERER	COLORIST

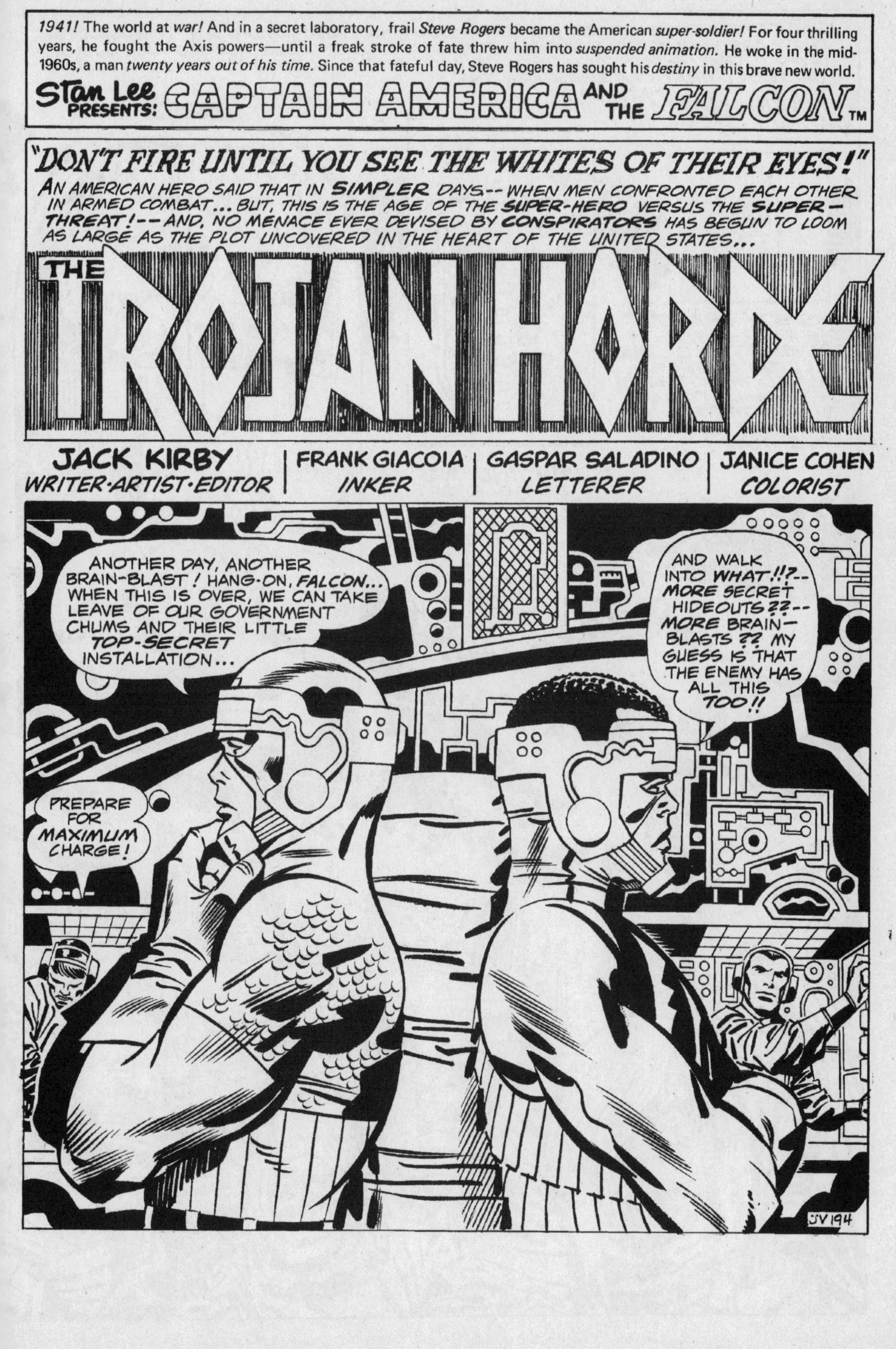
ANOTHER DAY, ANOTHER BRAIN-BLAST! HANG-ON, FALCON... WHEN THIS IS OVER, WE CAN TAKE LEAVE OF OUR GOVERNMENT CHUMS AND THEIR LITTLE TOP-SECRET INSTALLATION...
AND WALK INTO WHAT!!?-- MORE SECRET HIDEOUTS??-- MORE BRAIN-BLASTS?? MY GUESS IS THAT THE ENEMY HAS ALL THIS TOO!!
PREPARE FOR MAXIMUM CHARGE!
JV 194

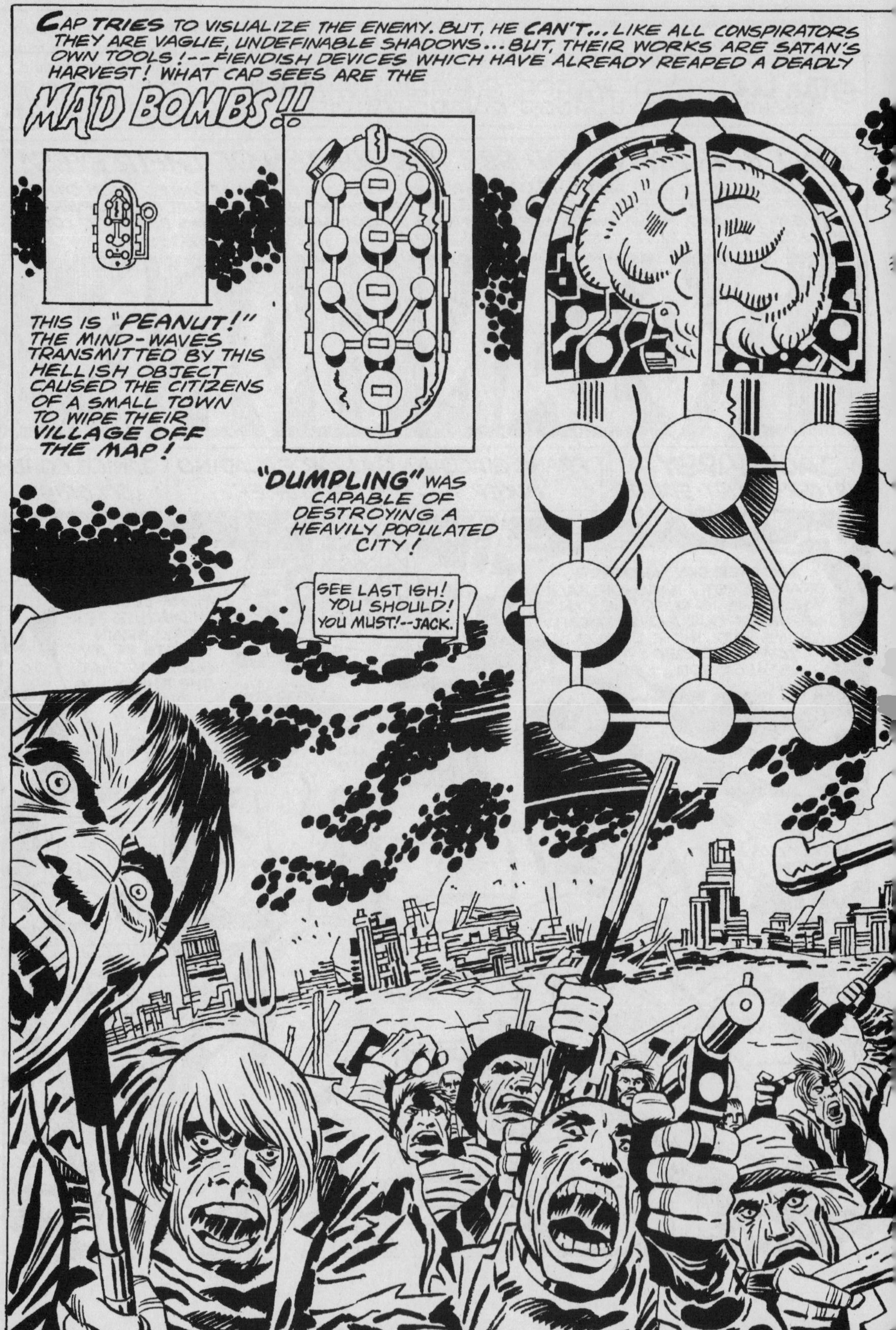

CAP TRIES TO VISUALIZE THE ENEMY. BUT, HE CAN'T... LIKE ALL CONSPIRATORS THEY ARE VAGUE, UNDEFINABLE SHADOWS... BUT, THEIR WORKS ARE SATAN'S OWN TOOLS! -- FIENDISH DEVICES WHICH HAVE ALREADY REAPED A DEADLY HARVEST! WHAT CAP SEES ARE THE
MAD BOMBS!!
THIS IS "PEANUT!" THE MIND-WAVES TRANSMITTED BY THIS HELLISH OBJECT CAUSED THE CITIZENS OF A SMALL TOWN TO WIPE THEIR VILLAGE OFF THE MAP!
"DUMPLING" WAS CAPABLE OF DESTROYING A HEAVILY POPULATED CITY!
SEE LAST ISH! YOU SHOULD! YOU MUST! --JACK.

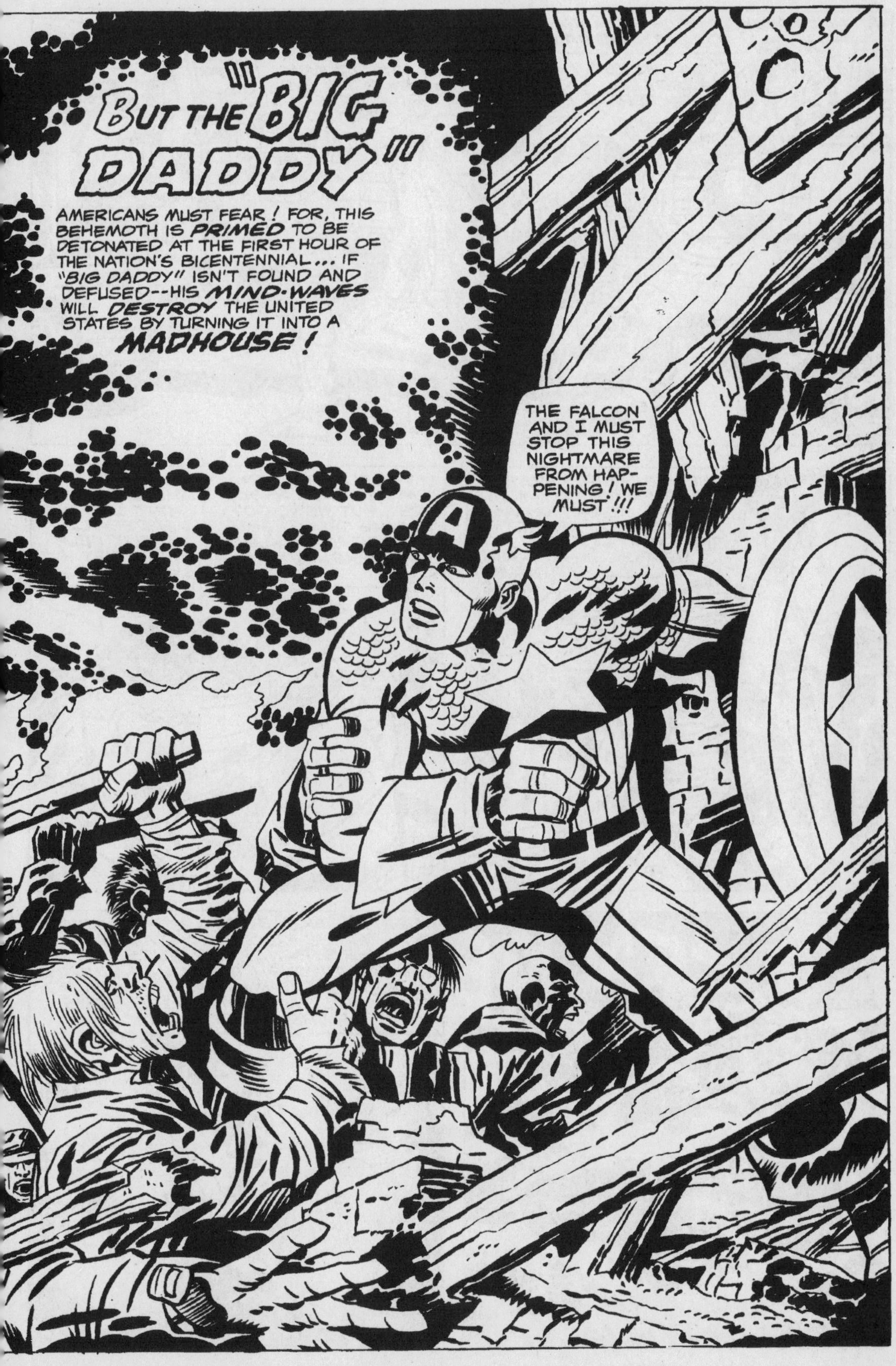

"BUT THE "BIG DADDY"
AMERICANS MUST FEAR! FOR, THIS BEHEMOTH IS PRIMED TO BE DETONATED AT THE FIRST HOUR OF THE NATION'S BICENTENNIAL... IF "BIG DADDY" ISN'T FOUND AND DEFUSED--HIS MIND-WAVES WILL DESTROY THE UNITED STATES BY TURNING IT INTO A MADHOUSE!
THE FALCON AND I MUST STOP THIS NIGHTMARE FROM HAPPENING! WE MUST!!!

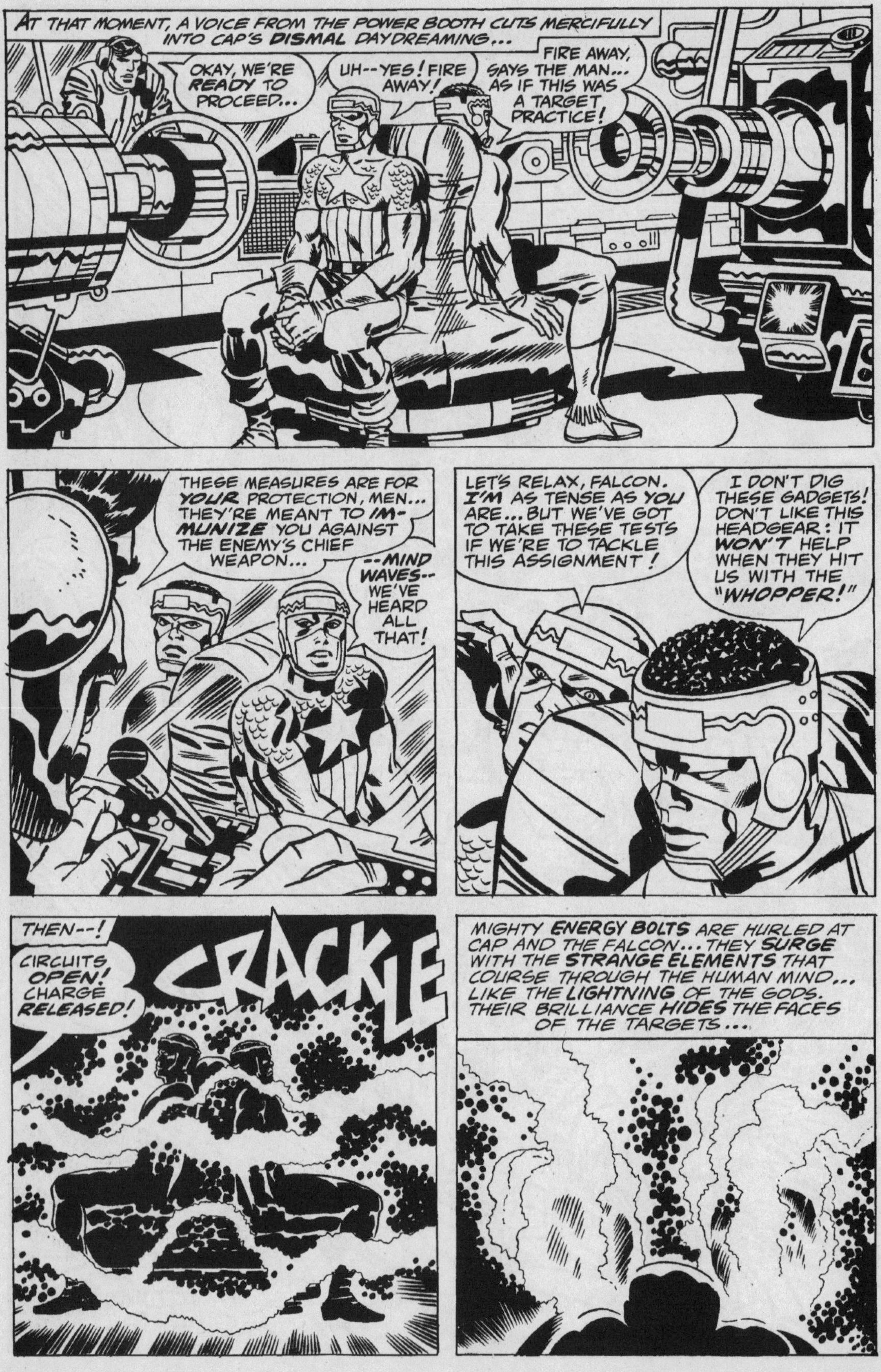
AT THAT MOMENT, A VOICE FROM THE POWER BOOTH CUTS MERCIFULLY INTO CAP'S DISMAL DAYDREAMING...
OKAY, WE'RE READY TO PROCEED...
UH--YES! FIRE AWAY!
FIRE AWAY, SAYS THE MAN... AS IF THIS WAS A TARGET PRACTICE!
THESE MEASURES ARE FOR YOUR PROTECTION, MEN... THEY'RE MEANT TO IMMUNIZE YOU AGAINST THE ENEMY'S CHIEF WEAPON...
--MIND WAVES-- WE'VE HEARD ALL THAT!
LET'S RELAX, FALCON. I'M AS TENSE AS YOU ARE... BUT WE'VE GOT TO TAKE THESE TESTS IF WE'RE TO TACKLE THIS ASSIGNMENT!
I DON'T DIG THESE GADGETS! DON'T LIKE THIS HEADGEAR: IT WON'T HELP WHEN THEY HIT US WITH THE "WHOPPER!"
THEN--!
CIRCUITS OPEN! CHARGE RELEASED!
CRACKLE
MIGHTY ENERGY BOLTS ARE HURLED AT CAP AND THE FALCON... THEY SURGE WITH THE STRANGE ELEMENTS THAT COURSE THROUGH THE HUMAN MIND... LIKE THE LIGHTNING OF THE GODS. THEIR BRILLIANCE HIDES THE FACES OF THE TARGETS...

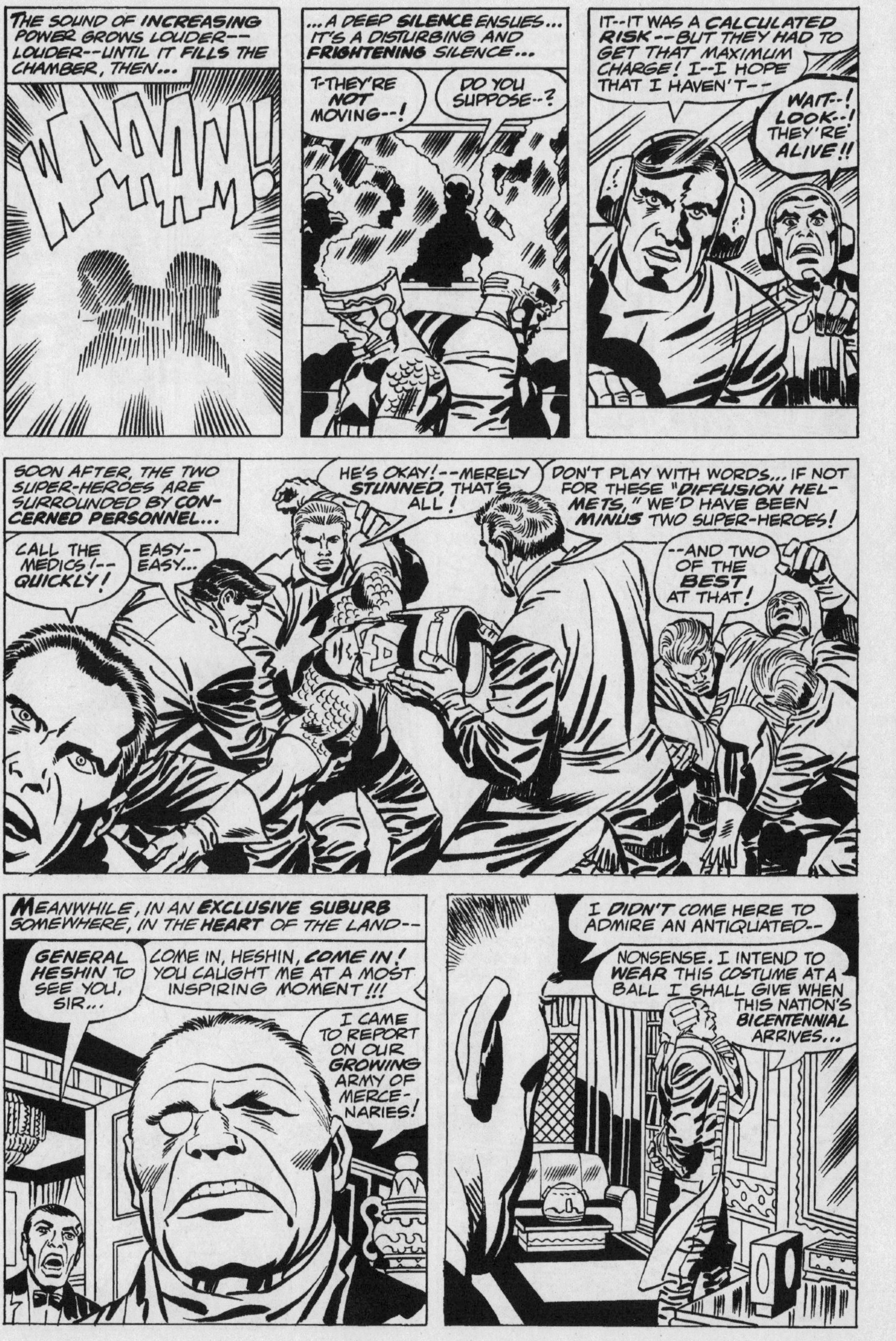
THE SOUND OF INCREASING POWER GROWS LOUDER-- LOUDER--UNTIL IT FILLS THE CHAMBER, THEN...
WHAAAM!
...A DEEP SILENCE ENSUES... IT'S A DISTURBING AND FRIGHTENING SILENCE...
T-THEY'RE NOT MOVING--!
DO YOU SUPPOSE--?
IT--IT WAS A CALCULATED RISK--BUT THEY HAD TO GET THAT MAXIMUM CHARGE! I--I HOPE THAT I HAVEN'T--
WAIT--! LOOK--! THEY'RE ALIVE!!
SOON AFTER, THE TWO SUPER-HEROES ARE SURROUNDED BY CONCERNED PERSONNEL...
CALL THE MEDICS!--QUICKLY!
EASY--EASY...
HE'S OKAY!--MERELY STUNNED, THAT'S ALL!
DON'T PLAY WITH WORDS... IF NOT FOR THESE "DIFFUSION HELMETS," WE'D HAVE BEEN MINUS TWO SUPER-HEROES!
--AND TWO OF THE BEST AT THAT!
MEANWHILE, IN AN EXCLUSIVE SUBURB SOMEWHERE, IN THE HEART OF THE LAND--
GENERAL HESHIN TO SEE YOU, SIR...
COME IN, HESHIN, COME IN! YOU CAUGHT ME AT A MOST INSPIRING MOMENT!!!
I CAME TO REPORT ON OUR GROWING ARMY OF MERCENARIES!
I DIDN'T COME HERE TO ADMIRE AN ANTIQUATED--
NONSENSE. I INTEND TO WEAR THIS COSTUME AT A BALL I SHALL GIVE WHEN THIS NATION'S BICENTENNIAL ARRIVES...

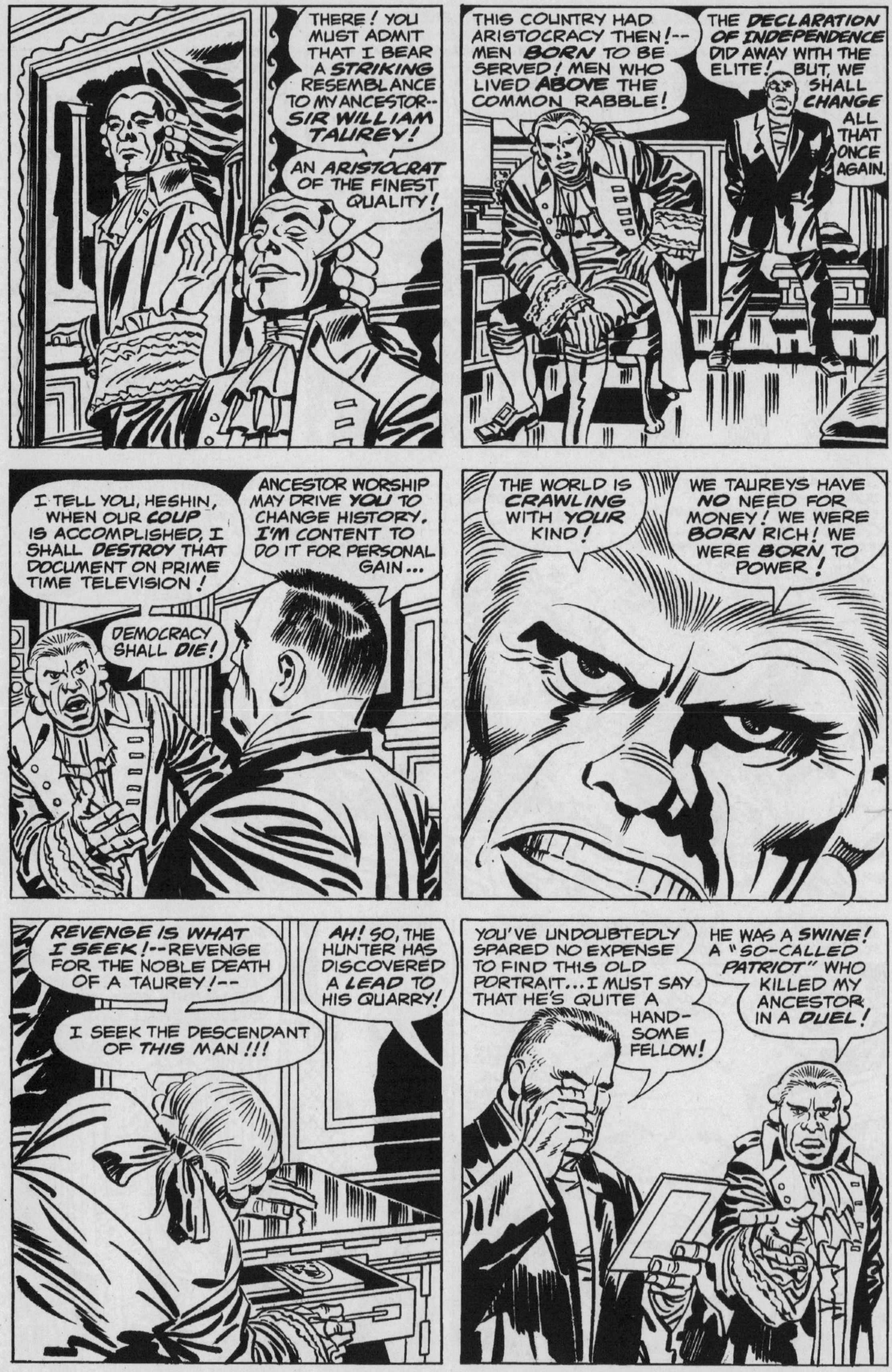
THERE! YOU MUST ADMIT THAT I BEAR A STRIKING RESEMBLANCE TO MY ANCESTOR-- SIR WILLIAM TAUREY!
AN ARISTOCRAT OF THE FINEST QUALITY!
THIS COUNTRY HAD ARISTOCRACY THEN!-- MEN BORN TO BE SERVED! MEN WHO LIVED ABOVE THE COMMON RABBLE!
THE DECLARATION OF INDEPENDENCE DID AWAY WITH THE ELITE! BUT, WE SHALL CHANGE ALL THAT ONCE AGAIN.
I TELL YOU, HESHIN, WHEN OUR COUP IS ACCOMPLISHED, I SHALL DESTROY THAT DOCUMENT ON PRIME TIME TELEVISION!
DEMOCRACY SHALL DIE!
ANCESTOR WORSHIP MAY DRIVE YOU TO CHANGE HISTORY. I'M CONTENT TO DO IT FOR PERSONAL GAIN...
THE WORLD IS CRAWLING WITH YOUR KIND!
WE TAUREYS HAVE NO NEED FOR MONEY! WE WERE BORN RICH! WE WERE BORN, TO POWER!
REVENGE IS WHAT I SEEK!--REVENGE FOR THE NOBLE DEATH OF A TAUREY!--
I SEEK THE DESCENDANT OF THIS MAN!!!
AH! SO, THE HUNTER HAS DISCOVERED A LEAD TO HIS QUARRY!
YOU'VE UNDOUBTEDLY SPARED NO EXPENSE TO FIND THIS OLD PORTRAIT...I MUST SAY THAT HE'S QUITE A HAND-SOME FELLOW!
HE WAS A SWINE! A "SO-CALLED PATRIOT" WHO KILLED MY ANCESTOR IN A DUEL!

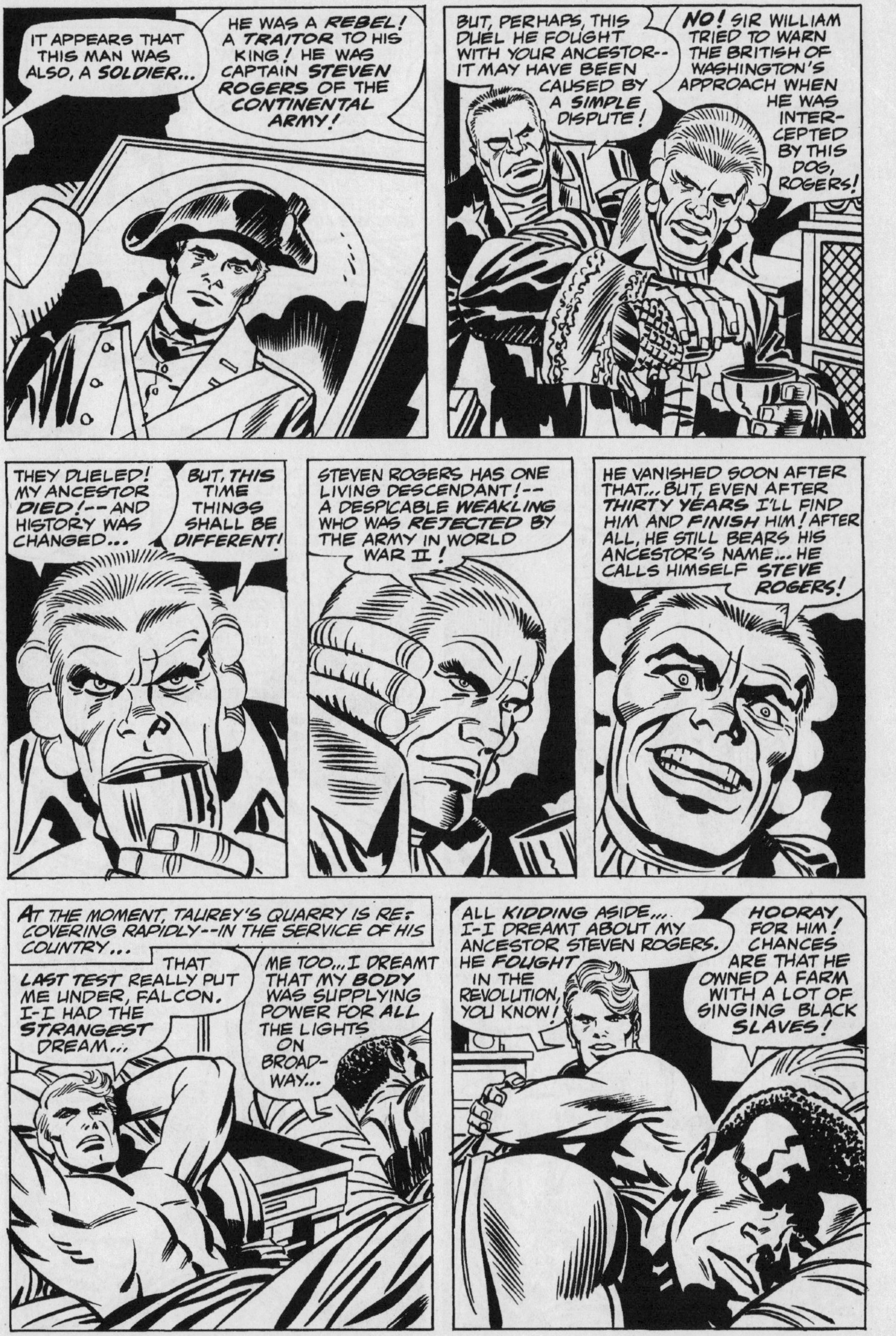
IT APPEARS THAT THIS MAN WAS ALSO, A SOLDIER...
HE WAS A REBEL! A TRAITOR TO HIS KING! HE WAS CAPTAIN STEVEN ROGERS OF THE CONTINENTAL ARMY!
BUT, PERHAPS, THIS DUEL HE FOUGHT WITH YOUR ANCESTOR-- IT MAY HAVE BEEN CAUSED BY A SIMPLE DISPUTE!
NO! SIR WILLIAM TRIED TO WARN THE BRITISH OF WASHINGTON'S APPROACH WHEN HE WAS INTERCEPTED BY THIS DOG, ROGERS!
THEY DUELED! MY ANCESTOR DIED!--AND HISTORY WAS CHANGED...
BUT, THIS TIME THINGS SHALL BE DIFFERENT!
STEVEN ROGERS HAS ONE LIVING DESCENDANT!-- A DESPICABLE WEAKLING WHO WAS REJECTED BY THE ARMY IN WORLD WAR II!
HE VANISHED SOON AFTER THAT... BUT, EVEN AFTER THIRTY YEARS I'LL FIND HIM AND FINISH HIM! AFTER ALL, HE STILL BEARS HIS ANCESTOR'S NAME... HE CALLS HIMSELF STEVE ROGERS!
AT THE MOMENT, TAUREY'S QUARRY IS RECOVERING RAPIDLY--IN THE SERVICE OF HIS COUNTRY...
THAT LAST TEST REALLY PUT ME UNDER, FALCON. I-I HAD THE STRANGEST DREAM...
ME TOO... I DREAMT THAT MY BODY WAS SUPPLYING POWER FOR ALL THE LIGHTS ON BROADWAY...
ALL KIDDING ASIDE... I-I DREAMT ABOUT MY ANCESTOR STEVEN ROGERS. HE FOUGHT IN THE REVOLUTION, YOU KNOW!
HOORAY FOR HIM! CHANCES ARE THAT HE OWNED A FARM WITH A LOT OF SINGING BLACK SLAVES!

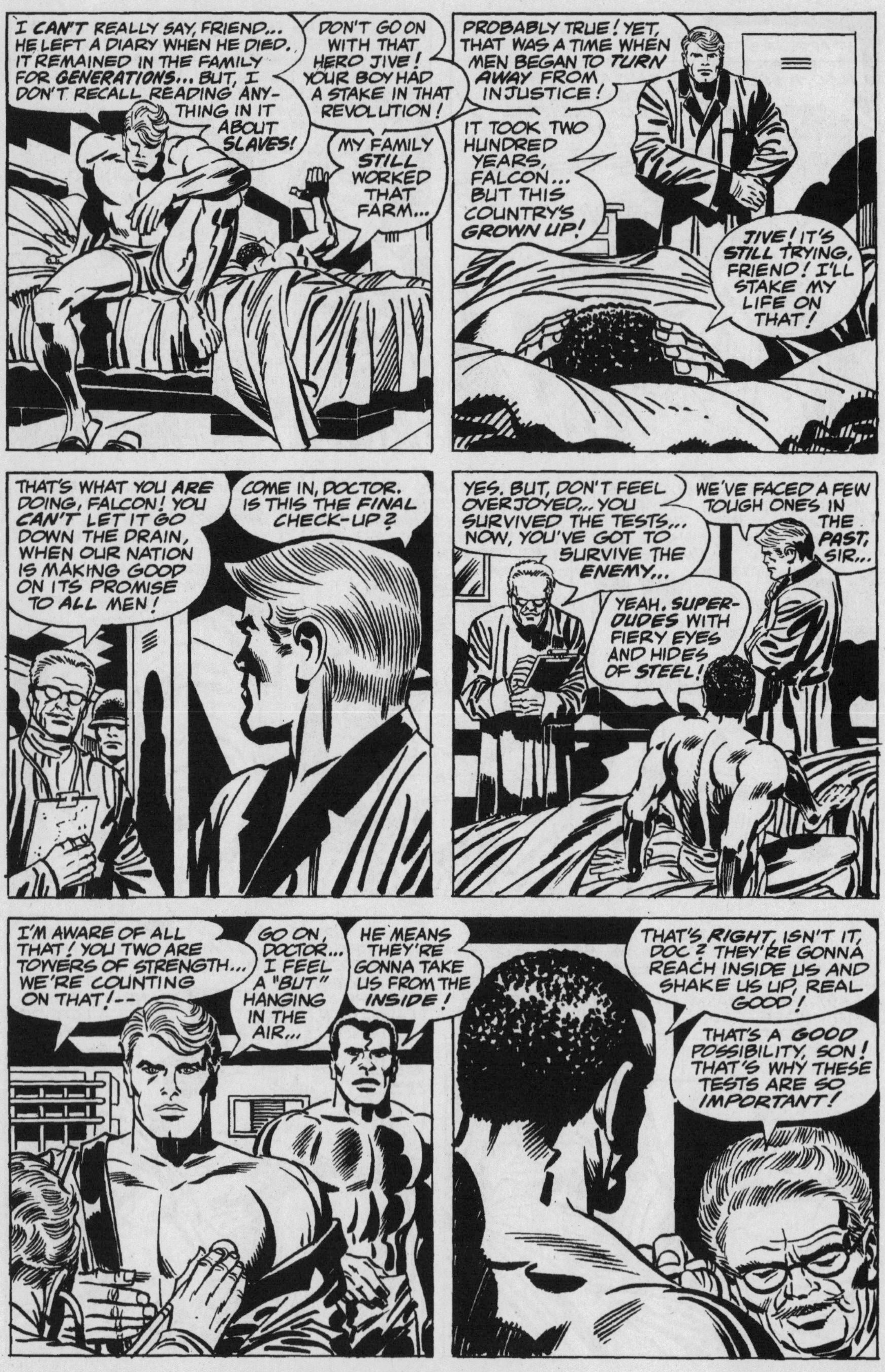
I CAN'T REALLY SAY, FRIEND... HE LEFT A DIARY WHEN HE DIED. IT REMAINED IN THE FAMILY FOR GENERATIONS... BUT, I DON'T RECALL READING ANYTHING IN IT ABOUT SLAVES!
DON'T GO ON WITH THAT HERO JIVE! YOUR BOY HAD A STAKE IN THAT REVOLUTION!
MY FAMILY STILL WORKED THAT FARM...
PROBABLY TRUE! YET, THAT WAS A TIME WHEN MEN BEGAN TO TURN AWAY FROM INJUSTICE!
IT TOOK TWO HUNDRED YEARS, FALCON... BUT THIS COUNTRY'S GROWN UP!
JIVE! IT'S STILL TRYING, FRIEND! I'LL STAKE MY LIFE ON THAT!
THAT'S WHAT YOU ARE DOING, FALCON! YOU CAN'T LET IT GO DOWN THE DRAIN, WHEN OUR NATION IS MAKING GOOD ON ITS PROMISE TO ALL MEN!
COME IN, DOCTOR. IS THIS THE FINAL CHECK-UP?
YES. BUT, DON'T FEEL OVERJOYED... YOU SURVIVED THE TESTS... NOW, YOU'VE GOT TO SURVIVE THE ENEMY...
WE'VE FACED A FEW TOUGH ONES IN THE PAST, SIR...
YEAH. SUPER-DUDES WITH FIERY EYES AND HIDES OF STEEL!
I'M AWARE OF ALL THAT! YOU TWO ARE TOWERS OF STRENGTH... WE'RE COUNTING ON THAT!--
GO ON, DOCTOR... I FEEL A "BUT" HANGING IN THE AIR...
HE MEANS THEY'RE GONNA TAKE US FROM THE INSIDE!
THAT'S RIGHT, ISN'T IT, DOC? THEY'RE GONNA REACH INSIDE US AND SHAKE US UP, REAL GOOD!
THAT'S A GOOD POSSIBILITY, SON! THAT'S WHY THESE TESTS ARE SO IMPORTANT!

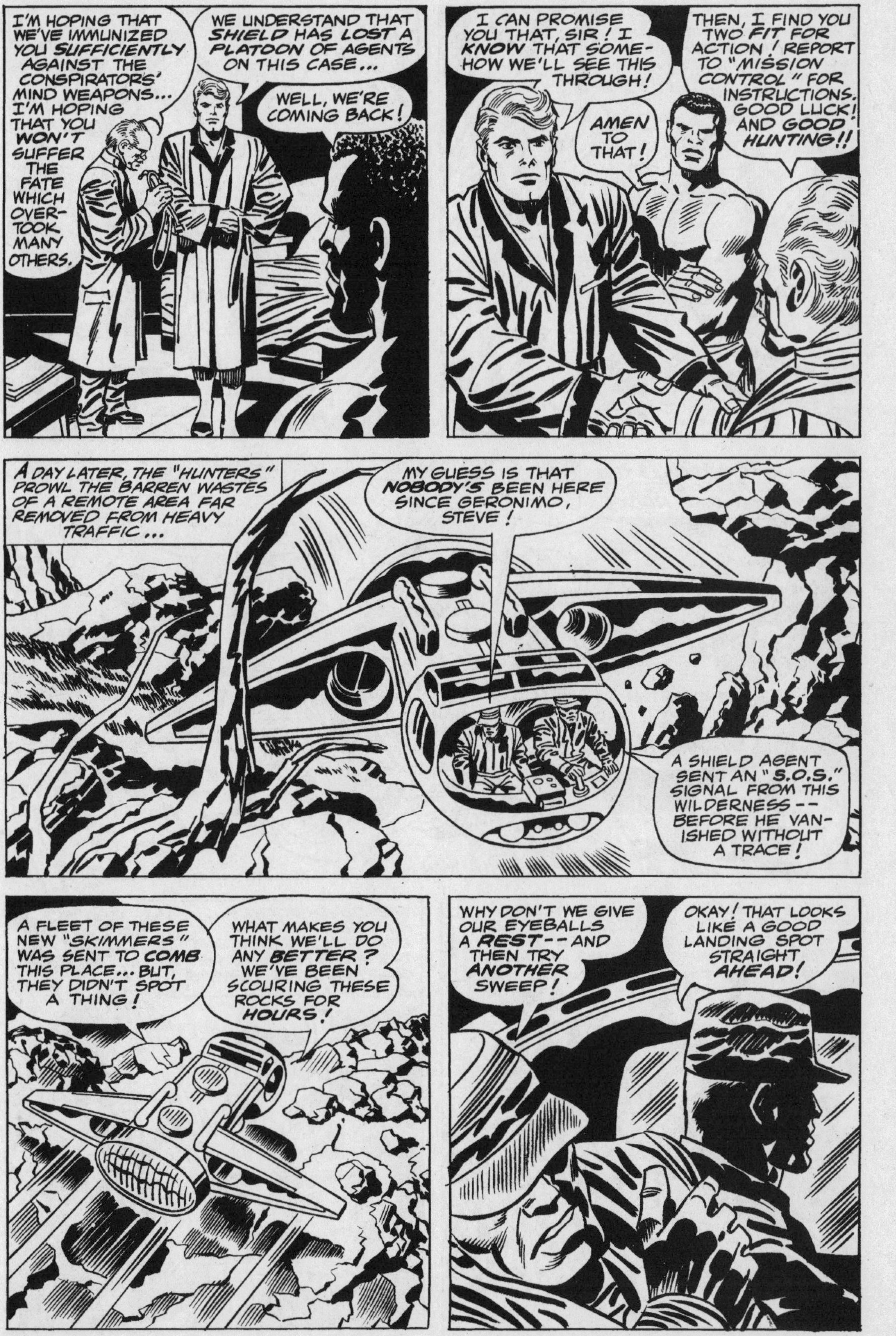
I'M HOPING THAT WE'VE IMMUNIZED YOU SUFFICIENTLY AGAINST THE CONSPIRATORS' MIND WEAPONS... I'M HOPING THAT YOU WON'T SUFFER THE FATE WHICH OVERTOOK MANY OTHERS.
WE UNDERSTAND THAT SHIELD HAS LOST A PLATOON OF AGENTS ON THIS CASE...
WELL, WE'RE COMING BACK!
I CAN PROMISE YOU THAT, SIR! I KNOW THAT SOMEHOW WE'LL SEE THIS THROUGH!
AMEN TO THAT!
THEN, I FIND YOU TWO FIT FOR ACTION! REPORT TO "MISSION CONTROL" FOR INSTRUCTIONS. GOOD LUCK! AND GOOD HUNTING!!
A DAY LATER, THE "HUNTERS" PROWL THE BARREN WASTES OF A REMOTE AREA FAR REMOVED FROM HEAVY TRAFFIC...
MY GUESS IS THAT NOBODY'S BEEN HERE SINCE GERONIMO, STEVE!
A SHIELD AGENT SENT AN "S.O.S." SIGNAL FROM THIS WILDERNESS-- BEFORE HE VANISHED WITHOUT A TRACE!
A FLEET OF THESE NEW "SKIMMERS" WAS SENT TO COMB THIS PLACE... BUT, THEY DIDN'T SPOT A THING!
WHAT MAKES YOU THINK WE'LL DO ANY BETTER? WE'VE BEEN SCOURING THESE ROCKS FOR HOURS!
WHY DON'T WE GIVE OUR EYEBALLS A REST-- AND THEN TRY ANOTHER SWEEP!
OKAY! THAT LOOKS LIKE A GOOD LANDING SPOT STRAIGHT AHEAD!

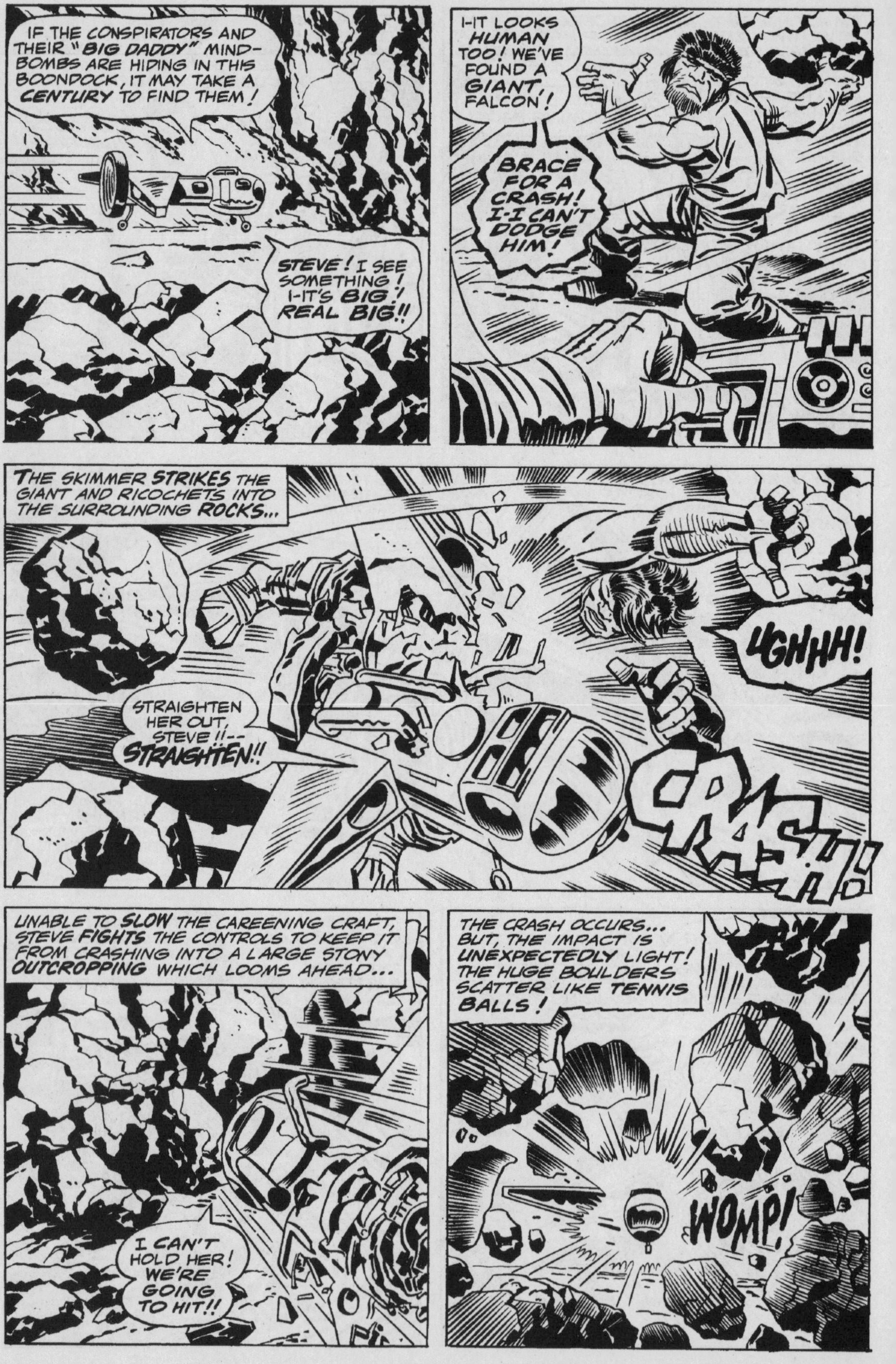
IF THE CONSPIRATORS AND THEIR "BIG DADDY" MIND-BOMBS ARE HIDING IN THIS BOONDOCK, IT MAY TAKE A CENTURY TO FIND THEM!
STEVE! I SEE SOMETHING! I-IT'S BIG! REAL BIG!!
I-IT LOOKS HUMAN TOO! WE'VE FOUND A GIANT, FALCON!
BRACE FOR A CRASH! I-I CAN'T DODGE HIM!
THE SKIMMER STRIKES THE GIANT AND RICOCHETS INTO THE SURROUNDING ROCKS...
UGHHH!
STRAIGHTEN HER OUT, STEVE!!-- STRAIGHTEN!!
CRASH!
UNABLE TO SLOW THE CAREENING CRAFT, STEVE FIGHTS THE CONTROLS TO KEEP IT FROM CRASHING INTO A LARGE STONY OUTCROPPING WHICH LOOMS AHEAD...
I CAN'T HOLD HER! WE'RE GOING TO HIT!!
THE CRASH OCCURS... BUT, THE IMPACT IS UNEXPECTEDLY LIGHT! THE HUGE BOULDERS SCATTER LIKE TENNIS BALLS!
WOMP!

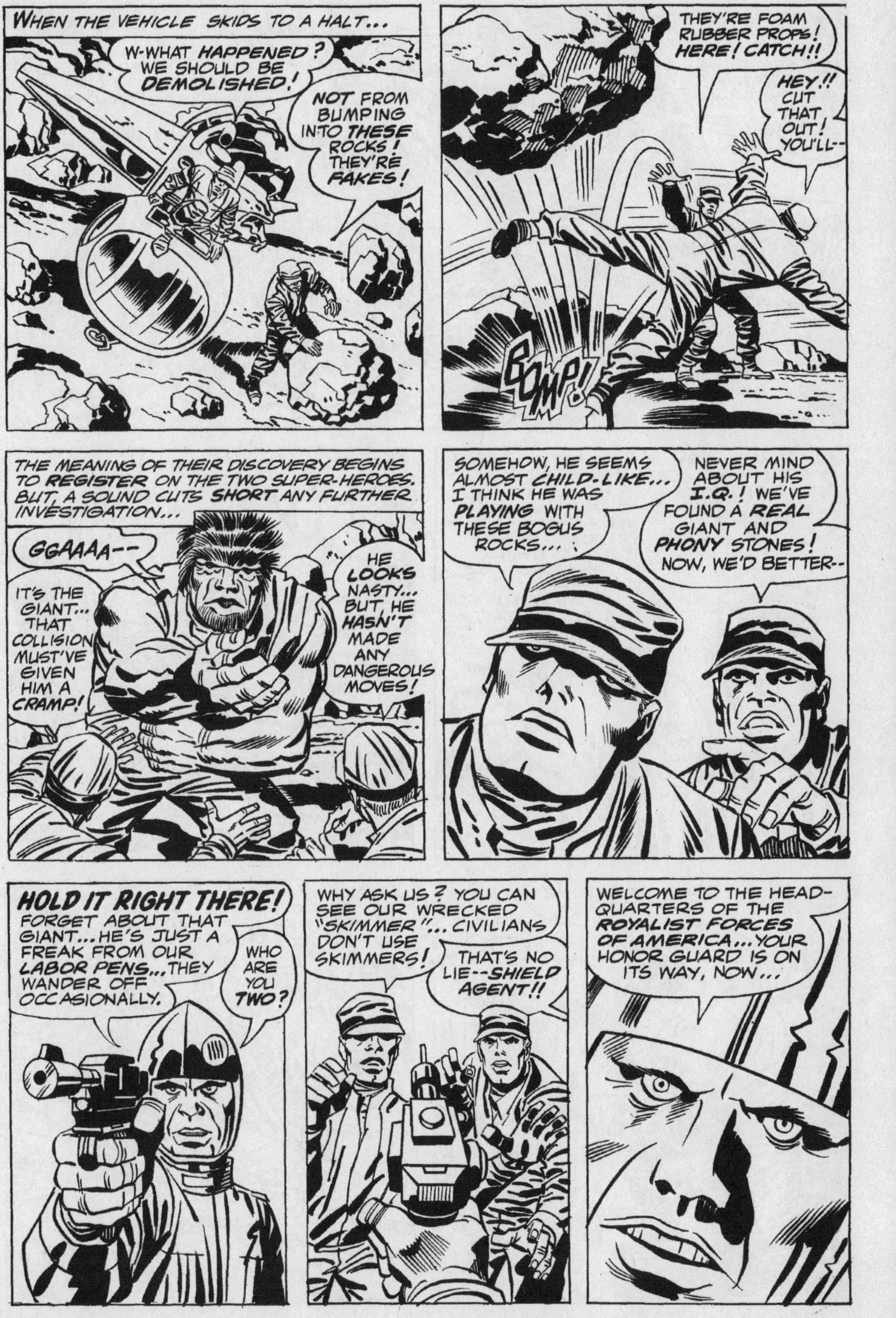
WHEN THE VEHICLE SKIDS TO A HALT...
W-WHAT HAPPENED? WE SHOULD BE DEMOLISHED!
NOT FROM BUMPING INTO THESE ROCKS! THEY'RE FAKES!
THEY'RE FOAM RUBBER PROPS! HERE! CATCH!!
HEY!! CUT THAT OUT! YOU'LL--
BOMP!
THE MEANING OF THEIR DISCOVERY BEGINS TO REGISTER ON THE TWO SUPER-HEROES. BUT, A SOUND CUTS SHORT ANY FURTHER INVESTIGATION...
GGAAAA--
IT'S THE GIANT... THAT COLLISION MUST'VE GIVEN HIM A CRAMP!
HE LOOKS NASTY... BUT, HE HASN'T MADE ANY DANGEROUS MOVES!
SOMEHOW, HE SEEMS ALMOST CHILD-LIKE... I THINK HE WAS PLAYING WITH THESE BOGUS ROCKS...
NEVER MIND ABOUT HIS I.Q.! WE'VE FOUND A REAL GIANT AND PHONY STONES! NOW, WE'D BETTER--
HOLD IT RIGHT THERE! FORGET ABOUT THAT GIANT... HE'S JUST A FREAK FROM OUR LABOR PENS... THEY WANDER OFF OCCASIONALLY.
WHO ARE YOU TWO?
WHY ASK US? YOU CAN SEE OUR WRECKED "SKIMMER"... CIVILIANS DON'T USE SKIMMERS!
THAT'S NO LIE--SHIELD AGENT!!
WELCOME TO THE HEAD-QUARTERS OF THE ROYALIST FORCES OF AMERICA... YOUR HONOR GUARD IS ON ITS WAY, NOW...

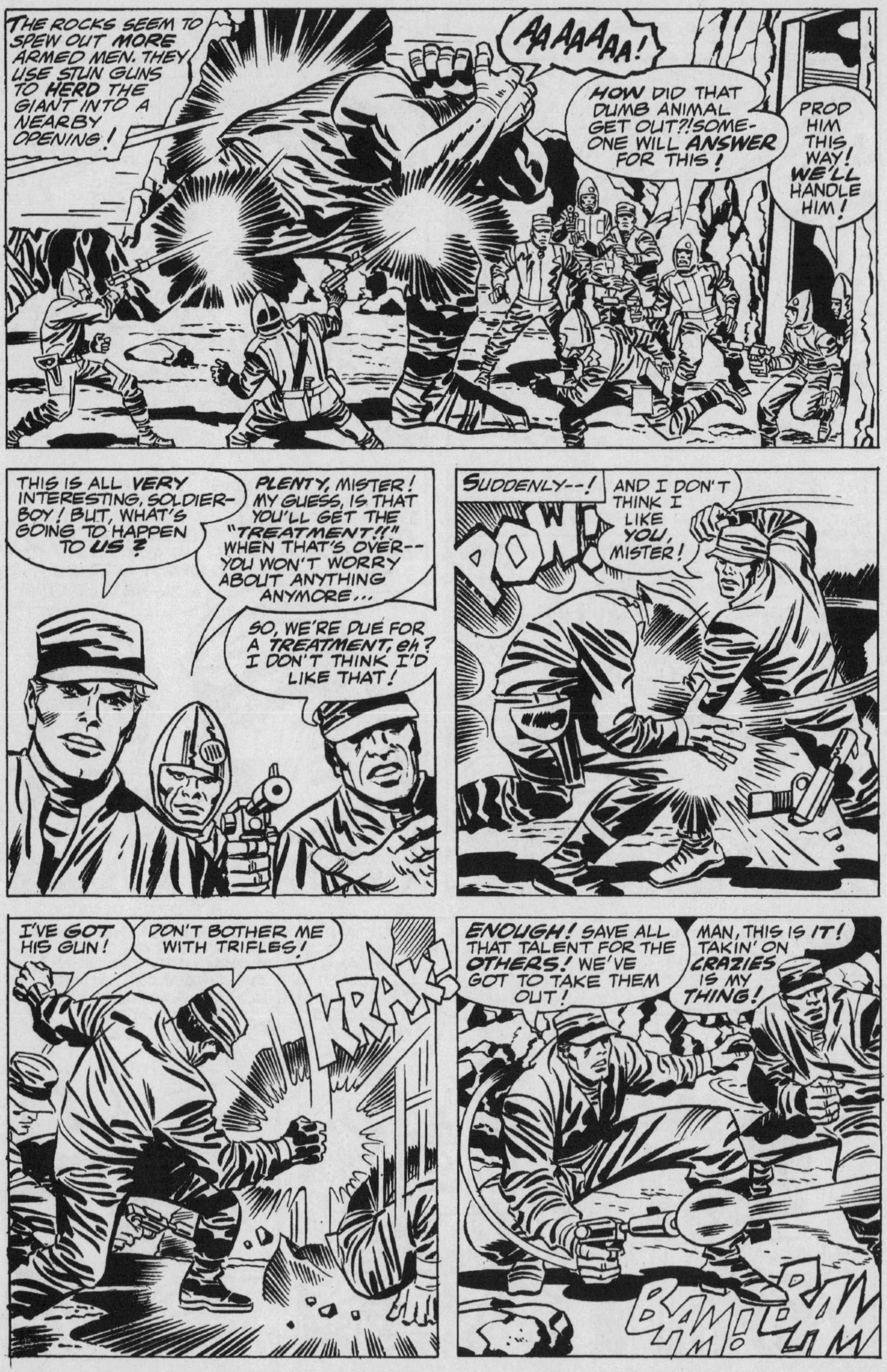
THE ROCKS SEEM TO SPEW OUT MORE ARMED MEN. THEY USE STUN GUNS TO HERD THE GIANT INTO A NEARBY OPENING!
AAAAAAA!
HOW DID THAT DUMB ANIMAL GET OUT?! SOMEONE WILL ANSWER FOR THIS!
PROD HIM THIS WAY! WE'LL HANDLE HIM!
THIS IS ALL VERY INTERESTING, SOLDIER-BOY! BUT, WHAT'S GOING TO HAPPEN TO US?
PLENTY, MISTER! MY GUESS, IS THAT YOU'LL GET THE "TREATMENT!!" WHEN THAT'S OVER-- YOU WON'T WORRY ABOUT ANYTHING ANYMORE...
SO, WE'RE DUE FOR A TREATMENT, eh? I DON'T THINK I'D LIKE THAT!
SUDDENLY--!
AND I DON'T THINK I LIKE YOU, MISTER!
POW!
I'VE GOT HIS GUN!
DON'T BOTHER ME WITH TRIFLES!
KRAK!
ENOUGH! SAVE ALL THAT TALENT FOR THE OTHERS! WE'VE GOT TO TAKE THEM OUT!
MAN, THIS IS IT! TAKIN' ON CRAZIES IS MY THING!
BAM! BAM!

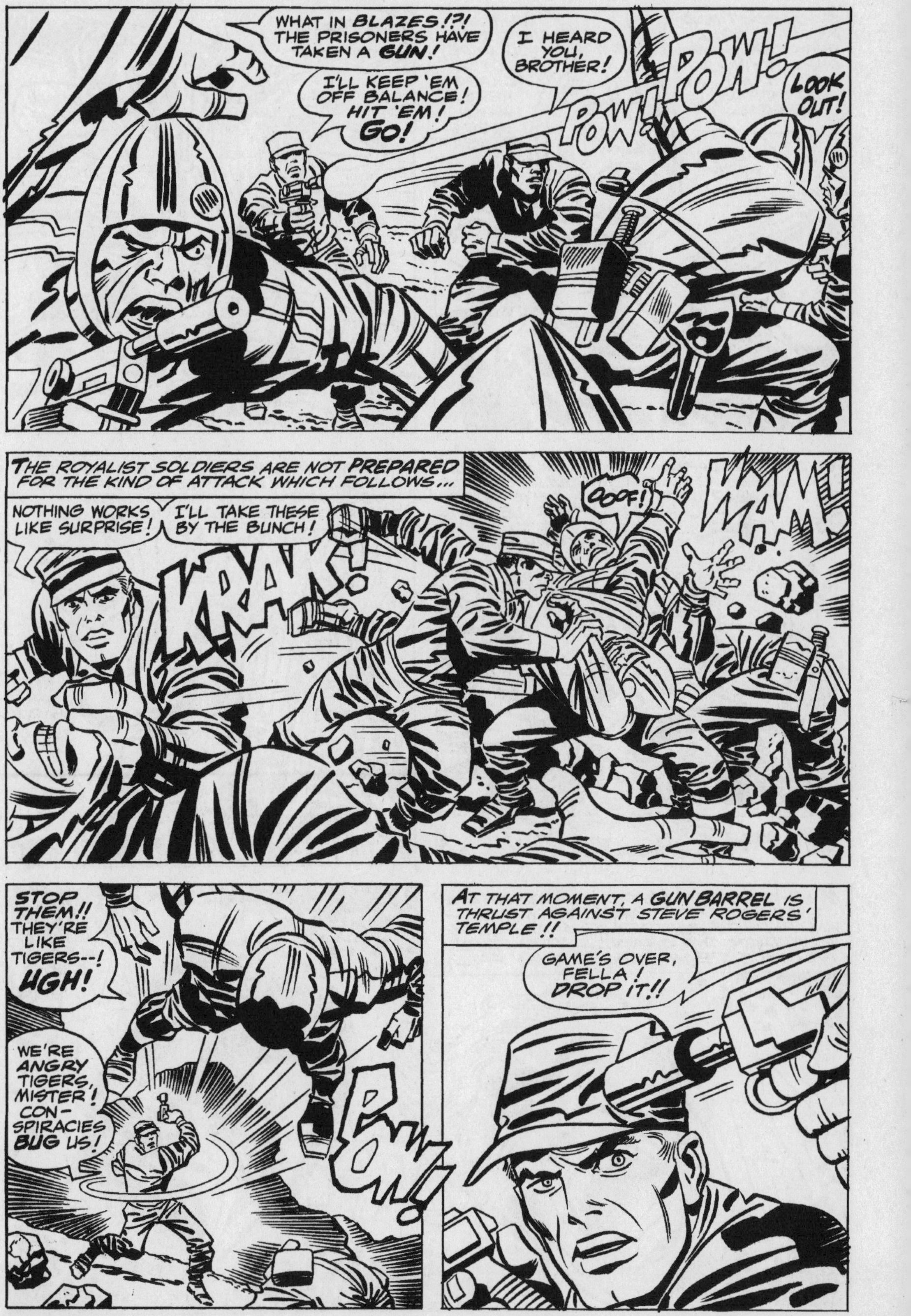

WHAT IN BLAZES!?! THE PRISONERS HAVE TAKEN A GUN!
I'LL KEEP 'EM OFF BALANCE! HIT 'EM! GO!
I HEARD YOU, BROTHER!
POW! POW!
LOOK OUT!
THE ROYALIST SOLDIERS ARE NOT PREPARED FOR THE KIND OF ATTACK WHICH FOLLOWS...
NOTHING WORKS LIKE SURPRISE!
I'LL TAKE THESE BY THE BUNCH!
KRAK!
OOOF!
WAM!
STOP THEM!! THEY'RE LIKE TIGERS--! UGH!
WE'RE ANGRY TIGERS, MISTER! CON-SPIRACIES BUG US!
POW!
AT THAT MOMENT, A GUN BARREL IS THRUST AGAINST STEVE ROGERS' TEMPLE!!
GAME'S OVER, FELLA! DROP IT!!

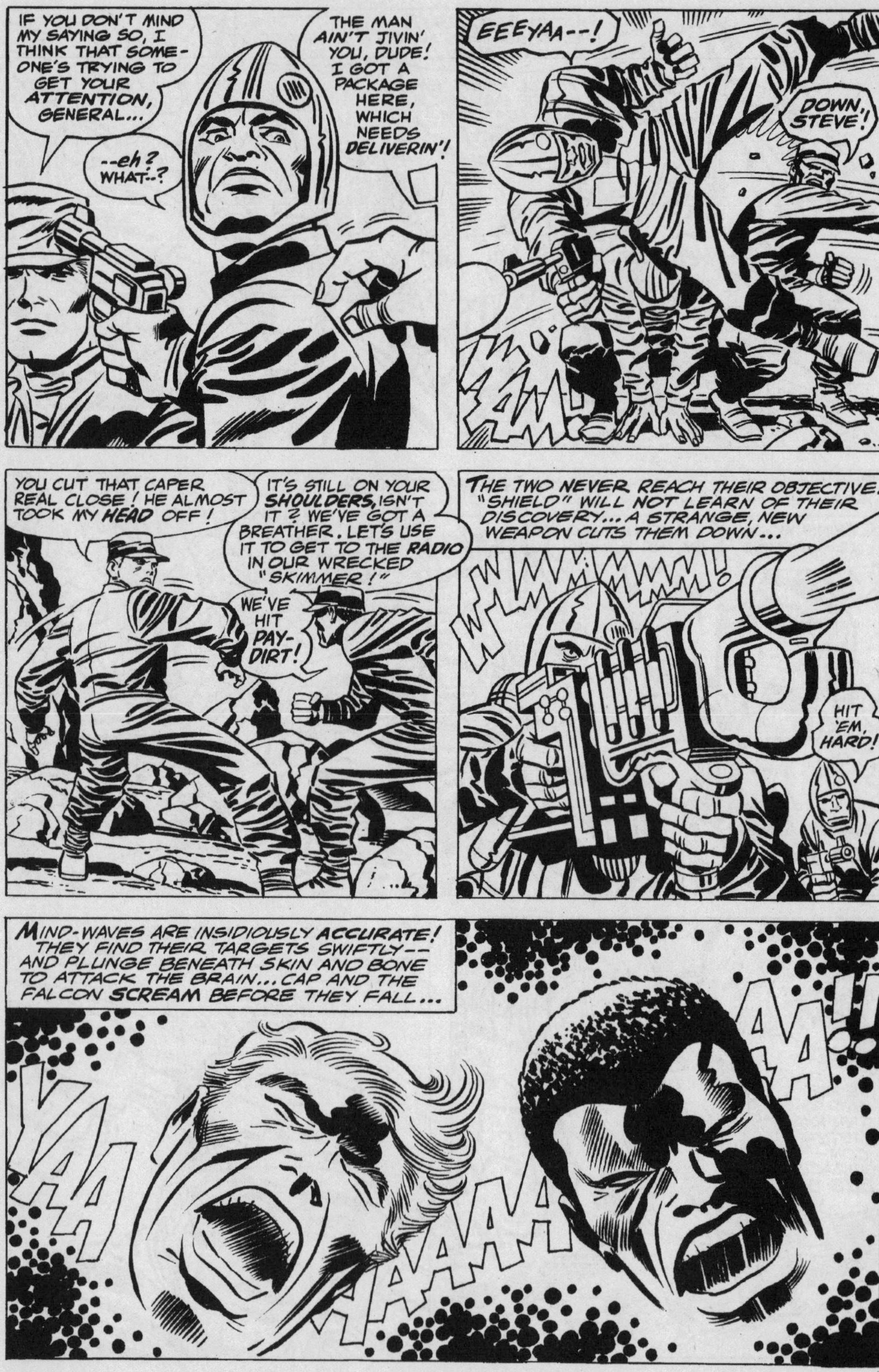
IF YOU DON'T MIND MY SAYING SO, I THINK THAT SOME-ONE'S TRYING TO GET YOUR ATTENTION, GENERAL...
--eh? WHAT--?
THE MAN AIN'T JIVIN' YOU, DUDE! I GOT A PACKAGE HERE, WHICH NEEDS DELIVERIN'!
EEEYAA--!
DOWN, STEVE!
YOU CUT THAT CAPER REAL CLOSE! HE ALMOST TOOK MY HEAD OFF!
IT'S STILL ON YOUR SHOULDERS, ISN'T IT? WE'VE GOT A BREATHER. LET'S USE IT TO GET TO THE RADIO IN OUR WRECKED "SKIMMER!"
WE'VE HIT PAY-DIRT!
THE TWO NEVER REACH THEIR OBJECTIVE. "SHIELD" WILL NOT LEARN OF THEIR DISCOVERY... A STRANGE, NEW WEAPON CUTS THEM DOWN...
HIT 'EM, HARD!
MIND-WAVES ARE INSIDIOUSLY ACCURATE! THEY FIND THEIR TARGETS SWIFTLY-- AND PLUNGE BENEATH SKIN AND BONE TO ATTACK THE BRAIN... CAP AND THE FALCON SCREAM BEFORE THEY FALL...
YAAAAAAAAA
AA!!

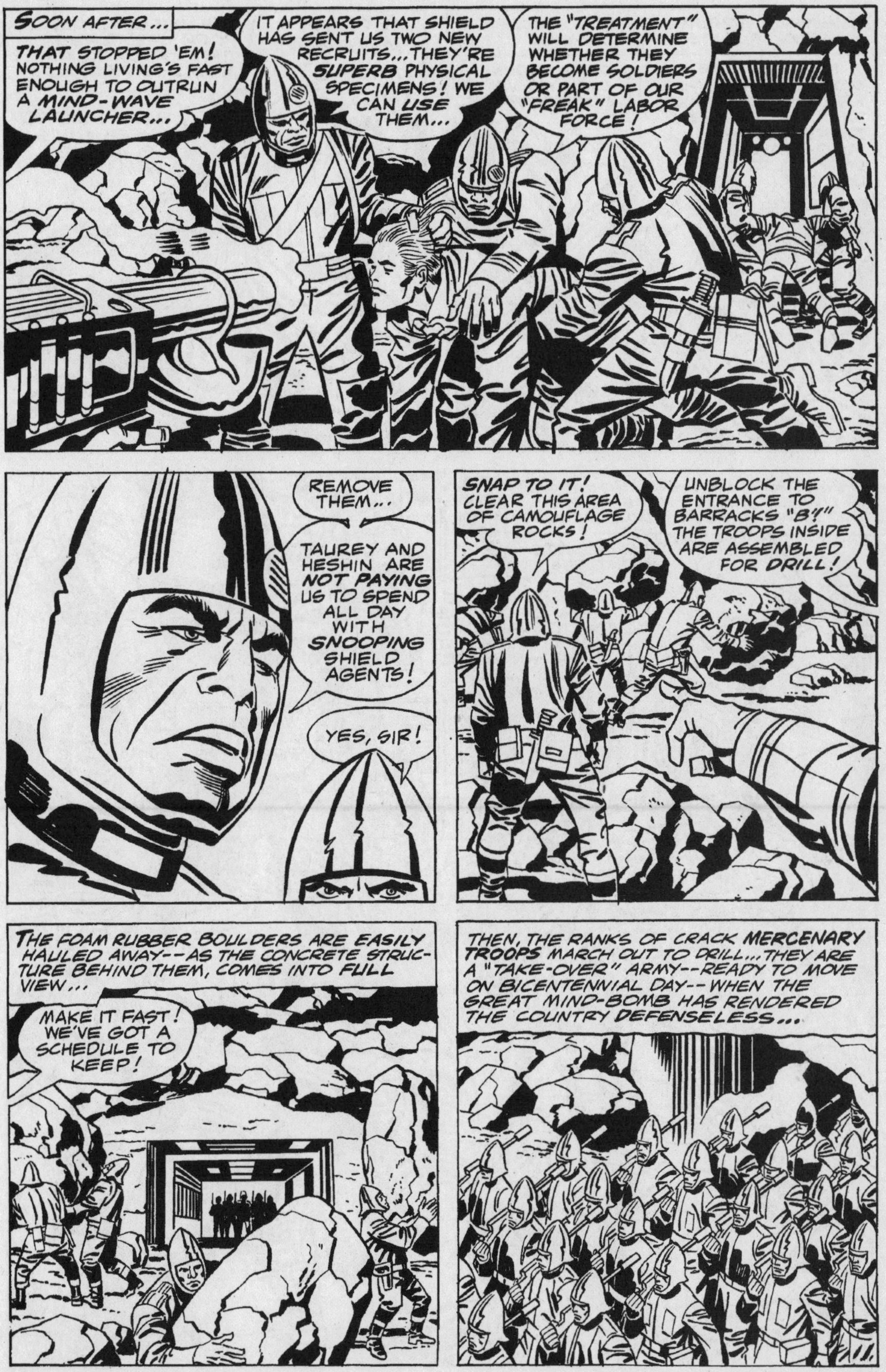
SOON AFTER...
THAT STOPPED 'EM! NOTHING LIVING'S FAST ENOUGH TO OUTRUN A MIND-WAVE LAUNCHER...
IT APPEARS THAT SHIELD HAS SENT US TWO NEW RECRUITS... THEY'RE SUPERB PHYSICAL SPECIMENS! WE CAN USE THEM...
THE "TREATMENT" WILL DETERMINE WHETHER THEY BECOME SOLDIERS OR PART OF OUR "FREAK" LABOR FORCE!
REMOVE THEM...
TAUREY AND HESHIN ARE NOT PAYING US TO SPEND ALL DAY WITH SNOOPING SHIELD AGENTS!
YES, SIR!
SNAP TO IT! CLEAR THIS AREA OF CAMOUFLAGE ROCKS!
UNBLOCK THE ENTRANCE TO BARRACKS "B"!" THE TROOPS INSIDE ARE ASSEMBLED FOR DRILL!
THE FOAM RUBBER BOULDERS ARE EASILY HAULED AWAY--AS THE CONCRETE STRUCTURE BEHIND THEM, COMES INTO FULL VIEW...
MAKE IT FAST! WE'VE GOT A SCHEDULE TO KEEP!
THEN, THE RANKS OF CRACK MERCENARY TROOPS MARCH OUT TO DRILL... THEY ARE A "TAKE-OVER" ARMY--READY TO MOVE ON BICENTENNIAL DAY--WHEN THE GREAT MIND-BOMB HAS RENDERED THE COUNTRY DEFENSELESS...

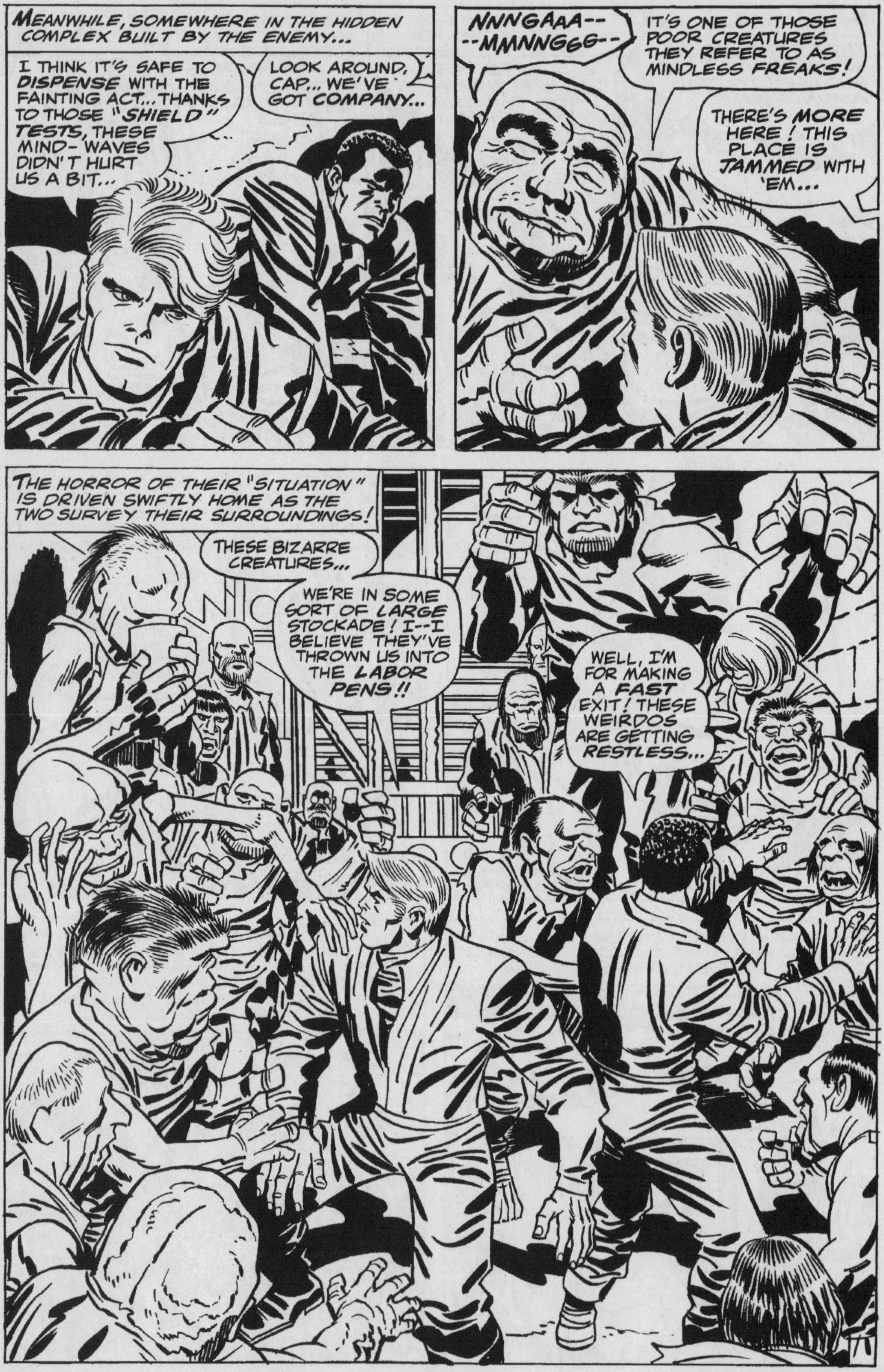
MEANWHILE, SOMEWHERE IN THE HIDDEN COMPLEX BUILT BY THE ENEMY...
I THINK IT'S SAFE TO DISPENSE WITH THE FAINTING ACT... THANKS TO THOSE "SHIELD" TESTS, THESE MIND-WAVES DIDN'T HURT US A BIT...
LOOK AROUND, CAP... WE'VE GOT COMPANY...
NNNGAAA-- --MMNNGGG--
IT'S ONE OF THOSE POOR CREATURES THEY REFER TO AS MINDLESS FREAKS!
THERE'S MORE HERE! THIS PLACE IS JAMMED WITH 'EM...
THE HORROR OF THEIR "SITUATION" IS DRIVEN SWIFTLY HOME AS THE TWO SURVEY THEIR SURROUNDINGS!
THESE BIZARRE CREATURES...
WE'RE IN SOME SORT OF LARGE STOCKADE! I--I BELIEVE THEY'VE THROWN US INTO THE LABOR PENS!!
WELL, I'M FOR MAKING A FAST EXIT! THESE WEIRDOS ARE GETTING RESTLESS...

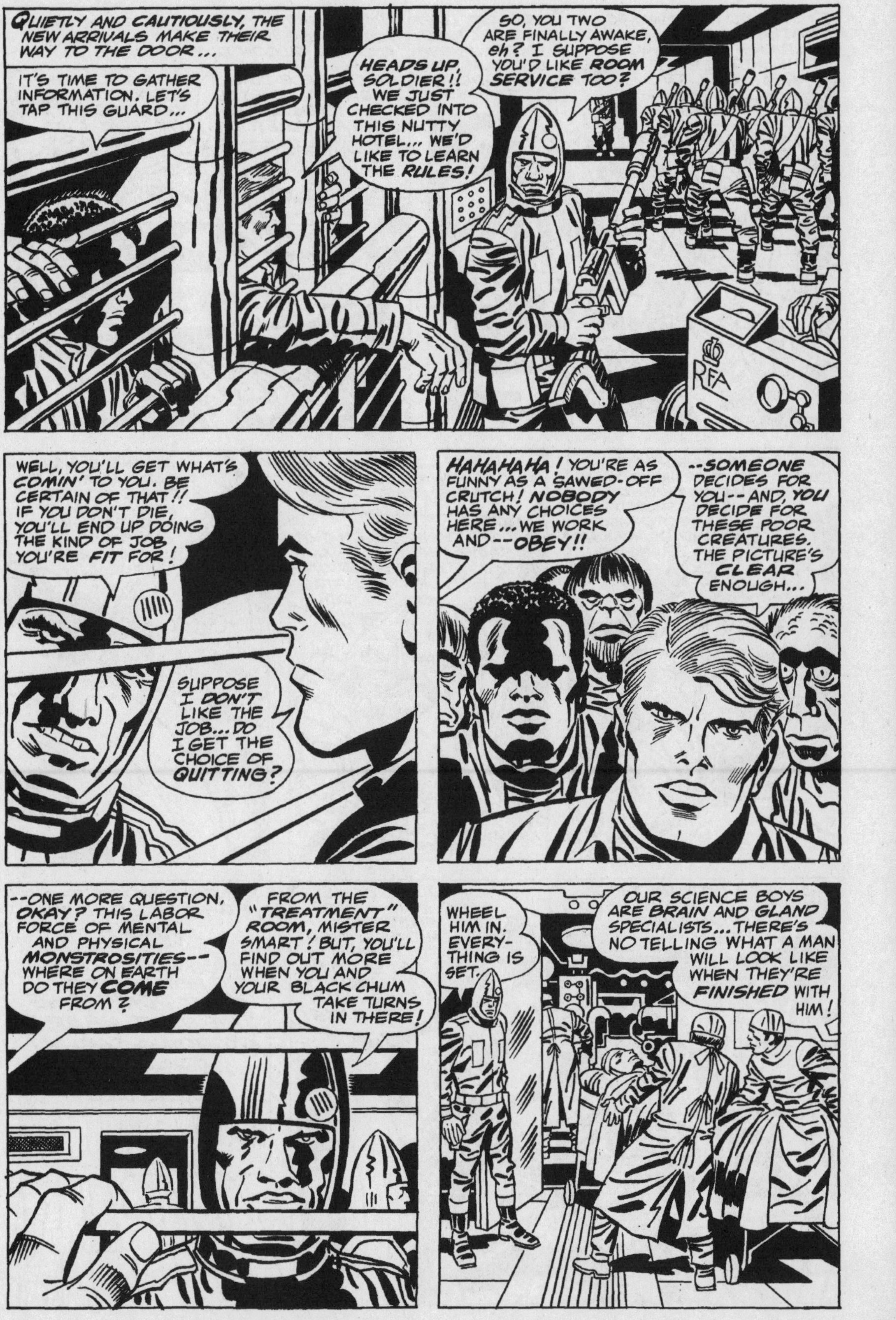
QUIETLY AND CAUTIOUSLY, THE NEW ARRIVALS MAKE THEIR WAY TO THE DOOR...
IT'S TIME TO GATHER INFORMATION. LET'S TAP THIS GUARD...
HEADS UP, SOLDIER!! WE JUST CHECKED INTO THIS NUTTY HOTEL... WE'D LIKE TO LEARN THE RULES!
SO, YOU TWO ARE FINALLY AWAKE, eh? I SUPPOSE YOU'D LIKE ROOM SERVICE TOO?
RFA
WELL, YOU'LL GET WHAT'S COMIN' TO YOU. BE CERTAIN OF THAT!! IF YOU DON'T DIE, YOU'LL END UP DOING THE KIND OF JOB YOU'RE FIT FOR!
SUPPOSE I DON'T LIKE THE JOB... DO I GET THE CHOICE OF QUITTING?
HAHAHAHA! YOU'RE AS FUNNY AS A SAWED-OFF CRUTCH! NOBODY HAS ANY CHOICES HERE... WE WORK AND--OBEY!!
--SOMEONE DECIDES FOR YOU--AND, YOU DECIDE FOR THESE POOR CREATURES. THE PICTURE'S CLEAR ENOUGH...
--ONE MORE QUESTION, OKAY? THIS LABOR FORCE OF MENTAL AND PHYSICAL MONSTROSITIES--WHERE ON EARTH DO THEY COME FROM?
FROM THE "TREATMENT" ROOM, MISTER SMART! BUT, YOU'LL FIND OUT MORE WHEN YOU AND YOUR BLACK CHUM TAKE TURNS IN THERE!
WHEEL HIM IN. EVERYTHING IS SET.
OUR SCIENCE BOYS ARE BRAIN AND GLAND SPECIALISTS... THERE'S NO TELLING WHAT A MAN WILL LOOK LIKE WHEN THEY'RE FINISHED WITH HIM!

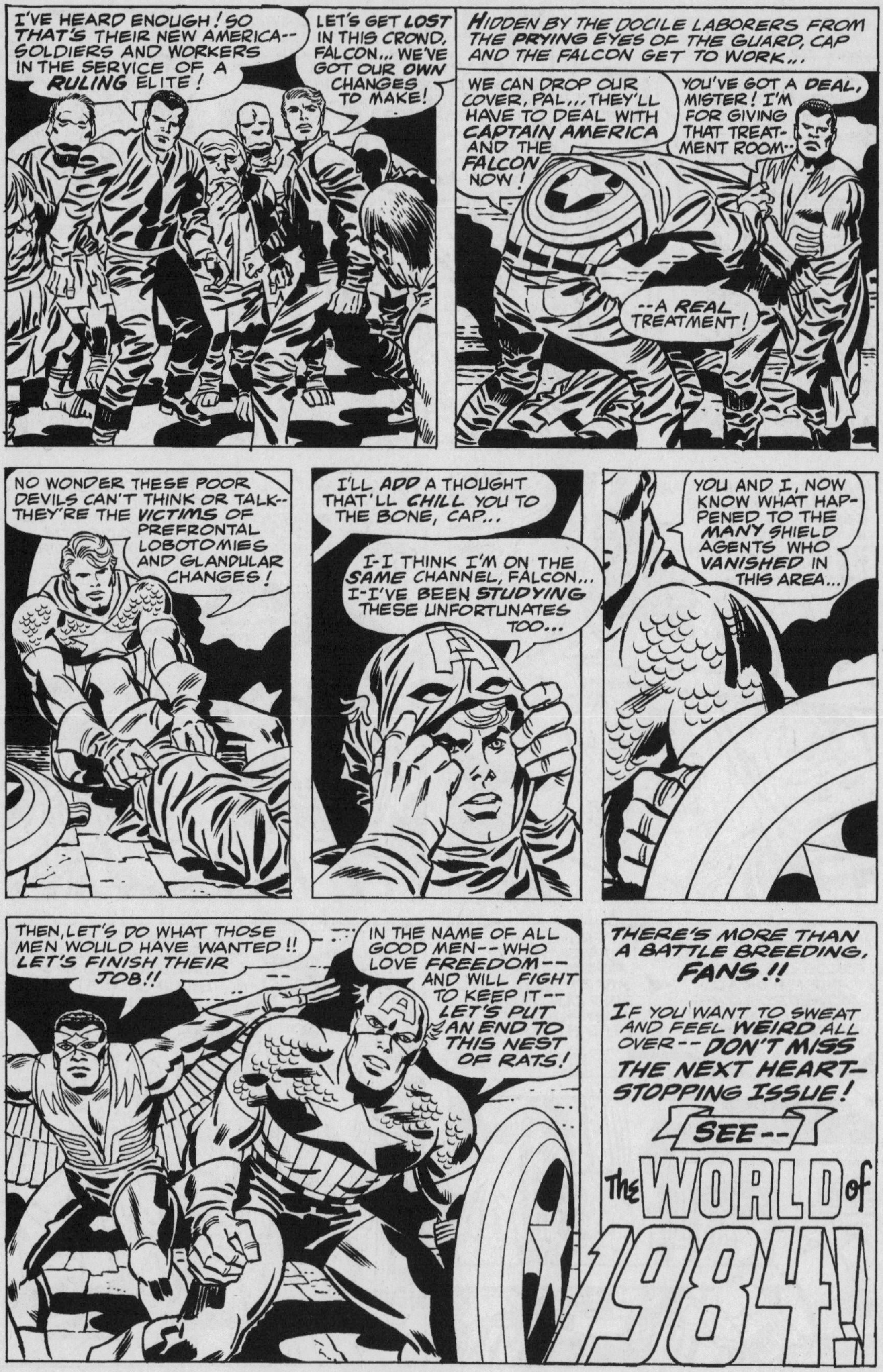
I'VE HEARD ENOUGH! SO THAT'S THEIR NEW AMERICA-- SOLDIERS AND WORKERS IN THE SERVICE OF A RULING ELITE!
LET'S GET LOST IN THIS CROWD, FALCON... WE'VE GOT OUR OWN CHANGES TO MAKE!
HIDDEN BY THE DOCILE LABORERS FROM THE PRYING EYES OF THE GUARD, CAP AND THE FALCON GET TO WORK...
WE CAN DROP OUR COVER, PAL... THEY'LL HAVE TO DEAL WITH CAPTAIN AMERICA AND THE FALCON NOW!
YOU'VE GOT A DEAL, MISTER! I'M FOR GIVING THAT TREATMENT ROOM--
--A REAL TREATMENT!
NO WONDER THESE POOR DEVILS CAN'T THINK OR TALK-- THEY'RE THE VICTIMS OF PREFRONTAL LOBOTOMIES AND GLANDULAR CHANGES!
I'LL ADD A THOUGHT THAT'LL CHILL YOU TO THE BONE, CAP...
I-I THINK I'M ON THE SAME CHANNEL, FALCON... I-I'VE BEEN STUDYING THESE UNFORTUNATES TOO...
YOU AND I, NOW KNOW WHAT HAPPENED TO THE MANY SHIELD AGENTS WHO VANISHED IN THIS AREA...
THEN, LET'S DO WHAT THOSE MEN WOULD HAVE WANTED!! LET'S FINISH THEIR JOB!!
IN THE NAME OF ALL GOOD MEN-- WHO LOVE FREEDOM-- AND WILL FIGHT TO KEEP IT-- LET'S PUT AN END TO THIS NEST OF RATS!
THERE'S MORE THAN A BATTLE BREEDING, FANS!!
IF YOU WANT TO SWEAT AND FEEL WEIRD ALL OVER-- DON'T MISS THE NEXT HEART-STOPPING ISSUE!
SEE--
THE WORLD OF 1984!

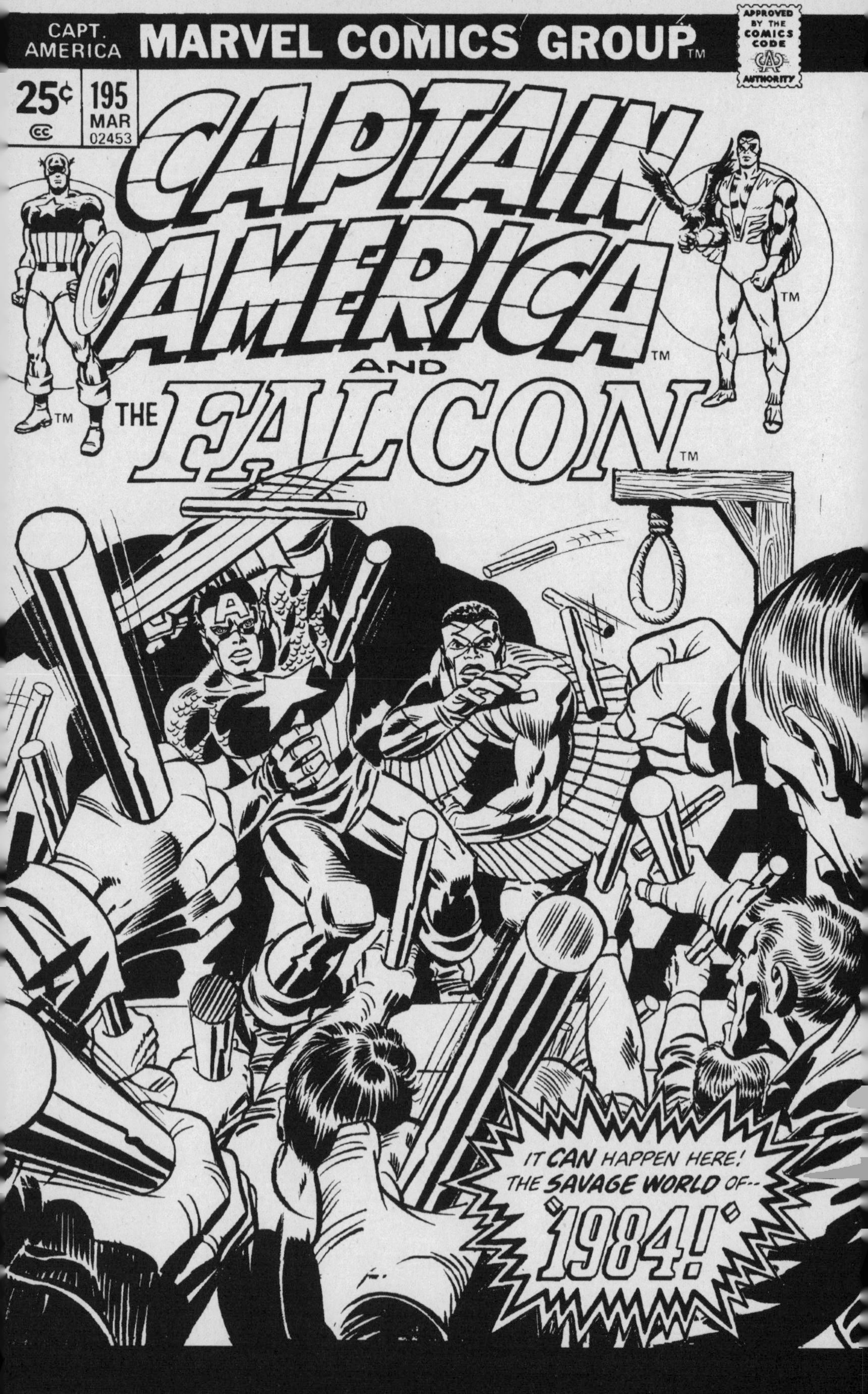
CAPT. AMERICA
MARVEL COMICS GROUP
APPROVED BY THE COMICS CODE AUTHORITY
25¢
195
MAR
02453
CAPTAIN AMERICA
AND
THE FALCON
IT CAN HAPPEN HERE! THE SAVAGE WORLD OF--
"1984!"

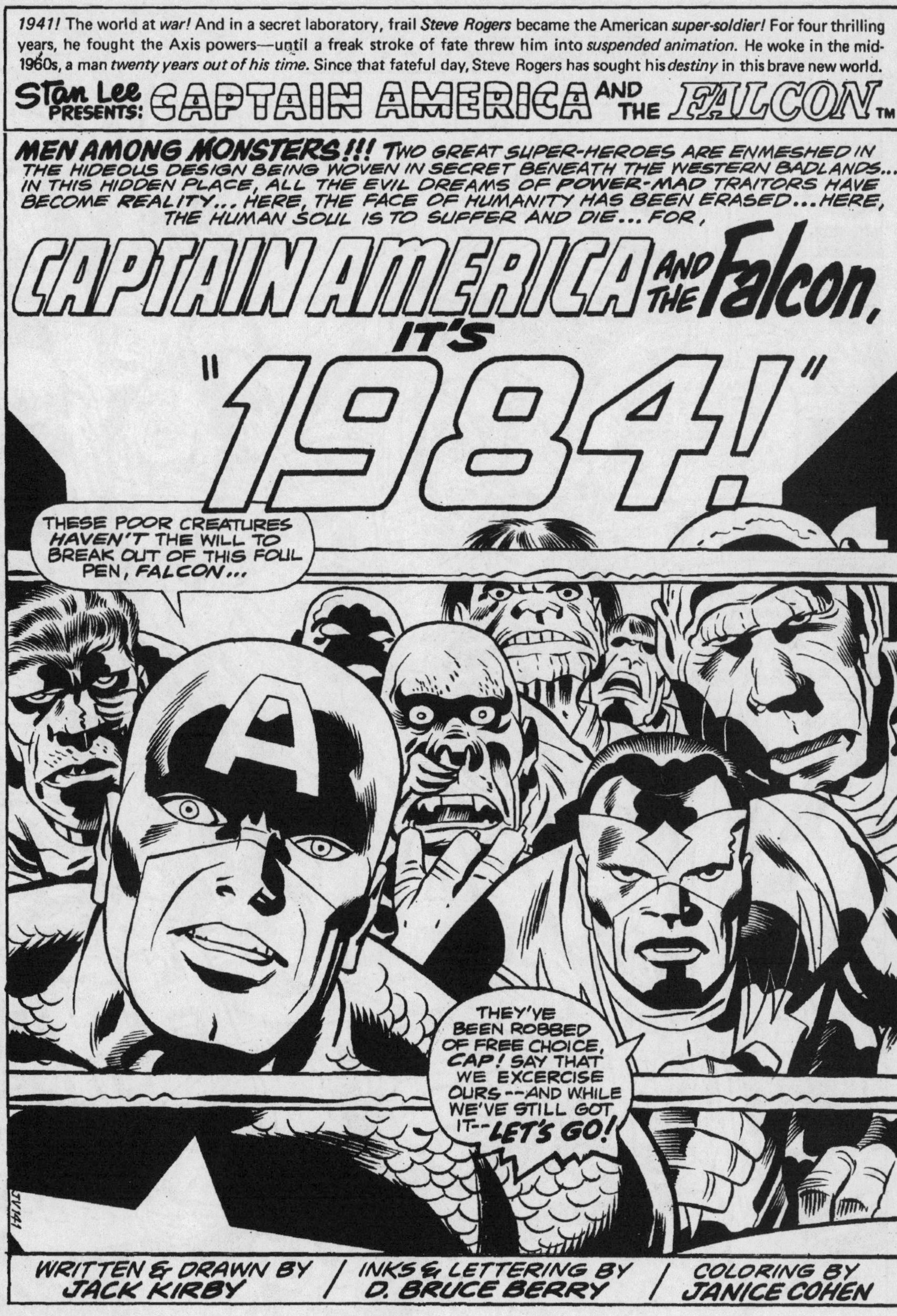
1941! The world at war! And in a secret laboratory, frail Steve Rogers became the American super-soldier! For four thrilling years, he fought the Axis powers—until a freak stroke of fate threw him into suspended animation. He woke in the mid-1960s, a man twenty years out of his time. Since that fateful day, Steve Rogers has sought his destiny in this brave new world.
Stan Lee PRESENTS: CAPTAIN AMERICA AND THE FALCON TM
MEN AMONG MONSTERS!!! TWO GREAT SUPER-HEROES ARE ENMESHED IN THE HIDEOUS DESIGN BEING WOVEN IN SECRET BENEATH THE WESTERN BADLANDS... IN THIS HIDDEN PLACE, ALL THE EVIL DREAMS OF POWER-MAD TRAITORS HAVE BECOME REALITY... HERE, THE FACE OF HUMANITY HAS BEEN ERASED... HERE, THE HUMAN SOUL IS TO SUFFER AND DIE... FOR,
CAPTAIN AMERICA AND THE Falcon, IT'S "1984!"
THESE POOR CREATURES HAVEN'T THE WILL TO BREAK OUT OF THIS FOUL PEN, FALCON...
THEY'VE BEEN ROBBED OF FREE CHOICE, CAP! SAY THAT WE EXCERCISE OURS--AND WHILE WE'VE STILL GOT IT--LET'S GO!
WRITTEN & DRAWN BY JACK KIRBY / INKS & LETTERING BY D. BRUCE BERRY / COLORING BY JANICE COHEN

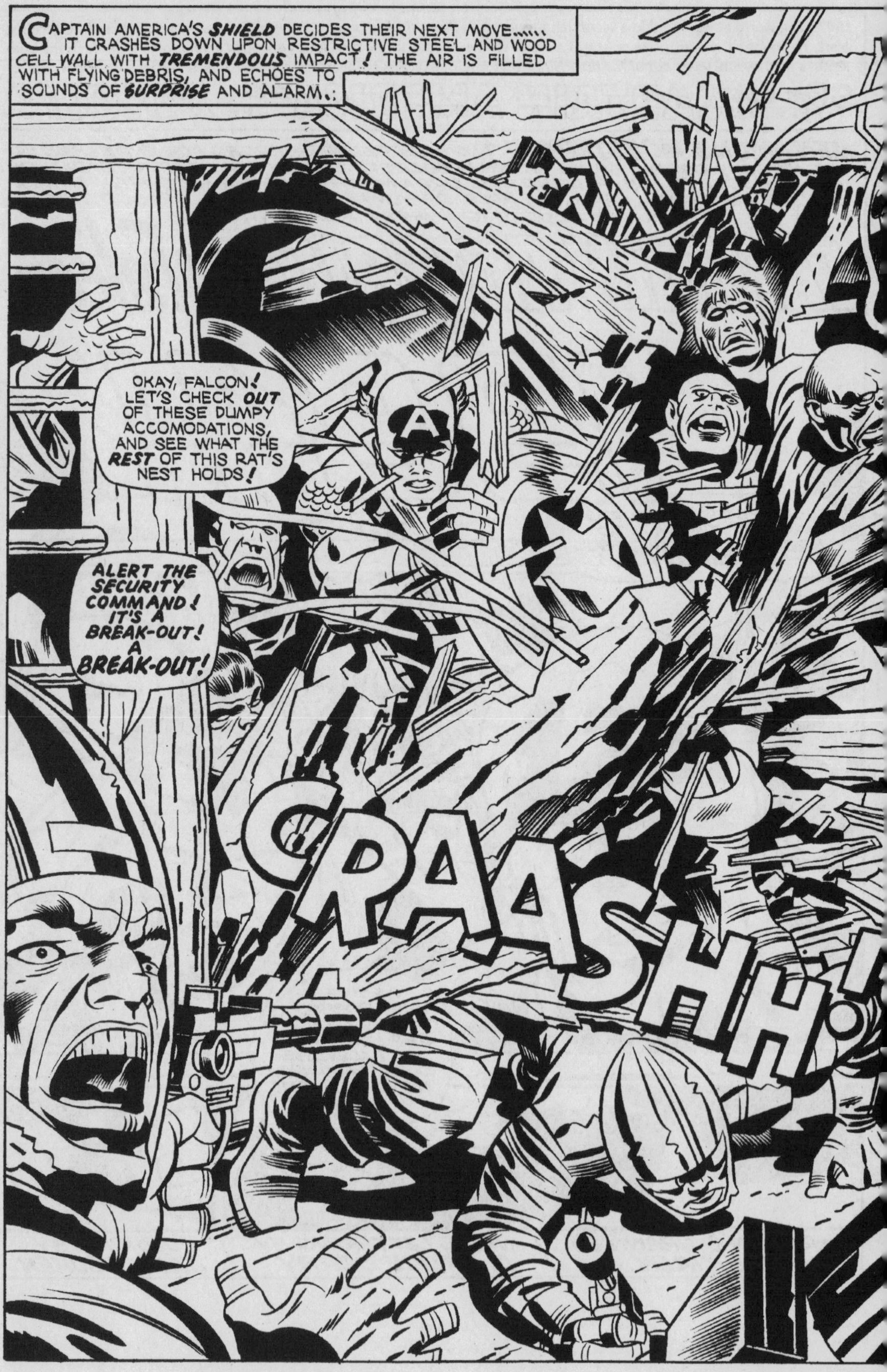
CAPTAIN AMERICA'S SHIELD DECIDES THEIR NEXT MOVE...... IT CRASHES DOWN UPON RESTRICTIVE STEEL AND WOOD CELL WALL WITH TREMENDOUS IMPACT! THE AIR IS FILLED WITH FLYING DEBRIS, AND ECHOES TO SOUNDS OF SURPRISE AND ALARM.:
OKAY, FALCON! LET'S CHECK OUT OF THESE DUMPY ACCOMODATIONS, AND SEE WHAT THE REST OF THIS RAT'S NEST HOLDS!
ALERT THE SECURITY COMMAND! IT'S A BREAK-OUT! A BREAK-OUT!
CRAASHH!

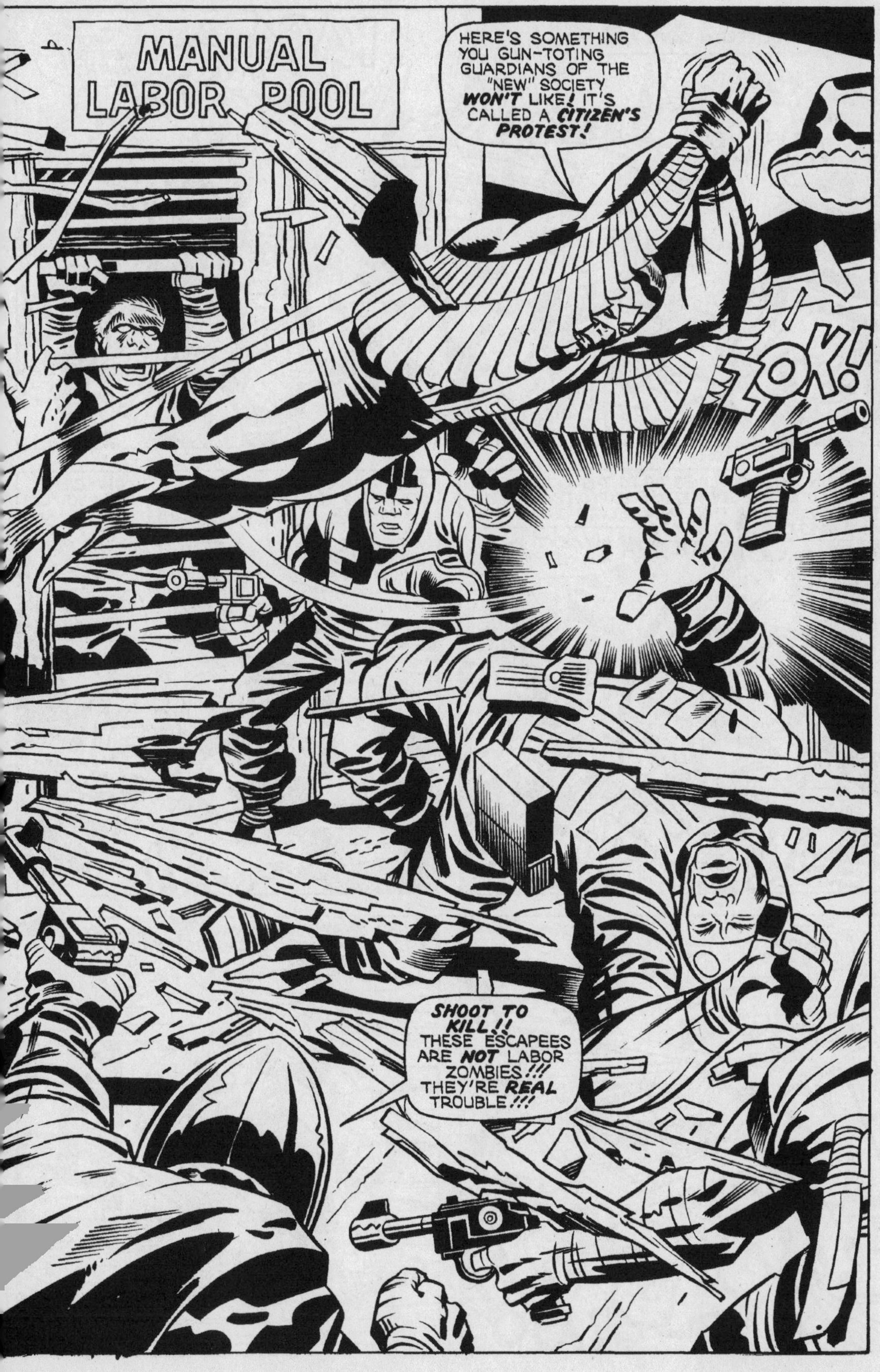
MANUAL LABOR POOL
HERE'S SOMETHING YOU GUN-TOTING GUARDIANS OF THE "NEW" SOCIETY WON'T LIKE! IT'S CALLED A CITIZEN'S PROTEST!
ZOK!
SHOOT TO KILL!! THESE ESCAPEES ARE NOT LABOR ZOMBIES!!! THEY'RE REAL TROUBLE!!!

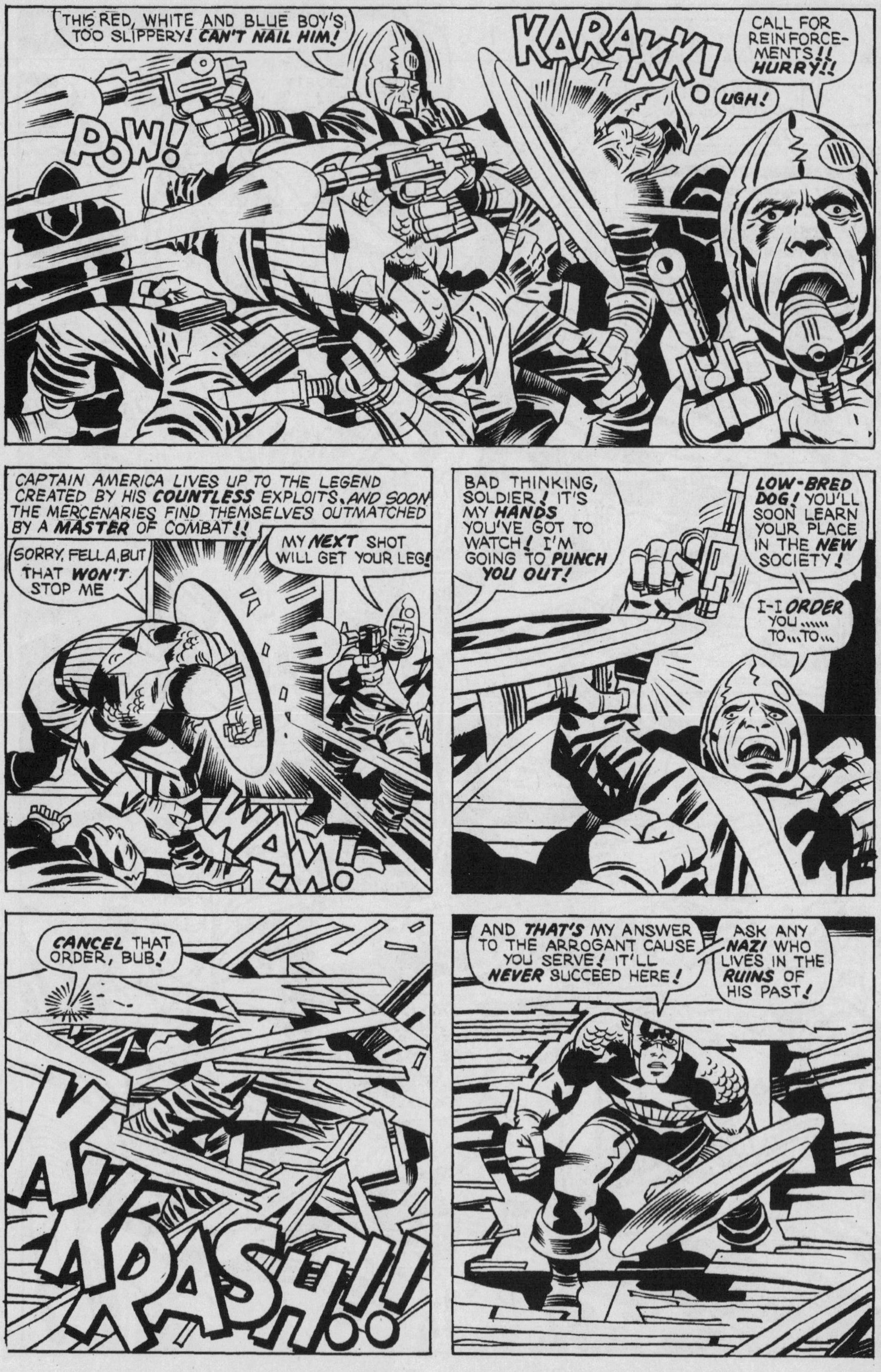

THIS RED, WHITE AND BLUE BOY'S TOO SLIPPERY! CAN'T NAIL HIM!
POW!
KARAKK!
UGH!
CALL FOR REINFORCE-MENTS!! HURRY!!
CAPTAIN AMERICA LIVES UP TO THE LEGEND CREATED BY HIS COUNTLESS EXPLOITS...AND SOON THE MERCENARIES FIND THEMSELVES OUTMATCHED BY A MASTER OF COMBAT!!
MY NEXT SHOT WILL GET YOUR LEG!
SORRY, FELLA, BUT THAT WON'T STOP ME
WAM!
BAD THINKING, SOLDIER! IT'S MY HANDS YOU'VE GOT TO WATCH! I'M GOING TO PUNCH YOU OUT!
LOW-BRED DOG! YOU'LL SOON LEARN YOUR PLACE IN THE NEW SOCIETY!
I-I ORDER YOU...... TO...TO...
CANCEL THAT ORDER, BUB!
KRASH!!
AND THAT'S MY ANSWER TO THE ARROGANT CAUSE YOU SERVE! IT'LL NEVER SUCCEED HERE!
ASK ANY NAZI WHO LIVES IN THE RUINS OF HIS PAST!

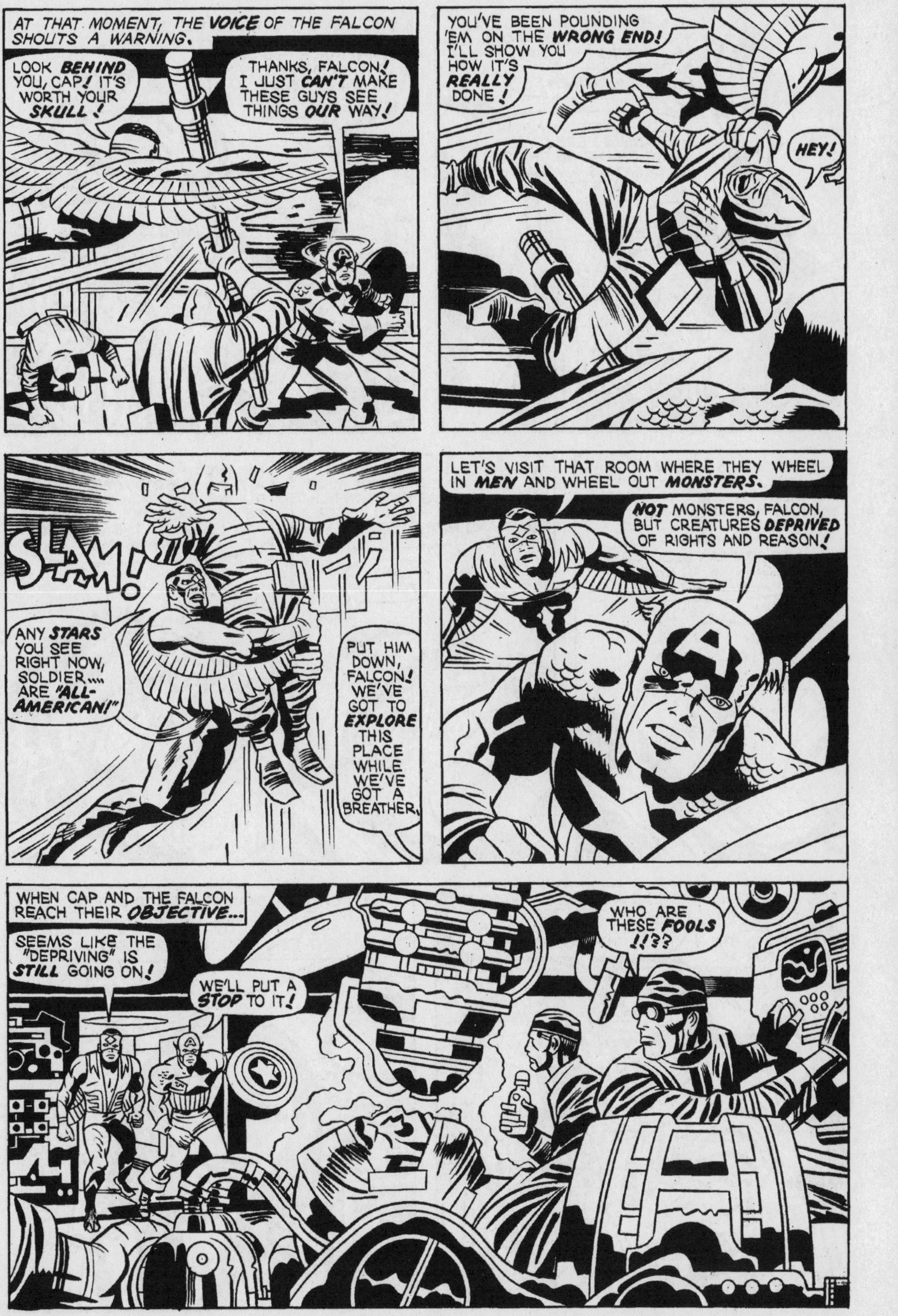
AT THAT MOMENT, THE VOICE OF THE FALCON SHOUTS A WARNING.
LOOK BEHIND YOU, CAP! IT'S WORTH YOUR SKULL!
THANKS, FALCON! I JUST CAN'T MAKE THESE GUYS SEE THINGS OUR WAY!
YOU'VE BEEN POUNDING 'EM ON THE WRONG END! I'LL SHOW YOU HOW IT'S REALLY DONE!
HEY!
SLAM!
ANY STARS YOU SEE RIGHT NOW, SOLDIER.... ARE "ALL-AMERICAN!"
PUT HIM DOWN, FALCON! WE'VE GOT TO EXPLORE THIS PLACE WHILE WE'VE GOT A BREATHER.
LET'S VISIT THAT ROOM WHERE THEY WHEEL IN MEN AND WHEEL OUT MONSTERS.
NOT MONSTERS, FALCON, BUT CREATURES DEPRIVED OF RIGHTS AND REASON!
WHEN CAP AND THE FALCON REACH THEIR OBJECTIVE...
SEEMS LIKE THE "DEPRIVING" IS STILL GOING ON!
WE'LL PUT A STOP TO IT!
WHO ARE THESE FOOLS !!??

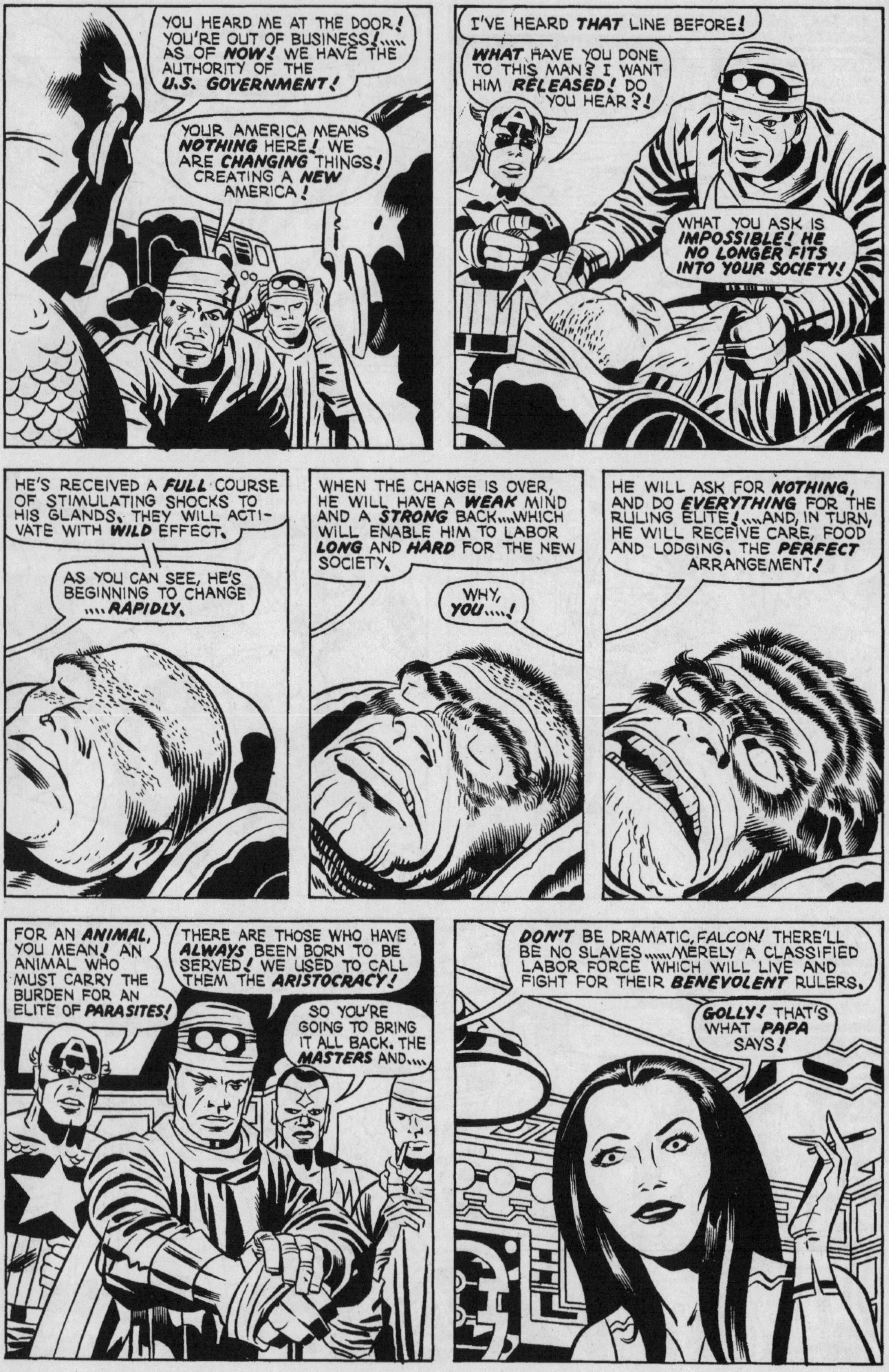

YOU HEARD ME AT THE DOOR! YOU'RE OUT OF BUSINESS!..... AS OF NOW! WE HAVE THE AUTHORITY OF THE U.S. GOVERNMENT!
YOUR AMERICA MEANS NOTHING HERE! WE ARE CHANGING THINGS! CREATING A NEW AMERICA!
I'VE HEARD THAT LINE BEFORE!
WHAT HAVE YOU DONE TO THIS MAN?! I WANT HIM RELEASED! DO YOU HEAR?!
WHAT YOU ASK IS IMPOSSIBLE! HE NO LONGER FITS INTO YOUR SOCIETY!
HE'S RECEIVED A FULL COURSE OF STIMULATING SHOCKS TO HIS GLANDS. THEY WILL ACTIVATE WITH WILD EFFECT.
AS YOU CAN SEE, HE'S BEGINNING TO CHANGE ....RAPIDLY.
WHEN THE CHANGE IS OVER, HE WILL HAVE A WEAK MIND AND A STRONG BACK....WHICH WILL ENABLE HIM TO LABOR LONG AND HARD FOR THE NEW SOCIETY.
WHY, YOU.....!
HE WILL ASK FOR NOTHING, AND DO EVERYTHING FOR THE RULING ELITE!.....AND, IN TURN, HE WILL RECEIVE CARE, FOOD AND LODGING. THE PERFECT ARRANGEMENT!
FOR AN ANIMAL, YOU MEAN! AN ANIMAL WHO MUST CARRY THE BURDEN FOR AN ELITE OF PARASITES!
THERE ARE THOSE WHO HAVE ALWAYS BEEN BORN TO BE SERVED! WE USED TO CALL THEM THE ARISTOCRACY!
SO YOU'RE GOING TO BRING IT ALL BACK. THE MASTERS AND....
DON'T BE DRAMATIC, FALCON! THERE'LL BE NO SLAVES......MERELY A CLASSIFIED LABOR FORCE WHICH WILL LIVE AND FIGHT FOR THEIR BENEVOLENT RULERS.
GOLLY! THAT'S WHAT PAPA SAYS!

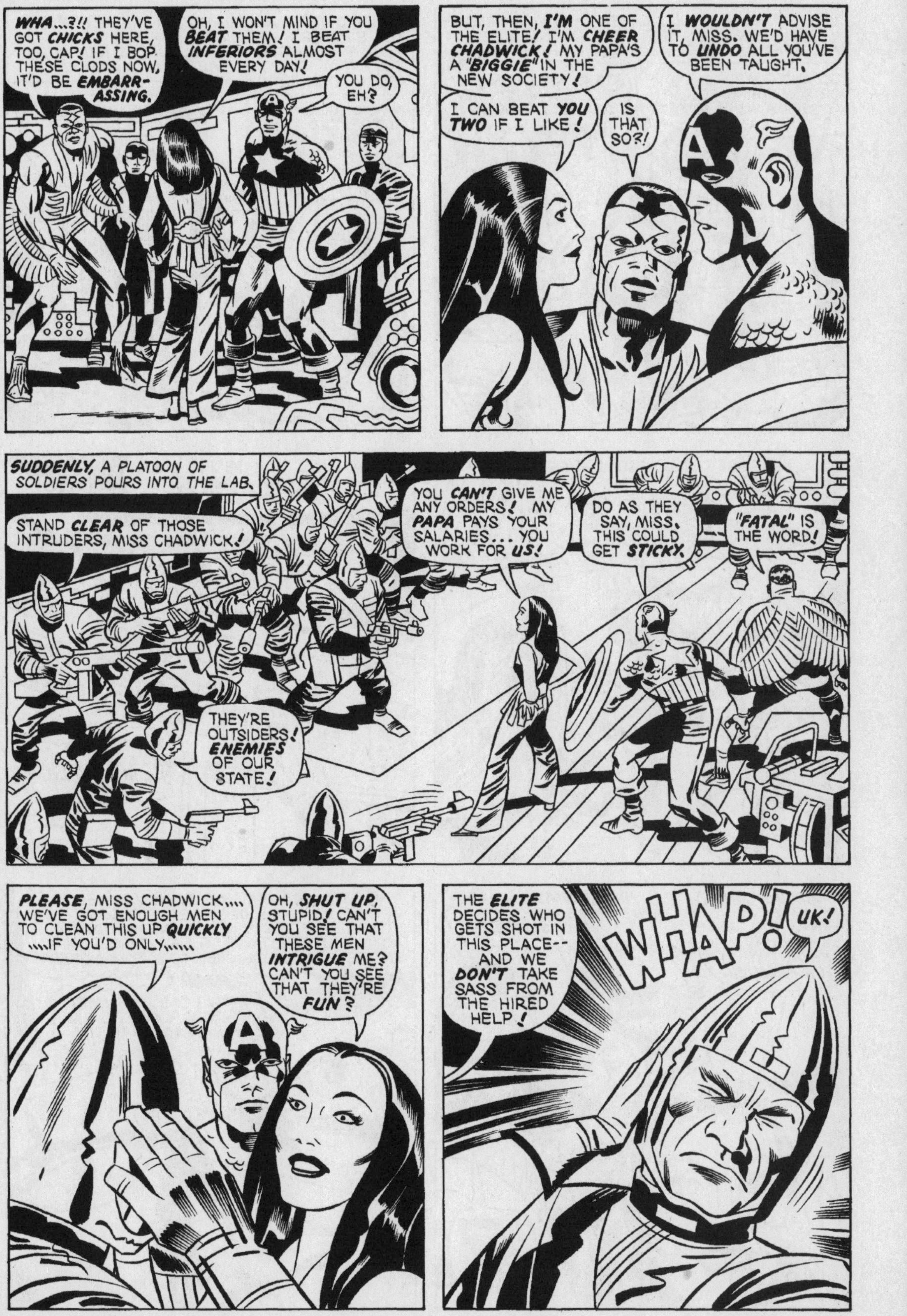
WHA...?!! THEY'VE GOT CHICKS HERE, TOO, CAP! IF I BOP THESE CLODS NOW, IT'D BE EMBARR-ASSING.
OH, I WON'T MIND IF YOU BEAT THEM! I BEAT INFERIORS ALMOST EVERY DAY!
YOU DO, EH?
BUT, THEN, I'M ONE OF THE ELITE! I'M CHEER CHADWICK! MY PAPA'S A "BIGGIE" IN THE NEW SOCIETY!
I CAN BEAT YOU TWO IF I LIKE!
IS THAT SO?!
I WOULDN'T ADVISE IT, MISS. WE'D HAVE TO UNDO ALL YOU'VE BEEN TAUGHT.
SUDDENLY, A PLATOON OF SOLDIERS POURS INTO THE LAB.
STAND CLEAR OF THOSE INTRUDERS, MISS CHADWICK!
YOU CAN'T GIVE ME ANY ORDERS! MY PAPA PAYS YOUR SALARIES... YOU WORK FOR US!
DO AS THEY SAY, MISS. THIS COULD GET STICKY.
"FATAL" IS THE WORD!
THEY'RE OUTSIDERS! ENEMIES OF OUR STATE!
PLEASE, MISS CHADWICK.... WE'VE GOT ENOUGH MEN TO CLEAN THIS UP QUICKLY ....IF YOU'D ONLY......
OH, SHUT UP, STUPID! CAN'T YOU SEE THAT THESE MEN INTRIGUE ME? CAN'T YOU SEE THAT THEY'RE FUN?
THE ELITE DECIDES WHO GETS SHOT IN THIS PLACE-- AND WE DON'T TAKE SASS FROM THE HIRED HELP!
WHAP!
UK!

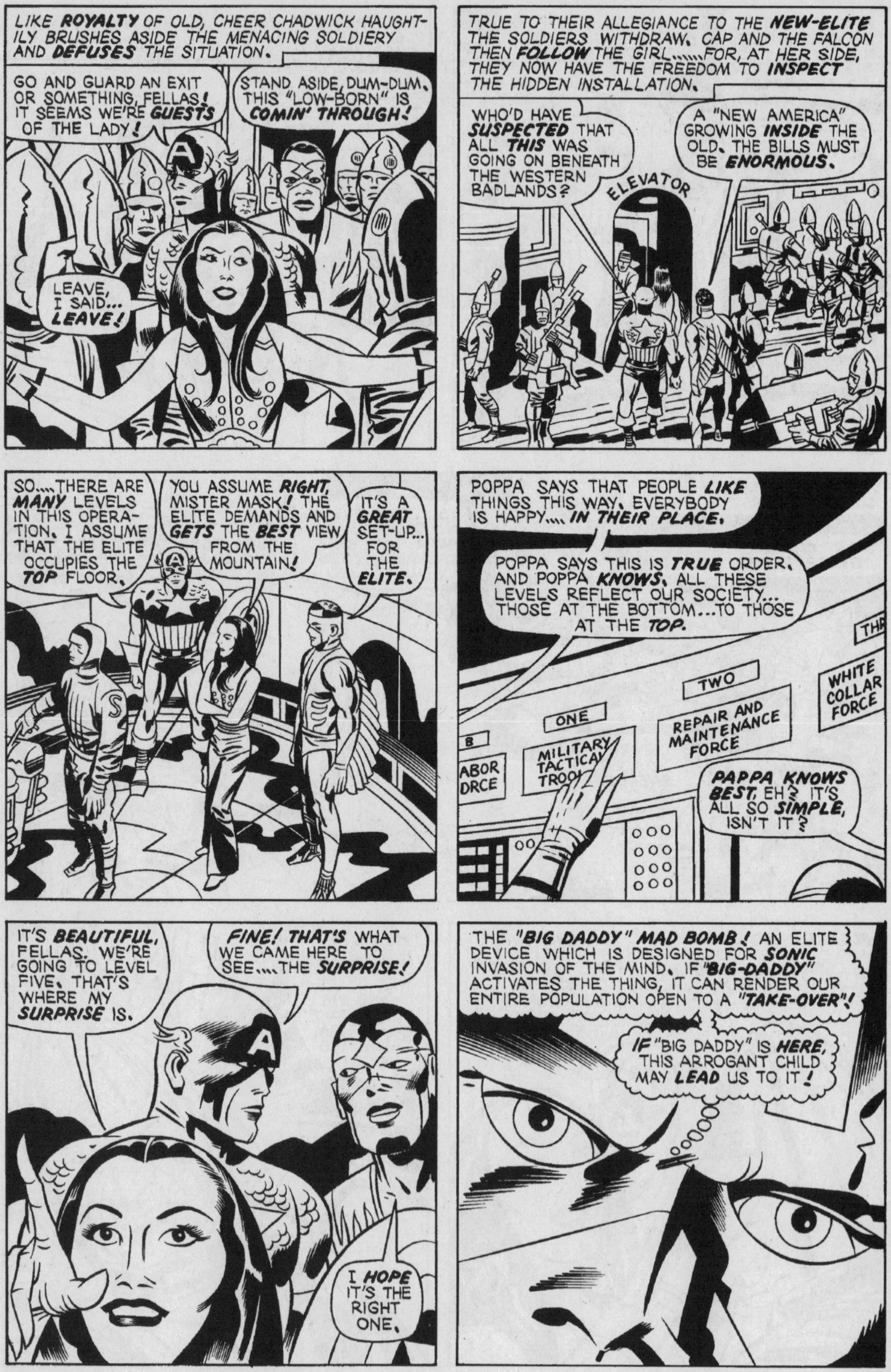
LIKE ROYALTY OF OLD, CHEER CHADWICK HAUGHTILY BRUSHES ASIDE THE MENACING SOLDIERY AND DEFUSES THE SITUATION.
GO AND GUARD AN EXIT OR SOMETHING, FELLAS! IT SEEMS WE'RE GUESTS OF THE LADY!
STAND ASIDE, DUM-DUM. THIS "LOW-BORN" IS COMIN' THROUGH!
LEAVE, I SAID... LEAVE!
TRUE TO THEIR ALLEGIANCE TO THE NEW-ELITE THE SOLDIERS WITHDRAW. CAP AND THE FALCON THEN FOLLOW THE GIRL......FOR, AT HER SIDE, THEY NOW HAVE THE FREEDOM TO INSPECT THE HIDDEN INSTALLATION.
WHO'D HAVE SUSPECTED THAT ALL THIS WAS GOING ON BENEATH THE WESTERN BADLANDS?
A "NEW AMERICA" GROWING INSIDE THE OLD. THE BILLS MUST BE ENORMOUS.
ELEVATOR
SO....THERE ARE MANY LEVELS IN THIS OPERATION. I ASSUME THAT THE ELITE OCCUPIES THE TOP FLOOR.
YOU ASSUME RIGHT, MISTER MASK! THE ELITE DEMANDS AND GETS THE BEST VIEW FROM THE MOUNTAIN!
IT'S A GREAT SET-UP... FOR THE ELITE.
POPPA SAYS THAT PEOPLE LIKE THINGS THIS WAY. EVERYBODY IS HAPPY.... IN THEIR PLACE.
POPPA SAYS THIS IS TRUE ORDER. AND POPPA KNOWS. ALL THESE LEVELS REFLECT OUR SOCIETY... THOSE AT THE BOTTOM...TO THOSE AT THE TOP.
THR
WHITE COLLAR FORCE
TWO
REPAIR AND MAINTENANCE FORCE
ONE
MILITARY TACTICAL TROO
B
ABOR ORCE
PAPPA KNOWS BEST, EH? IT'S ALL SO SIMPLE, ISN'T IT?
IT'S BEAUTIFUL, FELLAS. WE'RE GOING TO LEVEL FIVE. THAT'S WHERE MY SURPRISE IS.
FINE! THAT'S WHAT WE CAME HERE TO SEE....THE SURPRISE!
I HOPE IT'S THE RIGHT ONE.
THE "BIG DADDY" MAD BOMB! AN ELITE DEVICE WHICH IS DESIGNED FOR SONIC INVASION OF THE MIND. IF "BIG-DADDY" ACTIVATES THE THING, IT CAN RENDER OUR ENTIRE POPULATION OPEN TO A "TAKE-OVER"!
IF "BIG DADDY" IS HERE, THIS ARROGANT CHILD MAY LEAD US TO IT!

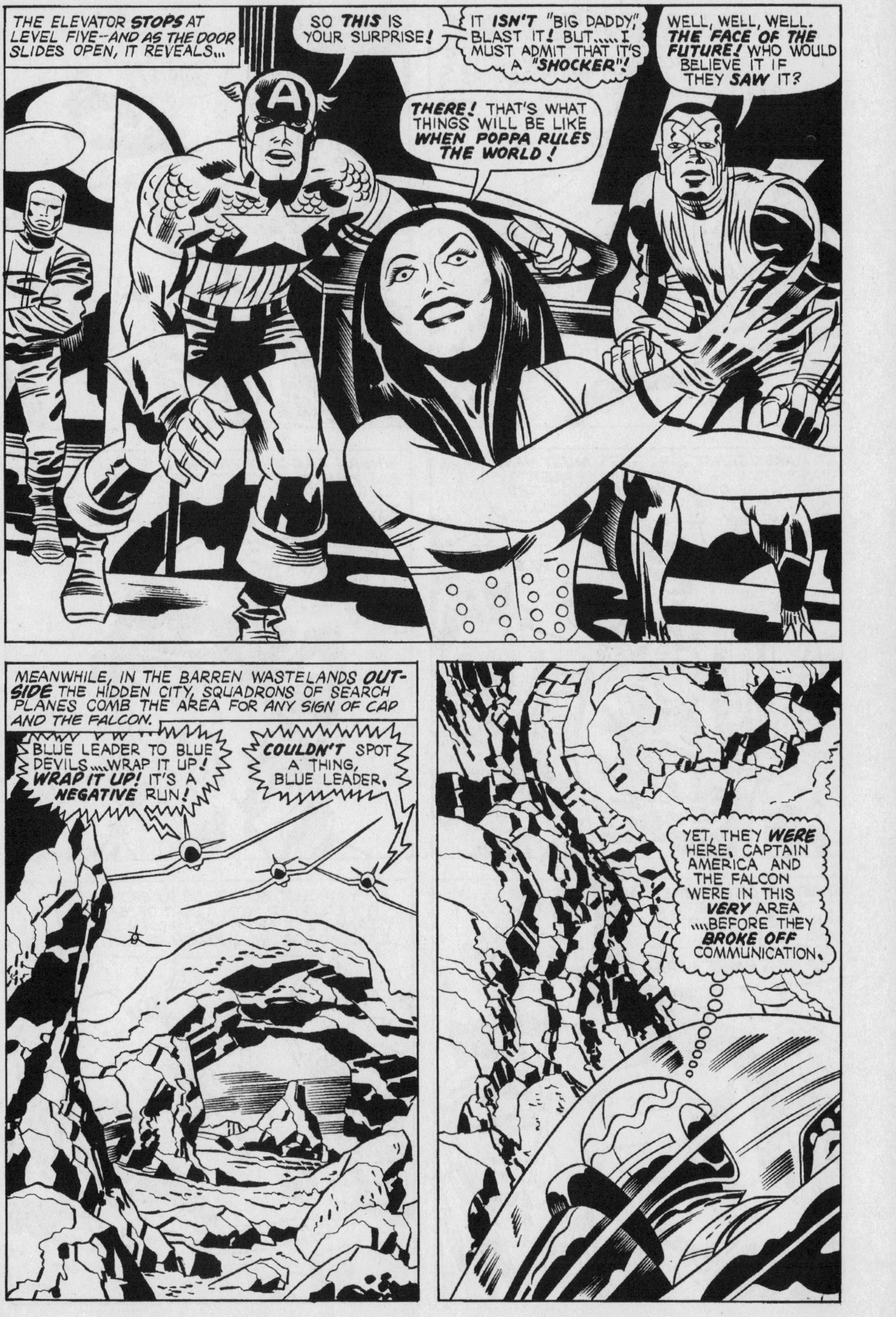
THE ELEVATOR STOPS AT LEVEL FIVE--AND AS THE DOOR SLIDES OPEN, IT REVEALS...
SO THIS IS YOUR SURPRISE!
IT ISN'T "BIG DADDY," BLAST IT! BUT..... I MUST ADMIT THAT IT'S A "SHOCKER"!
WELL, WELL, WELL. THE FACE OF THE FUTURE! WHO WOULD BELIEVE IT IF THEY SAW IT?
THERE! THAT'S WHAT THINGS WILL BE LIKE WHEN POPPA RULES THE WORLD!
MEANWHILE, IN THE BARREN WASTELANDS OUTSIDE THE HIDDEN CITY, SQUADRONS OF SEARCH PLANES COMB THE AREA FOR ANY SIGN OF CAP AND THE FALCON.
BLUE LEADER TO BLUE DEVILS.....WRAP IT UP! WRAP IT UP! IT'S A NEGATIVE RUN!
COULDN'T SPOT A THING, BLUE LEADER.
YET, THEY WERE HERE. CAPTAIN AMERICA AND THE FALCON WERE IN THIS VERY AREA ....BEFORE THEY BROKE OFF COMMUNICATION.

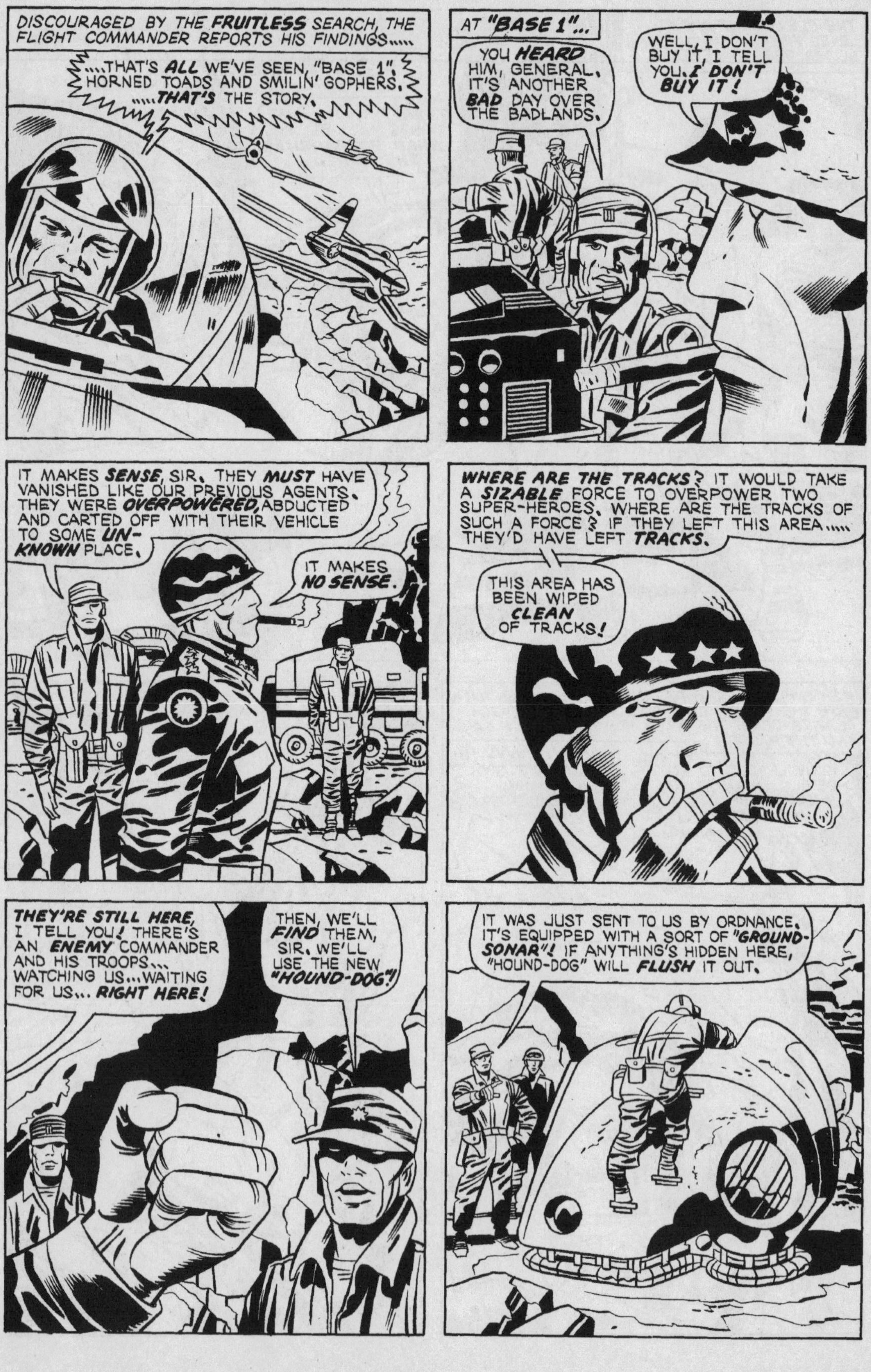
DISCOURAGED BY THE FRUITLESS SEARCH, THE FLIGHT COMMANDER REPORTS HIS FINDINGS.....
....THAT'S ALL WE'VE SEEN, "BASE 1". HORNED TOADS AND SMILIN' GOPHERS. .....THAT'S THE STORY.
AT "BASE 1"...
YOU HEARD HIM, GENERAL. IT'S ANOTHER BAD DAY OVER THE BADLANDS.
WELL, I DON'T BUY IT, I TELL YOU. I DON'T BUY IT!
IT MAKES SENSE, SIR. THEY MUST HAVE VANISHED LIKE OUR PREVIOUS AGENTS. THEY WERE OVERPOWERED, ABDUCTED AND CARTED OFF WITH THEIR VEHICLE TO SOME UNKNOWN PLACE.
IT MAKES NO SENSE.
WHERE ARE THE TRACKS? IT WOULD TAKE A SIZABLE FORCE TO OVERPOWER TWO SUPER-HEROES. WHERE ARE THE TRACKS OF SUCH A FORCE? IF THEY LEFT THIS AREA..... THEY'D HAVE LEFT TRACKS.
THIS AREA HAS BEEN WIPED CLEAN OF TRACKS!
THEY'RE STILL HERE, I TELL YOU! THERE'S AN ENEMY COMMANDER AND HIS TROOPS... WATCHING US... WAITING FOR US... RIGHT HERE!
THEN, WE'LL FIND THEM, SIR. WE'LL USE THE NEW "HOUND-DOG"!
IT WAS JUST SENT TO US BY ORDNANCE. IT'S EQUIPPED WITH A SORT OF "GROUND-SONAR"! IF ANYTHING'S HIDDEN HERE, "HOUND-DOG" WILL FLUSH IT OUT.

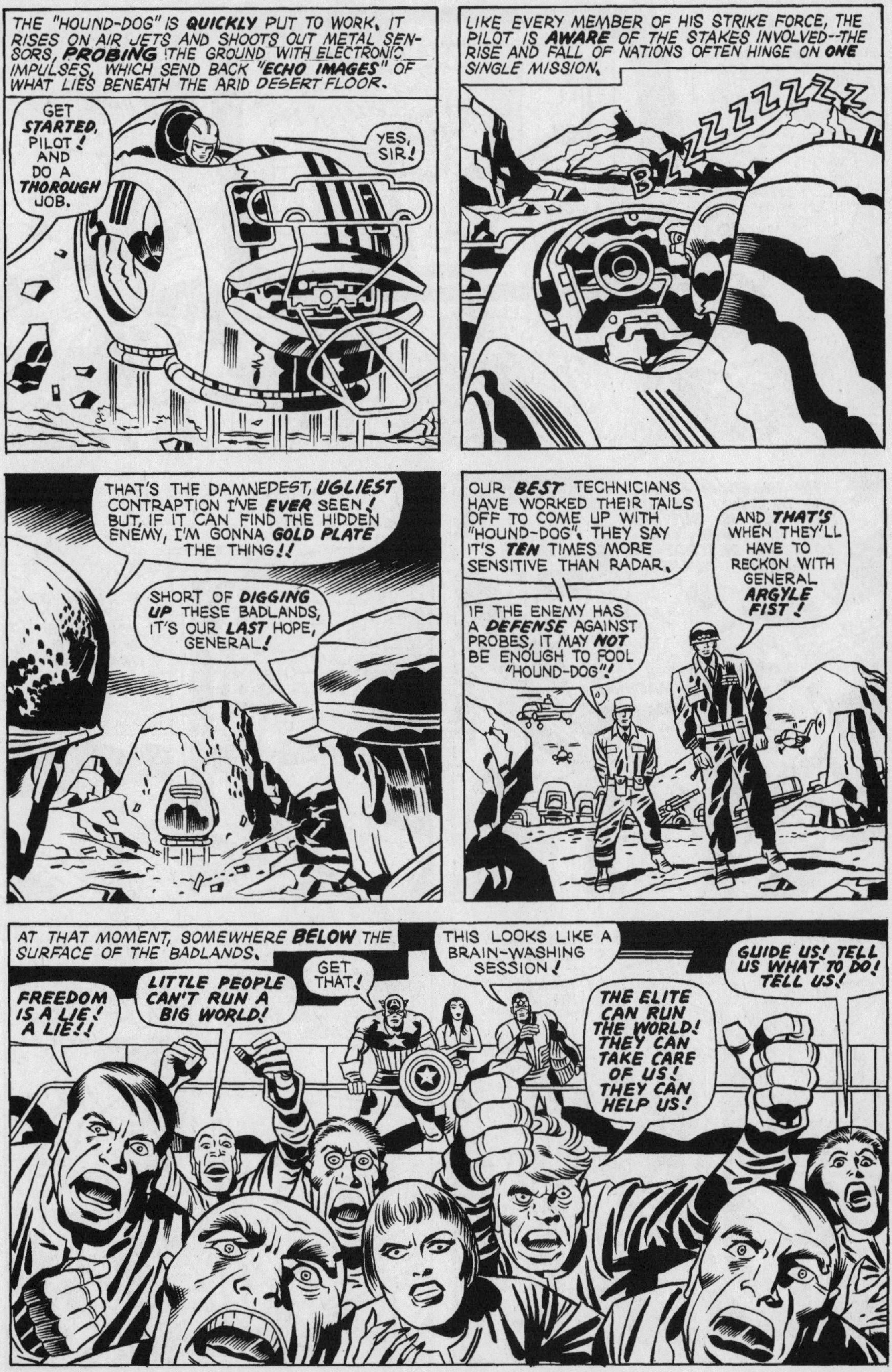

THE "HOUND-DOG" IS QUICKLY PUT TO WORK. IT RISES ON AIR JETS AND SHOOTS OUT METAL SENSORS, PROBING THE GROUND WITH ELECTRONIC IMPULSES, WHICH SEND BACK "ECHO IMAGES" OF WHAT LIES BENEATH THE ARID DESERT FLOOR.
GET STARTED, PILOT! AND DO A THOROUGH JOB.
YES, SIR!
LIKE EVERY MEMBER OF HIS STRIKE FORCE, THE PILOT IS AWARE OF THE STAKES INVOLVED--THE RISE AND FALL OF NATIONS OFTEN HINGE ON ONE SINGLE MISSION.
BZZZZZZZZZ
THAT'S THE DAMNEDEST, UGLIEST CONTRAPTION I'VE EVER SEEN! BUT, IF IT CAN FIND THE HIDDEN ENEMY, I'M GONNA GOLD PLATE THE THING!!
SHORT OF DIGGING UP THESE BADLANDS, IT'S OUR LAST HOPE, GENERAL!
OUR BEST TECHNICIANS HAVE WORKED THEIR TAILS OFF TO COME UP WITH "HOUND-DOG". THEY SAY IT'S TEN TIMES MORE SENSITIVE THAN RADAR.
IF THE ENEMY HAS A DEFENSE AGAINST PROBES, IT MAY NOT BE ENOUGH TO FOOL "HOUND-DOG"!
AND THAT'S WHEN THEY'LL HAVE TO RECKON WITH GENERAL ARGYLE FIST!
AT THAT MOMENT, SOMEWHERE BELOW THE SURFACE OF THE BADLANDS.
THIS LOOKS LIKE A BRAIN-WASHING SESSION!
GET THAT!
FREEDOM IS A LIE! A LIE!!
LITTLE PEOPLE CAN'T RUN A BIG WORLD!
THE ELITE CAN RUN THE WORLD! THEY CAN TAKE CARE OF US! THEY CAN HELP US!
GUIDE US! TELL US WHAT TO DO! TELL US!

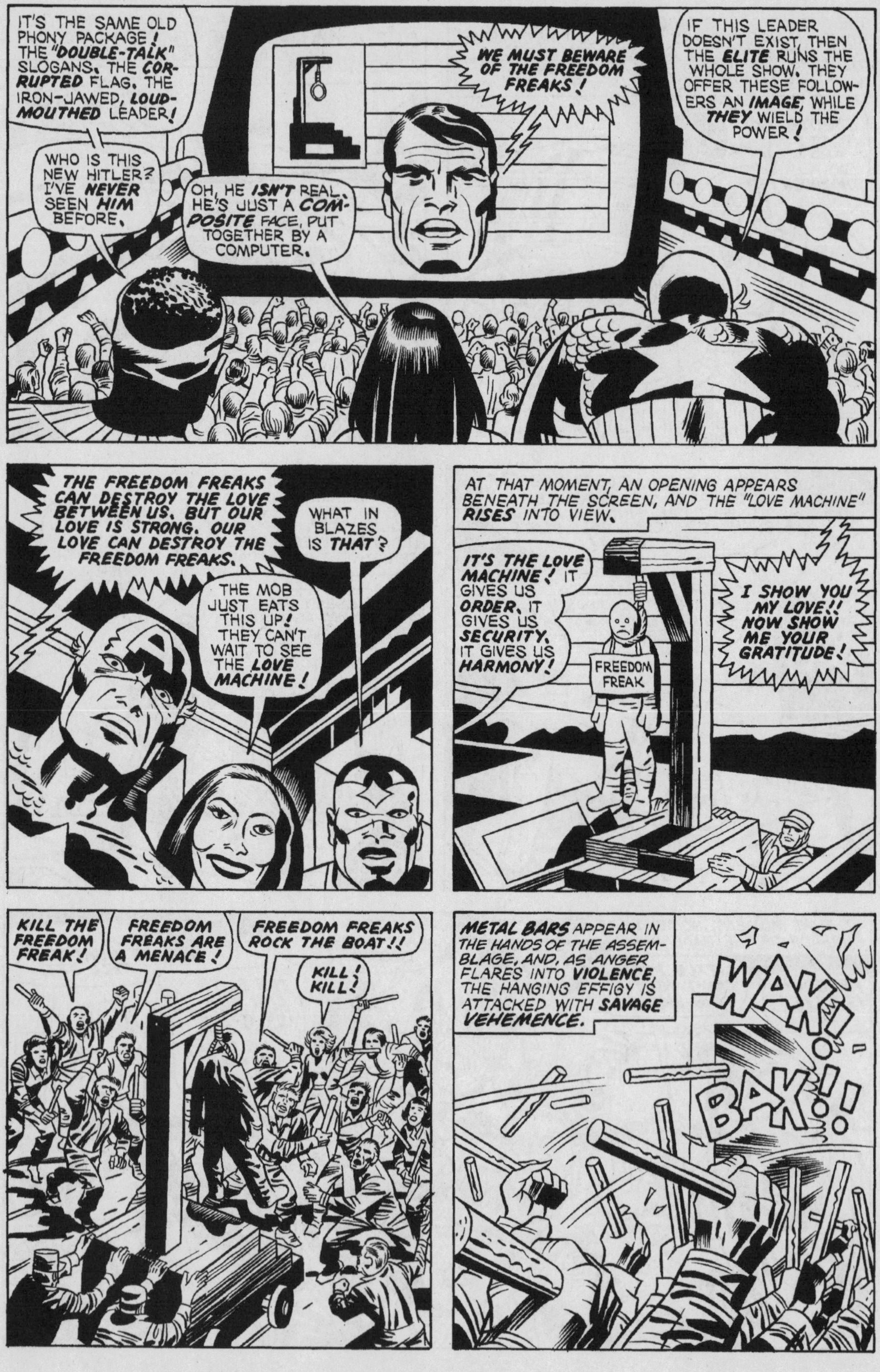
IT'S THE SAME OLD PHONY PACKAGE! THE "DOUBLE-TALK" SLOGANS, THE CORRUPTED FLAG, THE IRON-JAWED, LOUD-MOUTHED LEADER!
WE MUST BEWARE OF THE FREEDOM FREAKS!
IF THIS LEADER DOESN'T EXIST, THEN THE ELITE RUNS THE WHOLE SHOW. THEY OFFER THESE FOLLOWERS AN IMAGE, WHILE THEY WIELD THE POWER!
WHO IS THIS NEW HITLER? I'VE NEVER SEEN HIM BEFORE.
OH, HE ISN'T REAL. HE'S JUST A COMPOSITE FACE, PUT TOGETHER BY A COMPUTER.
THE FREEDOM FREAKS CAN DESTROY THE LOVE BETWEEN US. BUT OUR LOVE IS STRONG. OUR LOVE CAN DESTROY THE FREEDOM FREAKS.
WHAT IN BLAZES IS THAT?
THE MOB JUST EATS THIS UP! THEY CAN'T WAIT TO SEE THE LOVE MACHINE!
AT THAT MOMENT, AN OPENING APPEARS BENEATH THE SCREEN, AND THE "LOVE MACHINE" RISES INTO VIEW.
IT'S THE LOVE MACHINE! IT GIVES US ORDER. IT GIVES US SECURITY. IT GIVES US HARMONY!
FREEDOM FREAK
I SHOW YOU MY LOVE!! NOW SHOW ME YOUR GRATITUDE!
KILL THE FREEDOM FREAK!
FREEDOM FREAKS ARE A MENACE!
FREEDOM FREAKS ROCK THE BOAT!!
KILL! KILL!
METAL BARS APPEAR IN THE HANDS OF THE ASSEMBLAGE, AND, AS ANGER FLARES INTO VIOLENCE, THE HANGING EFFIGY IS ATTACKED WITH SAVAGE VEHEMENCE.
WAK!
BAK!!

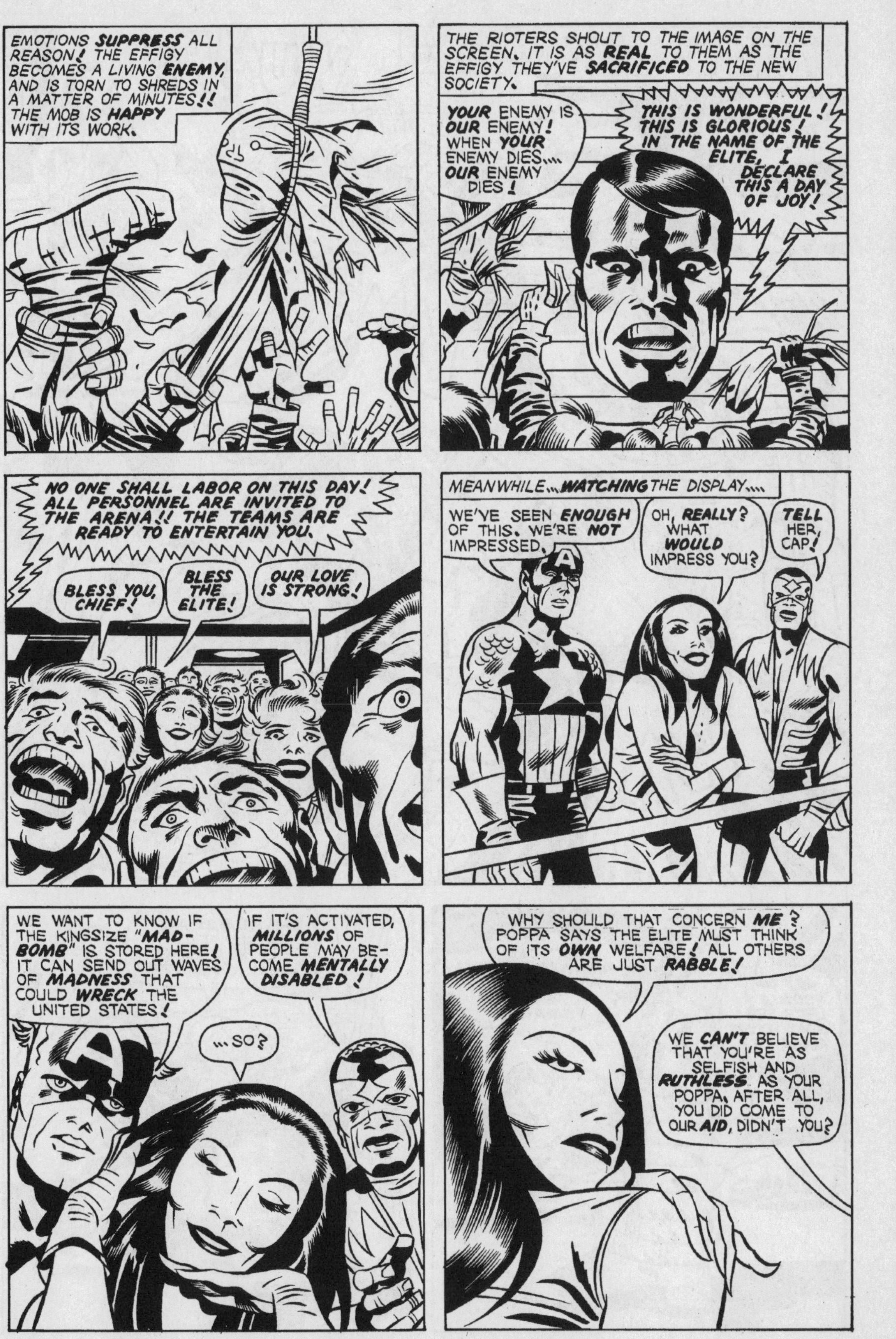
EMOTIONS SUPPRESS ALL REASON! THE EFFIGY BECOMES A LIVING ENEMY, AND IS TORN TO SHREDS IN A MATTER OF MINUTES!! THE MOB IS HAPPY WITH ITS WORK.
THE RIOTERS SHOUT TO THE IMAGE ON THE SCREEN. IT IS AS REAL TO THEM AS THE EFFIGY THEY'VE SACRIFICED TO THE NEW SOCIETY.
YOUR ENEMY IS OUR ENEMY! WHEN YOUR ENEMY DIES.... OUR ENEMY DIES!
THIS IS WONDERFUL! THIS IS GLORIOUS! IN THE NAME OF THE ELITE, I DECLARE THIS A DAY OF JOY!
NO ONE SHALL LABOR ON THIS DAY! ALL PERSONNEL ARE INVITED TO THE ARENA!! THE TEAMS ARE READY TO ENTERTAIN YOU.
BLESS YOU, CHIEF!
BLESS THE ELITE!
OUR LOVE IS STRONG!
MEANWHILE... WATCHING THE DISPLAY....
WE'VE SEEN ENOUGH OF THIS. WE'RE NOT IMPRESSED.
OH, REALLY? WHAT WOULD IMPRESS YOU?
TELL HER, CAP!
WE WANT TO KNOW IF THE KINGSIZE "MAD-BOMB" IS STORED HERE! IT CAN SEND OUT WAVES OF MADNESS THAT COULD WRECK THE UNITED STATES!
IF IT'S ACTIVATED, MILLIONS OF PEOPLE MAY BECOME MENTALLY DISABLED!
...SO?
WHY SHOULD THAT CONCERN ME? POPPA SAYS THE ELITE MUST THINK OF ITS OWN WELFARE! ALL OTHERS ARE JUST RABBLE!
WE CAN'T BELIEVE THAT YOU'RE AS SELFISH AND RUTHLESS AS YOUR POPPA. AFTER ALL, YOU DID COME TO OUR AID, DIDN'T YOU?

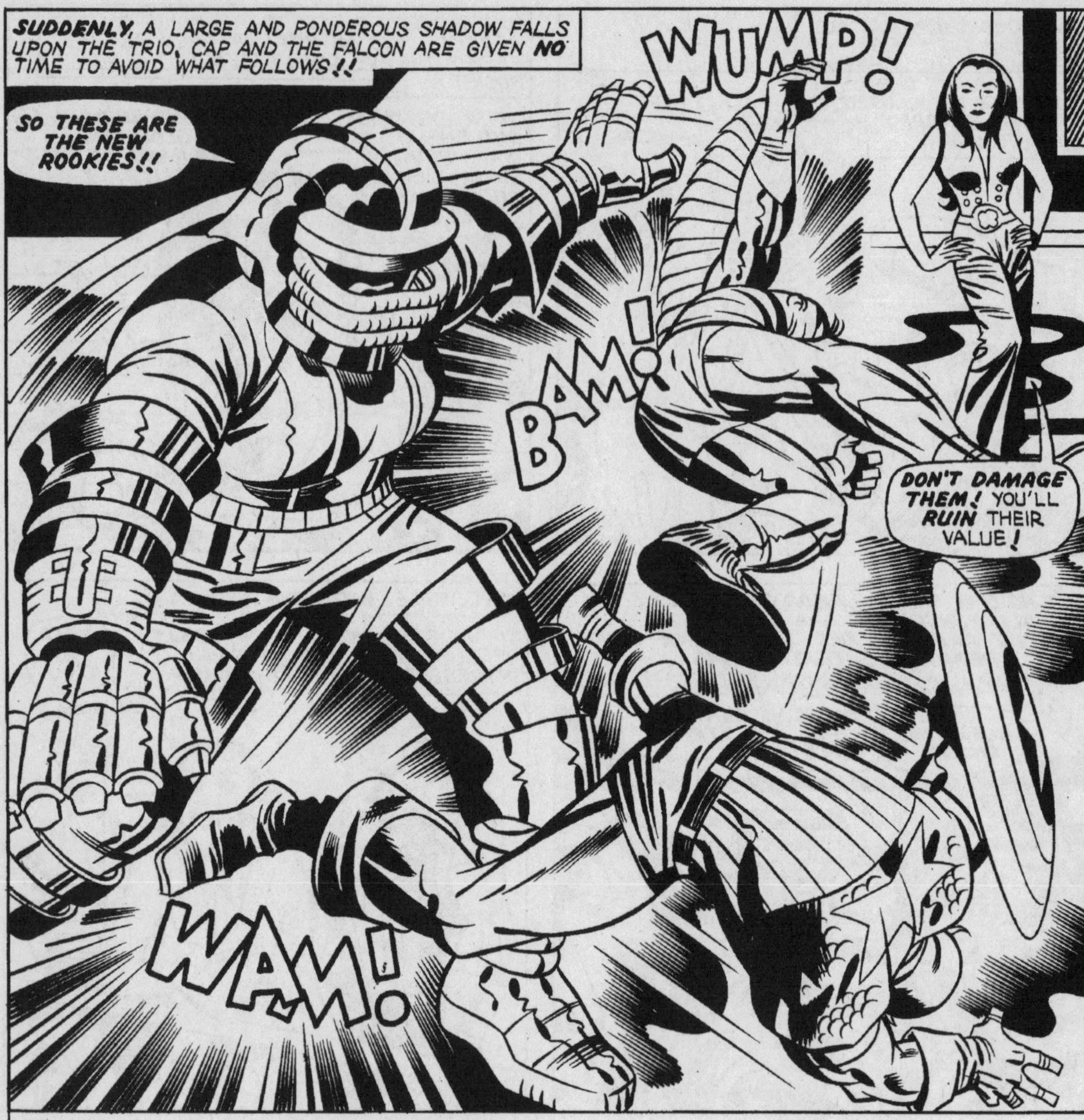
SUDDENLY, A LARGE AND PONDEROUS SHADOW FALLS UPON THE TRIO. CAP AND THE FALCON ARE GIVEN NO TIME TO AVOID WHAT FOLLOWS!!
WUMP!
SO THESE ARE THE NEW ROOKIES!!
BAM!
DON'T DAMAGE THEM! YOU'LL RUIN THEIR VALUE!
WAM!

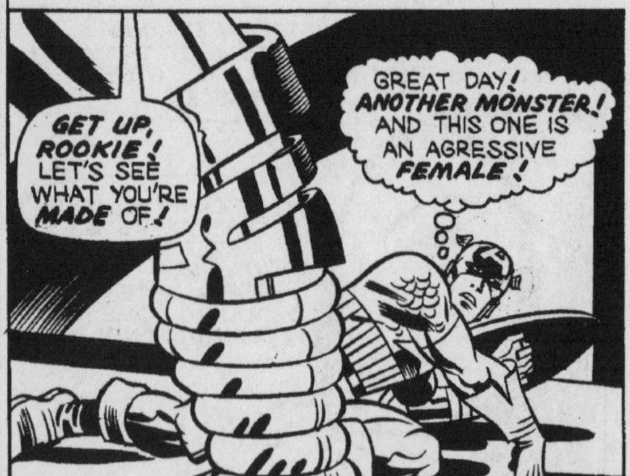
GET UP, ROOKIE! LET'S SEE WHAT YOU'RE MADE OF!
GREAT DAY! ANOTHER MONSTER! AND THIS ONE IS AN AGRESSIVE FEMALE!

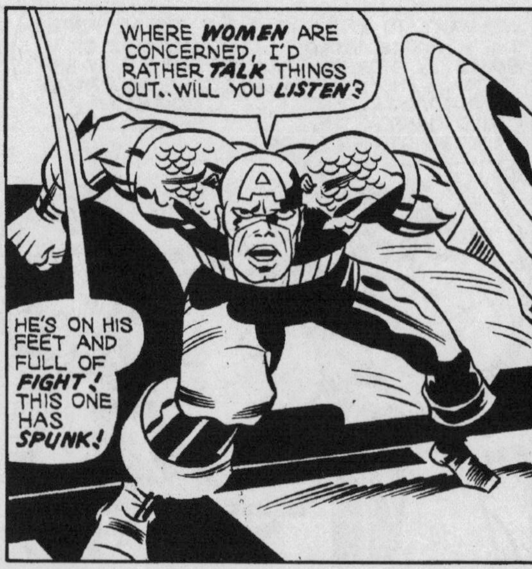
WHERE WOMEN ARE CONCERNED, I'D RATHER TALK THINGS OUT..WILL YOU LISTEN?
HE'S ON HIS FEET AND FULL OF FIGHT! THIS ONE HAS SPUNK!

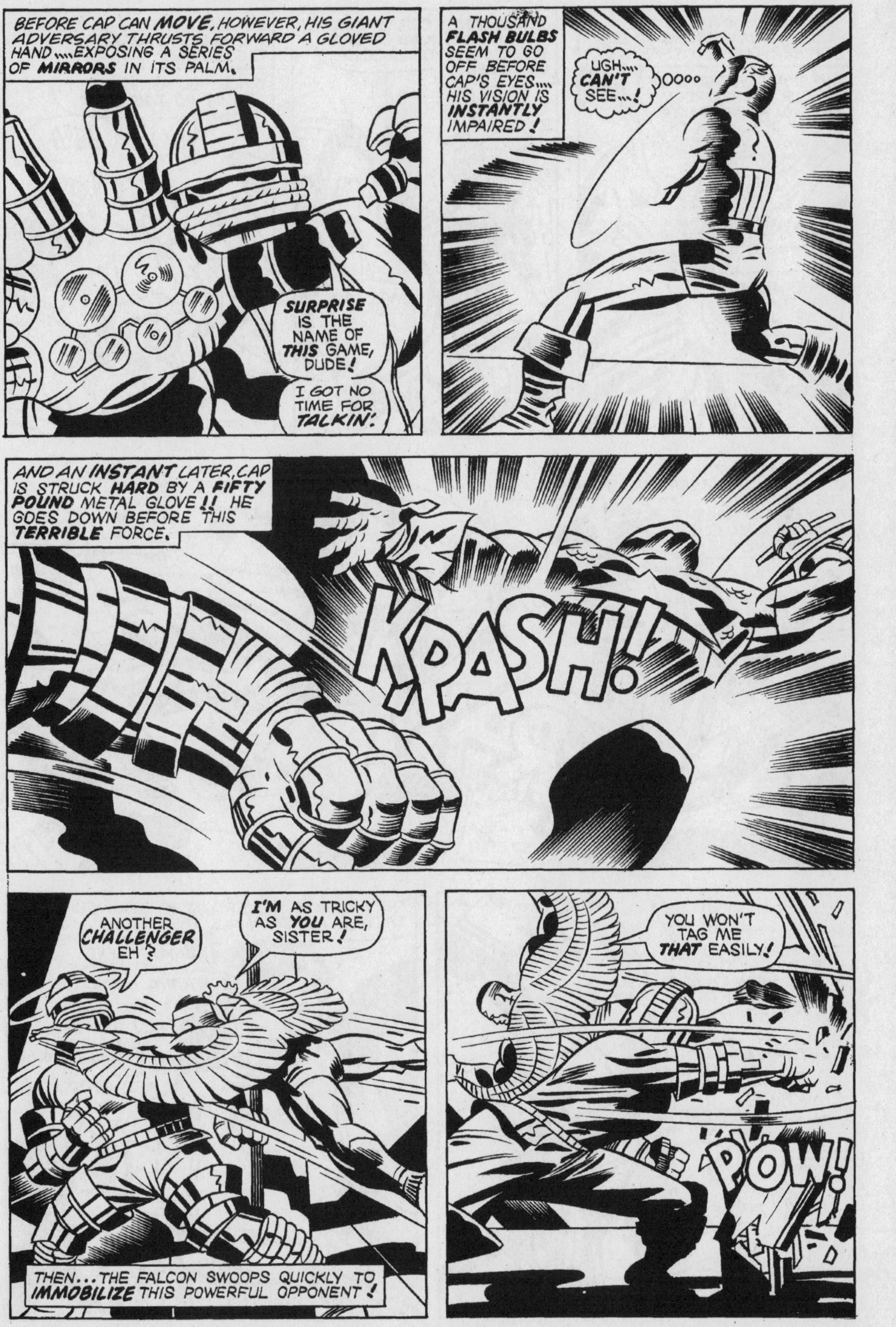
BEFORE CAP CAN MOVE, HOWEVER, HIS GIANT ADVERSARY THRUSTS FORWARD A GLOVED HAND.....EXPOSING A SERIES OF MIRRORS IN ITS PALM.
SURPRISE IS THE NAME OF THIS GAME, DUDE!
I GOT NO TIME FOR TALKIN'.
A THOUSAND FLASH BULBS SEEM TO GO OFF BEFORE CAP'S EYES..... HIS VISION IS INSTANTLY IMPAIRED!
UGH..... CAN'T SEE...!
AND AN INSTANT LATER, CAP IS STRUCK HARD BY A FIFTY POUND METAL GLOVE!! HE GOES DOWN BEFORE THIS TERRIBLE FORCE.
KRASH!
ANOTHER CHALLENGER EH?
I'M AS TRICKY AS YOU ARE, SISTER!
THEN... THE FALCON SWOOPS QUICKLY TO IMMOBILIZE THIS POWERFUL OPPONENT!
YOU WON'T TAG ME THAT EASILY!
POW!

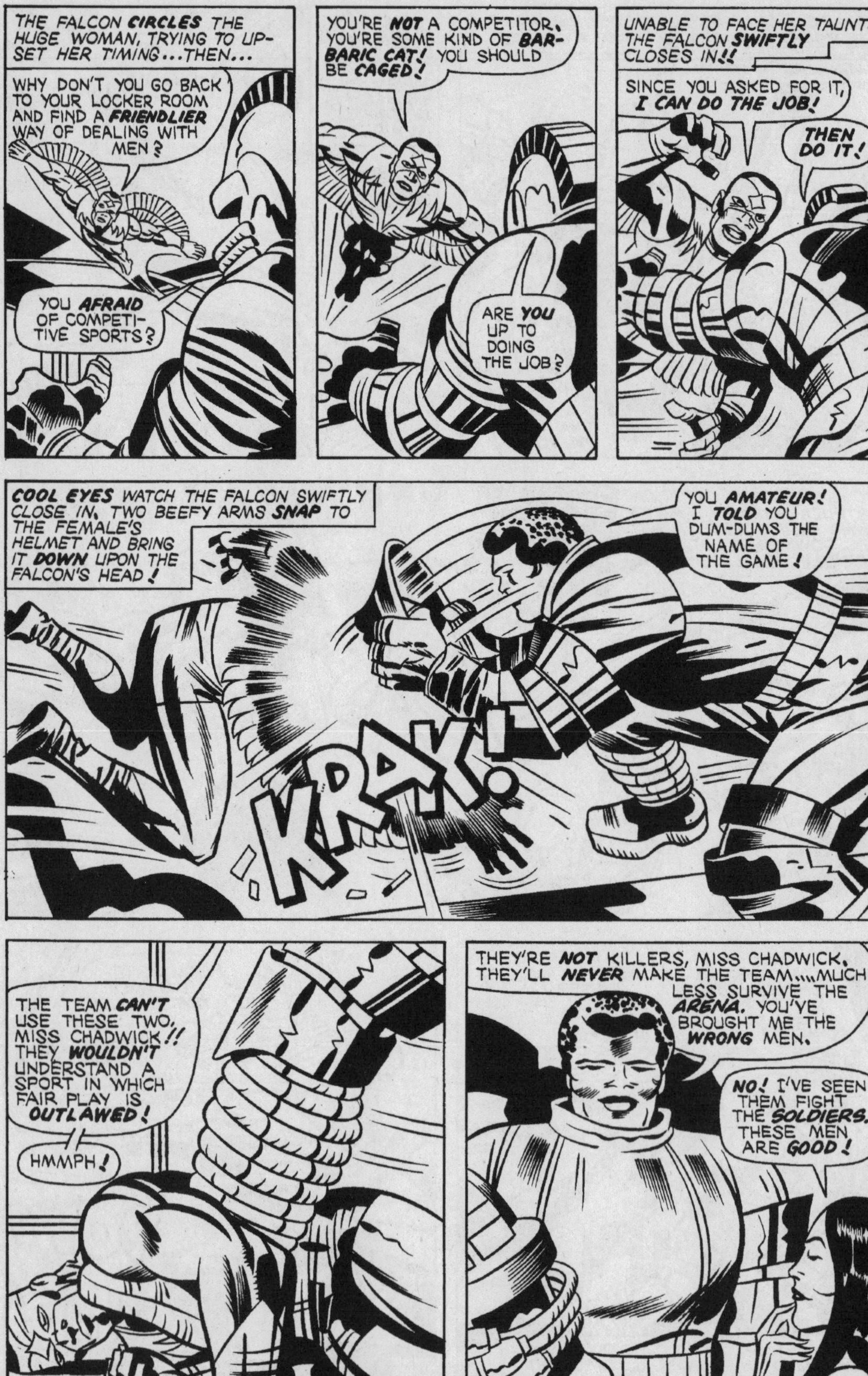

THE FALCON CIRCLES THE HUGE WOMAN, TRYING TO UPSET HER TIMING...THEN...
WHY DON'T YOU GO BACK TO YOUR LOCKER ROOM AND FIND A FRIENDLIER WAY OF DEALING WITH MEN?
YOU AFRAID OF COMPETITIVE SPORTS?
YOU'RE NOT A COMPETITOR. YOU'RE SOME KIND OF BARBARIC CAT! YOU SHOULD BE CAGED!
ARE YOU UP TO DOING THE JOB?
UNABLE TO FACE HER TAUNTS, THE FALCON SWIFTLY CLOSES IN!!
SINCE YOU ASKED FOR IT, I CAN DO THE JOB!
THEN DO IT!
COOL EYES WATCH THE FALCON SWIFTLY CLOSE IN. TWO BEEFY ARMS SNAP TO THE FEMALE'S HELMET AND BRING IT DOWN UPON THE FALCON'S HEAD!
YOU AMATEUR! I TOLD YOU DUM-DUMS THE NAME OF THE GAME!
KRAK!
THE TEAM CAN'T USE THESE TWO, MISS CHADWICK!! THEY WOULDN'T UNDERSTAND A SPORT IN WHICH FAIR PLAY IS OUTLAWED!
HMMPH!
THEY'RE NOT KILLERS, MISS CHADWICK. THEY'LL NEVER MAKE THE TEAM.....MUCH LESS SURVIVE THE ARENA. YOU'VE BROUGHT ME THE WRONG MEN.
NO! I'VE SEEN THEM FIGHT THE SOLDIERS. THESE MEN ARE GOOD!

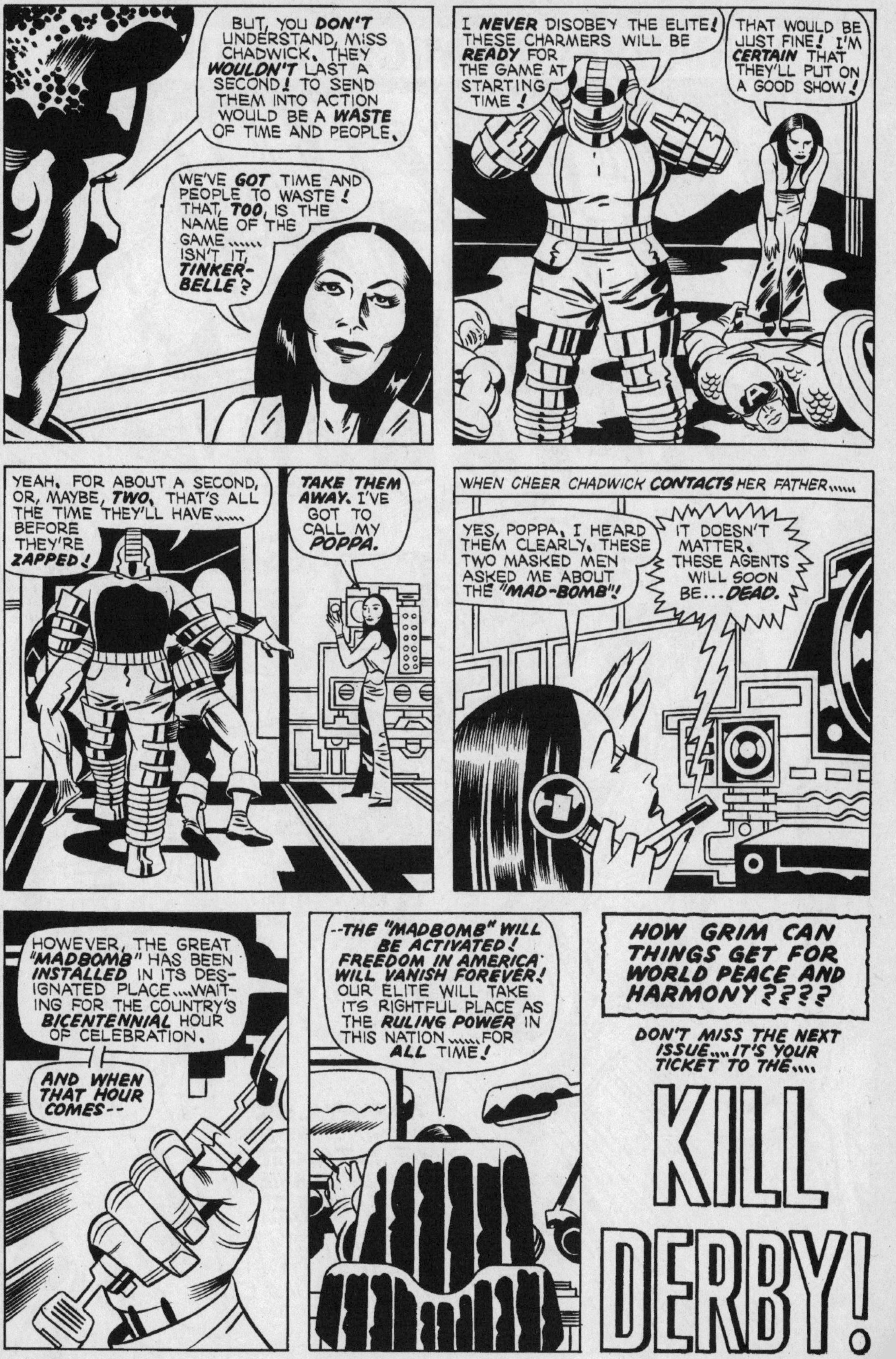
BUT, YOU DON'T UNDERSTAND, MISS CHADWICK. THEY WOULDN'T LAST A SECOND! TO SEND THEM INTO ACTION WOULD BE A WASTE OF TIME AND PEOPLE.
WE'VE GOT TIME AND PEOPLE TO WASTE! THAT, TOO, IS THE NAME OF THE GAME...... ISN'T IT, TINKER-BELLE?
I NEVER DISOBEY THE ELITE! THESE CHARMERS WILL BE READY FOR THE GAME AT STARTING TIME!
THAT WOULD BE JUST FINE! I'M CERTAIN THAT THEY'LL PUT ON A GOOD SHOW!
YEAH. FOR ABOUT A SECOND, OR, MAYBE, TWO. THAT'S ALL THE TIME THEY'LL HAVE...... BEFORE THEY'RE ZAPPED!
TAKE THEM AWAY. I'VE GOT TO CALL MY POPPA.
WHEN CHEER CHADWICK CONTACTS HER FATHER......
YES, POPPA, I HEARD THEM CLEARLY. THESE TWO MASKED MEN ASKED ME ABOUT THE "MAD-BOMB"!
IT DOESN'T MATTER. THESE AGENTS WILL SOON BE...DEAD.
HOWEVER, THE GREAT "MADBOMB" HAS BEEN INSTALLED IN ITS DES-IGNATED PLACE....WAIT-ING FOR THE COUNTRY'S BICENTENNIAL HOUR OF CELEBRATION.
AND WHEN THAT HOUR COMES--
--THE "MADBOMB" WILL BE ACTIVATED! FREEDOM IN AMERICA WILL VANISH FOREVER! OUR ELITE WILL TAKE ITS RIGHTFUL PLACE AS THE RULING POWER IN THIS NATION......FOR ALL TIME!
HOW GRIM CAN THINGS GET FOR WORLD PEACE AND HARMONY????
DON'T MISS THE NEXT ISSUE....IT'S YOUR TICKET TO THE....
KILL DERBY!

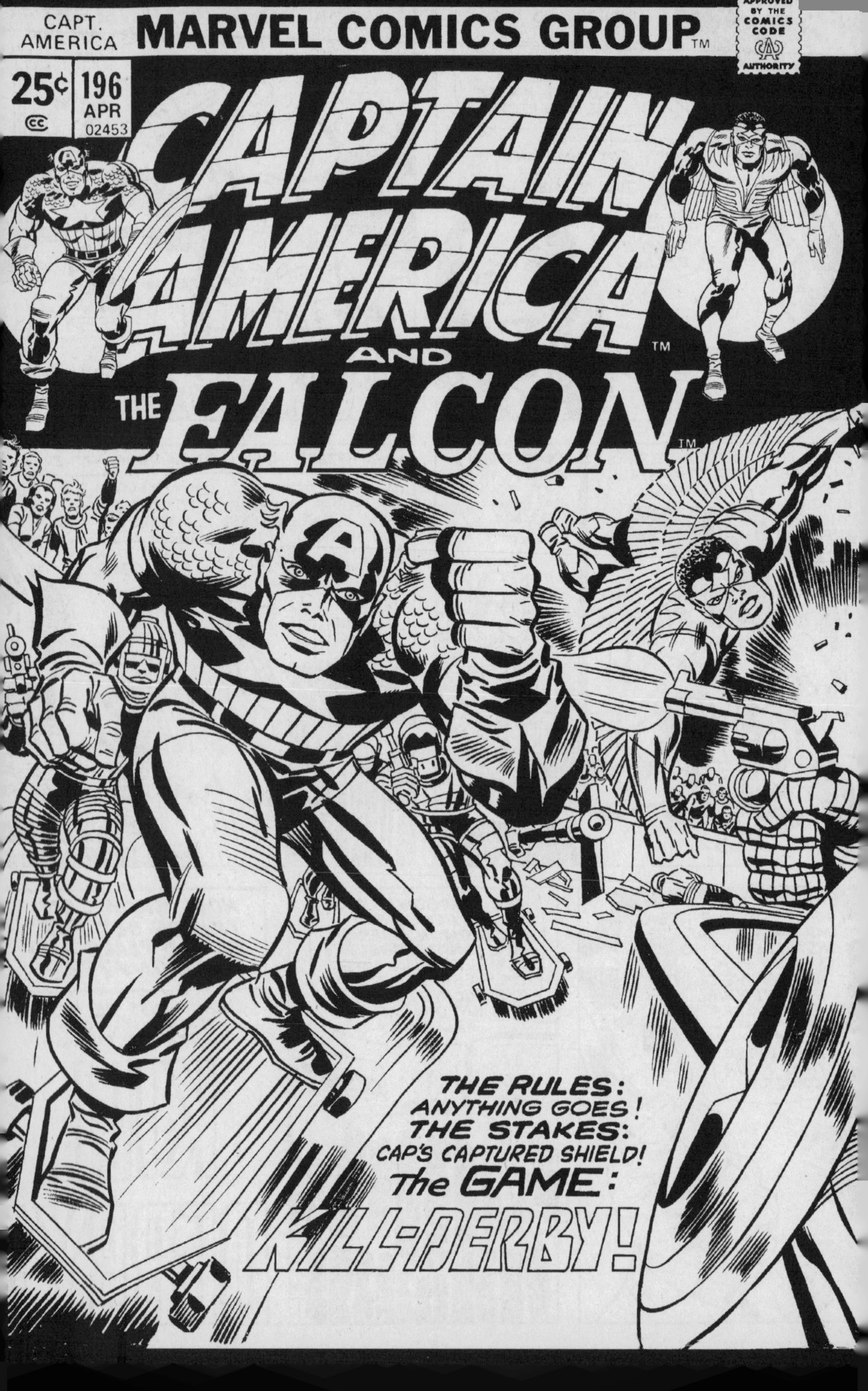
CAPT. AMERICA
MARVEL COMICS GROUP
APPROVED BY THE COMICS CODE AUTHORITY
25¢
196
APR
02453
CAPTAIN AMERICA AND THE FALCON
THE RULES: ANYTHING GOES!
THE STAKES: CAP'S CAPTURED SHIELD!
The GAME: KILL-DERBY!

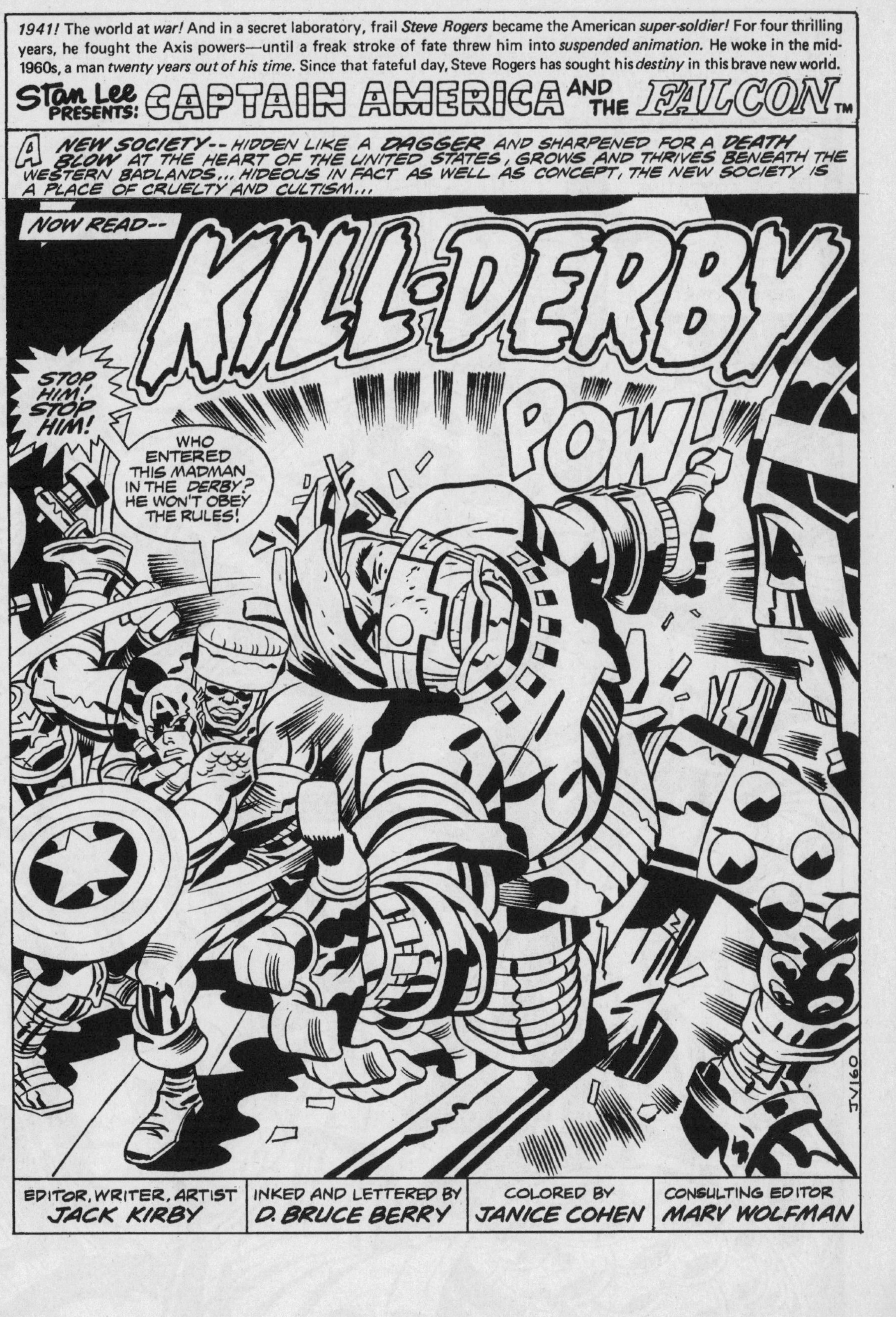
1941! The world at war! And in a secret laboratory, frail Steve Rogers became the American super-soldier! For four thrilling years, he fought the Axis powers—until a freak stroke of fate threw him into suspended animation. He woke in the mid-1960s, a man twenty years out of his time. Since that fateful day, Steve Rogers has sought his destiny in this brave new world.
Stan Lee PRESENTS: CAPTAIN AMERICA AND THE FALCON™
A NEW SOCIETY-- HIDDEN LIKE A DAGGER AND SHARPENED FOR A DEATH BLOW AT THE HEART OF THE UNITED STATES, GROWS AND THRIVES BENEATH THE WESTERN BADLANDS... HIDEOUS IN FACT AS WELL AS CONCEPT, THE NEW SOCIETY IS A PLACE OF CRUELTY AND CULTISM...
NOW READ--
KILL-DERBY
STOP HIM! STOP HIM!
WHO ENTERED THIS MADMAN IN THE DERBY? HE WON'T OBEY THE RULES!
POW!
EDITOR, WRITER, ARTIST JACK KIRBY
INKED AND LETTERED BY D. BRUCE BERRY
COLORED BY JANICE COHEN
CONSULTING EDITOR MARV WOLFMAN

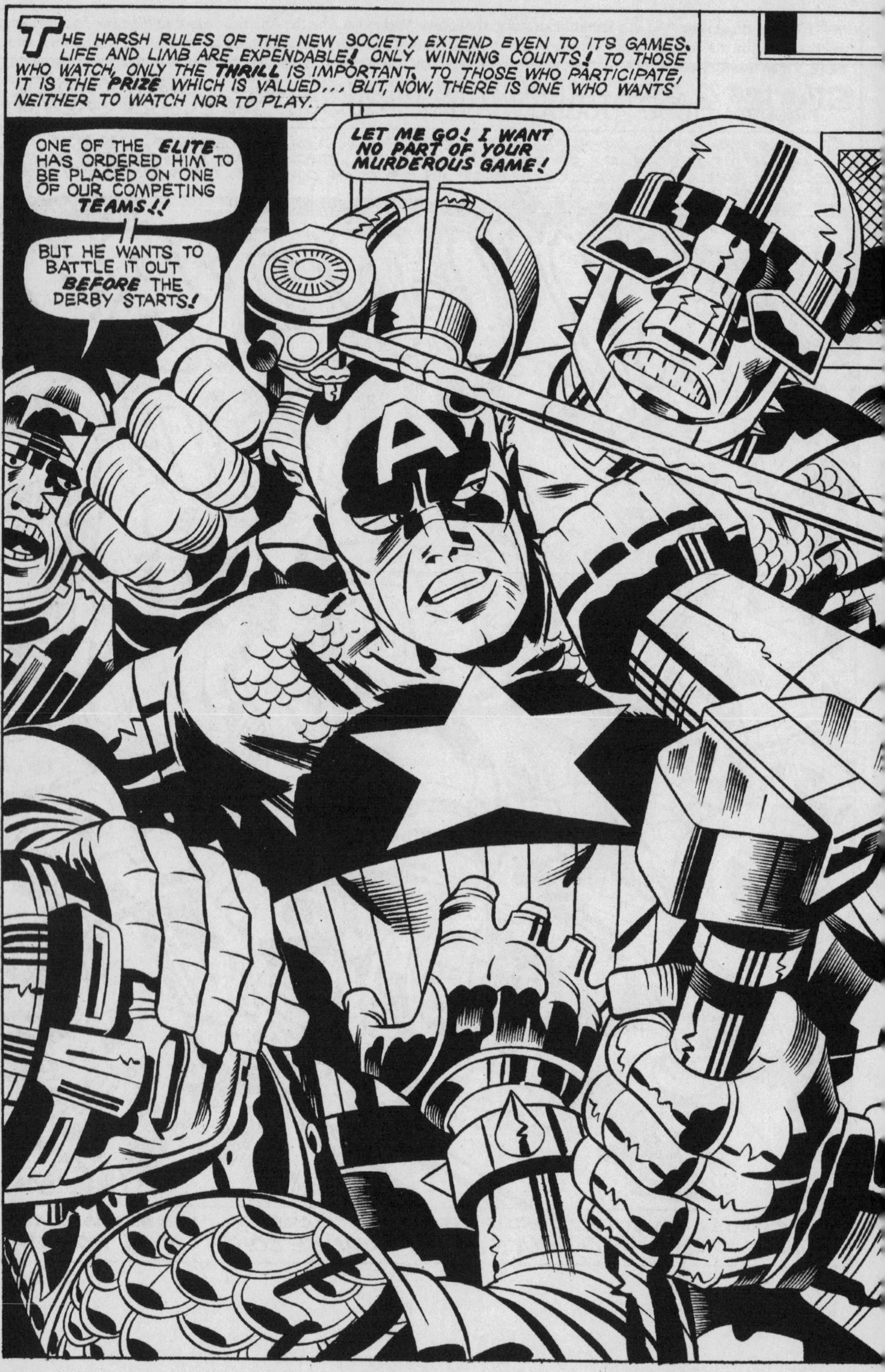
THE HARSH RULES OF THE NEW SOCIETY EXTEND EVEN TO ITS GAMES. LIFE AND LIMB ARE EXPENDABLE! ONLY WINNING COUNTS! TO THOSE WHO WATCH, ONLY THE THRILL IS IMPORTANT. TO THOSE WHO PARTICIPATE, IT IS THE PRIZE WHICH IS VALUED... BUT, NOW, THERE IS ONE WHO WANTS NEITHER TO WATCH NOR TO PLAY.
ONE OF THE ELITE HAS ORDERED HIM TO BE PLACED ON ONE OF OUR COMPETING TEAMS!!
BUT HE WANTS TO BATTLE IT OUT BEFORE THE DERBY STARTS!
LET ME GO! I WANT NO PART OF YOUR MURDEROUS GAME!

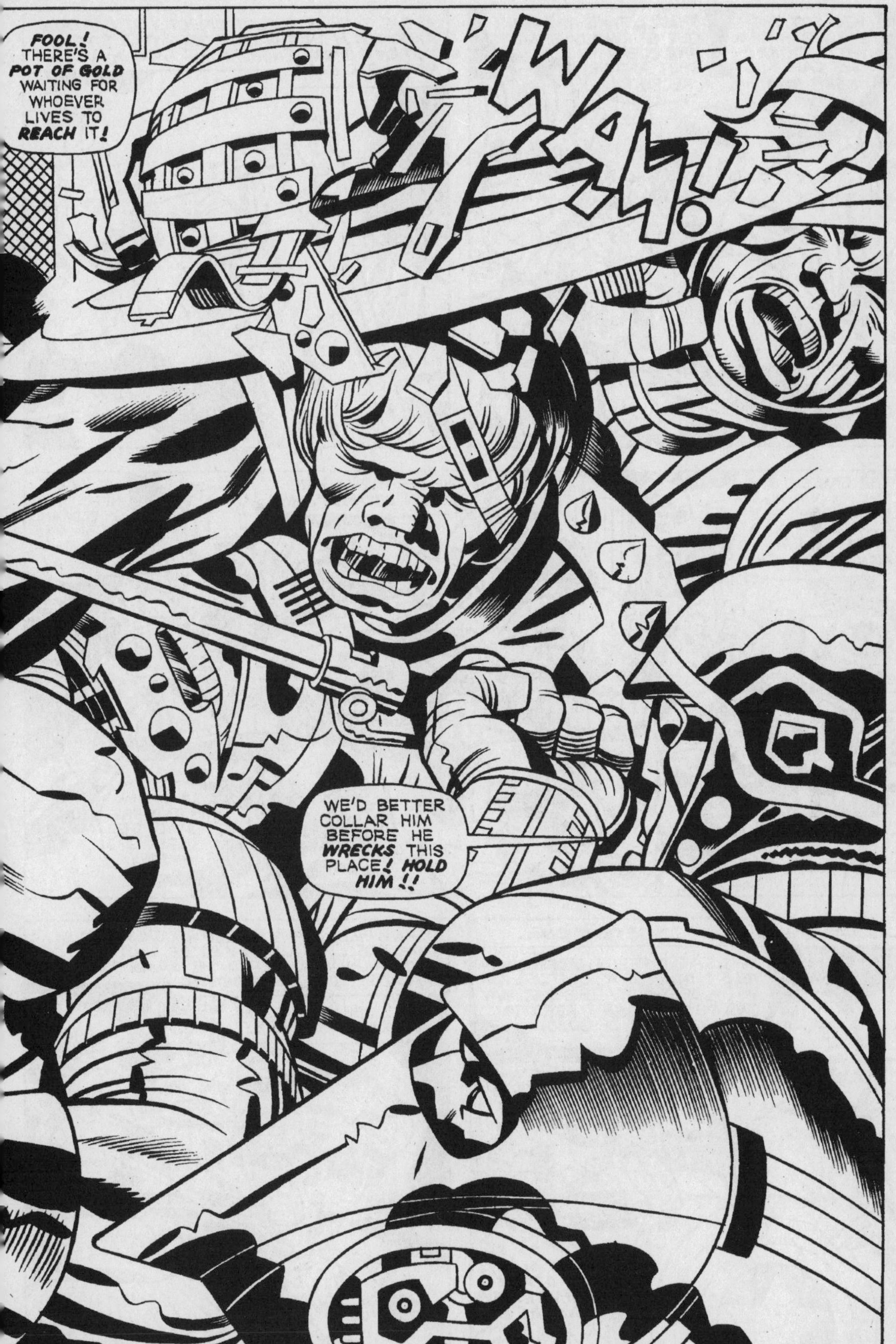
FOOL! THERE'S A POT OF GOLD WAITING FOR WHOEVER LIVES TO REACH IT!
WE'D BETTER COLLAR HIM BEFORE HE WRECKS THIS PLACE! HOLD HIM!!

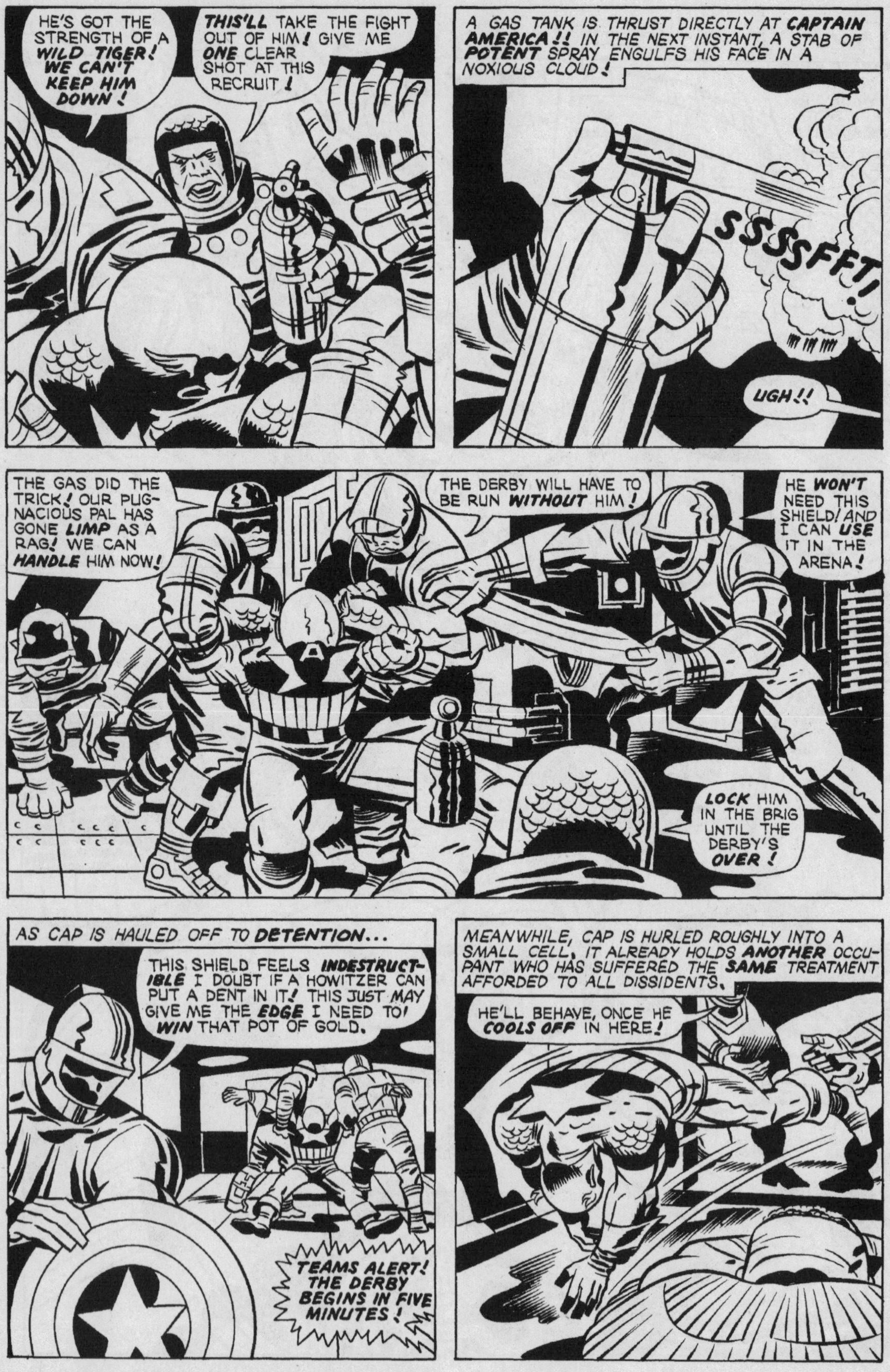
HE'S GOT THE STRENGTH OF A WILD TIGER! WE CAN'T KEEP HIM DOWN!
THIS'LL TAKE THE FIGHT OUT OF HIM! GIVE ME ONE CLEAR SHOT AT THIS RECRUIT!
A GAS TANK IS THRUST DIRECTLY AT CAPTAIN AMERICA!! IN THE NEXT INSTANT, A STAB OF POTENT SPRAY ENGULFS HIS FACE IN A NOXIOUS CLOUD!
SSSSFFT!
UGH!!
THE GAS DID THE TRICK! OUR PUG-NACIOUS PAL HAS GONE LIMP AS A RAG! WE CAN HANDLE HIM NOW!
THE DERBY WILL HAVE TO BE RUN WITHOUT HIM!
HE WON'T NEED THIS SHIELD! AND I CAN USE IT IN THE ARENA!
LOCK HIM IN THE BRIG UNTIL THE DERBY'S OVER!
AS CAP IS HAULED OFF TO DETENTION...
THIS SHIELD FEELS INDESTRUCT-IBLE I DOUBT IF A HOWITZER CAN PUT A DENT IN IT! THIS JUST MAY GIVE ME THE EDGE I NEED TO WIN THAT POT OF GOLD.
TEAMS ALERT! THE DERBY BEGINS IN FIVE MINUTES!
MEANWHILE, CAP IS HURLED ROUGHLY INTO A SMALL CELL, IT ALREADY HOLDS ANOTHER OCCU-PANT WHO HAS SUFFERED THE SAME TREATMENT AFFORDED TO ALL DISSIDENTS.
HE'LL BEHAVE, ONCE HE COOLS OFF IN HERE!

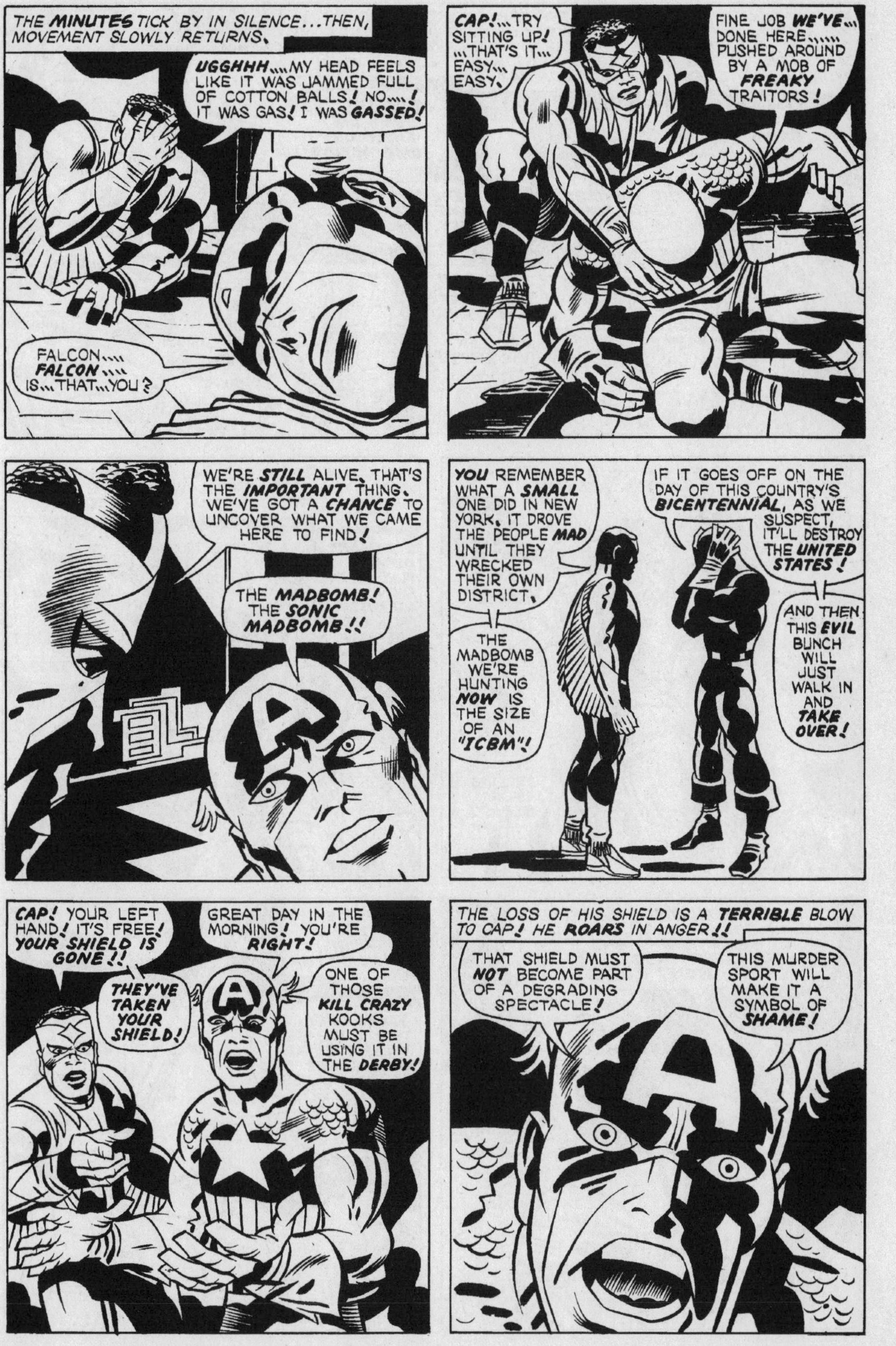
THE MINUTES TICK BY IN SILENCE...THEN, MOVEMENT SLOWLY RETURNS.
UGGHHH....MY HEAD FEELS LIKE IT WAS JAMMED FULL OF COTTON BALLS! NO....! IT WAS GAS! I WAS GASSED!
FALCON.... FALCON.... IS...THAT...YOU?
CAP!...TRY SITTING UP! ...THAT'S IT... EASY... EASY.
FINE JOB WE'VE... DONE HERE...... PUSHED AROUND BY A MOB OF FREAKY TRAITORS!
WE'RE STILL ALIVE. THAT'S THE IMPORTANT THING. WE'VE GOT A CHANCE TO UNCOVER WHAT WE CAME HERE TO FIND!
THE MADBOMB! THE SONIC MADBOMB!!
YOU REMEMBER WHAT A SMALL ONE DID IN NEW YORK. IT DROVE THE PEOPLE MAD UNTIL THEY WRECKED THEIR OWN DISTRICT.
THE MADBOMB WE'RE HUNTING NOW IS THE SIZE OF AN "ICBM"!
IF IT GOES OFF ON THE DAY OF THIS COUNTRY'S BICENTENNIAL, AS WE SUSPECT, IT'LL DESTROY THE UNITED STATES!
AND THEN THIS EVIL BUNCH WILL JUST WALK IN AND TAKE OVER!
CAP! YOUR LEFT HAND! IT'S FREE! YOUR SHIELD IS GONE!!
THEY'VE TAKEN YOUR SHIELD!
GREAT DAY IN THE MORNING! YOU'RE RIGHT!
ONE OF THOSE KILL CRAZY KOOKS MUST BE USING IT IN THE DERBY!
THE LOSS OF HIS SHIELD IS A TERRIBLE BLOW TO CAP! HE ROARS IN ANGER!!
THAT SHIELD MUST NOT BECOME PART OF A DEGRADING SPECTACLE!
THIS MURDER SPORT WILL MAKE IT A SYMBOL OF SHAME!

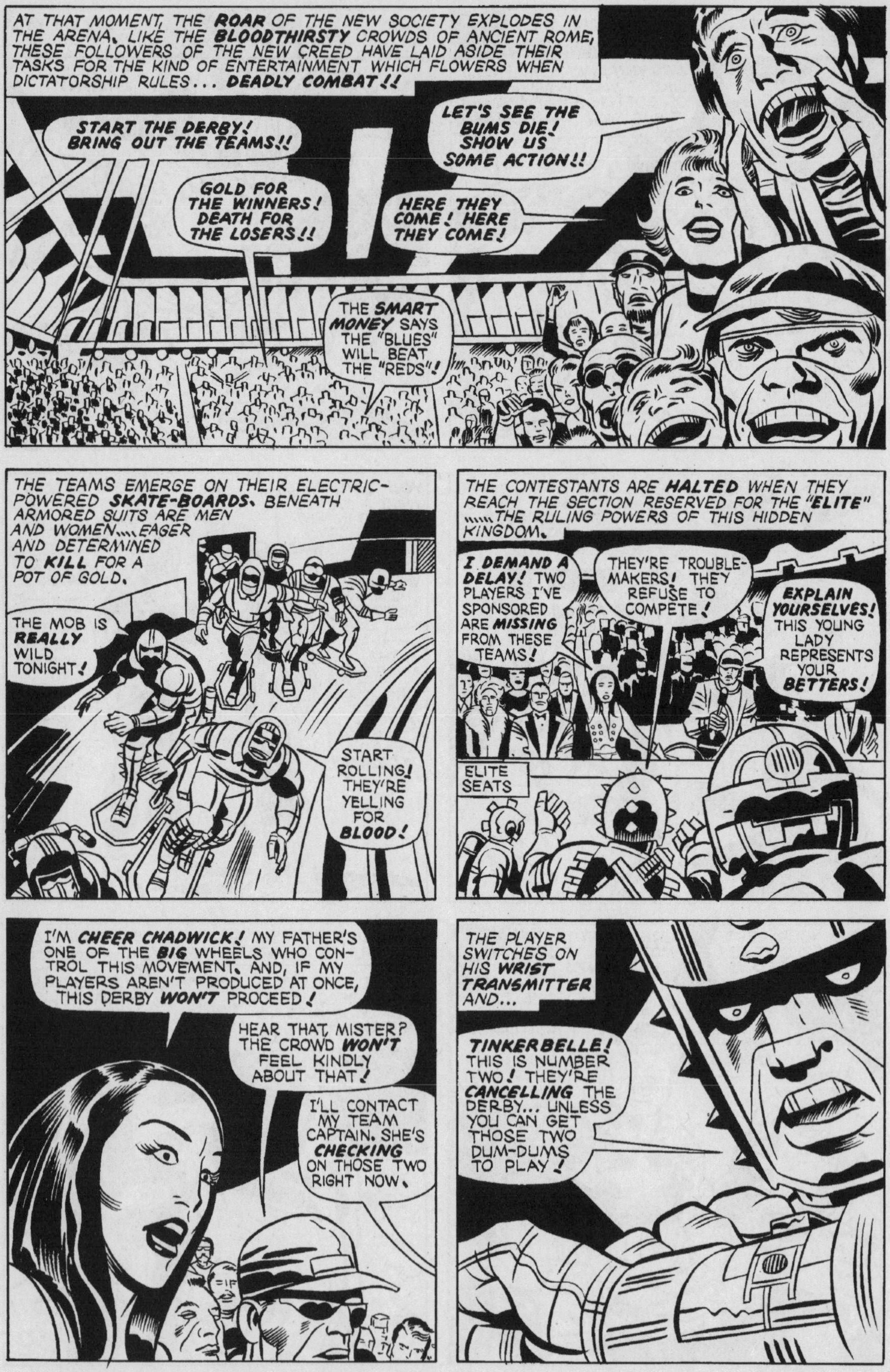
AT THAT MOMENT, THE ROAR OF THE NEW SOCIETY EXPLODES IN THE ARENA. LIKE THE BLOODTHIRSTY CROWDS OF ANCIENT ROME, THESE FOLLOWERS OF THE NEW CREED HAVE LAID ASIDE THEIR TASKS FOR THE KIND OF ENTERTAINMENT WHICH FLOWERS WHEN DICTATORSHIP RULES... DEADLY COMBAT!!
START THE DERBY! BRING OUT THE TEAMS!!
LET'S SEE THE BUMS DIE! SHOW US SOME ACTION!!
GOLD FOR THE WINNERS! DEATH FOR THE LOSERS!!
HERE THEY COME! HERE THEY COME!
THE SMART MONEY SAYS THE "BLUES" WILL BEAT THE "REDS"!
THE TEAMS EMERGE ON THEIR ELECTRIC-POWERED SKATE-BOARDS. BENEATH ARMORED SUITS ARE MEN AND WOMEN..... EAGER AND DETERMINED TO KILL FOR A POT OF GOLD.
THE MOB IS REALLY WILD TONIGHT!
START ROLLING! THEY'RE YELLING FOR BLOOD!
THE CONTESTANTS ARE HALTED WHEN THEY REACH THE SECTION RESERVED FOR THE "ELITE" ......THE RULING POWERS OF THIS HIDDEN KINGDOM.
I DEMAND A DELAY! TWO PLAYERS I'VE SPONSORED ARE MISSING FROM THESE TEAMS!
THEY'RE TROUBLE-MAKERS! THEY REFUSE TO COMPETE!
EXPLAIN YOURSELVES! THIS YOUNG LADY REPRESENTS YOUR BETTERS!
ELITE SEATS
I'M CHEER CHADWICK! MY FATHER'S ONE OF THE BIG WHEELS WHO CONTROL THIS MOVEMENT. AND, IF MY PLAYERS AREN'T PRODUCED AT ONCE, THIS DERBY WON'T PROCEED!
HEAR THAT, MISTER? THE CROWD WON'T FEEL KINDLY ABOUT THAT!
I'LL CONTACT MY TEAM CAPTAIN. SHE'S CHECKING ON THOSE TWO RIGHT NOW.
THE PLAYER SWITCHES ON HIS WRIST TRANSMITTER AND...
TINKERBELLE! THIS IS NUMBER TWO! THEY'RE CANCELLING THE DERBY... UNLESS YOU CAN GET THOSE TWO DUM-DUMS TO PLAY!

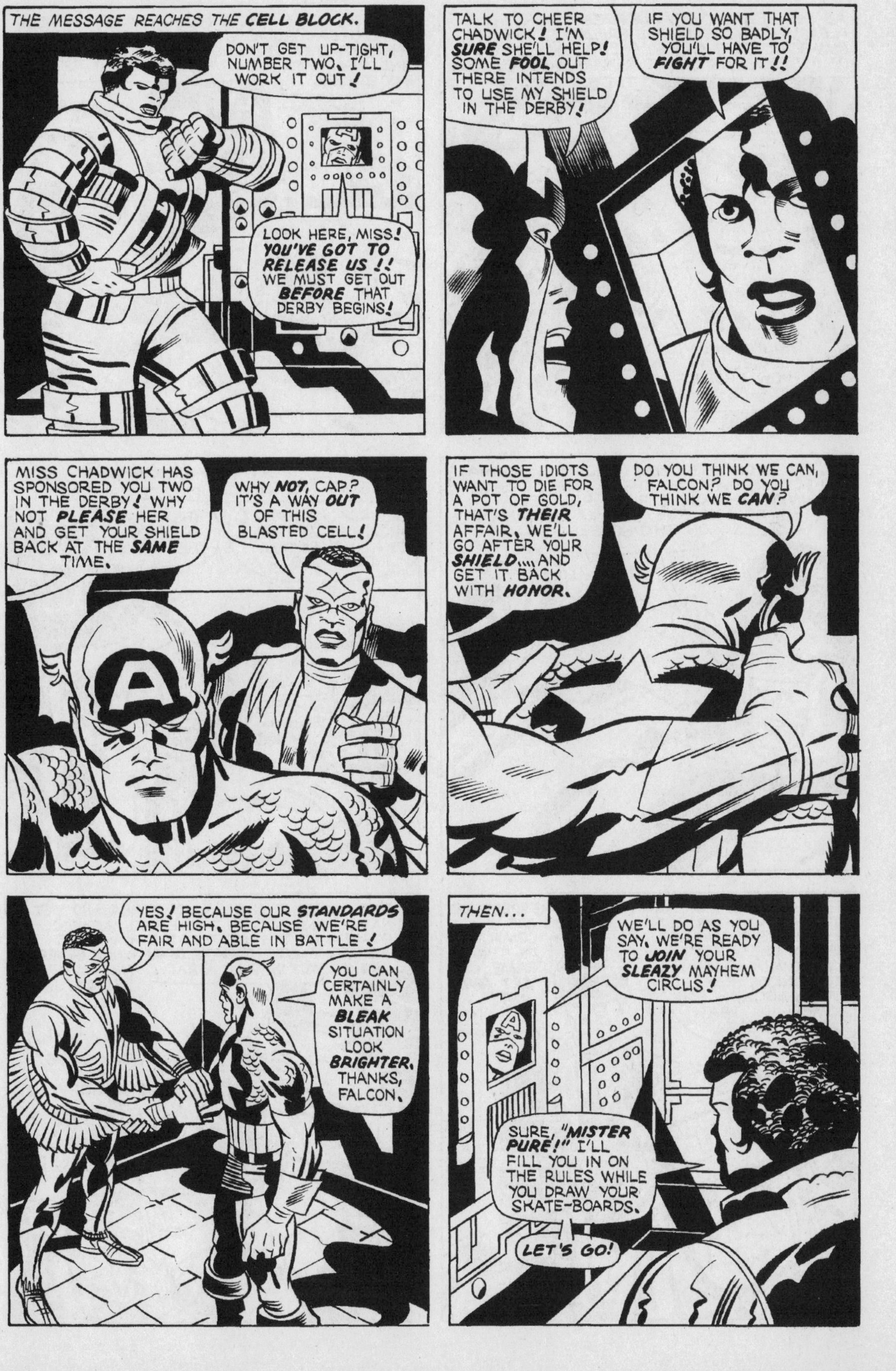
THE MESSAGE REACHES THE CELL BLOCK.
DON'T GET UP-TIGHT, NUMBER TWO. I'LL WORK IT OUT!
LOOK HERE, MISS! YOU'VE GOT TO RELEASE US!! WE MUST GET OUT BEFORE THAT DERBY BEGINS!
TALK TO CHEER CHADWICK! I'M SURE SHE'LL HELP! SOME FOOL OUT THERE INTENDS TO USE MY SHIELD IN THE DERBY!
IF YOU WANT THAT SHIELD SO BADLY, YOU'LL HAVE TO FIGHT FOR IT!!
MISS CHADWICK HAS SPONSORED YOU TWO IN THE DERBY! WHY NOT PLEASE HER AND GET YOUR SHIELD BACK AT THE SAME TIME.
WHY NOT, CAP? IT'S A WAY OUT OF THIS BLASTED CELL!
IF THOSE IDIOTS WANT TO DIE FOR A POT OF GOLD, THAT'S THEIR AFFAIR. WE'LL GO AFTER YOUR SHIELD.....AND GET IT BACK WITH HONOR.
DO YOU THINK WE CAN, FALCON? DO YOU THINK WE CAN?
YES! BECAUSE OUR STANDARDS ARE HIGH. BECAUSE WE'RE FAIR AND ABLE IN BATTLE!
YOU CAN CERTAINLY MAKE A BLEAK SITUATION LOOK BRIGHTER. THANKS, FALCON.
THEN...
WE'LL DO AS YOU SAY. WE'RE READY TO JOIN YOUR SLEAZY MAYHEM CIRCUS!
SURE, "MISTER PURE!" I'LL FILL YOU IN ON THE RULES WHILE YOU DRAW YOUR SKATE-BOARDS.
LET'S GO!

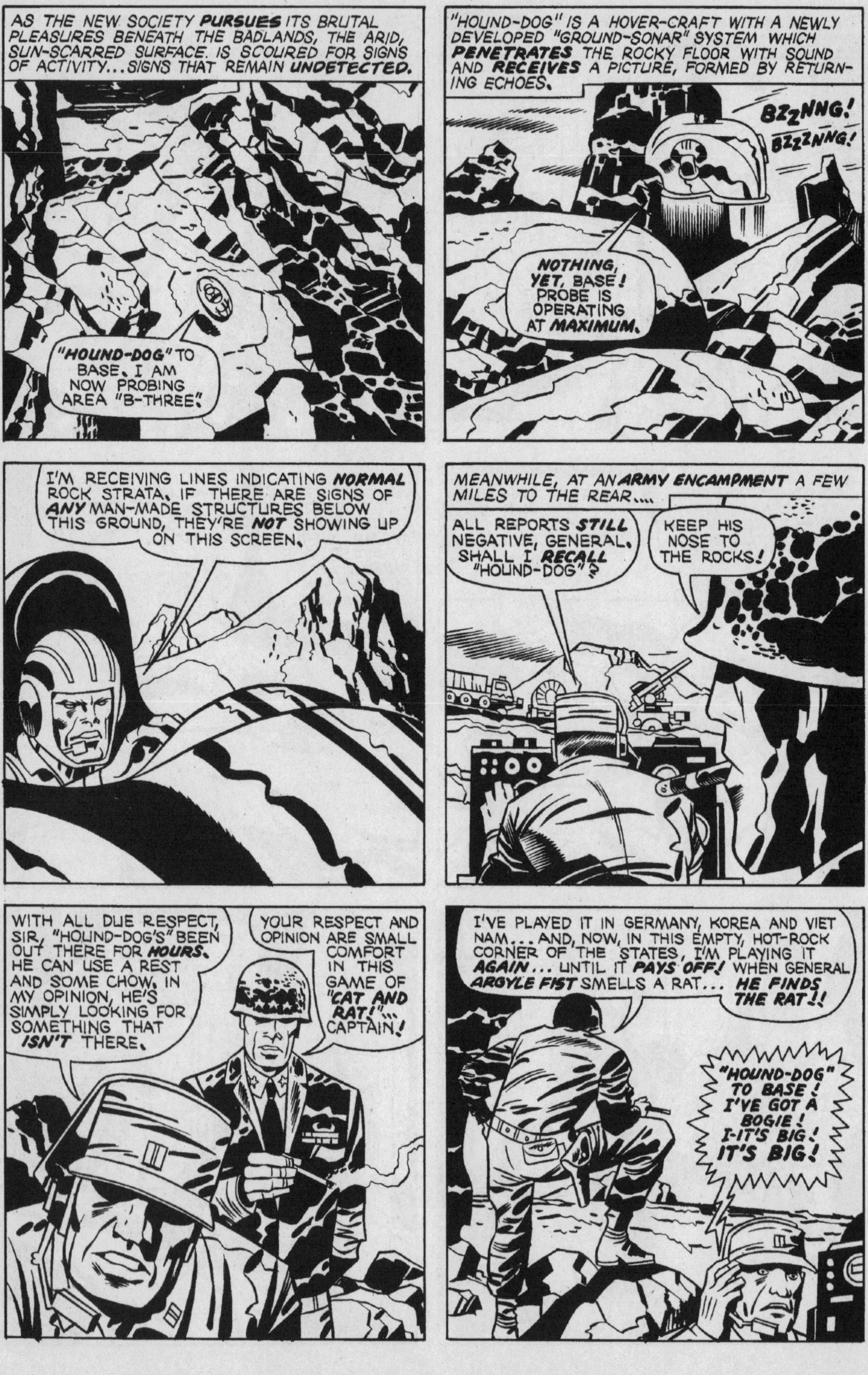
AS THE NEW SOCIETY PURSUES ITS BRUTAL PLEASURES BENEATH THE BADLANDS, THE ARID, SUN-SCARRED SURFACE IS SCOURED FOR SIGNS OF ACTIVITY... SIGNS THAT REMAIN UNDETECTED.
"HOUND-DOG" TO BASE. I AM NOW PROBING AREA "B-THREE".
"HOUND-DOG" IS A HOVER-CRAFT WITH A NEWLY DEVELOPED "GROUND-SONAR" SYSTEM WHICH PENETRATES THE ROCKY FLOOR WITH SOUND AND RECEIVES A PICTURE, FORMED BY RETURNING ECHOES.
BZZNNG!
BZZZNNG!
NOTHING, YET, BASE! PROBE IS OPERATING AT MAXIMUM.
I'M RECEIVING LINES INDICATING NORMAL ROCK STRATA. IF THERE ARE SIGNS OF ANY MAN-MADE STRUCTURES BELOW THIS GROUND, THEY'RE NOT SHOWING UP ON THIS SCREEN.
MEANWHILE, AT AN ARMY ENCAMPMENT A FEW MILES TO THE REAR....
ALL REPORTS STILL NEGATIVE, GENERAL. SHALL I RECALL "HOUND-DOG"?
KEEP HIS NOSE TO THE ROCKS!
WITH ALL DUE RESPECT, SIR, "HOUND-DOG'S" BEEN OUT THERE FOR HOURS. HE CAN USE A REST AND SOME CHOW. IN MY OPINION, HE'S SIMPLY LOOKING FOR SOMETHING THAT ISN'T THERE.
YOUR RESPECT AND OPINION ARE SMALL COMFORT IN THIS GAME OF "CAT AND RAT!"... CAPTAIN!
I'VE PLAYED IT IN GERMANY, KOREA AND VIET NAM... AND, NOW, IN THIS EMPTY, HOT-ROCK CORNER OF THE STATES, I'M PLAYING IT AGAIN... UNTIL IT PAYS OFF! WHEN GENERAL ARGYLE FIST SMELLS A RAT... HE FINDS THE RAT!!
"HOUND-DOG" TO BASE! I'VE GOT A BOGIE! I-IT'S BIG! IT'S BIG!

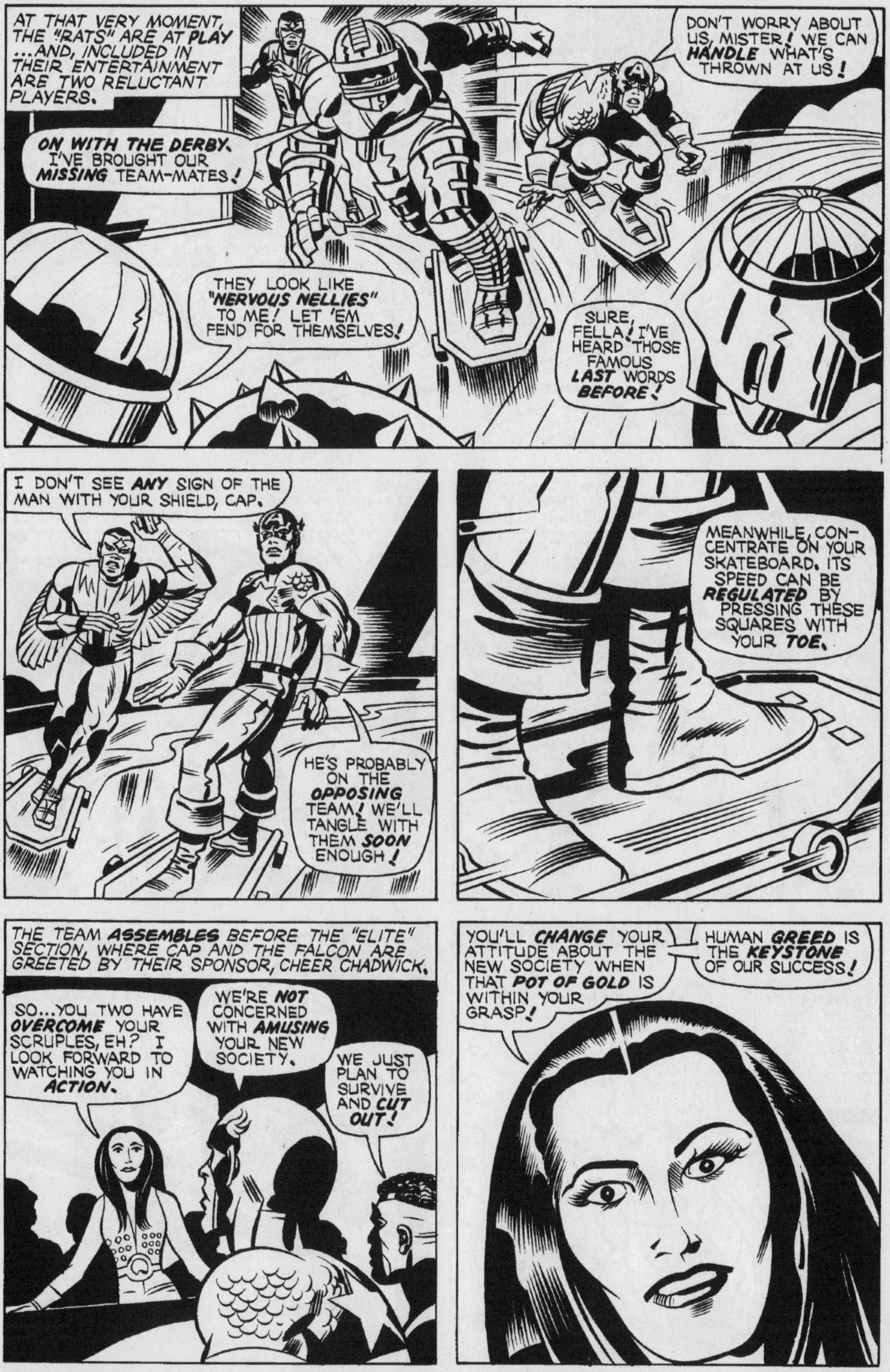
AT THAT VERY MOMENT, THE "RATS" ARE AT PLAY ...AND, INCLUDED IN THEIR ENTERTAINMENT ARE TWO RELUCTANT PLAYERS.
DON'T WORRY ABOUT US, MISTER! WE CAN HANDLE WHAT'S THROWN AT US!
ON WITH THE DERBY. I'VE BROUGHT OUR MISSING TEAM-MATES!
THEY LOOK LIKE "NERVOUS NELLIES" TO ME! LET 'EM FEND FOR THEMSELVES!
SURE, FELLA! I'VE HEARD THOSE FAMOUS LAST WORDS BEFORE!
I DON'T SEE ANY SIGN OF THE MAN WITH YOUR SHIELD, CAP.
HE'S PROBABLY ON THE OPPOSING TEAM! WE'LL TANGLE WITH THEM SOON ENOUGH!
MEANWHILE, CONCENTRATE ON YOUR SKATEBOARD. ITS SPEED CAN BE REGULATED BY PRESSING THESE SQUARES WITH YOUR TOE.
THE TEAM ASSEMBLES BEFORE THE "ELITE" SECTION, WHERE CAP AND THE FALCON ARE GREETED BY THEIR SPONSOR, CHEER CHADWICK.
SO...YOU TWO HAVE OVERCOME YOUR SCRUPLES, EH? I LOOK FORWARD TO WATCHING YOU IN ACTION.
WE'RE NOT CONCERNED WITH AMUSING YOUR NEW SOCIETY.
WE JUST PLAN TO SURVIVE AND CUT OUT!
YOU'LL CHANGE YOUR ATTITUDE ABOUT THE NEW SOCIETY WHEN THAT POT OF GOLD IS WITHIN YOUR GRASP!
HUMAN GREED IS THE KEYSTONE OF OUR SUCCESS!

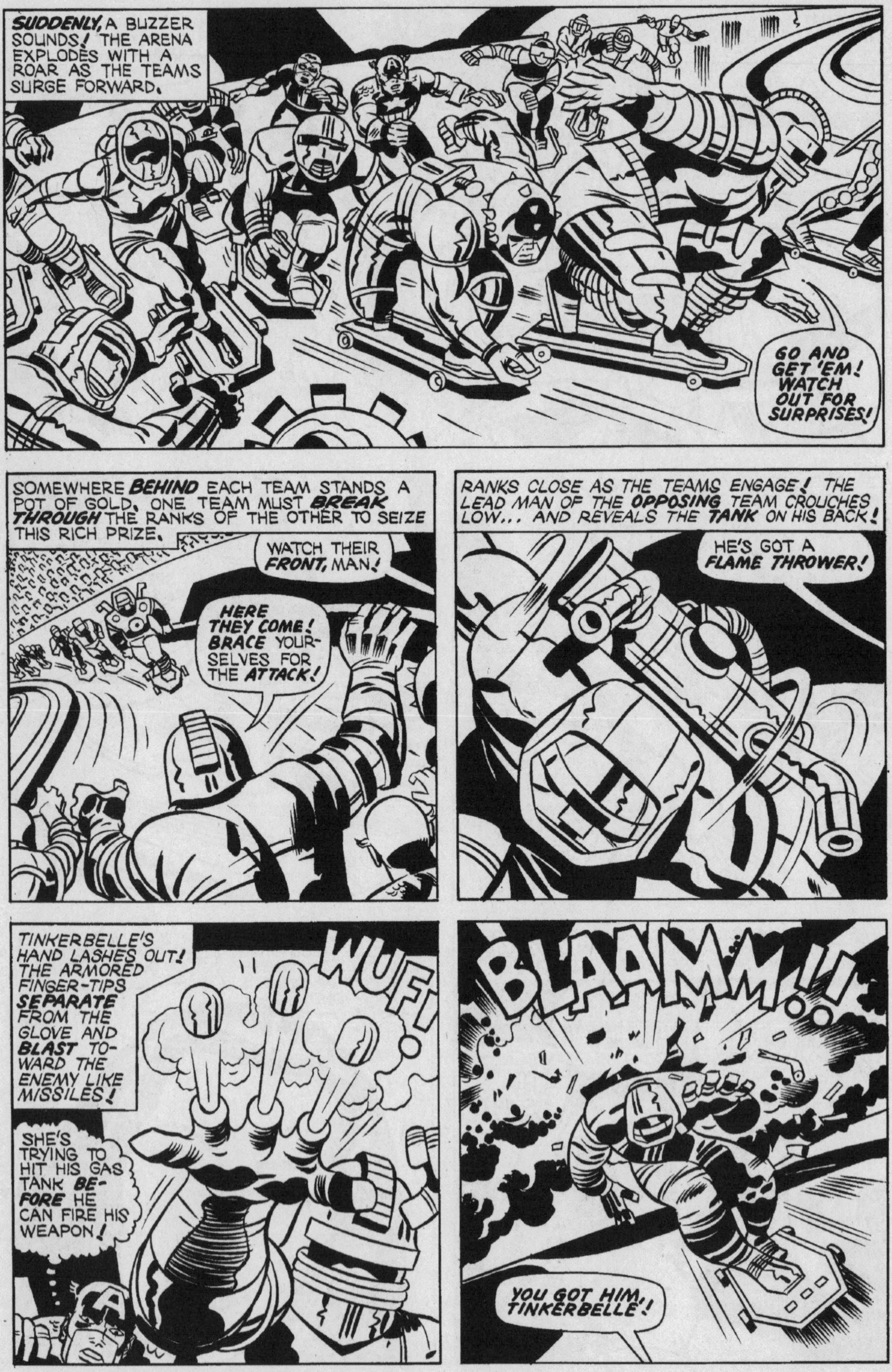
SUDDENLY, A BUZZER SOUNDS! THE ARENA EXPLODES WITH A ROAR AS THE TEAMS SURGE FORWARD.
GO AND GET 'EM! WATCH OUT FOR SURPRISES!
SOMEWHERE BEHIND EACH TEAM STANDS A POT OF GOLD. ONE TEAM MUST BREAK THROUGH THE RANKS OF THE OTHER TO SEIZE THIS RICH PRIZE.
WATCH THEIR FRONT, MAN!
HERE THEY COME! BRACE YOURSELVES FOR THE ATTACK!
RANKS CLOSE AS THE TEAMS ENGAGE! THE LEAD MAN OF THE OPPOSING TEAM CROUCHES LOW... AND REVEALS THE TANK ON HIS BACK!
HE'S GOT A FLAME THROWER!
TINKERBELLE'S HAND LASHES OUT! THE ARMORED FINGER-TIPS SEPARATE FROM THE GLOVE AND BLAST TOWARD THE ENEMY LIKE MISSILES!
WUFF
SHE'S TRYING TO HIT HIS GAS TANK BEFORE HE CAN FIRE HIS WEAPON!
BLAAMM!!
YOU GOT HIM, TINKERBELLE!

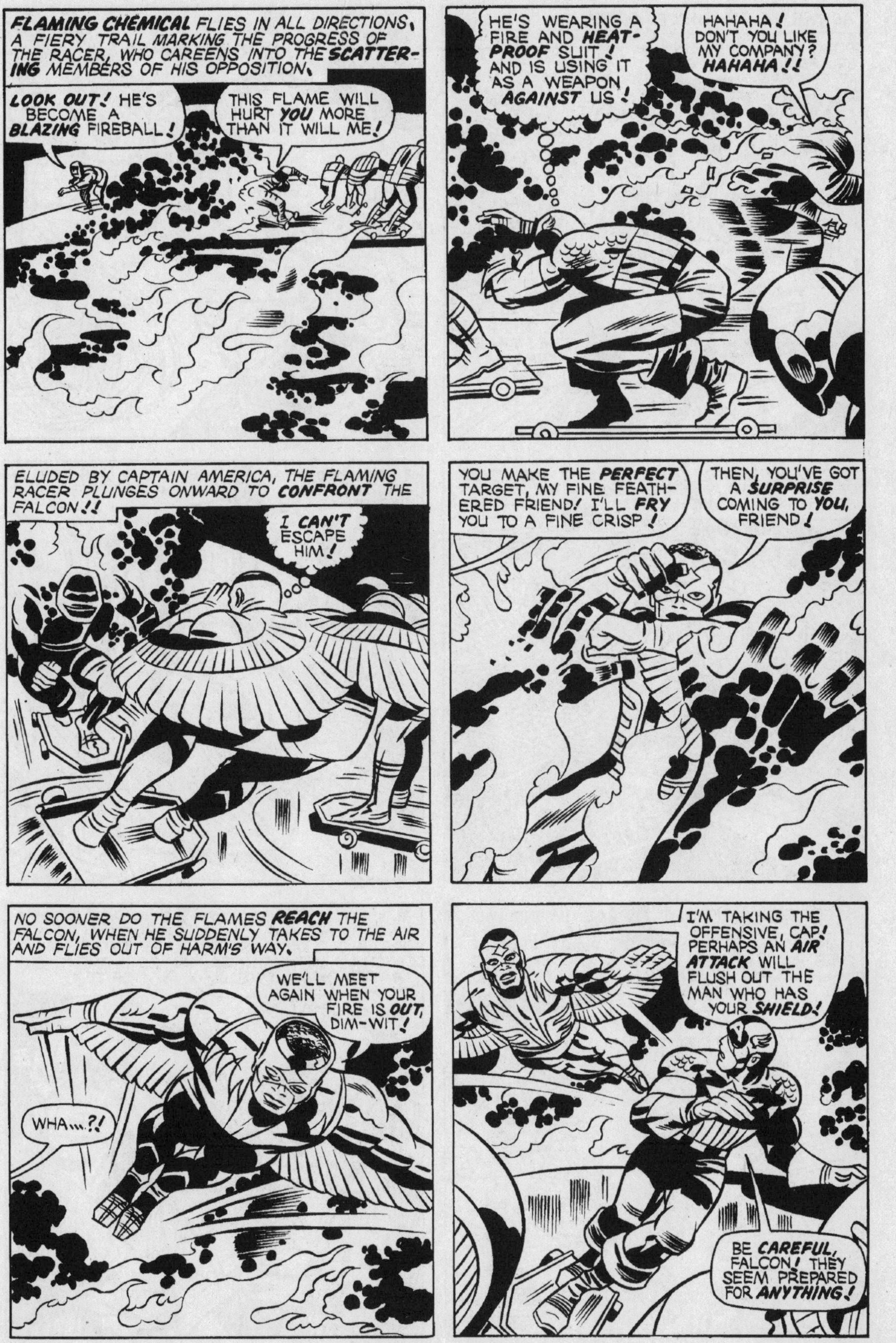
FLAMING CHEMICAL FLIES IN ALL DIRECTIONS, A FIERY TRAIL MARKING THE PROGRESS OF THE RACER, WHO CAREENS INTO THE SCATTERING MEMBERS OF HIS OPPOSITION.
LOOK OUT! HE'S BECOME A BLAZING FIREBALL!
THIS FLAME WILL HURT YOU MORE THAN IT WILL ME!
HE'S WEARING A FIRE AND HEAT-PROOF SUIT! AND IS USING IT AS A WEAPON AGAINST US!
HAHAHA! DON'T YOU LIKE MY COMPANY? HAHAHA!!
ELUDED BY CAPTAIN AMERICA, THE FLAMING RACER PLUNGES ONWARD TO CONFRONT THE FALCON!!
I CAN'T ESCAPE HIM!
YOU MAKE THE PERFECT TARGET, MY FINE FEATHERED FRIEND! I'LL FRY YOU TO A FINE CRISP!
THEN, YOU'VE GOT A SURPRISE COMING TO YOU, FRIEND!
NO SOONER DO THE FLAMES REACH THE FALCON, WHEN HE SUDDENLY TAKES TO THE AIR AND FLIES OUT OF HARM'S WAY.
WE'LL MEET AGAIN WHEN YOUR FIRE IS OUT, DIM-WIT!
WHA....?!
I'M TAKING THE OFFENSIVE, CAP! PERHAPS AN AIR ATTACK WILL FLUSH OUT THE MAN WHO HAS YOUR SHIELD!
BE CAREFUL, FALCON! THEY SEEM PREPARED FOR ANYTHING!

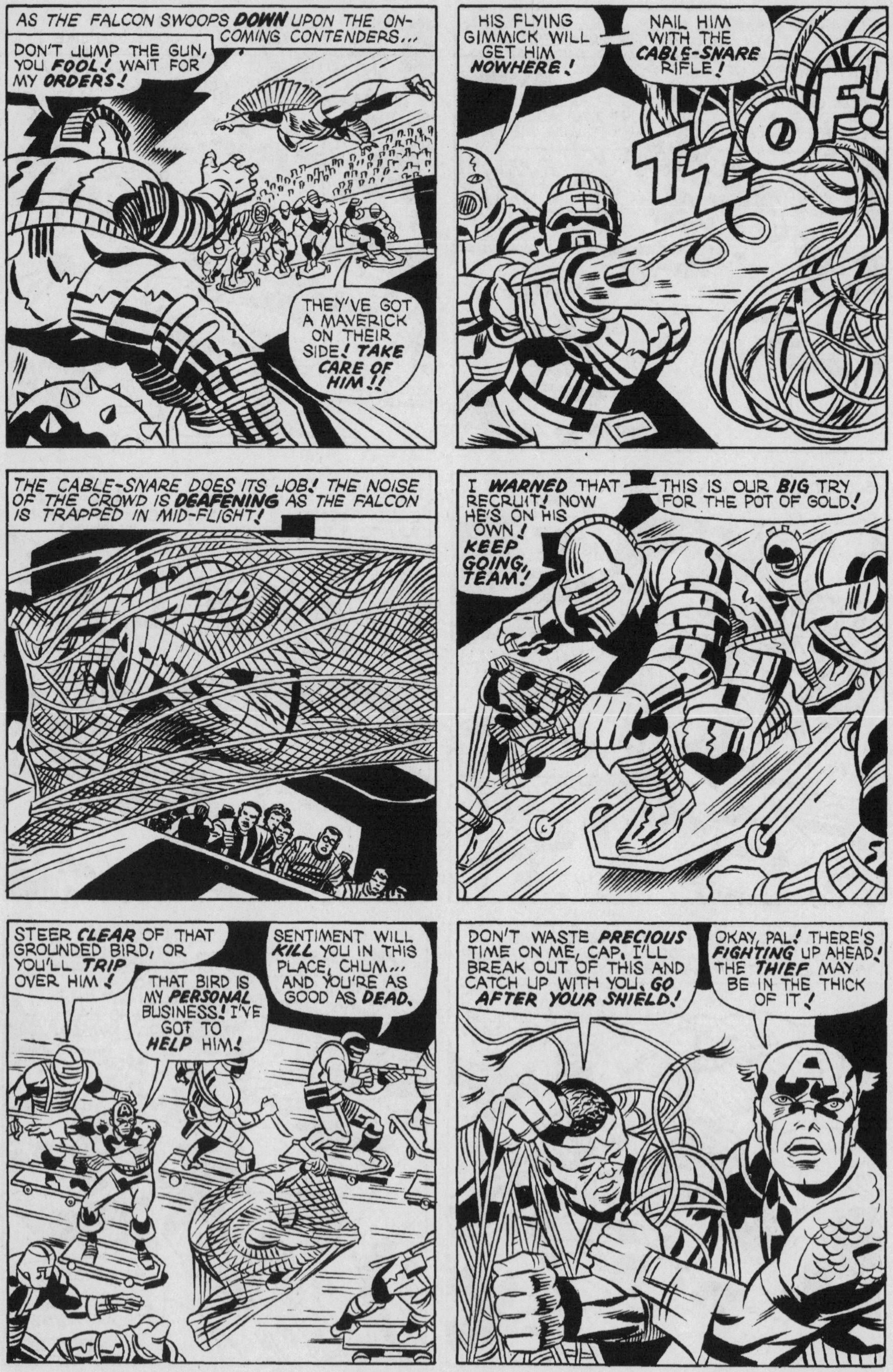
AS THE FALCON SWOOPS DOWN UPON THE ON-COMING CONTENDERS...
DON'T JUMP THE GUN, YOU FOOL! WAIT FOR MY ORDERS!
THEY'VE GOT A MAVERICK ON THEIR SIDE! TAKE CARE OF HIM!!
HIS FLYING GIMMICK WILL GET HIM NOWHERE!
NAIL HIM WITH THE CABLE-SNARE RIFLE!
TZOF!
THE CABLE-SNARE DOES ITS JOB! THE NOISE OF THE CROWD IS DEAFENING AS THE FALCON IS TRAPPED IN MID-FLIGHT!
I WARNED THAT RECRUIT! NOW HE'S ON HIS OWN! KEEP GOING, TEAM!
THIS IS OUR BIG TRY FOR THE POT OF GOLD!
STEER CLEAR OF THAT GROUNDED BIRD, OR YOU'LL TRIP OVER HIM!
THAT BIRD IS MY PERSONAL BUSINESS! I'VE GOT TO HELP HIM!
SENTIMENT WILL KILL YOU IN THIS PLACE, CHUM... AND YOU'RE AS GOOD AS DEAD.
DON'T WASTE PRECIOUS TIME ON ME, CAP. I'LL BREAK OUT OF THIS AND CATCH UP WITH YOU. GO AFTER YOUR SHIELD!
OKAY, PAL! THERE'S FIGHTING UP AHEAD! THE THIEF MAY BE IN THE THICK OF IT!

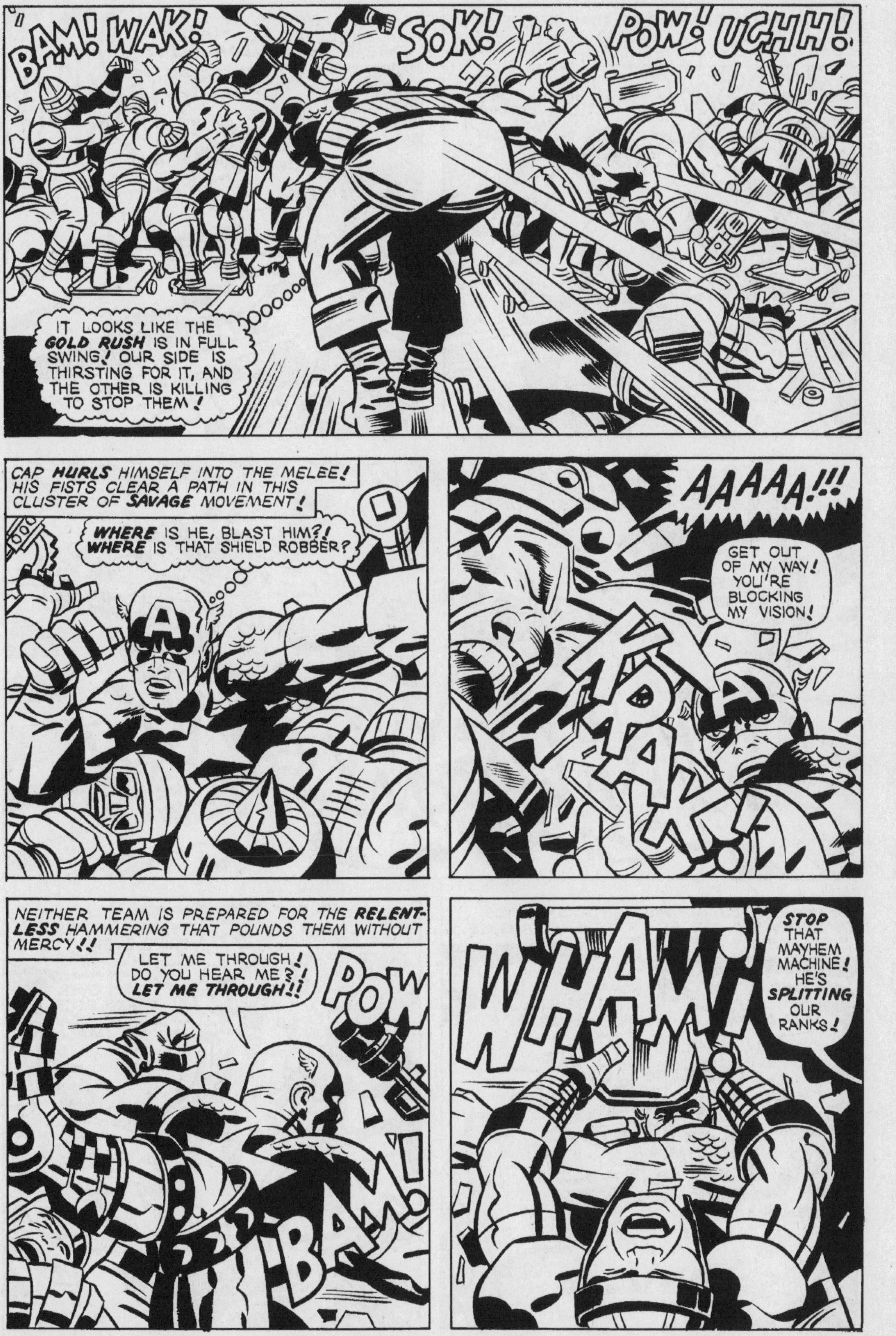
BAM! WAK!
SOK!
POW! UGHH!
IT LOOKS LIKE THE GOLD RUSH IS IN FULL SWING! OUR SIDE IS THIRSTING FOR IT, AND THE OTHER IS KILLING TO STOP THEM!
CAP HURLS HIMSELF INTO THE MELEE! HIS FISTS CLEAR A PATH IN THIS CLUSTER OF SAVAGE MOVEMENT!
WHERE IS HE, BLAST HIM?! WHERE IS THAT SHIELD ROBBER?
AAAAA!!!
GET OUT OF MY WAY! YOU'RE BLOCKING MY VISION!
KRAK!
NEITHER TEAM IS PREPARED FOR THE RELENTLESS HAMMERING THAT POUNDS THEM WITHOUT MERCY!!
LET ME THROUGH! DO YOU HEAR ME?! LET ME THROUGH!!
POW
BAM!
WHAM!
STOP THAT MAYHEM MACHINE! HE'S SPLITTING OUR RANKS!

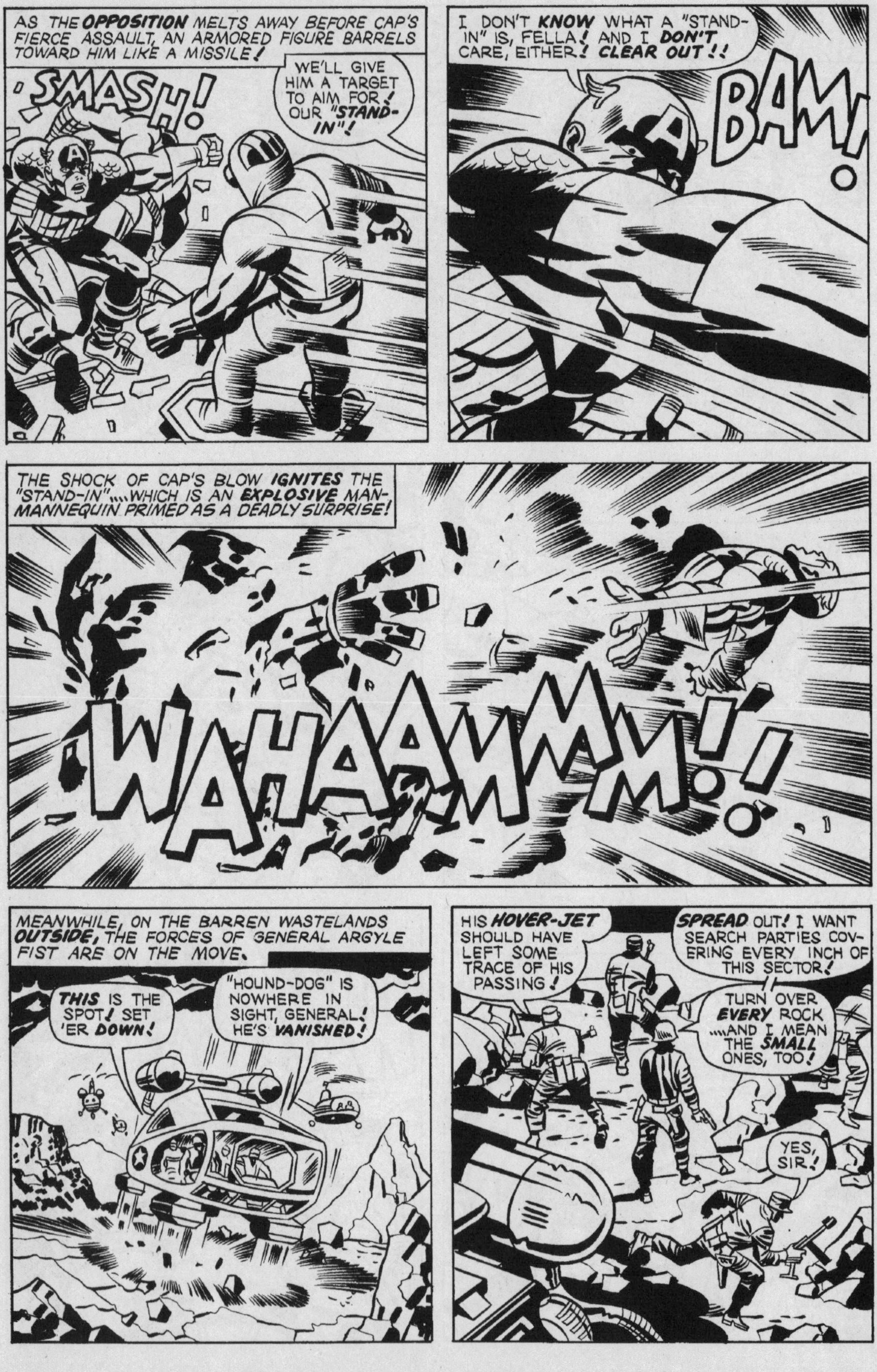
AS THE OPPOSITION MELTS AWAY BEFORE CAP'S FIERCE ASSAULT, AN ARMORED FIGURE BARRELS TOWARD HIM LIKE A MISSILE!
SMASH!
WE'LL GIVE HIM A TARGET TO AIM FOR! OUR "STAND-IN"!
I DON'T KNOW WHAT A "STAND-IN" IS, FELLA! AND I DON'T CARE, EITHER! CLEAR OUT!!
BAM!
THE SHOCK OF CAP'S BLOW IGNITES THE "STAND-IN"....WHICH IS AN EXPLOSIVE MAN-MANNEQUIN PRIMED AS A DEADLY SURPRISE!
WAHAAMM!!
MEANWHILE, ON THE BARREN WASTELANDS OUTSIDE, THE FORCES OF GENERAL ARGYLE FIST ARE ON THE MOVE.
THIS IS THE SPOT! SET 'ER DOWN!
"HOUND-DOG" IS NOWHERE IN SIGHT, GENERAL! HE'S VANISHED!
HIS HOVER-JET SHOULD HAVE LEFT SOME TRACE OF HIS PASSING!
SPREAD OUT! I WANT SEARCH PARTIES COV-ERING EVERY INCH OF THIS SECTOR!
TURN OVER EVERY ROCK ....AND I MEAN THE SMALL ONES, TOO!
YES, SIR!

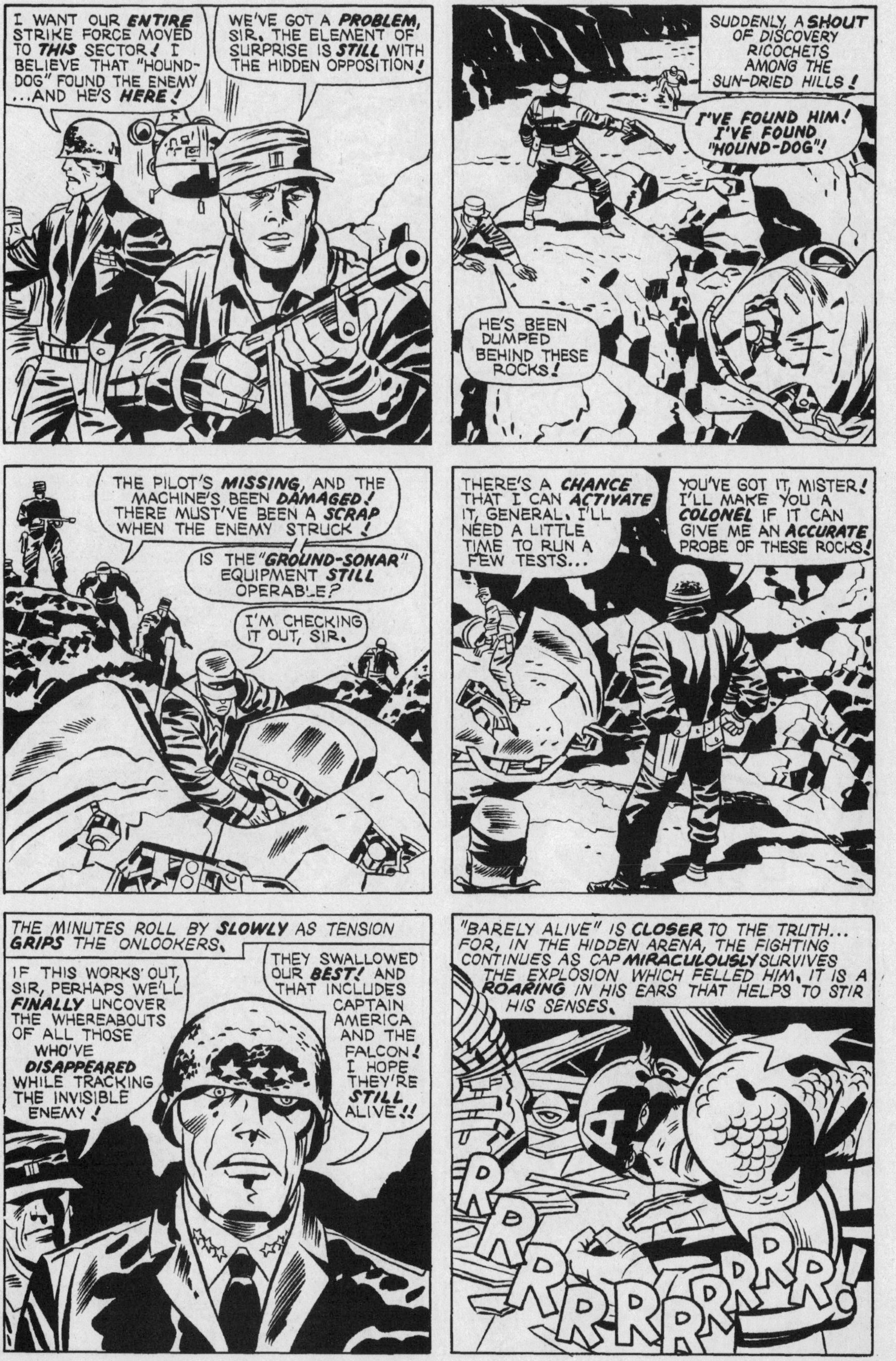
I WANT OUR ENTIRE STRIKE FORCE MOVED TO THIS SECTOR! I BELIEVE THAT "HOUND-DOG" FOUND THE ENEMY ...AND HE'S HERE!
WE'VE GOT A PROBLEM, SIR. THE ELEMENT OF SURPRISE IS STILL WITH THE HIDDEN OPPOSITION!
SUDDENLY, A SHOUT OF DISCOVERY RICOCHETS AMONG THE SUN-DRIED HILLS!
I'VE FOUND HIM! I'VE FOUND "HOUND-DOG"!
HE'S BEEN DUMPED BEHIND THESE ROCKS!
THE PILOT'S MISSING, AND THE MACHINE'S BEEN DAMAGED! THERE MUST'VE BEEN A SCRAP WHEN THE ENEMY STRUCK!
IS THE "GROUND-SONAR" EQUIPMENT STILL OPERABLE?
I'M CHECKING IT OUT, SIR.
THERE'S A CHANCE THAT I CAN ACTIVATE IT, GENERAL. I'LL NEED A LITTLE TIME TO RUN A FEW TESTS...
YOU'VE GOT IT, MISTER! I'LL MAKE YOU A COLONEL IF IT CAN GIVE ME AN ACCURATE PROBE OF THESE ROCKS!
THE MINUTES ROLL BY SLOWLY AS TENSION GRIPS THE ONLOOKERS.
IF THIS WORKS OUT, SIR, PERHAPS WE'LL FINALLY UNCOVER THE WHEREABOUTS OF ALL THOSE WHO'VE DISAPPEARED WHILE TRACKING THE INVISIBLE ENEMY!
THEY SWALLOWED OUR BEST! AND THAT INCLUDES CAPTAIN AMERICA AND THE FALCON! I HOPE THEY'RE STILL ALIVE!!
"BARELY ALIVE" IS CLOSER TO THE TRUTH... FOR, IN THE HIDDEN ARENA, THE FIGHTING CONTINUES AS CAP MIRACULOUSLY SURVIVES THE EXPLOSION WHICH FELLED HIM. IT IS A ROARING IN HIS EARS THAT HELPS TO STIR HIS SENSES.
RRRRRRRRRRR!

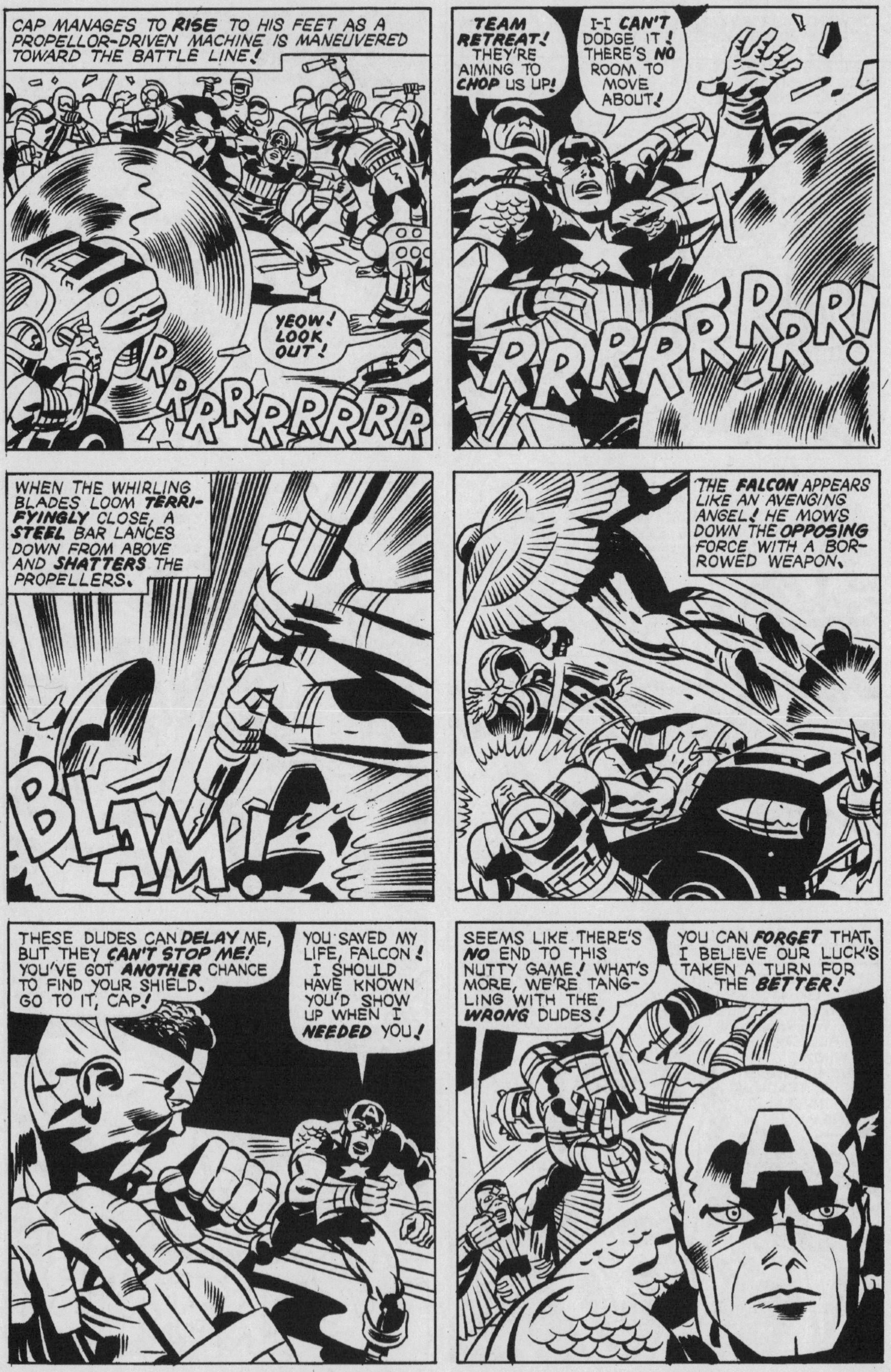
CAP MANAGES TO RISE TO HIS FEET AS A PROPELLOR-DRIVEN MACHINE IS MANEUVERED TOWARD THE BATTLE LINE!
YEOW! LOOK OUT!
RRRRRRRRRR
TEAM RETREAT! THEY'RE AIMING TO CHOP US UP!
I-I CAN'T DODGE IT! THERE'S NO ROOM TO MOVE ABOUT!
RRRRRRRRR!
WHEN THE WHIRLING BLADES LOOM TERRI-FYINGLY CLOSE, A STEEL BAR LANCES DOWN FROM ABOVE AND SHATTERS THE PROPELLERS.
BLAM!
THE FALCON APPEARS LIKE AN AVENGING ANGEL! HE MOWS DOWN THE OPPOSING FORCE WITH A BOR-ROWED WEAPON.
THESE DUDES CAN DELAY ME, BUT THEY CAN'T STOP ME! YOU'VE GOT ANOTHER CHANCE TO FIND YOUR SHIELD. GO TO IT, CAP!
YOU SAVED MY LIFE, FALCON! I SHOULD HAVE KNOWN YOU'D SHOW UP WHEN I NEEDED YOU!
SEEMS LIKE THERE'S NO END TO THIS NUTTY GAME! WHAT'S MORE, WE'RE TANG-LING WITH THE WRONG DUDES!
YOU CAN FORGET THAT. I BELIEVE OUR LUCK'S TAKEN A TURN FOR THE BETTER!

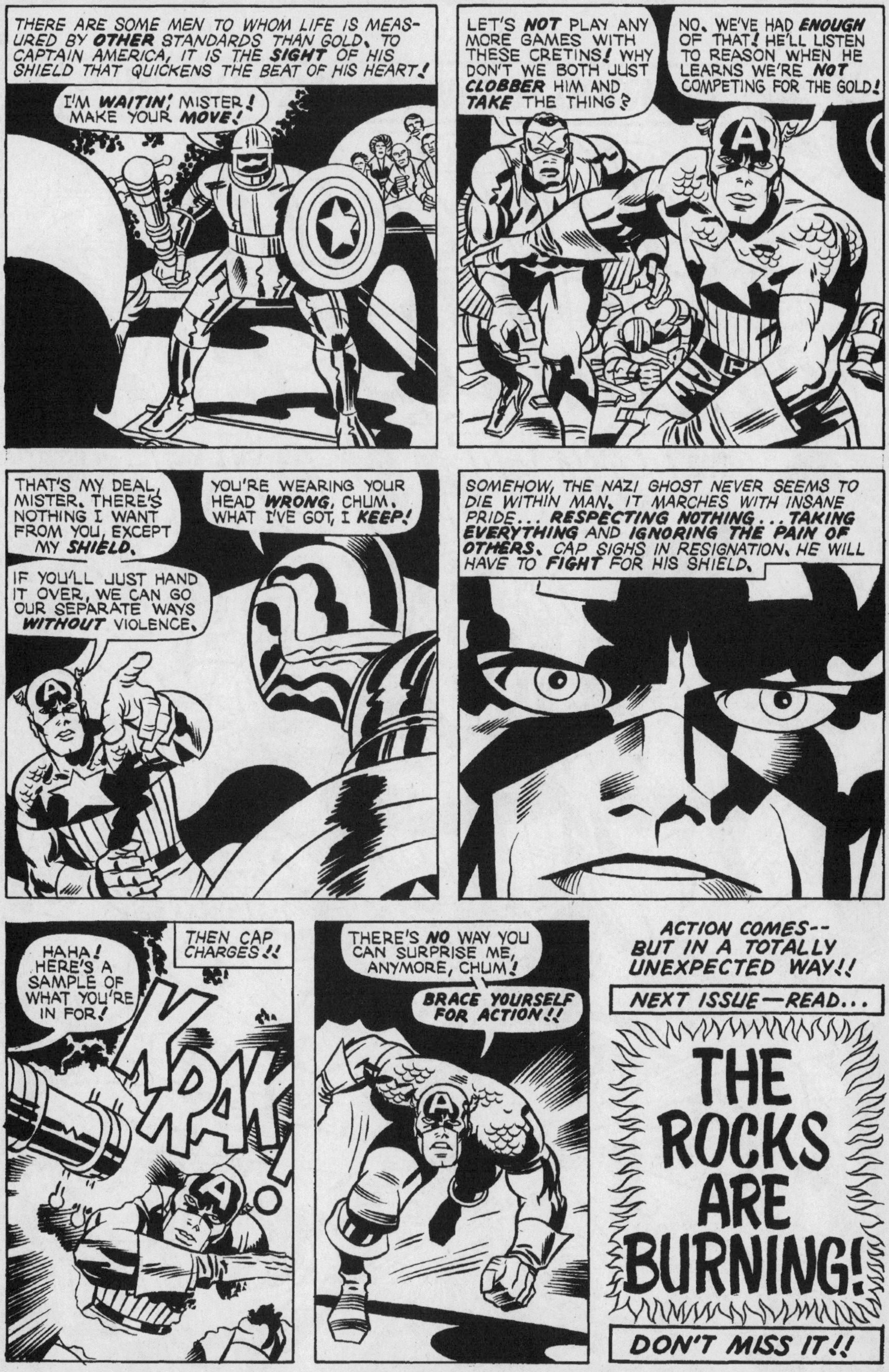
THERE ARE SOME MEN TO WHOM LIFE IS MEASURED BY OTHER STANDARDS THAN GOLD. TO CAPTAIN AMERICA, IT IS THE SIGHT OF HIS SHIELD THAT QUICKENS THE BEAT OF HIS HEART!
I'M WAITIN', MISTER! MAKE YOUR MOVE!
LET'S NOT PLAY ANY MORE GAMES WITH THESE CRETINS! WHY DON'T WE BOTH JUST CLOBBER HIM AND TAKE THE THING?
NO. WE'VE HAD ENOUGH OF THAT! HE'LL LISTEN TO REASON WHEN HE LEARNS WE'RE NOT COMPETING FOR THE GOLD!
THAT'S MY DEAL, MISTER. THERE'S NOTHING I WANT FROM YOU, EXCEPT MY SHIELD.
IF YOU'LL JUST HAND IT OVER, WE CAN GO OUR SEPARATE WAYS WITHOUT VIOLENCE.
YOU'RE WEARING YOUR HEAD WRONG, CHUM. WHAT I'VE GOT, I KEEP!
SOMEHOW, THE NAZI GHOST NEVER SEEMS TO DIE WITHIN MAN. IT MARCHES WITH INSANE PRIDE... RESPECTING NOTHING... TAKING EVERYTHING AND IGNORING THE PAIN OF OTHERS. CAP SIGHS IN RESIGNATION. HE WILL HAVE TO FIGHT FOR HIS SHIELD.
HAHA! HERE'S A SAMPLE OF WHAT YOU'RE IN FOR!
THEN CAP CHARGES!!
KRAK
THERE'S NO WAY YOU CAN SURPRISE ME, ANYMORE, CHUM!
BRACE YOURSELF FOR ACTION!!
ACTION COMES-- BUT IN A TOTALLY UNEXPECTED WAY!!
NEXT ISSUE—READ...
THE ROCKS ARE BURNING!
DON'T MISS IT!!

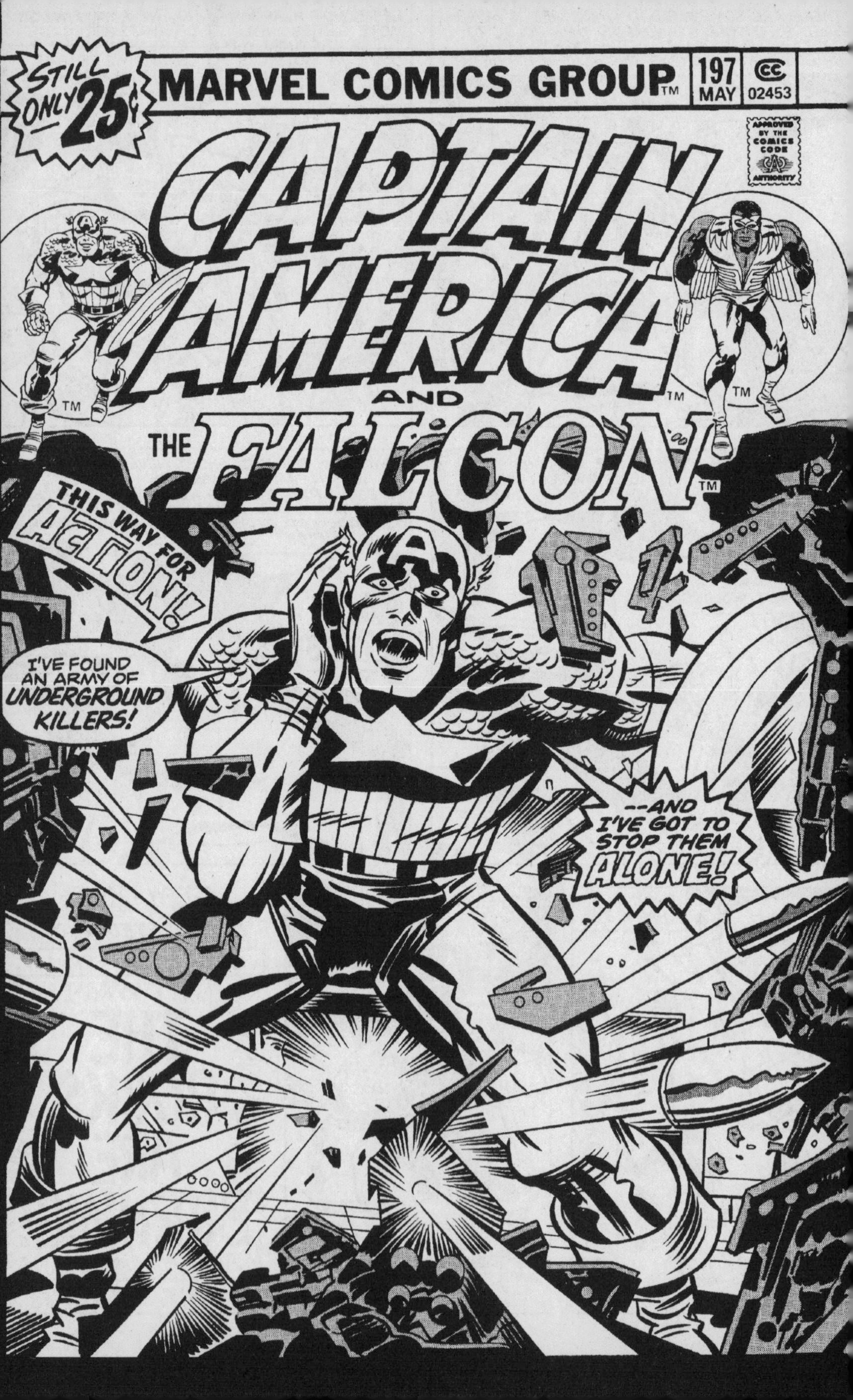

STILL ONLY 25¢
MARVEL COMICS GROUP
197 MAY
02453
APPROVED BY THE COMICS CODE AUTHORITY
CAPTAIN AMERICA AND THE FALCON
THIS WAY FOR ACTION!
I'VE FOUND AN ARMY OF UNDERGROUND KILLERS!
--AND I'VE GOT TO STOP THEM ALONE!

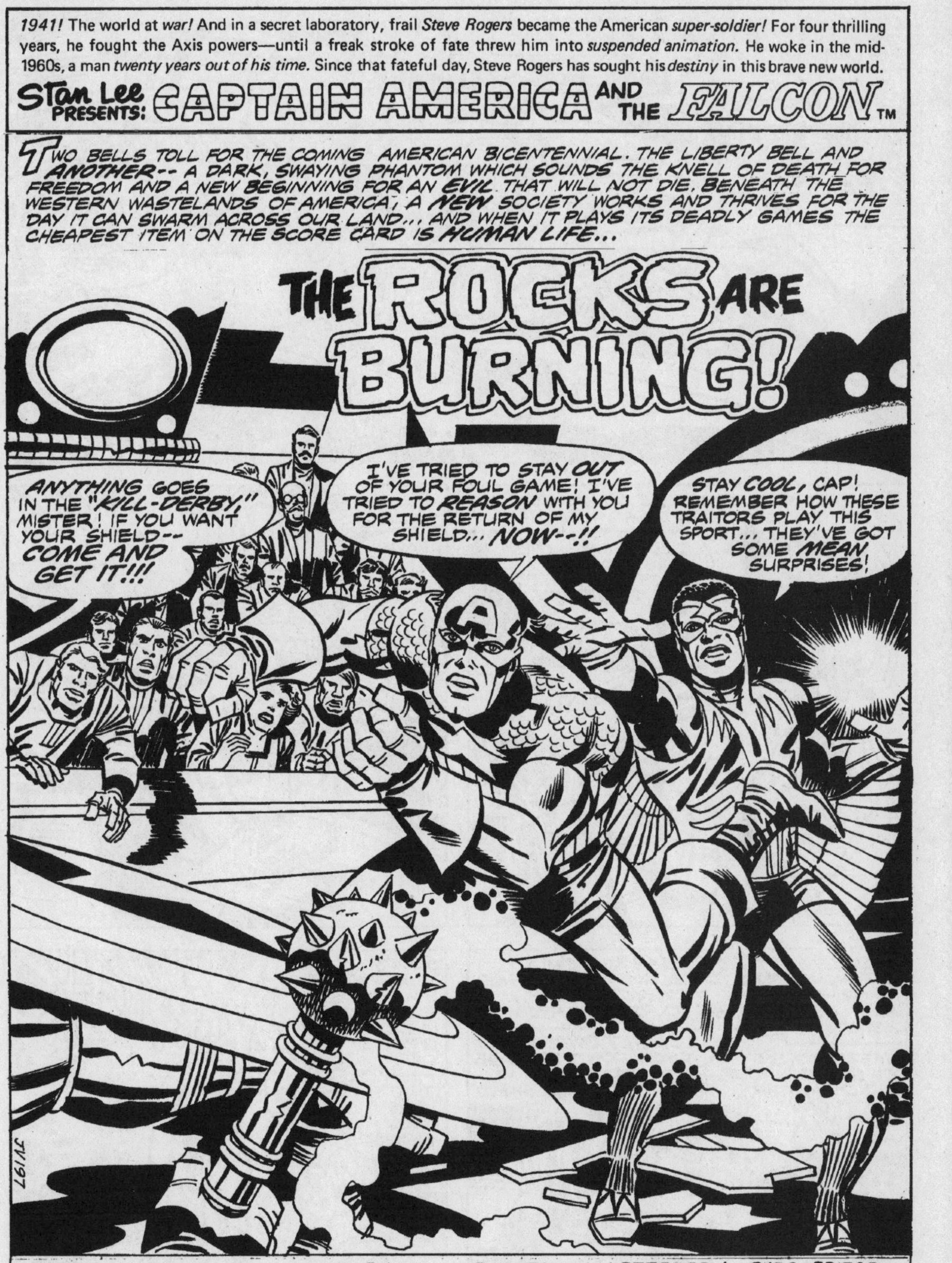
1941! The world at war! And in a secret laboratory, frail Steve Rogers became the American super-soldier! For four thrilling years, he fought the Axis powers—until a freak stroke of fate threw him into suspended animation. He woke in the mid-1960s, a man twenty years out of his time. Since that fateful day, Steve Rogers has sought his destiny in this brave new world.
STAN LEE PRESENTS: CAPTAIN AMERICA AND THE FALCON TM
TWO BELLS TOLL FOR THE COMING AMERICAN BICENTENNIAL. THE LIBERTY BELL AND ANOTHER-- A DARK, SWAYING PHANTOM WHICH SOUNDS THE KNELL OF DEATH FOR FREEDOM AND A NEW BEGINNING FOR AN EVIL THAT WILL NOT DIE. BENEATH THE WESTERN WASTELANDS OF AMERICA, A NEW SOCIETY WORKS AND THRIVES FOR THE DAY IT CAN SWARM ACROSS OUR LAND... AND WHEN IT PLAYS ITS DEADLY GAMES THE CHEAPEST ITEM ON THE SCORE CARD IS HUMAN LIFE...
THE ROCKS ARE BURNING!
ANYTHING GOES IN THE "KILL-DERBY," MISTER! IF YOU WANT YOUR SHIELD-- COME AND GET IT!!!
I'VE TRIED TO STAY OUT OF YOUR FOUL GAME! I'VE TRIED TO REASON WITH YOU FOR THE RETURN OF MY SHIELD... NOW--!!
STAY COOL, CAP! REMEMBER HOW THESE TRAITORS PLAY THIS SPORT... THEY'VE GOT SOME MEAN SURPRISES!
WRITTEN, DRAWN, & EDITED BY JACK KIRBY
INKED BY FRANK GIACOIA
J. COSTANZA, LETTERER P. RACHE, COLORIST
EXEC. EDITOR MARV WOLFMAN

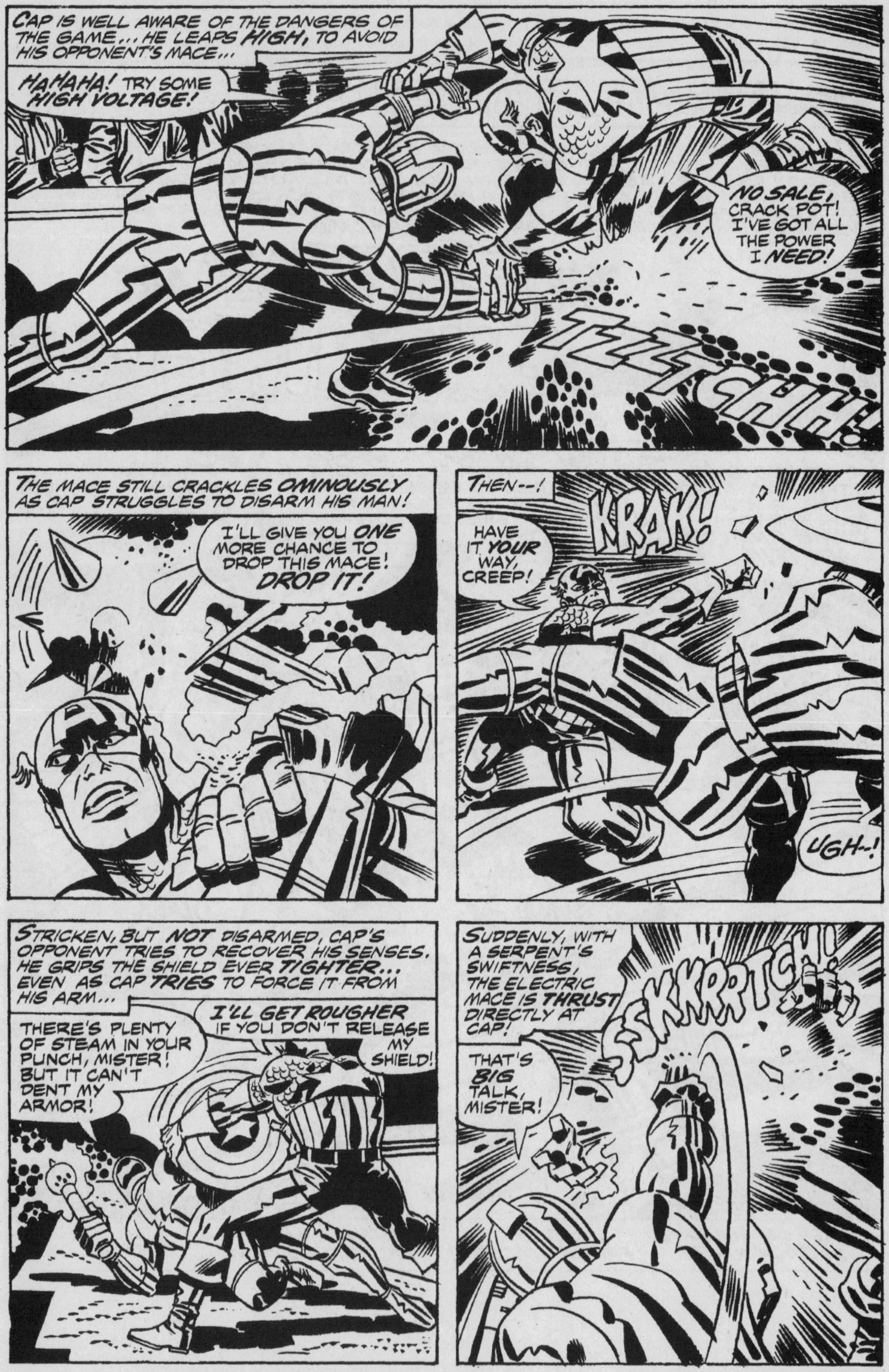
CAP IS WELL AWARE OF THE DANGERS OF THE GAME... HE LEAPS HIGH, TO AVOID HIS OPPONENT'S MACE...
HAHAHA! TRY SOME HIGH VOLTAGE!
NO SALE, CRACK POT! I'VE GOT ALL THE POWER I NEED!
TZZTCHH!
THE MACE STILL CRACKLES OMINOUSLY AS CAP STRUGGLES TO DISARM HIS MAN!
I'LL GIVE YOU ONE MORE CHANCE TO DROP THIS MACE! DROP IT!
THEN--!
KRAK!
HAVE IT YOUR WAY, CREEP!
UGH--!
STRICKEN, BUT NOT DISARMED, CAP'S OPPONENT TRIES TO RECOVER HIS SENSES. HE GRIPS THE SHIELD EVER TIGHTER... EVEN AS CAP TRIES TO FORCE IT FROM HIS ARM...
THERE'S PLENTY OF STEAM IN YOUR PUNCH, MISTER! BUT IT CAN'T DENT MY ARMOR!
I'LL GET ROUGHER IF YOU DON'T RELEASE MY SHIELD!
SUDDENLY, WITH A SERPENT'S SWIFTNESS, THE ELECTRIC MACE IS THRUST DIRECTLY AT CAP!
SSKKRRTCH!
THAT'S BIG TALK, MISTER!

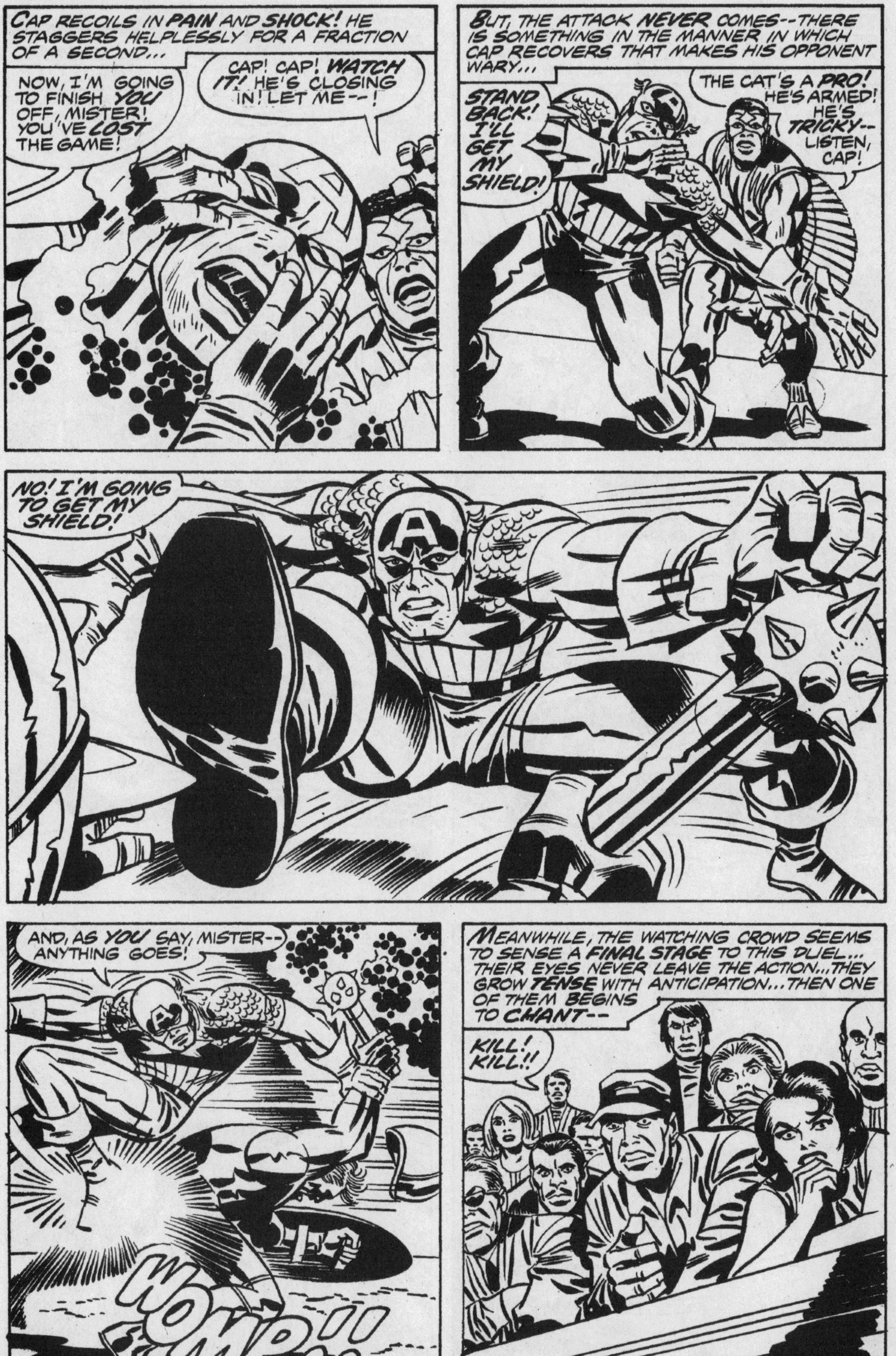
CAP RECOILS IN PAIN AND SHOCK! HE STAGGERS HELPLESSLY FOR A FRACTION OF A SECOND...
NOW, I'M GOING TO FINISH YOU OFF, MISTER! YOU'VE LOST THE GAME!
CAP! CAP! WATCH IT! HE'S CLOSING IN! LET ME--!
BUT, THE ATTACK NEVER COMES--THERE IS SOMETHING IN THE MANNER IN WHICH CAP RECOVERS THAT MAKES HIS OPPONENT WARY...
STAND BACK! I'LL GET MY SHIELD!
THE CAT'S A PRO! HE'S ARMED! HE'S TRICKY-- LISTEN, CAP!
NO! I'M GOING TO GET MY SHIELD!
AND, AS YOU SAY, MISTER-- ANYTHING GOES!
WOMP!!
MEANWHILE, THE WATCHING CROWD SEEMS TO SENSE A FINAL STAGE TO THIS DUEL... THEIR EYES NEVER LEAVE THE ACTION...THEY GROW TENSE WITH ANTICIPATION...THEN ONE OF THEM BEGINS TO CHANT--
KILL! KILL!!

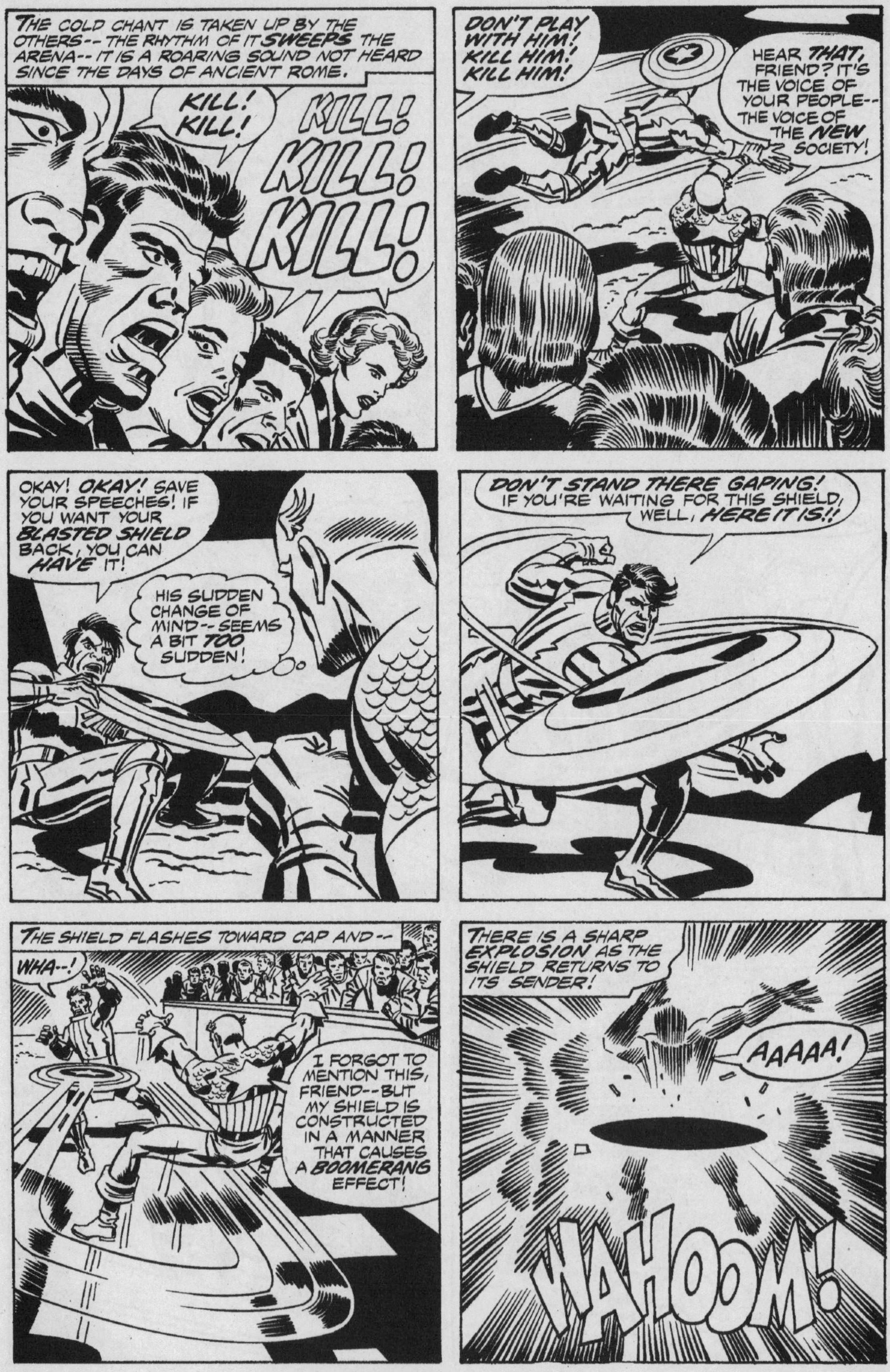
THE COLD CHANT IS TAKEN UP BY THE OTHERS-- THE RHYTHM OF IT SWEEPS THE ARENA-- IT IS A ROARING SOUND NOT HEARD SINCE THE DAYS OF ANCIENT ROME.
KILL! KILL!
KILL! KILL! KILL!
DON'T PLAY WITH HIM! KILL HIM! KILL HIM!
HEAR THAT, FRIEND? IT'S THE VOICE OF YOUR PEOPLE-- THE VOICE OF THE NEW SOCIETY!
OKAY! OKAY! SAVE YOUR SPEECHES! IF YOU WANT YOUR BLASTED SHIELD BACK, YOU CAN HAVE IT!
HIS SUDDEN CHANGE OF MIND-- SEEMS A BIT TOO SUDDEN!
DON'T STAND THERE GAPING! IF YOU'RE WAITING FOR THIS SHIELD, WELL, HERE IT IS!!
THE SHIELD FLASHES TOWARD CAP AND--
WHA--!
I FORGOT TO MENTION THIS, FRIEND--BUT MY SHIELD IS CONSTRUCTED IN A MANNER THAT CAUSES A BOOMERANG EFFECT!
THERE IS A SHARP EXPLOSION AS THE SHIELD RETURNS TO ITS SENDER!
AAAAA!
WAHOOM!

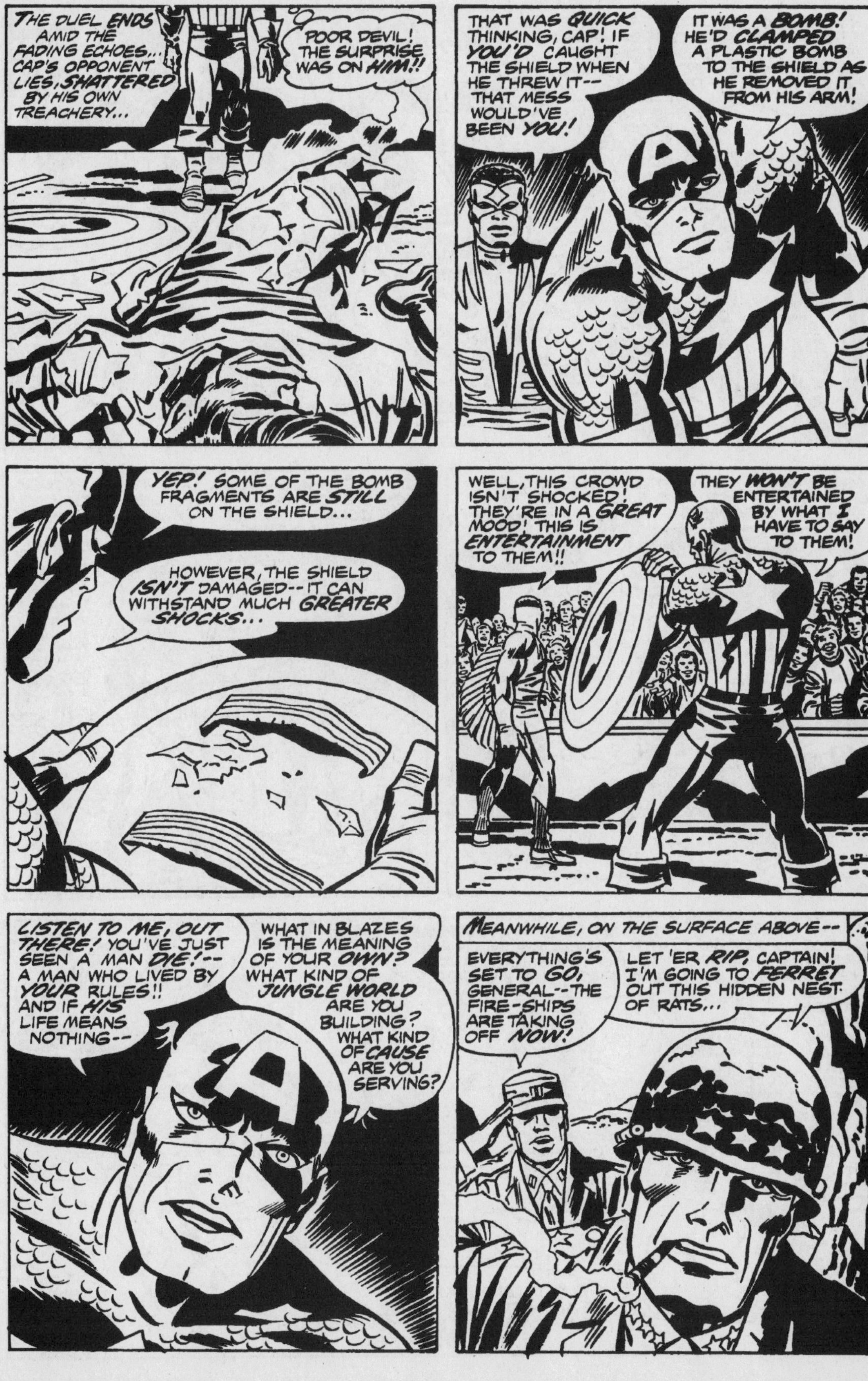
THE DUEL ENDS AMID THE FADING ECHOES... CAP'S OPPONENT LIES, SHATTERED BY HIS OWN TREACHERY...
POOR DEVIL! THE SURPRISE WAS ON HIM!!
THAT WAS QUICK THINKING, CAP! IF YOU'D CAUGHT THE SHIELD WHEN HE THREW IT-- THAT MESS WOULD'VE BEEN YOU!
IT WAS A BOMB! HE'D CLAMPED A PLASTIC BOMB TO THE SHIELD AS HE REMOVED IT FROM HIS ARM!
YEP! SOME OF THE BOMB FRAGMENTS ARE STILL ON THE SHIELD...
HOWEVER, THE SHIELD ISN'T DAMAGED-- IT CAN WITHSTAND MUCH GREATER SHOCKS...
WELL, THIS CROWD ISN'T SHOCKED! THEY'RE IN A GREAT MOOD! THIS IS ENTERTAINMENT TO THEM!!
THEY WON'T BE ENTERTAINED BY WHAT I HAVE TO SAY TO THEM!
LISTEN TO ME, OUT THERE! YOU'VE JUST SEEN A MAN DIE!-- A MAN WHO LIVED BY YOUR RULES!! AND IF HIS LIFE MEANS NOTHING--
WHAT IN BLAZES IS THE MEANING OF YOUR OWN? WHAT KIND OF JUNGLE WORLD ARE YOU BUILDING? WHAT KIND OF CAUSE ARE YOU SERVING?
MEANWHILE, ON THE SURFACE ABOVE--
EVERYTHING'S SET TO GO, GENERAL-- THE FIRE-SHIPS ARE TAKING OFF NOW!
LET 'ER RIP, CAPTAIN! I'M GOING TO FERRET OUT THIS HIDDEN NEST OF RATS...

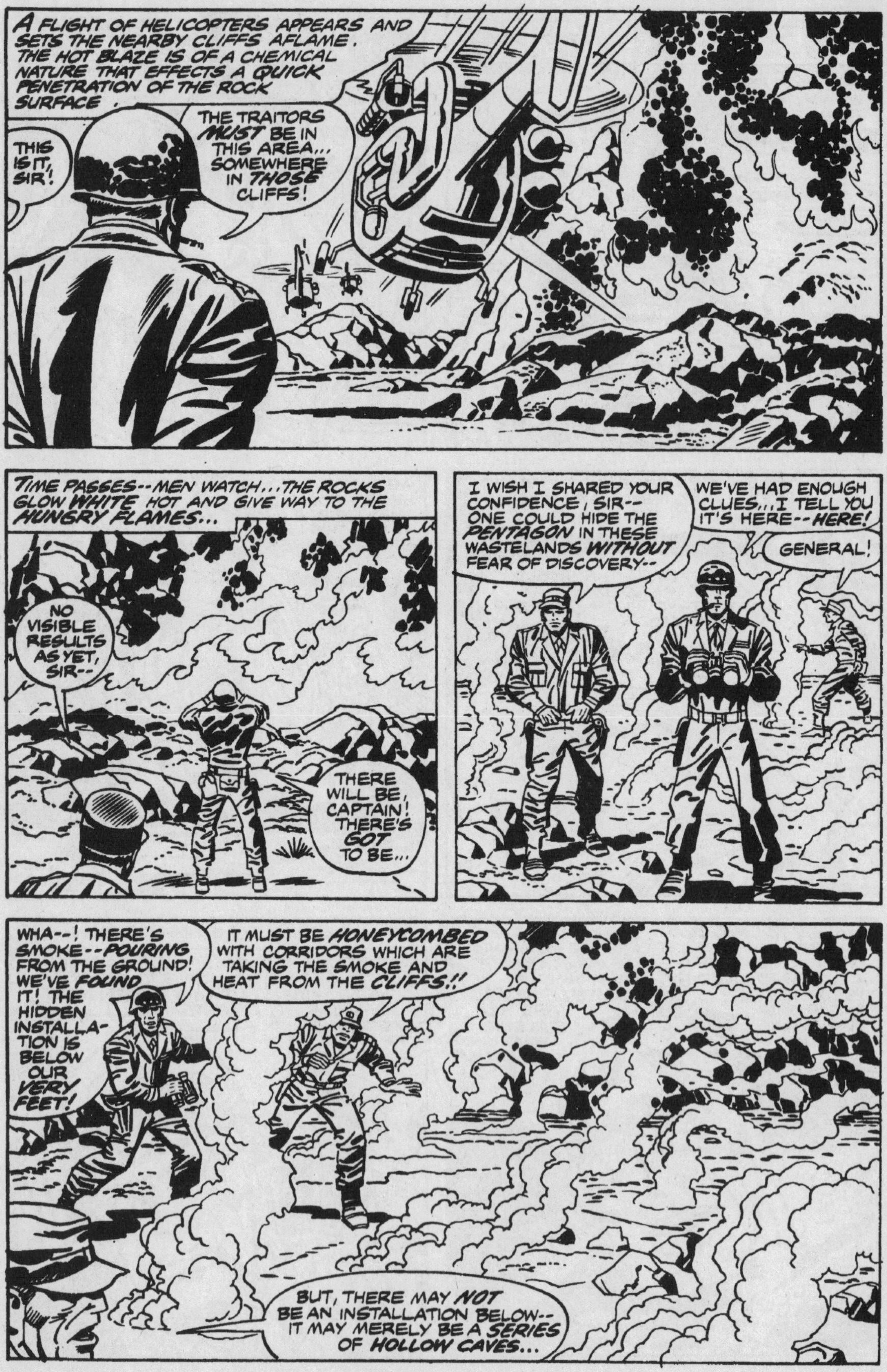
A FLIGHT OF HELICOPTERS APPEARS AND SETS THE NEARBY CLIFFS AFLAME. THE HOT BLAZE IS OF A CHEMICAL NATURE THAT EFFECTS A QUICK PENETRATION OF THE ROCK SURFACE.
THIS IS IT, SIR!
THE TRAITORS MUST BE IN THIS AREA... SOMEWHERE IN THOSE CLIFFS!
TIME PASSES--MEN WATCH...THE ROCKS GLOW WHITE HOT AND GIVE WAY TO THE HUNGRY FLAMES...
NO VISIBLE RESULTS AS YET, SIR--
THERE WILL BE, CAPTAIN! THERE'S GOT TO BE...
I WISH I SHARED YOUR CONFIDENCE, SIR-- ONE COULD HIDE THE PENTAGON IN THESE WASTELANDS WITHOUT FEAR OF DISCOVERY--
WE'VE HAD ENOUGH CLUES... I TELL YOU IT'S HERE--HERE!
GENERAL!
WHA--! THERE'S SMOKE--POURING FROM THE GROUND! WE'VE FOUND IT! THE HIDDEN INSTALLATION IS BELOW OUR VERY FEET!
IT MUST BE HONEYCOMBED WITH CORRIDORS WHICH ARE TAKING THE SMOKE AND HEAT FROM THE CLIFFS!!
BUT, THERE MAY NOT BE AN INSTALLATION BELOW-- IT MAY MERELY BE A SERIES OF HOLLOW CAVES...

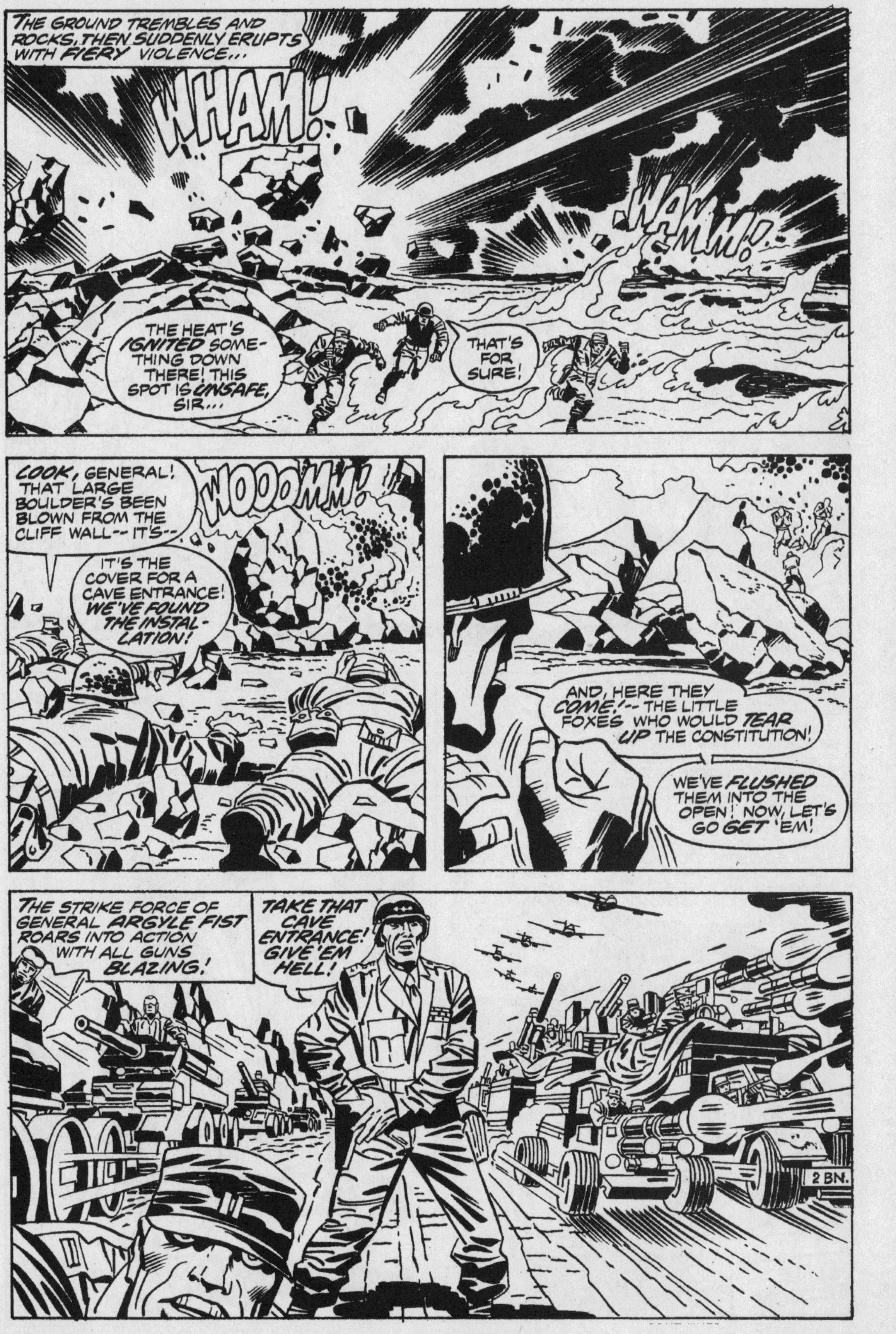
THE GROUND TREMBLES AND ROCKS, THEN SUDDENLY ERUPTS WITH FIERY VIOLENCE...
WHAM!
WAMM!
THE HEAT'S IGNITED SOMETHING DOWN THERE! THIS SPOT IS UNSAFE, SIR...
THAT'S FOR SURE!
LOOK, GENERAL! THAT LARGE BOULDER'S BEEN BLOWN FROM THE CLIFF WALL-- IT'S--
WOOOMM!
IT'S THE COVER FOR A CAVE ENTRANCE! WE'VE FOUND THE INSTALLATION!
AND, HERE THEY COME!-- THE LITTLE FOXES WHO WOULD TEAR UP THE CONSTITUTION!
WE'VE FLUSHED THEM INTO THE OPEN! NOW, LET'S GO GET 'EM!
THE STRIKE FORCE OF GENERAL ARGYLE FIST ROARS INTO ACTION WITH ALL GUNS BLAZING!
TAKE THAT CAVE ENTRANCE! GIVE 'EM HELL!
2 BN.

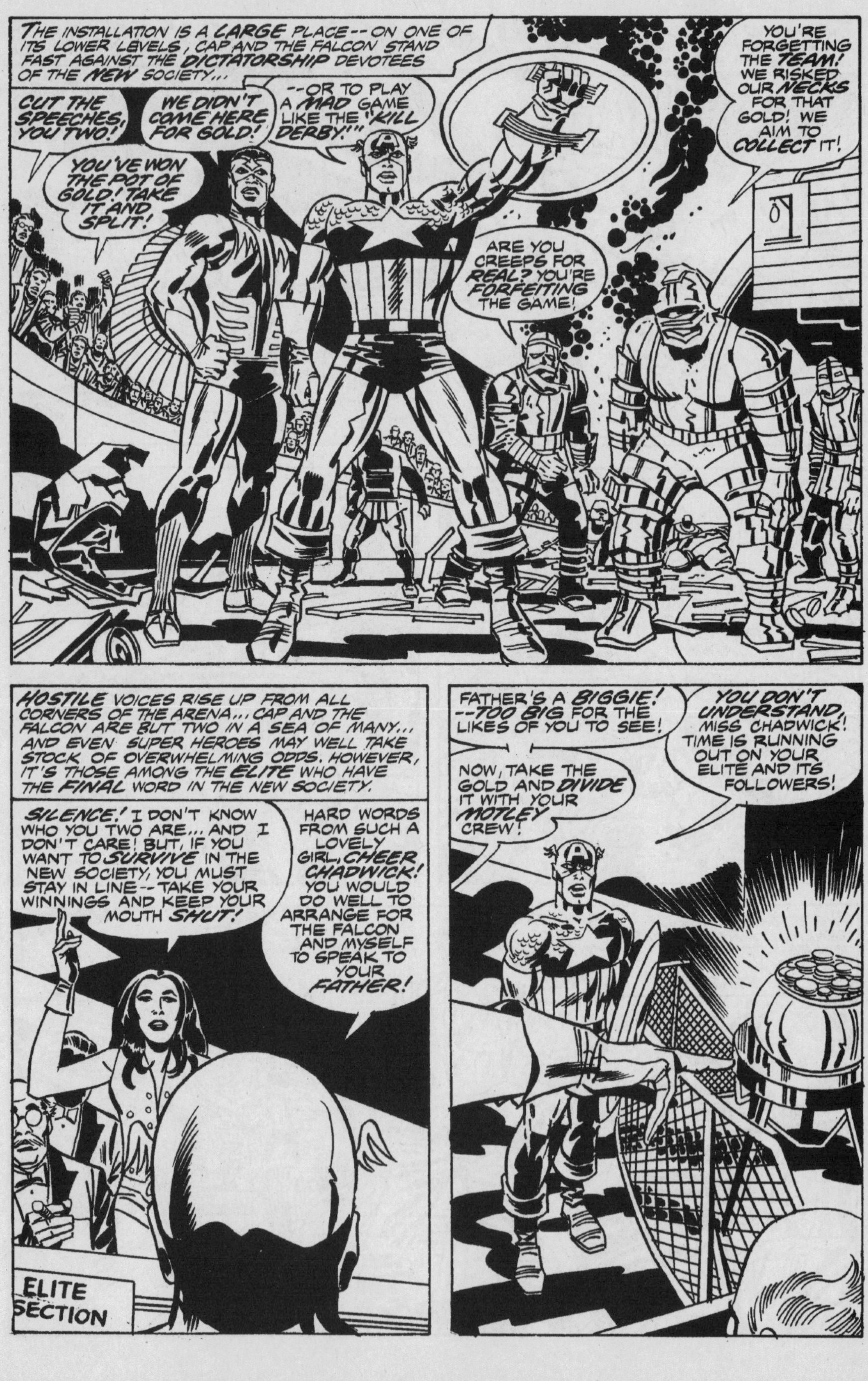
THE INSTALLATION IS A LARGE PLACE--ON ONE OF ITS LOWER LEVELS, CAP AND THE FALCON STAND FAST AGAINST THE DICTATORSHIP DEVOTEES OF THE NEW SOCIETY...
CUT THE SPEECHES, YOU TWO!
YOU'VE WON THE POT OF GOLD! TAKE IT AND SPLIT!
WE DIDN'T COME HERE FOR GOLD!
--OR TO PLAY A MAD GAME LIKE THE "KILL DERBY!"
YOU'RE FORGETTING THE TEAM! WE RISKED OUR NECKS FOR THAT GOLD! WE AIM TO COLLECT IT!
ARE YOU CREEPS FOR REAL? YOU'RE FORFEITING THE GAME!
HOSTILE VOICES RISE UP FROM ALL CORNERS OF THE ARENA... CAP AND THE FALCON ARE BUT TWO IN A SEA OF MANY... AND EVEN SUPER HEROES MAY WELL TAKE STOCK OF OVERWHELMING ODDS. HOWEVER, IT'S THOSE AMONG THE ELITE WHO HAVE THE FINAL WORD IN THE NEW SOCIETY.
SILENCE! I DON'T KNOW WHO YOU TWO ARE... AND I DON'T CARE! BUT, IF YOU WANT TO SURVIVE IN THE NEW SOCIETY, YOU MUST STAY IN LINE--TAKE YOUR WINNINGS AND KEEP YOUR MOUTH SHUT!
HARD WORDS FROM SUCH A LOVELY GIRL, CHEER CHADWICK! YOU WOULD DO WELL TO ARRANGE FOR THE FALCON AND MYSELF TO SPEAK TO YOUR FATHER!
ELITE SECTION
FATHER'S A BIGGIE! --TOO BIG FOR THE LIKES OF YOU TO SEE!
NOW, TAKE THE GOLD AND DIVIDE IT WITH YOUR MOTLEY CREW!
YOU DON'T UNDERSTAND, MISS CHADWICK! TIME IS RUNNING OUT ON YOUR ELITE AND ITS FOLLOWERS!

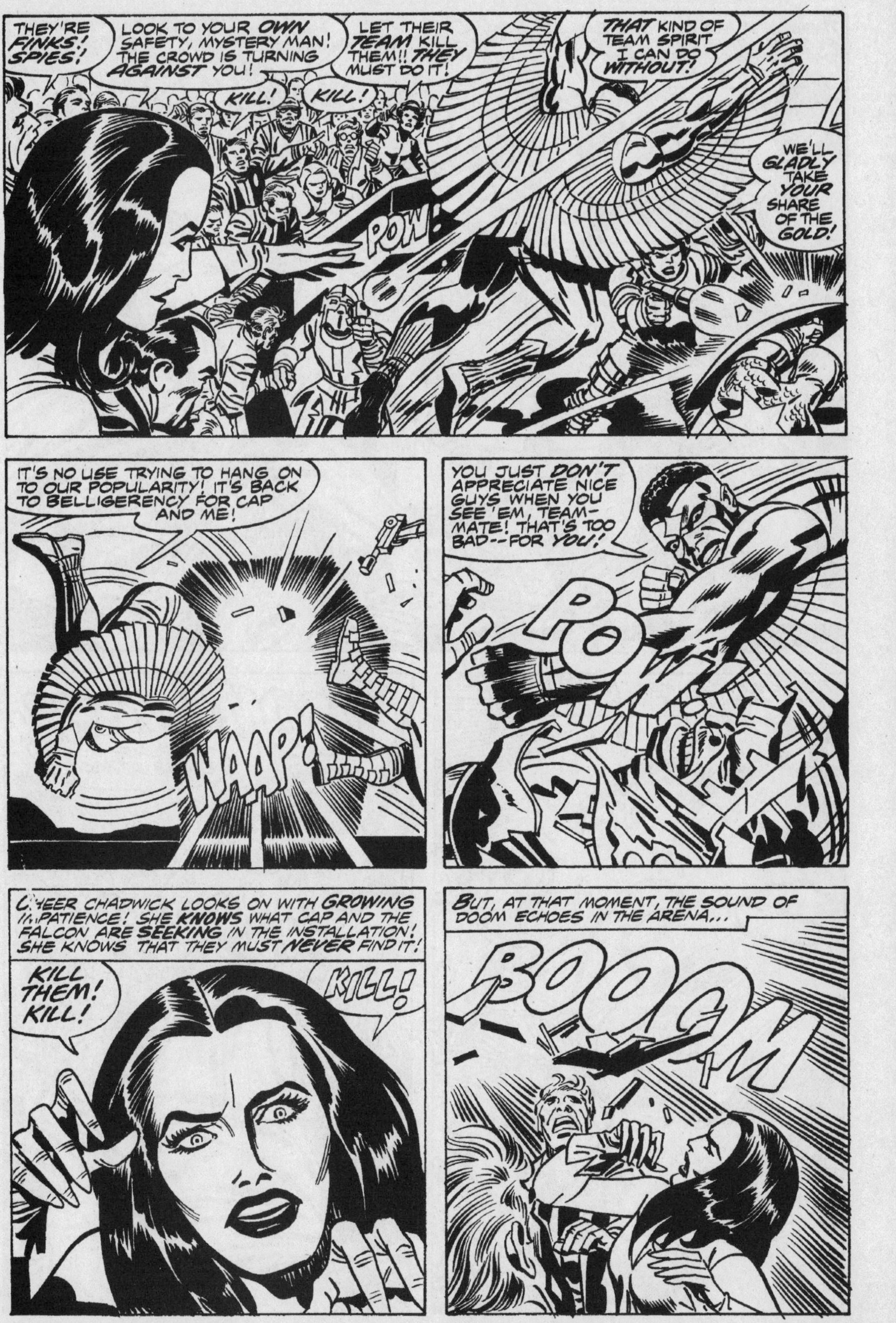
THEY'RE FINKS! SPIES!
LOOK TO YOUR OWN SAFETY, MYSTERY MAN! THE CROWD IS TURNING AGAINST YOU!
LET THEIR TEAM KILL THEM!! THEY MUST DO IT!
KILL!
KILL!
THAT KIND OF TEAM SPIRIT I CAN DO WITHOUT!
WE'LL GLADLY TAKE YOUR SHARE OF THE GOLD!
POW
IT'S NO USE TRYING TO HANG ON TO OUR POPULARITY! IT'S BACK TO BELLIGERENCY FOR CAP AND ME!
WAAP!
YOU JUST DON'T APPRECIATE NICE GUYS WHEN YOU SEE 'EM, TEAM-MATE! THAT'S TOO BAD--FOR YOU!
POW!
CHEER CHADWICK LOOKS ON WITH GROWING IMPATIENCE! SHE KNOWS WHAT CAP AND THE FALCON ARE SEEKING IN THE INSTALLATION! SHE KNOWS THAT THEY MUST NEVER FIND IT!
KILL THEM! KILL!
KILL!
BUT, AT THAT MOMENT, THE SOUND OF DOOM ECHOES IN THE ARENA...
BOOOM

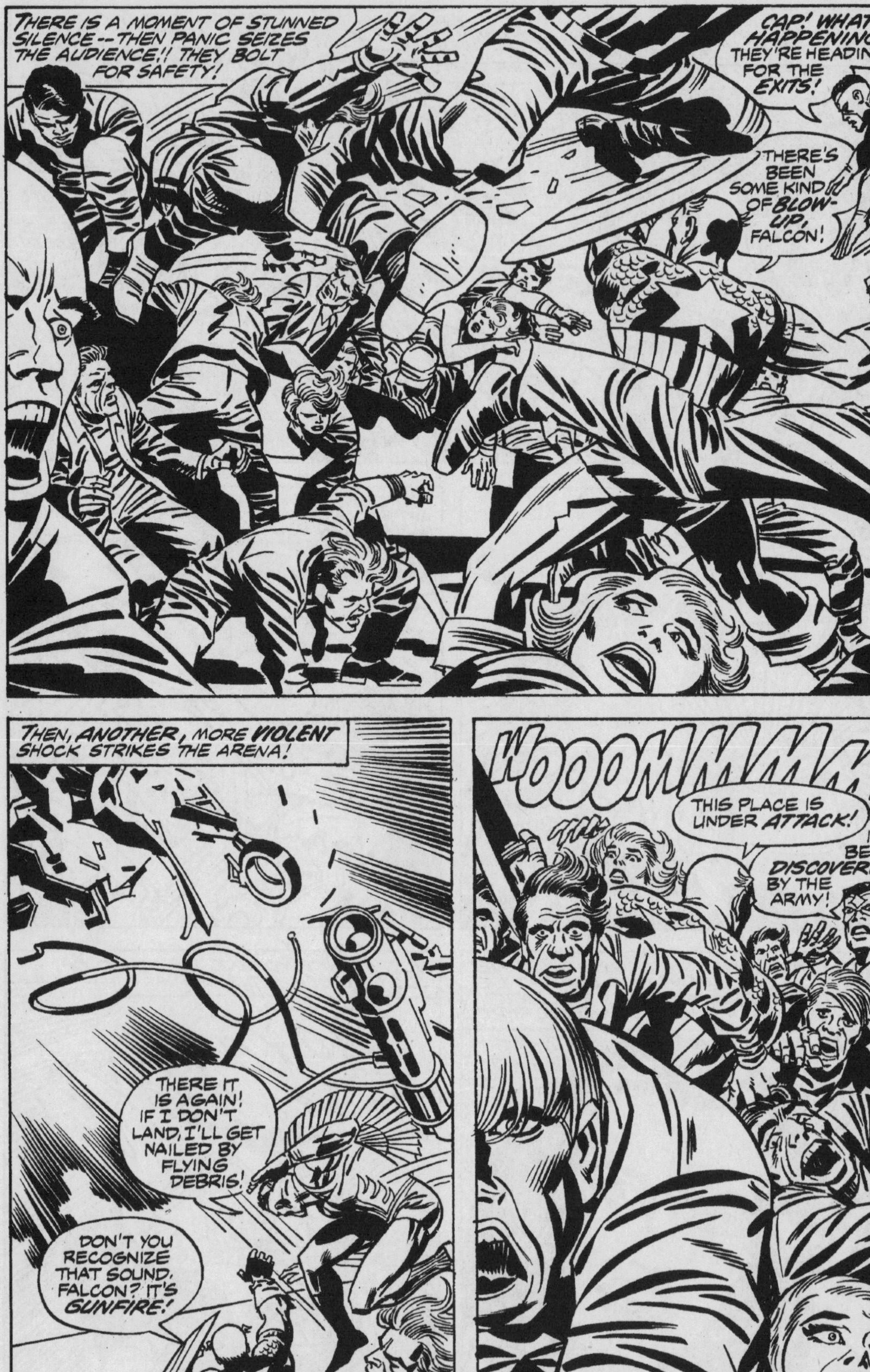
THERE IS A MOMENT OF STUNNED SILENCE--THEN PANIC SEIZES THE AUDIENCE!! THEY BOLT FOR SAFETY!
CAP! WHAT'S HAPPENING!? THEY'RE HEADING FOR THE EXITS!
THERE'S BEEN SOME KIND OF BLOW-UP, FALCON!
THEN, ANOTHER, MORE VIOLENT SHOCK STRIKES THE ARENA!
THERE IT IS AGAIN! IF I DON'T LAND, I'LL GET NAILED BY FLYING DEBRIS!
DON'T YOU RECOGNIZE THAT SOUND, FALCON? IT'S GUNFIRE!
WOOOMMMMM!
THIS PLACE IS UNDER ATTACK!
I-IT'S BEEN DISCOVERED! BY THE ARMY!

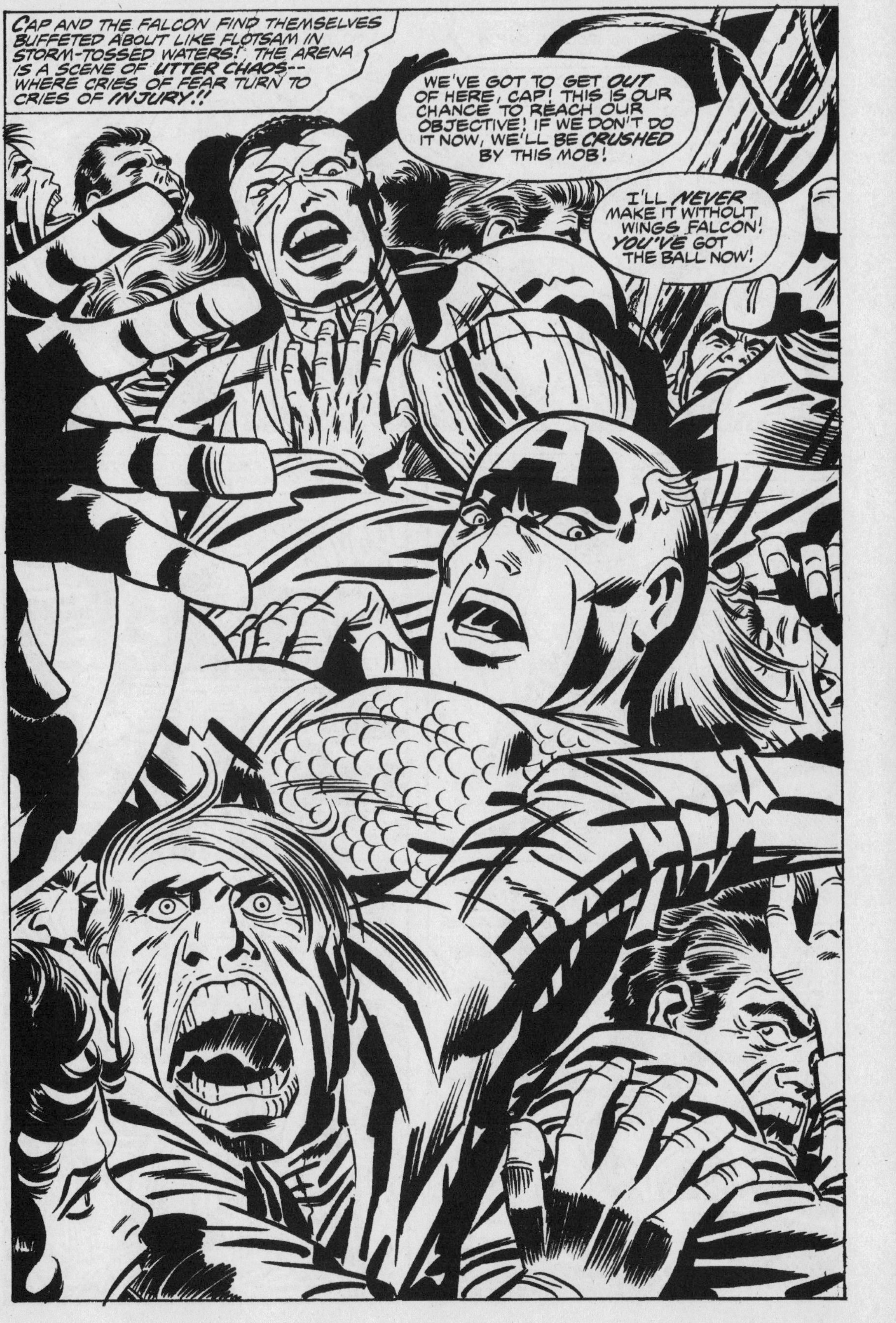
CAP AND THE FALCON FIND THEMSELVES BUFFETED ABOUT LIKE FLOTSAM IN STORM-TOSSED WATERS! THE ARENA IS A SCENE OF UTTER CHAOS-- WHERE CRIES OF FEAR TURN TO CRIES OF INJURY!!
WE'VE GOT TO GET OUT OF HERE, CAP! THIS IS OUR CHANCE TO REACH OUR OBJECTIVE! IF WE DON'T DO IT NOW, WE'LL BE CRUSHED BY THIS MOB!
I'LL NEVER MAKE IT WITHOUT WINGS, FALCON! YOU'VE GOT THE BALL NOW!

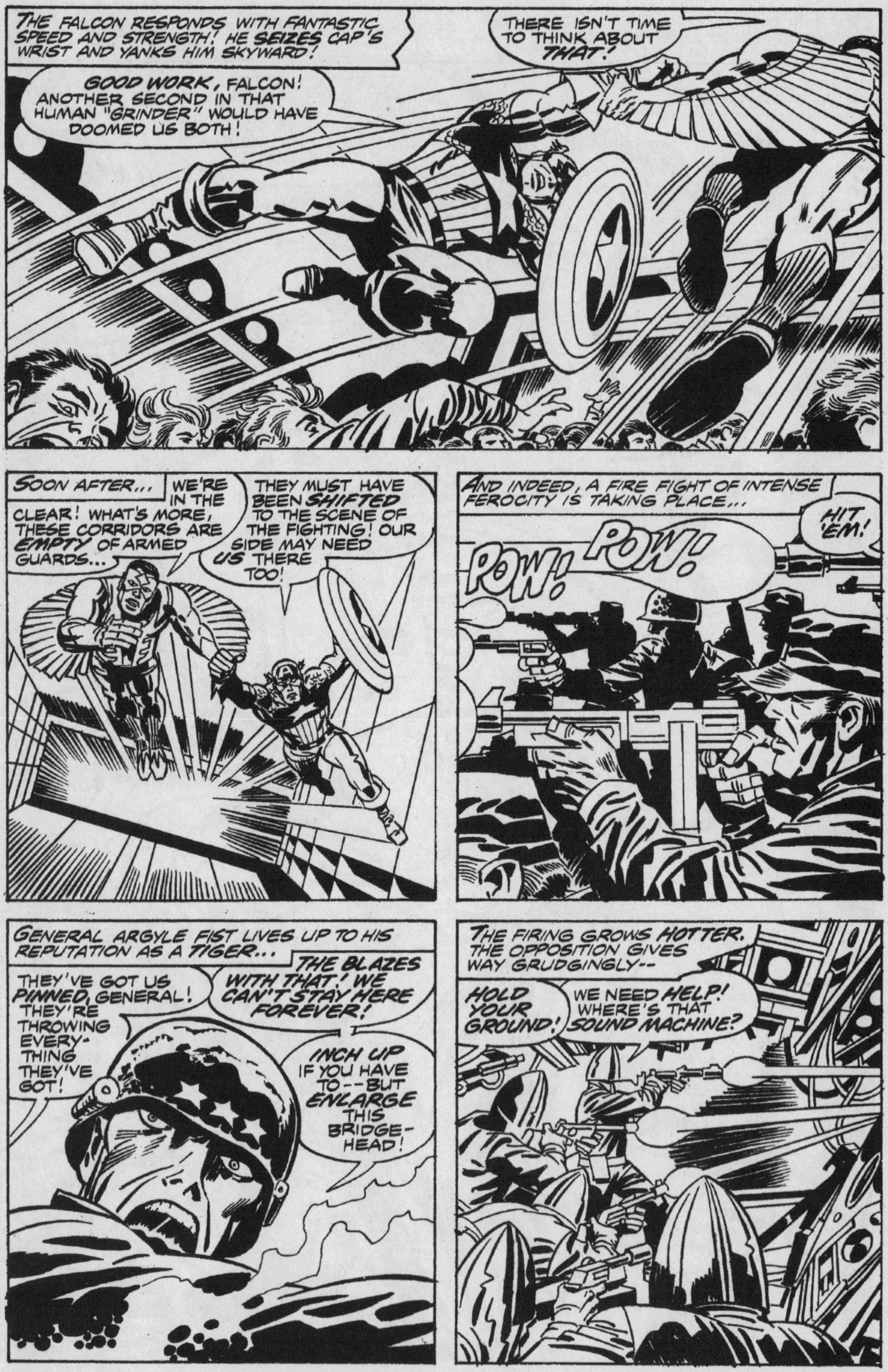
THE FALCON RESPONDS WITH FANTASTIC SPEED AND STRENGTH! HE SEIZES CAP'S WRIST AND YANKS HIM SKYWARD!
GOOD WORK, FALCON! ANOTHER SECOND IN THAT HUMAN "GRINDER" WOULD HAVE DOOMED US BOTH!
THERE ISN'T TIME TO THINK ABOUT THAT!
SOON AFTER...
WE'RE IN THE CLEAR! WHAT'S MORE, THESE CORRIDORS ARE EMPTY OF ARMED GUARDS...
THEY MUST HAVE BEEN SHIFTED TO THE SCENE OF THE FIGHTING! OUR SIDE MAY NEED US THERE TOO!
AND INDEED, A FIRE FIGHT OF INTENSE FEROCITY IS TAKING PLACE...
HIT 'EM!
POW!
POW!
GENERAL ARGYLE FIST LIVES UP TO HIS REPUTATION AS A TIGER...
THEY'VE GOT US PINNED, GENERAL! THEY'RE THROWING EVERY-THING THEY'VE GOT!
THE BLAZES WITH THAT! WE CAN'T STAY HERE FOREVER!
INCH UP IF YOU HAVE TO--BUT ENLARGE THIS BRIDGE-HEAD!
THE FIRING GROWS HOTTER. THE OPPOSITION GIVES WAY GRUDGINGLY--
HOLD YOUR GROUND!
WE NEED HELP! WHERE'S THAT SOUND MACHINE?

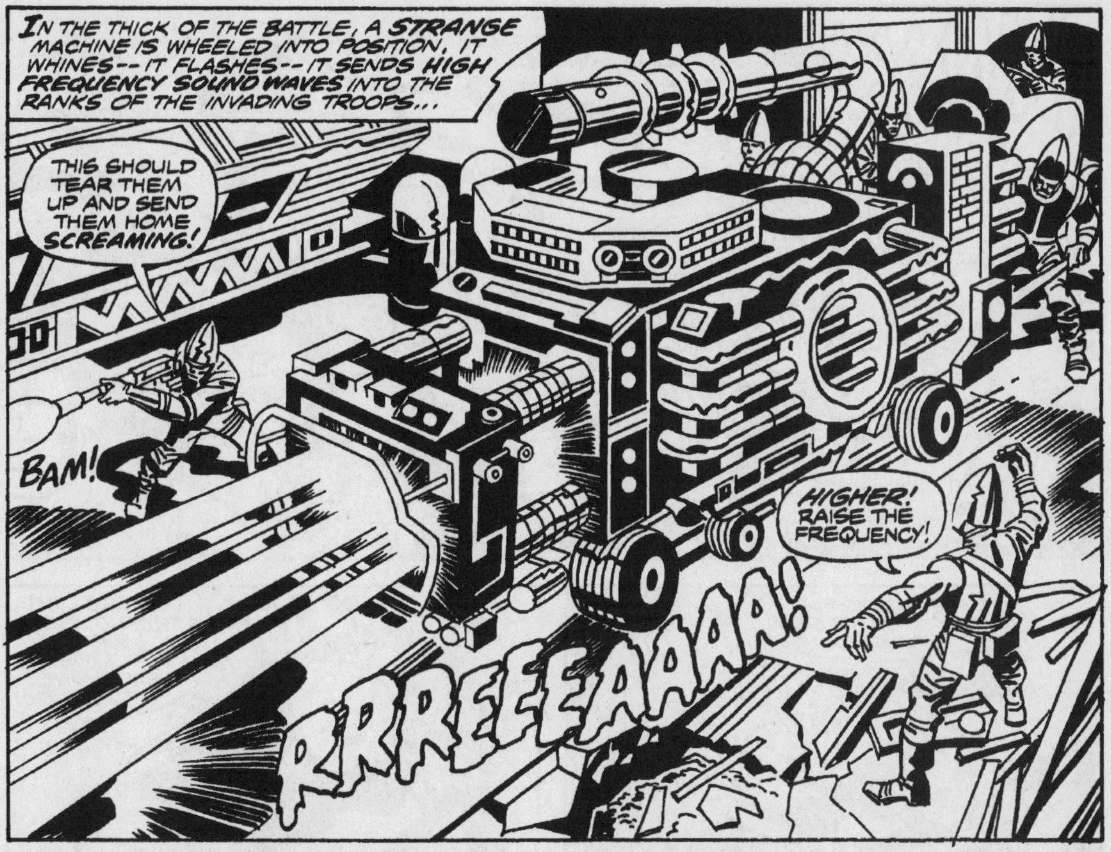
IN THE THICK OF THE BATTLE, A STRANGE MACHINE IS WHEELED INTO POSITION. IT WHINES-- IT FLASHES-- IT SENDS HIGH FREQUENCY SOUND WAVES INTO THE RANKS OF THE INVADING TROOPS...
THIS SHOULD TEAR THEM UP AND SEND THEM HOME SCREAMING!
BAM!
HIGHER! RAISE THE FREQUENCY!
RRREEEAAAA!

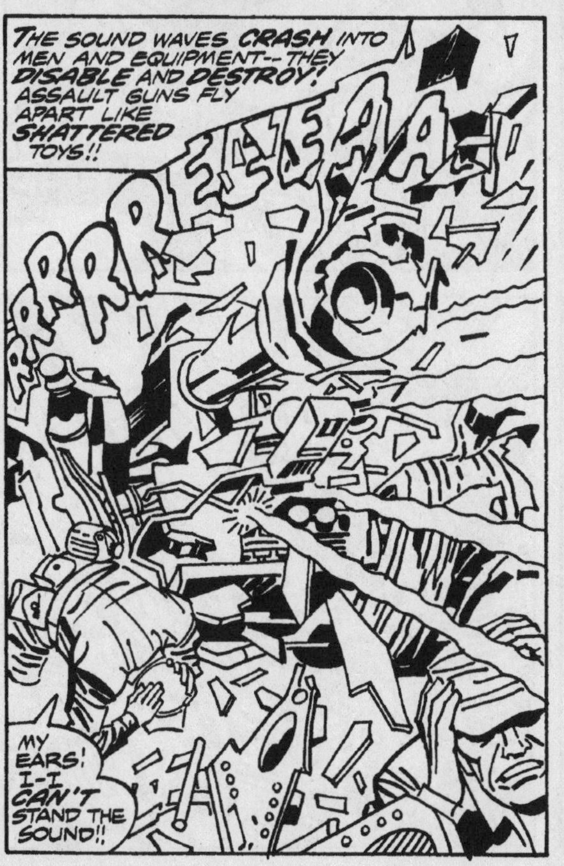
THE SOUND WAVES CRASH INTO MEN AND EQUIPMENT-- THEY DISABLE AND DESTROY! ASSAULT GUNS FLY APART LIKE SHATTERED TOYS!!
RRRREEEEAA!
MY EARS! I-I CAN'T STAND THE SOUND!!

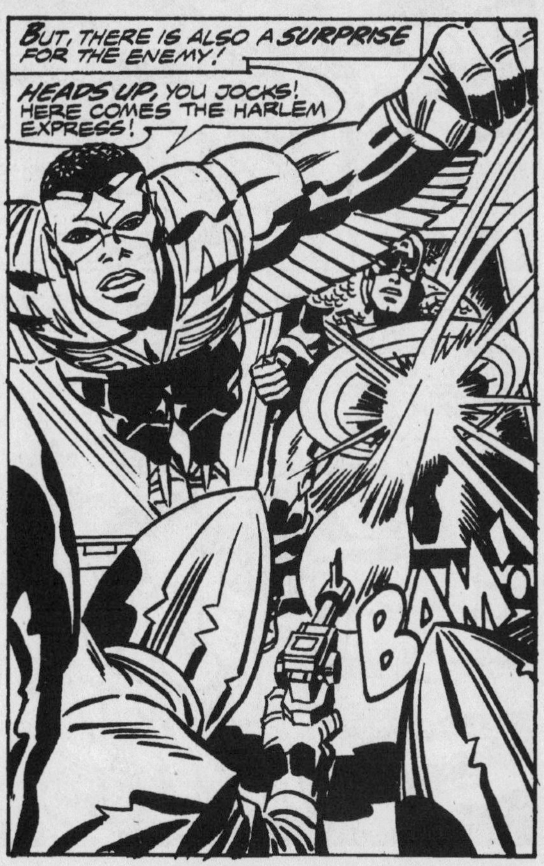
BUT, THERE IS ALSO A SURPRISE FOR THE ENEMY!
HEADS UP, YOU JOCKS! HERE COMES THE HARLEM EXPRESS!
BAM!

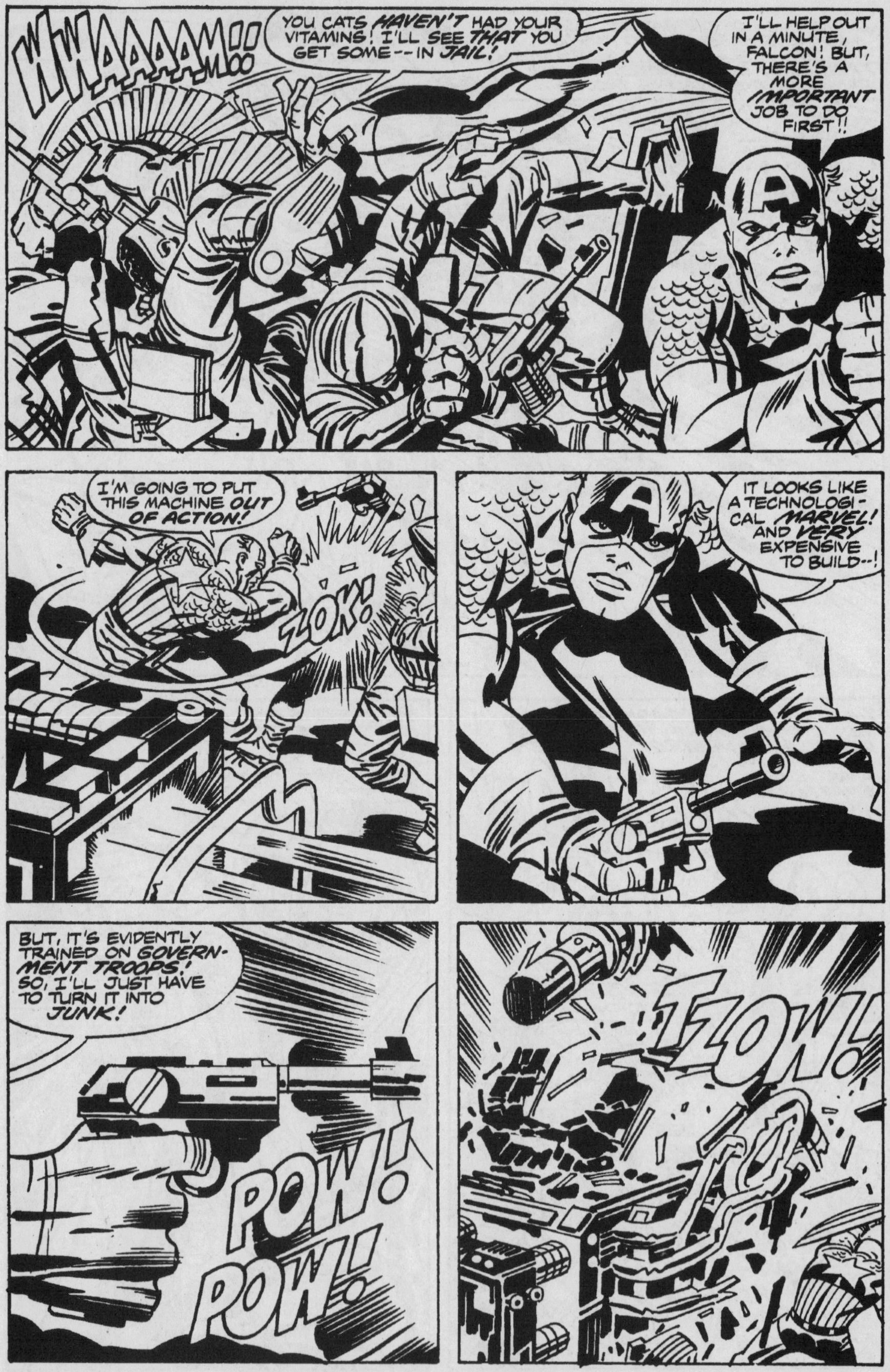

WHAAAAM!!
YOU CATS HAVEN'T HAD YOUR VITAMINS! I'LL SEE THAT YOU GET SOME--IN JAIL!
I'LL HELP OUT IN A MINUTE, FALCON! BUT, THERE'S A MORE IMPORTANT JOB TO DO FIRST!!
I'M GOING TO PUT THIS MACHINE OUT OF ACTION!
ZOK!
IT LOOKS LIKE A TECHNOLOGI-CAL MARVEL! AND VERY EXPENSIVE TO BUILD--!
BUT, IT'S EVIDENTLY TRAINED ON GOVERN-MENT TROOPS! SO, I'LL JUST HAVE TO TURN IT INTO JUNK!
POW! POW!
TZOW!

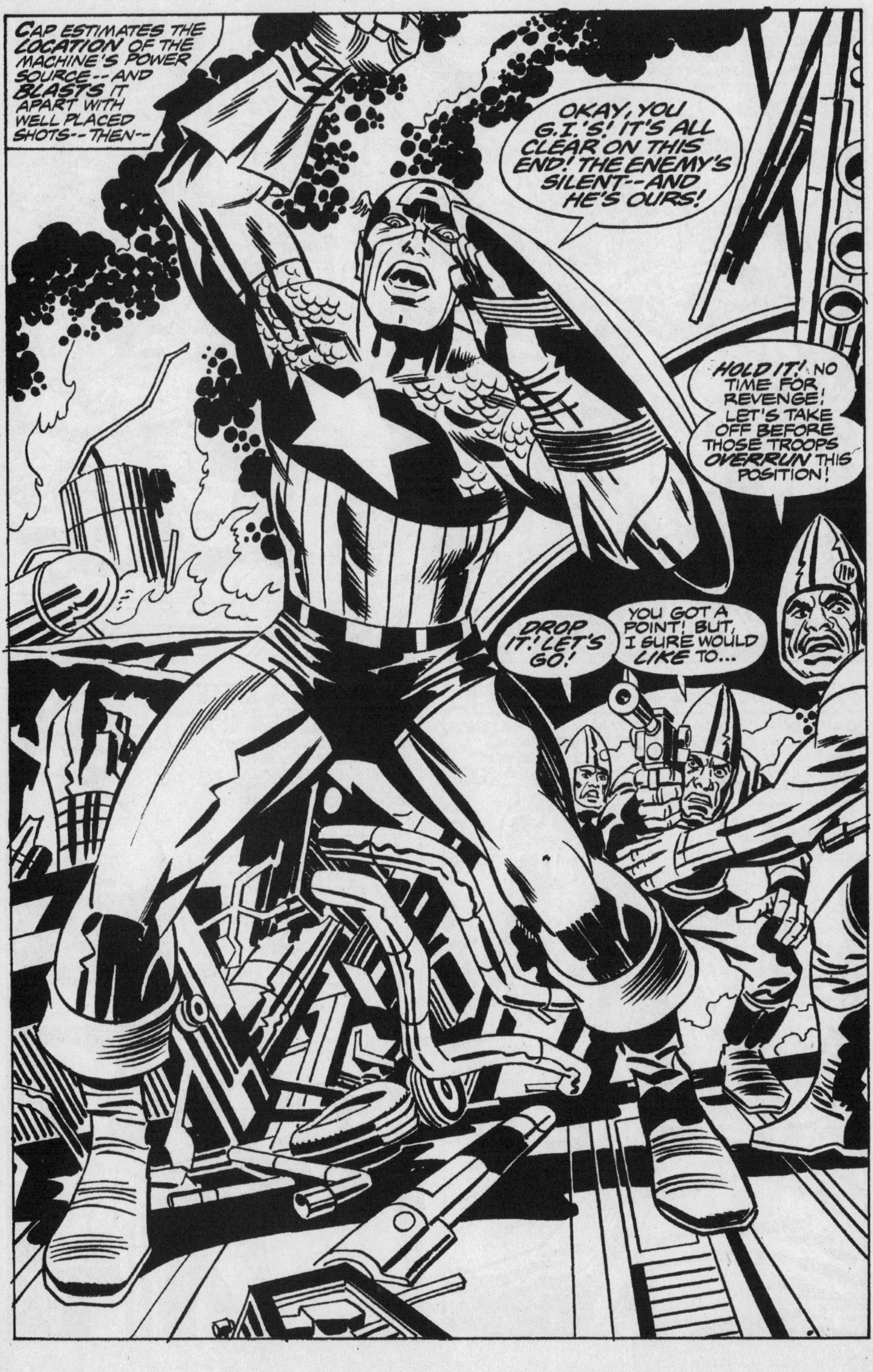
CAP ESTIMATES THE LOCATION OF THE MACHINE'S POWER SOURCE-- AND BLASTS IT APART WITH WELL PLACED SHOTS-- THEN--
OKAY, YOU G.I.'S! IT'S ALL CLEAR ON THIS END! THE ENEMY'S SILENT--AND HE'S OURS!
HOLD IT! NO TIME FOR REVENGE! LET'S TAKE OFF BEFORE THOSE TROOPS OVERRUN THIS POSITION!
YOU GOT A POINT! BUT, I SURE WOULD LIKE TO...
DROP IT! LET'S GO!

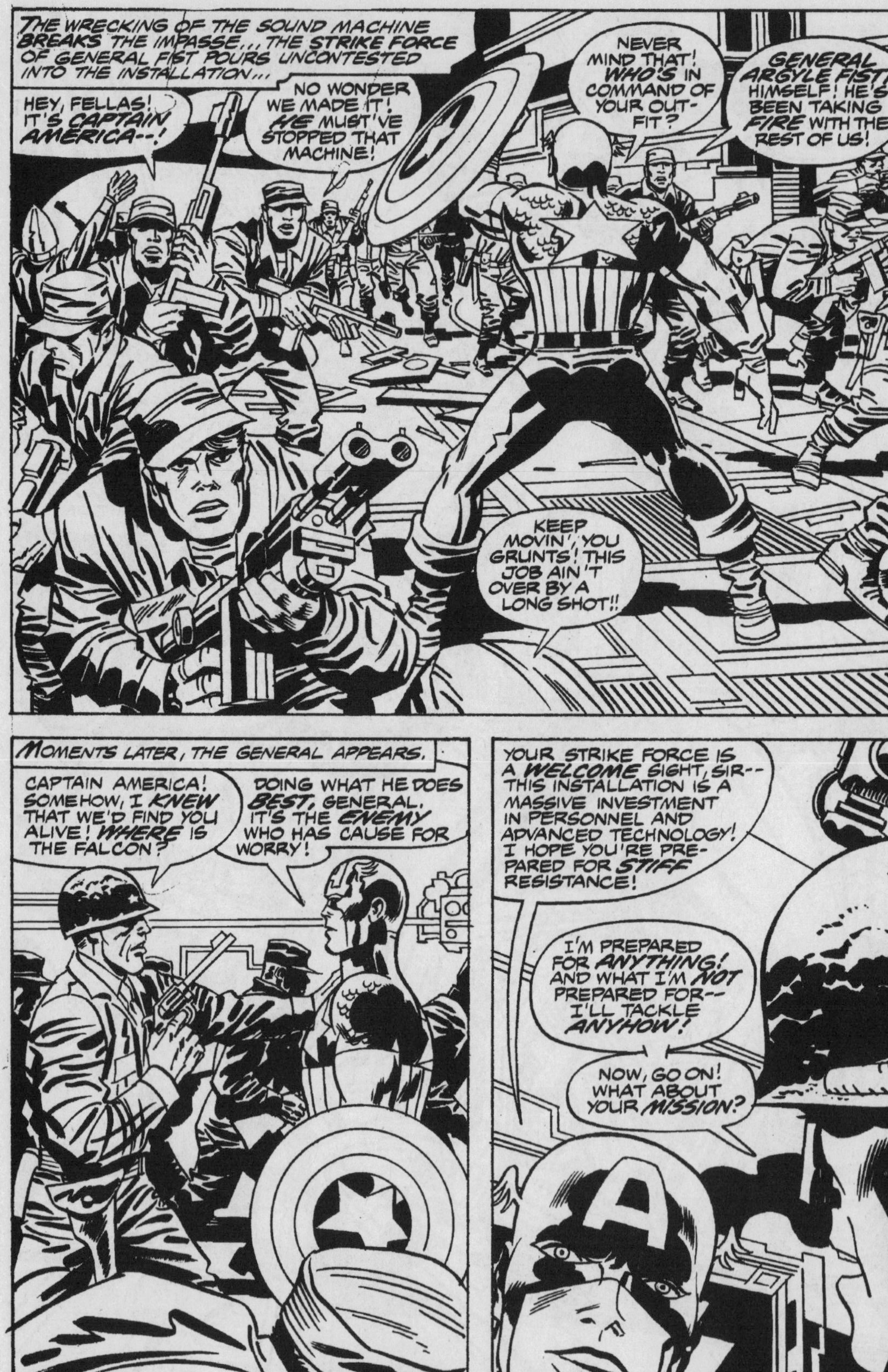
THE WRECKING OF THE SOUND MACHINE BREAKS THE IMPASSE... THE STRIKE FORCE OF GENERAL FIST POURS UNCONTESTED INTO THE INSTALLATION...
HEY, FELLAS! IT'S CAPTAIN AMERICA--!
NO WONDER WE MADE IT! HE MUST'VE STOPPED THAT MACHINE!
NEVER MIND THAT! WHO'S IN COMMAND OF YOUR OUT-FIT?
GENERAL ARGYLE FIST! HIMSELF! HE'S BEEN TAKING FIRE WITH THE REST OF US!
KEEP MOVIN', YOU GRUNTS! THIS JOB AIN'T OVER BY A LONG SHOT!!
MOMENTS LATER, THE GENERAL APPEARS.
CAPTAIN AMERICA! SOMEHOW, I KNEW THAT WE'D FIND YOU ALIVE! WHERE IS THE FALCON?
DOING WHAT HE DOES BEST, GENERAL. IT'S THE ENEMY WHO HAS CAUSE FOR WORRY!
YOUR STRIKE FORCE IS A WELCOME SIGHT, SIR-- THIS INSTALLATION IS A MASSIVE INVESTMENT IN PERSONNEL AND ADVANCED TECHNOLOGY! I HOPE YOU'RE PREPARED FOR STIFF RESISTANCE!
I'M PREPARED FOR ANYTHING! AND WHAT I'M NOT PREPARED FOR-- I'LL TACKLE ANYHOW!
NOW, GO ON! WHAT ABOUT YOUR MISSION?

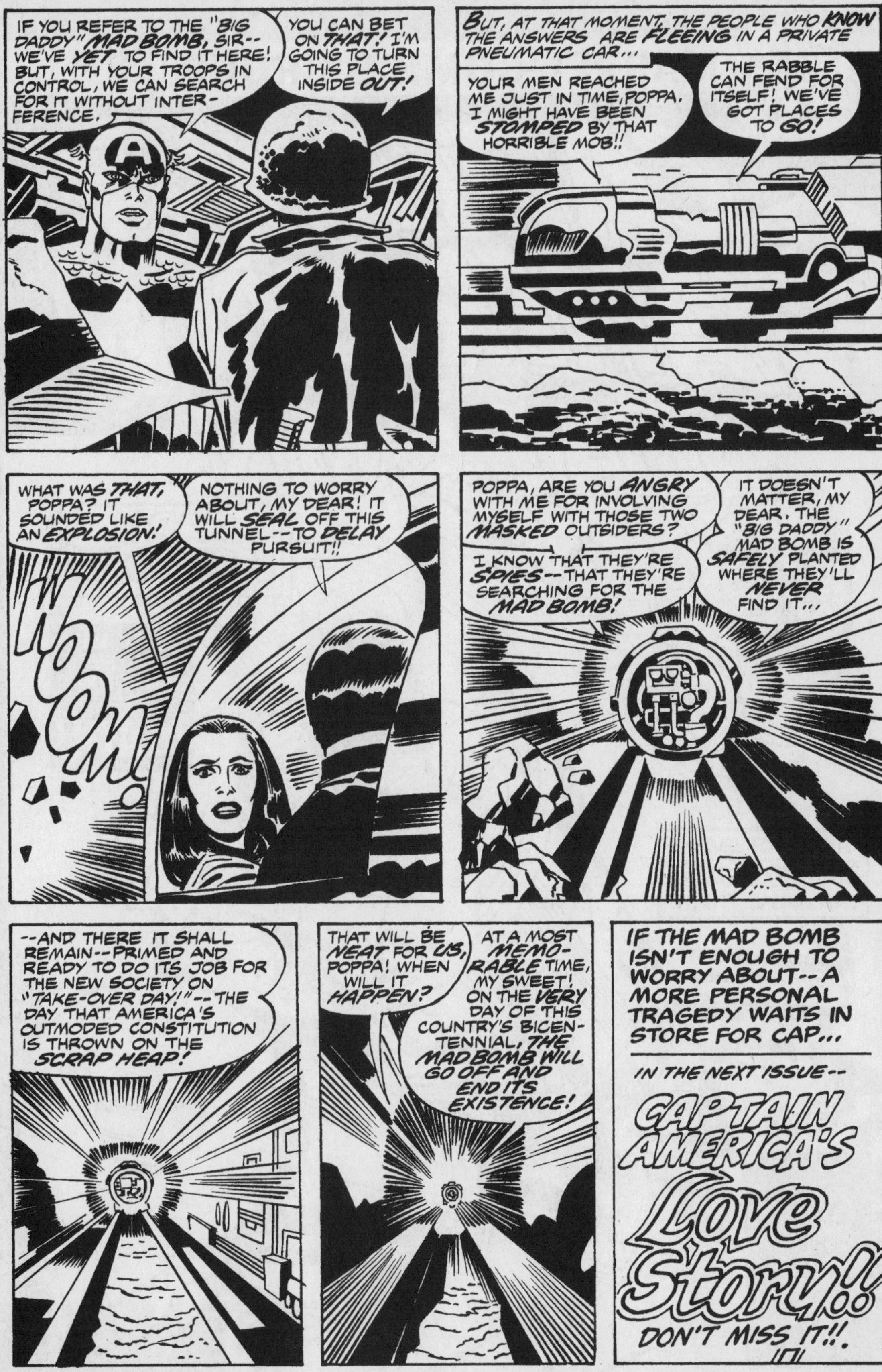
IF YOU REFER TO THE "BIG DADDY" MAD BOMB, SIR-- WE'VE YET TO FIND IT HERE! BUT, WITH YOUR TROOPS IN CONTROL, WE CAN SEARCH FOR IT WITHOUT INTER-FERENCE.
YOU CAN BET ON THAT! I'M GOING TO TURN THIS PLACE INSIDE OUT!
BUT, AT THAT MOMENT, THE PEOPLE WHO KNOW THE ANSWERS ARE FLEEING IN A PRIVATE PNEUMATIC CAR...
YOUR MEN REACHED ME JUST IN TIME, POPPA. I MIGHT HAVE BEEN STOMPED BY THAT HORRIBLE MOB!!
THE RABBLE CAN FEND FOR ITSELF! WE'VE GOT PLACES TO GO!
WHAT WAS THAT, POPPA? IT SOUNDED LIKE AN EXPLOSION!
NOTHING TO WORRY ABOUT, MY DEAR! IT WILL SEAL OFF THIS TUNNEL--TO DELAY PURSUIT!!
WHOOOM!
POPPA, ARE YOU ANGRY WITH ME FOR INVOLVING MYSELF WITH THOSE TWO MASKED OUTSIDERS?
I KNOW THAT THEY'RE SPIES--THAT THEY'RE SEARCHING FOR THE MAD BOMB!
IT DOESN'T MATTER, MY DEAR. THE "BIG DADDY" MAD BOMB IS SAFELY PLANTED WHERE THEY'LL NEVER FIND IT...
--AND THERE IT SHALL REMAIN--PRIMED AND READY TO DO ITS JOB FOR THE NEW SOCIETY ON "TAKE-OVER DAY!"--THE DAY THAT AMERICA'S OUTMODED CONSTITUTION IS THROWN ON THE SCRAP HEAP!
THAT WILL BE NEAT FOR US, POPPA! WHEN WILL IT HAPPEN?
AT A MOST MEMO-RABLE TIME, MY SWEET! ON THE VERY DAY OF THIS COUNTRY'S BICEN-TENNIAL, THE MAD BOMB WILL GO OFF AND END ITS EXISTENCE!
IF THE MAD BOMB ISN'T ENOUGH TO WORRY ABOUT--A MORE PERSONAL TRAGEDY WAITS IN STORE FOR CAP...
IN THE NEXT ISSUE--
CAPTAIN AMERICA'S
Love Story!!
DON'T MISS IT!!

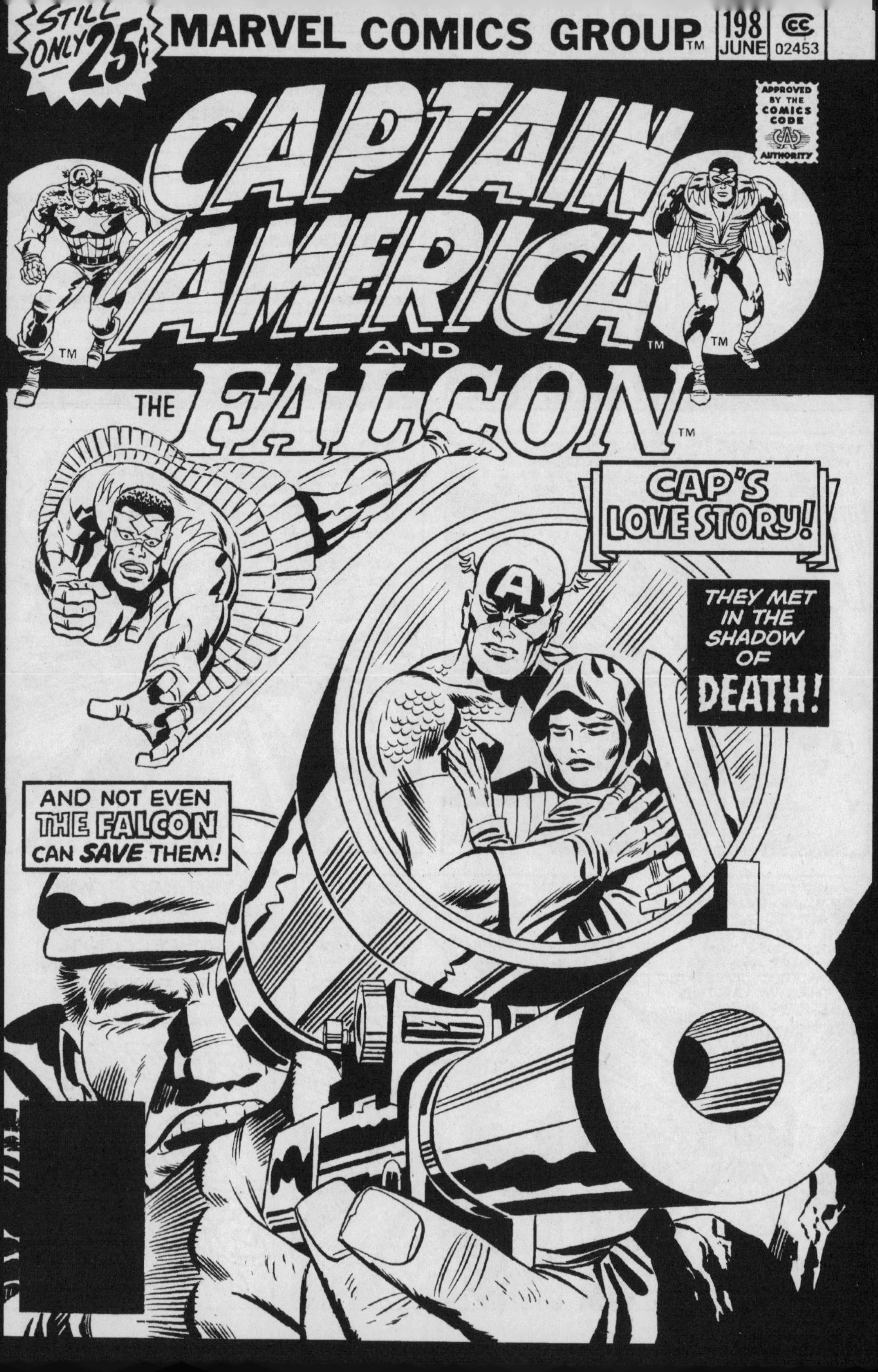
STILL ONLY 25¢
MARVEL COMICS GROUP™
198 JUNE
CC 02453
APPROVED BY THE COMICS CODE AUTHORITY
CAPTAIN AMERICA™
AND
THE FALCON™
CAP'S LOVE STORY!
THEY MET IN THE SHADOW OF DEATH!
AND NOT EVEN THE FALCON CAN SAVE THEM!

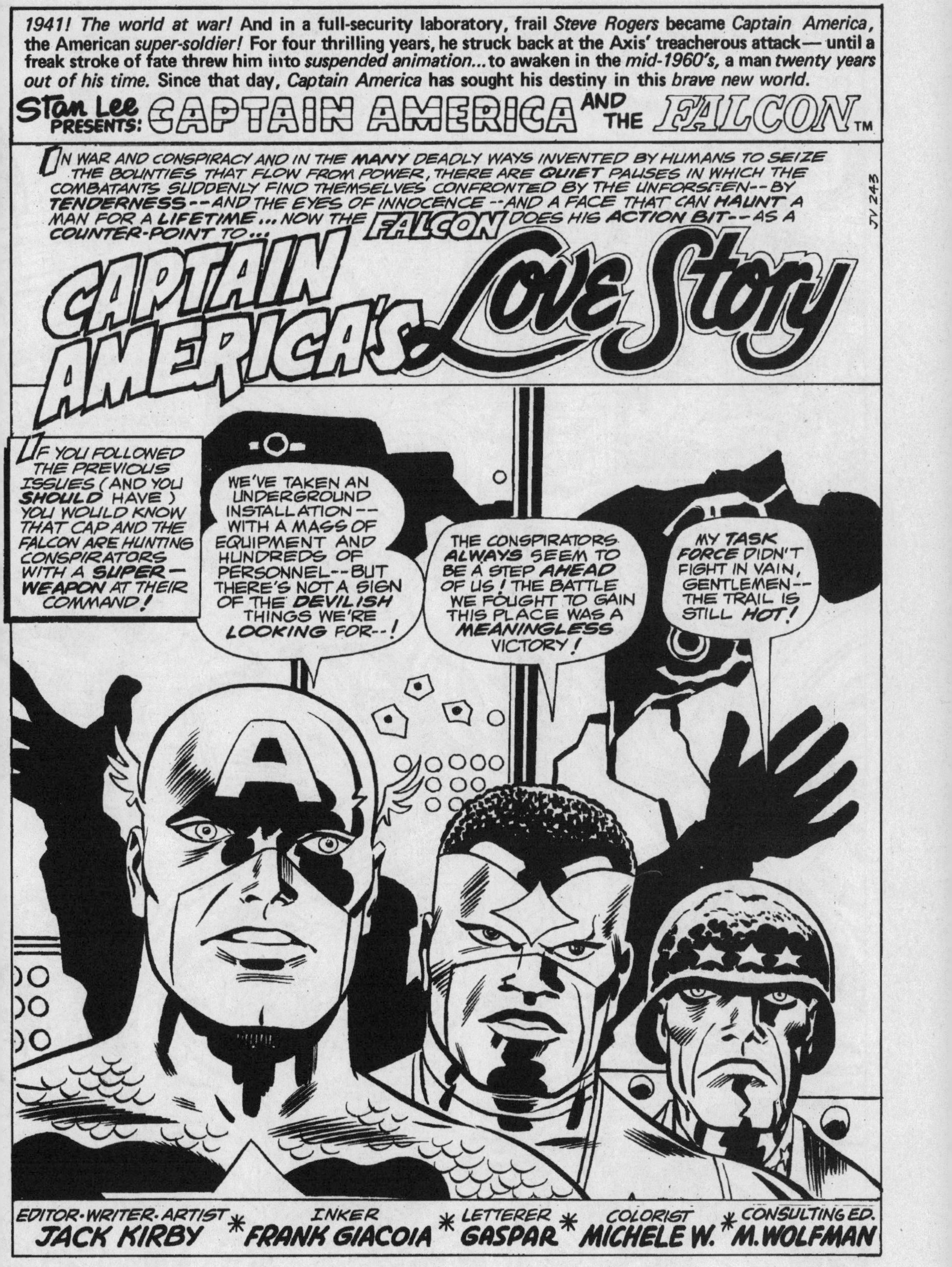
1941! The world at war! And in a full-security laboratory, frail Steve Rogers became Captain America, the American super-soldier! For four thrilling years, he struck back at the Axis' treacherous attack— until a freak stroke of fate threw him into suspended animation... to awaken in the mid-1960's, a man twenty years out of his time. Since that day, Captain America has sought his destiny in this brave new world.
Stan Lee PRESENTS: CAPTAIN AMERICA AND THE FALCON™
IN WAR AND CONSPIRACY AND IN THE MANY DEADLY WAYS INVENTED BY HUMANS TO SEIZE THE BOUNTIES THAT FLOW FROM POWER, THERE ARE QUIET PAUSES IN WHICH THE COMBATANTS SUDDENLY FIND THEMSELVES CONFRONTED BY THE UNFORSEEN-- BY TENDERNESS--AND THE EYES OF INNOCENCE--AND A FACE THAT CAN HAUNT A MAN FOR A LIFETIME... NOW THE FALCON DOES HIS ACTION BIT--AS A COUNTER-POINT TO...
CAPTAIN AMERICA'S LOVE STORY
IF YOU FOLLOWED THE PREVIOUS ISSUES (AND YOU SHOULD HAVE) YOU WOULD KNOW THAT CAP AND THE FALCON ARE HUNTING CONSPIRATORS WITH A SUPER-WEAPON AT THEIR COMMAND!
WE'VE TAKEN AN UNDERGROUND INSTALLATION--WITH A MASS OF EQUIPMENT AND HUNDREDS OF PERSONNEL--BUT THERE'S NOT A SIGN OF THE DEVILISH THINGS WE'RE LOOKING FOR--!
THE CONSPIRATORS ALWAYS SEEM TO BE A STEP AHEAD OF US! THE BATTLE WE FOUGHT TO GAIN THIS PLACE WAS A MEANINGLESS VICTORY!
MY TASK FORCE DIDN'T FIGHT IN VAIN, GENTLEMEN--THE TRAIL IS STILL HOT!
EDITOR-WRITER-ARTIST JACK KIRBY * INKER FRANK GIACOIA * LETTERER GASPAR * COLORIST MICHELE W. * CONSULTING ED. M.WOLFMAN

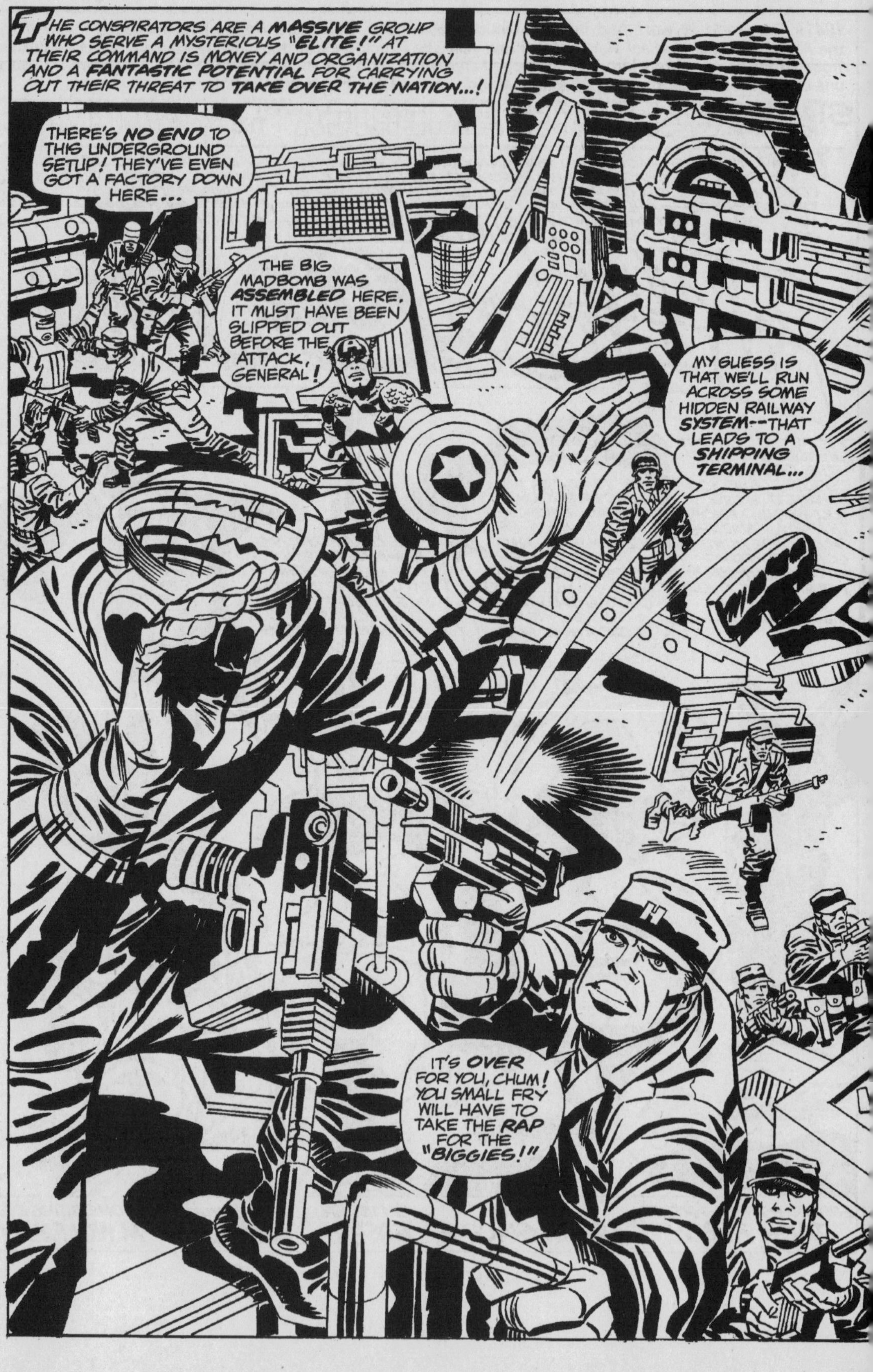
THE CONSPIRATORS ARE A MASSIVE GROUP WHO SERVE A MYSTERIOUS "ELITE!" AT THEIR COMMAND IS MONEY AND ORGANIZATION AND A FANTASTIC POTENTIAL FOR CARRYING OUT THEIR THREAT TO TAKE OVER THE NATION...!
THERE'S NO END TO THIS UNDERGROUND SETUP! THEY'VE EVEN GOT A FACTORY DOWN HERE...
THE BIG MADBOMB WAS ASSEMBLED HERE. IT MUST HAVE BEEN SLIPPED OUT BEFORE THE ATTACK, GENERAL!
MY GUESS IS THAT WE'LL RUN ACROSS SOME HIDDEN RAILWAY SYSTEM--THAT LEADS TO A SHIPPING TERMINAL...
IT'S OVER FOR YOU, CHUM! YOU SMALL FRY WILL HAVE TO TAKE THE RAP FOR THE "BIGGIES!"

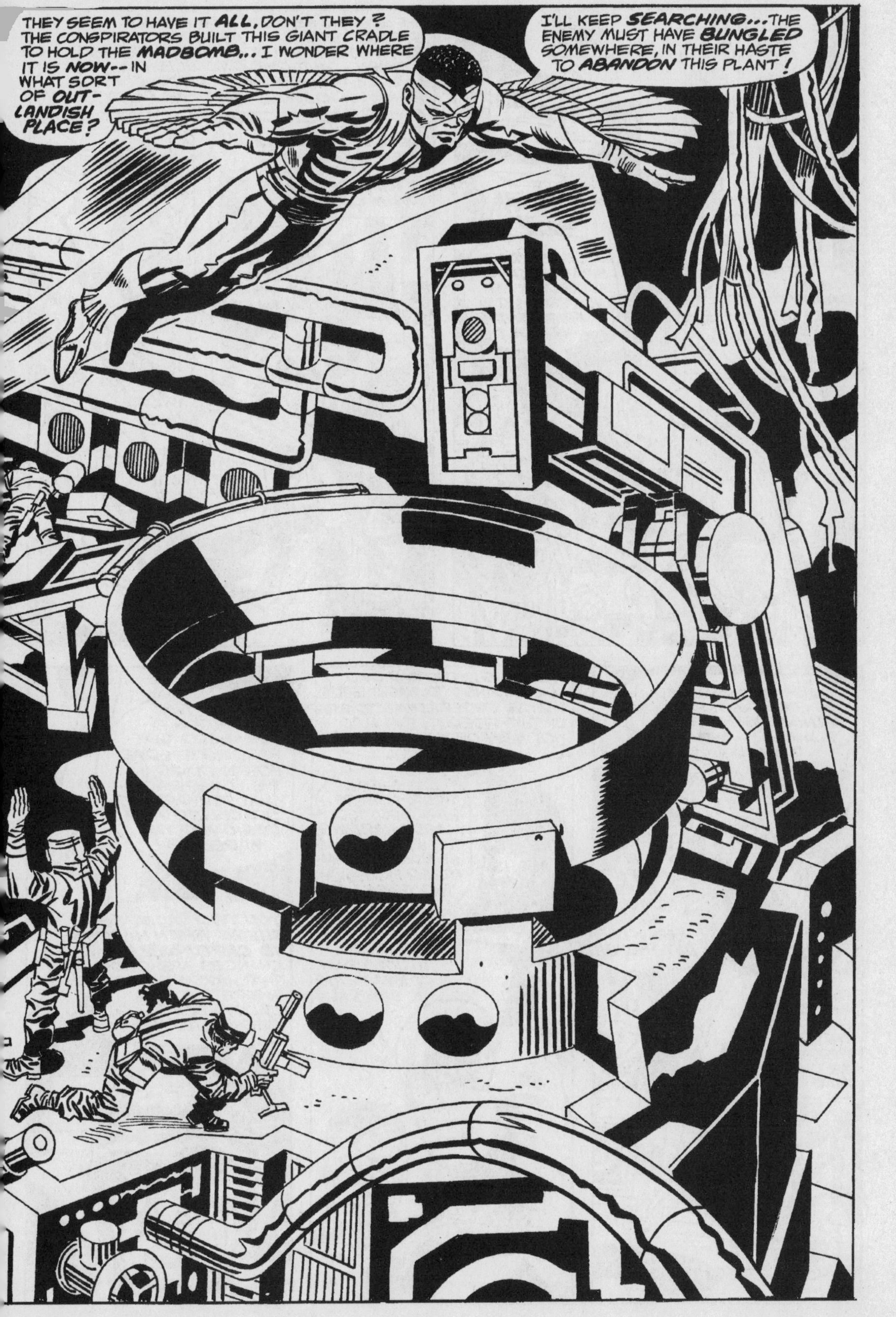
THEY SEEM TO HAVE IT ALL, DON'T THEY? THE CONSPIRATORS BUILT THIS GIANT CRADLE TO HOLD THE MADBOMB... I WONDER WHERE IT IS NOW-- IN WHAT SORT OF OUT-LANDISH PLACE?
I'LL KEEP SEARCHING... THE ENEMY MUST HAVE BUNGLED SOMEWHERE, IN THEIR HASTE TO ABANDON THIS PLANT!

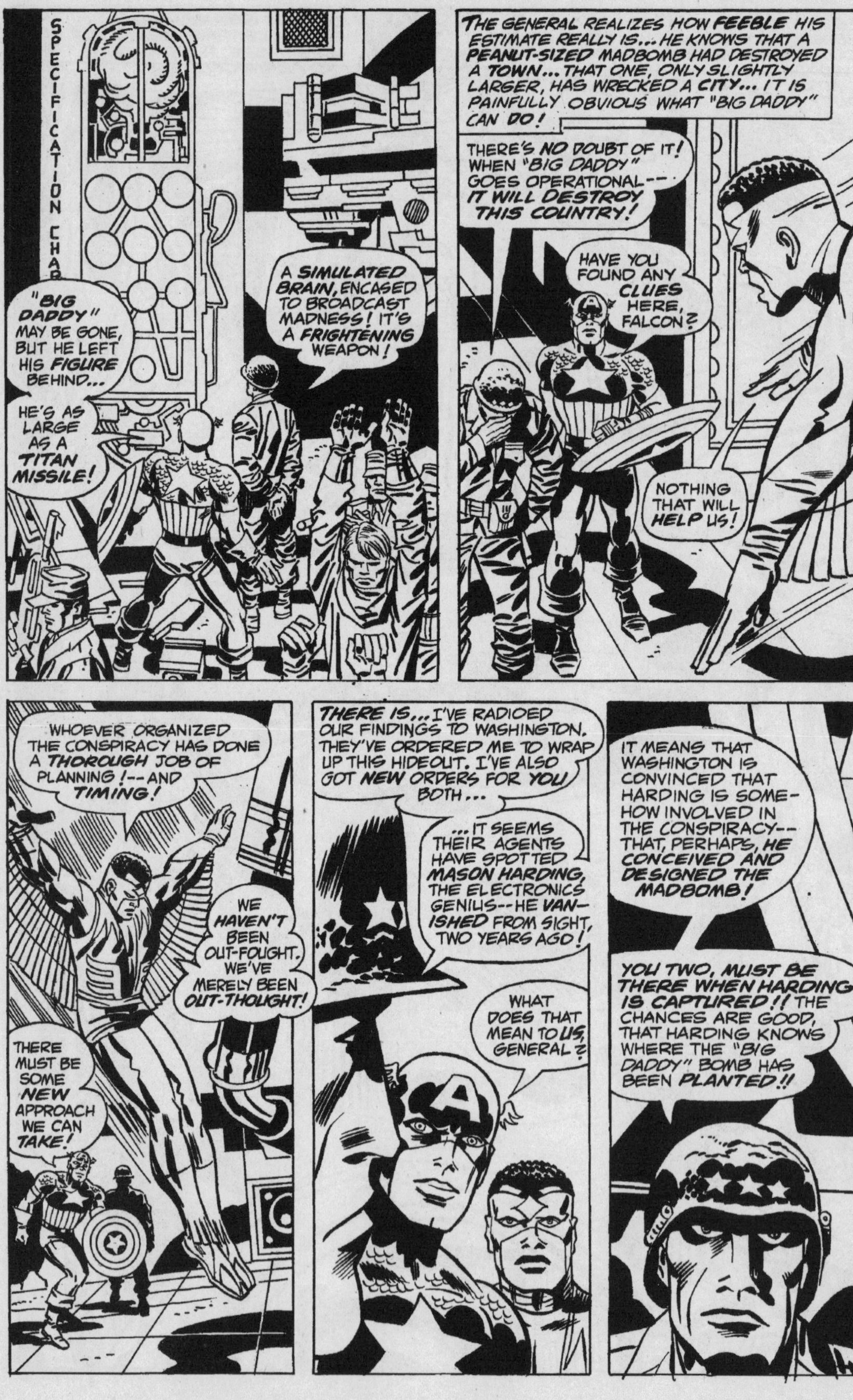
SPECIFICATION CHAR
"BIG DADDY" MAY BE GONE, BUT HE LEFT HIS FIGURE BEHIND...
HE'S AS LARGE AS A TITAN MISSILE!
A SIMULATED BRAIN, ENCASED TO BROADCAST MADNESS! IT'S A FRIGHTENING WEAPON!
THE GENERAL REALIZES HOW FEEBLE HIS ESTIMATE REALLY IS... HE KNOWS THAT A PEANUT-SIZED MADBOMB HAD DESTROYED A TOWN... THAT ONE, ONLY SLIGHTLY LARGER, HAS WRECKED A CITY... IT IS PAINFULLY OBVIOUS WHAT "BIG DADDY" CAN DO!
THERE'S NO DOUBT OF IT! WHEN "BIG DADDY" GOES OPERATIONAL-- IT WILL DESTROY THIS COUNTRY!
HAVE YOU FOUND ANY CLUES HERE, FALCON?
NOTHING THAT WILL HELP US!
WHOEVER ORGANIZED THE CONSPIRACY HAS DONE A THOROUGH JOB OF PLANNING!-- AND TIMING!
WE HAVEN'T BEEN OUT-FOUGHT. WE'VE MERELY BEEN OUT-THOUGHT!
THERE MUST BE SOME NEW APPROACH WE CAN TAKE!
THERE IS... I'VE RADIOED OUR FINDINGS TO WASHINGTON. THEY'VE ORDERED ME TO WRAP UP THIS HIDEOUT. I'VE ALSO GOT NEW ORDERS FOR YOU BOTH...
...IT SEEMS THEIR AGENTS HAVE SPOTTED MASON HARDING, THE ELECTRONICS GENIUS--HE VANISHED FROM SIGHT, TWO YEARS AGO!
WHAT DOES THAT MEAN TO US, GENERAL?
IT MEANS THAT WASHINGTON IS CONVINCED THAT HARDING IS SOMEHOW INVOLVED IN THE CONSPIRACY-- THAT, PERHAPS, HE CONCEIVED AND DESIGNED THE MADBOMB!
YOU TWO, MUST BE THERE WHEN HARDING IS CAPTURED!! THE CHANCES ARE GOOD, THAT HARDING KNOWS WHERE THE "BIG DADDY" BOMB HAS BEEN PLANTED!!

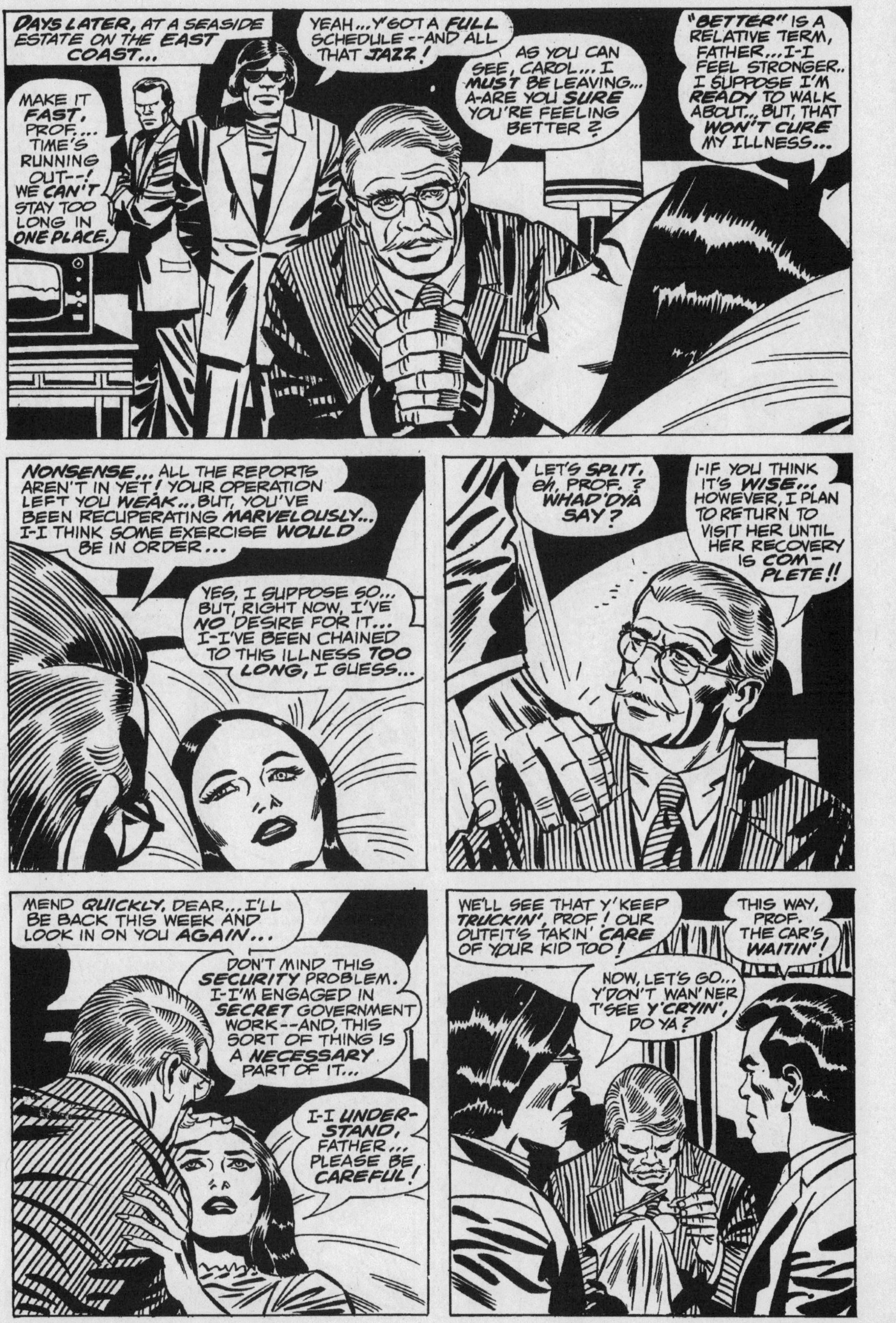
DAYS LATER, AT A SEASIDE ESTATE ON THE EAST COAST...
MAKE IT FAST, PROF.... TIME'S RUNNING OUT--! WE CAN'T STAY TOO LONG IN ONE PLACE.
YEAH...Y'GOT A FULL SCHEDULE--AND ALL THAT JAZZ!
AS YOU CAN SEE, CAROL... I MUST BE LEAVING... A-ARE YOU SURE YOU'RE FEELING BETTER?
"BETTER" IS A RELATIVE TERM, FATHER...I-I FEEL STRONGER.. I SUPPOSE I'M READY TO WALK ABOUT... BUT, THAT WON'T CURE MY ILLNESS...
NONSENSE... ALL THE REPORTS AREN'T IN YET! YOUR OPERATION LEFT YOU WEAK...BUT, YOU'VE BEEN RECUPERATING MARVELOUSLY... I-I THINK SOME EXERCISE WOULD BE IN ORDER...
YES, I SUPPOSE SO... BUT, RIGHT NOW, I'VE NO DESIRE FOR IT... I-I'VE BEEN CHAINED TO THIS ILLNESS TOO LONG, I GUESS...
LET'S SPLIT, eh, PROF.? WHAD'DYA SAY?
I-IF YOU THINK IT'S WISE... HOWEVER, I PLAN TO RETURN TO VISIT HER UNTIL HER RECOVERY IS COMPLETE!!
MEND QUICKLY, DEAR... I'LL BE BACK THIS WEEK AND LOOK IN ON YOU AGAIN...
DON'T MIND THIS SECURITY PROBLEM. I-I'M ENGAGED IN SECRET GOVERNMENT WORK--AND, THIS SORT OF THING IS A NECESSARY PART OF IT...
I-I UNDERSTAND, FATHER... PLEASE BE CAREFUL!
WE'LL SEE THAT Y'KEEP TRUCKIN', PROF! OUR OUTFIT'S TAKIN' CARE OF YOUR KID TOO!
THIS WAY, PROF. THE CAR'S WAITIN'!
NOW, LET'S GO... Y'DON'T WAN'NER T'SEE Y'CRYIN', DO YA?

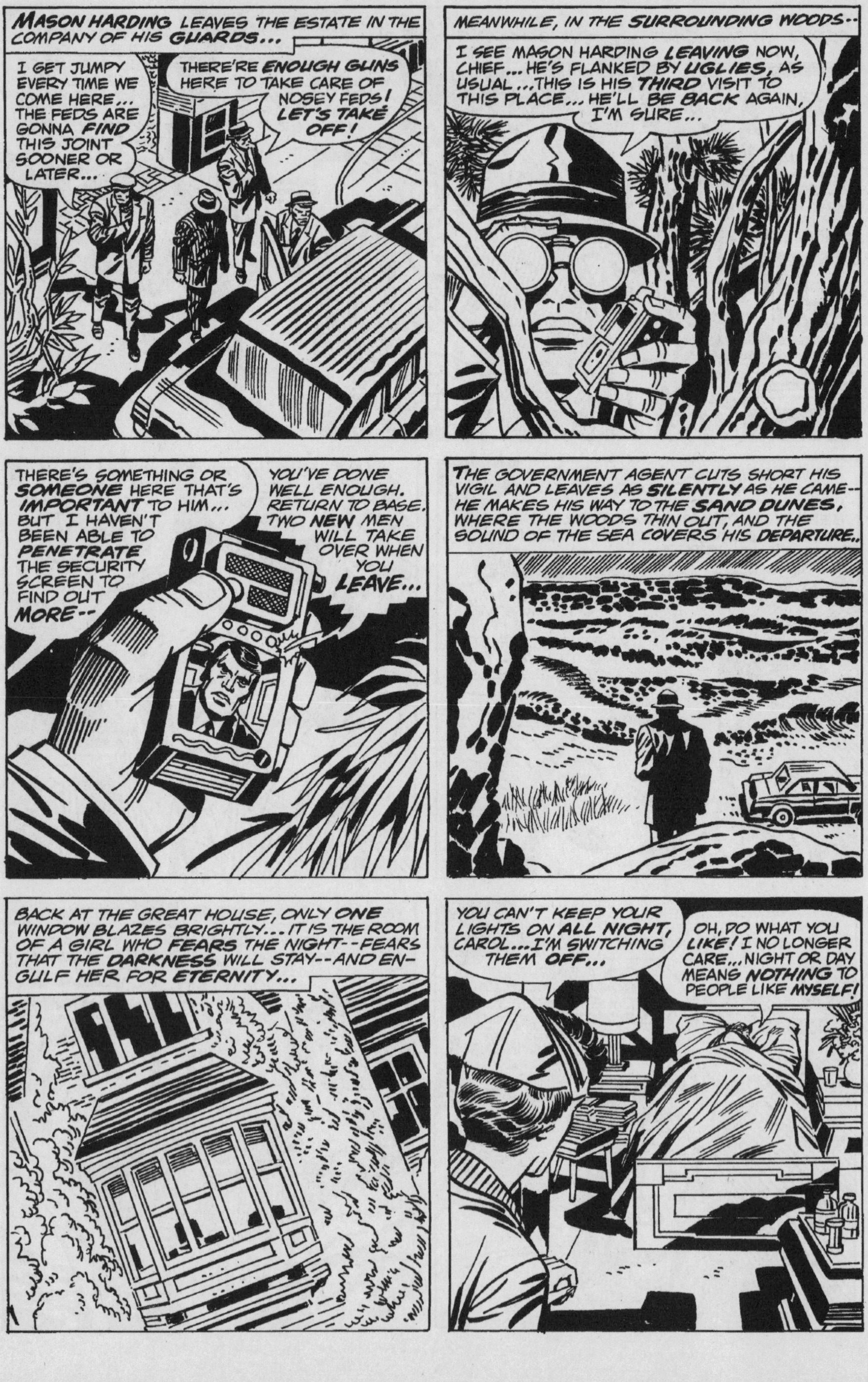
MASON HARDING LEAVES THE ESTATE IN THE COMPANY OF HIS GUARDS...
I GET JUMPY EVERY TIME WE COME HERE... THE FEDS ARE GONNA FIND THIS JOINT SOONER OR LATER...
THERE'RE ENOUGH GUNS HERE TO TAKE CARE OF NOSEY FEDS! LET'S TAKE OFF!
MEANWHILE, IN THE SURROUNDING WOODS...
I SEE MASON HARDING LEAVING NOW, CHIEF... HE'S FLANKED BY UGLIES, AS USUAL... THIS IS HIS THIRD VISIT TO THIS PLACE... HE'LL BE BACK AGAIN, I'M SURE...
THERE'S SOMETHING OR SOMEONE HERE THAT'S IMPORTANT TO HIM... BUT I HAVEN'T BEEN ABLE TO PENETRATE THE SECURITY SCREEN TO FIND OUT MORE--
YOU'VE DONE WELL ENOUGH. RETURN TO BASE. TWO NEW MEN WILL TAKE OVER WHEN YOU LEAVE...
THE GOVERNMENT AGENT CUTS SHORT HIS VIGIL AND LEAVES AS SILENTLY AS HE CAME-- HE MAKES HIS WAY TO THE SAND DUNES, WHERE THE WOODS THIN OUT, AND THE SOUND OF THE SEA COVERS HIS DEPARTURE...
BACK AT THE GREAT HOUSE, ONLY ONE WINDOW BLAZES BRIGHTLY... IT IS THE ROOM OF A GIRL WHO FEARS THE NIGHT--FEARS THAT THE DARKNESS WILL STAY--AND ENGULF HER FOR ETERNITY...
YOU CAN'T KEEP YOUR LIGHTS ON ALL NIGHT, CAROL... I'M SWITCHING THEM OFF...
OH, DO WHAT YOU LIKE! I NO LONGER CARE... NIGHT OR DAY MEANS NOTHING TO PEOPLE LIKE MYSELF!

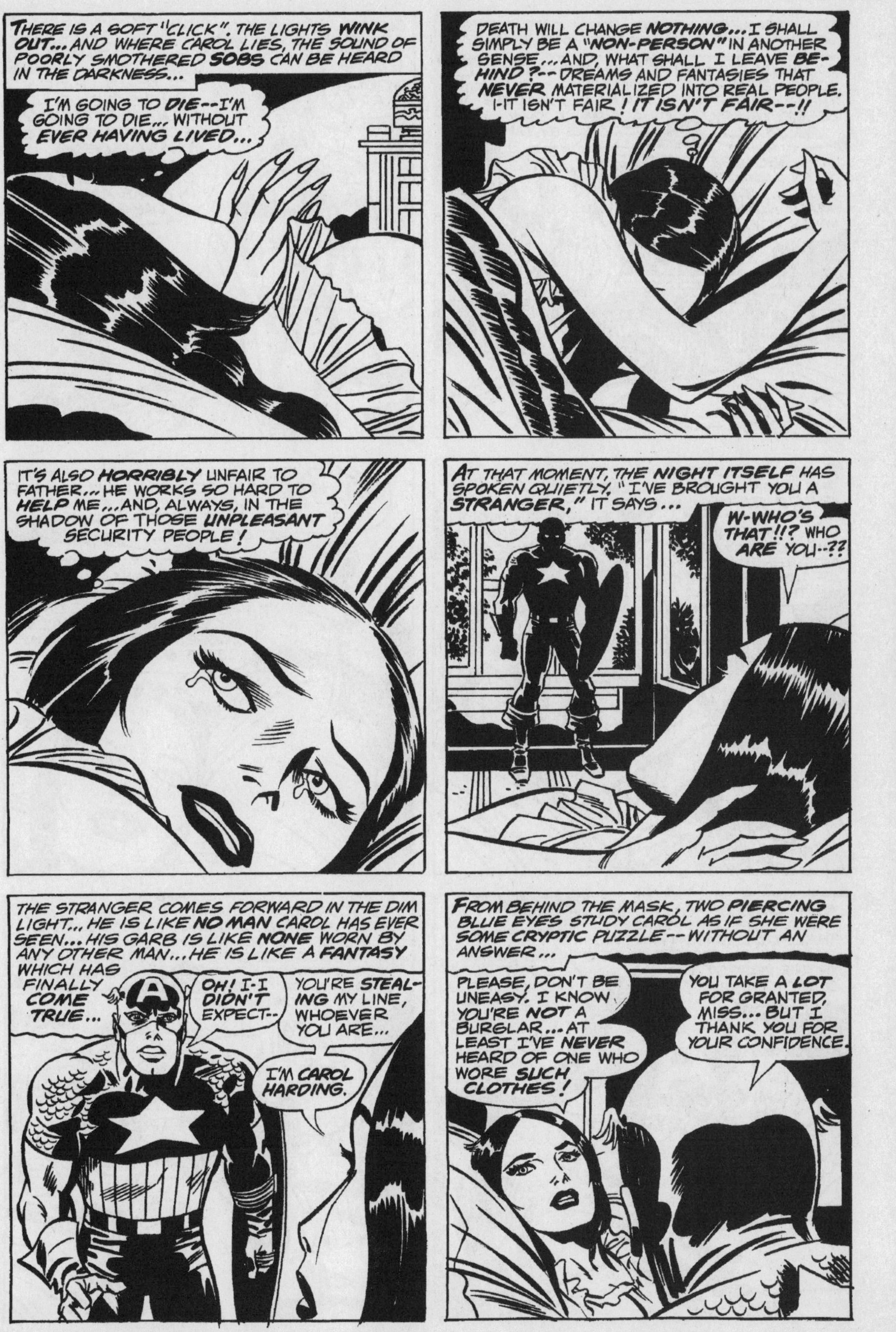

THERE IS A SOFT "CLICK". THE LIGHTS WINK OUT... AND WHERE CAROL LIES, THE SOUND OF POORLY SMOTHERED SOBS CAN BE HEARD IN THE DARKNESS...
I'M GOING TO DIE--I'M GOING TO DIE... WITHOUT EVER HAVING LIVED...
DEATH WILL CHANGE NOTHING... I SHALL SIMPLY BE A "NON-PERSON" IN ANOTHER SENSE... AND, WHAT SHALL I LEAVE BEHIND ?--DREAMS AND FANTASIES THAT NEVER MATERIALIZED INTO REAL PEOPLE. I-IT ISN'T FAIR ! IT ISN'T FAIR--!!
IT'S ALSO HORRIBLY UNFAIR TO FATHER... HE WORKS SO HARD TO HELP ME... AND, ALWAYS, IN THE SHADOW OF THOSE UNPLEASANT SECURITY PEOPLE !
AT THAT MOMENT, THE NIGHT ITSELF HAS SPOKEN QUIETLY. "I'VE BROUGHT YOU A STRANGER," IT SAYS...
W-WHO'S THAT!!? WHO ARE YOU--??
THE STRANGER COMES FORWARD IN THE DIM LIGHT... HE IS LIKE NO MAN CAROL HAS EVER SEEN... HIS GARB IS LIKE NONE WORN BY ANY OTHER MAN... HE IS LIKE A FANTASY WHICH HAS FINALLY COME TRUE...
OH! I-I DIDN'T EXPECT--
YOU'RE STEALING MY LINE, WHOEVER YOU ARE...
I'M CAROL HARDING.
FROM BEHIND THE MASK, TWO PIERCING BLUE EYES STUDY CAROL AS IF SHE WERE SOME CRYPTIC PUZZLE--WITHOUT AN ANSWER...
PLEASE, DON'T BE UNEASY. I KNOW YOU'RE NOT A BURGLAR... AT LEAST I'VE NEVER HEARD OF ONE WHO WORE SUCH CLOTHES !
YOU TAKE A LOT FOR GRANTED, MISS... BUT I THANK YOU FOR YOUR CONFIDENCE.

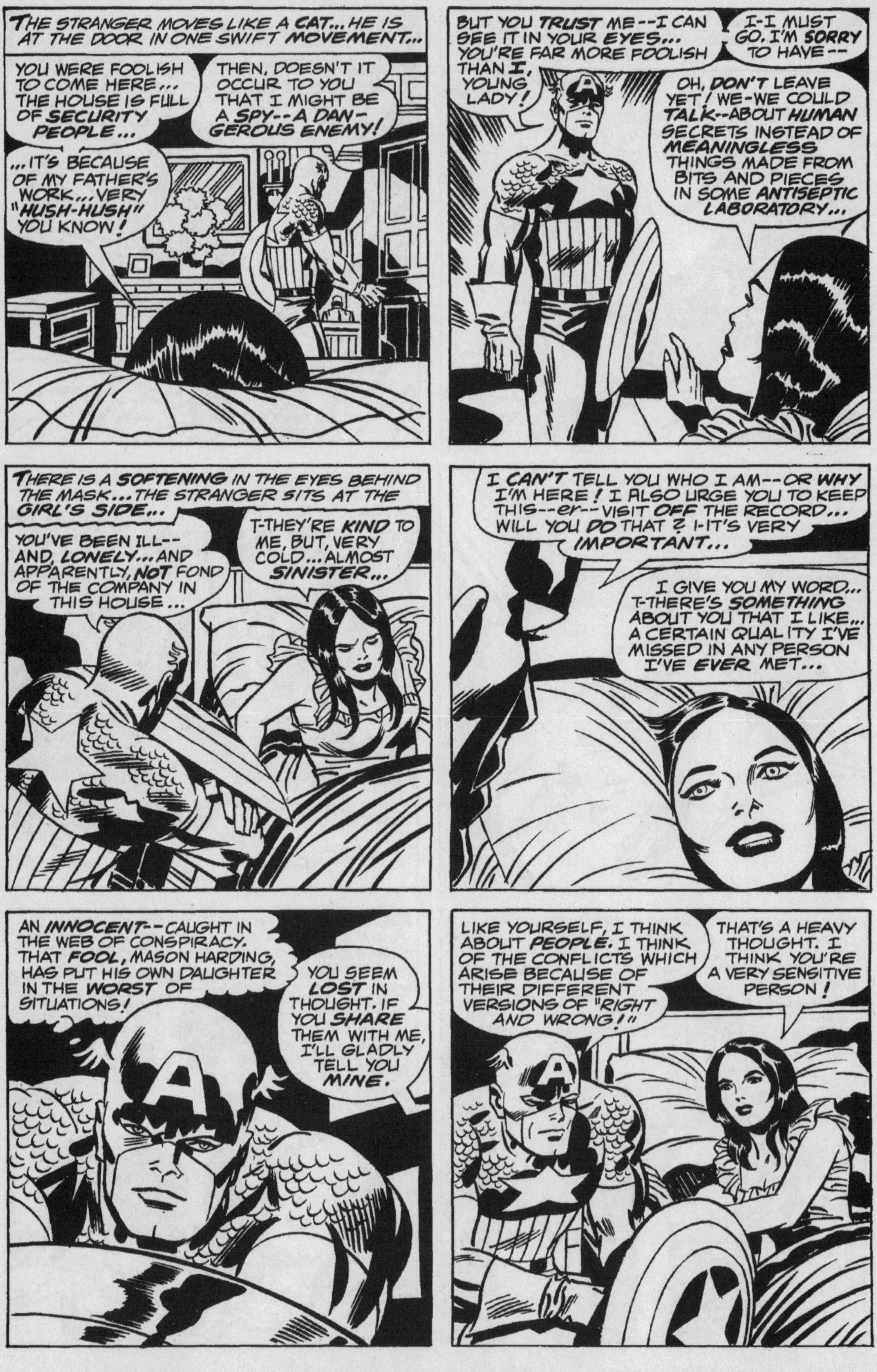

THE STRANGER MOVES LIKE A CAT... HE IS AT THE DOOR IN ONE SWIFT MOVEMENT...
YOU WERE FOOLISH TO COME HERE... THE HOUSE IS FULL OF SECURITY PEOPLE...
THEN, DOESN'T IT OCCUR TO YOU THAT I MIGHT BE A SPY--A DANGEROUS ENEMY!
...IT'S BECAUSE OF MY FATHER'S WORK... VERY "HUSH-HUSH" YOU KNOW!
BUT YOU TRUST ME--I CAN SEE IT IN YOUR EYES... YOU'RE FAR MORE FOOLISH THAN I, YOUNG LADY!
I-I MUST GO. I'M SORRY TO HAVE--
OH, DON'T LEAVE YET! WE-WE COULD TALK--ABOUT HUMAN SECRETS INSTEAD OF MEANINGLESS THINGS MADE FROM BITS AND PIECES IN SOME ANTISEPTIC LABORATORY...
THERE IS A SOFTENING IN THE EYES BEHIND THE MASK... THE STRANGER SITS AT THE GIRL'S SIDE...
YOU'VE BEEN ILL--AND, LONELY... AND APPARENTLY, NOT FOND OF THE COMPANY IN THIS HOUSE...
T-THEY'RE KIND TO ME, BUT, VERY COLD... ALMOST SINISTER...
I CAN'T TELL YOU WHO I AM--OR WHY I'M HERE! I ALSO URGE YOU TO KEEP THIS--er--VISIT OFF THE RECORD... WILL YOU DO THAT? I-IT'S VERY IMPORTANT...
I GIVE YOU MY WORD... T-THERE'S SOMETHING ABOUT YOU THAT I LIKE... A CERTAIN QUALITY I'VE MISSED IN ANY PERSON I'VE EVER MET...
AN INNOCENT--CAUGHT IN THE WEB OF CONSPIRACY. THAT FOOL, MASON HARDING, HAS PUT HIS OWN DAUGHTER IN THE WORST OF SITUATIONS!
YOU SEEM LOST IN THOUGHT. IF YOU SHARE THEM WITH ME, I'LL GLADLY TELL YOU MINE.
LIKE YOURSELF, I THINK ABOUT PEOPLE. I THINK OF THE CONFLICTS WHICH ARISE BECAUSE OF THEIR DIFFERENT VERSIONS OF "RIGHT AND WRONG!"
THAT'S A HEAVY THOUGHT. I THINK YOU'RE A VERY SENSITIVE PERSON!

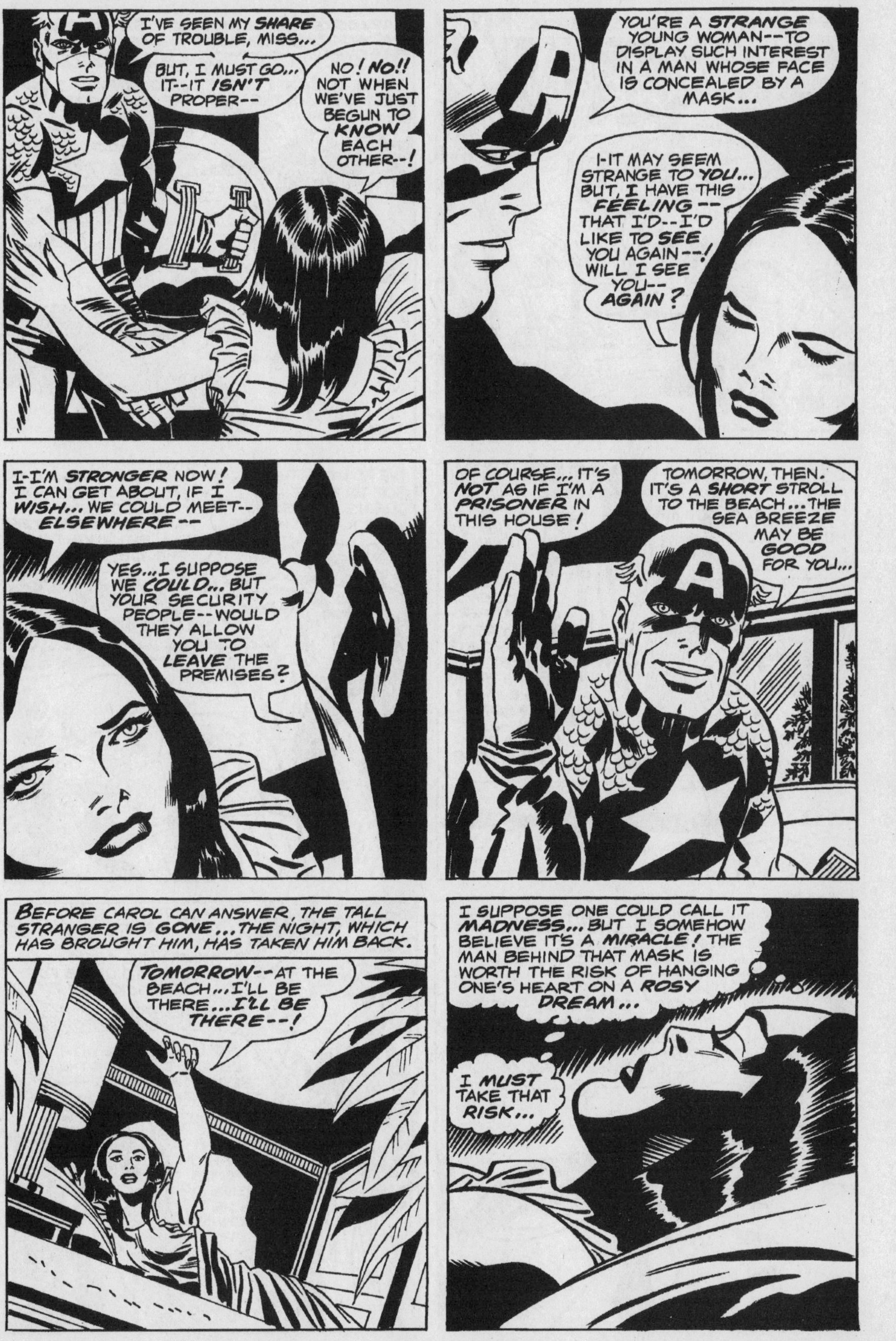
I'VE SEEN MY SHARE OF TROUBLE, MISS...
BUT, I MUST GO... IT--IT ISN'T PROPER--
NO! NO!! NOT WHEN WE'VE JUST BEGUN TO KNOW EACH OTHER--!
YOU'RE A STRANGE YOUNG WOMAN--TO DISPLAY SUCH INTEREST IN A MAN WHOSE FACE IS CONCEALED BY A MASK...
I-IT MAY SEEM STRANGE TO YOU... BUT, I HAVE THIS FEELING--THAT I'D--I'D LIKE TO SEE YOU AGAIN--! WILL I SEE YOU--AGAIN?
I-I'M STRONGER NOW! I CAN GET ABOUT, IF I WISH... WE COULD MEET--ELSEWHERE--
YES... I SUPPOSE WE COULD... BUT YOUR SECURITY PEOPLE--WOULD THEY ALLOW YOU TO LEAVE THE PREMISES?
OF COURSE... IT'S NOT AS IF I'M A PRISONER IN THIS HOUSE!
TOMORROW, THEN. IT'S A SHORT STROLL TO THE BEACH... THE SEA BREEZE MAY BE GOOD FOR YOU...
BEFORE CAROL CAN ANSWER, THE TALL STRANGER IS GONE... THE NIGHT, WHICH HAS BROUGHT HIM, HAS TAKEN HIM BACK.
TOMORROW--AT THE BEACH... I'LL BE THERE... I'LL BE THERE--!
I SUPPOSE ONE COULD CALL IT MADNESS... BUT I SOMEHOW BELIEVE IT'S A MIRACLE! THE MAN BEHIND THAT MASK IS WORTH THE RISK OF HANGING ONE'S HEART ON A ROSY DREAM...
I MUST TAKE THAT RISK...

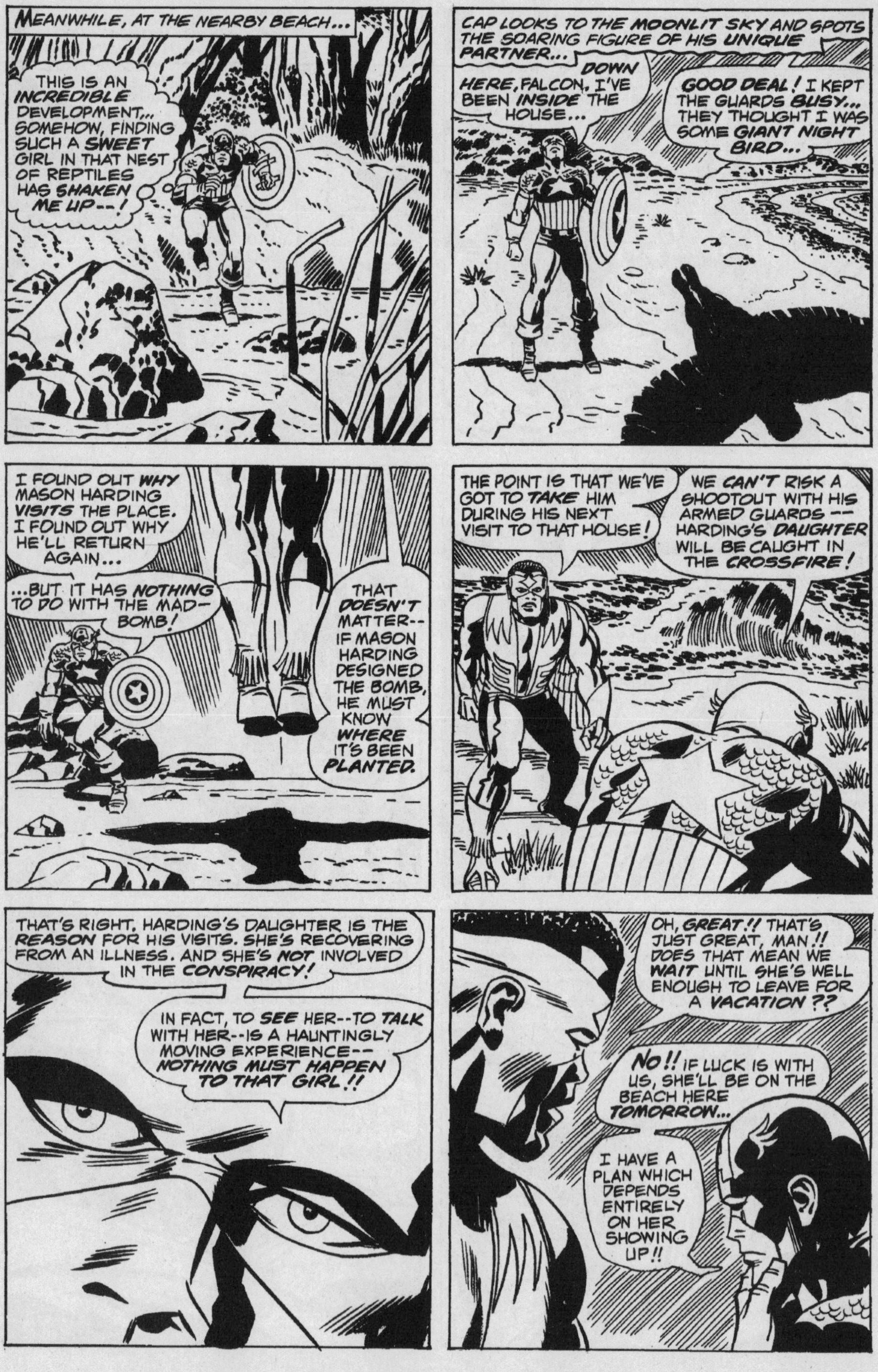
MEANWHILE, AT THE NEARBY BEACH...
THIS IS AN INCREDIBLE DEVELOPMENT... SOMEHOW, FINDING SUCH A SWEET GIRL IN THAT NEST OF REPTILES HAS SHAKEN ME UP--!
CAP LOOKS TO THE MOONLIT SKY AND SPOTS THE SOARING FIGURE OF HIS UNIQUE PARTNER...
DOWN HERE, FALCON. I'VE BEEN INSIDE THE HOUSE...
GOOD DEAL! I KEPT THE GUARDS BUSY... THEY THOUGHT I WAS SOME GIANT NIGHT BIRD...
I FOUND OUT WHY MASON HARDING VISITS THE PLACE. I FOUND OUT WHY HE'LL RETURN AGAIN...
...BUT IT HAS NOTHING TO DO WITH THE MAD-BOMB!
THAT DOESN'T MATTER-- IF MASON HARDING DESIGNED THE BOMB, HE MUST KNOW WHERE IT'S BEEN PLANTED.
THE POINT IS THAT WE'VE GOT TO TAKE HIM DURING HIS NEXT VISIT TO THAT HOUSE!
WE CAN'T RISK A SHOOTOUT WITH HIS ARMED GUARDS -- HARDING'S DAUGHTER WILL BE CAUGHT IN THE CROSSFIRE!
THAT'S RIGHT. HARDING'S DAUGHTER IS THE REASON FOR HIS VISITS. SHE'S RECOVERING FROM AN ILLNESS. AND SHE'S NOT INVOLVED IN THE CONSPIRACY!
IN FACT, TO SEE HER--TO TALK WITH HER--IS A HAUNTINGLY MOVING EXPERIENCE-- NOTHING MUST HAPPEN TO THAT GIRL!!
OH, GREAT!! THAT'S JUST GREAT, MAN!! DOES THAT MEAN WE WAIT UNTIL SHE'S WELL ENOUGH TO LEAVE FOR A VACATION??
NO!! IF LUCK IS WITH US, SHE'LL BE ON THE BEACH HERE TOMORROW...
I HAVE A PLAN WHICH DEPENDS ENTIRELY ON HER SHOWING UP!!

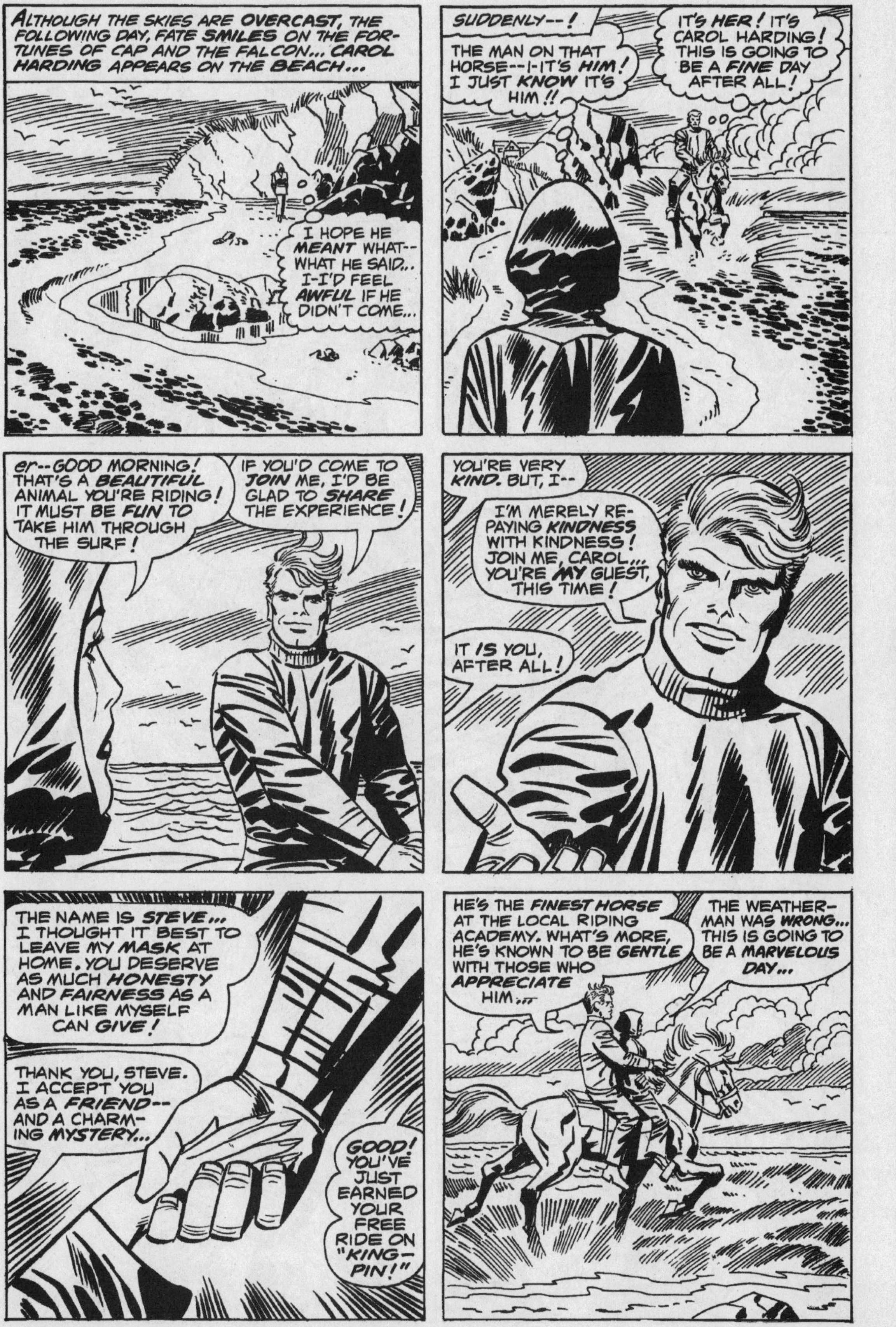
ALTHOUGH THE SKIES ARE OVERCAST, THE FOLLOWING DAY, FATE SMILES ON THE FORTUNES OF CAP AND THE FALCON... CAROL HARDING APPEARS ON THE BEACH...
I HOPE HE MEANT WHAT--WHAT HE SAID.. I-I'D FEEL AWFUL IF HE DIDN'T COME...
SUDDENLY--!
THE MAN ON THAT HORSE--I-IT'S HIM! I JUST KNOW IT'S HIM!!
IT'S HER! IT'S CAROL HARDING! THIS IS GOING TO BE A FINE DAY AFTER ALL!
er--GOOD MORNING! THAT'S A BEAUTIFUL ANIMAL YOU'RE RIDING! IT MUST BE FUN TO TAKE HIM THROUGH THE SURF!
IF YOU'D COME TO JOIN ME, I'D BE GLAD TO SHARE THE EXPERIENCE!
YOU'RE VERY KIND. BUT, I--
I'M MERELY REPAYING KINDNESS WITH KINDNESS! JOIN ME, CAROL... YOU'RE MY GUEST, THIS TIME!
IT IS YOU, AFTER ALL!
THE NAME IS STEVE... I THOUGHT IT BEST TO LEAVE MY MASK AT HOME. YOU DESERVE AS MUCH HONESTY AND FAIRNESS AS A MAN LIKE MYSELF CAN GIVE!
THANK YOU, STEVE. I ACCEPT YOU AS A FRIEND--AND A CHARMING MYSTERY...
GOOD! YOU'VE JUST EARNED YOUR FREE RIDE ON "KING-PIN!"
HE'S THE FINEST HORSE AT THE LOCAL RIDING ACADEMY. WHAT'S MORE, HE'S KNOWN TO BE GENTLE WITH THOSE WHO APPRECIATE HIM...
THE WEATHER-MAN WAS WRONG... THIS IS GOING TO BE A MARVELOUS DAY...

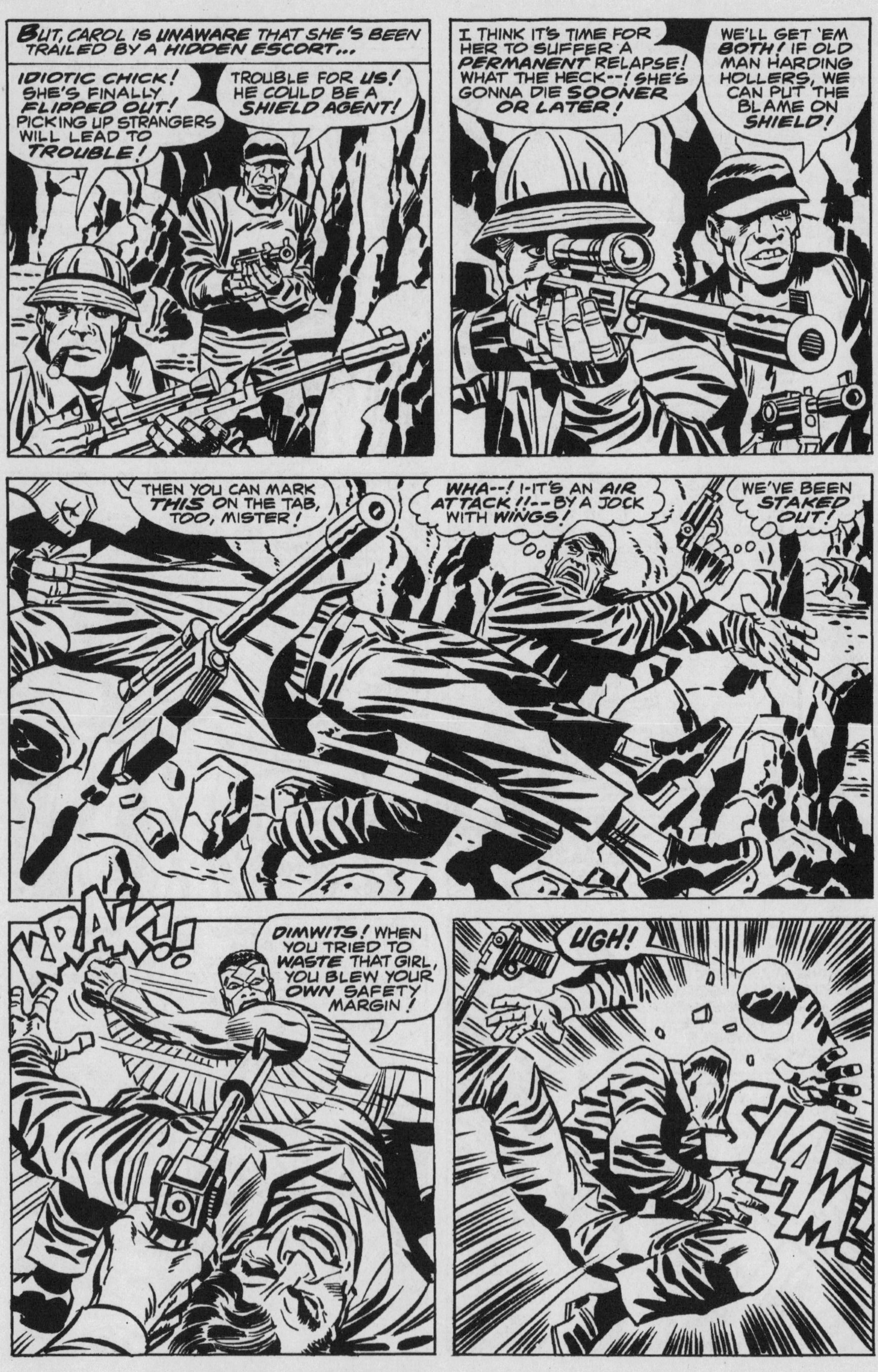
BUT, CAROL IS UNAWARE THAT SHE'S BEEN TRAILED BY A HIDDEN ESCORT...
IDIOTIC CHICK! SHE'S FINALLY FLIPPED OUT! PICKING UP STRANGERS WILL LEAD TO TROUBLE!
TROUBLE FOR US! HE COULD BE A SHIELD AGENT!
I THINK IT'S TIME FOR HER TO SUFFER A PERMANENT RELAPSE! WHAT THE HECK--! SHE'S GONNA DIE SOONER OR LATER!
WE'LL GET 'EM BOTH! IF OLD MAN HARDING HOLLERS, WE CAN PUT THE BLAME ON SHIELD!
THEN YOU CAN MARK THIS ON THE TAB, TOO, MISTER!
WHA--! I-IT'S AN AIR ATTACK!!--BY A JOCK WITH WINGS!
WE'VE BEEN STAKED OUT!
KRAK!!
DIMWITS! WHEN YOU TRIED TO WASTE THAT GIRL, YOU BLEW YOUR OWN SAFETY MARGIN!
UGH!
SLAM!

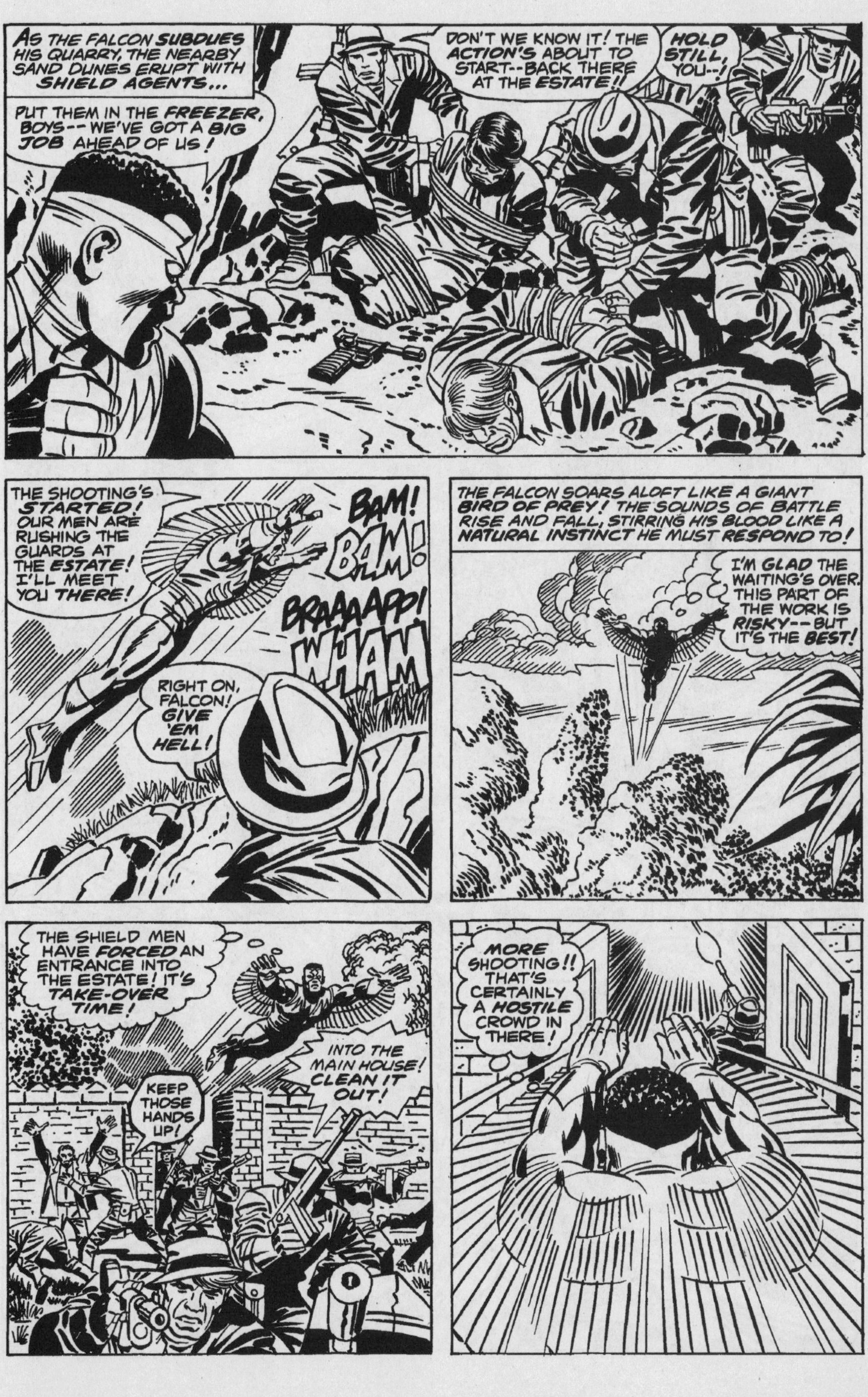
AS THE FALCON SUBDUES HIS QUARRY, THE NEARBY SAND DUNES ERUPT WITH SHIELD AGENTS...
PUT THEM IN THE FREEZER, BOYS-- WE'VE GOT A BIG JOB AHEAD OF US!
DON'T WE KNOW IT! THE ACTION'S ABOUT TO START--BACK THERE AT THE ESTATE!!
HOLD STILL, YOU--!
THE SHOOTING'S STARTED! OUR MEN ARE RUSHING THE GUARDS AT THE ESTATE! I'LL MEET YOU THERE!
BAM! BAM!
BRAAAAPP! WHAM
RIGHT ON, FALCON! GIVE 'EM HELL!
THE FALCON SOARS ALOFT LIKE A GIANT BIRD OF PREY! THE SOUNDS OF BATTLE RISE AND FALL, STIRRING HIS BLOOD LIKE A NATURAL INSTINCT HE MUST RESPOND TO!
I'M GLAD THE WAITING'S OVER. THIS PART OF THE WORK IS RISKY--BUT IT'S THE BEST!
THE SHIELD MEN HAVE FORCED AN ENTRANCE INTO THE ESTATE! IT'S TAKE-OVER TIME!
INTO THE MAIN HOUSE! CLEAN IT OUT!
KEEP THOSE HANDS UP!
MORE SHOOTING!! THAT'S CERTAINLY A HOSTILE CROWD IN THERE!

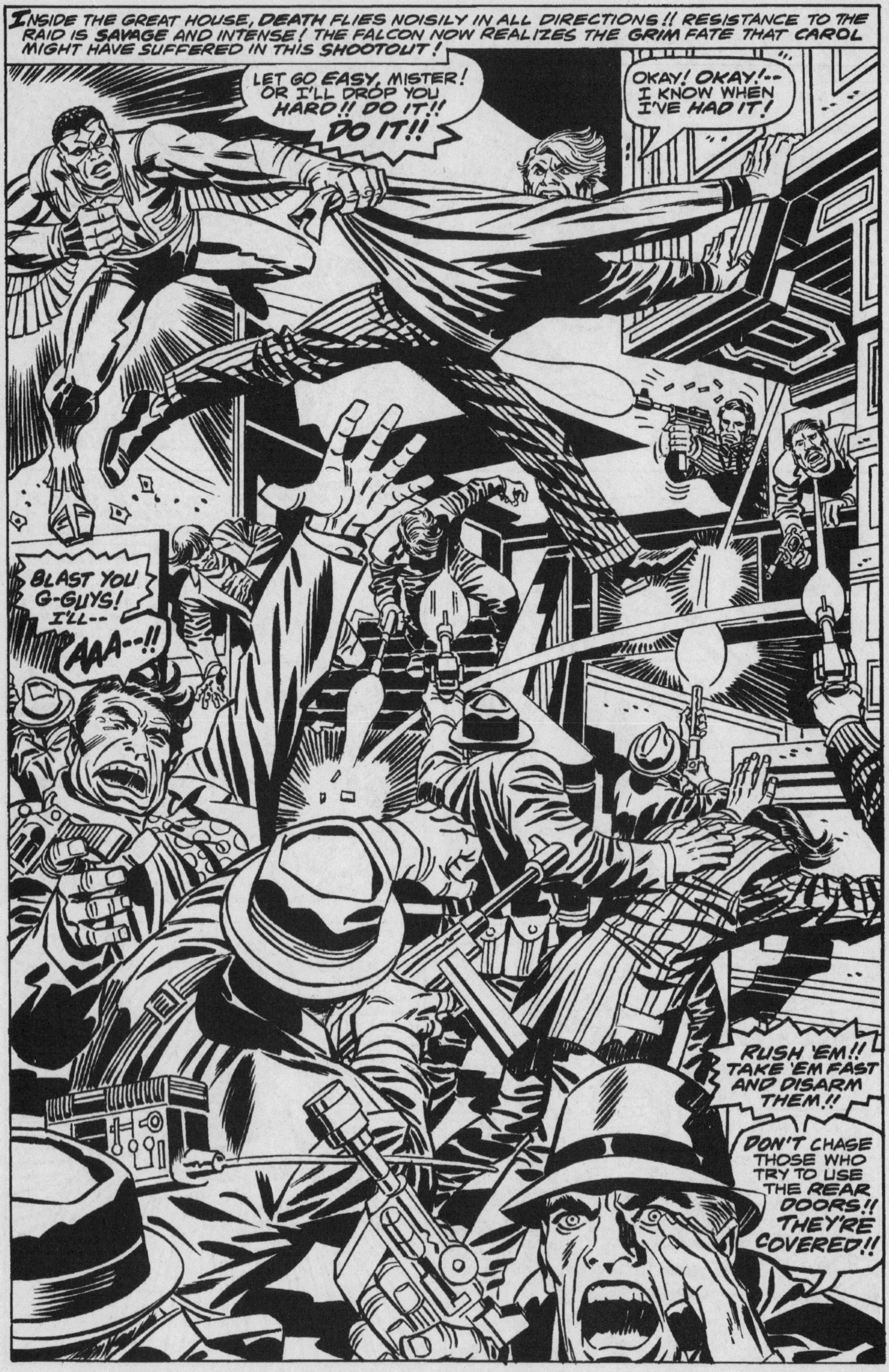
INSIDE THE GREAT HOUSE, DEATH FLIES NOISILY IN ALL DIRECTIONS!! RESISTANCE TO THE RAID IS SAVAGE AND INTENSE! THE FALCON NOW REALIZES THE GRIM FATE THAT CAROL MIGHT HAVE SUFFERED IN THIS SHOOTOUT!
LET GO EASY, MISTER! OR I'LL DROP YOU HARD!! DO IT!! DO IT!!
OKAY! OKAY!-- I KNOW WHEN I'VE HAD IT!
BLAST YOU G-GUYS! I'LL-- AAA--!!
RUSH 'EM!! TAKE 'EM FAST AND DISARM THEM!!
DON'T CHASE THOSE WHO TRY TO USE THE REAR DOORS!! THEY'RE COVERED!!

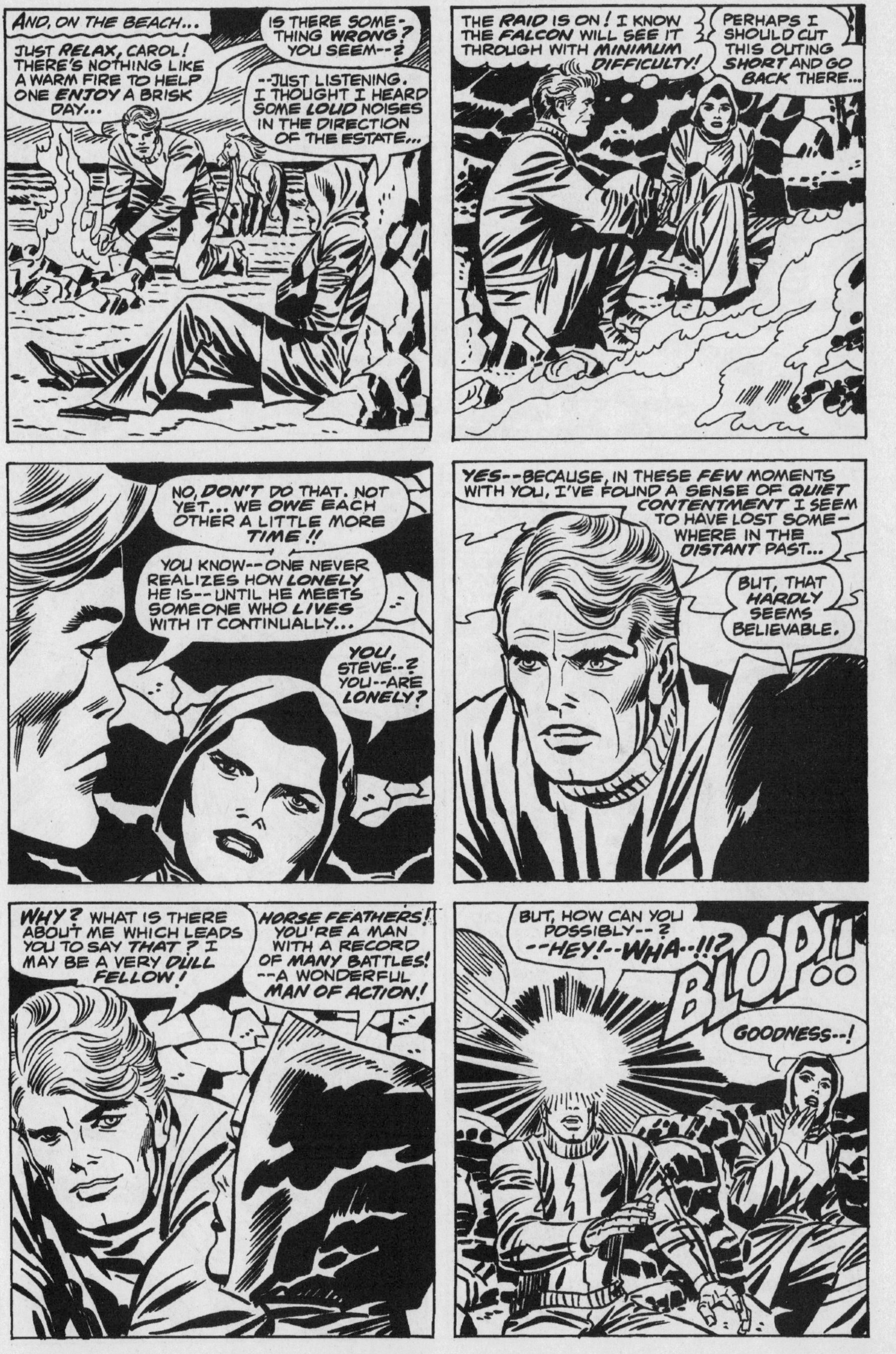
AND, ON THE BEACH...
JUST RELAX, CAROL! THERE'S NOTHING LIKE A WARM FIRE TO HELP ONE ENJOY A BRISK DAY...
IS THERE SOME-THING WRONG? YOU SEEM--?
--JUST LISTENING. I THOUGHT I HEARD SOME LOUD NOISES IN THE DIRECTION OF THE ESTATE...
THE RAID IS ON! I KNOW THE FALCON WILL SEE IT THROUGH WITH MINIMUM DIFFICULTY!
PERHAPS I SHOULD CUT THIS OUTING SHORT AND GO BACK THERE...
NO, DON'T DO THAT. NOT YET... WE OWE EACH OTHER A LITTLE MORE TIME!!
YOU KNOW--ONE NEVER REALIZES HOW LONELY HE IS--UNTIL HE MEETS SOMEONE WHO LIVES WITH IT CONTINUALLY...
YOU, STEVE--? YOU--ARE LONELY?
YES--BECAUSE, IN THESE FEW MOMENTS WITH YOU, I'VE FOUND A SENSE OF QUIET CONTENTMENT I SEEM TO HAVE LOST SOME-WHERE IN THE DISTANT PAST...
BUT, THAT HARDLY SEEMS BELIEVABLE.
WHY? WHAT IS THERE ABOUT ME WHICH LEADS YOU TO SAY THAT? I MAY BE A VERY DULL FELLOW!
HORSE FEATHERS! YOU'RE A MAN WITH A RECORD OF MANY BATTLES! --A WONDERFUL MAN OF ACTION!
BUT, HOW CAN YOU POSSIBLY--? --HEY!--WHA--!!?
BLOP!!
GOODNESS--!

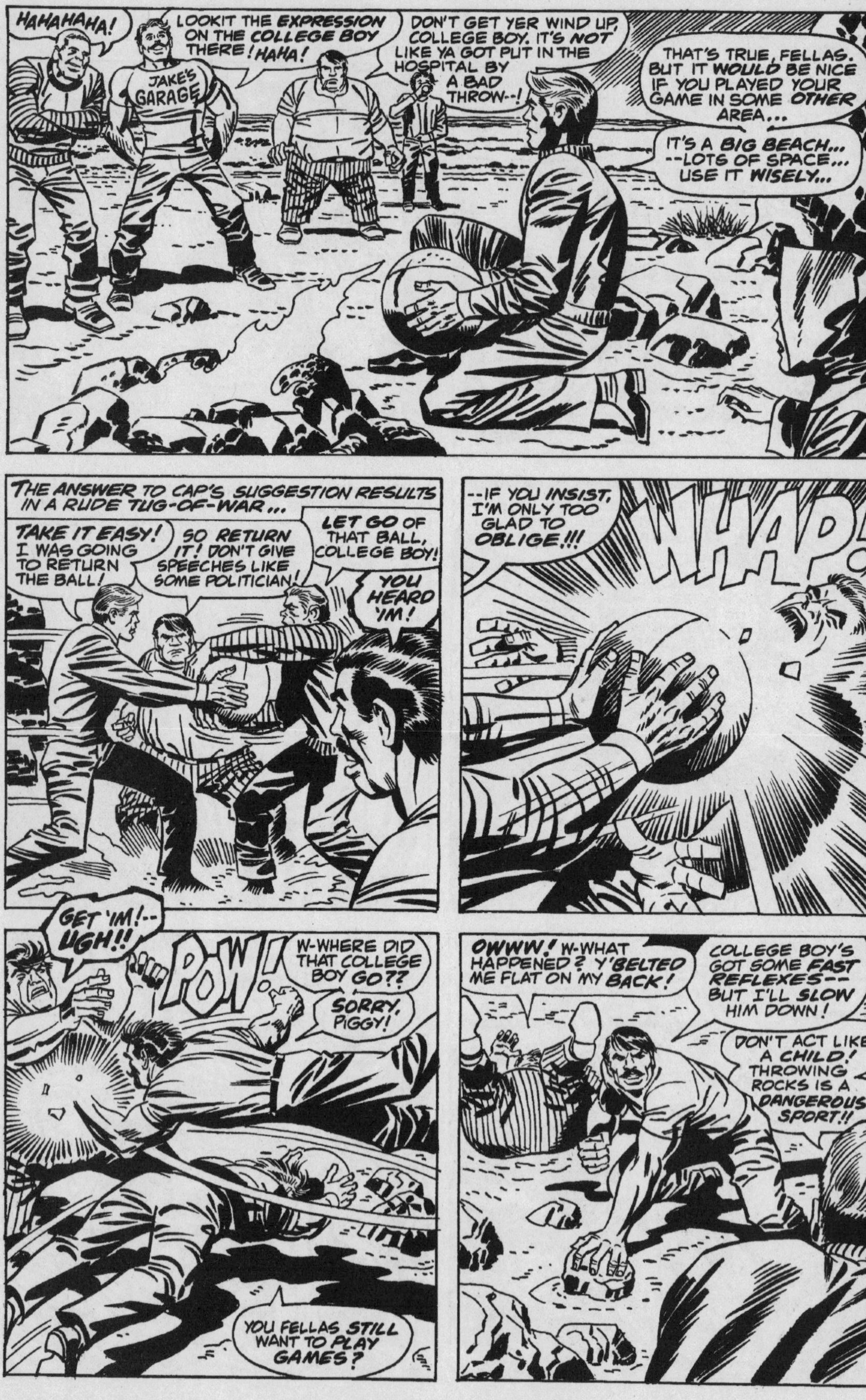
HAHAHAHA!
LOOKIT THE EXPRESSION ON THE COLLEGE BOY THERE! HAHA!
JAKE'S GARAGE
DON'T GET YER WIND UP, COLLEGE BOY. IT'S NOT LIKE YA GOT PUT IN THE HOSPITAL BY A BAD THROW--!
THAT'S TRUE, FELLAS. BUT IT WOULD BE NICE IF YOU PLAYED YOUR GAME IN SOME OTHER AREA...
IT'S A BIG BEACH... --LOTS OF SPACE... USE IT WISELY...
THE ANSWER TO CAP'S SUGGESTION RESULTS IN A RUDE TUG-OF-WAR...
TAKE IT EASY! I WAS GOING TO RETURN THE BALL!
SO RETURN IT! DON'T GIVE SPEECHES LIKE SOME POLITICIAN!
LET GO OF THAT BALL, COLLEGE BOY!
YOU HEARD 'IM!
--IF YOU INSIST, I'M ONLY TOO GLAD TO OBLIGE!!!
WHAP!
GET 'IM!-- UGH!!
POW!
W-WHERE DID THAT COLLEGE BOY GO??
SORRY, PIGGY!
YOU FELLAS STILL WANT TO PLAY GAMES?
OWWW! W-WHAT HAPPENED? Y'BELTED ME FLAT ON MY BACK!
COLLEGE BOY'S GOT SOME FAST REFLEXES-- BUT I'LL SLOW HIM DOWN!
DON'T ACT LIKE A CHILD! THROWING ROCKS IS A DANGEROUS SPORT!!

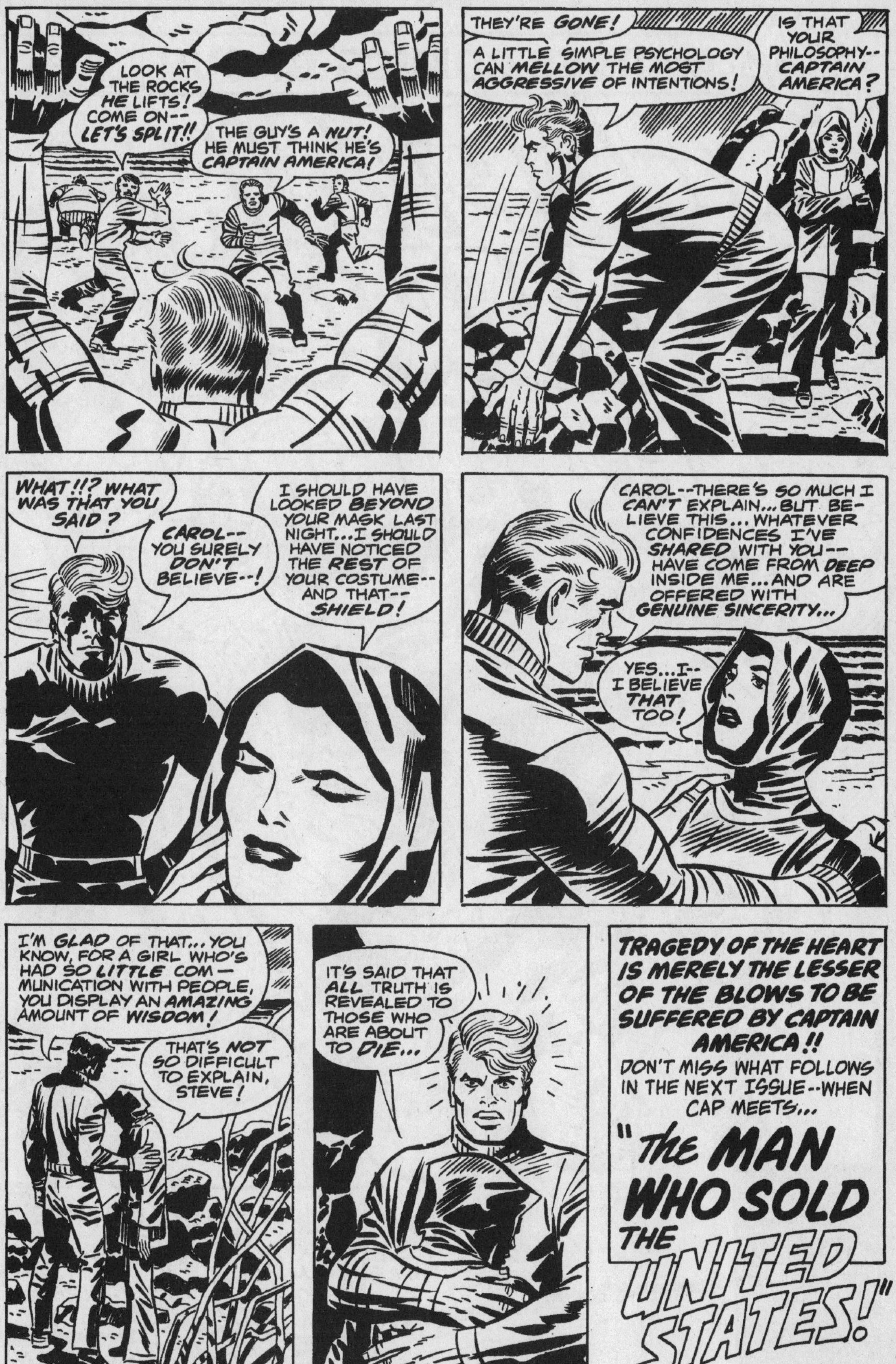
LOOK AT THE ROCKS HE LIFTS! COME ON--LET'S SPLIT!!
THE GUY'S A NUT! HE MUST THINK HE'S CAPTAIN AMERICA!
THEY'RE GONE!
A LITTLE SIMPLE PSYCHOLOGY CAN MELLOW THE MOST AGGRESSIVE OF INTENTIONS!
IS THAT YOUR PHILOSOPHY--CAPTAIN AMERICA?
WHAT!!? WHAT WAS THAT YOU SAID?
I SHOULD HAVE LOOKED BEYOND YOUR MASK LAST NIGHT...I SHOULD HAVE NOTICED THE REST OF YOUR COSTUME--AND THAT--SHIELD!
CAROL--YOU SURELY DON'T BELIEVE--!
CAROL--THERE'S SO MUCH I CAN'T EXPLAIN...BUT BELIEVE THIS...WHATEVER CONFIDENCES I'VE SHARED WITH YOU--HAVE COME FROM DEEP INSIDE ME...AND ARE OFFERED WITH GENUINE SINCERITY...
YES...I--I BELIEVE THAT TOO!
I'M GLAD OF THAT...YOU KNOW, FOR A GIRL WHO'S HAD SO LITTLE COMMUNICATION WITH PEOPLE, YOU DISPLAY AN AMAZING AMOUNT OF WISDOM!
THAT'S NOT SO DIFFICULT TO EXPLAIN, STEVE!
IT'S SAID THAT ALL TRUTH IS REVEALED TO THOSE WHO ARE ABOUT TO DIE...
TRAGEDY OF THE HEART IS MERELY THE LESSER OF THE BLOWS TO BE SUFFERED BY CAPTAIN AMERICA!!
DON'T MISS WHAT FOLLOWS IN THE NEXT ISSUE--WHEN CAP MEETS...
"THE MAN WHO SOLD THE UNITED STATES!"

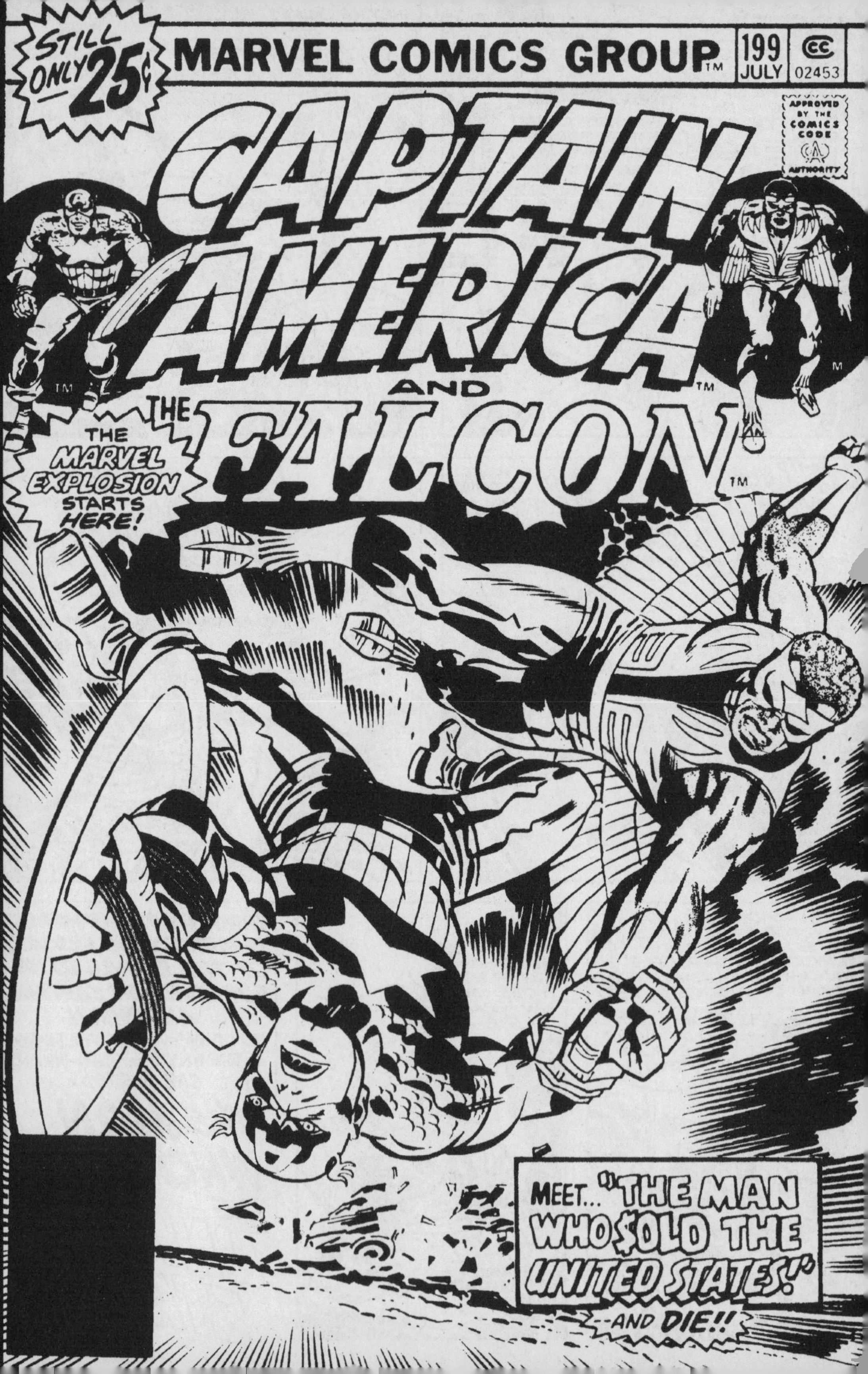
STILL ONLY 25¢
MARVEL COMICS GROUP™
199 JULY
CC 02453
APPROVED BY THE COMICS CODE AUTHORITY
CAPTAIN AMERICA™ AND THE FALCON™
THE MARVEL EXPLOSION STARTS HERE!
MEET... "THE MAN WHO $OLD THE UNITED STATES!"
--AND DIE!!

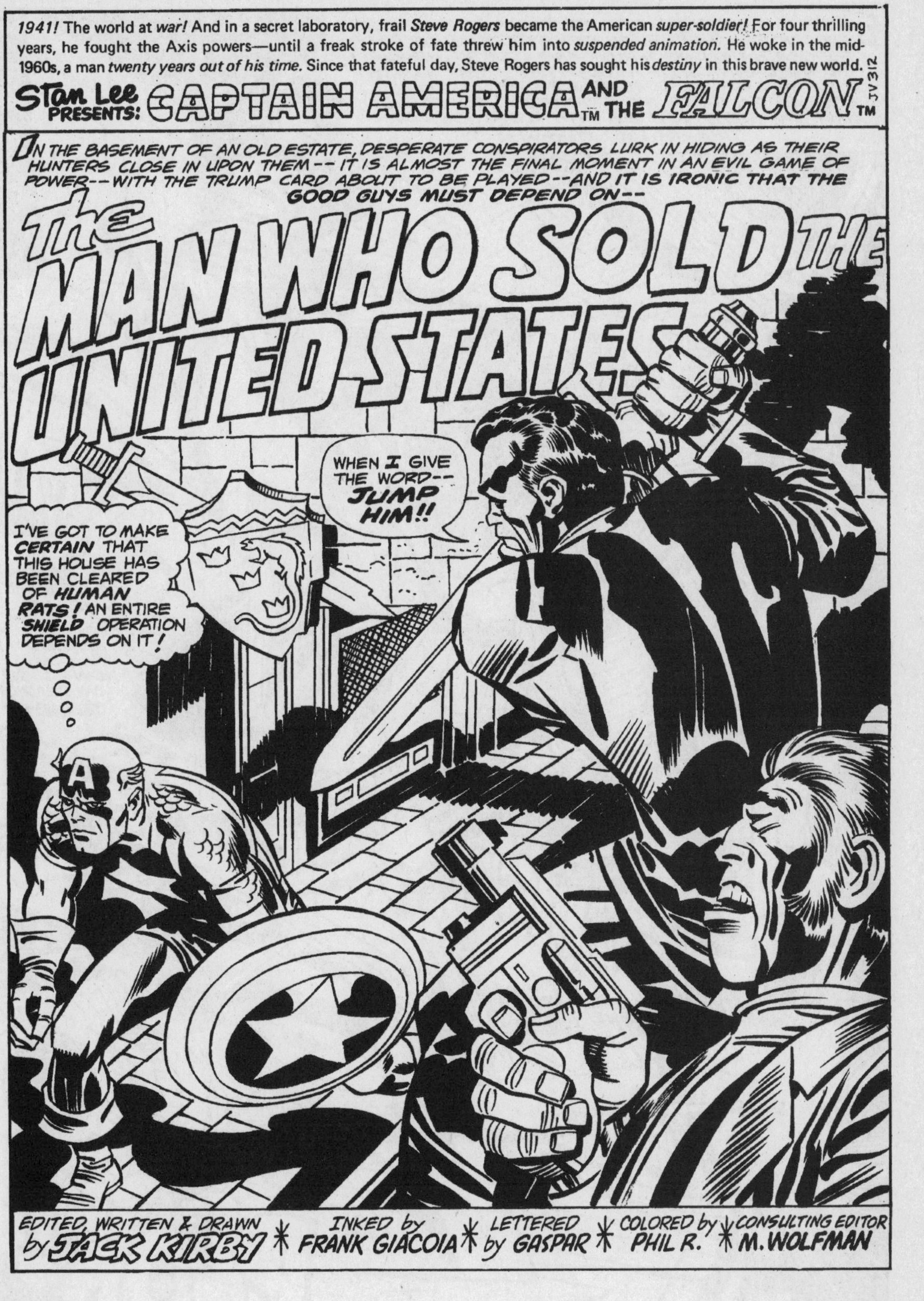
1941! The world at war! And in a secret laboratory, frail Steve Rogers became the American super-soldier! For four thrilling years, he fought the Axis powers—until a freak stroke of fate threw him into suspended animation. He woke in the mid-1960s, a man twenty years out of his time. Since that fateful day, Steve Rogers has sought his destiny in this brave new world.
Stan Lee PRESENTS: CAPTAIN AMERICA™ AND THE FALCON™
JV312
IN THE BASEMENT OF AN OLD ESTATE, DESPERATE CONSPIRATORS LURK IN HIDING AS THEIR HUNTERS CLOSE IN UPON THEM -- IT IS ALMOST THE FINAL MOMENT IN AN EVIL GAME OF POWER -- WITH THE TRUMP CARD ABOUT TO BE PLAYED -- AND IT IS IRONIC THAT THE GOOD GUYS MUST DEPEND ON --
THE MAN WHO SOLD THE UNITED STATES
WHEN I GIVE THE WORD -- JUMP HIM!!
I'VE GOT TO MAKE CERTAIN THAT THIS HOUSE HAS BEEN CLEARED OF HUMAN RATS! AN ENTIRE SHIELD OPERATION DEPENDS ON IT!
EDITED, WRITTEN & DRAWN by JACK KIRBY * INKED by FRANK GIACOIA * LETTERED by GASPAR * COLORED by PHIL R. * CONSULTING EDITOR M. WOLFMAN

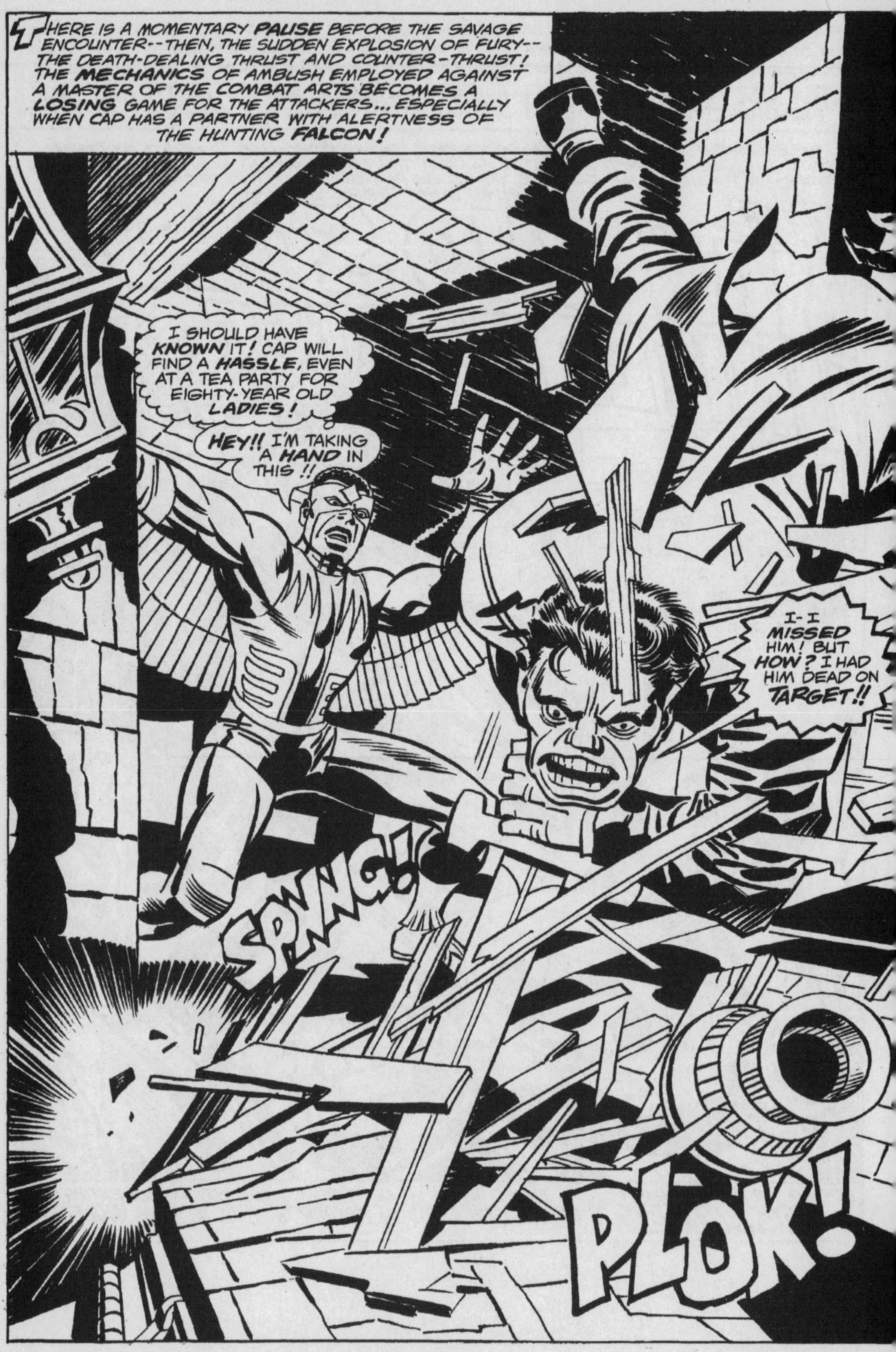
THERE IS A MOMENTARY PAUSE BEFORE THE SAVAGE ENCOUNTER--THEN, THE SUDDEN EXPLOSION OF FURY--THE DEATH-DEALING THRUST AND COUNTER-THRUST! THE MECHANICS OF AMBUSH EMPLOYED AGAINST A MASTER OF THE COMBAT ARTS BECOMES A LOSING GAME FOR THE ATTACKERS... ESPECIALLY WHEN CAP HAS A PARTNER WITH ALERTNESS OF THE HUNTING FALCON!
I SHOULD HAVE KNOWN IT! CAP WILL FIND A HASSLE, EVEN AT A TEA PARTY FOR EIGHTY-YEAR OLD LADIES!
HEY!! I'M TAKING A HAND IN THIS!!
I-I MISSED HIM! BUT HOW? I HAD HIM DEAD ON TARGET!!
SPWNG!
PLOK!

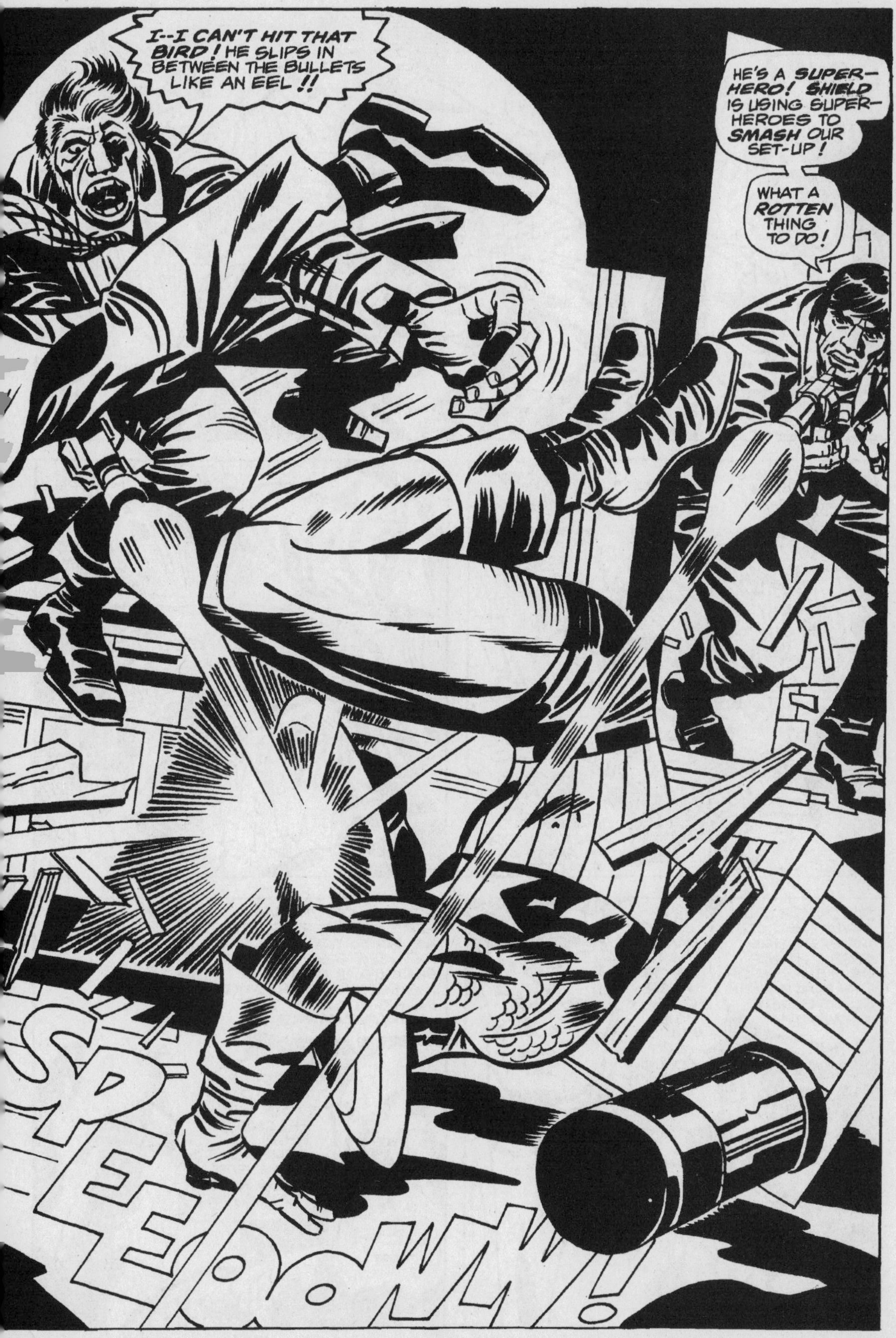
I--I CAN'T HIT THAT BIRD! HE SLIPS IN BETWEEN THE BULLETS LIKE AN EEL!!
HE'S A SUPER-HERO! SHIELD IS USING SUPER-HEROES TO SMASH OUR SET-UP!
WHAT A ROTTEN THING TO DO!
SPEEOWW!

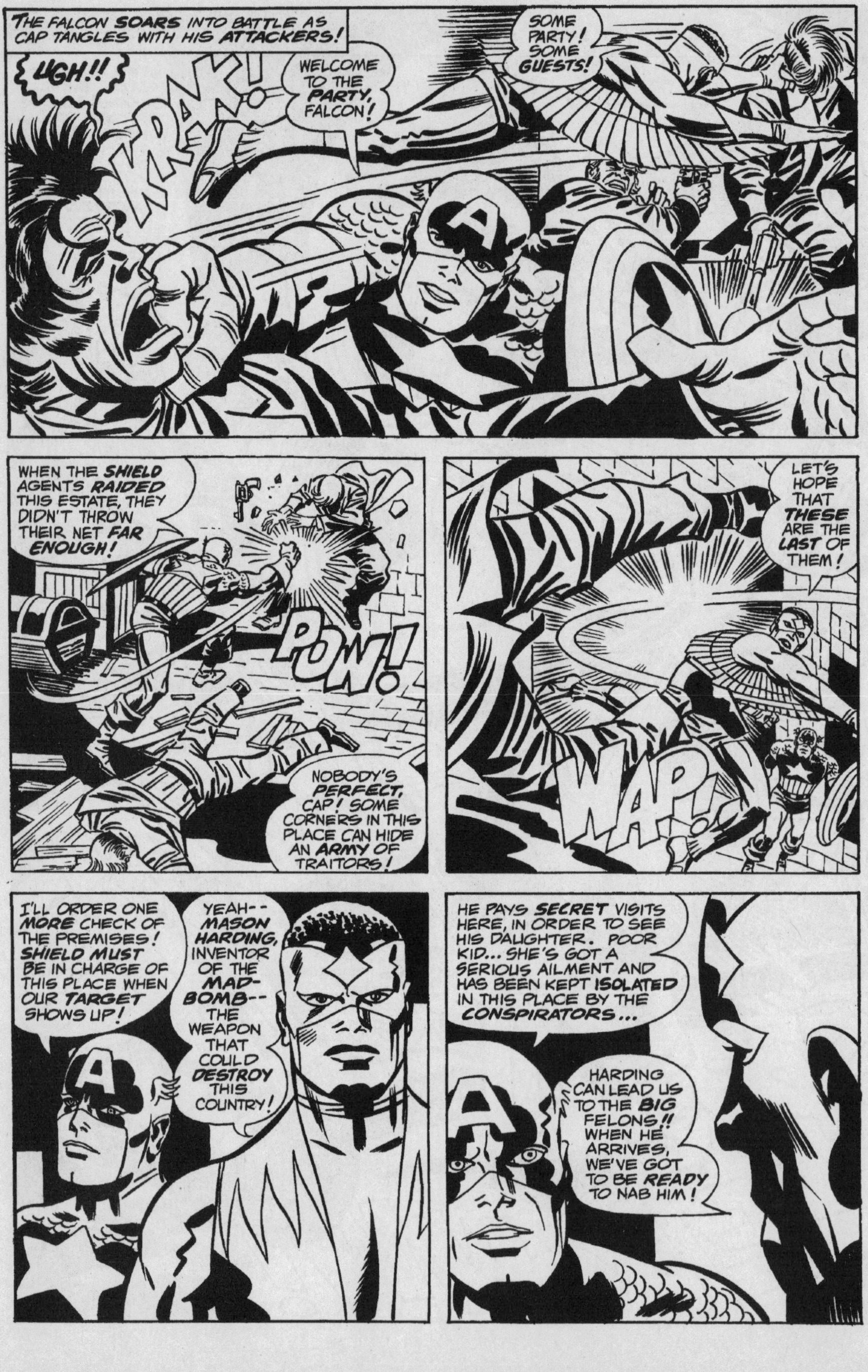
THE FALCON SOARS INTO BATTLE AS CAP TANGLES WITH HIS ATTACKERS!
UGH!!
KRAK!
WELCOME TO THE PARTY, FALCON!
SOME PARTY! SOME GUESTS!
WHEN THE SHIELD AGENTS RAIDED THIS ESTATE, THEY DIDN'T THROW THEIR NET FAR ENOUGH!
POW!
NOBODY'S PERFECT, CAP! SOME CORNERS IN THIS PLACE CAN HIDE AN ARMY OF TRAITORS!
LET'S HOPE THAT THESE ARE THE LAST OF THEM!
WAP!
I'LL ORDER ONE MORE CHECK OF THE PREMISES! SHIELD MUST BE IN CHARGE OF THIS PLACE WHEN OUR TARGET SHOWS UP!
YEAH-- MASON HARDING, INVENTOR OF THE MAD-BOMB-- THE WEAPON THAT COULD DESTROY THIS COUNTRY!
HE PAYS SECRET VISITS HERE, IN ORDER TO SEE HIS DAUGHTER. POOR KID... SHE'S GOT A SERIOUS AILMENT AND HAS BEEN KEPT ISOLATED IN THIS PLACE BY THE CONSPIRATORS...
HARDING CAN LEAD US TO THE BIG FELONS!! WHEN HE ARRIVES, WE'VE GOT TO BE READY TO NAB HIM!

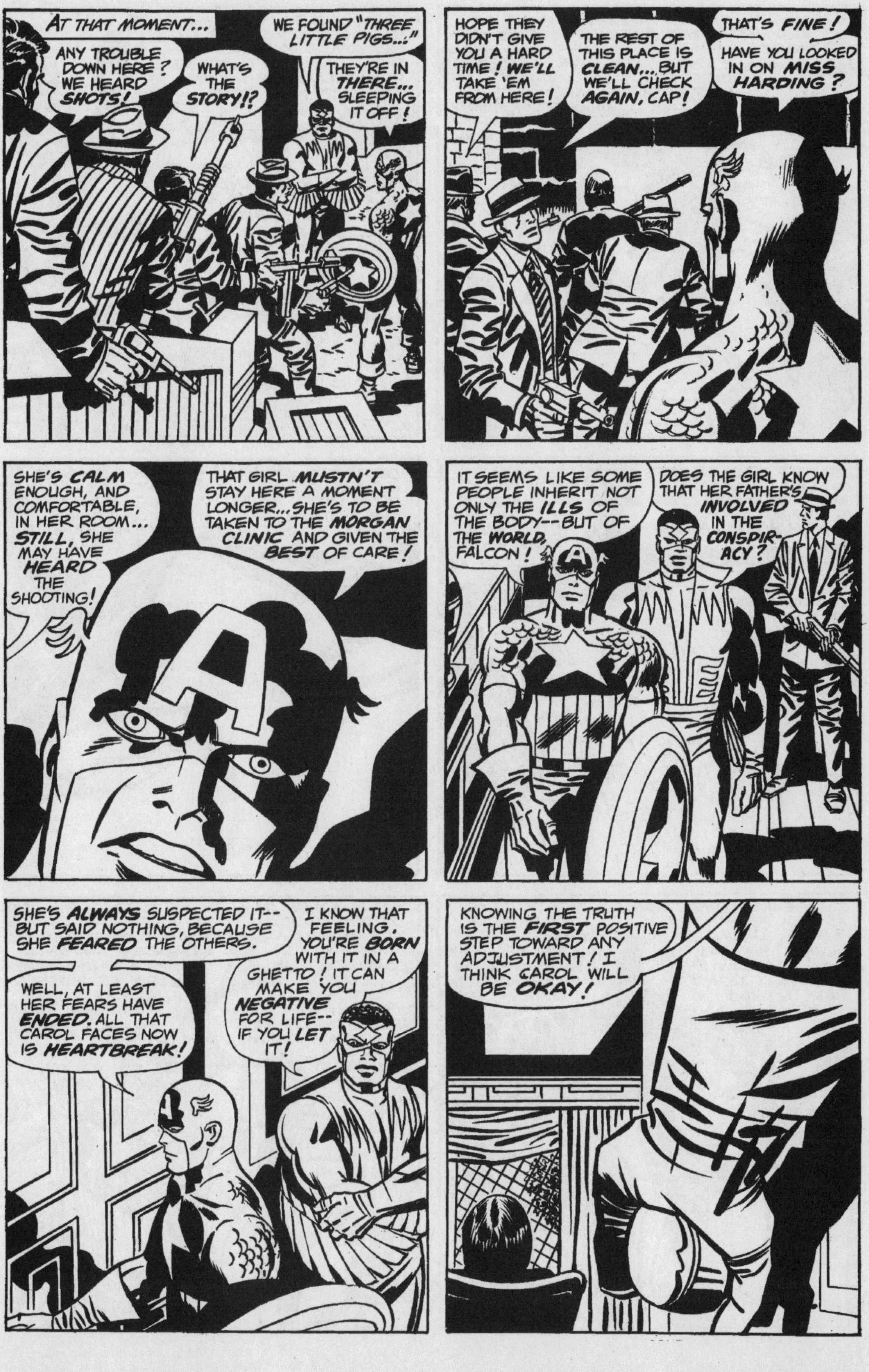
AT THAT MOMENT...
ANY TROUBLE DOWN HERE? WE HEARD SHOTS!
WHAT'S THE STORY!?
WE FOUND "THREE LITTLE PIGS...!"
THEY'RE IN THERE... SLEEPING IT OFF!
HOPE THEY DIDN'T GIVE YOU A HARD TIME! WE'LL TAKE 'EM FROM HERE!
THE REST OF THIS PLACE IS CLEAN... BUT WE'LL CHECK AGAIN, CAP!
THAT'S FINE!
HAVE YOU LOOKED IN ON MISS HARDING?
SHE'S CALM ENOUGH, AND COMFORTABLE, IN HER ROOM... STILL, SHE MAY HAVE HEARD THE SHOOTING!
THAT GIRL MUSTN'T STAY HERE A MOMENT LONGER... SHE'S TO BE TAKEN TO THE MORGAN CLINIC AND GIVEN THE BEST OF CARE!
IT SEEMS LIKE SOME PEOPLE INHERIT NOT ONLY THE ILLS OF THE BODY--BUT OF THE WORLD, FALCON!
DOES THE GIRL KNOW THAT HER FATHER'S INVOLVED IN THE CONSPIR-ACY?
SHE'S ALWAYS SUSPECTED IT--BUT SAID NOTHING, BECAUSE SHE FEARED THE OTHERS.
WELL, AT LEAST HER FEARS HAVE ENDED. ALL THAT CAROL FACES NOW IS HEARTBREAK!
I KNOW THAT FEELING. YOU'RE BORN WITH IT IN A GHETTO! IT CAN MAKE YOU NEGATIVE FOR LIFE--IF YOU LET IT!
KNOWING THE TRUTH IS THE FIRST POSITIVE STEP TOWARD ANY ADJUSTMENT! I THINK CAROL WILL BE OKAY!

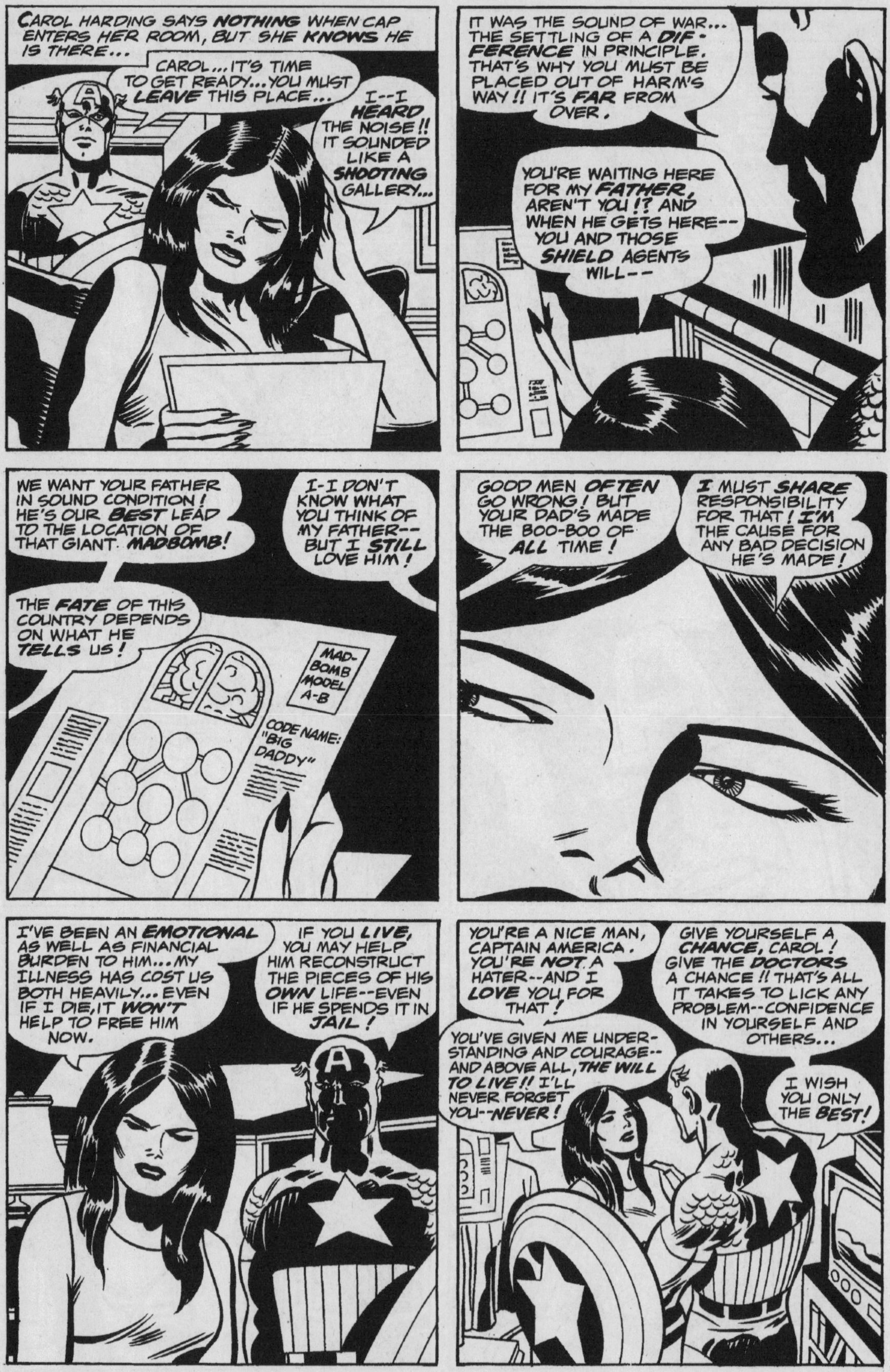
CAROL HARDING SAYS NOTHING WHEN CAP ENTERS HER ROOM, BUT SHE KNOWS HE IS THERE...
CAROL... IT'S TIME TO GET READY... YOU MUST LEAVE THIS PLACE...
I--I HEARD THE NOISE!! IT SOUNDED LIKE A SHOOTING GALLERY...
IT WAS THE SOUND OF WAR... THE SETTLING OF A DIFFERENCE IN PRINCIPLE. THAT'S WHY YOU MUST BE PLACED OUT OF HARM'S WAY!! IT'S FAR FROM OVER.
YOU'RE WAITING HERE FOR MY FATHER, AREN'T YOU!? AND WHEN HE GETS HERE-- YOU AND THOSE SHIELD AGENTS WILL--
WE WANT YOUR FATHER IN SOUND CONDITION! HE'S OUR BEST LEAD TO THE LOCATION OF THAT GIANT MADBOMB!
THE FATE OF THIS COUNTRY DEPENDS ON WHAT HE TELLS US!
I-I DON'T KNOW WHAT YOU THINK OF MY FATHER-- BUT I STILL LOVE HIM!
MAD-BOMB MODEL A-B
CODE NAME: "BIG DADDY"
GOOD MEN OFTEN GO WRONG! BUT YOUR DAD'S MADE THE BOO-BOO OF ALL TIME!
I MUST SHARE RESPONSIBILITY FOR THAT! I'M THE CAUSE FOR ANY BAD DECISION HE'S MADE!
I'VE BEEN AN EMOTIONAL AS WELL AS FINANCIAL BURDEN TO HIM... MY ILLNESS HAS COST US BOTH HEAVILY... EVEN IF I DIE, IT WON'T HELP TO FREE HIM NOW.
IF YOU LIVE, YOU MAY HELP HIM RECONSTRUCT THE PIECES OF HIS OWN LIFE--EVEN IF HE SPENDS IT IN JAIL!
YOU'RE A NICE MAN, CAPTAIN AMERICA. YOU'RE NOT A HATER--AND I LOVE YOU FOR THAT!
GIVE YOURSELF A CHANCE, CAROL! GIVE THE DOCTORS A CHANCE!! THAT'S ALL IT TAKES TO LICK ANY PROBLEM--CONFIDENCE IN YOURSELF AND OTHERS...
YOU'VE GIVEN ME UNDERSTANDING AND COURAGE-- AND ABOVE ALL, THE WILL TO LIVE!! I'LL NEVER FORGET YOU--NEVER!
I WISH YOU ONLY THE BEST!

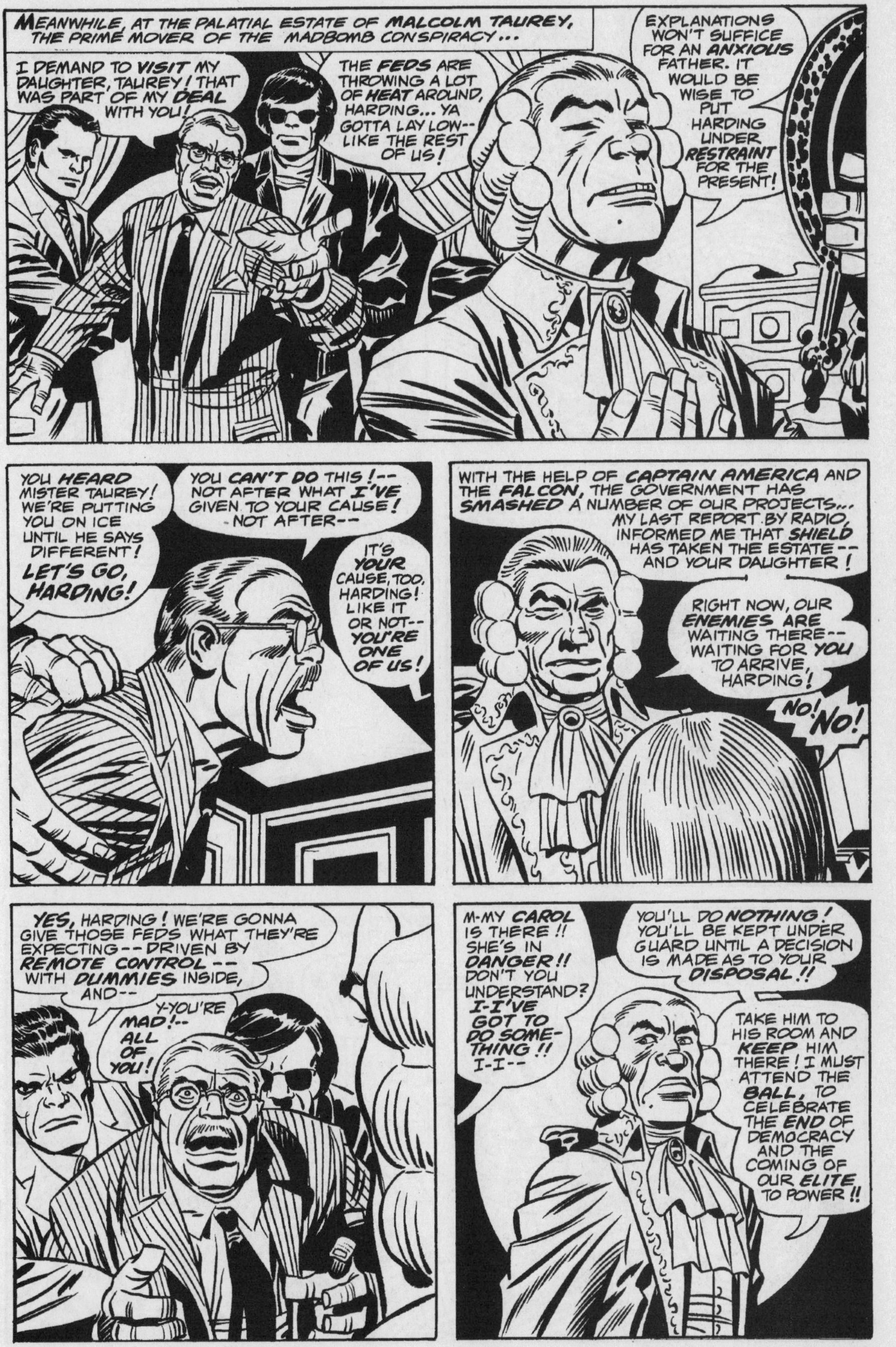

MEANWHILE, AT THE PALATIAL ESTATE OF MALCOLM TAUREY, THE PRIME MOVER OF THE MADBOMB CONSPIRACY...
I DEMAND TO VISIT MY DAUGHTER, TAUREY! THAT WAS PART OF MY DEAL WITH YOU!
THE FEDS ARE THROWING A LOT OF HEAT AROUND, HARDING... YA GOTTA LAY LOW-- LIKE THE REST OF US!
EXPLANATIONS WON'T SUFFICE FOR AN ANXIOUS FATHER. IT WOULD BE WISE TO PUT HARDING UNDER RESTRAINT FOR THE PRESENT!
YOU HEARD MISTER TAUREY! WE'RE PUTTING YOU ON ICE UNTIL HE SAYS DIFFERENT! LET'S GO, HARDING!
YOU CAN'T DO THIS!-- NOT AFTER WHAT I'VE GIVEN TO YOUR CAUSE! -NOT AFTER--
IT'S YOUR CAUSE, TOO, HARDING! LIKE IT OR NOT-- YOU'RE ONE OF US!
WITH THE HELP OF CAPTAIN AMERICA AND THE FALCON, THE GOVERNMENT HAS SMASHED A NUMBER OF OUR PROJECTS... MY LAST REPORT BY RADIO, INFORMED ME THAT SHIELD HAS TAKEN THE ESTATE-- AND YOUR DAUGHTER!
RIGHT NOW, OUR ENEMIES ARE WAITING THERE-- WAITING FOR YOU TO ARRIVE, HARDING!
NO! NO!
YES, HARDING! WE'RE GONNA GIVE THOSE FEDS WHAT THEY'RE EXPECTING-- DRIVEN BY REMOTE CONTROL-- WITH DUMMIES INSIDE, AND--
Y-YOU'RE MAD!-- ALL OF YOU!
M-MY CAROL IS THERE!! SHE'S IN DANGER!! DON'T YOU UNDERSTAND? I-I'VE GOT TO DO SOME-THING!! I-I--
YOU'LL DO NOTHING! YOU'LL BE KEPT UNDER GUARD UNTIL A DECISION IS MADE AS TO YOUR DISPOSAL!!
TAKE HIM TO HIS ROOM AND KEEP HIM THERE! I MUST ATTEND THE BALL, TO CELEBRATE THE END OF DEMOCRACY AND THE COMING OF OUR ELITE TO POWER!!

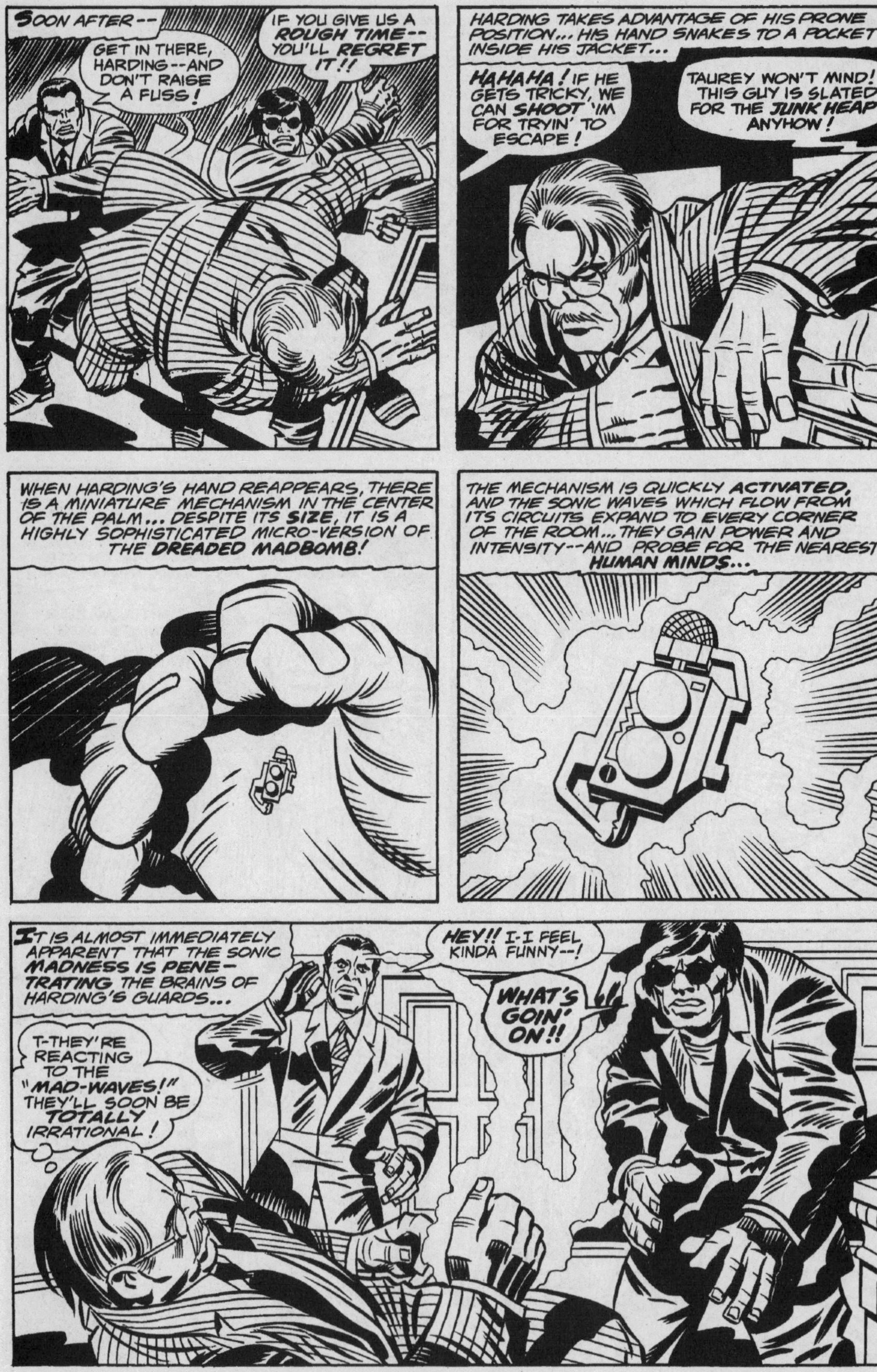

SOON AFTER--
GET IN THERE, HARDING--AND DON'T RAISE A FUSS!
IF YOU GIVE US A ROUGH TIME--YOU'LL REGRET IT!!
HARDING TAKES ADVANTAGE OF HIS PRONE POSITION... HIS HAND SNAKES TO A POCKET INSIDE HIS JACKET...
HAHAHA! IF HE GETS TRICKY, WE CAN SHOOT 'IM FOR TRYIN' TO ESCAPE!
TAUREY WON'T MIND! THIS GUY IS SLATED FOR THE JUNK HEAP ANYHOW!
WHEN HARDING'S HAND REAPPEARS, THERE IS A MINIATURE MECHANISM IN THE CENTER OF THE PALM... DESPITE ITS SIZE, IT IS A HIGHLY SOPHISTICATED MICRO-VERSION OF THE DREADED MADBOMB!
THE MECHANISM IS QUICKLY ACTIVATED, AND THE SONIC WAVES WHICH FLOW FROM ITS CIRCUITS EXPAND TO EVERY CORNER OF THE ROOM... THEY GAIN POWER AND INTENSITY--AND PROBE FOR THE NEAREST HUMAN MINDS...
IT IS ALMOST IMMEDIATELY APPARENT THAT THE SONIC MADNESS IS PENE-TRATING THE BRAINS OF HARDING'S GUARDS...
HEY!! I-I FEEL KINDA FUNNY--!
WHAT'S GOIN' ON!!
T-THEY'RE REACTING TO THE "MAD-WAVES!" THEY'LL SOON BE TOTALLY IRRATIONAL!

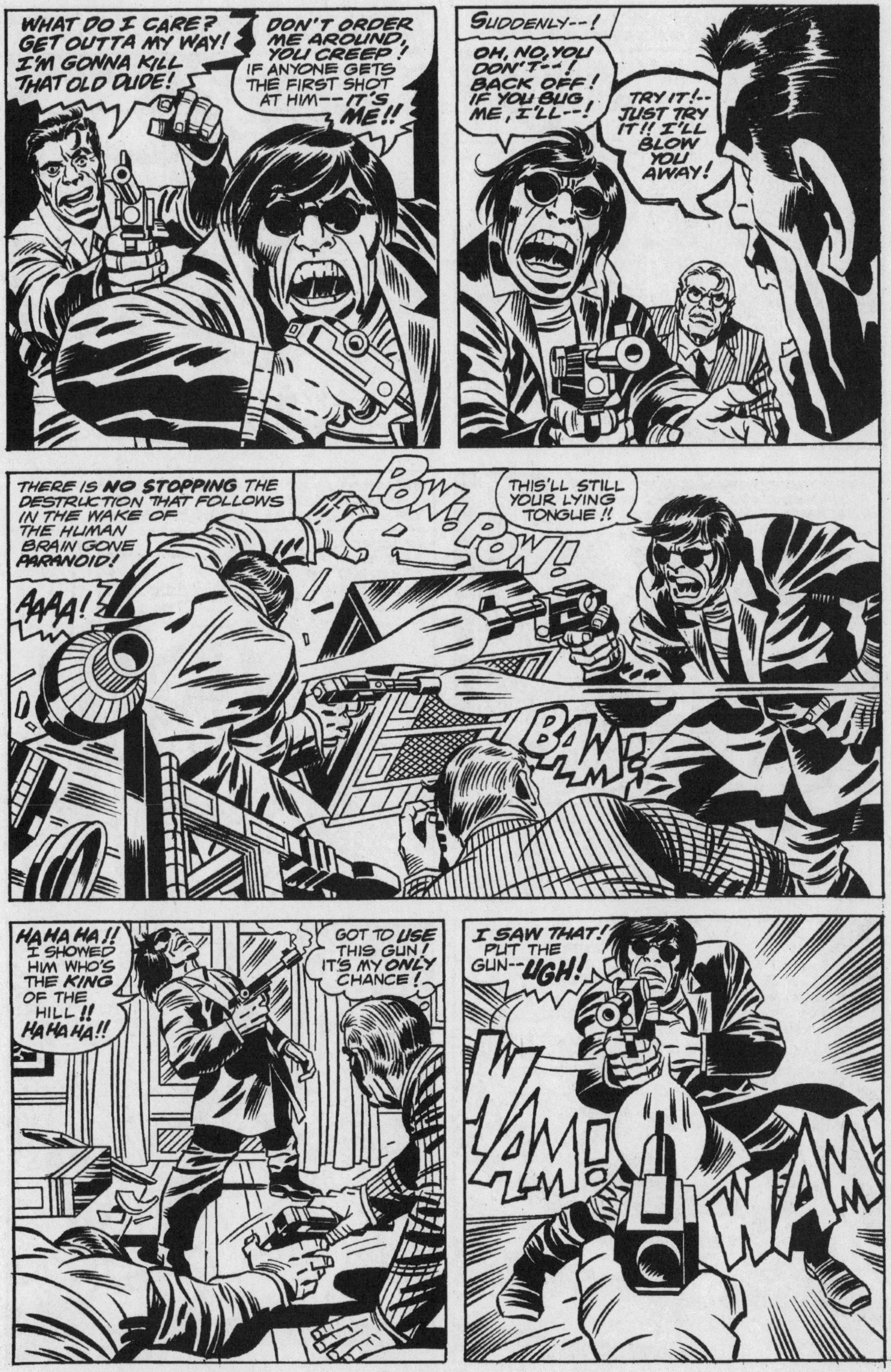
WHAT DO I CARE? GET OUTTA MY WAY! I'M GONNA KILL THAT OLD DUDE!
DON'T ORDER ME AROUND, YOU CREEP! IF ANYONE GETS THE FIRST SHOT AT HIM--IT'S ME!!
SUDDENLY--!
OH, NO, YOU DON'T--! BACK OFF! IF YOU BUG ME, I'LL--!
TRY IT!--JUST TRY IT!! I'LL BLOW YOU AWAY!
THERE IS NO STOPPING THE DESTRUCTION THAT FOLLOWS IN THE WAKE OF THE HUMAN BRAIN GONE PARANOID!
POW! POW!
THIS'LL STILL YOUR LYING TONGUE!!
AAAA!
BAM!
HAHAHA!! I SHOWED HIM WHO'S THE KING OF THE HILL!! HAHAHA!!
GOT TO USE THIS GUN! IT'S MY ONLY CHANCE!
I SAW THAT! PUT THE GUN--UGH!
WAM!
WAM!

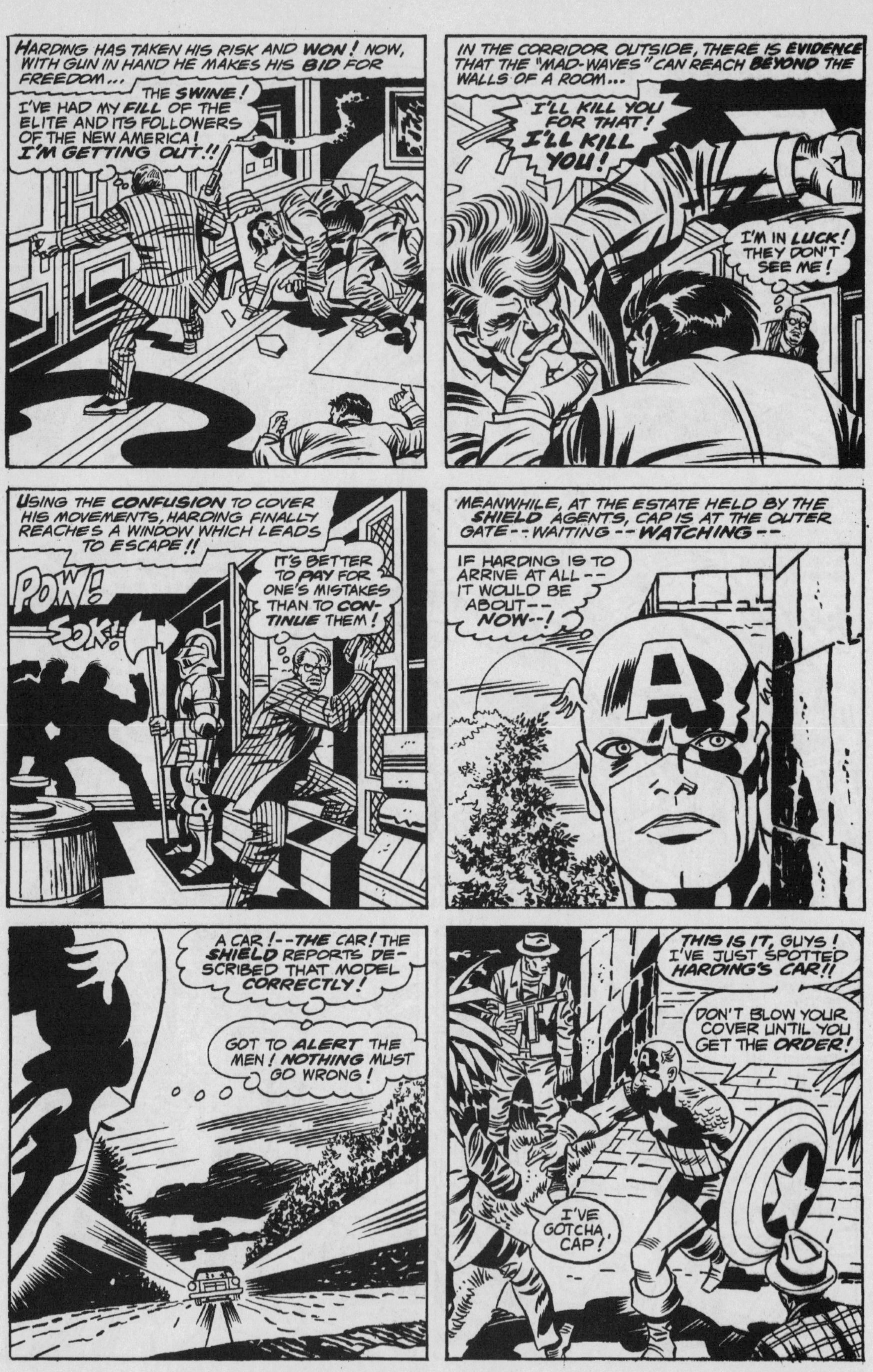
HARDING HAS TAKEN HIS RISK AND WON! NOW, WITH GUN IN HAND HE MAKES HIS BID FOR FREEDOM...
THE SWINE! I'VE HAD MY FILL OF THE ELITE AND ITS FOLLOWERS OF THE NEW AMERICA! I'M GETTING OUT!!
IN THE CORRIDOR OUTSIDE, THERE IS EVIDENCE THAT THE "MAD-WAVES" CAN REACH BEYOND THE WALLS OF A ROOM...
I'LL KILL YOU FOR THAT! I'LL KILL YOU!
I'M IN LUCK! THEY DON'T SEE ME!
USING THE CONFUSION TO COVER HIS MOVEMENTS, HARDING FINALLY REACHES A WINDOW WHICH LEADS TO ESCAPE!!
POW!
SOK!
IT'S BETTER TO PAY FOR ONE'S MISTAKES THAN TO CONTINUE THEM!
MEANWHILE, AT THE ESTATE HELD BY THE SHIELD AGENTS, CAP IS AT THE OUTER GATE--WAITING--WATCHING--
IF HARDING IS TO ARRIVE AT ALL--IT WOULD BE ABOUT--NOW--!
A CAR!--THE CAR! THE SHIELD REPORTS DESCRIBED THAT MODEL CORRECTLY!
GOT TO ALERT THE MEN! NOTHING MUST GO WRONG!
THIS IS IT, GUYS! I'VE JUST SPOTTED HARDING'S CAR!!
DON'T BLOW YOUR COVER UNTIL YOU GET THE ORDER!
I'VE GOTCHA, CAP!

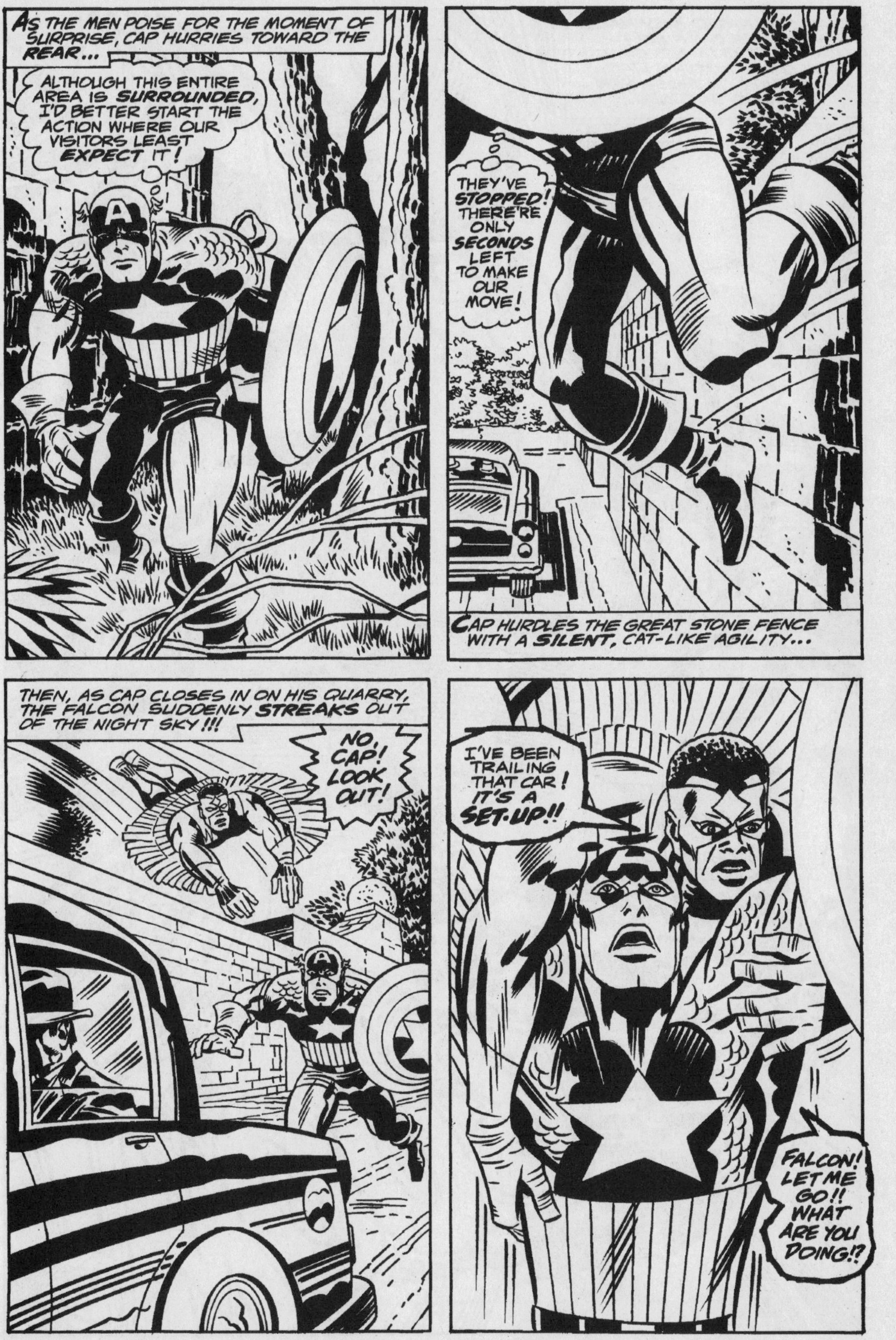
AS THE MEN POISE FOR THE MOMENT OF SURPRISE, CAP HURRIES TOWARD THE REAR...
ALTHOUGH THIS ENTIRE AREA IS SURROUNDED, I'D BETTER START THE ACTION WHERE OUR VISITORS LEAST EXPECT IT!
THEY'VE STOPPED! THERE'RE ONLY SECONDS LEFT TO MAKE OUR MOVE!
CAP HURDLES THE GREAT STONE FENCE WITH A SILENT, CAT-LIKE AGILITY...
THEN, AS CAP CLOSES IN ON HIS QUARRY, THE FALCON SUDDENLY STREAKS OUT OF THE NIGHT SKY!!!
NO, CAP! LOOK OUT!
I'VE BEEN TRAILING THAT CAR! IT'S A SET-UP!!
FALCON! LET ME GO!! WHAT ARE YOU DOING!?

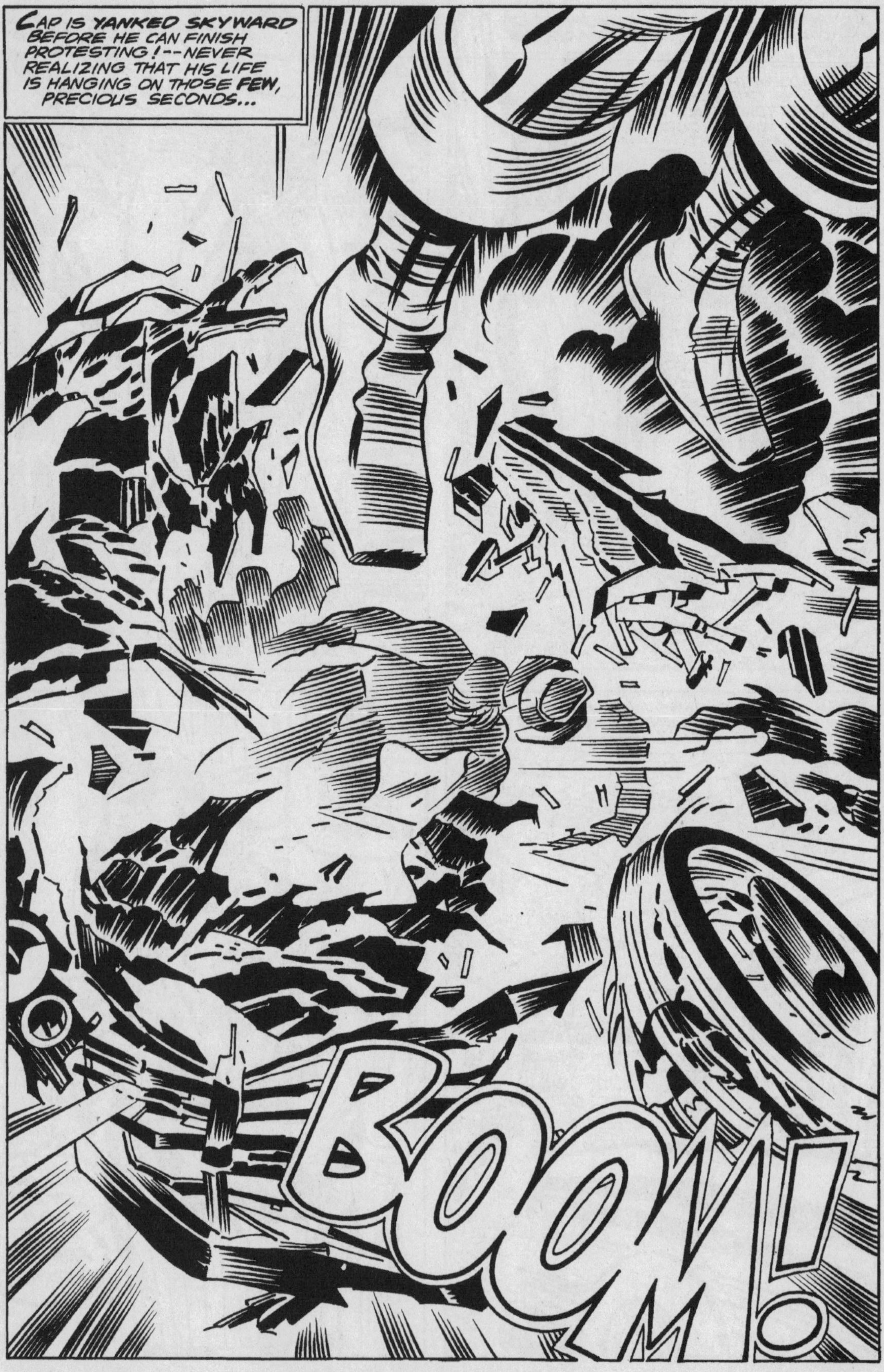
CAP IS YANKED SKYWARD BEFORE HE CAN FINISH PROTESTING! --NEVER REALIZING THAT HIS LIFE IS HANGING ON THOSE FEW, PRECIOUS SECONDS...
BOOOM!

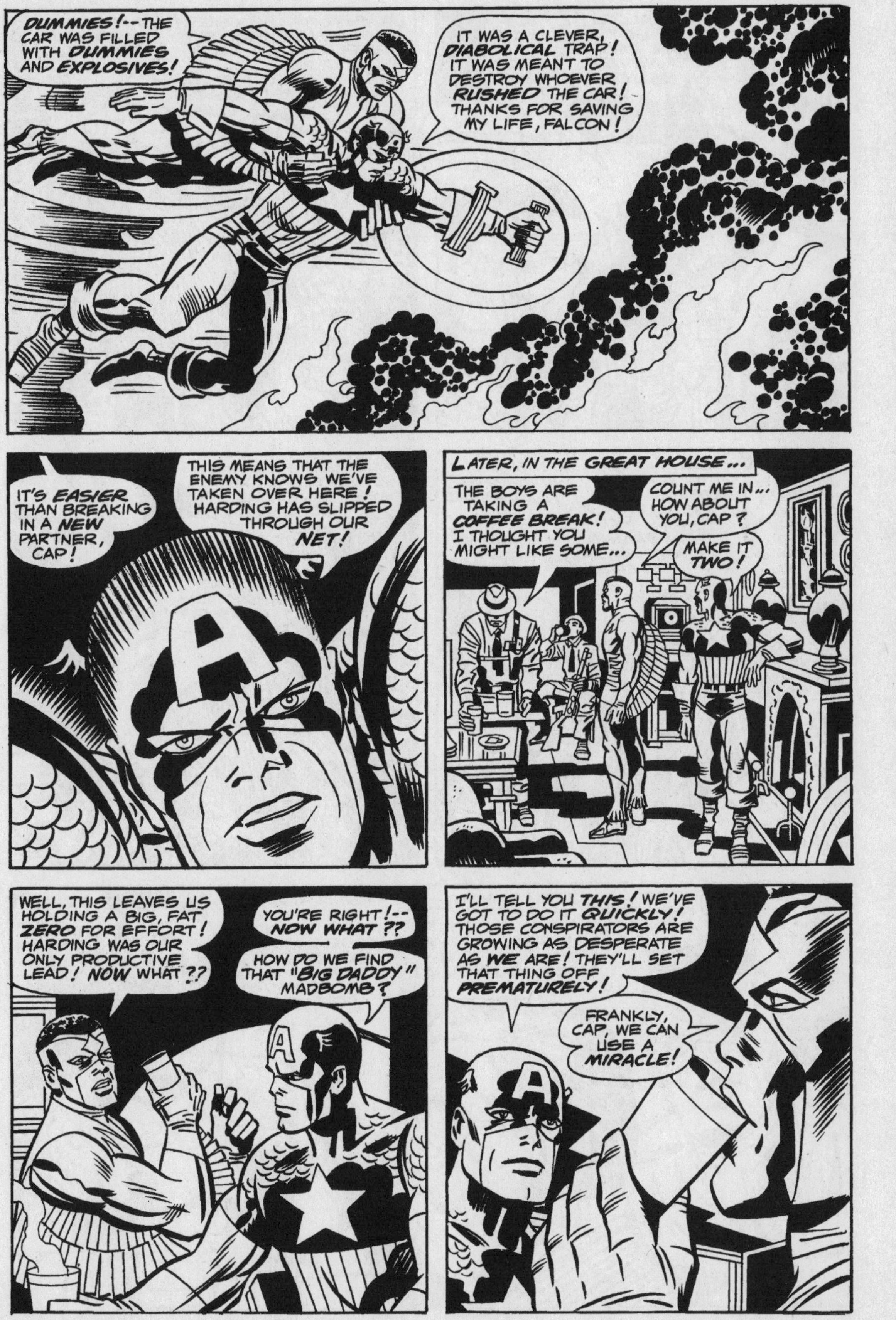
DUMMIES!-- THE CAR WAS FILLED WITH DUMMIES AND EXPLOSIVES!
IT WAS A CLEVER, DIABOLICAL TRAP! IT WAS MEANT TO DESTROY WHOEVER RUSHED THE CAR! THANKS FOR SAVING MY LIFE, FALCON!
IT'S EASIER THAN BREAKING IN A NEW PARTNER, CAP!
THIS MEANS THAT THE ENEMY KNOWS WE'VE TAKEN OVER HERE! HARDING HAS SLIPPED THROUGH OUR NET!
LATER, IN THE GREAT HOUSE...
THE BOYS ARE TAKING A COFFEE BREAK! I THOUGHT YOU MIGHT LIKE SOME...
COUNT ME IN... HOW ABOUT YOU, CAP?
MAKE IT TWO!
WELL, THIS LEAVES US HOLDING A BIG, FAT ZERO FOR EFFORT! HARDING WAS OUR ONLY PRODUCTIVE LEAD! NOW WHAT??
YOU'RE RIGHT!-- NOW WHAT??
HOW DO WE FIND THAT "BIG DADDY" MADBOMB?
I'LL TELL YOU THIS! WE'VE GOT TO DO IT QUICKLY! THOSE CONSPIRATORS ARE GROWING AS DESPERATE AS WE ARE! THEY'LL SET THAT THING OFF PREMATURELY!
FRANKLY, CAP, WE CAN USE A MIRACLE!

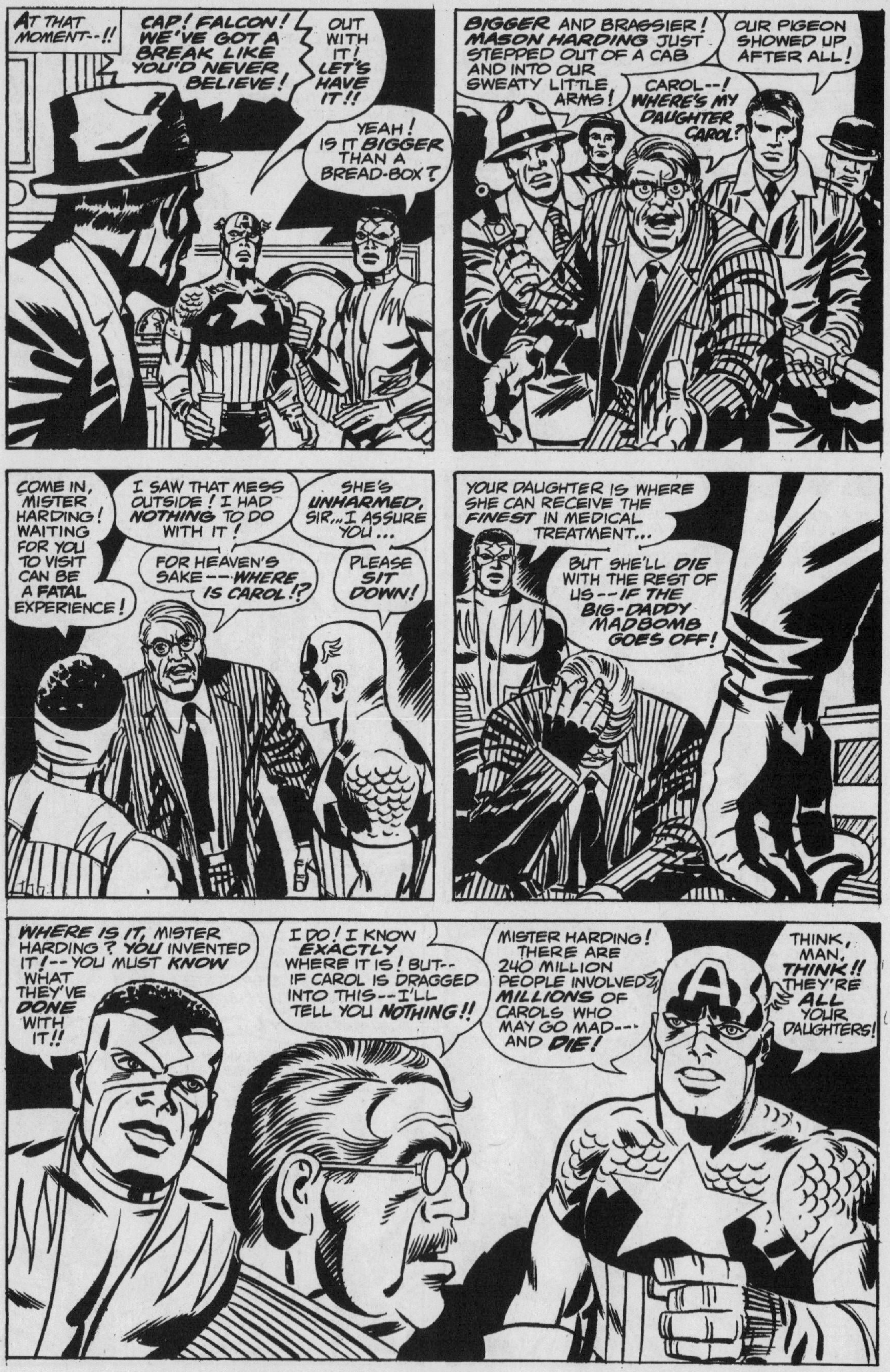
AT THAT MOMENT--!!
CAP! FALCON! WE'VE GOT A BREAK LIKE YOU'D NEVER BELIEVE!
OUT WITH IT! LET'S HAVE IT!!
YEAH! IS IT BIGGER THAN A BREAD-BOX?
BIGGER AND BRASSIER! MASON HARDING JUST STEPPED OUT OF A CAB AND INTO OUR SWEATY LITTLE ARMS!
OUR PIGEON SHOWED UP AFTER ALL!
CAROL--! WHERE'S MY DAUGHTER CAROL?
COME IN, MISTER HARDING! WAITING FOR YOU TO VISIT CAN BE A FATAL EXPERIENCE!
I SAW THAT MESS OUTSIDE! I HAD NOTHING TO DO WITH IT!
FOR HEAVEN'S SAKE--WHERE IS CAROL!?
SHE'S UNHARMED, SIR,...I ASSURE YOU...
PLEASE SIT DOWN!
YOUR DAUGHTER IS WHERE SHE CAN RECEIVE THE FINEST IN MEDICAL TREATMENT...
BUT SHE'LL DIE WITH THE REST OF US--IF THE BIG-DADDY MADBOMB GOES OFF!
WHERE IS IT, MISTER HARDING? YOU INVENTED IT!--YOU MUST KNOW WHAT THEY'VE DONE WITH IT!!
I DO! I KNOW EXACTLY WHERE IT IS! BUT--IF CAROL IS DRAGGED INTO THIS--I'LL TELL YOU NOTHING!!
MISTER HARDING! THERE ARE 240 MILLION PEOPLE INVOLVED! MILLIONS OF CAROLS WHO MAY GO MAD---AND DIE!
THINK, MAN, THINK!! THEY'RE ALL YOUR DAUGHTERS!

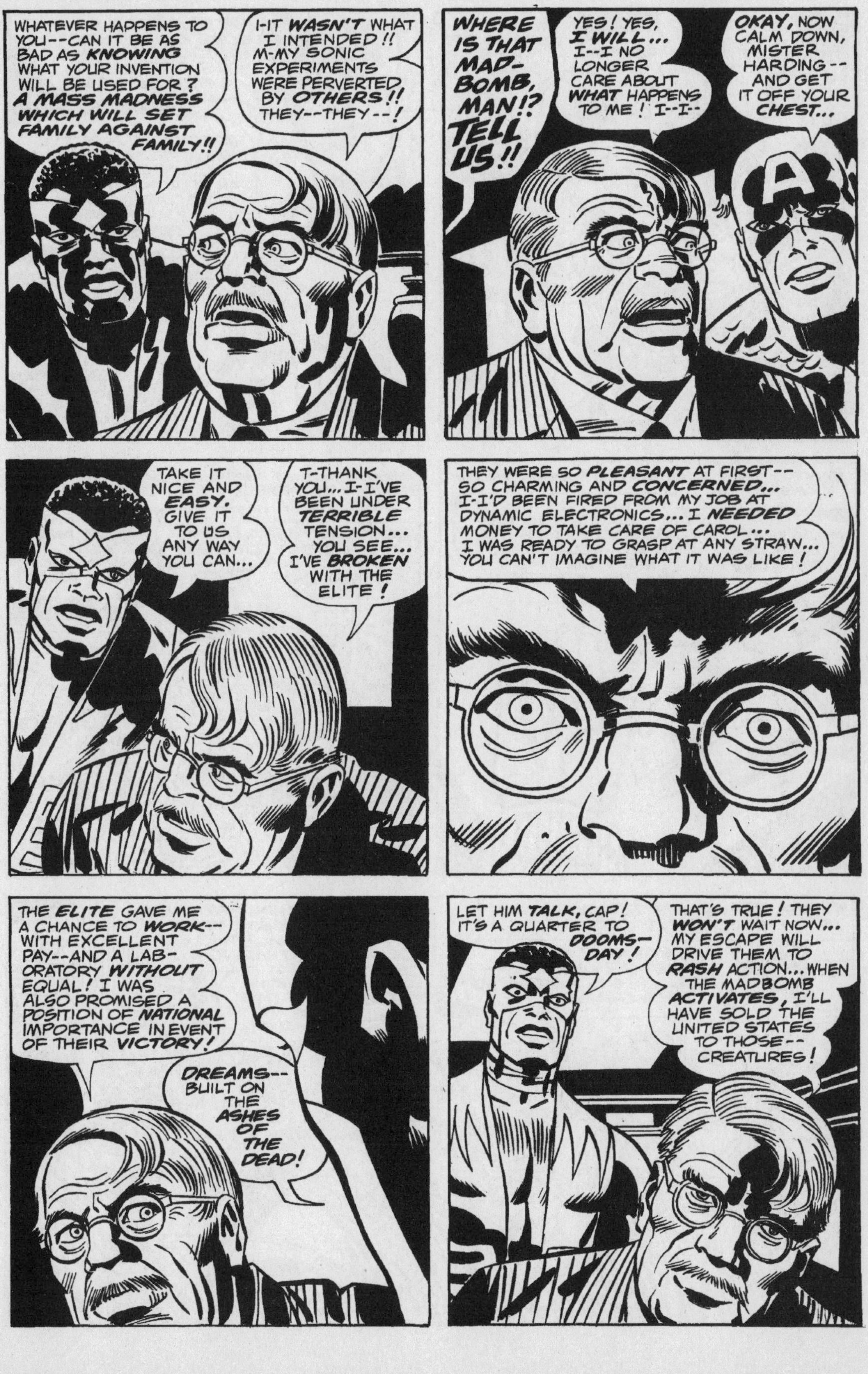
WHATEVER HAPPENS TO YOU--CAN IT BE AS BAD AS KNOWING WHAT YOUR INVENTION WILL BE USED FOR? A MASS MADNESS WHICH WILL SET FAMILY AGAINST FAMILY!!
I-IT WASN'T WHAT I INTENDED!! M-MY SONIC EXPERIMENTS WERE PERVERTED BY OTHERS!! THEY--THEY--!
WHERE IS THAT MAD-BOMB, MAN!? TELL US!!
YES! YES, I WILL... I--I NO LONGER CARE ABOUT WHAT HAPPENS TO ME! I--I--
OKAY, NOW CALM DOWN, MISTER HARDING--AND GET IT OFF YOUR CHEST...
TAKE IT NICE AND EASY. GIVE IT TO US ANY WAY YOU CAN...
T-THANK YOU...I-I'VE BEEN UNDER TERRIBLE TENSION... YOU SEE... I'VE BROKEN WITH THE ELITE!
THEY WERE SO PLEASANT AT FIRST--SO CHARMING AND CONCERNED... I-I'D BEEN FIRED FROM MY JOB AT DYNAMIC ELECTRONICS... I NEEDED MONEY TO TAKE CARE OF CAROL... I WAS READY TO GRASP AT ANY STRAW... YOU CAN'T IMAGINE WHAT IT WAS LIKE!
THE ELITE GAVE ME A CHANCE TO WORK--WITH EXCELLENT PAY--AND A LAB-ORATORY WITHOUT EQUAL! I WAS ALSO PROMISED A POSITION OF NATIONAL IMPORTANCE IN EVENT OF THEIR VICTORY!
DREAMS--BUILT ON THE ASHES OF THE DEAD!
LET HIM TALK, CAP! IT'S A QUARTER TO DOOMS-DAY!
THAT'S TRUE! THEY WON'T WAIT NOW... MY ESCAPE WILL DRIVE THEM TO RASH ACTION...WHEN THE MADBOMB ACTIVATES, I'LL HAVE SOLD THE UNITED STATES TO THOSE--CREATURES!

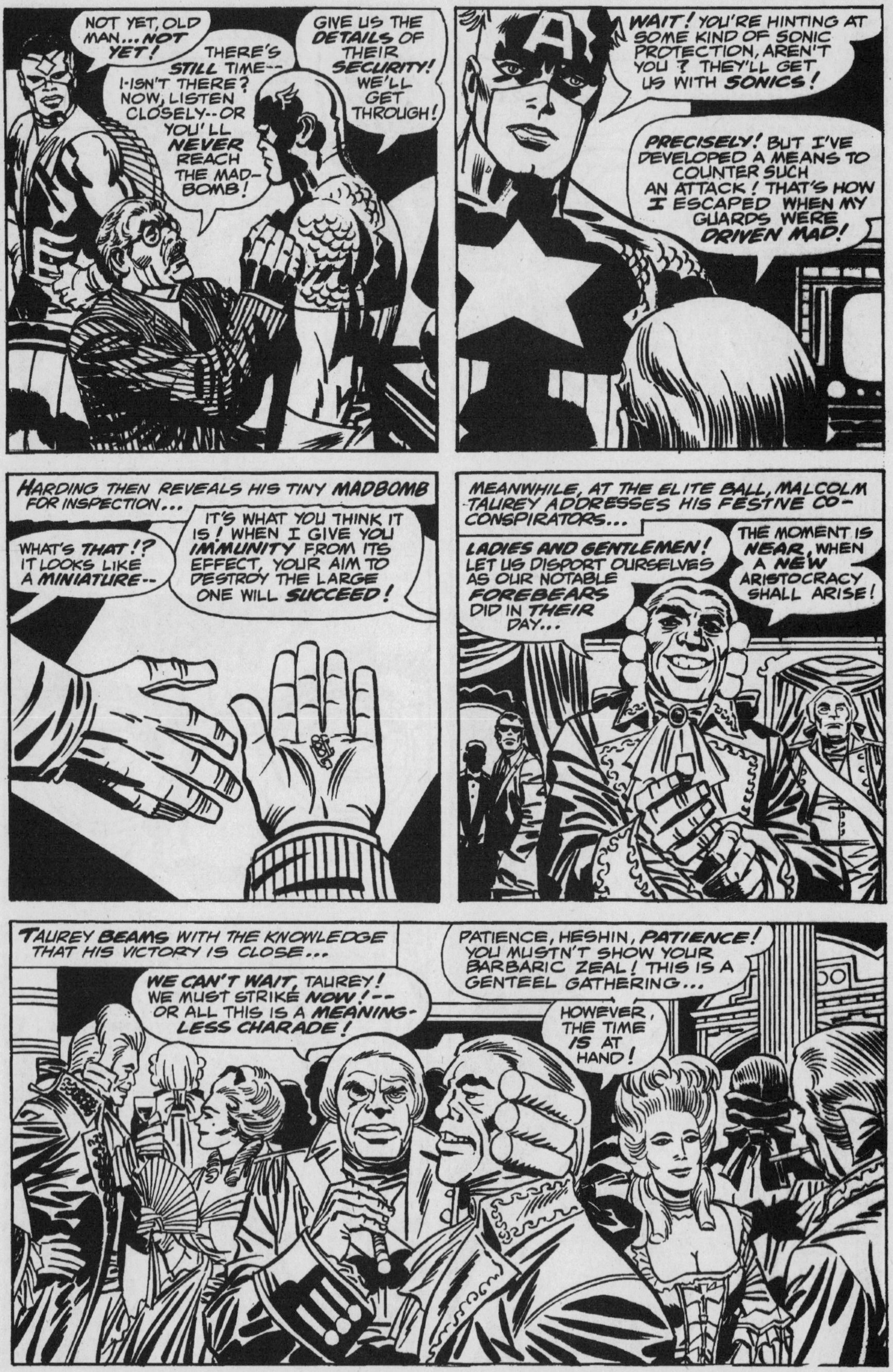
NOT YET, OLD MAN... NOT YET!
THERE'S STILL TIME-- I-ISN'T THERE? NOW, LISTEN CLOSELY--OR YOU'LL NEVER REACH THE MAD-BOMB!
GIVE US THE DETAILS OF THEIR SECURITY! WE'LL GET THROUGH!
WAIT! YOU'RE HINTING AT SOME KIND OF SONIC PROTECTION, AREN'T YOU? THEY'LL GET US WITH SONICS!
PRECISELY! BUT I'VE DEVELOPED A MEANS TO COUNTER SUCH AN ATTACK! THAT'S HOW I ESCAPED WHEN MY GUARDS WERE DRIVEN MAD!
HARDING THEN REVEALS HIS TINY MADBOMB FOR INSPECTION...
WHAT'S THAT!? IT LOOKS LIKE A MINIATURE--
IT'S WHAT YOU THINK IT IS! WHEN I GIVE YOU IMMUNITY FROM ITS EFFECT, YOUR AIM TO DESTROY THE LARGE ONE WILL SUCCEED!
MEANWHILE, AT THE ELITE BALL, MALCOLM TAUREY ADDRESSES HIS FESTIVE CO-CONSPIRATORS...
LADIES AND GENTLEMEN! LET US DISPORT OURSELVES AS OUR NOTABLE FOREBEARS DID IN THEIR DAY...
THE MOMENT IS NEAR, WHEN A NEW ARISTOCRACY SHALL ARISE!
TAUREY BEAMS WITH THE KNOWLEDGE THAT HIS VICTORY IS CLOSE...
WE CAN'T WAIT, TAUREY! WE MUST STRIKE NOW!--OR ALL THIS IS A MEANING-LESS CHARADE!
PATIENCE, HESHIN, PATIENCE! YOU MUSTN'T SHOW YOUR BARBARIC ZEAL! THIS IS A GENTEEL GATHERING...
HOWEVER, THE TIME IS AT HAND!

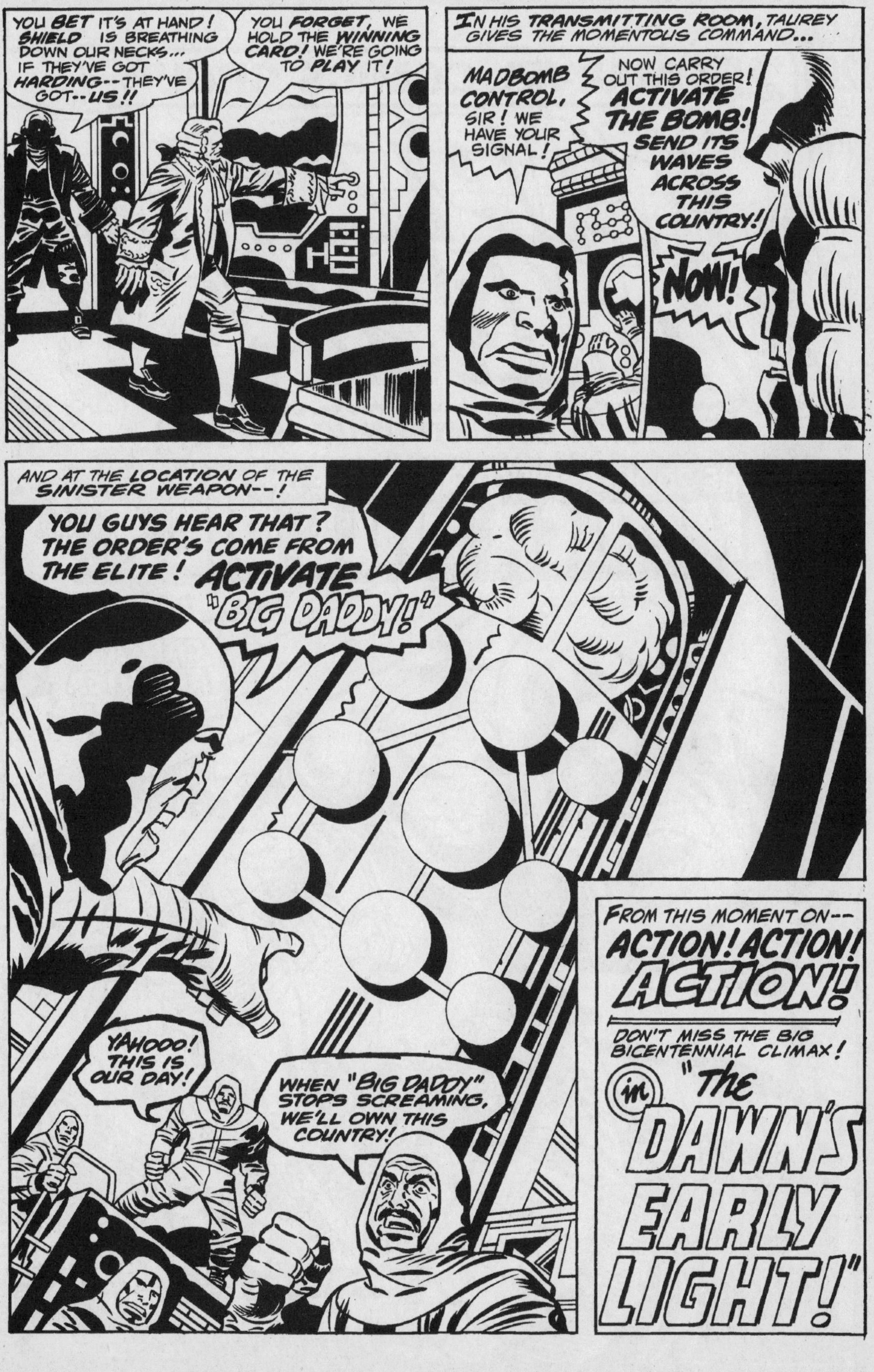
YOU BET IT'S AT HAND! SHIELD IS BREATHING DOWN OUR NECKS... IF THEY'VE GOT HARDING--THEY'VE GOT--US!!
YOU FORGET, WE HOLD THE WINNING CARD! WE'RE GOING TO PLAY IT!
IN HIS TRANSMITTING ROOM, TAUREY GIVES THE MOMENTOUS COMMAND...
MADBOMB CONTROL, SIR! WE HAVE YOUR SIGNAL!
NOW CARRY OUT THIS ORDER! ACTIVATE THE BOMB! SEND ITS WAVES ACROSS THIS COUNTRY!
NOW!
AND AT THE LOCATION OF THE SINISTER WEAPON--!
YOU GUYS HEAR THAT? THE ORDER'S COME FROM THE ELITE! ACTIVATE "BIG DADDY!"
YAHOOO! THIS IS OUR DAY!
WHEN "BIG DADDY" STOPS SCREAMING, WE'LL OWN THIS COUNTRY!
FROM THIS MOMENT ON-- ACTION! ACTION! ACTION!
DON'T MISS THE BIG BICENTENNIAL CLIMAX!
in "THE DAWN'S EARLY LIGHT!"

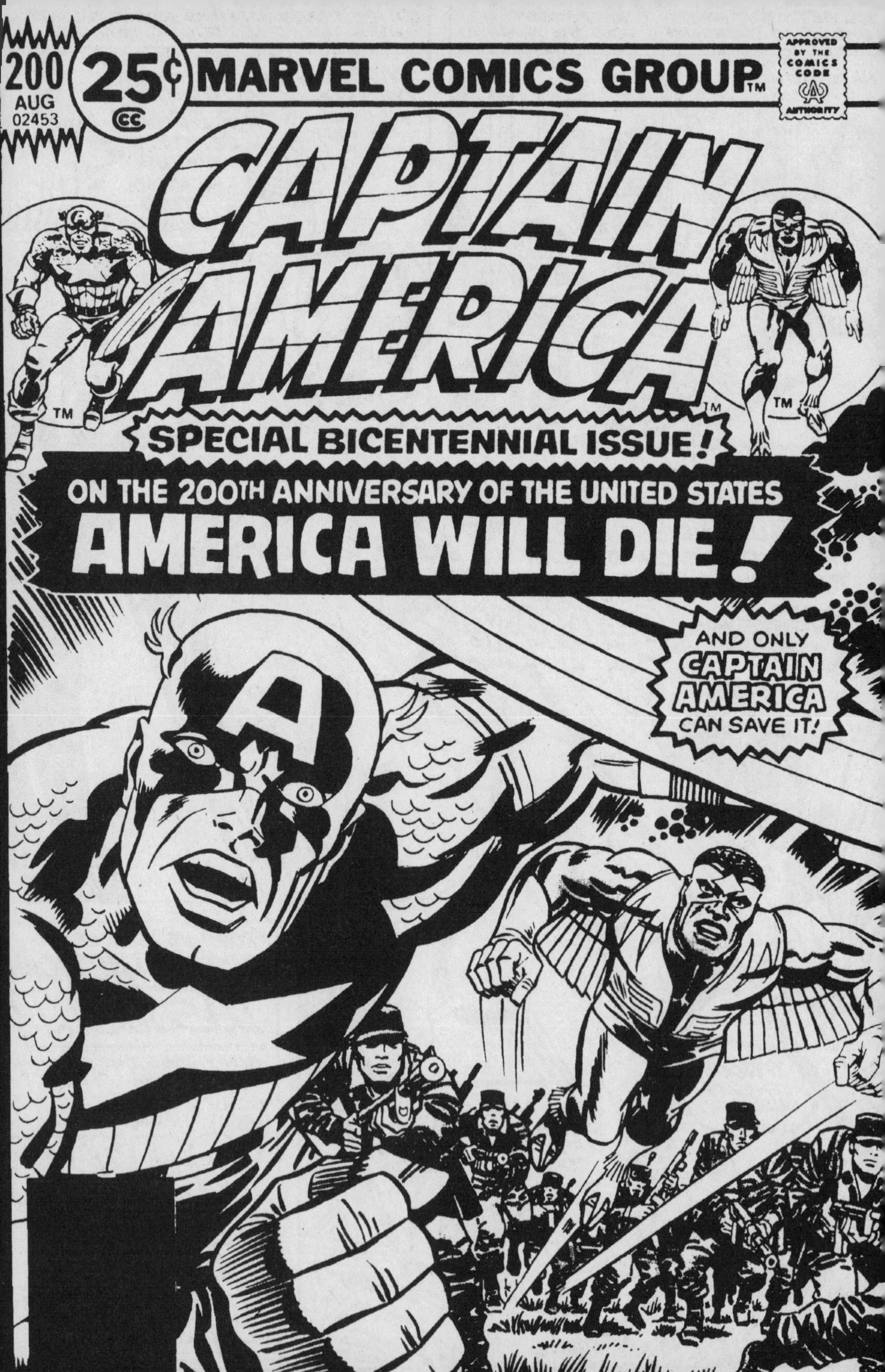
200
AUG
02453
25¢
CC
MARVEL COMICS GROUP
APPROVED BY THE COMICS CODE AUTHORITY
CAPTAIN AMERICA
SPECIAL BICENTENNIAL ISSUE!
ON THE 200TH ANNIVERSARY OF THE UNITED STATES
AMERICA WILL DIE!
AND ONLY CAPTAIN AMERICA CAN SAVE IT!

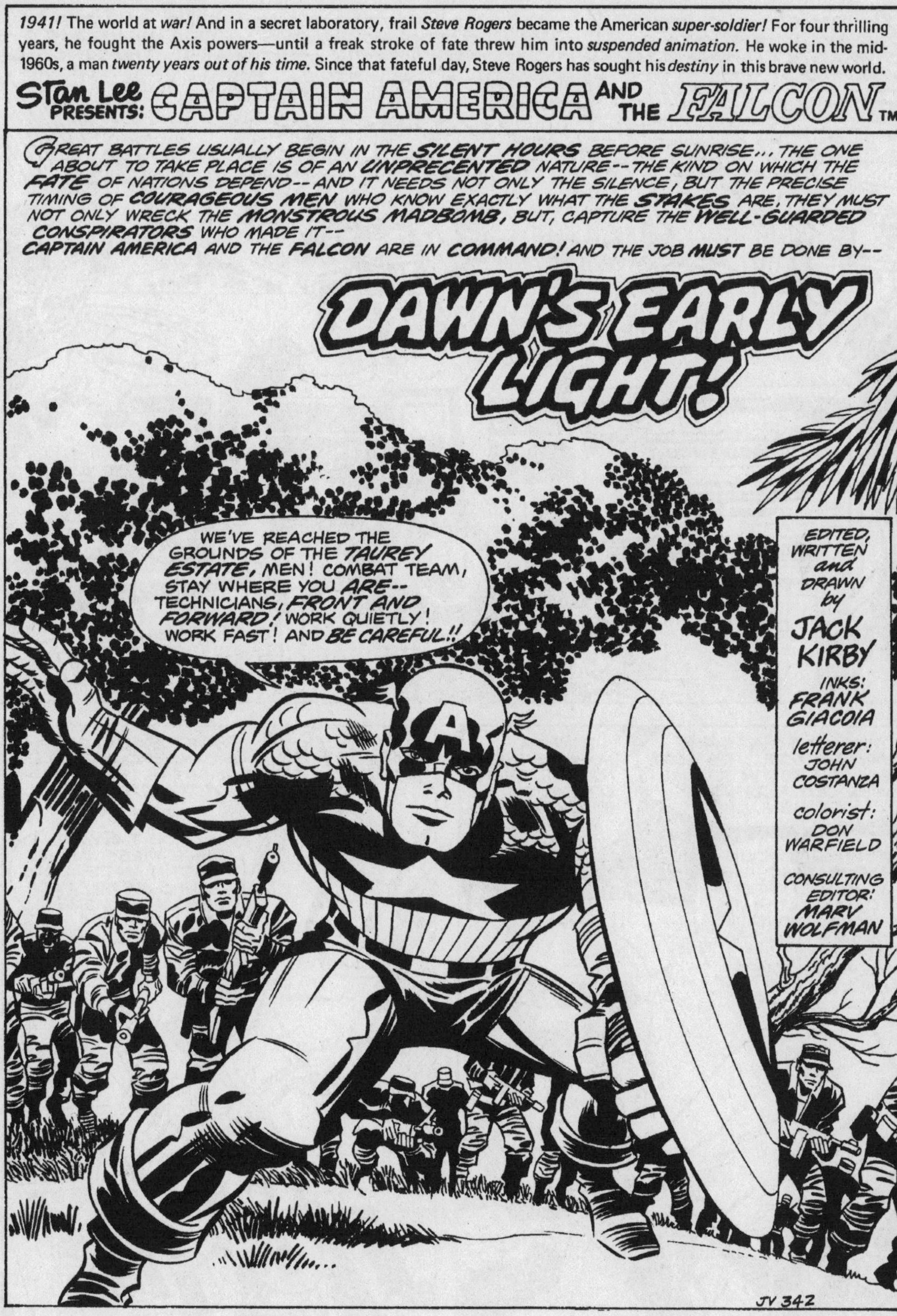

1941! The world at war! And in a secret laboratory, frail Steve Rogers became the American super-soldier! For four thrilling years, he fought the Axis powers—until a freak stroke of fate threw him into suspended animation. He woke in the mid-1960s, a man twenty years out of his time. Since that fateful day, Steve Rogers has sought his destiny in this brave new world.
Stan Lee PRESENTS: CAPTAIN AMERICA AND THE FALCON TM
GREAT BATTLES USUALLY BEGIN IN THE SILENT HOURS BEFORE SUNRISE... THE ONE ABOUT TO TAKE PLACE IS OF AN UNPRECENTED NATURE--THE KIND ON WHICH THE FATE OF NATIONS DEPEND--AND IT NEEDS NOT ONLY THE SILENCE, BUT THE PRECISE TIMING OF COURAGEOUS MEN WHO KNOW EXACTLY WHAT THE STAKES ARE. THEY MUST NOT ONLY WRECK THE MONSTROUS MADBOMB, BUT, CAPTURE THE WELL-GUARDED CONSPIRATORS WHO MADE IT--
CAPTAIN AMERICA AND THE FALCON ARE IN COMMAND! AND THE JOB MUST BE DONE BY--
DAWN'S EARLY LIGHT!
WE'VE REACHED THE GROUNDS OF THE TAUREY ESTATE, MEN! COMBAT TEAM, STAY WHERE YOU ARE-- TECHNICIANS, FRONT AND FORWARD! WORK QUIETLY! WORK FAST! AND BE CAREFUL!!
EDITED, WRITTEN and DRAWN by JACK KIRBY
INKS: FRANK GIACOIA
letterer: JOHN COSTANZA
colorist: DON WARFIELD
CONSULTING EDITOR: MARV WOLFMAN
JV 342

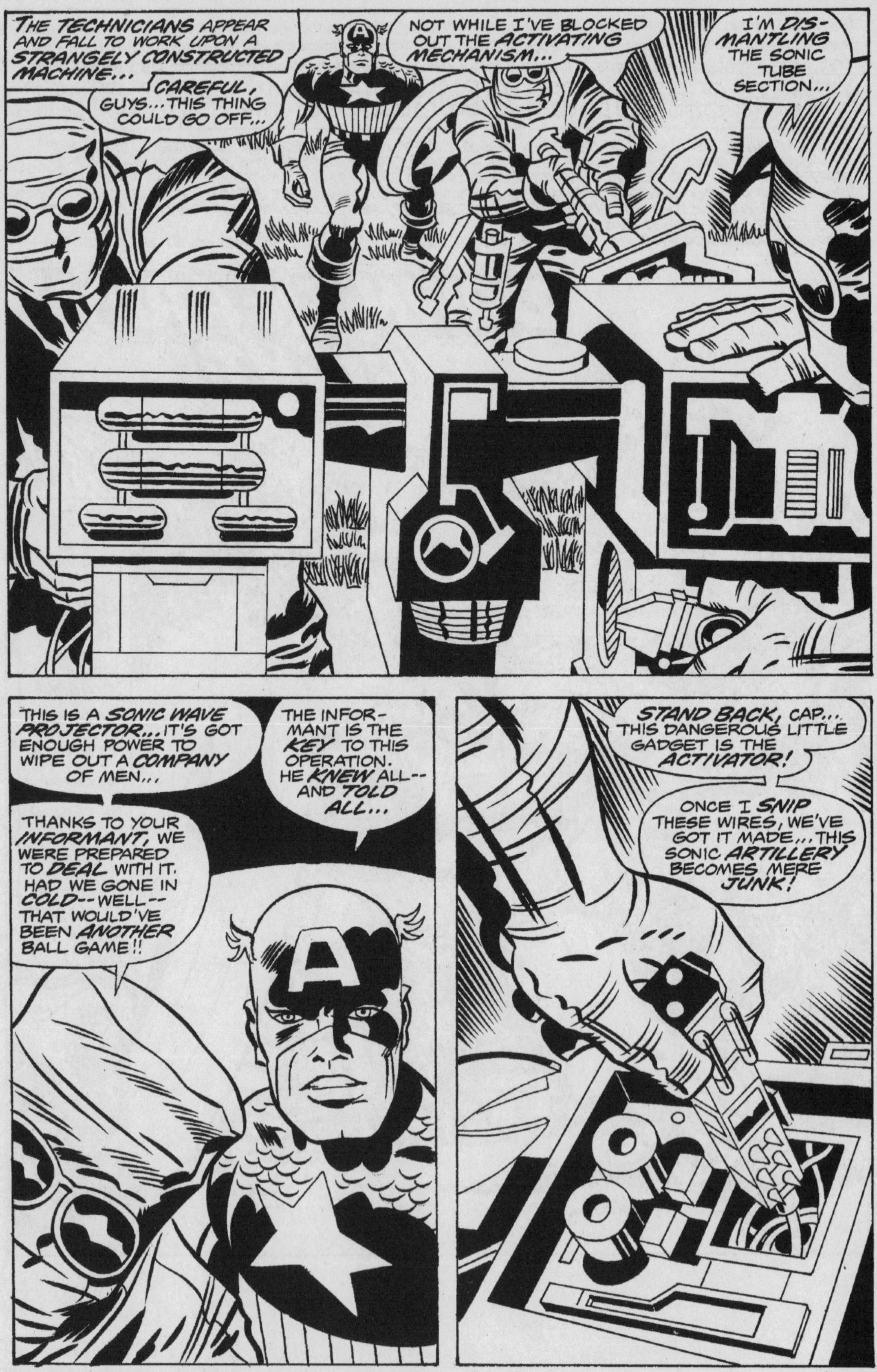
THE TECHNICIANS APPEAR AND FALL TO WORK UPON A STRANGELY CONSTRUCTED MACHINE...
CAREFUL, GUYS... THIS THING COULD GO OFF...
NOT WHILE I'VE BLOCKED OUT THE ACTIVATING MECHANISM...
I'M DIS-MANTLING THE SONIC TUBE SECTION...
THIS IS A SONIC WAVE PROJECTOR... IT'S GOT ENOUGH POWER TO WIPE OUT A COMPANY OF MEN...
THANKS TO YOUR INFORMANT, WE WERE PREPARED TO DEAL WITH IT. HAD WE GONE IN COLD-- WELL-- THAT WOULD'VE BEEN ANOTHER BALL GAME!!
THE INFOR-MANT IS THE KEY TO THIS OPERATION. HE KNEW ALL-- AND TOLD ALL...
STAND BACK, CAP... THIS DANGEROUS LITTLE GADGET IS THE ACTIVATOR!
ONCE I SNIP THESE WIRES, WE'VE GOT IT MADE... THIS SONIC ARTILLERY BECOMES MERE JUNK!

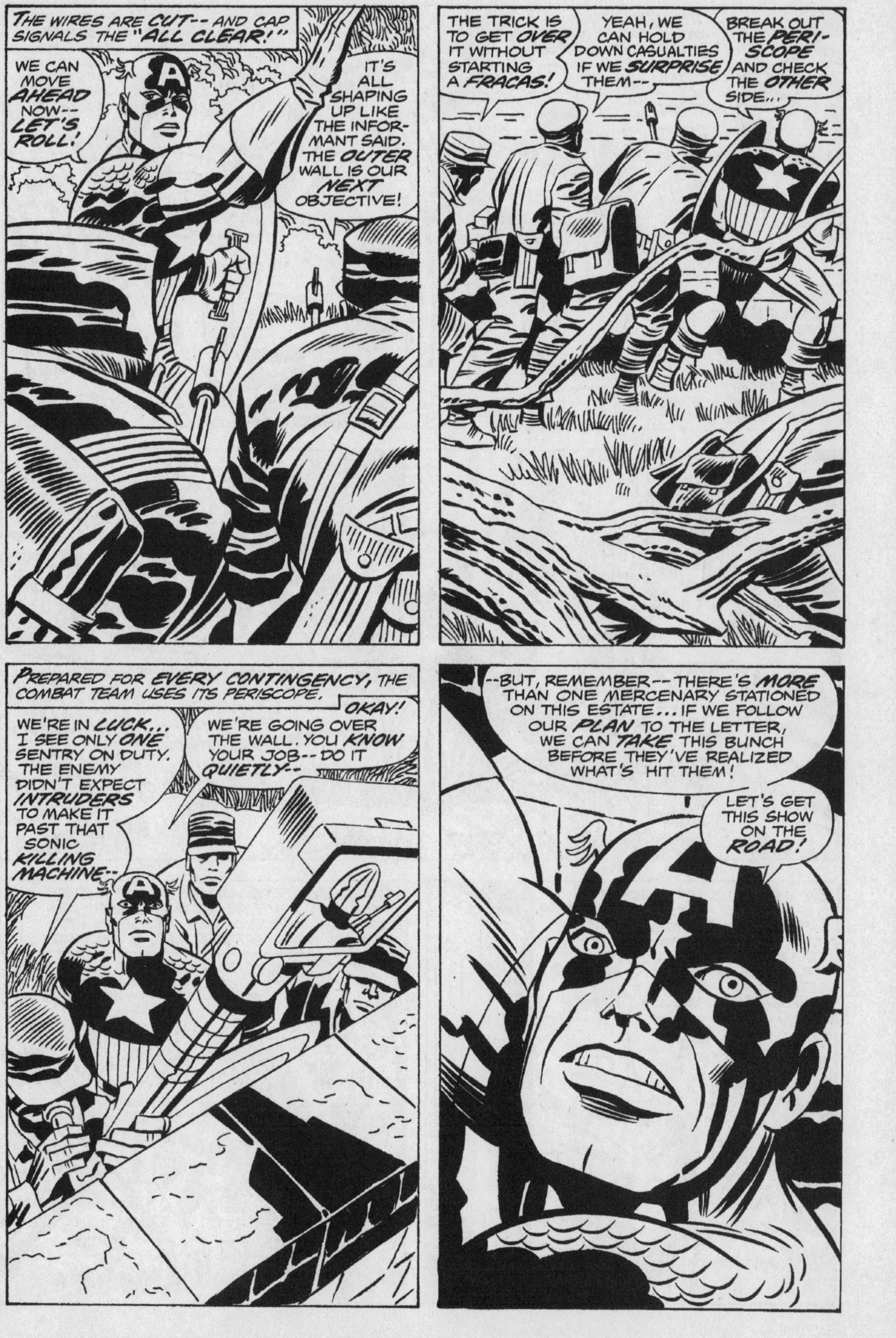
THE WIRES ARE CUT-- AND CAP SIGNALS THE "ALL CLEAR!"
WE CAN MOVE AHEAD NOW-- LET'S ROLL!
IT'S ALL SHAPING UP LIKE THE INFORMANT SAID. THE OUTER WALL IS OUR NEXT OBJECTIVE!
THE TRICK IS TO GET OVER IT WITHOUT STARTING A FRACAS!
YEAH, WE CAN HOLD DOWN CASUALTIES IF WE SURPRISE THEM--
BREAK OUT THE PERI-SCOPE AND CHECK THE OTHER SIDE...
PREPARED FOR EVERY CONTINGENCY, THE COMBAT TEAM USES ITS PERISCOPE.
WE'RE IN LUCK... I SEE ONLY ONE SENTRY ON DUTY. THE ENEMY DIDN'T EXPECT INTRUDERS TO MAKE IT PAST THAT SONIC KILLING MACHINE--
OKAY!
WE'RE GOING OVER THE WALL. YOU KNOW YOUR JOB-- DO IT QUIETLY--
--BUT, REMEMBER-- THERE'S MORE THAN ONE MERCENARY STATIONED ON THIS ESTATE... IF WE FOLLOW OUR PLAN TO THE LETTER, WE CAN TAKE THIS BUNCH BEFORE THEY'VE REALIZED WHAT'S HIT THEM!
LET'S GET THIS SHOW ON THE ROAD!

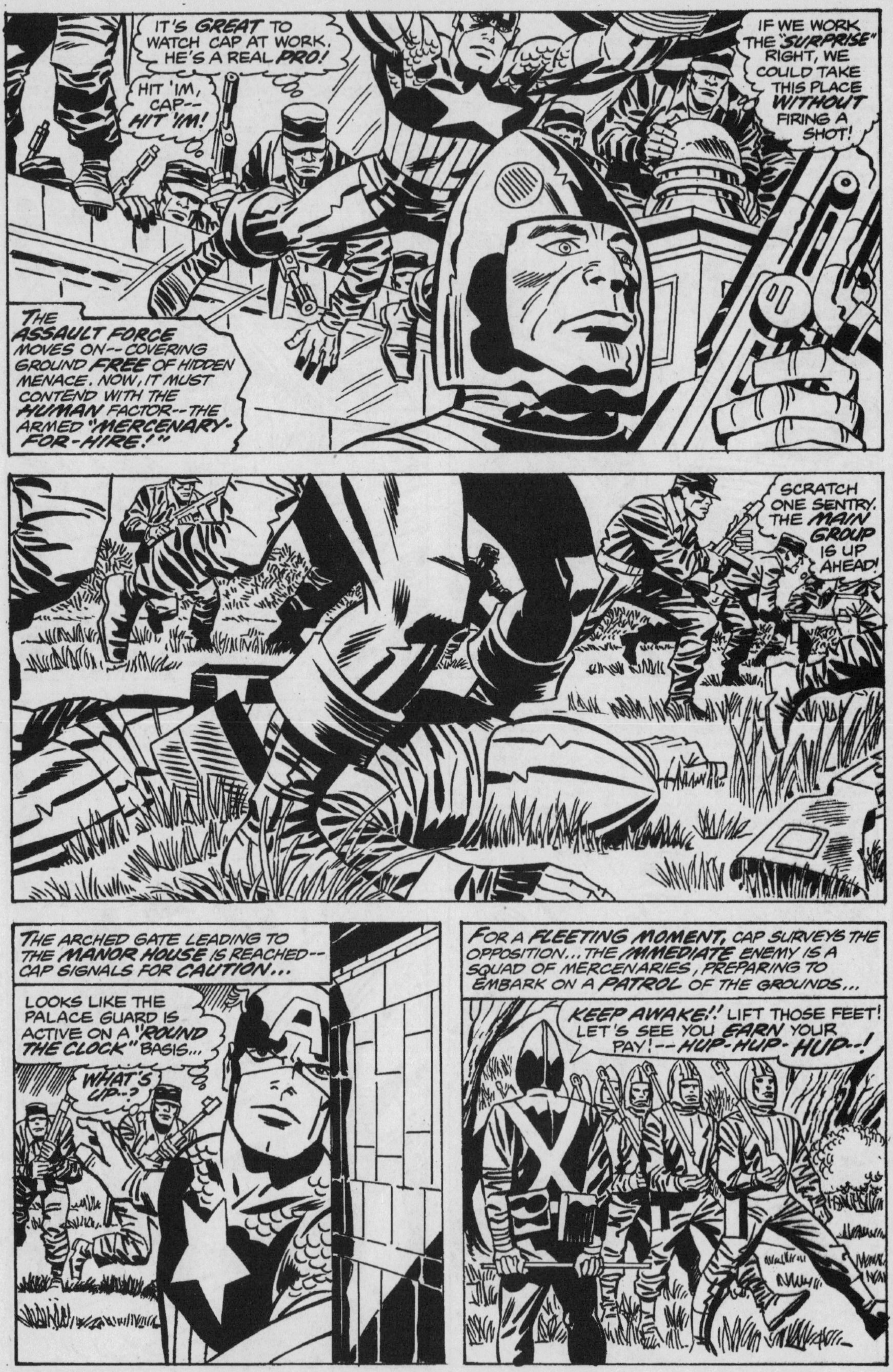
IT'S GREAT TO WATCH CAP AT WORK. HE'S A REAL PRO!
HIT 'IM, CAP-- HIT 'IM!
IF WE WORK THE "SURPRISE" RIGHT, WE COULD TAKE THIS PLACE WITHOUT FIRING A SHOT!
THE ASSAULT FORCE MOVES ON--COVERING GROUND FREE OF HIDDEN MENACE. NOW, IT MUST CONTEND WITH THE HUMAN FACTOR--THE ARMED "MERCENARY-FOR-HIRE!"
SCRATCH ONE SENTRY. THE MAIN GROUP IS UP AHEAD!
THE ARCHED GATE LEADING TO THE MANOR HOUSE IS REACHED-- CAP SIGNALS FOR CAUTION...
LOOKS LIKE THE PALACE GUARD IS ACTIVE ON A "ROUND THE CLOCK" BASIS...
WHAT'S UP--?
FOR A FLEETING MOMENT, CAP SURVEYS THE OPPOSITION... THE IMMEDIATE ENEMY IS A SQUAD OF MERCENARIES, PREPARING TO EMBARK ON A PATROL OF THE GROUNDS...
KEEP AWAKE!! LIFT THOSE FEET! LET'S SEE YOU EARN YOUR PAY!--HUP-HUP-HUP--!

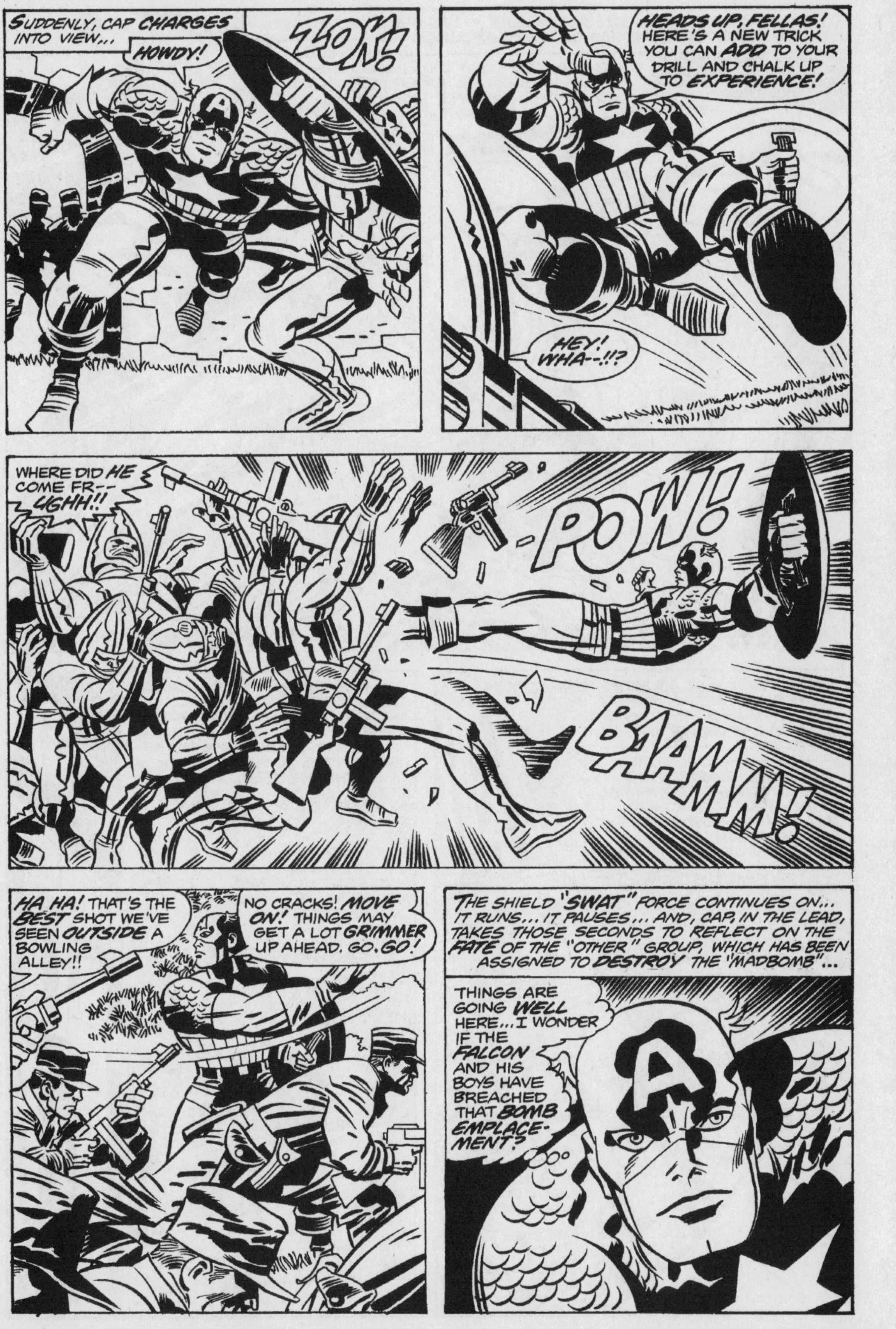
SUDDENLY, CAP CHARGES INTO VIEW...
HOWDY!
ZOK!
HEADS UP, FELLAS! HERE'S A NEW TRICK YOU CAN ADD TO YOUR DRILL AND CHALK UP TO EXPERIENCE!
HEY! WHA--!!?
WHERE DID HE COME FR-- UGHH!!
POW!
BAAMM!
HA HA! THAT'S THE BEST SHOT WE'VE SEEN OUTSIDE A BOWLING ALLEY!!
NO CRACKS! MOVE ON! THINGS MAY GET A LOT GRIMMER UP AHEAD. GO. GO!
THE SHIELD "SWAT" FORCE CONTINUES ON... IT RUNS... IT PAUSES... AND, CAP, IN THE LEAD, TAKES THOSE SECONDS TO REFLECT ON THE FATE OF THE "OTHER" GROUP, WHICH HAS BEEN ASSIGNED TO DESTROY THE "MADBOMB"...
THINGS ARE GOING WELL HERE... I WONDER IF THE FALCON AND HIS BOYS HAVE BREACHED THAT BOMB EMPLACEMENT?

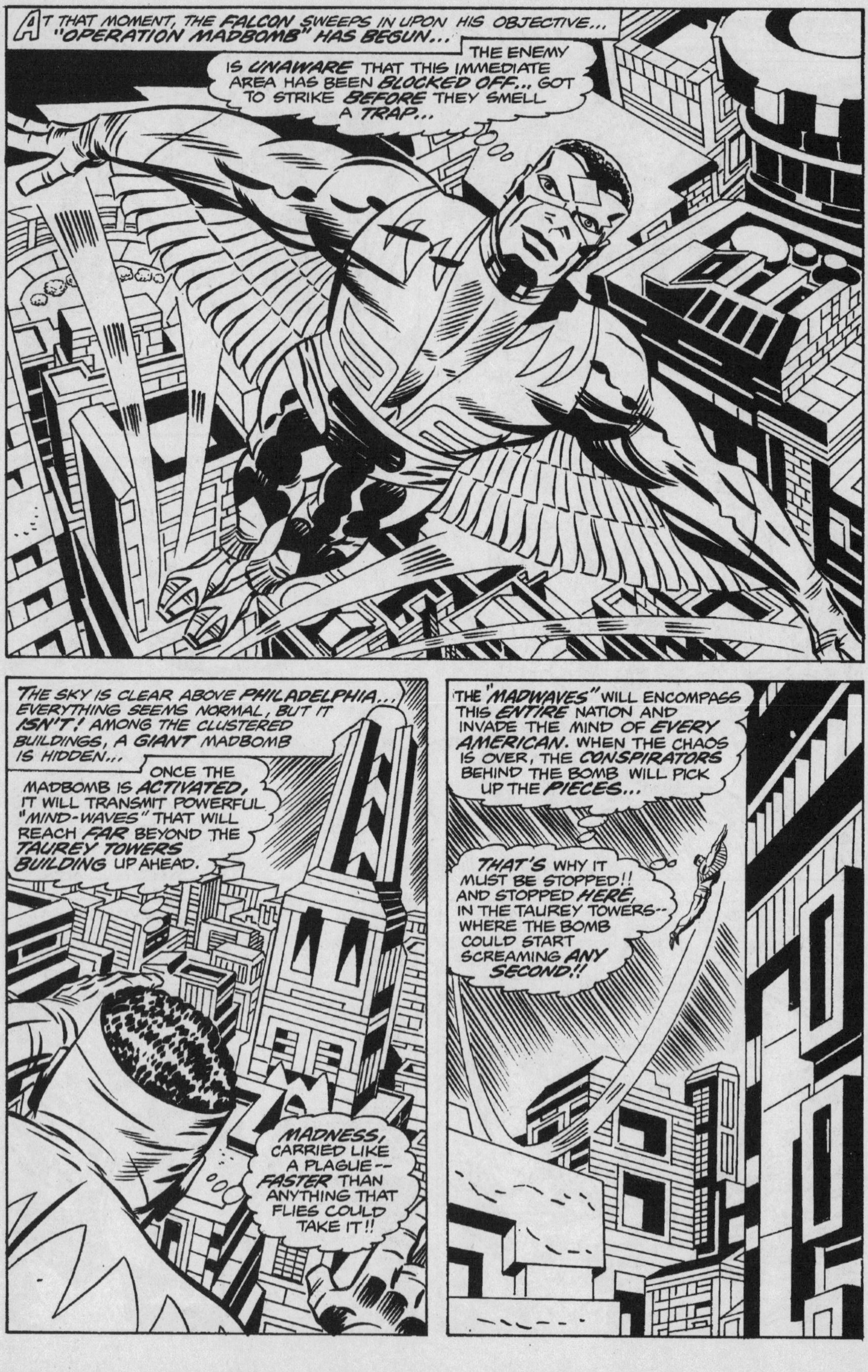
AT THAT MOMENT, THE FALCON SWEEPS IN UPON HIS OBJECTIVE... "OPERATION MADBOMB" HAS BEGUN...
THE ENEMY IS UNAWARE THAT THIS IMMEDIATE AREA HAS BEEN BLOCKED OFF... GOT TO STRIKE BEFORE THEY SMELL A TRAP...
THE SKY IS CLEAR ABOVE PHILADELPHIA... EVERYTHING SEEMS NORMAL, BUT IT ISN'T! AMONG THE CLUSTERED BUILDINGS, A GIANT MADBOMB IS HIDDEN...
ONCE THE MADBOMB IS ACTIVATED, IT WILL TRANSMIT POWERFUL "MIND-WAVES" THAT WILL REACH FAR BEYOND THE TAUREY TOWERS BUILDING UP AHEAD.
MADNESS, CARRIED LIKE A PLAGUE-- FASTER THAN ANYTHING THAT FLIES COULD TAKE IT!!
THE "MADWAVES" WILL ENCOMPASS THIS ENTIRE NATION AND INVADE THE MIND OF EVERY AMERICAN. WHEN THE CHAOS IS OVER, THE CONSPIRATORS BEHIND THE BOMB WILL PICK UP THE PIECES...
THAT'S WHY IT MUST BE STOPPED!! AND STOPPED HERE, IN THE TAUREY TOWERS-- WHERE THE BOMB COULD START SCREAMING ANY SECOND!!

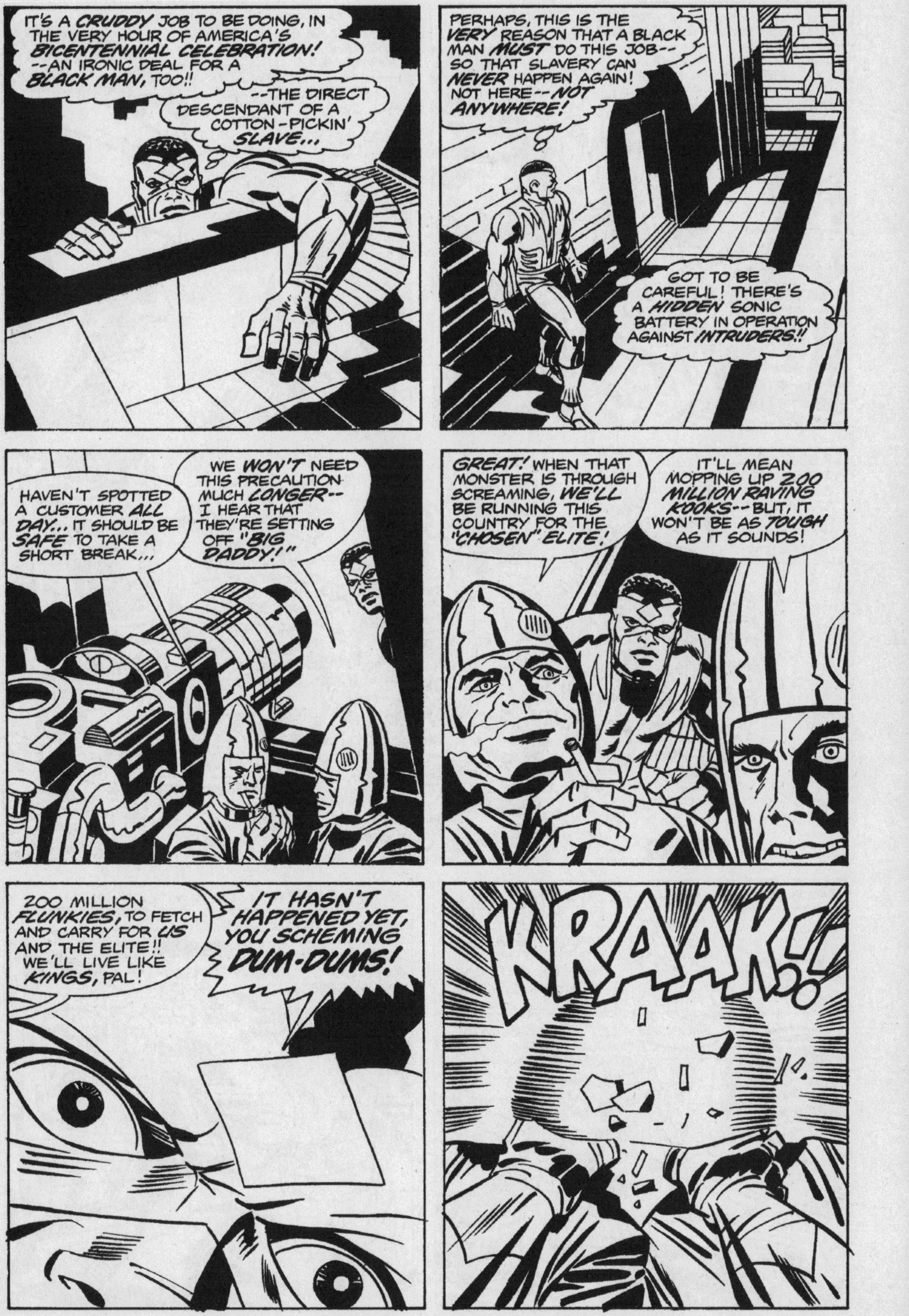
IT'S A CRUDDY JOB TO BE DOING, IN THE VERY HOUR OF AMERICA'S BICENTENNIAL CELEBRATION! --AN IRONIC DEAL FOR A BLACK MAN, TOO!!
--THE DIRECT DESCENDANT OF A COTTON-PICKIN' SLAVE...
PERHAPS, THIS IS THE VERY REASON THAT A BLACK MAN MUST DO THIS JOB-- SO THAT SLAVERY CAN NEVER HAPPEN AGAIN! NOT HERE--NOT ANYWHERE!
GOT TO BE CAREFUL! THERE'S A HIDDEN SONIC BATTERY IN OPERATION AGAINST INTRUDERS!!
HAVEN'T SPOTTED A CUSTOMER ALL DAY... IT SHOULD BE SAFE TO TAKE A SHORT BREAK...
WE WON'T NEED THIS PRECAUTION MUCH LONGER-- I HEAR THAT THEY'RE SETTING OFF "BIG DADDY!"
GREAT! WHEN THAT MONSTER IS THROUGH SCREAMING, WE'LL BE RUNNING THIS COUNTRY FOR THE "CHOSEN" ELITE!
IT'LL MEAN MOPPING UP 200 MILLION RAVING KOOKS--BUT, IT WON'T BE AS TOUGH AS IT SOUNDS!
200 MILLION FLUNKIES, TO FETCH AND CARRY FOR US AND THE ELITE!! WE'LL LIVE LIKE KINGS, PAL!
IT HASN'T HAPPENED YET, YOU SCHEMING DUM-DUMS!
KRAAK!!

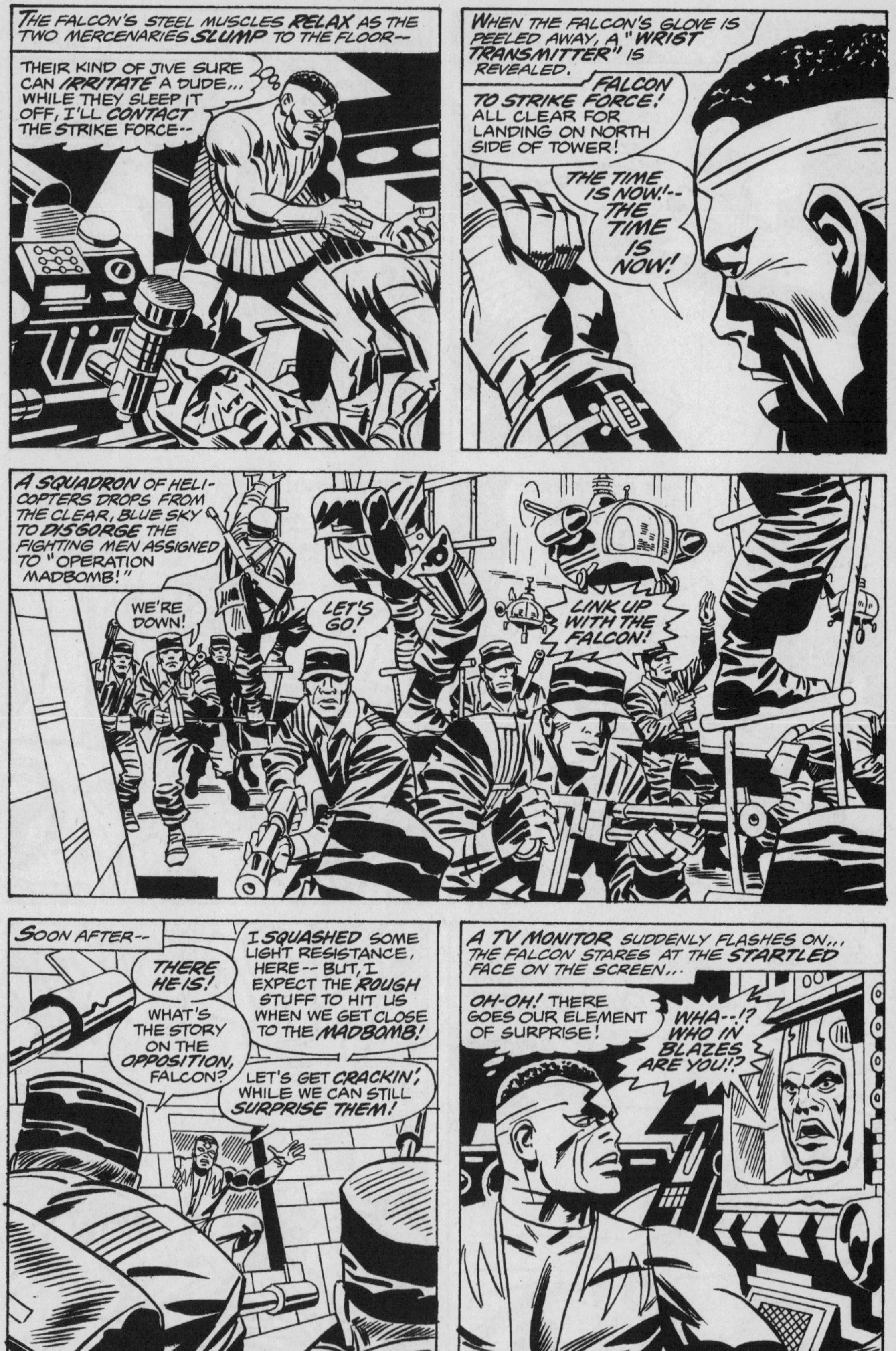
THE FALCON'S STEEL MUSCLES RELAX AS THE TWO MERCENARIES SLUMP TO THE FLOOR--
THEIR KIND OF JIVE SURE CAN IRRITATE A DUDE... WHILE THEY SLEEP IT OFF, I'LL CONTACT THE STRIKE FORCE--
WHEN THE FALCON'S GLOVE IS PEELED AWAY, A "WRIST TRANSMITTER" IS REVEALED.
FALCON TO STRIKE FORCE! ALL CLEAR FOR LANDING ON NORTH SIDE OF TOWER!
THE TIME IS NOW!-- THE TIME IS NOW!
A SQUADRON OF HELICOPTERS DROPS FROM THE CLEAR, BLUE SKY TO DISGORGE THE FIGHTING MEN ASSIGNED TO "OPERATION MADBOMB!"
WE'RE DOWN!
LET'S GO!
LINK UP WITH THE FALCON!
SOON AFTER--
THERE HE IS!
WHAT'S THE STORY ON THE OPPOSITION, FALCON?
I SQUASHED SOME LIGHT RESISTANCE, HERE-- BUT, I EXPECT THE ROUGH STUFF TO HIT US WHEN WE GET CLOSE TO THE MADBOMB!
LET'S GET CRACKIN', WHILE WE CAN STILL SURPRISE THEM!
A TV MONITOR SUDDENLY FLASHES ON... THE FALCON STARES AT THE STARTLED FACE ON THE SCREEN...
OH-OH! THERE GOES OUR ELEMENT OF SURPRISE!
WHA--!? WHO IN BLAZES ARE YOU!?

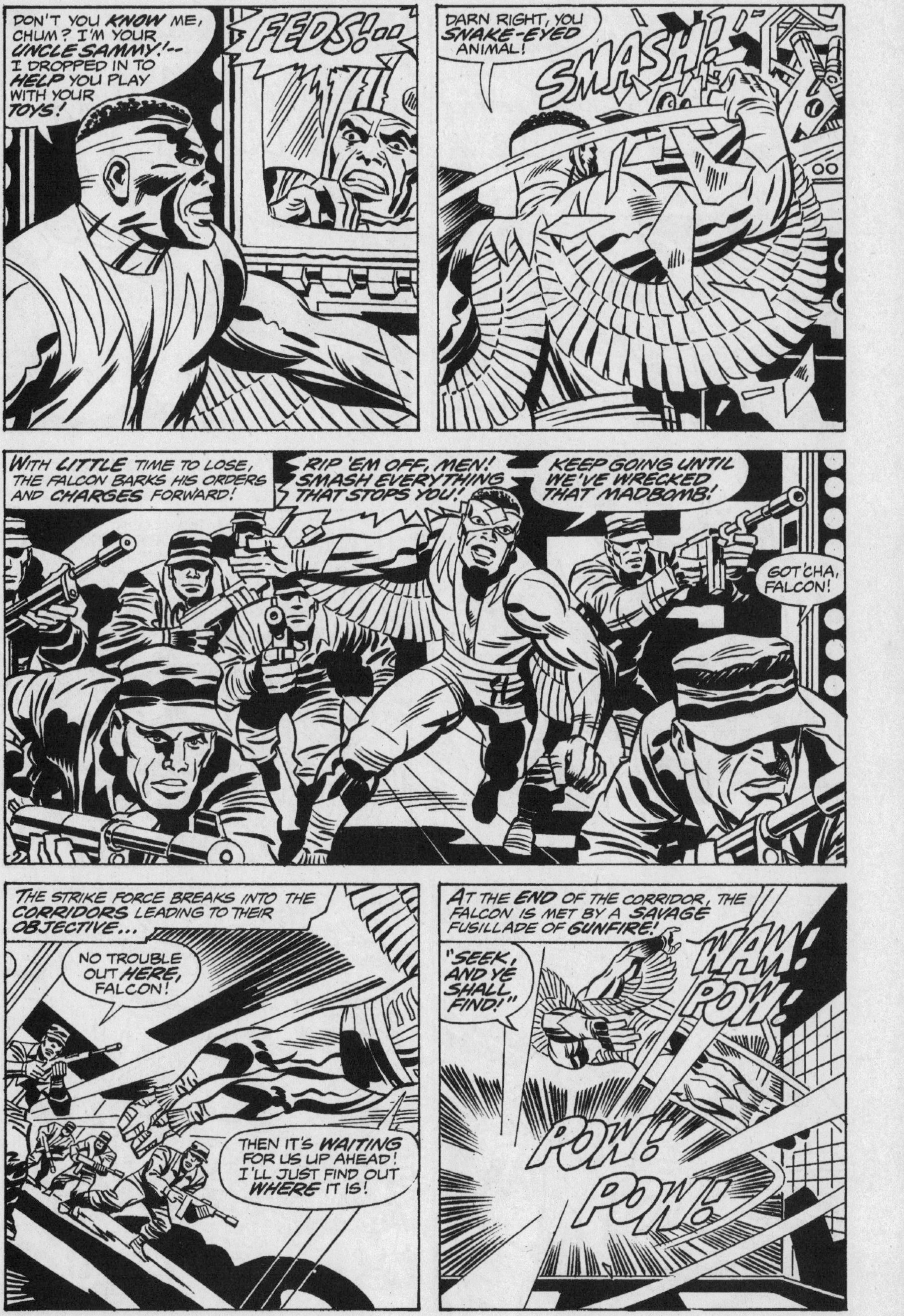
DON'T YOU KNOW ME, CHUM? I'M YOUR UNCLE SAMMY!-- I DROPPED IN TO HELP YOU PLAY WITH YOUR TOYS!
FEDS!
DARN RIGHT, YOU SNAKE-EYED ANIMAL!
SMASH!
WITH LITTLE TIME TO LOSE, THE FALCON BARKS HIS ORDERS AND CHARGES FORWARD!
RIP 'EM OFF, MEN! SMASH EVERYTHING THAT STOPS YOU!
KEEP GOING UNTIL WE'VE WRECKED THAT MADBOMB!
GOT'CHA, FALCON!
THE STRIKE FORCE BREAKS INTO THE CORRIDORS LEADING TO THEIR OBJECTIVE...
NO TROUBLE OUT HERE, FALCON!
THEN IT'S WAITING FOR US UP AHEAD! I'LL JUST FIND OUT WHERE IT IS!
AT THE END OF THE CORRIDOR, THE FALCON IS MET BY A SAVAGE FUSILLADE OF GUNFIRE!
"SEEK, AND YE SHALL FIND!"
WAM!
POW!
POW!
POW!

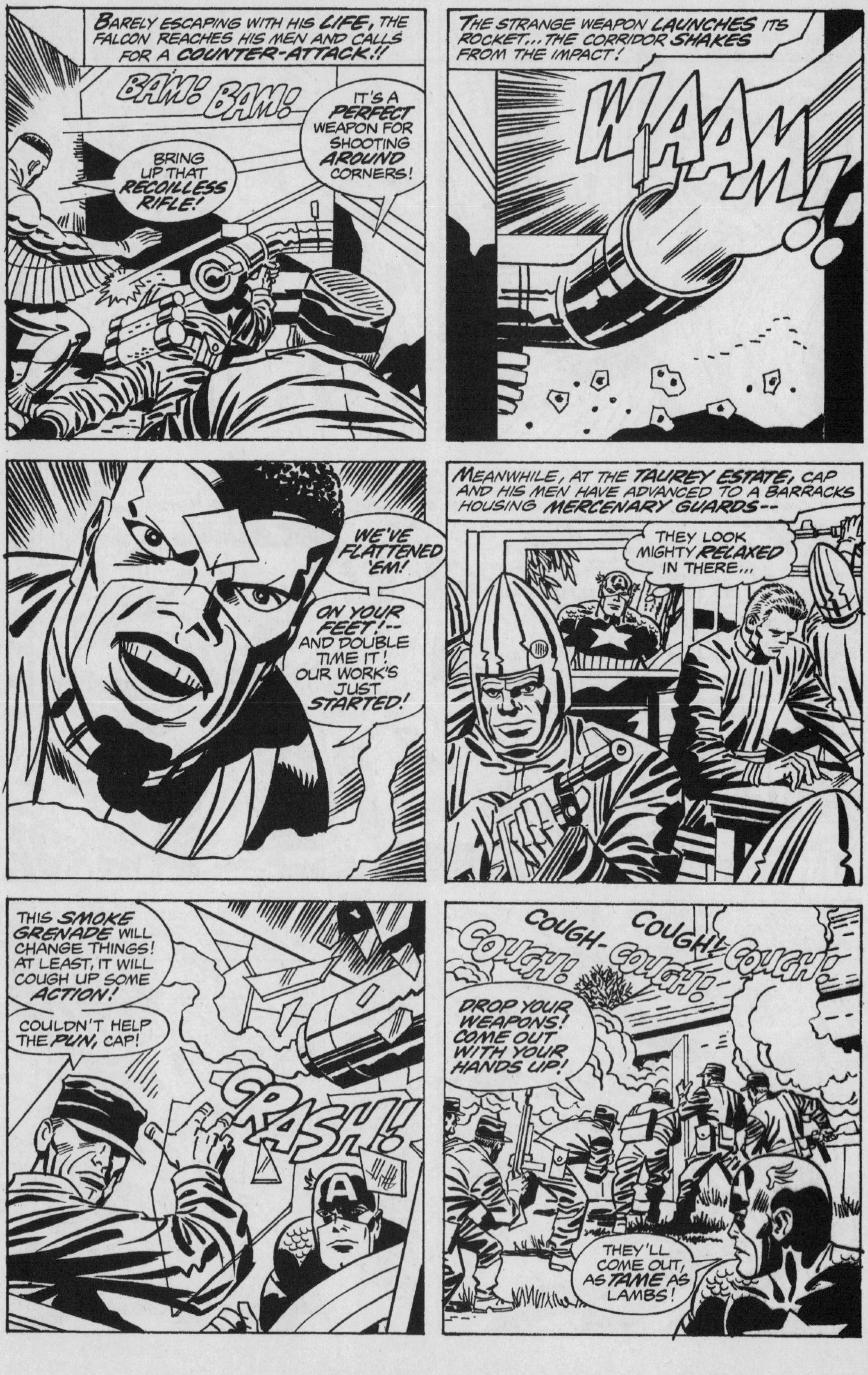
BARELY ESCAPING WITH HIS LIFE, THE FALCON REACHES HIS MEN AND CALLS FOR A COUNTER-ATTACK!!
BAM! BAM!
BRING UP THAT RECOILLESS RIFLE!
IT'S A PERFECT WEAPON FOR SHOOTING AROUND CORNERS!
THE STRANGE WEAPON LAUNCHES ITS ROCKET... THE CORRIDOR SHAKES FROM THE IMPACT!
WAAM!!
WE'VE FLATTENED 'EM!
ON YOUR FEET!-- AND DOUBLE TIME IT! OUR WORK'S JUST STARTED!
MEANWHILE, AT THE TAUREY ESTATE, CAP AND HIS MEN HAVE ADVANCED TO A BARRACKS HOUSING MERCENARY GUARDS--
THEY LOOK MIGHTY RELAXED IN THERE...
THIS SMOKE GRENADE WILL CHANGE THINGS! AT LEAST, IT WILL COUGH UP SOME ACTION!
COULDN'T HELP THE PUN, CAP!
CRASH!
COUGH! COUGH- COUGH! COUGH! COUGH! COUGH!
DROP YOUR WEAPONS! COME OUT WITH YOUR HANDS UP!
THEY'LL COME OUT, AS TAME AS LAMBS!

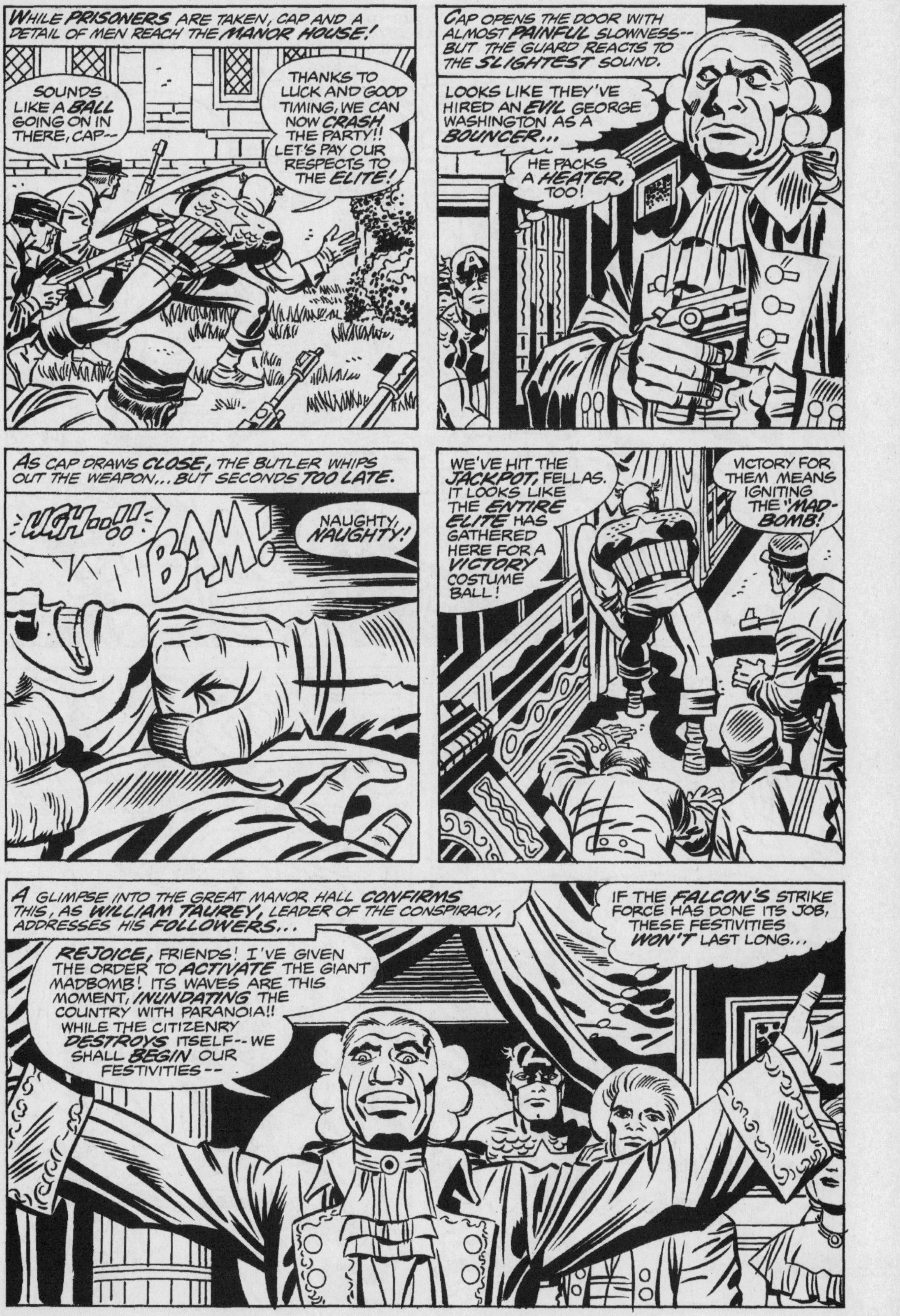
WHILE PRISONERS ARE TAKEN, CAP AND A DETAIL OF MEN REACH THE MANOR HOUSE!
SOUNDS LIKE A BALL GOING ON IN THERE, CAP--
THANKS TO LUCK AND GOOD TIMING, WE CAN NOW CRASH THE PARTY!! LET'S PAY OUR RESPECTS TO THE ELITE!
CAP OPENS THE DOOR WITH ALMOST PAINFUL SLOWNESS-- BUT THE GUARD REACTS TO THE SLIGHTEST SOUND.
LOOKS LIKE THEY'VE HIRED AN EVIL GEORGE WASHINGTON AS A BOUNCER...
HE PACKS A HEATER, TOO!
AS CAP DRAWS CLOSE, THE BUTLER WHIPS OUT THE WEAPON... BUT SECONDS TOO LATE.
UGHooo!!
BAM!
NAUGHTY, NAUGHTY!
WE'VE HIT THE JACKPOT, FELLAS. IT LOOKS LIKE THE ENTIRE ELITE HAS GATHERED HERE FOR A VICTORY COSTUME BALL!
VICTORY FOR THEM MEANS IGNITING THE "MAD-BOMB!
A GLIMPSE INTO THE GREAT MANOR HALL CONFIRMS THIS, AS WILLIAM TAUREY, LEADER OF THE CONSPIRACY, ADDRESSES HIS FOLLOWERS...
IF THE FALCON'S STRIKE FORCE HAS DONE ITS JOB, THESE FESTIVITIES WON'T LAST LONG...
REJOICE, FRIENDS! I'VE GIVEN THE ORDER TO ACTIVATE THE GIANT MADBOMB! ITS WAVES ARE THIS MOMENT, INUNDATING THE COUNTRY WITH PARANOIA!! WHILE THE CITIZENRY DESTROYS ITSELF--WE SHALL BEGIN OUR FESTIVITIES--

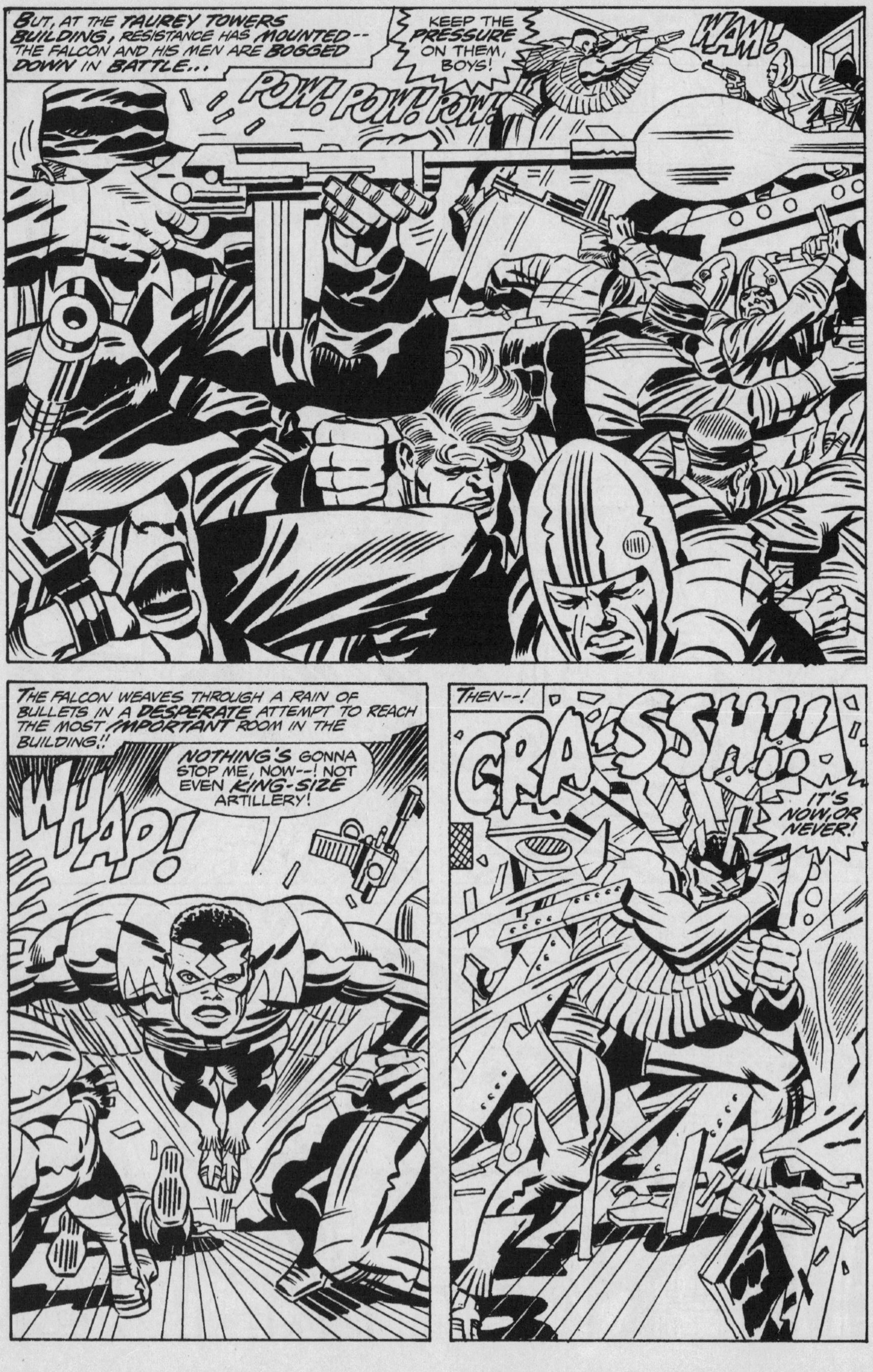

BUT, AT THE TAUREY TOWERS BUILDING, RESISTANCE HAS MOUNTED-- THE FALCON AND HIS MEN ARE BOGGED DOWN IN BATTLE...
KEEP THE PRESSURE ON THEM, BOYS!
WAM!
POW! POW! POW!
THE FALCON WEAVES THROUGH A RAIN OF BULLETS IN A DESPERATE ATTEMPT TO REACH THE MOST IMPORTANT ROOM IN THE BUILDING!!
NOTHING'S GONNA STOP ME, NOW--! NOT EVEN KING-SIZE ARTILLERY!
WHAP!
THEN--!
CRA-SSH!!
IT'S NOW, OR NEVER!

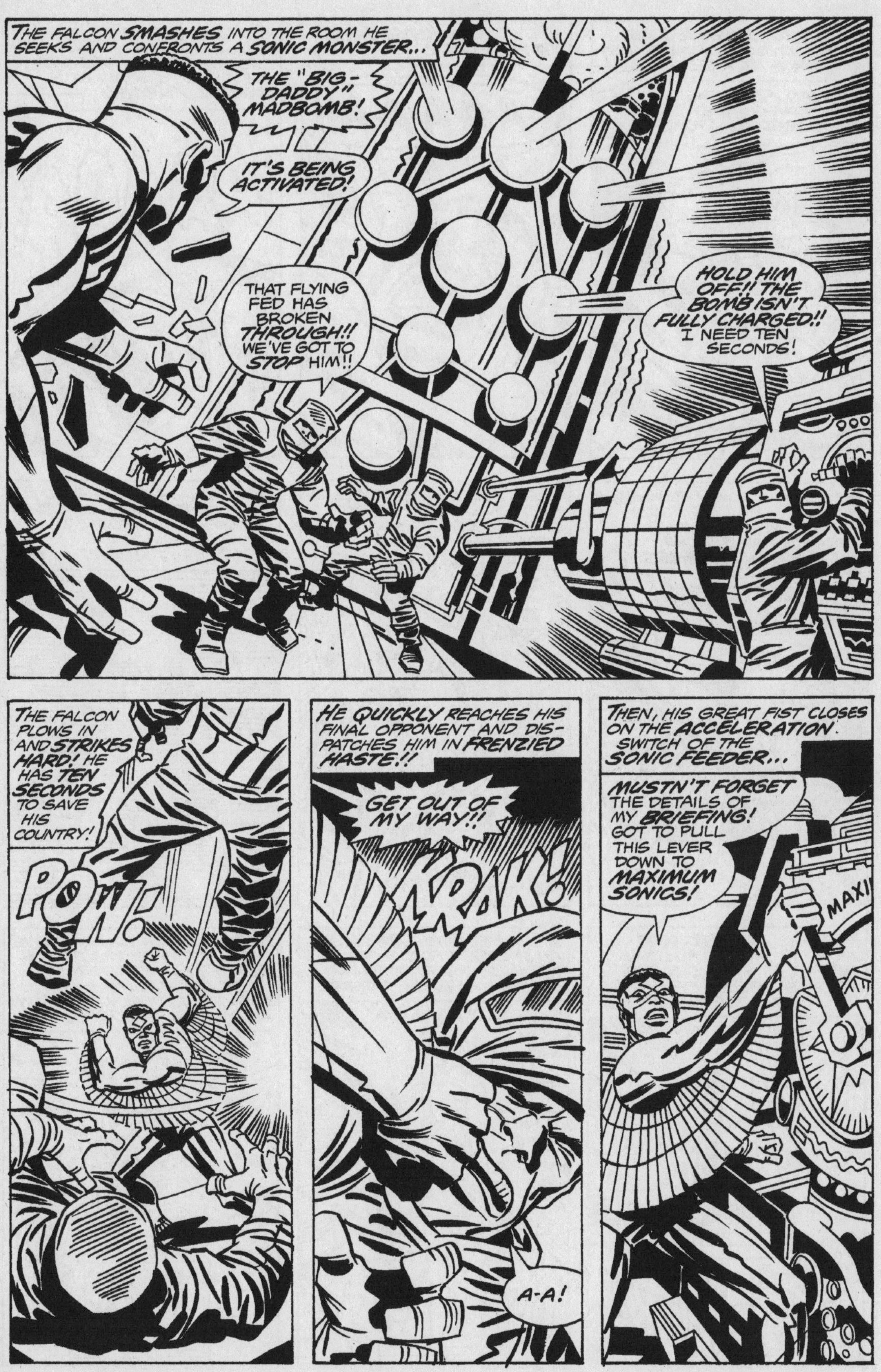
THE FALCON SMASHES INTO THE ROOM HE SEEKS AND CONFRONTS A SONIC MONSTER...
THE "BIG-DADDY" MADBOMB!
IT'S BEING ACTIVATED!
THAT FLYING FED HAS BROKEN THROUGH!! WE'VE GOT TO STOP HIM!!
HOLD HIM OFF!! THE BOMB ISN'T FULLY CHARGED!! I NEED TEN SECONDS!
THE FALCON PLOWS IN AND STRIKES HARD! HE HAS TEN SECONDS TO SAVE HIS COUNTRY!
POW!
HE QUICKLY REACHES HIS FINAL OPPONENT AND DISPATCHES HIM IN FRENZIED HASTE!!
GET OUT OF MY WAY!!
KRAK!
A-A!
THEN, HIS GREAT FIST CLOSES ON THE ACCELERATION SWITCH OF THE SONIC FEEDER...
MUSTN'T FORGET THE DETAILS OF MY BRIEFING! GOT TO PULL THIS LEVER DOWN TO MAXIMUM SONICS!
MAXI

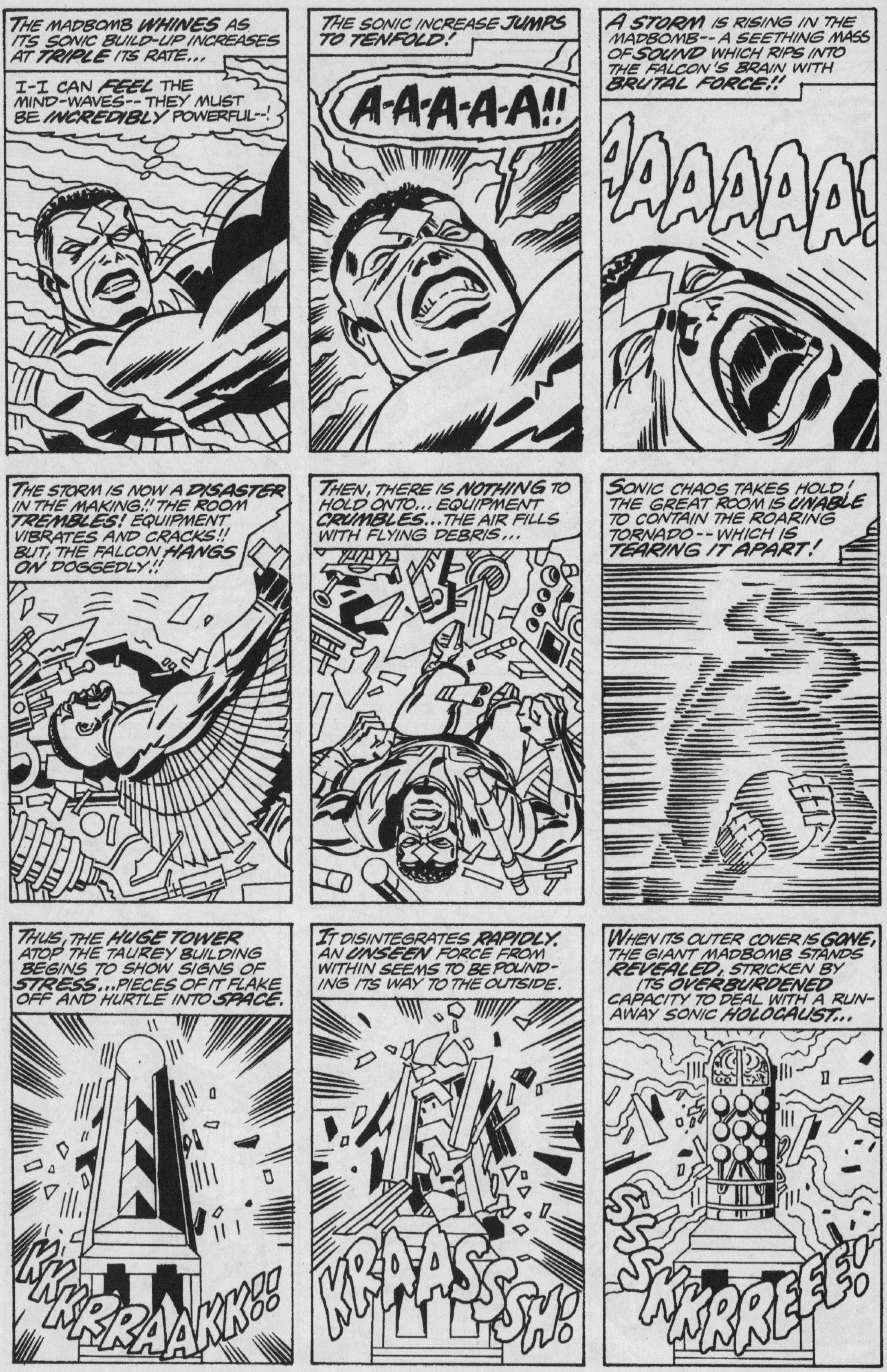
THE MADBOMB WHINES AS ITS SONIC BUILD-UP INCREASES AT TRIPLE ITS RATE...
I-I CAN FEEL THE MIND-WAVES--THEY MUST BE INCREDIBLY POWERFUL--!
THE SONIC INCREASE JUMPS TO TENFOLD!
A-A-A-A-A!!
A STORM IS RISING IN THE MADBOMB--A SEETHING MASS OF SOUND WHICH RIPS INTO THE FALCON'S BRAIN WITH BRUTAL FORCE!!
AAAAAAA!
THE STORM IS NOW A DISASTER IN THE MAKING!! THE ROOM TREMBLES! EQUIPMENT VIBRATES AND CRACKS!! BUT, THE FALCON HANGS ON DOGGEDLY!!
THEN, THERE IS NOTHING TO HOLD ONTO... EQUIPMENT CRUMBLES...THE AIR FILLS WITH FLYING DEBRIS...
SONIC CHAOS TAKES HOLD! THE GREAT ROOM IS UNABLE TO CONTAIN THE ROARING TORNADO--WHICH IS TEARING IT APART!
THUS, THE HUGE TOWER ATOP THE TAUREY BUILDING BEGINS TO SHOW SIGNS OF STRESS...PIECES OF IT FLAKE OFF AND HURTLE INTO SPACE.
KKKRRAAKK!!
IT DISINTEGRATES RAPIDLY. AN UNSEEN FORCE FROM WITHIN SEEMS TO BE POUNDING ITS WAY TO THE OUTSIDE.
KRAASSSH!
WHEN ITS OUTER COVER IS GONE, THE GIANT MADBOMB STANDS REVEALED, STRICKEN BY ITS OVERBURDENED CAPACITY TO DEAL WITH A RUN-AWAY SONIC HOLOCAUST...
SSSKKRREEE!

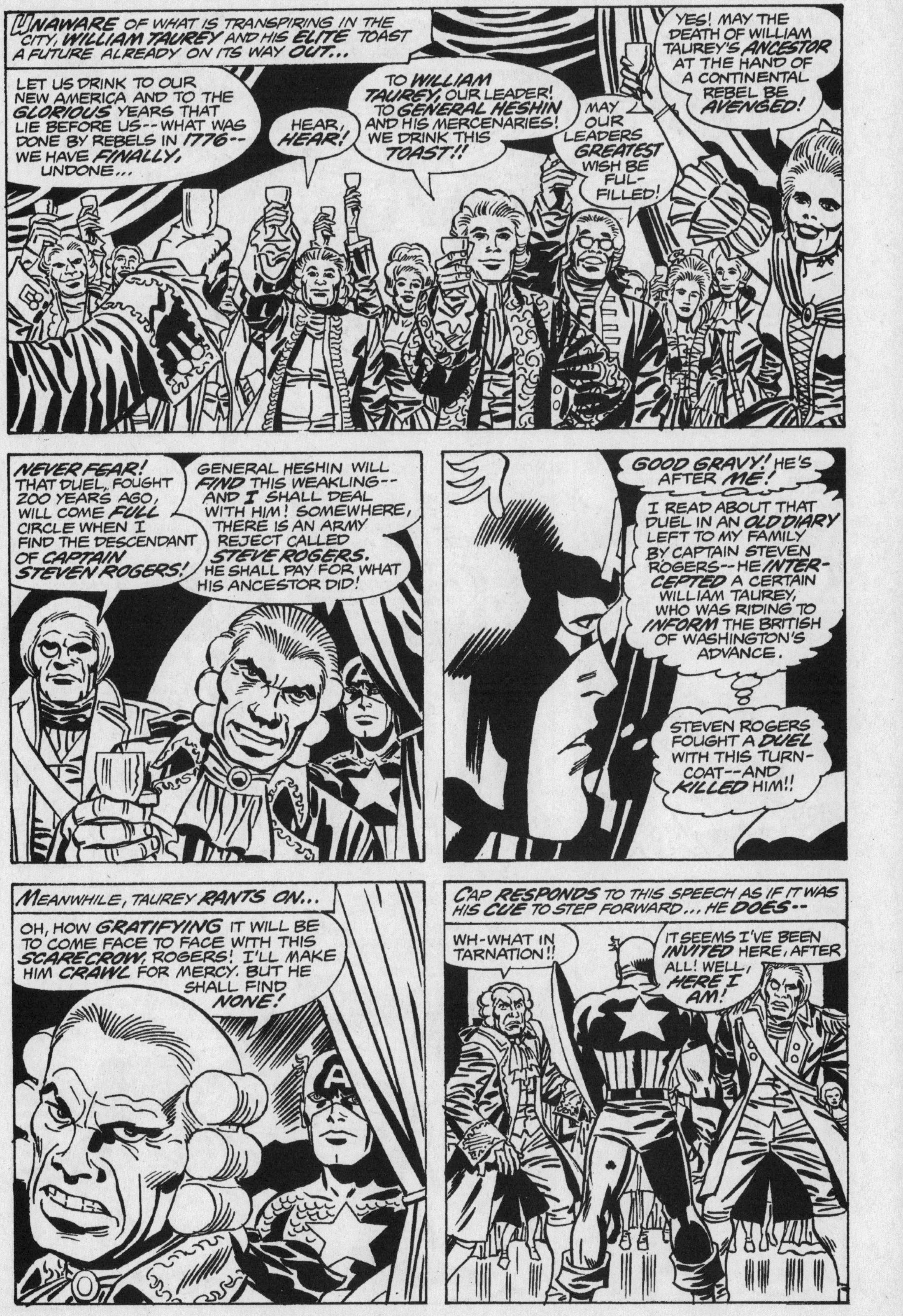
UNAWARE OF WHAT IS TRANSPIRING IN THE CITY, WILLIAM TAUREY AND HIS ELITE TOAST A FUTURE ALREADY ON ITS WAY OUT...
LET US DRINK TO OUR NEW AMERICA AND TO THE GLORIOUS YEARS THAT LIE BEFORE US-- WHAT WAS DONE BY REBELS IN 1776-- WE HAVE FINALLY, UNDONE...
HEAR, HEAR!
TO WILLIAM TAUREY, OUR LEADER! TO GENERAL HESHIN AND HIS MERCENARIES! WE DRINK THIS TOAST!!
MAY OUR LEADERS GREATEST WISH BE FUL-FILLED!
YES! MAY THE DEATH OF WILLIAM TAUREY'S ANCESTOR AT THE HAND OF A CONTINENTAL REBEL BE AVENGED!
NEVER FEAR! THAT DUEL, FOUGHT 200 YEARS AGO, WILL COME FULL CIRCLE WHEN I FIND THE DESCENDANT OF CAPTAIN STEVEN ROGERS!
GENERAL HESHIN WILL FIND THIS WEAKLING-- AND I SHALL DEAL WITH HIM! SOMEWHERE, THERE IS AN ARMY REJECT CALLED STEVE ROGERS. HE SHALL PAY FOR WHAT HIS ANCESTOR DID!
GOOD GRAVY! HE'S AFTER ME!
I READ ABOUT THAT DUEL IN AN OLD DIARY LEFT TO MY FAMILY BY CAPTAIN STEVEN ROGERS-- HE INTER-CEPTED A CERTAIN WILLIAM TAUREY, WHO WAS RIDING TO INFORM THE BRITISH OF WASHINGTON'S ADVANCE.
STEVEN ROGERS FOUGHT A DUEL WITH THIS TURN-COAT--AND KILLED HIM!!
MEANWHILE, TAUREY RANTS ON...
OH, HOW GRATIFYING IT WILL BE TO COME FACE TO FACE WITH THIS SCARECROW, ROGERS! I'LL MAKE HIM CRAWL FOR MERCY. BUT HE SHALL FIND NONE!
CAP RESPONDS TO THIS SPEECH AS IF IT WAS HIS CUE TO STEP FORWARD... HE DOES--
WH-WHAT IN TARNATION!!
IT SEEMS I'VE BEEN INVITED HERE, AFTER ALL! WELL, HERE I AM!

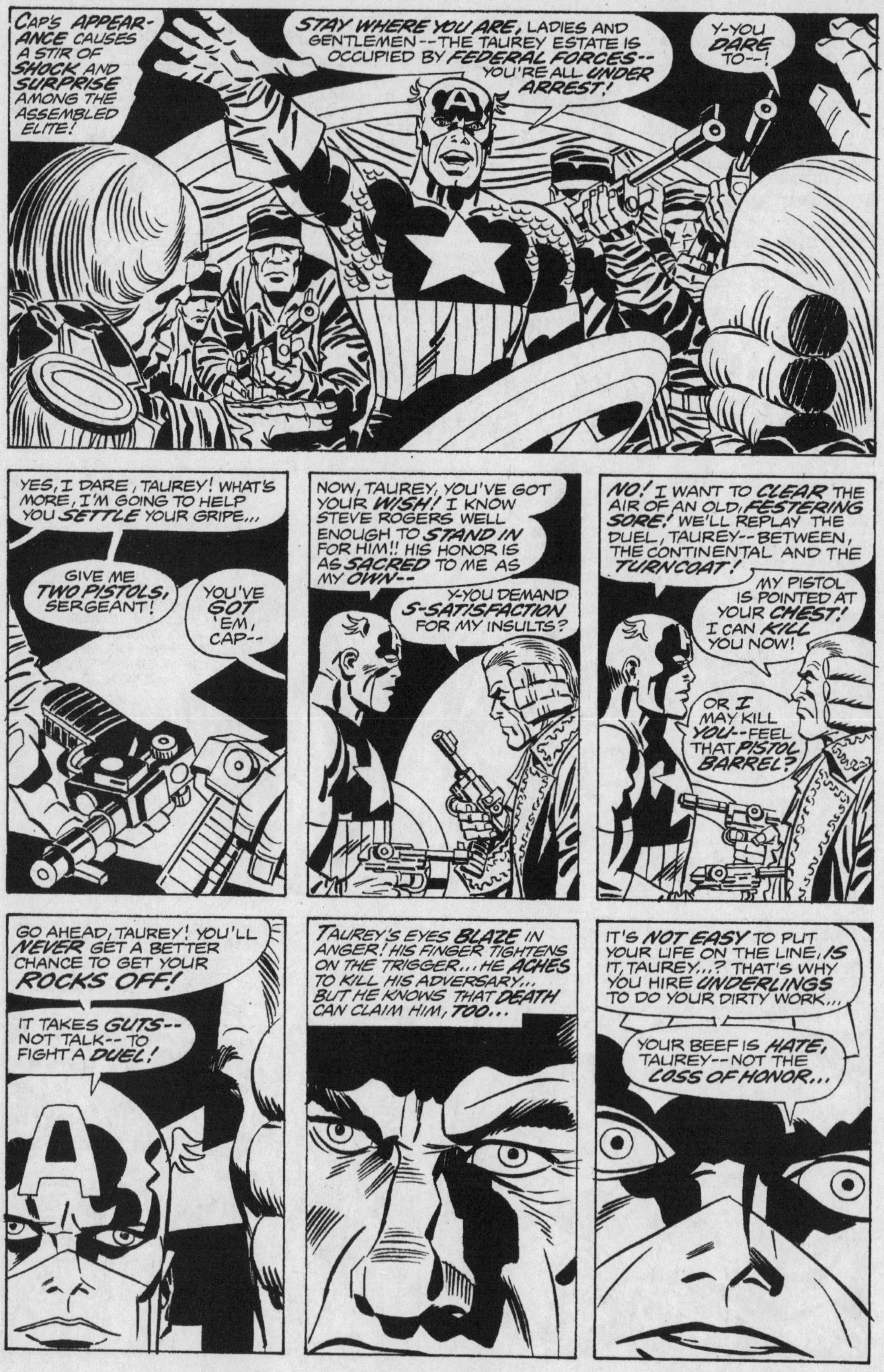
CAP'S APPEARANCE CAUSES A STIR OF SHOCK AND SURPRISE AMONG THE ASSEMBLED ELITE!
STAY WHERE YOU ARE, LADIES AND GENTLEMEN--THE TAUREY ESTATE IS OCCUPIED BY FEDERAL FORCES--YOU'RE ALL UNDER ARREST!
Y-YOU DARE TO--!
YES, I DARE, TAUREY! WHAT'S MORE, I'M GOING TO HELP YOU SETTLE YOUR GRIPE...
GIVE ME TWO PISTOLS, SERGEANT!
YOU'VE GOT 'EM, CAP--
NOW, TAUREY, YOU'VE GOT YOUR WISH! I KNOW STEVE ROGERS WELL ENOUGH TO STAND IN FOR HIM!! HIS HONOR IS AS SACRED TO ME AS MY OWN--
Y-YOU DEMAND S-SATISFACTION FOR MY INSULTS?
NO! I WANT TO CLEAR THE AIR OF AN OLD, FESTERING SORE! WE'LL REPLAY THE DUEL, TAUREY--BETWEEN, THE CONTINENTAL AND THE TURNCOAT!
MY PISTOL IS POINTED AT YOUR CHEST! I CAN KILL YOU NOW!
OR I MAY KILL YOU--FEEL THAT PISTOL BARREL?
GO AHEAD, TAUREY! YOU'LL NEVER GET A BETTER CHANCE TO GET YOUR ROCKS OFF!
IT TAKES GUTS--NOT TALK--TO FIGHT A DUEL!
TAUREY'S EYES BLAZE IN ANGER! HIS FINGER TIGHTENS ON THE TRIGGER... HE ACHES TO KILL HIS ADVERSARY... BUT HE KNOWS THAT DEATH CAN CLAIM HIM, TOO...
IT'S NOT EASY TO PUT YOUR LIFE ON THE LINE, IS IT, TAUREY...? THAT'S WHY YOU HIRE UNDERLINGS TO DO YOUR DIRTY WORK...
YOUR BEEF IS HATE, TAUREY--NOT THE LOSS OF HONOR...

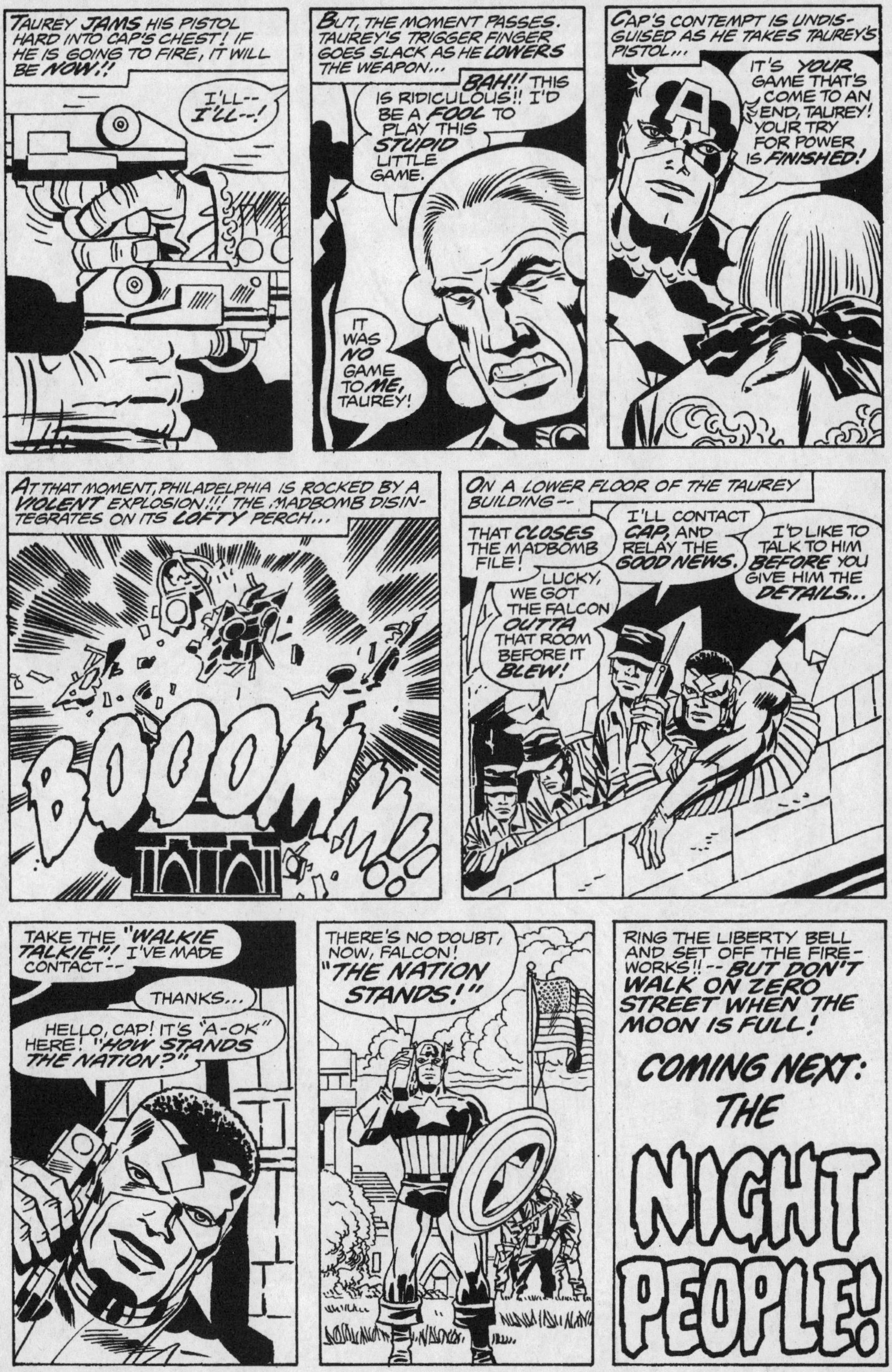
TAUREY JAMS HIS PISTOL HARD INTO CAP'S CHEST! IF HE IS GOING TO FIRE, IT WILL BE NOW!!
I'LL-- I'LL--!
BUT, THE MOMENT PASSES. TAUREY'S TRIGGER FINGER GOES SLACK AS HE LOWERS THE WEAPON...
BAH!! THIS IS RIDICULOUS!! I'D BE A FOOL TO PLAY THIS STUPID LITTLE GAME.
IT WAS NO GAME TO ME, TAUREY!
CAP'S CONTEMPT IS UNDISGUISED AS HE TAKES TAUREY'S PISTOL...
IT'S YOUR GAME THAT'S COME TO AN END, TAUREY! YOUR TRY FOR POWER IS FINISHED!
AT THAT MOMENT, PHILADELPHIA IS ROCKED BY A VIOLENT EXPLOSION!!! THE MADBOMB DISINTEGRATES ON ITS LOFTY PERCH...
BOOOMM!!
ON A LOWER FLOOR OF THE TAUREY BUILDING--
THAT CLOSES THE MADBOMB FILE!
I'LL CONTACT CAP, AND RELAY THE GOOD NEWS.
LUCKY, WE GOT THE FALCON OUTTA THAT ROOM BEFORE IT BLEW!
I'D LIKE TO TALK TO HIM BEFORE YOU GIVE HIM THE DETAILS...
TAKE THE "WALKIE TALKIE"! I'VE MADE CONTACT--
THANKS...
HELLO, CAP! IT'S "A-OK" HERE! "HOW STANDS THE NATION?"
THERE'S NO DOUBT, NOW, FALCON! "THE NATION STANDS!"
RING THE LIBERTY BELL AND SET OFF THE FIREWORKS!! -- BUT DON'T WALK ON ZERO STREET WHEN THE MOON IS FULL!
COMING NEXT: THE NIGHT PEOPLE!

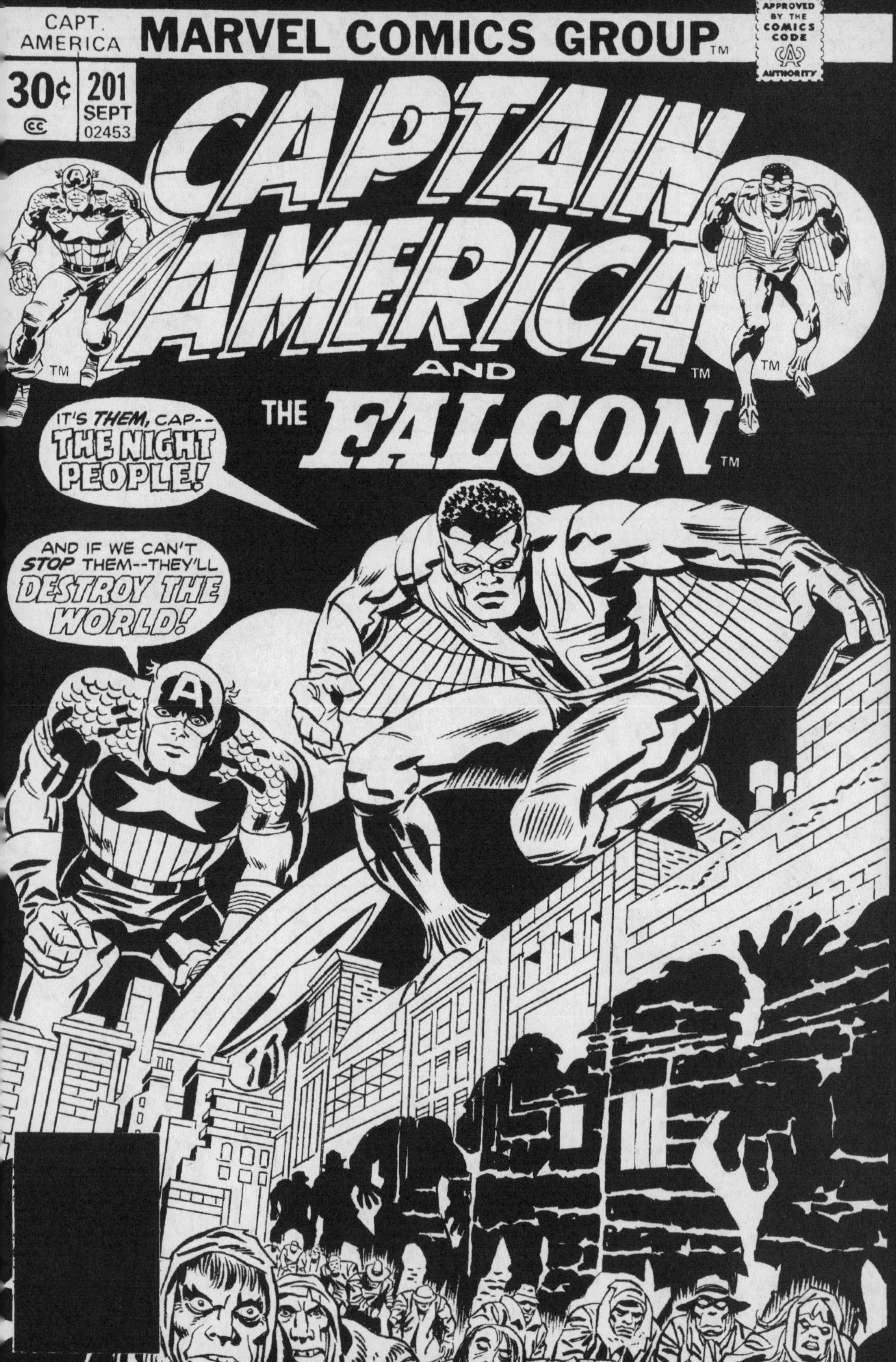
CAPT. AMERICA
MARVEL COMICS GROUP™
APPROVED BY THE COMICS CODE AUTHORITY
30¢
201
SEPT
02453
CAPTAIN AMERICA™
AND
THE FALCON™
IT'S THEM, CAP-- THE NIGHT PEOPLE!
AND IF WE CAN'T STOP THEM--THEY'LL DESTROY THE WORLD!

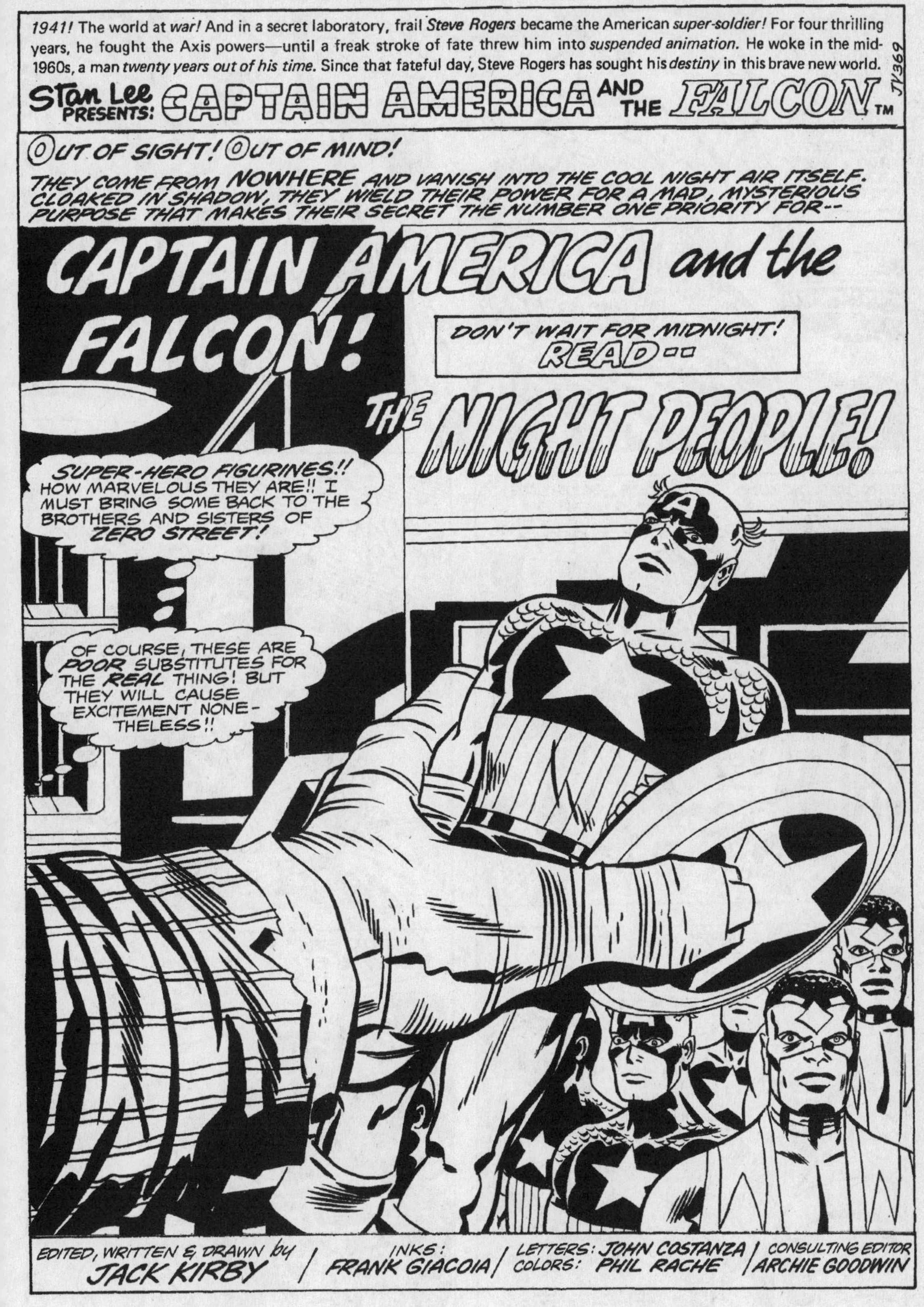

1941! The world at war! And in a secret laboratory, frail Steve Rogers became the American super-soldier! For four thrilling years, he fought the Axis powers—until a freak stroke of fate threw him into suspended animation. He woke in the mid-1960s, a man twenty years out of his time. Since that fateful day, Steve Rogers has sought his destiny in this brave new world.
STAN LEE PRESENTS: CAPTAIN AMERICA AND THE FALCON™
JV369
OUT OF SIGHT! OUT OF MIND!
THEY COME FROM NOWHERE AND VANISH INTO THE COOL NIGHT AIR ITSELF. CLOAKED IN SHADOW, THEY WIELD THEIR POWER FOR A MAD, MYSTERIOUS PURPOSE THAT MAKES THEIR SECRET THE NUMBER ONE PRIORITY FOR--
CAPTAIN AMERICA and the FALCON!
DON'T WAIT FOR MIDNIGHT! READ--
THE NIGHT PEOPLE!
SUPER-HERO FIGURINES!! HOW MARVELOUS THEY ARE!! I MUST BRING SOME BACK TO THE BROTHERS AND SISTERS OF ZERO STREET!
OF COURSE, THESE ARE POOR SUBSTITUTES FOR THE REAL THING! BUT THEY WILL CAUSE EXCITEMENT NONE-THELESS!!
EDITED, WRITTEN & DRAWN by JACK KIRBY | INKS: FRANK GIACOIA | LETTERS: JOHN COSTANZA COLORS: PHIL RACHE | CONSULTING EDITOR ARCHIE GOODWIN

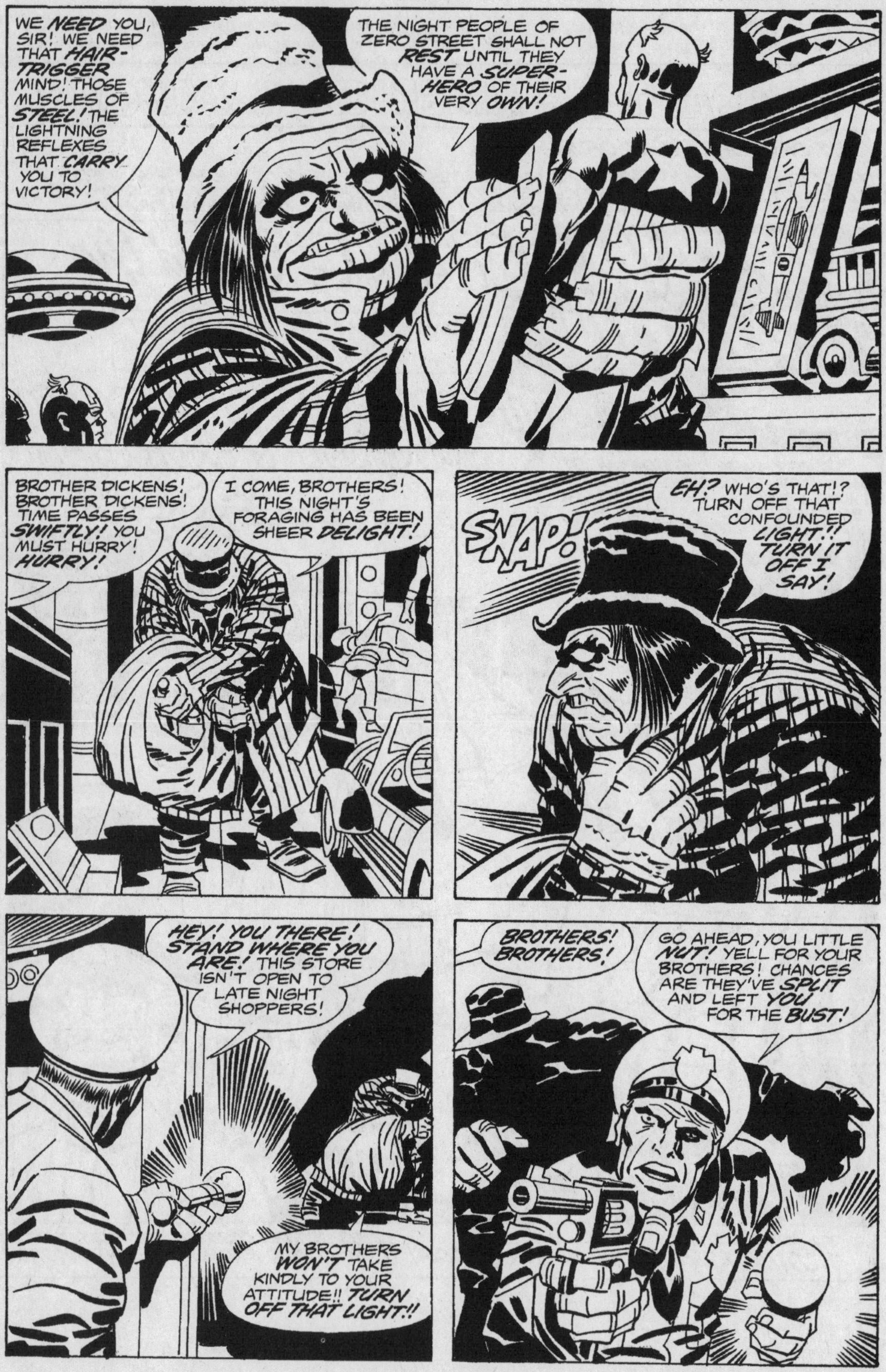
WE NEED YOU, SIR! WE NEED THAT HAIR-TRIGGER MIND! THOSE MUSCLES OF STEEL! THE LIGHTNING REFLEXES THAT CARRY YOU TO VICTORY!
THE NIGHT PEOPLE OF ZERO STREET SHALL NOT REST UNTIL THEY HAVE A SUPER-HERO OF THEIR VERY OWN!
BROTHER DICKENS! BROTHER DICKENS! TIME PASSES SWIFTLY! YOU MUST HURRY! HURRY!
I COME, BROTHERS! THIS NIGHT'S FORAGING HAS BEEN SHEER DELIGHT!
SNAP!
EH? WHO'S THAT!? TURN OFF THAT CONFOUNDED LIGHT!! TURN IT OFF I SAY!
HEY! YOU THERE! STAND WHERE YOU ARE! THIS STORE ISN'T OPEN TO LATE NIGHT SHOPPERS!
MY BROTHERS WON'T TAKE KINDLY TO YOUR ATTITUDE!! TURN OFF THAT LIGHT!!
BROTHERS! BROTHERS!
GO AHEAD, YOU LITTLE NUT! YELL FOR YOUR BROTHERS! CHANCES ARE THEY'VE SPLIT AND LEFT YOU FOR THE BUST!

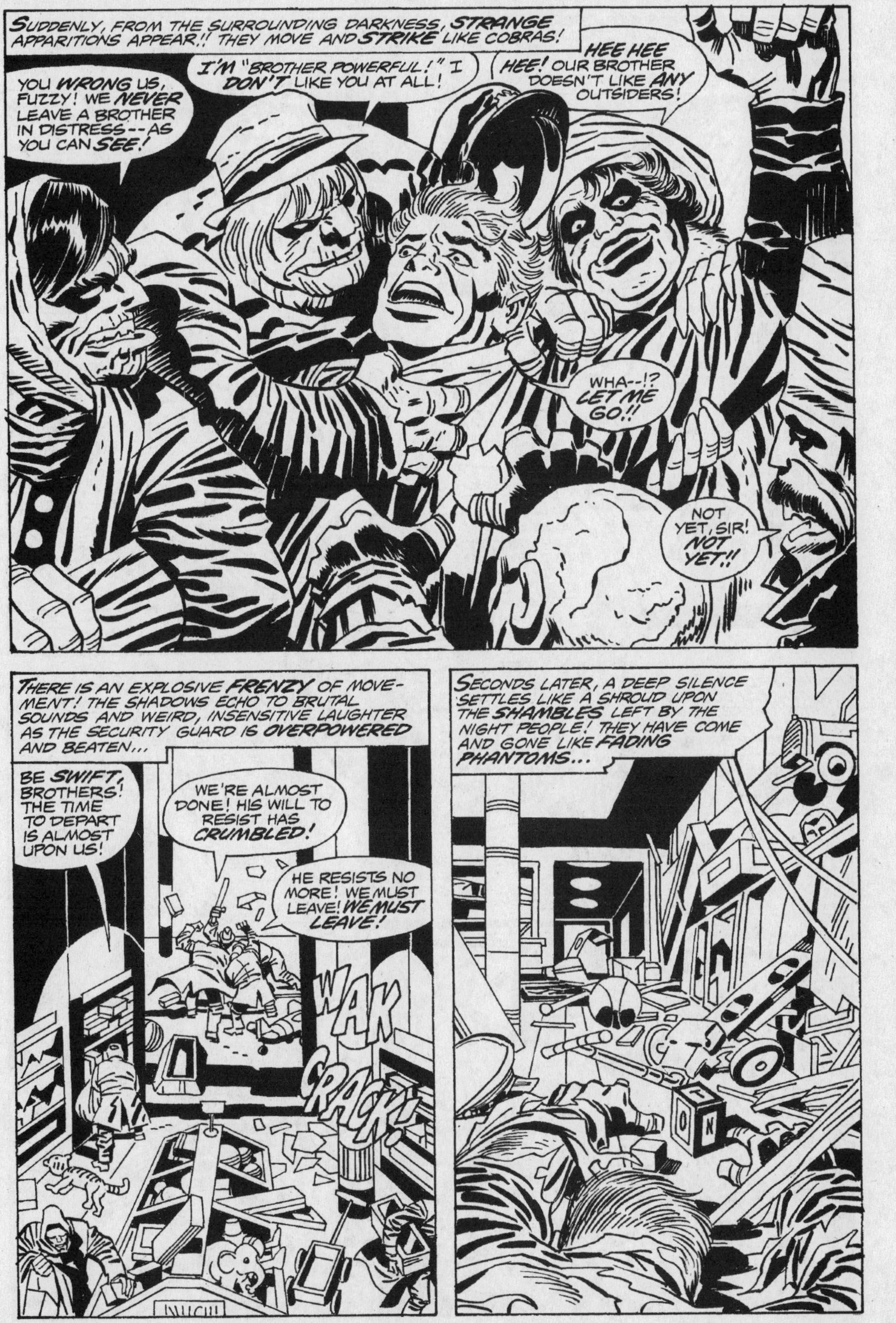
SUDDENLY, FROM THE SURROUNDING DARKNESS, STRANGE APPARITIONS APPEAR!! THEY MOVE AND STRIKE LIKE COBRAS!
YOU WRONG US, FUZZY! WE NEVER LEAVE A BROTHER IN DISTRESS--AS YOU CAN SEE!
I'M "BROTHER POWERFUL!" I DON'T LIKE YOU AT ALL!
HEE HEE HEE! OUR BROTHER DOESN'T LIKE ANY OUTSIDERS!
WHA--!? LET ME GO!!
NOT YET, SIR! NOT YET!!
THERE IS AN EXPLOSIVE FRENZY OF MOVEMENT! THE SHADOWS ECHO TO BRUTAL SOUNDS AND WEIRD, INSENSITIVE LAUGHTER AS THE SECURITY GUARD IS OVERPOWERED AND BEATEN...
BE SWIFT, BROTHERS! THE TIME TO DEPART IS ALMOST UPON US!
WE'RE ALMOST DONE! HIS WILL TO RESIST HAS CRUMBLED!
HE RESISTS NO MORE! WE MUST LEAVE! WE MUST LEAVE!
WAK
CRACK!
SECONDS LATER, A DEEP SILENCE SETTLES LIKE A SHROUD UPON THE SHAMBLES LEFT BY THE NIGHT PEOPLE! THEY HAVE COME AND GONE LIKE FADING PHANTOMS...

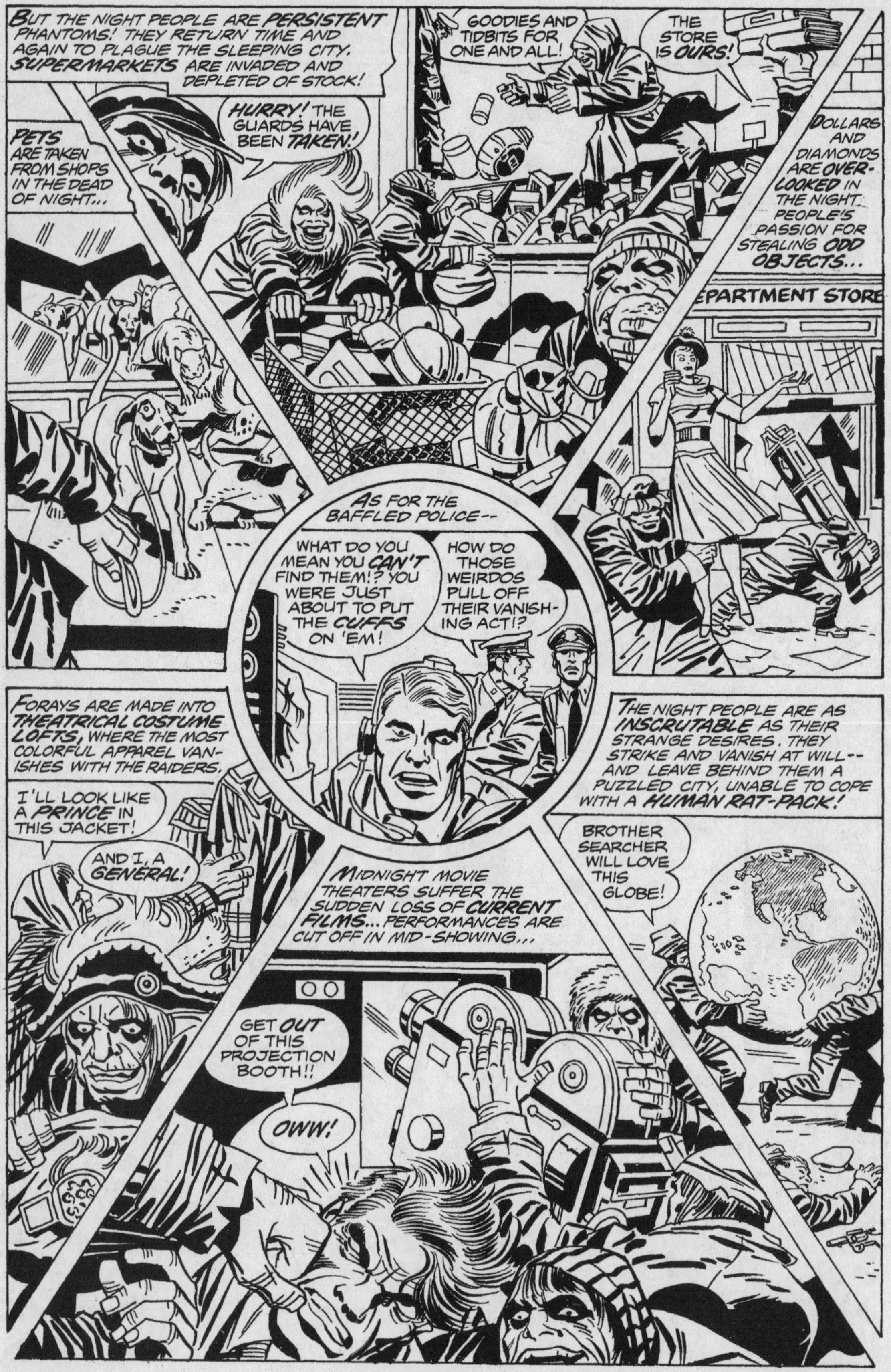

BUT THE NIGHT PEOPLE ARE PERSISTENT PHANTOMS! THEY RETURN TIME AND AGAIN TO PLAGUE THE SLEEPING CITY. SUPERMARKETS ARE INVADED AND DEPLETED OF STOCK!
GOODIES AND TIDBITS FOR ONE AND ALL!
THE STORE IS OURS!
HURRY! THE GUARDS HAVE BEEN TAKEN!
PETS ARE TAKEN FROM SHOPS IN THE DEAD OF NIGHT...
DOLLARS AND DIAMONDS ARE OVER-LOOKED IN THE NIGHT PEOPLE'S PASSION FOR STEALING ODD OBJECTS...
DEPARTMENT STORE
AS FOR THE BAFFLED POLICE--
WHAT DO YOU MEAN YOU CAN'T FIND THEM!? YOU WERE JUST ABOUT TO PUT THE CUFFS ON 'EM!
HOW DO THOSE WEIRDOS PULL OFF THEIR VANISHING ACT!?
FORAYS ARE MADE INTO THEATRICAL COSTUME LOFTS, WHERE THE MOST COLORFUL APPAREL VANISHES WITH THE RAIDERS.
I'LL LOOK LIKE A PRINCE IN THIS JACKET!
AND I, A GENERAL!
THE NIGHT PEOPLE ARE AS INSCRUTABLE AS THEIR STRANGE DESIRES. THEY STRIKE AND VANISH AT WILL-- AND LEAVE BEHIND THEM A PUZZLED CITY, UNABLE TO COPE WITH A HUMAN RAT-PACK!
BROTHER SEARCHER WILL LOVE THIS GLOBE!
MIDNIGHT MOVIE THEATERS SUFFER THE SUDDEN LOSS OF CURRENT FILMS... PERFORMANCES ARE CUT OFF IN MID-SHOWING...
GET OUT OF THIS PROJECTION BOOTH!!
OWW!

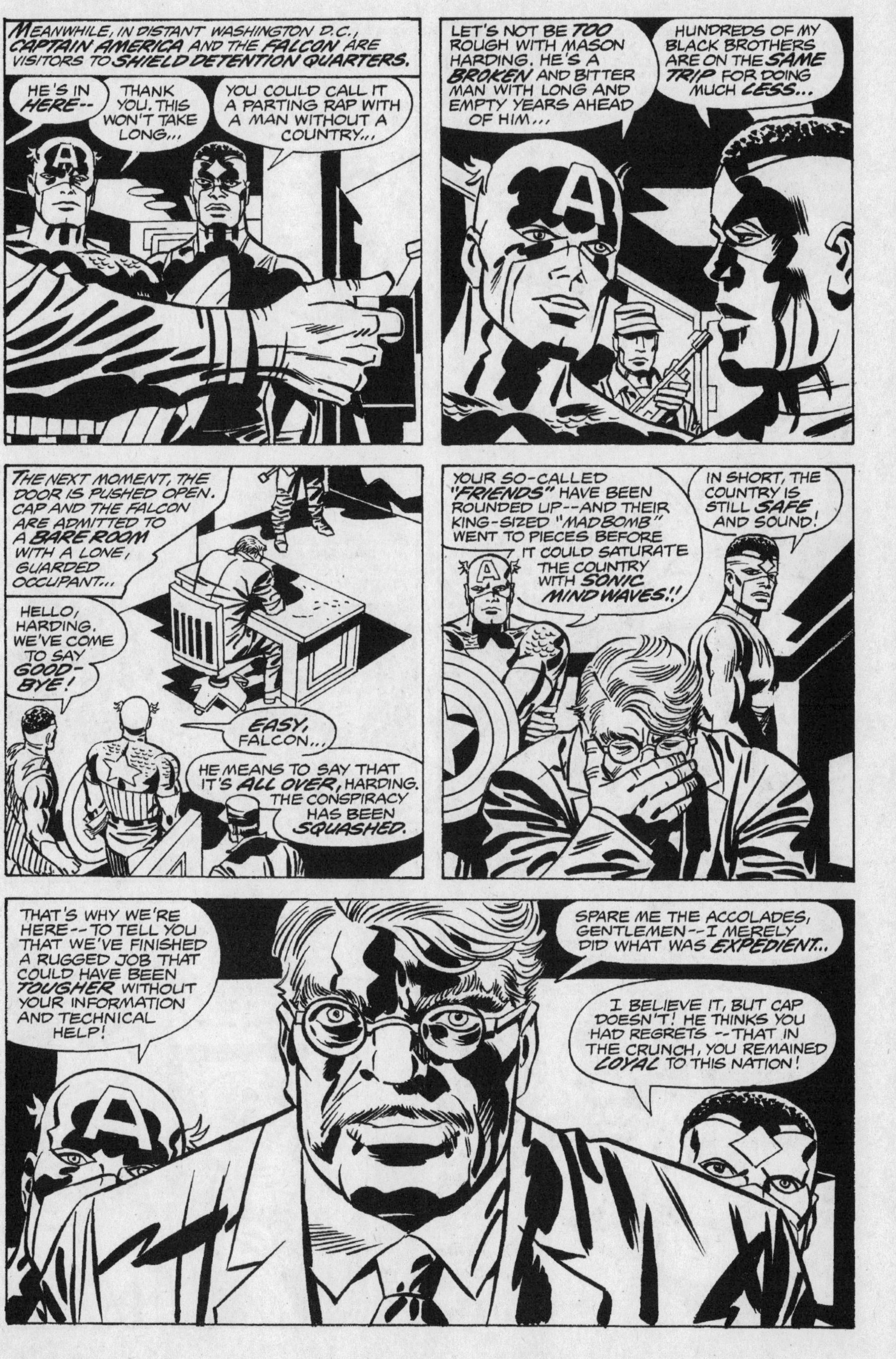
MEANWHILE, IN DISTANT WASHINGTON D.C., CAPTAIN AMERICA AND THE FALCON ARE VISITORS TO SHIELD DETENTION QUARTERS.
HE'S IN HERE--
THANK YOU. THIS WON'T TAKE LONG...
YOU COULD CALL IT A PARTING RAP WITH A MAN WITHOUT A COUNTRY...
LET'S NOT BE TOO ROUGH WITH MASON HARDING. HE'S A BROKEN AND BITTER MAN WITH LONG AND EMPTY YEARS AHEAD OF HIM...
HUNDREDS OF MY BLACK BROTHERS ARE ON THE SAME TRIP FOR DOING MUCH LESS...
THE NEXT MOMENT, THE DOOR IS PUSHED OPEN. CAP AND THE FALCON ARE ADMITTED TO A BARE ROOM WITH A LONE, GUARDED OCCUPANT...
HELLO, HARDING. WE'VE COME TO SAY GOOD-BYE!
EASY, FALCON...
HE MEANS TO SAY THAT IT'S ALL OVER, HARDING. THE CONSPIRACY HAS BEEN SQUASHED.
YOUR SO-CALLED "FRIENDS" HAVE BEEN ROUNDED UP--AND THEIR KING-SIZED "MADBOMB" WENT TO PIECES BEFORE IT COULD SATURATE THE COUNTRY WITH SONIC MIND WAVES!!
IN SHORT, THE COUNTRY IS STILL SAFE AND SOUND!
THAT'S WHY WE'RE HERE--TO TELL YOU THAT WE'VE FINISHED A RUGGED JOB THAT COULD HAVE BEEN TOUGHER WITHOUT YOUR INFORMATION AND TECHNICAL HELP!
SPARE ME THE ACCOLADES, GENTLEMEN--I MERELY DID WHAT WAS EXPEDIENT...
I BELIEVE IT, BUT CAP DOESN'T! HE THINKS YOU HAD REGRETS --THAT IN THE CRUNCH, YOU REMAINED LOYAL TO THIS NATION!

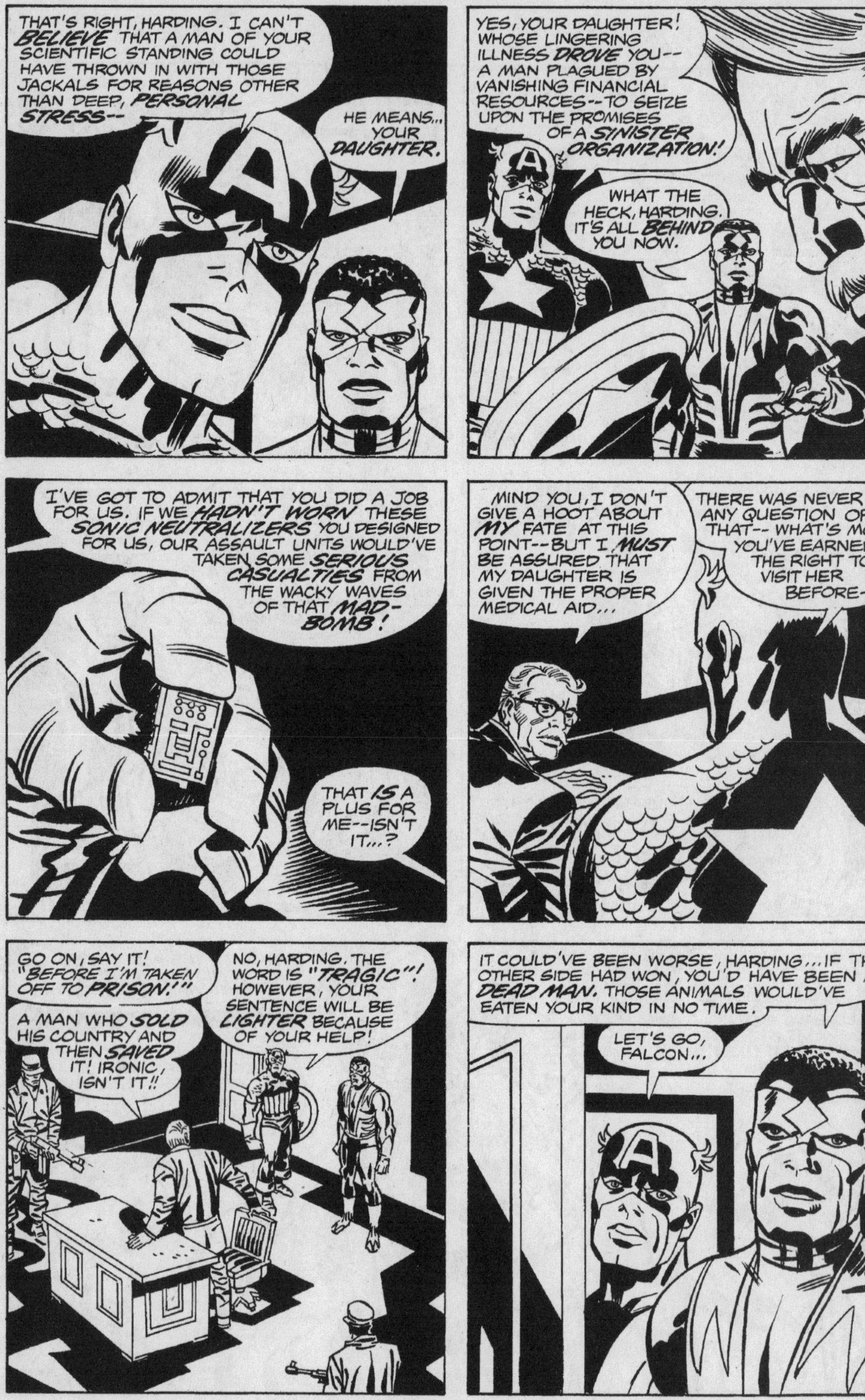
THAT'S RIGHT, HARDING. I CAN'T BELIEVE THAT A MAN OF YOUR SCIENTIFIC STANDING COULD HAVE THROWN IN WITH THOSE JACKALS FOR REASONS OTHER THAN DEEP, PERSONAL STRESS--
HE MEANS... YOUR DAUGHTER.
YES, YOUR DAUGHTER! WHOSE LINGERING ILLNESS DROVE YOU-- A MAN PLAGUED BY VANISHING FINANCIAL RESOURCES--TO SEIZE UPON THE PROMISES OF A SINISTER ORGANIZATION!
WHAT THE HECK, HARDING. IT'S ALL BEHIND YOU NOW.
I'VE GOT TO ADMIT THAT YOU DID A JOB FOR US. IF WE HADN'T WORN THESE SONIC NEUTRALIZERS YOU DESIGNED FOR US, OUR ASSAULT UNITS WOULD'VE TAKEN SOME SERIOUS CASUALTIES FROM THE WACKY WAVES OF THAT MAD-BOMB!
THAT IS A PLUS FOR ME--ISN'T IT...?
MIND YOU, I DON'T GIVE A HOOT ABOUT MY FATE AT THIS POINT--BUT I MUST BE ASSURED THAT MY DAUGHTER IS GIVEN THE PROPER MEDICAL AID...
THERE WAS NEVER ANY QUESTION OF THAT-- WHAT'S MORE, YOU'VE EARNED THE RIGHT TO VISIT HER BEFORE--
GO ON, SAY IT! "BEFORE I'M TAKEN OFF TO PRISON!"
A MAN WHO SOLD HIS COUNTRY AND THEN SAVED IT! IRONIC, ISN'T IT!!
NO, HARDING. THE WORD IS "TRAGIC"! HOWEVER, YOUR SENTENCE WILL BE LIGHTER BECAUSE OF YOUR HELP!
IT COULD'VE BEEN WORSE, HARDING... IF THE OTHER SIDE HAD WON, YOU'D HAVE BEEN A DEAD MAN. THOSE ANIMALS WOULD'VE EATEN YOUR KIND IN NO TIME.
LET'S GO, FALCON...

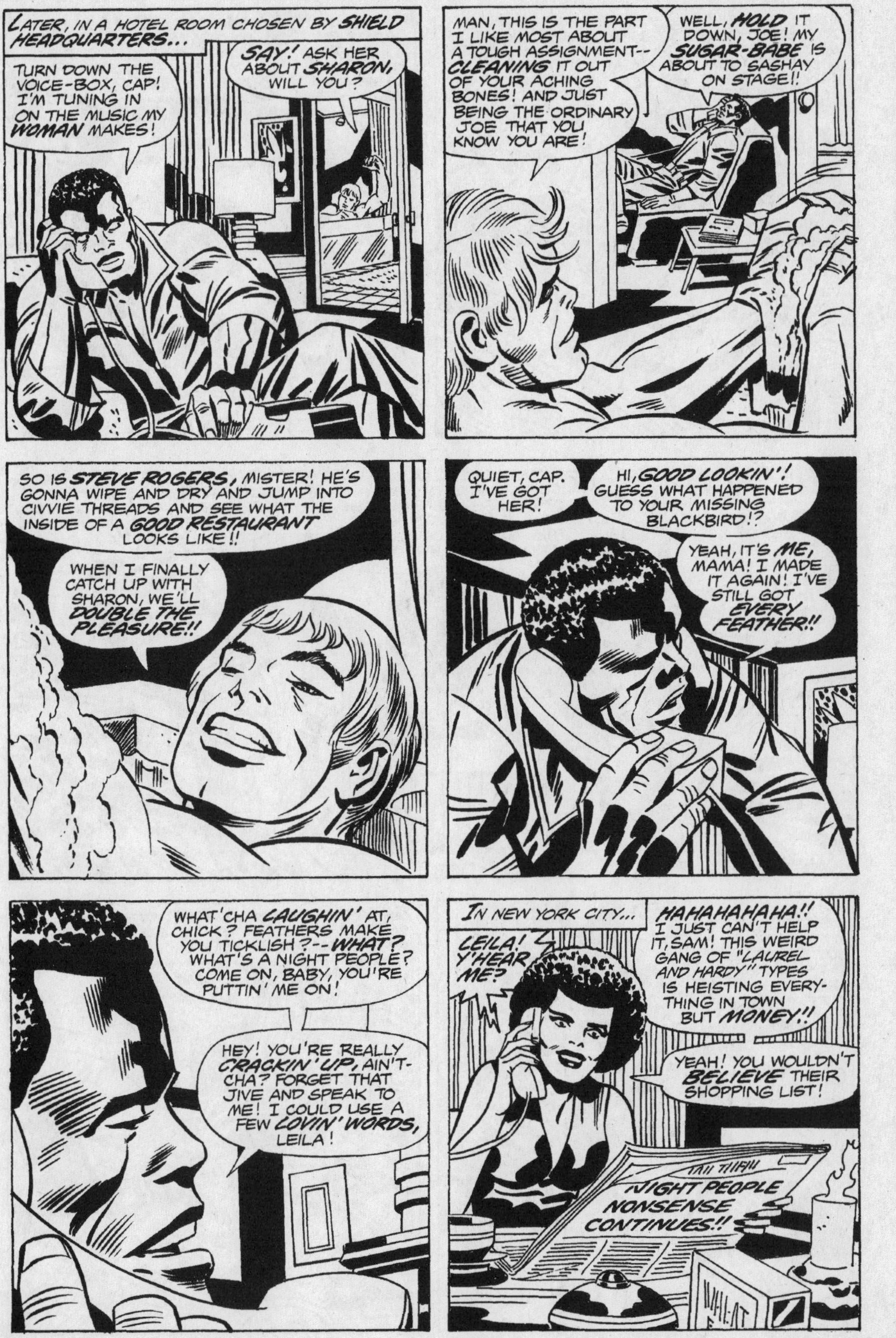
LATER, IN A HOTEL ROOM CHOSEN BY SHIELD HEADQUARTERS...
TURN DOWN THE VOICE-BOX, CAP! I'M TUNING IN ON THE MUSIC MY WOMAN MAKES!
SAY! ASK HER ABOUT SHARON, WILL YOU?
MAN, THIS IS THE PART I LIKE MOST ABOUT A TOUGH ASSIGNMENT-- CLEANING IT OUT OF YOUR ACHING BONES! AND JUST BEING THE ORDINARY JOE THAT YOU KNOW YOU ARE!
WELL, HOLD IT DOWN, JOE! MY SUGAR-BABE IS ABOUT TO SASHAY ON STAGE!!
SO IS STEVE ROGERS, MISTER! HE'S GONNA WIPE AND DRY AND JUMP INTO CIVVIE THREADS AND SEE WHAT THE INSIDE OF A GOOD RESTAURANT LOOKS LIKE!!
WHEN I FINALLY CATCH UP WITH SHARON, WE'LL DOUBLE THE PLEASURE!!
QUIET, CAP. I'VE GOT HER!
HI, GOOD LOOKIN'! GUESS WHAT HAPPENED TO YOUR MISSING BLACKBIRD!?
YEAH, IT'S ME, MAMA! I MADE IT AGAIN! I'VE STILL GOT EVERY FEATHER!!
WHAT'CHA LAUGHIN' AT, CHICK? FEATHERS MAKE YOU TICKLISH?--WHAT? WHAT'S A NIGHT PEOPLE? COME ON, BABY, YOU'RE PUTTIN' ME ON!
HEY! YOU'RE REALLY CRACKIN' UP, AIN'T-CHA? FORGET THAT JIVE AND SPEAK TO ME! I COULD USE A FEW LOVIN' WORDS, LEILA!
IN NEW YORK CITY...
LEILA! Y'HEAR ME?
HAHAHAHAHAHA!! I JUST CAN'T HELP IT, SAM! THIS WEIRD GANG OF "LAUREL AND HARDY" TYPES IS HEISTING EVERY-THING IN TOWN BUT MONEY!!
YEAH! YOU WOULDN'T BELIEVE THEIR SHOPPING LIST!
NIGHT PEOPLE NONSENSE CONTINUES!!

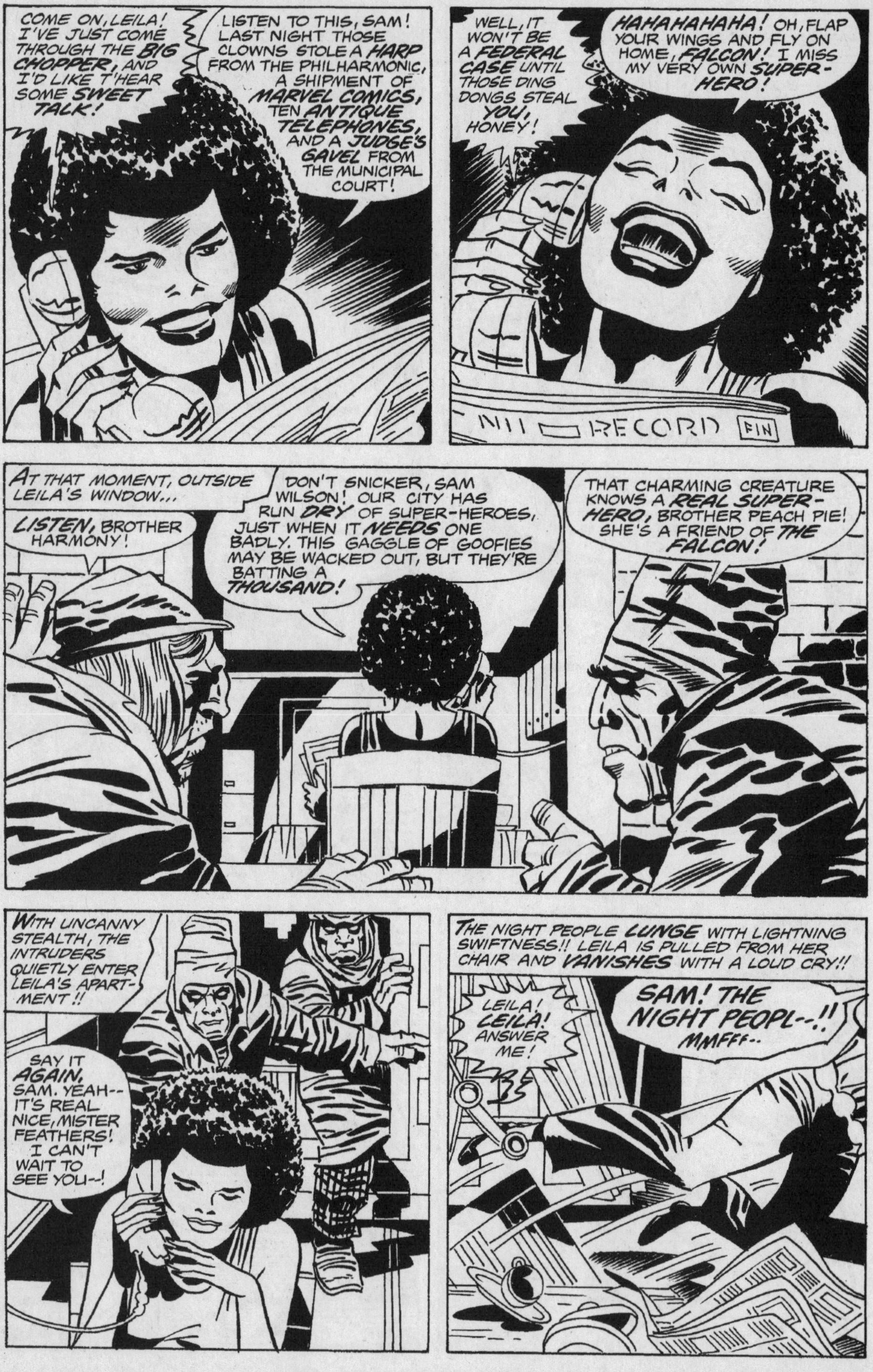
COME ON, LEILA! I'VE JUST COME THROUGH THE BIG CHOPPER, AND I'D LIKE T'HEAR SOME SWEET TALK!
LISTEN TO THIS, SAM! LAST NIGHT THOSE CLOWNS STOLE A HARP FROM THE PHILHARMONIC, A SHIPMENT OF MARVEL COMICS, TEN ANTIQUE TELEPHONES, AND A JUDGE'S GAVEL FROM THE MUNICIPAL COURT!
WELL, IT WON'T BE A FEDERAL CASE UNTIL THOSE DING DONGS STEAL YOU, HONEY!
HAHAHAHAHA! OH, FLAP YOUR WINGS AND FLY ON HOME, FALCON! I MISS MY VERY OWN SUPER-HERO!
RECORD
FIN
AT THAT MOMENT, OUTSIDE LEILA'S WINDOW...
LISTEN, BROTHER HARMONY!
DON'T SNICKER, SAM WILSON! OUR CITY HAS RUN DRY OF SUPER-HEROES, JUST WHEN IT NEEDS ONE BADLY. THIS GAGGLE OF GOOFIES MAY BE WACKED OUT, BUT THEY'RE BATTING A THOUSAND!
THAT CHARMING CREATURE KNOWS A REAL SUPER-HERO, BROTHER PEACH PIE! SHE'S A FRIEND OF THE FALCON!
WITH UNCANNY STEALTH, THE INTRUDERS QUIETLY ENTER LEILA'S APARTMENT!!
SAY IT AGAIN, SAM. YEAH-- IT'S REAL NICE, MISTER FEATHERS! I CAN'T WAIT TO SEE YOU--!
THE NIGHT PEOPLE LUNGE WITH LIGHTNING SWIFTNESS!! LEILA IS PULLED FROM HER CHAIR AND VANISHES WITH A LOUD CRY!!
LEILA! LEILA! ANSWER ME!
SAM! THE NIGHT PEOPL--!! MMFFF..

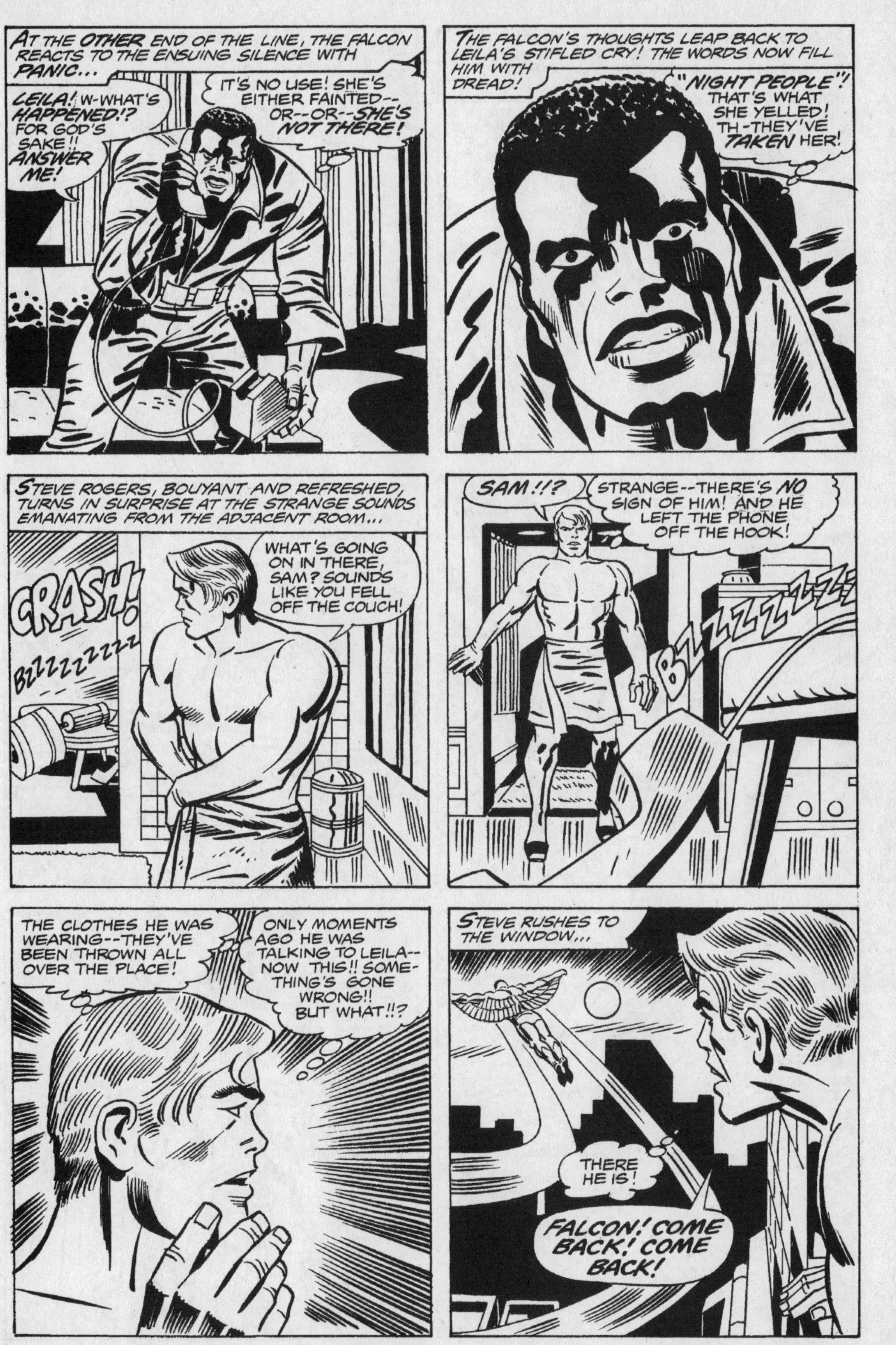
AT THE OTHER END OF THE LINE, THE FALCON REACTS TO THE ENSUING SILENCE WITH PANIC...
LEILA! W-WHAT'S HAPPENED!? FOR GOD'S SAKE!! ANSWER ME!
IT'S NO USE! SHE'S EITHER FAINTED-- OR--OR--SHE'S NOT THERE!
THE FALCON'S THOUGHTS LEAP BACK TO LEILA'S STIFLED CRY! THE WORDS NOW FILL HIM WITH DREAD!
"NIGHT PEOPLE"! THAT'S WHAT SHE YELLED! TH-THEY'VE TAKEN HER!
STEVE ROGERS, BOUYANT AND REFRESHED, TURNS IN SURPRISE AT THE STRANGE SOUNDS EMANATING FROM THE ADJACENT ROOM...
CRASH!
BZZZZZZZZZ
WHAT'S GOING ON IN THERE, SAM? SOUNDS LIKE YOU FELL OFF THE COUCH!
SAM!!?
STRANGE--THERE'S NO SIGN OF HIM! AND HE LEFT THE PHONE OFF THE HOOK!
BZZZZZZZZ
THE CLOTHES HE WAS WEARING--THEY'VE BEEN THROWN ALL OVER THE PLACE!
ONLY MOMENTS AGO HE WAS TALKING TO LEILA-- NOW THIS!! SOME-THING'S GONE WRONG!! BUT WHAT!!?
STEVE RUSHES TO THE WINDOW...
THERE HE IS!
FALCON! COME BACK! COME BACK!

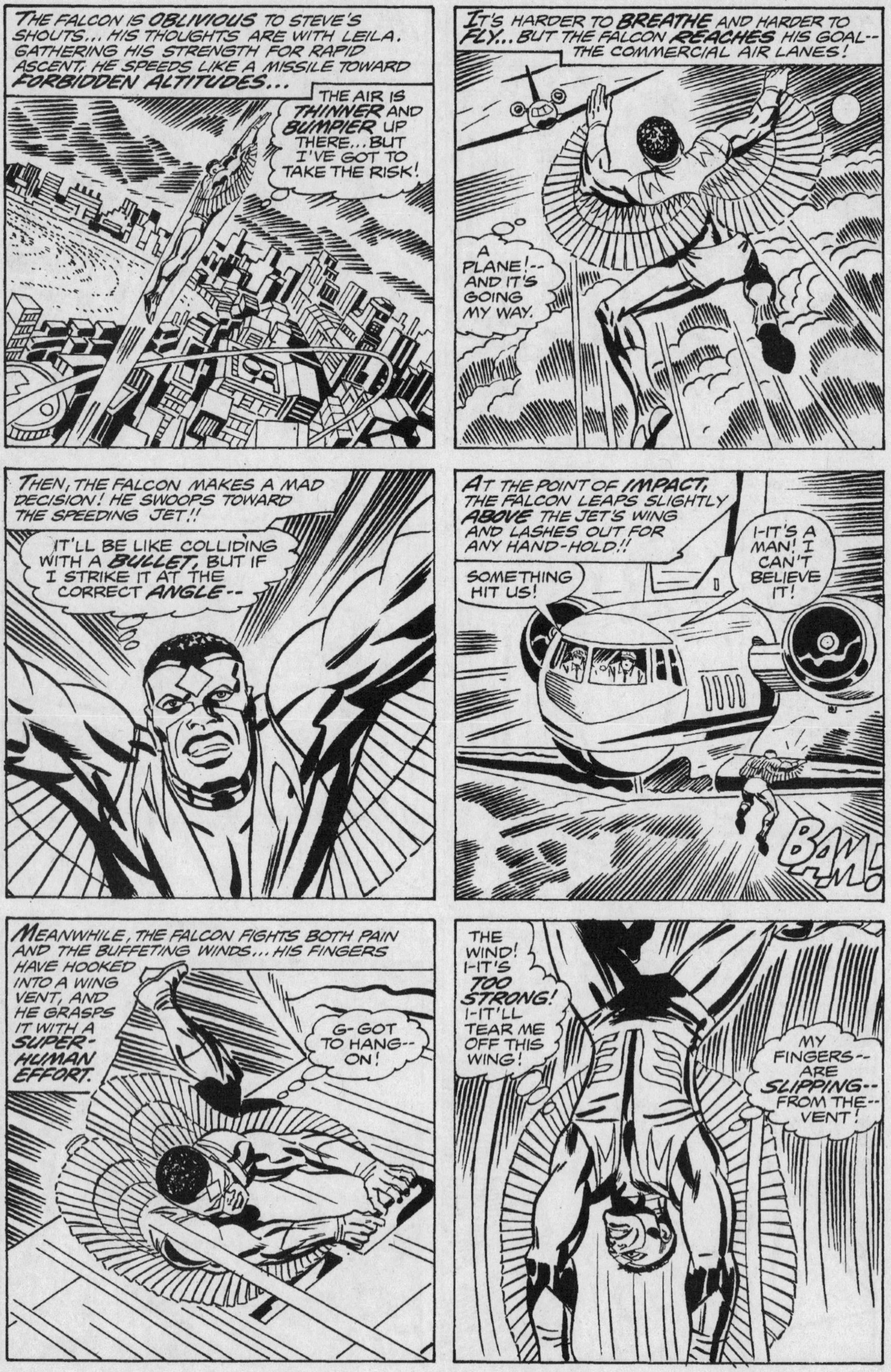
THE FALCON IS OBLIVIOUS TO STEVE'S SHOUTS... HIS THOUGHTS ARE WITH LEILA. GATHERING HIS STRENGTH FOR RAPID ASCENT, HE SPEEDS LIKE A MISSILE TOWARD FORBIDDEN ALTITUDES...
THE AIR IS THINNER AND BUMPIER UP THERE... BUT I'VE GOT TO TAKE THE RISK!
IT'S HARDER TO BREATHE AND HARDER TO FLY... BUT THE FALCON REACHES HIS GOAL-- THE COMMERCIAL AIR LANES!
A PLANE!-- AND IT'S GOING MY WAY.
THEN, THE FALCON MAKES A MAD DECISION! HE SWOOPS TOWARD THE SPEEDING JET!!
IT'LL BE LIKE COLLIDING WITH A BULLET, BUT IF I STRIKE IT AT THE CORRECT ANGLE--
AT THE POINT OF IMPACT, THE FALCON LEAPS SLIGHTLY ABOVE THE JET'S WING AND LASHES OUT FOR ANY HAND-HOLD!!
SOMETHING HIT US!
I-IT'S A MAN! I CAN'T BELIEVE IT!
BAM!
MEANWHILE, THE FALCON FIGHTS BOTH PAIN AND THE BUFFETING WINDS... HIS FINGERS HAVE HOOKED INTO A WING VENT, AND HE GRASPS IT WITH A SUPER-HUMAN EFFORT.
G-GOT TO HANG-- ON!
THE WIND! I-IT'S TOO STRONG! I-IT'LL TEAR ME OFF THIS WING!
MY FINGERS-- ARE SLIPPING-- FROM THE-- VENT!

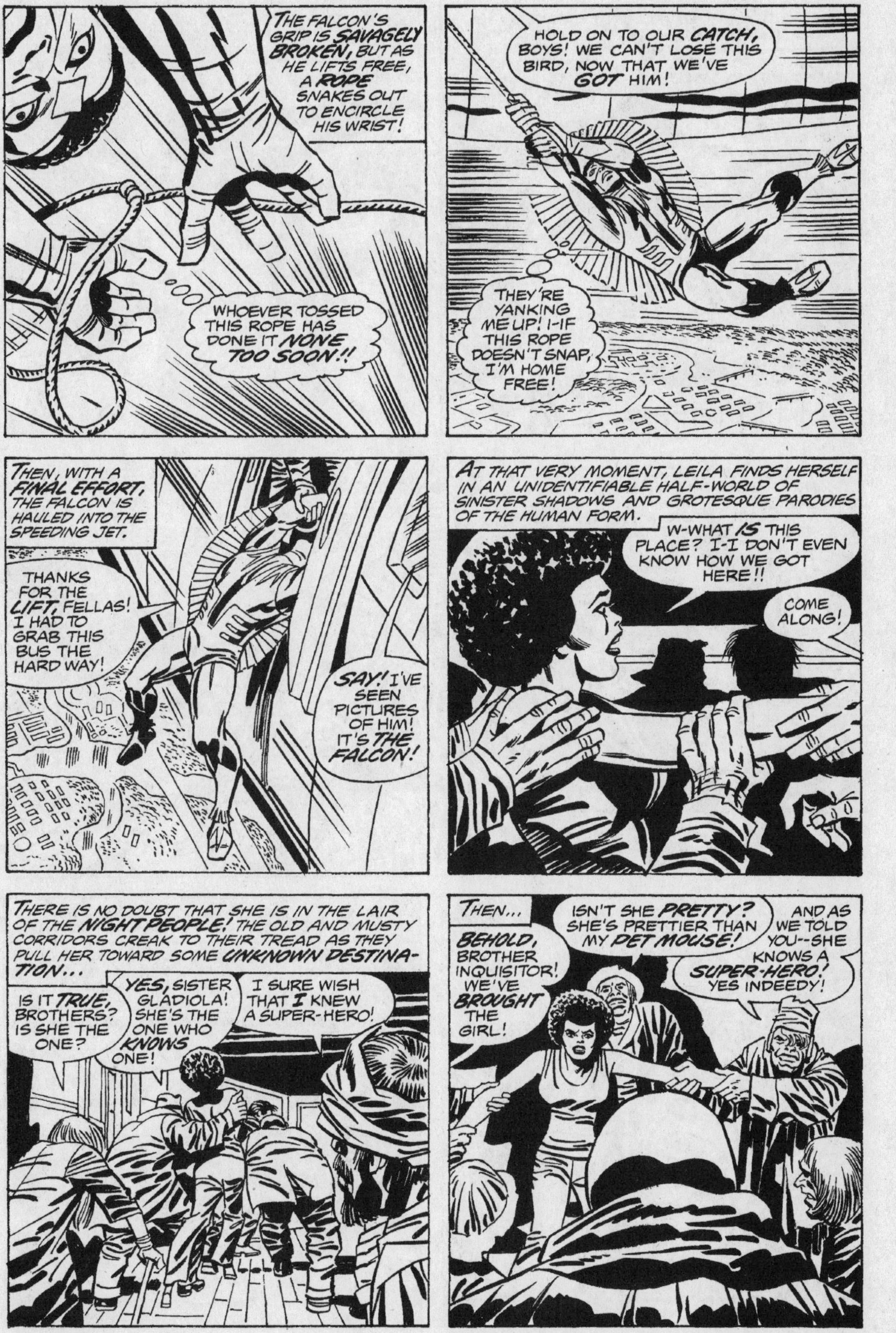
THE FALCON'S GRIP IS SAVAGELY BROKEN, BUT AS HE LIFTS FREE, A ROPE SNAKES OUT TO ENCIRCLE HIS WRIST!
WHOEVER TOSSED THIS ROPE HAS DONE IT NONE TOO SOON!!
HOLD ON TO OUR CATCH, BOYS! WE CAN'T LOSE THIS BIRD, NOW THAT WE'VE GOT HIM!
THEY'RE YANKING ME UP! I-IF THIS ROPE DOESN'T SNAP, I'M HOME FREE!
THEN, WITH A FINAL EFFORT, THE FALCON IS HAULED INTO THE SPEEDING JET.
THANKS FOR THE LIFT, FELLAS! I HAD TO GRAB THIS BUS THE HARD WAY!
SAY! I'VE SEEN PICTURES OF HIM! IT'S THE FALCON!
AT THAT VERY MOMENT, LEILA FINDS HERSELF IN AN UNIDENTIFIABLE HALF-WORLD OF SINISTER SHADOWS AND GROTESQUE PARODIES OF THE HUMAN FORM.
W-WHAT IS THIS PLACE? I-I DON'T EVEN KNOW HOW WE GOT HERE!!
COME ALONG!
THERE IS NO DOUBT THAT SHE IS IN THE LAIR OF THE NIGHT PEOPLE! THE OLD AND MUSTY CORRIDORS CREAK TO THEIR TREAD AS THEY PULL HER TOWARD SOME UNKNOWN DESTINATION...
IS IT TRUE, BROTHERS? IS SHE THE ONE?
YES, SISTER GLADIOLA! SHE'S THE ONE WHO KNOWS ONE!
I SURE WISH THAT I KNEW A SUPER-HERO!
THEN...
BEHOLD, BROTHER INQUISITOR! WE'VE BROUGHT THE GIRL!
ISN'T SHE PRETTY? SHE'S PRETTIER THAN MY PET MOUSE!
AND AS WE TOLD YOU--SHE KNOWS A SUPER-HERO! YES INDEEDY!

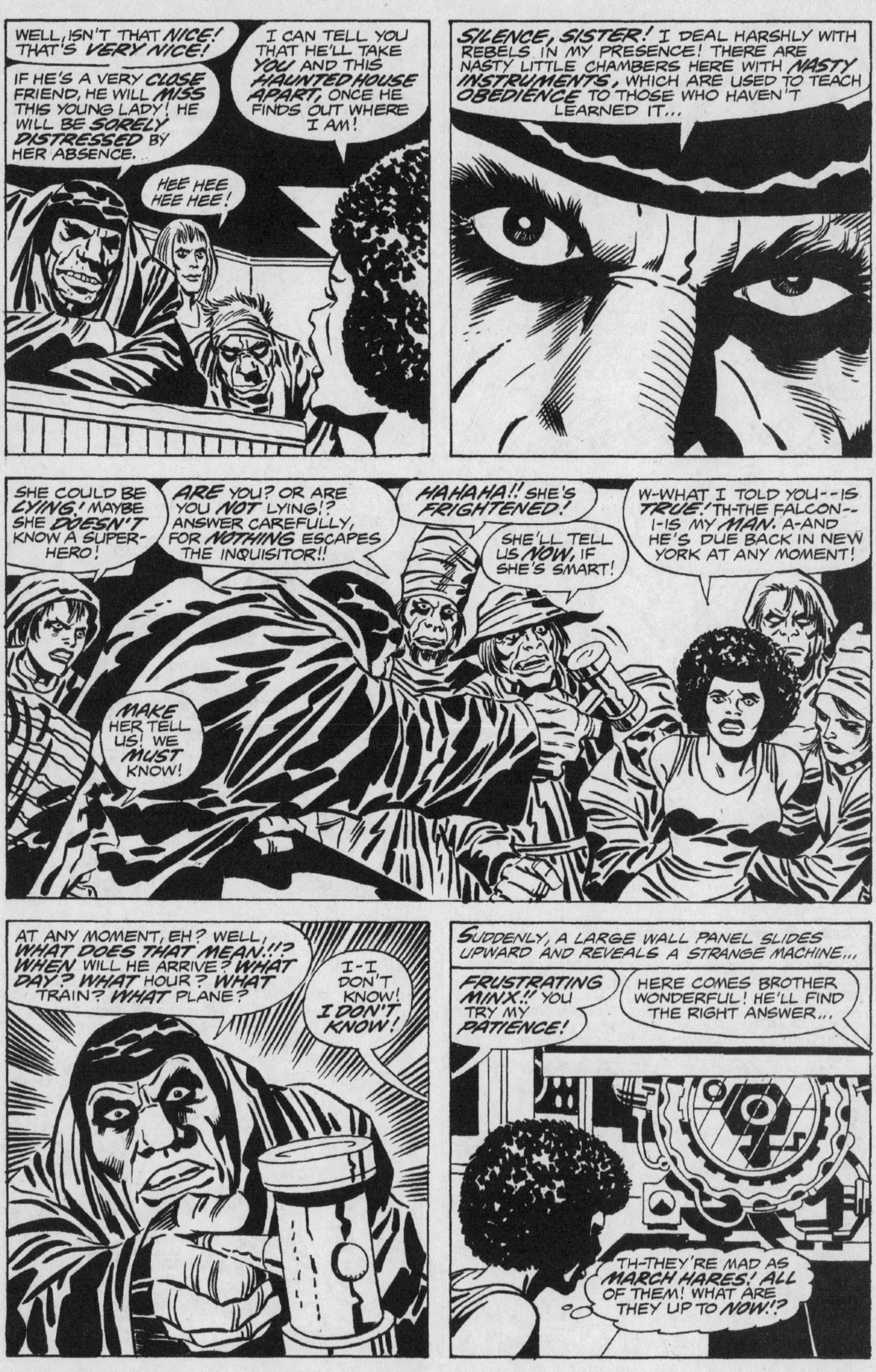
WELL, ISN'T THAT NICE! THAT'S VERY NICE!
IF HE'S A VERY CLOSE FRIEND, HE WILL MISS THIS YOUNG LADY! HE WILL BE SORELY DISTRESSED BY HER ABSENCE...
I CAN TELL YOU THAT HE'LL TAKE YOU AND THIS HAUNTED HOUSE APART, ONCE HE FINDS OUT WHERE I AM!
HEE HEE HEE HEE!
SILENCE, SISTER! I DEAL HARSHLY WITH REBELS IN MY PRESENCE! THERE ARE NASTY LITTLE CHAMBERS HERE WITH NASTY INSTRUMENTS, WHICH ARE USED TO TEACH OBEDIENCE TO THOSE WHO HAVEN'T LEARNED IT...
SHE COULD BE LYING! MAYBE SHE DOESN'T KNOW A SUPER-HERO!
ARE YOU? OR ARE YOU NOT LYING!? ANSWER CAREFULLY, FOR NOTHING ESCAPES THE INQUISITOR!!
HAHAHA!! SHE'S FRIGHTENED!
SHE'LL TELL US NOW, IF SHE'S SMART!
W-WHAT I TOLD YOU--IS TRUE! TH-THE FALCON--I-IS MY MAN. A-AND HE'S DUE BACK IN NEW YORK AT ANY MOMENT!
MAKE HER TELL US! WE MUST KNOW!
AT ANY MOMENT, EH? WELL, WHAT DOES THAT MEAN!!? WHEN WILL HE ARRIVE? WHAT DAY? WHAT HOUR? WHAT TRAIN? WHAT PLANE?
I-I DON'T KNOW! I DON'T KNOW!
SUDDENLY, A LARGE WALL PANEL SLIDES UPWARD AND REVEALS A STRANGE MACHINE...
FRUSTRATING MINX!! YOU TRY MY PATIENCE!
HERE COMES BROTHER WONDERFUL! HE'LL FIND THE RIGHT ANSWER...
TH-THEY'RE MAD AS MARCH HARES! ALL OF THEM! WHAT ARE THEY UP TO NOW!?

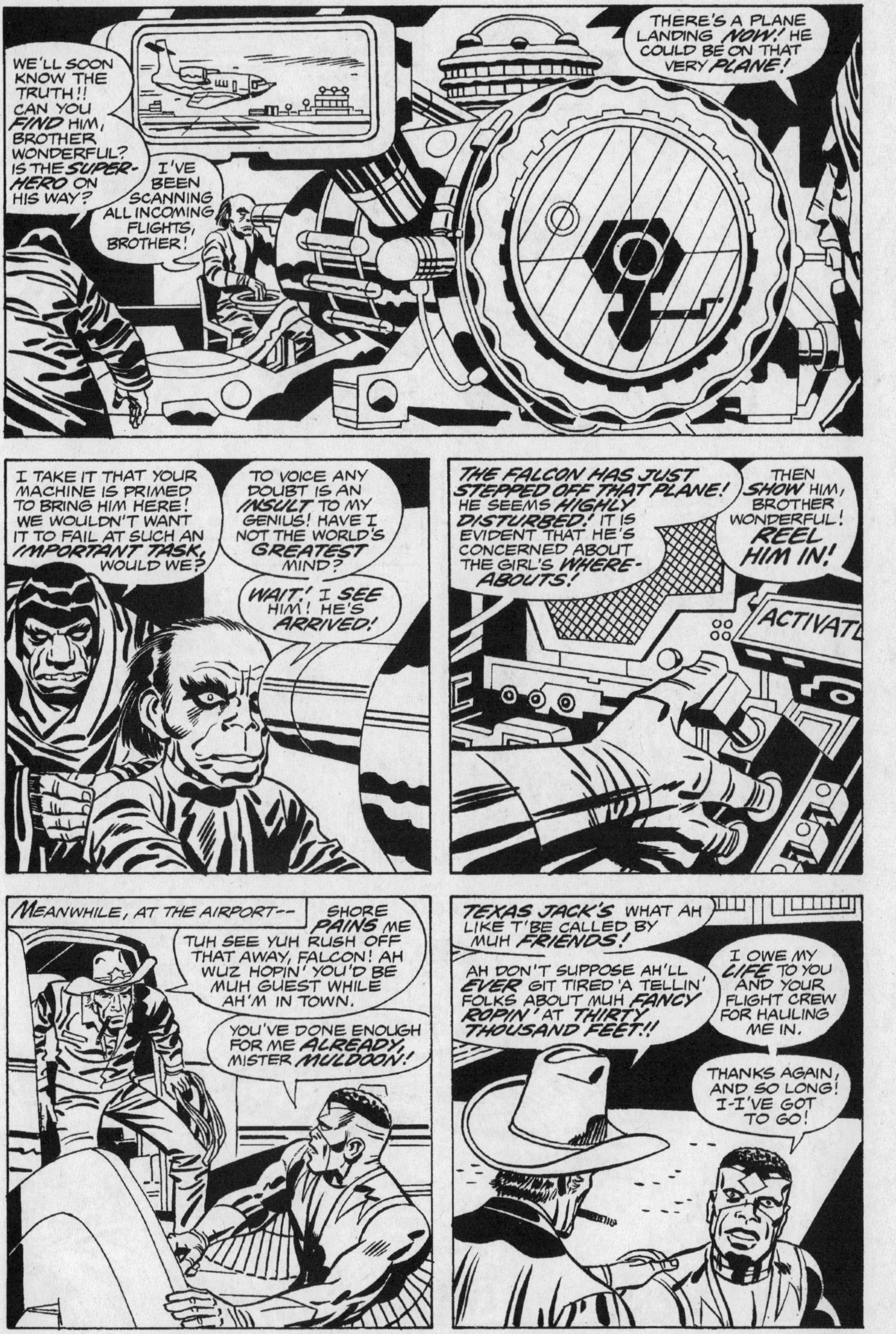
WE'LL SOON KNOW THE TRUTH!! CAN YOU FIND HIM, BROTHER WONDERFUL? IS THE SUPER-HERO ON HIS WAY?
I'VE BEEN SCANNING ALL INCOMING FLIGHTS, BROTHER!
THERE'S A PLANE LANDING NOW! HE COULD BE ON THAT VERY PLANE!
I TAKE IT THAT YOUR MACHINE IS PRIMED TO BRING HIM HERE! WE WOULDN'T WANT IT TO FAIL AT SUCH AN IMPORTANT TASK, WOULD WE?
TO VOICE ANY DOUBT IS AN INSULT TO MY GENIUS! HAVE I NOT THE WORLD'S GREATEST MIND?
WAIT! I SEE HIM! HE'S ARRIVED!
THE FALCON HAS JUST STEPPED OFF THAT PLANE! HE SEEMS HIGHLY DISTURBED! IT IS EVIDENT THAT HE'S CONCERNED ABOUT THE GIRL'S WHERE-ABOUTS!
THEN SHOW HIM, BROTHER WONDERFUL! REEL HIM IN!
ACTIVATE
MEANWHILE, AT THE AIRPORT--
SHORE PAINS ME TUH SEE YUH RUSH OFF THAT AWAY, FALCON! AH WUZ HOPIN' YOU'D BE MUH GUEST WHILE AH'M IN TOWN.
YOU'VE DONE ENOUGH FOR ME ALREADY, MISTER MULDOON!
TEXAS JACK'S WHAT AH LIKE T'BE CALLED BY MUH FRIENDS!
AH DON'T SUPPOSE AH'LL EVER GIT TIRED 'A TELLIN' FOLKS ABOUT MUH FANCY ROPIN' AT THIRTY THOUSAND FEET!!
I OWE MY LIFE TO YOU AND YOUR FLIGHT CREW FOR HAULING ME IN.
THANKS AGAIN, AND SO LONG! I-I'VE GOT TO GO!

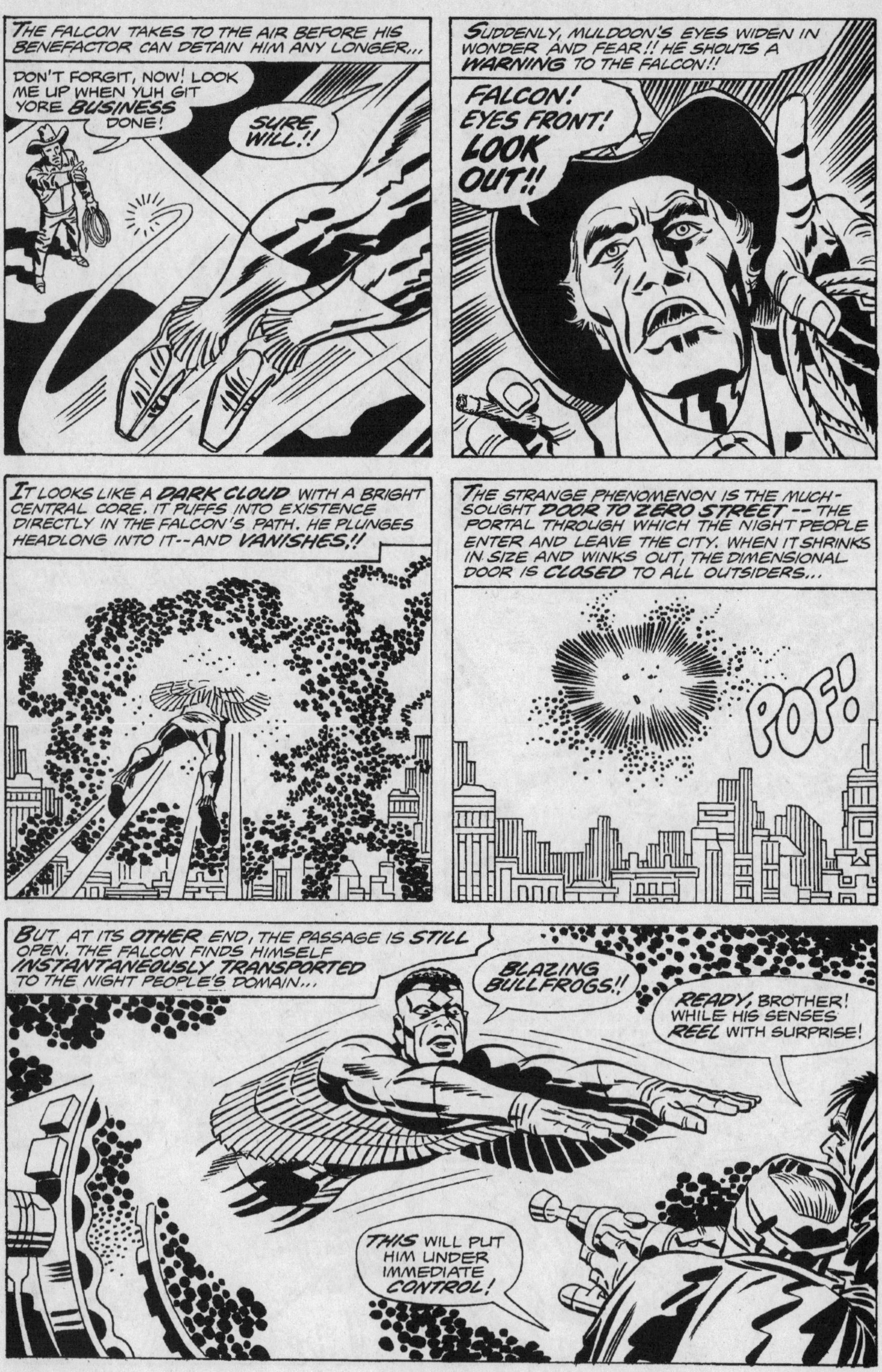

THE FALCON TAKES TO THE AIR BEFORE HIS BENEFACTOR CAN DETAIN HIM ANY LONGER...
DON'T FORGIT, NOW! LOOK ME UP WHEN YUH GIT YORE BUSINESS DONE!
SURE WILL!!
SUDDENLY, MULDOON'S EYES WIDEN IN WONDER AND FEAR!! HE SHOUTS A WARNING TO THE FALCON!!
FALCON! EYES FRONT! LOOK OUT!!
IT LOOKS LIKE A DARK CLOUD WITH A BRIGHT CENTRAL CORE. IT PUFFS INTO EXISTENCE DIRECTLY IN THE FALCON'S PATH. HE PLUNGES HEADLONG INTO IT--AND VANISHES!!
THE STRANGE PHENOMENON IS THE MUCH-SOUGHT DOOR TO ZERO STREET -- THE PORTAL THROUGH WHICH THE NIGHT PEOPLE ENTER AND LEAVE THE CITY. WHEN IT SHRINKS IN SIZE AND WINKS OUT, THE DIMENSIONAL DOOR IS CLOSED TO ALL OUTSIDERS...
POF!
BUT AT ITS OTHER END, THE PASSAGE IS STILL OPEN. THE FALCON FINDS HIMSELF INSTANTANEOUSLY TRANSPORTED TO THE NIGHT PEOPLE'S DOMAIN...
BLAZING BULLFROGS!!
READY, BROTHER! WHILE HIS SENSES REEL WITH SURPRISE!
THIS WILL PUT HIM UNDER IMMEDIATE CONTROL!

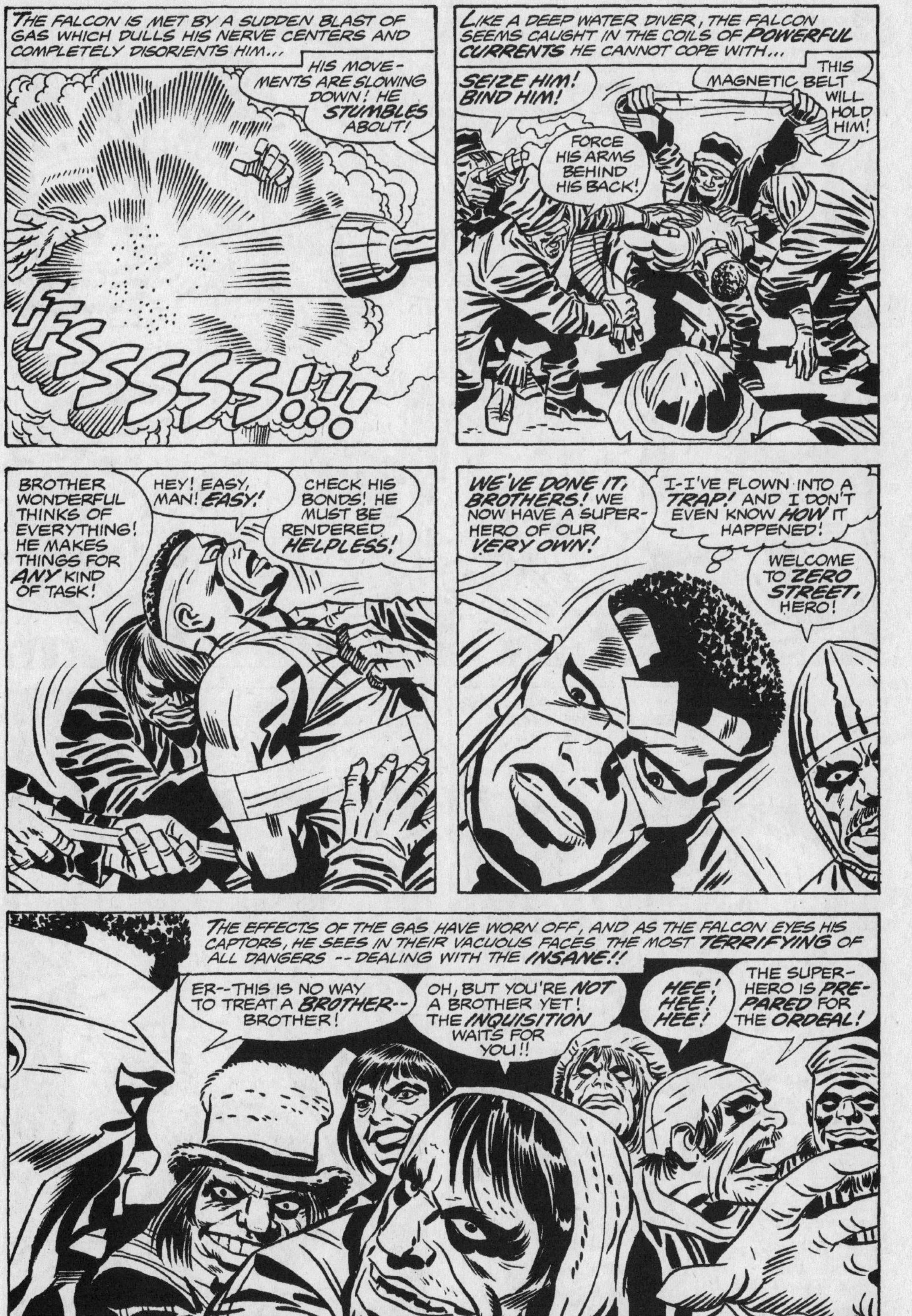
THE FALCON IS MET BY A SUDDEN BLAST OF GAS WHICH DULLS HIS NERVE CENTERS AND COMPLETELY DISORIENTS HIM...
HIS MOVE-MENTS ARE SLOWING DOWN! HE STUMBLES ABOUT!
FFSSSSSS!!!
LIKE A DEEP WATER DIVER, THE FALCON SEEMS CAUGHT IN THE COILS OF POWERFUL CURRENTS HE CANNOT COPE WITH...
SEIZE HIM! BIND HIM!
THIS MAGNETIC BELT WILL HOLD HIM!
FORCE HIS ARMS BEHIND HIS BACK!
BROTHER WONDERFUL THINKS OF EVERYTHING! HE MAKES THINGS FOR ANY KIND OF TASK!
HEY! EASY, MAN! EASY!
CHECK HIS BONDS! HE MUST BE RENDERED HELPLESS!
WE'VE DONE IT, BROTHERS! WE NOW HAVE A SUPER-HERO OF OUR VERY OWN!
I-I'VE FLOWN INTO A TRAP! AND I DON'T EVEN KNOW HOW IT HAPPENED!
WELCOME TO ZERO STREET, HERO!
THE EFFECTS OF THE GAS HAVE WORN OFF, AND AS THE FALCON EYES HIS CAPTORS, HE SEES IN THEIR VACUOUS FACES THE MOST TERRIFYING OF ALL DANGERS -- DEALING WITH THE INSANE!!
ER--THIS IS NO WAY TO TREAT A BROTHER--BROTHER!
OH, BUT YOU'RE NOT A BROTHER YET! THE INQUISITION WAITS FOR YOU!!
HEE! HEE! HEE!
THE SUPER-HERO IS PRE-PARED FOR THE ORDEAL!

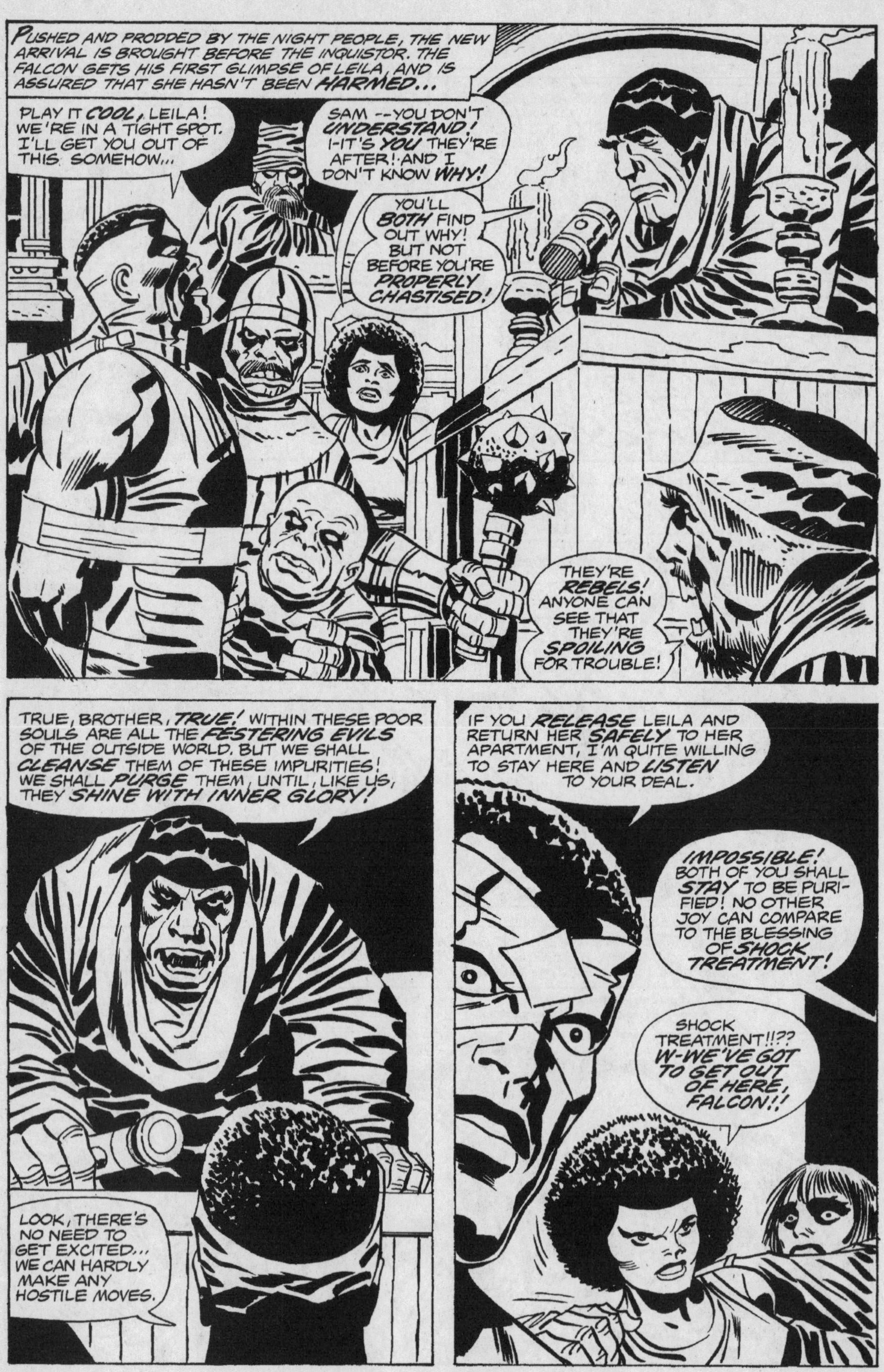
PUSHED AND PRODDED BY THE NIGHT PEOPLE, THE NEW ARRIVAL IS BROUGHT BEFORE THE INQUISTOR. THE FALCON GETS HIS FIRST GLIMPSE OF LEILA, AND IS ASSURED THAT SHE HASN'T BEEN HARMED...
PLAY IT COOL, LEILA! WE'RE IN A TIGHT SPOT. I'LL GET YOU OUT OF THIS SOMEHOW...
SAM --YOU DON'T UNDERSTAND! I-IT'S YOU THEY'RE AFTER! AND I DON'T KNOW WHY!
YOU'LL BOTH FIND OUT WHY! BUT NOT BEFORE YOU'RE PROPERLY CHASTISED!
THEY'RE REBELS! ANYONE CAN SEE THAT THEY'RE SPOILING FOR TROUBLE!
TRUE, BROTHER, TRUE! WITHIN THESE POOR SOULS ARE ALL THE FESTERING EVILS OF THE OUTSIDE WORLD. BUT WE SHALL CLEANSE THEM OF THESE IMPURITIES! WE SHALL PURGE THEM, UNTIL, LIKE US, THEY SHINE WITH INNER GLORY!
LOOK, THERE'S NO NEED TO GET EXCITED... WE CAN HARDLY MAKE ANY HOSTILE MOVES.
IF YOU RELEASE LEILA AND RETURN HER SAFELY TO HER APARTMENT, I'M QUITE WILLING TO STAY HERE AND LISTEN TO YOUR DEAL.
IMPOSSIBLE! BOTH OF YOU SHALL STAY TO BE PURIFIED! NO OTHER JOY CAN COMPARE TO THE BLESSING OF SHOCK TREATMENT!
SHOCK TREATMENT!!?? W-WE'VE GOT TO GET OUT OF HERE, FALCON!!

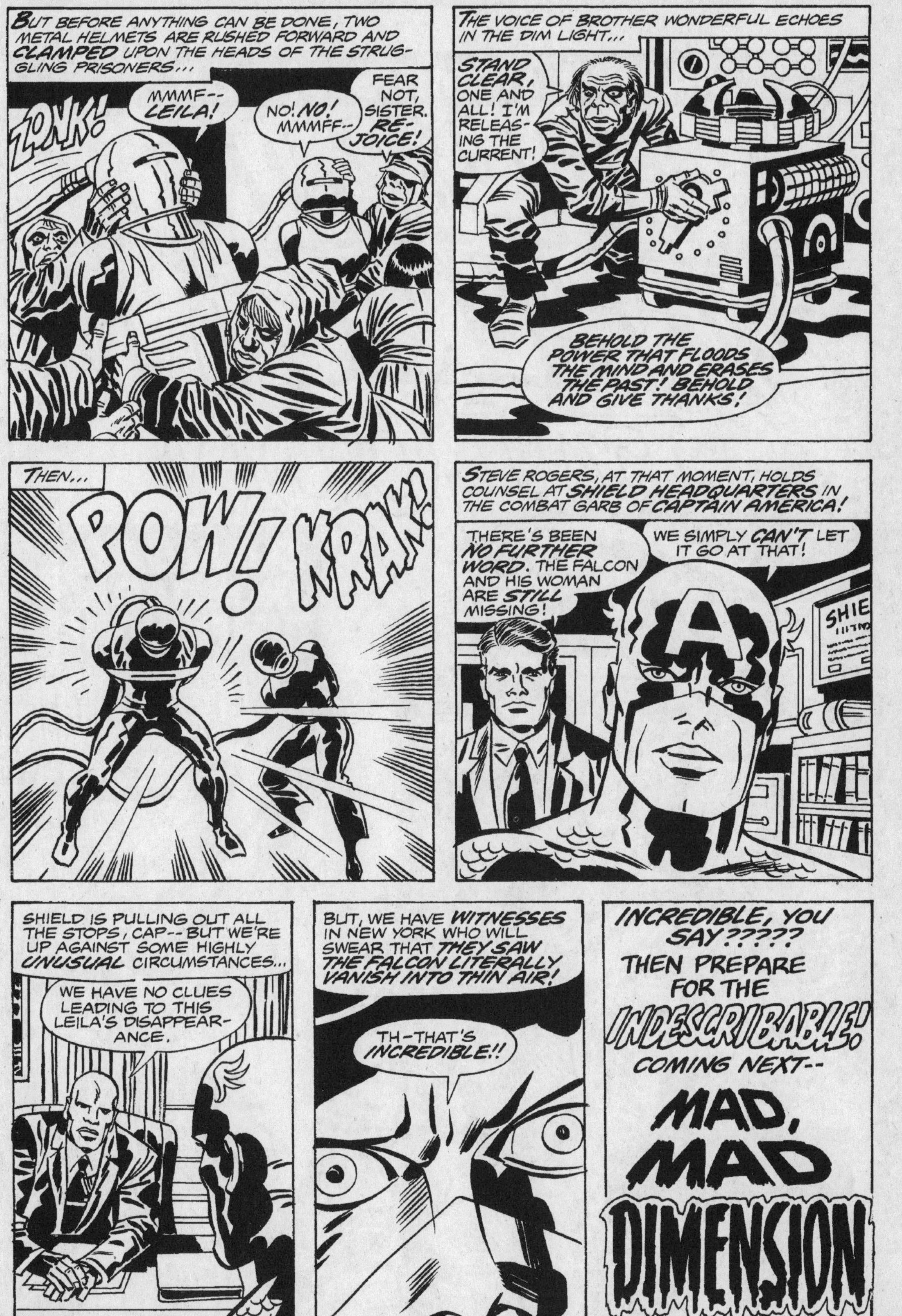

BUT BEFORE ANYTHING CAN BE DONE, TWO METAL HELMETS ARE RUSHED FORWARD AND CLAMPED UPON THE HEADS OF THE STRUGGLING PRISONERS...
ZONK!
MMMF-- LEILA!
NO! NO! MMMFF--
FEAR NOT, SISTER. REJOICE!
THE VOICE OF BROTHER WONDERFUL ECHOES IN THE DIM LIGHT...
STAND CLEAR, ONE AND ALL! I'M RELEASING THE CURRENT!
BEHOLD THE POWER THAT FLOODS THE MIND AND ERASES THE PAST! BEHOLD AND GIVE THANKS!
THEN...
POW! KRAK!
STEVE ROGERS, AT THAT MOMENT, HOLDS COUNSEL AT SHIELD HEADQUARTERS IN THE COMBAT GARB OF CAPTAIN AMERICA!
THERE'S BEEN NO FURTHER WORD. THE FALCON AND HIS WOMAN ARE STILL MISSING!
WE SIMPLY CAN'T LET IT GO AT THAT!
SHIELD IS PULLING OUT ALL THE STOPS, CAP-- BUT WE'RE UP AGAINST SOME HIGHLY UNUSUAL CIRCUMSTANCES...
WE HAVE NO CLUES LEADING TO THIS LEILA'S DISAPPEARANCE.
BUT, WE HAVE WITNESSES IN NEW YORK WHO WILL SWEAR THAT THEY SAW THE FALCON LITERALLY VANISH INTO THIN AIR!
TH-THAT'S INCREDIBLE!!
INCREDIBLE, YOU SAY?????
THEN PREPARE FOR THE INDESCRIBABLE!
COMING NEXT--
MAD, MAD DIMENSION

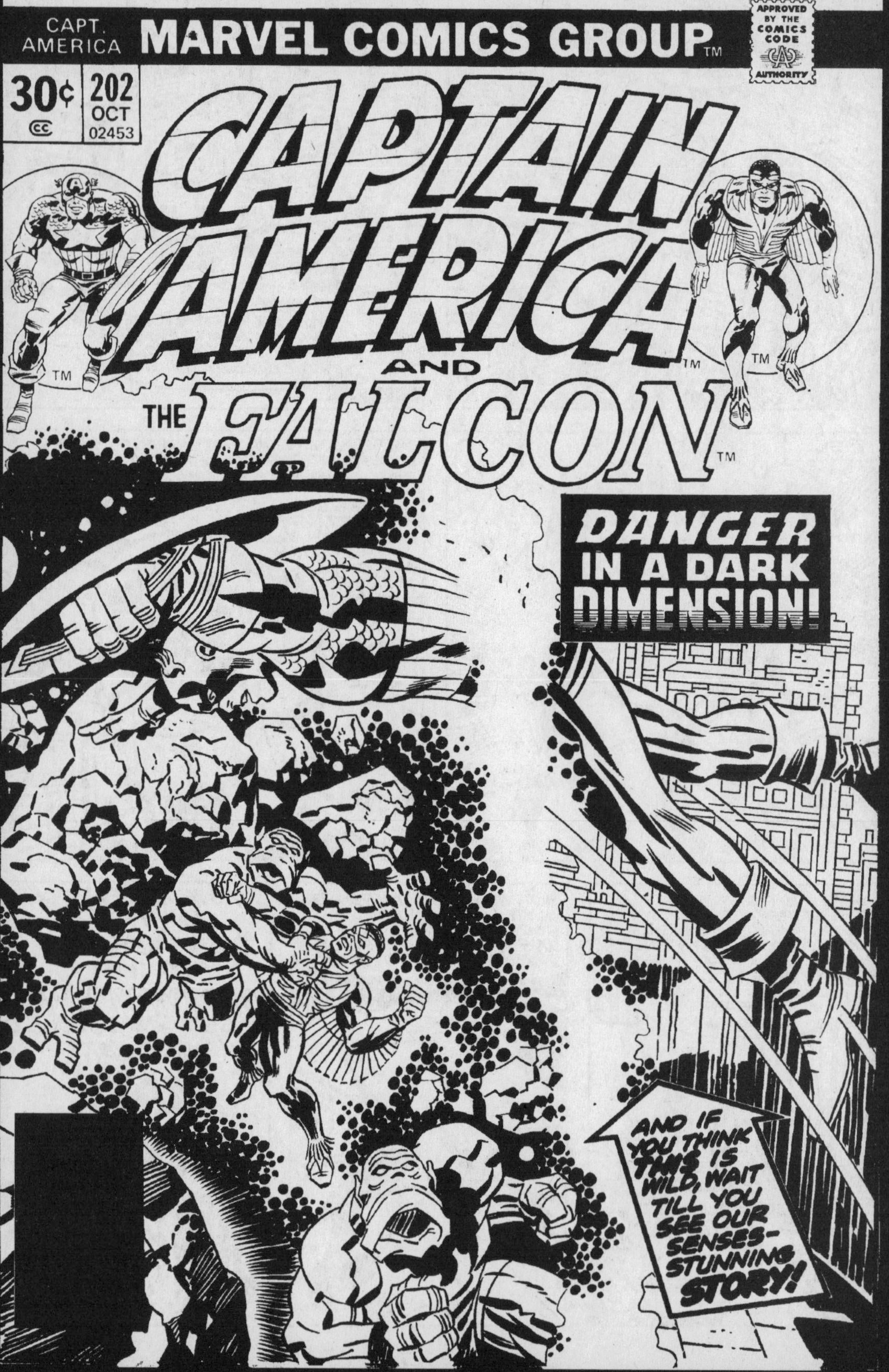
CAPT. AMERICA
MARVEL COMICS GROUP TM
APPROVED BY THE COMICS CODE CA AUTHORITY
30¢ CC
202 OCT 02453
CAPTAIN AMERICA TM
AND
THE FALCON TM
TM
TM
DANGER IN A DARK DIMENSION!
AND IF YOU THINK THIS IS WILD, WAIT TILL YOU SEE OUR SENSES-STUNNING STORY!

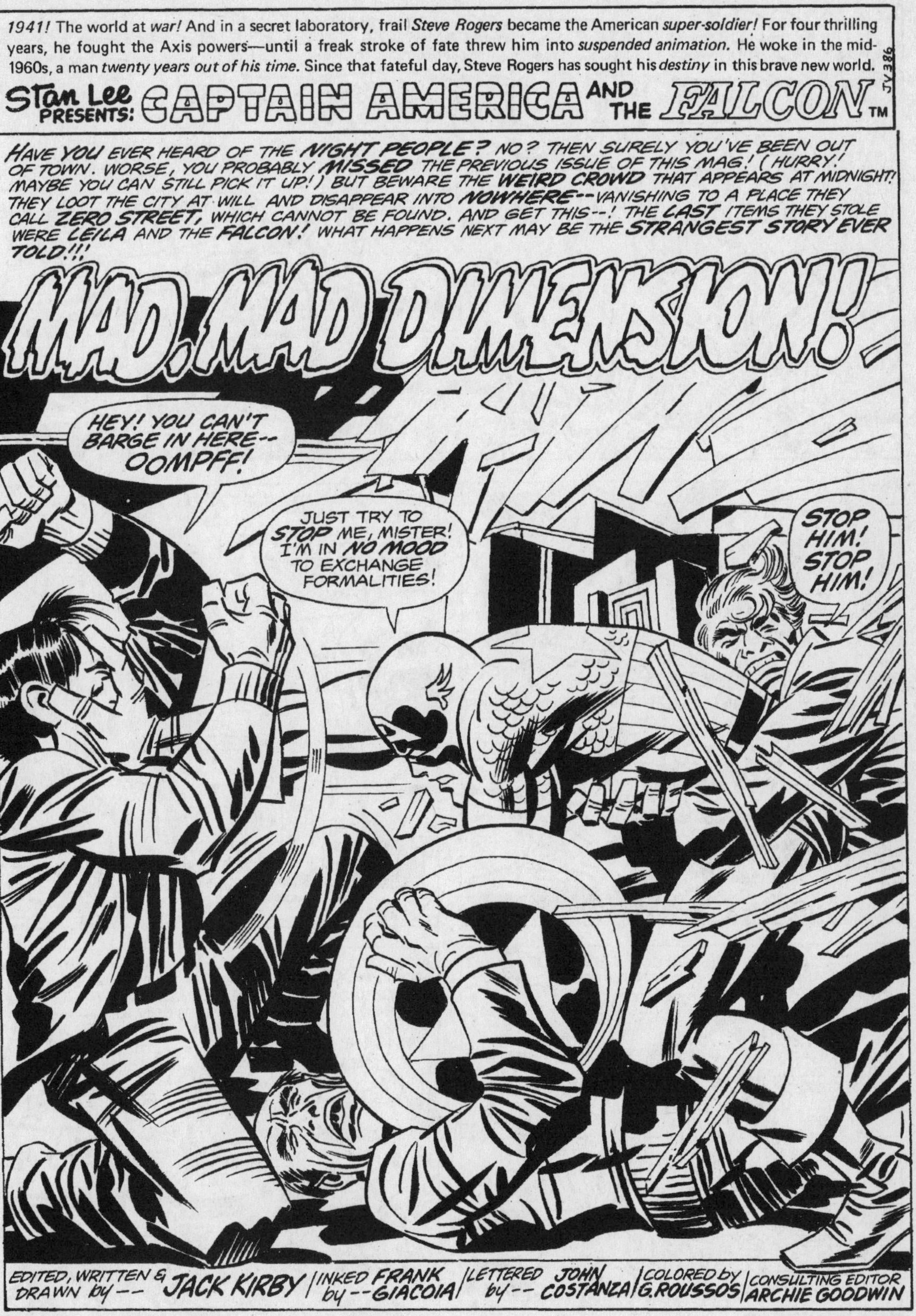
1941! The world at war! And in a secret laboratory, frail Steve Rogers became the American super-soldier! For four thrilling years, he fought the Axis powers—until a freak stroke of fate threw him into suspended animation. He woke in the mid-1960s, a man twenty years out of his time. Since that fateful day, Steve Rogers has sought his destiny in this brave new world.
JV 386
STAN LEE PRESENTS: CAPTAIN AMERICA AND THE FALCON ™
HAVE YOU EVER HEARD OF THE NIGHT PEOPLE? NO? THEN SURELY YOU'VE BEEN OUT OF TOWN. WORSE, YOU PROBABLY MISSED THE PREVIOUS ISSUE OF THIS MAG! (HURRY! MAYBE YOU CAN STILL PICK IT UP!) BUT BEWARE THE WEIRD CROWD THAT APPEARS AT MIDNIGHT! THEY LOOT THE CITY AT WILL AND DISAPPEAR INTO NOWHERE--VANISHING TO A PLACE THEY CALL ZERO STREET, WHICH CANNOT BE FOUND. AND GET THIS--! THE LAST ITEMS THEY STOLE WERE LEILA AND THE FALCON! WHAT HAPPENS NEXT MAY BE THE STRANGEST STORY EVER TOLD!!!
MAD, MAD DIMENSION!
HEY! YOU CAN'T BARGE IN HERE-- OOMPFF!
JUST TRY TO STOP ME, MISTER! I'M IN NO MOOD TO EXCHANGE FORMALITIES!
STOP HIM! STOP HIM!
EDITED, WRITTEN & DRAWN by -- JACK KIRBY | INKED by -- FRANK GIACOIA | LETTERED by -- JOHN COSTANZA | COLORED by G. ROUSSOS | CONSULTING EDITOR ARCHIE GOODWIN

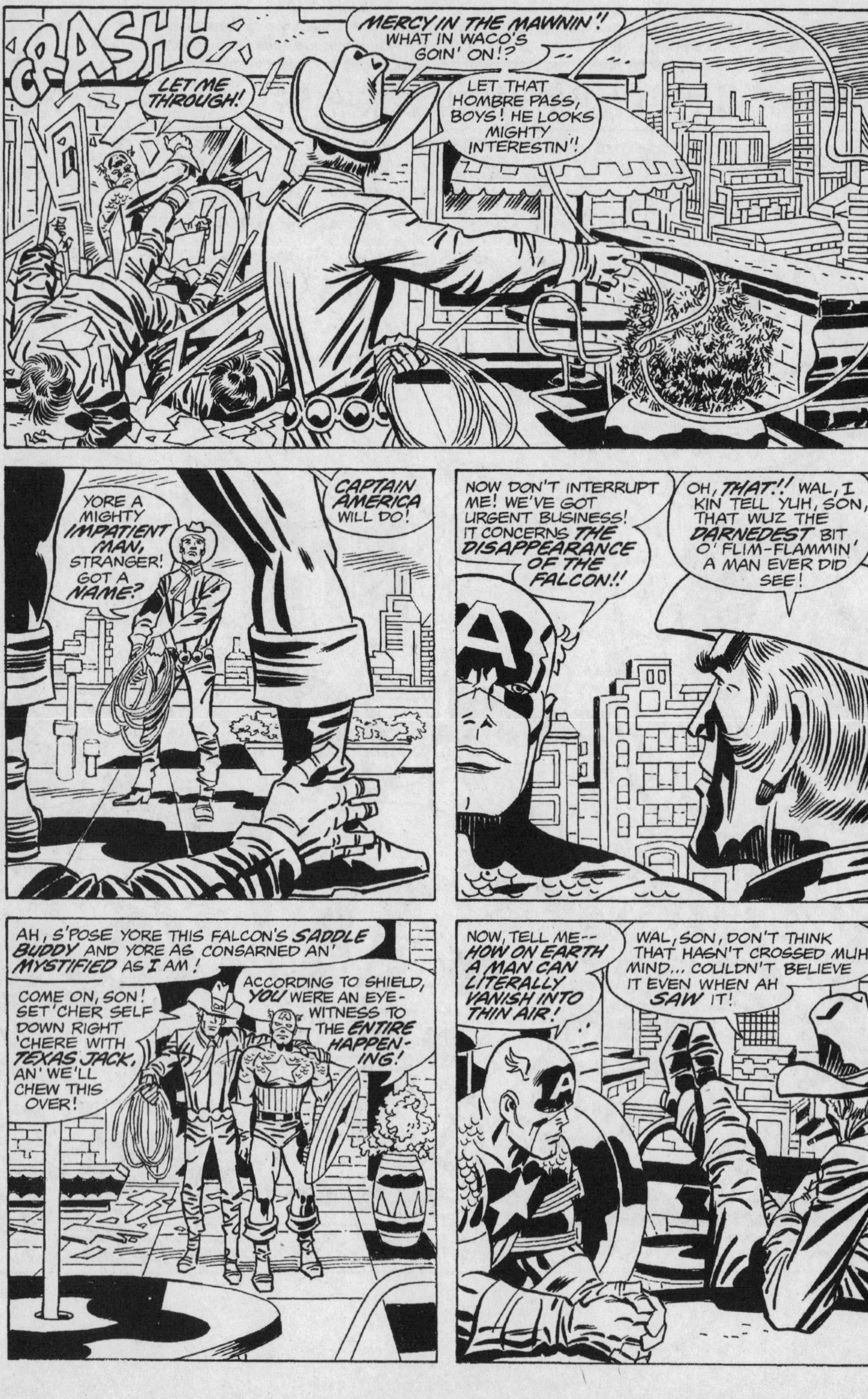
CRASH!
LET ME THROUGH!
MERCY IN THE MAWNIN'! WHAT IN WACO'S GOIN' ON!?
LET THAT HOMBRE PASS, BOYS! HE LOOKS MIGHTY INTERESTIN'!
YORE A MIGHTY IMPATIENT MAN, STRANGER! GOT A NAME?
CAPTAIN AMERICA WILL DO!
NOW DON'T INTERRUPT ME! WE'VE GOT URGENT BUSINESS! IT CONCERNS THE DISAPPEARANCE OF THE FALCON!!
OH, THAT!! WAL, I KIN TELL YUH, SON, THAT WUZ THE DARNEDEST BIT O' FLIM-FLAMMIN' A MAN EVER DID SEE!
AH, S'POSE YORE THIS FALCON'S SADDLE BUDDY AND YORE AS CONSARNED AN' MYSTIFIED AS I AM!
COME ON, SON! SET 'CHER SELF DOWN RIGHT 'CHERE WITH TEXAS JACK, AN' WE'LL CHEW THIS OVER!
ACCORDING TO SHIELD, YOU WERE AN EYE-WITNESS TO THE ENTIRE HAPPENING!
NOW, TELL ME-- HOW ON EARTH A MAN CAN LITERALLY VANISH INTO THIN AIR!
WAL, SON, DON'T THINK THAT HASN'T CROSSED MUH MIND... COULDN'T BELIEVE IT EVEN WHEN AH SAW IT!

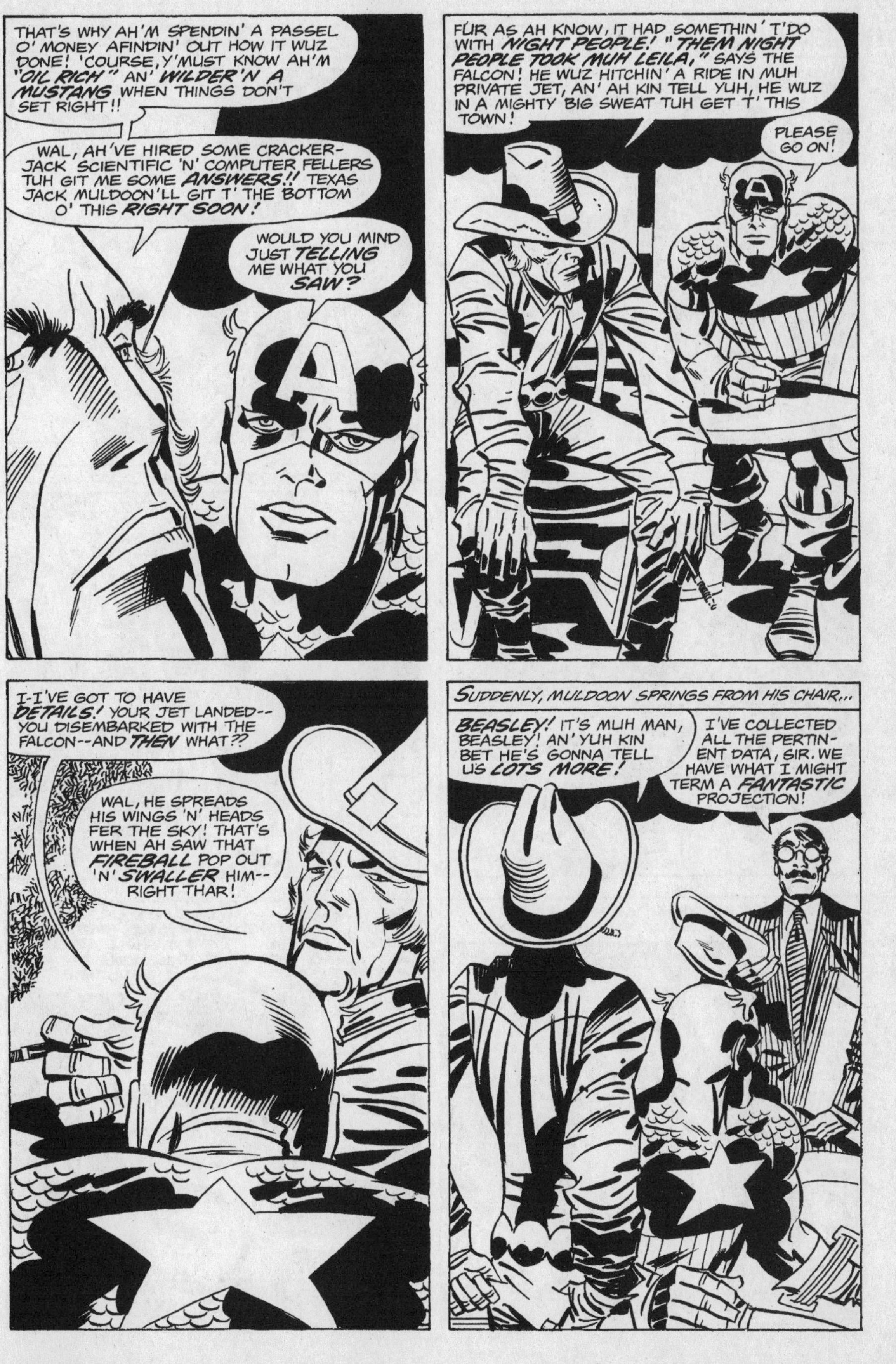
THAT'S WHY AH'M SPENDIN' A PASSEL O' MONEY AFINDIN' OUT HOW IT WUZ DONE! 'COURSE, Y'MUST KNOW AH'M "OIL RICH" AN' WILDER'N A MUSTANG WHEN THINGS DON'T SET RIGHT!!
WAL, AH'VE HIRED SOME CRACKER-JACK SCIENTIFIC 'N' COMPUTER FELLERS TUH GIT ME SOME ANSWERS!! TEXAS JACK MULDOON'LL GIT T' THE BOTTOM O' THIS RIGHT SOON!
WOULD YOU MIND JUST TELLING ME WHAT YOU SAW?
FUR AS AH KNOW, IT HAD SOMETHIN' T'DO WITH NIGHT PEOPLE! "THEM NIGHT PEOPLE TOOK MUH LEILA," SAYS THE FALCON! HE WUZ HITCHIN' A RIDE IN MUH PRIVATE JET, AN' AH KIN TELL YUH, HE WUZ IN A MIGHTY BIG SWEAT TUH GET T' THIS TOWN!
PLEASE GO ON!
I-I'VE GOT TO HAVE DETAILS! YOUR JET LANDED-- YOU DISEMBARKED WITH THE FALCON--AND THEN WHAT??
WAL, HE SPREADS HIS WINGS 'N' HEADS FER THE SKY! THAT'S WHEN AH SAW THAT FIREBALL POP OUT 'N' SWALLER HIM-- RIGHT THAR!
SUDDENLY, MULDOON SPRINGS FROM HIS CHAIR...
BEASLEY! IT'S MUH MAN, BEASLEY! AN' YUH KIN BET HE'S GONNA TELL US LOTS MORE!
I'VE COLLECTED ALL THE PERTINENT DATA, SIR. WE HAVE WHAT I MIGHT TERM A FANTASTIC PROJECTION!

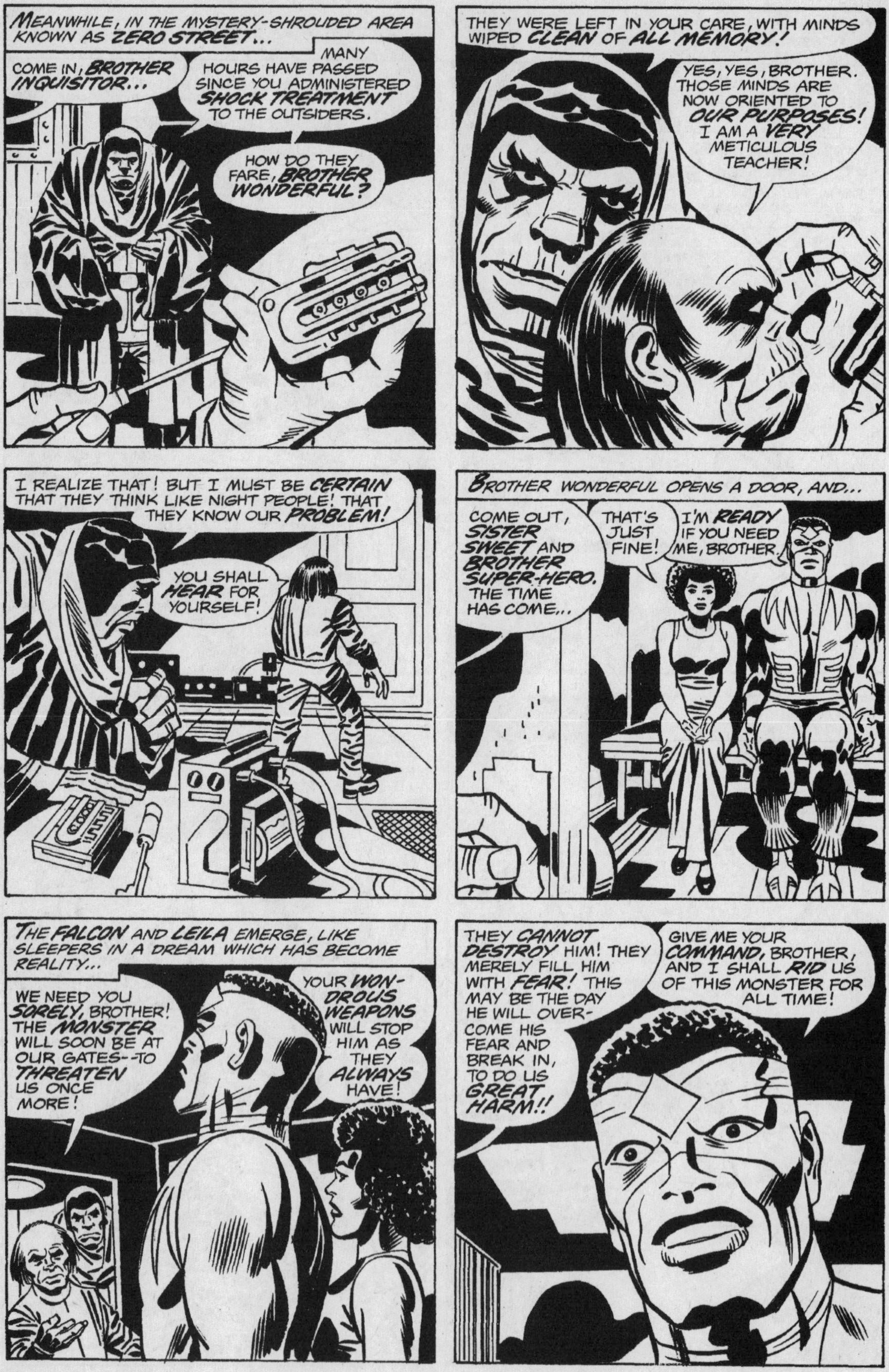
MEANWHILE, IN THE MYSTERY-SHROUDED AREA KNOWN AS ZERO STREET...
COME IN, BROTHER INQUISITOR...
MANY HOURS HAVE PASSED SINCE YOU ADMINISTERED SHOCK TREATMENT TO THE OUTSIDERS.
HOW DO THEY FARE, BROTHER WONDERFUL?
THEY WERE LEFT IN YOUR CARE, WITH MINDS WIPED CLEAN OF ALL MEMORY!
YES, YES, BROTHER. THOSE MINDS ARE NOW ORIENTED TO OUR PURPOSES! I AM A VERY METICULOUS TEACHER!
I REALIZE THAT! BUT I MUST BE CERTAIN THAT THEY THINK LIKE NIGHT PEOPLE! THAT THEY KNOW OUR PROBLEM!
YOU SHALL HEAR FOR YOURSELF!
BROTHER WONDERFUL OPENS A DOOR, AND...
COME OUT, SISTER SWEET AND BROTHER SUPER-HERO. THE TIME HAS COME...
THAT'S JUST FINE!
I'M READY IF YOU NEED ME, BROTHER.
THE FALCON AND LEILA EMERGE, LIKE SLEEPERS IN A DREAM WHICH HAS BECOME REALITY...
WE NEED YOU SORELY, BROTHER! THE MONSTER WILL SOON BE AT OUR GATES--TO THREATEN US ONCE MORE!
YOUR WONDROUS WEAPONS WILL STOP HIM AS THEY ALWAYS HAVE!
THEY CANNOT DESTROY HIM! THEY MERELY FILL HIM WITH FEAR! THIS MAY BE THE DAY HE WILL OVERCOME HIS FEAR AND BREAK IN, TO DO US GREAT HARM!!
GIVE ME YOUR COMMAND, BROTHER, AND I SHALL RID US OF THIS MONSTER FOR ALL TIME!

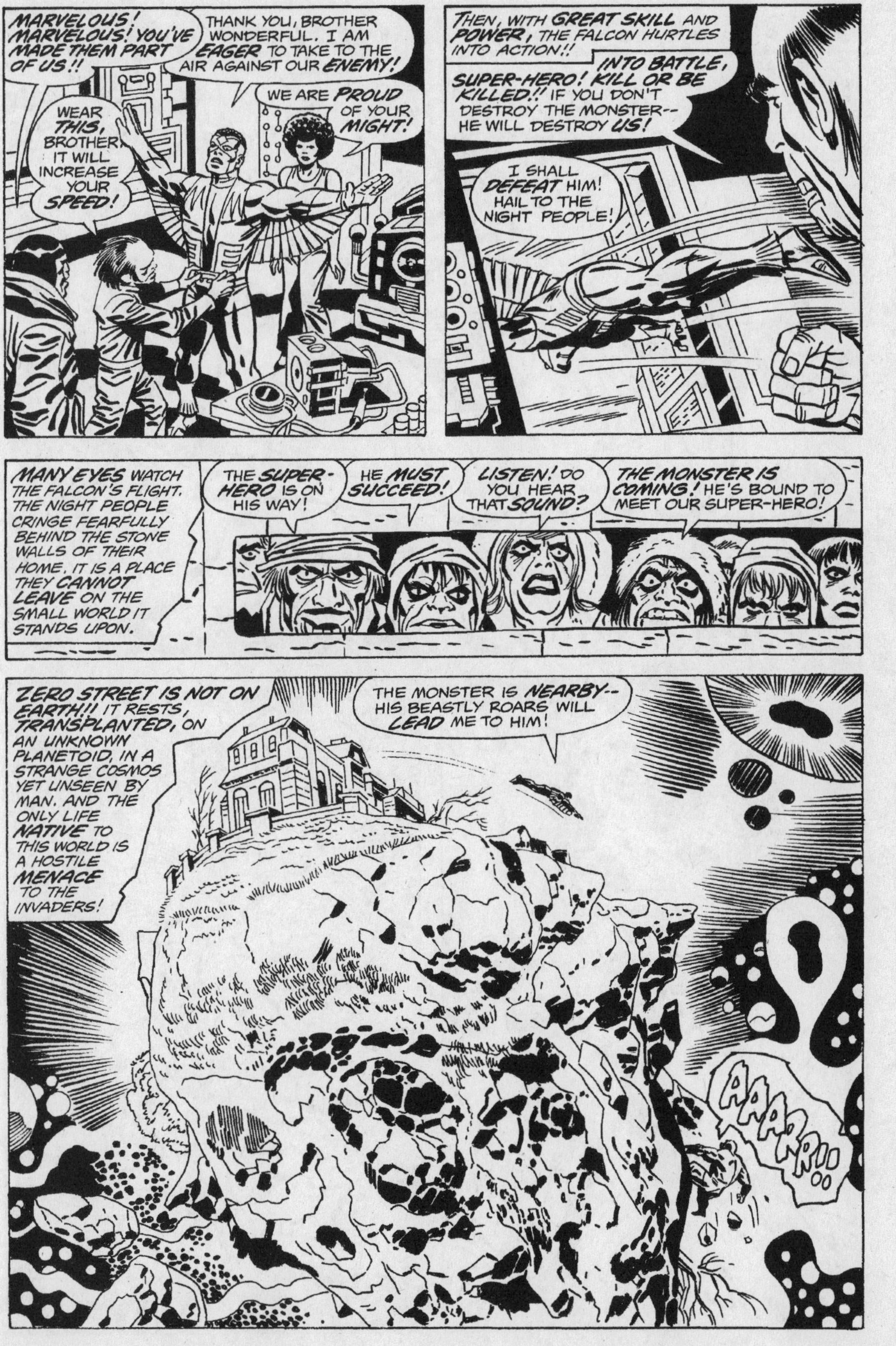

MARVELOUS! MARVELOUS! YOU'VE MADE THEM PART OF US!!
THANK YOU, BROTHER WONDERFUL. I AM EAGER TO TAKE TO THE AIR AGAINST OUR ENEMY!
WEAR THIS, BROTHER. IT WILL INCREASE YOUR SPEED!
WE ARE PROUD OF YOUR MIGHT!
THEN, WITH GREAT SKILL AND POWER, THE FALCON HURTLES INTO ACTION!!
INTO BATTLE, SUPER-HERO! KILL OR BE KILLED!! IF YOU DON'T DESTROY THE MONSTER-- HE WILL DESTROY US!
I SHALL DEFEAT HIM! HAIL TO THE NIGHT PEOPLE!
MANY EYES WATCH THE FALCON'S FLIGHT. THE NIGHT PEOPLE CRINGE FEARFULLY BEHIND THE STONE WALLS OF THEIR HOME. IT IS A PLACE THEY CANNOT LEAVE ON THE SMALL WORLD IT STANDS UPON.
THE SUPER-HERO IS ON HIS WAY!
HE MUST SUCCEED!
LISTEN! DO YOU HEAR THAT SOUND?
THE MONSTER IS COMING! HE'S BOUND TO MEET OUR SUPER-HERO!
ZERO STREET IS NOT ON EARTH!! IT RESTS, TRANSPLANTED, ON AN UNKNOWN PLANETOID, IN A STRANGE COSMOS YET UNSEEN BY MAN. AND THE ONLY LIFE NATIVE TO THIS WORLD IS A HOSTILE MENACE TO THE INVADERS!
THE MONSTER IS NEARBY-- HIS BEASTLY ROARS WILL LEAD ME TO HIM!
AAARRUOO

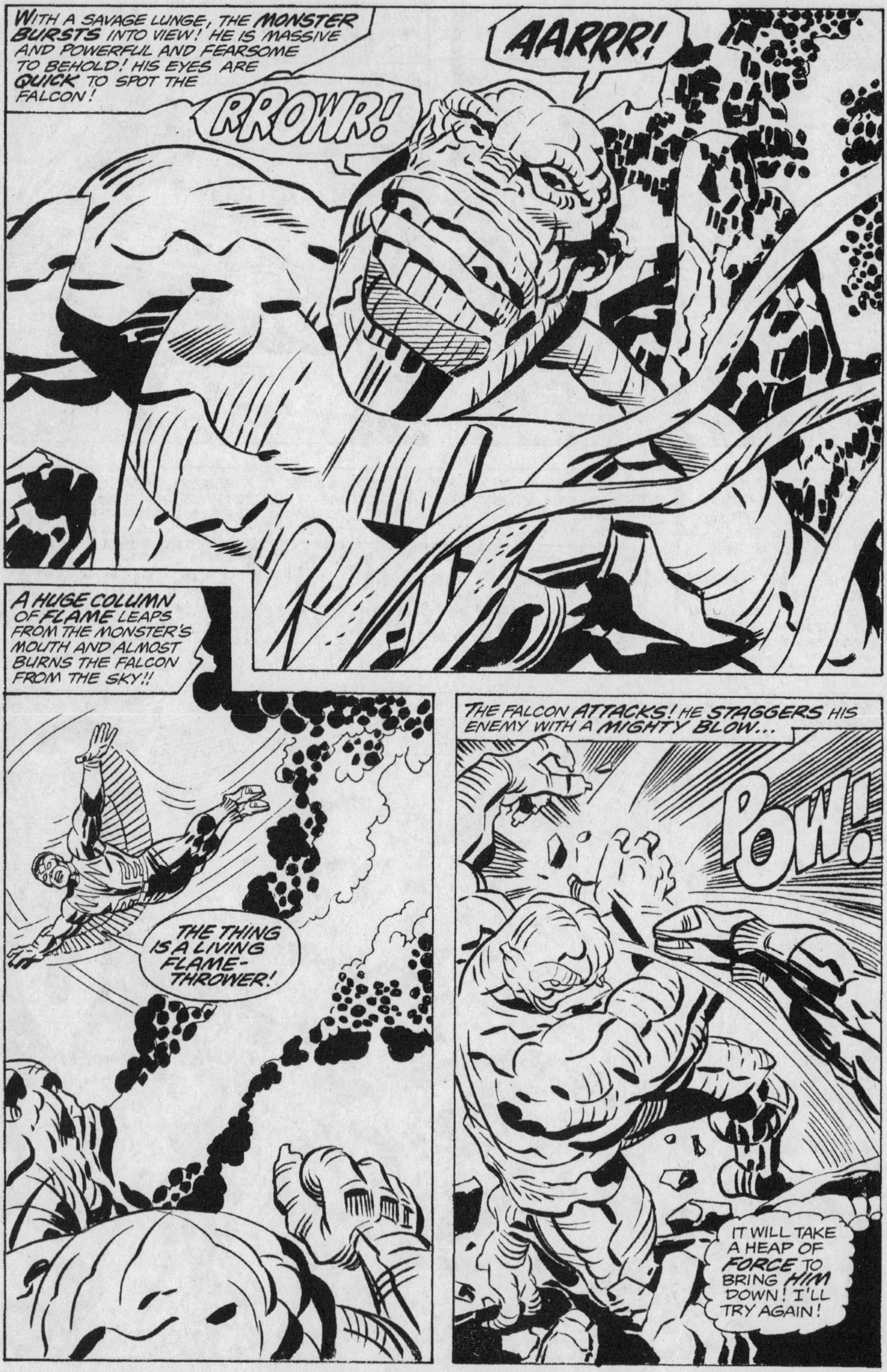
WITH A SAVAGE LUNGE, THE MONSTER BURSTS INTO VIEW! HE IS MASSIVE AND POWERFUL AND FEARSOME TO BEHOLD! HIS EYES ARE QUICK TO SPOT THE FALCON!
AARRR!
RROWR!
A HUGE COLUMN OF FLAME LEAPS FROM THE MONSTER'S MOUTH AND ALMOST BURNS THE FALCON FROM THE SKY!!
THE THING IS A LIVING FLAME-THROWER!
THE FALCON ATTACKS! HE STAGGERS HIS ENEMY WITH A MIGHTY BLOW...
POW!
IT WILL TAKE A HEAP OF FORCE TO BRING HIM DOWN! I'LL TRY AGAIN!

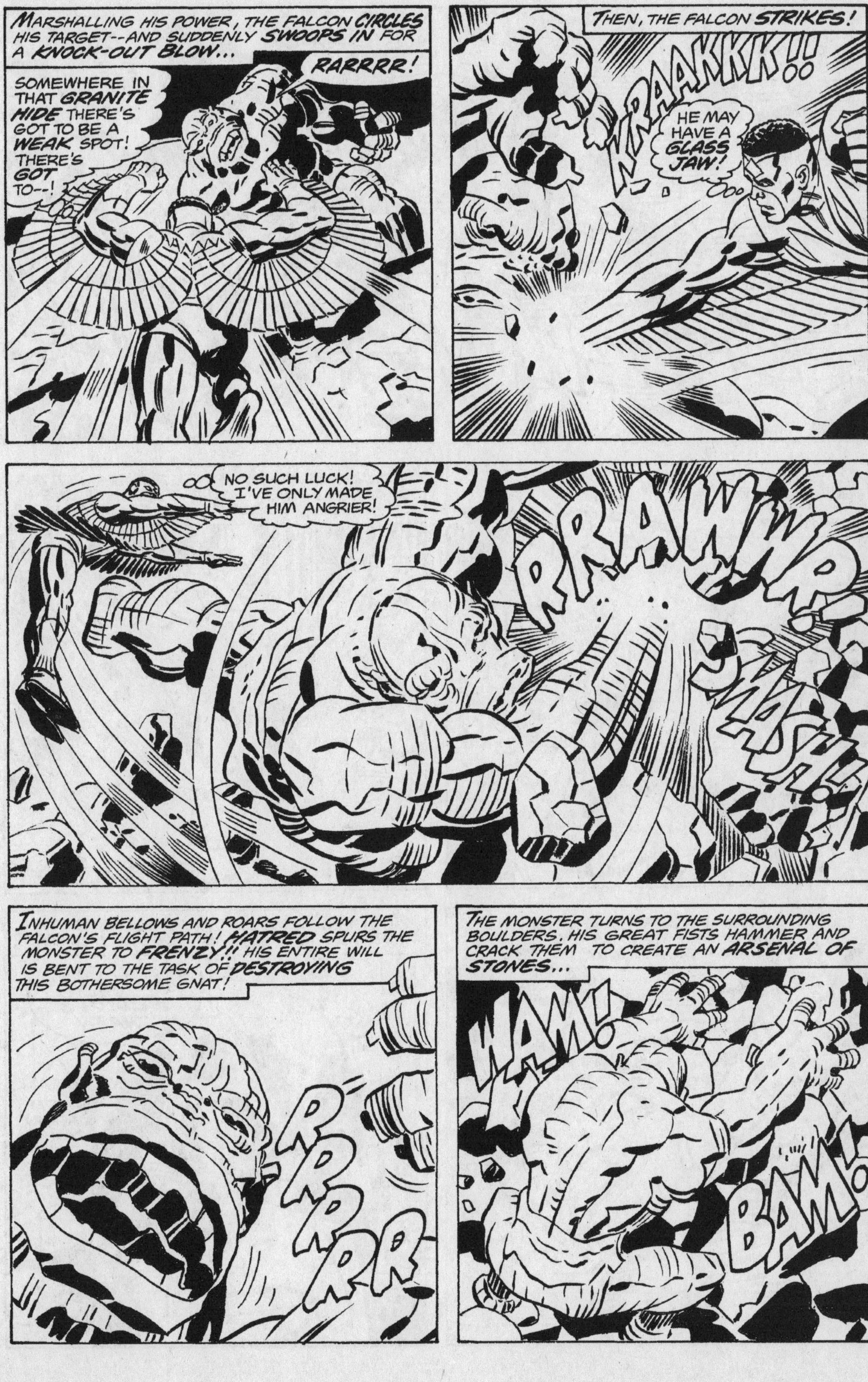

MARSHALLING HIS POWER, THE FALCON CIRCLES HIS TARGET--AND SUDDENLY SWOOPS IN FOR A KNOCK-OUT BLOW...
RARRRR!
SOMEWHERE IN THAT GRANITE HIDE THERE'S GOT TO BE A WEAK SPOT! THERE'S GOT TO--!
THEN, THE FALCON STRIKES!
KRAAKKK!!
HE MAY HAVE A GLASS JAW!
NO SUCH LUCK! I'VE ONLY MADE HIM ANGRIER!
RRAWWR!
SMASH!!
INHUMAN BELLOWS AND ROARS FOLLOW THE FALCON'S FLIGHT PATH! HATRED SPURS THE MONSTER TO FRENZY!! HIS ENTIRE WILL IS BENT TO THE TASK OF DESTROYING THIS BOTHERSOME GNAT!
RRRRR
THE MONSTER TURNS TO THE SURROUNDING BOULDERS. HIS GREAT FISTS HAMMER AND CRACK THEM TO CREATE AN ARSENAL OF STONES...
WAM!
BAM!

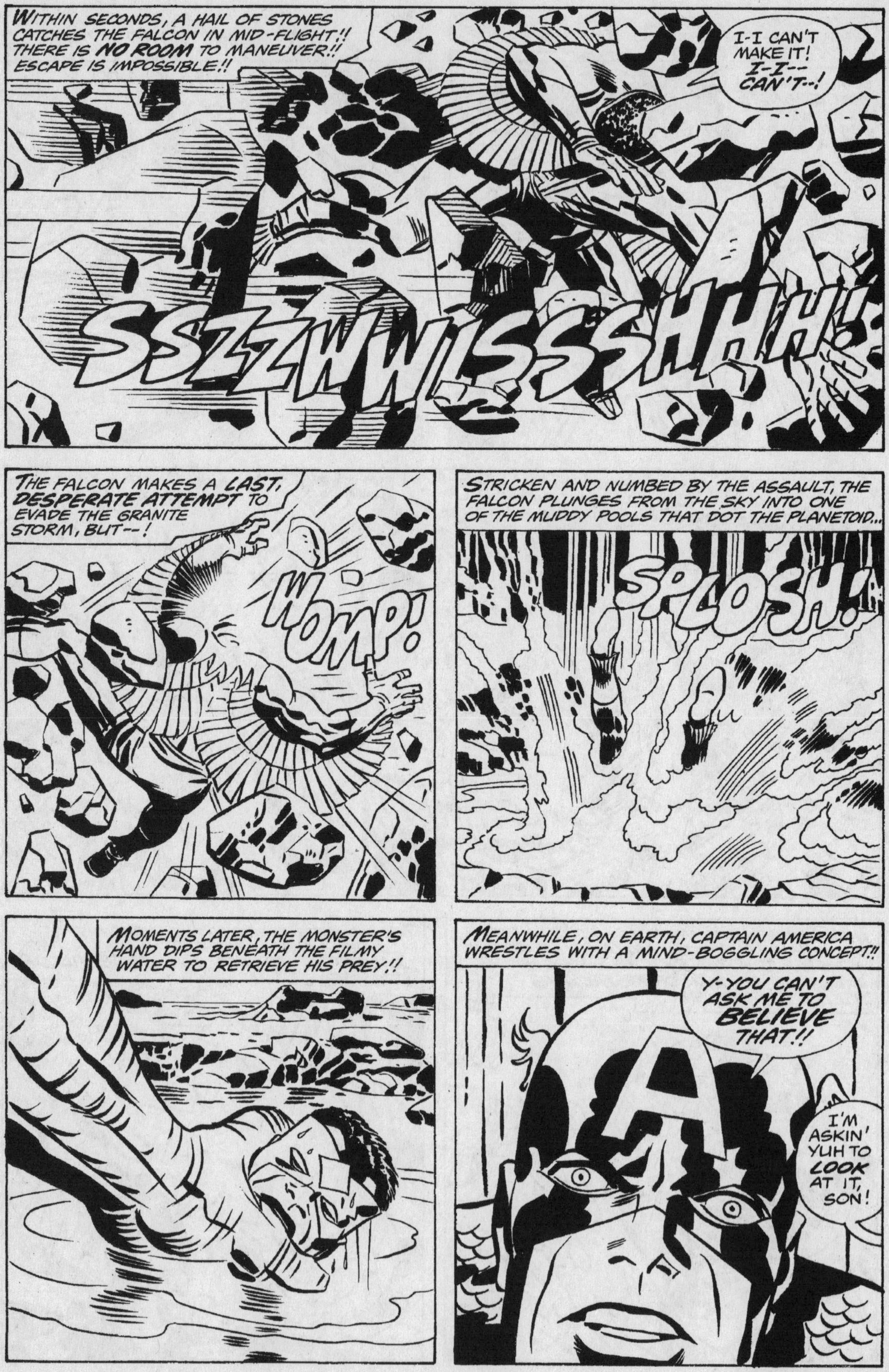
WITHIN SECONDS, A HAIL OF STONES CATCHES THE FALCON IN MID-FLIGHT!! THERE IS NO ROOM TO MANEUVER!! ESCAPE IS IMPOSSIBLE!!
I-I CAN'T MAKE IT! I-I-- CAN'T--!
SSZZWWLSSSHHH!
THE FALCON MAKES A LAST, DESPERATE ATTEMPT TO EVADE THE GRANITE STORM, BUT--!
WOMP!
STRICKEN AND NUMBED BY THE ASSAULT, THE FALCON PLUNGES FROM THE SKY INTO ONE OF THE MUDDY POOLS THAT DOT THE PLANETOID...
SPLOSH!
MOMENTS LATER, THE MONSTER'S HAND DIPS BENEATH THE FILMY WATER TO RETRIEVE HIS PREY!!
MEANWHILE, ON EARTH, CAPTAIN AMERICA WRESTLES WITH A MIND-BOGGLING CONCEPT!!
Y-YOU CAN'T ASK ME TO BELIEVE THAT!!
I'M ASKIN' YUH TO LOOK AT IT, SON!

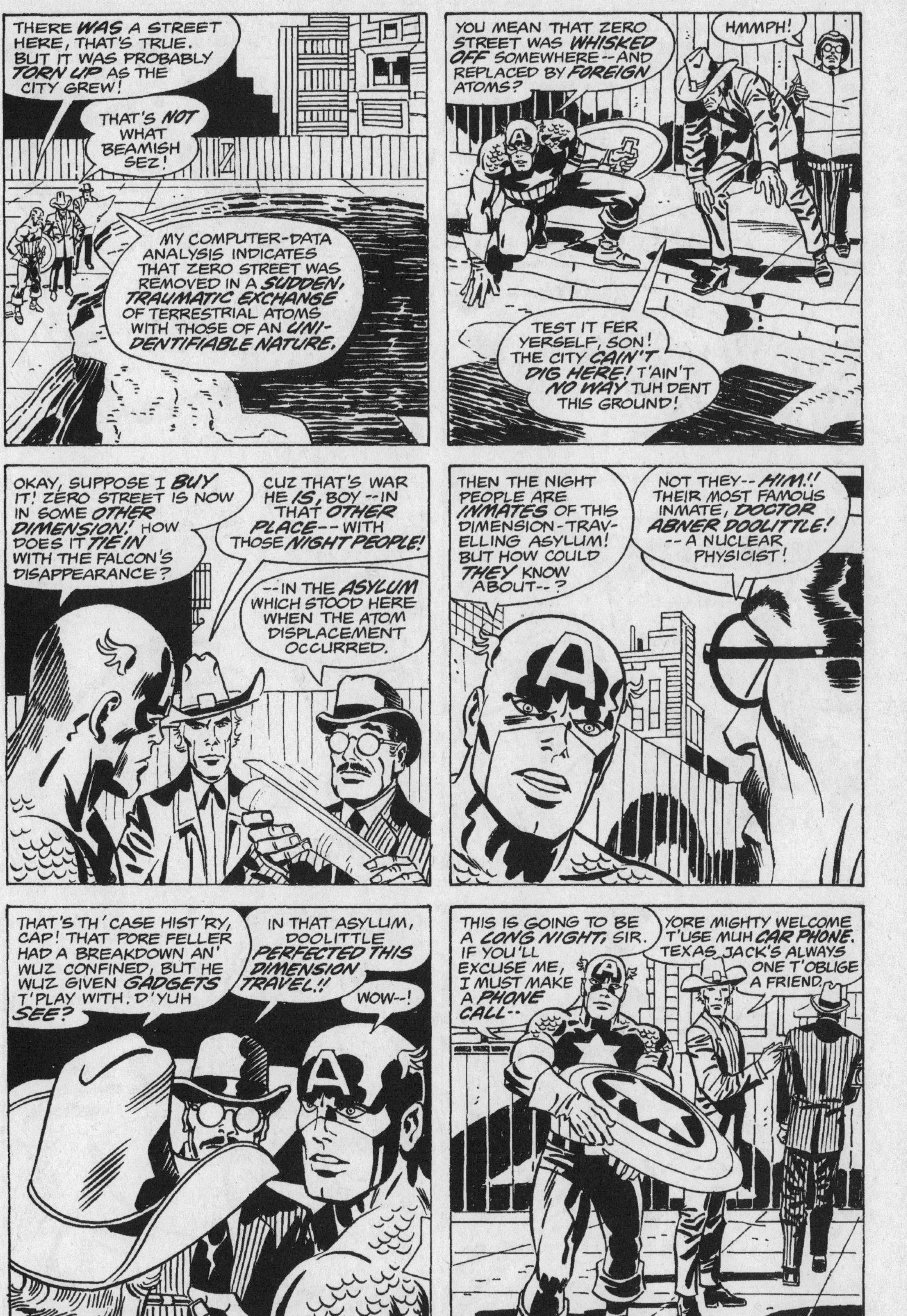
THERE WAS A STREET HERE, THAT'S TRUE. BUT IT WAS PROBABLY TORN UP AS THE CITY GREW!
THAT'S NOT WHAT BEAMISH SEZ!
MY COMPUTER-DATA ANALYSIS INDICATES THAT ZERO STREET WAS REMOVED IN A SUDDEN, TRAUMATIC EXCHANGE OF TERRESTRIAL ATOMS WITH THOSE OF AN UNI-DENTIFIABLE NATURE.
YOU MEAN THAT ZERO STREET WAS WHISKED OFF SOMEWHERE--AND REPLACED BY FOREIGN ATOMS?
HMMPH!
TEST IT FER YERSELF, SON! THE CITY CAIN'T DIG HERE! T'AIN'T NO WAY TUH DENT THIS GROUND!
OKAY, SUPPOSE I BUY IT! ZERO STREET IS NOW IN SOME OTHER DIMENSION! HOW DOES IT TIE IN WITH THE FALCON'S DISAPPEARANCE?
CUZ THAT'S WAR HE IS, BOY--IN THAT OTHER PLACE--WITH THOSE NIGHT PEOPLE!
--IN THE ASYLUM WHICH STOOD HERE WHEN THE ATOM DISPLACEMENT OCCURRED.
THEN THE NIGHT PEOPLE ARE INMATES OF THIS DIMENSION-TRAVELLING ASYLUM! BUT HOW COULD THEY KNOW ABOUT--?
NOT THEY--HIM!! THEIR MOST FAMOUS INMATE, DOCTOR ABNER DOOLITTLE! --A NUCLEAR PHYSICIST!
THAT'S TH' CASE HIST'RY, CAP! THAT PORE FELLER HAD A BREAKDOWN AN' WUZ CONFINED, BUT HE WUZ GIVEN GADGETS T'PLAY WITH. D'YUH SEE?
IN THAT ASYLUM, DOOLITTLE PERFECTED THIS DIMENSION TRAVEL!!
WOW--!
THIS IS GOING TO BE A LONG NIGHT, SIR. IF YOU'LL EXCUSE ME, I MUST MAKE A PHONE CALL--
YORE MIGHTY WELCOME T'USE MUH CAR PHONE. TEXAS JACK'S ALWAYS ONE T'OBLIGE A FRIEND.

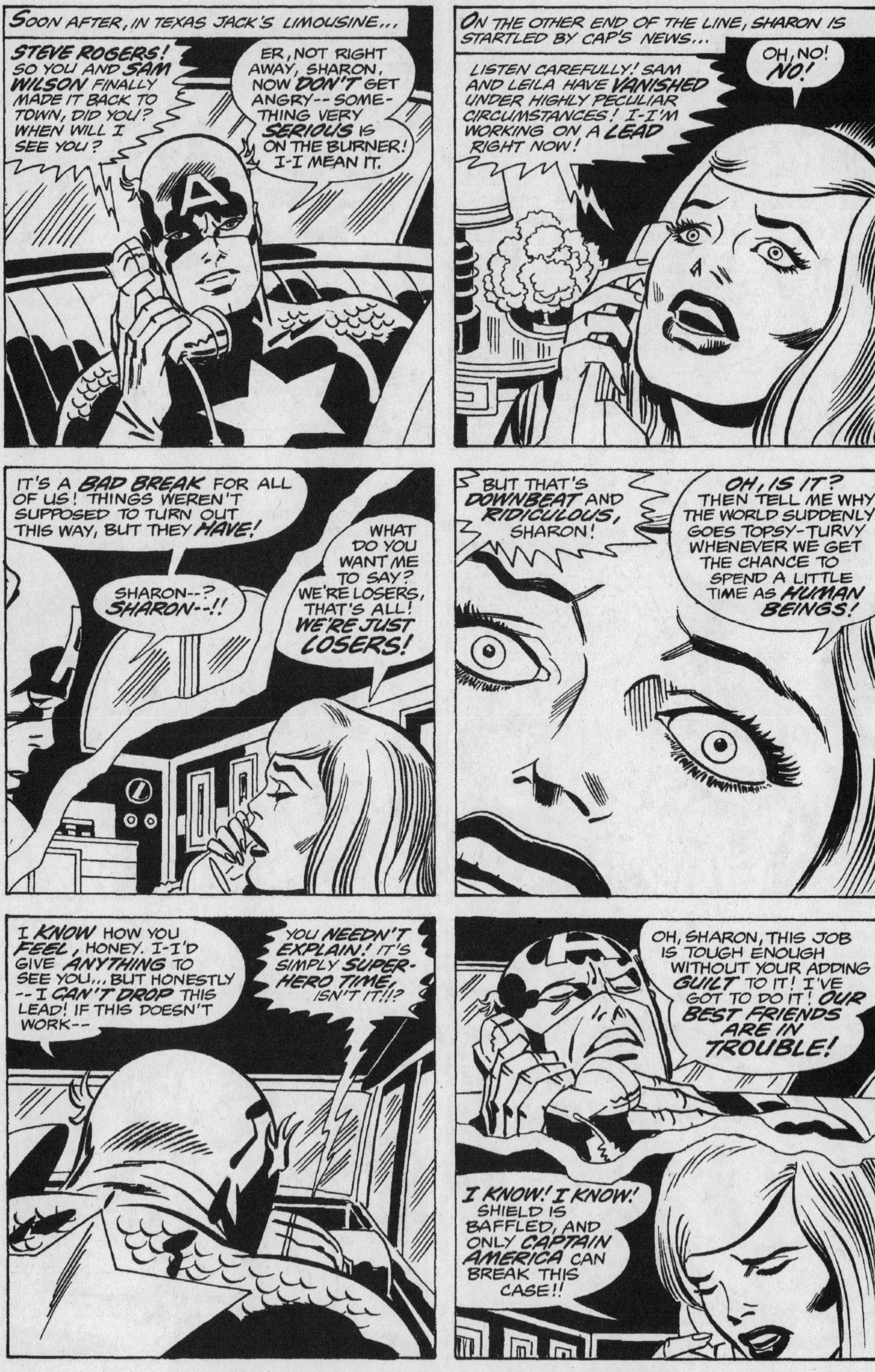

SOON AFTER, IN TEXAS JACK'S LIMOUSINE...
STEVE ROGERS! SO YOU AND SAM WILSON FINALLY MADE IT BACK TO TOWN, DID YOU? WHEN WILL I SEE YOU?
ER, NOT RIGHT AWAY, SHARON. NOW DON'T GET ANGRY-- SOMETHING VERY SERIOUS IS ON THE BURNER! I-I MEAN IT.
ON THE OTHER END OF THE LINE, SHARON IS STARTLED BY CAP'S NEWS...
LISTEN CAREFULLY! SAM AND LEILA HAVE VANISHED UNDER HIGHLY PECULIAR CIRCUMSTANCES! I-I'M WORKING ON A LEAD RIGHT NOW!
OH, NO! NO!
IT'S A BAD BREAK FOR ALL OF US! THINGS WEREN'T SUPPOSED TO TURN OUT THIS WAY, BUT THEY HAVE!
SHARON--? SHARON--!!
WHAT DO YOU WANT ME TO SAY? WE'RE LOSERS, THAT'S ALL! WE'RE JUST LOSERS!
BUT THAT'S DOWNBEAT AND RIDICULOUS, SHARON!
OH, IS IT? THEN TELL ME WHY THE WORLD SUDDENLY GOES TOPSY-TURVY WHENEVER WE GET THE CHANCE TO SPEND A LITTLE TIME AS HUMAN BEINGS!
I KNOW HOW YOU FEEL, HONEY. I-I'D GIVE ANYTHING TO SEE YOU... BUT HONESTLY --I CAN'T DROP THIS LEAD! IF THIS DOESN'T WORK--
YOU NEEDN'T EXPLAIN! IT'S SIMPLY SUPER-HERO TIME, ISN'T IT!!?
OH, SHARON, THIS JOB IS TOUGH ENOUGH WITHOUT YOUR ADDING GUILT TO IT! I'VE GOT TO DO IT! OUR BEST FRIENDS ARE IN TROUBLE!
I KNOW! I KNOW! SHIELD IS BAFFLED, AND ONLY CAPTAIN AMERICA CAN BREAK THIS CASE!!

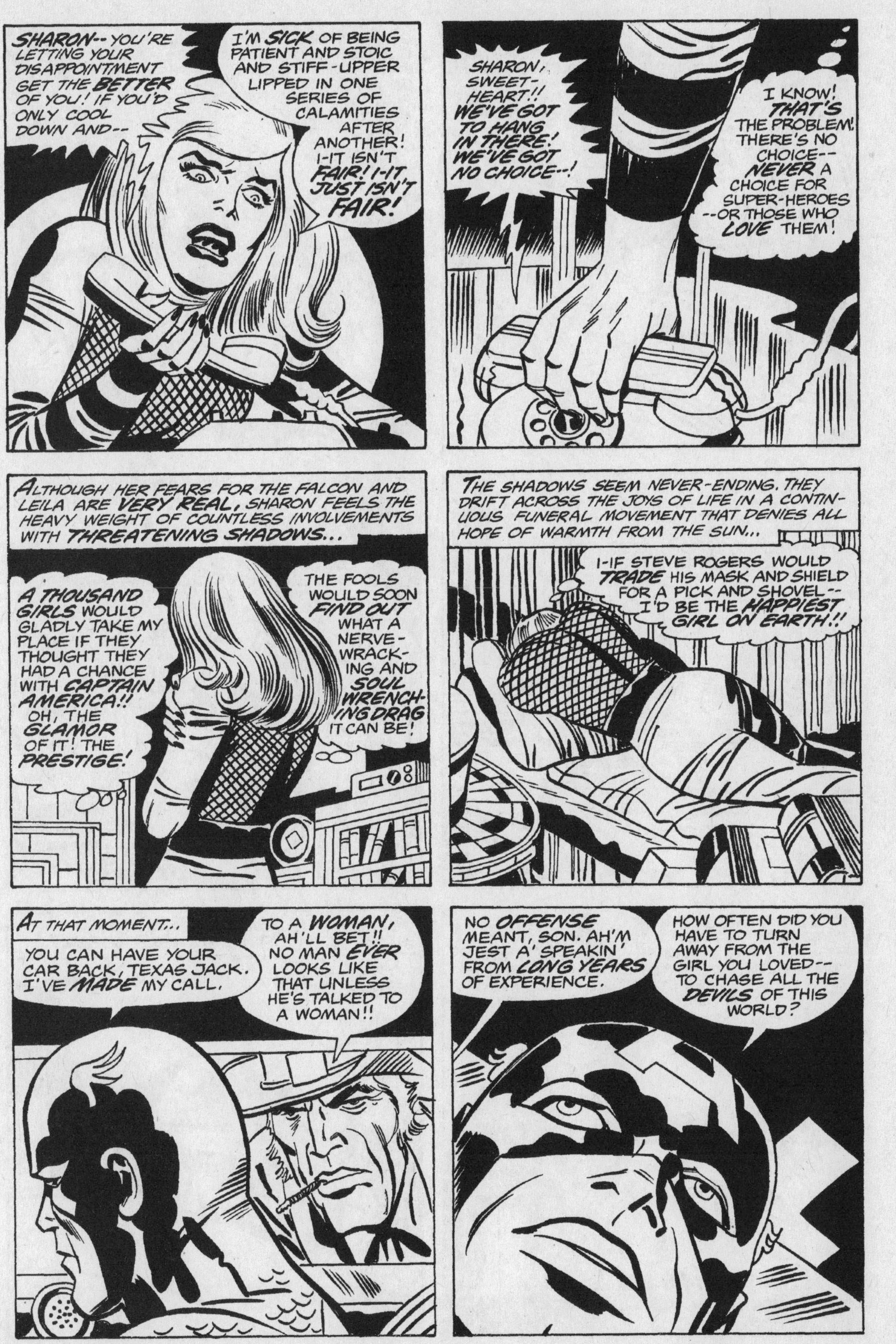
SHARON-- YOU'RE LETTING YOUR DISAPPOINTMENT GET THE BETTER OF YOU! IF YOU'D ONLY COOL DOWN AND--
I'M SICK OF BEING PATIENT AND STOIC AND STIFF-UPPER LIPPED IN ONE SERIES OF CALAMITIES AFTER ANOTHER! I-IT ISN'T FAIR! I-IT JUST ISN'T FAIR!
SHARON, SWEET-HEART!! WE'VE GOT TO HANG IN THERE! WE'VE GOT NO CHOICE--!
I KNOW! THAT'S THE PROBLEM! THERE'S NO CHOICE-- NEVER A CHOICE FOR SUPER-HEROES --OR THOSE WHO LOVE THEM!
ALTHOUGH HER FEARS FOR THE FALCON AND LEILA ARE VERY REAL, SHARON FEELS THE HEAVY WEIGHT OF COUNTLESS INVOLVEMENTS WITH THREATENING SHADOWS...
A THOUSAND GIRLS WOULD GLADLY TAKE MY PLACE IF THEY THOUGHT THEY HAD A CHANCE WITH CAPTAIN AMERICA!! OH, THE GLAMOR OF IT! THE PRESTIGE!
THE FOOLS WOULD SOON FIND OUT WHAT A NERVE-WRACKING AND SOUL WRENCHING DRAG IT CAN BE!
THE SHADOWS SEEM NEVER-ENDING. THEY DRIFT ACROSS THE JOYS OF LIFE IN A CONTINUOUS FUNERAL MOVEMENT THAT DENIES ALL HOPE OF WARMTH FROM THE SUN...
I-IF STEVE ROGERS WOULD TRADE HIS MASK AND SHIELD FOR A PICK AND SHOVEL-- I'D BE THE HAPPIEST GIRL ON EARTH!!
AT THAT MOMENT...
YOU CAN HAVE YOUR CAR BACK, TEXAS JACK. I'VE MADE MY CALL.
TO A WOMAN, AH'LL BET!! NO MAN EVER LOOKS LIKE THAT UNLESS HE'S TALKED TO A WOMAN!!
NO OFFENSE MEANT, SON. AH'M JEST A' SPEAKIN' FROM LONG YEARS OF EXPERIENCE.
HOW OFTEN DID YOU HAVE TO TURN AWAY FROM THE GIRL YOU LOVED-- TO CHASE ALL THE DEVILS OF THIS WORLD?

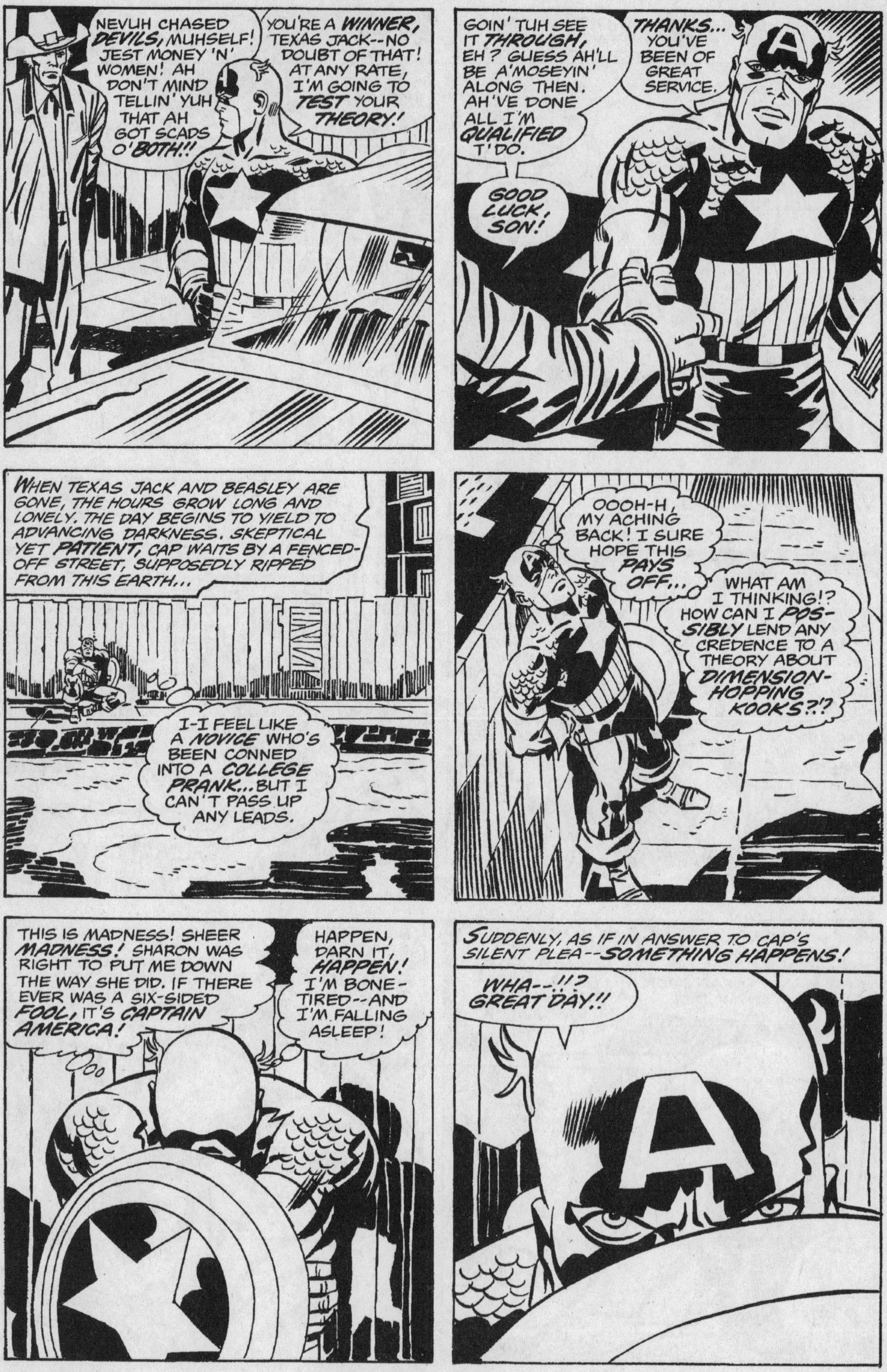
NEVUH CHASED DEVILS, MUHSELF! JEST MONEY 'N' WOMEN! AH DON'T MIND TELLIN' YUH THAT AH GOT SCADS O' BOTH!!
YOU'RE A WINNER, TEXAS JACK--NO DOUBT OF THAT! AT ANY RATE, I'M GOING TO TEST YOUR THEORY!
GOIN' TUH SEE IT THROUGH, EH? GUESS AH'LL BE A'MOSEYIN' ALONG THEN. AH'VE DONE ALL I'M QUALIFIED T'DO.
THANKS... YOU'VE BEEN OF GREAT SERVICE.
GOOD LUCK, SON!
WHEN TEXAS JACK AND BEASLEY ARE GONE, THE HOURS GROW LONG AND LONELY. THE DAY BEGINS TO YIELD TO ADVANCING DARKNESS. SKEPTICAL YET PATIENT, CAP WAITS BY A FENCED-OFF STREET, SUPPOSEDLY RIPPED FROM THIS EARTH...
I-I FEEL LIKE A NOVICE WHO'S BEEN CONNED INTO A COLLEGE PRANK... BUT I CAN'T PASS UP ANY LEADS.
OOOH-H, MY ACHING BACK! I SURE HOPE THIS PAYS OFF...
WHAT AM I THINKING!? HOW CAN I POSSIBLY LEND ANY CREDENCE TO A THEORY ABOUT DIMENSION-HOPPING KOOKS?!?
THIS IS MADNESS! SHEER MADNESS! SHARON WAS RIGHT TO PUT ME DOWN THE WAY SHE DID. IF THERE EVER WAS A SIX-SIDED FOOL, IT'S CAPTAIN AMERICA!
HAPPEN, DARN IT, HAPPEN! I'M BONE-TIRED--AND I'M FALLING ASLEEP!
SUDDENLY, AS IF IN ANSWER TO CAP'S SILENT PLEA--SOMETHING HAPPENS!
WHA--!!? GREAT DAY!!

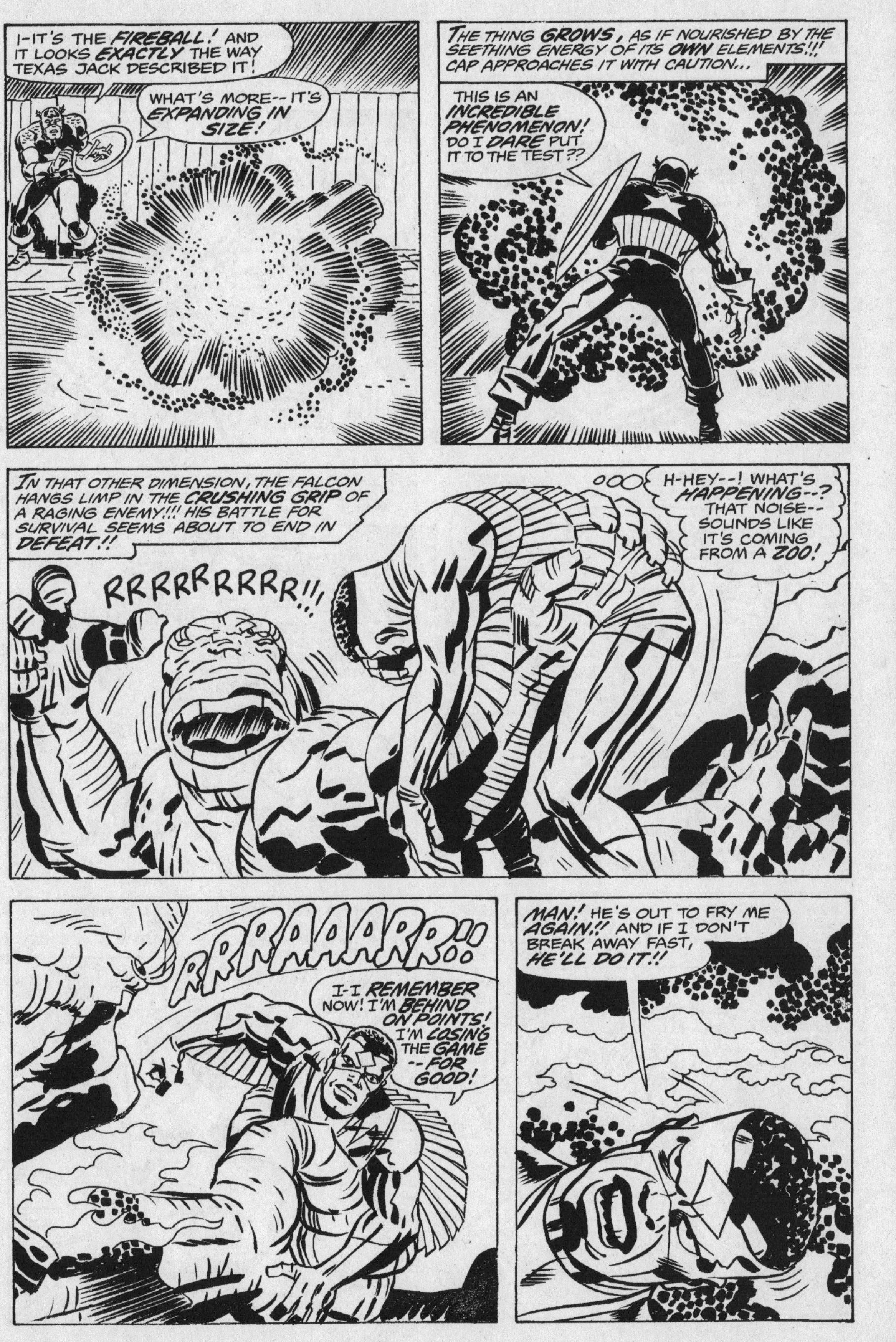

I-IT'S THE FIREBALL! AND IT LOOKS EXACTLY THE WAY TEXAS JACK DESCRIBED IT!
WHAT'S MORE-- IT'S EXPANDING IN SIZE!
THE THING GROWS, AS IF NOURISHED BY THE SEETHING ENERGY OF ITS OWN ELEMENTS!!! CAP APPROACHES IT WITH CAUTION...
THIS IS AN INCREDIBLE PHENOMENON! DO I DARE PUT IT TO THE TEST??
IN THAT OTHER DIMENSION, THE FALCON HANGS LIMP IN THE CRUSHING GRIP OF A RAGING ENEMY!!! HIS BATTLE FOR SURVIVAL SEEMS ABOUT TO END IN DEFEAT!!
H-HEY--! WHAT'S HAPPENING--? THAT NOISE-- SOUNDS LIKE IT'S COMING FROM A ZOO!
RRRRRRRRR!!!
RRRAAAARR!!
I-I REMEMBER NOW! I'M BEHIND ON POINTS! I'M COSING THE GAME --FOR GOOD!
MAN! HE'S OUT TO FRY ME AGAIN!! AND IF I DON'T BREAK AWAY FAST, HE'LL DO IT!!

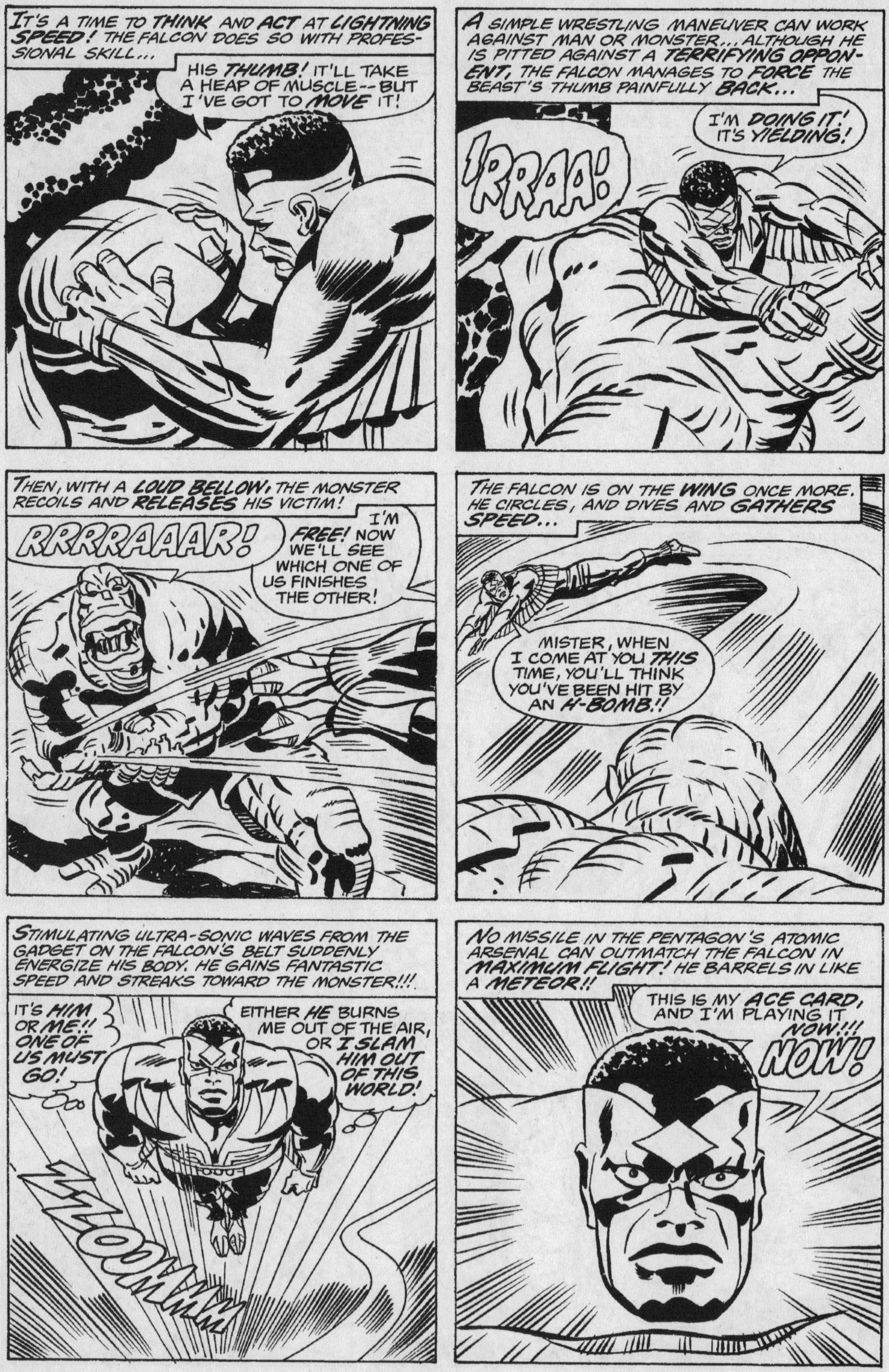

IT'S A TIME TO THINK AND ACT AT LIGHTNING SPEED! THE FALCON DOES SO WITH PROFESSIONAL SKILL...
HIS THUMB! IT'LL TAKE A HEAP OF MUSCLE--BUT I'VE GOT TO MOVE IT!
A SIMPLE WRESTLING MANEUVER CAN WORK AGAINST MAN OR MONSTER... ALTHOUGH HE IS PITTED AGAINST A TERRIFYING OPPONENT, THE FALCON MANAGES TO FORCE THE BEAST'S THUMB PAINFULLY BACK...
I'M DOING IT! IT'S YIELDING!
RRAA!
THEN, WITH A LOUD BELLOW, THE MONSTER RECOILS AND RELEASES HIS VICTIM!
RRRRAAAR!
I'M FREE! NOW WE'LL SEE WHICH ONE OF US FINISHES THE OTHER!
THE FALCON IS ON THE WING ONCE MORE. HE CIRCLES, AND DIVES AND GATHERS SPEED...
MISTER, WHEN I COME AT YOU THIS TIME, YOU'LL THINK YOU'VE BEEN HIT BY AN H-BOMB!!
STIMULATING ULTRA-SONIC WAVES FROM THE GADGET ON THE FALCON'S BELT SUDDENLY ENERGIZE HIS BODY. HE GAINS FANTASTIC SPEED AND STREAKS TOWARD THE MONSTER!!!
IT'S HIM OR ME!! ONE OF US MUST GO!
EITHER HE BURNS ME OUT OF THE AIR, OR I SLAM HIM OUT OF THIS WORLD!
WHOOMM
NO MISSILE IN THE PENTAGON'S ATOMIC ARSENAL CAN OUTMATCH THE FALCON IN MAXIMUM FLIGHT! HE BARRELS IN LIKE A METEOR!!
THIS IS MY ACE CARD, AND I'M PLAYING IT NOW!!!
NOW!

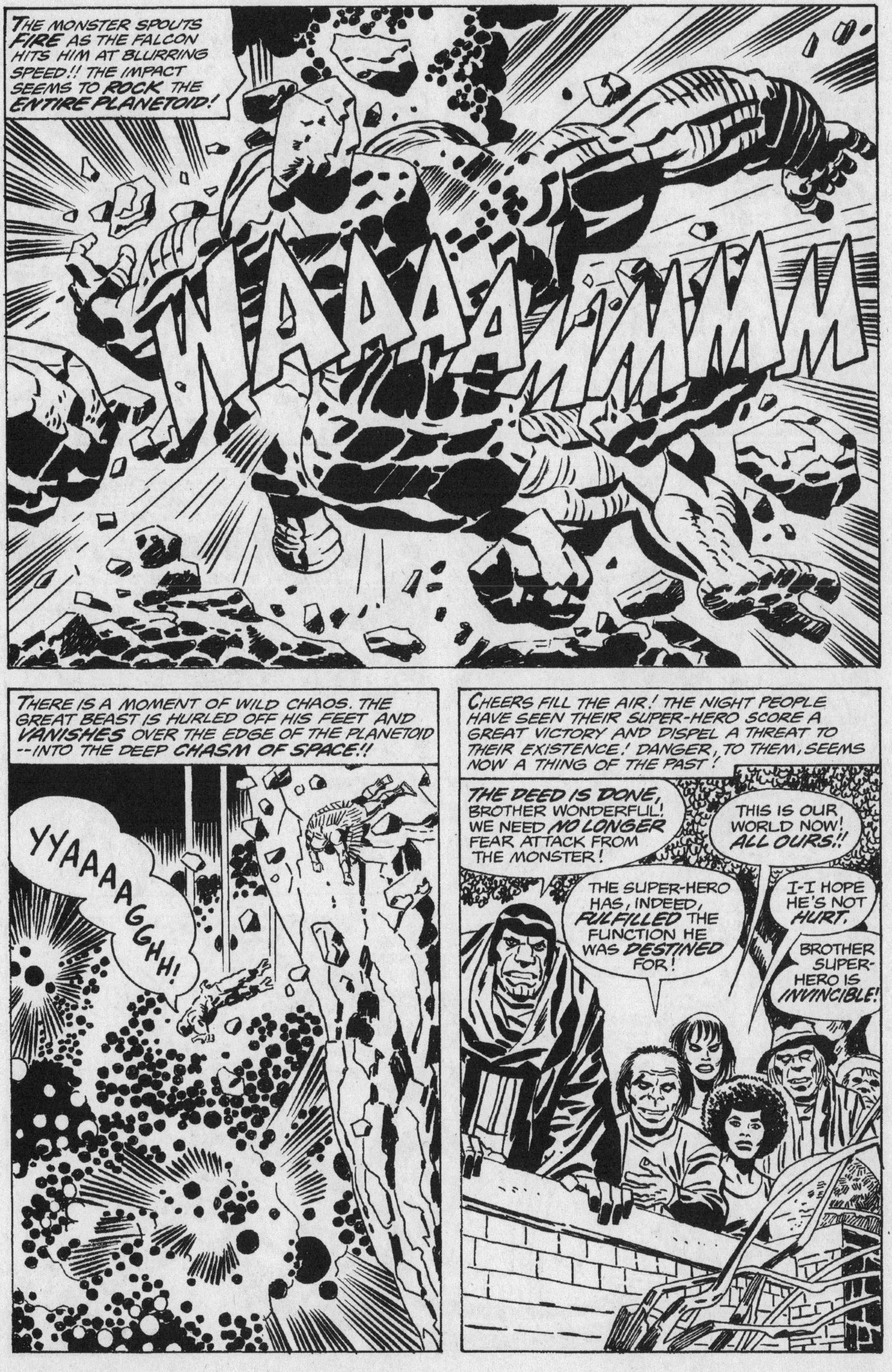
THE MONSTER SPOUTS FIRE AS THE FALCON HITS HIM AT BLURRING SPEED!! THE IMPACT SEEMS TO ROCK THE ENTIRE PLANETOID!
WAAAAHMMMM
THERE IS A MOMENT OF WILD CHAOS. THE GREAT BEAST IS HURLED OFF HIS FEET AND VANISHES OVER THE EDGE OF THE PLANETOID --INTO THE DEEP CHASM OF SPACE!!
YYAAAAAGGHH!
CHEERS FILL THE AIR! THE NIGHT PEOPLE HAVE SEEN THEIR SUPER-HERO SCORE A GREAT VICTORY AND DISPEL A THREAT TO THEIR EXISTENCE! DANGER, TO THEM, SEEMS NOW A THING OF THE PAST!
THE DEED IS DONE, BROTHER WONDERFUL! WE NEED NO LONGER FEAR ATTACK FROM THE MONSTER!
THIS IS OUR WORLD NOW! ALL OURS!!
THE SUPER-HERO HAS, INDEED, FULFILLED THE FUNCTION HE WAS DESTINED FOR!
I-I HOPE HE'S NOT HURT.
BROTHER SUPER-HERO IS INVINCIBLE!

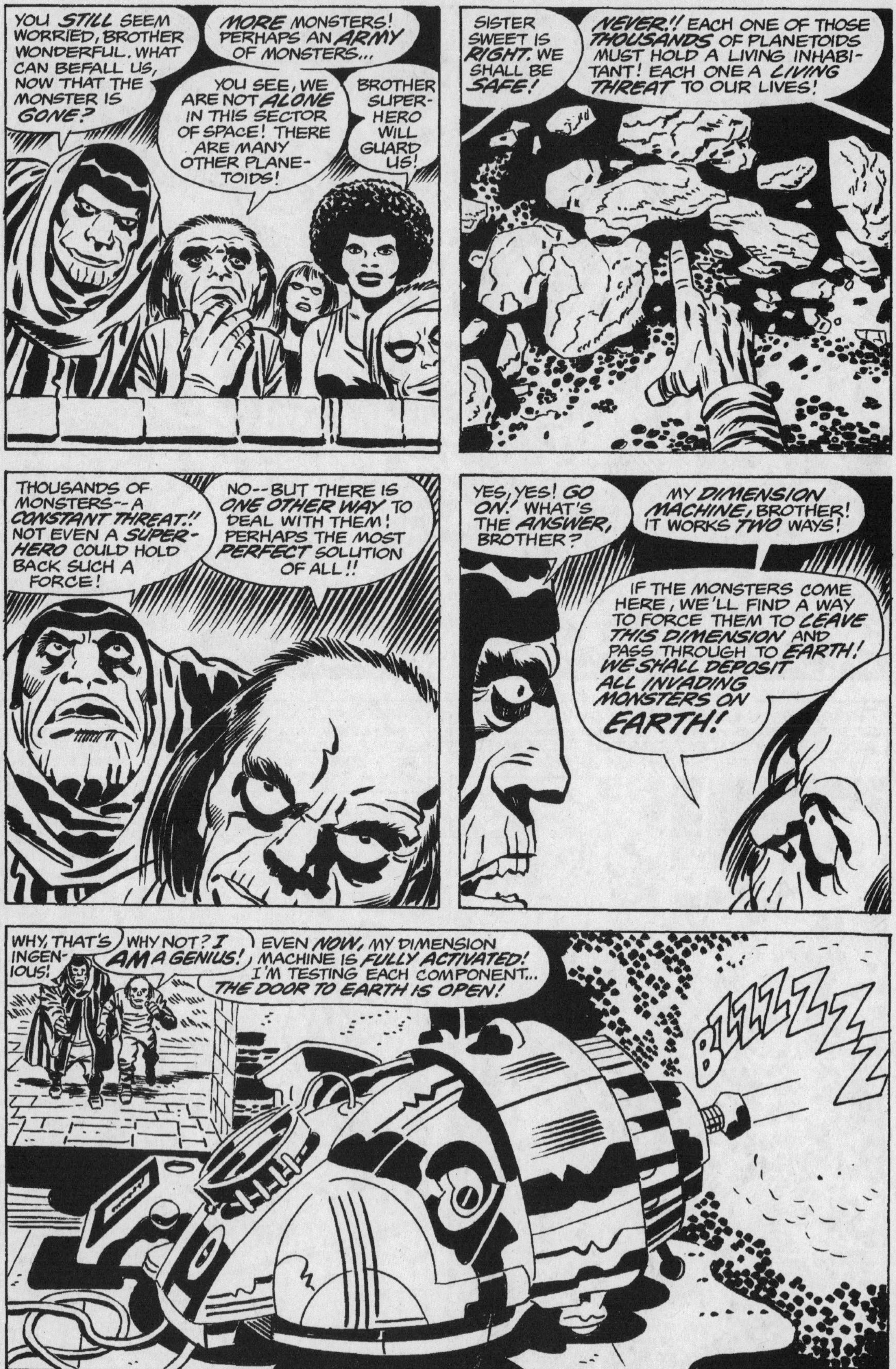
YOU STILL SEEM WORRIED, BROTHER WONDERFUL. WHAT CAN BEFALL US, NOW THAT THE MONSTER IS GONE?
MORE MONSTERS! PERHAPS AN ARMY OF MONSTERS...
YOU SEE, WE ARE NOT ALONE IN THIS SECTOR OF SPACE! THERE ARE MANY OTHER PLANE-TOIDS!
BROTHER SUPER-HERO WILL GUARD US!
SISTER SWEET IS RIGHT. WE SHALL BE SAFE!
NEVER!! EACH ONE OF THOSE THOUSANDS OF PLANETOIDS MUST HOLD A LIVING INHABI-TANT! EACH ONE A LIVING THREAT TO OUR LIVES!
THOUSANDS OF MONSTERS--A CONSTANT THREAT!! NOT EVEN A SUPER-HERO COULD HOLD BACK SUCH A FORCE!
NO--BUT THERE IS ONE OTHER WAY TO DEAL WITH THEM! PERHAPS THE MOST PERFECT SOLUTION OF ALL!!
YES, YES! GO ON! WHAT'S THE ANSWER, BROTHER?
MY DIMENSION MACHINE, BROTHER! IT WORKS TWO WAYS!
IF THE MONSTERS COME HERE, WE'LL FIND A WAY TO FORCE THEM TO LEAVE THIS DIMENSION AND PASS THROUGH TO EARTH! WE SHALL DEPOSIT ALL INVADING MONSTERS ON EARTH!
WHY, THAT'S INGEN-IOUS!
WHY NOT? I AM A GENIUS!
EVEN NOW, MY DIMENSION MACHINE IS FULLY ACTIVATED! I'M TESTING EACH COMPONENT... THE DOOR TO EARTH IS OPEN!
BZZZZZZZ

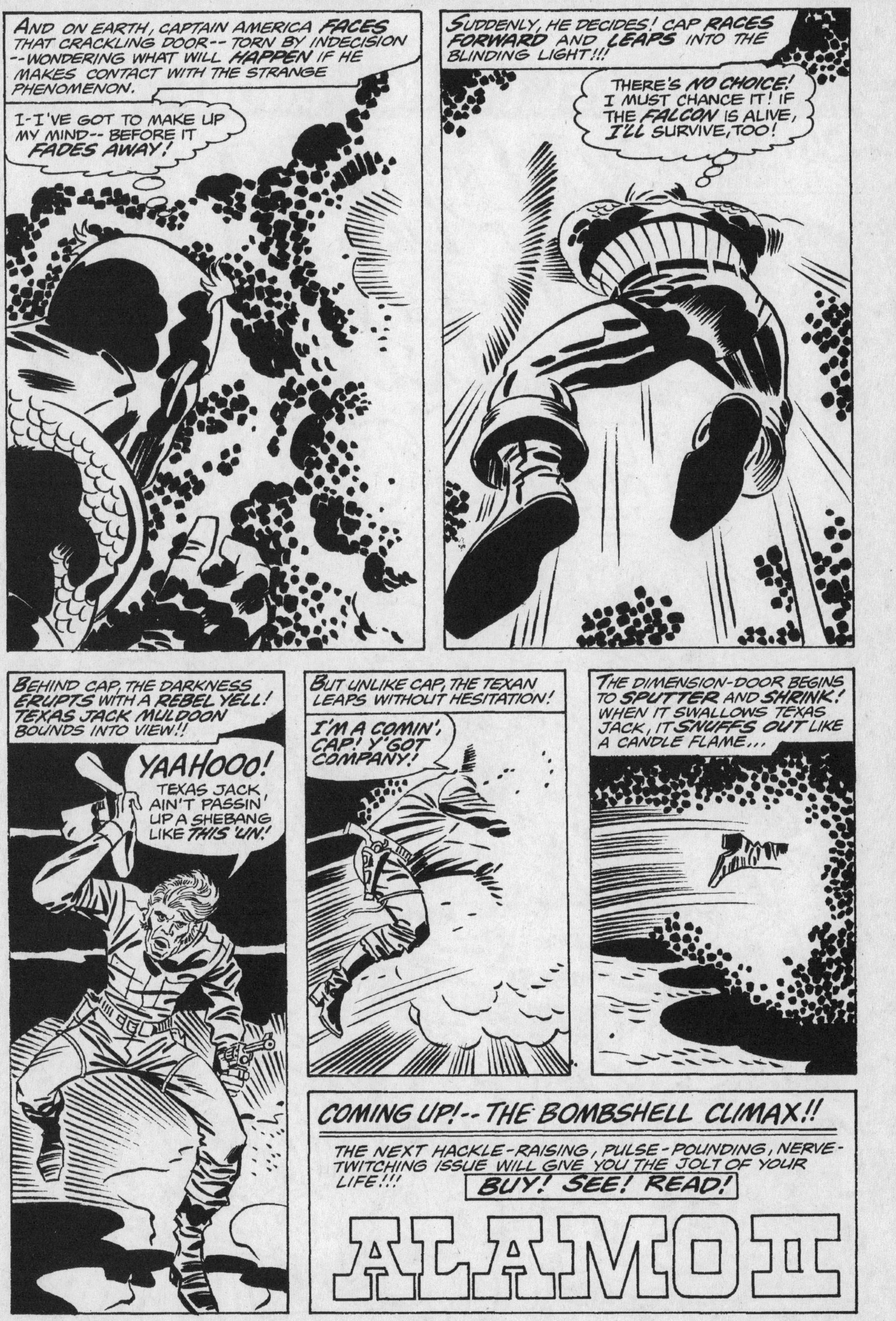
AND ON EARTH, CAPTAIN AMERICA FACES THAT CRACKLING DOOR-- TORN BY INDECISION --WONDERING WHAT WILL HAPPEN IF HE MAKES CONTACT WITH THE STRANGE PHENOMENON.
I-I'VE GOT TO MAKE UP MY MIND-- BEFORE IT FADES AWAY!
SUDDENLY, HE DECIDES! CAP RACES FORWARD AND LEAPS INTO THE BLINDING LIGHT!!!
THERE'S NO CHOICE! I MUST CHANCE IT! IF THE FALCON IS ALIVE, I'LL SURVIVE, TOO!
BEHIND CAP, THE DARKNESS ERUPTS WITH A REBEL YELL! TEXAS JACK MULDOON BOUNDS INTO VIEW!!
YAAHOOO! TEXAS JACK AIN'T PASSIN' UP A SHEBANG LIKE THIS 'UN!
BUT UNLIKE CAP, THE TEXAN LEAPS WITHOUT HESITATION!
I'M A COMIN', CAP! Y'GOT COMPANY!
THE DIMENSION-DOOR BEGINS TO SPUTTER AND SHRINK! WHEN IT SWALLOWS TEXAS JACK, IT SNUFFS OUT LIKE A CANDLE FLAME...
COMING UP!-- THE BOMBSHELL CLIMAX!!
THE NEXT HACKLE-RAISING, PULSE-POUNDING, NERVE-TWITCHING ISSUE WILL GIVE YOU THE JOLT OF YOUR LIFE!!!
BUY! SEE! READ!
ALAMO II

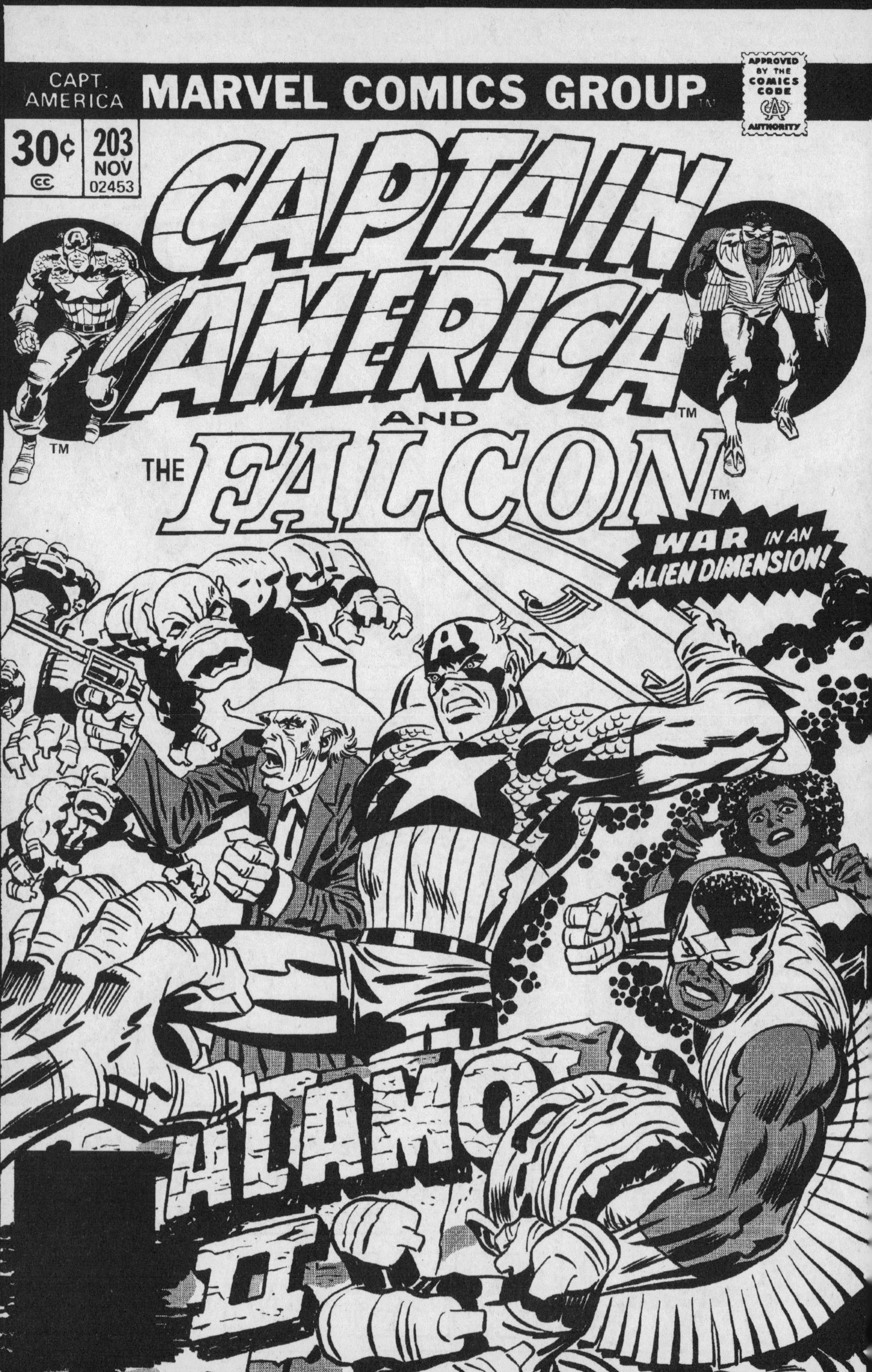
CAPT. AMERICA
MARVEL COMICS GROUP
APPROVED BY THE COMICS CODE AUTHORITY
30¢
203
NOV
02453
CAPTAIN AMERICA
AND
THE FALCON
WAR IN AN ALIEN DIMENSION!
ALAMO II

1941! The world at *war!* And in a secret laboratory, frail *Steve Rogers* became the American *super-soldier!* For four thrilling years, he fought the Axis powers—until a freak stroke of fate threw him into *suspended animation.* He woke in the mid-1960s, a man *twenty years out of his time.* Since that fateful day, Steve Rogers has sought his *destiny* in this brave new world.

STAN LEE PRESENTS: CAPTAIN AMERICA AND THE FALCON™

GET THIS!! SUPPOSE THE **INMATES** OF AN **ASYLUM** TOOK COMMAND OF THE PLACE! SUPPOSE ONE OF THOSE INMATES WAS A SCIENTIST NOTED FOR HIS RADICAL THEORIES--AND ONE OF THOSE THEORIES **WORKED!** THE RESULT--A DIMENSIONAL DOOR WHICH SWALLOWED THE ASYLUM, ITS INMATES, A SUPER-HEROE'S CHICK--AND...

CAPTAIN AMERICA AND THE FALCON!

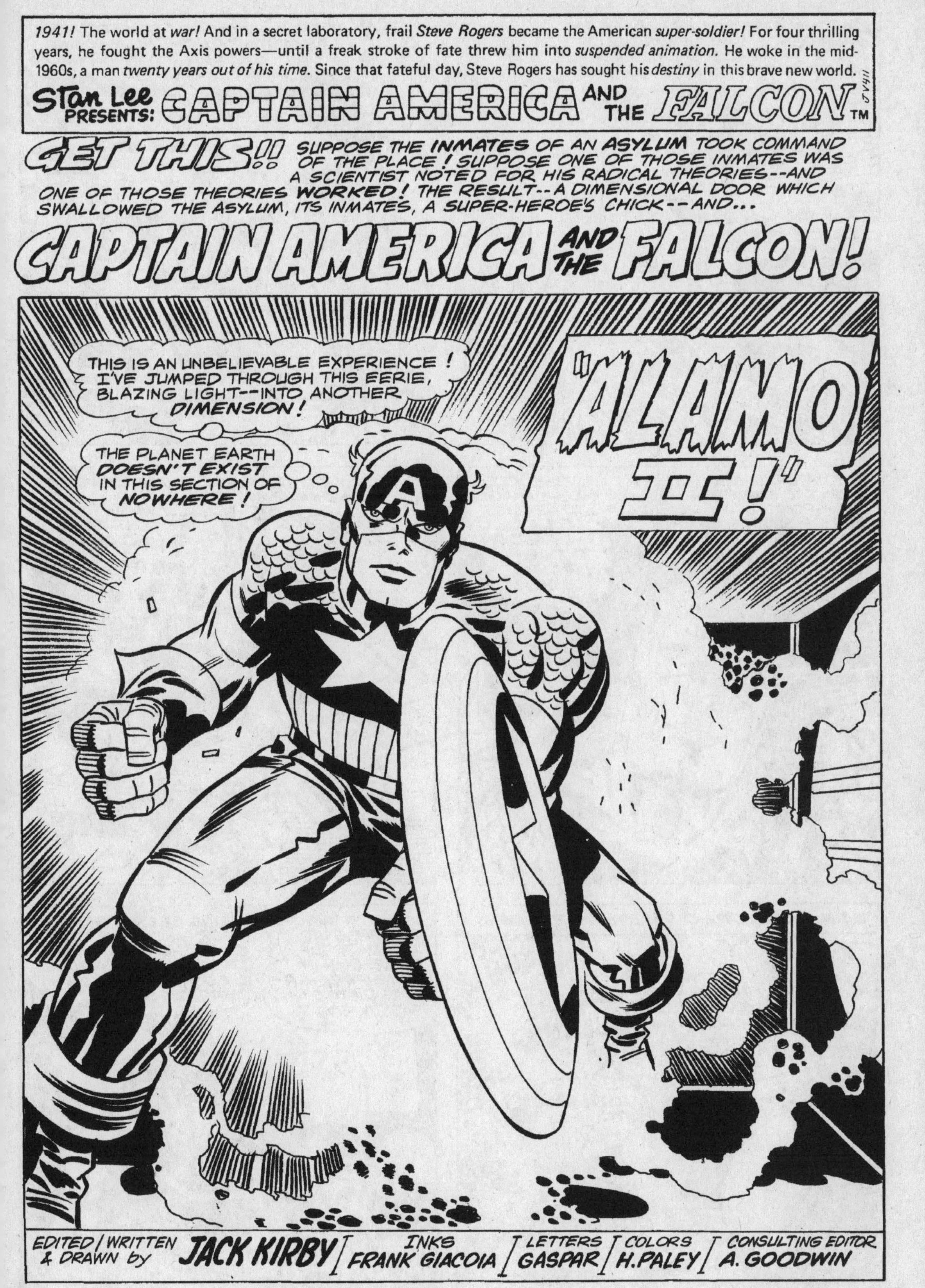

THIS IS AN UNBELIEVABLE EXPERIENCE! I'VE JUMPED THROUGH THIS EERIE, BLAZING LIGHT--INTO ANOTHER DIMENSION!
THE PLANET EARTH DOESN'T EXIST IN THIS SECTION OF NOWHERE!
"ALAMO II!"

EDITED / WRITTEN & DRAWN by JACK KIRBY | INKS FRANK GIACOIA | LETTERS GASPAR | COLORS H.PALEY | CONSULTING EDITOR A. GOODWIN

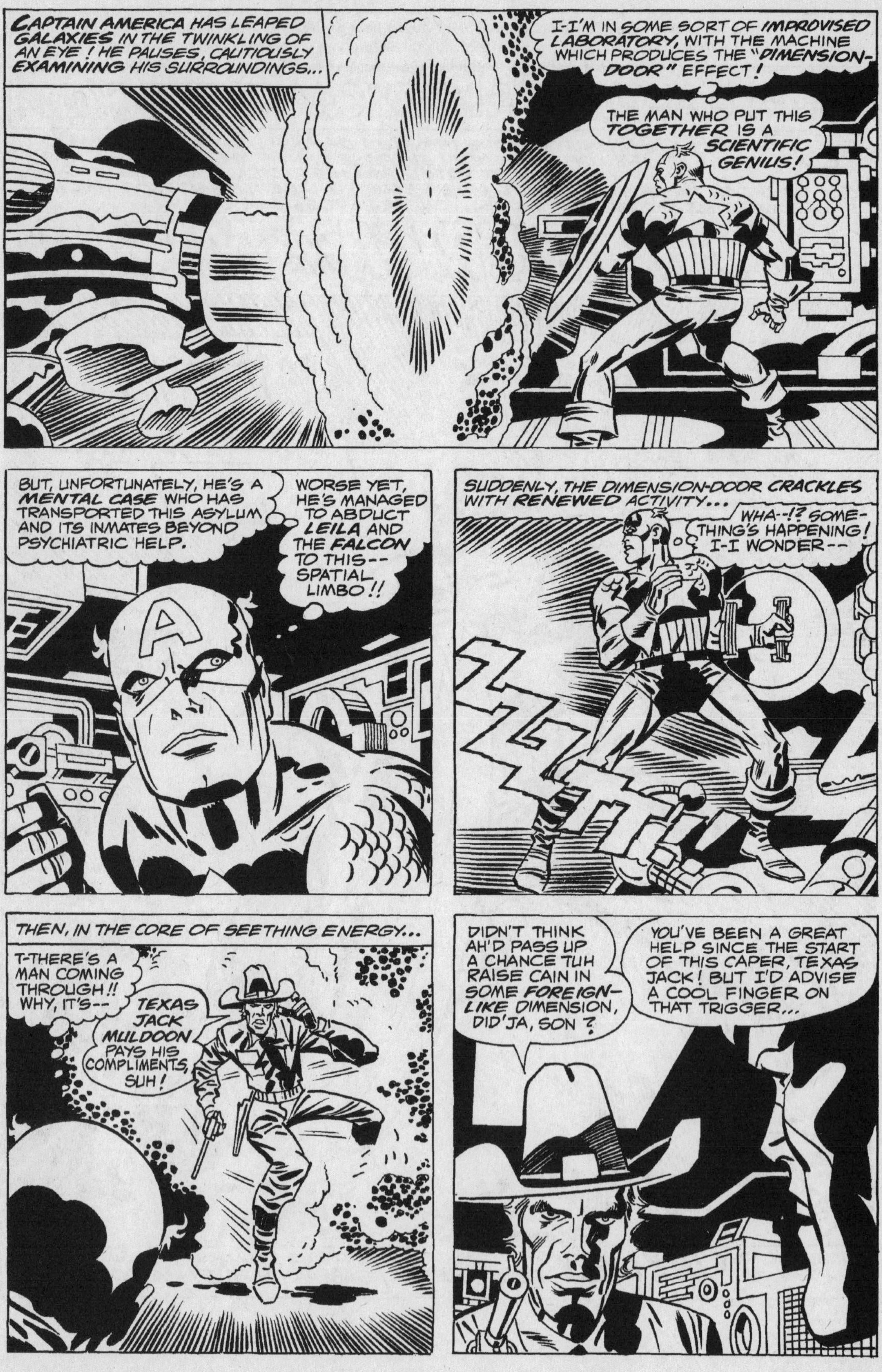
CAPTAIN AMERICA HAS LEAPED GALAXIES IN THE TWINKLING OF AN EYE! HE PAUSES, CAUTIOUSLY EXAMINING HIS SURROUNDINGS...
I-I'M IN SOME SORT OF IMPROVISED LABORATORY, WITH THE MACHINE WHICH PRODUCES THE "DIMENSION-DOOR" EFFECT!
THE MAN WHO PUT THIS TOGETHER IS A SCIENTIFIC GENIUS!
BUT, UNFORTUNATELY, HE'S A MENTAL CASE WHO HAS TRANSPORTED THIS ASYLUM AND ITS INMATES BEYOND PSYCHIATRIC HELP.
WORSE YET, HE'S MANAGED TO ABDUCT LEILA AND THE FALCON TO THIS-- SPATIAL LIMBO!!
SUDDENLY, THE DIMENSION-DOOR CRACKLES WITH RENEWED ACTIVITY...
WHA--!? SOMETHING'S HAPPENING! I-I WONDER--
ZZZTT!!
THEN, IN THE CORE OF SEETHING ENERGY...
T-THERE'S A MAN COMING THROUGH!! WHY, IT'S--
TEXAS JACK MULDOON PAYS HIS COMPLIMENTS, SUH!
DIDN'T THINK AH'D PASS UP A CHANCE TUH RAISE CAIN IN SOME FOREIGN-LIKE DIMENSION, DID'JA, SON?
YOU'VE BEEN A GREAT HELP SINCE THE START OF THIS CAPER, TEXAS JACK! BUT I'D ADVISE A COOL FINGER ON THAT TRIGGER...

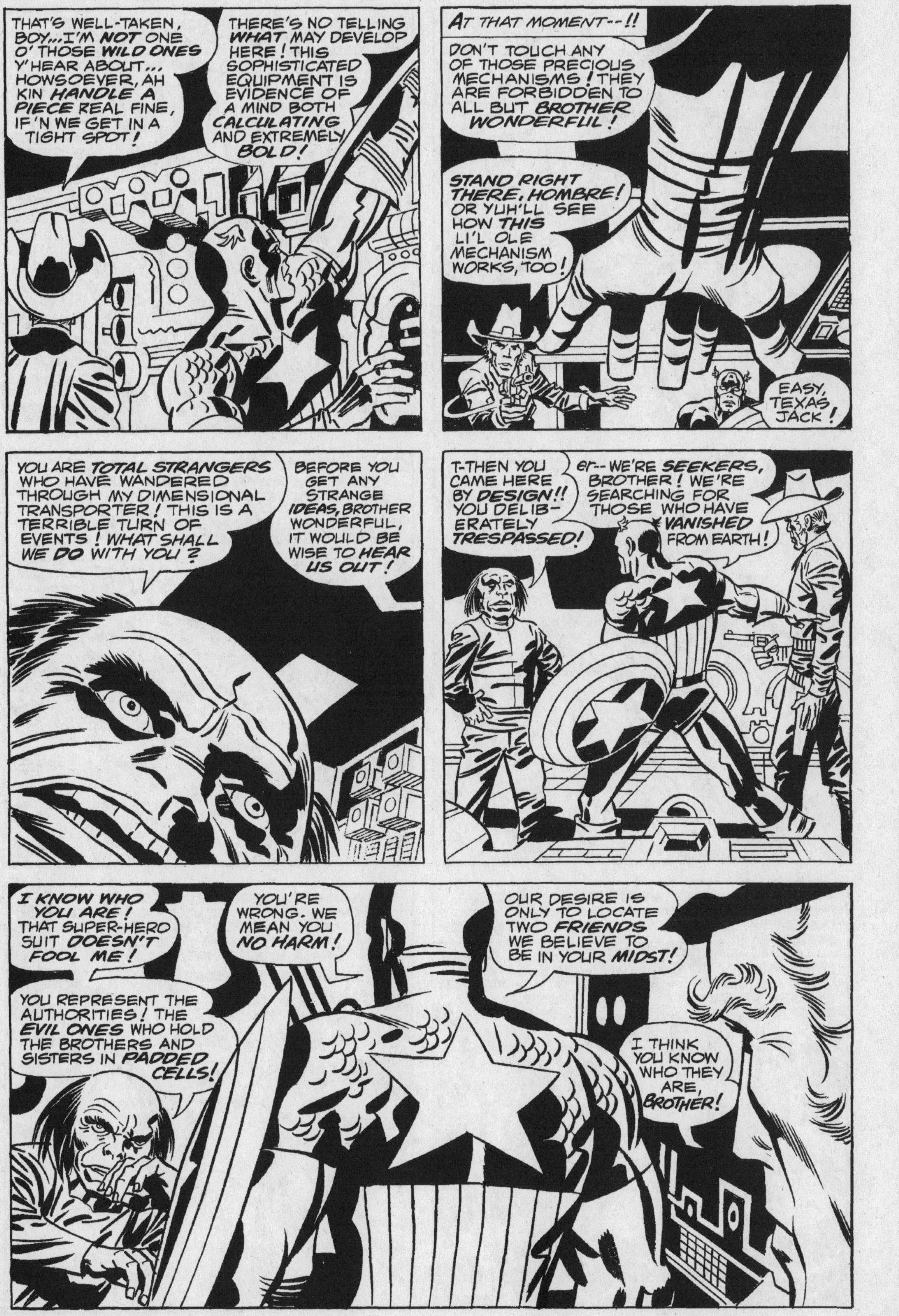
THAT'S WELL-TAKEN, BOY... I'M NOT ONE O' THOSE WILD ONES Y'HEAR ABOUT... HOWSOEVER, AH KIN HANDLE A PIECE REAL FINE, IF 'N WE GET IN A TIGHT SPOT!
THERE'S NO TELLING WHAT MAY DEVELOP HERE! THIS SOPHISTICATED EQUIPMENT IS EVIDENCE OF A MIND BOTH CALCULATING AND EXTREMELY BOLD!
AT THAT MOMENT--!!
DON'T TOUCH ANY OF THOSE PRECIOUS MECHANISMS! THEY ARE FORBIDDEN TO ALL BUT BROTHER WONDERFUL!
STAND RIGHT THERE, HOMBRE! OR YUH'LL SEE HOW THIS LI'L OLE MECHANISM WORKS, TOO!
EASY, TEXAS JACK!
YOU ARE TOTAL STRANGERS WHO HAVE WANDERED THROUGH MY DIMENSIONAL TRANSPORTER! THIS IS A TERRIBLE TURN OF EVENTS! WHAT SHALL WE DO WITH YOU?
BEFORE YOU GET ANY STRANGE IDEAS, BROTHER WONDERFUL, IT WOULD BE WISE TO HEAR US OUT!
T-THEN YOU CAME HERE BY DESIGN!! YOU DELIBERATELY TRESPASSED!
ER-- WE'RE SEEKERS, BROTHER! WE'RE SEARCHING FOR THOSE WHO HAVE VANISHED FROM EARTH!
I KNOW WHO YOU ARE! THAT SUPER-HERO SUIT DOESN'T FOOL ME!
YOU REPRESENT THE AUTHORITIES! THE EVIL ONES WHO HOLD THE BROTHERS AND SISTERS IN PADDED CELLS!
YOU'RE WRONG. WE MEAN YOU NO HARM!
OUR DESIRE IS ONLY TO LOCATE TWO FRIENDS WE BELIEVE TO BE IN YOUR MIDST!
I THINK YOU KNOW WHO THEY ARE, BROTHER!

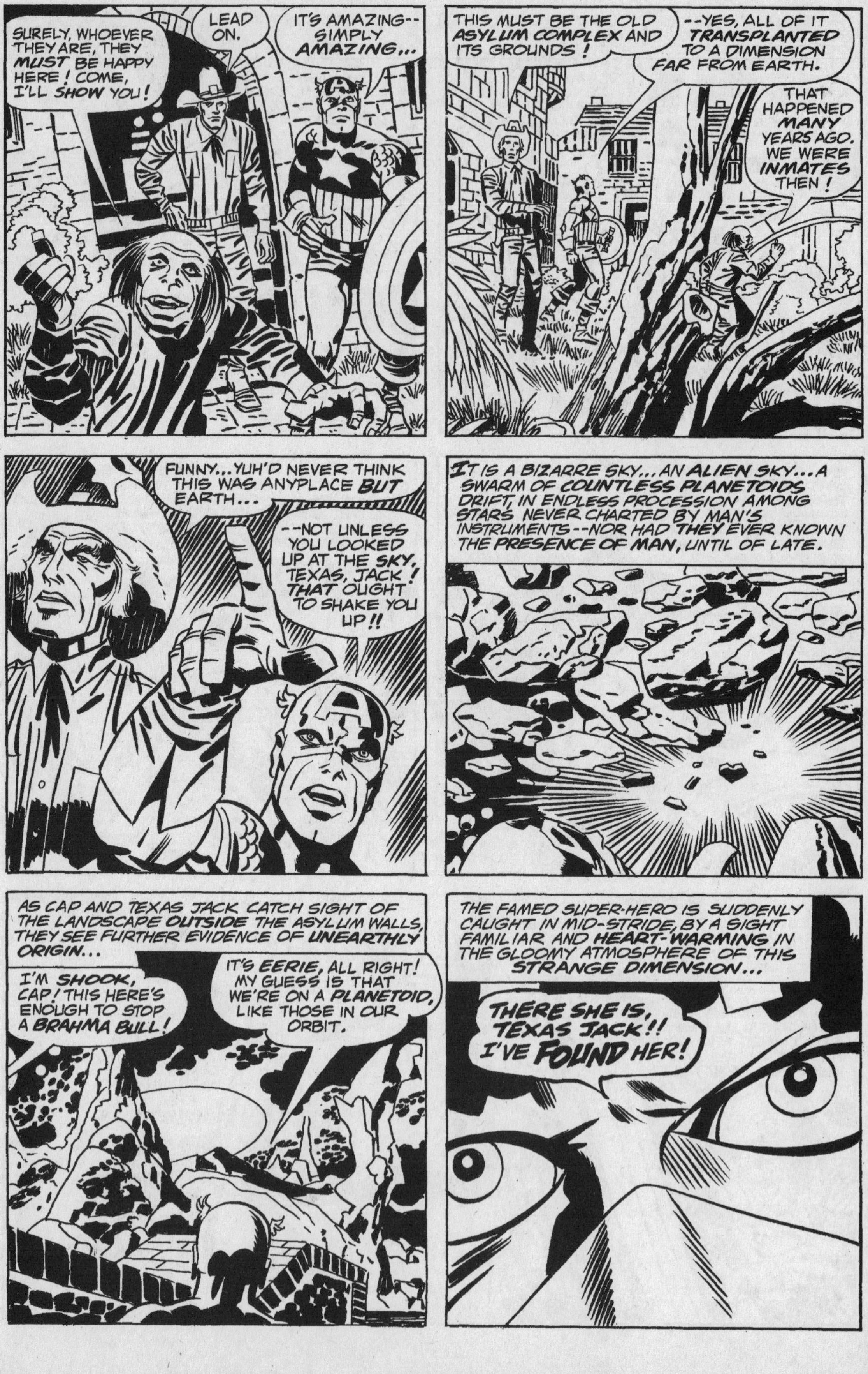

SURELY, WHOEVER THEY ARE, THEY MUST BE HAPPY HERE! COME, I'LL SHOW YOU!
LEAD ON.
IT'S AMAZING-- SIMPLY AMAZING...
THIS MUST BE THE OLD ASYLUM COMPLEX AND ITS GROUNDS!
--YES, ALL OF IT TRANSPLANTED TO A DIMENSION FAR FROM EARTH.
THAT HAPPENED MANY YEARS AGO. WE WERE INMATES THEN!
FUNNY...YUH'D NEVER THINK THIS WAS ANYPLACE BUT EARTH...
--NOT UNLESS YOU LOOKED UP AT THE SKY, TEXAS JACK! THAT OUGHT TO SHAKE YOU UP!!
IT IS A BIZARRE SKY...AN ALIEN SKY...A SWARM OF COUNTLESS PLANETOIDS DRIFT, IN ENDLESS PROCESSION AMONG STARS NEVER CHARTED BY MAN'S INSTRUMENTS--NOR HAD THEY EVER KNOWN THE PRESENCE OF MAN, UNTIL OF LATE.
AS CAP AND TEXAS JACK CATCH SIGHT OF THE LANDSCAPE OUTSIDE THE ASYLUM WALLS, THEY SEE FURTHER EVIDENCE OF UNEARTHLY ORIGIN...
I'M SHOOK, CAP! THIS HERE'S ENOUGH TO STOP A BRAHMA BULL!
IT'S EERIE, ALL RIGHT! MY GUESS IS THAT WE'RE ON A PLANETOID, LIKE THOSE IN OUR ORBIT.
THE FAMED SUPER-HERO IS SUDDENLY CAUGHT IN MID-STRIDE, BY A SIGHT FAMILIAR AND HEART-WARMING IN THE GLOOMY ATMOSPHERE OF THIS STRANGE DIMENSION...
THERE SHE IS, TEXAS JACK!! I'VE FOUND HER!

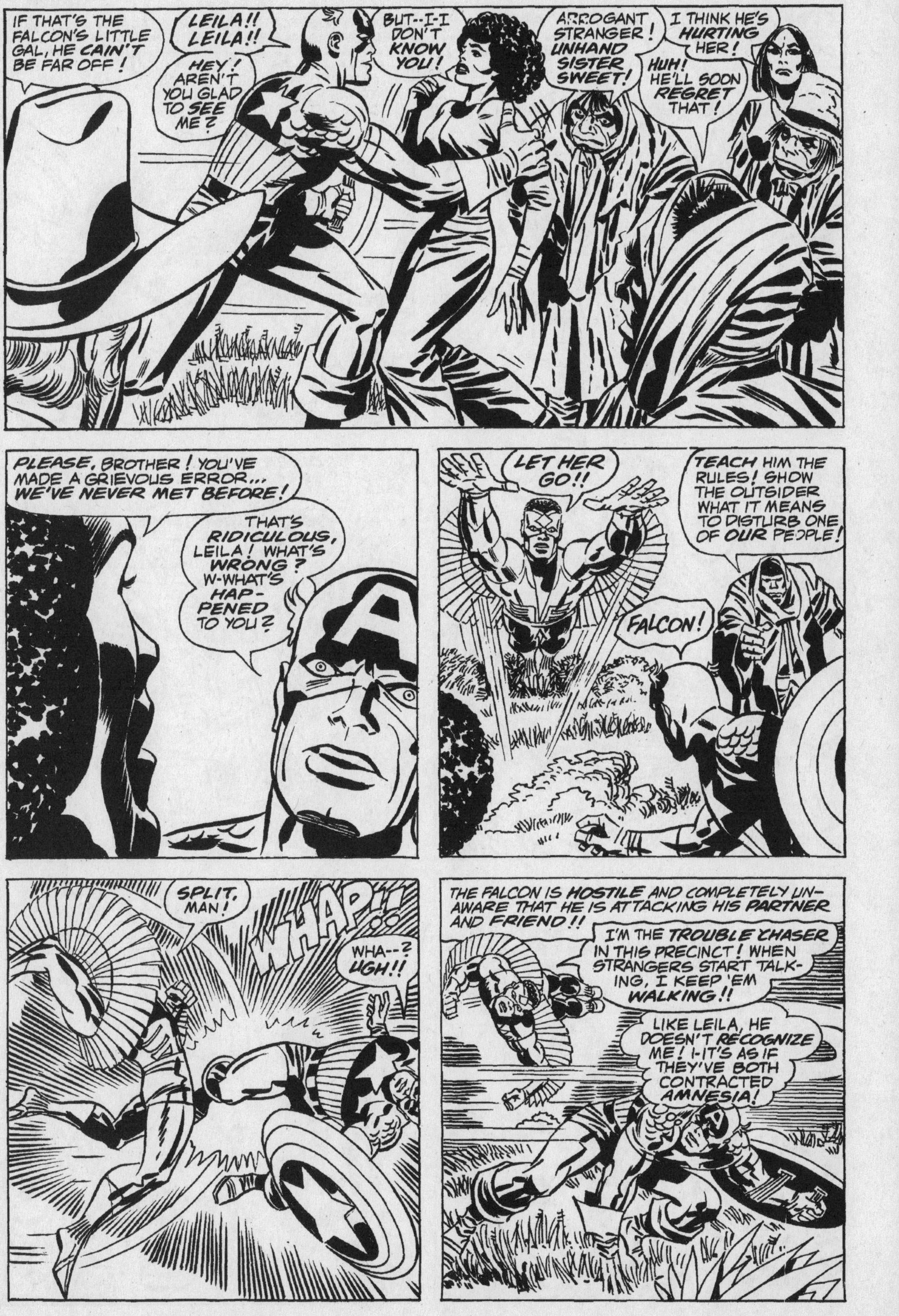
IF THAT'S THE FALCON'S LITTLE GAL, HE CAIN'T BE FAR OFF!
LEILA!! LEILA!!
HEY! AREN'T YOU GLAD TO SEE ME?
BUT--I-I DON'T KNOW YOU!
ARROGANT STRANGER! UNHAND SISTER SWEET!
I THINK HE'S HURTING HER!
HUH! HE'LL SOON REGRET THAT!
PLEASE, BROTHER! YOU'VE MADE A GRIEVOUS ERROR... WE'VE NEVER MET BEFORE!
THAT'S RIDICULOUS, LEILA! WHAT'S WRONG? W-WHAT'S HAPPENED TO YOU?
LET HER GO!!
TEACH HIM THE RULES! SHOW THE OUTSIDER WHAT IT MEANS TO DISTURB ONE OF OUR PEOPLE!
FALCON!
SPLIT, MAN!
WHAP!!
WHA--? UGH!!
THE FALCON IS HOSTILE AND COMPLETELY UNAWARE THAT HE IS ATTACKING HIS PARTNER AND FRIEND!!
I'M THE TROUBLE CHASER IN THIS PRECINCT! WHEN STRANGERS START TALKING, I KEEP 'EM WALKING!!
LIKE LEILA, HE DOESN'T RECOGNIZE ME! I-IT'S AS IF THEY'VE BOTH CONTRACTED AMNESIA!

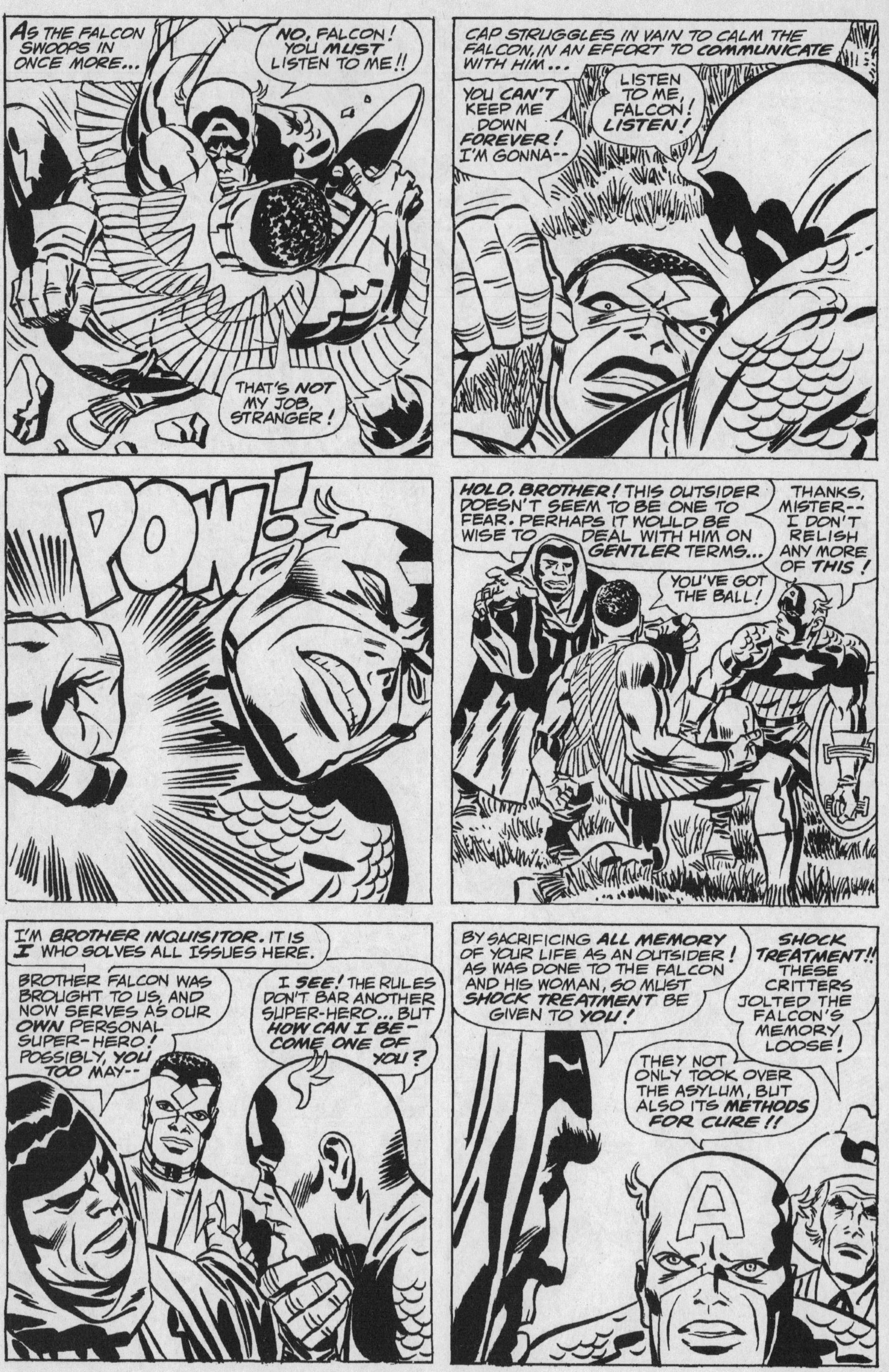
AS THE FALCON SWOOPS IN ONCE MORE...
NO, FALCON! YOU MUST LISTEN TO ME!!
THAT'S NOT MY JOB, STRANGER!
CAP STRUGGLES IN VAIN TO CALM THE FALCON, IN AN EFFORT TO COMMUNICATE WITH HIM...
YOU CAN'T KEEP ME DOWN FOREVER! I'M GONNA--
LISTEN TO ME, FALCON! LISTEN!
POW!
HOLD, BROTHER! THIS OUTSIDER DOESN'T SEEM TO BE ONE TO FEAR. PERHAPS IT WOULD BE WISE TO DEAL WITH HIM ON GENTLER TERMS...
THANKS, MISTER-- I DON'T RELISH ANY MORE OF THIS!
YOU'VE GOT THE BALL!
I'M BROTHER INQUISITOR. IT IS I WHO SOLVES ALL ISSUES HERE.
BROTHER FALCON WAS BROUGHT TO US, AND NOW SERVES AS OUR OWN PERSONAL SUPER-HERO! POSSIBLY, YOU TOO MAY--
I SEE! THE RULES DON'T BAR ANOTHER SUPER-HERO... BUT HOW CAN I BE-COME ONE OF YOU?
BY SACRIFICING ALL MEMORY OF YOUR LIFE AS AN OUTSIDER! AS WAS DONE TO THE FALCON AND HIS WOMAN, SO MUST SHOCK TREATMENT BE GIVEN TO YOU!
SHOCK TREATMENT!! THESE CRITTERS JOLTED THE FALCON'S MEMORY LOOSE!
THEY NOT ONLY TOOK OVER THE ASYLUM, BUT ALSO ITS METHODS FOR CURE!!

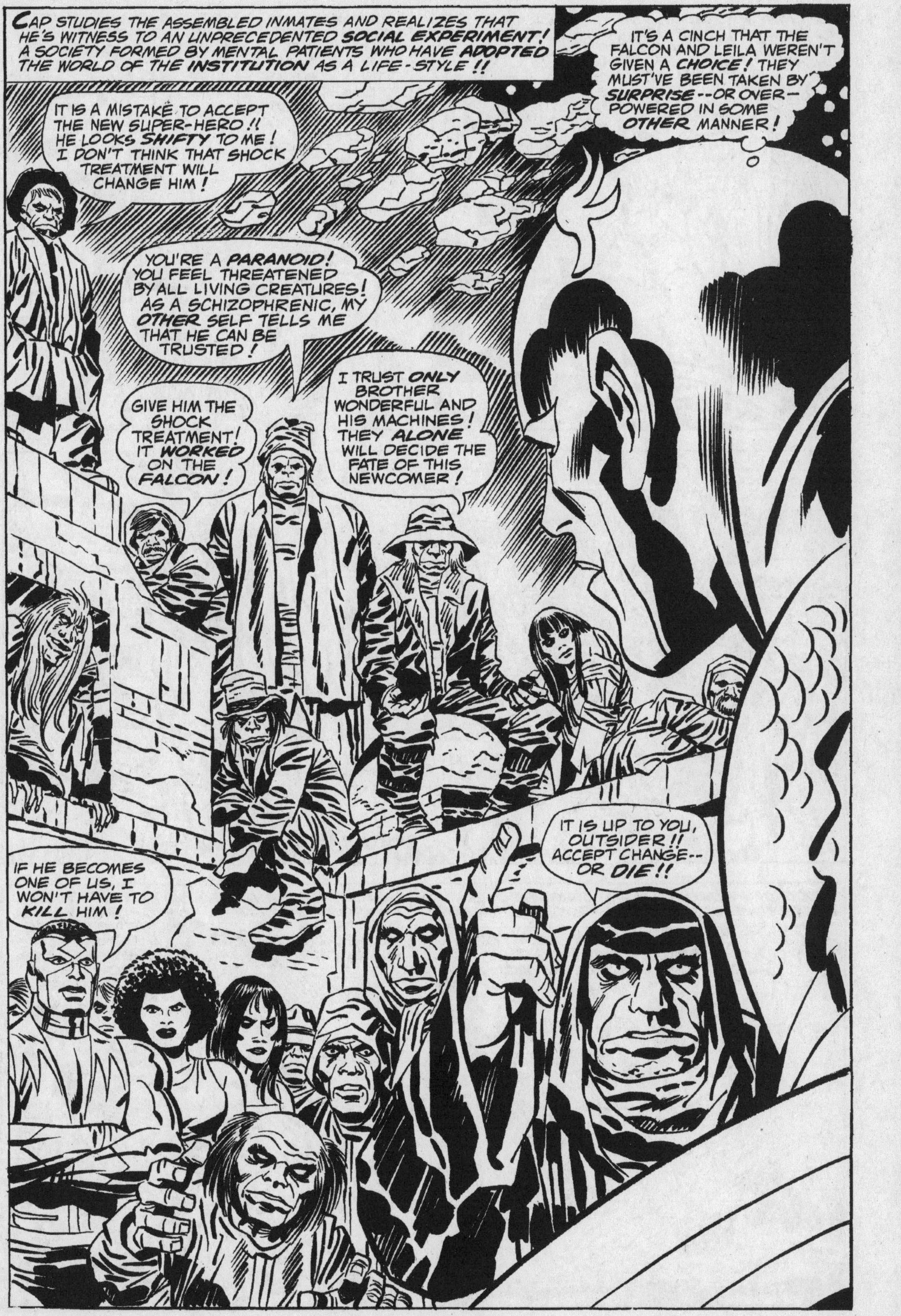
CAP STUDIES THE ASSEMBLED INMATES AND REALIZES THAT HE'S WITNESS TO AN UNPRECEDENTED SOCIAL EXPERIMENT! A SOCIETY FORMED BY MENTAL PATIENTS WHO HAVE ADOPTED THE WORLD OF THE INSTITUTION AS A LIFE-STYLE!!
IT'S A CINCH THAT THE FALCON AND LEILA WEREN'T GIVEN A CHOICE! THEY MUST'VE BEEN TAKEN BY SURPRISE--OR OVER-POWERED IN SOME OTHER MANNER!
IT IS A MISTAKE TO ACCEPT THE NEW SUPER-HERO!! HE LOOKS SHIFTY TO ME! I DON'T THINK THAT SHOCK TREATMENT WILL CHANGE HIM!
YOU'RE A PARANOID! YOU FEEL THREATENED BY ALL LIVING CREATURES! AS A SCHIZOPHRENIC, MY OTHER SELF TELLS ME THAT HE CAN BE TRUSTED!
GIVE HIM THE SHOCK TREATMENT! IT WORKED ON THE FALCON!
I TRUST ONLY BROTHER WONDERFUL AND HIS MACHINES! THEY ALONE WILL DECIDE THE FATE OF THIS NEWCOMER!
IF HE BECOMES ONE OF US, I WON'T HAVE TO KILL HIM!
IT IS UP TO YOU, OUTSIDER!! ACCEPT CHANGE-- OR DIE!!

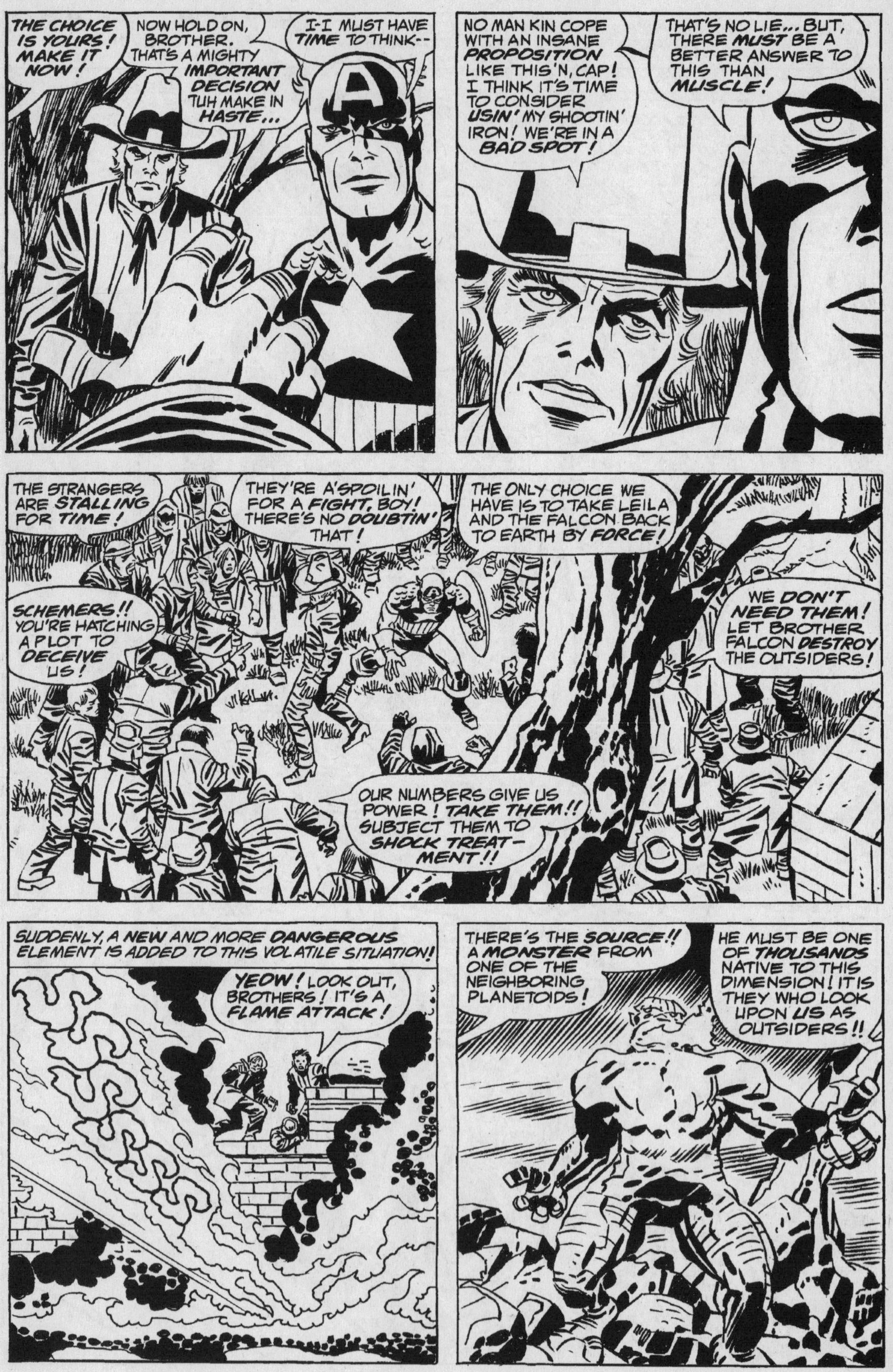
THE CHOICE IS YOURS! MAKE IT NOW!
NOW HOLD ON, BROTHER. THAT'S A MIGHTY IMPORTANT DECISION TUH MAKE IN HASTE...
I-I MUST HAVE TIME TO THINK--
NO MAN KIN COPE WITH AN INSANE PROPOSITION LIKE THIS'N, CAP! I THINK IT'S TIME TO CONSIDER USIN' MY SHOOTIN' IRON! WE'RE IN A BAD SPOT!
THAT'S NO LIE... BUT, THERE MUST BE A BETTER ANSWER TO THIS THAN MUSCLE!
THE STRANGERS ARE STALLING FOR TIME!
THEY'RE A'SPOILIN' FOR A FIGHT, BOY! THERE'S NO DOUBTIN' THAT!
THE ONLY CHOICE WE HAVE IS TO TAKE LEILA AND THE FALCON BACK TO EARTH BY FORCE!
SCHEMERS!! YOU'RE HATCHING A PLOT TO DECEIVE US!
WE DON'T NEED THEM! LET BROTHER FALCON DESTROY THE OUTSIDERS!
OUR NUMBERS GIVE US POWER! TAKE THEM!! SUBJECT THEM TO SHOCK TREAT-MENT!!
SUDDENLY, A NEW AND MORE DANGEROUS ELEMENT IS ADDED TO THIS VOLATILE SITUATION!
YEOW! LOOK OUT, BROTHERS! IT'S A FLAME ATTACK!
THERE'S THE SOURCE!! A MONSTER FROM ONE OF THE NEIGHBORING PLANETOIDS!
HE MUST BE ONE OF THOUSANDS NATIVE TO THIS DIMENSION! IT IS THEY WHO LOOK UPON US AS OUTSIDERS!!

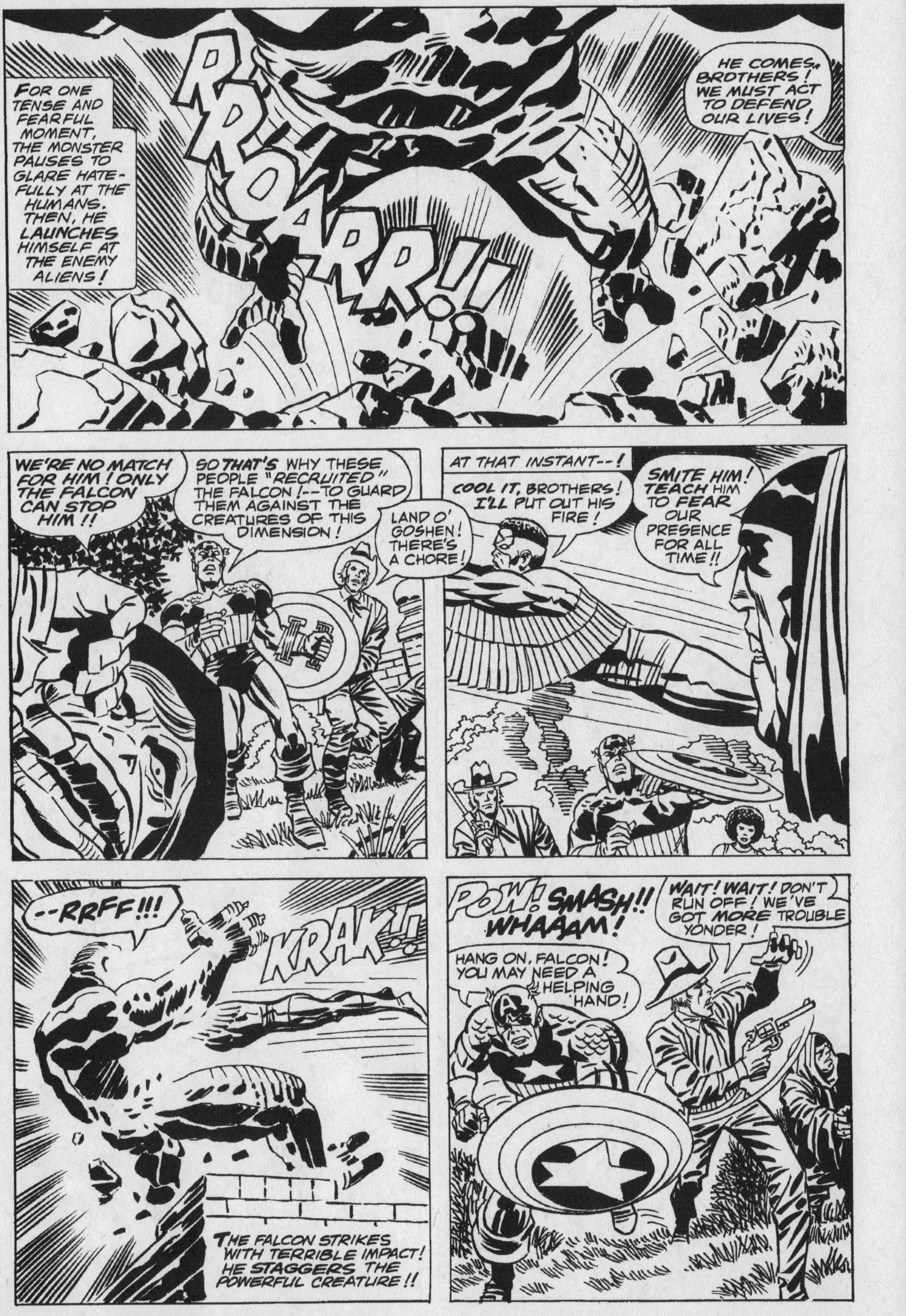

FOR ONE TENSE AND FEARFUL MOMENT, THE MONSTER PAUSES TO GLARE HATE-FULLY AT THE HUMANS. THEN, HE LAUNCHES HIMSELF AT THE ENEMY ALIENS!
RROARR!!
HE COMES, BROTHERS! WE MUST ACT TO DEFEND OUR LIVES!
WE'RE NO MATCH FOR HIM! ONLY THE FALCON CAN STOP HIM!!
SO THAT'S WHY THESE PEOPLE "RECRUITED" THE FALCON!--TO GUARD THEM AGAINST THE CREATURES OF THIS DIMENSION!
LAND O' GOSHEN! THERE'S A CHORE!
AT THAT INSTANT--!
COOL IT, BROTHERS! I'LL PUT OUT HIS FIRE!
SMITE HIM! TEACH HIM TO FEAR OUR PRESENCE FOR ALL TIME!!
--RRFF!!!
KRAK!!
THE FALCON STRIKES WITH TERRIBLE IMPACT! HE STAGGERS THE POWERFUL CREATURE!!
POW! SMASH!! WHAAAM!
WAIT! WAIT! DON'T RUN OFF! WE'VE GOT MORE TROUBLE YONDER!
HANG ON, FALCON! YOU MAY NEED A HELPING HAND!

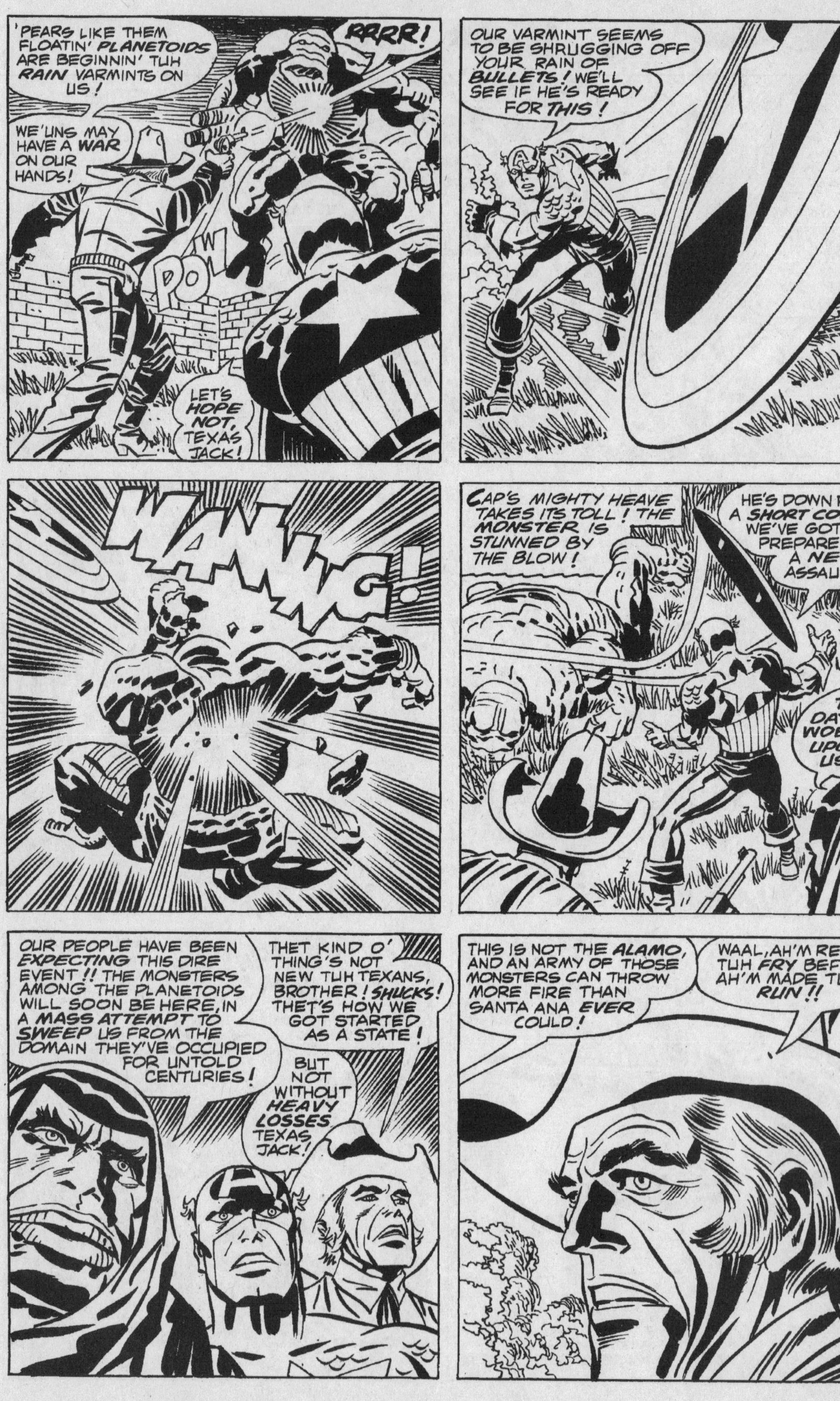
'PEARS LIKE THEM FLOATIN' PLANETOIDS ARE BEGINNIN' TUH RAIN VARMINTS ON US!
RRRR!
WE'UNS MAY HAVE A WAR ON OUR HANDS!
POW
LET'S HOPE NOT, TEXAS JACK!
OUR VARMINT SEEMS TO BE SHRUGGING OFF YOUR RAIN OF BULLETS! WE'LL SEE IF HE'S READY FOR THIS!
WANNG!
CAP'S MIGHTY HEAVE TAKES ITS TOLL! THE MONSTER IS STUNNED BY THE BLOW!
HE'S DOWN FOR A SHORT COUNT! WE'VE GOT TO PREPARE FOR A NEW ASSAULT!
THE DAY OF WOE IS UPON US!
OUR PEOPLE HAVE BEEN EXPECTING THIS DIRE EVENT!! THE MONSTERS AMONG THE PLANETOIDS WILL SOON BE HERE, IN A MASS ATTEMPT TO SWEEP US FROM THE DOMAIN THEY'VE OCCUPIED FOR UNTOLD CENTURIES!
THET KIND O' THING'S NOT NEW TUH TEXANS, BROTHER! SHUCKS! THET'S HOW WE GOT STARTED AS A STATE!
BUT NOT WITHOUT HEAVY LOSSES, TEXAS JACK!
THIS IS NOT THE ALAMO, AND AN ARMY OF THOSE MONSTERS CAN THROW MORE FIRE THAN SANTA ANA EVER COULD!
WAAL, AH'M READY TUH FRY BEFORE AH'M MADE TUH RUN!!

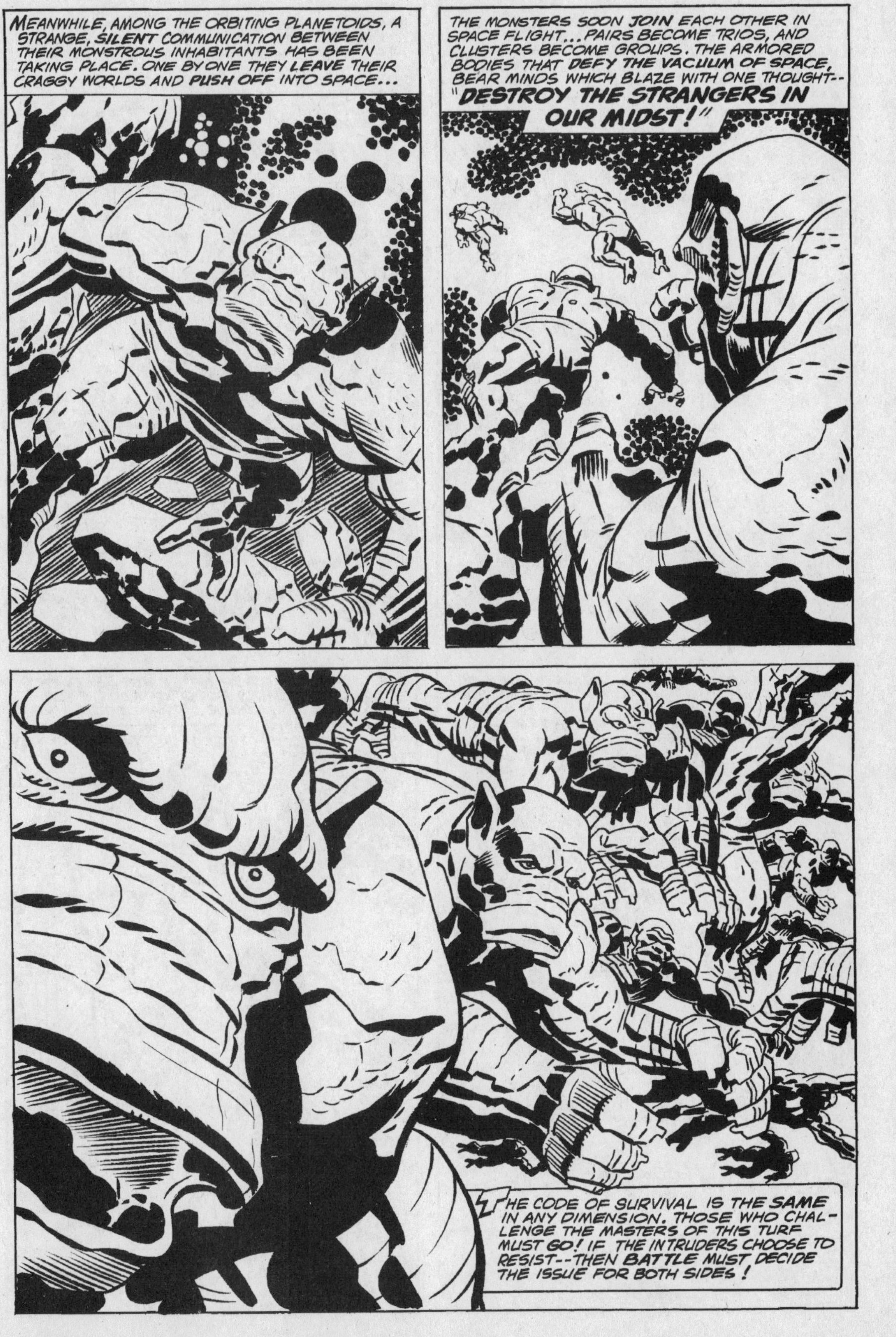
MEANWHILE, AMONG THE ORBITING PLANETOIDS, A STRANGE, SILENT COMMUNICATION BETWEEN THEIR MONSTROUS INHABITANTS HAS BEEN TAKING PLACE. ONE BY ONE THEY LEAVE THEIR CRAGGY WORLDS AND PUSH OFF INTO SPACE...
THE MONSTERS SOON JOIN EACH OTHER IN SPACE FLIGHT... PAIRS BECOME TRIOS, AND CLUSTERS BECOME GROUPS. THE ARMORED BODIES THAT DEFY THE VACUUM OF SPACE, BEAR MINDS WHICH BLAZE WITH ONE THOUGHT-- "DESTROY THE STRANGERS IN OUR MIDST!"
THE CODE OF SURVIVAL IS THE SAME IN ANY DIMENSION. THOSE WHO CHALLENGE THE MASTERS OF THIS TURF MUST GO! IF THE INTRUDERS CHOOSE TO RESIST--THEN BATTLE MUST DECIDE THE ISSUE FOR BOTH SIDES!

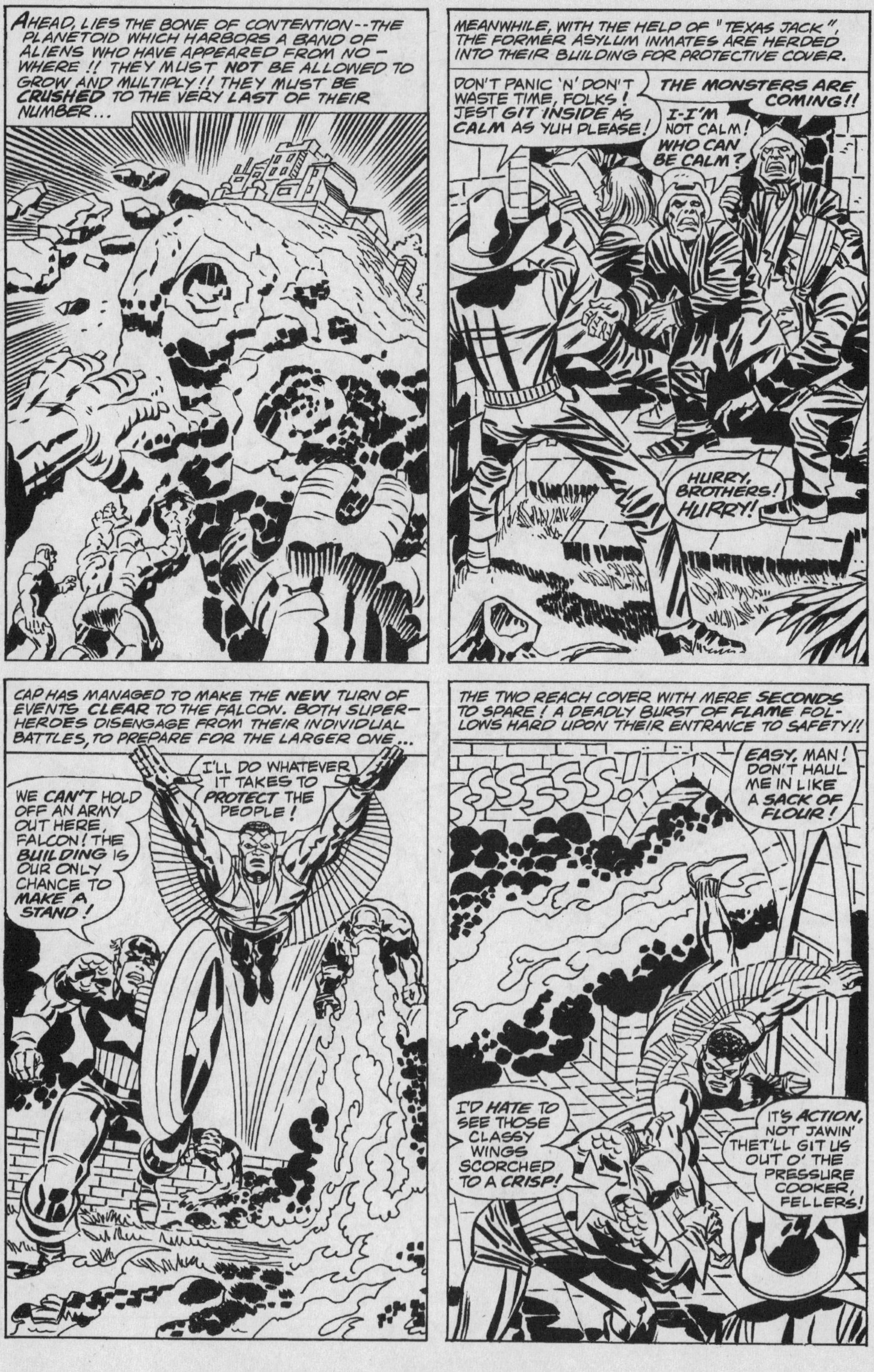
AHEAD, LIES THE BONE OF CONTENTION--THE PLANETOID WHICH HARBORS A BAND OF ALIENS WHO HAVE APPEARED FROM NO-WHERE!! THEY MUST NOT BE ALLOWED TO GROW AND MULTIPLY!! THEY MUST BE CRUSHED TO THE VERY LAST OF THEIR NUMBER...
MEANWHILE, WITH THE HELP OF "TEXAS JACK", THE FORMER ASYLUM INMATES ARE HERDED INTO THEIR BUILDING FOR PROTECTIVE COVER.
DON'T PANIC 'N' DON'T WASTE TIME, FOLKS! JEST GIT INSIDE AS CALM AS YUH PLEASE!
THE MONSTERS ARE COMING!!
I-I'M NOT CALM! WHO CAN BE CALM?
HURRY, BROTHERS! HURRY!
CAP HAS MANAGED TO MAKE THE NEW TURN OF EVENTS CLEAR TO THE FALCON. BOTH SUPER-HEROES DISENGAGE FROM THEIR INDIVIDUAL BATTLES, TO PREPARE FOR THE LARGER ONE...
WE CAN'T HOLD OFF AN ARMY OUT HERE, FALCON! THE BUILDING IS OUR ONLY CHANCE TO MAKE A STAND!
I'LL DO WHATEVER IT TAKES TO PROTECT THE PEOPLE!
THE TWO REACH COVER WITH MERE SECONDS TO SPARE! A DEADLY BURST OF FLAME FOLLOWS HARD UPON THEIR ENTRANCE TO SAFETY!!
SSSSSSS!
EASY, MAN! DON'T HAUL ME IN LIKE A SACK OF FLOUR!
I'D HATE TO SEE THOSE CLASSY WINGS SCORCHED TO A CRISP!
IT'S ACTION, NOT JAWIN' THET'LL GIT US OUT O' THE PRESSURE COOKER, FELLERS!

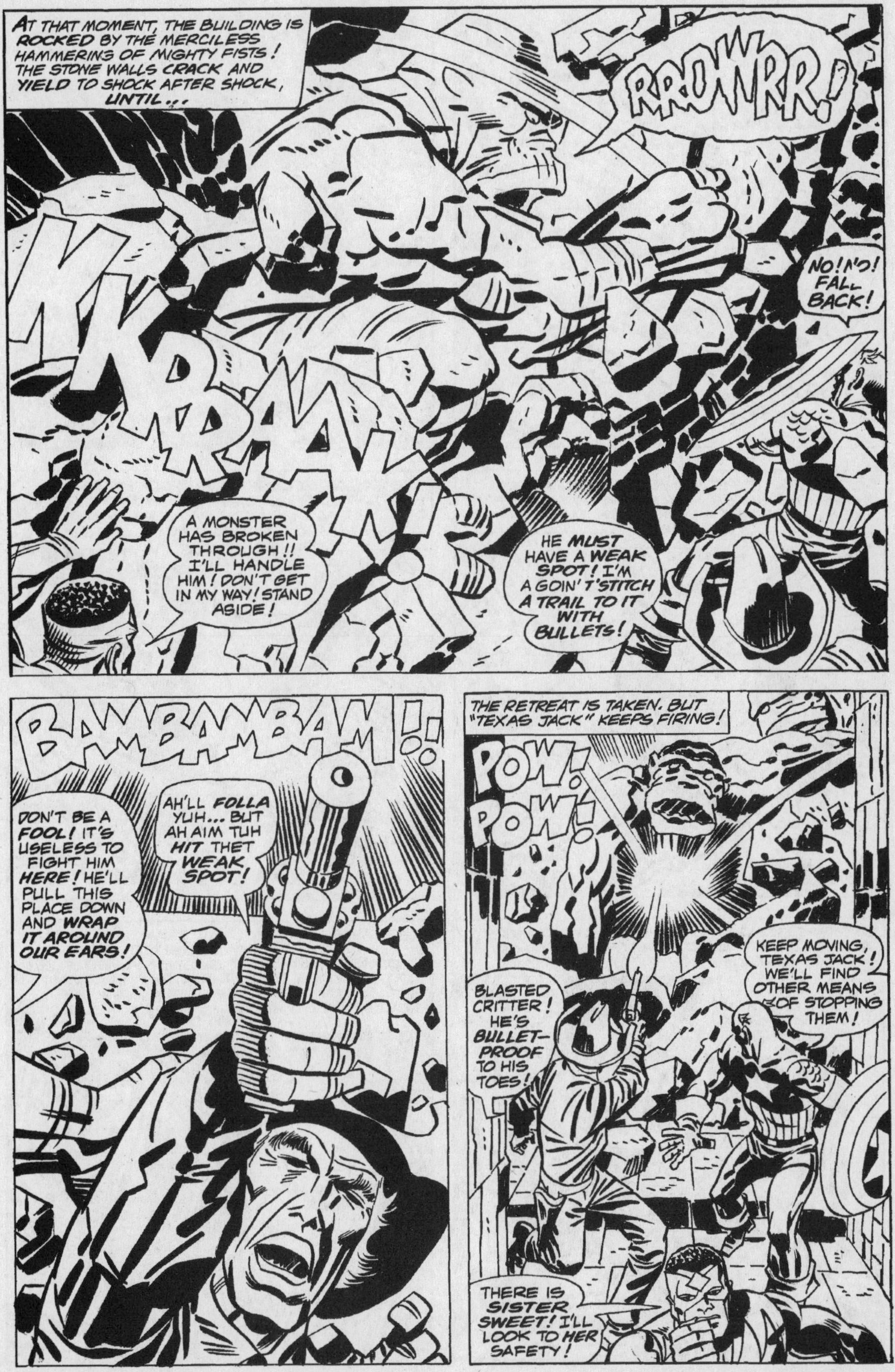

AT THAT MOMENT, THE BUILDING IS ROCKED BY THE MERCILESS HAMMERING OF MIGHTY FISTS! THE STONE WALLS CRACK AND YIELD TO SHOCK AFTER SHOCK, UNTIL...
RROWRR!
NO! NO! FALL BACK!
A MONSTER HAS BROKEN THROUGH!! I'LL HANDLE HIM! DON'T GET IN MY WAY! STAND ASIDE!
HE MUST HAVE A WEAK SPOT! I'M A GOIN' T'STITCH A TRAIL TO IT WITH BULLETS!
BAMBAMBAM!!
DON'T BE A FOOL! IT'S USELESS TO FIGHT HIM HERE! HE'LL PULL THIS PLACE DOWN AND WRAP IT AROUND OUR EARS!
AH'LL FOLLA YUH... BUT AH AIM TUH HIT THET WEAK SPOT!
THE RETREAT IS TAKEN. BUT "TEXAS JACK" KEEPS FIRING!
POW! POW!
KEEP MOVING, TEXAS JACK! WE'LL FIND OTHER MEANS OF STOPPING THEM!
BLASTED CRITTER! HE'S BULLET-PROOF TO HIS TOES!
THERE IS SISTER SWEET! I'LL LOOK TO HER SAFETY!

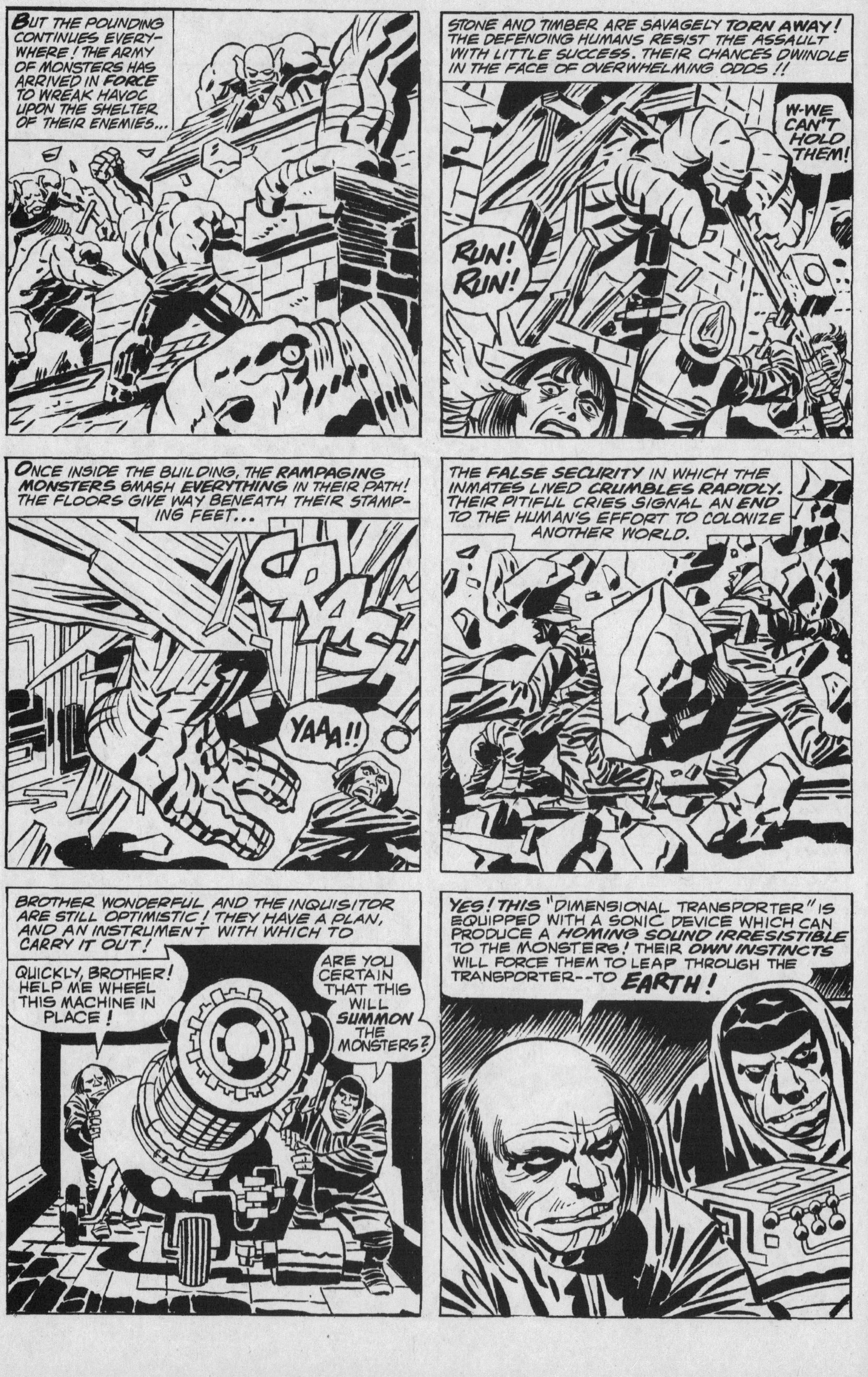
BUT THE POUNDING CONTINUES EVERYWHERE! THE ARMY OF MONSTERS HAS ARRIVED IN FORCE TO WREAK HAVOC UPON THE SHELTER OF THEIR ENEMIES...
STONE AND TIMBER ARE SAVAGELY TORN AWAY! THE DEFENDING HUMANS RESIST THE ASSAULT WITH LITTLE SUCCESS. THEIR CHANCES DWINDLE IN THE FACE OF OVERWHELMING ODDS!!
W-WE CAN'T HOLD THEM!
RUN! RUN!
ONCE INSIDE THE BUILDING, THE RAMPAGING MONSTERS SMASH EVERYTHING IN THEIR PATH! THE FLOORS GIVE WAY BENEATH THEIR STAMPING FEET...
CRASH
YAAA!!
THE FALSE SECURITY IN WHICH THE INMATES LIVED CRUMBLES RAPIDLY. THEIR PITIFUL CRIES SIGNAL AN END TO THE HUMAN'S EFFORT TO COLONIZE ANOTHER WORLD.
BROTHER WONDERFUL AND THE INQUISITOR ARE STILL OPTIMISTIC! THEY HAVE A PLAN, AND AN INSTRUMENT WITH WHICH TO CARRY IT OUT!
QUICKLY, BROTHER! HELP ME WHEEL THIS MACHINE IN PLACE!
ARE YOU CERTAIN THAT THIS WILL SUMMON THE MONSTERS?
YES! THIS "DIMENSIONAL TRANSPORTER" IS EQUIPPED WITH A SONIC DEVICE WHICH CAN PRODUCE A HOMING SOUND IRRESISTIBLE TO THE MONSTERS! THEIR OWN INSTINCTS WILL FORCE THEM TO LEAP THROUGH THE TRANSPORTER--TO EARTH!

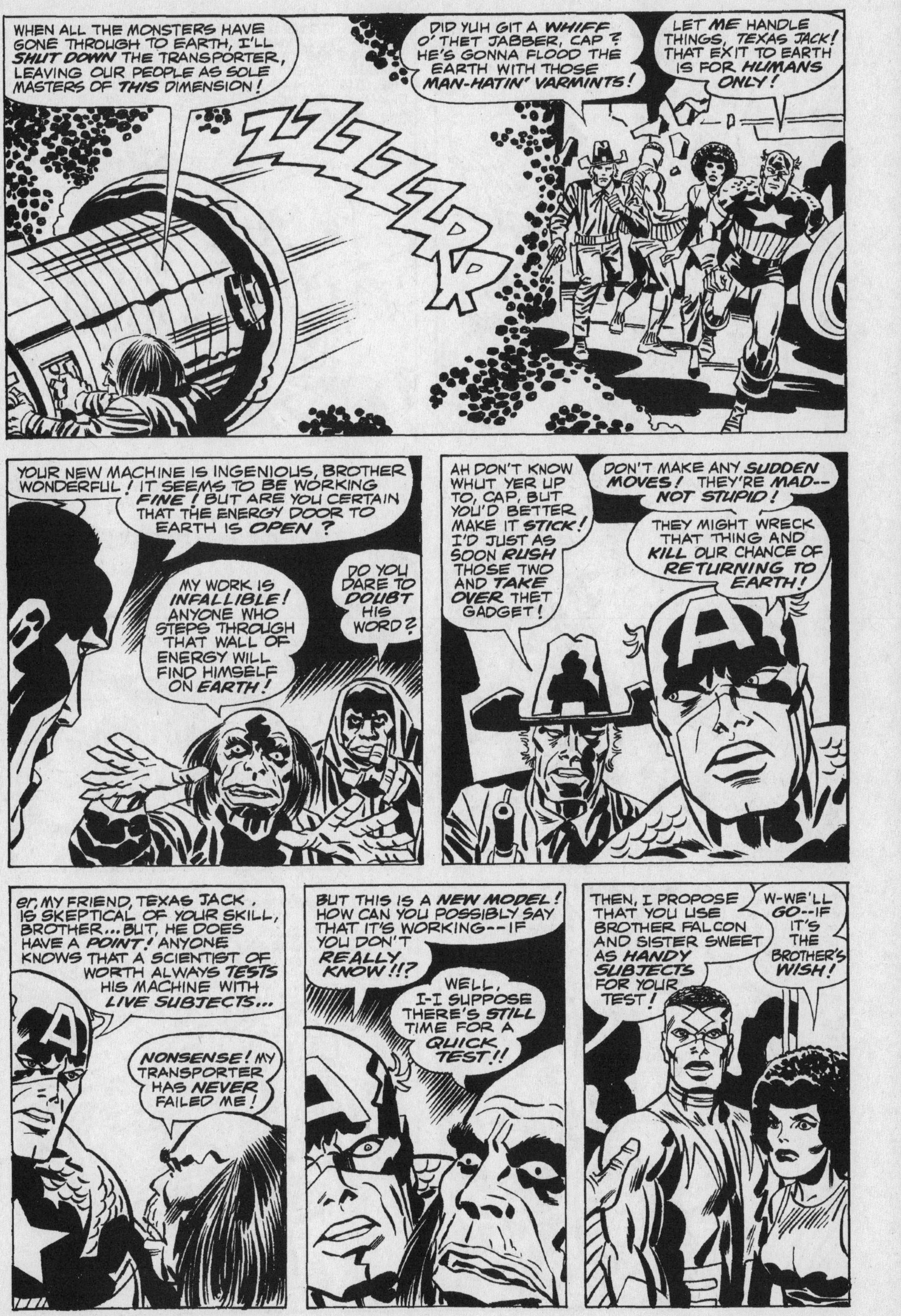
WHEN ALL THE MONSTERS HAVE GONE THROUGH TO EARTH, I'LL SHUT DOWN THE TRANSPORTER, LEAVING OUR PEOPLE AS SOLE MASTERS OF THIS DIMENSION!
DID YUH GIT A WHIFF O' THET JABBER, CAP? HE'S GONNA FLOOD THE EARTH WITH THOSE MAN-HATIN' VARMINTS!
LET ME HANDLE THINGS, TEXAS JACK! THAT EXIT TO EARTH IS FOR HUMANS ONLY!
YOUR NEW MACHINE IS INGENIOUS, BROTHER WONDERFUL! IT SEEMS TO BE WORKING FINE! BUT ARE YOU CERTAIN THAT THE ENERGY DOOR TO EARTH IS OPEN?
MY WORK IS INFALLIBLE! ANYONE WHO STEPS THROUGH THAT WALL OF ENERGY WILL FIND HIMSELF ON EARTH!
DO YOU DARE TO DOUBT HIS WORD?
AH DON'T KNOW WHUT YER UP TO, CAP, BUT YOU'D BETTER MAKE IT STICK! I'D JUST AS SOON RUSH THOSE TWO AND TAKE OVER THET GADGET!
DON'T MAKE ANY SUDDEN MOVES! THEY'RE MAD--NOT STUPID!
THEY MIGHT WRECK THAT THING AND KILL OUR CHANCE OF RETURNING TO EARTH!
er, MY FRIEND, TEXAS JACK, IS SKEPTICAL OF YOUR SKILL, BROTHER... BUT, HE DOES HAVE A POINT! ANYONE KNOWS THAT A SCIENTIST OF WORTH ALWAYS TESTS HIS MACHINE WITH LIVE SUBJECTS...
NONSENSE! MY TRANSPORTER HAS NEVER FAILED ME!
BUT THIS IS A NEW MODEL! HOW CAN YOU POSSIBLY SAY THAT IT'S WORKING--IF YOU DON'T REALLY KNOW!!?
WELL, I-I SUPPOSE THERE'S STILL TIME FOR A QUICK TEST!!
THEN, I PROPOSE THAT YOU USE BROTHER FALCON AND SISTER SWEET AS HANDY SUBJECTS FOR YOUR TEST!
W-WE'LL GO--IF IT'S THE BROTHER'S WISH!

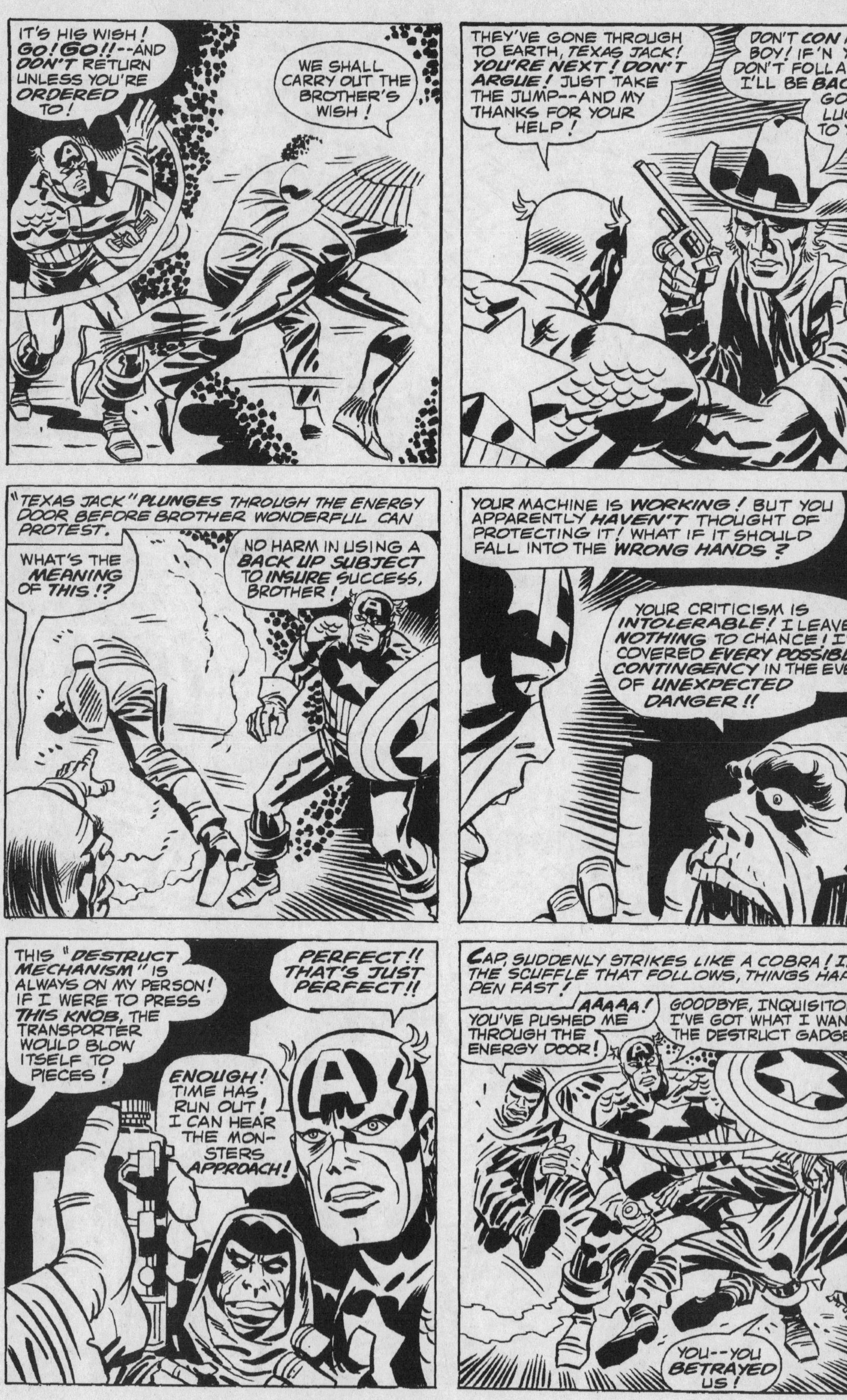
IT'S HIS WISH! GO! GO!!--AND DON'T RETURN UNLESS YOU'RE ORDERED TO!
WE SHALL CARRY OUT THE BROTHER'S WISH!
THEY'VE GONE THROUGH TO EARTH, TEXAS JACK! YOU'RE NEXT! DON'T ARGUE! JUST TAKE THE JUMP--AND MY THANKS FOR YOUR HELP!
DON'T CON ME, BOY! IF'N YOU DON'T FOLLA ME, I'LL BE BACK!--GOOD LUCK TO YUH!
"TEXAS JACK" PLUNGES THROUGH THE ENERGY DOOR BEFORE BROTHER WONDERFUL CAN PROTEST.
WHAT'S THE MEANING OF THIS!?
NO HARM IN USING A BACK UP SUBJECT TO INSURE SUCCESS, BROTHER!
YOUR MACHINE IS WORKING! BUT YOU APPARENTLY HAVEN'T THOUGHT OF PROTECTING IT! WHAT IF IT SHOULD FALL INTO THE WRONG HANDS?
YOUR CRITICISM IS INTOLERABLE! I LEAVE NOTHING TO CHANCE! I'VE COVERED EVERY POSSIBLE CONTINGENCY IN THE EVENT OF UNEXPECTED DANGER!!
THIS "DESTRUCT MECHANISM" IS ALWAYS ON MY PERSON! IF I WERE TO PRESS THIS KNOB, THE TRANSPORTER WOULD BLOW ITSELF TO PIECES!
PERFECT!! THAT'S JUST PERFECT!!
ENOUGH! TIME HAS RUN OUT! I CAN HEAR THE MON-STERS APPROACH!
CAP, SUDDENLY STRIKES LIKE A COBRA! IN THE SCUFFLE THAT FOLLOWS, THINGS HAP-PEN FAST!
AAAAA! YOU'VE PUSHED ME THROUGH THE ENERGY DOOR!
GOODBYE, INQUISITOR! I'VE GOT WHAT I WANTED-- THE DESTRUCT GADGET!
YOU--YOU BETRAYED US!

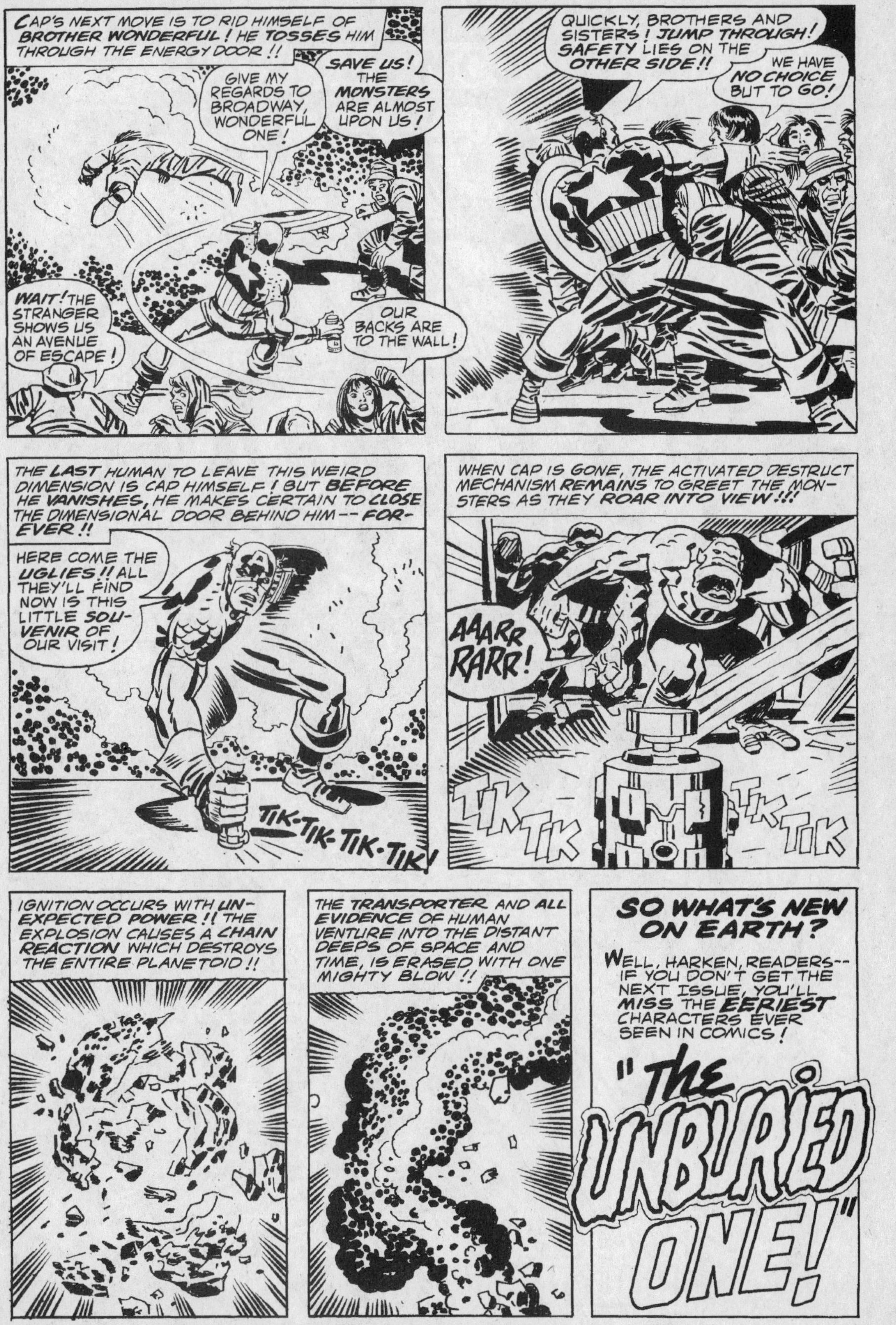
CAP'S NEXT MOVE IS TO RID HIMSELF OF BROTHER WONDERFUL! HE TOSSES HIM THROUGH THE ENERGY DOOR!!
GIVE MY REGARDS TO BROADWAY, WONDERFUL ONE!
SAVE US! THE MONSTERS ARE ALMOST UPON US!
WAIT! THE STRANGER SHOWS US AN AVENUE OF ESCAPE!
OUR BACKS ARE TO THE WALL!
QUICKLY, BROTHERS AND SISTERS! JUMP THROUGH! SAFETY LIES ON THE OTHER SIDE!!
WE HAVE NO CHOICE BUT TO GO!
THE LAST HUMAN TO LEAVE THIS WEIRD DIMENSION IS CAP HIMSELF! BUT BEFORE HE VANISHES, HE MAKES CERTAIN TO CLOSE THE DIMENSIONAL DOOR BEHIND HIM -- FOR-EVER!!
HERE COME THE UGLIES!! ALL THEY'LL FIND NOW IS THIS LITTLE SOU-VENIR OF OUR VISIT!
TIK-TIK-TIK-TIK!
WHEN CAP IS GONE, THE ACTIVATED DESTRUCT MECHANISM REMAINS TO GREET THE MON-STERS AS THEY ROAR INTO VIEW!!!
AAARR RARR!
TIK TIK TIK TIK
IGNITION OCCURS WITH UN-EXPECTED POWER!! THE EXPLOSION CAUSES A CHAIN REACTION WHICH DESTROYS THE ENTIRE PLANETOID!!
THE TRANSPORTER AND ALL EVIDENCE OF HUMAN VENTURE INTO THE DISTANT DEEPS OF SPACE AND TIME, IS ERASED WITH ONE MIGHTY BLOW!!
SO WHAT'S NEW ON EARTH?
WELL, HARKEN, READERS-- IF YOU DON'T GET THE NEXT ISSUE, YOU'LL MISS THE EERIEST CHARACTERS EVER SEEN IN COMICS!
"THE UNBURIED ONE!"

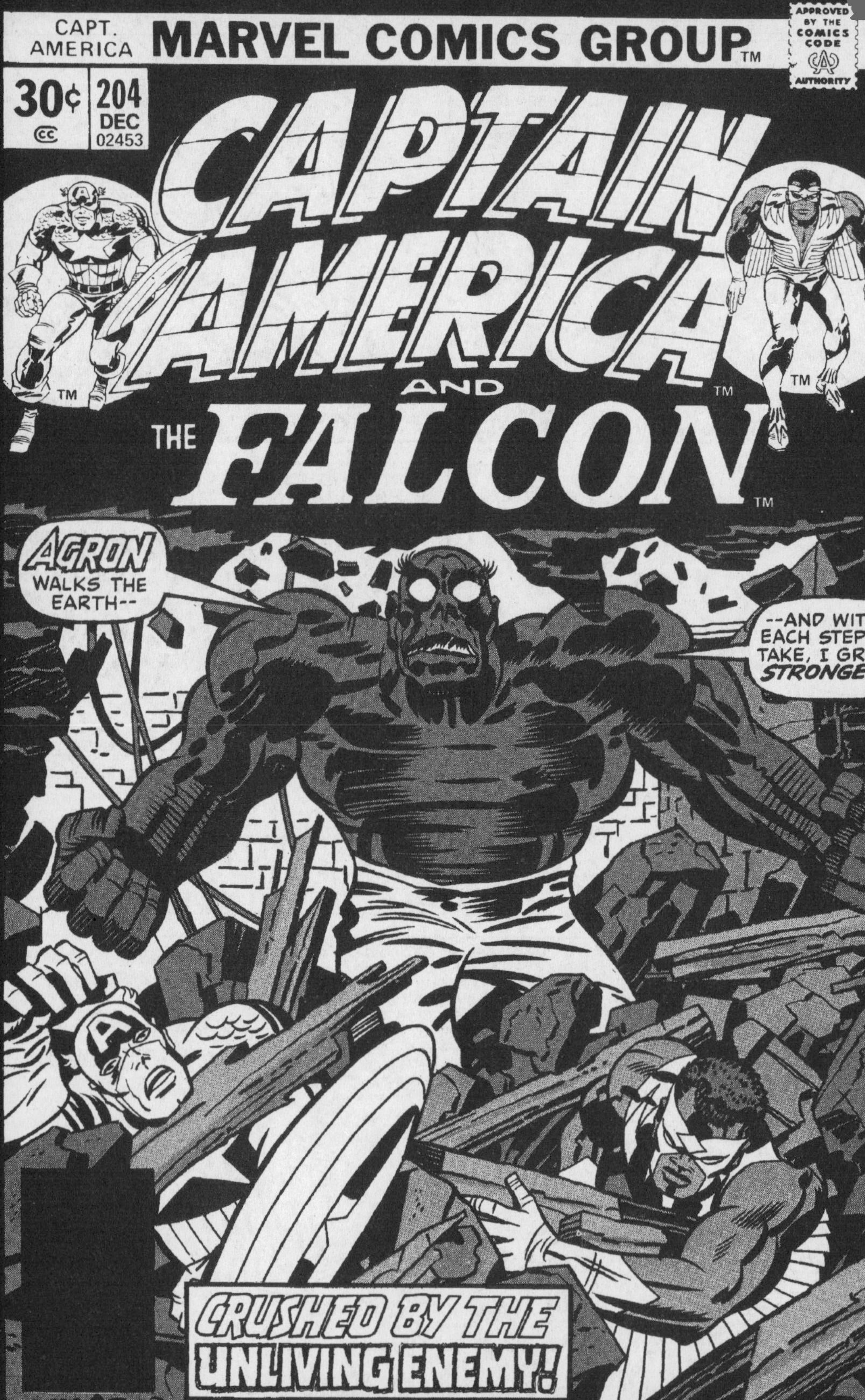
CAPT. AMERICA
MARVEL COMICS GROUP TM
APPROVED BY THE COMICS CODE AUTHORITY
30¢ CC
204 DEC 02453
CAPTAIN AMERICA AND THE FALCON
AGRON WALKS THE EARTH--
--AND WITH EACH STEP I TAKE, I GROW STRONGER!
CRUSHED BY THE UNLIVING ENEMY!

1941! The world at *war!* And in a secret laboratory, frail *Steve Rogers* became the American *super-soldier!* For four thrilling years, he fought the Axis powers—until a freak stroke of fate threw him into *suspended animation.* He woke in the mid-1960s, a man *twenty years out of his time.* Since that fateful day, Steve Rogers has sought his *destiny* in this brave new world.

STAN LEE PRESENTS: CAPTAIN AMERICA AND THE FALCON™

EDITED, WRITTEN AND DRAWN BY **JACK KIRBY** / INKS F. GIACOIA / LETTERS GASPAR / COLORS J. COHEN / CONSULTING EDITOR ARCHIE GOODWIN

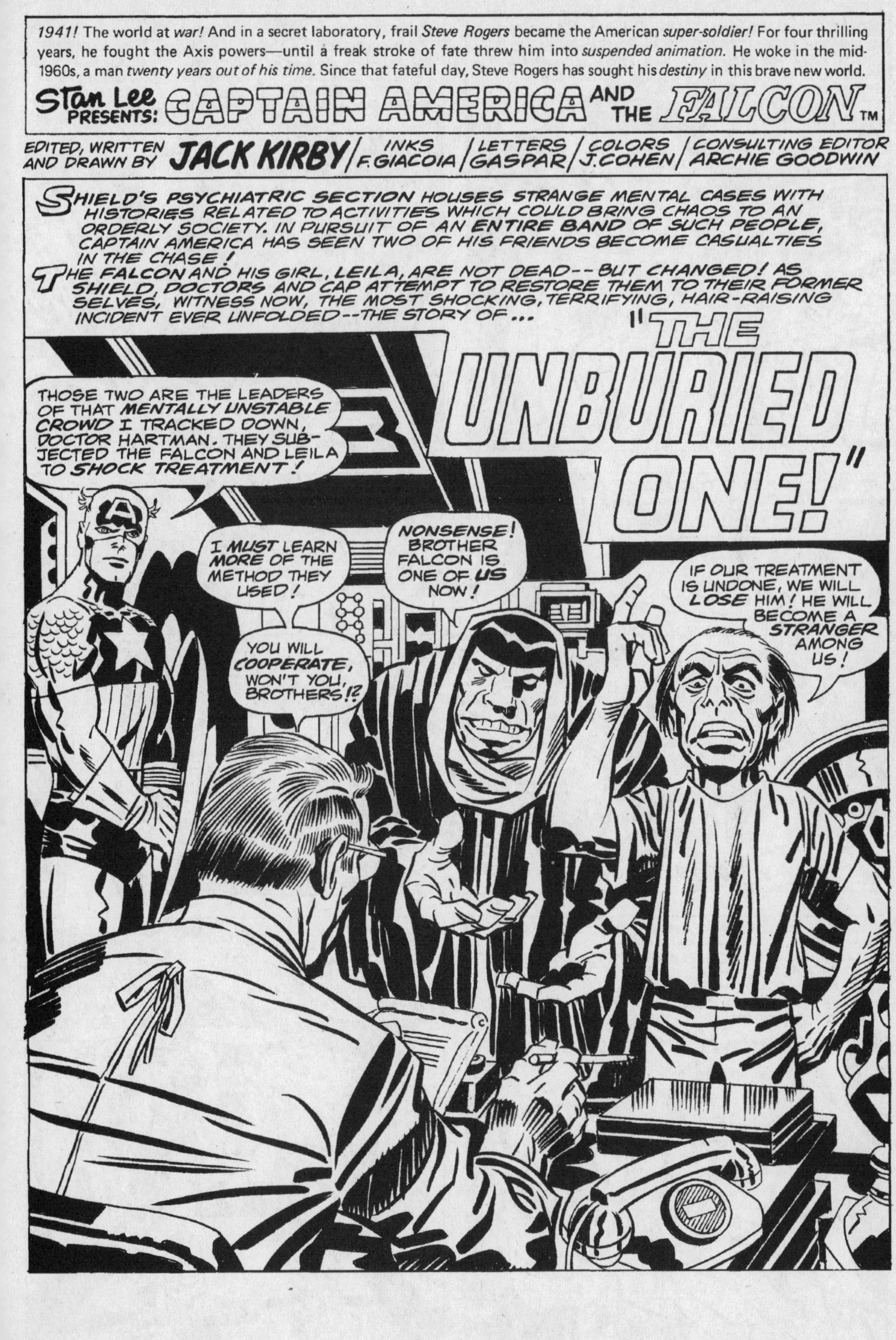
SHIELD'S PSYCHIATRIC SECTION HOUSES STRANGE MENTAL CASES WITH HISTORIES RELATED TO ACTIVITIES WHICH COULD BRING CHAOS TO AN ORDERLY SOCIETY. IN PURSUIT OF AN ENTIRE BAND OF SUCH PEOPLE, CAPTAIN AMERICA HAS SEEN TWO OF HIS FRIENDS BECOME CASUALTIES IN THE CHASE!
THE FALCON AND HIS GIRL, LEILA, ARE NOT DEAD--BUT CHANGED! AS SHIELD, DOCTORS AND CAP ATTEMPT TO RESTORE THEM TO THEIR FORMER SELVES, WITNESS NOW, THE MOST SHOCKING, TERRIFYING, HAIR-RAISING INCIDENT EVER UNFOLDED--THE STORY OF...
"THE UNBURIED ONE!"
THOSE TWO ARE THE LEADERS OF THAT MENTALLY UNSTABLE CROWD I TRACKED DOWN, DOCTOR HARTMAN. THEY SUBJECTED THE FALCON AND LEILA TO SHOCK TREATMENT!
I MUST LEARN MORE OF THE METHOD THEY USED!
YOU WILL COOPERATE, WON'T YOU, BROTHERS!?
NONSENSE! BROTHER FALCON IS ONE OF US NOW!
IF OUR TREATMENT IS UNDONE, WE WILL LOSE HIM! HE WILL BECOME A STRANGER AMONG US!

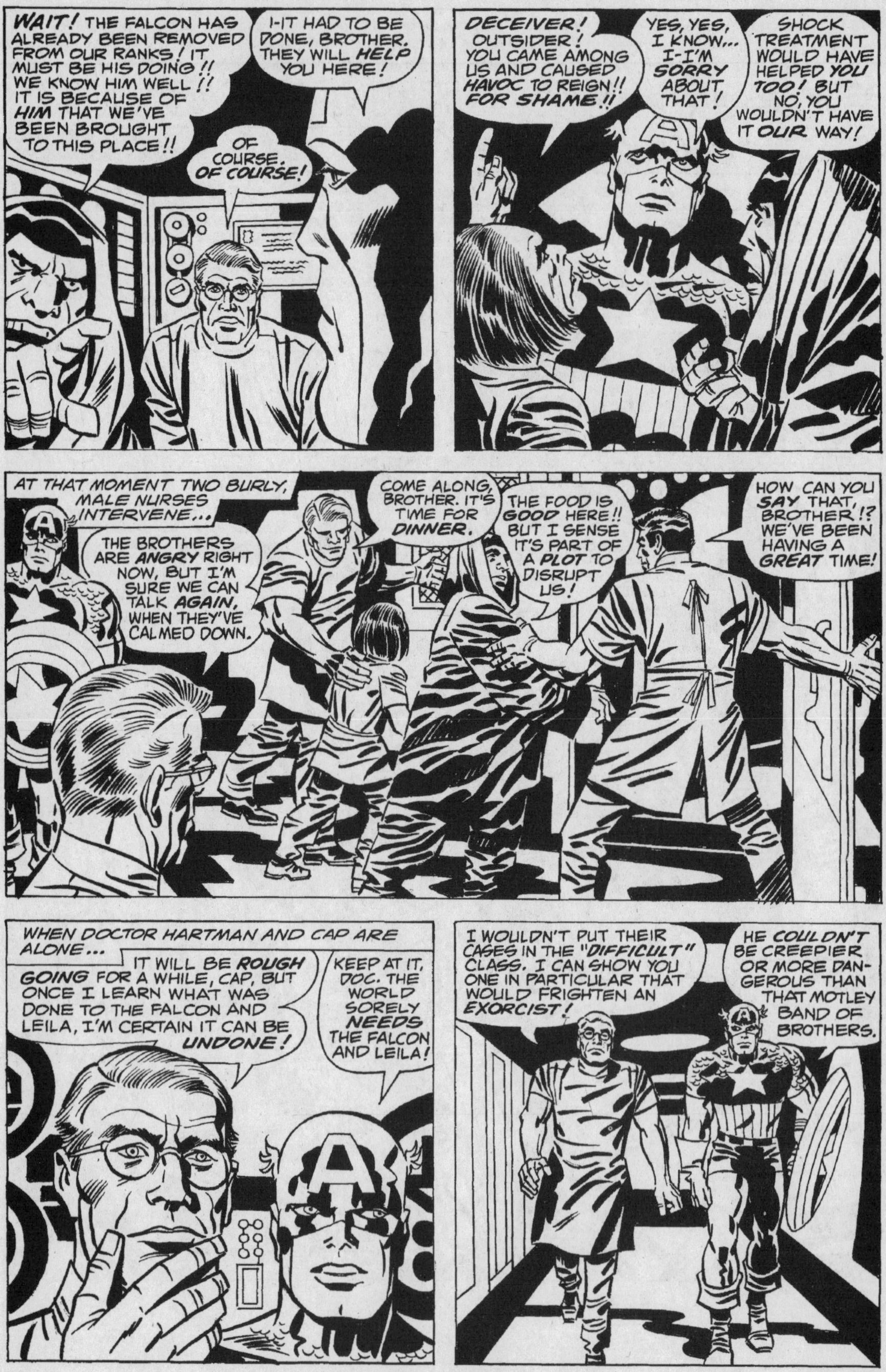
WAIT! THE FALCON HAS ALREADY BEEN REMOVED FROM OUR RANKS! IT MUST BE HIS DOING!! WE KNOW HIM WELL!! IT IS BECAUSE OF HIM THAT WE'VE BEEN BROUGHT TO THIS PLACE!!
I-IT HAD TO BE DONE, BROTHER. THEY WILL HELP YOU HERE!
OF COURSE. OF COURSE!
DECEIVER! OUTSIDER! YOU CAME AMONG US AND CAUSED HAVOC TO REIGN!! FOR SHAME!!
YES, YES, I KNOW... I-I'M SORRY ABOUT THAT!
SHOCK TREATMENT WOULD HAVE HELPED YOU TOO! BUT NO, YOU WOULDN'T HAVE IT OUR WAY!
AT THAT MOMENT TWO BURLY, MALE NURSES INTERVENE...
THE BROTHERS ARE ANGRY RIGHT NOW, BUT I'M SURE WE CAN TALK AGAIN, WHEN THEY'VE CALMED DOWN.
COME ALONG, BROTHER. IT'S TIME FOR DINNER.
THE FOOD IS GOOD HERE!! BUT I SENSE IT'S PART OF A PLOT TO DISRUPT US!
HOW CAN YOU SAY THAT, BROTHER!? WE'VE BEEN HAVING A GREAT TIME!
WHEN DOCTOR HARTMAN AND CAP ARE ALONE...
IT WILL BE ROUGH GOING FOR A WHILE, CAP, BUT ONCE I LEARN WHAT WAS DONE TO THE FALCON AND LEILA, I'M CERTAIN IT CAN BE UNDONE!
KEEP AT IT, DOC. THE WORLD SORELY NEEDS THE FALCON AND LEILA!
I WOULDN'T PUT THEIR CASES IN THE "DIFFICULT" CLASS. I CAN SHOW YOU ONE IN PARTICULAR THAT WOULD FRIGHTEN AN EXORCIST!
HE COULDN'T BE CREEPIER OR MORE DAN-GEROUS THAN THAT MOTLEY BAND OF BROTHERS.

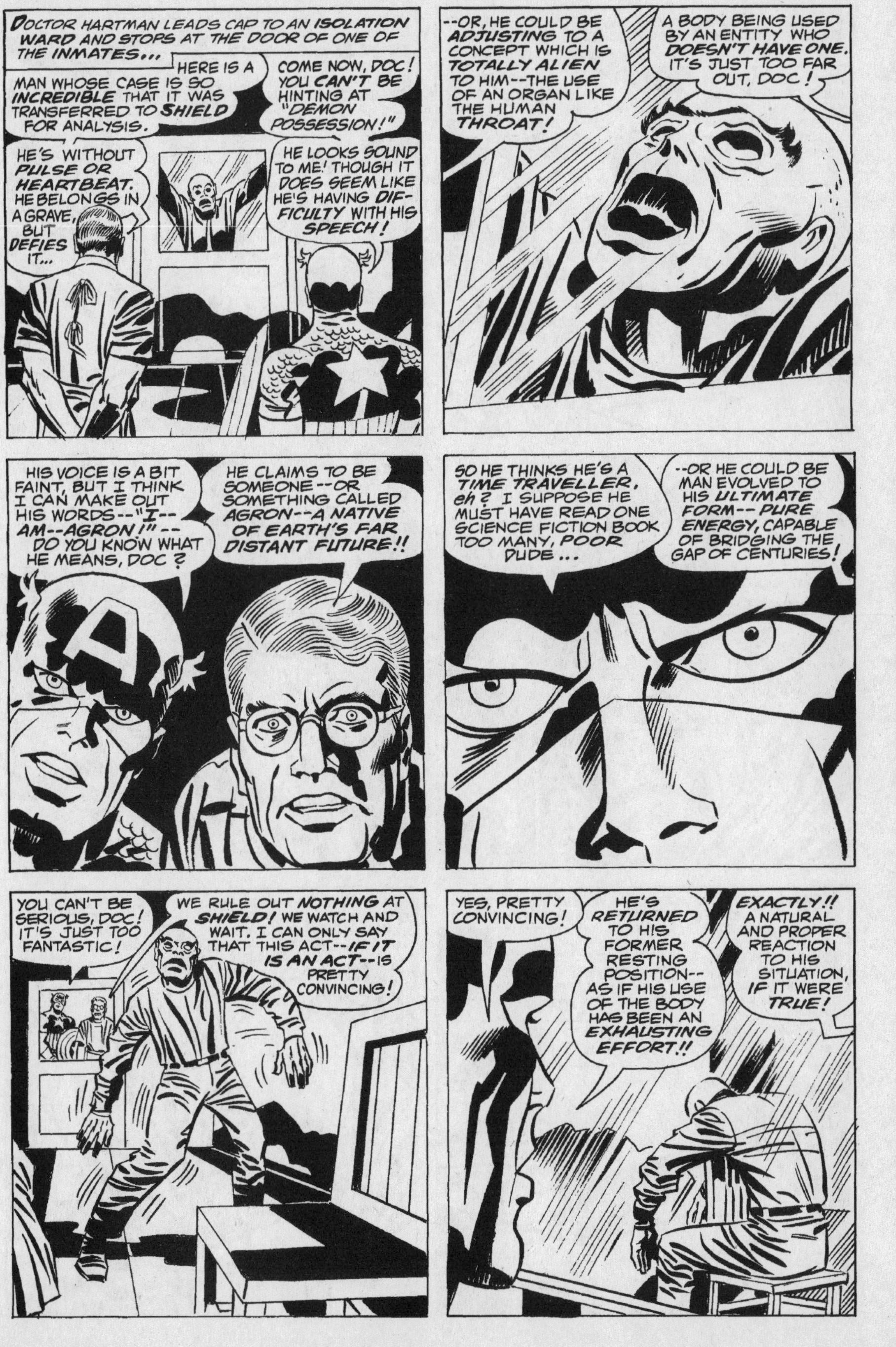
DOCTOR HARTMAN LEADS CAP TO AN ISOLATION WARD AND STOPS AT THE DOOR OF ONE OF THE INMATES...
HERE IS A MAN WHOSE CASE IS SO INCREDIBLE THAT IT WAS TRANSFERRED TO SHIELD FOR ANALYSIS.
COME NOW, DOC! YOU CAN'T BE HINTING AT "DEMON POSSESSION!"
HE'S WITHOUT PULSE OR HEARTBEAT. HE BELONGS IN A GRAVE, BUT DEFIES IT...
HE LOOKS SOUND TO ME! THOUGH IT DOES SEEM LIKE HE'S HAVING DIFFICULTY WITH HIS SPEECH!
--OR, HE COULD BE ADJUSTING TO A CONCEPT WHICH IS TOTALLY ALIEN TO HIM--THE USE OF AN ORGAN LIKE THE HUMAN THROAT!
A BODY BEING USED BY AN ENTITY WHO DOESN'T HAVE ONE. IT'S JUST TOO FAR OUT, DOC!
HIS VOICE IS A BIT FAINT, BUT I THINK I CAN MAKE OUT HIS WORDS--"I--AM--AGRON!"--DO YOU KNOW WHAT HE MEANS, DOC?
HE CLAIMS TO BE SOMEONE--OR SOMETHING CALLED AGRON--A NATIVE OF EARTH'S FAR DISTANT FUTURE!!
SO HE THINKS HE'S A TIME TRAVELLER, eh? I SUPPOSE HE MUST HAVE READ ONE SCIENCE FICTION BOOK TOO MANY, POOR DUDE...
--OR HE COULD BE MAN EVOLVED TO HIS ULTIMATE FORM--PURE ENERGY, CAPABLE OF BRIDGING THE GAP OF CENTURIES!
YOU CAN'T BE SERIOUS, DOC! IT'S JUST TOO FANTASTIC!
WE RULE OUT NOTHING AT SHIELD! WE WATCH AND WAIT. I CAN ONLY SAY THAT THIS ACT--IF IT IS AN ACT--IS PRETTY CONVINCING!
YES, PRETTY CONVINCING!
HE'S RETURNED TO HIS FORMER RESTING POSITION--AS IF HIS USE OF THE BODY HAS BEEN AN EXHAUSTING EFFORT!!
EXACTLY!! A NATURAL AND PROPER REACTION TO HIS SITUATION, IF IT WERE TRUE!

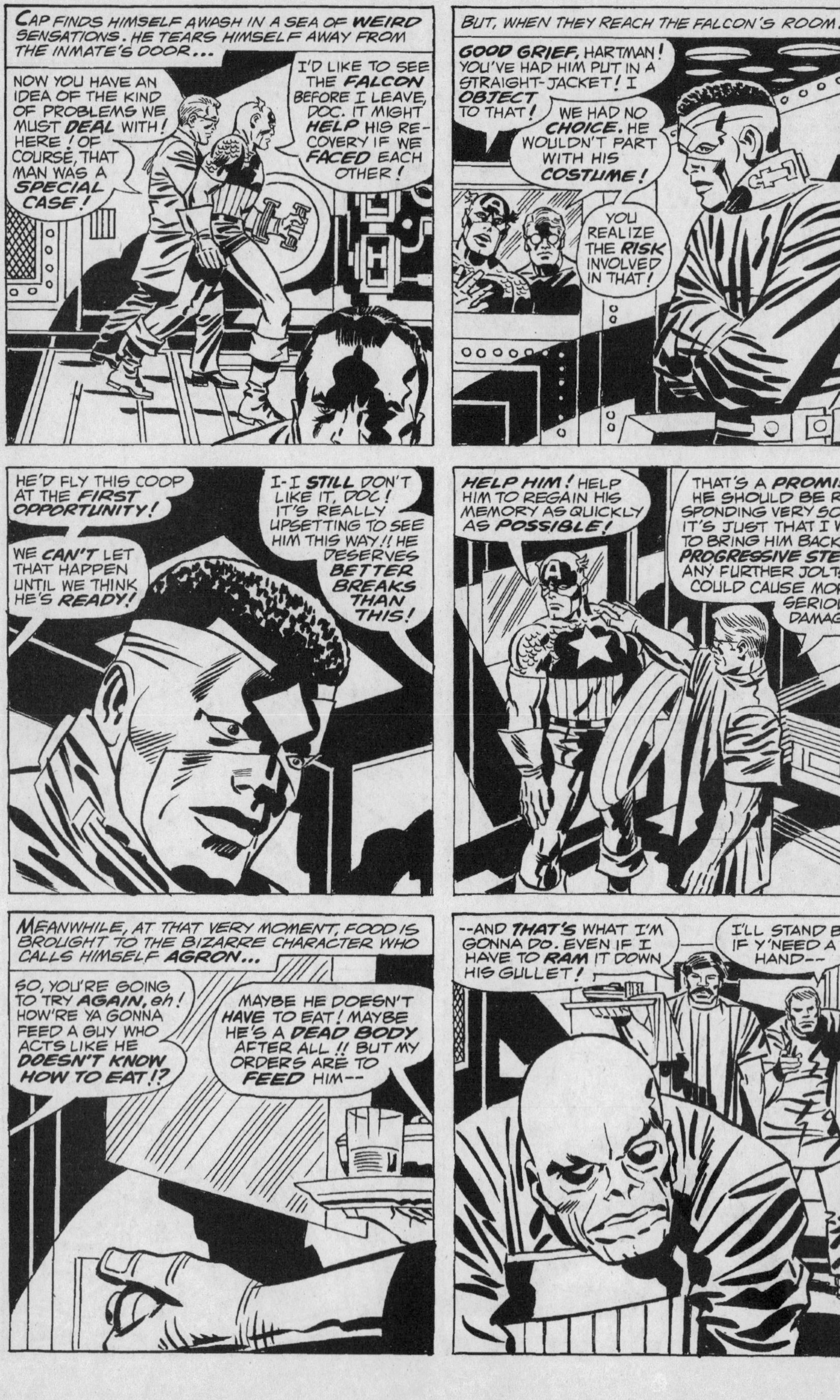
CAP FINDS HIMSELF AWASH IN A SEA OF WEIRD SENSATIONS. HE TEARS HIMSELF AWAY FROM THE INMATE'S DOOR...
NOW YOU HAVE AN IDEA OF THE KIND OF PROBLEMS WE MUST DEAL WITH! HERE! OF COURSE, THAT MAN WAS A SPECIAL CASE!
I'D LIKE TO SEE THE FALCON BEFORE I LEAVE, DOC. IT MIGHT HELP HIS RE-COVERY IF WE FACED EACH OTHER!
BUT, WHEN THEY REACH THE FALCON'S ROOM...
GOOD GRIEF, HARTMAN! YOU'VE HAD HIM PUT IN A STRAIGHT-JACKET! I OBJECT TO THAT!
WE HAD NO CHOICE. HE WOULDN'T PART WITH HIS COSTUME!
YOU REALIZE THE RISK INVOLVED IN THAT!
HE'D FLY THIS COOP AT THE FIRST OPPORTUNITY!
WE CAN'T LET THAT HAPPEN UNTIL WE THINK HE'S READY!
I-I STILL DON'T LIKE IT, DOC! IT'S REALLY UPSETTING TO SEE HIM THIS WAY!! HE DESERVES BETTER BREAKS THAN THIS!
HELP HIM! HELP HIM TO REGAIN HIS MEMORY AS QUICKLY AS POSSIBLE!
THAT'S A PROMISE! HE SHOULD BE RE-SPONDING VERY SOON! IT'S JUST THAT I WANT TO BRING HIM BACK IN PROGRESSIVE STEPS. ANY FURTHER JOLTS COULD CAUSE MORE SERIOUS DAMAGE!
MEANWHILE, AT THAT VERY MOMENT, FOOD IS BROUGHT TO THE BIZARRE CHARACTER WHO CALLS HIMSELF AGRON...
SO, YOU'RE GOING TO TRY AGAIN, eh! HOW'RE YA GONNA FEED A GUY WHO ACTS LIKE HE DOESN'T KNOW HOW TO EAT!?
MAYBE HE DOESN'T HAVE TO EAT! MAYBE HE'S A DEAD BODY AFTER ALL!! BUT MY ORDERS ARE TO FEED HIM--
--AND THAT'S WHAT I'M GONNA DO. EVEN IF I HAVE TO RAM IT DOWN HIS GULLET!
I'LL STAND BY-- IF Y'NEED A HAND--

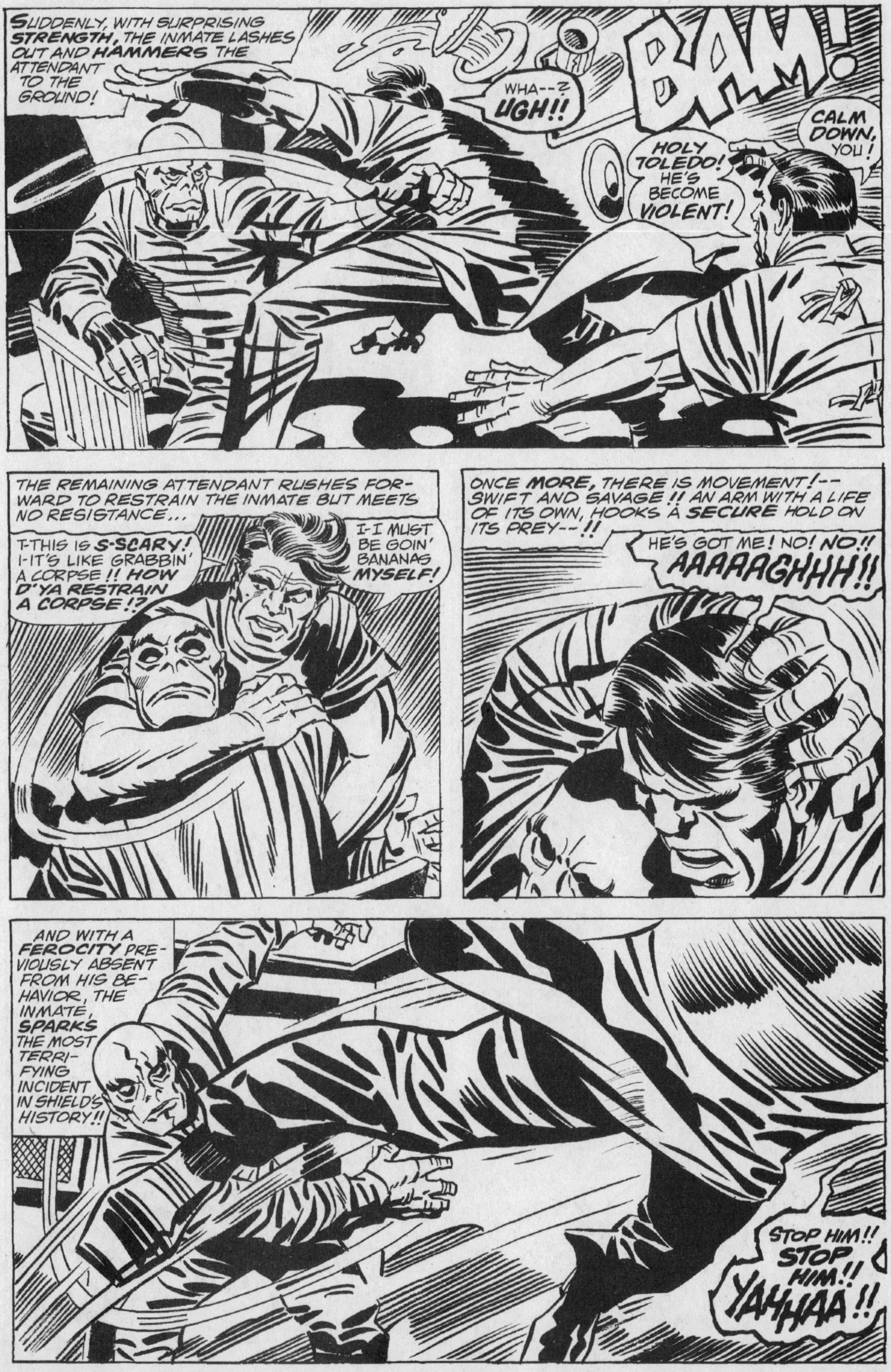
SUDDENLY, WITH SURPRISING STRENGTH, THE INMATE LASHES OUT AND HAMMERS THE ATTENDANT TO THE GROUND!
BAM!
WHA--? UGH!!
HOLY TOLEDO! HE'S BECOME VIOLENT!
CALM DOWN, YOU!
THE REMAINING ATTENDANT RUSHES FORWARD TO RESTRAIN THE INMATE BUT MEETS NO RESISTANCE...
T-THIS IS S-SCARY! I-IT'S LIKE GRABBIN' A CORPSE!! HOW D'YA RESTRAIN A CORPSE!?
I-I MUST BE GOIN' BANANAS MYSELF!
ONCE MORE, THERE IS MOVEMENT!-- SWIFT AND SAVAGE!! AN ARM WITH A LIFE OF ITS OWN, HOOKS A SECURE HOLD ON ITS PREY--!!
HE'S GOT ME! NO! NO!! AAAARAGHHH!!
AND WITH A FEROCITY PREVIOUSLY ABSENT FROM HIS BEHAVIOR, THE INMATE, SPARKS THE MOST TERRIFYING INCIDENT IN SHIELD'S HISTORY!!
STOP HIM!! STOP HIM!! YAHHAA!!

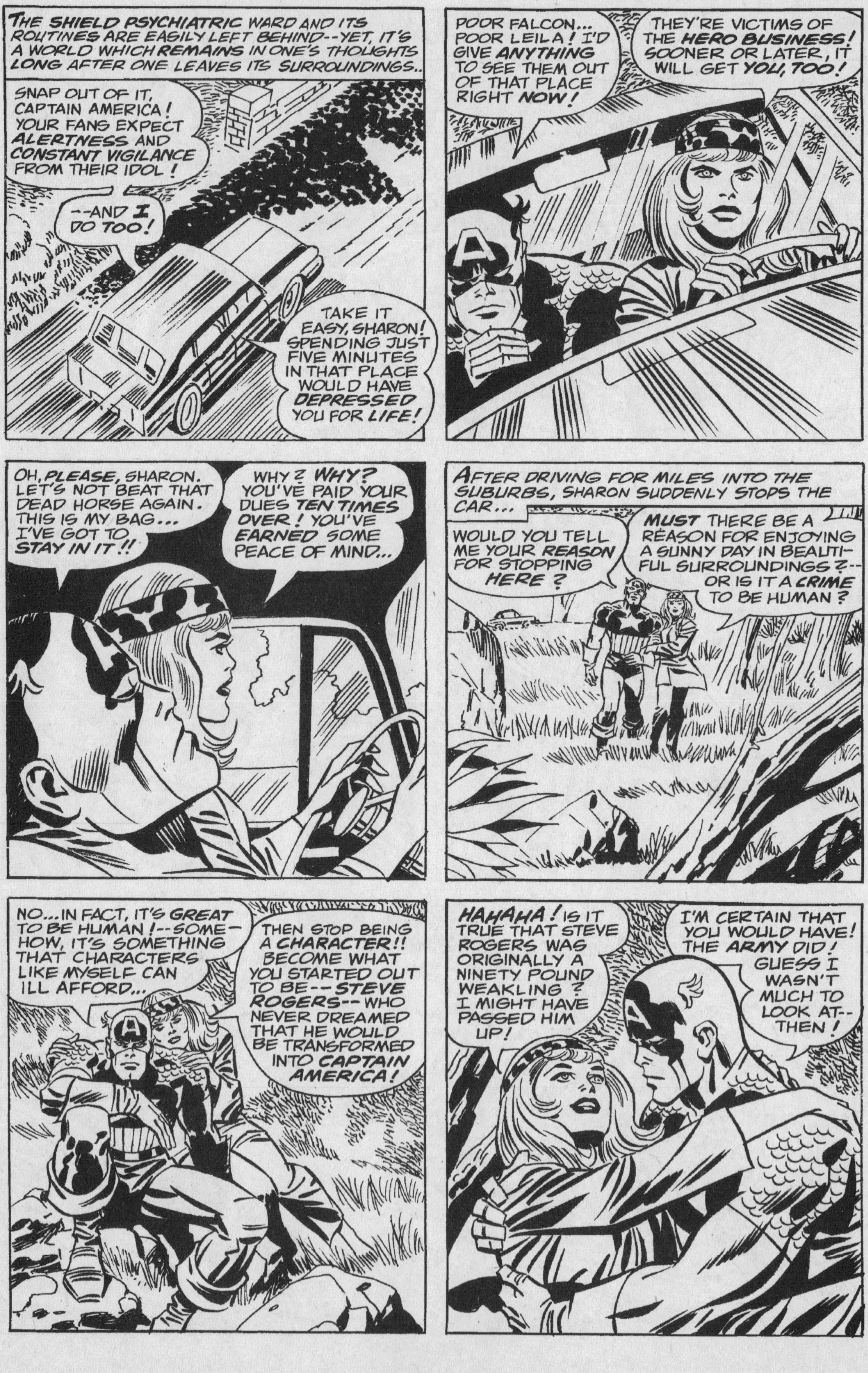
THE SHIELD PSYCHIATRIC WARD AND ITS ROUTINES ARE EASILY LEFT BEHIND--YET, IT'S A WORLD WHICH REMAINS IN ONE'S THOUGHTS LONG AFTER ONE LEAVES ITS SURROUNDINGS..
SNAP OUT OF IT, CAPTAIN AMERICA! YOUR FANS EXPECT ALERTNESS AND CONSTANT VIGILANCE FROM THEIR IDOL!
--AND I DO TOO!
TAKE IT EASY, SHARON! SPENDING JUST FIVE MINUTES IN THAT PLACE WOULD HAVE DEPRESSED YOU FOR LIFE!
POOR FALCON... POOR LEILA! I'D GIVE ANYTHING TO SEE THEM OUT OF THAT PLACE RIGHT NOW!
THEY'RE VICTIMS OF THE HERO BUSINESS! SOONER OR LATER, IT WILL GET YOU, TOO!
OH, PLEASE, SHARON. LET'S NOT BEAT THAT DEAD HORSE AGAIN. THIS IS MY BAG... I'VE GOT TO STAY IN IT!!
WHY? WHY? YOU'VE PAID YOUR DUES TEN TIMES OVER! YOU'VE EARNED SOME PEACE OF MIND...
AFTER DRIVING FOR MILES INTO THE SUBURBS, SHARON SUDDENLY STOPS THE CAR...
WOULD YOU TELL ME YOUR REASON FOR STOPPING HERE?
MUST THERE BE A REASON FOR ENJOYING A SUNNY DAY IN BEAUTIFUL SURROUNDINGS?--OR IS IT A CRIME TO BE HUMAN?
NO...IN FACT, IT'S GREAT TO BE HUMAN!--SOMEHOW, IT'S SOMETHING THAT CHARACTERS LIKE MYSELF CAN ILL AFFORD...
THEN STOP BEING A CHARACTER!! BECOME WHAT YOU STARTED OUT TO BE--STEVE ROGERS--WHO NEVER DREAMED THAT HE WOULD BE TRANSFORMED INTO CAPTAIN AMERICA!
HAHAHA! IS IT TRUE THAT STEVE ROGERS WAS ORIGINALLY A NINETY POUND WEAKLING? I MIGHT HAVE PASSED HIM UP!
I'M CERTAIN THAT YOU WOULD HAVE! THE ARMY DID! GUESS I WASN'T MUCH TO LOOK AT--THEN!

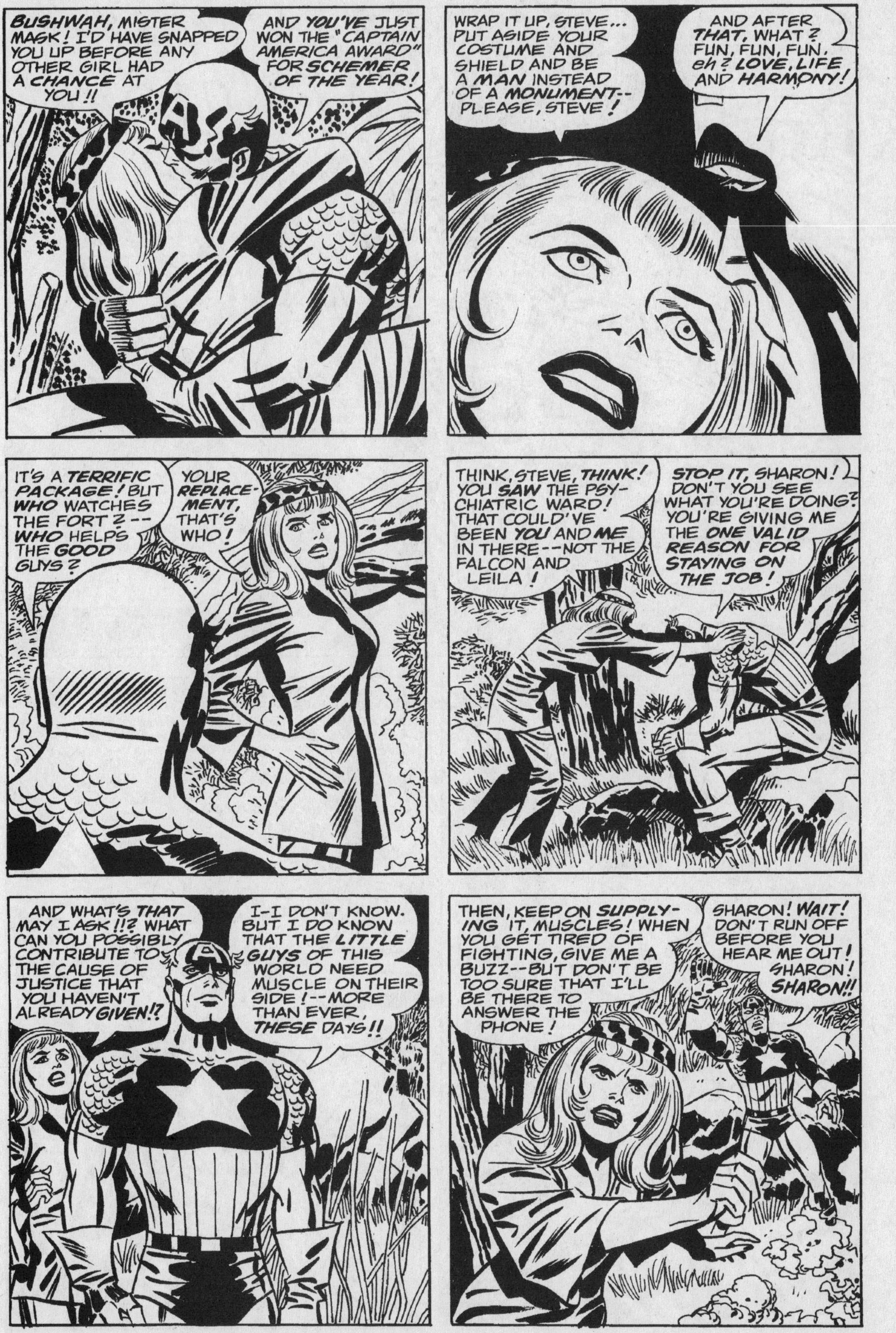
BUSHWAH, MISTER MASK! I'D HAVE SNAPPED YOU UP BEFORE ANY OTHER GIRL HAD A CHANCE AT YOU!!
AND YOU'VE JUST WON THE "CAPTAIN AMERICA AWARD" FOR SCHEMER OF THE YEAR!
WRAP IT UP, STEVE... PUT ASIDE YOUR COSTUME AND SHIELD AND BE A MAN INSTEAD OF A MONUMENT-- PLEASE, STEVE!
AND AFTER THAT, WHAT? FUN, FUN, FUN, eh? LOVE, LIFE AND HARMONY!
IT'S A TERRIFIC PACKAGE! BUT WHO WATCHES THE FORT? --WHO HELPS THE GOOD GUYS?
YOUR REPLACEMENT, THAT'S WHO!
THINK, STEVE, THINK! YOU SAW THE PSYCHIATRIC WARD! THAT COULD'VE BEEN YOU AND ME IN THERE--NOT THE FALCON AND LEILA!
STOP IT, SHARON! DON'T YOU SEE WHAT YOU'RE DOING? YOU'RE GIVING ME THE ONE VALID REASON FOR STAYING ON THE JOB!
AND WHAT'S THAT MAY I ASK!!? WHAT CAN YOU POSSIBLY CONTRIBUTE TO THE CAUSE OF JUSTICE THAT YOU HAVEN'T ALREADY GIVEN!?
I-I DON'T KNOW. BUT I DO KNOW THAT THE LITTLE GUYS OF THIS WORLD NEED MUSCLE ON THEIR SIDE!--MORE THAN EVER, THESE DAYS!!
THEN, KEEP ON SUPPLYING IT, MUSCLES! WHEN YOU GET TIRED OF FIGHTING, GIVE ME A BUZZ--BUT DON'T BE TOO SURE THAT I'LL BE THERE TO ANSWER THE PHONE!
SHARON! WAIT! DON'T RUN OFF BEFORE YOU HEAR ME OUT! SHARON! SHARON!!

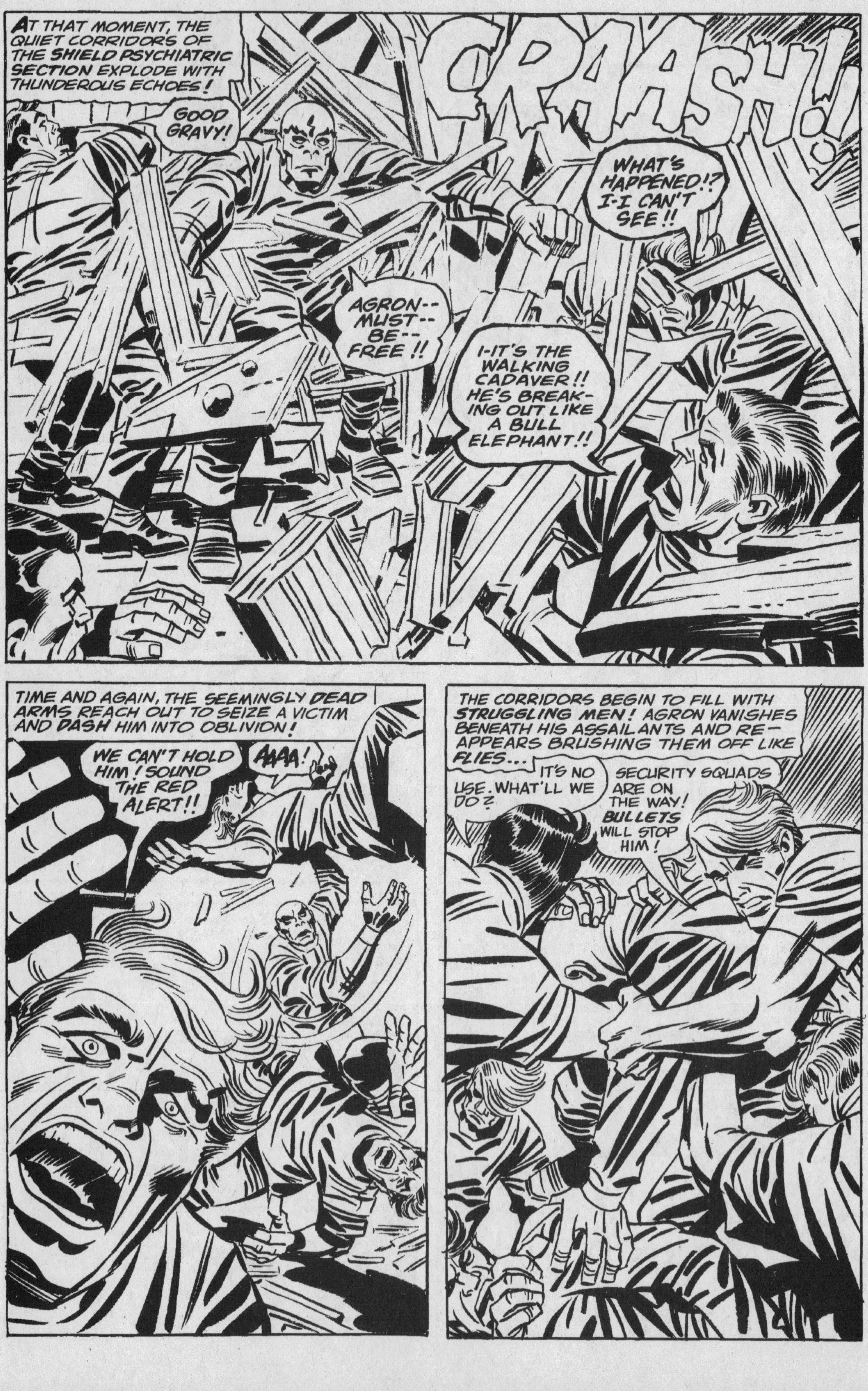
AT THAT MOMENT, THE QUIET CORRIDORS OF THE SHIELD PSYCHIATRIC SECTION EXPLODE WITH THUNDEROUS ECHOES!
CRAASH!!
GOOD GRAVY!
WHAT'S HAPPENED!? I-I CAN'T SEE!!
AGRON-- MUST-- BE-- FREE!!
I-IT'S THE WALKING CADAVER!! HE'S BREAKING OUT LIKE A BULL ELEPHANT!!
TIME AND AGAIN, THE SEEMINGLY DEAD ARMS REACH OUT TO SEIZE A VICTIM AND DASH HIM INTO OBLIVION!
WE CAN'T HOLD HIM! SOUND THE RED ALERT!!
AAAA!
THE CORRIDORS BEGIN TO FILL WITH STRUGGLING MEN! AGRON VANISHES BENEATH HIS ASSAILANTS AND RE-APPEARS BRUSHING THEM OFF LIKE FLIES...
IT'S NO USE. WHAT'LL WE DO?
SECURITY SQUADS ARE ON THE WAY! BULLETS WILL STOP HIM!

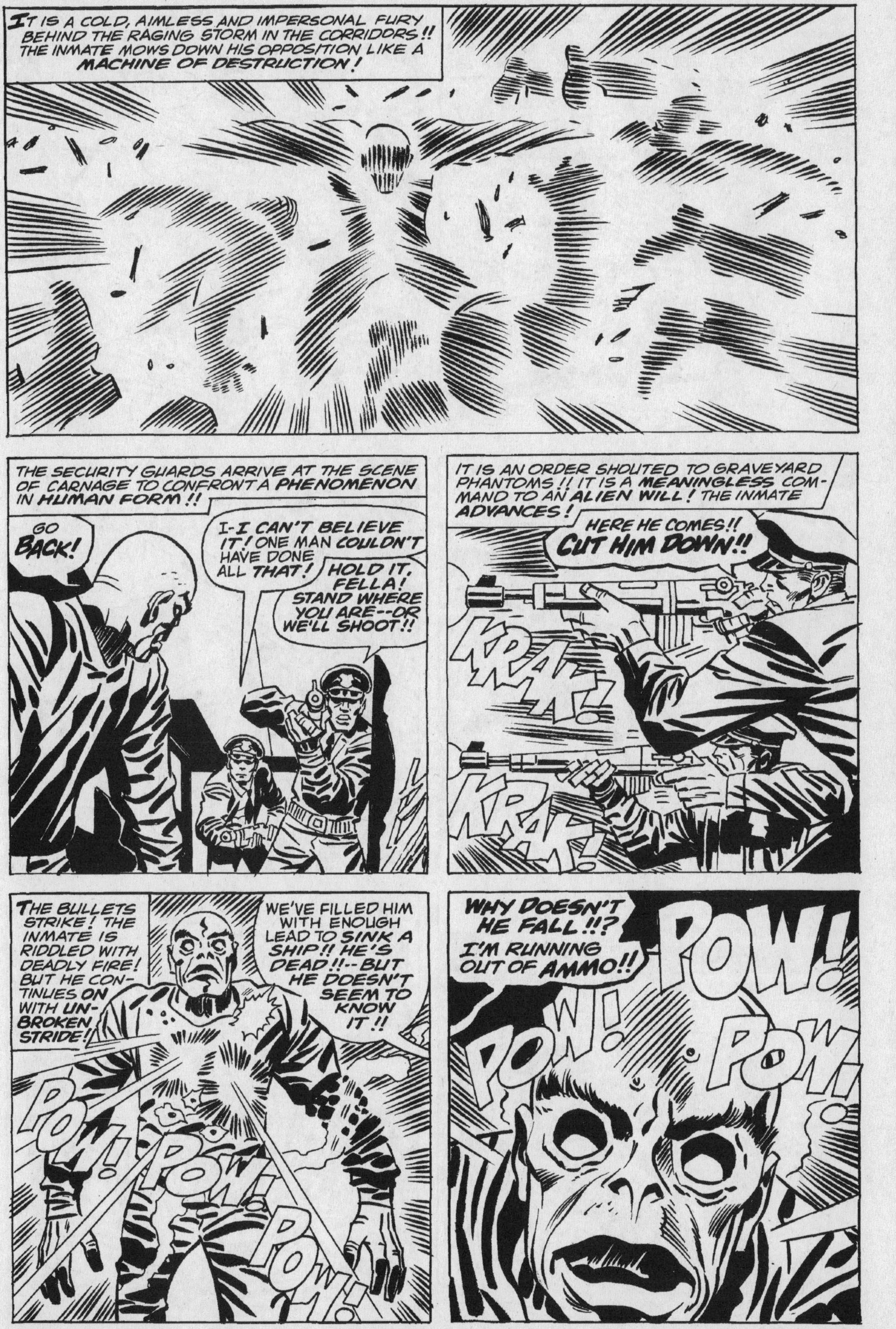
IT IS A COLD, AIMLESS AND IMPERSONAL FURY BEHIND THE RAGING STORM IN THE CORRIDORS!! THE INMATE MOWS DOWN HIS OPPOSITION LIKE A MACHINE OF DESTRUCTION!
THE SECURITY GUARDS ARRIVE AT THE SCENE OF CARNAGE TO CONFRONT A PHENOMENON IN HUMAN FORM!!
GO BACK!
I-I CAN'T BELIEVE IT! ONE MAN COULDN'T HAVE DONE ALL THAT!
HOLD IT, FELLA! STAND WHERE YOU ARE--OR WE'LL SHOOT!!
IT IS AN ORDER SHOUTED TO GRAVEYARD PHANTOMS!! IT IS A MEANINGLESS COMMAND TO AN ALIEN WILL! THE INMATE ADVANCES!
HERE HE COMES!! CUT HIM DOWN!!
KRAK!
KRAK!
THE BULLETS STRIKE! THE INMATE IS RIDDLED WITH DEADLY FIRE! BUT HE CONTINUES ON WITH UNBROKEN STRIDE!
WE'VE FILLED HIM WITH ENOUGH LEAD TO SINK A SHIP!! HE'S DEAD!!--BUT HE DOESN'T SEEM TO KNOW IT!!
POW!
POW!
POW!
WHY DOESN'T HE FALL!!? I'M RUNNING OUT OF AMMO!!
POW!
POW!
POW!

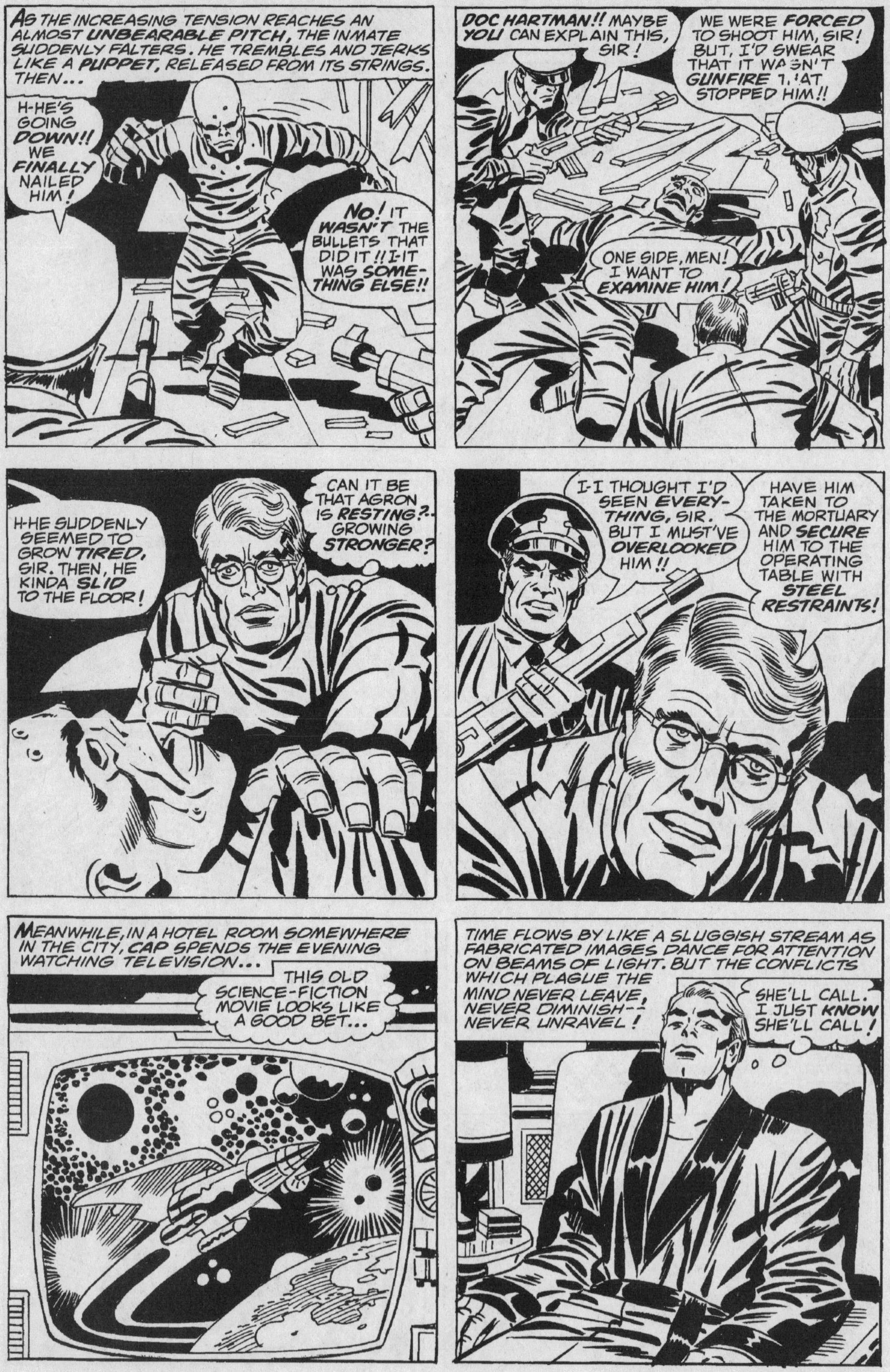

AS THE INCREASING TENSION REACHES AN ALMOST UNBEARABLE PITCH, THE INMATE SUDDENLY FALTERS. HE TREMBLES AND JERKS LIKE A PUPPET, RELEASED FROM ITS STRINGS. THEN...
H-HE'S GOING DOWN!! WE FINALLY NAILED HIM!
NO! IT WASN'T THE BULLETS THAT DID IT!! I-IT WAS SOMETHING ELSE!!
DOC HARTMAN!! MAYBE YOU CAN EXPLAIN THIS, SIR!
WE WERE FORCED TO SHOOT HIM, SIR! BUT, I'D SWEAR THAT IT WASN'T GUNFIRE THAT STOPPED HIM!!
ONE SIDE, MEN! I WANT TO EXAMINE HIM!
H-HE SUDDENLY SEEMED TO GROW TIRED, SIR. THEN, HE KINDA SLID TO THE FLOOR!
CAN IT BE THAT AGRON IS RESTING?-- GROWING STRONGER?
I-I THOUGHT I'D SEEN EVERYTHING, SIR. BUT I MUST'VE OVERLOOKED HIM!!
HAVE HIM TAKEN TO THE MORTUARY AND SECURE HIM TO THE OPERATING TABLE WITH STEEL RESTRAINTS!
MEANWHILE, IN A HOTEL ROOM SOMEWHERE IN THE CITY, CAP SPENDS THE EVENING WATCHING TELEVISION...
THIS OLD SCIENCE-FICTION MOVIE LOOKS LIKE A GOOD BET...
TIME FLOWS BY LIKE A SLUGGISH STREAM AS FABRICATED IMAGES DANCE FOR ATTENTION ON BEAMS OF LIGHT. BUT THE CONFLICTS WHICH PLAGUE THE MIND NEVER LEAVE, NEVER DIMINISH-- NEVER UNRAVEL!
SHE'LL CALL. I JUST KNOW SHE'LL CALL!

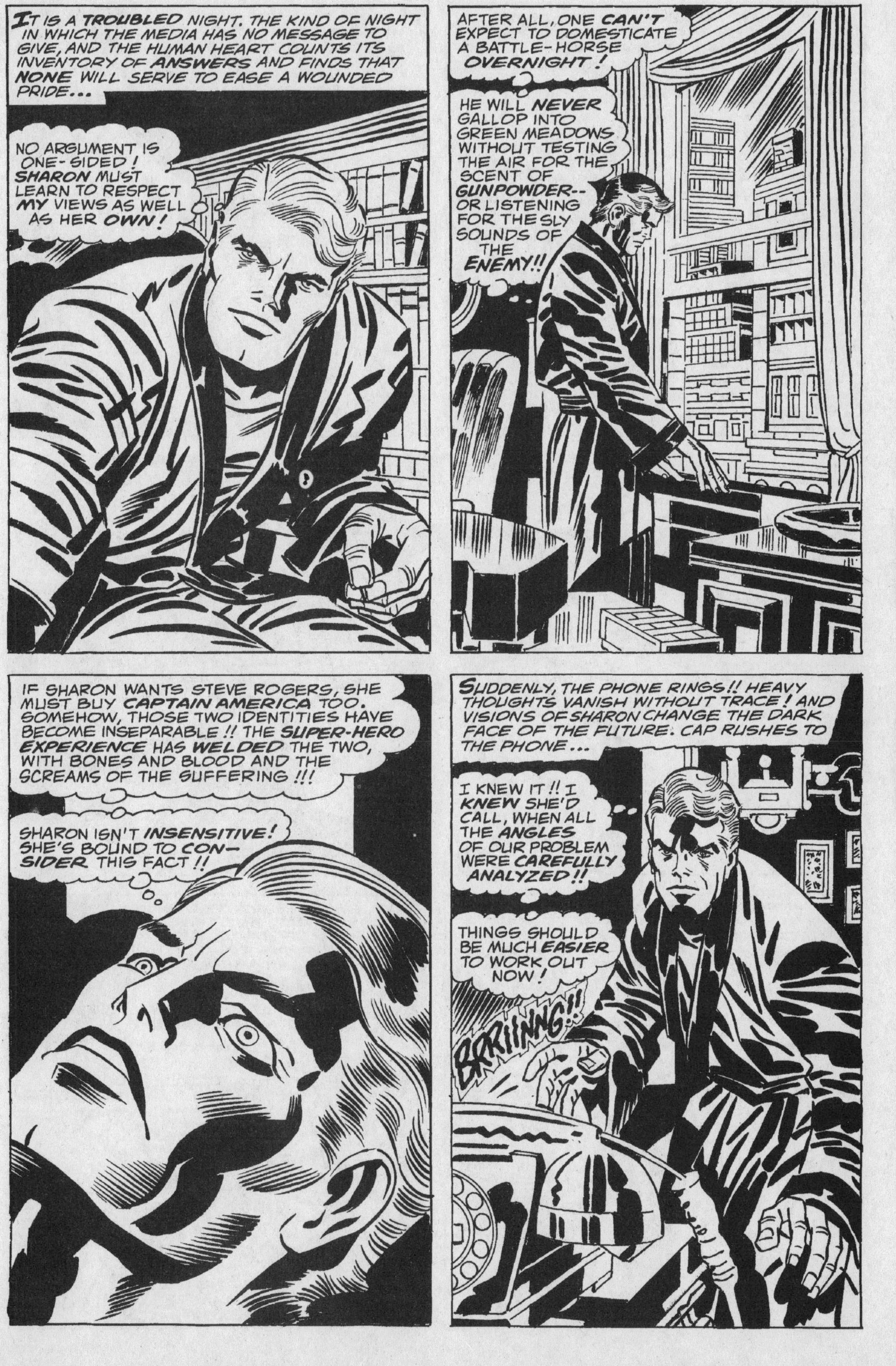
IT IS A TROUBLED NIGHT. THE KIND OF NIGHT IN WHICH THE MEDIA HAS NO MESSAGE TO GIVE, AND THE HUMAN HEART COUNTS ITS INVENTORY OF ANSWERS AND FINDS THAT NONE WILL SERVE TO EASE A WOUNDED PRIDE...
NO ARGUMENT IS ONE-SIDED! SHARON MUST LEARN TO RESPECT MY VIEWS AS WELL AS HER OWN!
AFTER ALL, ONE CAN'T EXPECT TO DOMESTICATE A BATTLE-HORSE OVERNIGHT!
HE WILL NEVER GALLOP INTO GREEN MEADOWS WITHOUT TESTING THE AIR FOR THE SCENT OF GUNPOWDER-- OR LISTENING FOR THE SLY SOUNDS OF THE ENEMY!!
IF SHARON WANTS STEVE ROGERS, SHE MUST BUY CAPTAIN AMERICA TOO. SOMEHOW, THOSE TWO IDENTITIES HAVE BECOME INSEPARABLE!! THE SUPER-HERO EXPERIENCE HAS WELDED THE TWO, WITH BONES AND BLOOD AND THE SCREAMS OF THE SUFFERING!!!
SHARON ISN'T INSENSITIVE! SHE'S BOUND TO CON-SIDER THIS FACT!!
SUDDENLY, THE PHONE RINGS!! HEAVY THOUGHTS VANISH WITHOUT TRACE! AND VISIONS OF SHARON CHANGE THE DARK FACE OF THE FUTURE. CAP RUSHES TO THE PHONE...
I KNEW IT!! I KNEW SHE'D CALL, WHEN ALL THE ANGLES OF OUR PROBLEM WERE CAREFULLY ANALYZED!!
THINGS SHOULD BE MUCH EASIER TO WORK OUT NOW!
BRRIIING!!

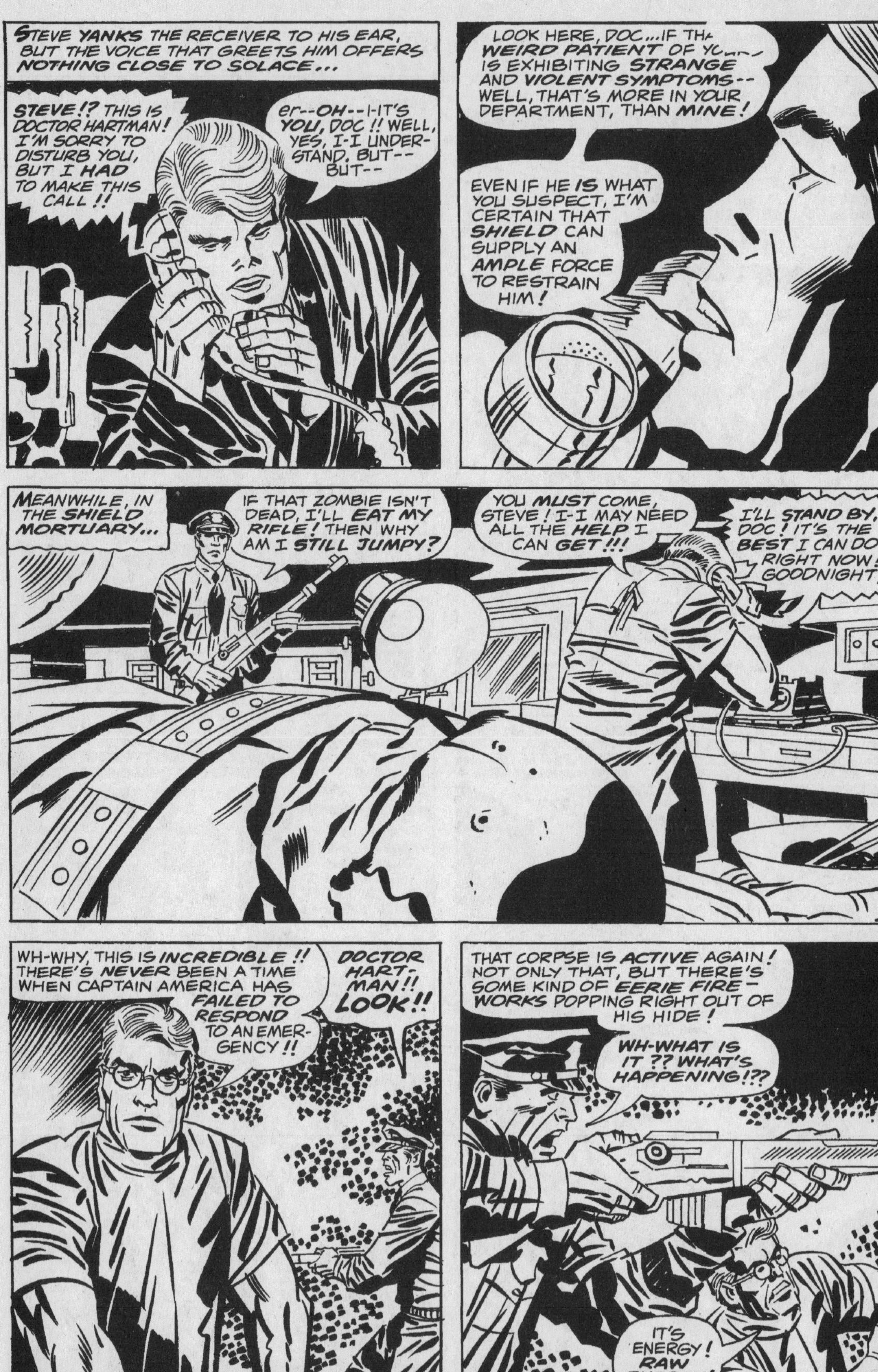
STEVE YANKS THE RECEIVER TO HIS EAR, BUT THE VOICE THAT GREETS HIM OFFERS NOTHING CLOSE TO SOLACE...
STEVE!? THIS IS DOCTOR HARTMAN! I'M SORRY TO DISTURB YOU, BUT I HAD TO MAKE THIS CALL!!
er--OH--I-IT'S YOU, DOC!! WELL, YES, I-I UNDERSTAND, BUT--BUT--
LOOK HERE, DOC...IF THA WEIRD PATIENT OF YOU IS EXHIBITING STRANGE AND VIOLENT SYMPTOMS--WELL, THAT'S MORE IN YOUR DEPARTMENT, THAN MINE!
EVEN IF HE IS WHAT YOU SUSPECT, I'M CERTAIN THAT SHIELD CAN SUPPLY AN AMPLE FORCE TO RESTRAIN HIM!
MEANWHILE, IN THE SHIELD MORTUARY...
IF THAT ZOMBIE ISN'T DEAD, I'LL EAT MY RIFLE! THEN WHY AM I STILL JUMPY?
YOU MUST COME, STEVE! I-I MAY NEED ALL THE HELP I CAN GET!!!
I'LL STAND BY, DOC! IT'S THE BEST I CAN DO RIGHT NOW! GOODNIGHT!
WH-WHY, THIS IS INCREDIBLE!! THERE'S NEVER BEEN A TIME WHEN CAPTAIN AMERICA HAS FAILED TO RESPOND TO AN EMERGENCY!!
DOCTOR HARTMAN!! LOOK!!
THAT CORPSE IS ACTIVE AGAIN! NOT ONLY THAT, BUT THERE'S SOME KIND OF EERIE FIREWORKS POPPING RIGHT OUT OF HIS HIDE!
WH-WHAT IS IT?? WHAT'S HAPPENING!??
IT'S ENERGY! RAW ENERGY!

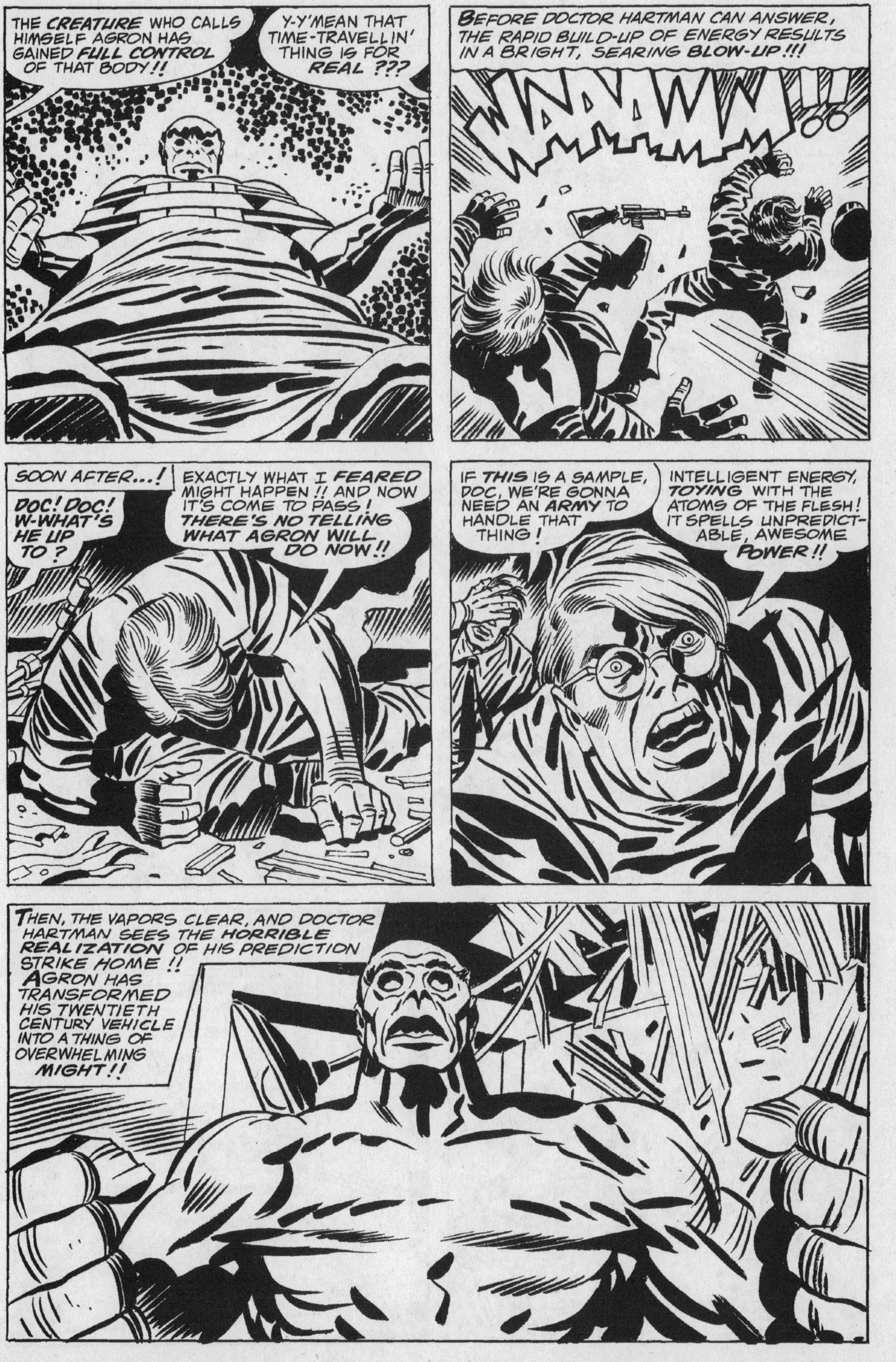
THE CREATURE WHO CALLS HIMSELF AGRON HAS GAINED FULL CONTROL OF THAT BODY!!
Y-Y'MEAN THAT TIME-TRAVELLIN' THING IS FOR REAL ???
BEFORE DOCTOR HARTMAN CAN ANSWER, THE RAPID BUILD-UP OF ENERGY RESULTS IN A BRIGHT, SEARING BLOW-UP!!!
WAAAWW!!!
SOON AFTER...!
DOC! DOC! W-WHAT'S HE UP TO?
EXACTLY WHAT I FEARED MIGHT HAPPEN!! AND NOW IT'S COME TO PASS! THERE'S NO TELLING WHAT AGRON WILL DO NOW!!
IF THIS IS A SAMPLE, DOC, WE'RE GONNA NEED AN ARMY TO HANDLE THAT THING!
INTELLIGENT ENERGY, TOYING WITH THE ATOMS OF THE FLESH! IT SPELLS UNPREDICTABLE, AWESOME POWER!!
THEN, THE VAPORS CLEAR, AND DOCTOR HARTMAN SEES THE HORRIBLE REALIZATION OF HIS PREDICTION STRIKE HOME!! AGRON HAS TRANSFORMED HIS TWENTIETH CENTURY VEHICLE INTO A THING OF OVERWHELMING MIGHT!!

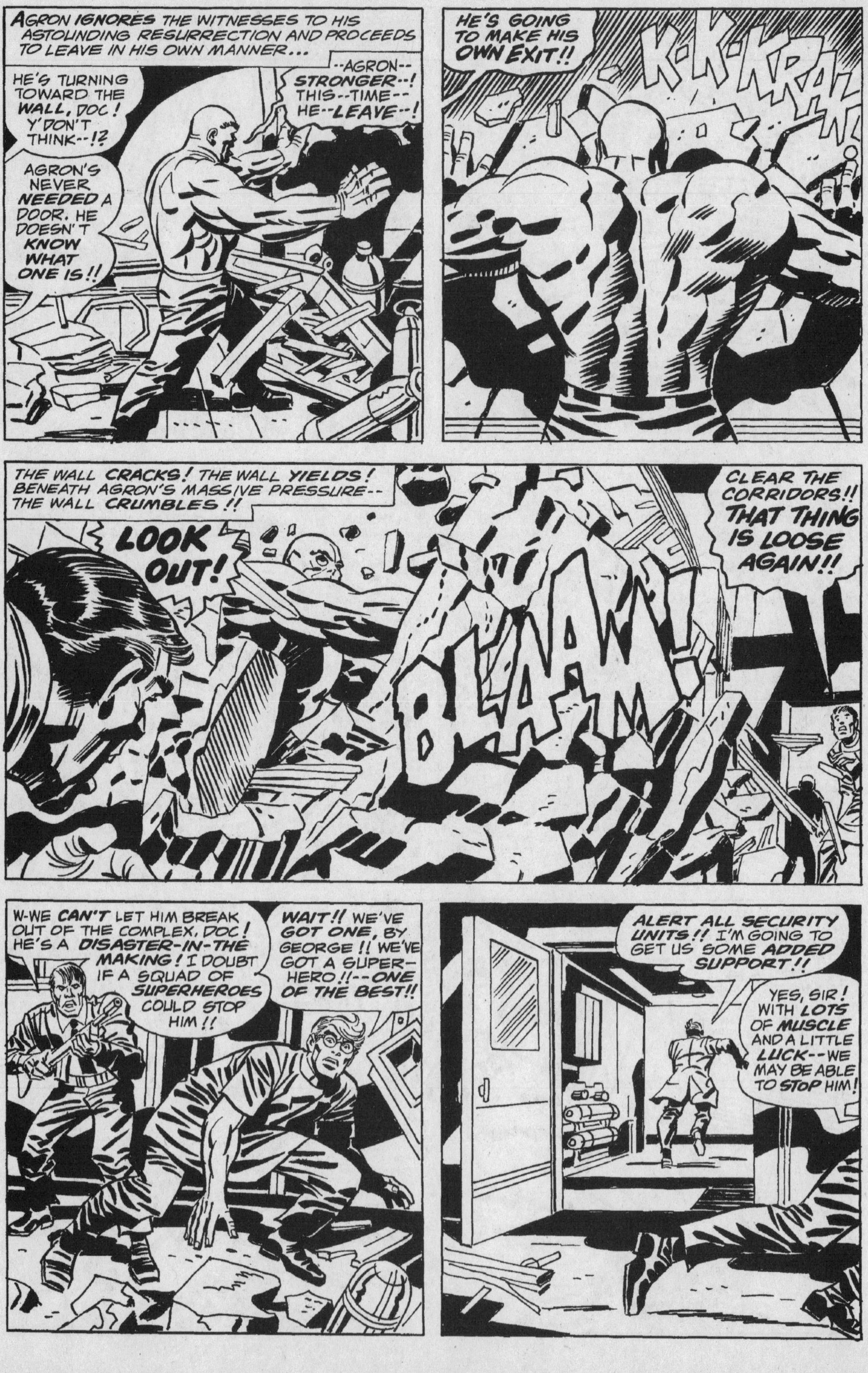
AGRON IGNORES THE WITNESSES TO HIS ASTOUNDING RESURRECTION AND PROCEEDS TO LEAVE IN HIS OWN MANNER...
HE'S TURNING TOWARD THE WALL, DOC! Y'DON'T THINK--!?
--AGRON-- STRONGER--! THIS--TIME-- HE--LEAVE--!
AGRON'S NEVER NEEDED A DOOR. HE DOESN'T KNOW WHAT ONE IS!!
HE'S GOING TO MAKE HIS OWN EXIT!!
K-K-KRAK
THE WALL CRACKS! THE WALL YIELDS! BENEATH AGRON'S MASSIVE PRESSURE-- THE WALL CRUMBLES!!
LOOK OUT!
CLEAR THE CORRIDORS!! THAT THING IS LOOSE AGAIN!!
BLAAM!
W-WE CAN'T LET HIM BREAK OUT OF THE COMPLEX, DOC! HE'S A DISASTER-IN-THE MAKING! I DOUBT IF A SQUAD OF SUPERHEROES COULD STOP HIM!!
WAIT!! WE'VE GOT ONE, BY GEORGE!! WE'VE GOT A SUPER-HERO!!--ONE OF THE BEST!!
ALERT ALL SECURITY UNITS!! I'M GOING TO GET US SOME ADDED SUPPORT!!
YES, SIR! WITH LOTS OF MUSCLE AND A LITTLE LUCK--WE MAY BE ABLE TO STOP HIM!

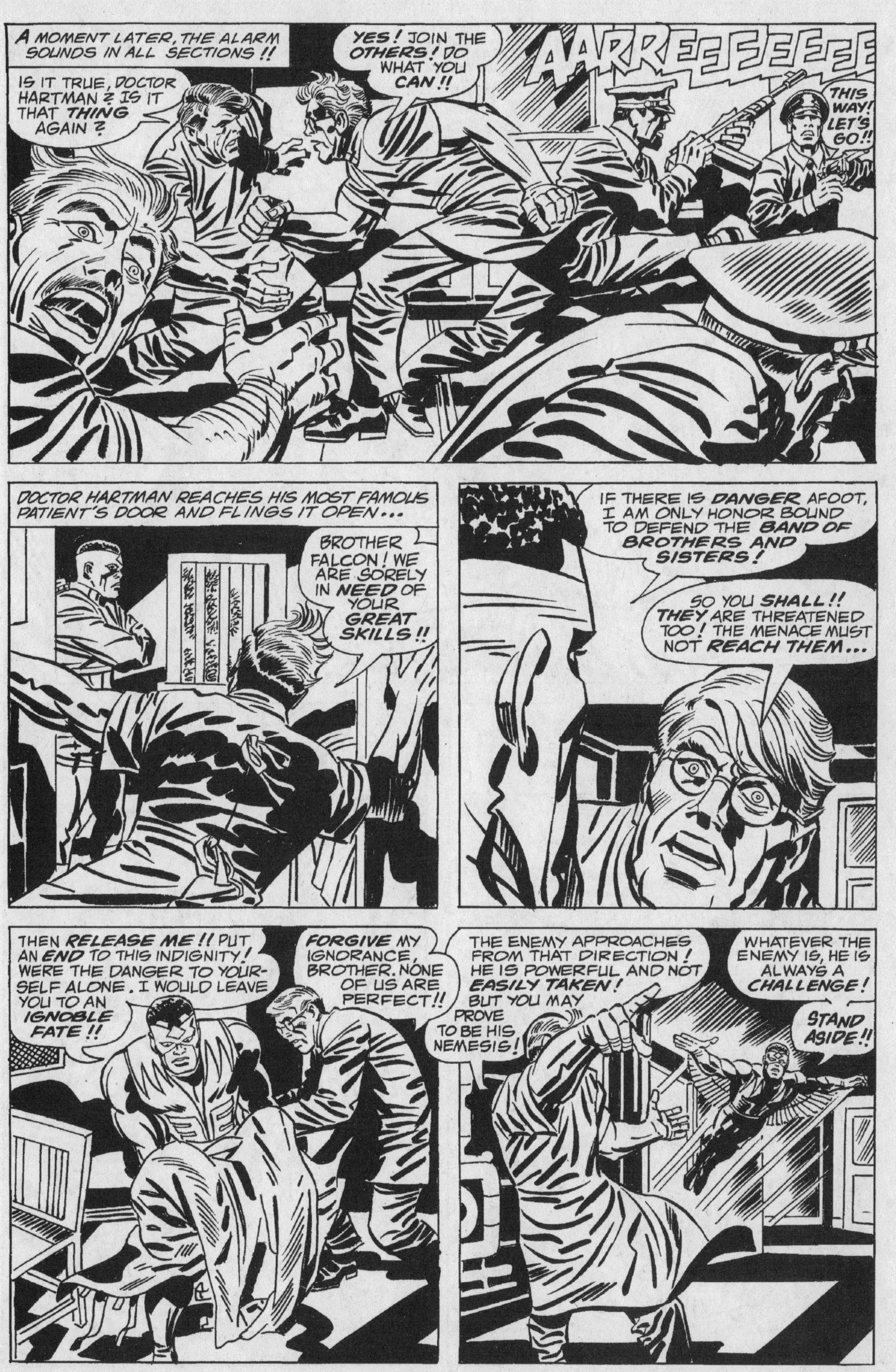
A MOMENT LATER, THE ALARM SOUNDS IN ALL SECTIONS!!
IS IT TRUE, DOCTOR HARTMAN? IS IT THAT THING AGAIN?
YES! JOIN THE OTHERS! DO WHAT YOU CAN!!
AARREEEEEEEE
THIS WAY! LET'S GO!!
DOCTOR HARTMAN REACHES HIS MOST FAMOUS PATIENT'S DOOR AND FLINGS IT OPEN...
BROTHER FALCON! WE ARE SORELY IN NEED OF YOUR GREAT SKILLS!!
IF THERE IS DANGER AFOOT, I AM ONLY HONOR BOUND TO DEFEND THE BAND OF BROTHERS AND SISTERS!
SO YOU SHALL!! THEY ARE THREATENED TOO! THE MENACE MUST NOT REACH THEM...
THEN RELEASE ME!! PUT AN END TO THIS INDIGNITY! WERE THE DANGER TO YOURSELF ALONE. I WOULD LEAVE YOU TO AN IGNOBLE FATE!!
FORGIVE MY IGNORANCE, BROTHER. NONE OF US ARE PERFECT!!
THE ENEMY APPROACHES FROM THAT DIRECTION! HE IS POWERFUL AND NOT EASILY TAKEN! BUT YOU MAY PROVE TO BE HIS NEMESIS!
WHATEVER THE ENEMY IS, HE IS ALWAYS A CHALLENGE!
STAND ASIDE!!

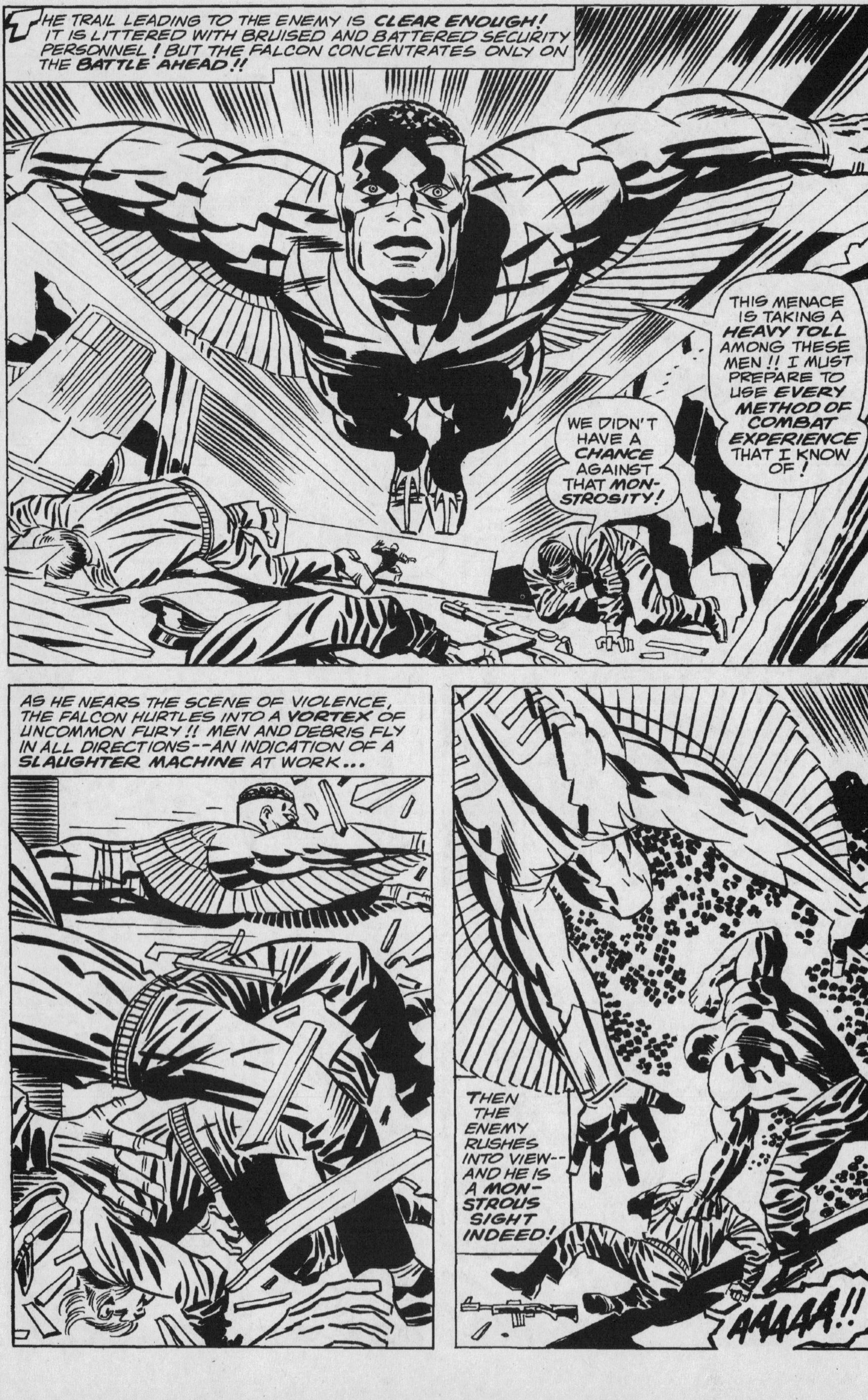
THE TRAIL LEADING TO THE ENEMY IS CLEAR ENOUGH! IT IS LITTERED WITH BRUISED AND BATTERED SECURITY PERSONNEL! BUT THE FALCON CONCENTRATES ONLY ON THE BATTLE AHEAD!!
THIS MENACE IS TAKING A HEAVY TOLL AMONG THESE MEN!! I MUST PREPARE TO USE EVERY METHOD OF COMBAT EXPERIENCE THAT I KNOW OF!
WE DIDN'T HAVE A CHANCE AGAINST THAT MONSTROSITY!
AS HE NEARS THE SCENE OF VIOLENCE, THE FALCON HURTLES INTO A VORTEX OF UNCOMMON FURY!! MEN AND DEBRIS FLY IN ALL DIRECTIONS--AN INDICATION OF A SLAUGHTER MACHINE AT WORK...
THEN THE ENEMY RUSHES INTO VIEW--AND HE IS A MONSTROUS SIGHT INDEED!
AAAAA!!

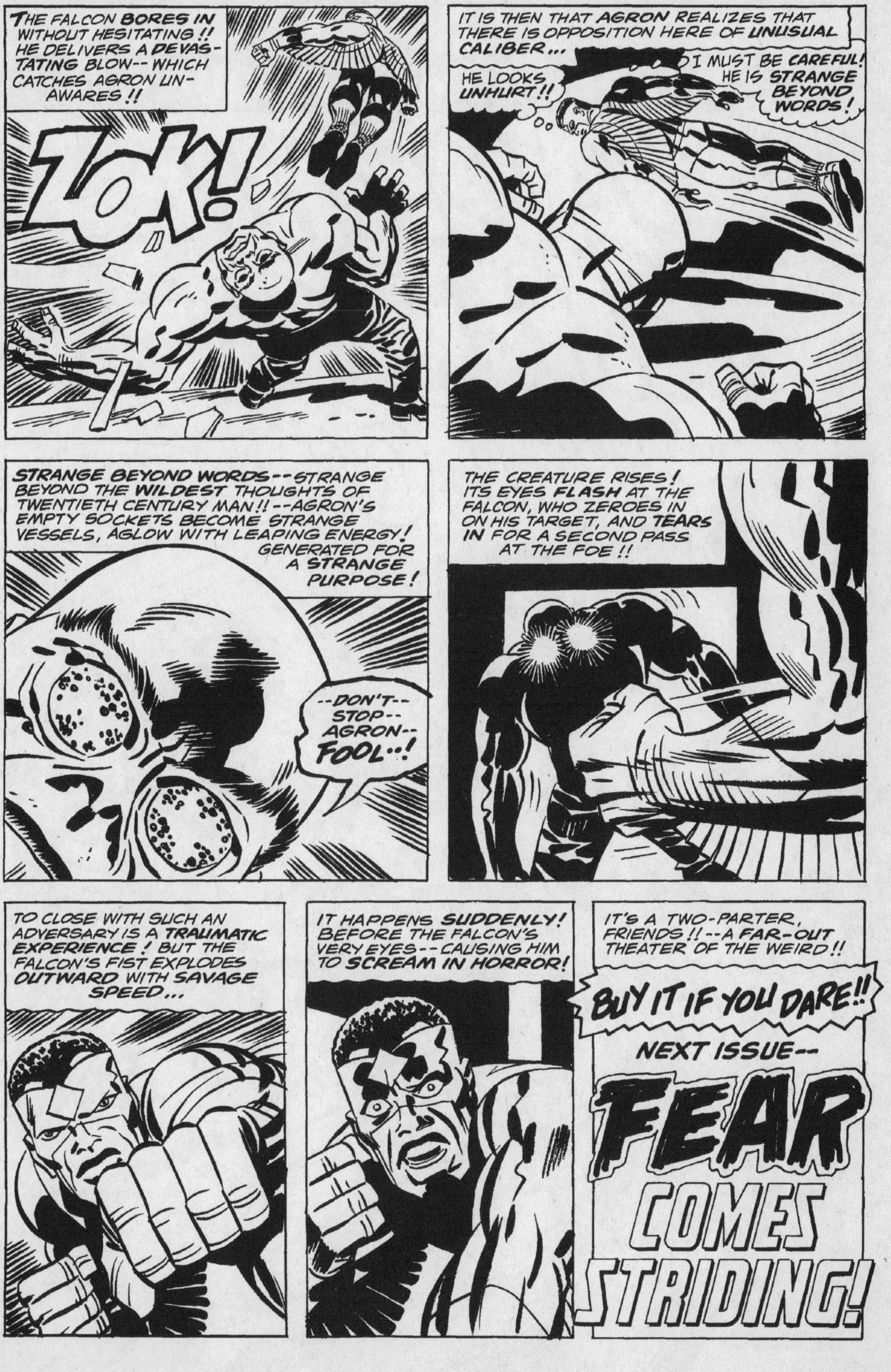
THE FALCON BORES IN WITHOUT HESITATING!! HE DELIVERS A DEVASTATING BLOW--WHICH CATCHES AGRON UNAWARES!!
ZOK!
IT IS THEN THAT AGRON REALIZES THAT THERE IS OPPOSITION HERE OF UNUSUAL CALIBER...
HE LOOKS UNHURT!!
I MUST BE CAREFUL! HE IS STRANGE BEYOND WORDS!
STRANGE BEYOND WORDS--STRANGE BEYOND THE WILDEST THOUGHTS OF TWENTIETH CENTURY MAN!!--AGRON'S EMPTY SOCKETS BECOME STRANGE VESSELS, AGLOW WITH LEAPING ENERGY! GENERATED FOR A STRANGE PURPOSE!
--DON'T--STOP--AGRON--FOOL--!
THE CREATURE RISES! ITS EYES FLASH AT THE FALCON, WHO ZEROES IN ON HIS TARGET, AND TEARS IN FOR A SECOND PASS AT THE FOE!!
TO CLOSE WITH SUCH AN ADVERSARY IS A TRAUMATIC EXPERIENCE! BUT THE FALCON'S FIST EXPLODES OUTWARD WITH SAVAGE SPEED...
IT HAPPENS SUDDENLY! BEFORE THE FALCON'S VERY EYES--CAUSING HIM TO SCREAM IN HORROR!
IT'S A TWO-PARTER, FRIENDS!!--A FAR-OUT THEATER OF THE WEIRD!!
BUY IT IF YOU DARE!!
NEXT ISSUE--
FEAR COMES STRIDING!

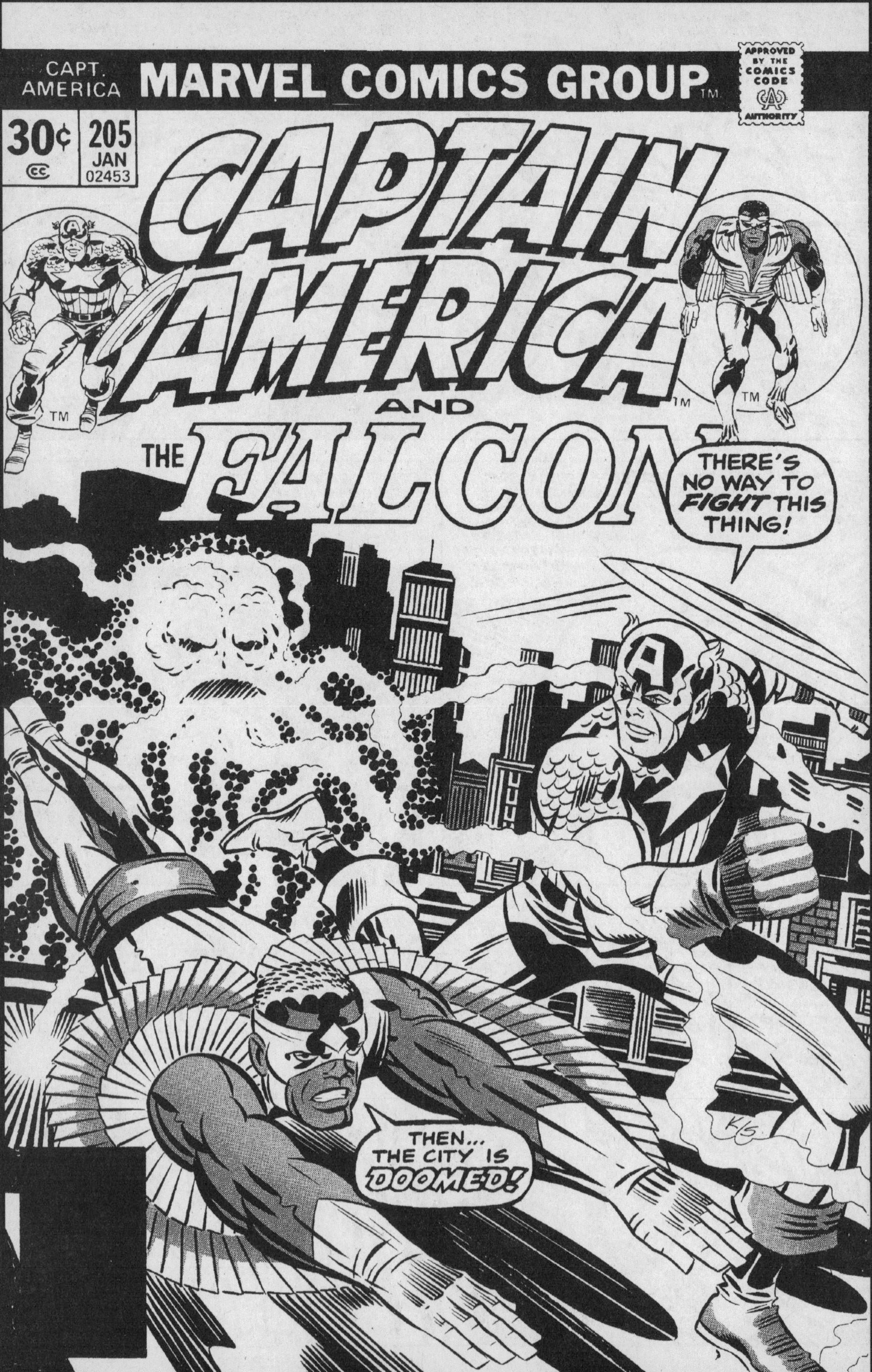
CAPT. AMERICA
MARVEL COMICS GROUP
APPROVED BY THE COMICS CODE AUTHORITY
30¢
205
JAN
02453
CAPTAIN AMERICA
AND
THE FALCON
THERE'S NO WAY TO FIGHT THIS THING!
THEN... THE CITY IS DOOMED!
K/S

1941! The world at *war!* And in a secret laboratory, frail *Steve Rogers* became the American *super-soldier!* For four thrilling years, he fought the Axis powers—until a freak stroke of fate threw him into *suspended animation.* He woke in the mid-1960s, a man *twenty years out of his time.* Since that fateful day, Steve Rogers has sought his *destiny* in this brave new world.

Stan Lee PRESENTS: CAPTAIN AMERICA AND THE FALCON™

EDITED, WRITTEN, & DRAWN BY **JACK KIRBY** INKED BY **JOHN VERPOORTEN** COLORED BY **MICHELE W.** LETTERED BY **JIM NOVAK** PERUSED BY **ARCHIE GOODWIN**

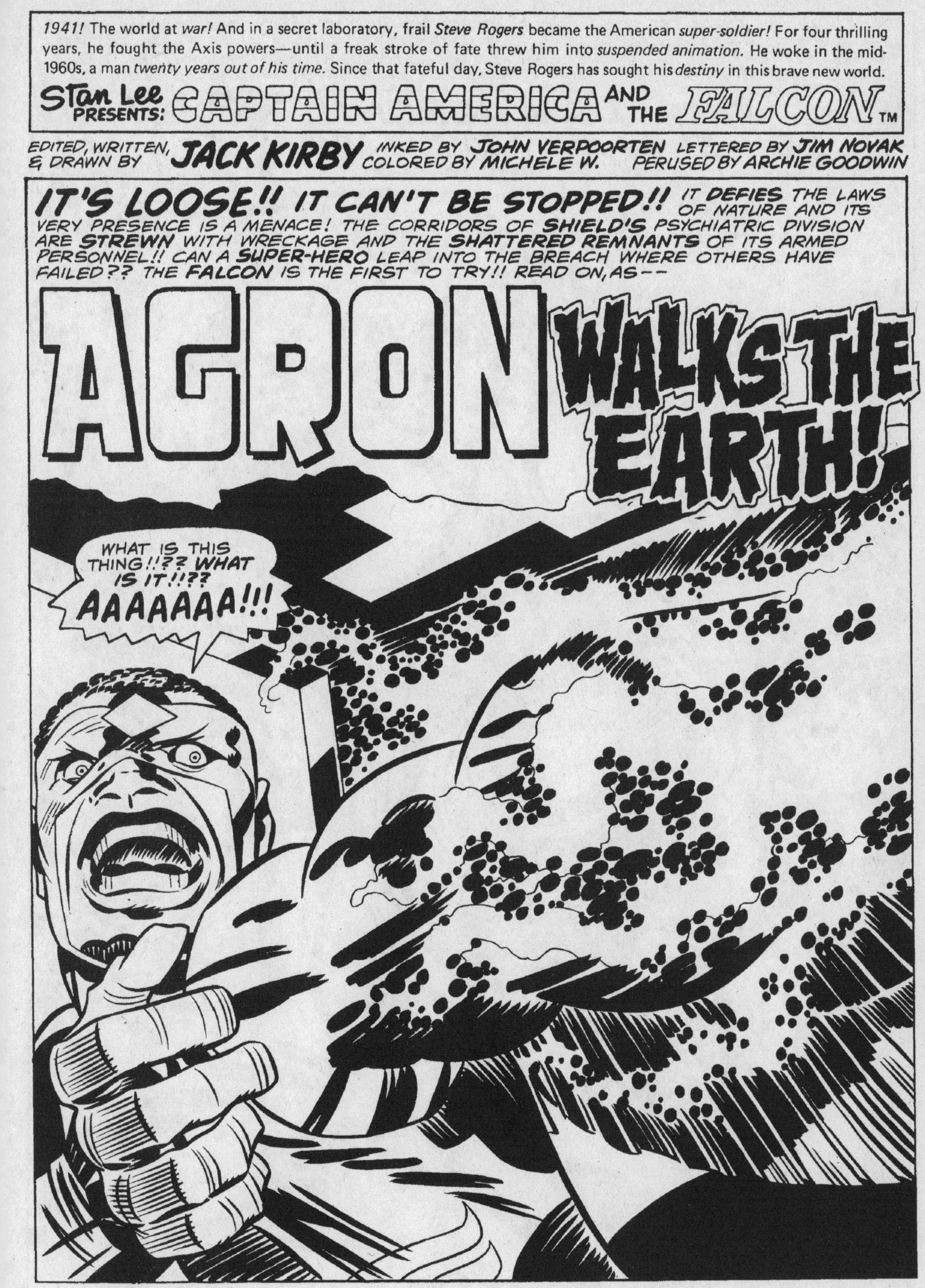
IT'S LOOSE!! IT CAN'T BE STOPPED!! IT DEFIES THE LAWS OF NATURE AND ITS VERY PRESENCE IS A MENACE! THE CORRIDORS OF SHIELD'S PSYCHIATRIC DIVISION ARE STREWN WITH WRECKAGE AND THE SHATTERED REMNANTS OF ITS ARMED PERSONNEL!! CAN A SUPER-HERO LEAP INTO THE BREACH WHERE OTHERS HAVE FAILED?? THE FALCON IS THE FIRST TO TRY!! READ ON, AS--
AGRON WALKS THE EARTH!
WHAT IS THIS THING!!?? WHAT IS IT!!?? AAAAAAA!!!

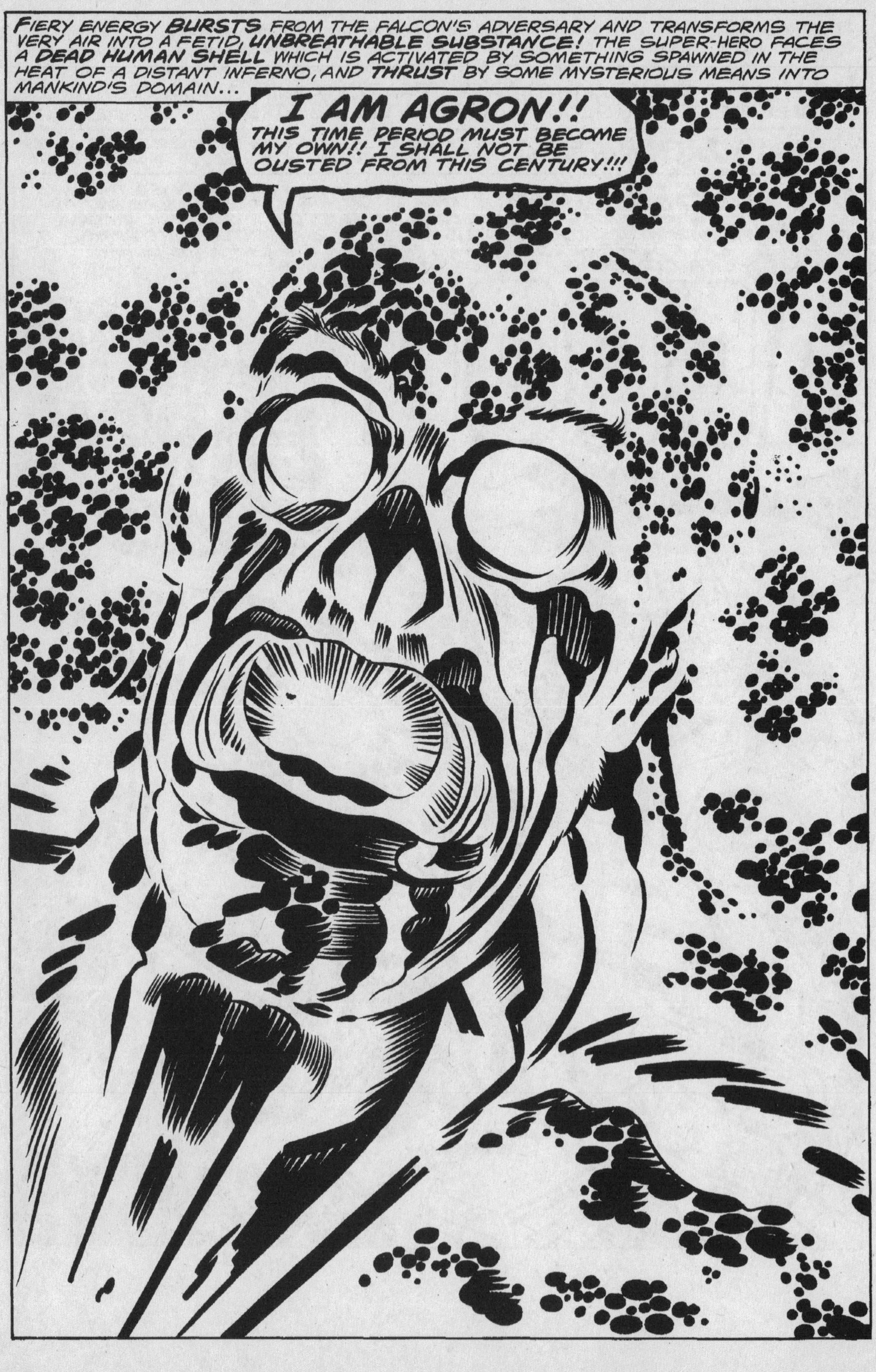

FIERY ENERGY BURSTS FROM THE FALCON'S ADVERSARY AND TRANSFORMS THE VERY AIR INTO A FETID, UNBREATHABLE SUBSTANCE! THE SUPER-HERO FACES A DEAD HUMAN SHELL WHICH IS ACTIVATED BY SOMETHING SPAWNED IN THE HEAT OF A DISTANT INFERNO, AND THRUST BY SOME MYSTERIOUS MEANS INTO MANKIND'S DOMAIN...
I AM AGRON!! THIS TIME PERIOD MUST BECOME MY OWN!! I SHALL NOT BE OUSTED FROM THIS CENTURY!!!

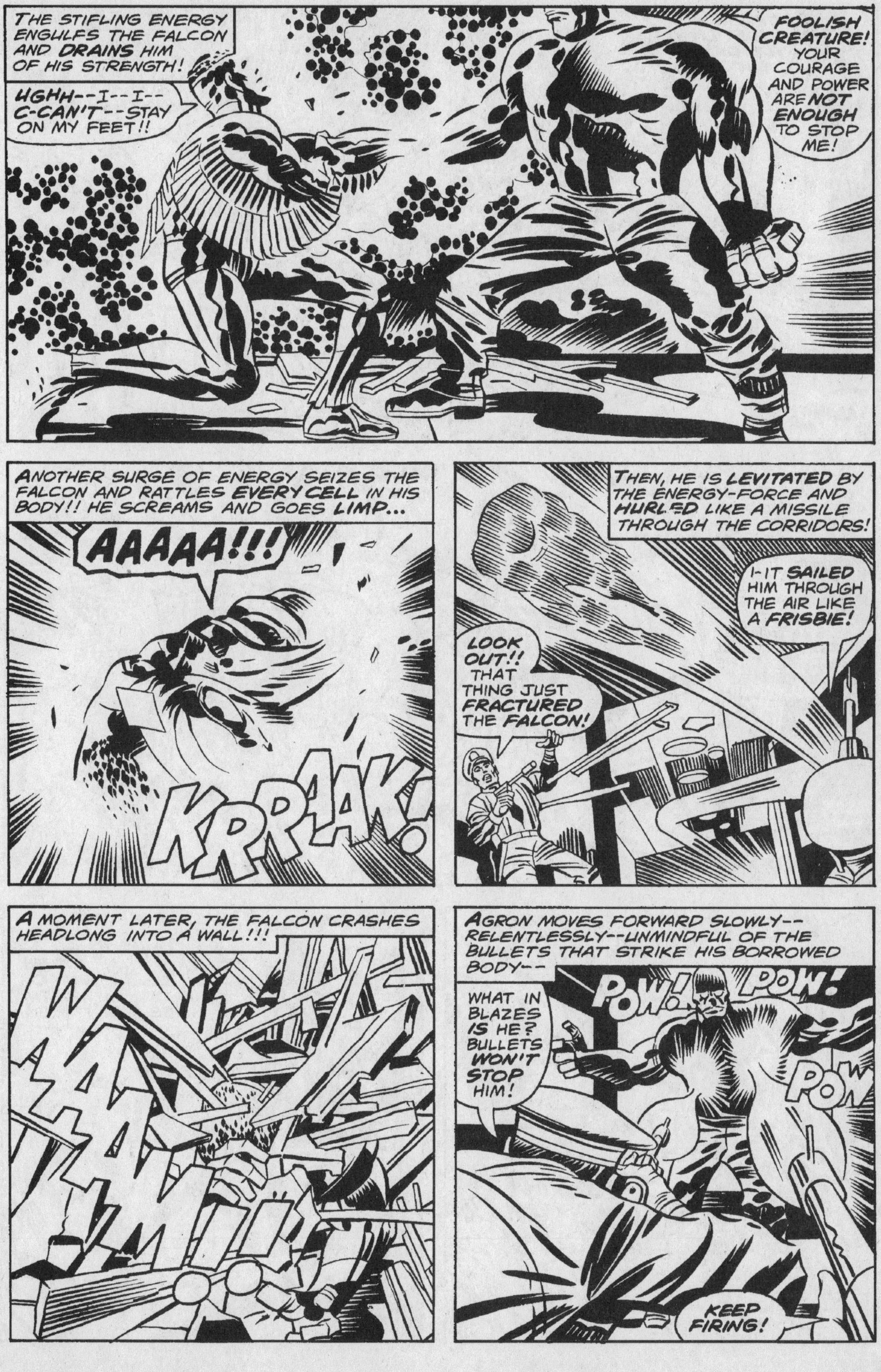
THE STIFLING ENERGY ENGULFS THE FALCON AND DRAINS HIM OF HIS STRENGTH!
UGHH--I--I-- C-CAN'T--STAY ON MY FEET!!
FOOLISH CREATURE! YOUR COURAGE AND POWER ARE NOT ENOUGH TO STOP ME!
ANOTHER SURGE OF ENERGY SEIZES THE FALCON AND RATTLES EVERY CELL IN HIS BODY!! HE SCREAMS AND GOES LIMP...
AAAAA!!!
KRRAAK!
THEN, HE IS LEVITATED BY THE ENERGY-FORCE AND HURLED LIKE A MISSILE THROUGH THE CORRIDORS!
I-IT SAILED HIM THROUGH THE AIR LIKE A FRISBIE!
LOOK OUT!! THAT THING JUST FRACTURED THE FALCON!
A MOMENT LATER, THE FALCON CRASHES HEADLONG INTO A WALL!!!
WHAAM!!
AGRON MOVES FORWARD SLOWLY-- RELENTLESSLY--UNMINDFUL OF THE BULLETS THAT STRIKE HIS BORROWED BODY--
POW! POW!
WHAT IN BLAZES IS HE? BULLETS WON'T STOP HIM!
KEEP FIRING!

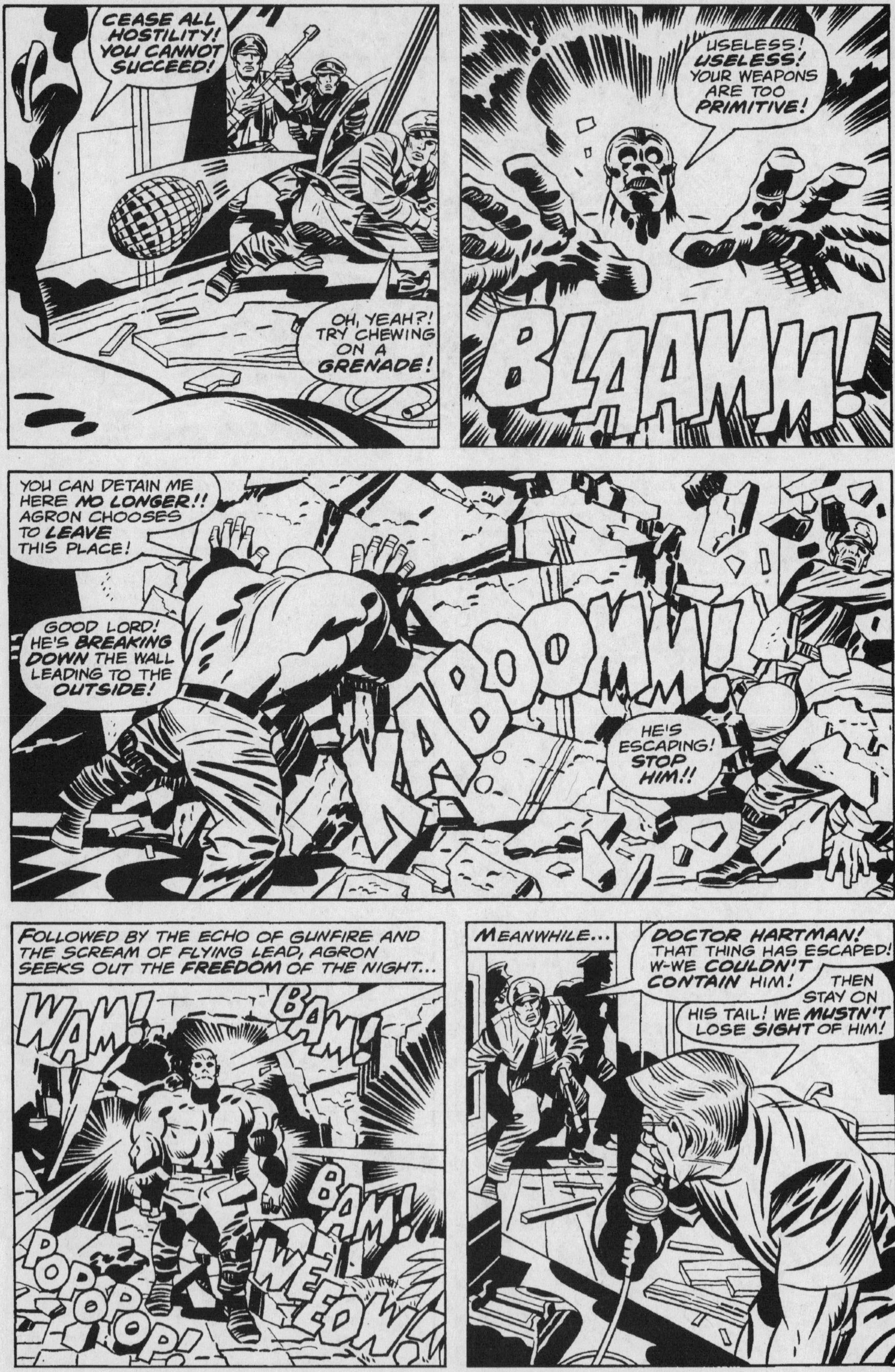
CEASE ALL HOSTILITY! YOU CANNOT SUCCEED!
OH, YEAH?! TRY CHEWING ON A GRENADE!
USELESS! USELESS! YOUR WEAPONS ARE TOO PRIMITIVE!
BLAAMM!
YOU CAN DETAIN ME HERE NO LONGER!! AGRON CHOOSES TO LEAVE THIS PLACE!
GOOD LORD! HE'S BREAKING DOWN THE WALL LEADING TO THE OUTSIDE!
KABOOMM!
HE'S ESCAPING! STOP HIM!!
FOLLOWED BY THE ECHO OF GUNFIRE AND THE SCREAM OF FLYING LEAD, AGRON SEEKS OUT THE FREEDOM OF THE NIGHT...
WAM!
BAM!
BAM!
POP POP POP!
WEEOW!
MEANWHILE...
DOCTOR HARTMAN! THAT THING HAS ESCAPED! W-WE COULDN'T CONTAIN HIM!
THEN STAY ON HIS TAIL! WE MUSTN'T LOSE SIGHT OF HIM!

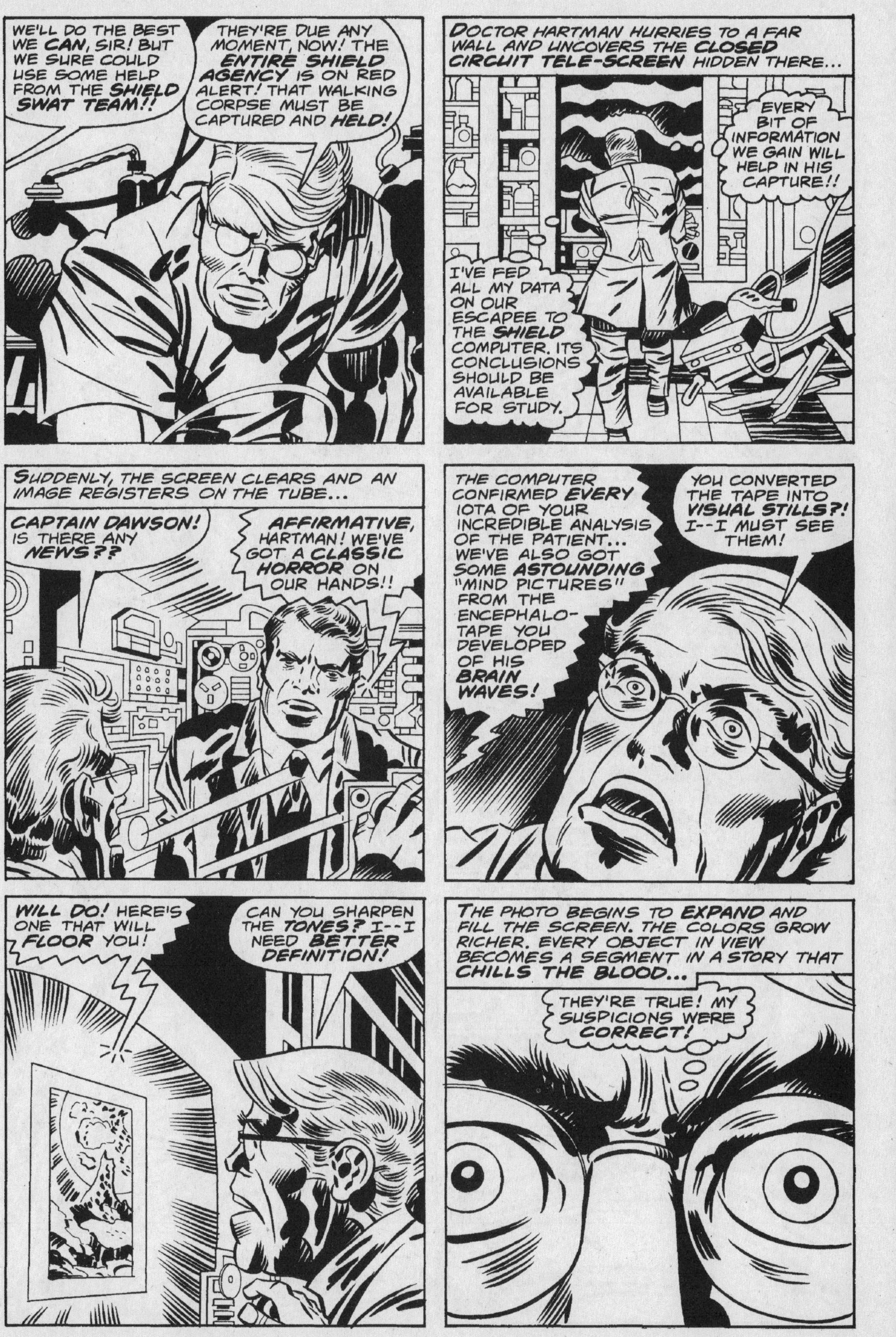

WE'LL DO THE BEST WE CAN, SIR! BUT WE SURE COULD USE SOME HELP FROM THE SHIELD SWAT TEAM!!
THEY'RE DUE ANY MOMENT, NOW! THE ENTIRE SHIELD AGENCY IS ON RED ALERT! THAT WALKING CORPSE MUST BE CAPTURED AND HELD!
DOCTOR HARTMAN HURRIES TO A FAR WALL AND UNCOVERS THE CLOSED CIRCUIT TELE-SCREEN HIDDEN THERE...
EVERY BIT OF INFORMATION WE GAIN WILL HELP IN HIS CAPTURE!!
I'VE FED ALL MY DATA ON OUR ESCAPEE TO THE SHIELD COMPUTER. ITS CONCLUSIONS SHOULD BE AVAILABLE FOR STUDY.
SUDDENLY, THE SCREEN CLEARS AND AN IMAGE REGISTERS ON THE TUBE...
CAPTAIN DAWSON! IS THERE ANY NEWS??
AFFIRMATIVE, HARTMAN! WE'VE GOT A CLASSIC HORROR ON OUR HANDS!!
THE COMPUTER CONFIRMED EVERY IOTA OF YOUR INCREDIBLE ANALYSIS OF THE PATIENT... WE'VE ALSO GOT SOME ASTOUNDING "MIND PICTURES" FROM THE ENCEPHALO-TAPE YOU DEVELOPED OF HIS BRAIN WAVES!
YOU CONVERTED THE TAPE INTO VISUAL STILLS?! I--I MUST SEE THEM!
WILL DO! HERE'S ONE THAT WILL FLOOR YOU!
CAN YOU SHARPEN THE TONES? I--I NEED BETTER DEFINITION!
THE PHOTO BEGINS TO EXPAND AND FILL THE SCREEN. THE COLORS GROW RICHER. EVERY OBJECT IN VIEW BECOMES A SEGMENT IN A STORY THAT CHILLS THE BLOOD...
THEY'RE TRUE! MY SUSPICIONS WERE CORRECT!

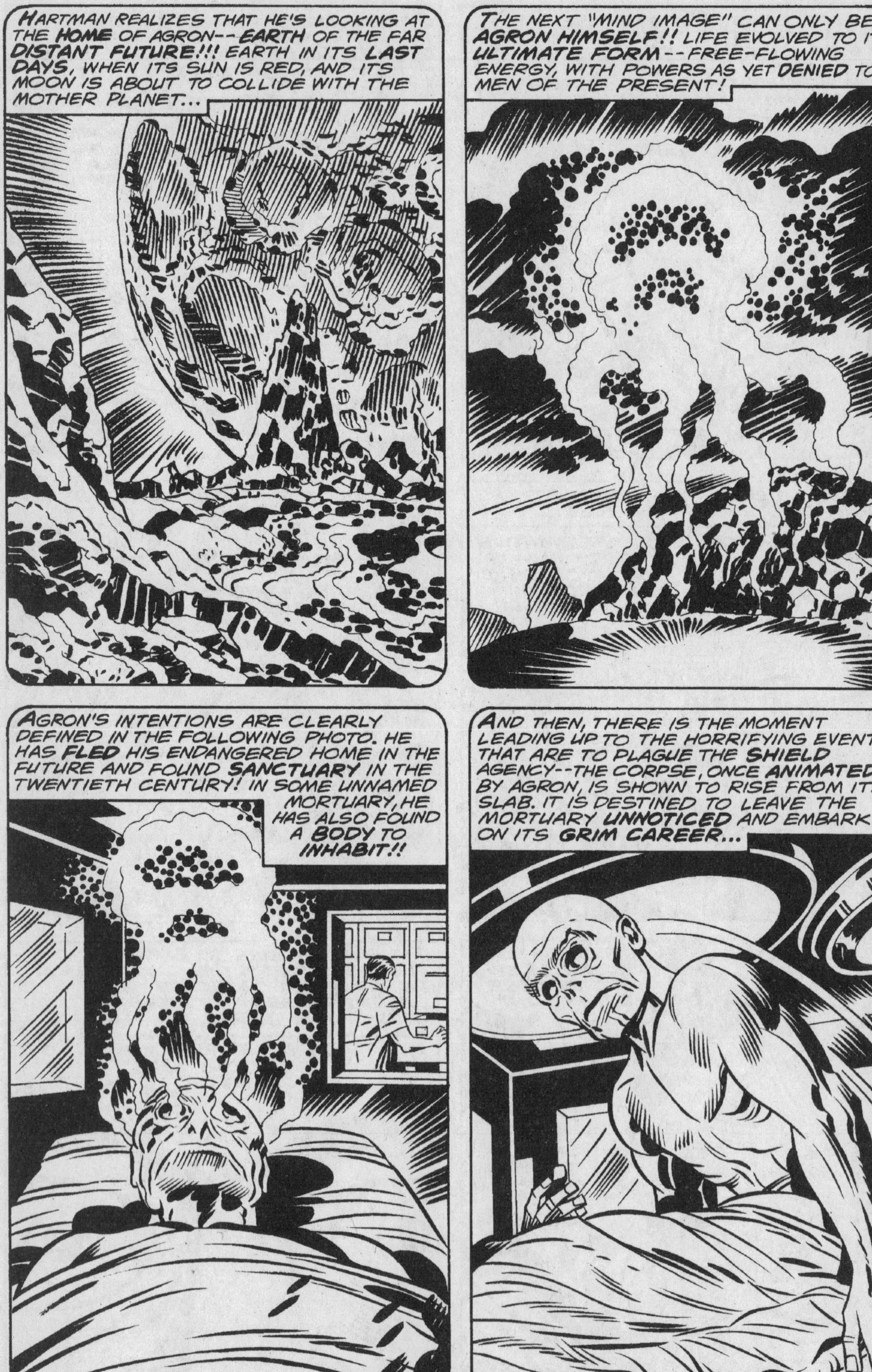
HARTMAN REALIZES THAT HE'S LOOKING AT THE HOME OF AGRON--EARTH OF THE FAR DISTANT FUTURE!!! EARTH IN ITS LAST DAYS, WHEN ITS SUN IS RED, AND ITS MOON IS ABOUT TO COLLIDE WITH THE MOTHER PLANET...
THE NEXT "MIND IMAGE" CAN ONLY BE AGRON HIMSELF!! LIFE EVOLVED TO ITS ULTIMATE FORM--FREE-FLOWING ENERGY, WITH POWERS AS YET DENIED TO MEN OF THE PRESENT!
AGRON'S INTENTIONS ARE CLEARLY DEFINED IN THE FOLLOWING PHOTO. HE HAS FLED HIS ENDANGERED HOME IN THE FUTURE AND FOUND SANCTUARY IN THE TWENTIETH CENTURY! IN SOME UNNAMED MORTUARY, HE HAS ALSO FOUND A BODY TO INHABIT!!
AND THEN, THERE IS THE MOMENT LEADING UP TO THE HORRIFYING EVENTS THAT ARE TO PLAGUE THE SHIELD AGENCY--THE CORPSE, ONCE ANIMATED BY AGRON, IS SHOWN TO RISE FROM ITS SLAB. IT IS DESTINED TO LEAVE THE MORTUARY UNNOTICED AND EMBARK ON ITS GRIM CAREER...

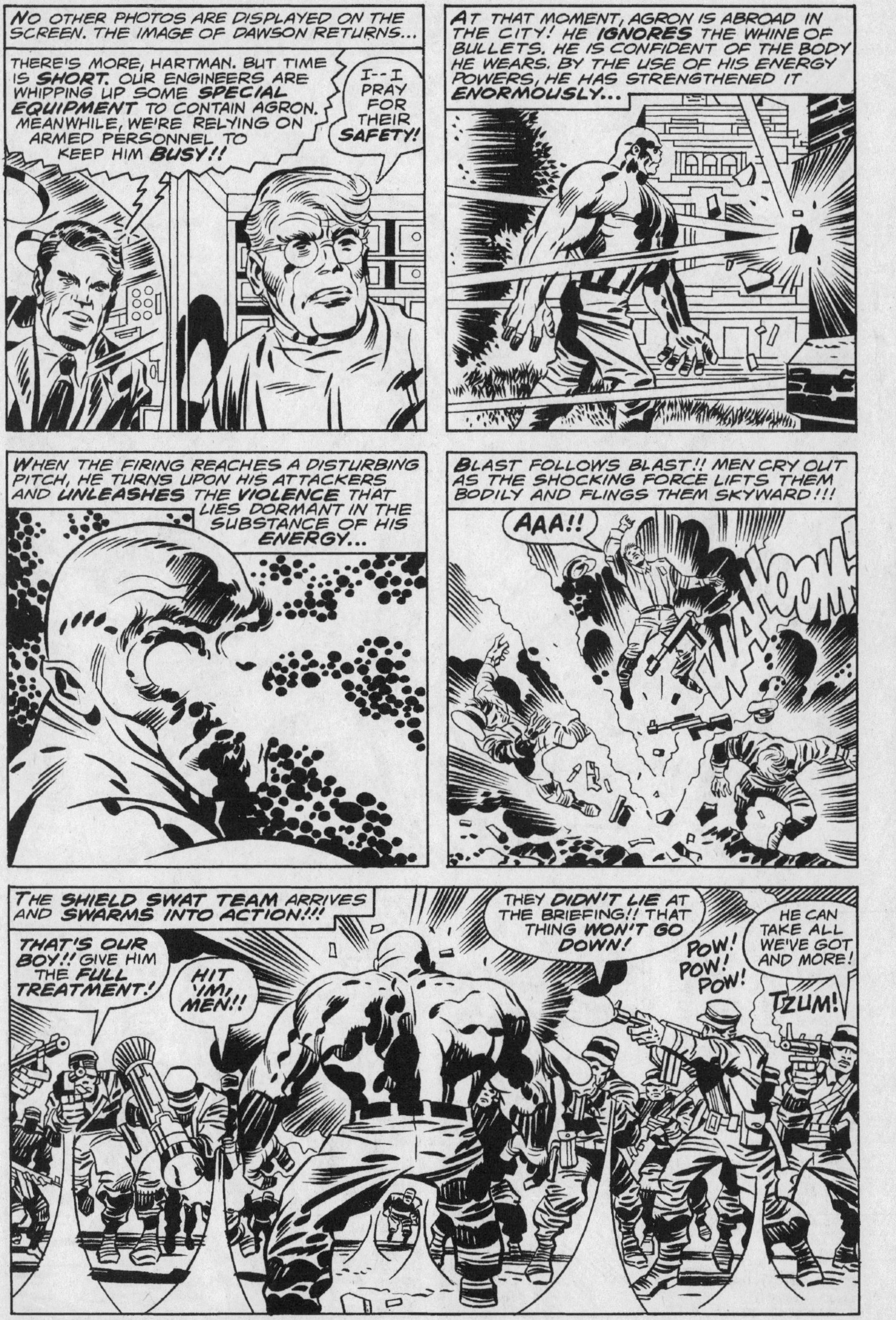
NO OTHER PHOTOS ARE DISPLAYED ON THE SCREEN. THE IMAGE OF DAWSON RETURNS...
THERE'S MORE, HARTMAN. BUT TIME IS SHORT. OUR ENGINEERS ARE WHIPPING UP SOME SPECIAL EQUIPMENT TO CONTAIN AGRON. MEANWHILE, WE'RE RELYING ON ARMED PERSONNEL TO KEEP HIM BUSY!!
I-- I PRAY FOR THEIR SAFETY!
AT THAT MOMENT, AGRON IS ABROAD IN THE CITY! HE IGNORES THE WHINE OF BULLETS. HE IS CONFIDENT OF THE BODY HE WEARS. BY THE USE OF HIS ENERGY POWERS, HE HAS STRENGTHENED IT ENORMOUSLY...
WHEN THE FIRING REACHES A DISTURBING PITCH, HE TURNS UPON HIS ATTACKERS AND UNLEASHES THE VIOLENCE THAT LIES DORMANT IN THE SUBSTANCE OF HIS ENERGY...
BLAST FOLLOWS BLAST!! MEN CRY OUT AS THE SHOCKING FORCE LIFTS THEM BODILY AND FLINGS THEM SKYWARD!!!
AAA!!
WAHOOM!
THE SHIELD SWAT TEAM ARRIVES AND SWARMS INTO ACTION!!!
THAT'S OUR BOY!! GIVE HIM THE FULL TREATMENT!
HIT 'IM, MEN!!
THEY DIDN'T LIE AT THE BRIEFING!! THAT THING WON'T GO DOWN!
POW! POW! POW!
HE CAN TAKE ALL WE'VE GOT AND MORE!
TZUM!

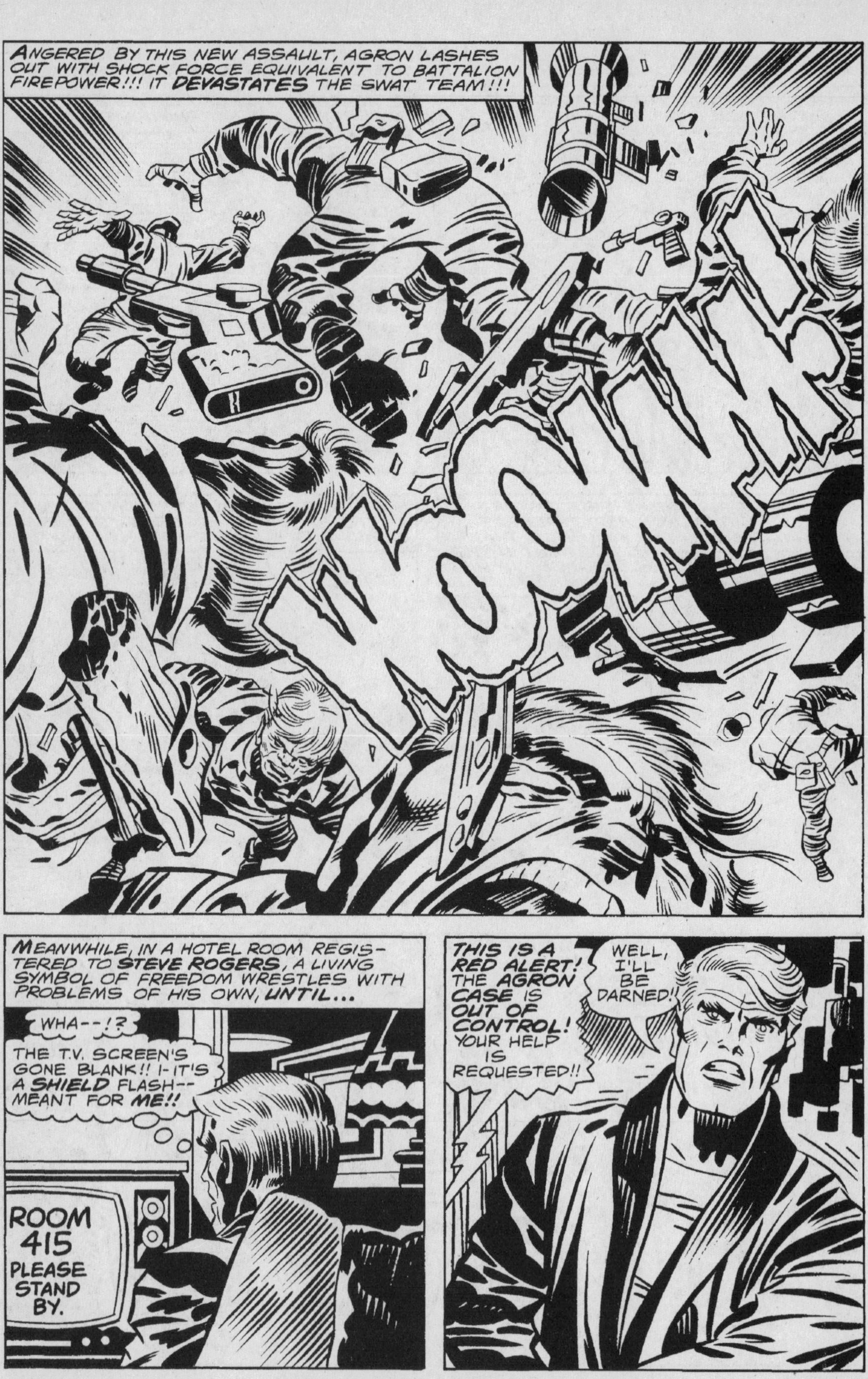
ANGERED BY THIS NEW ASSAULT, AGRON LASHES OUT WITH SHOCK FORCE EQUIVALENT TO BATTALION FIREPOWER!!! IT DEVASTATES THE SWAT TEAM!!!
MEANWHILE, IN A HOTEL ROOM REGISTERED TO STEVE ROGERS, A LIVING SYMBOL OF FREEDOM WRESTLES WITH PROBLEMS OF HIS OWN, UNTIL...
WHA--!?
THE T.V. SCREEN'S GONE BLANK!! I-IT'S A SHIELD FLASH-- MEANT FOR ME!!
ROOM 415 PLEASE STAND BY.
THIS IS A RED ALERT! THE AGRON CASE IS OUT OF CONTROL! YOUR HELP IS REQUESTED!!
WELL, I'LL BE DARNED!!

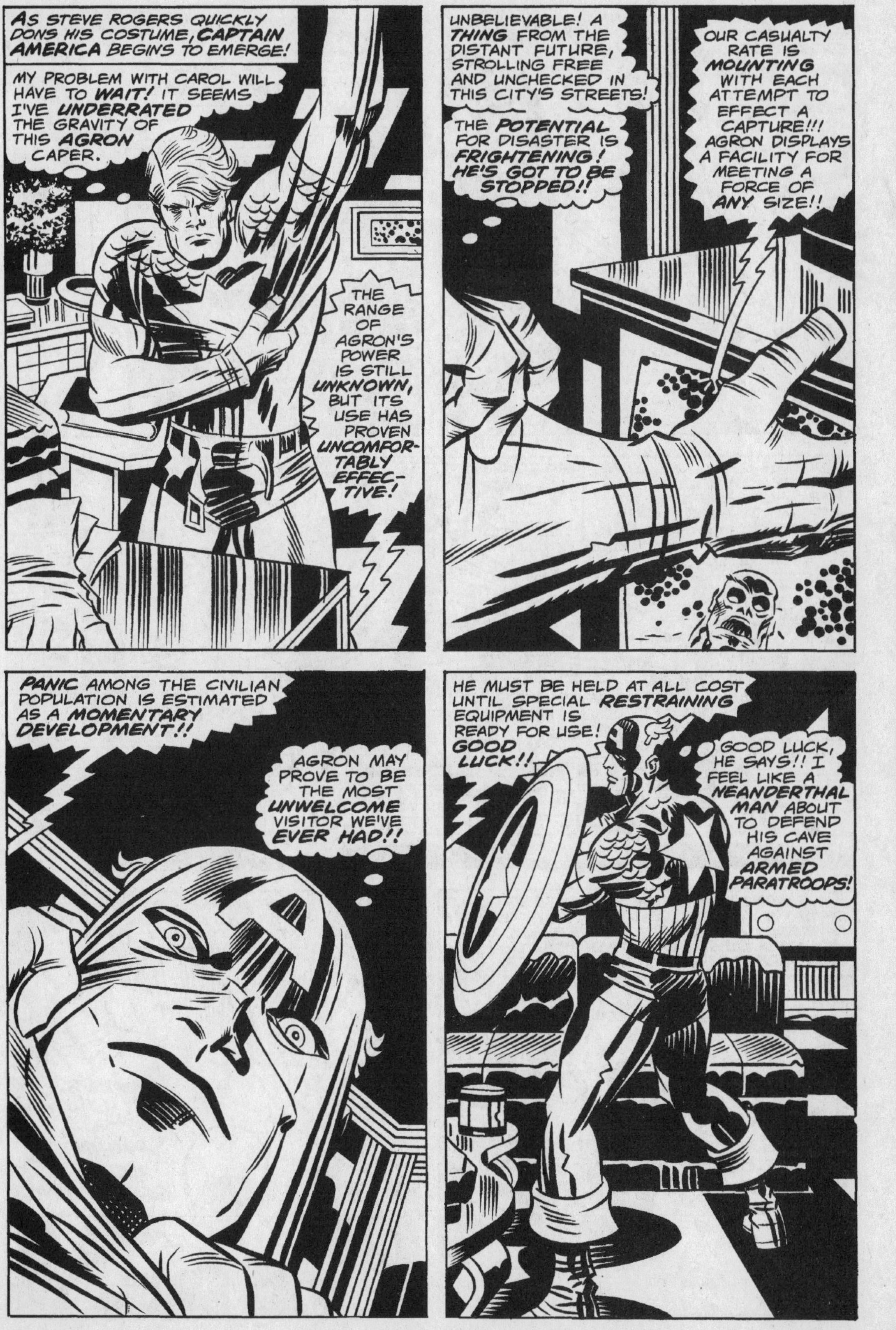
AS STEVE ROGERS QUICKLY DONS HIS COSTUME, CAPTAIN AMERICA BEGINS TO EMERGE!
MY PROBLEM WITH CAROL WILL HAVE TO WAIT! IT SEEMS I'VE UNDERRATED THE GRAVITY OF THIS AGRON CAPER.
THE RANGE OF AGRON'S POWER IS STILL UNKNOWN, BUT ITS USE HAS PROVEN UNCOMFORTABLY EFFECTIVE!
UNBELIEVABLE! A THING FROM THE DISTANT FUTURE, STROLLING FREE AND UNCHECKED IN THIS CITY'S STREETS!
THE POTENTIAL FOR DISASTER IS FRIGHTENING! HE'S GOT TO BE STOPPED!!
OUR CASUALTY RATE IS MOUNTING WITH EACH ATTEMPT TO EFFECT A CAPTURE!!! AGRON DISPLAYS A FACILITY FOR MEETING A FORCE OF ANY SIZE!!
PANIC AMONG THE CIVILIAN POPULATION IS ESTIMATED AS A MOMENTARY DEVELOPMENT!!
AGRON MAY PROVE TO BE THE MOST UNWELCOME VISITOR WE'VE EVER HAD!!
HE MUST BE HELD AT ALL COST UNTIL SPECIAL RESTRAINING EQUIPMENT IS READY FOR USE! GOOD LUCK!!
GOOD LUCK, HE SAYS!! I FEEL LIKE A NEANDERTHAL MAN ABOUT TO DEFEND HIS CAVE AGAINST ARMED PARATROOPS!

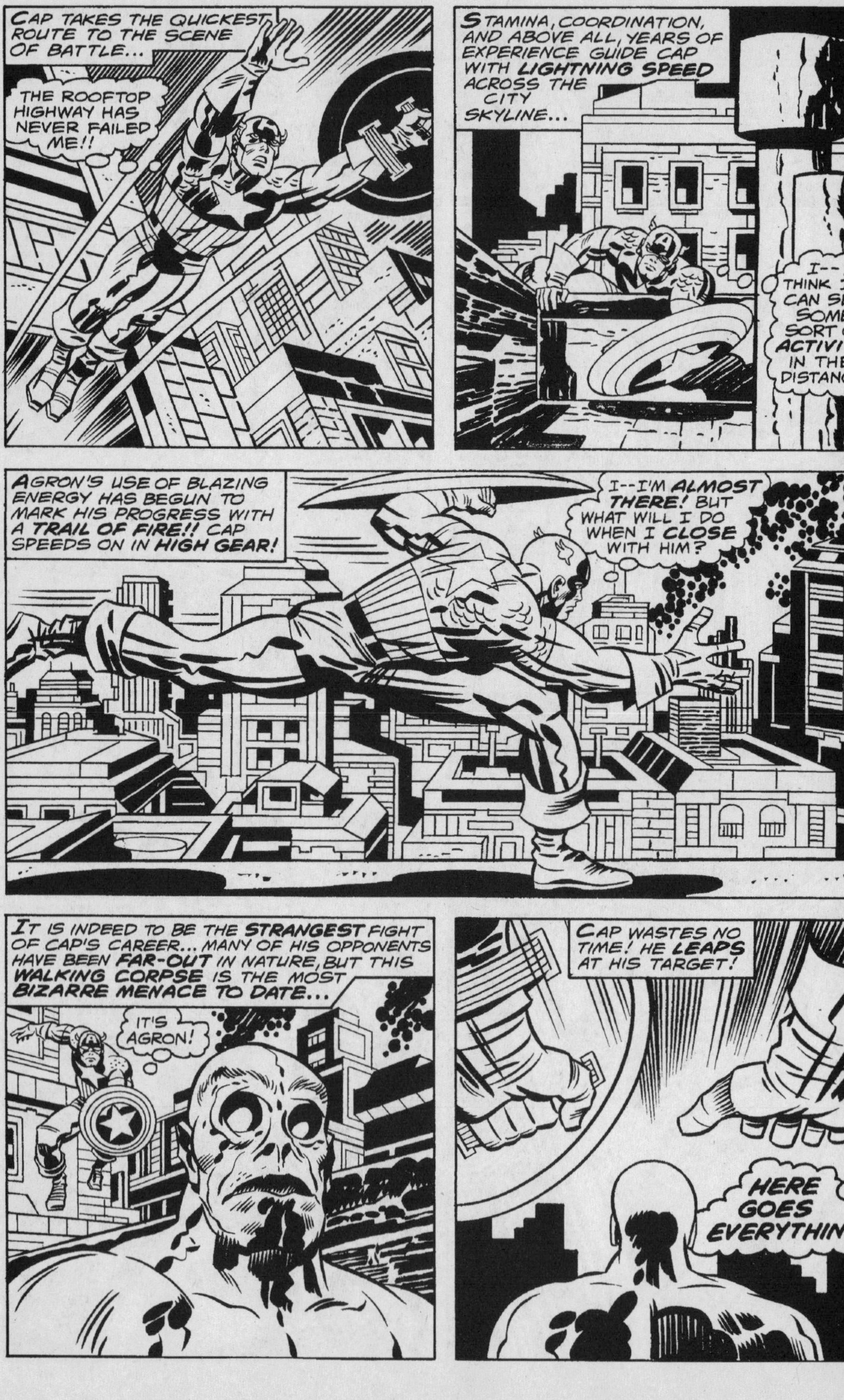
CAP TAKES THE QUICKEST ROUTE TO THE SCENE OF BATTLE...
THE ROOFTOP HIGHWAY HAS NEVER FAILED ME!!
STAMINA, COORDINATION, AND ABOVE ALL, YEARS OF EXPERIENCE GUIDE CAP WITH LIGHTNING SPEED ACROSS THE CITY SKYLINE...
I--I THINK I CAN SEE SOME SORT OF ACTIVITY IN THE DISTANCE!
AGRON'S USE OF BLAZING ENERGY HAS BEGUN TO MARK HIS PROGRESS WITH A TRAIL OF FIRE!! CAP SPEEDS ON IN HIGH GEAR!
I--I'M ALMOST THERE! BUT WHAT WILL I DO WHEN I CLOSE WITH HIM?
IT IS INDEED TO BE THE STRANGEST FIGHT OF CAP'S CAREER... MANY OF HIS OPPONENTS HAVE BEEN FAR-OUT IN NATURE, BUT THIS WALKING CORPSE IS THE MOST BIZARRE MENACE TO DATE...
IT'S AGRON!
CAP WASTES NO TIME! HE LEAPS AT HIS TARGET!
HERE GOES EVERYTHING!

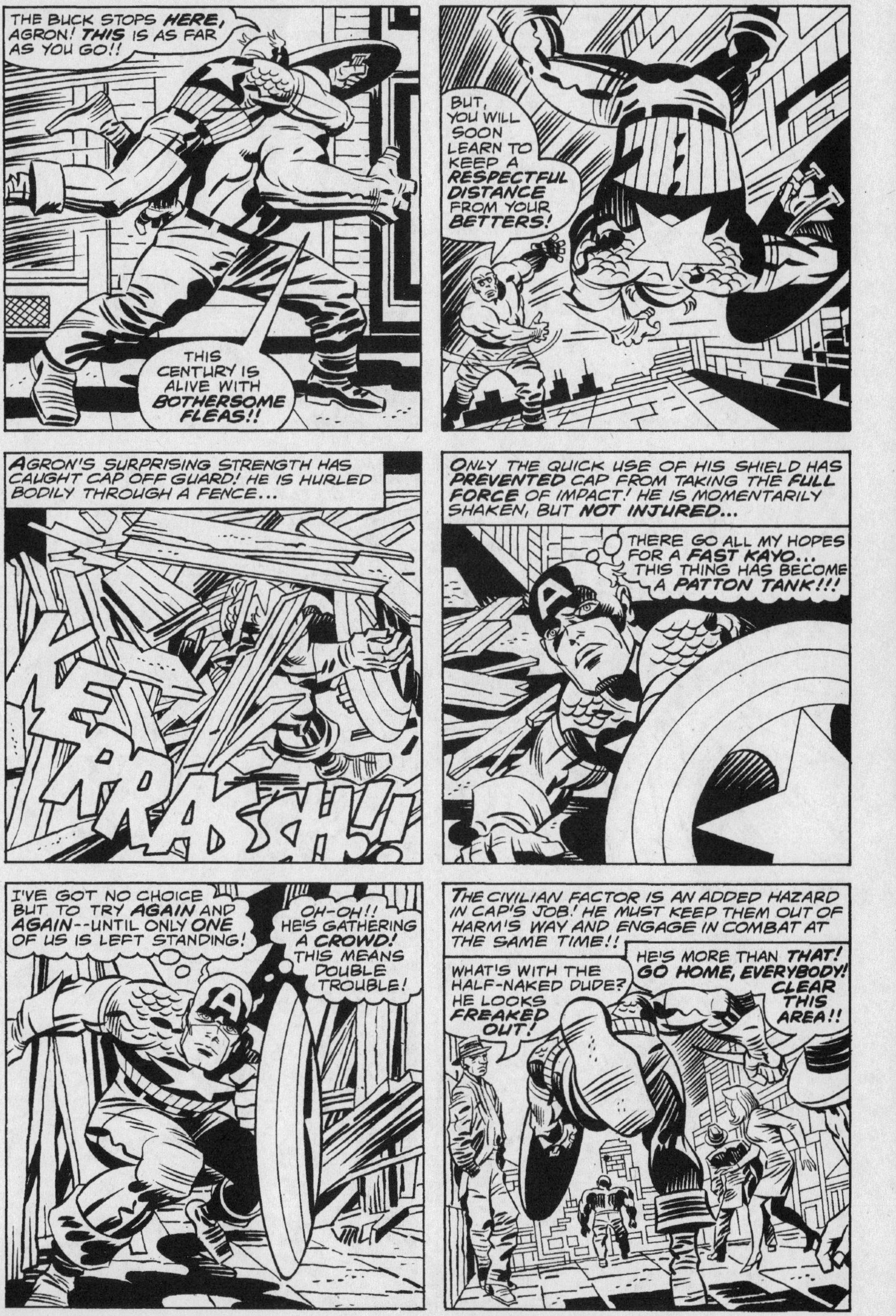
THE BUCK STOPS HERE, AGRON! THIS IS AS FAR AS YOU GO!!
THIS CENTURY IS ALIVE WITH BOTHERSOME FLEAS!!
BUT, YOU WILL SOON LEARN TO KEEP A RESPECTFUL DISTANCE FROM YOUR BETTERS!
AGRON'S SURPRISING STRENGTH HAS CAUGHT CAP OFF GUARD! HE IS HURLED BODILY THROUGH A FENCE...
KRRASSH!!
ONLY THE QUICK USE OF HIS SHIELD HAS PREVENTED CAP FROM TAKING THE FULL FORCE OF IMPACT! HE IS MOMENTARILY SHAKEN, BUT NOT INJURED...
THERE GO ALL MY HOPES FOR A FAST KAYO... THIS THING HAS BECOME A PATTON TANK!!!
I'VE GOT NO CHOICE BUT TO TRY AGAIN AND AGAIN--UNTIL ONLY ONE OF US IS LEFT STANDING!
OH-OH!! HE'S GATHERING A CROWD! THIS MEANS DOUBLE TROUBLE!
THE CIVILIAN FACTOR IS AN ADDED HAZARD IN CAP'S JOB! HE MUST KEEP THEM OUT OF HARM'S WAY AND ENGAGE IN COMBAT AT THE SAME TIME!!
WHAT'S WITH THE HALF-NAKED DUDE? HE LOOKS FREAKED OUT!
HE'S MORE THAN THAT! GO HOME, EVERYBODY! CLEAR THIS AREA!!

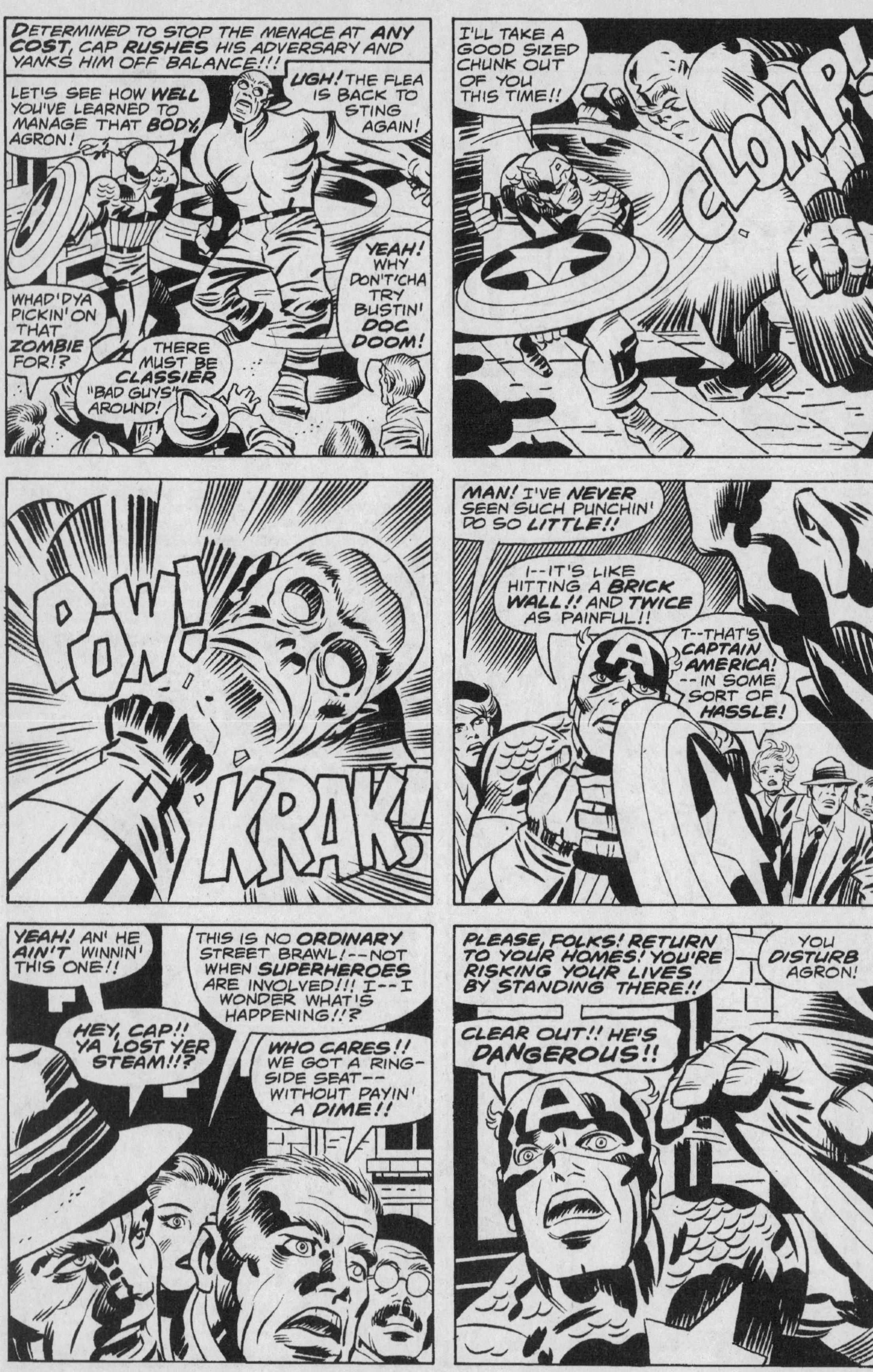
DETERMINED TO STOP THE MENACE AT ANY COST, CAP RUSHES HIS ADVERSARY AND YANKS HIM OFF BALANCE!!!
LET'S SEE HOW WELL YOU'VE LEARNED TO MANAGE THAT BODY, AGRON!
UGH! THE FLEA IS BACK TO STING AGAIN!
YEAH! WHY DON'T'CHA TRY BUSTIN' DOC DOOM!
WHAD'DYA PICKIN' ON THAT ZOMBIE FOR!?
THERE MUST BE CLASSIER "BAD GUYS" AROUND!
I'LL TAKE A GOOD SIZED CHUNK OUT OF YOU THIS TIME!!
CLOMP!
POW!
KRAK!
MAN! I'VE NEVER SEEN SUCH PUNCHIN' DO SO LITTLE!!
I--IT'S LIKE HITTING A BRICK WALL!! AND TWICE AS PAINFUL!!
T--THAT'S CAPTAIN AMERICA! --IN SOME SORT OF HASSLE!
YEAH! AN' HE AIN'T WINNIN' THIS ONE!!
THIS IS NO ORDINARY STREET BRAWL!--NOT WHEN SUPERHEROES ARE INVOLVED!!! I--I WONDER WHAT'S HAPPENING!!?
HEY, CAP!! YA LOST YER STEAM!!?
WHO CARES!! WE GOT A RING-SIDE SEAT-- WITHOUT PAYIN' A DIME!!
PLEASE, FOLKS! RETURN TO YOUR HOMES! YOU'RE RISKING YOUR LIVES BY STANDING THERE!!
YOU DISTURB AGRON!
CLEAR OUT!! HE'S DANGEROUS!!

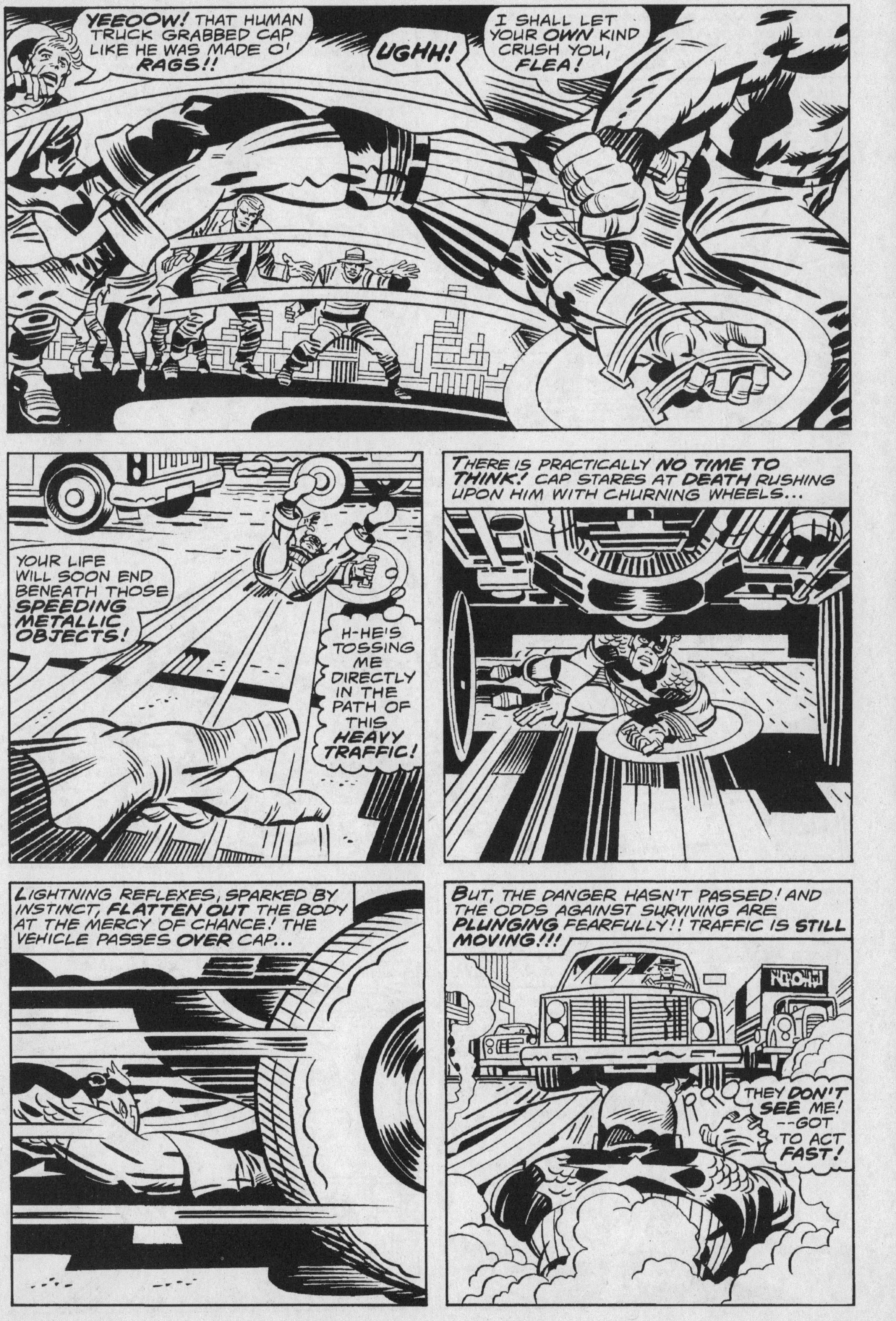
YEEOOW! THAT HUMAN TRUCK GRABBED CAP LIKE HE WAS MADE O' RAGS!!
UGHH!
I SHALL LET YOUR OWN KIND CRUSH YOU, FLEA!
YOUR LIFE WILL SOON END BENEATH THOSE SPEEDING METALLIC OBJECTS!
H-HE'S TOSSING ME DIRECTLY IN THE PATH OF THIS HEAVY TRAFFIC!
THERE IS PRACTICALLY NO TIME TO THINK! CAP STARES AT DEATH RUSHING UPON HIM WITH CHURNING WHEELS...
LIGHTNING REFLEXES, SPARKED BY INSTINCT, FLATTEN OUT THE BODY AT THE MERCY OF CHANCE! THE VEHICLE PASSES OVER CAP...
BUT, THE DANGER HASN'T PASSED! AND THE ODDS AGAINST SURVIVING ARE PLUNGING FEARFULLY!! TRAFFIC IS STILL MOVING!!!
THEY DON'T SEE ME! --GOT TO ACT FAST!

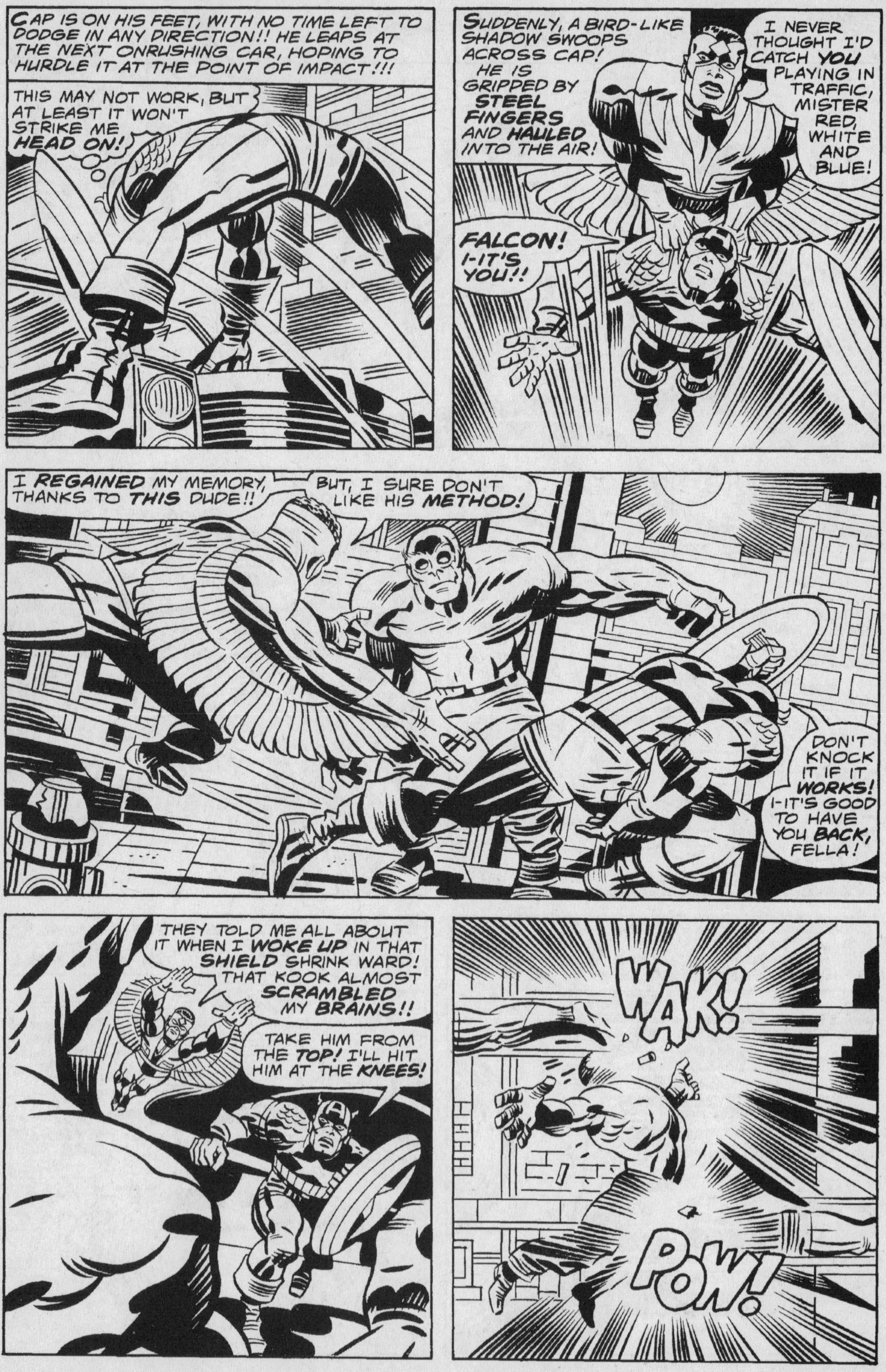

CAP IS ON HIS FEET, WITH NO TIME LEFT TO DODGE IN ANY DIRECTION!! HE LEAPS AT THE NEXT ONRUSHING CAR, HOPING TO HURDLE IT AT THE POINT OF IMPACT!!!
THIS MAY NOT WORK, BUT AT LEAST IT WON'T STRIKE ME HEAD ON!
SUDDENLY, A BIRD-LIKE SHADOW SWOOPS ACROSS CAP! HE IS GRIPPED BY STEEL FINGERS AND HAULED INTO THE AIR!
I NEVER THOUGHT I'D CATCH YOU PLAYING IN TRAFFIC, MISTER RED, WHITE AND BLUE!
FALCON! I-IT'S YOU!!
I REGAINED MY MEMORY, THANKS TO THIS DUDE!!
BUT, I SURE DON'T LIKE HIS METHOD!
DON'T KNOCK IT IF IT WORKS! I-IT'S GOOD TO HAVE YOU BACK, FELLA!
THEY TOLD ME ALL ABOUT IT WHEN I WOKE UP IN THAT SHIELD SHRINK WARD! THAT KOOK ALMOST SCRAMBLED MY BRAINS!!
TAKE HIM FROM THE TOP! I'LL HIT HIM AT THE KNEES!
WAK!
POW!

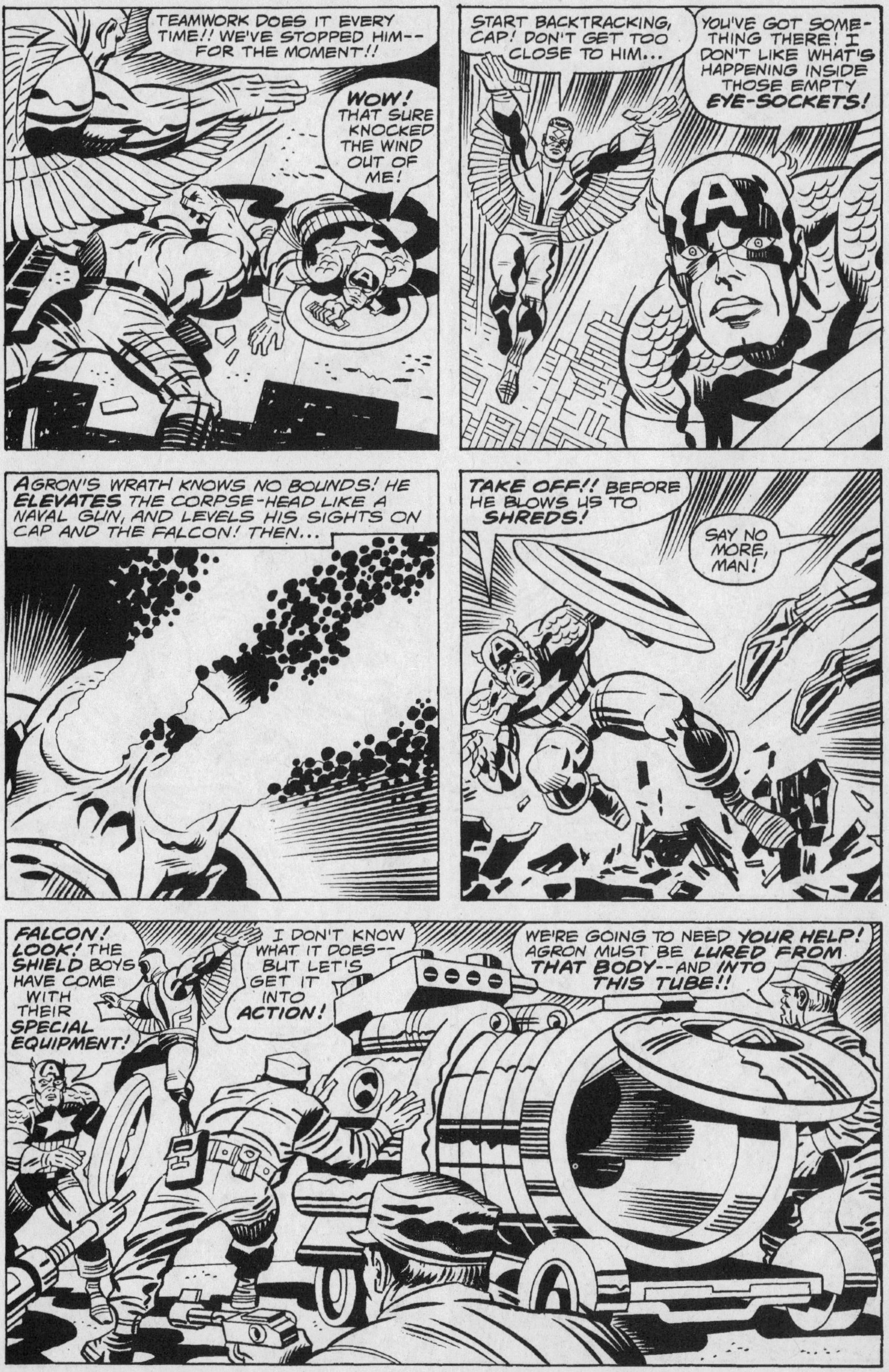
TEAMWORK DOES IT EVERY TIME!! WE'VE STOPPED HIM-- FOR THE MOMENT!!
WOW! THAT SURE KNOCKED THE WIND OUT OF ME!
START BACKTRACKING, CAP! DON'T GET TOO CLOSE TO HIM...
YOU'VE GOT SOMETHING THERE! I DON'T LIKE WHAT'S HAPPENING INSIDE THOSE EMPTY EYE-SOCKETS!
AGRON'S WRATH KNOWS NO BOUNDS! HE ELEVATES THE CORPSE-HEAD LIKE A NAVAL GUN, AND LEVELS HIS SIGHTS ON CAP AND THE FALCON! THEN...
TAKE OFF!! BEFORE HE BLOWS US TO SHREDS!
SAY NO MORE, MAN!
FALCON! LOOK! THE SHIELD BOYS HAVE COME WITH THEIR SPECIAL EQUIPMENT!
I DON'T KNOW WHAT IT DOES-- BUT LET'S GET IT INTO ACTION!
WE'RE GOING TO NEED YOUR HELP! AGRON MUST BE LURED FROM THAT BODY--AND INTO THIS TUBE!!

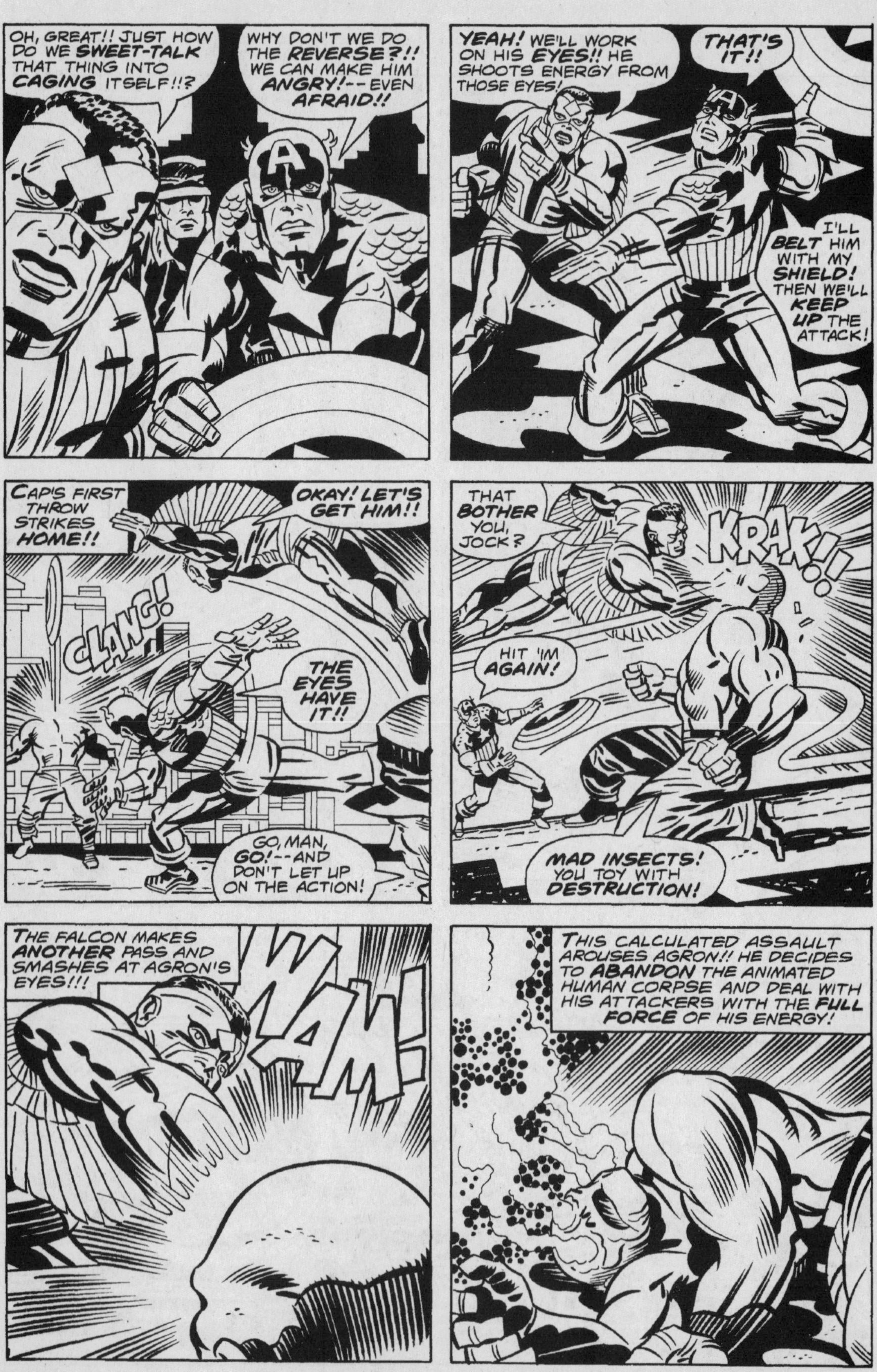

OH, GREAT!! JUST HOW DO WE SWEET-TALK THAT THING INTO CAGING ITSELF!!?
WHY DON'T WE DO THE REVERSE?!! WE CAN MAKE HIM ANGRY!--EVEN AFRAID!!
YEAH! WE'LL WORK ON HIS EYES!! HE SHOOTS ENERGY FROM THOSE EYES!
THAT'S IT!!
I'LL BELT HIM WITH MY SHIELD! THEN WE'LL KEEP UP THE ATTACK!
CAP'S FIRST THROW STRIKES HOME!!
OKAY! LET'S GET HIM!!
CLANG!
THE EYES HAVE IT!!
GO, MAN, GO!--AND DON'T LET UP ON THE ACTION!
THAT BOTHER YOU, JOCK?
KRAK!!
HIT 'IM AGAIN!
MAD INSECTS! YOU TOY WITH DESTRUCTION!
THE FALCON MAKES ANOTHER PASS AND SMASHES AT AGRON'S EYES!!!
WAM!
THIS CALCULATED ASSAULT AROUSES AGRON!! HE DECIDES TO ABANDON THE ANIMATED HUMAN CORPSE AND DEAL WITH HIS ATTACKERS WITH THE FULL FORCE OF HIS ENERGY!

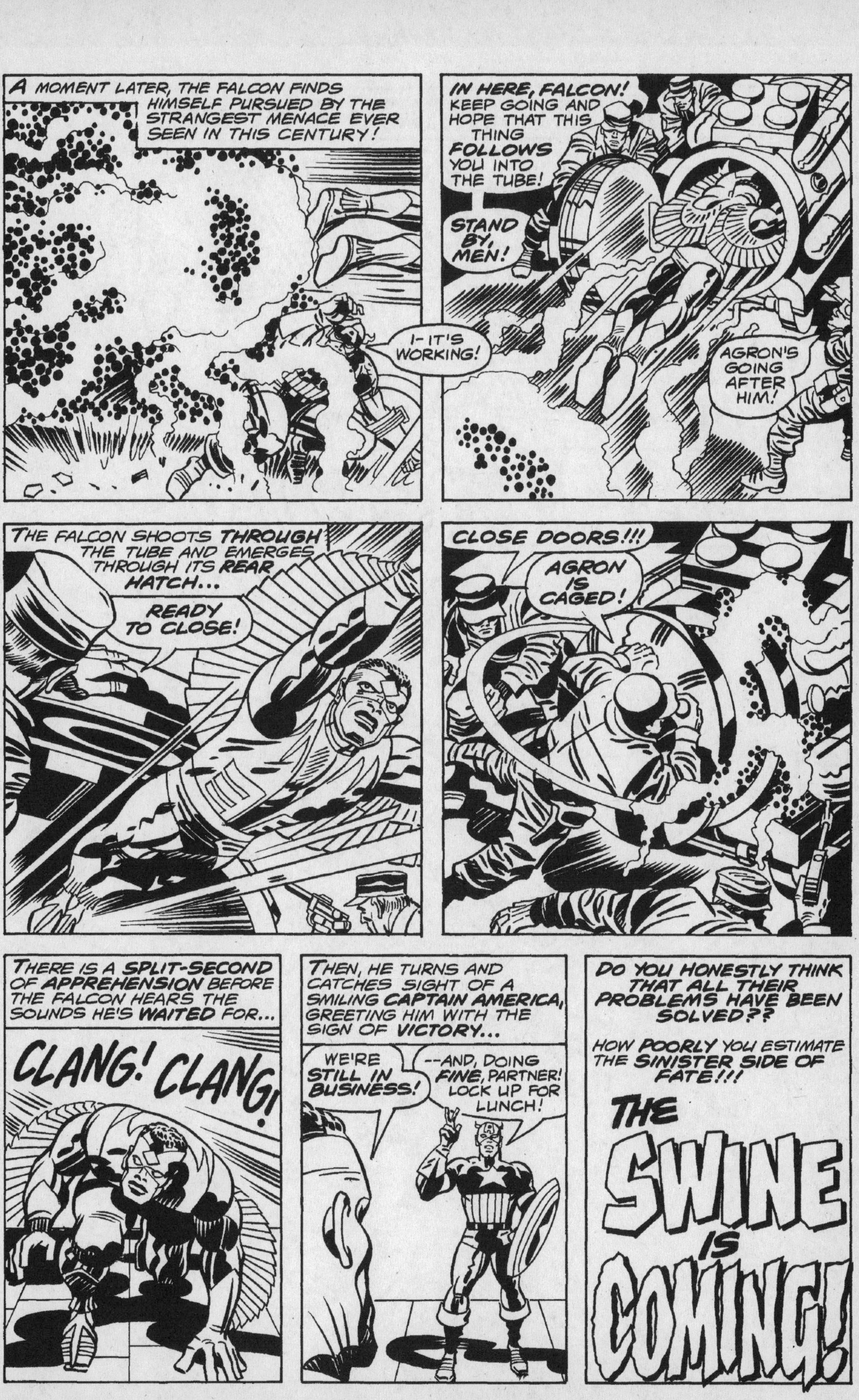
A MOMENT LATER, THE FALCON FINDS HIMSELF PURSUED BY THE STRANGEST MENACE EVER SEEN IN THIS CENTURY!
I-IT'S WORKING!
IN HERE, FALCON! KEEP GOING AND HOPE THAT THIS THING FOLLOWS YOU INTO THE TUBE!
STAND BY, MEN!
AGRON'S GOING AFTER HIM!
THE FALCON SHOOTS THROUGH THE TUBE AND EMERGES THROUGH ITS REAR HATCH...
READY TO CLOSE!
CLOSE DOORS!!!
AGRON IS CAGED!
THERE IS A SPLIT-SECOND OF APPREHENSION BEFORE THE FALCON HEARS THE SOUNDS HE'S WAITED FOR...
CLANG! CLANG!
THEN, HE TURNS AND CATCHES SIGHT OF A SMILING CAPTAIN AMERICA, GREETING HIM WITH THE SIGN OF VICTORY...
WE'RE STILL IN BUSINESS!
--AND, DOING FINE, PARTNER! LOCK UP FOR LUNCH!
DO YOU HONESTLY THINK THAT ALL THEIR PROBLEMS HAVE BEEN SOLVED??
HOW POORLY YOU ESTIMATE THE SINISTER SIDE OF FATE!!!
THE SWINE IS COMING!

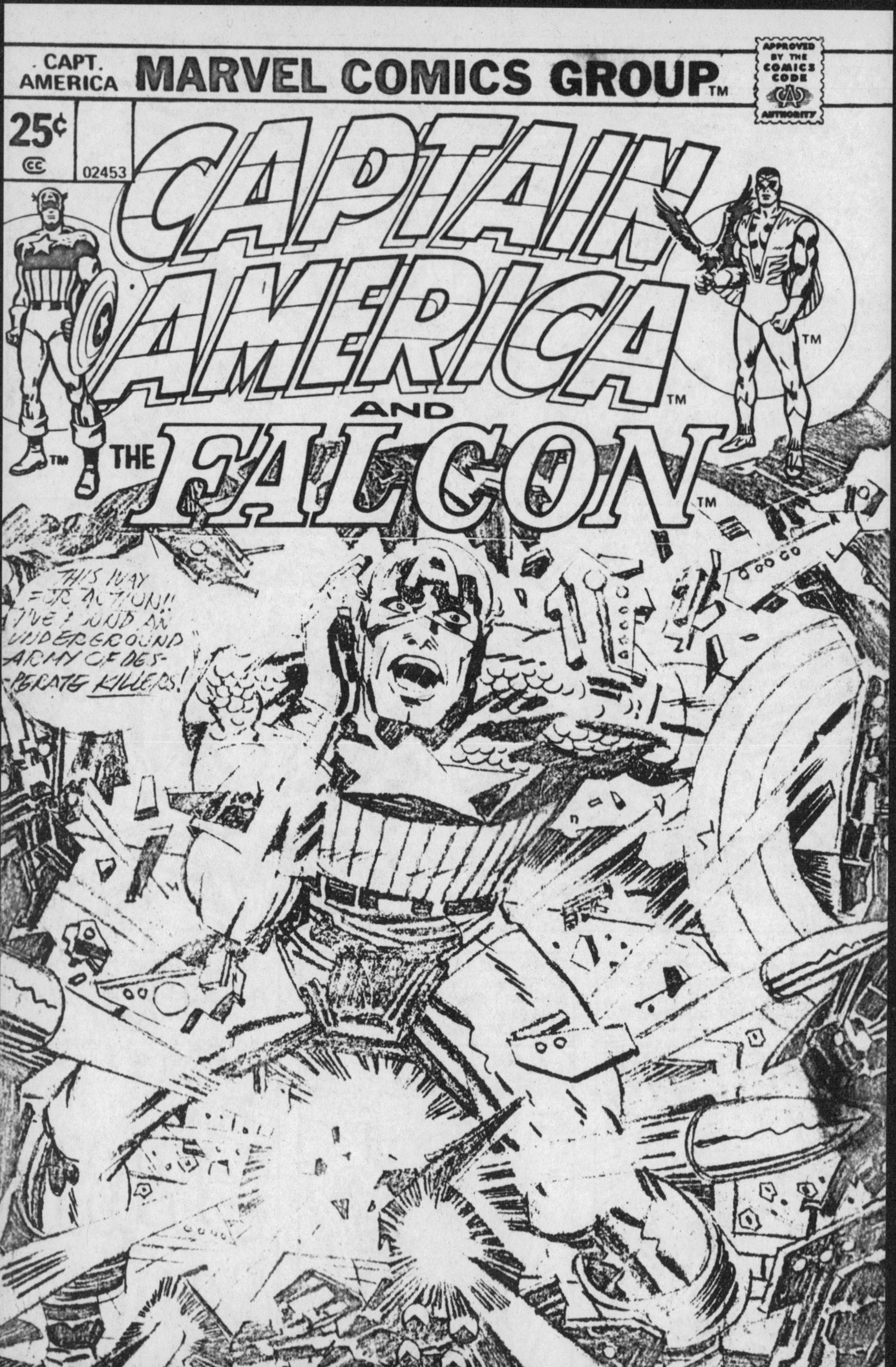
CAPT. AMERICA
MARVEL COMICS GROUP
APPROVED BY THE COMICS CODE AUTHORITY
25¢
02453
CAPTAIN AMERICA AND THE FALCON
THIS WAY FOR ACTION!! I'VE FOUND AN UNDERGROUND ARMY OF DES-PERATE KILLERS!

Captain America #197 Cover Pencils by Jack Kirby

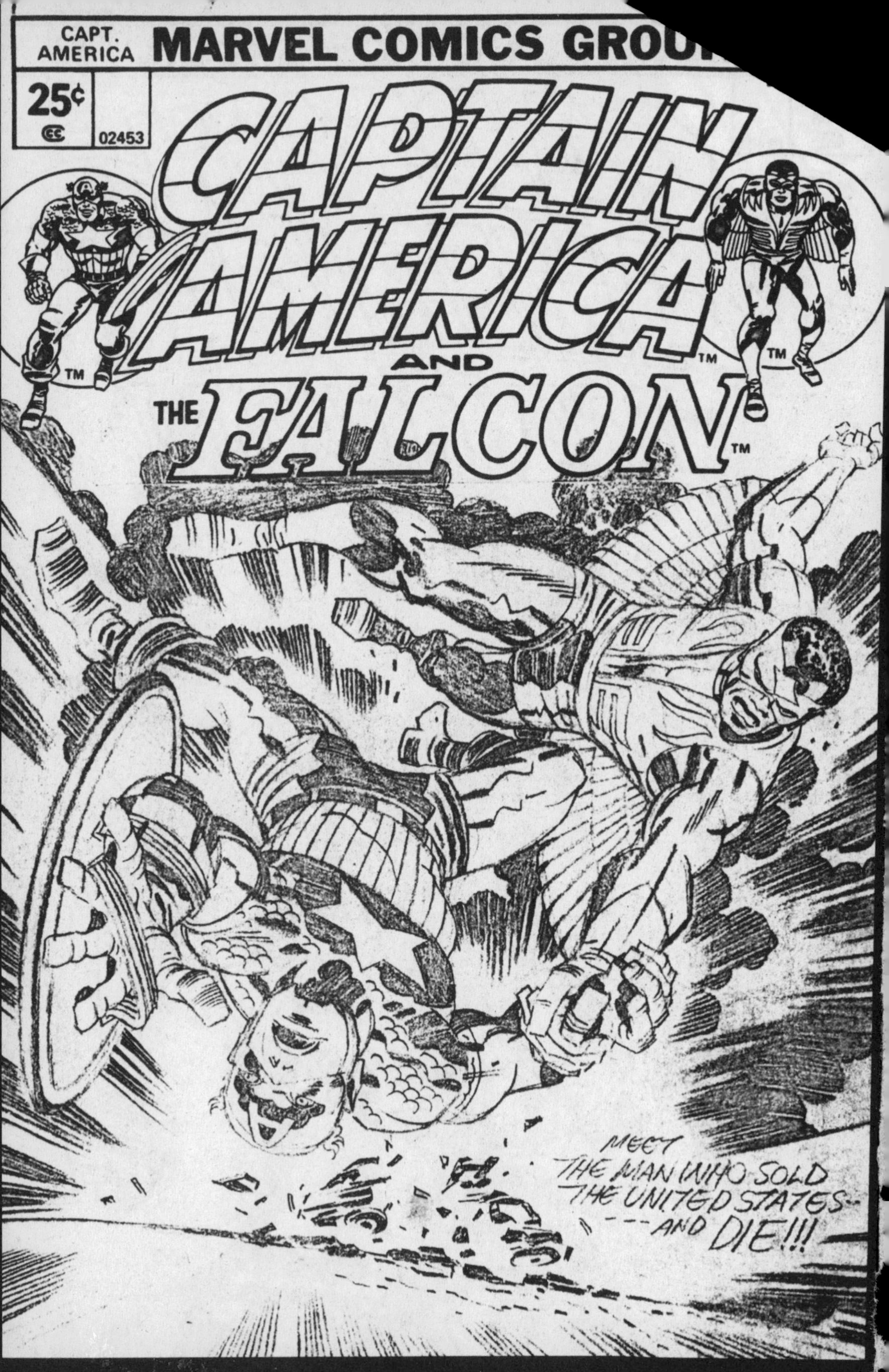
CAPT. AMERICA
MARVEL COMICS GROUP
25¢
02453
CAPTAIN AMERICA
AND
THE FALCON
MEET THE MAN WHO SOLD THE UNITED STATES---AND DIE!!!

Captain America #199 Cover Pencils by Jack Kirby

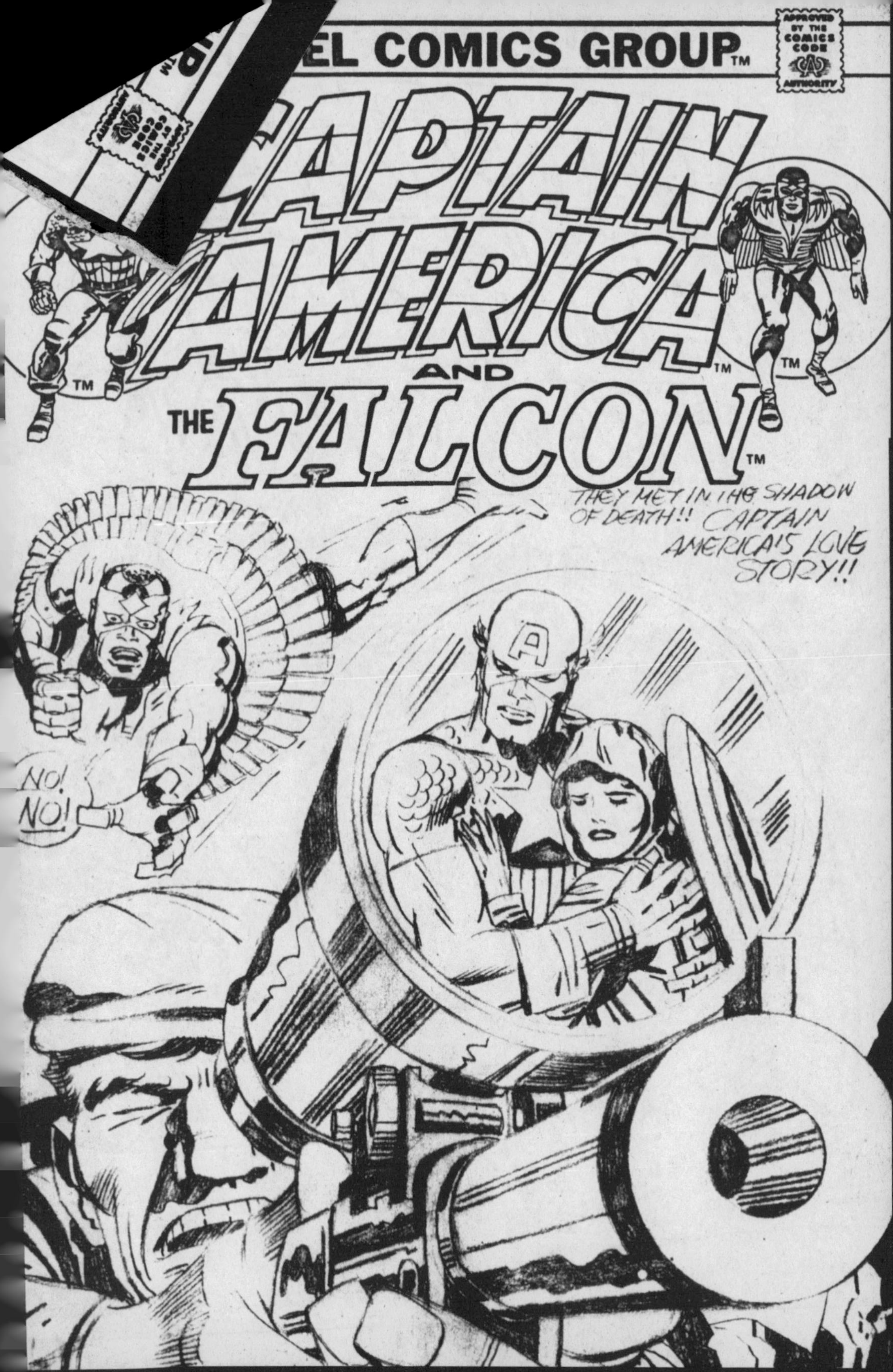

EL COMICS GROUP™
APPROVED BY THE COMICS CODE AUTHORITY
CAPTAIN AMERICA™
AND
THE FALCON™
THEY MET IN THE SHADOW OF DEATH!! CAPTAIN AMERICA'S LOVE STORY!!
NO! NO!

Captain America #198 **Cover Pencils by Jack Kirby**